D0755897

The Oxford

Colour

German Dictionary

Revised Edition

GERMAN–ENGLISH
ENGLISH–GERMAN

DEUTSCH–ENGLISCH
ENGLISCH–DEUTSCH

Gunhild Prowe

Jill Schneider

Word games prepared by
Neil and Roswitha Morris

Oxford   New York

OXFORD UNIVERSITY PRESS

1998

Oxford University Press, Great Clarendon Street, Oxford, OX2 6DP
Oxford New York
Athens Auckland Bangkok Bogota Bombay Buenos Aires
Calcutta Cape Town Dar es Salaam Delhi
Florence Hong Kong Istanbul Karachi
Kuala Lumpur Madras Madrid Melbourne
Mexico City Nairobi Paris Singapore
Taipei Tokyo Toronto Warsaw
and associated companies in
Berlin Ibadan

Oxford is a trade mark of Oxford University Press

© Oxford University Press 1998

First published 1997 as The Oxford–Duden Paperback
German dictionary
First published 1998 as The Oxford Colour German Dictionary

British Library Cataloguing in Publication Data
Data available

Library of Congress Cataloging in Publication Data
Data available

ISBN 0-19-860188-3
10 9 8 7 6 5 4 3 2 1

Printed in Spain by
Mateu Cromo Artes Graficas S.A.
Madrid

Contents

Preface

The Oxford Colour German Dictionary is a dictionary designed for beginners of German. Its clear presentation and use of colour headwords make it easily accessible. This new edition includes word games which are specifically designed to build key skills in using your dictionary more effectively, and to improve knowledge of German vocabulary and usage in a fun and entertaining way. You will find answers to all puzzles and games at the end of the section.

Introduction

As an aid to easy reference all main headwords, compounds, and derivatives appear in blue. The text of this new edition reflects recent changes to the spelling of German ratified in July 1996. The symbol (NEW) has been introduced to refer from the old spelling to the new, preferred one:

Ạs *nt* -ses, -se (NEW) **Ass**
Diät *f* -,-en (*Med*) diet; **D~ leben** be on a
  diet. **d~** *adv* **d~ leben** (NEW) **D~ leben**,
  s. **Diät.**
ạbsein† *vi sep* (*sein*) (NEW) **ab sein**, *s.* **ab**
schneuzen (**sich**) *vr* (NEW) **schnäuzen**
  (**sich**)
Rọlladen *m* (NEW) **Rollladen**

When the two forms follow each other alphabetically or are used in phrases, the old form is shown in brackets after the new, preferred one:

Ạbfluss (**Ạbfluß**) *m* drainage;
  (*Öffnung*) drain. **A~rohr** *nt* drain-pipe
ạrm *a* (**ärmer, ärmst**) poor; **Arm und**
  Reich (**arm und reich**) rich and poor

Where both the old and new forms are valid, an equals sign = is used to refer to the preferred form:

ạufwändig *a* = **aufwendig**
Tụnfisch *m* = **Thunfisch**
Rạnd *m* . . . **zu R~e kommen mit** =
  zurande kommen mit, *s.* **zurande**
Stạnd *m* . . . **in S~ halten/setzen** =
  instand halten/setzen, *s.* **instand**

When such forms follow each other alphabetically, they are given with commas, with the preferred form in first place:

Pạnther, Pạnter *m* -s, - panther

In phrases, *od* (oder) is used:

. . . **d~e(r,s)** *poss pron* yours; **die D~en** *od*
  d~en *pl* your family *sg.*
. . . **s~e(r,s)** *poss pron* his; **das S~e** *od*
  seine tun do one's share

On the English–German side, only the preferred German form is given.

- A swung dash ~ represents the headword or that part of the headword preceding a vertical bar |. The initial letter of a German headword is given to show whether or not it is a capital.
- The vertical bar | follows the part of the headword which is not repeated in compounds or derivatives.
- Square brackets [ ] are used for optional material.
- Angled brackets < > are used after a verb translation to indicate the object; before a verb translation to indicate the subject; before an adjective to indicate a typical noun which it qualifies.
- Round brackets ( ) are used for field or style labels (see list on page vii) and for explanatory matter.
- A box □ indicates a new part of speech within an entry.
- *od* (oder) and *or* denote that words or portions of a phrase are synonymous. An oblique stroke / is used where there is a difference in usage or meaning.
- ≈ is used where no exact equivalent exists in the other language.
- A dagger † indicates that a German verb is irregular and that the parts can be found in the verb table on page 503. Compound verbs are not listed there as they follow the pattern of the basic verb.
- The stressed vowel is marked in a German headword by ‗ (long) or ˳ (short). A phonetic transcription is only given for words which do not follow the normal rules of pronunciation. These rules can be found on page 501.
- Phonetics are given for all English headwords and for derivatives where there is a change of pronunciation or stress. In blocks of compounds, if no stress is shown, it falls on the first element.
- A change in pronunciation or stress shown within a block of compounds applies only to that particular word (subsequent entries revert to the pronunciation and stress of the headword).
- German headword nouns are followed by the gender and, with the exception of compound nouns, by the genitive and plural. These are only given at compound nouns if they

present some difficulty. Otherwise the user should refer to the final element.

- Nouns that decline like adjectives are entered as follows: **-e(r)** *m/f*, **-e(s)** *nt*.
- Adjectives which have no undeclined form are entered in the feminine form with the masculine and neuter in brackets **-e(r,s)**.
- The reflexive pronoun **sich** is accusative unless marked (*dat*).

Proprietary terms

This dictionary includes some words which are, or are asserted to be, proprietary names or trademarks. Their inclusion does not imply that they have acquired for legal purposes a non-proprietary or general significance, nor is any other judgement implied concerning their legal status. In cases where the editor has some evidence that a word is used as a proprietary name or trademark this is indicated by the letter (P), but no judgement concerning the legal status of such words is made or implied thereby.

Abbreviations • Abkürzungen

adjective	a	Adjektiv
abbreviation	abbr	Abkürzung
accusative	acc	Akkusativ
Administration	Admin	Administration
adverb	adv	Adverb
American	Amer	amerikanisch
Anatomy	Anat	Anatomie
Archaeology	Archaeol	Archäologie
Architecture	Archit	Architektur
Astronomy	Astr	Astronomie
attributive	attrib	attributiv
Austrian	Aust	österreichisch
Motor vehicles	Auto	Automobil
Aviation	Aviat	Luftfahrt
Biology	Biol	Biologie
Botany	Bot	Botanik
Chemistry	Chem	Chemie
collective	coll	Kollektivum
Commerce	Comm	Handel
conjunction	conj	Konjunktion
Cookery	Culin	Kochkunst
dative	dat	Dativ
definite article	def art	bestimmter Artikel
demonstrative	dem	Demonstrativ-
dialect	dial	Dialekt
Electricity	Electr	Elektrizität
something	etw	etwas
feminine	f	Femininum
familiar	fam	familiär
figurative	fig	figurativ
genitive	gen	Genitiv
Geography	Geog	Geographie
Geology	Geol	Geologie
Geometry	Geom	Geometrie
Grammar	Gram	Grammatik
Horticulture	Hort	Gartenbau
impersonal	impers	unpersönlich
indefinite article	indef art	unbestimmter Artikel

indefinite pronoun	indef pron	unbestimmtes Pronomen
infinitive	inf	Infinitiv
inseparable	insep	untrennbar
interjection	int	Interjektion
invariable	inv	unveränderlich
irregular	irreg	unregelmäßig
someone	jd	jemand
someone	jdm	jemandem
someone	jdn	jemanden
someone's	jds	jemandes
Journalism	Journ	Journalismus
Law	Jur	Jura
Language	Lang	Sprache
literary	liter	dichterisch
masculine	m	Maskulinum
Mathematics	Math	Mathematik
Medicine	Med	Medizin
Meteorology	Meteorol	Meteorologie
Military	Mil	Militär
Mineralogy	Miner	Mineralogie
Music	Mus	Musik
noun	n	Substantiv
Nautical	Naut	nautisch
North German	N Ger	Norddeutsch
nominative	nom	Nominativ
neuter	nt	Neutrum
or	od	oder
Proprietary term	P	Warenzeichen
pejorative	pej	abwertend
Photography	Phot	Fotografie
Physics	Phys	Physik
plural	pl	Plural
Politics	Pol	Politik
possessive	poss	Possessiv-
past participle	pp	zweites Partizip
predicative	pred	prädikativ
prefix	pref	Präfix
preposition	prep	Präposition
present	pres	Präsens
present participle	pres p	erstes Partizip
pronoun	pron	Pronomen
Psychology	Psych	Psychologie

past tense	pt	Präteritum
Railway	Rail	Eisenbahn
reflexive	refl	reflexiv
regular	reg	regelmäßig
relative	rel	Relativ-
Religion	Relig	Religion
see	s.	siehe
School	Sch	Schule
separable	sep	trennbar
singular	sg	Singular
South German	S Ger	Süddeutsch
slang	sl	salopp
someone	s.o.	jemand
something	sth	etwas
Technical	Techn	Technik
Telephone	Teleph	Telefon
Textiles	Tex	Textilien
Theatre	Theat	Theater
Television	TV	Fernsehen
Typography	Typ	Typographie
University	Univ	Universität
auxiliary verb	v aux	Hilfsverb
intransitive verb	vi	intransitives Verb
reflexive verb	vr	reflexives Verb
transitive verb	vt	transitives Verb
vulgar	vulg	vulgär
Zoology	Zool	Zoologie

Pronunciation of the alphabet •
Aussprache des Alphabets

English/Englisch		*German/Deutsch*
eɪ	a	aː
biː	b	beː
siː	c	t͜seː
diː	d	deː
iː	e	eː
ef	f	ɛf
dʒiː	g	geː
eɪtʃ	h	haː
aɪ	i	iː
dʒeɪ	j	jɔt
keɪ	k	kaː
el	l	ɛl
em	m	ɛm
en	n	ɛn
əʊ	o	oː
piː	p	peː
kjuː	q	kuː
ɑː(r)	r	ɛr
es	s	ɛs
tiː	t	teː
juː	u	uː
viː	v	faʊ
'dʌbljuː	w	veː
eks	x	ɪks
waɪ	y	'ʏpsilɔn
zed	z	t͜sɛt
eɪ umlaut	ä	ɛː
əʊ umlaut	ö	øː
juː umlaut	ü	yː
es'zed	ß	ɛs't͜sɛt

A

Aal *m* -[e]s,-e eel. a~en (sich) *vr* laze; (*ausgestreckt*) stretch out

Aas *nt* -es carrion; (*sl*) swine

ab *prep* (+ *dat*) from; ab Montag from Monday □ *adv* off; (*weg*) away; (*auf Fahrplan*) departs; ab sein (*fam*) have come off; (*erschöpft*) be worn out; von jetzt ab from now on; ab und zu now and then; auf und ab up and down

abändern *vt sep* alter; (*abwandeln*) modify

abarbeiten *vt sep* work off; sich a~ slave away

Abart *f* variety. a~ig *a* abnormal

Abbau *m* dismantling; (*Kohlen-*) mining; (*fig*) reduction. a~en *vt sep* dismantle; mine (*Kohle*); (*fig*) reduce, cut

abbeißen† *vt sep* bite off

abbeizen *vt sep* strip

abberufen† *vt sep* recall

abbestellen *vt sep* cancel; jdn a~ put s.o. off

abbiegen† *vi sep* (*sein*) turn off; [nach] links a~ turn left

Abbild *nt* image. a~en *vt sep* depict, portray. A~ung *f* -,-en illustration

Abbitte *f* A~ leisten apologize

abblättern *vi sep* (*sein*) flake off

abblend|en *vt/i sep* (*haben*) [die Scheinwerfer] a~en dip one's headlights. A~licht *nt* dipped headlights *pl*

abbrechen† *v sep* □ *vt* break off; (*abreißen*) demolish □ *vi* (*sein/haben*) break off

abbrennen† *v sep* □ *vt* burn off; (*niederbrennen*) burn down; let off (*Feuerwerkskörper*) □ *vi* (*sein*) burn down

abbringen† *vt sep* dissuade (von from)

Abbruch *m* demolition; (*Beenden*) breaking off; etw (*dat*) keinen A~ tun do no harm to sth

abbuchen *vt sep* debit

abbürsten *vt sep* brush down; (*entfernen*) brush off

abdanken *vi sep* (*haben*) resign; (*Herrscher:*) abdicate. A~ung *f* -,-en resignation; abdication

abdecken *vt sep* uncover; (*abnehmen*) take off; (*zudecken*) cover; den Tisch a~ clear the table

abdichten *vt sep* seal

abdrehen *vt sep* turn off

Abdruck *m* (*pl* -e) impression; (*Finger-*) print; (*Nachdruck*) reprint. a~en *vt sep* print

abdrücken *vt/i sep* (*haben*) fire; sich a~ leave an impression

Abend *m* -s,-e evening; am A~ in the evening; heute A~ this evening, tonight; gestern A~ yesterday evening, last night. a~ *adv* heute/gestern a~ (NEW) heute/gestern A~, s. Abend. A~brot *nt* supper. A~essen *nt* dinner; (*einfacher*) supper. A~kurs[us] *m* evening class. A~mahl *nt* (*Relig*) [Holy] Communion. a~s *adv* in the evening

Abenteuer *nt* -s,- adventure; (*Liebes-*) affair. a~lich *a* fantastic; (*gefährlich*) hazardous

Abenteurer *m* -s,- adventurer

aber *conj* but; oder a~ or else □ *adv* (*wirklich*) really; a~ ja! but of course! Tausende und a~ Tausende thousands upon thousands

Aber|glaube *m* superstition. a~gläubisch *a* superstitious

aber|mals *adv* once again. a~tausende, a~tausende *pl* thousands upon thousands

abfahr|en† *v sep* □ *vi* (*sein*) leave; (*Auto:*) drive off □ *vt* take away; (*entlangfahren*) drive along; use (*Fahrkarte*); abgefahrene Reifen worn tyres. A~t *f* departure; (*Talfahrt*) descent; (*Piste*) run; (*Ausfahrt*) exit

Abfall *m* refuse, rubbish, (*Amer*) garbage; (*auf der Straße*) litter; (*Industrie-*) waste. A~eimer *m* rubbish-bin; litter-bin

abfallen† *vi sep* (*sein*) drop, fall; (*übrig bleiben*) be left (für for); (*sich neigen*) slope away; (*fig*) compare badly (gegen with); vom Glauben a~ renounce one's faith. a~d *a* sloping

Abfallhaufen *m* rubbish-dump

abfällig *a* disparaging, *adv* -ly

abfangen† *vt sep* intercept; (*beherrschen*) bring under control

abfärben *vi sep* (*haben*) (*Farbe:*) run; (*Stoff:*) not be colour-fast; a~ auf (+ *acc*) (*fig*) rub off on

abfassen *vt sep* draft

abfertigen *vt sep* attend to; (*zollamtlich*) clear; jdn kurz a~ (*fam*) give s.o. short shrift

abfeuern *vt sep* fire

abfind|en† *vt sep* pay off; (*entschädigen*) compensate; sich a~en mit come to terms with. A~ung *f* -,-en compensation

abflauen *vi sep* (sein) decrease

abfliegen† *vi sep* (sein) fly off; (*Aviat*) take off

abfließen† *vi sep* (sein) drain *or* run away

Abflug *m* (*Aviat*) departure

Abfluss (Abfluß) *m* drainage; (*Öffnung*) drain. A~rohr *nt* drain-pipe

abfragen *vt sep* jdn *od* jdm Vokabeln a~ test s.o. on vocabulary

Abfuhr *f* - removal; (*fig*) rebuff

abführ|en *vt sep* take *or* lead away. a~end a laxative. A~mittel *nt* laxative

abfüllen *vt sep* auf *od* in Flaschen a~ bottle

Abgabe *f* handing in; (*Verkauf*) sale; (*Fußball*) pass; (*Steuer*) tax

Abgang *m* departure; (*Theat*) exit; (*Schul-*) leaving

Abgase *ntpl* exhaust fumes

abgeben† *vt sep* hand in; (*abliefern*) deliver; (*verkaufen*) sell; (*zur Aufbewahrung*) leave; (*Fußball*) pass; (*ausströmen*) give off; (*abfeuern*) fire; (*verlauten lassen*) give; cast (*Stimme*); jdm etw a~ give s.o. a share of sth; sich a~ mit occupy oneself with

abgedroschen *a* hackneyed

abgehen† *v sep* □ *vi* (sein) leave; (*Theat*) exit; (*sich lösen*) come off; (*abgezogen werden*) be deducted; (*abbiegen*) turn off; (*verlaufen*) go off; ihr geht jeglicher Humor ab she totally lacks a sense of humour □ *vt* walk along

abgehetzt *a* harassed. **abgelegen** *a* remote. **abgeneigt** *a* etw (*dat*) nicht abgeneigt sein not be averse to sth. **abgenutzt** *a* worn. **Abgeordnete(r)** *m/f* deputy; (*Pol*) Member of Parliament. **abgepackt** *a* pre-packed. **abgerissen** *a* ragged

abgeschieden *a* secluded. A~heit *f* - seclusion

abgeschlossen *a* (*fig*) complete; (*Wohnung*) self-contained. **abgeschmackt** *a* (*fig*) tasteless. **abgesehen** *prep* apart (from von). **abgespannt** *a* exhausted. **abgestanden** *a* stale. **abgestorben** *a* dead; (*Glied*) numb. **abgetragen** *a* worn. **abgewetzt** *a* threadbare

abgewinnen† *vt sep* win (jdm from s.o.); etw (*dat*) Geschmack a~ get a taste for sth

abgewöhnen *vt sep* jdm/sich das Rauchen a~ cure s.o. of/ give up smoking

abgezehrt *a* emaciated

abgießen† *vt sep* pour off; drain (*Gemüse*)

abgleiten† *vi sep* (sein) slip

Abgott *m* idol

abgöttisch *adv* a~ lieben idolize

abgrenz|en *vt sep* divide off; (*fig*) define. A~ung *f* - demarcation

Abgrund *m* abyss; (*fig*) depths *pl*

abgucken *vt sep* (*fam*) copy

Abguss (Abguß) *m* cast

abhacken *vt sep* chop off

abhaken *vt sep* tick off

abhalten† *vt sep* keep off; (*hindern*) keep, prevent (von from); (*veranstalten*) hold

Abhandlung *f* treatise

Abhang *m* slope

abhängen[1] *vt sep* (*reg*) take down; (*abkuppeln*) uncouple

abhäng|en[2]† *vi sep* (haben) depend (von on). a~ig a dependent (von on). A~igkeit *f* - dependence

abhärten *vt sep* toughen up

abhauen† *v sep* □ *vt* chop off □ *vi* (sein) (*fam*) clear off

abheben† *v sep* □ *vt* take off; (*vom Konto*) withdraw; sich a~ stand out (gegen against) □ *vi* (haben) (*Cards*) cut [the cards]; (*Aviat*) take off, (*Rakete:*) lift off

abheften *vt sep* file

abhelfen† *vt sep* (+ *dat*) remedy

Abhilfe *f* remedy; A~ schaffen take [remedial] action

abholen *vt sep* collect; call for (*Person*); jdn am Bahnhof a~ meet s.o. at the station

abhorchen *vt sep* (*Med*) sound

abhör|en *vt sep* listen to; (*überwachen*) tap; jdn *od* jdm Vokabeln a~en test s.o. on vocabulary. A~gerät *nt* bugging device

Abitur *nt* -s ≈ A levels *pl*. A~ient(in) *m* -en,-en (f -,-nen) pupil taking the '*Abitur*'

abkanzeln *vt sep* (*fam*) reprimand

abkaufen† *vt sep* buy (*dat* from)

abkehren (sich) *vr sep* turn away

abkette[l]n *vt/i sep* (haben) cast off

abklingen† *vi sep* (sein) die away; (*nachlassen*) subside

abkochen *vt sep* boil

abkommen† *vi sep* (sein) a~ von stray from; (*aufgeben*) give up; vom Thema a~ digress. A~ *nt* -s,- agreement

abkömmlich *a* available

Abkömmling *m* -s,-e descendant

abkratzen *v sep* □ *vt* scrape off □ *vi* (sein) (*sl*) die

abkühlen *vt/i sep* (sein) cool; sich a~ cool [down]; (*Wetter:*) turn cooler

Abkunft f - origin

abkuppeln vt sep uncouple

abkürz|en vt sep shorten; abbreviate ⟨Wort⟩. A∼ung f short cut; ⟨Wort⟩ abbreviation

abladen† vt sep unload

Ablage f shelf; ⟨für Akten⟩ tray

ablager|n vt sep deposit; sich a∼n be deposited. A∼ung f -,-en deposit

ablassen† v sep □ vt drain [off]; let off ⟨Dampf⟩; ⟨vom Preis⟩ knock off □ vi ⟨haben⟩ von give up; von jdm a∼ leave s.o. alone

Ablauf m drain; ⟨Verlauf⟩ course; ⟨Ende⟩ end; ⟨einer Frist⟩ expiry. a∼en† v sep □ vi ⟨sein⟩ run or drain off; ⟨verlaufen⟩ go off; ⟨enden⟩ expire; ⟨Zeit:⟩ run out; ⟨Uhrwerk:⟩ run down □ vt walk along; ⟨absuchen⟩ scour ⟨nach for⟩; ⟨abnutzen⟩ wear down

ableg|en v sep □ vt put down; discard ⟨Karte⟩; ⟨abheften⟩ file; ⟨ausziehen⟩ take off; ⟨aufgeben⟩ give up; sit, take ⟨Prüfung⟩; abgelegte Kleidung cast-offs pl □ vi ⟨haben⟩ take off one's coat; ⟨Naut⟩ cast off. A∼er m -s,- ⟨Bot⟩ cutting; ⟨Schössling⟩ shoot

ablehn|en vt sep refuse; ⟨missbilligen⟩ reject. A∼ung f -,-en refusal; rejection

ableit|en vt sep divert; sich a∼en be derived ⟨von/aus from⟩. A∼ung f derivation; ⟨Wort⟩ derivative

ablenk|en vt sep deflect; divert ⟨Aufmerksamkeit⟩; ⟨zerstreuen⟩ distract. A∼ung f -,-en distraction

ablesen† vt sep read; ⟨absuchen⟩ pick off

ableugnen vt sep deny

ablichten vt sep photocopy. A∼ung f photocopy

abliefern vt sep deliver

ablös|en vt sep detach; ⟨abwechseln⟩ relieve; ⟨sich abwechseln⟩ sich abwechseln⟩ take turns. A∼ung f relief

abmach|en vt sep remove; ⟨ausmachen⟩ arrange; ⟨vereinbaren⟩ agree; abgemacht! agreed! A∼ung f -,-en agreement

abmager|n vi sep ⟨sein⟩ lose weight. A∼ungskur f slimming diet

abmarschieren vi sep ⟨sein⟩ march off

abmelden vt sep cancel ⟨Zeitung⟩; sich a∼ report that one is leaving; ⟨im Hotel⟩ check out

abmess|en† vt sep measure. A∼ungen fpl measurements

abmühen (sich) vr sep struggle

abnäh|en† vt sep take in. A∼er m -s,- dart

Abnahme f - removal; ⟨Kauf⟩ purchase; ⟨Verminderung⟩ decrease

abnehm|en† v sep □ vt take off, remove; pick up ⟨Hörer⟩; jdm etw a∼en take/

⟨kaufen⟩ buy sth from s.o. □ vi ⟨haben⟩ decrease; ⟨nachlassen⟩ decline; ⟨Person:⟩ lose weight; ⟨Mond:⟩ wane. A∼er m -s,- buyer

Abneigung f dislike ⟨gegen of⟩

abnorm a abnormal, adv -ly

abnutz|en vt sep wear out; sich a∼en wear out. A∼ung f - wear [and tear]

Abon|nement /abɔnə'mãː/ nt -s,-s subscription. A∼nent m -en,-en subscriber. a∼nieren vt take out a subscription to

Abordnung f -,-en deputation

abpassen vt sep wait for; gut a∼ time well

abprallen vi sep ⟨sein⟩ rebound; ⟨Geschoss:⟩ ricochet

abraten† vt sep ⟨haben⟩ jdm von etw a∼ advise s.o. against sth

abräumen vt/i ⟨haben⟩ clear away; clear ⟨Tisch⟩

abrechn|en v sep □ vt deduct □ vi ⟨haben⟩ settle up; ⟨fig⟩ get even. A∼ung f settlement [of accounts]; ⟨Rechnung⟩ account

Abreise f departure. a∼n vi sep ⟨sein⟩ leave

abreißen† v sep □ vt tear off; ⟨demolieren⟩ pull down □ vi ⟨sein⟩ come off; ⟨fig⟩ break off

abrichten vt sep train

abriegeln vt sep bolt; ⟨absperren⟩ seal off

Abriss (Abriß) m demolition; ⟨Übersicht⟩ summary

abrufen† vt sep call away; ⟨Computer⟩ retrieve

abrunden vt sep round off; nach unten/oben a∼ round down/up

abrupt a abrupt, adv -ly

abrüst|en vi sep ⟨haben⟩ disarm. A∼ung f disarmament

abrutschen vi sep ⟨sein⟩ slip

Absage f -,-n cancellation; ⟨Ablehnung⟩ refusal. a∼n v sep □ vt cancel □ vi ⟨haben⟩ [jdm] a∼n cancel an appointment [with s.o.]; ⟨auf Einladung⟩ refuse [s.o.'s invitation]

absägen vt sep saw off; ⟨fam⟩ sack

Absatz m heel; ⟨Abschnitt⟩ paragraph; ⟨Verkauf⟩ sale

abschaff|en vt sep abolish; get rid of ⟨Auto, Hund⟩. A∼ung f abolition

abschalten vt/i sep ⟨haben⟩ switch off

abschätzig a disparaging, adv -ly

Abschaum m ⟨fig⟩ scum

Abscheu m - revulsion

abscheulich a revolting; ⟨fam⟩ horrible, adv -bly

abschicken vt sep send off

Abschied m -[e]s,-e farewell; ⟨Trennung⟩ parting; A∼ nehmen say goodbye ⟨von to⟩

abschießen† *vt sep* shoot down; (*abtrennen*) shoot off; (*abfeuern*) fire; launch ⟨*Rakete*⟩

abschirmen *vt sep* shield

abschlagen† *vt sep* knock off; (*verweigern*) refuse; (*abwehren*) repel

abschlägig *a* negative; a∼e Antwort refusal

Abschlepp|dienst *m* breakdown service. a∼en *vt sep* tow away. A∼seil *nt* tow-rope. A∼wagen *m* breakdown vehicle

abschließen† *v sep* □ *vt* lock; (*beenden, abmachen*) conclude; make ⟨*Wette*⟩; balance ⟨*Bücher*⟩; sich a∼ (*fig*) cut oneself off □ *vi* (*haben*) lock up; (*enden*) end. a∼d *adv* in conclusion

Abschluss (**Abschluß**) *m* conclusion. A∼prüfung *f* final examination. A∼zeugnis *nt* diploma

abschmecken *vt sep* season

abschmieren *vt sep* lubricate

abschneiden† *v sep* □ *vt* cut off; den Weg a∼ take a short cut □ *vi* (*haben*) gut/schlecht a∼ do well/badly

Abschnitt *m* section; (*Stadium*) stage; (*Absatz*) paragraph; (*Kontroll-*) counterfoil

abschöpfen *vt sep* skim off

abschrauben *vt sep* unscrew

abschreck|en *vt sep* deter; (*Culin*) put in cold water ⟨*Ei*⟩. a∼end *a* repulsive, *adv* -ly; a∼endes Beispiel warning. A∼ungsmittel *nt* deterrent

abschreib|en† *v sep* □ *vt* copy; (*Comm & fig*) write off □ *vi* (*haben*) copy. A∼ung *f* (*Comm*) depreciation

Abschrift *f* copy

Abschuss (**Abschuß**) *m* shooting down; (*Abfeuern*) firing; (*Raketen-*) launch

abschüssig *a* sloping; (*steil*) steep

abschwächen *vt sep* lessen; sich a∼ lessen; (*schwächer werden*) weaken

abschweifen *vi sep* (*sein*) digress

abschwellen† *vi sep* (*sein*) go down

abschwören† *vi sep* (*haben*) (+ *dat*) renounce

abseh|bar *a* in a∼barer Zeit in the foreseeable future. a∼en† *vt/i sep* (*haben*) copy; (*voraussehen*) foresee; a∼en von disregard; (*aufgeben*) refrain from; es abgesehen haben auf (+ *acc*) have one's eye on; (*schikanieren*) have it in for

absein† *vi sep* (*sein*) NEW ab sein, s. ab

abseits *adv* apart; (*Sport*) offside □ *prep* (+ *gen*) away from. A∼ *nt* - (*Sport*) offside

absend|en† *vt sep* send off. A∼er *m* sender

absetzen *v sep* □ *vt* put *or* set down; (*ablagern*) deposit; (*abnehmen*) take off; (*absagen*) cancel; (*abbrechen*) stop; (*entlassen*) dismiss; (*verkaufen*) sell; (*abziehen*) deduct; sich a∼ be deposited; (*fliehen*) flee □ *vi* (*haben*) pause

Absicht *f* -,-en intention; mit A∼ intentionally, on purpose

absichtlich *a* intentional, *adv* -ly, deliberate, *adv* -ly

absitzen† *v sep* □ *vi* (*sein*) dismount □ *vt* (*fam*) serve ⟨*Strafe*⟩

absolut *a* absolute, *adv* -ly

Absolution /-'tsjo:n/ *f* - absolution

absolvieren *vt* complete; (*bestehen*) pass

absonderlich *a* odd

absonder|n *vt sep* separate; (*ausscheiden*) secrete; sich a∼n keep apart (von from). A∼ung *f* -,-en secretion

absorbieren *vt* absorb. A∼ption /-'tsjo:n/ *f* - absorption

abspeisen *vt sep* fob off (mit with)

abspenstig *a* a∼ machen take (jdm from s.o.)

absperr|en *vt sep* cordon off; (*abstellen*) turn off; (*SGer*) lock. A∼ung *f* -,-en barrier

abspielen *vt sep* play; (*Fußball*) pass; sich a∼ take place

Absprache *f* agreement

absprechen† *vt sep* arrange; sich a∼ agree; jdm etw a∼ deny s.o. sth

abspringen† *vi sep* (*sein*) jump off; (*mit Fallschirm*) parachute; (*abgehen*) come off; (*fam: zurücktreten*) back out

Absprung *m* jump

abspülen *vt sep* rinse; (*entfernen*) rinse off

abstamm|en *vi sep* (*haben*) be descended (von from). A∼ung *f* - descent

Abstand *m* distance; (*zeitlich*) interval; A∼ halten keep one's distance; A∼ nehmen von (*fig*) refrain from

abstatten *vt sep* jdm einen Besuch a∼ pay s.o. a visit

abstauben *vt sep* dust

abstech|en† *vi sep* (*haben*) stand out. A∼er *m* -s,- detour

abstehen† *vi sep* (*haben*) stick out; a∼ von be away from

absteigen† *vi sep* (*sein*) dismount; (*niedersteigen*) descend; (*Fußball*) be relegated

abstell|en *vt sep* put down; (*lagern*) store; (*parken*) park; (*abschalten*) turn off; (*fig: beheben*) remedy. A∼gleis *nt* siding. A∼raum *m* box-room

absterben† *vi sep* (*sein*) die; (*gefühllos werden*) go numb

Abstieg *m* -[e]s,-e descent; (*Fußball*) relegation

abstimm|en *v sep* □ *vi (haben)* vote (über + *acc* on) □ *vt* coordinate (auf + *acc* with). A~ung *f* vote

Abstinenz /-st-/ *f* - abstinence. A~ler *m* -s,- teetotaller

abstoßen† *vt sep* knock off; *(abschieben)* push off; *(verkaufen)* sell; *(fig: ekeln)* repel. a~d *a* repulsive, *adv* -ly

abstrakt *a* abstract

abstreifen *vt sep* remove; slip off *(Kleidungsstück, Schuhe)*

abstreiten† *vt sep* deny

Abstrich *m (Med)* smear; *(Kürzung)* cut

abstufen *vt sep* grade

Absturz *m* fall; *(Aviat)* crash

abstürzen *vi sep (sein)* fall; *(Aviat)* crash

absuchen *vt sep* search; *(ablesen)* pick off

absurd *a* absurd

Abszess *m* -es,-e (Abszeß *m* -sses,-sse) abscess

Abt *m* -[e]s,¨e abbot

abtasten *vt sep* feel; *(Techn)* scan

abtauen *vt/i sep (sein)* thaw; *(entfrosten)* defrost

Abtei *f* -,-en abbey

Abteil *nt* compartment

abteilen *vt sep* divide off

Abteilung *f* -,-en section; *(Admin, Comm)* department

abtragen† *vt sep* clear; *(einebnen)* level; *(abnutzen)* wear out; *(abzahlen)* pay off

abträglich *a* detrimental *(dat* to)

abtreiben† *v sep* □ *vt (Naut)* drive off course; ein Kind a~en lassen have an abortion □ *vi (sein)* drift off course. A~ung *f* -,-en abortion

abtrennen *vt sep* detach; *(abteilen)* divide off

abtret|en† *v sep* □ *vt* cede (an + *acc* to); sich *(dat)* die Füße a~en wipe one's feet □ *vi (sein) (Theat)* exit; *(fig)* resign. A~er *m* -s,- doormat

abtrocknen *vt/i sep (haben)* dry; sich a~ dry oneself

abtropfen *vi sep (sein)* drain

abtrünnig *a* renegade; a~ werden (+ *dat)* desert

abtun† *vt sep (fig)* dismiss

abverlangen *vt sep* demand *(dat* from)

abwägen† *vt sep (fig)* weigh

abwandeln *vt sep* modify

abwandern *vi sep (sein)* move away

abwarten *v sep* □ *vt* wait for □ *vi (haben)* wait [and see]

abwärts *adv* down[wards]

Abwasch *m* -[e]s washing-up; *(Geschirr)* dirty dishes *pl*. a~en† *v sep* □ *vt* wash;

wash up *(Geschirr)*; *(entfernen)* wash off □ *vi (haben)* wash up. A~lappen *m* dish-cloth

Abwasser *nt* -s,¨ sewage. A~kanal *m* sewer

abwechseln *vi/r sep (haben)* [sich] a~ alternate; *(Personen:)* take turns. a~d *a* alternate, *adv* -ly

Abwechslung *f* -,-en change; zur A~ for a change. a~sreich *a* varied

Abweg *m* auf A~e geraten *(fig)* go astray. a~ig *a* absurd

Abwehr *f* - defence; *(Widerstand)* resistance; *(Pol)* counter-espionage. a~en *vt sep* ward off; *(Mil)* repel; *(zurückweisen)* dismiss. A~system *nt* immune system

abweich|en† *vi sep (sein)* deviate/*(von Regel)* depart (von from); *(sich unterscheiden)* differ (von from). a~end *a* divergent; *(verschieden)* different. A~ung *f* -,-en deviation; difference

abweis|en† *vt sep* turn down; turn away *(Person)*; *(abwehren)* repel. a~end *a* unfriendly. A~ung *f* rejection; *(Abfuhr)* rebuff

abwenden† *vt sep* turn away; *(verhindern)* avert; sich a~ turn away; den Blick a~ look away

abwerfen† *vt sep* throw off; throw *(Reiter)*; *(Aviat)* drop; *(Kartenspiel)* discard; shed *(Haut, Blätter)*; yield *(Gewinn)*

abwert|en *vt sep* devalue. a~end *a* pejorative, *adv* -ly. A~ung *f* -,-en devaluation

abwesen|d *a* absent; *(zerstreut)* absent-minded. A~heit *f* - absence; absent-mindedness

abwickeln *vt sep* unwind; *(erledigen)* settle

abwischen *vt sep* wipe; *(entfernen)* wipe off

abwürgen *vt sep* stall *(Motor)*

abzahlen *vt sep* pay off

abzählen *vt sep* count

Abzahlung *f* instalment

abzapfen *vt sep* draw

Abzeichen *nt* badge

abzeichnen *vt sep* copy; *(unterzeichnen)* initial; sich a~ stand out

Abzieh|bild *nt* transfer. a~en† *v sep* □ *vt* pull off; take off *(Laken)*; strip *(Bett)*; *(häuten)* skin; *(Phot)* print; run off *(Kopien)*; *(zurückziehen)* withdraw; *(abrechnen)* deduct □ *vi (sein)* go away; *(Rauch:)* escape

abzielen *vi sep (haben)* a~ auf (+ *acc) (fig)* be aimed at

Abzug *m* withdrawal; *(Abrechnung)* deduction; *(Phot)* print; *(Korrektur-)* proof;

(*am Gewehr*) trigger; (A~*söffnung*) vent; A~*e pl* deductions

abzüglich *prep* (+ *gen*) less

Abzugshaube *f* [cooker] hood

abzweig|en *v sep* □ *vi* (*sein*) branch off □ *vt* divert. A~**ung** *f* -,-en junction; (*Gabelung*) fork

ach *int* oh; a~ je! oh dear! a~ so I see; mit A~ und Krach (*fam*) by the skin of one's teeth

Achse *f* -,-n axis; (*Rad-*) axle

Achsel *f* -,-n shoulder; die A~n zucken shrug one's shoulders. A~**höhle** *f* armpit. A~**zucken** *nt* -s shrug

acht[1] *inv a*, A~[1] *f* -,-en eight; heute in a~ Tagen a week today

acht[2] außer a~ lassen/sich in a~ nehmen (NEW) außer Acht lassen/sich in Acht nehmen, s. Acht[2]

Acht[2] *f* A~ geben be careful; A~ geben auf (+ *acc*) look after; außer A~ lassen disregard; sich in A~ nehmen be careful

acht|e(r,s) *a* eighth. a~**eckig** *a* octagonal. a~**el** *inv a* eighth. A~**el** *nt* -s,- eighth. A~**elnote** *f* quaver, (*Amer*) eighth note

achten *vt* respect □ *vi* (*haben*) a~ auf (+ *acc*) pay attention to; (*aufpassen*) look after; darauf a~, dass take care that

ächten *vt* ban; ostracize (*Person*)

Achter|bahn *f* roller-coaster. a~**n** *adv* (*Naut*) aft

achtgeben† *vi sep* (*haben*) (NEW) Acht geben, s. Acht[2]

achtlos *a* careless, *adv* -ly

achtsam *a* careful, *adv* -ly

Achtung *f* - respect (vor + *dat* for); A~! look out! (*Mil*) attention! 'A~ Stufe' 'mind the step'

acht|zehn *inv a* eighteen. a~**zehnte(r,s)** *a* eighteenth. a~**zig** *a* inv eighty. a~**zigste(r,s)** *a* eightieth

ächzen *vi* (*haben*) groan

Acker *m* -s,- field. A~**bau** *m* agriculture. A~**land** *nt* arable land

addieren *vt/i* (*haben*) add; (*zusammenzählen*) add up

Addition /-'tsjo:n/ *f* -,-en addition

ade *int* goodbye

Adel *m* -s nobility

Ader *f* -,-n vein; künstlerische A~ artistic bent

Adjektiv *nt* -s,-e adjective

Adler *m* -s,- eagle

adlig *a* noble. A~**e(r)** *m* nobleman

Administration /-'tsjo:n/ *f* - administration

Admiral *m* -s,-e admiral

adop|tieren *vt* adopt. A~**tion** /-'tsjo:n/ *f* -,-en adoption. a~**tiveltern** *pl* adoptive parents. A~**tivkind** *nt* adopted child

Adrenalin *nt* -s adrenalin

Adres|se *f* -,-n address. a~**sieren** *vt* address

adrett *a* neat, *adv* -ly

Adria *f* - Adriatic

Advent *m* -s Advent. A~**skranz** *m* Advent wreath

Adverb *nt* -s,-ien /-jə:n/ adverb

Affäre *f* -,-n affair

Affe *m* -n,-n monkey; (*Menschen-*) ape

Affekt *m* -[e]s,-e im A~ in the heat of the moment

affektiert *a* affected. A~**heit** *f* - affectation

affig *a* affected; (*eitel*) vain

Afrika *nt* -s Africa

Afrikan|er(in) *m* -s,- (*f* -,-nen) African. a~**isch** *a* African

After *m* -s,- anus

Agen|t(in) *m* -en,-en (*f* -,-nen) agent. A~**tur** *f* -,-en agency

Aggres|sion *f* -,-en aggression. a~**siv** *a* aggressive, *adv* -ly. A~**sivität** *f* - aggressiveness

Agitation /-'tsjo:n/ *f* - agitation

Agnostiker *m* -s,- agnostic

Ägypt|en /ɛ'gyptən/ *nt* -s Egypt. Ä~**er(in)** *m* -s,- (*f* -,-nen) Egyptian. ä~**isch** *a* Egyptian

ähneln *vi* (*haben*) (+ *dat*) resemble; sich ä~ be alike

ahnen *vt* have a presentiment of; (*vermuten*) suspect

Ahnen *mpl* ancestors. A~**forschung** *f* genealogy. A~**tafel** *f* family tree

ähnlich *a* similar, *adv* -ly; jdm ä~ sehen resemble s.o.; (*typisch sein*) be just like s.o. Ä~**keit** *f* -,-en similarity; resemblance

Ahnung *f* -,-en premonition; (*Vermutung*) idea, hunch; keine A~ (*fam*) no idea. a~**slos** *a* unsuspecting

Ahorn *m* -s,-e maple

Ähre *f* -,-n ear [of corn]

Aids /e:ts/ *nt* - Aids

Akademie *f* -,-n academy

Akadem|iker(in) *m* -s,- (*f* -,-nen) university graduate. a~**isch** *a* academic, *adv* -ally

akklimatisieren (sich) *vr* become acclimatized

Akkord *m* -[e]s,-e (*Mus*) chord; im A~ arbeiten be on piece-work. A~**arbeit** *f* piece-work

Akkordeon *nt* -s,-s accordion

Akkumulator *m* -s,-en /-'to:rən/ (*Electr*) accumulator

Akkusativ *m* -s,-e accusative. A~objekt *nt* direct object

Akrobat|(in) *m* -en,-en (*f* -,-nen) acrobat. a~isch *a* acrobatic

Akt *m* -[e]s,-e act; (*Kunst*) nude

Akte *f* -,-n file; A~n documents. A~ndeckel *m* folder. A~nkoffer *m* attaché case. A~nschrank *m* filing cabinet. A~ntasche *f* briefcase

Aktie /'aktsjə/ *f* -,-n (*Comm*) share. A~ngesellschaft *f* joint-stock company

Aktion /ak'tsjo:n/ *f* -,-en action; (*Kampagne*) campaign. A~är *m* -s,-e shareholder

aktiv *a* active, *adv* -ly. a~ieren *vt* activate. A~ität *f* -,-en activity

Aktualität *f* -,-en topicality; A~en current events

aktuell *a* topical; (*gegenwärtig*) current; nicht mehr a~ no longer relevant

Akupunktur *f* - acupuncture

Akust|ik *f* - acoustics *pl*. a~isch *a* acoustic, *adv* -ally

akut *a* acute

Akzent *m* -[e]s,-e accent

akzept|abel *a* acceptable. a~ieren *vt* accept

Alarm *m* -s alarm; (*Mil*) alert; A~schlagen raise the alarm. a~ieren *vt* alert; (*beunruhigen*) alarm. a~ierend *a* alarming

Albdruck *m* = Alpdruck

albern *a* silly □ *adv* in a silly way □ *vi* (*haben*) play the fool

Albtraum *m* = Alptraum

Album *nt* -s,-ben album

Algebra *f* - algebra

Algen *fpl* algae

Algerien /-jən/ *nt* -s Algeria

Alibi *nt* -s,-s alibi

Alimente *pl* maintenance *sg*

Alkohol *m* -s alcohol. a~frei *a* non-alcoholic

Alkohol|iker(in) *m* -s,- (*f* -,-nen) alcoholic. a~isch *a* alcoholic. A~ismus *m* - alcoholism

all *inv pron* all das/mein Geld all the/my money; all dies all this

All *nt* -s universe

alle *pred a* finished, (*fam*) all gone; a~ machen finish up

all|e(r,s) *pron* all; (*jeder*) every; a~es everything, all; (*alle Leute*) everyone; a~e *pl* all; a~es Geld all the money; a~e meine Freunde all my friends; a~e beide both [of them/us]; wir a~e we all;

a~e Tage every day; a~e drei Jahre every three years; in a~er Unschuld in all innocence; ohne a~en Grund without any reason; vor a~em above all; a~es in a~em all in all; a~es aussteigen! all change! a~edem *pron* bei/trotz a~edem with/despite all that

Allee *f* -,-n avenue

Alleg|orie *f* -,-n allegory. a~orisch *a* allegorical

allein *adv* alone; (*nur*) only; a~ stehend single; a~ der Gedanke the mere thought; von a~[e] of its/(*Person*) one's own accord; (*automatisch*) automatically; einzig und a~ solely □ *conj* but. A~erziehende(r) *m/f* single parent. a~ig *a* sole. a~stehend *a* (NEW) a~ stehend, *s.* allein. A~stehende *pl* single people

allemal *adv* every time; (*gewiss*) certainly; ein für a~ (NEW) ein für allemal, *s.* Mal¹

allenfalls *adv* at most; (*eventuell*) possibly

aller|beste(r,s) *a* very best; am a~besten best of all. a~dings *adv* indeed; (*zwar*) admittedly. a~erste(r,s) *a* very first

Allergie *f* -,-n allergy

allergisch *a* allergic (gegen to)

aller|hand *inv a* all sorts of □ *pron* all sorts of things; das ist a~hand! that's quite something! (*empört*) that's a bit much! A~heiligen *nt* -s All Saints Day. a~höchstens *adv* at the very most. a~lei *inv a* all sorts of □ *pron* all sorts of things. a~letzte(r,s) *a* very last. a~liebst *a* enchanting. a~liebste(r,s) *a* favourite □ *adv* am a~liebsten for preference; am a~liebsten haben like best of all. a~meiste(r,s) *a* most □ *adv* am a~meisten most of all. A~seelen *nt* -s All Souls Day. a~seits *adv* generally; guten Morgen a~seits! good morning everyone! a~wenigste(r,s) *a* very least □ *adv* am a~wenigsten least of all

alle|s *s.* alle(r,s). a~samt *adv* all. A~swisser *m* -s,- (*fam*) know-all

allgemein *a* general, *adv* -ly; im A~en (a~en) in general. A~heit *f* - community; (*Öffentlichkeit*) general public

Allheilmittel *nt* panacea

Allianz *f* -,-en alliance

Alligator *m* -s,-en /-'to:rən/ alligator

alliiert *a* allied; die A~en *pl* the Allies

all|jährlich *a* annual, *adv* -ly. a~mächtig *a* almighty; der A~mächtige the Almighty. a~mählich *a* gradual, *adv* -ly

Alltag *m* working day; der A~ (*fig*) everyday life

alltäglich *a* daily; (*gewöhnlich*) everyday; (*Mensch*) ordinary □ *adv* daily

alltags *adv* on weekdays

allzu adv [far] too; a~ bald/oft all too soon/often; a~ sehr/viel far too much; a~ vorsichtig over-cautious. a~bald adv (NEW)a~ bald, s. allzu. a~oft adv (NEW)a~ oft, s. allzu. a~sehr adv (NEW)a~ sehr, s. allzu. a~viel adv (NEW)a~ viel, s. allzu

Alm f -,-en alpine pasture

Almosen ntpl alms

Alpdruck m nightmare

Alpen pl Alps. A~veilchen nt cyclamen

Alphabet nt -[e]s,-e alphabet. a~isch a alphabetical, adv -ly

Alptraum m nightmare

als conj as; (zeitlich) when; (mit Komparativ) than; nichts als nothing but; als ob as if or though; so tun als ob (fam) pretend

also adv & conj so; a~ gut all right then; na a~! there you are!

alt a (älter, ältest) old; (gebraucht) second-hand; (ehemalig) former; alt werden grow old; alles beim A~en (a~en) lassen leave things as they are

Alt m -s (Mus) contralto

Altar m -s,-̈e altar

Alt|e(r) m/f old man/woman; die A~en old people. A~eisen nt scrap iron. A~enheim nt old people's home

Alter nt -s,- age; (Bejahrtheit) old age; im A~ von at the age of; im A~ in old age

älter a older; mein ä~er Bruder my elder brother

altern vi (sein) age

Alternative f -,-n alternative

Alters|grenze f age limit. A~heim nt old people's home. A~rente f old-age pension. a~schwach a old and infirm; ⟨Ding⟩ decrepit

Alter|tum nt -s,-̈er antiquity. a~tümlich a old; (altmodisch) old-fashioned

ältest|e(r,s) a oldest; der ä~e Sohn the eldest son

althergebracht a traditional

altklug a precocious, adv -ly

ältlich a elderly

alt|modisch a old-fashioned □ adv in an old-fashioned way. A~papier nt waste paper. A~stadt f old [part of a] town. A~warenhändler m second-hand dealer. A~weibermärchen nt old wives' tale. A~weibersommer m Indian summer; (Spinnfäden) gossamer

Alufolie f [aluminium] foil

Aluminium nt -s aluminium, (Amer) aluminum

am prep = an dem; am Montag on Monday; am Morgen in the morning; am besten/meisten [the] best/most; am teuersten sein to be the most expensive

Amateur /-'tøːɐ̯/ m -s,-e amateur

Ambition /-'tsjoːn/ f -,-en ambition

Amboss m -es,-e (Amboß m -sses,-sse) anvil

ambulan|t a out-patient ... □ adv a~t behandeln treat as an out-patient. A~z f -,-en out-patients' department; (Krankenwagen) ambulance

Ameise f -,-n ant

amen int, A~ nt -s amen

Amerika nt -s America

Amerika|ner(in) m -s,- (f -,-nen) American. a~isch a American

Ami m -s,-s (fam) Yank

Ammoniak nt -s ammonia

Amnestie f -,-n amnesty

amoralisch a amoral

Ampel f -,-n traffic lights pl; (Blumen-) hanging basket

Amphib|ie /-jə/ f -,-n amphibian. a~isch a amphibious

Amphitheater nt amphitheatre

Amput|ation /-'tsjoːn/ f -,-en amputation. a~ieren vt amputate

Amsel f -,-n blackbird

Amt nt -[e]s,-̈er office; (Aufgabe) task; (Teleph) exchange. a~ieren vi (haben) hold office; a~ierend acting. a~lich a official, adv -ly. A~szeichen nt dialling tone

Amulett nt -[e]s,-e [lucky] charm

amüs|ant a amusing, adv -ly. a~ieren vt amuse; sich a~ieren be amused (über + acc at); (sich vergnügen) enjoy oneself

an prep (+ dat/acc) at; (haftend, berührend) on; (gegen) against; (+ acc) ⟨schicken⟩ to; an der/die Universität at/to university; an dem Tag on that day; es ist an mir it is up to me; an [und für] sich actually; die Arbeit an sich the work as such □ adv (angeschaltet) on; (auf Fahrplan) arriving; an die zwanzig Mark/Leute about twenty marks/people; von heute an from today

analog a analogous; (Computer) analog. A~ie f -,-n analogy

Analphabet m -en,-en illiterate person. A~entum nt -s illiteracy

Analy|se f -,-n analysis. a~sieren vt analyse. A~tiker m -s,- analyst. a~tisch a analytical

Anämie f - anaemia

Ananas f -,-[se] pineapple

Anarch|ie f - anarchy. A~ist m -en,-en anarchist

Anat|omie f - anatomy. a~omisch a anatomical, adv -ly

anbahnen (sich) vr sep develop

Anbau *m* cultivation; *(Gebäude)* extension. a~en *vt sep* build on; *(anpflanzen)* cultivate, grow

anbehalten† *vt sep* keep on

anbei *adv* enclosed

anbeißen† *v sep* □ *vt* take a bite of □ *vi (haben)* ⟨*Fisch:*⟩ bite; *(fig)* take the bait

anbelangen *vt sep* = anbetreffen

anbellen *vt sep* bark at

anbeten *vt sep* worship

Anbetracht *m* in A~ (+ *gen*) in view of

anbetreffen† *vt sep* was mich/das anbetrifft as far as I am/that is concerned

Anbetung *f* - worship

anbiedern (sich) *vr sep* ingratiate oneself (bei with)

anbieten† *vt sep* offer; sich a~ offer (zu to)

anbinden† *vt sep* tie up

Anblick *m* sight. a~en *vt sep* look at

anbrechen† *v sep* □ *vt* start on; break into ⟨*Vorräte*⟩ □ *vi (sein)* begin; ⟨*Tag:*⟩ break; ⟨*Nacht:*⟩ fall

anbrennen† *v sep* □ *vt* light □ *vi (sein)* burn; *(Feuer fangen)* catch fire

anbringen† *vt sep* bring [along]; *(befestigen)* fix

Anbruch *m (fig)* dawn; bei A~ des Tages/der Nacht at daybreak/nightfall

anbrüllen *vt sep (fam)* bellow at

Andacht *f* -,-en reverence; *(Gottesdienst)* prayers *pl*

andächtig *a* reverent, *adv* -ly; *(fig)* rapt, *adv* -ly

andauern *vi sep (haben)* last; *(anhalten)* continue. a~d a persistent, *adv* -ly; *(ständig)* constant, *adv* -ly

Andenken *nt* -s,- memory; *(Souvenir)* souvenir; zum A~ an (+ *acc*) in memory of

ander|e(r,s) *a* other; *(verschieden)* different; *(nächste)* next; ein a~er, eine a~e another □ *pron* der a~e/die a~e the other/others; ein a~er another [one]; *(Person)* someone else; kein a~er no one else; einer nach dem a~en one after the other; alles a~e/nichts a~es everything/nothing else; etwas ganz a~es something quite different; alles a~e als anything but; unter a~em among other things. a~enfalls *adv* otherwise. a~erseits *adv* on the other hand. a~mal *adv* ein a~mal another time

ändern *vt* alter; *(wechseln)* change; sich ä~ change

andernfalls *adv* otherwise

anders *pred a* different; a~ werden change □ *adv* differently; ⟨*riechen, schmecken*⟩ different; *(sonst)* else; jemand/niemand/irgendwo a~ someone/no one/somewhere else

anderseits *adv* on the other hand

anders|herum *adv* the other way round. a~wo *adv (fam)* somewhere else

anderthalb *inv a* one and a half; a~ Stunden an hour and a half

Änderung *f* -,-en alteration; *(Wechsel)* change

anderweitig *a* other □ *adv* otherwise; *(anderswo)* elsewhere

andeut|en *vt sep* indicate; *(anspielen)* hint at. A~ung *f* -,-en indication; hint

andicken *vt sep (Culin)* thicken

Andrang *m* rush (nach for); *(Gedränge)* crush

andre *a & pron* = andere

andrehen *vt sep* turn on; jdm etw a~ *(fam)* palm sth off on s.o.

andrerseits *adv* = andererseits

androhen *vt sep* jdm etw a~ threaten s.o. with sth

aneignen *vt sep* sich (*dat*) a~ appropriate; *(lernen)* learn

aneinander *adv & pref* together; ⟨*denken*⟩ of one another; a~ vorbei past one another; a~ geraten quarrel. a~geraten† *vi sep (sein)* (NEW) a~ geraten, *s.* aneinander

Anekdote *f* -,-n anecdote

anekeln *vt sep* nauseate

anerkannt *a* acknowledged

anerkenn|en† *vt sep* acknowledge, recognize; *(würdigen)* appreciate. a~end *a* approving, *adv* -ly. A~ung *f* - acknowledgement, recognition; appreciation

anfahren† *v sep* □ *vt* deliver; *(streifen)* hit; *(schimpfen)* snap at □ *vi (sein)* start; angefahren kommen drive up

Anfall *m* fit, attack. a~en† *v sep* □ *vt* attack □ *vi (sein)* arise; *(Zinsen:)* accrue

anfällig *a* susceptible (für to); *(zart)* delicate. A~keit *f* - susceptibility (für to)

Anfang *m* -s,-̈e beginning, start; zu od am A~ at the beginning; *(anfangs)* at first. a~en† *vt/i sep (haben)* begin, start; *(tun)* do

Anfäng|er(in) *m* -s,- (*f* -,-nen) beginner. a~lich *a* initial, *adv* -ly

anfangs *adv* at first. A~buchstabe *m* initial letter. A~gehalt *nt* starting salary. A~gründe *mpl* rudiments

anfassen *v sep* □ *vt* touch; *(behandeln)* treat; tackle ⟨*Arbeit*⟩; jdn a~ take s.o.'s hand; sich a~ hold hands; sich weich a~

feel soft □ *vi* (*haben*) mit a~ lend a hand

anfechten† *vt sep* contest; (*fig: beunruhigen*) trouble

anfeinden *vt sep* be hostile to

anfertigen *vt sep* make

anfeuchten *vt sep* moisten

anfeuern *vt sep* spur on

anflehen *vt sep* implore, beg

Anflug *m* (*Aviat*) approach; (*fig: Spur*) trace

anforder|n *vt sep* demand; (*Comm*) order. A~ung *f* demand

Anfrage *f* enquiry. a~n *vi sep* (*haben*) enquire, ask

anfreunden (sich) *vr sep* make friends (mit with); (*miteinander*) become friends

anfügen *vt sep* add

anfühl|en *vt sep* feel; sich weich a~ feel soft

anführ|en *vt sep* lead; (*zitieren*) quote; (*angeben*) give; jdn a~en (*fam*) have s.o. on. A~er *m* leader. A~ungszeichen *ntpl* quotation marks

Angabe *f* statement; (*Anweisung*) instruction; (*Tennis*) service; (*fam: Angeberei*) showing-off; nähere A~n particulars

angeb|en *v sep* □ *vt* state; give (*Namen, Grund*); (*anzeigen*) indicate; set (*Tempo*) □ *vi* (*haben*) (*Tennis*) serve; (*fam: protzen*) show off. A~er(in) *m* -s,- (*f* -,-nen) (*fam*) show-off. A~erei *f* - (*fam*) showing-off

angeblich *a* alleged, *adv* -ly

angeboren *a* innate; (*Med*) congenital

Angebot *nt* offer; (*Auswahl*) range; A~ und Nachfrage supply and demand

angebracht *a* appropriate

angebunden *a* kurz a~ curt

angegriffen *a* worn out; (*Gesundheit*) poor

angeheiratet *a* (*Onkel, Tante*) by marriage

angeheitert *a* (*fam*) tipsy

angehen† *v sep* □ *vi* (*sein*) begin, start; (*Licht, Radio*:) come on; (*anwachsen*) take root; a~ gegen fight □ *vt* attack; tackle (*Arbeit*); (*bitten*) ask (um for); (*betreffen*) concern; das geht dich nichts an it's none of your business. a~d *a* future; (*Künstler*) budding

angehör|en *vi sep* (*haben*) (+ *dat*) belong to. A~ige(r) *m/f* relative; (*Mitglied*) member

Angeklagte(r) *m/f* accused

Angel *f* -,-n fishing-rod; (*Tür-*) hinge

Angelegenheit *f* matter; auswärtige A~en foreign affairs

Angel|haken *m* fish-hook. a~n *vi* (*haben*) fish (nach for); a~n gehen go

fishing □ *vt* (*fangen*) catch. A~rute *f* fishing-rod

angelsächsisch *a* Anglo-Saxon

angemessen *a* commensurate (*dat* with); (*passend*) appropriate, *adv* -ly

angenehm *a* pleasant, *adv* -ly; (*bei Vorstellung*) a~! delighted to meet you!

angenommen *a* (*Kind*) adopted; (*Name*) assumed

angeregt *a* animated, *adv* -ly

angesehen *a* respected; (*Firma*) reputable

angesichts *prep* (+ *gen*) in view of

angespannt *a* intent, *adv* -ly; (*Lage*) tense

Angestellte(r) *m/f* employee

angetan *a* a~ sein von be taken with

angetrunken *a* slightly drunk

angewandt *a* applied

angewiesen *a* dependent (auf + *acc* on); auf sich selbst a~ on one's own

angewöhnen *vt sep* jdm etw a~ get s.o. used to sth; sich (*dat*) etw a~ get into the habit of doing sth

Angewohnheit *f* habit

Angina *f* - tonsillitis

angleichen† *vt sep* adjust (*dat* to)

Angler *m* -s,- angler

anglikanisch *a* Anglican

Anglistik *f* - English [language and literature]

Angorakatze *f* Persian cat

angreif|en *vt sep* attack; tackle (*Arbeit*); (*schädigen*) damage; (*anbrechen*) break into; (*anfassen*) touch. A~er *m* -s,- attacker; (*Pol*) aggressor

angrenzen *vi sep* (*haben*) adjoin (an etw *acc* sth). a~d *a* adjoining

Angriff *m* attack; in A~ nehmen tackle. a~slustig *a* aggressive

Angst *f* -,-e fear; (*Psych*) anxiety; (*Sorge*) worry (um about); A~ haben be afraid (vor + *dat* of); (*sich sorgen*) be worried (um about); jdm A~ machen frighten s.o. □ mir ist a~ I am frightened; I am worried (um about); jdm a~ machen (NEW) jdm A~ machen

ängstigen *vt* frighten; (*Sorge machen*) worry; sich ä~ be frightened; be worried (um about)

ängstlich *a* nervous, *adv* -ly; (*scheu*) timid, *adv* -ly; (*verängstigt*) frightened, scared; (*besorgt*) anxious, *adv* -ly. Ä~keit *f* - nervousness; timidity; anxiety

angstvoll *a* anxious, *adv* -ly; (*verängstigt*) frightened

angucken *vt sep* (*fam*) look at

angurten (sich) *vr sep* fasten one's seat-belt

anhaben† *vt sep* have on; er/es kann mir nichts a~ (*fig*) he/it cannot hurt me

anhalt|en† *v sep* □ *vt* stop; hold ⟨*Atem*⟩; jdn zur Arbeit/Ordnung a~en urge s.o. to work/be tidy □ *vi* (*haben*) stop; (*andauern*) continue. a~end *a* persistent, *adv* -ly; ⟨*Beifall*⟩ prolonged. A~er(in) *m* -s,- (*f* -,-nen) hitchhiker; per A~er fahren hitchhike. A~spunkt *m* clue

anhand *prep* (+ *gen*) with the aid of

Anhang *m* appendix; (*fam: Angehörige*) family

anhängen¹ *vt sep* (*reg*) hang up; (*befestigen*) attach; (*hinzufügen*) add

anhäng|en²† *vi* (*haben*) be a follower (*dat*). A~er *m* -s,- follower; (*Auto*) trailer; (*Schild*) [tie-on] label; (*Schmuck*) pendant; (*Aufhänger*) loop. A~erin *f* -,-nen follower. A~erschaft *f* - following, followers *pl*. a~lich *a* affectionate. A~sel *nt* -s,- appendage

anhäufen *vt sep* pile up; sich a~ pile up, accumulate

anheben† *vt sep* lift; (*erhöhen*) raise

Anhieb *m* auf A~ straight away

Anhöhe *f* hill

anhören *vt sep* listen to; mit a~ overhear; sich gut a~ sound good

animieren *vt* encourage (zu to)

Anis *m* -es aniseed

Anker *m* -s,- anchor; vor A~ gehen drop anchor. a~n *vi* (*haben*) anchor; (*liegen*) be anchored

anketten *vt sep* chain up

Anklage *f* accusation; (*Jur*) charge; (*Ankläger*) prosecution. A~bank *f* dock. a~n *vt sep* accuse (*gen* of); (*Jur*) charge (*gen* with)

Ankläger *m* accuser; (*Jur*) prosecutor

anklammern *vt sep* clip on; peg on the line (*Wäsche*); sich a~ cling (an + *acc* to)

Anklang *m* bei jdm A~ finden meet with s.o.'s approval

ankleben *v sep* □ *vt* stick on □ *vi* (*sein*) stick (an + *dat* to)

Ankleide|kabine *f* changing cubicle; (*zur Anprobe*) fitting-room. a~n *vt sep* dress; sich a~n dress

anklopfen *vi sep* (*haben*) knock

anknipsen *vt sep* (*fam*) switch on

anknüpfen *v sep* □ *vt* tie on; (*fig*) enter into ⟨*Gespräch, Beziehung*⟩ □ *vi* (*haben*) refer (an + *acc* to)

ankommen† *vi sep* (*sein*) arrive; (*sich nähern*) approach; gut a~ arrive safely; (*fig*) go down well (bei with); nicht a~ gegen (*fig*) be no match for; a~ auf (+ *acc*) depend on; es a~ lassen auf (+ *acc*)

risk; das kommt darauf an it [all] depends

ankreuzen *vt sep* mark with a cross

ankündig|en *vt sep* announce. A~ung *f* announcement

Ankunft *f* - arrival

ankurbeln *vt sep* (*fig*) boost

anlächeln *vt sep* smile at

anlachen *vt sep* smile at

Anlage *f* -,-n installation; (*Industrie-*) plant; (*Komplex*) complex; (*Geld-*) investment; (*Plan*) layout; (*Beilage*) enclosure; (*Veranlagung*) aptitude; (*Neigung*) predisposition; [öffentliche] A~n [public] gardens; als A~ enclosed

Anlass *m* -es,⸚e ⟨*Anlaß m* -sses,⸚sse⟩ reason; (*Gelegenheit*) occasion; A~ geben zu give cause for

anlass|en† *vt sep* (*Auto*) start; (*fam*) leave on ⟨*Licht*⟩; keep on ⟨*Mantel*⟩; sich gut/ schlecht a~en start off well/badly. A~er *m* -s,- starter

anlässlich ⟨**anläßlich**⟩ *prep* (+ *gen*) on the occasion of

Anlauf *m* (*Sport*) run-up; (*fig*) attempt. a~en† *v sep* □ *vi* (*sein*) start; (*beschlagen*) mist up; ⟨*Metall:*⟩ tarnish; rot a~en go red; (*erröten*) blush; angelaufen kommen come running up □ *vt* (*Naut*) call at

anlegen *v sep* □ *vt* put (an + *acc* against); put on ⟨*Kleidung, Verband*⟩; lay back ⟨*Ohren*⟩; aim ⟨*Gewehr*⟩; (*investieren*) invest; (*ausgeben*) spend (für on); (*erstellen*) build; (*gestalten*) lay out; draw up ⟨*Liste*⟩; [mit] Hand a~ lend a hand; es darauf a~ (*fig*) aim (zu to); sich a~ mit quarrel with □ *vi* (*haben*) ⟨*Schiff:*⟩ moor; a~ auf (+ *acc*) aim at

anlehnen *vt sep* lean (an + *acc* against); sich a~ lean (an + *acc* on); eine Tür angelehnt lassen leave a door ajar

Anleihe *f* -,-n loan

anleinen *vt sep* put on a lead

anleit|en *vt sep* instruct. A~ung *f* instructions *pl*

anlernen *vt sep* train

Anliegen *nt* -s,- request; (*Wunsch*) desire

anlieg|en† *vi sep* (*haben*) ⟨*eng*⟩ a~en fit closely; ⟨*eng*⟩ a~end close-fitting. A~er *mpl* residents; 'A~er frei' 'access for residents only'

anlocken *vt sep* attract

anlügen† *vt sep* lie to

anmachen *vt sep* (*fam*) fix; (*anschalten*) turn on; (*anzünden*) light; (*Culin*) dress ⟨*Salat*⟩

anmalen *vt sep* paint

Anmarsch *m* (*Mil*) approach

anmaß|en vt sep sich (dat) a~en presume (zu to); sich (dat) ein Recht a~en claim a right. a~end a presumptuous, adv -ly; (arrogant) arrogant, adv -ly. A~ung f - presumption; arrogance

anmeld|en vt sep announce; (Admin) register; sich a~en say that one is coming; (Admin) register; (Sch) enrol; (im Hotel) check in; (beim Arzt) make an appointment. A~ung f announcement; (Admin) registration; (Sch) enrolment; (Termin) appointment

anmerk|en vt sep mark; sich (dat) etw a~en lassen show sth. A~ung f -,-en note

Anmut f - grace; (Charme) charm

anmuten vt sep es mutet mich seltsam/ vertraut an it seems odd/familiar to me

anmutig a graceful, adv -ly; (lieblich) charming, adv -ly

annähen vt sep sew on

annäher|nd a approximate, adv -ly. A~ungsversuche mpl advances

Annahme f -,-n acceptance; (Adoption) adoption; (Vermutung) assumption

annehm|bar a acceptable. a~en† vt sep accept; (adoptieren) adopt; acquire (Gewohnheit); (sich zulegen, vermuten) assume; sich a~en (+ gen) take care of; angenommen, dass assuming that. A~lichkeiten fpl comforts

annektieren vt annex

Anno adv A~ 1920 in the year 1920

Annonce /a'nõ:sə/ f -,-n advertisement. a~cieren /-'si:-/ vt/i (haben) advertise

annullieren vt annul; cancel (Flug)

anöden vt sep (fam) bore

Anomalie f -,-n anomaly

anonym a anonymous, adv -ly

Anorak m -s,-s anorak

anordn|en vt sep arrange; (befehlen) order. A~ung f arrangement; order

anorganisch a inorganic

anormal a abnormal

anpacken v sep □ vt grasp; tackle (Arbeit, Problem) □ vi (haben) mit a~en lend a hand

anpass|en vt sep try on; (angleichen) adapt (dat to); sich a~ adapt (dat to). A~ung f - adaptation. a~ungsfähig a adaptable. A~ungsfähigkeit f adaptability

Anpfiff m (Sport) kick-off; (fam: Rüge) reprimand

anpflanzen vt sep plant; (anbauen) grow

Anprall m -[e]s impact. a~en vi sep (sein) strike (an etw acc sth)

anprangern vt sep denounce

anpreisen† vt sep commend

Anprob|e f fitting. a~ieren vt sep try on

anrechnen vt sep count (als as); (berechnen) charge for; (verrechnen) allow (Summe); ich rechne ihm seine Hilfe hoch an I very much appreciate his help

Anrecht nt right (auf + acc to)

Anrede f [form of] address. a~n vt sep address; (ansprechen) speak to

anreg|en vt sep stimulate; (ermuntern) encourage (zu to); (vorschlagen) suggest. a~end a stimulating. A~ung f stimulation; (Vorschlag) suggestion

anreichern vt sep enrich

Anreise f journey; (Ankunft) arrival. a~n vi sep (sein) arrive

Anreiz m incentive

anrempeln vt sep jostle

Anrichte f -,-n sideboard. a~n vt sep (Culin) prepare; (garnieren) garnish (mit with); (verursachen) cause

anrüchig a disreputable

Anruf m call. A~beantworter m -s,- answering machine. a~en† v sep □ vt call to; (bitten) call on (um for); (Teleph) ring □ vi (haben) ring (bei jdm s.o.)

anrühren vt sep touch; (verrühren) mix

ans prep = an das

Ansage f announcement. a~n vt sep announce; sich a~n say that one is coming. A~r(in) m -s,- (f -,-nen) announcer

ansamm|eln vt sep collect; (anhäufen) accumulate; sich a~eln collect; (sich häufen) accumulate; (Leute:) gather. A~lung f collection; (Menschen-) crowd

ansässig a resident

Ansatz m beginning; (Haar-) hairline; (Versuch) attempt; (Techn) extension

anschaff|en vt sep [sich dat] etw a~en acquire/(kaufen) buy sth. A~ung f -,-en acquisition; (Kauf) purchase

anschalten vt sep switch on

anschau|en vt sep look at. a~lich a vivid, adv -ly. A~ung f -,-en (fig) view

Anschein m appearance; den A~ haben seem. a~end adv apparently

anschicken (sich) vr sep be about (zu to)

anschicken (sich) vr sep be about (zu to)

anschirren vt sep harness

Anschlag m notice; (Vor-) estimate; (Überfall) attack (auf + acc on); (Mus) touch; (Techn) stop; 240 A~e in der Minute ≈ 50 words per minute. A~brett nt notice board. a~en† v sep □ vt put up (Aushang); strike (Note, Taste); cast on (Masche); (beschädigen) chip □ vi (haben) strike/(stoßen) knock (an + acc against); (Hund:) bark; (wirken) be effective □ vi (sein) knock (an + acc against); mit dem Kopf a~en hit one's head. A~zettel m notice

anschließen† *v sep* □ *vt* connect (an + *acc* to); (*zufügen*) add; sich a~ an (+ *acc*) (*anstoßen*) adjoin; (*folgen*) follow; (*sich anfreunden*) become friendly with; sich jdm a~ join s.o. □ *vi* (*haben*) a~ an (+ *acc*) adjoin; (*folgen*) follow. a~d *a* adjoining; (*zeitlich*) following □ *adv* afterwards; a~d an (+ *acc*) after

Anschluss (Anschluß) *m* connection; (*Kontakt*) contact; A~ finden make friends; im A~ an (+ *acc*) after

anschmieg|en (sich) *vr sep* snuggle up/ (*Kleid:*) cling (an + *acc* to). a~sam *a* affectionate

anschmieren *vt sep* smear; (*fam: täuschen*) cheat

anschnallen *vt sep* strap on; sich a~ fasten one's seat-belt

anschneiden† *vt sep* cut into; broach (*Thema*)

anschreiben† *vt sep* write (an + *acc* on); (*Comm*) put on s.o.'s account; (*sich wenden*) write to; bei jdm gut/schlecht angeschrieben sein be in s.o.'s good/bad books

anschreien† *vt sep* shout at

Anschrift *f* address

anschuldig|en *vt sep* accuse. A~ung *f* -,-en accusation

anschwellen† *vi sep* (*sein*) swell

anschwemmen *vt sep* wash up

anschwindeln *vt sep* (*fam*) lie to

ansehen† *vt sep* look at; (*einschätzen*) regard (als as); [sich *dat*]etw a~ look at sth; (*TV*) watch sth. A~ *nt* -s respect; (*Ruf*) reputation

ansehnlich *a* considerable

ansetzen *v sep* □ *vt* join (an + *acc* to); (*festsetzen*) fix; (*veranschlagen*) estimate; Rost a~ get rusty; sich a~ form □ *vi* (*haben*) (*anbrennen*) burn; zum Sprung a~ get ready to jump

Ansicht *f* view; meiner A~ nach in my view; zur A~ (*Comm*) on approval. A~s[post]karte *f* picture postcard. A~ssache *f* matter of opinion

ansiedeln (sich) *vr sep* settle

ansonsten *adv* apart from that

anspannen *vt sep* hitch up; (*anstrengen*) strain; tense (*Muskel*)

anspiel|en *vi sep* (*haben*) a~en auf (+ *acc*) allude to; (*versteckt*) hint at. A~ung *f* -,-en allusion; hint

Anspitzer *m* -s,- pencil-sharpener

Ansporn *m* (*fig*) incentive. a~en *vt sep* spur on

Ansprache *f* address

ansprechen† *v sep* □ *vt* speak to; (*fig*) appeal to □ *vi* (*haben*) respond (auf + *acc* to). a~d *a* attractive

anspringen† *v sep* □ *vt* jump at □ *vi* (*sein*) (*Auto*) start

Anspruch *m* claim/(*Recht*) right (auf + *acc* to); A~ haben be entitled (auf + *acc* to); in A~ nehmen make use of; (*erfordern*) demand; take up (*Zeit*); occupy (*Person*); hohe A~e stellen be very demanding. a~slos *a* undemanding; (*bescheiden*) unpretentious. a~svoll *a* demanding; (*kritisch*) discriminating; (*vornehm*) up-market

anspucken *vt sep* spit at

anstacheln *vt sep* (*fig*) spur on

Anstalt *f* -,-en institution; A~en/keine A~en machen prepare/make no move (zu to)

Anstand *m* decency; (*Benehmen*) [good] manners *pl*

anständig *a* decent, *adv* -ly; (*ehrbar*) respectable, *adv* -bly; (*fam: beträchtlich*) considerable, *adv* -bly; (*richtig*) proper, *adv* -ly

Anstands|dame *f* chaperon. a~los *adv* without any trouble; (*bedenkenlos*) without hesitation

anstarren *vt sep* stare at

anstatt *conj & prep* (+ *gen*) instead of; a~ zu arbeiten instead of working

anstechen† *vt sep* tap (*Fass*)

ansteck|en *v sep* □ *vt* pin (an + *acc* to/on); put on (*Ring*); (*anzünden*) light; (*in Brand stecken*) set fire to; (*Med*) infect; sich a~en catch an infection (bei from) □ *vi* (*haben*) be infectious. a~end *a* infectious, (*fam*) catching. A~ung *f* -,-en infection

anstehen† *vi sep* (*haben*) queue, (*Amer*) stand in line

ansteigen† *vi sep* (*sein*) climb; (*Gelände, Preise:*) rise

anstelle *prep* (+ *gen*) instead of

anstell|en *vt sep* put, stand (an + *acc* against); (*einstellen*) employ; (*anschalten*) turn on; (*tun*) do; sich a~en queue [up], (*Amer*) stand in line; (*sich haben*) make a fuss. A~ung *f* employment; (*Stelle*) job

Anstieg *m* -[e]s,-e climb; (*fig*) rise

anstift|en *vt sep* cause; (*anzetteln*) instigate; jdn a~n put s.o. up (zu to). A~r *m* instigator

Anstoß *m* (*Anregung*) impetus; (*Stoß*) knock; (*Fußball*) kick-off; A~ erregen/ nehmen give/take offence (an + *dat* at). a~en† *v sep* □ *vt* knock; (*mit dem Ellbogen*) nudge □ *vi* (*sein*) knock (an + *acc* against) □ *vi* (*haben*) adjoin (an etw *acc* sth); [mit den Gläsern] a~en clink glasses; a~en auf (+ acc) drink to; mit der Zunge a~en lisp

anstößig a offensive, adv -ly

anstrahlen vt sep floodlight; (anlachen) beam at

anstreiche|n† vt sep paint; (anmerken) mark. A~r m -s,- painter

anstreng|en vt sep strain; (ermüden) tire; sich a~en exert oneself; (sich bemühen) make an effort (zu to). a~end a strenuous; (ermüdend) tiring. A~ung f -,-en strain; (Mühe) effort

Anstrich m coat [of paint]

Ansturm m rush; (Mil) assault

Ansuchen nt -s,- request

Antagonismus m - antagonism

Antarktis f - Antarctic

Anteil m share; A~ nehmen take an interest (an + dat in); (mitfühlen) sympathize. A~nahme f - interest (an + dat in); (Mitgefühl) sympathy

Antenne f -,-n aerial

Anthologie f -,-n anthology

Anthropologie f - anthropology

Anti|alkoholiker m teetotaller. A~biotikum nt -s,-ka antibiotic

antik a antique. A~e f - [classical] antiquity

Antikörper m antibody

Antilope f -,-n antelope

Antipathie f - antipathy

Anti|quariat nt -[e]s,-e antiquarian bookshop. a~quarisch a & adv secondhand

Antiquitäten fpl antiques. A~händler m antique dealer

Antisemitismus m - anti-Semitism

Antisept|ikum nt -s,-ka antiseptic. a~isch a antiseptic

Antrag m -[e]s,-e proposal; (Pol) motion; (Gesuch) application. A~steller m -s,- applicant

antreffen† vt sep find

antreiben† v sep □ vt urge on; (Techn) drive; (anschwemmen) wash up □ vi (sein) be washed up

antreten† v sep □ vt start; take up ⟨Amt⟩ □ vi (sein) line up; (Mil) fall in

Antrieb m urge; (Techn) drive; aus eigenem A~ of one's own accord

antrinken† vt sep sich (dat) einen Rausch a~ get drunk; sich (dat) Mut a~ give oneself Dutch courage

Antritt m start; bei A~ eines Amtes when taking office. A~srede f inaugural address

antun† vt sep jdm etw a~ do sth to s.o.; sich (dat) etwas a~ take one's own life; es jdm angetan haben appeal to s.o.

Antwort f -,-en answer, reply (auf + acc to). a~en vt/i (haben) answer (jdm s.o.)

anvertrauen vt sep entrust/(mitteilen) confide (jdm to s.o.); sich jdm a~ confide in s.o.

anwachsen† vi sep (sein) take root; (zunehmen) grow

Anwalt m -[e]s,-e, **Anwältin** f -,-nen lawyer; (vor Gericht) counsel

Anwandlung f -,-en fit (von of)

Anwärter(in) m(f) candidate

anweis|en† vt sep assign (dat to); (beauftragen) instruct. A~ung f instruction; (Geld-) money order

anwend|en† vt sep apply (auf + acc to); (gebrauchen) use. A~ung f application; use

anwerben† vt sep recruit

Anwesen nt -s,- property

anwesen|d a present (bei at); die A~den those present. A~heit f - presence

anwidern vt sep disgust

Anwohner mpl residents

Anzahl f number

anzahl|en vt sep pay a deposit on; pay on account ⟨Summe⟩. A~ung f deposit

anzapfen vt sep tap

Anzeichen nt sign

Anzeige f -,-n announcement; (Inserat) advertisement; A~ erstatten gegen jdn report s.o. to the police. a~n vt sep announce; (inserieren) advertise; (melden) report [to the police]; (angeben) indicate, show. A~r m indicator

anzieh|en† vt sep □ vt attract; (festziehen) tighten; put on ⟨Kleider, Bremse⟩; draw up ⟨Beine⟩; (ankleiden) dress; sich a~en get dressed; was soll ich a~en? what shall I wear? gut angezogen well-dressed □ vi (haben) start pulling; ⟨Preise:⟩ go up. a~end a attractive. A~ung f -attraction. A~ungskraft f attraction; (Phys) gravity

Anzug m suit; im A~ sein (fig) be imminent

anzüglich a suggestive; ⟨Bemerkung⟩ personal

anzünden vt sep light; (in Brand stecken) set fire to

anzweifeln vt sep question

apart a striking, adv -ly

Apathie f - apathy

apathisch a apathetic, adv -ally

Aperitif m -s,-s aperitif

Apfel m -s,- apple. A~mus nt apple purée

Apfelsine f -,-n orange

Apostel m -s,- apostle

Apostroph m -s,-e apostrophe

Apothek|e f -,-n pharmacy. A~er(in) m -s,- (f -,-nen) pharmacist, [dispensing] chemist

Apparat m -[e]s,-e device; (Phot) camera; (Radio, TV) set; (Teleph) telephone; am A~! speaking! A~ur f -,-en apparatus

Appell m -s,-e appeal; (Mil) roll-call. a~ieren vi (haben) appeal (an + acc to)

Appetit m -s appetite; guten A~! enjoy your meal! a~lich a appetizing, adv -ly

applaudieren vi (haben) applaud

Applaus m -es applause

Aprikose f -,-n apricot

April m -[s] April; in den A~ schicken (fam) make an April fool of

Aquarell nt -s,-e water-colour

Aquarium nt -s,-ien aquarium

Äquator m -s equator

Ära f -era

Araber(in) m -s,- (f -,-nen) Arab

arabisch a Arab; (Geog) Arabian; ⟨Ziffer⟩ Arabic

Arbeit f -,-en work; (Anstellung) employment, job; (Aufgabe) task; (Sch) [written] test; (Abhandlung) treatise; (Qualität) workmanship; bei der A~ at work; zur A~ gehen go to work; an die A~ gehen, sich an die A~ machen set to work; sich (dat) viel A~ machen go to a lot of trouble. a~en v sep a vi (haben) work (an + dat on) ◻ vt make; einen Anzug a~en lassen have a suit made; sich durch etw a~en work one's way through sth. A~er(in) m -s,- (f -,-nen) worker; (Land-, Hilfs-) labourer. A~erklasse f working class

Arbeit|geber m -s,- employer. A~nehmer m -s,- employee. a~sam a industrious

Arbeits|amt nt employment exchange. A~erlaubnis, A~genehmigung f work permit. A~kraft f worker; Mangel an A~kräften shortage of labour. a~los a unemployed; a~los sein be out of work. A~lose(r) m/f unemployed person; die A~losen the unemployed pl. A~losenunterstützung f unemployment benefit. A~losigkeit f - unemployment

arbeitsparend a labour-saving

Arbeits|platz m job. A~tag m working day. A~zimmer nt study

Archäo|loge m -n,-n archaeologist. A~logie f - archaeology. a~logisch a archaeological

Arche f - die A~ Noah Noah's Ark

Architekt|in m -en,-en (f -,-nen) architect. a~tonisch a architectural. A~tur f - architecture

Archiv nt -s,-e archives pl

Arena f -,-nen arena

arg a (ärger, ärgst) bad; (groß) terrible; sein ärgster Feind his worst enemy ◻ adv badly; (sehr) terribly

Argentin|ien /-jən/ nt -s Argentina. a~isch a Argentinian

Ärger m -s annoyance; (Unannehmlichkeit) trouble. ä~lich a annoyed; (leidig) annoying; ä~lich sein be annoyed. ä~n vt annoy; (necken) tease; sich ä~n get annoyed (über jdn/etw with s.o./about sth). Ä~nis nt -ses, -se annoyance; öffentliches Ä~nis public nuisance

Arglist f - malice. a~ig a malicious, adv -ly

arglos a unsuspecting; (unschuldig) innocent, adv -ly

Argument nt -[e]s,-e argument. a~ieren vi (haben) argue (dass that)

Argwohn m -s suspicion

argwöhn|en vt suspect. a~isch a suspicious, adv -ly

Arie /'a:rjə/ f -,-n aria

Aristo|krat m -en,-en aristocrat. A~kratie f - aristocracy. a~kratisch a aristocratic

Arithmetik f - arithmetic

Arkt|is f - Arctic. a~isch a Arctic

arm a (ärmer, ärmst) poor; Arm und Reich (arm und reich) rich and poor

Arm m -[e]s,-e arm; jdn auf den Arm nehmen (fam) pull s.o.'s leg

Armaturenbrett nt instrument panel; (Auto) dashboard

Armband nt (pl -bänder) bracelet; (Uhr-) watch-strap. A~uhr f wrist-watch

Arm|e(r) m/f poor man/woman; die A~en the poor pl; du A~e(r) od Ärmste! you poor thing!

Armee f -,-n army

Ärmel m -s,- sleeve. Ä~kanal m [English] Channel. ä~los a sleeveless

Arm|lehne f arm. A~leuchter m candelabra

ärmlich a poor, adv -ly; (elend) miserable, adv -bly

armselig a miserable, adv -bly

Armut f - poverty

Arom|a nt -s,-men &-mas aroma; (Culin) essence. a~atisch a aromatic

Arran|gement /arãʒə'mã:/ nt -s,-s arrangement. a~gieren /-'ʒi:rən/ vt arrange; sich a~gieren come to an arrangement

Arrest m -[e]s (Mil) detention

arrogan|t a arrogant, adv -ly. A~z f - arrogance

Arsch m -[e]s,-̈e (vulg) arse

Arsen nt -s arsenic

Art f -,-en manner; (Weise) way; (Natur) nature; (Sorte) kind; (Biol) species; auf diese Art in this way. a∼en vi (sein) a∼en nach take after

Arterie /-jə/ f -,-n artery

Arthritis f - arthritis

artig a well-behaved; (höflich) polite, adv -ly; sei a∼! be good!

Artikel m -s,- article

Artillerie f - artillery

Artischocke f -,-n artichoke

Artist(in) m -en,-en (f -,-nen) [circus] artiste

Arznei f -,-en medicine. A∼mittel nt drug

Arzt m -es,-̈e doctor

Ärztin f -,-nen [woman] doctor. ä∼lich a medical

As nt -ses,-se (NEW) Ass

Asbest m -[e]s asbestos

Asche f - ash. A∼nbecher m ashtray. A∼rmittwoch m Ash Wednesday

Asiat(in) m -en,-en (f -,-nen) Asian. a∼isch a Asian

Asien /'a:zjən/ nt -s Asia

asozial a antisocial

Aspekt m -[e]s aspect

Asphalt m -[e]s asphalt. a∼ieren vt asphalt

Ass nt -es,-̈e ace

Assistent(in) m -en,-en (f -,-nen) assistant

Ast m -[e]s,-̈e branch

ästhetisch a aesthetic

Asthma nt -s asthma. a∼tisch a asthmatic

Astro|loge m -n,-n astrologer. A∼logie f - astrology. A∼naut m -en,-en astronaut. A∼nom m -en,-en astronomer. A∼nomie f - astronomy. a∼nomisch a astronomical

Asyl nt -s,-e home; (Pol) asylum. A∼ant m -en,-en asylum-seeker

Atelier /-'lje:/ nt -s,-s studio

Atem m -s breath; tief A∼ holen take a deep breath. a∼beraubend a breath-taking. a∼los a breathless, adv -ly. A∼pause f breather. A∼zug m breath

Atheist m -en,-en atheist

Äther m -s ether

Äthiopien /-jən/ nt -s Ethiopia

Athlet|(in) m -en,-en (f -,-nen) athlete. a∼isch a athletic

Atlantik m -s Atlantic. a∼isch a Atlantic; der A∼ische Ozean the Atlantic Ocean

Atlas m -lasses,-lanten atlas

atmen vt/i (haben) breathe

Atmosphär|e f -,-n atmosphere. a∼isch a atmospheric

Atmung f - breathing

Atom nt -s,-e atom. a∼ar a atomic. A∼bombe f atom bomb. A∼krieg m nuclear war

Attentat nt -[e]s,-e assassination attempt. A∼täter m [would-be] assassin

Attest nt -[e]s,-e certificate

Attrak|tion /-'tsjo:n/ f -,-en attraction. a∼tiv a attractive, adv -ly

Attrappe f -,-n dummy

Attribut nt -[e]s,-e attribute. a∼iv a attributive, adv -ly

ätzen vt corrode; (Med) cauterize; (Kunst) etch. ä∼d a corrosive; (Spott) caustic

au int ouch; au fein! oh good!

Aubergine /ober'ʒi:nə/ f -,-n aubergine

auch adv & conj also, too; (außerdem) what's more; (selbst) even; a∼ wenn even if; ich mag ihn—ich a∼ I like him—so do I; ich bin nicht müde—ich a∼ nicht I'm not tired—nor or neither am I; sie weiß es a∼ nicht she doesn't know either; wer/wie/was a∼ immer whoever/however/whatever; ist das a∼ wahr? is that really true?

Audienz f -,-en audience

audiovisuell a audiovisual

Auditorium nt -s,-ien (Univ) lecture hall

auf prep (+ dat) on; (+ acc) on [to]; (bis) until, till; (Proportion) to; auf Deutsch/ Englisch in German/English; auf einer/ eine Party at/to a party; auf der Straße in the street; auf seinem Zimmer in one's room; auf einem Ohr taub deaf in one ear; auf einen Stuhl steigen climb on [to] a chair; auf die Toilette gehen go to the toilet; auf ein paar Tage verreisen go away for a few days; auf 10 Kilometer zu sehen visible for 10 kilometres □ adv open; (in die Höhe) up; auf sein be open; (Person:) be up; auf und ab up and down; sich auf und davon machen make off; Tür auf! open the door!

aufarbeiten vt sep do up; Rückstände a∼ clear arrears [of work]

aufatmen vi sep (haben) heave a sigh of relief

aufbahren vt sep lay out

Aufbau m construction; (Struktur) structure. a∼en v sep □ vt construct, build; (errichten) erect; (schaffen) build up; (arrangieren) arrange; wieder a∼en reconstruct; sich a∼en (fig) be based (auf + dat on) □ vi (haben) be based (auf + dat on)

aufbäumen (sich) vr sep rear [up]; (fig) rebel

aufbauschen vt sep puff out; (fig) exaggerate

aufbehalten† vt sep keep on

aufbekommen† vt sep get open; (Sch) be given [as homework]

aufbessern vt sep improve; (erhöhen) increase

aufbewahr|en vt sep keep; (lagern) store. A~ung f - safe keeping; storage; (Gepäck-) left-luggage office

aufbieten† vt sep mobilize; (fig) summon up

aufblas|bar a inflatable. a~en† vt sep inflate; sich a~en (fig) give oneself airs

aufbleiben† vi sep (sein) stay open; (Person.) stay up

aufblenden vt/i sep (haben) (Auto) switch to full beam

aufblicken vi sep (haben) look up (zu at/(fig) to)

aufblühen vi sep (sein) flower; (Knospe:) open

aufbocken vt sep jack up

aufbraten† vt sep fry up

aufbrauchen vt sep use up

aufbrausen vi sep (sein) (fig) flare up. a~d a quick-tempered

aufbrechen† v sep ▫ vt break open ▫ vi (sein) (Knospe:) open; (sich aufmachen) set out, start

aufbringen† vt sep raise (Geld); find (Kraft); (wütend machen) infuriate

Aufbruch m start, departure

aufbrühen vt sep make (Tee)

aufbürden vt sep jdm etw a~ (fig) burden s.o. with sth

aufdecken vt sep (auflegen) put on; (abdecken) uncover; (fig) expose

aufdrängen vt sep force (dat on); sich jdm a~ force one's company on s.o.

aufdrehen vt sep turn on

aufdringlich a persistent

aufeinander adv one on top of the other; (schießen) at each other; (warten) for each other; a~ folgen follow one another; a~folgend successive; (Tage) consecutive. a~folgen (NEW)a~ folgen, s. aufeinander. a~folgend a (NEW)a~folgend, s. aufeinander

Aufenthalt m stay; 10 Minuten A~ haben (Zug:) stop for 10 minutes. A~serlaubnis, A~sgenehmigung f residence permit. A~sraum m recreation room; (im Hotel) lounge

auferlegen vt sep impose (dat on)

auferstehlen† vi sep (sein) rise from the dead. A~ung f - resurrection

aufessen† vt sep eat up

auffahr|en† vi sep (sein) drive up; (aufprallen) crash, run (auf + acc into); (aufschrecken) start up; (aufbrausen) flare up. A~t f drive; (Autobahn-) access road, slip road; (Bergfahrt) ascent

auffallen† vi sep (sein) be conspicuous; unangenehm a~ make a bad impression; jdm a~ strike s.o. a~d a striking, adv -ly

auffällig a conspicuous, adv -ly; (grell) gaudy, adv -ily

auffangen† vt sep catch; pick up (Funkspruch)

auffass|en vt sep understand; (deuten) take; falsch a~en misunderstand. A~ung f understanding; (Ansicht) view. A~ungsgabe f grasp

aufforder|n vt sep ask; (einladen) invite; jdn zum Tanz a~n ask s.o. to dance. A~ung f request; invitation

auffrischen v sep ▫ vt freshen up; revive (Erinnerung); seine Englischkenntnisse a~ brush up one's English

aufführ|en vt sep perform; (angeben) list; sich a~en behave. A~ung f performance

auffüllen vt sep fill up; [wieder] a~ replenish

Aufgabe f task; (Rechen-) problem; (Verzicht) giving up; A~n (Sch) homework sg

Aufgang m way up; (Treppe) stairs pl; (Astr) rise

aufgeben† v sep ▫ vt give up; post (Brief); send (Telegramm); place (Bestellung); register (Gepäck); put in the paper (Annonce); jdm eine Aufgabe/ein Rätsel a~ set s.o. a task/a riddle; jdm Suppe a~ serve s.o. with soup ▫ vi (haben) give up

aufgeblasen a (fig) conceited

Aufgebot nt contingent (an + dat of); (Relig) banns pl; unter A~ aller Kräfte with all one's strength

aufgebracht a (fam) angry

aufgedunsen a bloated

aufgehen† vi sep (sein) open; (sich lösen) come undone; (Teig, Sonne:) rise; (Saat:) come up; (Math) come out exactly; in Flammen a~ go up in flames; in etw (dat) a~ (fig) be wrapped up in sth; ihm ging auf (fam) he realized (dass that)

aufgelegt a a~ sein zu be in the mood for; gut/schlecht a~ sein be in a good/bad mood

aufgelöst a (fig) distraught; in Tränen a~ in floods of tears

aufgeregt a excited, adv -ly; (erregt) agitated, adv -ly

aufgeschlossen a (fig) openminded

aufgesprungen a chapped

aufgeweckt *a* (*fig*) bright

aufgießen† *vt sep* (*haben*) pour on; (*aufbrühen*) make 〈*Tee*〉

aufgreifen† *vt sep* pick up; take up 〈*Vorschlag, Thema*〉

aufgrund *prep* (+ *gen*) on the strength of

Aufguss 〈*Aufguß*〉 *m* infusion

aufhaben† *v sep* □ *vt* have on; den Mund a∼ have one's mouth open; viel a∼ (*Sch*) have a lot of homework □ *vi* (*haben*) be open

aufhalsen *vt sep* (*fam*) saddle with

aufhalten† *vt sep* hold up; (*anhalten*) stop; (*abhalten*) keep, detain; (*offen halten*) hold open; hold out 〈*Hand*〉; sich a∼ stay; (*sich befassen*) spend one's time (mit on)

aufhängen *vt/i sep* (*haben*) hang up; (*henken*) hang; sich a∼en hang oneself. A∼er *m* -s,- loop. A∼ung *f* - (*Auto*) suspension

aufheben† *vt sep* pick up; (*hochheben*) raise; (*aufbewahren*) keep; (*beenden*) end; (*rückgängig machen*) lift; (*abschaffen*) abolish; (*Jur*) quash 〈*Urteil*〉; repeal 〈*Gesetz*〉; (*ausgleichen*) cancel out; sich a∼ cancel each other out; gut aufgehoben sein be well looked after. A∼ *nt* -s viel A∼s machen make a great fuss (von about)

aufheitern *vt sep* cheer up; sich a∼ 〈*Wetter:*〉 brighten up

aufhellen *vt sep* lighten; sich a∼ 〈*Himmel:*〉 brighten

aufhetzen *vt sep* incite

aufholen *v sep* □ *vt* make up □ *vi* (*haben*) catch up; (*zeitlich*) make up time

aufhorchen *vi sep* (*haben*) prick up one's ears

aufhören *vi sep* (*haben*) stop; mit der Arbeit a∼, a∼ zu arbeiten stop working

aufklappen *vt/i sep* (*sein*) open

aufklären *vt sep* solve; jdn a∼en enlighten s.o.; (*sexuell*) tell s.o. the facts of life; sich a∼en be solved; 〈*Wetter:*〉 clear up. A∼ung *f* solution; enlightenment; (*Mil*) reconnaissance; sexuelle A∼ung *f* sex education

aufkleben *vt sep* stick on. A∼er *m* -s,- sticker

aufknöpfen *vt sep* unbutton

aufkochen *v sep* □ *vt* bring to the boil □ *vi* (*sein*) come to the boil

aufkommen† *vi sep* (*sein*) start; 〈*Wind:*〉 spring up; 〈*Mode:*〉 come in; a∼ für pay for

aufkrempeln *vt sep* roll up

aufladen† *vt sep* load; (*Electr*) charge

Auflage *f* impression; (*Ausgabe*) edition; (*Zeitungs-*) circulation; (*Bedingung*) condition; (*Überzug*) coating

auflassen† *vt sep* leave open; leave on 〈*Hut*〉

auflauern *vi sep* (*haben*) jdm a∼ lie in wait for s.o.

Auflauf *m* crowd; (*Culin*) ≈ soufflé. a∼en† *vi sep* (*sein*) 〈*Naut*〉 run aground

auflegen *v sep* □ *vt* apply (auf + *acc* to); put down 〈*Hörer*〉; neu a∼ reprint □ *vi* (*haben*) ring off

auflehnen (sich) *vr sep* (*fig*) rebel. A∼ung *f* - rebellion

auflesen† *vt sep* pick up

aufleuchten *vi sep* (*haben*) light up

aufliegen† *vt sep* (*haben*) rest (auf + *dat* on)

auflisten *vt sep* list

auflockern *vt sep* break up; (*entspannen*) relax; (*fig*) liven up

auflös|en *vt sep* dissolve; close 〈*Konto*〉; sich a∼en dissolve; 〈*Nebel:*〉 clear. A∼ung dissolution; (*Lösung*) solution

aufmach|en *v sep* □ *vt* open; (*lösen*) undo; sich a∼en set out (nach for); (*sich schminken*) make oneself up □ *vi* (*haben*) open; jdm a∼en open the door to s.o. A∼ung *f* -,-en get-up; (*Comm*) presentation

aufmerksam *a* attentive, *adv* -ly; a∼ werden auf (+ *acc*) notice; jdn a∼ machen auf (+ *acc*) draw s.o.'s attention to. A∼keit *f* -,-en attention; (*Höflichkeit*) courtesy

aufmucken *vi sep* (*haben*) rebel

aufmuntern *vt sep* cheer up

Aufnahme *f* -,-n acceptance; (*Empfang*) reception; (in Klub, Krankenhaus) admission; (*Einbeziehung*) inclusion; (*Beginn*) start; (*Foto*) photograph; (*Film-*) shot; (*Mus*) recording; (*Band-*) tape recording. a∼fähig *a* receptive. A∼prüfung *f* entrance examination

aufnehmen† *vt sep* pick up; (*absorbieren*) absorb; take 〈*Nahrung, Foto*〉; (*fassen*) hold; (*annehmen*) accept; (*leihen*) borrow; (*empfangen*) receive; (in Klub, Krankenhaus) admit; (*beherbergen, geistig erfassen*) take in; (*einbeziehen*) include; (*beginnen*) take up; (*niederschreiben*) take down; (*filmen*) film, shoot; (*Mus*) record; auf Band a∼ tape[-record]; etw gelassen a∼ take sth calmly; es a∼ können mit (*fig*) be a match for

aufopfer|n *vt sep* sacrifice; sich a∼n sacrifice oneself. a∼nd *a* devoted, *adv* -ly. A∼ung *f* self-sacrifice

aufpassen *vi sep* (*haben*) pay attention; (*sich vorsehen*) take care; a∼ auf (+ *acc*) look after

aufpflanzen (sich) *vr sep* (*fam*) plant oneself

aufplatzen *vi sep* (sein) split open

aufplustern (sich) *vr sep* ⟨*Vogel:*⟩ ruffle up its feathers

Aufprall *m* -[e]s impact. a~en *vi sep* (sein) a~en auf (+ *acc*) hit

aufpumpen *vt sep* pump up, inflate

aufputsch|en *vt sep* incite; sich a~en take stimulants. A~mittel *nt* stimulant

aufquellen† *vi sep* (sein) swell

aufraffen *vt sep* pick up; sich a~ pick oneself up; (*fig*) pull oneself together; (*sich aufschwingen*) find the energy (zu for)

aufragen *vi sep* (sein) rise [up]

aufräumen *vt/i sep* (haben) tidy up; (*wegräumen*) put away; a~ mit (*fig*) get rid of

aufrecht *a & adv* upright. a~erhalten† *vt sep* (fig) maintain

aufreg|en *vt sep* excite; (*beunruhigen*) upset; (*ärgern*) annoy; sich a~en get excited; (*sich erregen*) get worked up. a~end *a* exciting. A~ung *f* excitement

aufreiben† *vt sep* chafe; (fig) wear down; sich a~ wear oneself out. a~d *a* trying, wearing

aufreißen† *v sep* □ *vt* tear open; dig up ⟨*Straße*⟩; open wide ⟨*Augen, Mund*⟩ □ *vi* (sein) split open

aufreizend *a* provocative, *adv* -ly

aufrichten *vt sep* erect; (fig: *trösten*) comfort; sich a~ straighten up; (*sich setzen*) sit up

aufrichtig *a* sincere, *adv* -ly. A~keit *f* - sincerity

aufriegeln *vt sep* unbolt

aufrollen *vt sep* roll up; (*entrollen*) unroll

aufrücken *vi sep* (sein) move up; (fig) be promoted

Aufruf *m* appeal (an + *dat* to). a~en† *vt sep* call out ⟨*Namen*⟩; jdn a~en call s.o.'s name; (fig) call on s.o. (zu to)

Aufruhr *m* -s,-e turmoil; (*Empörung*) revolt

aufrühr|en *vt sep* stir up. A~er *m* -s,- rebel. a~erisch *a* inflammatory; (*rebellisch*) rebellious

aufrunden *vt sep* round up

aufrüsten *vi sep* (haben) arm

aufs *prep* = auf das

aufsagen *vt sep* recite

aufsammeln *vt sep* gather up

aufsässig *a* rebellious

Aufsatz *m* top; (*Sch*) essay

aufsaugen† *vt sep* soak up

aufschauen *vi sep* (haben) look up (zu at/(fig) to)

aufschichten *vt sep* stack up

aufschieben† *vt sep* slide open; (*verschieben*) put off, postpone

Aufschlag *m* impact; (*Tennis*) service; (*Hosen-*) turn-up; (*Ärmel*) upturned cuff; (*Revers*) lapel; (*Comm*) surcharge. a~en† *v sep* □ *vt* open; crack ⟨*Ei*⟩; (*hochschlagen*) turn up; (*errichten*) put up; (*erhöhen*) increase; cast on ⟨*Masche*⟩; sich (*dat*) das Knie a~en cut [open] one's knee □ *vi* (haben) hit (auf etw *acc/dat* sth); (*Tennis*) serve; (*teurer werden*) go up

aufschließen† *v sep* □ *vt* unlock □ *vi* (haben) unlock the door

aufschlitzen *vt sep* slit open

Aufschluss (Aufschluß) *m* A~ geben give information (über + *acc* on). a~reich *a* revealing; (*lehrreich*) informative

aufschneid|en† *v sep* □ *vt* cut open; (*in Scheiben*) slice; carve ⟨*Braten*⟩ □ *vi* (haben) (fam) exaggerate. A~er *m* -s,- (fam) showoff

Aufschnitt *m* sliced sausage, cold meat [and cheese]

aufschrauben *vt sep* screw on; (*abschrauben*) unscrew

aufschrecken *v sep* □ *vt* startle □ *vi†* (sein) start up; aus dem Schlaf a~ wake up with a start

Aufschrei *m* [sudden] cry

aufschreiben† *vt sep* write down; (fam: *verschreiben*) prescribe; jdn a~ ⟨*Polizist:*⟩ book s.o.

aufschreien† *vi sep* (haben) cry out

Aufschrift *f* inscription; (*Etikett*) label

Aufschub *m* delay; (*Frist*) grace

aufschürfen *vt sep* sich (*dat*) das Knie a~ graze one's knee

aufschwatzen *vt sep* jdm etw a~ talk s.o. into buying sth

aufschwingen† (sich) *vr sep* find the energy (zu for)

Aufschwung *m* (fig) upturn

aufsehen† *vi sep* (haben) look up (zu at/(fig) to). A~ *nt* -s A~ erregen cause a sensation; A~ erregend sensational. a~erregend *a* NEW A~ erregend, s. Aufsehen

Aufseher(in) *m* -s,- (*f* -,-nen) supervisor; (*Gefängnis-*) warder

aufsein† *vi sep* (sein) NEW auf sein, s. auf

aufsetzen *vt sep* put on; (*verfassen*) draw up; (*entwerfen*) draft; sich a~ sit up

Aufsicht *f* supervision; (*Person*) supervisor. A~srat *m* board of directors

aufsitzen† *vi sep* (sein) mount

aufspannen *vt sep* put up

aufsparen *vt sep* save, keep

aufsperren *vt sep* open wide

aufspielen *v sep* □ *vi* (haben) play □ *vr* sich a~ show off; sich als Held a~ play the hero

aufspießen vt sep spear

aufspringen† vi sep (sein) jump up; (aufprallen) bounce; (sich öffnen) burst open; (Haut:) become chapped; a~ auf (+ acc) jump on

aufspüren vt sep track down

aufstacheln vt sep incite

aufstampfen vi sep (haben) mit dem Fuß a~ stamp one's foot

Aufstand m uprising, rebellion

aufständisch a rebellious. A~e(r) m rebel, insurgent

aufstapeln vt sep stack up

aufstauen vt sep dam [up]

aufstehen† vi sep (sein) get up; (offen sein) be open; (fig) rise up

aufsteigen† vi sep (sein) get on; (Reiter:) mount; (Bergsteiger:) climb up; (hochsteigen) rise [up]; (fig: befördert werden) rise (zu to); (Sport) be promoted

aufstell|en vt sep put up; (Culin) put on; (postieren) post; (in einer Reihe) line up; (nominieren) nominate; (Sport) select (Mannschaft); make out (Liste); lay down (Regel); make (Behauptung); set up (Rekord); sich a~en rise [up]; (in einer Reihe) line up. A~ung f nomination; (Liste) list

Aufstieg m -[e]s, -e ascent; (fig) rise; (Sport) promotion

aufstöbern vt sep flush out; (fig) track down

aufstoßen† v sep □ vt push open □ vi (haben) burp; a~ auf (+ acc) strike. A~ nt -s burping

aufstrebend a (fig) ambitious

Aufstrich m [sandwich] spread

aufstützen vt sep rest (auf + acc on); sich a~ lean (auf + acc on)

aufsuchen vt sep look for; (besuchen) go to see

Auftakt m (fig) start

auftauchen vi sep (sein) emerge; (U-Boot:) surface; (fig) turn up; (Frage:) crop up

auftauen vt/i sep (sein) thaw

aufteil|en vt sep divide [up]. A~ung f division

auftischen vt sep serve [up]

Auftrag m -[e]s, -e task; (Kunst) commission; (Comm) order; im A~ (+ gen) on behalf of. a~en† v sep □ vt apply; (servieren) serve; (abtragen) wear out; jdm a~en instruct s.o. (zu to) □ vi (haben) dick a~en (fam) exaggerate. A~ geber m -s,- client

auftreiben† vt sep distend; (fam: beschaffen) get hold of

auftrennen vt sep unpick, undo

auftreten† v sep □ vi (sein) tread; (sich benehmen) behave, act; (Theat) appear; (die Bühne betreten) enter; (vorkommen) occur □ vt kick open. A~ nt -s occurrence; (Benehmen) manner

Auftrieb m buoyancy; (fig) boost

Auftritt m (Theat) appearance; (auf die Bühne) entrance; (Szene) scene

auftun† vt sep jdm Suppe a~ serve s.o. with soup; sich (dat) etw a~ help oneself to sth; sich a~ open

aufwachen vi sep (sein) wake up

aufwachsen† vi sep (sein) grow up

Aufwand m -[e]s expenditure; (Luxus) extravagance; (Mühe) trouble; A~ treiben be extravagant

aufwändig a = aufwendig

aufwärmen vt sep heat up; (fig) rake up; sich a~ warm oneself; (Sport) warm up

Aufwartefrau f cleaner

aufwärts adv upwards; (bergauf) uphill; es geht a~ mit jdm/etw s.o./sth is improving. a~gehen† vi sep (sein) (NEW) a~ gehen, s. aufwärts

Aufwartung f - cleaner; jdm seine A~ machen call on s.o.

aufwaschen† vt/i sep (haben) wash up

aufwecken vt sep wake up

aufweichen v sep □ vt soften □ vi (sein) become soft

aufweisen† vt sep have, show

aufwend|en† vt sep spend; Mühe a~en take pains. a~ig a lavish, adv -ly; (teuer) expensive, adv -ly

aufwerfen† vt sep (fig) raise

aufwert|en vt sep revalue. A~ung f revaluation

aufwickeln vt sep roll up; (auswickeln) unwrap

aufwiegeln vt sep stir up

aufwiegen† vt sep compensate for

Aufwiegler m -s,- agitator

aufwirbeln vt sep Staub a~ stir up dust; (fig) cause a stir

aufwisch|en vt sep wipe up; wash (Fußboden). A~lappen m floorcloth

aufwühlen vt sep churn up; (fig) stir up

aufzähl|en vt sep enumerate, list. A~ung f list

aufzeichn|en vt sep record; (zeichnen) draw. A~ung f recording; A~ungen notes

aufziehen† v sep □ vt pull up; hoist (Segel); (öffnen) open; draw (Vorhang); (auftrennen) undo; (großziehen) bring up; rear (Tier); mount (Bild); thread (Perlen); wind up (Uhr); (arrangieren) organize; (fam: necken) tease □ vi (sein) approach

Aufzucht f rearing

Aufzug m hoist; (*Fahrstuhl*) lift, (*Amer*) elevator; (*Prozession*) procession; (*Theat*) act; (*fam: Aufmachung*) get-up

Augapfel m eyeball

Auge nt -s,-n eye; (*Punkt*) spot; vier A∼n werfen throw a four; gute A∼n good eyesight; unter vier A∼n in private; aus den A∼n verlieren lose sight of; im A∼ behalten keep in sight; (*fig*) bear in mind

Augenblick m moment; im/jeden A∼ at the/at any moment; A∼! just a moment! a∼lich a immediate; (*derzeitig*) present □ adv immediately; (*derzeit*) at present

Augen|braue f eyebrow. A∼höhle f eye socket. A∼licht nt sight. A∼lid nt eyelid. A∼schein m in A∼schein nehmen inspect. A∼zeuge m eyewitness

August m -[s] August

Auktion /'tsjo:n/ f -,-en auction. A∼ator m -s,-en /-'to:rən/ auctioneer

Aula f -,-len (*Sch*) [assembly] hall

Aupairmädchen /o'pɛ:r-/ nt au pair

aus prep (+ dat) out of; (*von*) from; (*bestehend*) [made] of; aus Angst from or out of fear; aus Spaß for fun □ adv out of; (*Licht, Radio*) off; aus sein be out; (*Licht, Radio:*) be off; (*zu Ende sein*) be over; aus sein auf (+ acc) be after; mit ihm ist es aus he's had it; aus und ein in and out; nicht mehr aus noch ein wissen be at one's wits' end; von . . . aus from; von sich aus of one's own accord; von mir aus as far as I'm concerned

ausarbeiten vt sep work out

ausarten vi sep (sein) degenerate (in + acc into)

ausatmen vt/i sep (haben) breathe out

ausbaggern vt sep excavate; dredge (*Fluss*)

ausbauen vt sep remove; (*vergrößern*) extend; (*fig*) expand

ausbedingen† vt sep sich (dat) a∼ insist on; (*zur Bedingung machen*) stipulate

ausbessern vt sep mend, repair. A∼ung f repair

ausbeulen vt sep remove the dents from; (*dehnen*) make baggy

Ausbeut|e f yield. a∼en vt sep exploit. A∼ung f -exploitation

ausbild|en vt sep train; (*formen*) form; (*entwickeln*) develop; sich a∼en train (als/zu as); (*entstehen*) develop. A∼er m -s,- instructor. A∼ung f training; (*Sch*) education

ausbitten† vt sep sich (dat) a∼ ask for; (*verlangen*) insist on

ausblasen† vt sep blow out

ausbleiben vi sep (sein) fail to appear/ (*Erfolg:*) materialize; (*nicht heimkommen*) stay out; es konnte nicht a∼ it was inevitable. A∼ nt -s absence

Ausblick m view

ausbrech|en vi sep (sein) break out; (*Vulkan:*) erupt; (*fliehen*) escape; in Tränen a∼en burst into tears. A∼er m runaway

ausbreit|en vt sep spread [out]; sich a∼en spread. A∼ung f spread

ausbrennen† v sep □ vt cauterize □ vi (sein) burn out; (*Haus:*) be gutted [by fire]

Ausbruch m outbreak; (*Vulkan-*) eruption; (*Wut-*) outburst; (*Flucht*) escape, break-out

ausbrüten vt sep hatch

Ausbund m A∼ der Tugend paragon of virtue

ausbürsten vt sep brush; (*entfernen*) brush out

Ausdauer f perseverance; (*körperlich*) stamina. a∼nd a persevering; (*unermüdlich*) untiring; (*Bot*) perennial □ adv with perseverance; untiringly

ausdehn|en vt sep stretch; (*fig*) extend; sich a∼en stretch; (*Phys & fig*) expand; (*dauern*) last. A∼ung f expansion; (*Umfang*) extent

ausdenken† vt sep sich (dat) a∼ think up; (*sich vorstellen*) imagine

ausdrehen vt sep turn off

Ausdruck m expression; (*Fach-*) term; (*Computer*) printout. a∼en vt sep print

ausdrück|en vt sep squeeze out; squeeze (*Zitrone*); stub out (*Zigarette*); (*äußern*) express; sich a∼en express oneself. a∼lich a express, adv -ly

ausdrucks|los a expressionless. a∼voll a expressive, adv -ly

auseinander adv apart; (*entzwei*) in pieces; a∼ falten unfold; a∼ gehen part; (*Linien, Meinungen:*) diverge; (*Menge:*) disperse; (*Ehe:*) break up; (*entzweigehen*) come apart; a∼ halten tell apart; a∼ nehmen take apart or to pieces; a∼ setzen place apart; (*erklären*) explain (jdm to s.o.); sich a∼ setzen sit apart; (*sich aussprechen*) have it out (mit jdm with s.o.); come to grips (mit einem Problem with a problem). a∼falten vt sep [NEW] a∼ falten, s. auseinander. a∼gehen† vi sep (sein) [NEW] a∼ gehen, s. auseinander. a∼halten† vt sep [NEW] a∼ halten, s. auseinander. a∼nehmen† vt sep [NEW] a∼ nehmen, s. auseinander. a∼setzen vt sep [NEW] a∼ setzen, s. auseinander. A∼setzung f -,-en discussion; (*Streit*) argument

auserlesen a select, choice

ausfahr|en v sep □ vt take for a drive; take out (*Baby*) [in the pram] □ vi (sein) go for a drive. A∼t f drive; ⟨Autobahn-, Garagen-⟩ exit

Ausfall m failure; ⟨Absage⟩ cancellation; ⟨Comm⟩ loss. a∼en† vi sep (sein) fall out; ⟨versagen⟩ fail; ⟨abgesagt werden⟩ be cancelled; gut/schlecht a∼en turn out to be good/poor

ausfallend, ausfällig a abusive

ausfertig|en vt sep make out. A∼ung f -,-en in doppelter/dreifacher A∼ung in duplicate/triplicate

ausfindig a a∼ machen find

ausflippen vi (sein) freak out

Ausflucht f -,-̈e excuse

Ausflug m excursion, outing

Ausflügler m -s,- [day-]tripper

Ausfluss (Ausfluß) m outlet; ⟨Abfluss⟩ drain; ⟨Med⟩ discharge

ausfragen vt sep question

ausfransen vi sep (sein) fray

Ausfuhr f -,-en ⟨Comm⟩ export

ausführ|en vt sep take out; ⟨Comm⟩ export; ⟨durchführen⟩ carry out; ⟨erklären⟩ explain.a∼lich a detailed □ adv in detail. A∼ung f execution; ⟨Comm⟩ version; ⟨äußere⟩ finish; ⟨Qualität⟩ workmanship; ⟨Erklärung⟩ explanation

Ausgabe f issue; ⟨Buch-⟩ edition; ⟨Comm⟩ version

Ausgang m way out, exit; ⟨Flugsteig⟩ gate; ⟨Ende⟩ end; ⟨Ergebnis⟩ outcome, result; A∼ haben have time off. A∼spunkt m starting-point. A∼sperre f curfew

ausgeb|en† vt sep hand out; issue ⟨Fahrkarten⟩; spend ⟨Geld⟩; buy ⟨Runde Bier⟩; sich a∼ als pretend to be

ausgebeult a baggy

ausgebildet a trained

ausgebucht a fully booked; ⟨Vorstellung⟩ sold out

ausgedehnt a extensive; ⟨lang⟩ long

ausgedient a worn out; ⟨Person⟩ retired

ausgefallen a unusual

ausgefranst a frayed

ausgeglichen a [well-]balanced; ⟨gelassen⟩ even-tempered

ausgeh|en† vi sep (sein) go out; ⟨Haare:⟩ fall out; ⟨Vorräte, Geld:⟩ run out; ⟨verblassen⟩ fade; ⟨herrühren⟩ come (von from); ⟨abzielen⟩ aim (auf + acc at); gut/schlecht a∼en end well/badly; leer a∼en come away empty-handed; davon a∼en, dass assume that. A∼verbot nt curfew

ausgelassen a high-spirited; a∼ sein be in high spirits

ausgelernt a [fully] trained

ausgemacht a agreed; ⟨fam: vollkommen⟩ utter

ausgenommen conj except; a∼ wenn unless

ausgeprägt a marked

ausgerechnet adv a∼ heute today of all days; a∼er/Rom he of all people/Rome of all places

ausgeschlossen pred a out of the question

ausgeschnitten a low-cut

ausgesprochen a marked □ adv decidedly

ausgestorben a extinct; [wie] a∼ ⟨Straße:⟩ deserted

Ausgestoßene(r) m/f outcast

ausgewachsen a fully-grown

ausgewogen a [well-]balanced

ausgezeichnet a excellent, adv -ly

ausgiebig a extensive; ⟨lang⟩ long; ⟨ausgedehnt⟩ long; a∼ Gebrauch machen von make full use of; a∼ frühstücken have a really good breakfast

ausgießen† vt sep pour out; ⟨leeren⟩ empty

Ausgleich m -[e]s balance; ⟨Entschädigung⟩ compensation. a∼en† v sep □ vt balance; even out ⟨Höhe⟩; ⟨wettmachen⟩ compensate for; sich a∼en balance out □ vi (haben) equalize. A∼sgymnastik f keep-fit exercises pl. A∼streffer m equalizer

ausgleiten† vi sep (sein) slip

ausgrab|en† vt sep dig up; ⟨Archaeol⟩ excavate. A∼ung f -,-en excavation

Ausguck m -[e]s,-e look-out post; ⟨Person⟩ look-out

Ausguss (Ausguß) m ⟨kitchen⟩ sink

aushaben† vt sep have finished ⟨Buch⟩; wann habt ihr Schule aus? when do you finish school?

aushalten† v sep □ vt bear, stand; hold ⟨Note⟩; ⟨Unterhalt zahlen für⟩ keep; nicht auszuhalten, nicht zum A∼ unbearable □ vi (haben) hold out

aushandeln vt sep negotiate

aushändigen vt sep hand over

Aushang m [public] notice

aushängen¹ vt sep (reg) display; take off its hinges ⟨Tür⟩

aushäng|en²† vi sep (haben) be displayed. A∼eschild nt sign

ausharren vi sep (haben) hold out

ausheben† vt sep excavate; take off its hinges ⟨Tür⟩

aushecken vt sep ⟨fig⟩ hatch

aushelfen† vi sep (haben) help out (jdm s.o.)

Aushilf|e f [temporary] assistant; zur A∼e to help out. A∼skraft f temporary worker. a∼sweise adv temporarily

aushöhlen vt sep hollow out

ausholen vi sep (haben) [zum Schlag] a~ raise one's arm [ready to strike]

aushorchen vt sep sound out

auskennen†(sich) vr sep know one's way around; sich mit/in etw (dat) a~ know all about sth

auskleiden vt sep undress; (Techn) line; sich a~ undress

ausknipsen vi sep switch off

auskommen† vi sep (sein) manage (mit/ohne with/without); (sich vertragen) get on (gut well). A~ nt -s sein A~/ ein gutes A~haben get by/be well off

auskosten vt sep enjoy [to the full]

auskugeln vt sep sich (dat) den Arm a~ dislocate one's shoulder

auskühlen vt/i sep (sein) cool

auskundschaften vt sep spy out; (erfahren) find out

Auskunft f -,ːe information; (A~sstelle) information desk/ (Büro) bureau; (Teleph) enquiries pl; eine A~ a piece of information. A~sbüro nt information bureau

auslachen vt sep laugh at

ausladen† vt sep unload; (fam: absagen) put off ⟨Gast⟩. a~d a projecting

Auslage f [window] display; A~n expenses

Ausland nt im/ins A~ abroad

Ausländ|er(in) m -s,- (f -,-nen) foreigner. a~isch a foreign

Auslandsgespräch nt international call

auslass|en vt sep let out; let down ⟨Saum⟩; (weglassen) leave out; (versäumen) miss; (Culin) melt; (fig) vent ⟨Ärger⟩ (an + dat on); sich a~en über (+ acc) go on about. A~ungszeichen nt apostrophe

Auslauf m run. a~en† vi sep (sein) run out; (Farbe:) run; (Naut) put to sea; (leer laufen) run dry; (enden) end; ⟨Modell:⟩ be discontinued

Ausläufer m (Geog) spur; (Bot) runner, sucker

ausleeren vt sep empty [out]

ausleg|en vt sep lay out; display ⟨Waren⟩; (bedecken) cover/ (auskleiden) line (mit with); (bezahlen) pay; (deuten) interpret. A~ung f -,-en interpretation

ausleihen† vt sep lend; sich (dat) a~ borrow

auslernen vi sep (haben) finish one's training

Auslese f - selection; (fig) pick; (Elite) élite. a~n† vt sep finish reading ⟨Buch⟩; (auswählen) pick out, select

ausliefer|n vt sep hand over; (Jur) extradite; ausgeliefert sein (+ dat) be at the mercy of. A~ung f handing over; (Jur) extradition; (Comm) distribution

ausliegen† vi sep (haben) be on display

auslöschen vt sep extinguish; (abwischen) wipe off; (fig) erase

auslosen vt sep draw lots for

auslös|en vt sep set off, trigger; (fig) cause; arouse ⟨Begeisterung⟩; (einlösen) redeem; pay a ransom for ⟨Gefangene⟩. A~er m -s,- trigger; (Phot) shutter release

Auslosung f draw

auslüften vt/i sep (haben) air

ausmachen vt sep put out; (abschalten) turn off; (abmachen) arrange; (erkennen) make out; (betragen) amount to; (darstellen) represent; (wichtig sein) matter; das macht mir nichts aus I don't mind

ausmalen vt sep paint; (fig) describe; sich (dat) a~ imagine

Ausmaß nt extent; A~e dimensions

ausmerzen vt sep eliminate

ausmessen† vt sep measure

Ausnahme f -,-n exception. A~zustand m state of emergency. a~slos adv without exception. a~sweise adv as an exception

ausnehmen† vt sep take out; gut ⟨Fisch⟩; draw ⟨Huhn⟩; (ausschließen) exclude; (fam: schröpfen) fleece; sich gut a~ look good. a~d adv exceptionally

ausnutz|en, ausnütz|en vt sep exploit; make the most of ⟨Gelegenheit⟩. A~ung f exploitation

auspacken v sep □ vt unpack; (auswickeln) unwrap □ vi (haben) (fam) talk

auspeitschen vt sep flog

auspfeifen vt sep whistle and boo

ausplaudern vt sep let out, blab

ausplündern vt sep loot; rob ⟨Person⟩

ausprobieren vt sep try out

Auspuff m -s exhaust [system]. A~gase ntpl exhaust fumes. A~rohr nt exhaust pipe

auspusten vt sep blow out

ausradieren vt sep rub out

ausrangieren vt sep (fam) discard

ausrauben vt sep rob

ausräuchern vt sep smoke out; fumigate ⟨Zimmer⟩

ausräumen vt sep clear out

ausrechnen vt sep work out, calculate

Ausrede f excuse. a~n v sep □ vi (haben) finish speaking; lass mich a~n! let me finish! □ vt jdm etw a~n talk s.o. out of sth

aus|reichen vi sep (haben) be enough; a~ mit have enough. a~d a adequate, adv -ly; (Sch) ≈ pass

Ausreise f departure [from a country]. a~n vi sep (sein) leave the country. A~visum nt exit visa

ausreiß|en† v sep □ vt pull or tear out □ vi (sein) (fam) run away. A~er m (fam) runaway

ausrenken vt sep dislocate; sich (dat) den Arm a~ dislocate one's shoulder

ausrichten vt sep align; (bestellen) deliver; (erreichen) achieve; jdm a~ tell s.o. (dass that); kann ich etwas a~? can I take a message? ich soll Ihnen Grüße von X a~ X sends [you] his regards

ausrotten vt sep exterminate; (fig) eradicate

ausrücken vi sep (sein) (Mil) march off; (fam) run away

Ausruf m exclamation. a~en† vt sep exclaim; call out ⟨Namen⟩; (verkünden) proclaim; call ⟨Streik⟩; jdn a~en lassen have s.o. paged. A~ezeichen nt exclamation mark

ausruhen vt/i sep (haben) rest; sich a~ have a rest

ausrüst|en† vt sep equip. A~ung f equipment; (Mil) kit

ausrutschen vi sep (sein) slip

Aussage f · -.n statement; (Jur) testimony, evidence; (Gram) predicate. a~n vt/i sep (haben) state; (Jur) give evidence, testify

Aussatz m leprosy

Aussätzige(r) m/f leper

ausschachten vt sep excavate

ausschalten vt sep switch or turn off; (fig) eliminate

Ausschank m sale of alcoholic drinks; (Bar) bar

Ausschau f · A~ halten nach look out for. a~en vi sep (haben) (SGer) look; a~en nach look out for

ausscheiden† v sep □ vi (sein) leave; (Sport) drop out; (nicht in Frage kommen) be excluded; aus dem Dienst a~ retire □ vt eliminate; (Med) excrete

ausschenken vt sep pour out; (verkaufen) sell

ausscheren vi sep (sein) (Auto) pull out

ausschildern vt sep signpost

ausschimpfen vt sep tell off

ausschlachten vt sep (fig) exploit

ausschlafen† v sep □ vi/r (haben) [sich] a~ get enough sleep; (morgens) sleep late; nicht ausgeschlafen haben or sein be still tired □ vt sleep off ⟨Rausch⟩

Ausschlag m (Med) rash; den A~ geben (fig) tip the balance. a~en† v sep □ vi

(haben) kick [out]; (Bot) sprout; ⟨Baum:⟩ come into leaf □ vt knock out; (auskleiden) line; (ablehnen) refuse. a~gebend a decisive

ausschließ|en† vt sep lock out; (fig) exclude; (entfernen) expel. a~lich a exclusive, adv -ly

ausschlüpfen vi sep (sein) hatch

Ausschluss (**Ausschluß**) m exclusion; expulsion; unter A~ der Öffentlichkeit in camera

ausschmücken vt sep decorate; (fig) embellish

ausschneiden† vt sep cut out

Ausschnitt m excerpt, extract; ⟨Zeitungs-⟩ cutting; (Hals-) neckline

ausschöpfen vt sep ladle out; (Naut) bail out; exhaust ⟨Möglichkeiten⟩

ausschreiben† vt sep write out; (ausstellen) make out; (bekanntgeben) announce; put out to tender ⟨Auftrag⟩

Ausschreitungen fpl riots; (Exzesse) excesses

Ausschuss (**Ausschuß**) m committee; (Comm) rejects pl

ausschütten vt sep tip out; (verschütten) spill; (leeren) empty; sich vor Lachen a~ (fam) be in stitches

ausschweif|end a dissolute. A~ung f -,-en debauchery; A~ungen excesses

ausschwenken vt sep rinse [out]

aussehen† vi sep (haben) look; es sieht nach Regen aus it looks like rain; wie sieht er/es aus? what does he/it look like? ein gut a~der Mann a good-looking man. A~ nt -s appearance

aussein† vi sep (sein) (NEW) aus sein, s. aus

außen adv [on the] outside; nach a~ outwards. A~bordmotor m outboard motor. A~handel m foreign trade. A~minister m Foreign Minister. A~politik f foreign policy. A~seite f outside. A~seiter m -s,- outsider; (fig) misfit. A~stände mpl outstanding debts. A~stehende(r) m/f outsider

außer prep (+ dat) except [for], apart from; (außerhalb) out of; a~ Atem/Sicht out of breath/sight; a~ sich (fig) beside oneself □ conj except; a~ wenn unless. a~dem adv in addition, as well □ conj moreover

äußer|e(r,s) a external; ⟨Teil, Schicht⟩ outer. Ä~e(s) nt exterior; (Aussehen) appearance

außer|ehelich a extramarital. a~gewöhnlich a exceptional, adv -ly. a~halb prep (+ gen) outside □ adv a~halb wohnen live outside town

äußer|lich a external, adv -ly; (fig) outward, adv -ly. ä~n vt express; sich ä~n comment; (sich zeigen) manifest itself

außerordentlich *a* extraordinary, *adv*
-ily; *(außergewöhnlich)* exceptional, *adv*
-ly

äußerst *adv* extremely

außerstande *pred a* unable (zu to)

äußerste(r,s) *a* outermost; *(weiteste)*
furthest; *(höchste)* utmost, extreme;
(letzte) last; *(schlimmste)* worst; am ä∼n
Ende at the very end; aufs ä∼ = aufs
Ä∼, *s.* Äußerste(s). Ä∼(s) *nt* das Ä∼ the
limit; *(Schlimmste)* the worst; sein Ä∼s
tun do one's utmost; aufs Ä∼ extremely

Äußerung *f* -,-en comment; *(Bemerkung)*
remark

aussetzen *v sep* □ *vt* expose (*dat* to); abandon *(Kind, Hund)*; launch *(Boot)*; offer *(Belohnung)*; etwas auszusetzen haben an
(+ *dat*) find fault with □ *vi* (haben) stop;
(Motor:) cut out

Aussicht *f* -,-en view/*(fig)* prospect (auf
+ *acc* of); in A∼ stellen promise; weitere
A∼en *(Meteorol)* further outlook *sg.*
a∼slos *a* hopeless, *adv* -ly. a∼sreich *a*
promising

aussöhnen *vt sep* reconcile; sich a∼ become reconciled

aussortieren *vt sep* pick out; *(ausscheiden)* eliminate

ausspann|en *v sep* □ *vt* spread out; un-
hitch *(Pferd)*; *(fam: wegnehmen)* take (*dat*
from) □ *vi* (haben) rest. A∼ung *f* rest

aussperr|en *vt sep* lock out. A∼ung *f*
-,-en lock-out

ausspielen *v sep* □ *vt* play *(Karte)*; *(fig)*
play off (gegen against) □ *vi* (haben) *(Kartenspiel)* lead

Aussprache *f* pronunciation; *(Sprech-
weise)* diction; *(Gespräch)* talk

aussprechen† *v sep* □ *vt* pronounce;
(äußern) express; sich a∼ talk; come out
(für/gegen in favour of/against) □ *vi*
(haben) finish [speaking]

Ausspruch *m* saying

ausspucken *v sep* □ *vt* spit out □ *vi*
(haben) spit

ausspülen *vt sep* rinse out

ausstaffieren *vt sep (fam)* kit out

Ausstand *m* strike; in den A∼ treten go
on strike

ausstatt|en *vt sep* equip; mit Möbeln
a∼en furnish. A∼ung *f* -,-en equipment;
(Innen-) furnishings *pl*; *(Theat)* scenery
and costumes *pl*; *(Aufmachung)* get-up

ausstehen† *v sep* □ *vt* suffer; Angst a∼
be frightened; ich kann sie nicht a∼ I
can't stand her □ *vi* (haben) be outstanding

aussteigen† *vi sep* (sein) get out; *(aus Bus,
Zug)* get off; *(fam: ausscheiden)* opt out;

(aus einem Geschäft) back out; alles
a∼en! all change! A∼er(in) *m* -s,- *(f*
-,-nen) *(fam)* drop-out

ausstell|en *vt sep* exhibit; *(Comm)* dis-
play; *(ausfertigen)* make out; issue *(Pass)*.
A∼er *m* -s,- exhibitor. A∼ung *f* exhibition; *(Comm)* display. A∼ungsstück *nt*
exhibit

aussterben† *vi sep* (sein) die out; *(Biol)*
become extinct. A∼ *nt* -s extinction

Aussteuer *f* trousseau

Ausstieg *m* -[e]s,-e exit

ausstopfen *vt sep* stuff

ausstoßen† *vt sep* emit; utter *(Fluch)*;
heave *(Seufzer)*; *(ausschließen)* expel

ausstrahl|en *vt/i sep* (sein) radiate, emit;
(Radio, TV) broadcast. A∼ung *f* radiation; *(fig)* charisma

ausstrecken *vt sep* stretch out; put out
(Hand); sich a∼ stretch out

ausstreichen† *vt sep* cross out

ausstreuen *vt sep* scatter; spread
(Gerüchte)

ausströmen *v sep* □ *vi* (sein) pour out;
(entweichen) escape □ *vt* emit; *(ausstrahlen)* radiate

aussuchen *vt sep* pick, choose

Austausch *m* exchange. a∼bar *a* inter-
changeable. a∼en *vt sep* exchange; *(auswechseln)* replace

austeilen *vt sep* distribute; *(ausgeben)*
hand out

Auster *f* -,-n oyster

austoben (sich) *vr sep (Sturm:)* rage; *(Person:)* let off steam; *(Kinder:)* romp about

austragen† *vt sep* deliver; hold
(Wettkampf); play *(Spiel)*

Austral|ien /-jən/ *nt* -s Australia.
A∼ier(in) *m* -s,- *(f* -,-nen) Australian.
a∼isch *a* Australian

austreiben† *v sep* □ *vt* drive out; *(Relig)*
exorcize □ *vi* (haben) *(Bot)* sprout

austreten† *v sep* □ *vt* stamp out; *(abnutzen)* wear down □ *vi* (sein) come out;
(ausscheiden) leave (aus etw sth); [mal]
a∼ *(fam)* go to the loo; *(Sch)* be excused

austrinken† *vt/i sep* (haben) drink up;
(leeren) drain

Austritt *m* resignation

austrocknen *vt/i sep* (sein) dry out

ausüben *vt sep* practise; carry on
(Handwerk); exercise *(Recht)*; exert
(Druck, Einfluss); have *(Wirkung)*

Ausverkauf *m* [clearance] sale. a∼t *a*
sold out; a∼tes Haus full house

auswachsen† *vt sep* outgrow

Auswahl *f* choice, selection; *(Comm)*
range; *(Sport)* team

auswählen vt sep choose, select

Auswander|er m emigrant. a∼n vi sep (sein) emigrate. A∼ung f emigration

auswärt|ig a non-local; (ausländisch) foreign. a∼s adv outwards; (Sport) away; a∼s essen eat out; a∼s arbeiten nicht work locally. A∼ sspiel nt away game

auswaschen† vt sep wash out

auswechseln vt sep change; (ersetzen) replace; (Sport) substitute

Ausweg m (fig) way out. a∼los a (fig) hopeless

ausweich|en† vi sep (sein) get out of the way; jdm/etw a∼en avoid/ (sich entziehen) evade s.o./sth. a∼end a evasive, adv -ly

ausweinen vt sep sich (dat) die Augen a∼ cry one's eyes out; sich a∼ have a good cry

Ausweis m -es,-e pass; (Mitglieds-, Studenten-) card. a∼en† vt sep deport; sich a∼en prove one's identity. A∼papiere ntpl identification papers. A∼ung f deportation

ausweiten vt sep stretch; (fig) expand

auswendig adv by heart

auswerten vt sep evaluate; (nutzen) utilize

auswickeln vt sep unwrap

auswirk|en (sich) vr sep have an effect (auf + acc on). A∼ung f effect; (Folge) consequence

auswischen vt sep wipe out; jdm eins a∼ (fam) play a nasty trick on s.o.

auswringen† vt sep wring out

Auswuchs m excrescence; Auswüchse (fig) excesses

auszahlen vt sep pay out; (entlohnen) pay off; (abfinden) buy out; sich a∼ (fig) pay off

auszählen vt sep count; (Boxen) count out

Auszahlung f payment

auszeichn|en vt sep (Comm) price; (ehren) honour; (mit einem Preis) award a prize to; (Mil) decorate; sich a∼en distinguish oneself. A∼ung f honour; (Preis) award; (Mil) decoration; (fig) distinction

ausziehen† v sep □ vt pull out; (auskleiden) undress; take off (Mantel, Schuhe); sich a∼ take off one's coat; (sich entkleiden) undress □ vi (sein) move out; (sich aufmachen) set out

Auszubildende(r) m/f trainee

Auszug m departure; (Umzug) move; (Ausschnitt) extract, excerpt; (Bank-) statement

authentisch a authentic

Auto nt -s,-s car; A∼ fahren drive; (mitfahren) go in the car. A∼bahn f motorway, (Amer) freeway

Autobiographie f autobiography

Auto|bus m bus. A∼fähre f car ferry. A∼fahrer(in) m(f) driver, motorist. A∼fahrt f drive

Autogramm nt -s,-e autograph

autokratisch a autocratic

Automat m -en,-en automatic device; (Münz-) slot-machine; (Verkaufs-) vending-machine; (Fahrkarten-) machine; (Techn) robot. A∼ik f - automatic mechanism; (Auto) automatic transmission

Auto|mation /-'tsio:n/ f - automation. a∼matisch a automatic, adv -ally

autonom a autonomous. A∼ie f - autonomy

Autonummer f registration number

Autopsie f -,-n autopsy

Autor m -s,-en /-'to:rən/ author

Auto|reisezug m Motorail. A∼rennen nt motor race

Autorin f -,-nen author[ess]

Autori|sation /-'tsio:n/ f -authorization. a∼sieren vt authorize. a∼tär a authoritarian. A∼tät f -,-en authority

Auto|schlosser m motor mechanic. A∼skooter /-sku:tɐ/ m -s,- dodgem. A∼stopp m -s per A∼stopp fahren hitchhike. A∼verleih m car hire [firm]. A∼waschanlage f car wash

autsch int ouch

Aversion f -,-en aversion (gegen to)

Axt f -,-e axe

B

B, b /be:/ nt - (Mus) B flat

Baby /'be:bi/ nt -s,-s baby. B∼ausstattung f layette. B∼sitter /-sɪtɐ/ m -s,-babysitter

Bach m -[e]s,-e stream

Backbord nt -[e]s port [side]

Backe f -,-n cheek

backen v □ vt/i† (haben) bake; (braten) fry □ vi (reg) (haben) (kleben) stick (an + dat to)

Backenzahn m molar

Bäcker m -s,- baker. B∼ei f -,-en, B∼laden m baker's shop .

Back|form f baking tin. B∼obst nt dried fruit. B∼ofen m oven. B∼pfeife f (fam) slap in the face. B∼pflaume f prune.

B~pulver nt baking-powder. B~rohr nt oven. B~stein m brick. B~werk nt cakes and pastries pl

Bad nt -[e]s,˙er bath; (im Meer) bathe; (Zimmer) bathroom; (Schwimm-) pool; (Ort) spa

Bade|anstalt f swimming baths pl. B~anzug m swim-suit. B~hose f swimming trunks pl. B~kappe f bathing-cap. B~mantel m bathrobe. B~matte f bath-mat. B~mütze f bathing-cap. b~n vi (haben) have a bath; (im Meer) bathe □ vt bath; (waschen) bathe. B~ort m seaside resort; (Kurort) spa. B~tuch nt bathtowel. B~wanne f bath. B~zimmer nt bathroom

Bagatelle f -,-n trifle; (Mus) bagatelle

Bagger m -s,- excavator; (Nass-) dredger. b~n vt/i (haben) excavate; dredge. B~see m flooded gravel-pit

Bahn f -,-en path; (Astr) orbit; (Sport) track; (einzelne) lane; (Rodel-) run; (Stoff-, Papier-) width; (Rock-) panel; (Eisen-) railway; (Zug) train; (Straßen-) tram; auf die schiefe B~ kommen (fig) get into bad ways. b~brechend a (fig) pioneering. b~en vt sich (dat) einen Weg b~en clear a way (durch through). B~hof m [railway] station. B~steig m -[e]s,-e platform. B~übergang m level crossing, (Amer) grade crossing

Bahre f -,-n stretcher; (Toten-) bier

Baiser /bɛˈzeː/ nt -s,-s meringue

Bajonett nt -[e]s,-e bayonet

Bake f -,-n (Naut, Aviat) beacon

Bakterien /-jən/ fpl bacteria

Balance /baˈlãːsə/ f - balance; die B~e halten/verlieren keep/lose one's balance. b~ieren vt/i (haben/sein) balance

bald adv soon; (fast) almost; b~ . . . b~ . . . now . . . now . . .

Baldachin /-xiːn/ m -s,-e canopy

bald|ig a early; (Besserung) speedy. b~möglichst adv as soon as possible

Balg nt & m -[e]s,˙er (fam) brat. b~en (sich) vr tussle. B~erei f -,-en tussle

Balkan m -s Balkans pl

Balken m -s,- beam

Balkon /balˈkõ:/ m -s,-s balcony; (Theat) circle

Ball¹ m -[e]s,˙e ball

Ball² m -[e]s,˙e (Tanz) ball

Ballade f -,-n ballad

Ballast m -[e]s ballast. B~stoffe mpl roughage sg

ballen vt die [Hand zur] Faust b~ clench one's fist; sich b~ gather, mass. B~ m -s,- bale; (Anat) ball of the hand/(Fuß-) foot; (Med) bunion

Ballerina f -,-nen ballerina

Ballett nt -s,-e ballet

Balletttänzer(in) (Ballettänzer(in)) m(f) ballet dancer

ballistisch a ballistic

Ballon /baˈlõ:/ m -s,-s balloon

Ball|saal m ballroom. B~ungsgebiet nt conurbation. B~wechsel m (Tennis) rally

Balsam m -s balm

Balt|ikum nt -s Baltic States pl. b~isch a Baltic

Balustrade f -,-n balustrade

Bambus m -ses,-se bamboo

banal a banal. B~ität f -,-en banality

Banane f -,-n banana

Banause m -n,-n philistine

Band¹ nt -[e]s,˙er ribbon; (Naht-, Ton-, Ziel-) tape; (Anat) ligament; auf B~ aufnehmen tape; laufendes B~ conveyor belt; am laufenden B~ (fam) non-stop

Band² m -[e]s,˙e volume

Band³ nt -[e]s,-e (fig) bond; B~e der Freundschaft bonds of friendship

Band⁴ /bɛnt/ f -,-s [jazz] band

Bandag|e /banˈdaːʒə/ f -,-n bandage. b~ieren vt bandage

Bande f -,-n gang

bändigen vt control, restrain; (zähmen) tame

Bandit m -en,-en bandit

Band|maß nt tape-measure. B~nudeln fpl noodles. B~scheibe f (Anat) disc. B~scheibenvorfall m slipped disc. B~wurm m tapeworm

bang|[e] a (bänger, bängst) anxious; jdm b~e machen (NEW) jdm B~e machen, s. Bange. B~e f B~e haben be afraid; jdm B~e machen frighten s.o. b~en vi (haben) fear (um for); mir b~t davor I dread it

Banjo nt -s,-s banjo

Bank¹ f -,˙e bench

Bank² f -,-en (Comm) bank. B~einzug m direct debit

Bankett nt -[e]s,-e banquet

Bankier /baŋˈkje:/ m -s,-s banker

Bank|konto nt bank account. B~note f banknote

Bankrott m -s,-e bankruptcy; B~ machen od gehen go bankrupt. b~ a bankrupt

Bankwesen nt banking

Bann m -[e]s,-e (fig) spell; in jds B~ under s.o.'s spell. b~en vt exorcize; (abwenden) avert; [wie] gebannt spellbound

Banner nt -s,- banner

Baptist(in) m -en,-en (f -,-nen) Baptist

bar a (rein) sheer; (Gold) pure; b~es Geld cash; [in] bar bezahlen pay cash; etw für b~e Münze nehmen (fig) take sth as gospel

Bar_ f -,-s bar

Bär m -en,-en bear; jdm einen B~en aufbinden (fam) pull s.o.'s leg

Baracke f -,-n (Mil) hut

Barb|ar m -en,-en barbarian. b~arisch a barbaric

bar|fuß adv barefoot. B~geld nt cash

Bariton m -s,-e /-'to:nə/ baritone

Barkasse f -,-n launch

Barmann m (pl -männer) barman

barmherzig a merciful. B~keit f - mercy

barock a baroque. B~ nt & m -[s] baroque

Barometer nt -s,- barometer

Baron m -s,-e baron. B~in f -,-nen baroness

Barren m -s,- (Gold-) bar, ingot; (Sport) parallel bars pl. B~gold nt gold bullion

Barriere f -,-n barrier

Barrikade f -,-n barricade

barsch a gruff, adv -ly; (kurz) curt, adv -ly

Barsch m -[e]s,-e (Zool) perch

Barschaft f - meine ganze B~ all I have/had on me

Bart m -[e]s,-e beard; (der Katze) whiskers pl

bärtig a bearded

Barzahlung f cash payment

Basar m -s,-e bazaar

Base¹ f -,-n [female] cousin

Base² f -,-n (Chem) alkali, base

Basel nt -s Basle

basieren vi (haben) be based (auf + dat on)

Basilikum nt -s basil

Basis f -,Basen base; (fig) basis

basisch a (Chem) alkaline

Bask|enmütze f beret. b~isch a Basque

Bass m -es,-e (Baß m -sses,-sse) bass; (Kontra-) double-bass

Bassin /ba'sɛ:/ nt -s,-s pond; (Brunnen-) basin; (Schwimm-) pool

Bassist m -en,-en bass player; (Sänger) bass

Bassstimme (Baßstimme) f bass voice

Bast m -[e]s raffia

basta int [und damit] b~! and that's that!

bast|eln vt make □ vi (haben) do handicrafts; (herum-) tinker (an + dat with). B~ler m -s,- amateur craftsman; (Heim-) do-it-yourselfer

Bataillon /batal'jo:n/ nt -s,-e battalion

Batterie f -,-n battery

Bau¹ m -[e]s,-e burrow; (Fuchs-) earth

Bau² m -[e]s,-ten construction; (Gebäude) building; (Auf-) structure; (Körper-) build; (B~stelle) building site; im Bau under construction. B~arbeiten fpl building work sg; (Straßen-) road-works. B~art f design; (Stil) style

Bauch m -[e]s, Bäuche abdomen, belly; (Magen) stomach; (Schmer-) paunch; (Bauchung) bulge. b~ig a bulbous. B~nabel m navel. B~redner m ventriloquist. B~schmerzen mpl stomach-ache sg. B~speicheldrüse f pancreas. B~weh nt stomach-ache

bauen vt build; (konstruieren) construct; (an-) grow; einen Unfall b~ (fam) have an accident □ vi (haben) (auf etw dat sth); b~ auf (+ acc) (fig) rely on

Bauer¹ m -s,-n farmer; (Schach) pawn

Bauer² nt -s,- [bird]cage

Bäuer|in f -,-nen farmer's wife. b~lich a rustic

Bauern|haus nt farmhouse. B~hof m farm

bau|fällig a dilapidated. B~genehmigung f planning permission. B~gerüst nt scaffolding. B~jahr nt year of construction; B~jahr 1985 (Auto) 1985 model. B~kasten m box of building bricks; (Modell-) model kit. B~klotz m building brick. B~kunst f architecture. b~lich a structural, adv -ly. B~lichkeiten fpl buildings

Baum m -[e]s, Bäume tree

baumeln vi (haben) dangle; die Beine b~ lassen dangle one's legs

bäumen (sich) vr rear [up]

Baum|schule f [tree] nursery. B~stamm m tree-trunk. B~wolle f cotton. b~wollen a cotton

Bauplatz m building plot

bäurisch a rustic; (plump) uncouth

Bausch m -[e]s, Bäusche wad; in B~ und Bogen (fig) wholesale. b~en vt puff out; sich b~en billow [out]. b~ig a puffed [out]; (Ärmel) full

Bau|sparkasse f building society. B~stein m building brick; (fig) element. B~stelle f building site; (Straßen-) road-works pl. B~unternehmer m building contractor. B~werk nt building. B~zaun m hoarding

Bayer|(in) m -s,-n (f -,-nen) Bavarian. B~n nt -s Bavaria

bay[e]risch a Bavarian

Bazillus m -,-len bacillus; (fam: Keim) germ

beabsichtig|en vt intend. b~t a intended; (absichtlich) intentional

beacht|en vt take notice of; (einhalten) observe; (folgen) follow; nicht b∼en ignore. b∼lich a considerable. B∼ung f -observance; etw (dat) keine B∼ung schenken take no notice of sth

Beamte(r) m, **Beamtin** f -,-nen official; (Staats-) civil servant; (Schalter-) clerk

beängstigend a alarming

beanspruchen vt claim; (erfordern) demand; (brauchen) take up; (Techn) stress; die Arbeit beansprucht ihn sehr his work is very demanding

beanstand|en vt find fault with; (Comm) make a complaint about. B∼ung f -,-en complaint

beantragen vt apply for

beantworten vt answer

bearbeiten vt work; (weiter-) process; (behandeln) treat (mit with); (Admin) deal with; (redigieren) edit; (Theat) adapt; (Mus) arrange; (fam: bedrängen) pester; (fam: schlagen) pummel

Beatmung f künstliche B∼ artificial respiration. B∼sgerät nt ventilator

beaufsichtig|en vt supervise. B∼ung f - supervision

beauftrag|en vt instruct; commission (Künstler); jdn mit einer Arbeit b∼en assign a task to s.o. B∼te(r) m/f representative

bebauen vt build on; (bestellen) cultivate

beben vi (haben) tremble

bebildert a illustrated

Becher m -s,- beaker; (Henkel-) mug; (Joghurt-, Sahne-) carton

Becken nt -s,- basin; (Schwimm-) pool; (Mus) cymbals pl; (Anat) pelvis

bedacht a careful; b∼ auf (+ acc) concerned about; darauf b∼ anxious (zu to)

bedächtig a careful, adv -ly; (langsam) slow, adv -ly

bedanken (sich) vr thank (bei jdm s.o.)

Bedarf m - need/(Comm) demand (an + dat for); bei B∼ if required. B∼sartikel mpl requisites. B∼shaltestelle f request stop

bedauer|lich a regrettable. b∼licherweise** adv unfortunately. b∼n vt regret; (bemitleiden) feel sorry for; bedaure! sorry! B∼n nt -s regret; (Mitgefühl) sympathy. b∼nswert a pitiful; (bedauerlich) regrettable

bedeck|en vt cover; sich b∼en (Himmel:) cloud over. b∼t a covered; (Himmel:) overcast

bedenken† vt consider; (überlegen) think over; jdn b∼ give s.o. a present; sich b∼ consider. B∼ pl misgivings; ohne B∼

without hesitation. b∼los a unhesitating, adv -ly

bedenklich a doubtful; (verdächtig) dubious; (bedrohlich) worrying; (ernst) serious

bedeut|en vi (haben) mean; jdm viel/ nichts b∼en mean a lot/nothing to s.o.; es hat nichts zu b∼en it is of no significance. b∼end a important; (beträchtlich) considerable. b∼sam a = b∼ungsvoll. B∼ung f -,-en meaning; (Wichtigkeit) importance. b∼ungslos a meaningless; (unwichtig) unimportant. b∼ungsvoll a significant; (vielsagend) meaningful, adv -ly

bedien|en vt serve; (betätigen) operate; sich [selbst] b∼en help oneself. B∼ung f -,-en service; (Betätigung) operation; (Kellner) waiter; (Kellnerin) waitress. B∼ungsgeld nt, B∼ungszuschlag m service charge

bedingt a conditional; (eingeschränkt) qualified

Bedingung f -,-en condition; B∼en conditions; (Comm) terms. b∼slos a unconditional, adv -ly; (unbedingt) unquestioning, adv -ly

bedrängen vt press; (belästigen) pester

bedroh|en vt threaten. b∼lich a threatening. B∼ung f threat

bedrück|en vt depress. b∼end a depressing. b∼t a depressed

bedruckt a printed

bedürf|en† vi (haben) (+ gen) need. B∼nis nt -ses,-se need. B∼nisanstalt f public convenience. b∼tig a needy

Beefsteak /'bi:fste:k/ nt -s,-s steak; deutsches B∼ hamburger

beeilen (sich) vr hurry; hasten (zu to); beeilt euch! hurry up!

beeindrucken vt impress

beeinflussen vt influence

beeinträchtigen vt mar; (schädigen) impair

beend[ig]en vt end

beengen vt restrict; beengt wohnen live in cramped conditions

beerben vt jdn b∼ inherit s.o.'s property

beerdig|en vt bury. B∼ung f -,-en funeral

Beere f -,-n berry

Beet nt -[e]s,-e (Hort) bed

Beete f -,-n rote B∼ beetroot

befähig|en vt enable; (qualifizieren) qualify. B∼ung f - qualification; (Fähigkeit) ability

befahr|bar a passable. b∼en† vt drive along; stark b∼ene Straße busy road

befallen† vt attack; (Angst:) seize

befangen a shy; (*gehemmt*) self-conscious; (*Jur*) biased. B~heit f- shyness; self-consciousness; bias

befassen (sich) vr concern oneself/ (*behandeln*) deal (mit with)

Befehl m -[e]s,-e order; (*Leitung*) command (über + acc of). b~en† vt jdm etw b~en order s.o. to do sth a vi (*haben*) give the orders. b~igen vt (*Mil*) command. B~sform f (*Gram*) imperative. B~shaber m -s,- commander

befestig|en vt fasten (an + dat to); (*stärken*) strengthen; (*Mil*) fortify. B~ung f-,-en fastening; (*Mil*) fortification

befeuchten vt moisten

befinden† (sich) vr be. B~ nt -s [state of] health

beflecken vt stain

beflissen a assiduous, adv -ly

befolgen vt follow

beförder|n vt transport; (*im Rang*) promote. B~ung f-,-en transport; promotion

befragen vt question

befrei|en vt free; (*räumen*) clear (von of); (*freistellen*) exempt (von from); sich b~en free oneself. B~er m -s,- liberator. b~t a (*erleichtert*) relieved. B~ung f- liberation; exemption

befremd|en vt disconcert. B~en nt -s surprise. b~lich a strange

befreunden (sich) vr make friends; befreundet sein be friends

befriedig|en vt satisfy. b~end a satisfying; (*zufrieden stellend*) satisfactory. B~ung f- satisfaction

befruchten vt fertilize. B~ung f- fertilization; künstliche B~ung artificial insemination

Befug|nis f-,-se authority. b~t a authorized

Befund m result

befürchten vt fear. B~ung f-,-en fear

befürworten vt support

begab|t a gifted. B~ung f-,-en gift, talent

begatten (sich) vr mate

begeben† (sich) vr go; (*liter: geschehen*) happen; sich in Gefahr b~ expose oneself to danger. B~heit f-,-en incident

begegn|en vi (*sein*) jdm/etw b~en meet s.o./sth; sich b~en meet. B~ung f-,-en meeting; (*Sport*) encounter

begehen† vt walk along; (*verüben*) commit; (*feiern*) celebrate

begehr|en vt desire. b~enswert a desirable. b~t a sought-after

begeister|n vt jdn b~n arouse s.o.'s enthusiasm; sich b~n be enthusiastic (für

about). b~t a enthusiastic, adv -ally; (*eifrig*) keen. B~ung f- enthusiasm

Begier|de f-,-n desire. b~ig a eager (auf + acc for)

begießen† vt water; (*Culin*) baste; (*fam: feiern*) celebrate

Beginn m -s beginning; zu B~ at the beginning. b~en† vt/i (*haben*) start, begin; (*anstellen*) do

beglaubigen vt authenticate

begleichen† vt settle

begleit|en vt accompany. B~er m -s,-, B~erin f -,-nen companion; (*Mus*) accompanist. B~ung f-,-en company; (*Gefolge*) entourage; (*Mus*) accompaniment

beglück|en vt make happy. b~t a happy. b~wünschen vt congratulate (zu on)

begnadig|en vt (*Jur*) pardon. B~ung f -,-en (*Jur*) pardon

begnügen (sich) vr content oneself (mit with)

Begonie /-jə/ f-,-n begonia

begraben† vt bury

Begräbnis n -ses,-se burial; (*Feier*) funeral

begreif|en† vt understand; nicht zu b~en incomprehensible. b~lich a understandable; jdm etw b~lich machen make s.o. understand sth. b~licherweise adv understandably

begrenz|en vt form the boundary of; (*beschränken*) restrict. b~t a limited. B~ung f-,-en restriction; (*Grenze*) boundary

Begriff m -[e]s,-e concept; (*Ausdruck*) term; (*Vorstellung*) idea; für meine B~e to my mind; im B~ sein etw zu tun be about (zu to); schwer von B~ (*fam*) slow on the uptake. b~sstutzig a obtuse

begründ|en vt give one's reason for; (*gründen*) establish. b~et a justified. B~ung f-,-en reason

begrüß|en vt greet; (*billigen*) welcome. b~enswert a welcome. B~ung f- greeting; welcome

begünstigen vt favour; (*fördern*) encourage

begutachten vt give an opinion on; (*fam: ansehen*) look at

begütert a wealthy

begütigen vt placate

behaart a hairy

behäbig a portly; (*gemütlich*) comfortable, adv -bly

behagen vi (*haben*) please (jdm s.o.). B~en nt -s contentment; (*Genuss*) enjoyment. b~lich a comfortable, adv -bly. B~lichkeit f- comfort

behalten† vt keep; (sich merken) remember; etw für sich b~ (verschweigen) keep sth to oneself

Behälter m -s,- container

behände a nimble, adv -bly

behandeln vt treat; (sich befassen) deal with. B~lung f treatment

beharr|en vi (haben) persist (auf + dat in). b~lich a persistent, adv -ly; (hartnäckig) dogged, adv -ly. B~lichkeit f - persistence

behaupt|en vt maintain; (vorgeben) claim; (sagen) say; (bewahren) retain; sich b~en hold one's own. B~ung f -,-en assertion; claim; (Äußerung) statement

beheben† vt remedy; (beseitigen) remove

behelf|en (sich) vr make do (mit with). b~smäßig a make-shift □ adv provisionally

behelligen vt bother

behende a (NEW) behände

beherbergen vt put up

beherrsch|en vt rule over; (dominieren) dominate; (meistern, zügeln) control; (können) know; sich b~en control oneself. b~ta self-controlled. B~ung f -control; (Selbst-) self-control; (Können) mastery

beherzigen vt heed. b~t a courageous, adv -ly

behilflich a jdm b~ sein help s.o.

behinder|n vt hinder; (blockieren) obstruct. b~t a handicapped; (schwer) disabled. B~te(r) m/f handicapped/disabled person. B~ung f -,-en obstruction; (Med) handicap; disability

Behörde f -,-n [public] authority

behüte|n vt protect; Gott behüte! heaven forbid! b~t a sheltered

behutsam a careful, adv -ly; (zart) gentle, adv -ly

bei prep (+ dat) near; (dicht) by; at (Firma, Veranstaltung); bei der Hand nehmen take by the hand; bei sich haben have with one; bei mir at my place; in (in meinem Fall) in my case; Herr X bei Meyer Mr X c/o Meyer; bei Regen when/(falls) if it rains; bei Feuer in case of fire; bei Tag/Nacht by day/night; bei der Ankunft on arrival; bei Tisch/der Arbeit at table/work; bei guter Gesundheit in good health; bei der hohen Miete [what] with the high rent; bei all seiner Klugheit for all his cleverness

beibehalten† vt sep keep

beibringen† vt sep jdm etw b~ teach s.o. sth; (mitteilen) break sth to s.o.; (zufügen) inflict sth on s.o.

Beicht|e f -,-n confession. b~en vt/i (haben) confess. B~stuhl m confessional

beide a & pron both; die b~n Brüder the two brothers; b~s both; dreißig b~ (Tennis) thirty all. b~rseitig a mutual. b~rseits adv & prep (+ gen) on both sides (of)

beidrehen vi sep (haben) heave to

beieinander adv together

Beifahrer|(in) m(f) [front-seat] passenger; (Lkw) driver's mate; (Motorrad) pillion passenger. B~sitz m passenger seat

Beifall m -[e]s applause; (Billigung) approval; B~ klatschen applaud

beifällig a approving, adv -ly

beifügen vt sep add; (beilegen) enclose

beige /be:ʒ/ inv a beige

beigeben† v sep □ vt add □ vi (haben) klein b~ give in

Beigeschmack m [slight] taste

Beihilfe f financial aid; (Studien-) grant; (Jur) aiding and abetting

beikommen† vi sep (sein) jdm b~ get the better of s.o.

Beil nt -[e]s,-e hatchet, axe

Beilage f supplement; (Gemüse) vegetable; als B~ Reis (Culin) served with rice

beiläufig a casual, adv -ly

beilegen vt sep enclose; (schlichten) settle

beileibe adv b~ nicht by no means

Beileid nt condolences pl. B~sbrief m letter of condolence

beiliegend a enclosed

beim prep = bei dem; b~ Militär in the army; b~ Frühstück at breakfast; b~ Lesen when reading; b~ Lesen sein be reading

beimessen† vt sep (fig) attach (dat to)

Bein nt -[e]s,-e leg; jdm ein B~ stellen trip s.o. up

beinah[e] adv nearly, almost

Beiname m epithet

beipflichten vi sep (haben) agree (dat with)

Beirat m advisory committee

beirren vt sich nicht b~ lassen not let oneself be put off

beisammen adv together; b~ sein be together. b~sein† vi sep (sein) (NEW) b~ sein, s. beisammen. B~sein nt -s getting-together

Beisein nt presence

beiseite adv aside; (abseits) apart; b~ legen put aside; (sparen) put by; Spaß od Scherz b~ joking apart

beisetz|en vt sep bury. B~ung f -,-en funeral

Beispiel nt example; zum B~ for example. b~haft a exemplary. b~los a unprecedented. b~weise adv for example

beispringen† *vi sep* (*sein*) jdm b~ come to s.o.'s aid

beißen| *vt/i* (*haben*) bite; (*brennen*) sting; sich b~en (*Farben:*) clash. b~end *a* (*fig*) biting; (*Bemerkung*) caustic. B~zange *f* pliers *pl*

Bei|stand *m* -[e]s help; jdm B~stand leisten help s.o. b~stehen† *vi sep* (*haben*) jdm b~stehen help s.o.

beisteuern *vt sep* contribute

beistimmen *vi sep* (*haben*) agree

Beistrich *m* comma

Beitrag *m* -[e]s,⸚e contribution; (*Mitglieds-*) subscription; (*Versicherungs-*) premium; (*Zeitungs-*) article. b~en† *vt/i sep* (*haben*) contribute

bei|treten† *vi sep* (*sein*) (+ *dat*) join. B~tritt *m* joining

beiwohnen *vi sep* (*haben*) (+ *dat*) be present at

Beize *f* -,-n (*Holz-*) stain; (*Culin*) marinade

beizeiten *adv* in good time

beizen *vt* stain (*Holz*)

bejahen *vt* answer in the affirmative; (*billigen*) approve of

bejahrt *a* aged, old

bejubeln *vt* cheer

bekämpf|en *vt* fight. B~ung *f·* fight (*gegen* against)

bekannt *a* well-known; (*vertraut*) familiar; jdm b~ sein be known to s.o.; jdm b~ machen introduce s.o.; etw b~ machen *od* geben announce sth; b~ werden become known. B~e(r) *m/f* acquaintance; (*Freund*) friend. B~gabe *f* (NEW) announcement. b~geben† *vt sep* (NEW) b~ geben, *s.* bekannt. b~lich *adv* as is well known. b~machen *vt sep* (NEW) b~ machen, *s.* bekannt. B~machung *f* -,-en announcement; (*Anschlag*) notice. B~schaft *f* - acquaintance; (*Leute*) acquaintances *pl*; (*Freunde*) friends *pl*. b~werden† *vi sep* (*sein*) (NEW) b~ werden, *s.* bekannt

bekehr|en *vt* convert; sich b~en become converted. B~ung *f* -,-en conversion

bekenn|en† *vt* confess, profess (*Glauben*); sich [für] schuldig b~en admit one's guilt; sich b~en zu confess to (*Tat*); profess (*Glauben*); (*stehen zu*) stand by. B~tnis *nt* -ses,-se confession; (*Konfession*) denomination

beklag|en *vt* lament; (*bedauern*) deplore; sich b~en complain. b~enswert *a* unfortunate. B~te(r) *m/f* (*Jur*) defendant

beklatschen *vt* applaud

bekleid|en *vt* hold (*Amt*). b~et *a* dressed (mit in). B~ung *f* clothing

Beklemmung *f* -,-en feeling of oppression

beklommen *a* uneasy; (*ängstlich*) anxious, *adv* -ly

bekommen† *vt* get; have (*Baby*); catch (*Erkältung*); Angst/Hunger b~ get frightened/hungry; etw geliehen b~ be lent sth □ *vi* (*sein*) jdm gut b~ do s.o. good; (*Essen:*) agree with s.o.

bekömmlich *a* digestible

beköstig|en *vt* feed; sich selbst b~en cater for oneself. B~ung *f·* board; (*Essen*) food

bekräftigen *vt* reaffirm; (*bestätigen*) confirm

bekreuzigen (sich) *vr* cross oneself

bekümmert *a* troubled; (*besorgt*) worried

bekunden *vt* show; (*bezeugen*) testify

belächeln *vt* laugh at

beladen† *vt* load □ *a* laden

Belag *m* -[e]s,⸚e coating; (*Fußboden-*) covering; (*Brot-*) topping; (*Zahn-*) tartar; (*Brems-*) lining

belager|n *vt* besiege. B~ung *f* -,-en siege

Belang *m* von/ohne B~ of/of no importance; B~e *pl* interests. b~en *vt* (*Jur*) sue. b~los *a* irrelevant; (*unwichtig*) trivial. B~losigkeit *f* -,-en triviality

belassen† *vt* leave; es dabei b~ leave it at that

belasten *vt* load; (*fig*) burden; (*beanspruchen*) put a strain on; (*Comm*) debit; (*Jur*) incriminate

belästigen *vt* bother; (*bedrängen*) pester; (*unsittlich*) molest

Belastung *f* -,-en load; (*fig*) strain; (*Last*) burden; (*Comm*) debit. B~smaterial *nt* incriminating evidence. B~szeuge *m* prosecution witness

belaufen†(sich) *vr* amount (auf + *acc* to)

belauschen *vt* eavesdrop on

beleb|en *vt* (*fig*) revive; (*lebhaft machen*) enliven; wieder b~en (*Med*) revive, resuscitate; (*fig*) revive (*Handel*); sich b~en revive; (*Stadt:*) come to life. b~t *a* lively; (*Straße*) busy

Beleg *m* -[e]s,-e evidence; (*Beispiel*) instance (für of); (*Quittung*) receipt. b~en *vt* cover/(*garnieren*) garnish (mit with); (*besetzen*) reserve; (*Univ*) enrol for; (*nachweisen*) provide evidence for; den ersten Platz b~en (*Sport*) take first place. B~schaft *f* -,-en work-force. b~t *a* occupied; (*Zunge*) coated; (*Stimme*) husky; b~te Brote open sandwiches; der Platz ist b~t this seat is taken

belehren *vt* instruct; (*aufklären*) inform

beleibt *a* corpulent

beleidig|en vt offend; (absichtlich) insult. B~ung f -,-en insult

belesen a well-read

beleucht|en vt light; (anleuchten) illuminate. B~ung f -,-en illumination; (elektrisch) lighting; (Licht) light

Belgi|en /-jən/ nt -s Belgium. B~ier(in) m -s,- (f -,-nen) Belgian. b~isch a Belgian

belicht|en vt (Phot) expose. B~ung f - exposure

Belieb|en nt -s nach B~en [just] as one likes; (Culin) if liked. b~ig a eine b~ige Zahl/Farbe any number/colour you like □ adv b~ig lange/oft as long/often as one likes. b~t a popular. B~theit f - popularity

beliefern vt supply (mit with)

bellen vi (haben) bark

belohn|en vt reward. B~ung f -,-en reward

belüften vt ventilate

belügen† vt lie to; sich [selbst] b~ deceive oneself

belustig|en vt amuse. B~ung f -,-en amusement

bemächtigen (sich) vr (+ gen) seize

bemalen vt paint

bemängeln vt criticize

bemannt a manned

bemerk|bar a sich b~bar machen attract attention; (Ding:) become noticeable. b~en vt notice; (äußern) remark. b~ enswert a remarkable, adv -bly. B~ung f -,-en remark

bemitleiden vt pity

bemittelt a well-to-do

bemüh|en vt trouble; sich b~en try (zu to; um etw to get sth); (sich kümmern) attend (um to); b~t sein endeavour (zu to). B~ung f -,-en effort; (Mühe) trouble

bemuttern vt mother

benachbart a neighbouring

benachrichtig|en vt inform; (amtlich) notify. B~ung f -,-en notification

benachteilig|en vt discriminate against; (ungerecht sein) treat unfairly. B~ung f -,-en discrimination (gen against)

benehmen† (sich) vr behave. B~ nt -s behaviour

beneiden vt envy (um etw sth). b~swert a enviable

Bengel m -s,- boy; (Rüpel) lout

benommen a dazed

benötigen vt need

benutz|en, (SGer) **benützen** vt use; take (Bahn). B~er m -s,- user. b~erfreundlich a user-friendly. B~ung f use

Benzin nt -s petrol, (Amer) gasoline. B~tank m petrol tank

beobacht|en vt observe. B~er m -s,- observer. B~ung f -,-en observation

bepacken vt load (mit with)

bepflanzen vt plant (mit with)

bequem a comfortable, adv -bly; (mühelos) easy, adv -ily; (faul) lazy. b~en (sich) vr deign (zu to). B~lichkeit f -,-en comfort; (Faulheit) laziness

berat|en† vt advise; (überlegen) discuss; sich b~en confer; sich b~en lassen get advice □ vi (haben) discuss (über etw acc sth); (beratschlagen) confer. B~er(in) m -s,- (f -,-nen) adviser. b~schlagen vi (haben) confer. B~ung f -,-en guidance; (Rat) advice; (Besprechung) discussion; (Med, Jur) consultation. B~ungsstelle f advice centre

berauben vt rob (gen of)

berauschen vt intoxicate. b~d a intoxicating, heady

berechn|en vt calculate; (anrechnen) charge for; (abfordern) charge. b~end a (fig) calculating. B~ung f calculation

berechtig|en vt entitle; (befugen) authorize; (fig) justify. b~t a justified, justifiable. B~ung f -,-en authorization; (Recht) right; (Rechtmäßigkeit) justification

bered|en vt talk about; (klatschen) gossip about; (überreden) talk round; sich b~en talk. B~samkeit f - eloquence

beredt a eloquent, adv -ly

Bereich m -[e]s,-e area; (fig) realm; (Fach-) field

bereichern vt enrich; sich b~ grow rich (an + dat on)

Bereifung f - tyres pl

bereinigen vt (fig) settle

bereit a ready. b~en vt prepare; (verursachen) cause; give (Überraschung). b~halten† vt sep have (ständig) keep ready. b~legen vt sep put out [ready]. b~machen vt sep get ready; sich b~machen get ready. b~s adv already

Bereitschaft f -,-en readiness; (Einheit) squad. B~sdienst m B~sdienst haben (Mil) be on stand-by; (Arzt:) be on call; (Apotheke:) be open for out-of-hours dispensing. B~spolizei f riot police

bereit|stehen† vi sep (haben) be ready. b~stellen vt sep put out ready; (verfügbar machen) make available. B~ung f - preparation. b~willig a willing, adv -ly. B~willigkeit f - willingness

bereuen vt regret

Berg m -[e]s,-e mountain; (Anhöhe) hill; in den B~en in the mountains. b~ab adv downhill. b~an adv uphill. B~arbeiter *m* miner. b~auf *adv* uphill; es geht b~auf *(fig)* things are looking up. B~bau *m* -[e]s mining

bergen† *vt* recover; *(Naut)* salvage; *(retten)* rescue

Berg|führer *m* mountain guide. b~ig *a* mountainous. B~kette *f* mountain range. B~mann *m* *(pl* -leute) miner. B~steigen *nt* -s mountaineering. B~steiger(in) *m* -s, *(f* -,-nen) mountaineer, climber. B~-und-Talbahn *f* roller-coaster

Bergung *f* - recovery; *(Naut)* salvage; *(Rettung)* rescue

Berg|wacht *f* mountain rescue service. B~werk *nt* mine

Bericht *m* -[e]s,-e report; *(Reise-)* account; B~ erstatten report (über + *acc* on). b~en *vt/i* *(haben)* report; *(erzählen)* tell (von of). B~erstatter(in) *m* -s,- *(f*-,-nen) reporter; *(Korrespondent)* correspondent

berichtig|en *vt* correct. B~ung *f* -,-en correction

berieseln|n *vt* irrigate. B~ungsanlage *f* sprinkler system

beritten *a* ⟨*Polizei*⟩ mounted

Berlin *nt* -s Berlin. B~er *m* -s,- Berliner; *(Culin)* doughnut □ *a* Berlin . . .

Bernhardiner *m* -s,- St Bernard

Bernstein *m* amber

bersten† *vi* *(sein)* burst

berüchtigt *a* notorious

berückend *a* entrancing

berücksichtig|en *vt* take into consideration. B~ung *f* - consideration

Beruf *m* profession; *(Tätigkeit)* occupation; *(Handwerk)* trade. b~en† *vt* appoint; sich b~en refer (auf + *acc* to); *(vorgeben)* plead (auf etw *acc* sth) □ *a* competent; b~en sein be destined (zu to). b~lich *a* professional; *(Ausbildung)* vocational □ *adv* professionally; b~lich tätig sein work, have a job. B~saussichten *fpl* career prospects. B~sberater(in) *m(f)* careers officer. B~sberatung *f* vocational guidance. b~smäßig *adv* professionally. B~sschule *f* vocational school. B~ssoldat *m* regular soldier. b~stätig *a* working; b~stätig sein work, have a job. B~stätige(r) *m/f* working man/woman. B~sverkehr *m* rush-hour traffic. B~ung *f* -,-en appointment; *(Bestimmung)* vocation; *(Jur)* appeal; B~ung einlegen appeal. B~ungsgericht *nt* appeal court

beruhen *vi* *(haben)* be based (auf + *dat* on); eine Sache auf sich b~ lassen let a matter rest

beruhig|en *vt* calm [down]; *(zuversichtlich machen)* reassure; sich b~en calm

down. b~end *a* calming; *(tröstend)* reassuring; *(Med)* sedative. B~ung *f* - calming; reassurance; *(Med)* sedation. B~ungsmittel *nt* sedative; *(bei Psychosen)* tranquillizer

berühmt *a* famous. B~heit *f* -,-en fame; *(Person)* celebrity

berühr|en *vt* touch; *(erwähnen)* touch on; *(beeindrucken)* affect; sich b~en touch. B~ung *f* -,-en touch; *(Kontakt)* contact

besag|en *vt* say; *(bedeuten)* mean. b~t *a* [afore]said

besänftigen *vt* soothe; sich b~ calm down

Besatz *m* -es,¨e trimming

Besatzung *f* -,-en crew; *(Mil)* occupying force

besaufen† (sich) *vr* *(sl)* get drunk

beschädig|en *vt* damage. B~ung *f* -,-en damage

beschaffen *vt* obtain, get □ *a* so b~ sein, dass be such that; wie ist es b~ mit? what about? B~heit *f* - consistency; *(Art)* nature

beschäftig|en *vt* occupy; ⟨*Arbeitgeber:*⟩ employ; sich b~en occupy oneself. b~t *a* busy; *(angestellt)* employed (bei at). B~te(r) *m/f* employee. B~ung *f* -,-en occupation; *(Anstellung)* employment. b~ungslos *a* unemployed. B~ungstherapie *f* occupational therapy

beschäm|en *vt* make ashamed. b~end *a* shameful; *(demütigend)* humiliating. b~t *a* ashamed; *(verlegen)* embarrassed

beschatten *vt* shade; *(überwachen)* shadow

beschau|en *vt* *(SGer)* [sich *(dat)*] etw b~en look at sth. b~lich *a* tranquil; *(Relig)* contemplative

Bescheid *m* -[e]s information; jdm B~ sagen *od* geben let s.o. know; B~ wissen know

bescheiden *a* modest, *adv* -ly. B~heit *f* - modesty

bescheinen† *vt* shine on; von der Sonne beschienen sunlit

bescheinig|en *vt* certify. B~ung *f* -,-en [written] confirmation; *(Schein)* certificate

beschenken *vt* give a present/presents to

bescher|en *vt* jdn b~en give s.o. presents; jdm etw b~en give s.o. sth. B~ung *f* -,-en distribution of Christmas presents; *(fam: Schlamassel)* mess

beschießen† *vt* fire at; *(mit Artillerie)* shell, bombard

beschildern *vt* signpost

beschimpf|en *vt* abuse, swear at. B~ung *f* -,-en abuse

beschirmen *vt* protect

Beschlag *m* in B~ nehmen, mit B~ belegen monopolize. **b~en†** *vt* shoe □ *vi* (*sein*) steam *or* mist up □ *a* steamed *or* misted up; (*erfahren*) knowledgeable (in + *dat* about). **B~nahme** *f* -,-n confiscation; (*Jur*) seizure. **b~nahmen** *vt* confiscate; (*Jur*) seize; (*fam*) monopolize

beschleunig|en *vt* hasten; (*schneller machen*) speed up; quicken (*Schritt, Tempo*); sich b~en speed up; quicken □ *vi* (*haben*) accelerate. **B~ung** *f* -acceleration

beschließen† *vt* decide; (*beenden*) end □ *vi* (*haben*) decide (über + *acc* about)

Beschluss (Beschluß) *m* decision

beschmieren *vt* smear/(*bestreichen*) spread (mit with)

beschmutzen *vt* make dirty; sich b~ get [oneself] dirty

beschneid|en† *vt* trim; (*Hort*) prune; (*fig: kürzen*) cut back; (*Relig*) circumcise. **B~ung** *f* - circumcision

beschneit *a* snow-covered

beschnüffeln, beschnuppern *vt* sniff at

beschönigen *vt* (*fig*) gloss over

beschränken *vt* limit, restrict; sich b~ auf (+ *acc*) confine oneself to; (*Sache:*) be limited to

beschrankt *a* (*Bahnübergang*) with barrier[s]

beschränk|t *a* limited; (*geistig*) dull-witted; (*borniert*) narrow-minded. **B~ung** *f* -,-en limitation, restriction

beschreib|en† *vt* describe; (*schreiben*) write on. **B~ung** *f* -,-en description

beschuldig|en *vt* accuse. **B~ung** *f* -,-en accusation

beschummeln *vt* (*fam*) cheat

Beschuss (Beschuß) *m* (*Mil*) fire; (*Artillerie-*) shelling

beschütz|en *vt* protect. **B~er** *m* -s,- protector

Beschwer|de *f* -,-n complaint; **B~den** (*Med*) trouble *sg.* **b~en** *vt* weight down; sich b~en complain. **b~lich** *a* difficult

beschwichtigen *vt* placate

beschwindeln *vt* cheat (um out of); (*belügen*) lie to

beschwingt *a* elated; (*munter*) lively

beschwipst *a* (*fam*) tipsy

beschwören† *vt* swear to; (*anflehen*) implore; (*herauf-*) invoke

beseh|en† *vt* look at

beseitig|en *vt* remove. **B~ung** *f* - removal

Besen *m* -s,- broom. **B~ginster** *m* (*Bot*) broom. **B~stiel** *m* broomstick

besessen *a* obsessed (von by)

besetz|en *vt* occupy; fill (*Posten*); (*Theat*) cast (*Rolle*); (*verzieren*) trim (mit with). **b~t** *a* occupied; (*Toilette, Leitung*) engaged; (*Zug, Bus*) full up; der Platz ist b~t this seat is taken; mit Perlen b~t set with pearls. **B~tzeichen** *nt* engaged tone. **B~ung** *f* -,-en occupation; (*Theat*) cast

besichtig|en *vt* look round (*Stadt, Museum*); (*prüfen*) inspect; (*besuchen*) visit. **B~ung** *f* -,-en visit; (*Prüfung*) inspection; (*Stadt-*) sightseeing

besiedelt *a* dünn/dicht b~ sparsely/densely populated

besiegeln *vt* (*fig*) seal

besieg|en *vt* defeat; (*fig*) overcome. **B~te(r)** *m/f* loser

besinn|en† (sich) *vr* think, reflect; (*sich erinnern*) remember (auf jdn/etw s.o./sth); sich anders b~en change one's mind. **b~lich** *a* contemplative; (*nachdenklich*) thoughtful. **B~ung** *f* - reflection; (*Bewusstsein*) consciousness; bei/ohne B~ung conscious/unconscious; zur B~ung kommen regain consciousness; (*fig*) come to one's senses. **b~ungslos** *a* unconscious

Besitz *m* possession; (*Eigentum, Land-*) property; (*Gut*) estate. **b~anzeigend** *a* (*Gram*) possessive. **b~en†** *vt* own, possess; (*haben*) have. **B~er(in)** *m* -s,- (*f* -,-nen) owner; (*Comm*) proprietor. **B~ung** *f* -,-en [landed] property; (*Gut*) estate

besoffen *a* (*sl*) drunken; b~ sein be drunk

besohlen *vt* sole

besold|en *vt* pay. **B~ung** *f* - pay

besonder|e(r,s) *a* special; (*bestimmt*) particular; (*gesondert*) separate; nichts B~es nothing special. **B~heit** *f* -,-en peculiarity. **b~s** *adv* [e]specially, particularly; (*gesondert*) separately

besonnen *a* calm, *adv* -ly

besorg|en *vt* get; (*kaufen*) buy; (*erledigen*) attend to; (*versorgen*) look after. **B~nis** *f* -,-se anxiety; (*Sorge*) worry. **b~niserregend** *a* worrying. **b~t** *a* worried/(*bedacht*) concerned (um about). **B~ung** *f* -,-en errand; **B~ungen machen** do shopping

bespielt *a* recorded

bespitzeln *vt* spy on

besprech|en† *vt* discuss; (*rezensieren*) review; sich b~en confer; ein Tonband b~en make a tape recording. **B~ung** *f* -,-en discussion; review; (*Konferenz*) meeting

bespritzen *vt* splash

besser a & adv better. b~n vt improve; sich b~n get better, improve. B~ung f - improvement; gute B~ung! get well soon! B~wisser m -s,- know-all

Bestand m -[e]s,:-e existence; (Vorrat) stock (an + dat of); B~haben, von B~ sein last

beständig a constant, adv -ly; (Wetter) settled; b~ gegen resistant to

Bestand|saufnahme f stocktaking. B~teil m part

bestärken vt (fig) strengthen

bestätig|en vt confirm; acknowledge (Empfang); sich b~en prove to be true. B~ung f -,-en confirmation

bestatt|en vt bury. B~ung f -,-en funeral. B~ungsinstitut nt [firm of] undertakers pl, (Amer) funeral home

bestäuben vt pollinate

bestaubt a dusty

Bestäubung f - pollination

bestaunen vt gaze at in amazement; (bewundern) admire

best|e(r,s) a best; b~en Dank! many thanks! am b~en sein be best; zum b~en geben/halten (NEW) zum B~en geben/halten, s. Beste(r,s). B~e(r,s) m/f/nt best; sein B~es tun do one's best; zum B~en geben recite (Gedicht); tell (Geschichte, Witz); sing (Lied); jdn zum B~n halten (fam) pull s.o.'s leg

bestech|en vt bribe; (bezaubern) captivate. b~end a captivating. b~lich a corruptible. B~ung f - bribery. B~ungsgeld nt bribe

Besteck nt -[e]s,-e [set of] knife, fork and spoon; (coll) cutlery

bestehen† vt (haben) exist; (fortdauern) last; (bei Prüfung) pass; ~ aus consist of; (gemacht sein) be made of; ~ auf (+ dat) insist on □ vt pass (Prüfung). B~ nt -s existence

bestehlen† vt rob

besteig|en vt climb; (einsteigen) board; (aufsteigen) mount; ascend (Thron). B~ung f ascent

bestell|en vt order; (vor-) book; (ernennen) appoint; (bebauen) cultivate; (ausrichten) tell; zu sich b~en send for; b~t sein have an appointment; kann ich etwas b~en? can I take a message? b~en Sie Ihrer Frau Grüße von mir give my regards to your wife. B~schein m order form. B~ung f order; (Botschaft) message; (Bebauung) cultivation

besten|falls adv at best. b~s adv very well

besteuer|n vt tax. B~ung f - taxation

bestialisch /-st-/ a bestial

Bestie /ˈbɛstjə/ f -,-n beast

bestimm|en vt fix; (entscheiden) decide; (vorsehen) intend; (ernennen) appoint; (ermitteln) determine; (definieren) define; (Gram) qualify □ vi (haben) be in charge (über + acc of). □ a definite, adv -ly; (gewiss) certain, adv -ly; (fest) firm, adv -ly. B~theit f - firmness; mit B~theit for certain. B~ung f fixing; (Vorschrift) regulation; (Ermittlung) determination; (Definition) definition; (Zweck) purpose; (Schicksal) destiny. B~ungsort m destination

Bestleistung f (Sport) record

bestraf|en vt punish. B~ung f -,-en punishment

bestrahl|en vt shine on; (Med) treat with radiotherapy; irradiate (Lebensmittel). B~ung f radiotherapy

Bestreb|en nt -s endeavour; (Absicht) aim. b~t a b~t sein endeavour (zu to). B~ung f -,-en effort

bestreichen† vt spread (mit with)

bestreikt a strike-hit

bestreiten† vt dispute; (leugnen) deny; (bezahlen) pay for

bestreuen vt sprinkle (mit with)

bestürmen vt (fig) besiege

bestürz|t a dismayed; (erschüttert) stunned. B~ung f - dismay, consternation

Bestzeit f (Sport) record [time]

Besuch m -[e]s,-e visit; (kurz) call; (Schul-) attendance; (Gast) visitor; (Gäste) visitors pl; B~ haben have a visitor/visitors; bei jdm zu od auf B~ sein be staying with s.o. b~en vt visit; (kurz) call on; (teilnehmen) attend; go to (Schule, Ausstellung); gut b~t well attended. B~er(in) m -s,- (f -,-nen) visitor; caller; (Theat) patron. B~szeit f visiting hours pl

betagt a aged, old

betasten vt feel

betätig|en vt operate; sich b~en work (als as); sich politisch b~en engage in politics. B~ung f -,-en operation; (Tätigkeit) activity

betäub|en vt stun; (Lärm:) deafen; (Med) anaesthetize; (lindern) ease; deaden (Schmerz); wie b~t dazed. B~ung f - daze; (Med) anaesthesia; unter örtlicher B~ung under local anaesthetic. B~ungsmittel nt anaesthetic

Bete f -,-n rote B~ beetroot

beteilig|en vt give a share to; sich b~en take part (an + dat in); (beitragen) contribute (an + dat to). b~t a b~t sein take part/(an Unfall) be involved/(Comm) have a share (an + dat in); alle B~ten all those involved. B~ung f -,-en participation; involvement; (*Anteil*) share □ vt say

b**eten** vi (*haben*) pray; (*bei Tisch*) say grace □ vt say

be**teuer**|n vt protest. B~ung f -,-en protestation

Beton /be'tɔŋ/ m -s concrete

be**tonen** vt stressed, emphasize

beto**nieren** vt concrete

be**ton**|t a stressed; (*fig*) pointed, adv ·ly. B~ung f -,-en stress, emphasis

be**tören** vt bewitch

betr., Betr. abbr (betreffs) re

Be**tracht** m in B~ ziehen consider; außer B~ lassen disregard; nicht in B~ kommen be out of the question. b~en vt look at; (*fig*) regard (als as)

be**trächtlich** a considerable, adv ·bly

Be**trachtung** f -,-en contemplation; (*Überlegung*) reflection

Be**trag** m -[e]s,·̈e amount. b~en† vt amount to; sich b~en behave. B~en nt -s behaviour; (*Sch*) conduct

be**trauen** vt entrust (mit with)

be**trauern** vt mourn

be**treff**|en† vt affect; (*angehen*) concern; was mich betrifft as far as I am concerned. b~end a relevant; der b~ende Brief the letter in question. b~s prep (+ gen) concerning

be**treiben**† vt (*leiten*) run; (*ausüben*) carry on; (*vorantreiben*) pursue; (*antreiben*) run (mit on)

be**treten**† vt step on; (*eintreten*) enter; 'B~ verboten 'no entry'; (*bei Rasen*) 'keep off [the grass]' □ a embarrassed □ adv in embarrassment

be**treu**|en vt look after. B~er(in) m -s,· (f -,-nen) helper; (*Kranken-*) nurse. B~ung f - care

Be**trieb** m business; (*Firma*) firm; (*Treiben*) activity; (*Verkehr*) traffic; in B~ working; (*in Gebrauch*) in use; außer B~ not in use; (*defekt*) out of order

Be**triebs**|anleitung, B~anweisung f operating instructions pl. B~ferien pl firm's holiday; 'B~ferien 'closed for the holidays'. B~leitung f management. B~rat m works committee. B~ruhe f montags B~ruhe' 'closed on Mondays'. B~störung f breakdown

be**trinken**† (sich) vr get drunk

be**troffen** a disconcerted; b~ sein be affected (von by); die B~en those affected □ adv in consternation

be**trüb**|en vt sadden. b~lich a sad. b~t a sad, adv ·ly

Be**trug** m -[e]s deception; (*Jur*) fraud

be**trüg**|en† vt cheat, swindle; (*Jur*) defraud; (*in der Ehe*) be unfaithful to; sich selbst b~en deceive oneself. B~er(in) m -s,· (f -,-nen) swindler. B~erei f -,-en fraud. b~erisch a fraudulent; (*Person*) deceitful

be**trunken** a drunken; b~ sein be drunk. B~e(r) m drunk

Bett nt -[e]s,-en bed; im B~ in bed; ins od zu B~ gehen go to bed. B~couch f sofabed. B~decke f blanket; (*Tages-*) bedspread

bettel|arm a destitute. B~ei f - begging. b~n vi (*haben*) beg

bett|en vt lay, put; sich b~en lie down. b~lägerig a bedridden. B~laken nt sheet

Bettler(in) m -s,· (f -,-nen) beggar

Bettpfanne f bedpan

Betttuch (Bettuch) nt sheet

Bett|vorleger m bedside rug. B~wäsche f bed linen. B~zeug nt bedding

be**tupfen** vt dab (mit with)

beug|en vt bend; (*Gram*) decline; conjugate (*Verb*); sich b~en bend; (*lehnen*) lean; (*sich fügen*) submit (dat to). B~ung f -,-en (*Gram*) declension; conjugation

Beule f -,-n bump; (*Delle*) dent

be**unruhig**|en vt worry; sich b~en worry. B~ung f - worry

be**urlauben** vt give leave to; (*des Dienstes entheben*) suspend

be**urteil**|en vt judge. B~ung f -,-en judgement; (*Ansicht*) opinion

Beute f - booty, haul; (*Jagd-*) bag; (*B~tier*) quarry; (*eines Raubtiers*) prey

Beutel m -s,· bag; (*Geld-*) purse; (*Tabak- & Zool*) pouch. B~tier nt marsupial

be**völker**|n vt populate. B~ung f -,-en population

be**vollmächtig**|en vt authorize. B~te(r) m/f [authorized] agent

bevor conj before; b~ nicht until

be**vormunden** vt treat like a child

be**vorstehen**† vi sep (*haben*) approach; (*unmittelbar*) be imminent; jdm b~ be in store for s.o. b~d a approaching, forthcoming; unmittelbar b~d imminent

be**vorzug**|en vt prefer; (*begünstigen*) favour. b~t a privileged; (*Behandlung*) preferential; (*beliebt*) favoured

be**wachen** vt guard; bewachter Parkplatz car park with an attendant

be**wachsen** a covered (mit with)

Be**wachung** f - guard; unter B~ under guard

be**waffn**|en vt arm. b~et a armed. B~ung f - armament; (*Waffen*) arms pl

bewahren vt protect (vor + dat from); (behalten) keep; die Ruhe b~ keep calm; Gott bewahre! heaven forbid!

bewähren (sich) vr prove one's/⟨Ding:⟩ its worth; (erfolgreich sein) prove a success

bewahrheiten (sich) vr prove to be true

bewähr|t a reliable; (erprobt) proven. B~ung f -(Jur) probation. B~ungsfrist f [period of] probation. B~ungsprobe f (fig) test

bewaldet a wooded

bewältigen vt cope with; (überwinden) overcome; (schaffen) manage

bewandert a knowledgeable

bewässer|n vt irrigate. B~ung f - irrigation

bewegen¹ vt (reg) move; sich b~ move; (körperlich) take exercise

bewegen² vt jdn dazu b~, etw zu tun induce s.o. to do sth

Beweg|grund m motive. b~lich a movable, mobile; (wendig) agile. B~lichkeit f -mobility; agility. b~t a moved; (ergnisreich) eventful; ⟨See⟩ rough. B~ung f -,-en movement; (Phys) motion; (Rührung) emotion; (Gruppe) movement; körperliche B~ung physical exercise; sich in B~ung setzen [start to] move. B~ungsfreiheit f freedom of movement/(fig) of action. b~ungslos a motionless

beweinen vt mourn

Beweis m -es,-e proof; (Zeichen) token; B~evidence sg. b~en† vt prove; (zeigen) show; sich b~en prove oneself/⟨Ding:⟩ itself. B~material nt evidence

bewenden vi es dabei b~lassen leave it at that

bewerb|en (sich) vr apply (um for; bei to). B~er(in) m -s,- (f -,-nen) applicant. B~ung f -,-en application

bewerkstelligen vt manage

bewerten vt value; (einschätzen) rate; (Sch) mark, grade

bewilligen vt grant

bewirken vt cause; (herbeiführen) bring about; (erreichen) achieve

bewirt|en vt entertain. B~ung f -hospitality

bewohn|bar a habitable. b~en vt inhabit, live in. B~er(in) m -s,- (f -,-nen) resident, occupant; (Einwohner) inhabitant

bewölk|en (sich) vr cloud over; b~t cloudy. B~ung f -clouds pl

bewunder|n vt admire. b~nswert a admirable. B~ung f - admiration

bewusst (bewußt) a conscious (gen of); (absichtlich) deliberate, adv -ly; (besagt) said; sich (dat) etw (gen) b~ sein/ werden be/become aware of sth. b~los a unconscious. B~losigkeit f - unconsciousness; B~sein n -s consciousness; (Gewissheit) awareness; bei [vollem] B~sein [fully] conscious; mir kam zum B~sein I realized (dass that)

bez. abbr (bezahlt) paid; (bezüglich) re

bezahl|en vt/i (haben) pay; pay for (Ware, Essen); gut b~te Arbeit well-paid work; sich b~t machen (fig) pay off. B~ung f - payment; (Lohn) pay

bezähmen vt control; (zügeln) restrain; sich b~ restrain oneself

bezaubern vt enchant. b~d a enchanting

bezeichn|en vt mark; (bedeuten) denote; (beschreiben, nennen) describe (als as). b~end a typical. B~ung f marking; (Beschreibung) description (als as); (Ausdruck) term; (Name) name

bezeugen vt testify to

bezichtigen vt accuse (gen of)

bezieh|en† vt cover; (einziehen) move into; (beschaffen) obtain; (erhalten) get, receive; take ⟨Zeitung⟩; (in Verbindung bringen) relate (auf + acc to); sich b~en (bewölken) cloud over; sich b~en auf (+ acc) refer to; das Bett frisch b~en put clean sheets on the bed. B~ung f -,-en relation; (Verhältnis) relationship; (Bezug) respect; in dieser B~ung in this respect; [gute] B~ungen haben have [good] connections. b~ungsweise adv respectively; (vielmehr) or rather

beziffern (sich) vr amount (auf + acc to)

Bezirk m -[e]s,-e district

Bezug m cover; (Kissen-) case; (Beschaffung) obtaining; (Kauf) purchase; (Zusammenhang) reference; B~e pl earnings; B~ nehmen refer (auf + acc to); in B~ (b~) auf (+ acc) regarding, concerning

bezüglich prep (+ gen) regarding, concerning □ a relating (auf + acc to);(Gram) relative

bezwecken vt (fig) aim at

bezweifeln vt doubt

bezwingen† vt conquer

BH /be:'ha:/ m -[s],-[s] bra

bibbern vi (haben) tremble; (vor Kälte) shiver

Bibel f -,-n Bible

Biber¹ m -s,- beaver

Biber² m & nt -s flannelette

Biblio|graphie B~grafie f -,-n bibliography. B~thek f -,-en library. B~thekar(in) m -s,- (f -,-nen) librarian

biblisch a biblical

bieder a honest, upright; (*ehrenwert*) worthy; (*einfach*) simple

biegen† vt bend; sich b∼en bend; sich vor Lachen b∼en (*fam*) double up with laughter □ vi (*sein*) curve (nach to); um die Ecke b∼en turn the corner. b∼sam a flexible, supple. B∼ung f -,-en bend

Biene f -,-n bee. B∼nhonig m natural honey. B∼nstock m beehive. B∼nwabe f honeycomb

Bier nt -s,-e beer. B∼deckel m beer-mat. B∼krug m beer-mug

Biest nt -[e]s,-er (*fam*) beast

bieten† vt offer; (*bei Auktion*) bid; (*zeigen*) present; das lasse ich mir nicht b∼ I won't stand for that

Bifokalbrille f bifocals pl

Biga|mie f - bigamy. B∼ mist m -en,-en bigamist

bigott a over-pious

Bikini m -s,-s bikini

Bilanz f -,-en balance sheet; (*fig*) result; die B∼ ziehen (*fig*) draw conclusions (aus from)

Bild nt -[e]s,-er picture; (*Theat*) scene; jdn ins B∼ setzen put s.o. in the picture

bilden vt form; (*sein*) be; (*erziehen*) educate; sich b∼ form; (*geistig*) educate oneself

Bild|erbuch nt picture-book. B∼ergalerie f picture gallery. B∼fläche f screen; von der B∼fläche verschwinden disappear from the scene. B∼hauer m -s,-sculptor. B∼hauerei f - sculpture. b∼hübsch a very pretty. b∼lich a pictorial; (*figurativ*) figurative, adv -ly. B∼nis nt -ses,-se portrait. B∼schirm m (*TV*) screen. B∼schirmgerät nt visual display unit, VDU. b∼schön a very beautiful

Bildung f -formation; (*Erziehung*) education; (*Kultur*) culture

Billard /'bɪljart/ nt -s billiards sg. B∼tisch m billiard table

Billett /bɪl'jɛt/ nt -[e]s,-e & -s ticket

Billiarde f -,-n thousand million million

billig a cheap, adv -ly; (*dürftig*) poor; (*gerecht*) just; recht und b∼ right and proper. b∼en vt approve. B∼ung f - approval

Billion /bɪljo:n/ f -,-en million million, billion

bimmeln vi (*haben*) tinkle

Bimsstein m pumice stone

bin s. sein; ich bin I am

Binde f -,-n band; (*Verband*) bandage; (*Damen-*) sanitary towel. B∼hautentzündung f conjunctivitis. b∼n† vt tie

(an + acc to); make ⟨*Strauß*⟩; bind ⟨*Buch*⟩; (*fesseln*) tie up; (*Culin*) thicken; sich b∼n commit oneself. b∼nd a (*fig*) binding. B∼strich m hyphen. B∼wort nt (pl -wörter) (*Gram*) conjunction

Bind|faden m string; ein B∼faden a piece of string. B∼ung f -,-en (*fig*) tie, bond; (*Beziehung*) relationship; (*Verpflichtung*) commitment; (*Ski-*) binding; (*Tex*) weave

binnen prep (+ dat) within; b∼ kurzem shortly. B∼handel m home trade

Binse f -,-n rush. B∼nwahrheit, B∼nweisheit f truism

Bio- pref organic

Bio|chemie f biochemistry. b∼dynamisch m organic. B∼graphie, B∼grafie f -,-biography

Bio|hof m organic farm. B∼laden m health-food store

Biolog|e m -n,-n biologist. B∼ie f - biology. b∼isch a biological, adv -ly; b∼ischer Anbau organic farming; b∼isch angebaut organically grown

Birke f -,-n birch [tree]

Birm|a nt -s Burma. b∼anisch a Burmese

Birn|baum m pear-tree. B∼e f -,-n pear; (*Electr*) bulb

bis prep (+ acc) as far as, [up] to; (*zeitlich*) until, till; (*spätestens*) by; bis zu up to; bis jetzt up to now, so far; bis dahin until/ (*spätestens*) then; bis auf (+ acc) (*einschließlich*) [down] to; (*ausgenommen*) except [for]; drei bis vier Mark three to four marks; bis morgen! see you tomorrow! □ conj until

Bischof m -s,-e bishop

bisher adv so far, up to now. b∼ig attrib a ⟨*Präsident*⟩ outgoing; meine b∼igen Erfahrungen my experiences so far

Biskuit|rolle /bɪs'kvi:t-/ f Swiss roll. B∼teig m sponge mixture

bislang adv so far, up to now

Biss m -es,-e (*Biß m -sses,-sse*) bite

bisschen (*bißchen*) inv pron ein b∼ a bit, a little; ein b∼ Brot a bit of bread; kein b∼ not a bit

Biss|en m -s,-. bite, mouthful. b∼ig a vicious; (*fig*) caustic

bist s. sein; du b∼ you are

Bistum nt -s,-er diocese, see

bisweilen adv from time to time

bitte adv please; (*nach Klopfen*) come in; (*als Antwort auf 'danke'*) don't mention it, you're welcome; wie b∼e? pardon? (*empört*) I beg your pardon? möchten Sie Kaffee?—ja b∼e would you like some coffee?—yes please. B∼e f -,-n request/(*dringend*) plea (um for). b∼en† vt/i (*haben*) ask/(*dringend*) beg (um for); (*einladen*) invite, ask; ich b∼e dich! I beg [of] you! (*empört*) I ask you! b∼end *a* pleading, *adv* -ly

bitter *a* bitter, *adv* -ly. B∼keit *f* - bitterness. b∼lich *adv* bitterly

Bittschrift *f* petition

bizarr *a* bizarre, *adv* -ly

bläh|en *vt* swell; puff out (*Vorhang*); sich b∼en swell; (*Vorhang, Segel:*) billow ◻ *vi* (*haben*) cause flatulence. B∼ungen *fpl* flatulence *sg*, (*fam*) wind *sg*

Blamage /bla'ma:ʒə/ *f* -,-n humiliation; (*Schande*) disgrace

blamieren *vt* disgrace; sich b∼ disgrace oneself; (*sich lächerlich machen*) make a fool of oneself

blanchieren /blã'ʃi:rən/ *vt* (*Culin*) blanch

blank *a* shiny; (*nackt*) bare; b∼ sein (*fam*) be broke. B∼oscheck *m* blank cheque

Blase *f* -,-n bubble; (*Med*) blister; (*Anat*) bladder. B∼balg *m* -[e]s,¨e bellows *pl.* b∼n† *vt/i* (*haben*) blow; play (*Flöte*). B∼nentzündung *f* cystitis

Bläser *m* -s,- (*Mus*) wind player; die B∼ the wind section *sg*

blasiert *a* blasé

Blas|instrument *nt* wind instrument. B∼kapelle *f* brass band

Blasphemie *f* - blasphemy

blass (blaß) *a* (blasser, blassest) pale; (*schwach*) faint; b∼ werden turn pale

Blässe *f* - pallor

Blatt *nt* -[e]s,¨er (*Bot*) leaf; (*Papier*) sheet; (*Zeitung*) paper; kein B∼ vor den Mund nehmen (*fig*) not mince one's words

blätter|n *vi* (*haben*) b∼n in (+ *dat*) leaf through. B∼teig *m* puff pastry

Blattlaus *f* greenfly

blau *a*, B∼ *nt*-s,- blue; b∼er Fleck bruise; b∼es Auge black eye; b∼ sein (*fam*) be tight; Fahrt ins B∼e mystery tour. B∼beere *f* bilberry. B∼licht *nt* blue flashing light. b∼machen *vi sep* (*haben*) (*fam*) skive off work

Blech *nt* -[e]s,-e sheet metal; (*Weiß-*) tin; (*Platte*) metal sheet; (*Back-*) baking sheet; (*Mus*) brass; (*fam: Unsinn*) rubbish. b∼en *vt/i* (*haben*) (*fam*) pay. B∼[blas]instrument *nt* brass instrument. B∼schaden *m* (*Auto*) damage to the bodywork

Blei *nt* -[e]s lead

Bleibe *f* - place to stay. b∼n† *vi* (*sein*) remain, stay; (*übrig-*) be left; ruhig b∼n keep calm; bei etw b∼n (*fig*) stick to sth; b∼n Sie am Apparat hold the line; etw b∼n lassen not do sth; (*aufhören*) stop

doing sth. b∼nd *a* permanent; (*anhaltend*) lasting. b∼nlassen† *vt sep* (NEW) b∼n lassen, *s.* bleiben

bleich *a* pale. b∼en† *vi* (*sein*) bleach; (*ver-*) fade ◻ *vt* (*reg*) bleach. B∼mittel *nt* bleach

blei|ern *a* leaden. b∼frei *a* unleaded. B∼stift *m* pencil. B∼stiftabsatz *m* stiletto heel. B∼stiftspitzer *m* -s,- pencil-sharpener

Blende *f* -,-n shade, shield; (*Sonnen-*) [sun]visor; (*Phot*) diaphragm; (*Öffnung*) aperture; (*an Kleid*) facing. b∼n *vt* dazzle, blind. b∼nd *a* (*fig*) dazzling; (*prima*) marvellous, *adv* -ly

Blick *m* -[e]s,-e look; (*kurz*) glance; (*Aussicht*) view; auf den ersten B∼ at first sight; einen B∼ für etw haben (*fig*) have an eye for sth. b∼en *vi* (*haben*) look; (*kurz*) glance (auf + *acc* at). B∼punkt *m* (*fig*) point of view

blind *a* blind; (*trübe*) dull; b∼er Alarm false alarm; b∼er Passagier stowaway. B∼darm *m* appendix. B∼darmentzündung *f* appendicitis. B∼e(r) *m/f* blind man/woman; die B∼en the blind *pl.* B∼enhund *m* guidedog. B∼enschrift *f* braille. B∼gänger *m* -s,- (*Mil*) dud. B∼heit *f* - blindness. b∼lings *adv* blindly

blink|en *vi* (*haben*) flash; (*funkeln*) gleam; (*Auto*) indicate. B∼er *m* -s,- (*Auto*) indicator. B∼licht *nt* flashing light

blinzeln *vi* (*haben*) blink

Blitz *m* -es,-e [flash of] lightning; (*Phot*) flash; ein B∼ aus heiterem Himmel (*fig*) a bolt from the blue. B∼ableiter *m* lightning-conductor. b∼artig *a* lightning ... ◻ *adv* like lightning. B∼birne *f* flashbulb. b∼en *vi* (*haben*) flash; (*funkeln*) sparkle; es hat geblitzt there was a flash of lightning. B∼gerät *nt* flash [unit]. B∼licht *nt* (*Phot*) flash. b∼sauber *a* spick and span. b∼schnell *a* lightning ... ◻ *adv* like lightning. B∼strahl *m* flash of lightning

Block *m* -[e]s,¨e block ◻ -[e]s,-s & ¨e (*Schreib-*) [note]pad; (*Häuser-*) block; (*Pol*) bloc

Blockade *f* -,-n blockade

Blockflöte *f* recorder

blockieren *vt* block; (*Mil*) blockade

Blockschrift *f* block letters *pl*

blöd[e] *a* feeble-minded; (*dumm*) stupid, *adv* -ly

Blödsinn *m* -[e]s idiocy; (*Unsinn*) nonsense. b∼ig *a* feeble-minded; (*verrückt*) idiotic

blöken *vi* (*haben*) bleat

blond *a* fair-haired; (*Haar*) fair. B∼ine *f* -,-n blonde

bloß *a* bare; (*alleinig*) mere; mit b~em Auge with the naked eye □ *adv* only, just; was mache ich b~? whatever shall I do?

Blöße *f* -,-n nakedness; sich (*dat*) eine B~ geben (*fig*) show a weakness

bloß|legen *vt sep* uncover. B~stellen *vt sep* compromise; sich b~stellen show oneself up

Bluff *m* -s,-s bluff. b~en *vt/i* (*haben*) bluff

blühen *vi* (*haben*) flower; (*fig*) flourish. b~d a flowering; (*fig*) flourishing, thriving; (*Phantasie*) fertile

Blume *f* -,-n flower; (*vom Wein*) bouquet. B~nbeet *n* flower-bed. B~ngeschäft *nt* flower-shop, florist's [shop]. B~nkohl *m* cauliflower. B~nmuster *nt* floral design. B~nstrauß *m* bunch of flowers. B~ntopf *m* flowerpot; (*Pflanze*) [flowering] pot plant. B~nzwiebel *f* bulb

blumig *a* (*fig*) flowery

Bluse *f* -,-n blouse

Blut *nt* -[e]s blood. b~arm *a* anaemic. B~bahn *f* blood-stream. b~befleckt *a* blood-stained. B~bild *nt* blood count. B~buche *f* copper beech. B~druck *m* blood pressure. b~dürstig *a* bloodthirsty

Blüte *f* -,-n flower, bloom; (*vom Baum*) blossom; (*B~zeit*) flowering period; (*Baum-*) blossom time; (*fig*) flowering; (*Höhepunkt*) peak, prime; (*fam: Banknote*) forged note, (*fam*) dud

Blut|egel *m* -s,- leech. b~en *vi* (*haben*) bleed

Blüten|blatt *nt* petal. B~staub *m* pollen

Blut|er *m* -s,- haemophiliac. B~erguss (B~erguß) *m* bruise. B~gefäß *nt* blood-vessel. B~gruppe *f* blood group. B~hund *m* bloodhound. b~ig *a* bloody. b~jung *a* very young. B~körperchen *nt* -s,- [blood] corpuscle. B~probe *f* blood test. b~rünstig *a* (*fig*) bloody, gory; (*Person*) blood-thirsty. B~schande *f* incest. B~spender *m* blood donor. B~sturz *m* haemorrhage. B~sverwandte(r) *m/f* blood relation. B~transfusion, B~übertragung *f* blood transfusion. B~ung *f* -,-en bleeding; (*Med*) haemorrhage; (*Regel-*) period. b~unterlaufen *a* bruised; (*Auge*) bloodshot. B~vergießen *nt* -s bloodshed. B~vergiftung *f* blood-poisoning. B~wurst *f* black pudding

Bö *f* -,-en gust; (*Regen-*) squall

Bob *m* -s,-s bob[-sleigh]

Bock *m* -[e]s,⸗e buck; (*Ziege*) billy goat; (*Schaf*) ram; (*Gestell*) support; einen B~ schießen (*fam*) make a blunder. b~en *vi* (*haben*) (*Pferd*:) buck; (*Kind*:) be stubborn. b~ig *a* (*fam*) stubborn. B~springen *nt* leap-frog

Boden *m* -s,⸗ ground; (*Erde*) soil; (*Fuß-*) floor; (*Grundfläche*) bottom; (*Dach-*) loft, attic. B~kammer *f* attic [room]. b~los *a* bottomless; (*fam*) incredible. B~satz *m* sediment. B~schätze *mpl* mineral deposits. B~see (der) Lake Constance

Bogen *m* -s,- & ⸗ curve; (*Geom*) arc; (*beim Skilauf*) turn; (*Archit*) arch; (*Waffe, Geigen-*) bow; (*Papier*) sheet; einen großen B~ um jdn/etw machen (*fam*) give s.o./sth a wide berth. B~gang *m* arcade. B~schießen *nt* archery

Bohle *f* -,-n [thick] plank

Böhm|en *nt* -s Bohemia. b~isch *a* Bohemian

Bohne *f* -,-n bean; grüne B~n French beans. B~nkaffee *m* real coffee

bohner|n *vt* polish. B~wachs *nt* floor-polish

bohr|en *vt/i* (*haben*) drill (nach for); drive (*Tunnel*); sink (*Brunnen*); (*Insekt*:) bore; in der Nase b~en pick one's nose. B~er *m* -s,- drill. B~insel *f* [offshore] drilling rig. B~maschine *f* electric drill. B~turm *m* derrick

Boje *f* -,-n buoy

Böllerschuss *m* gun salute

Bolzen *m* -s,- bolt; (*Stift*) pin

bombardieren *vt* bomb; (*fig*) bombard (mit with)

bombastisch *a* bombastic

Bombe *f* -,-n bomb. B~nangriff *m* bombing raid. B~nerfolg *m* huge success. B~r *m* -s,- (*Aviat*) bomber

Bon /bɔŋ/ *m* -s,-s voucher; (*Kassen-*) receipt

Bonbon /bɔŋ'bɔŋ/ *m & nt* -s,-s sweet

Bonus *m* -[sses],-[sse] bonus

Boot *nt* -[e]s,-e boat. B~ssteg *m* landing-stage

Bord[1] *nt* -[e]s,-e shelf

Bord[2] *m* (*Naut*) an B~ aboard, on board; über B~ overboard. B~buch *nt* log [-book]

Bordell *nt* -s,-e brothel

Bord|karte *f* boarding-pass. B~stein *m* kerb

borgen *vt* borrow; jdm etw b~ lend s.o. sth

Borke *f* -,-n bark

borniert *a* narrow-minded

Börse *f* -,-n purse; (*Comm*) stock exchange. B~nmakler *m* stockbroker

Borst|e *f* -,-n bristle. b~ig *a* bristly

Borte *f* -,-n braid

bösartig *a* vicious; (*Med*) malignant

Böschung *f* -,-en embankment; (*Hang*) slope

böse a wicked, evil; (*unartig*) naughty; (*schlimm*) bad, adv -ly; (*zornig*) cross; jdm od auf jdn b~ sein be cross with s.o. B~wicht m -[e]s,-e villain; (*Schlingel*) rascal

bos|haft a malicious, adv -ly; (*gehässig*) spiteful, adv -ly. B~heit f -,-en malice; spite; (*Handlung*) spiteful act/(*Bemerkung*) remark

böswillig a malicious, adv -ly. B~keit f - malice

Bota̱ni|k f - botany. B~ker(in) m -s,- (f -,-nen) botanist. b~sch a botanical

Bot|e m -n,-n messenger. B~engang m errand. B~schaft f -,-en message; (*Pol*) embassy. B~schafter m -s,- ambassador

Bottich m -[e]s,-e vat; (*Wasch-*) tub

Bouillon /bul'jɔŋ/ f -,-s clear soup. B~würfel m stock cube

Bowle /'bo:lə/ f -,-n punch

box|en vi (*haben*) box □ vt punch. B~en nt -s boxing. B~er m -s,- boxer. B~kampf m boxing match; (*Boxen*) boxing

Boykott m -[e]s,-s boycott. b~ie̱ren vt boycott; (*Comm*) black

brachliegen† vi sep (*haben*) lie fallow

Branche /'brã:ʃə/ f -,-n [line of] business. B~nverzeichnis nt (*Teleph*) classified directory

Brand m -[e]s,-e fire; (*Med*) gangrene; (*Bot*) blight; in B~ geraten catch fire; in B~ setzen od stecken set on fire. B~bombe f incendiary bomb

branden vi (*haben*) surge; (*sich brechen*) break

Brand|geruch m smell of burning. b~marken vt (*fig*) brand. B~stifter m arsonist. B~stiftung f arson

Brandung f - surf. B~sreiten nt surfing

Brand|wunde f burn. B~zeichen nt brand

Branntwein m spirit; (*coll*) spirits pl. B~brennerei f distillery

bras|ilia̱nisch a Brazilian. B~ilien /-jən/ nt -s Brazil

Brat|apfel m baked apple. b~en† vt/i (*haben*) roast; (*in der Pfanne*) fry. B~en m -s,- roast; (*B~stück*) joint. B~ensoße f gravy. b~fertig a oven-ready. B~hähnchen, B~huhn nt roast/(*zum Braten*) roasting chicken. B~kartoffeln fpl fried potatoes. B~klops m rissole. B~pfanne f frying-pan

Bratsche f -,-n (*Mus*) viola

Brat|spieß m spit. B~wurst f sausage for frying; (*gebraten*) fried sausage

Brauch m -[e]s,Bräuche custom. b~bar a usable; (*nützlich*) useful. b~en vt need; (*ge-, verbrauchen*) use; take (*Zeit*); er b~t

es nur zu sagen he only has to say; du b~st nicht zu gehen you needn't go

Braue f -,-n eyebrow

brau|en vt brew. B~er m -s,- brewer. B~erei f -,-en brewery

braun a, B~ nt -s,- brown; b~ werden (*Person:*) get a tan; b~ [gebrannt] sein be [sun-]tanned

Bräune f - [sun-]tan. b~n vt/i (*haben*) brown; (*in der Sonne*) tan

braungebrannt a (NEW) braun gebrannt, s. braun

Braunschweig nt -s Brunswick

Brause f -,-n (*Dusche*) shower; (*an Gießkanne*) rose; (*B~limonade*) fizzy drink. b~n vi (*haben*) roar; (*duschen*) shower □ vi (*sein*) rush [along] □ vr sich b~n shower. b~nd a roaring; (*sprudelnd*) effervescent

Braut f -,-e bride; (*Verlobte*) fiancée

Bräutigam m -s,-e bridegroom; (*Verlobter*) fiancé

Brautkleid nt wedding dress

bräutlich a bridal

Brautpaar nt bridal couple; (*Verlobte*) engaged couple

brav a good, well-behaved; (*redlich*) honest □ adv dutifully; (*redlich*) honestly

bravo int bravo!

BRD abbr (Bundesrepublik Deutschland) FRG

Brech|eisen nt jemmy; (*B~stange*) crowbar. b~en† vt break; (*Phys*) refract (*Licht*); (*erbrechen*) vomit; sich b~en (*Wellen:*) break; (*Licht:*) be refracted; sich (*dat*) den Arm b~en break one's arm □ vi (*sein*) break □ vi (*haben*) vomit, be sick; mit jdm b~en (*fig*) break with s.o. B~er m -s,- breaker. B~reiz m nausea. B~stange f crowbar

Brei m -[e]s,-e paste; (*Culin*) purée; (*Grieß-*) pudding; (*Hafer-*) porridge. b~ig a mushy

breit a wide; (*Schultern, Grinsen*) broad □ adv b~ grinsen grin broadly; b~beinig a & adv with legs apart. B~e f -,-n width; breadth; (*Geog*) latitude. b~en vt spread (über + acc over). b~engrad m [degree of] latitude. B~enkreis m parallel. B~ seite f long side; (*Naut*) broadside

Bremse¹ f -,-n horsefly

Bremse² f -,-n brake. b~n vt slow down; (*fig*) restrain □ vi (*haben*) brake

Bremslicht nt brake-light

brenn|bar a combustible; leicht b~bar highly [in]flammable. b~en† vi (*haben*) burn; (*Licht:*) be on; (*Zigarette:*) be alight; (*weh tun*) smart, sting; es b~t there's a fire in X; darauf b~en, etw zu tun be dying to do sth □ vt burn; (*rösten*) roast;

(im *Brennofen*) fire; (*destillieren*) distil. b~end *a* burning; (*angezündet*) lighted; (*fig*) fervent ❑ *adv* ich würde b~end gern ... I'd love to ... B~erei *f* -,-en distillery

Brennessel *f* (NEW)Brennnessel

Brenn|holz *nt* firewood. B~nessel *f* stinging nettle. B~ofen *m* kiln. B~punkt *m* (*Phys*) focus; im B~punkt des Interesses stehen be the focus of attention. B~spiritus *m* methylated spirits. B~stoff *m* fuel

brenzlig *a* (*fam*) risky; b~er Geruch smell of burning

Bresche *f* -,-n (*fig*) breach

Bretagne /bre'tanjə/ (die) - Brittany

Brett *nt* -[e]s,-er board; (im *Regal*) shelf; schwarzes B~ notice board. B~chen *nt* -s,- slat; (*Frühstücks-*) small board (*used as plate*). B~spiel *nt* board game

Brezel *f* -,-n pretzel

Bridge /britʃ/ *nt* - (*Spiel*) bridge

Brief *m* -[e]s,-e letter. B~beschwerer *m* -s,- paperweight. B~block *m* writing pad. B~freund(in) *m(f)* pen-friend. B~kasten *m* letter-box, (*Amer*) mailbox. B~kopf *m* letter-head. b~lich *a* & *adv* by letter. B~marke *f* [postage] stamp. B~öffner *m* paper-knife. B~papier *nt* notepaper. B~porto *nt* letter rate. B~tasche *f* wallet. B~träger *m* postman, (*Amer*) mailman. B~umschlag *m* envelope. B~wahl *f* postal vote. B~wechsel *m* correspondence

Brigade *f* -,-n brigade

Brikett *nt* -s,-s briquette

brillan|t /bril'jant/ *a* brilliant, *adv* -ly. B~t *m* -en,-en [cut] diamond. B~z *f* - brilliance

Brille *f* -,-n glasses *pl*, spectacles *pl*; (*Schutz-*) goggles *pl*; (*Klosett-*) toilet seat

bringen† *vt* bring; (*fort-*) take; (*ein-*) yield; (*veröffentlichen*) publish; (im *Radio*) broadcast; show (*Film*); ins Bett b~ put to bed; jdn nach Hause b~ take/(*begleiten*) see s.o. home; an sich (*acc*) b~ get possession of; mit sich b~ entail; um etw b~ deprive of sth; etw hinter sich (*acc*) b~ get sth over [and done] with; jdn dazu b~, etw zu tun get s.o. to do sth; es weit b~ (*fig*) go far

brisant *a* explosive

Brise *f* -,-n breeze

Brit|e *m* -n,-n Briton. B~in *f* -,-nen Briton. b~isch *a* British

Bröck|chen *nt* -s,- (*Culin*) crouton. b~elig *a* crumbly; (*Gestein*) friable. b~eln *vt/i* (*haben/sein*) crumble

Brocken *m* -s,- chunk; (*Erde, Kohle*) lump; ein paar B~ Englisch (*fam*) a smattering of English

Brokat *m* -[e]s,-e brocade

Brokkoli *pl* broccoli *sg*

Brombeer|e *f* blackberry. B~strauch *m* bramble [bush]

Bronchitis *f* - bronchitis

Bronze /'brõ:sə/ *f* -,-n bronze

Brosch|e *f* -,-n brooch. b~iert *a* paperback. B~üre *f* -,-n brochure; (*Heft*) booklet

Brösel *mpl* (*Culin*) breadcrumbs

Brot *n* -[e]s,-e bread; ein B~ a loaf [of bread]; (*Scheibe*) a slice of bread; sein B~ verdienen (*fig*) earn one's living (mit by)

Brötchen *n* -s,- [bread] roll

Brot|krümel *m* breadcrumb. B~verdiener *m* breadwinner

Bruch *m* -[e]s,-̈e break; (*Brechen*) breaking; (*Rohr-*) burst; (*Med*) fracture; (*Eingeweide-*) rupture, hernia; (*Math*) fraction; (*fig*) breach; (in *Beziehung*) break-up

brüchig *a* brittle

Bruch|landung *f* crash-landing. B~rechnung *f* fractions *pl*. B~stück *nt* fragment. b~stückhaft *a* fragmentary. B~teil *m* fraction

Brücke *f* -,-n bridge; (*Teppich*) rug

Bruder *m* -s,-̈ brother

brüderlich *a* brotherly, fraternal

Brügge *nt* -s Bruges

Brüh|e *f* -,-n broth; (*Knochen-*) stock; klare B~e clear soup. b~en *vt* scald; (*auf-*) make (*Kaffee*). B~würfel *m* stock cube

brüllen *vt/i* (*haben*) roar; (*Kuh:*) moo; (*fam: schreien*) bawl

brumm|eln *vt/i* (*haben*) mumble. b~en *vi* (*haben*) (*Insekt:*) buzz; (*Bär:*) growl; (*Motor:*) hum; (*murren*) grumble ❑ *vt* mutter. B~er *m* -s,- (*fam*) bluebottle. b~ig *a* (*fam*) grumpy, *adv* -ily

brünett *a* dark-haired. B~e *f* -,-n brunette

Brunnen *m* -s,- well; (*Spring-*) fountain; (*Heil-*) spa water. B~kresse *f* watercress

brüsk *a* brusque, *adv* -ly. b~ieren *vt* snub

Brüssel *nt* -s Brussels

Brust *f* -,-̈e chest; (*weibliche, Culin: B~stück*) breast. B~bein *nt* breastbone. B~beutel *m* purse worn round the neck

brüsten (sich) *vr* boast

Brust|fellentzündung *f* pleurisy. B~schwimmen *nt* breaststroke

Brüstung *f* -,-en parapet

Brustwarze *f* nipple

Brut f -,-en incubation; (*Junge*) brood; (*Fisch-*) fry

brutal a brutal, adv -ly. B~ität f -,-en brutality

brüten vi (haben) sit (on eggs); (*fig*) ponder (über + dat over); b~de Hitze oppressive heat

Brutkasten m (*Med*) incubator

brutto adv, B~- pref gross

brutzeln vi (haben) sizzle □ vt fry

Bub m -en,-en (SGer) boy. B~e m -n,-n (*Karte*) jack, knave

Bubikopf m bob

Buch nt -[e]s,¨er book; B~ führen keep a record (über + acc of); die B~er führen keep the accounts. B~drucker m printer

Buche f -,-n beech

buchen vt book; (*Comm*) enter

Bücher|bord, f bookshelf. B~brett nt bookshelf. B~ei f -,-en library. B~regal nt bookcase, bookshelves pl. B~schrank m bookcase. B~wurm m bookworm

Buchfink m chaffinch

Buch|führung f bookkeeping. B~halter(in) m -s,- (f -,-nen) bookkeeper, accountant. B~haltung f bookkeeping, accountancy; (*Abteilung*) accounts department. B~händler(in) m(f) bookseller. B~handlung f bookshop. B~macher m -s,- bookmaker. B~prüfer m auditor

Büchse f -,-n box; (*Konserven-*) tin, can; (*Gewehr*) [sporting] gun. B~nmilch f evaporated milk. B~nöffner m tin or can opener

Buch|stabe m -n,-n letter. b~stabieren vt spell [out]. b~stäblich adv literally

Buchstützen fpl book-ends

Bucht f -,-en (*Geog*) bay

Buchung f -,-en booking, reservation; (*Comm*) entry

Buckel m -s,- hump; (*Beule*) bump; (*Hügel*) hillock; einen B~ machen (*Katze:*) arch its back

bücken (sich) vr bend down

bucklig a hunchbacked. B~e(r) m/f hunchback

Bückling m -s,-e smoked herring; (*fam: Verbeugung*) bow

buddeln vt/i (haben) (*fam*) dig

Buddhis|mus m - Buddhism. B~t(in) m -en,-en (f -,-nen) Buddhist. b~tisch a Buddhist

Bude f -,-n hut; (*Kiosk*) kiosk; (*Markt-*) stall; (*fam: Zimmer*) room; (*Studenten-*) digs pl

Budget /by'dʒe:/ nt -s,-s budget

Büfett nt -[e]s,-e sideboard; (*Theke*) bar; kaltes B~ cold buffet

Büffel m -s,- buffalo. b~n vt/i (haben) (*fam*) swot

Bug m -[e]s,-e (*Naut*) bow[s pl]

Bügel m -s,- frame; (*Kleider-*) coathanger; (*Steig-*) stirrup; (*Brillen-*) sidepiece. B~brett nt ironing-board. B~eisen nt iron. B~falte f crease. b~frei a non-iron. b~n vt/i (haben) iron

bugsieren vt (*fam*) manoeuvre

buhen vi (haben) (*fam*) boo

Buhne f -,-n breakwater

Bühne f -,-n stage. B~nbild nt set. B~n-eingang m stage door

Buhrufe mpl boos

Bukett nt -[e]s,-e bouquet

Bulette f -,-n [meat] rissole

Bulgarien /-jən/ nt -s Bulgaria

Bull|auge nt (*Naut*) porthole. B~dogge f bulldog. B~dozer /-do:ze/ m -s,- bulldozer. B~e m -n,-n bull; (*sl: Polizist*) cop

Bummel m -s,- (*fam*) stroll. B~lant m -en,-en (*fam*) dawdler; (*Faulenzer*) loafer. B~lei f - (*fam*) dawdling; (*Nachlässigkeit*) carelessness

bummel|ig a (*fam*) slow; (*nachlässig*) careless. b~n vi (sein) (*fam*) stroll □ vi (haben) (*fam*) dawdle. B~streik m go-slow. B~zug m (*fam*) slow train

Bums m -es,-e bump, thump

Bund[1] nt -[e]s,-e bunch; (*Stroh-*) bundle

Bund[2] m -[e]s,¨e association; (*Bündnis*) alliance; (*Pol*) federation; (*Rock-, Hosen-*) waistband; im B~e sein be in league (mit with); der B~ the Federal Government; (*fam: Bundeswehr*) the [German] Army

Bündel nt -s,- bundle. b~n vt bundle [up]

Bundes|- pref Federal. B~genosse m ally. B~kanzler m Federal Chancellor. B~land nt [federal] state; (*Aust*) province. B~liga f German national league. B~rat m Upper House of Parliament. B~regierung f Federal Government. B~republik f die B~republik Deutschland the Federal Republic of Germany. B~straße f ≈ A road. B~tag m Lower House of Parliament. B~wehr f [Federal German] Army

bünd|ig a & adv kurz und b~ig short and to the point. B~nis nt -sses,-sse alliance

Bunker m -s,- bunker; (*Luftschutz-*) shelter

bunt a coloured; (*farbenfroh*) colourful; (*grell*) gaudy; (*gemischt*) varied; (*wirr*) confused; b~er Abend social evening; b~e Platte assorted cold meats □ adv b~ durcheinander higgledy-piggledy; es zu b~ treiben (*fam*) go too far. B~stift m crayon

Bürde f -,-n (fig) burden

Burg f -,-en castle

Bürge m -n,-n guarantor. b∼n vi (haben) b∼n für vouch for; (fig) guarantee

Bürger|(in) m -s,- (f -,-nen) citizen. B∼krieg m civil war. b∼lich a civil; (Pflicht) civic; (mittelständisch) middle-class; b∼liche Küche plain cooking. B∼liche(r) m/f commoner. B∼meister m mayor. B∼rechte npl civil rights. B∼steig m -[e]s, -e pavement, (Amer) sidewalk

Burggraben m moat

Bürgschaft f -,-en surety; B∼ leisten stand surety

Burgunder m -s,- (Wein) Burgundy

Burleske f -,-n burlesque

Büro nt -s,-s office. B∼angestellte(r) m/f office-worker. B∼klammer f paper-clip. B∼krat m -en,-en bureaucrat. B∼kratie f -,-n bureaucracy. b∼kratisch a bureaucratic

Bursch|e m -n,-n lad, youth; (fam: Kerl) fellow. b∼ikos a hearty; (männlich) mannish

Bürste f -,-n brush. b∼n vt brush. B∼nschnitt m crew cut

Bus m -ses,-se bus; (Reise-) coach. B∼bahnhof m bus and coach station

Busch m -[e]s,-e bush

Büschel nt -s,- tuft

buschig a bushy

Busen m -s,- bosom

Bussard m -s,-e buzzard

Buße f -,-n penance; (Jur) fine

büßen vt/i (haben) [für] etw b∼ atone for sth; (fig: bezahlen) pay for sth

bußfertig a penitent. B∼geld nt (Jur) fine

Büste f -,-n bust; (Schneider-) dummy. B∼nhalter m -s,- bra

Butter f - butter. B∼blume f buttercup. B∼brot nt slice of bread and butter. B∼brotpapier nt grease-proof paper. B∼fass (B∼faß) nt churn. B∼milch f buttermilk. b∼n vi (haben) make butter □ vt butter

b.w. abbr (bitte wenden) P.T.O.

bzgl. abbr s. bezüglich

bzw. abbr s. beziehungsweise

C

ca. abbr (circa) about

Café /ka'fe:/ nt -s,-s café

Cafeteria /kafete'ri:a/ f -,-s cafeteria

camp|en /'kɛmpən/ vi (haben) go camping. C∼ing nt -s camping. C∼ingplatz m campsite

Cape /ke:p/ nt -s,-s cape

Caravan /'ka[:]ravan/ m -s,-s (Auto) caravan; (Kombi) estate car

Cassette /ka'sɛtə/ f -,-n cassette. C∼nrecorder /-rekɔrdɐ/ m -s,- cassette recorder

CD /tse:'de:/ f -,-s compact disc, CD

Cell|ist(in) /tʃɛ'lıst(ın)/ m -en, -en (f -,-nen) cellist. C∼o /'tʃɛlo/ nt -s,-los & -li cello

Celsius /'tsɛlzjos/ inv Celsius, centigrade

Cembalo /'tʃɛmbalo/ nt -s,-los & -li harpsichord

Champagner /ʃam'panjɐ/ m -s champagne

Champignon /'ʃampınjɔn/ m -s,-s [field] mushroom

Chance /'ʃã:s[ə]/ f -,-n chance

Chaos /'ka:ɔs/ nt -chaos

chaotisch /ka'o:tıʃ/ a chaotic

Charakter /ka'rakte/ m -s,-e /-'te:rə/ character. c∼isieren vt characterize. c∼istisch a characteristic (für of), adv -ally

Charism|a /ka'rısma/ nt -s charisma. c∼atisch a charismatic

charm|ant /ʃar'mant/ a charming, adv -ly. C∼e /ʃarm/ m -s charm

Charter|flug /'tʃ-, 'ʃartɐ-/ m charter flight. c∼n vt charter

Chassis /ʃa'si:/ nt -,- /-'si:[s], -'si:s/ chassis

Chauffeur /ʃɔ'fø:ɐ/ m -s,-e chauffeur; (Taxi-) driver

Chauvinis|mus /ʃovi'nısmos/ m - chauvinism. C∼t m -en,-en chauvinist

Chef /ʃɛf/ m -s,-s head; (fam) boss

Chem|ie /çe'mi:/ f - chemistry. C∼ikalien /-jən/ fpl chemicals

Chem|iker(in) /'çe:-/ m -s,- (f -,-nen) chemist. c∼isch a chemical, adv -ly; c∼ische Reinigung dry-cleaning; (Geschäft) dry-cleaner's

Chicorée /'ʃıkore:/ m -s chicory

Chiffr|e /'ʃıfɐ, 'ʃıfrə/ f -,-n cipher; (bei Annonce) box number. c∼iert a coded

Chile /'çi:le/ nt -s Chile

Chin|a /'çi:na/ nt -s China. C∼ese m -n, -n, C∼esin f -,-nen Chinese. c∼esisch a Chinese. C∼esisch nt -[s] (Lang) Chinese

Chip /tʃıp/ m -s,-s [micro]chip. C∼s pl crisps, (Amer) chips

Chirurg /çi'rork/ m -en,-en surgeon. C∼ie /-'gi:/ f - surgery. c∼isch a /-g-/ a surgical, adv -ly

Chlor /kloːɐ̯/ nt -s chlorine. C~oform /kloroˈfɔrm/ nt -s chloroform

Choke /tʃoːk/ m -s,-s (Auto) choke

Cholera /ˈkoːlera/ f -cholera

cholerisch /koˈleːrɪʃ/ a irascible

Cholesterin /ço-, koleste'riːn/ nt -s cholesterol

Chor /koːɐ̯/ m -[e]s,ˑe choir; (Theat) chorus; im C~ in chorus

Choral /koˈraːl/ m -[e]s,ˑe chorale

Choreographie, Choreografie /koreogra'fiː/ f -,-n choreography

Chor|knabe /ˈkoːɐ̯-/ m choirboy. C~musik f choral music

Christ /krɪst/ m -en,-en Christian. C~baum m Christmas tree. C~entum nt -s Christianity. C~in f -,-nen Christian. C~kind nt Christ-child; (als Geschenk-bringer) ≈ Father Christmas. c~lich a Christian

Christus /ˈkrɪstus/ m -ti Christ

Chrom /kroːm/ nt -s chromium

Chromosom /kromoˈzoːm/ nt -s,-en chromosome

Chronik /ˈkroːnɪk/ f -,-en chronicle

chron|isch /ˈkroːnɪʃ/ a chronic, adv -ally. c~ologisch a chronological, adv -ly

Chrysantheme /kryzanˈteːmə/ f -,-n chrysanthemum

circa /ˈtsɪrka/ adv about

Clique /ˈklɪkə/ f -,-n clique

Clou /kluː/ m -s,-s highlight, (fam) high spot

Clown /klaʊn/ m -s,-s clown. c~en vi (haben) clown

Club /klʊp/ m -s,-s club

Cocktail /ˈkɔkteːl/ m -s,-s cocktail

Code /koːt/ m -s,-s code

Cola /ˈkoːla/ f -,- (fam) Coke (P)

Comic-Heft /ˈkɔmɪk-/ nt comic

Computer /kɔmˈpjuːtɐ/ m -s,- computer. c~isieren vt computerize

Conférencier /kõˈferãˈsjeː/ m -s,- compère

Cord /kɔrt/ m -s, C~samt m corduroy. C~[samt]hose f cords pl

Couch /kaʊtʃ/ f -,-s settee. C~tisch m coffee-table

Coupon /kuˈpõ/ m -s,-s = Kupon

Cousin /kuˈzɛ̃/ m -s,-s [male] cousin. C~e /-'ziːnə/ f -,-n [female] cousin

Crem|e /kreːm/ f -,-s cream; (Speise) cream dessert. c~efarben a cream. c~ig a creamy

Curry /ˈkari, ˈkœri/ nt & m -s curry powder. ▭ nt -s,-s (Gericht) curry

D

da adv there; (hier) here; (zeitlich) then; (in dem Fall) in that case; von da an from then on; da sein be there/(hier) here; (existieren) exist; wieder da sein be back; noch nie da gewesen unprecedented. ▭ conj as, since

dabehalten† vt sep keep there

dabei (emphatic: dabei) adv nearby; (daran) with it; (eingeschlossen) included; (hinsichtlich) about it; (während dem) during this; (gleichzeitig) at the same time; (doch) and yet; dicht d~ close by; d~ sein be present; (mitmachen) be involved; d~ sein, etw zu tun be just doing sth; d~ bleiben (fig) remain adamant; was ist denn d~? (fam) so what? d~sein† vi sep (sein) NEW d~ sein, s. dabei

dableiben† vi sep (sein) stay there

Dach nt -[e]s,ˑer roof. D~boden m loft. D~gepäckträger m roof-rack. D~kammer f attic room. D~luke f sky-light. D~rinne f gutter

Dachs m -es,ˑe badger

Dach|sparren m -s,- rafter. D~ziegel m [roofing] tile

Dackel m -s,- dachshund

dadurch (emphatic: dadurch) adv through it/them; (Ursache) by it; (deshalb) because of that; d~, dass because

dafür (emphatic: dafür) adv for it/them; (anstatt) instead; (als Ausgleich) but [on the other hand]; d~, dass considering that; ich kann nichts dafür it's not my fault. d~können† vi sep (haben) NEW d~können, s. dafür

dagegen (emphatic: dagegen) adv against it/them; (Mittel, Tausch) for it; (verglichen damit) by comparison; (jedoch) however; hast du was d~? do you mind? d~halten† vt sep argue (dass that)

daheim adv at home

daher (emphatic: daher) adv from there; (deshalb) for that reason; das kommt d~, weil that's because; d~ meine Eile hence my hurry. ▭ conj that is why

dahin (emphatic: dahin) adv there; bis d~ up to there; (bis dann) until/(Zukunft) by then; jdn d~ bringen, dass er etw tut get s.o. to do sth; d~ sein (fam) be gone. d~gehen† vi sep (sein) walk along; (Zeit:) pass. d~gestellt a d~gestellt lassen (fig) leave open; das bleibt d~gestellt that remains to be seen

dahinten *adv* back there

dahinter (*emphatic:* dahinter) *adv* behind it/them; d~ kommen (*fig*) get to the bottom of it. d~kommen† *vi sep* (*sein*) (NEWD)~ kommen, *s.* dahinter

Dahlie /-jə/ *f* -,-n dahlia

dalassen† *vt sep* leave there

daliegen† *vi sep* (*haben*) lie there

damalig *a* at that time; der d~e Minister the then minister

damals *adv* at that time

Damast *m* -es,-e damask

Dame *f* -,-n lady; (*Karte, Schach*) queen; (D~spiel) draughts *sg*, (*Amer*) checkers *sg*; (*Doppelstein*) king. D~n- *pref* ladies'/lady's ... d~nhaft *a* ladylike

damit (*emphatic:* damit) *adv* with it/them; (*dadurch*) by it; hör auf d~! stop it! □ *conj* so that

dämlich *a* (*fam*) stupid, *adv* -ly

Damm *m* -[e]s,-e dam; (*Insel-*) causeway; nicht auf dem D~ (*fam*) under the weather

dämmerig *a* dim; es wird d~ig dusk is falling. D~licht *nt* twilight. d~n *vi* (*haben*) (*Morgen:*) dawn; der Abend d~t dusk is falling; es d~t it is getting light/(*abends*) dark. D~ung *f* dawn; (*Abend-*) dusk

Dämon *m* -s,-en /-'mo:nən/ demon

Dampf *m* -es,-e steam; (*Chem*) vapour. d~en *vi* (*haben*) steam

dämpfen *vt* (*Culin*) steam; (*fig*) muffle (*Ton*); lower (*Stimme*); dampen (*Enthusiasmus*)

Dampf|er *m* -s,- steamer. D~kochtopf *m* pressure-cooker. D~maschine *f* steam engine. D~walze *f* steamroller

Damwild *nt* fallow deer *pl*

danach (*emphatic:* danach) *adv* after it/them; (*suchen*) for it/them; (*riechen*) of it; (*später*) afterwards; (*entsprechend*) accordingly; es sieht d~ aus it looks like it

Däne *m* -n,-n Dane

daneben (*emphatic:* daneben) *adv* beside it/them; (*außerdem*) in addition; (*verglichen damit*) by comparison. d~gehen† *vi sep* (*sein*) miss; (*scheitern*) fail

Dän|emark *nt* -s Denmark. D~in *f* -,-nen Dane. d~isch *a* Danish

Dank *m* -es thanks *pl*; vielen D~! thank you very much! □ *prep* (+ *dat or gen*) thanks to. d~bar *a* grateful, *adv* -ly; (*erleichtert*) thankful, *adv* -ly; (*lohnend*) rewarding. D~barkeit *f* - gratitude. d~e *adv* d~e [schön od sehr]! thank you [very much]! [nein] d~e! no thank you! d~en *vi* (*haben*) thank (jdm s.o.); (*ablehnen*) decline; ich d~e! no thank you! nichts zu d~en! don't mention it!

dann *adv* then; d~ und wann now and then; nur/selbst d~, wenn only/even if

daran (*emphatic:* daran) *adv* on it/them; at it/them; (*denken*) of it; nahe d~ on the point (etw zu tun of doing sth); denkt d~! remember! d~gehen† *vi sep* (*sein*), d~machen (sich) *vr sep* set about (etw zu tun doing sth). d~setzen *vt sep* alles d~setzen do one's utmost (zu to)

darauf (*emphatic:* darauf) *adv* on it/them; (*warten*) for it; (*antworten*) to it; (*danach*) after that; (d~hin) as a result; am Tag d~ the day after; am d~folgenden Tag the following *or* next day. d~folgend *a* (NEW) d~ folgend, *s.* darauf. d~hin *adv* as a result

daraus (*emphatic:* daraus) *adv* out of *or* from it/them; er macht sich nichts d~ he doesn't care for it; was ist d~ geworden? what has become of it?

Darbietung *f* -,-en performance; (*Nummer*) item

darin (*emphatic:* darin) *adv* in it/them

darlegen *vt sep* expound; (*erklären*) explain

Darlehen *nt* -s,- loan

Darm *m* -[e]s,-e intestine; (*Wurst-*) skin. D~grippe *f* gastric flu

darstell|en *vt sep* represent; (*bildlich*) portray; (*Theat*) interpret; (*spielen*) play; (*schildern*) describe. D~er *m* -s,- actor. D~erin *f* -,-nen actress. D~ung *f* representation; interpretation; description; (*Bericht*) account

darüber (*emphatic:* darüber) *adv* over it/them; (*höher*) above it/them; (*sprechen, lachen, sich freuen*) about it; (*mehr*) more; (*inzwischen*) in the meantime; d~hinaus beyond [it]; (*dazu*) on top of that

darum (*emphatic:* darum) *adv* round it/them; (*bitten, kämpfen*) for it; (*deshalb*) that is why; d~, weil because

darunter (*emphatic:* darunter) *adv* under it/them; (*tiefer*) below it/them; (*weniger*) less; (*dazwischen*) among them

das *def art & pron s.* der

dasein† *vi sep* (*sein*) (NEWD)da sein, *s.* da. D~ *nt* -s existence

dasitzen† *vi sep* (*haben*) sit there

dasjenige *pron s.* derjenige

dass (daß) *conj* that; d~ du nicht fällst! mind you don't fall!

dasselbe *pron s.* derselbe

dastehen† *vi sep* (*haben*) stand there; allein d~ (*fig*) be alone

Daten|sichtgerät *nt* visual display unit, VDU. D~verarbeitung *f* data processing

datieren *vt/i* (*haben*) date

Dativ *m* -s,-e dative. D~objekt *nt* indirect object

Dattel *f* -,-n date

Datum *nt* -s,-ten date; Daten dates; (*Angaben*) data

Dauer f -duration, length; (*Jur*) term; von D∼ lasting; auf die D∼ in the long run. D∼auftrag m standing order. d∼haft a lasting, enduring; (*fest*) durable. D∼karte f season ticket. D∼lauf m im Dauerlauf at a jog. D∼milch f long-life milk. d∼n vi (haben) last; lange d∼n take a long time. d∼nd a lasting; (*ständig*) constant, adv -ly; d∼nd fragen keep asking. D∼stellung f permanent position. D∼welle f perm. D∼wurst f salami-type sausage

Daumen m -s,- thumb; jdm den D∼ drücken od halten keep one's fingers crossed for s.o.

Daunen fpl down sg. D∼decke f [down-filled] duvet

davon (*emphatic*: davon) adv from it/ them; (*dadurch*) by it; (*damit*) with it/ them; (*darüber*) about it; (*Menge*) of it/ them; die Hälfte d∼ half of it/them; das kommt d∼! it serves you right! d∼kommen† vi sep (sein) escape (mit dem Leben with one's life). d∼laufen† vi sep (sein) run away. d∼machen (sich) vr sep (fam) make off. d∼tragen† vt sep carry off; (*erleiden*) suffer; (*gewinnen*) win

davor (*emphatic*: davor) adv in front of it/them; (*sich fürchten*) of it; (*zeitlich*) before it/them

dazu (*emphatic*: dazu) adv to it/them; (*damit*) with it/them; (*dafür*) for it; noch d∼ in addition to that; jdn d∼ bringen, etw zu tun get s.o. to do sth; ich kam nicht d∼ I didn't get round to [doing] it. d∼gehören vi sep (haben) belong to it/them; alles, was d∼gehört everything that goes with it. d∼kommen† vi sep (sein) arrive [on the scene]; (*hinzukommen*) be added; d∼ kommt, dass er krank ist on top of that he is ill. d∼rechnen vt sep add to it/them

dazwischen (*emphatic*: dazwischen) adv between them; in between; (*darunter*) among them. d∼fahren† vi sep (sein) (fig) intervene. d∼kommen† vi sep (sein) (fig) crop up; wenn nichts d∼kommt if all goes well. d∼reden vi sep (haben) interrupt. d∼treten† vi sep (sein) (fig) intervene

DDR f -abbr (Deutsche Demokratische Republik) GDR

Debatte f -,-n debate; zur D∼te stehen be at issue. d∼tieren vt/i (haben) debate

Debüt /de'by:/ nt -s,-s début

dechiffrieren /deʃɪ'fri:rən/ vt decipher

Deck nt -[e]s,-s (*Naut*) deck; an D∼ on deck. D∼bett nt duvet

Decke f -,-n cover; (*Tisch-*) table-cloth; (*Bett-*) blanket; (*Reise-*) rug; (*Zimmer-*) ceiling; unter einer D∼stecken (*fam*) be in league

Deckel m -s,- lid; (*Flaschen-*) top; (*Buch-*) cover

decken vt cover; tile (*Dach*); lay (*Tisch*); (*schützen*) shield; (*Sport*) mark; meet (*Bedarf*); jdn d∼ (fig) cover up for s.o.; sich d∼ (fig) cover oneself (gegen against); (*übereinstimmen*) coincide

Deck|mantel m (fig) pretence. D∼name m pseudonym

Deckung f -(*Mil*) cover; (*Sport*) defence; (*Mann-*) marking; (*Boxen*) guard; (*Sicherheit*) security; in D∼ gehen take cover

Defekt m -[e]s,-e defect. d∼a defective

defensiv a defensive. D∼e f -defensive

defilieren vi (sein/haben) file past

defin|ieren vt define. D∼ition /-'tsjo:n/ f -,-en definition. d∼itiv a definite, adv -ly

Defizit nt -s,-e deficit

Deflation /-'tsjo:n/ f -deflation

deformiert a deformed

deftig a (fam) (*Mahlzeit*) hearty; (*Witz*) coarse

Degen m -s,-sword; (*Fecht-*) épée

degenerier|en vi (sein) degenerate. d∼t a (fig) degenerate

degradieren vt (*Mil*) demote; (fig) degrade

dehn|bar a elastic. d∼en vt stretch; lengthen (*Vokal*); sich d∼en stretch

Deich m -[e]s,-e dike

Deichsel f -,-n pole; (*Gabel-*) shafts pl

dein poss pron your. d∼e(r,s) poss pron yours; die D∼en od d∼en pl your family sg. d∼erseits adv for your part. d∼etwegen adv for your sake; (*wegen dir*) because of you, on your account. d∼etwillen adv um d∼etwillen for your sake. d∼ige poss pron der/die/das d∼ige yours. d∼s poss pron yours

Deka nt -[s]-. (*Aust*) = Dekagramm

dekaden|t a decadent. D∼z f -decadence

Dekagramm nt (*Aust*) 10 grams; 10 D∼ 100 grams

Dekan m -s,-e dean

Deklin|ation /-'tsjo:n/ f -,-en declension. d∼ieren vt decline

Dekolleté, Dekolletee /dekɔl'te:/ nt -s,-s low neckline

Dekor m & nt -s decoration. D∼ateur /-'tø:ɐ/ m -s,-e interior decorator; (*Schaufenster-*) window-dresser. D∼ation /-'tsjo:n/ f -,-en decoration; (*Schaufenster-*) window-dressing; (*Auslage*) display; D∼ationen (*Theat*) scenery sg. d∼ativ a decorative. d∼ieren vt decorate; dress (*Schaufenster*)

Delegation /-'tsjo:n/ f -,-en delegation. d∼ieren vt delegate. D∼ierte(r) m/f delegate

Delfin *m* -s,-e = Delphin

delikat *a* delicate; (*lecker*) delicious; (*taktvoll*) tactful, *adv* -ly. D∼**esse** *f* -,-n delicacy. D∼**essengeschäft** *nt* delicatessen

Delikt *nt* -[e]s,-e offence

Delinquent *m* -en,-en offender

Delirium *nt* -s delirium

Delle *f* -,-n dent

Delphin *m* -s,-e dolphin

Delta *nt* -s,-s delta

dem *def art & pron s.* der

Dement|i *nt* -s,-s denial. d∼**ieren** *vt* deny

dem|entsprechend *a* corresponding; (*passend*) appropriate, *adv* accordingly; (*passend*) appropriately. d∼**gemäß** *adv* accordingly. d∼**nach** *adv* according to that; (*folglich*) consequently. d∼**nächst** *adv* soon; (*in Kürze*) shortly

Demokrat *m* -en,-en democrat. D∼**ie** *f* -,-n democracy. d∼**isch** *a* democratic, *adv* -ally

demolieren *vt* wreck

Demonstr|ant *m* -en,-en demonstrator. D∼**ation** /-'tsjo:n/ *f* -,-en demonstration. d∼**ativ** *a* pointed, *adv* -ly; (*Gram*) demonstrative. D∼**ativpronomen** *nt* demonstrative pronoun. d∼**ieren** *vt/i* (*haben*) demonstrate

demontieren *vt* dismantle

demoralisieren *vt* demoralize

Demoskopie *f* - opinion research

Demut *f* - humility

demütig *a* humble, *adv* -bly. d∼**en** *vt* humiliate; sich d∼**en** humble oneself. D∼**ung** *f* -,-en humiliation

demzufolge *adv* = demnach

den *def art & pron s.* der. d∼**en** *pron s.* der

denk|bar *a* conceivable. d∼**en†** *vt/i* (*haben*) think (an + *acc* of); (*sich erinnern*) remember (an etw *acc* sth); für jdn gedacht meant for s.o.; das kann ich mir d∼**en** I can imagine [that]; ich d∼**e** nicht daran I have no intention of doing it; d∼**t** daran! don't forget! D∼**mal** *nt* memorial; (*Monument*) monument. d∼**würdig** *a* memorable. D∼**zettel** *m* jdm einen D∼**zettel** geben (*fam*) teach s.o. a lesson

denn *conj* for; besser/mehr d∼ je better/more than ever d∼ wie/wo d∼? but how/where? warum d∼ nicht? why ever not? es sei d∼ [, dass] unless

dennoch *adv* nevertheless

Denunz|iant *m* -en,-en informer. d∼**ieren** *vt* denounce

Deodorant *nt* -s,-s deodorant

deplaciert (deplaziert) /-'tsi:ɐt/ *a* (*fig*) out of place

Deponie *f* -,-n dump. d∼**ren** *vt* deposit

deportieren *vt* deport

Depot /de'po:/ *nt* -s,-s depot; (*Lager*) warehouse; (*Bank*) safe deposit

Depression *f* -,-en depression

deprimieren *vt* depress. d∼**d** *a* depressing

Deputation /-'tsjo:n/ *f* -,-en deputation

der, **die**, **das**, *pl* **die** *def art* (*acc* den, die, das, *pl* die; *gen* des, der, des, *pl* der; *dat* dem, der, dem, *pl* den) the; der Mensch man; die Natur nature; das Leben life; das Lesen/Tanzen reading/dancing; sich (*dat*) das Gesicht/die Hände waschen wash one's face/hands; 5 Mark das Pfund 5 marks a pound □ *pron* (*acc* den, die, das, *pl* die; *gen* dessen, deren, dessen, *pl* deren; *dat* dem, der, dem, *pl* denen) □ *dem pron* that; (*pl*) those; (*substantivisch*) he, she, it; (*Ding*) it; (*betont*) that; (*d∼jenige*) the one; (*pl*) they, those; (*Dinge*) those; (*diejenigen*) the ones; der und der such and such; um die und die Zeit at such and such a time; das waren Zeiten! those were the days! □ *rel pron* who; (*Ding*) which, that

derart *adv* so; (*so sehr*) so much. d∼**ig** *a* such □ *adv* = derart

derb *a* tough; (*kräftig*) strong; (*grob*) coarse, *adv* -ly; (*unsanft*) rough, *adv* -ly

deren *pron s.* der

dergleichen *inv a* such □ *pron* such a thing/such things; nichts d∼ nothing of the kind; und d∼ and the like

der-/die-/dasjenige, *pl* **diejenigen** *pron* the one; (*Person*) he, she; (*Ding*) it; (*pl*) those, the ones

dermaßen *adv* = derart

der-/die-/dasselbe, *pl* **dieselben** *pron* the same; ein- und dasselbe one and the same thing

derzeit *adv* at present

des *def art s.* der

Desert|eur /-'tø:ɐ/ *m* -s,-e deserter. d∼**ieren** *vi* (*sein/haben*) desert

desgleichen *adv* likewise □ *pron* the like

deshalb *adv* for this reason; (*also*) therefore

Designer(in) /di'zajnɐ, -nərın/ *m* -s,- (*f* -,-nen) designer

Desin|fektion /dɛs'ınfɛk'tsjo:n/ *f* disinfecting. D∼**fektionsmittel** *nt* disinfectant. d∼**fizieren** *vt* disinfect

Desodorant *nt* -s,-s deodorant

Despot *m* -en,-en despot

dessen *pron s.* der

Dessert /dɛ'se:ɐ/ *nt* -s,-s dessert, sweet. D∼**löffel** *m* dessertspoon

Destill|ation /-'tsjo:n/ *f* - distillation. d∼**ieren** *vt* distil

desto adv je mehr/eher, d~ besser the more/sooner the better

destruktiv a (fig) destructive

deswegen adv = deshalb

Detail /de'taj/ nt -s,-s detail

Detektiv m -s,-e detective. D~roman m detective story

Detonation /-'tsjo:n/ f -,-en explosion. d~ieren vi (sein) explode

deuten vt interpret; predict ⟨Zukunft⟩ □ vi (haben) point (auf + acc at/⟨fig⟩ to). d~lich a clear, adv -ly; ⟨eindeutig⟩ plain, adv -ly. D~lichkeit f -clarity

deutsch a German; auf d~ NEW auf D~, s. Deutsch. D~ nt -[s] ⟨Lang⟩ German; auf D~ in German. D~e(r) m/f German. D~land nt -s Germany

Deutung f -,-en interpretation

Devise f -,-n motto. D~n pl foreign currency or exchange sg

Dezember m -s,- December

dezent a unobtrusive, adv -ly; ⟨diskret⟩ discreet, adv -ly

Dezernat nt -[e]s,-e department

Dezimal|system nt decimal system. D~zahl f decimal

dezimieren vt decimate

dgl. abbr s. dergleichen

d.h. abbr ⟨das heißt⟩ i.e.

Dia nt -s,-s ⟨Phot⟩ slide

Diabet|es m - diabetes. D~iker m -s,-diabetic

Diadem nt -s,-e tiara

Diagnose f -,-n diagnosis. d~tizieren vt diagnose

diagonal a diagonal, adv -ly. D~e f -,-n diagonal

Diagramm nt -s,-e diagram; ⟨Kurven-⟩ graph

Diakon m -s,-e deacon

Dialekt m -[e]s,-e dialect

Dialog m -[e]s,-e dialogue

Diamant m -en,-en diamond

Diameter m -s,- diameter

Diapositiv nt -s,-e ⟨Phot⟩ slide

Diaprojektor m slide projector

Diät f -,-en ⟨Med⟩ diet; D~ leben be on a diet. d~ adv d~ leben NEW D~ leben, s. Diät. D~assistent(in) m(f) dietician

dich pron ⟨acc of du⟩ you; ⟨refl⟩ yourself

dicht a dense; ⟨dick⟩ thick; ⟨undurchlässig⟩ airtight; ⟨wasser-⟩ watertight □ adv densely; thickly; ⟨nahe⟩ close (bei to). D~e f -density. d~en¹ vt make watertight; ⟨ab-⟩ seal

dicht|en² vi (haben) write poetry □ vt write, compose. D~er(in) m -s,- (f -,-en)

poet. d~erisch a poetic. D~ung¹ f -,-en poetry; ⟨Gedicht⟩ poem

Dichtung² f -,-en seal; ⟨Ring⟩ washer; ⟨Auto⟩ gasket

dick a thick, adv -ly; ⟨beleibt⟩ fat; ⟨geschwollen⟩ swollen; ⟨fam; eng⟩ close; d~ werden get fat; d~ machen be fattening; ein d~es Fell haben be thick-skinned. D~e f -,-n thickness; ⟨D~leibigkeit⟩ fatness. d~fellig a ⟨fam⟩ thick-skinned. d~flüssig a thick; ⟨Phys⟩ viscous. D~kopf m ⟨fam⟩ stubborn person; einen D~kopf haben be stubborn. d~köpfig a ⟨fam⟩ stubborn

didaktisch a didactic

die def art & pron s. der

Dieb|(in) m -[e]s,-e (f -,-nen) thief. d~isch a thieving; ⟨Freude⟩ malicious. D~stahl m -[e]s,-e theft; ⟨geistig⟩ plagiarism

diejenige pron s. derjenige

Diele f -,-n floorboard; ⟨Flur⟩ hall

dien|en vi (haben) serve. D~er m -s,- servant; ⟨Verbeugung⟩ bow. D~erin f -,-nen maid, servant. d~lich a helpful

Dienst m -[e]s,-e service; ⟨Arbeit⟩ work; ⟨Amtsausübung⟩ duty; außer D~ off duty; ⟨pensioniert⟩ retired; D~ haben work; ⟨Soldat, Arzt:⟩ be on duty; der D~ habende Arzt the duty doctor; jdm einen schlechten D~ erweisen do s.o. a disservice

Dienstag m Tuesday. d~s adv on Tuesdays

Dienst|alter nt seniority. d~bereit a obliging; ⟨Apotheke⟩ open. D~bote m servant. d~eifrig a zealous, adv -ly. d~frei a d~freier Tag day off; d~frei haben have time off; ⟨Soldat, Arzt:⟩ be off duty. D~grad m rank. d~habend a NEW D~ habend, s. Dienst. D~leistung f service. d~lich a official □ adv d~lich verreist away on business. D~mädchen nt maid. D~reise f business trip. D~stelle f office. D~stunden fpl office hours. D~weg m official channels pl

dies inv pron this. d~bezüglich a relevant □ adv regarding this matter. d~e(r,s) pron this; ⟨pl⟩ these; ⟨substantivisch⟩ this [one]; ⟨pl⟩ these; d~e Nacht tonight; ⟨letzte⟩ last night

Diesel m -[s],- ⟨fam⟩ diesel

dieselbe pron s. derselbe

Diesel|kraftstoff m diesel [oil]. D~motor m diesel engine

diesig a hazy, misty

dies|mal adv this time. d~seits adv & prep (+ gen) this side (of)

Dietrich m -s,-e skeleton key

Diffam|ation /-'tsjo:n/ f - defamation. **d~ierend** a defamatory

Differential /-'tsja:l/ nt -s,-e (NEW) Differenzial

Differenz f -,-en difference. **D~ial** nt -s,-e differential. **d~ieren** vt/i (haben) differentiate (zwischen + dat between)

Digital- pref digital. **D~uhr** f digital clock/watch

Dikt|at nt -[e]s,-e dictation. **D~ator** m -s,-en /-'ta:rən/ dictator. **d~atorisch** a dictatorial. **D~atur** f -,-en dictatorship. **d~ieren** vt/i (haben) dictate

Dilemma nt -s,-s dilemma

Dilettant|(in) m -en,-en (f -,-nen) dilettante. **d~isch** a amateurish

Dill m -s dill

Dimension f -,-en dimension

Ding nt -[e]s,-e & (fam) -er thing; guter **D~e** sein be cheerful; vor allen **D~en** above all

Dinghi /'dıŋgi/ nt -s,-s dinghy

Dinosaurier /-jɐ/ m -s,- dinosaur

Diözese f -,-n diocese

Diphtherie f - diphtheria

Diplom nt -[e]s,-e diploma; (Univ) degree

Diplomat m -en,-en diplomat. **D~ie** f - diplomacy. **d~isch** a diplomatic, adv -ally

dir pron (dat of du) [to] you; (refl) yourself; ein Freund von dir a friend of yours

direkt a direct □ adv directly; (wirklich) really. **D~ion** /-'tsjo:n/ f - management; (Vorstand) board of directors. **D~or** m -s,-en /-'to:rən/, **D~orin** f -,-nen director; (Bank-, Theater-) manager; (Sch) head; (Gefängnis) governor. **D~übertragung** f live transmission

Dirigent m -en,-en (Mus) conductor. **d~ieren** vt direct; (Mus) conduct

Dirndl nt -s,- dirndl [dress]

Dirne f -,-n prostitute

Diskant m -s,-e (Mus) treble

Diskette f -,-n floppy disc

Disko f -,-s (fam) disco. **D~thek** f -,-en discothèque

Diskrepanz f -,-en discrepancy

diskret a discreet, adv -ly. **D~ion** /-'tsjo:n/ f - discretion

diskriminier|en vt discriminate against. **D~ung** f - discrimination

Diskus m -,-se & Disken discus

Diskussion f -,-en discussion. **d~tieren** vt/i (haben) discuss

disponieren vi (haben) make arrangements; **d~** [können] über (+ acc) have at one's disposal

Disput m -[e]s,-e dispute

Disqualifi|kation /-'tsjo:n/ f disqualification. **d~zieren** vt disqualify

Dissertation /-'tsjo:n/ f -,-en dissertation

Dissident m -en,-en dissident

Dissonanz f -,-en dissonance

Distanz f -,-en distance. **d~ieren (sich)** vr dissociate oneself (von from). **d~iert** a aloof

Distel f -,-n thistle

distinguiert /dıstıŋ'gi:ɐt/ a distinguished

Disziplin f -,-en discipline. **d~arisch** a disciplinary. **d~iert** a disciplined

dito adv ditto

diverse attrib a pl various

Divid|ende f -,-en dividend. **d~ieren** vt divide (durch by)

Division f -,-en division

DJH abbr (Deutsche Jugendherberge) [German] youth hostel

DM abbr (Deutsche Mark) DM

doch conj & adv but; (dennoch) yet; (trotzdem) after all; wenn **d~** ...! if only ...! nicht **d~**! don't [do that]! er kommt **d~**? he is coming, isn't he? kommst du nicht? —**d~**! aren't you coming?—yes, I am!

Docht m -[e]s,-e wick

Dock nt -s,-s dock. **d~en** vt/i (haben) dock

Dogge f -,-n Great Dane

Dogma nt -s,-men dogma. **d~atisch** a dogmatic, adv -ally

Dohle f -,-n jackdaw

Doktor m -s,-en /-'to:rən/ doctor. **D~arbeit** f [doctoral] thesis. **D~würde** f doctorate

Doktrin f -,-en doctrine

Dokument nt -[e]s,-e document. **D~arbericht** m documentary. **D~arfilm** m documentary film

Dolch m -[e]s,-e dagger

doll a (fam) fantastic; (schlimm) awful □ adv beautifully; (sehr) very; (schlimm) badly

Dollar m -s,- dollar

dolmetsch|en vt/i (haben) interpret. **D~er(in)** m -s,- (f -,-nen) interpreter

Dom m -[e]s,-e cathedral

dominant a dominant. **d~ieren** vi (haben) dominate; (vorherrschen) predominate

Domino nt -s,-s dominoes sg. **D~stein** m domino

Dompfaff m -en,-en bullfinch

Donau f - Danube

Donner m -s thunder. **d~n** vi (haben) thunder

Donnerstag m Thursday. d~s adv on
Thursdays

Donnerwetter nt (fam) telling-off;
(Krach) row □ int /'--'--/ wow! (Fluch)
damn it!

doof a (fam) stupid, adv -ly

Doppel nt -s,- duplicate; (Tennis) doubles
pl. D~bett nt double bed. D~decker m
-s,- doubledecker [bus]. d~deutig a ambiguous. D~gänger m -s,- double.
D~kinn nt double chin. D~name m
double-barrelled name. D~punkt m
(Gram) colon. D~schnitte f sandwich.
d~sinnig a ambiguous. D~stecker m
two-way adaptor. d~t a double; (Boden)
false; in d~ter Ausfertigung in duplicate; die d~te Menge twice the amount
□ adv doubly; (zweimal) twice; d~t so
viel twice as much. D~zimmer nt double
room

Dorf nt -[e]s,"er village. D~bewohner m
villager

dörflich a rural

Dorn m -[e]s,-en thorn. d~ig a thorny

Dörrobst nt dried fruit

Dorsch m -[e]s,-e cod

dort adv there; d~ drüben over there.
d~her adv [von] d~her from there.
d~hin adv there. d~ig a local

Dose f -,-n tin, can; (Schmuck-) box

dösen vi (haben) doze

Dosen|milch f evaporated milk.
D~öffner m tin or can opener

dosieren vt measure out

Dosis f -, Dosen dose

Dotter m & nt -s,- [egg] yolk

Dozent(in) m -en,-en (f -,-nen) (Univ) lec-
turer

Dr. abbr (Doktor) Dr

Drache m -n,-n dragon. D~n m -s,- kite;
(fam: Frau) dragon. D~nfliegen nt hang-
gliding. D~nflieger m hang-glider

Draht m -[e]s,"e wire; auf D~ (fam) on
the ball. d~ig a (fig) wiry. D~seilbahn
f cable railway

drall a plump; (Frau) buxom

Dram|a nt -s,-men drama. D~atik f -
drama. D~atiker m -s,- dramatist. d~a-
tisch a dramatic, adv -ally. d~atisieren
vt dramatize

dran adv (fam) = daran; gut/schlecht
d~ sein be well off/in a bad way; ich bin
d~ it's my turn

Dränage /-'na:ʒə/ f drainage

Drang m -[e]s urge; (Druck) pressure

dräng|eln vt/i (haben) push; (bedrängen)
pester. d~en vt push; (bedrängen) urge;
sich d~en crowd (um round) □ vi (haben)

push; (eilen) be urgent; (Zeit.) press; d~en
auf (+ acc) press for

dran|halten† (sich) vr sep hurry.
d~kommen† vi sep (sein) have one's turn;
wer kommt dran? whose turn is it?

drapieren vt drape

drastisch a drastic, adv -ally

drauf adv (fam) = darauf; d~ und dran
sein be on the point (etw zu tun of doing
sth). D~gänger m -s,- daredevil. d~gän-
gerisch a reckless

draus adv (fam) = daraus

draußen adv outside; (im Freien) out of
doors

drechseln vt (Techn) turn

Dreck m -s dirt; (Morast) mud; (fam: Kleinigkeit) trifle; in den D~ ziehen (fig)
denigrate. d~ig a dirty; muddy

Dreh m -s (fam) knack; den D~ heraus-
haben have got the hang of it. D~bank
f lathe. D~bleistift m propelling pencil.
D~buch nt screenplay, script. d~en vt
turn; (im Kreis) rotate; (verschlingen)
twist; roll (Zigarette); shoot (Film); lauter/
leiser d~en turn up/down; sich d~en
turn; (im Kreis) rotate; (schnell) spin;
(Wind:) change; sich d~en um revolve
around; (sich handeln) be about □ vi
(haben) turn; (Wind:) change; an etw (dat)
d~en turn sth. D~orgel f barrel organ.
D~stuhl m swivel chair. D~tür f revolv-
ing door. D~ung f -,-en turn; (im Kreis)
rotation. D~zahl f number of revolu-
tions

drei inv a, D~ f -,-en three; (Sch) ≈ pass.
D~eck nt -[e]s,-e triangle. d~eckig a tri-
angular. D~einigkeit f - die [Heilige]
D~einigkeit the [Holy] Trinity. d~erlei
inv a three kinds of □ pron three things.
d~fach a triple; in d~facher Ausfertigung in triplicate. D~faltigkeit f - =
D~einigkeit. d~mal adv three times.
D~rad nt tricycle

dreißig inv a thirty. d~ste(r,s) a thirtieth

dreist a impudent, adv -ly; (verwegen)
audacious, adv -ly. D~igkeit f - impudence; audacity

dreiviertel inv a (NEW)drei viertel, s.
viertel. D~stunde f three-quarters of an
hour

dreizehn inv a thirteen. d~te(r,s) a thir-
teenth

dreschen† vt thresh

dress|ieren vt train. D~ur f - training

dribbeln vi (haben) dribble

Drill m -[e]s (Mil) drill. d~en vt drill

Drillinge mpl triplets

drin adv (fam) = darin; (drinnen) inside

dring|en† vi (sein) penetrate (in + acc
into; durch etw sth); (heraus-) come (aus

out of); d∼en auf(+ acc) insist on. d∼end
a urgent, adv -ly. d∼lich a urgent.
D∼lichkeit f - urgency

Drink m -[s],-s [alcoholic] drink

drinnen adv inside; (im Haus) indoors

dritt adv zu d∼ in threes; wir waren zu
d∼ there were three of us. d∼e(r,s) a
third; ein D∼er a third person. d∼el inv
a third; ein d∼el Apfel a third of an apple.
D∼el nt -s,- third. d∼ens adv thirdly.
d∼rangig a third-rate

Drog|e f -,-n drug. D∼enabhängige(r)
m/f drug addict. D∼erie f -,-n chemist's
shop, (Amer) drugstore. D∼ist m -en,-en
chemist

drohen vi (haben) threaten (jdm s.o.).
d∼d a threatening; (Gefahr) imminent

dröhnen vi (haben) resound; (tönen) boom

Drohung f -,-en threat

drollig a funny; (seltsam) odd

Drops m -,- [fruit] drop

Droschke f -,-n cab

Drossel f -,-n thrush

drosseln vt (Techn) throttle; (fig) cut back

drüb|en adv over there. D∼er adv (fam) =
darüber

Druck[1] m -[e]s,-e pressure; unter D∼
setzen (fig) pressurize

Druck[2] m -[e]s,-e printing; (Schrift, Repro-
duktion) print. D∼buchstabe m block letter

Drückeberger m -s,- shirker

drucken vt print

drücken vt/i (haben) press; (aus-)
squeeze; (Schuh:) pinch; (umarmen) hug;
(fig: belasten) weigh down; Preise d∼
force down prices; (an Tür) ∼ push; sich
d∼ (fam) make oneself scarce; sich d∼
vor (+ dat) shirk. d∼d a heavy;
(schwül) oppressive

Drucker m -s,- printer

Drücker m -s,- push-button; (Tür-) door
knob

Druckerei f -,-en printing works

Druck|fehler m misprint. D∼knopf m
press-stud; (Drücker) push-button.
D∼luft f compressed air. D∼sache f
printed matter. D∼schrift f type; (Veröffentlichung) publication; in D∼schrift in
block letters pl

drucksen vi (haben) hum and haw

Druck|stelle f bruise. D∼taste f push-
button. D∼topf m pressure-cooker

drum adv (fam) = darum

drunter adv (fam) = darunter; alles
geht d∼ und drüber (fam) everything is
topsy-turvy

Drüse f -,-n (Anat) gland

Dschungel m -s,- jungle

du pron (familiar address) you; auf Du und
Du (auf du und du) on familiar terms

Dübel m -s,- plug

duck|en vt duck; (fig: demütigen) humili-
ate; sich d∼en duck; (fig) cringe.
D∼mäuser m -s,- moral coward

Dudelsack m bagpipes pl

Duell nt -s,-e duel

Duett nt -s,-e [vocal] duet

Duft m -[e]s,-e fragrance, scent; (Aroma)
aroma. d∼en vi (haben) smell (nach of).
d∼ig a fine; (zart) delicate

duld|en vt tolerate; (erleiden) suffer □ vi
(haben) suffer. d∼sam a tolerant

dumm a (dümmer, dümmst) stupid, adv
-ly; (unklug) foolish, adv -ly; (fam: lästig)
awkward; wie d∼! what a nuisance! der
D∼e sein (fig) be the loser. d∼erweise
adv stupidly; (leider) unfortunately.
D∼heit f -,-en stupidity; (Torheit) fool-
ishness; (Handlung) folly. D∼kopf m
(fam) fool.

dumpf a dull, adv -y; (muffig) musty. d∼ig
a musty

Düne f -,-n dune

Dung m -s manure

Düng|emittel nt fertilizer. d∼en vt fertil-
ize. D∼er m -s,- fertilizer

dunk|el a dark; (vage) vague, adv -ly;
(fragwürdig) shady; d∼les Bier brown
ale; im D∼eln in the dark

Dünkel m -s conceit

dunkel|blau a dark blue. d∼braun a
dark brown

dünkelhaft a conceited

Dunkel|heit f - darkness. D∼kammer f
dark-room. d∼n vi (haben) get dark.
d∼rot a dark red

dünn a thin, adv -ly; (Buch) slim; (spärlich)
sparse; (schwach) weak

Dunst m -es,-e mist, haze; (Dampf) vapour

dünsten vt steam

dunstig a misty, hazy

Dünung f - swell

Duo nt -s,-s [instrumental] duet

Duplikat nt -[e]s,-e duplicate

Dur nt - (Mus) major [key]; in A-Dur in A
major

durch prep (+ acc) through; (mittels) by;
[geteilt] d∼ (Math) divided by □ adv die
Nacht d∼ throughout the night; sechs
Uhr d∼ (fam) gone six o'clock; d∼ und
d∼ nass wet through

durcharbeiten vt sep work through; sich
d∼ work one's way through

durchaus adv absolutely; d∼ nicht by no
means

durchbeißen† *vt sep* bite through

durchblättern *vt sep* leaf through

durchblicken *vi sep* (*haben*) look through; d∼ lassen (*fig*) hint at

Durchblutung *f* circulation

durchbohren *vt insep* pierce

durchbrechen†¹ *vt/i sep* (*haben*) break [in two]

durchbrechen†² *vt insep* break through; break ⟨*Schallmauer*⟩

durchbrennen† *vi sep* (*sein*) burn through; ⟨*Sicherung:*⟩ blow; (*fam: weglaufen*) run away

durchbringen† *vt sep* get through; (*verschwenden*) squander; (*versorgen*) support; sich d∼ mit make a living by

Durchbruch *m* breakthrough

durchdacht *a* gut d∼ well thought out

durchdrehen *v sep* □ *vt* mince □ *vi* (*haben/sein*) (*fam*) go crazy

durchdringen†¹ *vt insep* penetrate

durchdringen†² *vi sep* (*sein*) penetrate; (*sich durchsetzen*) get one's way. d∼d *a* penetrating; ⟨*Schrei*⟩ piercing

durcheinander *adv* in a muddle; (*Person*) confused; d∼ bringen muddle [up]; confuse ⟨*Person*⟩; d∼ geraten get mixed up; d∼ reden all talk at once. D∼ *nt* -s muddle. d∼bringen† *v sep* NEW d∼ bringen, *s.* durcheinander. d∼geraten† *vi sep* (*sein*) NEW d∼ geraten, *s.* durcheinander. d∼reden *vi sep* (*haben*) NEW d∼ reden, *s.* durcheinander

durchfahren†¹ *vi sep* (*sein*) drive through; ⟨*Zug:*⟩ go through

durchfahren†² *vt insep* drive/go through; jdn d∼ ⟨*Gedanke:*⟩ flash through s.o.'s mind

Durchfahrt *f* journey/drive through; auf der D∼ passing through; 'D∼ verboten' 'no thoroughfare'

Durchfall *m* diarrhoea; (*fam: Versagen*) flop. d∼en *vi sep* (*sein*) fall through; (*fam: versagen*) flop; (*bei Prüfung*) fail

durchfliegen†¹ *vi sep* (*sein*) fly through; (*fam: durchfallen*) fail

durchfliegen†² *vt insep* fly through; (*lesen*) skim through

durchfroren *a* frozen

Durchfuhr *f* · (*Comm*) transit

durchführ|bar *a* feasible. d∼en *vt sep* carry out

Durchgang *m* passage; (*Sport*) round; 'D∼ verboten' 'no entry'. D∼sverkehr *m* through traffic

durchgeben† *vt sep* (*übermitteln*) transmit; (*Radio, TV*) broadcast

durchgebraten *a* gut d∼ well done

durchgehen† *v sep* □ *vi* (*sein*) go through; (*davonlaufen*) run away; ⟨*Pferd:*⟩ bolt; jdm etw d∼ lassen let s.o. get away with sth □ *vt* go through. d∼d *a* continuous, *adv* -ly; d∼d geöffnet open all day; d∼der Wagen/Zug through carriage/train

durchgreifen† *vi sep* (*haben*) reach through; (*vorgehen*) take drastic action. d∼d *a* drastic

durchhalte|n† *v sep* (*fig*) □ *vi* (*haben*) hold out □ *vt* keep up. D∼vermögen *nt* stamina

durchhängen† *vi sep* (*haben*) sag

durchkommen† *vi sep* (*sein*) come through; (*gelangen, am Telefon*) get through; (*bestehen*) pass; (*überleben*) pull through; (*finanziell*) get by (mit on)

durchkreuzen *vt insep* thwart

durchlassen† *vt sep* let through

durchlässig *a* permeable; (*undicht*) leaky

durchlaufen†¹ *v sep* □ *vi* (*sein*) run through □ *vt* wear out

durchlaufen†² *vt insep* pass through

Durchlauferhitzer *m* -s,- geyser

durchleben *vt insep* live through

durchlesen† *vt sep* read through

durchleuchten *vt insep* X-ray

durchlöchert *a* riddled with holes

durchmachen *vt sep* go through; (*erleiden*) undergo; have ⟨*Krankheit*⟩

Durchmesser *m* -s,- diameter

durchnässt (**durchnäßt**) *a* wet through

durchnehmen† *vt sep* (*Sch*) do

durchnummeriert (**durchnumeriert**) *a* numbered consecutively

durchpausen *vt sep* trace

durchqueren *vt insep* cross

Durchreiche *f* -,-n [serving] hatch. d∼n *vt sep* pass through

Durchreise *f* journey through; auf der D∼ passing through. d∼n *vi sep* (*sein*) pass through

durchreißen† *vt/i sep* (*sein*) tear

durchs *adv* = durch das

Durchsage *f* -,-n announcement. d∼n *vt sep* announce

durchschauen *vt insep* (*fig*) see through

durchscheinend *a* translucent

Durchschlag *m* carbon copy; (*Culin*) colander. d∼en†¹ *v sep* □ *vt* (*Culin*) rub through a sieve; sich d∼en (*fig*) struggle through □ *vi* (*sein*) ⟨*Sicherung:*⟩ blow

durchschlagen†² *vt insep* smash

durchschlagend *a* (*fig*) effective; ⟨*Erfolg*⟩ resounding

durchschneiden† *vt sep* cut

Durchschnitt m average; im D∼ on average. d∼lich a average □ adv on average. D∼s- pref average

Durchschrift f carbon copy

durchsehen† v sep □ vi (haben) see through □ vt look through

durchseihen vt sep strain

durchsetzen¹ vt sep force through; sich d∼ assert oneself; ⟨Mode:⟩ catch on

durchsetzen² vt insep intersperse; ⟨infiltrieren⟩ infiltrate

Durchsicht f check

durchsichtig a transparent

durchsickern vi sep (sein) seep through; ⟨Neuigkeit:⟩ leak out

durchsprechen† vt sep discuss

durchstehen† vt sep ⟨fig⟩ come through

durchstreichen† vt sep cross out

durchsuch|en vt insep search. D∼ung f -,-en search

durchtrieben a cunning

durchwachsen a ⟨Speck⟩ streaky; ⟨fam: gemischt⟩ mixed

durchwacht a sleepless ⟨Nacht⟩

durchwählen vi sep (haben) (Teleph) dial direct

durchweg adv without exception

durchweicht a soggy

durchwühlen vt insep rummage through; ransack ⟨Haus⟩

durchziehen† v sep □ vt pull through □ vi (sein) pass through

durchzucken vt insep ⟨fig⟩ shoot through; jdn d∼ ⟨Gedanke:⟩ flash through s.o.'s mind

Durchzug m through draught

dürfen† vt & v aux etw [tun] d∼ be allowed to do sth; darf ich? may I? sie darf es nicht sehen she must not see it; ich hätte es nicht tun/sagen d∼ I ought not to have done/said it; das dürfte nicht allzu schwer sein that should not be too difficult

dürftig a poor; ⟨Mahlzeit⟩ scanty

dürr a dry; ⟨Boden⟩ arid; ⟨mager⟩ skinny. D∼e f -,-n drought

Durst m -[e]s thirst; D∼ haben be thirsty. d∼en vi (haben) be thirsty. d∼ig a thirsty

Dusche f -,-n shower. d∼n vi/r (haben) [sich] d∼n have a shower

Düse f -,-n nozzle. D∼nflugzeug nt jet

düster a gloomy, adv -ily; ⟨dunkel⟩ dark

Dutzend nt -s,-e dozen. d∼weise adv by the dozen

duzen vt jdn d∼ call s.o. 'du'

Dynam|ik f - dynamics sg; ⟨fig⟩ dynamism. d∼isch a dynamic; ⟨Rente⟩ index-linked

Dynamit nt -es dynamite

Dynamo m -s,-s dynamo

Dynastie f -,-n dynasty

D-Zug /'de:-/ m express [train]

E

Ebbe f -,-n low tide

eben a level; ⟨glatt⟩ smooth; zu e∼er Erde on the ground floor □ adv just; ⟨genau⟩ exactly; e∼ noch only just; ⟨gerade vorhin⟩ just now; das ist es e∼! that's just it! [na] e∼ exactly! E∼bild nt image. e∼bürtig a equal; jdm e∼bürtig sein be s.o.'s equal

Ebene f -,-n ⟨Geog⟩ plain; ⟨Geom⟩ plane; ⟨fig: Niveau⟩ level

eben|falls adv also; danke, e∼falls thank you, [the] same to you. E∼holz nt ebony. e∼mäßig a regular, adv -ly. e∼so adv just the same; ⟨ebenso sehr⟩ just as much; e∼so schön/teuer just as beautiful/expensive; e∼so gut just as good; adv just as well; e∼so sehr just as much; e∼so viel just as much/many; e∼so wenig just as little/few; ⟨noch⟩ no more. e∼sogut adv NEW e∼so gut, s. ebenso. e∼sosehr adv NEW e∼so sehr, s. ebenso. e∼soviel adv NEW e∼so viel, s. ebenso. e∼sowenig adv NEW e∼so wenig, s. ebenso

Eber m -s,- boar. E∼esche f rowan

ebnen vt level; ⟨fig⟩ smooth

Echo nt -s,-s echo. e∼en vt/i (haben) echo

echt a genuine, real; ⟨authentisch⟩ authentic; ⟨Farbe⟩ fast; ⟨typisch⟩ typical □ adv ⟨fam⟩ really; typically. E∼heit f - authenticity

Eck|ball m ⟨Sport⟩ corner. E∼e f -,-n corner; um die E∼e bringen ⟨fam⟩ bump off. e∼ig a angular, adv -ly; ⟨Klammern⟩ square; ⟨unbeholfen⟩ awkward. E∼stein m corner-stone. E∼stoß m = E∼ball. E∼zahn m canine tooth

Ecu, ECU /e'ky:/ m -[s],-[s] ecu

edel a noble, adv -bly; ⟨wertvoll⟩ precious; ⟨fein⟩ fine. E∼mann m ⟨pl -leute⟩ nobleman. E∼mut m magnanimity. e∼mütig a magnanimous, adv -ly. E∼stahl m stainless steel. E∼stein m precious stone

Efeu m -s ivy

Effekt m -[e]s,-e effect. E∼en pl securities. e∼iv a actual, adv -ly; ⟨wirksam⟩ effective, adv -ly. e∼voll a effective

EG f · abbr (Europäische Gemeinschaft) EC

egal a das ist mir e~ (fam) it's all the same to me □ adv e~ wie/wo no matter how/where. e~itär a egalitarian

Egge f -,-n harrow

Ego|ismus m - selfishness. E~ist(in) m -en,-en (f -,-nen) egoist. e~istisch a selfish, adv -ly. e~zentrisch a egocentric

eh adv (Aust fam) anyway; seit eh und je from time immemorial

ehe conj before; ehe nicht until

Ehe f -,-n marriage. E~bett nt double bed. E~bruch m adultery. E~frau f wife. E~leute pl married couple sg. e~lich a marital; (Recht) conjugal; (Kind) legitimate

ehemal|ig a former. e~s adv formerly

Ehe|mann m (pl -männer) husband. E~paar nt married couple

eher adv earlier, sooner; (lieber, vielmehr) rather; (mehr) more

Ehering m wedding ring

ehr|bar a respectable. E~e f -,-n honour; jdm E~e machen do credit to s.o. e~en vt honour. e~enamtlich a honorary □ adv in an honorary capacity. E~endoktorat nt honorary doctorate. E~engast m guest of honour. e~enhaft a honourable, adv -bly. E~enmann m (pl -männer) man of honour. E~enmitglied nt honorary member. e~enrührig a defamatory. E~enrunde f lap of honour. E~ensache f point of honour. e~enwert a honourable. E~enwort nt word of honour. e~erbietig a deferential, adv -ly. E~erbietung f - deference. E~furcht f reverence; (Scheu) awe. e~fürchtig a reverent, adv -ly. E~gefühl nt sense of honour. E~geiz m ambition. e~geizig a ambitious. e~lich a honest, adv -ly; e~lich gesagt to be honest. E~lichkeit f - honesty. e~los a dishonourable. e~sam a respectable. E~würdig a venerable; (als Anrede) Reverend

Ei nt -[e]s,-er egg

Eibe f -,-n yew

Eiche f -,-n oak. E~l f -,-n acorn. E~lhäher m -s,- jay

eichen vt standardize

Eichhörnchen nt -s,- squirrel

Eid m -[e]s,-e oath

Eidechse f -,-n lizard

eidlich a sworn □ adv on oath

Eidotter m & nt egg yolk

Eier|becher m egg-cup. E~kuchen m pancake; (Omelett) omelette. E~schale f eggshell. E~schnee m beaten egg-white. E~stock m ovary. E~uhr f egg-timer

Eifer m -s eagerness; (Streben) zeal. E~sucht f jealousy. e~süchtig a jealous, adv -ly

eiförmig a egg-shaped; (oval) oval

eifrig a eager, adv -ly; (begeistert) keen, adv -ly

Eigelb nt -[e]s,-e [egg] yolk

eigen a own; (typisch) characteristic (dat of); (seltsam) odd, adv -ly; (genau) particular. E~art f peculiarity. e~artig a peculiar, adv -ly; (seltsam) odd. E~brötler m -s,- crank. e~händig a personal, adv -ly; (Unterschrift) own. E~heit f -,-en peculiarity. e~mächtig a high-handed; (unbefugt) unauthorized □ adv high-handedly; without authority. E~name m proper name. E~nutz m self-interest. e~nützig a selfish, adv -ly. e~s adv specially. E~schaft f -,-en quality; (Phys) property; (Merkmal) characteristic; (Funktion) capacity. E~schaftswort nt (pl -wörter) adjective. E~sinn m obstinacy. e~sinnig a obstinate, adv -ly

eigentlich a actual, real; (wahr) true □ adv actually, really; (streng genommen) strictly speaking; wie geht es ihm e~? by the way, how is he?

Eigen|tor nt own goal. E~tum nt -s property. E~tümer(in) m -s,- (f -,-nen) owner. e~tümlich a odd, adv -ly; (typisch) characteristic. E~tumswohnung f freehold flat. e~willig a self-willed; (Stil) highly individual

eign|en (sich) vr be suitable. E~ung f - suitability

Eil|brief m express letter. E~e f - hurry; E~e haben be in a hurry; (Sache:) be urgent. e~en vi (sein) hurry □ (haben) (drängen) be urgent. e~ends adv hurriedly. e~ig a hurried, adv -ly; (dringend) urgent, adv -ly; es e~ig haben be in a hurry. E~zug m semi-fast train

Eimer m -s,- bucket; (Abfall-) bin

ein[1] adj one; e~es Tages/ Abends one day/ evening; mit jdm in einem Zimmer schlafen sleep in the same room as s.o. □ indef art a, (vor Vokal) an; so ein such a; was für ein (Frage) what kind of a? (Ausruf) what a!

ein[2] adv ein und aus in and out; nicht mehr ein noch aus wissen (fam) be at one's wits' end

einander pron one another

einarbeiten vt sep train

einäscher|n vt sep reduce to ashes; cremate (Leiche). E~ung f -,-en cremation

einatmen vt/i sep (haben) inhale, breathe in

ein|äugig a one-eyed. E~bahnstraße f one-way street

einbalsamieren vt sep embalm

Einband m binding

Einbau m installation; ⟨Montage⟩ fitting. e~en vt sep install; ⟨montieren⟩ fit. E~küche f fitted kitchen

einbegriffen pred a included

einberuf|en† vt sep convene; ⟨Mil⟩ call up, ⟨Amer⟩ draft. E~ung f call-up, ⟨Amer⟩ draft

Einbettzimmer nt single room

einbeulen vt sep dent

einbeziehen† vt sep [mit] e~ include; ⟨berücksichtigen⟩ take into account

einbiegen† vi sep (sein) turn

einbild|en vt sep sich ⟨dat⟩ etw e~en imagine sth; sich ⟨dat⟩ viel e~en be conceited. E~ung f imagination; ⟨Dünkel⟩ conceit. E~ungskraft f imagination

einbläuen vt sep jdm etw e~ ⟨fam⟩ drum sth into s.o.

einblenden vt sep fade in

einbleuen vt sep (NEW) einbläuen

Einblick m insight

einbrech|en† vt sep (haben/sein) break in; bei uns ist eingebrochen worden we have been burgled ◻ (sein) set in; ⟨Nacht:⟩ fall. E~er m burglar

einbring|en† vt sep get in; bring in ⟨Geld⟩; das bringt nichts ein it's not worth while. e~lich a profitable

Einbruch m burglary; bei E~ der Nacht at nightfall

einbürger|n vt sep naturalize; sich e~n become naturalized. E~ung f naturalization

Ein|buße f loss (an + dat of). e~büßen vt sep lose

einchecken /-tʃɛkən/ vt/i sep (haben) check in

eindecken (sich) vr sep stock up

eindeutig a unambiguous; ⟨deutlich⟩ clear, adv -ly

eindicken vt sep ⟨Culin⟩ thicken

eindring|en† vi sep (sein) e~en in (+ acc) penetrate into; ⟨mit Gewalt⟩ force one's ⟨Wasser:⟩ its way into; ⟨Mil⟩ invade; auf jdn e~en ⟨fig⟩ press s.o.; ⟨bittend⟩ plead with s.o. e~lich a urgent, adv -ly. E~ling m -s,-e intruder

Eindruck m impression; E~ machen impress (auf jdn s.o.)

eindrücken vt sep crush

eindrucksvoll a impressive

ein|e(r,s) pron one; ⟨jemand⟩ someone; ⟨man⟩ one, you; e~er von uns one of us; es macht e~lich a müde it makes you tired

einebnen vt sep level

eineiig a ⟨Zwillinge⟩ identical

eineinhalb inv a one and a half; e~ Stunden an hour and a half

Einelternfamilie f one-parent family

einengen vt sep restrict

Einer m -s,- ⟨Math⟩ unit. e~ pron s. eine(r,s). e~lei inv a ◻ attrib a one kind of; ⟨eintönig, einheitlich⟩ the same ◻ pred a ⟨fam⟩ immaterial; es ist mir e~lei it's all the same to me. E~lei nt -s monotony. e~seits adv on the one hand

einfach a simple, adv -ly; ⟨Essen⟩ plain; ⟨Faden, Fahrt, Fahrkarte⟩ single; e~er Soldat private. E~heit f -- simplicity

einfädeln vt sep thread; ⟨fig; arrangieren⟩ arrange; sich e~ filter in

einfahr|en† vt sep ◻ vi (sein) arrive; ⟨Zug:⟩ pull in ◻ vt ⟨Auto⟩ run in; die Ernte e~en get in the harvest. E~t f arrival; ⟨Eingang⟩ entrance, way in; ⟨Auffahrt⟩ drive; ⟨Autobahn-⟩ access road; keine E~t no entry

Einfall m idea; ⟨Mil⟩ invasion. e~en† vi sep ⟨sein⟩ collapse; ⟨eindringen⟩ invade; ⟨einstimmen⟩ join in; jdm e~en occur to s.o.; sein Name fällt mir nicht ein I can't think of his name; was fällt ihm ein! what does he think he is doing! e~sreich a imaginative

Einfalt f -- naïvety

einfältig a simple; ⟨naiv⟩ naïve

Einfaltspinsel m simpleton

einfangen† vt sep catch

einfarbig a of one colour; ⟨Stoff, Kleid⟩ plain

einfass|en vt sep edge; set ⟨Edelstein⟩. E~ung f border, edging

einfetten vt sep grease

einfind|en† (sich) vr sep turn up

einfließen† vi sep (sein) flow in

einflößen† vt sep etw e~ give s.o. sips of sth; jdm Angst e~ ⟨fig⟩ frighten s.o.

Einfluss (Einfluß) m influence. e~reich a influential

einförmig a monotonous, adv -ly. E~keit f -- monotony

einfried[ig]|en vt sep enclose. E~ung f -,-en enclosure

einfrieren† vt/i sep (sein) freeze

einfügen vt sep insert; ⟨einschieben⟩ interpolate; sich e~ fit in

einfühl|en (sich) vr sep empathize (in + acc with). e~sam a sensitive

Einfuhr f -,-en import

einführ|en† vt sep introduce; ⟨einstecken⟩ insert; ⟨einweisen⟩ initiate; ⟨Comm⟩ import. e~end a introductory. E~ung f introduction; ⟨Einweisung⟩ initiation

Eingabe f petition; ⟨Computer⟩ input

Eingang m entrance, way in; ⟨Ankunft⟩ arrival

eingebaut a built-in; ⟨Schrank⟩ fitted

eingeben† vt sep hand in; ⟨einflößen⟩ give (jdm s.o.); ⟨Computer⟩ feed in

eingebildet a imaginary; ⟨überheblich⟩ conceited

Eingeborene(r) m/f native

Eingebung f -,-en inspiration

eingedenk prep (+ gen) mindful of

eingefleischt a e~er Junggeselle confirmed bachelor

eingehakt adv arm in arm

eingehen† v sep □ vi (sein) come in; ⟨ankommen⟩ arrive; ⟨einlaufen⟩ shrink; ⟨sterben⟩ die; ⟨Zeitung, Firma:⟩ fold; auf etw(acc) e~go into sth; ⟨annehmen⟩ agree to sth □ vt enter into; contract ⟨Ehe⟩; make ⟨Wette⟩; take ⟨Risiko⟩. e~d a detailed; ⟨gründlich⟩ thorough, adv -ly

eingelegt a inlaid; ⟨Culin⟩ pickled; ⟨mariniert⟩ marinaded

eingemacht a ⟨Culin⟩ bottled

eingenommen pred a ⟨fig⟩ taken ⟨von with⟩; prejudiced ⟨gegen against⟩; von sich e~ conceited

eingeschneit a snowbound

eingeschrieben a registered

Einge|ständnis nt admission. e~stehen†** vt sep admit

eingetragen a registered

Eingeweide pl bowels, entrails

eingewöhnen (sich) vr sep settle in

eingießen† vt sep pour in; ⟨einschenken⟩ pour

eingleisig a single-track

eingliedern vt sep integrate. E~ung f integration

eingraben† vt sep bury

eingravieren vt sep engrave

eingreifen† vi sep (haben) intervene. E~ nt -s intervention

Eingriff m intervention; ⟨Med⟩ operation

einhaken vt/r sep jdn e~od sich bei jdm e~ take s.o.'s arm

einhalten† v sep □ vt keep; ⟨befolgen⟩ observe □ vi (haben) stop

einhändigen vt sep hand in

einhängen v sep □ vt hang; put down ⟨Hörer⟩; sich bei jdm e~ take s.o.'s arm □ vi (haben) hang up

einheimisch a local; ⟨eines Landes⟩ native; ⟨Comm⟩ home-produced. E~e(r) m/f local; native

Einheit f -,-en unity; ⟨Maß-, Mil⟩ unit. e~lich a uniform, adv -ly; ⟨vereinheitlicht⟩ standard. E~spreis m standard price; ⟨Fahrpreis⟩ flat fare

einhellig a unanimous, adv -ly

einholen vt sep catch up with; ⟨aufholen⟩ make up for; ⟨erbitten⟩ seek; ⟨einkaufen⟩ buy; e~ gehen go shopping

einhüllen vt sep wrap

einhundert inv a one hundred

einig a united; [sich ⟨dat⟩] e~ werden/ sein come to an/be in agreement

einig|e(r,s) pron some; ⟨ziemlich viel⟩ quite a lot of; ⟨substantivisch⟩ e~e pl some; ⟨mehrere⟩ several; ⟨ziemlich viele⟩ quite a lot; e~es sg some things; vor e~er Zeit some time ago. e~emal adv (NEW) e~e Mal, s. Mal¹

einigen vt unite; unify ⟨Land⟩; sich e~ come to an agreement; ⟨ausmachen⟩ agree (auf + acc on)

einigermaßen adv to some extent; ⟨ziemlich⟩ fairly; ⟨ziemlich gut⟩ fairly well

Einig|keit f - unity; ⟨Übereinstimmung⟩ agreement. E~ung f - unification; ⟨Übereinkunft⟩ agreement

einjährig a one-year-old; ⟨ein Jahr dauernd⟩ one year's ...; e~e Pflanze annual

einkalkulieren vt sep take into account

einkassieren vt sep collect

Einkauf m purchase; ⟨Einkaufen⟩ shopping; Einkäufe machen do some shopping. e~en vt sep buy; e~en gehen go shopping. E~skorb m shopping/⟨im Geschäft⟩ wire basket. E~stasche f shopping bag. E~swagen m shopping trolley. E~szentrum nt shopping centre

einkehren vi sep (sein) [in einem Lokal] e~ stop for a meal/drink [at an inn]

einklammern vt sep bracket

Einklang m harmony; in E~ stehen be in accord ⟨mit with⟩

einkleben vt sep stick in

einkleiden vt sep fit out

einklemmen vt sep clamp; sich ⟨dat⟩ den Finger in der Tür e~ catch one's finger in the door

einkochen v sep □ vi (sein) boil down □ vt preserve, bottle

Einkommen nt -s income. E~[s]steuer f income tax

einkreisen vt sep encircle; rot e~ ring in red

Einkünfte pl income sg; ⟨Einnahmen⟩ revenue sg

einlad|en† vt sep load; ⟨auffordern⟩ invite; ⟨bezahlen für⟩ treat. e~end a inviting. E~ung f invitation

Einlage f enclosure; ⟨Schuh-⟩ arch support; ⟨Zahn-⟩ temporary filling;

(*Programm-*) interlude; (*Comm*) investment; (*Bank-*) deposit; Suppe mit E~ soup with noodles/dumplings

Ein|lass *m* -es (**Einlaß** *m* -sses) admittance. e~lassen† *vt sep* let in; run (*Bad, Wasser*); sich auf etw (*acc*)/mit jdm e~lassen get involved in sth/with s.o.

einlaufen† *vi sep* (*sein*) come in; (*ankommen*) arrive; (*Wasser:*) run in; (*schrumpfen*) shrink; [in den Hafen] e~ enter port

einleben (sich) *vr sep* settle in

Einlege|arbeit *f* inlaid work. e~n *vt sep* put in; lay in (*Vorrat*); lodge (*Protest, Berufung*); (*einfügen*) insert; (*Auto*) engage (*Gang*); (*verzieren*) inlay; (*Culin*) pickle; (*marinieren*) marinade; eine Pause e~ have a break. E~sohle *f* insole

einleit|en *vt sep* initiate; (*eröffnen*) begin. e~end *a* introductory. E~ung *f* introduction

einlenken *vi sep* (*haben*) (*fig*) relent

einleuchten *vi sep* (*haben*) be clear (*dat* to). e~d *a* convincing

einliefer|n *vt sep* take (ins Krankenhaus to hospital). E~ung *f* admission

einlösen *vt sep* cash (*Scheck*); redeem (*Pfand*); (*fig*) keep

einmachen *vt sep* preserve

einmal *adv* once; (*eines Tages*) one or some day; noch/schon e~ again/before; noch e~ so teuer twice as expensive; auf e~ at the same time; (*plötzlich*) suddenly; nicht e~ not even; es geht nun e~ nicht it's just not possible. E~eins *nt* -[multiplication] tables *pl*. e~ig *a* single; (*einzigartig*) unique; (*fam: großartig*) fantastic, *adv* -ally

einmarschieren *vi sep* (*sein*) march in

einmisch|en (sich) *vr sep* interfere. E~ung *f* interference

einmütig *a* unanimous, *adv* -ly

Einnahme *f* -,-n taking; (*Mil*) capture; E~n *pl* income *sg*; (*Einkünfte*) revenue *sg*; (*Comm*) receipts; (*eines Ladens*) takings

einnehmen† *vt sep* take; have (*Mahlzeit*); (*Mil*) capture; take up (*Platz*); (*fig*) prejudice (gegen against); jdn für sich e~ win s.o. over. e~d *a* engaging

einnicken *vi sep* (*sein*) nod off

Einöde *f* wilderness

einordnen *vt sep* put in its proper place; (*klassifizieren*) classify; sich e~ fit in; (*Auto*) get in lane

einpacken *vt sep* pack; (*einhüllen*) wrap

einparken *vt sep* park

einpauken *vt sep* jdm etw e~ (*fam*) drum sth into s.o.

einpflanzen *vt sep* plant; implant (*Organ*)

einplanen *vt sep* allow for

einprägen *vt sep* impress (jdm [up]on s.o.); sich (*dat*) etw e~en memorize sth. e~sam *a* easy to remember; (*Melodie*) catchy

einquartieren *vt sep* (*Mil*) billet (bei on); sich in einem Hotel e~ put up at a hotel

einrahmen *vt sep* frame

einrasten *vi sep* (*sein*) engage

einräumen *vt sep* put away; (*zugeben*) admit; (*zugestehen*) grant

einrechnen *vt sep* include

einreden *v sep* □ *vt* jdm/sich (*dat*) etw e~ persuade s.o./oneself of sth □ *vi* (*haben*) auf jdn e~ talk insistently to s.o.

einreib|en† *vt sep* rub (mit with). E~mittel *nt* liniment

einreichen *vt sep* submit; die Scheidung e~ file for divorce

Einreih|er *m* -s,- single-breasted suit. e~ig *a* single-breasted

Einreise *f* entry. e~n *vi sep* (*sein*) enter (nach Irland Ireland). E~visum *nt* entry visa

einreißen† *v sep* □ *vt* tear; (*abreißen*) pull down □ *vi* (*sein*) tear; (*Sitte:*) become a habit

einrenken *vt sep* (*Med*) set

einricht|en *vt sep* fit out; (*möblieren*) furnish; (*anordnen*) arrange; (*Med*) set (*Bruch*); (*eröffnen*) set up; sich e~en furnish one's home; (*sich einschränken*) economize; (*sich vorbereiten*) prepare (auf *acc* for). E~ung *f* furnishing; (*Möbel*) furnishings *pl*; (*Techn*) equipment; (*Vorrichtung*) device; (*Eröffnung*) setting up; (*Institution*) institution; (*Gewohnheit*) practice. E~ungsgegenstand *m* piece of equipment/(*Möbelstück*) furniture

einrollen *vt sep* roll up; put in rollers (*Haare*)

einrosten *vi sep* (*sein*) rust; (*fig*) get rusty

einrücken *v sep* □ *vi* (*sein*) (*Mil*) be called up; (*einmarschieren*) move in □ *vt* indent

eins *inv a & pron* one; noch e~ one other thing; mir ist alles e~ (*fam*) it's all the same to me. E~ *f* -,-en one; (*Sch*) ≈ A

einsam *a* lonely; (*allein*) solitary; (*abgelegen*) isolated. E~keit *f* -loneliness; solitude; isolation

einsammeln *vt sep* collect

Einsatz *m* use; (*Mil*) mission; (*Wett-*) stake; (*E~teil*) insert; im E~ in action. e~bereit *a* ready for action

einschalt|en *vt sep* switch on; (*einschieben*) interpolate; (*fig: beteiligen*) call in; sich e~en (*fig*) intervene. E~quote *f* (*TV*) viewing figures *pl*; ≈ ratings *pl*

einschärfen vt sep jdm etw e~ impress sth [up]on s.o.

einschätz|en vt sep assess; (bewerten) rate. E~ung f assessment; estimation

einschenken vt sep pour

einscheren vi sep (sein) pull in

einschicken vt sep send in

einschieben† vt sep push in; (einfügen) insert; (fig) interpolate

einschiff|en (sich) vr sep embark. E~ung f - embarkation

einschlafen† vi sep (sein) go to sleep; (aufhören) peter out

einschläfern vt sep lull to sleep; (betäuben) put out; (töten) put to sleep. e~d a soporific

Einschlag m impact; (fig: Beimischung) element. e~en† v sep □ vt knock in; (zerschlagen) smash; (einwickeln) wrap; (falten) turn up; (drehen) turn; take (Weg); take up (Laufbahn). □ vi (haben) hit/ (Blitz:) strike (in etw acc sth); (zustimmen) shake hands [on a deal]; (Erfolg haben) be a hit; auf jdn e~en beat s.o.

einschlägig a relevant

einschleusen vt sep infiltrate

einschließ|en† vt sep lock in; (umgeben) enclose; (einkreisen) surround; (einbeziehen) include; sich e~en lock oneself in; Bedienung eingeschlossen service included. e~lich adv inclusive □ prep (+ gen) including

einschmeicheln (sich) vr sep ingratiate oneself (bei with)

einschnappen vi sep (sein) click shut; eingeschnappt sein (fam) be in a huff

einschneiden† vt/i sep (haben) [in] etw acc e~ cut into sth. e~d a (fig) drastic, adv -ally

Einschnitt m cut; (Med) incision; (Lücke) gap; (fig) decisive event

einschränk|en vt sep restrict; (reduzieren) cut back; sich e~en economize. E~ung f -,-en restriction; (Reduzierung) reduction; (Vorbehalt) reservation

Einschreib[e]brief m registered letter. e~en† vt sep enter; register (Brief); sich e~en put one's name down; (sich anmelden) enrol. E~en nt registered letter/packet; als od per E~en by registered post

einschreiten† vi sep (sein) intervene

einschüchter|n vt sep intimidate. E~ung f - intimidation

einsegn|en vt sep (Relig) confirm. E~ung f -,-en confirmation

einsehen† vt sep inspect; (lesen) consult; (begreifen) see. E~ nt -s ein E~ haben

show some understanding; (vernünftig sein) see reason

einseitig a one-sided; (Pol) unilateral. □ adv on one side; (fig) one-sidedly; (Pol) unilaterally

einsenden† vt sep send in

einsetzen v sep □ vt put in; (einfügen) insert; (verwenden) use; put on (Zug); call out (Truppen); (Mil) deploy; (ernennen) appoint; (wetten) stake; (riskieren) risk; sich e~ für support □ vi (haben) start; (Winter, Regen:) set in

Einsicht f insight; (Verständnis) understanding; (Vernunft) reason; zur E~ kommen see reason. e~ig a understanding; (vernünftig) sensible

Einsiedler m hermit

einsilbig a monosyllabic; (Person) taciturn

einsinken† vi sep (sein) sink in

einspannen vt sep harness; jdn e~ (fam) rope s.o. in; sehr eingespannt (fam) very busy

einsparen vt sep save

einsperren vt sep shut/(im Gefängnis) lock up

einspielen (sich) vr sep warm up; gut aufeinander eingespielt sein work well together

einsprachig a monolingual

einspringen† vi sep (sein) step in (für for)

einspritzen vt sep inject

Einspruch m objection; E~ erheben object; (Jur) appeal

einspurig a single-track; (Auto) single-lane

einst adv once; (Zukunft) one day

Einstand m (Tennis) deuce

einstecken vt sep put in; post (Brief); (Electr) plug in; (fam: behalten) pocket; (fam: hinnehmen) take; suffer (Niederlage); etw e~ put sth in one's pocket

einstehen† vi sep (haben) e~ für vouch for; answer for (Folgen)

einsteigen† vi sep (sein) get in; (in Bus/Zug) get on

einstell|en vt sep put in; (anstellen) employ; (aufhören) stop; (regulieren) adjust, set; (Optik) focus; tune (Motor, Zündung); tune to (Sender); sich e~en turn up; (ankommen) arrive; (eintreten) occur; (Schwierigkeiten:) arise; sich e~en auf (+ acc) adjust to; (sich vorbereiten) prepare for. E~ung f employment; (Aufhören) cessation; (Regulierung) adjustment; (Optik) focusing; (TV, Auto) tuning; (Haltung) attitude

Einstieg m -[e]s,-e entrance

einstig a former

einstimmen *vi sep* (*haben*) join in

einstimmig *a* unanimous, *adv* -ly. E~keit *f* unanimity

einstöckig *a* single-storey

einstudieren *vt sep* rehearse

einstufen *vt sep* classify

Ein|sturz *m* collapse. e~stürzen *vi sep* (*sein*) collapse

einstweil|en *adv* for the time being; (*inzwischen*) meanwhile. e~ig *a* temporary

eintasten *vt sep* key in

eintauchen *vt/i sep* (*sein*) dip in; (*heftiger*) plunge in

eintauschen *vt sep* exchange

eintausend *inv a* one thousand

einteil|en *vt sep* divide (in + *acc* into); (*Biol*) classify; sich (*dat*) seine Zeit gut e~en organize one's time well. e~ig *a* one-piece. E~ung *f* division; classification

eintönig *a* monotonous, *adv* -ly. E~keit *f* monotony

Eintopf *m*, E~gericht *nt* stew

Ein|tracht *f* · harmony. e~trächtig *a* harmonious □ *adv* in harmony

Eintrag *m* -[e]s,-̈e entry. e~en† *vt sep* enter; (*Admin*) register; (*einbringen*) bring in; sich e~en put one's name down

einträglich *a* profitable

Eintragung *f* -,-en registration; (*Eintrag*) entry

eintreffen† *vi sep* (*sein*) arrive; (*fig*) come true; (*geschehen*) happen. E~ *nt* -s arrival

eintreiben† *vt sep* drive in; (*einziehen*) collect

eintreten† *v sep* □ *vi* (*sein*) enter; (*geschehen*) occur; in einen Klub e~ join a club; e~ für (*fig*) stand up for □ *vt* kick in

Eintritt *m* entrance; (*zu Veranstaltung*) admission; (*Beitritt*) joining; (*Beginn*) beginning. E~skarte *f* (admission) ticket

eintrocknen *vi sep* (*sein*) dry up

einüben *vt sep* practise

einundachtzig *inv a* eighty-one

einverleiben *vt sep* incorporate (*dat* into); sich (*dat*) etw e~ (*fam*) consume sth

Einvernehmen *nt* -s understanding; (*Übereinstimmung*) agreement; in bestem E~ on the best of terms

einverstanden *a* e~ sein agree

Einverständnis *nt* agreement; (*Zustimmung*) consent

Einwand *m* -[e]s,-̈e objection

Einwander|er *m* immigrant. e~n *vi sep* (*sein*) immigrate. E~ung *f* immigration

einwandfrei *a* perfect, *adv* -ly; (*untadelig*) impeccable, *adv* -bly; (*eindeutig*) indisputable, *adv* -bly

einwärts *adv* inwards

einwechseln *vt sep* change

einwecken *vt sep* preserve, bottle

Einweg- *pref* non-returnable; (*Feuerzeug*) throw-away

einweichen *vt sep* soak

einweih|en *vt sep* inaugurate; (*Relig*) consecrate; (*einführen*) initiate; (*fam*) use for the first time; in ein Geheimnis e~en let into a secret. E~ung *f* -,-en inauguration; consecration; initiation

einweisen† *vt sep* direct; (*einführen*) initiate; ins Krankenhaus e~ send to hospital

einwenden† *vt sep* etwas e~ object (gegen to); dagegen hätte ich nichts einzuwenden (*fam*) I wouldn't say no

einwerfen† *vt sep* insert; post (*Brief*); (*Sport*) throw in; (*vorbringen*) interject; (*zertrümmern*) smash

einwickeln *vt sep* wrap [up]

einwillig|en *vi sep* (*haben*) consent, agree (in + *acc* to). E~ung *f* · consent

einwirken *vi sep* (*haben*) e~ auf (+ *acc*) have an effect on; (*beeinflussen*) influence

Einwohner|in *f* (*f* -,-nen) inhabitant. E~zahl *f* population

Einwurf *m* interjection; (*Einwand*) objection; (*Sport*) throw-in; (*Münz-*) slot

Einzahl *f* (*Gram*) singular

einzahl|en *vt sep* pay in. E~ung *f* payment; (*Einlage*) deposit

einzäunen *vt sep* fence in

Einzel *nt* -s,- (*Tennis*) singles *pl*. E~bett *nt* single bed. E~fall *m* individual;(*Sonderfall*) isolated case. E~gänger *m* -s,- loner. E~haft *f* solitary confinement. E~handel *m* retail trade. E~händler *m* retailer. E~haus *nt* detached house. E~heit *f* -,-en detail. E~karte *f* single ticket. E~kind *nt* only child

einzeln *a* single, *adv* -gly; (*individuell*) individual, *adv* -ly; (*gesondert*) separate, *adv* -ly; odd (*Handschuh, Socken*); e~e Fälle some cases. E~e(r,s) (e~e(r,s)) *pron* der/die E~e (e~e) the individual; ein E~er (e~er) a single one; (*Person*) one individual; jeder E~e (e~e) every single one; (*Person*) each individual; E~e (e~e) *pl* some; im E~en (e~en) in detail; ins E~e (e~e) gehen go into detail

Einzel|person *f* single person. E~teil *nt* [component] part. E~zimmer *nt* single room

einziehen† *v sep* □ *vt* pull in; draw in (*Atem, Krallen*); (*Zool, Techn*) retract; indent (*Zeile*); (*aus dem Verkehr ziehen*) withdraw; (*beschlagnahmen*) confiscate; (*eintreiben*) collect; make (*Erkundigungen*); (*Mil*) call up; (*einfügen*) insert; (*einbauen*) put in; den Kopf e~ duck [one's head] □ *vi* (*sein*) enter; (*umziehen*) move in; (*eindringen*) penetrate

einzig *a* only; (*einmalig*) unique; eine/ keine e~e Frage a/not a single question; ein e~es Mal only once □ *adv* only; e~ und allein solely. e~artig *a* unique (*unvergleichlich*) unparalleled. E~e(r,s) (e~e(r,s)) *pron* der/die/das E~e (e~e) the only one; ein/kein E~er (e~er) a/not a single one; das E~e (e~e), was mich stört the only thing that bothers me

Einzug *m* entry; (*Umzug*) move (in + *acc* into). E~sgebiet *nt* catchment area

Eis *nt* -es ice; (*Speise*) ice-cream; Eis am Stiel ice lolly; Eis laufen skate. E~bahn *f* ice rink. E~bär *m* polar bear. E~becher *m* ice-cream sundae. E~bein *nt* (*Culin*) knuckle of pork. E~berg *m* iceberg. E~diele *f* ice-cream parlour

Eisen *nt* -s,- iron. E~bahn *f* railway. E~bahner *m* -s,- railwayman

eisern *a* iron; (*fest*) resolute, *adv* -ly; e~er Vorhang (*Theat*) safety curtain; (*Pol*) Iron Curtain

Eis|fach *nt* freezer compartment. e~gekühlt *a* chilled. e~ig *a* icy. E~kaffee *m* iced coffee. e~kalt *a* ice cold; (*fig*) icy, *adv* -ily. E~kunstlauf *m* figure skating. E~lauf *m* skating. e~laufen† *vi sep* (*sein*) [NEW]Eis laufen, s. Eis. E~läufer(in) *m(f)* skater. E~pickel *m* ice-axe. E~scholle *f* ice-floe. E~schrank *m* refrigerator. E~vogel *m* kingfisher. E~würfel *m* icecube. E~zapfen *m* icicle. E~zeit *f* ice age

eitel *a* vain; (*rein*) pure. E~keit *f* - vanity

Eiter *m* -s pus. e~n *vi* (*haben*) discharge pus

Eiweiß *nt* -es,- egg-white; (*Chem*) protein

Ekel¹ *m* -s disgust; (*Widerwille*) revulsion

Ekel² *nt* -s,- (*fam*) beast

ekel|erregend *a* nauseating. e~haft *a* nauseating; (*widerlich*) repulsive. e~n *vt/i* (*haben*) mich od mir e~t [es] davor it makes me feel sick □ *vr* sich e~n vor (+ *dat*) find repulsive

eklig *a* disgusting, repulsive

Ekstase *f* - ecstasy. e~tisch *a* ecstatic, *adv* -ally

Ekzem *nt* -s,-e eczema

elasti|sch *a* elastic; (*federnd*) springy; (*fig*) flexible. E~zität *f* - elasticity; flexibility

Elch *m* -[e]s,-e elk

Elefant *m* -en,-en elephant

elegan|t *a* elegant, *adv* -ly. E~z *f* - elegance

elektrifizieren *vt* electrify

Elektri|ker *m* -s,- electrician. e~sch *a* electric, *adv* -ally

elektrisieren *vt* electrify; sich e~ get an electric shock

Elektrizität *f* - electricity. E~swerk *nt* power station

Elektr|oartikel *mpl* electrical appliances. E~ode *f* -,-n electrode. E~oherd *m* electric cooker. E~on *nt* -s,-en /-'tro:nən/ electron. E~onik *f* - electronics *sg*. e~onisch *a* electronic

Element *nt* -[e]s,-e element; (*Anbau-*) unit. e~ar *a* elementary

Elend *nt* -s misery; (*Armut*) poverty. e~ *a* miserable, *adv* -bly, wretched, *adv* -ly; (*krank*) poorly; (*gemein*) contemptible; (*fam: schrecklich*) dreadful, *adv* -ly. E~sviertel *nt* slum

elf *inv a*, E~ *f* -,-en eleven

Elfe *f* -,-n fairy

Elfenbein *nt* ivory

Elfmeter *m* (*Fußball*) penalty

elfte(r,s) *a* eleventh

eliminieren *vt* eliminate

Elite *f* -,-n élite

Elixier *nt* -s,-e elixir

Ell[en]bogen *m* elbow

Ellip|se *f* -,-n ellipse. e~tisch *a* elliptical

Elsass (Elsaß) *nt* - Alsace

elsässisch *a* Alsatian

Elster *f* -,-n magpie

elter|lich *a* parental. E~n *pl* parents. E~nhaus *nt* [parental] home. e~nlos *a* orphaned. E~nteil *m* parent

Email /e'maj/ *nt* -s,-s, E~le /e'maljə/ *f* -,-n enamel. e~lieren /ema[l]'ji:rən/ *vt* enamel

Emanzi|pation /-'tsjo:n/ *f* - emancipation. e~piert *a* emancipated

Embargo *nt* -s,-s embargo

Emblem *nt* -s,-e emblem

Embryo *m* -s,-s embryo

Emigr|ant(in) *m* -en,-en (*f* -,-nen) emigrant. E~ation /-'tsjo:n/ *f* - emigration. e~ieren *vi* (*sein*) emigrate

eminent *a* eminent, *adv* -ly

Emission *f* -,-en emission; (*Comm*) issue

Emotion /-'tsjo:n/ *f* -,-en emotion. e~al *a* emotional

Empfang *m* -[e]s,:e reception; (*Erhalt*) receipt; in E~ nehmen receive; (*annehmen*) accept. e~en† *vt* receive; (*Biol*) conceive

Empfäng|er *m* -s,- recipient; (*Post-*) addressee; (*Zahlungs-*) payee; (*Radio, TV*)

receiver. e∼lich *a* receptive/(*Med*) susceptible (für to). E∼nis *f* - (*Biol*) conception

Empfängnisverhütung *f* contraception. E∼smittel *nt* contraceptive

Empfangs|bestätigung *f* receipt. E∼chef *m* reception manager. E∼dame *f* receptionist. E∼halle *f* [hotel] foyer

empfehl|en† *vt* recommend; sich e∼en be advisable; (*verabschieden*) take one's leave. e∼enswert *a* to be recommended; (*ratsam*) advisable. E∼ung *f* -,-en recommendation; (*Gruß*) regards *pl*

empfind|en† *vt* feel. e∼lich *a* sensitive (gegen to); (*zart*) delicate; (*wund*) tender; (*reizbar*) touchy; (*hart*) severe, *adv* -ly. E∼lichkeit *f* - sensitivity; delicacy; tenderness; touchiness. e∼sam *a* sensitive; (*sentimental*) sentimental. E∼ung *f* -,-en sensation; (*Regung*) feeling

emphatisch *a* emphatic, *adv* -ally

empor *adv* (*liter*) up[wards]

empören *vt* incense; sich e∼ be indignant; (*sich auflehnen*) rebel. e∼d *a* outrageous

Empor|kömmling *m* -s,-e upstart. e∼ragen *vi sep* (*haben*) rise [up]

empör|t *a* indignant, *adv* -ly. E∼ung *f* - indignation; (*Auflehnung*) rebellion

emsig *a* busy, *adv* -ily

Ende *nt* -s,-n end; (*eines Films, Romans*) ending; (*fam: Stück*) bit; E∼ Mai at the end of May; zu E∼sein/gehen be finished/come to an end; etw zu E∼ schreiben finish writing sth; am E∼ at the end; (*schließlich*) in the end; (*fam: vielleicht*) perhaps; (*fam: erschöpft*) at the end of one's tether

end|en *vi* (*haben*) end. e∼gültig *a* final, *adv* -ly; (*bestimmt*) definite, *adv* -ly

Endivie /-iə/ *f* -,-n endive

end|lich *adv* at last, finally; (*schließlich*) in the end. e∼los *a* endless, *adv* -ly. E∼resultat *nt* final result. E∼spiel *nt* final. E∼spurt *m* -[e]s final spurt. E∼station *f* terminus. E∼ung *f* -,-en (*Gram*) ending

Energie *f* - energy

energisch *a* resolute, *adv* -ly; (*nachdrücklich*) vigorous, *adv* -ly; e∼ werden put one's foot down

eng *a* narrow; (*beengt*) cramped; (*anliegend*) tight; (*nah*) close, *adv* -ly; e∼ anliegend tight-fitting

Enga|gement /ãgaʒə'mã:/ *nt* -s,-s (*Theat*) engagement; (*fig*) commitment. e∼gieren /-'ʒi:rən/ *vt* (*Theat*) engage; sich e∼gieren become involved; e∼giert committed

eng|anliegend *a* (NEW)e∼ anliegend, *s.* eng. E∼e *f* - narrowness; in die E∼e treiben (*fig*) drive into a corner

Engel *m* -s,- angel. e∼haft *a* angelic

engherzig *a* petty

England *nt* -s England

Engländer *m* -s,- Englishman; (*Techn*) monkey-wrench; die E∼ the English *pl.* E∼in *f* -,-nen Englishwoman

englisch *a* English; auf e∼ (NEW)auf E∼, *s.* Englisch. E∼ *nt* -[s] (*Lang*) English; auf E∼ in English

Engpass (Engpaß) *m* (*fig*) bottle-neck

en gros /ã'gro:/ *adv* wholesale

engstirnig *a* (*fig*) narrowminded

Enkel *m* -s,- grandson; E∼ *pl* grandchildren. E∼in *f* -,-nen granddaughter. E∼kind *nt* grandchild. E∼sohn *m* grandson. E∼tochter *f* granddaughter

enorm *a* enormous, *adv* -ly; (*fam: großartig*) fantastic

Ensemble /ã'sã:bəl/ *nt* -s,-s ensemble; (*Theat*) company

entart|en *vi* (*sein*) degenerate. e∼et *a* degenerate

entbehr|en *vt* do without; (*vermissen*) miss. e∼lich *a* dispensable; (*überflüssig*) superfluous. E∼ung *f* -,-en privation

entbind|en† *vt* release (von from); (*Med*) deliver (von of) □ *vi* (*haben*) give birth. E∼ung *f* delivery. E∼ungsstation *f* maternity ward

entblöß|en *vt* bare. e∼t *a* bare

entdeck|en *vt* discover. E∼er *m* -s,- discoverer; (*Forscher*) explorer. E∼ung *f* -,-en discovery

Ente *f* -,-n duck

entehren *vt* dishonour

enteignen *vt* dispossess; expropriate (*Eigentum*)

enterben *vt* disinherit

Enterich *m* -s,-e drake

entfachen *vt* kindle

entfallen† *vi* (*sein*) not apply; jdm e∼ slip from s.o.'s hand; (*aus dem Gedächtnis*) slip s.o.'s mind; auf jdn e∼ be s.o.'s share

entfalt|en *vt* unfold; (*entwickeln*) develop; (*zeigen*) display; sich e∼en unfold; develop. E∼ung *f* - development

entfern|en *vt* remove; sich e∼en leave. e∼t *a* distant; (*schwach*) vague, *adv* -ly; 2 Kilometer e∼t 2 kilometres away; e∼t verwandt distantly related; nicht im E∼testen (e∼testen) not in the least. E∼ung *f* -,-en removal; (*Abstand*) distance; (*Reichweite*) range. E∼ungsmesser *m* range-finder

entfesseln *vt* (*fig*) unleash

entfliehen† *vi* (*sein*) escape

entfremd|en *vt* alienate. E~ung *f* - alienation

entfrosten *vt* defrost

entführ|en *vt* abduct, kidnap; hijack ⟨*Flugzeug.*⟩ E~er *m* abductor, kidnapper; hijacker. E~ung *f* abduction, kidnapping; hijacking

entgegen *adv* towards □ *prep* (+ *dat*) contrary to. e~gehen† *vi sep* (*sein*) (+ *dat*) go to meet; ⟨*fig*⟩ be heading for. e~gesetzt *a* opposite; (*gegensätzlich*) opposing. e~halten† *vt sep* (*fig*) object. e~kommen† *vi sep* (*sein*) (+ *dat*) come to meet; (*zukommen auf*) come towards; (*fig*) oblige. E~kommen *nt* -s helpfulness; (*Zugeständnis*) concession. e~kommend *a* approaching; ⟨*Verkehr*⟩ oncoming; (*fig*) obliging. e~nehmen† *vt sep* accept. e~sehen† *vt sep* (*fig*) await; (*freudig*) look forward to. e~setzen *vt sep* Widerstand e~setzen (+ *dat*) resist. e~treten† *vi sep* (*sein*) (+ *dat*) (*fig*) confront; (*bekämpfen*) fight. e~wirken *vi sep* (*haben*) (+ *dat*) counteract; (*fig*) oppose

entgegn|en *vt* reply (auf + *acc* to). E~ung *f* -,-en reply

entgehen† *vi sep* (*sein*) (+ *dat*) escape; jdm e~ (*unbemerkt bleiben*) escape s.o.'s notice; sich (*dat*) etw e~ lassen miss sth

entgeistert *a* flabbergasted

Entgelt *nt* -[e]s payment; gegen E~ for money. e~en *vt* jdn etw e~en lassen (*fig*) make s.o. pay for sth

entgleis|en *vi* (*sein*) be derailed; (*fig*) make a gaffe. E~ung *f* -,-en derailment; (*fig*) gaffe

entgleiten† *vi sep* (*sein*) jdm e~ slip from s.o.'s grasp

entgräten *vt* fillet, bone

Enthaarungsmittel *nt* depilatory

enthalt|en† *vt* contain; in etw (*dat*) e~en sein be contained/ (*eingeschlossen*) included in sth; sich der Stimme e~en (*Pol*) abstain. e~sam *a* abstemious. E~samkeit *f* - abstinence. E~ung *f* (*Pol*) abstention

enthaupten *vt* behead

entheben† *vt* jdn seines Amtes e~ relieve s.o. of his post

enthüll|en *vt* unveil; (*fig*) reveal. E~ung *f* -,-en revelation

Enthusias|mus *m* - enthusiast. E~t *m* -en,-en enthusiast. e~tisch *a* enthusiastic, *adv* -ally

entkernen *vt* stone; core ⟨*Apfel*⟩

entkleid|en *vt* undress; sich e~en undress. E~ungsnummer *f* strip-tease [act]

entkommen† *vi* (*sein*) escape

entkorken *vt* uncork

entkräft|en *vt* weaken; (*fig*) invalidate. E~ung *f* - debility

entkrampfen *vt* relax; sich e~ relax

entlad|en† *vt* unload; ⟨*Electr*⟩ discharge; sich e~ discharge; ⟨*Gewitter.*⟩ break; ⟨*Zorn.*⟩ explode

entlang *adv* & *prep* (+ *preceding acc or following dat*) along; die Straße e~, e~ der Straße along the road; an etw (*dat*) e~ along sth. e~fahren† *vi sep* (*sein*) drive along. e~gehen† *vi sep* (*sein*) walk along

entlarven *vt* unmask

entlass|en† *vt* dismiss; (*aus Krankenhaus*) discharge; (*aus der Haft*) release; aus der Schule e~en werden leave school. E~ung *f* -,-en dismissal; discharge; release

entlast|en *vt* relieve the strain on; ease ⟨*Gewissen, Verkehr.*⟩; relieve (von of); ⟨*Jur*⟩ exonerate. E~ung *f* - relief; exoneration. E~ungszug *m* relief train

entlaufen† *vi* (*sein*) run away

entledigen (sich) *vr* (+ *gen*) rid oneself of; (*ausziehen*) take off; (*erfüllen*) discharge

entleeren *vt* empty

entlegen *a* remote

entleihen† *vt* borrow (von from)

entlocken *vt* coax (*dat* from)

entlohnen *vt* pay

entlüft|en *vt* ventilate. E~er *m* -s,- extractor fan. E~ung *f* ventilation

entmündigen *vt* declare incapable of managing his own affairs

entmutigen *vt* discourage

entnehmen† *vt* take (*dat* from); (*schließen*) gather (*dat* from)

Entomologie *f* - entomology

entpuppen (sich) *vr* (*fig*) turn out (als etw to be sth)

entrahmt *a* skimmed

entreißen† *vt* snatch (*dat* from)

entrichten *vt* pay

entrinnen† *vi* (*sein*) escape

entrollen *vt* unroll; unfurl ⟨*Fahne*⟩; sich e~ unroll; unfurl

entrüst|en *vt* fill with indignation; sich e~en be indignant (über + *acc* at). e~et *a* indignant, *adv* -ly. E~ung *f* - indignation

entsaft|en *vt* extract the juice from. E~er *m* -s,- juice extractor

entsag|en *vi* (*haben*) (+ *dat*) renounce. E~ung *f* - renunciation

entschädig|en *vt* compensate. E~ung *f* -,-en compensation

entschärfen *vt* defuse

entscheid|en† *vt/i (haben)* decide; sich e~en decide; *(Sache:)* be decided. e~end *a* decisive, *adv* -ly; *(kritisch)* crucial. E~ung *f* decision

entschieden *a* decided, *adv* -ly; *(fest)* firm, *adv* -ly

entschlafen† *vi (sein) (liter)* pass away

entschließen† (sich) *vr* decide, make up one's mind; sich anders e~ change one's mind

entschlossen *a* determined; *(energisch)* resolute, *adv* -ly; kurz e~ without hesitation; *(spontan)* on the spur of the moment. E~heit *f* determination

Entschluss (Entschluß) *m* decision; einen E~ fassen make a decision

entschlüsseln *vt* decode

entschuld|bar *a* excusable. e~igen *vt* excuse; sich e~igen apologize (bei to); e~igen Sie [bitte]! sorry! *(bei Frage)* excuse me. E~igung *f* -,-en apology; *(Ausrede)* excuse; [jdn] um E~igung bitten apologize [to s.o.]; E~igung! sorry! *(bei Frage)* excuse me

entsetz|en *vt* horrify. E~en *nt* -s horror. e~lich *a* horrible, *adv* -bly; *(schrecklich)* terrible, *adv* -bly. e~t *a* horrified

entsinnen† (sich) *vr* (+ *Kize*) remember

Entsorgung *f* - waste disposal

entspann|en *vt* relax; sich e~en relax; *(Lage:)* ease. E~ung *f* -relaxation; easing; *(Pol)* détente

entsprech|en† *vi (haben)* (+ *dat*) correspond to; *(übereinstimmen)* agree with; *(nachkommen)* comply with. e~end *a* corresponding; *(angemessen)* appropriate; *(zuständig)* relevant □ *adv* correspondingly; appropriately; *(demgemäß)* accordingly □ *prep* (+ *dat*) in accordance with. E~ung *f* -,-en equivalent

entspringen† *vi (sein) (Fluss:)* rise; *(fig)* arise, spring *(dat* from); *(entfliehen)* escape

entstammen *vi (sein)* come in/*(abstammen)* be descended *(dat* from)

entsteh|en† *vi (sein)* come into being; *(sich bilden)* form; *(sich entwickeln)* develop; *(Brand:)* start; *(stammen)* originate/*(sich ergeben)* result (aus from). E~ung *f* - origin; formation; development; *(fig)* birth

entsteinen *vt* stone

entstell|en *vt* disfigure; *(verzerren)* distort. E~ung *f* disfigurement; distortion

entstört *a (Electr)* suppressed

enttäusch|en *vt* disappoint. E~ung *f* disappointment

entvölkern *vt* depopulate

entwaffnen *vt* disarm. e~d *a (fig)* disarming

Entwarnung *f* all-clear [signal]

entwässer|n *vt* drain. E~ung *f* - drainage

entweder *conj* & *adv* either

entweichen† *vi (sein)* escape

entweihen *vt* desecrate. E~ung *f* - desecration

entwenden *vt* steal *(dat* from)

entwerfen† *vt* design; *(aufsetzen)* draft; *(skizzieren)* sketch

entwert|en *vt* devalue; *(ungültig machen)* cancel. E~er *m* -s,- ticket-cancelling machine. E~ung *f* devaluation; cancelling

entwick|eln *vt* develop; sich e~eln develop. E~lung *f* -,-en development; *(Biol)* evolution. E~lungsland *nt* developing country

entwinden† *vt* wrench *(dat* from)

entwirren *vt* disentangle; *(fig)* unravel

entwischen *vi (sein)* jdm e~ *(fam)* give s.o. the slip

entwöhnen *vt* wean *(gen* from); cure *(Süchtige)*

entwürdigend *a* degrading

Entwurf *m* design; *(Konzept)* draft; *(Skizze)* sketch

entwurzeln *vt* uproot

entzie|hen† *vt* take away *(dat* from); jdm den Führerschein e~hen disqualify s.o. from driving; sich e~hen (+ *dat*) withdraw from; *(entgehen)* evade. E~hungskur *f* treatment for drug/alcohol addiction

entziffern *vt* decipher

entzücken *vt* delight. E~ *nt* -s delight. e~d *a* delightful

Entzug *m* withdrawal; *(Vorenthaltung)* deprivation. E~serscheinungen *fpl* withdrawal symptoms

entzünd|en *vt* ignite; *(anstecken)* light; *(fig: erregen)* inflame; sich e~en ignite; *(Med)* become inflamed. e~et *a (Med)* inflamed. e~lich *a* inflammable. E~ung *f (Med)* inflammation

entzwei *a* broken. e~en (sich) *vr* quarrel. e~gehen† *vi sep (sein)* break

Enzian *m* -s,-e gentian

Enzyklo|pädie *f* -,-en encyclopaedia. e~pädisch *a* encyclopaedic

Enzym *nt* -s,-e enzyme

Epidemie *f* -,-n epidemic

Epi|lepsie *f* - epilepsy. E~leptiker(in) *m* -s,- *(f* -,-nen) epileptic. e~leptisch *a* epileptic

Epilog *m* -s,-e epilogue

episch *a* epic

Episode *f* -,-n episode

Epitaph nt -s,-e epitaph

Epoche f -,-n epoch. e~machend a epoch-making

Epos nt -/Epen epic

er pron he; ⟨Ding, Tier⟩ it

erachten vt consider (für nötig necessary). E~ nt -s meines E~s in my opinion

erbarmen (sich) vr have pity/⟨Gott:⟩ mercy (gen on). E~ nt -s pity; mercy

erbärmlich a wretched, adv -ly; ⟨stark⟩ terrible, adv -bly

erbarmungslos a merciless, adv -ly

erbauen vt build; (fig) edify; sich e~en be edified (an + dat by); nicht e~t von ⟨fam⟩ not pleased about. e~lich a edifying

Erbe[1] m -n,-n heir

Erbe[2] nt -s inheritance; (fig) heritage. e~n vt inherit

erbeuten vt get; (Mil) capture

Erbfolge f (Jur) succession

erbieten† (sich) vr offer (zu to)

Erbin f -,-nen heiress

erbitten† vt ask for

erbittert a bitter; ⟨heftig⟩ fierce, adv -ly

erblassen vi (sein) turn pale

erblich a hereditary

erblicken vt catch sight of

erblinden vi (sein) go blind

erbost a angry, adv -ily

erbrechen† vt vomit □ vi/r [sich] e~ vomit. E~ nt -s vomiting

Erbschaft f -,-en inheritance

Erbse f -,-n pea

Erb|stück nt heirloom. E~teil nt inheritance

Erd|apfel m (Aust) potato. E~beben nt -s,- earthquake. E~beere f strawberry. E~boden m ground

Erde f -,-n earth; ⟨Erdboden⟩ ground; ⟨Fußboden⟩ floor; auf der E~ on earth; ⟨auf dem Boden⟩ on the ground/floor. e~n vt (Electr) earth

erdenklich a imaginable

Erd|gas nt natural gas. E~geschoss (E~geschoß) nt ground floor, (Amer) first floor. e~ig a earthy. E~kugel f globe. E~kunde f geography. E~nuss (E~nuß) f peanut. E~öl nt [mineral] oil. E~reich nt soil

erdreisten (sich) vr have the audacity (zu to)

erdrosseln vt strangle

erdrücken vt crush to death. e~d a (fig) overwhelming

Erd|rutsch m landslide. E~teil m continent

erdulden vt endure

ereifern (sich) vr get worked up

ereignen (sich) vr happen

Ereignis nt -ses,-se event. e~los a uneventful. e~reich a eventful

Eremit m -en,-en hermit

ererbt a inherited

erfahr|en† vt learn, hear; ⟨erleben⟩ experience □ a experienced. E~ung f -,-en experience; in E~ung bringen find out

erfassen vt seize; ⟨begreifen⟩ grasp; ⟨einbeziehen⟩ include; ⟨aufzeichnen⟩ record; von einem Auto erfasst werden be struck by a car

erfind|en† vt invent. E~er m -s,- inventor. e~erisch a inventive. E~ung f -,-en invention

Erfolg m -[e]s,-e success; ⟨Folge⟩ result; E~ haben be successful; E~ versprechend promising. e~en vi (sein) take place; ⟨geschehen⟩ happen. e~los a unsuccessful, adv -ly. e~reich a successful, adv -ly. e~versprechend a ⟨NEW⟩ E~ versprechend, s. Erfolg

erforder|lich a required, necessary. e~n vt require, demand. E~nis nt -ses,-se requirement

erforsch|en vt explore; ⟨untersuchen⟩ investigate. E~ung f exploration; investigation

erfreu|en vt please; sich guter Gesundheit e~en enjoy good health. e~lich a pleasing, gratifying; ⟨willkommen⟩ welcome. e~licherweise adv happily. e~t a pleased

erfrier|en† vi (sein) freeze to death; ⟨Glied:⟩ become frostbitten; ⟨Pflanze:⟩ be killed by the frost. E~ung f -,-en frostbite

erfrisch|en vt refresh; sich e~en refresh oneself. e~end a refreshing. E~ung f -,-en refreshment

erfüll|en vt fill; ⟨nachkommen⟩ fulfil; serve ⟨Zweck⟩; discharge ⟨Pflicht:⟩; sich e~en come true. E~ung f fulfilment; in E~ung gehen come true

erfunden invented; ⟨fiktiv⟩ fictitious

ergänz|en vt complement; ⟨nachtragen⟩ supplement; ⟨auffüllen⟩ replenish; ⟨vervollständigen⟩ complete; ⟨hinzufügen⟩ add; sich e~en complement each other. E~ung f complement; supplement; ⟨Zusatz⟩ addition. E~ungsband m supplement

ergeben† vt produce; ⟨zeigen⟩ show, establish; sich e~en result; ⟨Schwierigkeit:⟩ arise; ⟨kapitulieren⟩ surrender; ⟨sich fügen⟩ submit; es ergab sich it turned out (dass that) □ a devoted, adv -ly; ⟨resigniert⟩ resigned, adv -ly. E~heit f- devotion

Ergebnis nt -ses,-se result. e∼los a
fruitless, adv -ly

ergehen† vi (sein) be issued; etw über
sich (acc) e∼ lassen submit to sth; wie
ist es dir ergangen? how did you get on?
□ vr sich e∼ in (+ dat) indulge in

ergiebig a productive; (fig) rich

ergötzen vt amuse

ergreifen† vt seize; take ⟨Maßnahme, Ge-
legenheit⟩; take up ⟨Beruf⟩; (rühren) move;
die Flucht e∼ flee. e∼d a moving

ergriffen a deeply moved. E∼heit f -
emotion

ergründen vt (fig) get to the bottom of

erhaben a raised; (fig) sublime; über etw
(acc) e∼ sein (fig) be above sth

Erhalt m -[e]s receipt. e∼en† vt receive,
get; (gewinnen) obtain; (bewahren) preserve, keep; (instand halten) maintain;
(unterhalten) support; am Leben e∼en
keep alive □ a gut/schlecht e∼en in
good/bad condition; e∼en bleiben survive

erhältlich a obtainable

Erhaltung f - (s. erhalten) preservation;
maintenance

erhängen (sich) vr hang oneself

erhärten vt (fig) substantiate

erheben† vt raise; levy ⟨Steuer⟩; charge
⟨Gebühr⟩; Anspruch e∼en lay claim (auf
+ acc to); Protest e∼en protest; sich
e∼en rise; ⟨Frage:⟩ arise; (sich empören)
rise up. e∼lich a considerable, adv -bly.
E∼ung f -,-en elevation; ⟨Anhöhe⟩ rise;
(Aufstand) uprising; (Ermittlung) survey

erheiter|n vt amuse. E∼ung f - amuse-
ment

erhitzen vt heat; sich e∼ get hot; (fig) get
heated

erhoffen vt sich (dat) etw e∼ hope for sth

erhöh|en vt raise; (fig) increase; sich
e∼en rise, increase. E∼ung f -,-en increase. E∼ungszeichen nt (Mus) sharp

erhol|en (sich) vr recover (von from);
(nach Krankheit) convalesce, recuperate;
(sich ausruhen) have a rest. e∼sam a restful. E∼ung f - recovery; convalescence;
(Ruhe) rest. E∼ungsheim nt convalescent home

erhören vt (fig) answer

erinner|n vt remind (an + acc of); sich
e∼n remember (an jdn/etw s.o./sth).
E∼ung f -,-en memory; (Andenken) souvenir

erkält|en (sich) vr catch a cold; e∼et sein
have a cold. E∼ung f -,-en cold

erkenn|bar a recognizable; (sichtbar) vis-
ible. e∼en† vt recognize; (wahrnehmen)
distinguish; (einsehen) realize. e∼tlich a

sich e∼tlich zeigen show one's apprecia-
tion. E∼tnis f -,-se recognition; realization; (Wissen) knowledge; die neuesten
E∼tnisse the latest findings

Erker m -s,- bay

erklär|en vt declare; (erläutern) explain;
sich bereit e∼en agree (zu to); ich kann
es mir nicht e∼en I can't explain it.
e∼end a explanatory. e∼lich a explic-
able; (verständlich) understandable. e∼
licherweise adv understandably. e∼t
attrib a declared. E∼ung f -,-en declaration; explanation; öffentliche E∼ung
public statement

erklingen† vi (sein) ring out

erkrank|en vi (sein) fall ill; be taken ill
(an + dat with). E∼ung f -,-en illness

erkunden vt explore; (Mil) reconnoitre

erkundig|en (sich) vr enquire (nach
jdm/etw after s.o./about sth). E∼ung f
-,-en enquiry

erlahmen vi (sein) tire; ⟨Kraft, Eifer:⟩ flag

erlangen vt attain, get

Erlass m -es,-̈e ⟨Erlaß m -sses,-̈sse⟩ (Admin) decree; (Befreiung) exemption;
(Straf-) remission

erlassen† vt (Admin) issue; jdm etw e∼
exempt s.o. from sth; let s.o. off ⟨Strafe⟩

erlaub|en vt allow, permit; sich e∼, etw
zu tun take the liberty of doing sth; ich
kann es mir nicht e∼ I can't afford it.
E∼nis f - permission. E∼schein m
permit

erläuter|n vt explain. E∼ung f -,-en ex-
planation

Erle f -,-n alder

erleb|en vt experience; (mit-) see; have
⟨Überraschung, Enttäuschung⟩; etw nicht
mehr e∼en not live to see sth. E∼nis nt
-ses,-se experience

erledig|en vt do; (sich befassen mit) deal
with; (beenden) finish; (entscheiden) settle;
(töten) kill; e∼t sein be
done/settled/⟨fam: müde⟩ worn out/⟨fam:
ruiniert⟩ finished

erleichter|n vt lighten; (vereinfachen)
make easier; (befreien) relieve; (lindern)
ease; sich e∼n (fig) unburden oneself.
e∼t a relieved. E∼ung f - relief

erleiden† vt suffer

erlernen vt learn

erlesen a exquisite; (auserlesen) choice,
select

erleucht|en vt illuminate; hell e∼et
brightly lit. E∼ung f -,-en (fig) inspiration

erliegen† vi (sein) succumb (dat to);
seinen Verletzungen e∼ die of one's in-
juries

erlogen a untrue, false

Erlös m -es proceeds pl

erlöschen vi (sein) go out; (vergehen) die; (aussterben) die out; (ungültig werden) expire; erloschener Vulkan extinct volcano

erlös|en vt save; (befreien) release (von from); (Relig) redeem. e~t a relieved. E~ung f release; (Erleichterung) relief; (Relig) redemption

ermächtig|en vt authorize. E~ung f -,-en authorization

ermahn|en vt exhort; (zurechtweisen) admonish. E~ung f exhortation; admonition

ermäßig|en vt reduce. E~ung f -,-en reduction

ermatt|en vi (sein) grow weary □ vt weary. E~ung f - weariness

ermessen vt judge; (begreifen) appreciate. E~ nt -s discretion; (Urteil) judgement; nach eigenem E~ at one's own discretion

ermitt|eln vt establish; (herausfinden) find out □ vi (haben) investigate (gegen jdn s.o.). E~lungen fpl investigations. E~lungsverfahren nt (Jur) preliminary inquiry

ermöglichen vt make possible

ermord|en vt murder. E~ung f -,-en murder

ermüd|en vt tire □ vi (sein) get tired. E~ung f - tiredness

ermunter|n vt encourage; sich e~n rouse oneself. E~ung f - encouragement

ermutigen vt encourage. e~d a encouraging

ernähr|en vt feed; (unterhalten) support, keep; sich e~en von live/(Tier:) feed on. E~er m -s,- breadwinner. E~ung f - nourishment; nutrition; (Kost) diet

ernenn|en vt appoint. E~ung f -,-en appointment

erneu|ern vt renew; (auswechseln) replace; change (Verband); (renovieren) renovate. E~erung f renewal; replacement; renovation. e~t a renewed; (neu) new □ adv again

erniedrig|en vt degrade; sich e~en lower oneself. e~end a degrading. E~ungszeichen nt (Mus) flat

ernst a serious, adv -ly; e~ nehmen take seriously; im E~ seriously; mit einer Drohung E~ machen carry out a threat; ist das dein E~? are you serious? E~fall m im E~ fall when the real thing happens. e~haft a serious, adv -ly. e~lich a serious, adv -ly

Ernte f -,-n harvest; (Ertrag) crop. E~dankfest nt harvest festival. e~n vt harvest; (fig) reap, win

ernüchter|n vt sober up; (fig) bring down to earth; (enttäuschen) disillusion. e~nd a (fig) sobering. E~ung f - disillusionment

Erober|er m -s,- conqueror. e~n vt conquer. E~ung f -,-en conquest

eröffn|en vt open; jdm etw e~en announce sth to s.o.; sich jdm e~en (Aussicht:) present itself to s.o. E~ung f opening; (Mitteilung) announcement. E~ungsansprache f opening address

erörter|n vt discuss. E~ung f -,-en discussion

Erosion f -,-en erosion

Erot|ik f - eroticism. e~isch a erotic

Erpel m -s,- drake

erpicht a e~ auf (+ acc) keen on

erpress|en vt extort; blackmail (Person). E~er m -s,- blackmailer. E~ung f - extortion; blackmail

erprob|en vt test. e~t a proven

erquicken vt refresh

errat|en vt guess

erreg|bar a excitable. e~en vt excite; (hervorrufen) arouse; sich e~en get worked up. e~end a exciting. E~er m -s,- (Med) germ. e~t a agitated; (hitzig) heated. E~ung f - excitement; (Erregtheit) agitation

erreich|bar a within reach; (Ziel) attainable; (Person) available. e~en vt reach; catch (Zug); live to (Alter); (durchsetzen) achieve

erretten vt save

errichten vt erect

erring|en vt gain, win

erröten vi (sein) blush

Errungenschaft f -,-en achievement; (fam: Anschaffung) acquisition; E~en der Technik technical advances

Ersatz m -es replacement, substitute; (Entschädigung) compensation. E~dienst m = Zivildienst. E~reifen m spare tyre. E~spieler(in) m(f) substitute. E~teil nt spare part

ersäufen vt drown

erschaffen vt create

erschallen vi (sein) ring out

erschein|en vi (sein) appear; (Buch:) be published; jdm merkwürdig e~en seem odd to s.o. E~en nt -s appearance; publication. E~ung f -,-en appearance; (Person) figure; (Phänomen) phenomenon; (Symptom) symptom; (Geist) apparition

erschieß|en vt shoot [dead]. E~ungskommando nt firing squad erschlaffen *vi* (sein) go limp; ⟨*Haut, Muskeln:*⟩ become flabby

erschlagen† *vt* beat to death; (*tödlich treffen*) strike dead; vom Blitz e~ werden be killed by lightning □ *a* (*fam*) (*erschöpft*) worn out; (*fassungslos*) stunned

erschließen† *vt* develop; (*zugänglich machen*) open up; (*nutzbar machen*) tap

erschöpf|en *vt* exhaust. e~end *a* exhausting; (*fig: vollständig*) exhaustive. e~t *a* exhausted. E~ung *f* - exhaustion

erschreck|en¹ *vi* (sein) get a fright □ *vt* (*reg*) startle; (*beunruhigen*) alarm; du hast mich e~t you gave me a fright □ *vr* (*reg* & *irreg*) sich e~en get a fright. e~end *a* alarming, *adv* -ly

erschrocken *a* frightened; (*erschreckt*) startled; (*bestürzt*) dismayed

erschütter|n *vt* shake; (*ergreifen*) upset deeply. E~ung *f* -,-en shock

erschweren *vt* make more difficult

erschwinglich *a* affordable

ersehen† *vt* (*fig*) see (aus from)

ersetzen *vt* replace; make good ⟨*Schaden*⟩; refund ⟨*Kosten*⟩; jdm etw e~ compensate s.o. for sth

ersichtlich *a* obvious, apparent

erspar|en *vt* save; jdm etw e~en save/(*fern halten*) spare s.o. sth. E~nis *f* -,-se saving; E~nisse savings

erst *adv* (*zuerst*) first; (*noch nicht mehr als*) only; (*nicht vor*) not until; e~ dann only then; eben *od* gerade e~ [only] just; das machte ihn e~ recht wütend it made him all the more angry

erstarren *vi* (sein) solidify; (*gefrieren*) freeze; (*steif werden*) go stiff; (*vor Schreck*) be paralysed

erstatten *vt* (*zurück-*) refund; Bericht e~ report (jdm to s.o.)

Erstaufführung *f* first performance, première

erstaun|en *vt* amaze, astonish. E~en *nt* amazement, astonishment. e~lich *a* amazing, *adv* -ly. e~licherweise *adv* amazingly

Erst|ausgabe *f* first edition. e~e(r,s) *a* first; (*beste*) best; e~e (E~e) Hilfe first aid; der e~e Beste (beste) the first one to come along; (*fam*) any Tom, Dick or Harry; als e~es/fürs e~e ⟨NEW⟩ als E~es/fürs E~e, *s.* Erste(r,s). E~e(r) *m/f* first; (*Beste*) best; fürs E~e for the time being; als E~es first of all; er kam als E~er he arrived first; er ist der/sie ist die E~e in Latein he/she is top in Latin

erstechen† *vt* stab to death

erstehen† *vt* buy

ersteigern *vt* buy at an auction

erst|emal *adv* das e~emal/zum e~enmal ⟨NEW⟩ das erste Mal/zum ersten Mal, *s.* Mal¹. e~ens *adv* firstly, in the first place. e~ere(r,s) *a* the former; der/ die/das E~ere (e~ere) the former

ersticken *vt* suffocate; smother ⟨*Flammen*⟩; (*unterdrücken*) suppress □ *vi* (sein) suffocate. E~ *nt* -s suffocation; zum E~ stifling

erstklassig *a* first-class. e~mals *adv* for the first time

erstreben *vt* strive for. e~swert *a* desirable

erstrecken (sich) *vr* stretch; sich e~auf (+ *acc*) ⟨*fig*⟩ apply to

ersuchen *vt* ask, request. E~ *nt* -s request

ertappen *vt* (*fam*) catch

erteilen *vt* give (jdm s.o.)

ertönen *vi* (sein) sound; (*erschallen*) ring out

Ertrag *m* -[e]s,˙e yield. e~en† *vt* bear

erträglich *a* bearable; (*leidlich*) tolerable

ertränken *vt* drown

ertrinken† *vi* (sein) drown

erübrigen (sich) *vr* be unnecessary

erwachen *vi* (sein) awake

erwachsen *a* grown-up. E~e(r) *m/f* adult, grown-up

erwäg|en† *vt* consider. E~ung *f* -,-en consideration; in E~ung ziehen consider

erwähn|en *vt* mention. E~ung *f* -,-en mention

erwärmen *vt* warm; sich e~ warm up; ⟨*fig*⟩ warm (für to)

erwart|en *vt* expect; (*warten auf*) wait for. E~ung *f* -,-en expectation. e~ungsvoll *a* expectant, *adv* -ly

erwecken *vt* ⟨*fig*⟩ arouse; give ⟨*Anschein*⟩

erweichen *vt* soften; ⟨*fig*⟩ move; sich e~ lassen ⟨*fig*⟩ relent

erweisen† *vt* prove; (*bezeigen*) do ⟨*Gefallen, Dienst, Ehre*⟩; sich e~ als prove to be

erweitern *vt* widen; dilate ⟨*Pupille*⟩; ⟨*fig*⟩ extend, expand

Erwerb *m* -[e]s acquisition; (*Kauf*) purchase; (*Brot-*) livelihood; (*Verdienst*) earnings *pl.* e~en† *vt* acquire; (*kaufen*) purchase; (*fig: erlangen*) gain. e~slos *a* unemployed. e~stätig *a* [gainfully] employed. E~ung *f* -,-en acquisition

erwider|n *vt* reply; return ⟨*Besuch, Gruß*⟩. E~ung *f* -,-en reply

erwirken *vt* obtain

erwischen *vt* (*fam*) catch

erwünscht *a* desired

erwürgen *vt* strangle

Erz nt -es,-e ore

erzähl|en vt tell (jdm s.o.). □ vi (haben) talk (von about). **E∼er** m -s,- narrator. **E∼ung** f -,-en story, tale

Erzbischof m archbishop

erzeug|en vt produce; (Electr) generate; (fig) create. **E∼er** m -s,- producer; (Vater) father. **E∼nis** nt -ses,-se product; landwirtschaftliche **E∼nisse** farm produce sg. **E∼ung** f - production; generation

Erz|feind m arch-enemy. **E∼herzog** m archduke

erzieh|en† vt bring up; (Sch) educate. **E∼er** m -s,- [private] tutor. **E∼erin** f -,-nen governess. **E∼ung** f - upbringing; education

erzielen vt achieve; score ⟨Tor⟩

erzogen a gut/schlecht e∼ well/badly brought up

erzürnt a angry

erzwingen† vt force

es pron it; (Mädchen) she; (acc) her; impers es regnet it is raining; es gibt there is/(pl) are; ich hoffe es I hope so

Esche f -,-n ash

Esel m -s,- donkey; (fam: Person) ass. **E∼sohr** nt **E∼sohren haben** ⟨Buch:⟩ be dog-eared

Eskalation /-'tsĭo:n/ f - escalation. **e∼ieren** vt/i (haben) escalate

Eskimo m -[s],-[s] Eskimo

Eskort|e f -,-n (Mil) escort. **e∼ieren** vt escort

essbar (eßbar) a edible. **Essecke** (Eßecke) f dining area

essen† vt/i (haben) eat; zu Mittag/Abend e∼ have lunch/supper; [auswärts] e∼ gehen eat out; chinesisch e∼ have a Chinese meal. **E∼** nt -s,- food; (Mahl) meal; (festlich) dinner

Essenz f -,-en essence

Esser(in) m -s,- (f -,-nen) eater

Essig m -s vinegar. **E∼gurke** f [pickled] gherkin

Esskastanie (Eßkastanie) f sweet chestnut. **Esslöffel** (Eßlöffel) m ≈ dessertspoon. **Essstäbchen** (Eßstäbchen) ntpl chopsticks. **Esstisch** (Eßtisch) m dining-table. **Esswaren** (Eßwaren) fpl food sg; (Vorräte) provisions. **Esszimmer** (Eßzimmer) nt dining-room

Estland nt -s Estonia

Estragon m -s tarragon

etablieren (sich) vr establish oneself/ ⟨Geschäft:⟩ itself

Etage /e'ta:ʒə/ f -,-n storey. **E∼nbett** nt bunk-beds pl. **E∼nwohnung** f flat, (Amer) apartment

Etappe f -,-n stage

Etat /e'ta:/ m -s,-s budget

etepetete a (fam) fussy

Eth|ik f - ethic; (Sittenlehre) ethics sg. **e∼isch** a ethical

Etikett nt -[e]s,-e[n] label; (Preis-) tag. **E∼e** f -,-n etiquette; (Aust) = Etikett. **e∼ieren** vt label

etlich|e(r,s) pron some; (mehrere) several; e∼e Mal several times; e∼es a number of things; (ziemlich viel) quite a lot. **e∼emal** adv (NEW) e∼e Mal, s. etliche(r,s)

Etui /e'tvi:/ nt -s,-s case

etwa adv (ungefähr) about; (zum Beispiel) for instance; (womöglich) perhaps; nicht e∼, dass . . . not that . . .; denkt nicht e∼ . . . don't imagine . . .; du hast doch nicht e∼ Angst? you're not afraid, are you? **e∼ig** a possible

etwas pron something; (fragend/verneint) anything; (ein bisschen) some, a little; ohne e∼ zu sagen without saying anything; sonst noch e∼? anything else? noch e∼ Tee? some more tea? so e∼ Ärgerliches! what a nuisance! □ adv a bit

Etymologie f - etymology

euch pron (acc of ihr pl) you; (dat) [to] you; (refl) yourselves; (einander) each other; ein Freund von e∼ a friend of yours

euer poss pron pl your. **e∼e, e∼t-** s. eure, euret-

Eule f -,-n owl

Euphorie f - euphoria

eur|e poss pron pl your. **e∼e(r,s)** poss pron yours. **e∼erseits** adv for your part. **e∼etwegen** adv for your sake; (wegen euch) because of you, on your account. **e∼etwillen** adv um e∼etwillen for your sake. **e∼ige** poss pron der/die/das e∼ige yours

Euro m -[s]/-[s] Euro. **E∼-** pref Euro-

Europa nt -s Europe. **E∼-** pref Euro-

Europä|er(in) m -s,- (f -,-nen) European. **e∼isch** a European; **E∼ische Gemeinschaft** European Community

Euro|paß m Europasport. **E∼scheck** m Eurocheque

Euter nt -s,- udder

evakuier|en vt evacuate. **E∼ung** f - evacuation

evan|gelisch a Protestant. **E∼gelist** m -en,-en evangelist. **E∼gelium** nt -s,-ien gospel

evaporieren vt/i (sein) evaporate

Eventu|alität f -,-en eventuality. **e∼ell** a possible □ adv possibly; (vielleicht) perhaps

Evolution /-'tsĭo:n/ f - evolution

evtl. *abbr s.* eventuell

ewig *a* eternal, *adv* -ly; *(fam: ständig)* constant, *adv* -ly; *(endlos)* never-ending; e∼
dauern *(fam)* take ages. E∼keit *f* - eternity; eine E∼keit *(fam)* ages

exakt *a* exact, *adv* -ly. E∼heit *f* - exactitude

Examen *nt* -s, & -mina *(Sch)* examination

Exekutive *f* - *(Pol)* executive

Exempel *nt* -s,- example; ein E∼ an jdm statuieren make an example of s.o.

Exemplar *nt* -s,-e specimen; *(Buch)* copy. e∼isch *a* exemplary

exerzieren *vt/i (haben) (Mil)* drill; *(üben)* practise

exhumieren *vt* exhume

Exil *nt* -s exile

Existenz *f* -,-en existence; *(Lebensgrundlage)* livelihood; *(pej: Person)* individual

existieren *vi (haben)* exist

exklusiv *a* exclusive. e∼e *prep* (+ *gen*) excluding

exkommunizieren *vt* excommunicate

Exkremente *npl* excrement *sg*

exotisch *a* exotic

expandieren *vt/i (haben)* expand. E∼sion *f* -,-en expansion

Expedition /-'tsjo:n/ *f* -,-en expedition

Experiment *nt* -[e]s,-e experiment. e∼ell *a* experimental. e∼ieren *vi (haben)* experiment

Experte *m* -n,-n expert

explodieren *vi (sein)* explode. E∼sion *f* -,-en explosion. e∼siv *a* explosive

Export|t *m* -[e]s,-e export. E∼teur /-'tø:ɐ/ *m* -s,-e exporter. e∼tieren *vt* export

Express *m* -es,-e (Expreß *m* -sses,-sse) express

extra *adv* separately; *(zusätzlich)* extra; *(eigens)* specially; *(fam: absichtlich)* on purpose

Extrakt *m* -[e]s,-e extract

Extras *ntpl (Auto)* extras

extravagant *a* flamboyant, *adv* -ly; *(übertrieben)* extravagant. E∼z *f* -,-en flamboyance; extravagance; *(Überspanntheit)* folly

extravertiert *a* extrovert

extrem *a* extreme, *adv* -ly. E∼ *nt* -s,-e extreme. E∼ist *m* -en,-en extremist. E∼itäten *fpl* extremities

Exzellenz *f* - *(title)* Excellency

Exzentriker *m* -s,- eccentric. e∼isch *a* eccentric

Exzess *m* -es,-e (Exzeß *ß* -sses, -sse) excess

F

Fabel *f* -,-n fable. f∼haft *a (fam)* fantastic, *adv* -ally

Fabrik *f* -,-en factory. F∼ant *m* -en,-en manufacturer. F∼at *nt* -[e]s,-e product; *(Marke)* make. F∼ation /-'tsjo:n/ *f* - manufacture

Facette /fa'sɛtə/ *f* -,-n facet

Fach *nt* -[e]s,-er compartment; *(Schub-)* drawer; *(Gebiet)* field; *(Sch)* subject. F∼arbeiter *m* skilled worker. F∼arzt *m*, F∼ärztin *f* specialist. F∼ausdruck *m* technical term

fächeln (sich) *vr* fan oneself. F∼er *m* -s,- fan

Fach|gebiet *nt* field. f∼gemäß, f∼gerecht *a* expert, *adv* -ly. F∼hochschule *f* ≈ technical university. f∼kundig *a* expert, *adv* -ly. f∼lich *a* technical, *adv* -ly; *(beruflich)* professional. F∼mann *m (pl* -leute) expert. f∼männisch *a* expert, *adv* -ly. F∼schule *f* technical college. f∼simpeln *vi (haben) (fam)* talk shop. F∼werkhaus *nt* half-timbered house. F∼wort *nt (pl* -wörter) technical term

Fackel *f* -,-n torch. F∼zug *m* torchlight procession

fade *a* insipid; *(langweilig)* dull

Faden *m* -s,- thread; *(Bohnen-)* string; *(Naut)* fathom. f∼scheinig *a* threadbare; *(Grund)* flimsy

Fagott *nt* -[e]s,-e bassoon

fähig *a* capable (zu/gen of); *(tüchtig)* able, competent. F∼keit *f* -,-en ability; competence

fahl *a* pale

fahnd|en *vi (haben)* search (nach for). F∼ung *f* -,-en search

Fahne *f* -,-n flag; *(Druck-)* galley [proof]; eine F∼ haben *(fam)* reek of alcohol. F∼nflucht *f* desertion. f∼nflüchtig *a* f∼nflüchtig werden desert

Fahr|ausweis *m* ticket. F∼bahn *f* carriageway; *(Straße)* road. f∼bar *a* mobile

Fähre *f* -,-n ferry

fahren† *vi (sein)* go, travel; *(Fahrer:)* drive; *(Radfahrer:)* ride; *(verkehren)* run, *(ab-)* leave; *(Schiff:)* sail; mit dem Auto/Zug f∼en go by car/train; in die Höhe f∼en start up; in die Kleider f∼en throw on one's clothes; mit der Hand über etw *(acc)* f∼en run one's hand over sth; was ist in ihn gefahren? *(fam)* what has got into him? □ *vt* drive; ride *(Fahrrad)*; take

⟨Kurve⟩. f∼end a moving; (f∼bar) mobile; (nicht sesshaft) travelling, itinerant. F∼er m -s,- driver. F∼erflucht f failure to stop after an accident. F∼erhaus nt driver's cab. F∼erin f -,-nen woman driver. F∼gast m passenger; (im Taxi) fare. F∼geld nt fare. F∼gestell nt chassis; (Aviat) undercarriage. f∼ig a nervy; (zerstreut) distracted. F∼karte f ticket. F∼kartenausgabe f, F∼kartenschalter m ticket office. f∼lässig a negligent, adv -ly. F∼lässigkeit f - negligence. F∼lehrer m driving instructor. F∼plan m timetable. f∼planmäßig a scheduled □ adv according to/(pünktlich) on schedule. F∼preis m fare. F∼prüfung f driving test. F∼rad nt bicycle. F∼schein m ticket

Fährschiff nt ferry

Fahr|schule f driving school. F∼schüler(in) m(f) learner driver. F∼spur f [traffic] lane. F∼stuhl m lift, (Amer) elevator. F∼stunde f driving lesson

Fahrt f -,-en journey; (Auto) drive; (Ausflug) trip; (Tempo) speed; in voller F∼ at full speed. F∼ausweis m ticket

Fährte f -,-n track; (Witterung) scent; auf der falschen F∼ (fig) on the wrong track

Fahr|tkosten pl travelling expenses. F∼werk nt undercarriage. F∼zeug nt -[e]s,-e vehicle; (Wasser-) craft, vessel

fair /fɛːɐ/ a fair, adv -ly. F∼ness (F∼neß) f - fairness

Fakten pl facts

Faktor m -s,-en /-'toːrən/ factor

Fakul|tät f -,-en faculty. f∼tativ a optional

Falke m -n,-n falcon

Fall m -[e]s,¨e fall; (Jur, Med, Gram) case; im F∼[e] in case (gen of); auf jeden F∼, auf alle F∼e in any case; (bestimmt) definitely; für alle F∼e just in case; auf keinen F∼ on no account

Falle f -,-n trap; eine F∼ stellen set a trap (dat for)

fallen vi (sein) fall; (sinken) go down; [im Krieg] f∼ be killed in the war; f∼ lassen drop (etw, fig: Plan, jdn); make (Bemerkung)

fällen vt fell; (fig) pass (Urteil); make (Entscheidung)

fallenlassen† vt sep (NEW) fallen lassen, s. fallen

fällig a due; (Wechsel) mature; längst f∼ long overdue. F∼keit f - (Comm) maturity

Fallobst nt windfalls pl

falls conj in case; (wenn) if

Fallschirm m parachute. F∼jäger m paratrooper. F∼springer m parachutist

Falltür f trapdoor

falsch a wrong; (nicht echt, unaufrichtig) false; (gefälscht) forged; (Geld) counterfeit; (Schmuck) fake □ adv wrongly; falsely; (singen) out of tune; f∼ gehen ⟨Uhr:⟩ be wrong

fälsch|en vt forge, fake. F∼er m -s,- forger

Falsch|geld nt counterfeit money. F∼heit f - falseness

fälschlich a wrong, adv -ly; (irrtümlich) mistaken, adv -ly. f∼erweise adv by mistake

Falsch|meldung f false report; (absichtlich) hoax report. F∼münzer m -s,- counterfeiter

Fälschung f -,-en forgery, fake; (Fälschen) forging

Falte f -,-n fold; (Rock-) pleat; (Knitter-) crease; (im Gesicht) line; (Runzel) wrinkle

falten vt fold; sich f∼ ⟨Haut:⟩ wrinkle. F∼rock m pleated skirt

Falter m -s,- butterfly; (Nacht-) moth

faltig a creased; (Gesicht) lined; (runzlig) wrinkled

familiär a family …; (vertraut, zudringlich) familiar; (zwanglos) informal

Familie /-jə/ f -,-n family. F∼nanschluss (F∼nanschluß) m F∼nanschluss haben live as one of the family. F∼nforschung f genealogy. F∼nleben nt family life. F∼nname m surname. F∼nplanung f family planning. F∼nstand m marital status

Fan /fɛn/ m -s,-s fan

Fana|tiker m -s,- fanatic. f∼tisch a fanatical, adv -ly. F∼tismus m - fanaticism

Fanfare f -,-n trumpet; (Signal) fanfare

Fang m -[e]s,¨e capture; (Beute) catch; F∼e (Krallen) talons; (Zähne) fangs. F∼arm m tentacle. f∼en† vt catch; (ein-) capture; sich f∼en get caught (in + dat in); (fig) regain one's balance/(seelisch) composure; gefangen nehmen take prisoner; gefangen halten hold prisoner; keep in captivity ⟨Tier:⟩. F∼en nt -s F∼en spielen play tag. F∼frage f catch question. F∼zahn m fang

Fantasie f -,-n = Phantasie

fantastisch a = phantastisch

Farb|aufnahme f colour photograph. F∼band nt (pl -bänder) typewriter ribbon. F∼e f -,-n colour; (Maler-) paint; (zum Färben) dye; (Karten) suit. f∼echt a colour-fast

färben vt colour; dye (Textilien, Haare); (fig) slant ⟨Bericht⟩; sich [rot] f∼ turn [red] □ vi (haben) not be colour-fast

farb|enblind a colour-blind. f∼enfroh a colourful. F∼fernsehen nt colour television. F∼film m colour film. F∼foto nt colour photo. f~ig *a* coloured □ *adv* in colour. F~ige(r) *m/f* coloured man/woman. F~kasten *m* box of paints. f~los *a* colourless. F~stift *m* crayon. F~stoff *m* dye; (*Lebensmittel-*) colouring. F~ton *m* shade

Färbung *f* -,-en colouring; (*fig: Anstrich*) bias

Farce /'farsə/ *f* -,-n farce; (*Culin*) stuffing

Farn *m* -[e]s,-e, F~kraut *nt* fern

Färse *f* -,-n heifer

Fasan *m* -[e]s,-e[n] pheasant

Faschierte(s) *nt* (*Aust*) mince

Fasching *m* -s (*SGer*) carnival

Faschis|mus *m* - fascism. F~t *m* -en,-en fascist. f~tisch *a* fascist

faseln *vt/i* (*haben*) (*fam*) [Unsinn] f~ talk nonsense

Faser *f* -,-n fibre. f~n *vi* (*haben*) fray

Fass *nt* -es,̈-er (*Faß nt* -sses,̈-sser) barrel, cask; Bier vom F~ draught beer; F~ ohne Boden (*fig*) bottomless pit

Fassade *f* -,-n façade

fassbar (*faßbar*) *a* comprehensible; (*greifbar*) tangible

fassen *vt* take [hold of], grasp; (*ergreifen*) seize; (*fangen*) catch; (*ein-*) set; (*enthalten*) hold; (*fig: begreifen*) take in, grasp; conceive (*Plan*); make (*Entschluss*); sich f~ compose oneself; sich kurz/in Geduld f~ be brief/patient; in Worte f~ put into words; nicht zu f~ (*fig*) unbelievable □ *vi* (*haben*) f~ an (+ *acc*) touch; f~ nach reach for

fasslich (*faßlich*) *a* comprehensible

Fasson /fa'sõ:/ *f* -,-style; (*Form*) shape; (*Weise*) way

Fassung *f* -,-en mount; (*Edelstein-*) setting; (*Electr*) socket; (*Version*) version; (*Beherrschung*) composure; aus der F~ bringen disconcert. f~slos *a* shaken; (*erstaunt*) flabbergasted. F~svermögen *nt* capacity

fast *adv* almost, nearly; f~ nie hardly ever

fast|en *vi* (*haben*) fast. F~enzeit *f* Lent. F~nacht *f* Shrovetide; (*Karneval*) carnival. F~nachtsdienstag *m* Shrove Tuesday. F~tag *m* fast-day

Faszin|ation /-'tsjo:n/ *f* - fascination. f~ieren *vt* fascinate; f~ierend fascinating

fatal *a* fatal; (*peinlich*) embarrassing. F~ismus *m* - fatalism. F~ist *m* -en,-en fatalist

Fata Morgana *f* --, --nen mirage

fauchen *vi* (*haben*) spit, hiss □ *vt* snarl

faul *a* lazy; (*verdorben*) rotten, bad; (*Ausrede*) lame; (*zweifelhaft*) bad; (*verdächtig*) fishy

Fäule *f* - decay

faul|en *vi* (*sein*) rot; (*Zahn:*) decay; (*verwesen*) putrefy. F~enzen *vi* (*haben*) be lazy. F~enzer *m* -s,- lazy-bones *sg*. F~heit *f* - laziness. f~ig *a* rotting; (*Geruch*) putrid

Fäulnis *f* - decay

Faulpelz *m* (*fam*) lazy-bones *sg*

Fauna *f* - fauna

Faust *f* -,Fäuste fist; auf eigene F~ (*fig*) off one's own bat. F~handschuh *m* mitten. F~schlag *m* punch

Fauxpas /fo'pa/ *m* -,- /-[s],-s/ gaffe

Favorit(in) /favo'ri:t(in)/ *m* -en, -en (*f* -,-nen) (*Sport*) favourite

Fax *nt* -,-[e] fax. f~en *vt* fax

Faxen *fpl* (*fam*) antics; F~ machen fool about; F~ schneiden pull faces

Faxgerät *nt* fax machine

Feber *m* -s,- (*Aust*) February

Februar *m* -s,-e February

fecht|en *vi* (*haben*) fence. F~er *m* -s,- fencer

Feder *f* -,-n feather; (*Schreib-*) pen; (*Spitze*) nib; (*Techn*) spring. F~ball *m* shuttlecock; (*Spiel*) badminton. F~busch *m* plume. f~leicht *a* as light as a feather. F~messer *nt* penknife. f~nd *vi* (*haben*) be springy; (*nachgeben*) give; (*hoch-*) bounce. F~nd *a* springy; (*elastisch*) elastic. F~ung *f* - (*Techn*) springs *pl*; (*Auto*) suspension

Fee *f* -,-n fairy

Fegefeuer *nt* purgatory

fegen *vt* sweep □ *vi* (*sein*) (*rasen*) tear

Fehde *f* -,-n feud

fehl *a* f~ am Platze out of place. F~betrag *m* deficit. f~en *vi* (*haben*) be missing/(*Sch*) absent; (*mangeln*) be lacking; es f~t an (+ *dat*) there is a shortage of; mir f~t die Zeit I haven't got the time; sie/es f~t mir sehr I miss her/it very much; was f~t ihm? what's the matter with him? es f~te nicht viel und er ... he very nearly ...; das hat uns noch gefehlt! that's all we need! f~end *a* missing; (*Sch*) absent

Fehler *m* -s,- mistake, error; (*Sport & fig*) fault; (*Makel*) flaw. f~frei *a* faultless, *adv* -ly. f~haft *a* faulty. f~los *a* flawless, *adv* -ly

Fehl|geburt *f* miscarriage. f~gehen† *vi sep* (*sein*) go wrong; (*Schuss:*) miss; (*fig*) be mistaken. F~griff *m* mistake. F~kalkulation *f* miscalculation. F~schlag *m* failure. f~schlagen† *vi sep* (*sein*) fail. F~start *m* (*Sport*) false start. F~tritt *m* false step; (*fig*) [moral] lapse. F~zündung *f* (*Auto*) misfire

Feier f -,-n celebration; (*Zeremonie*) ceremony; (*Party*) party. F∼abend m end of the working day; F∼abend machen stop work, (*fam*) knock off; nach F∼abend after work. f∼lich a solemn, adv -ly; (*förmlich*) formal, adv -ly. F∼lichkeit f -,-en solemnity; F∼lichkeiten festivities. f∼n vt celebrate; hold (*Fest*); (*ehren*) fête □ vi (*haben*) celebrate; (*lustig sein*) make merry. F∼tag m [public] holiday; (*kirchlicher*) feast-day; erster/zweiter F∼tag Christmas Day / Boxing Day. f∼tags adv on public holidays

feige a cowardly; f∼ sein be a coward □ adv in a cowardly way

Feige f -,-n fig. F∼nbaum m fig tree

Feig|heit f - cowardice. F∼ling m -s,-e coward

Feile f -,-n file. f∼n vt/i (*haben*) file

feilschen vi (*haben*) haggle

Feilspäne mpl filings

fein a fine, adv -ly; (*zart*) delicate, adv -ly; (*Strümpfe*) sheer; (*Unterschied*) subtle; (*scharf*) keen; (*vornehm*) refined; (*elegant*) elegant; (*prima*) great; sich f∼ machen dress up. F∼arbeit f precision work

feind a jdm f∼ sein NEW jdm F∼ sein, s. Feind. F∼(in) m -es,-e (f -,-nen) enemy; jdm F∼ sein be hostile towards s.o. f∼lich a enemy; (*f∼selig*) hostile. F∼schaft f -,-en enmity. f∼selig a hostile. F∼seligkeit f -,-en hostility

fein|fühlig a sensitive. F∼gefühl nt sensitivity; (*Takt*) delicacy. F∼heit f -,-en (s. fein) fineness; delicacy; subtlety; keenness; refinement; F∼heiten subtleties. F∼kostgeschäft nt delicatessen [shop]. F∼schmecker m -s,- gourmet

feist a fat

feixen vi (*haben*) smirk

Feld nt -[e]s,-er field; (*Fläche*) ground; (*Sport*) pitch; (*Schach-*) square; (*auf Formular*) box. F∼bau m agriculture. F∼bett nt camp-bed, (*Amer*) cot. F∼forschung f fieldwork. F∼herr m commander. F∼marschall m Field Marshal. F∼stecher m -s,- field-glasses pl. F∼webel m -s,- (*Mil*) sergeant. F∼zug m campaign

Felge f -,-n [wheel] rim

Fell nt -[e]s,-e (*Zool*) coat; (*Pelz*) fur; (*abgezogen*) skin, pelt; ein dickes F∼ haben (*fam*) be thick-skinned

Fels m -en,-en rock. F∼block m boulder. F∼en m -s,- rock. f∼enfest a (*fig*) firm, adv -ly. f∼ig a rocky

feminin a feminine; (*weibisch*) effeminate

Femininum nt -s,-na (*Gram*) feminine

Feminist|(in) m -en,-en (f -,-nen) feminist. f∼isch a feminist

Fenchel m -s fennel

Fenster nt -s,- window. F∼brett nt window-sill. F∼laden m [window] shutter. F∼leder nt chamois[-leather]. F∼putzer m -s,- window-cleaner. F∼scheibe f [window-]pane

Ferien /'fe:rjən/ pl holidays; (*Univ*) vacation sg; F∼ haben be on holiday. F∼ort m holiday resort

Ferkel nt -s,- piglet

fern a distant; der F∼e Osten the Far East; f∼ halten keep away; sich f∼ halten keep away □ adv keep away; von f∼ from a distance □ prep (+ dat) far [away] from. F∼bedienung f remote control. F∼bleiben† vi sep (*sein*) stay away (*dat* from). F∼e f - distance; in/aus der F∼e in/from a distance; in weiter F∼e far away; (*zeitlich*) in the distant future. F∼er a further □ adv (*außerdem*) furthermore; (*in Zukunft*) in future. f∼gelenkt a remote-controlled; (*Rakete*) guided. F∼gespräch nt long-distance call. F∼gesteuert a = f∼gelenkt. F∼glas nt binoculars pl. f∼halten† vt sep NEW f∼ halten, s. fern. F∼kopierer m -s,- fax machine. F∼kurs[us] m correspondence course. F∼lenkung f remote control. F∼licht nt (*Auto*) full beam. F∼meldewesen nt telecommunications pl. F∼rohr nt telescope. F∼schreiben nt telex. F∼schreiber m -s,- telex [machine]

Fernseh|apparat m television set. f∼en† vi sep (*haben*) watch television. F∼en nt -s television. F∼er m -s,- [television] viewer; (*Gerät*) television set. F∼gerät nt television set

Fernsprech|amt nt telephone exchange, (*Amer*) central. F∼er m telephone. F∼nummer f telephone number. F∼zelle f telephone box

Fernsteuerung f remote control

Ferse f -,-n heel. F∼ngeld nt F∼ngeld geben (*fam*) take to one's heels

fertig a finished; (*bereit*) ready; (*Comm*) ready-made; (*Gericht*) ready-to-serve; f∼ werden mit finish; (*bewältigen*) cope with; f∼ sein have finished; (*fig*) be through (mit jdm with s.o.); (*fam: erschöpft*) be all in; (*seelisch*) shattered; etw f∼ bringen od (*fam*) kriegen manage to do sth; (*beenden*) finish sth; ich bringe od (*fam*) kriege es nicht f∼ I can't bring myself to do it; etw jdn f∼ machen finish sth; (*bereitmachen*) get sth/s.o. ready; (*fam: erschöpfen*) wear s.o. out; (*seelisch*) shatter s.o.; (*fam: abkanzeln*) carpet s.o.; sich f∼ machen get ready; etw f∼ stellen complete sth □ adv f∼ essen/lesen finish eating/reading. F∼bau m (pl -bauten) prefabricated building.

f~bringen† *vt sep* NEW f~ bringen, *s.* fertig. f~en *vt* make. F~gericht *nt* ready-to-serve meal. F~haus *nt* prefabricated house. F~keit *f* -,-en skill. f~kriegen *vt sep (fam)* NEW f~ kriegen, *s.* fertig. f~machen *vt sep* NEW f~ machen, *s.* fertig. f~stellen *vt sep* NEW f~ stellen, *s.* fertig. F~stellung *f* completion. F~ung *f* · manufacture

fesch *a (fam)* attractive; *(flott)* smart; *(Aust: nett)* kind

Fessel *f* -,-n ankle

fesseln *vt* tie up; tie (an + *acc* to); *(fig)* fascinate; ans Bett gefesselt confined to bed. F~ *fpl* bonds. f~d *a (fig)* fascinating; *(packend)* absorbing

fest *a* firm; *(nicht flüssig)* solid; *(erstarrt)* set; *(haltbar)* strong; *(nicht locker)* tight; *(feststehend)* fixed; *(ständig)* steady; *(Anstellung)* permanent; *(Schlaf)* sound; *(Blick, Stimme)* steady; f~ werden harden; *(Gelee:)* set; f~e Nahrung solids *pl* □ *adv* firmly; tightly; steadily; soundly; *(kräftig, tüchtig)* hard; f~ schlafen be fast asleep; f~ angestellt permanent

Fest *nt* -[e]s,-e celebration; *(Party)* party; *(Relig)* festival; frohes F~! happy Christmas!

fest|angestellt *a* NEW f~ angestellt, *s.* fest. f~binden† *vt sep* tie (an + *dat* to). f~bleiben† *vi sep (sein) (fig)* remain firm. f~e *adv (fam)* hard. F~essen *nt* = F~mahl. f~fahren† *vi/r sep (sein)* [sich] f~fahren get stuck; *(Verhandlungen:)* reach deadlock. f~halten† *v sep* □ *vt* hold on to; *(aufzeichnen)* record; sich f~halten hold on □ *vi (haben)* f~halten an (+ *dat) (fig)* stick to; cling to *(Tradition)*. f~igen *vt* strengthen; sich f~igen grow stronger. F~iger *m* -s,- styling lotion/*(Schaum:)* mousse. F~igkeit *f* - *(s. fest)* firmness; solidity; strength; steadiness. f~klammern *vt sep* clip (an + *dat* to); sich f~klammern cling (an + *dat* to). F~land *nt* mainland; *(Kontinent)* continent. f~legen *vt sep (fig)* fix, settle; lay down *(Regeln)*; tie up *(Geld)*; sich f~legen commit oneself

festlich *a* festive, *adv* -ly. F~keiten *fpl* festivities

fest|liegen† *vi sep (haben)* be fixed, settled. f~machen *v sep* □ *vt* fasten; *(binden)* tie (an + *dat* to); *(f~legen)* fix, settle □ *vi (haben) (Naut)* moor. F~mahl *nt* feast; *(Bankett)* banquet. F~nahme *f* -,-n arrest. f~nehmen† *vt sep* arrest. F~ordner *m* steward. f~setzen *vt sep* fix, settle; *(inhaftieren)* gaol; sich f~setzen collect. f~sitzen† *vi sep (haben)* be firm/*(Schraube:)* tight; *(haften)* stick; *(nicht weiterkommen)* be stuck. F~spiele

npl festival *sg.* f~stehen† *vi sep (haben)* be certain. f~stellen *vt sep* fix; *(ermitteln)* establish; *(bemerken)* notice; *(sagen)* state. F~stellung *f* establishment; *(Aussage)* statement; *(Erkenntnis)* realization. F~tag *m* special day

Festung *f* -,-en fortress

Fest|zelt *nt* marquee. f~ziehen† *vt sep* pull tight. F~zug *m* [grand] procession

Fete /'fe:tə, 'fɛ:tə/ *f* -,-n party

fett *a* fat; *(f~reich)* fatty; *(fettig)* greasy; *(üppig)* rich; *(Druck)* bold; f~ gedruckt bold. F~ *nt* -[e]s,-e fat; *(flüssig)* grease. f~arm *a* low-fat. f~en *vt* grease □ *vi (haben)* be greasy. F~fleck *m* grease mark. f~ig *a* greasy. f~leibig *a* obese. F~näpfchen *nt* ins F~näpfchen treten *(fam)* put one's foot in it

Fetzen *m* -s,- scrap; *(Stoff)* rag; in F~ in shreds

feucht *a* damp, moist; *(Luft)* humid. f~heiß *a* humid. F~igkeit *f* · dampness; *(Nässe)* moisture; *(Luft-)* humidity. F~igkeitscreme *f* moisturizer

feudal *a (fam: vornehm)* sumptuous, *adv* -ly. F~ismus *m* · feudalism

Feuer *nt* -s,- fire; *(für Zigarette)* light; *(Begeisterung)* passion; F~ machen light a fire; F~ fangen catch fire; *(fam: sich verlieben)* be smitten; jdm F~ geben give s.o. a light; F~ speiender Berg volcano. F~alarm *m* fire alarm. F~bestattung *f* cremation. f~gefährlich *a* [in]flammable. F~leiter *f* fire-escape. F~löscher *m* -s,- fire extinguisher. F~melder *m* -s,- fire alarm. f~n *vi (haben)* fire (auf + *acc* on) □ *vt (fam) (schleudern)* fling; *(entlassen)* fire. F~probe *f (fig)* test. f~rot *a* crimson. f~speiend *a* NEW F~ speiend, *s.* Feuer. F~stein *m* flint. F~stelle *f* hearth. F~treppe *f* fire-escape. F~wache *f* fire station. F~waffe *f* firearm. F~wehr *f* -,-en fire brigade. F~wehrauto *nt* fire-engine. F~wehrmann *m (pl* -männer & -leute) fireman. F~werk *nt* firework display, fireworks *pl.* F~werkskörper *m* firework. F~zeug *nt* lighter

feurig *a* fiery; *(fig)* passionate

Fiaker *m* -s,- *(Aust)* horse-drawn cab

Fichte *f* -,-n spruce

fidel *a* cheerful

Fieber *nt* -s [raised] temperature; F~ haben have a temperature. f~haft *a (fig)* feverish, *adv* -ly. f~n *vi (haben)* be feverish. F~thermometer *nt* thermometer

fiebrig *a* feverish

fies *a (fam)* nasty, *adv* -ily

Figur *f* -,-en figure; *(Roman-, Film-)* character; *(Schach-)* piece

Fik|tion /-'tsio:n/ f -,-en fiction. f~tiv a fictitious

Filet /fi'le:/ nt -s,-s fillet

Filial|e f -,-n, F~geschäft nt (Comm) branch

Filigran nt -s filigree

Film m -[e]s,-e film; (Kino-) film, (Amer) movie; (Schicht) coating. f~en vt/i (haben) film. F~kamera f cine/(für Kinofilm) film camera

Filt|er m & (Techn) nt -s,- filter; (Zigaretten-) filter-tip. f~ern vt filter. F~erzigarette f filter-tipped cigarette. f~rieren vt filter

Filz m -es felt. f~en vi (haben) become matted □ vt (fam) (durchsuchen) frisk; (stehlen) steal. F~schreiber m -s,-, F~stift m felt-tipped pen

Fimmel m -s,- (fam) obsession

Fina|le nt -s,- (Mus) finale; (Sport) final. F~list(in) m -en,-en (f -,-nen) finalist

Finanz f -,-en finance. F~amt nt tax office. f~iell a financial, adv -ly. f~ieren vt finance. F~minister m minister of finance

find|en† vt find; (meinen) think; den Tod f~en meet one's death; wie f~est du das? what do you think of that? f~est du? do you think so? es wird sich f~en it'll turn up; (fig) it'll be all right □ vi (haben) find one's way. F~er m -s,- finder. F~erlohn m reward. f~ig a resourceful. F~ling m -s,-e boulder

Finesse f -,-n (Kniff) trick; F~n (Techn) refinements

Finger m -s,- finger; die F~ lassen von (fam) leave alone; etw im kleinen F~ haben (fam) have sth at one's fingertips. F~abdruck m finger-mark; (Admin) fingerprint. F~hut m thimble. F~nagel m finger-nail. F~ring m ring. F~spitze f finger-tip. F~zeig m -[e]s,-e hint

fingier|en vt fake. f~t a fictitious

Fink m -en,-en finch

Finn|e m -n,-n, F~in f -,-nen Finn. f~isch a Finnish. F~land nt -s Finland

finster a dark; (düster) gloomy; (unheildrohend) sinister; im F~n in the dark. F~nis f -,darkness; (Astr) ecluse

Finte f -,-n trick; (Boxen) feint

Firma f -,-men firm, company

firmen vt (Relig) confirm

Firmen|wagen m company car. F~zeichen nt trade mark, logo

Firmung f -,-en (Relig) confirmation

Firnis m -ses,-se varnish. f~sen vt varnish

First m -[e]s,-e [roof] ridge

Fisch m -[e]s,-e fish; F~e (Astr) Pisces. F~dampfer m trawler. f~en vt/i (haben) fish; aus dem Wasser f~en (fam) fish out of the water. F~er m -s,- fisherman. F~erei f -, F~fang m fishing. F~gräte f fishbone. F~händler m fishmonger. F~otter m otter. F~reiher m heron. F~stäbchen nt -s,- fish finger. F~teich m fish-pond

Fiskus m - der F~ the Treasury

Fisole f -,-n (Aust) French bean

fit a fit. Fitness (Fitneß) f - fitness

fix a (fam) quick, adv -ly; (geistig) bright; f~e Idee obsession; fix und fertig all finished; (bereit) all ready; (fam: erschöpft) shattered. F~er m -s,- (sl) junkie

fixieren vt stare at; (Phot) fix

Fjord m -[e]s,-e fiord

FKK abbr (Freikörperkultur) naturism

flach a flat; (eben) level; (niedrig) low; (nicht tief) shallow; f~er Teller dinner plate; die f~e Hand the flat of the hand

Fläche f -,-n area; (Ober-) surface; (Seite) face. F~nmaß nt square measure

Flachs m -es flax. f~blond a flaxen-haired; (Haar) flaxen

flackern vi (haben) flicker

Flagge f -,-n flag

flagrant a flagrant

Flair /fle:ʁ/ nt -s air, aura

Flak f -,-[s] anti-aircraft artillery/(Geschütz) gun

flämisch a Flemish

Flamme f -,-n flame; (Koch-) burner; in F~n in flames

Flanell m -s (Tex) flannel

Flank|e f -,-n flank. f~ieren vt flank

Flasche f -,-n bottle. F~nbier nt bottled beer. F~nöffner m bottle-opener

flatter|haft a fickle. f~n vi (sein/haben) flutter; (Segel:) flap

flau a (schwach) faint; (Comm) slack; mir ist f~ I feel sick

Flaum m -[e]s down. f~ig a downy; f~ig rühren (Aust Culin) cream

flauschig a fleecy; (Spielzeug) fluffy

Flausen fpl (fam) silly ideas; (Ausflüchte) silly excuses

Flaute f -,-n (Naut) calm; (Comm) slack period; (Schwäche) low

fläzen (sich) vr (fam) sprawl

Flechte f -,-n (Med) eczema; (Bot) lichen; (Zopf) plait. f~n† vt plait; weave (Korb)

Fleck m -[e]s,-e[n] spot; (größer) patch; (Schmutz-) stain, mark; blauer F~ bruise; nicht vom F~ kommen (fam) make no progress. f~en vi (haben) stain. F~en m -s,- = Fleck; (Ortschaft) small town. f∼enlos a spotless. F∼entferner m -s, stain remover. f∼ig a stained; ⟨Haut⟩ blotchy

Fledermaus f bat

Flegel m -s, lout. f∼haft a loutish. F∼jahre npl ⟨fam⟩ awkward age sg. f∼n (sich) vr loll

flehen vi (haben) beg (um for). f∼tlich a pleading, adv -ly

Fleisch nt -[e]s flesh; ⟨Culin⟩ meat; ⟨Frucht-⟩ pulp; F∼ fressend carnivorous. F∼er m -s, butcher. F∼erei f -,-en, F∼erladen m butcher's shop. f∼fressend a (NEW) F∼ fressend, s. Fleisch. F∼fresser m -s, carnivore. F∼hauer m -s, ⟨Aust⟩ butcher. f∼ig a fleshy. f∼lich a carnal. F∼wolf m mincer. F∼wunde f flesh-wound

Fleiß m -es diligence; mit F∼ diligently; ⟨absichtlich⟩ on purpose. f∼ig a diligent, adv -ly; ⟨arbeitsam⟩ industrious, adv -ly

flektieren vt ⟨Gram⟩ inflect

fletschen vt die Zähne f∼ ⟨Tier:⟩ bare its teeth

flex|ibel a flexible; ⟨Einband⟩ limp. F∼ibilität f - flexibility. F∼ion f -,-en ⟨Gram⟩ inflexion

flicken vt mend; ⟨mit Flicken⟩ patch. F∼ m -s, patch

Flieder m -s lilac. f∼farben a lilac

Fliege f -,-n fly; ⟨Schleife⟩ bow-tie; zwei F∼n mit einer Klappe schlagen kill two birds with one stone. f∼n† vi (sein) fly; ⟨geworfen werden⟩ be thrown; ⟨fam: fallen⟩ fall; ⟨fam: entlassen werden⟩ be fired/⟨von der Schule⟩ expelled; in die Luft f∼n blow up ◻ vt fly. f∼nd a flying; ⟨Händler⟩ itinerant; in f∼nder Eile in great haste. F∼r m -s, airman; ⟨Pilot⟩ pilot; ⟨fam: Flugzeug⟩ plane. F∼rangriff m air raid

flieh|en vi (sein) flee (vor + dat from); ⟨entweichen⟩ escape ◻ vt shun. f∼end a fleeing; ⟨Kinn, Stirn⟩ receding. F∼kraft f centrifugal force

Fliese f -,-n tile

Fließ|band nt assembly line. f∼en† vi (sein) flow; ⟨aus Wasserhahn⟩ run. f∼end a flowing; ⟨Wasser⟩ running; ⟨Verkehr⟩ moving; ⟨geläufig⟩ fluent, adv -ly. F∼heck nt fastback. F∼wasser nt running water

flimmern vi (haben) shimmer; ⟨TV⟩ flicker; es flimmert mir vor den Augen everything is dancing in front of my eyes

flink a nimble, adv -bly; ⟨schnell⟩ quick, adv -ly

Flinte f -,-n shotgun

Flirt /flœrt/ m -s,-s flirtation. f∼en vi (haben) flirt

Flitter m -s sequins pl; ⟨F∼schmuck⟩ tinsel. F∼wochen fpl honeymoon sg

flitzen vi (sein) ⟨fam⟩ dash; ⟨Auto:⟩ whizz

Flock|e f -,-n flake; ⟨Wolle⟩ tuft. f∼ig a fluffy

Floh m -[e]s,ˆe flea. F∼markt m flea market. F∼spiel nt tiddly-winks sg

Flor m -s gauze; ⟨Trauer-⟩ crape; ⟨Samt-, Teppich-⟩ pile

Flora f - flora

Florett nt -[e]s,-e foil

florieren vi (haben) flourish

Floskel f -,-n [empty] phrase

Floß nt -es,ˆe raft

Flosse f -,-n fin; ⟨Seehund-, Gummi-⟩ flipper; ⟨sl: Hand⟩ paw

Flöt|e f -,-n flute; ⟨Block-⟩ recorder. f∼en vi (haben) play the flute/recorder; ⟨fam: pfeifen⟩ whistle ◻ vt play on the flute/recorder. F∼ist[in] m -en,-en (f -,-nen) flautist

flott a quick, adv -ly; ⟨lebhaft⟩ lively; ⟨schick⟩ smart, adv -ly; f∼ leben live it up

Flotte f -,-n fleet

flottmachen vt sep wieder f∼ ⟨Naut⟩ refloat; get going again ⟨Auto⟩; put back on its feet ⟨Unternehmen⟩

Flöz nt -es,-e [coal] seam

Fluch m -[e]s,ˆe curse. f∼en vi (haben) curse, swear

Flucht[1] f -,-en ⟨Reihe⟩ line; ⟨Zimmer-⟩ suite

Flucht[2] f - flight; ⟨Entweichen⟩ escape; die F∼ ergreifen take flight. f∼artig a hasty, adv -ily

flücht|en vi (sein) flee (vor + dat from); ⟨entweichen⟩ escape ◻ vr sich f∼en take refuge. f∼ig a fugitive; ⟨kurz⟩ brief, adv -ly; ⟨Blick, Gedanke⟩ fleeting; ⟨Bekanntschaft⟩ passing; ⟨oberflächlich⟩ cursory, adv -ily; ⟨nicht sorgfältig⟩ careless, adv -ly; ⟨Chem⟩ volatile; f∼ig sein be on the run; f∼ig kennen know slightly. F∼igkeitsfehler m slip. F∼ling m -s,-e fugitive; ⟨Pol⟩ refugee

Fluchwort nt (pl -wörter) swear-word

Flug m -[e]s,ˆe flight. F∼abwehr f anti-aircraft defence. F∼ball m ⟨Tennis⟩ volley. F∼blatt nt pamphlet

Flügel m -s, wing; ⟨Fenster-⟩ casement; ⟨Mus⟩ grand piano

Fluggast m [air] passenger

flügge a fully-fledged

Flug|gesellschaft f airline. F∼hafen m airport. F∼lotse m air-traffic controller. F∼platz m airport; ⟨klein⟩ airfield. F∼preis m air fare. F∼schein m air ticket. F∼schneise f flight path. F∼schreiber m -s, flight recorder. F∼

schrift f pamphlet. F~steig m -[e]s,-e gate. F~wesen nt aviation. F~zeug nt -[e]s,-e aircraft, plane

Fluidum nt -s aura

Flunder f -,-n flounder

flunkern vi (haben) (fam) tell fibs; (aufschneiden) tell tall stories

Flunsch m -[e]s,-e pout

fluoreszierend a fluorescent

Flur m -[e]s,-e [entrance] hall; (Gang) corridor

Flusen fpl fluff sg

Fluss m -es,ᵕe (Fluß m -sses,-sse) river; (Fließen) flow; im F~ (fig) in a state of flux. f~abwärts adv down-stream. f~aufwärts adv up-stream. f~bett nt river-bed

flüssig a liquid; (Lava) molten; (fließend) fluent, adv -ly; (Verkehr) freely moving. F~keit f -,-en liquid; (Anat) fluid

Flusspferd (Flußpferd) nt hippopotamus

flüstern vt/i (haben) whisper

Flut f -,-en high tide; (fig) flood; F~en waters. F~licht nt flood-light. F~welle f tidal wave

Föderation /-'tsi̯o:n/ f -,-en federation

Fohlen nt -s,- foal

Föhn m -s föhn [wind]; (Haartrockner) hair-drier. f~en vt [blow-]dry

Folge f -,-n consequence; (Reihe) succession; (Fortsetzung) instalment; (Teil) part; F~e leisten (+ dat) obey (Befehl). f~en vi (sein) follow (jdm/etw s.o./sth); (zuhören) listen (dat to); daraus f~t, dass it follows that; wie f~t as follows □ (haben) (gehorchen) obey (jdm s.o.). f~end a following; F~endes (f~endes) the following. f~endermaßen adv as follows

folger|n vt conclude (aus from). F~ung f -,-en conclusion

folg|lich adv consequently. f~sam a obedient, adv -ly

Folie /'fo:li̯ə/ f -,-n foil; (Plastik-) film

Folklore f -, folklore

Folter f -,-n torture; auf die F~ spannen (fig) keep on tenterhooks. f~n vt torture

Fön (P) m -s,-e hair-drier

Fonds /fõ:/ m -,- //-[s],-s// fund

fönen vt (NEW) föhnen

Fontäne f -,-n jet; (Brunnen) fountain

Förder|band nt (pl -bänder) conveyor belt. f~lich a beneficial

fordern vt demand; (beanspruchen) claim; (zum Kampf) challenge; gefordert werden (fig) be stretched

fördern vt promote; (unterstützen) encourage; (finanziell) sponsor; (gewinnen) extract

Forderung f -,-en demand; (Anspruch) claim

Förderung f -(s. fördern) promotion; encouragement; (Techn) production

Forelle f -,-n trout

Form f -,-en form; (Gestalt) shape; (Culin, Techn) mould; (Back-) tin; [gut] in F~ in good form

Formalität f -,-en formality

Format nt -[e]s,-e format; (Größe) size; (fig: Bedeutung) stature

Formation /-'tsi̯o:n/ f -,-en formation

Formel f -,-n formula

formell a formal, adv -ly

formen vt shape, mould; (bilden) form; sich f~ take shape

förmlich a formal, adv -ly; (regelrecht) virtual, adv -ly. F~keit f -,-en formality

form|los a shapeless; (zwanglos) informal, adv -ly. F~sache f formality

Formular nt -s,-e [printed] form

formulier|en vt formulate, word. F~ung f -,-en wording

forsch a brisk, adv -ly; (schneidig) dashing, adv -ly

forsch|en vi (haben) search (nach for). f~end a searching. F~er m -s,- research scientist; (Reisender) explorer. F~ung f -,-en research. F~ungsreisende(r) m explorer

Forst m -[e]s,-e forest

Förster m -s,- forester

Forstwirtschaft f forestry

Forsythie /-tsi̯ə/ f -,-n forsythia

Fort nt -s,-s (Mil) fort

fort adv away; f~ sein be away; (gegangen/verschwunden) have gone; und so f~ and so on; in einem f~ continuously. f~bewegen vt sep move; sich f~bewegen move. F~bewegung f locomotion. F~bildung f further education/training. f~bleiben† vi sep (sein) stay away. f~bringen† vt sep take away. f~fahren† vi sep (sein) go away □ (haben/sein) continue (zu to). f~fallen† vi sep (sein) be dropped/ (ausgelassen) omitted; (entfallen) no longer apply; (aufhören) cease. f~führen vt sep continue. F~gang m departure; (Verlauf) progress. f~gehen† vi sep (sein) leave, go away; (ausgehen) go out; (andauern) go on. f~geschritten a advanced; (spät) late. F~geschrittene(r) m/f advanced student. f~gesetzt a constant, adv -ly. f~jagen vt sep chase away. f~lassen† *sep* let go; ⟨*auslassen*⟩ omit. f~laufent† *vi sep* (*sein*) run away; ⟨*sich f~setzen*⟩ continue. f~laufend *a* consecutive, *adv* -ly. f~nehment† *vt sep* take away. f~pflanzen (sich) *vr sep* reproduce; ⟨*Ton, Licht:*⟩ travel. F~pflanzung *f* - reproduction. F~pflanzungsorgan *nt* reproductive organ. f~reißent† *vt sep* carry away; ⟨*entreißen*⟩ tear away. f~schaffen *vt sep* take away. f~schicken *vt sep* send away; ⟨*abschicken*⟩ send off. f~schreiten† *vi sep* (*sein*) continue; ⟨*Fortschritte machen*⟩ progress, advance. f~schreitend *a* progressive; ⟨*Alter*⟩ advancing. F~schritt *m* progress; F~schritte machen make progress. f~schrittlich *a* progressive. f~setzen *vt sep* continue; sich f~setzen continue. F~setzung *f* -,-en continuation; ⟨*Folge*⟩ instalment; F~setzung folgt to be continued. F~setzungsroman *m* serialized novel, serial. f~während *a* constant, *adv* -ly. f~werfent† *vt sep* throw away. f~ziehent† *v sep* □ *vt* pull away □ *vi* (*sein*) move away

Fossil *nt* -,-ien /-jən/ fossil

Foto *nt* -s,-s photo. F~apparat *m* camera. f~gen *a* photogenic

Fotograf|in /-in/ *m* -en,-en (*f* -,-nen) photographer. F~ie *f* -,-n photography; ⟨*Bild*⟩ photograph. f~ieren *vt* take a photo [graph] of; sich f~ieren lassen have one's photo[graph] taken □ *vi* (*haben*) take photographs. f~isch *a* photographic

Fotokopie *f* photocopy. f~ren *vt* photocopy. F~rgerät *nt* photocopier

Fötus *m* -,-ten foetus

Foul /faul/ *nt* -s,-s (*Sport*) foul. f~en *vt* foul

Foyer /fŏa'je:/ *nt* -s,-s foyer

Fracht *f* -,-en freight. F~er *m* -s,- freighter. F~gut *nt* freight. F~schiff *nt* cargo boat

Frack *m* -[e]s,⸚e & -s tailcoat; im F~ in tails *pl*

Frage *f* -,-n question; ohne F~ undoubtedly; eine F~ stellen ask a question; etw in F~ stellen = etw infrage stellen, *s.* infrage; nicht in F~ kommen = nicht infrage kommen, *s.* infrage. F~bogen *m* questionnaire. f~n *vt* (*haben*) ask; sich f~n wonder (ob whether). f~nd *a* questioning, *adv* -ly; (*Gram*) interrogative. F~zeichen *nt* question mark

frag|lich *a* doubtful; ⟨*Person, Sache*⟩ in question. f~los *adv* undoubtedly

Fragment *nt* -[e]s,-e fragment. f~arisch *a* fragmentary

fragwürdig *a* questionable; ⟨*verdächtig*⟩ dubious

fraisefarben /'frɛ:s-/ *a* strawberry-pink

Fraktion /-'tsjo:n/ *f* -,-en parliamentary party

Franken¹ *m* -s,- (*Swiss*) franc

Franken² *nt* -s Franconia

Frankfurter *f* -,- frankfurter

frankieren *vt* stamp, frank

Frankreich *nt* -s France

Fransen *fpl* fringe *sg*

Franz|ose *m* -n,-n Frenchman; die F~osen the French *pl*. F~ösin *f* -,-nen Frenchwoman. f~ösisch *a* French. F~ösisch *nt* -[s] (*Lang*) French

frapp|ant *a* striking. f~ieren *vt* (*fig*) strike; f~ierend striking

fräsen *vt* (*Techn*) mill

Fraß *m* -es feed; (*pej: Essen*) muck

Fratze *f* -,-n grotesque face; ⟨*Grimasse*⟩ grimace; (*pej: Gesicht*) face; F~n schneiden pull faces

Frau *f* -,-en woman; (*Ehe-*) wife; F~ Thomas Mrs/(*unverheiratet*) Miss/(*Admin*) Ms Thomas; Unsere Liebe F~ (*Relig*) Our Lady. F~chen *nt* -s,- mistress

Frauen|arzt *m*, F~ärztin *f* gynaecologist. F~rechtlerin *f* -,-nen feminist. F~zimmer *nt* woman

Fräulein *nt* -s,- single woman; (*jung*) young lady; (*Anrede*) Miss

fraulich *a* womanly

frech *a* cheeky, *adv* -ily; (*unverschämt*) impudent, *adv* -ly. F~dachs *m* (*fam*) cheeky monkey. F~heit *f* -,-en cheekiness; impudence; ⟨*Äußerung, Handlung*⟩ impertinence

frei *a* free; (*freischaffend*) freelance; ⟨*Künstler*⟩ independent; (*nicht besetzt*) vacant; (*offen*) open; (*bloß*) bare; f~er Tag day off; sich (*dat*) f~ nehmen take time off; f~ machen (*räumen*) clear; vacate ⟨*Platz*⟩; (*befreien*) liberate; f~ lassen leave free; jdm f~e Hand lassen give s.o. a free hand; ist dieser Platz f~? is this seat taken? 'Zimmer f~' 'vacancies' □ *adv* freely; (*ohne Notizen*) without notes; (*umsonst*) free

Frei|bad *nt* open-air swimming pool. f~bekomment† *vt sep* get released; einen Tag f~bekommen get a day off. F~beruflich *a & adv* freelance. F~e *nt* im F~en in the open air, out of doors. F~frau *f* baroness. F~gabe *f* release. f~geben† *v sep* □ *vt* release; (*eröffnen*) open; jdm einen Tag f~geben give s.o. a day off □ *vi* (*haben*) jdm f~geben give s.o. time off. f~gebig *a* generous, *adv* -ly. F~gebigkeit *f* - generosity. f~haben† *v sep* □ *vt* eine Stunde f~haben have an hour off; (*Sch*) have a free period □ *vi* (*haben*) be off work/(*Sch*) school; (*beurlaubt sein*) have time off. f~halten† *vt sep* keep clear;

(*belegen*) keep; einen Tag/sich f~halten keep a day/oneself free; jdn f~halten treat s.o. [to a meal/drink]. F~handelszone *f* free-trade area. f~händig *adv* without holding on

Freiheit *f* -,-en freedom, liberty; sich (*dat*) F~en erlauben take liberties. F~sstrafe *f* prison sentence

freiheraus *adv* frankly

Frei|herr *m* baron. F~karte *f* free ticket. F~körperkultur *f* naturism. f~lassen† *vt sep* release, set free. F~lassung *f* - release. F~lauf *m* free-wheel. f~legen *vt sep* expose. f~lich *adv* admittedly; (*natürlich*) of course. F~lichttheater *nt* open-air theatre. f~machen *v sep* □ *vt* (*frankieren*) frank; (*entkleiden*) bare; einen Tag f~machen take a day off □ *vi/r* (*haben*) [sich] f~machen take time off. F~marke *f* [postage] stamp. F~maurer *m* Freemason. f~mütig *a* candid, *adv* -ly. F~platz *m* free seat; (*Sch*) free place. f~schaffend *a* freelance. f~schwimmen† (sich) *v sep* pass one's swimming test. f~setzen *vt sep* release; (*entlassen*) make redundant. f~sprechen† *vt sep* acquit. F~spruch *m* acquittal. f~stehen† *vi sep* (*haben*) stand empty; es steht ihm f~ (*fig*) he is free (zu to). f~stellen *vt sep* exempt (von from); jdm etw f~stellen leave sth up to s.o. F~stempeln *vt sep* frank. F~stil *m* freestyle. F~stoß *m* free kick. f~willig *a* (*Sch*) free period

Freitag *m* Friday. f~s *adv* on Fridays

Frei|tod *m* suicide. F~übungen *fpl* [physical] exercises. F~umschlag *m* stamped envelope. f~weg *adv* freely; (*offen*) openly. f~willig *a* voluntary, *adv* -ily. F~willige(r) *m/f* volunteer. F~zeichen *nt* ringing tone; (*Rufzeichen*) dialling tone. F~zeit *f* free *or* spare time; (*Muße*) leisure; (*Tagung*) [weekend/holiday] course. F~zeit- *pref* leisure ... F~zeitbekleidung *f* casual wear. f~zügig *a* unrestricted; (*großzügig*) liberal; (*moralisch*) permissive

fremd *a* foreign; (*unbekannt, ungewohnt*) strange; (*nicht das eigene*) other people's; ein f~er Mann a stranger; f~e Leute strangers; unter f~em Namen under an assumed name; jdm f~ sein be unknown/(*wesens-*) alien to s.o.; ich bin hier f~ I'm a stranger here. f~artig *a* strange, *adv* -ly; (*exotisch*) exotic. F~e *f* - in der F~e away from home; (*im Ausland*) in a foreign country. F~e(r) *m/f* stranger; (*Ausländer*) foreigner; (*Tourist*) tourist. F~enführer *m* [tourist] guide. F~enverkehr *m* tourism. F~enzimmer *nt* room [to let]; (*Gäste-*) guest room.

f~gehen† *vi sep* (*sein*) (*fam*) be unfaithful. F~körper *m* foreign body. f~ländisch *a* foreign; (*exotisch*) exotic. F~ling *m* -s,-e stranger. F~sprache *f* foreign language. F~wort *nt* (*pl* -wörter) foreign word

frenetisch *a* frenzied

frequ|entieren *vt* frequent. F~enz *f* -,-en frequency

Freske *f* -,-n, **Fresko** *nt* -s,-ken fresco

Fresse *f* -,-n (*sl*) (*Mund*) gob; (*Gesicht*) mug; halt die F~! shut your trap! f~n† *vt/i* (*haben*) eat. F~n *nt* -s feed; (*sl: Essen*) grub

Fressnapf (**Freßnapf**) *m* feeding bowl

Freud|e *f* -,-n pleasure; (*innere*) joy; mit F~en with pleasure; jdm eine F~e machen please s.o. f~ig *a* joyful, *adv* -ly; f~iges Ereignis (*fig*) happy event. f~los *a* cheerless; (*traurig*) sad

freuen *vt* please; sich f~ be pleased (über + *acc* about); sich f~ auf (+ *acc*) look forward to; es freut mich, ich freue mich I'm glad *or* pleased (dass that)

Freund *m* -es,-e friend; (*Verehrer*) boyfriend; (*Anhänger*) lover (gen of). F~in *f* -,-nen friend; (*Liebste*) girlfriend; (*Anhängerin*) lover (gen of). f~lich *a* kind, *adv* -ly; (*umgänglich*) friendly; (*angenehm*) pleasant; wären Sie so f~lich? would you be so kind? f~licherweise *adv* kindly. F~lichkeit *f* -,-en kindness; friendliness; pleasantness

Freundschaft *f* -,-en friendship; F~ schließen become friends. f~lich *a* friendly

Frevel /'fre:fəl/ *m* -s,- (*liter*) outrage. f~haft *a* (*liter*) wicked

Frieden *m* -s peace; F~ schließen make peace; im F~ in peace-time; laß mich in F~! leave me alone! F~srichter *m* ≈ magistrate. F~svertrag *m* peace treaty

fried|fertig *a* peaceable. F~hof *m* cemetery. f~lich *a* peaceful, *adv* -ly; (*verträglich*) peaceable. f~liebend *a* peace-loving

frieren† *vi* (*haben*) (*Person:*) be cold; *impers* es friert/hat gefroren it is freezing/ there has been a frost; frierst du? friert [es] dich? are you cold? □ (*sein*) (*gefrieren*) freeze

Fries *m* -es,-e frieze

Frikadelle *f* -,-n (*meat*) rissole

frisch *a* fresh; (*sauber*) clean; (*leuchtend*) bright; (*munter*) lively; (*rüstig*) fit; sich f~ machen freshen up □ *adv* freshly, newly; f~ gelegte Eier new-laid eggs; ein Bett f~ beziehen put clean sheets on a bed; f~ gestrichen! wet paint! F~e *f* - freshness; brightness; liveliness; fitness. F~haltepackung *f* vacuum pack.

F~käse *m* ≈ cottage cheese. f~weg *adv* freely

Fri|seur /fri'zøːɐ/ *m* -s,-e hairdresser; (*Herren-*) barber. F~seursalon *m* hairdressing salon. F~seuse /-'zøːzə/ *f* -,-n hairdresser

frisier|en *vt* jdn/sich f~en do s.o.'s/one's hair; die Bilanz/einen Motor f~en (*fam*) fiddle the accounts/soup up an engine. F~kommode *f* dressing-table. F~salon *m* = Friseursalon. F~tisch *m* dressing-table

Frisör *m* -s,-e = Friseur

Frist *f* -,-en period; (*Termin*) deadline; (*Aufschub*) time; drei Tage F~ three days' grace. f~en *vt* sein Leben f~en eke out an existence. f~los *a* instant, *adv* -ly

Frisur *f* -,-en hairstyle

frittieren (fritieren) *vt* deep-fry

frivol /fri'voːl/ *a* frivolous, *adv* -ly; (*schlüpfrig*) smutty

froh *a* happy; (*freudig*) joyful; (*erleichtert*) glad; f~e Ostern! happy Easter!

fröhlich *a* cheerful, *adv* -ly; (*vergnügt*) merry, *adv* -ily; f~e Weihnachten! merry Christmas! F~keit *f* - cheerfulness; merriment

frohlocken *vi* (*haben*) rejoice; (*schadenfroh*) gloat

Frohsinn *m* - cheerfulness

fromm *a* (frömmer, frömmst) devout, *adv* -ly; (*gutartig*) docile, *adv* -ly; f~er Wunsch idle wish

Frömmig|keit *f* - devoutness, piety. f~lerisch *a* sanctimonious, *adv* -ly

frönen *vi* (*haben*) indulge (*dat* in)

Fronleichnam *m* Corpus Christi

Front *f* -,-en front. f~al *a* frontal; (*Zusammenstoß*) head-on □ *adv* from the front; (*zusammenstoßen*) head-on. F~alzusammenstoß *m* head-on collision

Frosch *m* -[e]s,-e frog. F~laich *m* frogspawn. F~mann *m* (*pl* -männer) frogman

Frost *m* -[e]s,-e frost. F~beule *f* chilblain

fröst|eln *vi* (*haben*) shiver; mich fröstelte [es] I shivered/(*fror*) felt chilly

frost|ig *a* frosty, *adv* -ily. F~schutzmittel *nt* antifreeze

Frottee *nt* & *m* -s towelling

frottier|en *vt* rub down. F~[hand]tuch *nt* terry towel

frotzeln *vt/i* (*haben*) [über] jdn f~ make fun of s.o.

Frucht *f* -,-e fruit; F~ tragen bear fruit. f~bar *a* fertile; (*fig*) fruitful. F~barkeit *f* -fertility. f~en *vi* (*haben*) wenig/nichts f~en have little/no effect. f~ig *a* fruity.

f~los *a* fruitless, *adv* -ly. F~saft *m* fruit juice

frugal *a* frugal, *adv* -ly

früh *a* early □ *adv* early; (*morgens*) in the morning; heute/gestern/morgen f~ this/yesterday/tomorrow morning; von f~ an *od auf* from an early age. f~auf *adv* von f~auf (NEW) von f~ auf, *s.* früh. F~aufsteher *m* -s,- early riser. F~e *f* - in aller F~e bright and early; in der F~e (*SGer*) in the morning. f~er *adv* earlier; (*eher*) sooner; (*ehemals*) formerly; (*vor langer Zeit*) previously; f~er oder später sooner or later; ich wohnte f~er in X I used to live in X. f~ere(r,s) *a* earlier; (*ehemalig*) former; (*vorige*) previous; in f~eren Zeiten in former times. f~estens *adv* at the earliest. F~geburt *f* premature birth/(*Kind*) baby. F~jahr *nt* spring. F~jahrsputz *m* spring-cleaning. F~ling *m* -s,-e spring. f~morgens *adv* early in the morning. f~reif *a* precocious

Frühstück *nt* breakfast. f~en *vi* (*haben*) have breakfast

frühzeitig *a* & *adv* early; (*vorzeitig*) premature, *adv* -ly

Frustr|ation /-'tsjoːn/ *f* -,-en frustration. f~ieren *vt* frustrate; f~ierend frustrating

Fuchs *m* -es,-e fox; (*Pferd*) chestnut. f~en *vt* (*fam*) annoy

Füchsin *f* -,-nen vixen

fuchteln *vi* (*haben*) mit etw f~ (*fam*) wave sth about

Fuder *nt* -s,- cart-load

Fuge [1] *f* -,-n joint; aus den F~n gehen fall apart

Fuge [2] *f* -,-n (*Mus*) fugue

füg|en *vt* fit (in + *acc* into); (*an-*) join (an + *acc* on to); (*dazu-*) add (zu to); (*fig: bewirken*) ordain; sich f~en fit (in + *acc* into); adjoin/(*folgen*) follow (an etw *acc* sth); (*fig: gehorchen*) submit (*dat* to); sich in sein Schicksal f~en resign oneself to one's fate; es f~te sich it so happened (dass that). f~sam *a* obedient, *adv* -ly. F~ung *f* -,-en eine F~ung des Schicksals a stroke of fate

fühl|bar *a* noticeable. f~en *vt/i* (*haben*) feel; sich f~en feel (krank/einsam ill/lonely); (*fam: stolz sein*) fancy oneself; sich [nicht] wohl f~en [not] feel well. F~er *m* -s,- feeler. F~ung *f* - contact; F~ung aufnehmen get in touch

Fuhre *f* -,-n load

führ|en *vt* lead; guide (*Tourist*); (*geleiten*) take; (*leiten*) run; (*befehligen*) command; (*verkaufen*) stock; bear (*Namen, Titel*); keep (*Liste, Bücher, Tagebuch*); bei *od* mit sich f~en carry; sich gut/schlecht f~en conduct oneself well/badly □ vi (haben) lead; (verlaufen) go, run; zu etw f~en lead to sth. f~end a leading. F~er m -s,- leader; (Fremden-) guide; (Buch) guide(book). F~erhaus nt driver's cab. F~erschein m driving licence; den F~erschein machen take one's driving test. F~erscheinentzug m disqualification from driving. F~ung f -,-en leadership; (Leitung) management; (Mil) command; (Betragen) conduct; (Besichtigung) guided tour; (Vorsprung) lead; in F~ung gehen go into the lead

Fuhr|unternehmer m haulage contractor. F~werk nt cart

Fülle f -,-n abundance, wealth (an + dat of); (Körper-) plumpness. f~n vt fill; (Culin) stuff; sich f~n fill [up]

Füllen nt -s,- foal

Füll|er m -s,- (fam), F~federhalter m fountain pen. f~ig a plump; (Busen) ample. F~ung f -,-en filling; (Kissen-, Braten-) stuffing; (Pralinen-) centre

fummeln vi (haben) fumble (an + dat with)

Fund m -[e]s,-e find

Fundament nt -[e]s,-e foundations pl. f~al a fundamental

Fund|büro nt lost-property office. F~grube f (fig) treasure trove. F~sachen fpl lost property sg

fünf inv a, F~ f -,-en five; (Sch) ≈ fail mark. F~linge mpl quintuplets. f~te(r,s) a fifth. f~zehn inv a fifteen. f~zehnte(r,s) a fifteenth. f~zig inv a fifty. F~ziger m -s,- man in his fifties; (Münze) 50-pfennig piece. f~zigste(r,s) a fiftieth

fungieren vi (haben) act (als as)

Funk m -s radio; über F~ over the radio. F~e m -n,-n spark. f~eln vi (haben) sparkle; (Stern-) twinkle. f~elnagelneu a (fam) brand-new. F~en m -s,- spark. f~en vt radio. F~er m -s,- radio operator. F~sprechgerät nt walkie-talkie. F~spruch m radio message. F~streife f [police] radio patrol

Funktion /-'tsjo:n/ f -,-en function; (Stellung) position; (Funktionieren) working; außer F~ out of action. F~är m -s,-e official. f~ieren vi (haben) work

für prep (+ acc) for; Schritt für Schritt step by step; was für [ein] what [a]! (fragend) what sort of [a]? für sich by oneself/(Ding-) itself. Für nt das Für und Wider the pros and cons pl. F~bitte f intercession

Furche f -,-n furrow

Furcht f - fear (vor + dat of); F~ erregend terrifying. f~bar a terrible, adv -bly

fürcht|en vt/i (haben) fear; sich f~en be afraid (vor + dat of); ich f~e, das geht nicht I'm afraid that's impossible. f~erlich a dreadful, adv -ly

furcht|erregend a NEW F~ erregend, s. Furcht. f~los a fearless, adv -ly. f~sam a timid, adv -ly

füreinander adv for each other

Furnier nt -s,-e veneer. f~t a veneered

fürs prep = für das

Fürsorg|e f care; (Admin) welfare; (fam: Geld) ≈ social security. f~er(in) m -s,-(f -,-nen) social worker. f~lich a solicitous

Fürsprache f intercession; F~ einlegen intercede

Fürsprecher m (fig) advocate

Fürst m -en,-en prince. F~entum nt -s, -er principality. F~in f -,-nen princess. f~lich a princely; (üppig) lavish, adv -ly

Furt f -,-en ford

Furunkel m -s,- (Med) boil

Fürwort nt (pl -wörter) pronoun

Furz m -es,-e (vulg) fart. f~en vi (haben) (vulg) fart

Fusion f -,-en fusion; (Comm) merger. f~ieren vi (haben) (Comm) merge

Fuß m -es,-e foot; (Aust: Bein) leg; (Lampen-) base; (von Weinglas) stem; zu Fuß on foot; zu Fuß gehen walk; auf freiem Fuß free; auf freundschaftlichem/großem Fuß on friendly terms/in grand style. F~abdruck m footprint. F~abtreter m -s,- doormat. F~bad nt footbath. F~ball m football. F~ballspieler m footballer. F~balltoto nt football pools pl. F~bank f footstool. F~boden m floor. F~bremse f footbrake

Fussel f -,-n & m -s,-[n] piece of fluff; F~n fluff sg. f~n vi (haben) shed fluff

fuß|en vi (haben) be based (auf + dat on). F~ende nt foot

Fußgänger|(in) m -s,- (f -,-nen) pedestrian. F~brücke f footbridge. F~überweg m pedestrian crossing. F~zone f pedestrian precinct

Fuß|geher m -s,- (Aust) = F~gänger. F~gelenk nt ankle. F~hebel m pedal. F~nagel m toenail. F~note f footnote. F~pflege f chiropody. F~pfleger(in) m(f) chiropodist. F~rücken m instep. F~sohle f sole of the foot. F~stapfen pl in jds F~stapfen treten (fig) follow in s.o.'s footsteps. F~tritt m kick. F~weg m footpath; eine Stunde F~weg an hour's walk

futsch pred a (fam) gone

Futter[1] nt -s feed; (Trocken-) fodder

Futter² nt -s,- (Kleider-) lining

Futteral nt -s,-e case

füttern¹ vt feed

füttern² vt line

Futur nt -s (Gram) future; zweites F~ future perfect. f~istisch a futuristic

G

Gabe f -,-n gift; (Dosis) dose

Gabel f -,-n fork. g~n (sich) vr fork. G~stapler m -s,- fork-lift truck. G~ung f -,-en fork

gackern vi (haben) cackle

gaffen vi (haben) gape, stare

Gag /gɛk/ m -s,-s (Theat) gag

Gage /ˈgaːʒə/ f -,-n (Theat) fee

gähnen vi (haben) yawn. G~ nt -s yawn; (wiederholt) yawning

Gala f - ceremonial dress

galant a gallant, adv -ly

Galavorstellung f gala performance

Galerie f -,-n gallery

Galgen m -s,- gallows sg. G~frist f (fam) reprieve

Galionsfigur f figurehead

Galle f - bile; (G~nblase) gall-bladder. G~nblase f gall-bladder. G~nstein m gallstone

Gallert nt -[e]s,-e, **Gallerte** f -,-n [meat] jelly

Galopp m -s gallop; im G~ at a gallop. g~ieren vi (sein) gallop

galvanisieren vt galvanize

gammeln vi (haben) (fam) loaf around. G~ler(in) m -s,- (f -,-nen) drop-out

Gams f -,-en (Aust) chamois

Gämse f -,-n chamois

gang pred a g~ und gäbe quite usual

Gang m -[e]s,-e walk; (G~art) gait; (Boten-) errand; (Funktionieren) running; (Verlauf, Culin) course; (Durch-) passage; (Korridor) corridor; (zwischen Sitzreihen) aisle, gangway; (Anat) duct; (Auto) gear; in G~ bringen/halten get/keep going; in G~ kommen get going/(fig) under way; im G~e/in vollem G~e sein be in progress/in full swing; Essen mit vier G~en four-course meal. G~art f gait

gängig a common; (Comm) popular

Gangschaltung f gear change

Gangster /ˈgɛŋstɐ/ m -s,- gangster

Gangway /ˈgɛŋweː/ f -,-s gangway

Ganove m -n,-n (fam) crook

Gans f -,-e goose

Gänse|blümchen nt -s,- daisy. G~füßchen ntpl inverted commas. G~haut f goose-pimples pl. G~marsch m im G~marsch in single file. G~rich m -s,-e gander

ganz a whole, entire; (vollständig) complete; (fam: heil) undamaged, intact; die g~e Zeit all the time, the whole time; eine g~e Weile/Menge quite a while/lot; g~e zehn Mark all of ten marks; meine g~en Bücher all my books; inv g~ Deutschland the whole of Germany; g~ bleiben (fam) remain intact; wieder g~ machen (fam) mend; im g~en (fam) in all, altogether; im Großen und G~en (im großen und g~en) on the whole □ adv quite; (völlig) completely, entirely; (sehr) very; nicht g~ not quite; g~ allein all on one's own; ein g~ alter Mann a very old man; g~ wie du willst just as you like; es war g~ nett it was quite nice; g~ und gar completely, totally; g~ und gar nicht not at all. G~e(s) nt whole; es geht ums G~e it's all or nothing. g~jährig adv all the year round

gänzlich adv completely, entirely

ganz|tägig a & adv full-time; (geöffnet) all day. g~tags adv all day; (arbeiten) full-time

gar¹ a done, cooked

gar² adv gar nicht/nichts/niemand not/nothing/no one at all; oder gar or even

Garage /gaˈraːʒə/ f -,-n garage

Garantie f -,-n guarantee. g~ren vt/i (haben) [für] etw g~ren guarantee sth; er kommt g~rt zu spät (fam) he's sure to be late. G~schein m guarantee

Garbe f -,-n sheaf

Garderobe f -,-n (Kleider-) wardrobe; (Ablage) cloakroom, (Amer) checkroom; (Flur-) coat-rack; (Künstler-) dressing-room. G~nfrau f cloakroom attendant

Gardine f -,-n curtain. G~nstange f curtain rail

garen vt/i (haben) cook

gären vi (haben) ferment; (fig) seethe

Garn nt -[e]s,-e yarn; (Näh-) cotton

Garnele f -,-n shrimp; (rote) prawn

garnieren vt decorate; (Culin) garnish

Garnison f -,-en garrison

Garnitur f -,-en set; (Wäsche) set of matching underwear; (Möbel-) suite; erste/zweite G~ sein (fam) be first-rate/second-best

garstig a nasty

Garten m -s,- garden; botanischer G~ botanical gardens pl. G~arbeit f gardening. G~bau m horticulture. G~haus nt, G~laube f summerhouse. G~lokal *nt* open-air café. G~schere *f* secateurs *pl*

Gärtner|(in) *m* -s,- (*f* -,-nen) gardener. G~ei *f* -,-en nursery; (*fam: Gartenarbeit*) gardening

Gärung *f* - fermentation

Gas *nt* -es,-e gas; Gas geben (*fam*) accelerate. G~herd *m* gas cooker. G~maske *f* gas mask. G~pedal *nt* (*Auto*) accelerator

Gasse *f* -,-n alley; (*Aust*) street

Gast *m* -[e]s,-̈e guest; (*Hotel-, Urlaubs-*) visitor; (*im Lokal*) patron; zum Mittag G~e haben have people to lunch; bei jdm zu G~ sein be staying with s.o. G~arbeiter *m* foreign worker. G~bett *nt* spare bed

Gäste|bett *nt* spare bed. G~buch *nt* visitors' book. G~zimmer *nt* [hotel] room; (*privat*) spare room; (*Aufenthaltsraum*) residents' lounge

gast|frei, g~freundlich *a* hospitable, *adv* -bly. G~freundschaft *f* hospitality. G~geber *m* -s,- host. G~geberin *f* -,-nen hostess. G~haus *nt*, G~hof *m* inn, hotel

gastieren *vi* (*haben*) make a guest appearance; ⟨*Truppe, Zirkus:*⟩ perform (in + *dat* in)

gastlich *a* hospitable, *adv* -bly. G~keit *f* - hospitality

Gastro|nomie *f* - gastronomy. g~nomisch *a* gastronomic

Gast|spiel *nt* guest performance. G~spielreise *f* (*Theat*) tour. G~stätte *f* restaurant. G~stube *f* bar; (*Restaurant*) restaurant. G~wirt *m* landlord. G~wirtin *f* landlady. G~wirtschaft *f* restaurant

Gas|werk *nt* gasworks *sg*. G~zähler *m* gas-meter

Gatte *m* -n,-n husband

Gatter *nt* -s,- gate; (*Gehege*) pen

Gattin *f* -,-nen wife

Gattung *f* -,-en kind; (*Biol*) genus; (*Kunst*) genre. G~sbegriff *m* generic term

Gaudi *f* - (*Aust, fam*) fun

Gaul *m* -[e]s, Gäule [old] nag

Gaumen *m* -s,- palate

Gauner *m* -s,- crook, swindler. G~ei *f* -,-en swindle

Gaze /'ɡɑːzə/ *f* - gauze

Gazelle *f* -,-n gazelle

geachtet *a* respected

geädert *a* veined

geartet *a* gut g~ good-natured; anders g~ different

Gebäck *nt* -s [cakes and] pastries *pl*; (*Kekse*) biscuits *pl*

Gebälk *nt* -s timbers *pl*

geballt *a* ⟨*Faust*⟩ clenched

Gebärde *f* -,-n gesture. g~n (sich) *vr* behave (wie like)

Gebaren *nt* -s behaviour

gebär|en† *vt* give birth to, bear; geboren werden be born. G~mutter *f* womb, uterus

Gebäude *nt* -s,- building

Gebeine *ntpl* [mortal] remains

Gebell *nt* -s barking

geben† *vt* give; (*tun, bringen*) put; (*Karten*) deal; (*aufführen*) perform; (*unterrichten*) teach; etw verloren g~ give up as lost; von sich g~ utter; (*fam: erbrechen*) bring up; viel/wenig g~ auf (+ *acc*) set great/little store by; sich g~ (*nachlassen*) wear off; (*besser werden*) get better; (*sich verhalten*) behave; sich geschlagen g~ admit defeat □ *impers* es gibt there is/are; was gibt es Neues/zum Mittag/im Kino? what's the news/for lunch/on at the cinema? es wird Regen g~ it's going to rain; das gibt es nicht there's no such thing □ *vi* (*haben*) (*Karten*) deal

Gebet *nt* -[e]s,-e prayer

Gebiet *nt* -[e]s,-e area; (*Hoheits-*) territory; (*Sach-*) field

gebiet|en† *vt* command; (*erfordern*) demand □ *vi* (*haben*) rule. G~er *m* -s,- master; (*Herrscher*) ruler. g~erisch *a* imperious, *adv* -ly; (*Ton*) peremptory

Gebilde *nt* -s,- structure

gebildet *a* educated; (*kultiviert*) cultured

Gebirg|e *nt* -s,- mountains *pl*. g~ig *a* mountainous

Gebiss *nt* -es,-e (Gebiß *nt* -sses, -sse) teeth *pl*; (*künstliches*) false teeth *pl*, dentures *pl*; (*des Zaumes*) bit

geblümt *a* floral, flowered

gebogen *a* curved

geboren *a* born; g~er Deutscher German by birth; Frau X, g~e Y Mrs X, née Y

geborgen *a* safe, secure. G~heit *f* - security

Gebot *nt* -[e]s,-e rule; (*Relig*) commandment; (*bei Auktion*) bid

gebraten *a* fried

Gebrauch *m* use; (*Sprach-*) usage; Gebräuche customs; in G~ in use; G~ machen von make use of. g~en *vt* use; ich kann es nicht/gut g~en I have no use for/can make good use of it; zu nichts zu g~en useless

gebräuchlich *a* common; ⟨*Wort*⟩ in common use

Gebrauch|sanleitung, G~sanweisung *f* directions *pl* for use. g~t *a* used; (*Comm*) secondhand. G~twagen *m* used car

gebrechlich *a* frail, infirm

gebrochen *a* broken ◻ *adv* g~ Englisch sprechen speak broken English

Gebrüll *nt* -s roaring; (*fam: Schreien*) bawling

Gebrumm *nt* -s buzzing; (*Motoren-*) humming

Gebühr *f* -,-en charge, fee; über G~ excessively. g~en *vi* (*haben*) ihm g~t Respekt he deserves respect; wie es sich g~t as is right and proper. g~end *a* due, *adv* duly; (*geziemend*) proper, *adv* -ly. g~enfrei *a* free ◻ *adv* free of charge. g~enpflichtig *a* & *adv* subject to a charge; g~enpflichtige Straße toll road

gebunden *a* bound; (*Suppe*) thickened

Geburt *f* -,-en birth; von G~ by birth. G~enkontrolle, G~enregelung *f* birthcontrol. G~enziffer *f* birth-rate

gebürtig *a* native (aus of); g~er Deutscher German by birth

Geburts|datum *nt* date of birth. G~helfer *m* obstetrician. G~hilfe *f* obstetrics *sg*. G~ort *m* place of birth. G~tag *m* birthday. G~urkunde *f* birth certificate

Gebüsch *nt* -[e]s,-e bushes *pl*

Gedächtnis *nt* -ses memory; aus dem G~ from memory

gedämpft *a* (*Ton*) muffled; (*Stimme*) hushed; (*Musik*) soft; (*Licht, Stimmung*) subdued

Gedanke *m* -ns,-n thought (an + *acc* of); (*Idee*) idea; sich (*dat*) G~n machen worry (über + *acc* about). G~nblitz *m* brainwave. g~nlos *a* thoughtless, *adv* -ly; (*zerstreut*) absent-minded, *adv* -ly. G~nstrich *m* dash. G~nübertragung *f* telepathy. g~nvoll *a* pensive, *adv* -ly

Gedärme *ntpl* intestines; (*Tier-*) entrails

Gedeck *nt* -[e]s,-e place setting; (*auf Speisekarte*) set meal; ein G~ auflegen set a place. g~t *a* covered; (*Farbe*) muted

gedeihen† *vi* (*sein*) thrive, flourish

gedenken† *vi* (*haben*) propose (etw zu tun to do sth); jds/etw g~ remember s.o./sth. G~ *nt* -s memory; zum G~ an (+ *acc*) in memory of

Gedenk|feier *f* commemoration. G~gottesdienst *m* memorial service. G~stätte *f* memorial. G~tafel *f* commemorative plaque. G~tag *m* day of remembrance; (*Jahrestag*) anniversary

Gedicht *nt* -[e]s,-e poem

gediegen *a* quality . . .; (*solide*) well-made; (*Charakter*) upright; (*Gold*) pure ◻ *adv* g~ gebaut well built

Gedräng|e *nt* -s crush, crowd. g~t *a* (*knapp*) concise ◻ *adv* g~t voll packed

gedrückt *a* depressed

gedrungen *a* stocky

Geduld *f* -patience; G~ haben be patient. g~en (sich) *vr* be patient. g~ig *a* patient, *adv* -ly. G~[s]spiel *nt* puzzle

gedunsen *a* bloated

geehrt *a* honoured; Sehr g~er Herr X Dear Mr X

geeignet *a* suitable; im g~en Moment at the right moment

Gefahr *f* -,-en danger; in/außer G~ in/out of danger; auf eigene G~ at one's own risk; G~ laufen run the risk (etw zu tun of doing sth)

gefähr|den *vt* endanger; (*fig*) jeopardize. g~lich *a* dangerous, *adv* -ly; (*riskant*) risky

gefahrlos *a* safe

Gefährt *nt* -[e]s,-e vehicle

Gefährte *m* -n,-n, **Gefährtin** *f* -,-nen companion

gefahrvoll *a* dangerous, perilous

Gefälle *nt* -s,- slope; (*Straßen-*) gradient

gefallen† *vi* (*haben*) jdm g~ please s.o.; er/es gefällt mir I like him/it; sich (*dat*) etw g~ lassen put up with sth

Gefallen[1] *m* -s,- favour

Gefallen[2] *nt* -s pleasure (an + *dat* in); G~ finden an (+ *dat*) like; dir zu G~ to please you

Gefallene(r) *m* soldier killed in the war

gefällig *a* pleasing; (*hübsch*) attractive, *adv* -ly; (*hilfsbereit*) obliging; jdm g~ sein do s.o. a good turn; [sonst] noch etwas g~? will there be anything else? G~keit *f* -,-en favour; (*Freundlichkeit*) kindness. g~st *adv* (*fam*) kindly

Gefangen|e(r) *m/f* prisoner. g~halten† *vt sep* (NEW) g~ halten, s. fangen. G~nahme *f* - capture. g~nehmen† *vt sep* (NEW) g~ nehmen, s. fangen. G~schaft *f* - captivity; in G~schaft geraten be taken prisoner

Gefängnis *nt* -ses,-se prison; (*Strafe*) imprisonment. G~strafe *f* imprisonment; (*Urteil*) prison sentence. G~wärter *m* [prison] warder, (*Amer*) guard

Gefäß *nt* -es,-e container, receptacle; (*Blut-*) vessel

gefasst (gefaßt) *a* composed; (*ruhig*) calm, *adv* -ly; g~ sein auf (+ *acc*) be prepared for

Gefecht *nt* -[e]s,-e fight; (*Mil*) engagement; außer G~ setzen put out of action

gefedert *a* sprung

gefeiert *a* celebrated

Gefieder *nt* -s plumage. g~t *a* feathered

Geflecht *nt* -[e]s,-e network; (*Gewirr*) tangle; (*Korb-*) wicker-work

gefleckt *a* spotted

geflissentlich *adv* studiously

Geflügel *nt* -s poultry. **G~klein** *nt* -s giblets *pl*. **g~t** *a* winged; **g~tes** Wort familiar quotation

Geflüster *nt* -s whispering

Gefolge *nt* -s retinue, entourage. **G~schaft** *f* - followers *pl*, following; (*Treue*) allegiance

gefragt *a* popular; **g~** sein be in demand

gefräßig *a* voracious; ⟨*Mensch*⟩ greedy

Gefreite(r) *m* lance-corporal

gefrier|en† *vi* (*sein*) freeze. **G~fach** *nt* freezer compartment. **G~punkt** *m* freezing point. **G~schrank** *m* upright freezer. **G~truhe** *f* chest freezer

gefroren *a* frozen. **G~e(s)** *nt* (*Aust*) ice-cream

Gefüge *nt* -s,- structure; (*fig*) fabric

gefügig *a* compliant; (*gehorsam*) obedient

Gefühl *nt* -[e]s,-e feeling; (*Empfindung*) sensation; (*G~sregung*) emotion; im **G~** haben know instinctively. **g~los** *a* insensitive; (*herzlos*) unfeeling; (*taub*) numb. **g~sbetont** *a* emotional. **g~skalt** *a* (*fig*) cold. **g~smäßig** *a* emotional, *adv* -ly; (*instinktiv*) instinctive, *adv* -ly. **G~sregung** *f* emotion. **g~voll** *a* sensitive, *adv* -ly; (*sentimental*) sentimental, *adv* -ly

gefüllt *a* filled; (*voll*) full; (*Bot*) double; (*Culin*) stuffed; ⟨*Schokolade*⟩ with a filling

gefürchtet *a* feared, dreaded

gefüttert *a* lined

gegeben *a* given; (*bestehend*) present; (*passend*) appropriate; zu **g~er** Zeit at the proper time. **g~enfalls** *adv* if need be. **G~heiten** *fpl* realities, facts

gegen *prep* (+ *acc*) against; (*Sport*) versus; (*g~über*) to[wards]; (*Vergleich*) compared with; (*Richtung, Zeit*) towards; (*ungefähr*) around; ein Mittel **g~** a remedy for □ *adv* **g~** 100 Leute about 100 people. **G~angriff** *m* counter-attack

Gegend *f* -,-en area, region; (*Umgebung*) neighbourhood

gegeneinander *adv* against/(*gegenüber*) towards one another

Gegen|fahrbahn *f* opposite carriageway. **G~gift** *nt* antidote. **G~leistung** *f* als **G~leistung** in return. **G~maßnahme** *f* countermeasure. **G~satz** *m* contrast; (*Widerspruch*) contradiction; (*G~teil*) opposite; im **G~satz** zu unlike. **g~sätzlich** *a* contrasting; (*widersprüchlich*) opposing. **g~seitig** *a* mutual, *adv* -ly; sich **g~seitig** hassen hate one another. **G~spieler** *m* opponent. **G~sprechanlage** *f* intercom. **G~stand** *m* object; (*Gram, Gesprächs-*) subject. **g~standslos** *a* unfounded; (*überflüssig*)

irrelevant; (*abstrakt*) abstract. **G~stück** *nt* counterpart; (*G~teil*) opposite. **G~teil** *nt* opposite, contrary; im **G~teil** on the contrary. **g~teilig** *a* opposite

gegenüber *prep* (+ *dat*) opposite; (*Vergleich*) compared with; jdm **g~** höflich sein be polite to s.o. □ *adv* opposite. **G~** *nt* -s person opposite. **g~liegen†** *vi sep* (*haben*) be opposite (etw *dat* sth). **g~liegend** *a* opposite. **g~stehen†** *vi sep* (*haben*) (+ *dat*) face; feindlich **g~stehen** (+ *dat*) be hostile to. **g~stellen** *vt sep* confront; (*vergleichen*) compare. **g~treten†** *vi sep* (*sein*) (+ *dat*) face

Gegen|verkehr *m* oncoming traffic. **G~vorschlag** *m* counter-proposal. **G~wart** *f* - present; (*Anwesenheit*) presence. **g~wärtig** *a* present □ *adv* at present. **G~wehr** *f* - resistance. **G~wert** *m* equivalent. **G~wind** *m* head wind. **g~zeichnen** *vt sep* countersign

geglückt *a* successful

Gegner|(in) *m* -s,- (*f* -,-nen) opponent. **g~isch** *a* opposing

Gehabe *nt* -s affected behaviour

Gehackte(s) *nt* mince, (*Amer*) ground meat

Gehalt¹ *m* -[e]s content

Gehalt² *nt* -[e]s,-̈er salary. **G~serhöhung** *f* rise, (*Amer*) raise

gehaltvoll *a* nourishing

gehässig *a* spiteful, *adv* -ly

gehäuft *a* heaped

Gehäuse *nt* -s,- case; (*TV, Radio*) cabinet; (*Schnecken-*) shell; (*Kern-*) core

Gehege *nt* -s,- enclosure

geheim *a* secret; **g~** halten keep secret; im **g~en** (**g~en**) secretly. **G~dienst** *m* Secret Service. **g~halten†** *vt sep* (NEW) **g~** halten, s. geheim. **G~nis** *nt* -ses,-se secret. **g~nisvoll** *a* mysterious, *adv* -ly. **G~polizei** *f* secret police

gehemmt *a* (*fig*) inhibited

gehen† *vi* (*sein*) go; (*zu Fuß*) walk; (*fort-*) leave; (*funktionieren*) work; ⟨*Teig:*⟩ rise; tanzen/einkaufen **g~** go dancing/shopping; an die Arbeit **g~** set to work; in Schwarz [gekleidet] **g~** dress in black; nach Norden **g~** (*Fenster:*) face north; wenn es nach mir ginge if I had my way; über die Straße **g~** cross the road; was geht hier vor sich? what is going on here? das geht zu weit (*fam*) that's going too far; *impers* wie geht es [Ihnen]? how are you? es geht mir gut/besser/schlecht he is well/better/not well; (*geschäftlich*) he is doing well/better/ badly; ein gut **g~des** Geschäft a flourishing *or* thriving business; es geht nicht/nicht anders it's impossible/there is no other way; es ging ganz schnell it was very quick; es geht um it concerns; es geht ihr nur ums Geld she is only interested in the money; es geht [so] (*fam*) not too bad; sich g~ lassen lose one's self-control; (*sich vernachlässigen*) let oneself go □ *vt* walk. g~lassen† (sich) *vr sep* (NEW) g~ lassen (sich), s. gehen

geheuer *a* nicht g~ eerie; (*verdächtig*) suspicious; mir ist nicht g~ I feel uneasy

Geheul *nt* -s howling

Gehilfe *m* -n,-n, Gehilfin *f* -,-nen trainee; (*Helfer*) assistant

Gehirn *nt* -s brain; (*Verstand*) brains *pl*. G~erschütterung *f* concussion. G~hautentzündung *f* meningitis. G~wäsche *f* brainwashing

gehoben *a* (*fig*) superior; ⟨*Sprache*⟩ elevated

Gehöft *nt* -[e]s,-e farm

Gehölz *nt* -es,-e coppice, copse

Gehör *nt* -s hearing; G~ schenken (+ *dat*) listen to

gehorchen *vi* (*haben*) (+ *dat*) obey

gehören *vi* (*haben*) belong (*dat* to); zu den Besten g~ be one of the best; dazu gehört Mut that takes courage; sich g~ be [right and] proper; es gehört sich nicht it isn't done

gehörig *a* proper, *adv* -ly; jdn g~ verprügeln give s.o. a good hiding

gehörlos *a* deaf

Gehörn *nt* -s,-e horns *pl*; (*Geweih*) antlers *pl*

gehorsam *a* obedient, *adv* -ly. G~ *m* -s obedience

Geh|steig *m* -[e]s,-e pavement, (*Amer*) sidewalk. G~weg *m* = Gehsteig; (*Fußweg*) footpath

Geier *m* -s,- vulture

Geig|e *f* -,-n violin. g~en *vi* (*haben*) play the violin □ *vt* play on the violin. G~er(in) *m* -s,- (*f* -,-nen) violinist

geil *a* lecherous; (*fam*) randy; (*fam: toll*) great

Geisel *f* -,-n hostage

Geiß *f* -,-en (*SGer*) [nanny-]goat. G~blatt *nt* honeysuckle

Geißel *f* -,-n scourge

Geist *m* -[e]s,-er mind; (*Witz*) wit; (*Gesinnung*) spirit; (*Gespenst*) ghost; der Heilige G~ the Holy Ghost *or* Spirit; im G~ in one's mind. G~erhaft *a* ghostly

geistes|abwesend *a* absent-minded, *adv* -ly. G~blitz *m* brainwave. G~gegenwart *f* presence of mind. g~gegenwärtig *adv* with great presence of mind. g~gestört *a* [mentally] deranged. g~krank *a* mentally ill. G~krankheit

f mental illness. G~wissenschaften *fpl* arts. G~zustand *m* mental state

geist|ig *a* mental, *adv* -ly; (*intellektuell*) intellectual, *adv* -ly; g~ige Getränke spirits. g~lich *a* spiritual, *adv* -ly; (*religiös*) religious; (*Musik*) sacred; (*Tracht*) clerical. G~liche(r) *m* clergyman. G~lichkeit *f* - clergy. g~los *a* uninspired. g~reich *a* clever; (*witzig*) witty

Geiz *m* -es meanness. g~en *vi* (*haben*) be mean (mit with). G~hals *m* (*fam*) miser. g~ig *a* mean, miserly. G~kragen *m* (*fam*) miser

Gekicher *nt* -s giggling

geknickt *a* (*fam*) dejected, *adv* -ly

gekonnt *a* accomplished □ *adv* expertly

Gekrakel *nt* -s scrawl

gekränkt *a* offended, hurt

Gekritzel *nt* -s scribble

gekünstelt *a* affected, *adv* -ly

Gelächter *nt* -s laughter

geladen *a* loaded; (*fam: wütend*) furious

Gelage *nt* -s,- feast

gelähmt *a* paralysed

Gelände *nt* -s,- terrain; (*Grundstück*) site. G~lauf *m* cross-country run

Geländer *nt* -s,- railings *pl*; (*Treppen-*) banisters *pl*; (*Brücken-*) parapet

gelangen *vi* (*sein*) reach/(*fig*) attain (zu etw/an etw *acc* sth); in jds Besitz g~ come into s.o.'s possession

gelassen *a* composed; (*ruhig*) calm, *adv* -ly. G~heit *f* - equanimity; (*Fassung*) composure

Gelatine /ʒela-/ *f* - gelatine

geläufig *a* common, current; (*fließend*) fluent, *adv* -ly; jdm g~ sein be familiar to s.o.

gelaunt *a* gut/schlecht g~e Leute good-humoured/bad-tempered people; gut/schlecht g~ sein be in a good/bad mood

gelb *a* yellow; (*bei Ampel*) amber; g~e Rübe (*SGer*) carrot; das G~e vom Ei the yolk of the egg. G~ *nt* -s,- yellow; bei G~ (*Auto*) on [the] amber. g~lich *a* yellowish. G~sucht *f* jaundice

Geld *nt* -es,-er money; öffentliche G~er public funds. G~beutel *m*, G~börse *f* purse. G~geber *m* -s,- backer. g~lich *a* financial, *adv* -ly. G~mittel *ntpl* funds. G~schein *m* banknote. G~schrank *m* safe. G~strafe *f* fine. G~stück *nt* coin

Gelee /ʒe'le:/ *nt* -s,-s jelly

gelegen *a* situated; (*passend*) convenient; jdm sehr g~ sein *od* kommen suit s.o. well; mir ist viel/wenig daran g~ I'm very/not keen on it; (*es ist wichtig*) it matters a lot/little to me

Gelegenheit f -,-en opportunity, chance; (*Anlass*) occasion; (*Comm*) bargain; bei G~ some time. G~sarbeit f casual work. G~sarbeiter m casual worker. G~skauf m bargain

gelegentlich a occasional □ adv occasionally; (*bei Gelegenheit*) some time □ prep (+ gen) on the occasion of

gelehrt a learned. G~e(r) m/f scholar

Geleise nt -s,- = Gleis

Geleit nt -[e]s escort; freies G~ safe conduct. g~en vt escort. G~zug m (*Naut*) convoy

Gelenk nt -[e]s,-e joint. g~ig a supple; (*Techn*) flexible

gelernt a skilled

Geliebte(r) m/f lover; (*liter*) beloved

gelieren /ʒe-/ vi (haben) set

gelinde a mild, adv -ly; g~ gesagt to put it mildly

gelingen† vi (sein) succeed, be successful; es gelang ihm, zu entkommen he succeeded in escaping. G~ nt -s success

gell int (SGer) = gelt

gellend a shrill, adv -y

geloben vt promise [solemnly]; sich (dat) g~ vow (zu to); das Gelobte Land the Promised Land

Gelöbnis nt -ses,-se vow

gelöst a (fig) relaxed

Gelse f -,-n (Aust) mosquito

gelt nt (SGer) das ist schön, g~? it's nice, isn't it? ihr kommt doch, g~? you are coming, aren't you?

gelten† vi (haben) be valid; (*Regel:*) apply; g~ als be regarded as; etw nicht g~ lassen not accept sth; wenig/viel g~ be worth/(fig) count for little/a lot; jdm g~ be meant for s.o.; das gilt nicht that doesn't count. g~d a valid; (*Preise*) current; (*Meinung*) prevailing; g~d machen assert (*Recht, Forderung*); bring to bear (*Einfluss*)

Geltung f validity; (*Ansehen*) prestige; G~ haben be valid; zur G~ bringen/kommen set off/show to advantage

Gelübde nt -s,- vow

gelungen a successful

Gelüst nt -[e]s,-e desire/(stark) craving (nach for)

gemächlich a leisurely □ adv in a leisurely manner

Gemahl m -s,-e husband. G~in f -,-nen wife

Gemälde nt -s,- painting. G~galerie f picture gallery

gemäß prep (+ dat) in accordance with □ a etw (dat) g~ sein be in keeping with sth

gemäßigt a moderate; (*Klima*) temperate

gemein a common; (*unanständig*) vulgar; (*niederträchtig*) mean; g~er Soldat private; etw g~ haben have sth in common □ adv shabbily; (*fam: schrecklich*) terribly

Gemeinde f -,-n [local] community; (*Admin*) borough; (*Pfarr-*) parish; (*bei Gottesdienst*) congregation. G~rat m local council/(*Person*) councillor. G~wahlen fpl local elections

gemein|gefährlich a dangerous. G~heit f -,-en (s. gemein) commonness; vulgarity; meanness; (*Bemerkung, Handlung*) mean thing [to say/do]; so eine G~heit! how mean! (*wie ärgerlich*) what a nuisance! G~kosten pl overheads. g~nützig a charitable. G~platz m platitude. g~sam a common; etw g~sam haben have sth in common □ adv together

Gemeinschaft f -,-en community. g~lich a joint; (*Besitz*) communal □ adv jointly; (*zusammen*) together. G~sarbeit f team-work

Gemenge nt -s,- mixture

gemessen a measured; (*würdevoll*) dignified

Gemetzel nt -s,- carnage

Gemisch nt -[e]s,-e mixture. g~t a mixed

Gemme f -,-n engraved gem

Gemse f -,-n (NEW) Gämse

Gemurmel nt -s murmuring

Gemüse nt -s,- vegetable; (*coll*) vegetables pl. G~händler m greengrocer

gemustert a patterned

Gemüt nt -[e]s,-er nature, disposition; (*Gefühl*) feelings pl; (*Person*) soul

gemütlich a cosy; (*gemächlich*) leisurely; (*zwanglos*) informal; (*Person*) genial; es sich (dat) g~ machen make oneself comfortable □ adv cosily; in a leisurely manner; informally. G~keit f -: cosiness; leisureliness

Gemüts|art f nature, disposition. G~mensch m (fam) placid person. G~ruhe f in aller G~ruhe (fam) calmly. G~verfassung f frame of mind

Gen nt -s,-e gene

genau a exact, adv -ly, precise, adv -ly; (*Waage, Messung*) accurate, adv -ly; (*sorgfältig*) meticulous, adv -ly; (*ausführlich*) detailed; nichts G~es wissen not know any details; es nicht so g~ nehmen not be too particular; g~ genommen strictly speaking; g~! exactly! g~genommen adv (NEW) g~ genommen, s. genau. G~igkeit f -: exactitude; precision; accuracy; meticulousness

genauso *adv* just the same; (*g~ sehr*) just as much; g~ schön/teuer just as beautiful/expensive; g~ gut just as good; *adv* just as well; g~ sehr just as much; g~ viel just as much/many; g~ wenig just as little/few; (*noch*) no more. g~gut *adv* (NEW) g~ gut, s. genauso. g~sehr *adv* (NEW) g~ sehr, s. genauso. g~viel *adv* (NEW) g~ viel, s. genauso. g~wenig *adv* (NEW) g~ wenig, s. genauso

Gendarm /ʒãˈdarm/ *m* -en,-en (*Aust*) policeman

Genealogie *f* - genealogy

genehmig|en *vt* grant; approve (*Plan*). G~ung *f* -,-en permission; (*Schein*) permit

geneigt *a* sloping, inclined; (*fig*) well-disposed (*dat* towards); (*nicht*) g~ sein (*fig*) [not] feel inclined (zu to)

General *m* -s,-e general. G~direktor *m* managing director. g~isieren *vt* (*haben*) generalize. G~probe *f* dress rehearsal. G~streik *m* general strike. g~überholen *vt insep* (*inf & pp only*) completely overhaul

Generation /-ˈtsjoːn/ *f* -,-en generation

Generator *m* -s,-en /-ˈtoːrən/ generator

generell *a* general, *adv* -ly

genes|en† *vi* (*sein*) recover. G~ung *f* - recovery; (*Erholung*) convalescence

Genet|ik *f* - genetics *sg*. g~isch *a* genetic, *adv* -ally

Genf *nt* -s Geneva. G~er *a* Geneva ...; G~er See Lake Geneva

genial *a* brilliant, *adv* -ly; ein g~er Mann a man of genius. G~ität *f* - genius

Genick *nt* -s,-e [back of the] neck; sich (*dat*) das G~ brechen break one's neck

Genie /ʒeˈniː/ *nt* -s,-s genius

genieren /ʒeˈniːrən/ *vt* embarrass; sich g~ feel *or* be embarrassed

genieß|bar *a* fit to eat/drink. g~en† *vt* enjoy; (*verzehren*) eat/drink. G~er *m* -s,-, gourmet. g~erisch *a* appreciative □ *adv* with relish

Genitiv *m* -s,-e genitive

Genosse *m* -n,-n (*Pol*) comrade. G~nschaft *f* -,-en cooperative

Genre /ˈʒãːrə/ *nt* -s,-s genre

Gentechnologie *f* genetic engineering

genug *inv a & adv* enough

Genüge *f* zur G~ sufficiently. g~n *vi* (*haben*) be enough; jds Anforderungen g~n meet s.o.'s requirements. g~nd *inv a* sufficient, enough; (*Sch*) fair □ *adv* sufficiently, enough

genügsam *a* frugal, *adv* -ly; (*bescheiden*) modest, *adv* -ly

Genugtuung *f* - satisfaction

Genuss *m* -es,̈-e (Genuß *m* -sses,̈-sse) enjoyment; (*Vergnügen*) pleasure; (*Verzehr*) consumption. genüsslich (genüßlich) *a* pleasurable □ *adv* with relish

geöffnet *a* open

Geo|graphie, G~grafie *f* - geography. g~graphisch, g~grafisch *a* geographical, *adv* -ly. G~loge *m* -n,-n geologist. G~logie *f* - geology. g~logisch *a* geological. *adv* -ly. G~meter *m* -s,- surveyor. G~metrie *f* - geometry. g~metrisch *a* geometric[al]

geordnet *a* well-ordered; (*stabil*) stable; alphabetisch g~ in alphabetical order

Gepäck *nt* -s luggage, baggage. G~ablage *f* luggage-rack. G~aufbewahrung *f* left-luggage office. G~schalter *m* luggage office. G~schein *m* left-luggage ticket; (*Aviat*) baggage check. G~stück *nt* piece of luggage. G~träger *m* porter; (*Fahrrad-*) luggage carrier; (*Dach-*) roof-rack. G~wagen *m* luggage-van

Gepard *m* -s,-e cheetah

gepflegt *a* well-kept; (*Person*) well-groomed; (*Hotel*) first-class

Gepflogenheit *f* -,-en practice; (*Brauch*) custom

Gepolter *nt* -s [loud] noise

gepunktet *a* spotted

gerade *a* straight; (*direkt*) direct; (*aufrecht*) upright; (*aufrichtig*) straightforward; (*Zahl*) even; etw g~ biegen straighten sth; sich g~ halten hold oneself straight □ *adv* straight; directly; (*eben*) just; (*genau*) exactly; (*besonders*) especially; g~ sitzen/stehen sit/stand [up] straight; nicht g~ billig not exactly cheap; g~ erst only just; g~ an dem Tag on that very day. G~ *f* -,-n straight line. g~aus *adv* straight ahead/on

gerade|biegen† *vt sep* (NEW) g~ biegen, s. gerade. g~halten† (sich) *vr sep* (NEW) sich g~ halten, s. gerade. g~heraus *adv* (*fig*) straight out. g~sitzen† *vi sep* (*haben*) (NEW) g~ sitzen, s. gerade. g~so *adv* just the same; g~so gut just as good; *adv* just as well. g~sogut *adv* (NEW) g~so gut, s. geradeso. g~stehen† *vi sep* (*haben*) (*fig*) accept responsibility (für for); (*aufrecht stehen*) (NEW) g~ stehen, s. gerade. g~wegs *adv* directly, straight. g~zu *adv* virtually; (*wirklich*) absolutely

Geranie /-jə/ *f* -,-n geranium

Gerät *nt* -[e]s,-e tool; (*Acker-*) implement; (*Küchen-*) utensil; (*Elektro-*) appliance; (*Radio-, Fernseh-*) set; (*Turn-*) piece of apparatus; (*coll*) equipment

geraten† *vi* (*sein*) get; in Brand g~ catch fire; in Wut g~ get angry; in Streit g~ start quarrelling; gut/schlecht g~ turn out well/badly; nach jdm g~ take after s.o.

Geratewohl nt aufs G~ at random

geräuchert a smoked

geräumig a spacious, roomy

Geräusch nt -[e]s,-e noise. g~los a noiseless, adv -ly. g~voll a noisy, adv -ily

gerben vt tan

gerecht a just, adv -ly; (fair) fair, adv -ly; g~ werden (+ dat) do justice to. g~fertigt a justified. G~igkeit f - justice; fairness

Gerede nt -s talk; (Klatsch) gossip

geregelt a regular

gereift a mature

gereizt a irritable, adv -bly. G~heit f - irritability

gereuen vt es gereut mich nicht I don't regret it

Geriatrie f - geriatrics sg

Gericht[1] nt -[e]s,-e (Culin) dish

Gericht[2] nt -[e]s,-e court [of law]; vor G~ in court; das Jüngste G~ the Last Judgement; jdn ins G~ gehen take s.o. to task. g~lich a judicial; ⟨Verfahren⟩ legal □ adv g~lich vorgehen take legal action. G~sbarkeit f - jurisdiction. G~shof m court of justice. G~smedizin f forensic medicine. G~ssaal m court-room. G~svollzieher m -s,- bailiff

gerieben a grated; (fam: schlau) crafty

gering a small; (niedrig) low; (g~fügig) slight; jdn/etw g~ achten have little regard for s.o./sth; (verachten) despise s.o./sth. g~achten vt sep (NEW) g~ achten, s. gering. g~fügig a slight, adv -ly. g~schätzig a contemptuous, adv -ly; (Bemerkung) disparaging. g~ste(r,s) a least; nicht im G~sten ⟨g~sten⟩ not in the least

gerinnen† vi (sein) curdle; ⟨Blut:⟩ clot

Gerippe nt -s,- skeleton; (fig) framework

gerissen a (fam) crafty

Germ m -[e]s & (Aust) f - yeast

German|e m -n,-n [ancient] German. g~isch a Germanic. G~ist(in) m -en,-en (f -,-nen) Germanist. G~istik f - German [language and literature]

gern[e] adv gladly; g~ haben like; (lieben) be fond of; ich tanze/schwimme g~ I like dancing/swimming; das kannst du g~ tun you're welcome to do that; willst du mit?—g~! do you want to come?—I'd love to!

gerötet a red

Gerste f - barley. G~nkorn nt (Med) stye

Geruch m -[e]s,:e smell (von/nach of). g~los a odourless. G~ssinn m sense of smell

Gerücht nt -[e]s,-e rumour

geruhen vi (haben) deign (zu to)

gerührt a (fig) moved, touched

Gerümpel nt -s lumber, junk

Gerüst nt -[e]s,-e scaffolding; (fig) framework

gesalzen a salted; (fam: hoch) steep

gesammelt a collected; (gefasst) composed

gesamt a entire, whole. G~ausgabe f complete edition. G~betrag m total amount. G~eindruck m overall impression. G~heit f - whole. G~schule f comprehensive school. G~summe f total

Gesandte(r) m/f envoy

Gesang m -[e]s,:e singing; (Lied) song; (Kirchen-) hymn. G~buch nt hymn-book. G~verein m choral society

Gesäß nt -es buttocks pl. G~tasche f hip pocket

Geschäft nt -[e]s,-e business; (Laden) shop; (Amer) store; (Transaktion) deal; (fam: Büro) office; schmutzige G~e shady dealings; ein gutes G~ machen do very well (mit out of); sein G~ verstehen know one's job. g~ehalber adv on business. g~ig a busy, adv -ily; ⟨Treiben⟩ bustling. G~igkeit f - activity. g~lich a business ... □ adv on business

Geschäfts|brief m business letter. G~führer m manager; (Vereins-) secretary. G~mann m (pl -leute) businessman. G~reise f business trip. G~stelle f office; (Zweigstelle) branch. g~tüchtig a g~tüchtig sein be a good businessman/-woman. G~viertel nt shopping area. G~zeiten fpl hours of business

geschehen† vi (sein) happen (dat to); es ist ein Unglück g~ there has been an accident; es ist um uns g~ we are done for; das geschieht dir recht! it serves you right! gern g~! you're welcome! G~ nt -s events pl

gescheit a clever; daraus werde ich nicht g~ I can't make head or tail of it

Geschenk nt -[e]s,-e present, gift. G~korb m gift hamper

Geschichte f -,-n history; (Erzählung) story; (fam: Sache) business. g~lich a historical, adv -ly

Geschick nt -[e]s fate; (Talent) skill; G~ haben be good (zu at). G~lichkeit f - skilfulness, skill. g~t a skilful, adv -ly; (klug) clever, adv -ly

geschieden a divorced. G~e(r) m/f divorcee

Geschirr nt -s,-e (coll) crockery; (Porzellan) china; (Service) service; (Pferde-) harness; schmutziges G~ dirty dishes pl.

G~spülmaschine f dishwasher. G~tuch nt tea-towel

Geschlecht nt -[e]s,-er sex; (Gram) gender; (Familie) family; (Generation) generation. g~lich a sexual, adv -ly. G~skrankheit f venereal disease. G~steile ntpl genitals. G~sverkehr m sexual intercourse. G~swort nt (pl -wörter) article

geschliffen a (fig) polished

geschlossen a closed □ adv unanimously; (vereint) in a body

Geschmack m -[e]s,-̈e taste; (Aroma) flavour; (G~ssinn) sense of taste; einen guten G~ haben (fig) have good taste; G~ finden an (+ dat) acquire a taste for. g~los a tasteless, adv -ly; G~los sein (fig) be in bad taste. G~ssache f matter of taste. g~voll a (fig) tasteful, adv -ly

geschmeidig a supple; (weich) soft

Geschöpf nt -[e]s,-e creature

Geschoss nt -es,-e (Geschoßnt -sses,-sse) missile; (Stockwerk) storey, floor

geschraubt a (fig) stilted

Geschrei nt -s screaming; (fig) fuss

Geschütz nt -es,-e gun, cannon

geschützt a protected; (Stelle) sheltered

Geschwader nt -s,- squadron

Geschwätz nt -es talk. g~ig a garrulous

geschweift a curved

geschweige conj g~ denn let alone

geschwind a quick, adv -ly

Geschwindigkeit f -,-en speed; (Phys) velocity. G~sbegrenzung, G~sbeschränkung f speed limit

Geschwister pl brother[s] and sister[s]; siblings

geschwollen a swollen; (fig) pompous, adv -ly

Geschworene|(r) m/f juror; die G~n the jury sg

Geschwulst f -,-̈e swelling; (Tumor) tumour

geschwungen a curved

Geschwür nt -s,-e ulcer

Geselle m -n,-n fellow; (Handwerks-) journeyman

gesellig a sociable; (Zool) gregarious; (unterhaltsam) convivial; g~er Abend social evening. G~keit f -,-en entertaining; die G~keit lieben love company

Gesellschaft f -,-en company; (Veranstaltung) party; die G~ society; jdm G~ leisten keep s.o. company. g~lich a social, adv -ly. G~sreise f group tour. G~sspiel nt party game

Gesetz nt -es,-e law. G~entwurf m bill. g~gebend a legislative. G~gebung f -legislation. g~lich a legal, adv -ly. g~los

a lawless. g~mäßig a lawful, adv -ly; (gesetzlich) legal, adv -ly

gesetzt a staid; (Sport) seeded □ conj g~ den Fall supposing

gesetzwidrig a illegal, adv -ly

gesichert a secure

Gesicht nt -[e]s,-er face; (Aussehen) appearance; zu G~ bekommen set eyes on. G~sausdruck m [facial] expression. G~sfarbe f complexion. G~spunkt m point of view. G~szüge mpl features

Gesindel nt -s riff-raff

gesinnt a gut/übel g~ well/ill disposed (dat towards)

Gesinnung f -,-en mind; (Einstellung) attitude; politische G~ political convictions pl

gesittet a well-mannered; (zivilisiert) civilized

gesondert a separate, adv -ly

Gespann nt -[e]s,-e team; (Wagen) horse and cart/carriage

gespannt a taut; (fig) tense, adv -ly; (Beziehungen) strained; (neugierig) eager, adv -ly; (erwartungsvoll) expectant, adv -ly; g~ sein, ob wonder whether; auf etw/jdn g~ sein look forward eagerly to sth/to seeing s.o.

Gespenst nt -[e]s,-er ghost. g~isch a ghostly; (unheimlich) eerie

Gespött nt -[e]s mockery; zum G~ werden become a laughing-stock

Gespräch nt -[e]s-e conversation; (Telefon-) call; ins G~ kommen get talking; im G~ sein be under discussion. g~ig a talkative. G~sgegenstand m, G~sthema nt topic of conversation

gesprenkelt a speckled

Gespür nt -s feeling; (Instinkt) instinct

Gestalt f -,-en figure; (Form) shape, form; G~ annehmen (fig) take shape. g~en vt shape; (organisieren) arrange; (schaffen) create; (entwerfen) design; sich g~en turn out

geständig a confessed; g~ sein have confessed. G~nis nt -ses,-se confession

Gestank m -s stench, [bad] smell

gestatten vt allow, permit; nicht gestattet prohibited; g~ Sie? may I?

Geste /'ge-, 'ge:stə/ f -,-n gesture

Gesteck nt -[e]s-e flower arrangement

gestehen vt/i (haben) confess; confess to (Verbrechen); offen gestanden to tell the truth

Gestein nt -[e]s,-e rock

Gestell nt -[e]s,-e stand; (Flaschen-) rack; (Rahmen) frame

gestellt a gut/schlecht g∼ well/badly off; auf sich (acc) selbst g∼ sein be thrown on one's own resources

gestelzt a (fig) stilted

gesteppt a quilted

gestern adv yesterday; g∼ Nacht (nacht) last night

Gestik /'gɛstɪk/ f - gestures pl. g∼ulieren vi (haben) gesticulate

gestrandet a stranded

gestreift a striped

gestrichelt a ⟨Linie⟩ dotted

gestrichen a g∼er Teelöffel level tea-spoon[ful]

gestrig /'gɛstrɪç/ a yesterday's; am g∼en Tag yesterday

Gestrüpp nt -s,-e undergrowth

Gestüt nt -[e]s,-e stud [farm]

Gesuch nt -[e]s,-e request; (Admin) application. g∼t a (gekünstelt) contrived

gesund a healthy, adv -ily; g∼ sein be in good health; ⟨Sport, Getränk:⟩ be good for one; wieder g∼ werden get well again

Gesundheit f - health; g∼! (bei Niesen) bless you! g∼lich a health ...; g∼licher Zustand state of health □ adv es geht ihm g∼lich gut/schlecht he is in good/poor health. g∼shalber adv for health reasons. g∼sschädlich a harmful. G∼szustand m state of health

getäfelt a panelled

getigert a tabby

Getöse nt -s racket, din

getragen a solemn, adv -ly

Getränk nt -[e]s,-e drink. G∼ekarte f wine-list

getrauen vt sich (dat) etw g∼ dare [to] do sth; sich g∼ dare

Getreide nt -s (coll) grain

getrennt a separate, adv -ly; g∼ leben live apart; g∼ schreiben write as two words. g∼schreiben† vt sep (NEW)g∼ schreiben, s. getrennt

getreu a faithful, adv -ly □ prep (+ dat) true to; der Wahrheit g∼ truthfully. g∼lich adv faithfully

Getriebe nt -s,-, bustle; (Techn) gear; (Auto) transmission; (Gehäuse) gearbox

getrost adv with confidence

Getto nt -s,-s ghetto

Getue nt -s (fam) fuss

Getümmel nt -s tumult

getüpfelt a spotted

geübt a skilled; ⟨Auge, Hand⟩ practised

Gewächs nt -es,-e plant; (Med) growth

gewachsen a jdm/etw g∼ sein (fig) be a match for s.o./be equal to sth

Gewächshaus nt greenhouse; (Treibhaus) hothouse

gewagt a daring

gewählt a refined

gewahr a g∼ werden become aware (acc/gen of)

Gewähr f - guarantee

gewahren vt notice

gewähr|en vt grant; (geben) offer; jdn g∼en lassen let s.o. have his way. g∼leisten vt guarantee

Gewahrsam m -s safekeeping; (Haft) custody

Gewährsmann m (pl -männer & -leute) informant, source

Gewalt f -,-en power; (Kraft) force; (Brutalität) violence; mit G∼ by force; G∼ anwenden use force; sich in der G∼ haben be in control of oneself. G∼herrschaft f tyranny. g∼ig a powerful; (fam: groß) enormous, adv -ly; (stark) tremendous, adv -ly. g∼sam a forcible, adv -bly; (Tod) violent. g∼tätig a violent. G∼tätigkeit f -,-en violence; (Handlung) act of violence

Gewand nt -[e]s,-er robe

gewandt a skilful, adv -ly; (flink) nimble, adv -bly. G∼heit f - skill; nimbleness

Gewässer nt -s,- body of water; G∼ pl waters

Gewebe nt -s,- fabric; (Anat) tissue

Gewehr nt -s,-e rifle, gun

Geweih nt -[e]s,-e antlers pl

Gewerb|e nt -s,-, trade. g∼lich a commercial, adv -ly. g∼smäßig a professional, adv -ly

Gewerkschaft f -,-en trade union. G∼ler(in) m -s,- (f -,-nen) trade unionist

Gewicht nt -[e]s,-e weight; (Bedeutung) importance. G∼heben nt -s weight-lifting. g∼ig a important

gewieft a (fam) crafty

gewillt a g∼ sein be willing

Gewinde nt -s,- [screw] thread

Gewinn m -[e]s,-e profit; (fig) gain, benefit; (beim Spiel) winnings pl; (Preis) prize; (Los) winning ticket; G∼ bringend profitable, adv -bly. G∼beteiligung f profit-sharing. g∼bringend a (NEW)G∼ bringend, s. Gewinn. g∼en† vt win; (erlangen) gain; (fördern) extract; jdn für sich g∼en win s.o. over □ vi (haben) win; g∼en an (+ dat) gain in. g∼end a engaging. G∼er(in) m -s,- (f -,-nen) winner

Gewirr nt -s,-e tangle; (Straßen-) maze; G∼ von Stimmen hubbub of voices

gewiss (gewiß) a (gewisser, gewissest) certain, adv -ly

Gewissen nt -s,- conscience. g~haft a conscientious, adv -ly. g~los a unscrupulous. G~sbisse mpl pangs of conscience

gewissermaßen adv to a certain extent; (sozusagen) as it were

Gewissheit (Gewißheit) f - certainty

Gewitter nt -s,- thunderstorm. g~n vi (haben) es g~ert it is thundering. g~rig a thundery

gewogen a (fig) well-disposed (dat towards)

gewöhnen vt jdn/sich g~ an (+ acc) get s.o. used to/get used to; [an] jdn/etw gewöhnt sein be used to s.o./sth

Gewohnheit f -,-en habit. g~smäßig a habitual, adv -ly. G~srecht nt common law

gewöhnlich a ordinary, adv -ily; (üblich) usual, adv -ly; (ordinär) common

gewohnt a customary; (vertraut) familiar; (üblich) usual; etw (acc) g~ sein be used to sth

Gewöhnung f - getting used (an + acc to); (Süchtigkeit) addiction

Gewölbe nt -s,- vault. g~t a curved; (Archit) vaulted

gewollt a forced

Gewühl nt -[e]s crush

gewunden a winding

gewürfelt a check[ed]

Gewürz nt -es,-e spice. G~nelke f clove

gezackt a serrated

gezähnt a serrated; (Säge) toothed

Gezeiten fpl tides

gezielt a specific; (Frage) pointed

geziemend a proper, adv -ly

geziert a affected, adv -ly

gezwungen a forced □ adv g~ lachen give a forced laugh. g~ermaßen adv of necessity; etw g~ermaßen tun be forced to do sth

Gicht f - gout

Giebel m -s,- gable

Gier f - greed (nach for). g~ig a greedy, adv -ily

gießen† vt pour; water (Blumen, Garten); (Techn) cast □ v impers es g~t it is pouring [with rain]. G~erei f -,-en foundry. G~kanne f watering-can

Gift nt -[e]s,-e poison; (Schlangen-) venom; (Biol, Med) toxin. g~ig a poisonous; (Schlange) venomous; (Med, Chem) toxic; (fig) spiteful, adv -ly. G~müll m toxic waste. G~pilz m poisonous fungus, toadstool. G~zahn m [poison] fang

gigantisch a gigantic

Gilde f -,-n guild

Gimpel m -s,- bullfinch; (fam: Tölpel) simpleton

Gin /dʒɪn/ m -s gin

Ginster m -s (Bot) broom

Gipfel m -s,- summit, top; (fig) peak. G~konferenz f summit conference. g~n vi (haben) culminate (in + dat in)

Gips m -es plaster. G~abguss (G~abguß) m plaster cast. G~er m -s,- plasterer. G~verband m (Med) plaster cast

Giraffe f -,-n giraffe

Girlande f -,-n garland

Girokonto /ˈʒiːro-/ nt current account

Gischt m -[e]s & f - spray

Gitar|re f -,-n guitar. G~rist(in) m -en, -en (f -,-nen) guitarist

Gitter nt -s,- bars pl; (Rost) grating, grid; (Geländer, Zaun) railings pl; (Fenster-) grille; (Draht-) wire screen; hinter G~n (fam) behind bars. G~netz nt grid

Glanz m -es shine; (von Farbe, Papier) gloss; (Seiden-) sheen; (Politur) polish; (fig) brilliance; (Pracht) splendour

glänzen vi (haben) shine. g~d a shining, bright; (Papier, Haar) glossy; (fig) brilliant, adv -ly

glanz|los a dull. G~stück nt masterpiece; (einer Sammlung) show-piece. g~voll a (fig) brilliant, adv -ly; (prachtvoll) splendid, adv -ly. G~zeit f heyday

Glas nt -es,-̈er glass; (Brillen-) lens; (Fern-) binoculars pl; (Marmeladen-) [glass] jar. G~er m -s,- glazier

gläsern a glass …

Glashaus nt greenhouse

glasieren vt glaze; ice (Kuchen)

glas|ig a glassy; (durchsichtig) transparent. G~scheibe f pane

Glasur f -,-en glaze; (Culin) icing

glatt a smooth; (eben) even; (Haar) straight; (rutschig) slippery; (einfach) straightforward; (eindeutig) downright; (Absage) flat; g~ streichen smooth out □ adv smoothly; evenly; (fam: völlig) completely; (gerade) straight; (leicht) easily; (ablehnen) flatly; g~ rasiert clean-shaven; g~ gehen od verlaufen go off smoothly; das ist g~ gelogen it's a downright lie

Glätte f - smoothness; (Rutschigkeit) slipperiness

Glatteis nt [black] ice; aufs G~ führen (fam) take for a ride

glätten vt smooth; sich g~ become smooth; (Wellen:) subside

glatt|gehen† vi sep (sein) (NEW) g~ gehen, s. glatt. g~rasiert a (NEW) g~ rasiert, s. glatt. g~streichen† vt sep (NEW) g~

streichen, s. glatt. g~weg adv (fam) outright

Glatz|e f -,-n bald patch; (Voll-) bald head;
eine G~e bekommen go bald. g~köpfig
a bald

Glaube m -ns belief (an + acc in); (Relig)
faith; in gutem G~n in good faith; G~n
schenken (+ dat) believe. g~n vt/i
(haben) believe (an + acc in); (vermuten)
think; jdm n~ believe s.o; nicht zu
g~n unbelievable, incredible. G~nsbe-
kenntnis nt creed

glaubhaft a credible; (überzeugend) convincing, adv -ly

gläubig a religious; (vertrauend) trusting,
adv -ly. G~e(r) m/f (Relig) believer; die
G~en the faithful. G~er m -s,- (Comm)
creditor

glaub|lich a kaum n~lich scarcely be-
lievable. g~würdig a credible; (Person)
reliable. G~würdigkeit f - credibility;
reliability

gleich a same; (identisch) identical;
(g~wertig) equal; g~ bleibend constant;
2 mal 5 [ist] g~ 10 two times 5 equals 10;
das ist mir g~ it's all the same to me;
ganz g~, wo/wer no matter where/who
□ adv equally; (übereinstimmend) identi-
cally, the same; (sofort) immediately; (in
Kürze) in a minute; (fast) nearly; (direkt)
right; g~ gesinnt like-minded. g~
alt/schwer sein be the same age/weight.
g~altrig a [of] the same age. g~artig
a similar. g~bedeutend a synonymous.
g~berechtigt a equal. g~berechtigung
f equality. g~bleibend a (NEW) g~ bleibend, s. gleich

gleichen† vi (haben) jdm/etw g~ be like
or resemble s.o./sth; sich g~ be alike

gleich|ermaßen adv equally. g~falls
adv also, likewise; danke g~falls thank
you, the same to you. g~förmig a uniform, adv -ly; (eintönig) monotonous, adv
-ly. G~förmigkeit f uniformity; monotony. g~gesinnt a (NEW) g~ gesinnt, s.
gleich. G~gewicht nt balance; (Phys &
fig) equilibrium. g~gültig a indifferent,
adv -ly; (unwichtig) unimportant. G~gül-
tigkeit f indifference. G~heit f -
equality; (Ähnlichkeit) similarity.
g~machen vt equal make equal; dem Erd-
boden g~machen raze to the ground.
g~mäßig a even, adv -ly, regular, adv -ly;
(beständig) constant, adv -ly. G~mäßig-
keit f- regularity. G~mut m equanimity.
g~mütig a calm, adv -ly

Gleichnis nt -ses,-se parable

gleich|sam adv as it were. G~schritt m
im G~schritt in step. g~sehen† vt sep
(haben) jdm g~sehen look like s.o.; (fam:
typisch sein) be just like s.o. g~setzen vt

sep equate/(g~stellen) place on a par (dat/
mit with). g~stellen vt sep place on a par
(dat with). G~strom m direct current.
g~tun† vi sep (haben) es jdm g~tun
emulate s.o.

Gleichung f -,-en equation

gleich|viel adv no matter (ob/wer
whether/who). g~wertig a of equal
value. g~zeitig a simultaneous, adv -ly

Gleis nt -es,-e track; (Bahnsteig) platform;
G~ 5 platform 5

gleiten† vi (sein) glide; (rutschen) slide.
g~d a sliding; (g~de Arbeitszeit flexitime

Gleitzeit f flexitime

Gletscher m -s,- glacier. G~spalte f crevasse

Glied nt -[e]s,-er limb; (Teil) part; (Ketten-)
link; (Mitglied) member; (Mil) rank.
g~ern vt arrange; (einteilen) divide; sich
g~ern be divided (in + acc into).
G~maßen fpl limbs

glimmen† vi (haben) glimmer

glimpflich a lenient, adv -ly; g~ davonkommen get off lightly

glitschig a slippery

glitzern vi (haben) glitter

global a global, adv -ly

Globus m - & -busses,-ben & -busse globe

Glocke f -,-n bell. G~nturm m bell-tower,
belfry

glorifizieren vt glorify

glorreich a glorious

Glossar nt -s,-e glossary

Glosse f -,-n comment

glotzen vi (haben) stare

Glück nt -[e]s [good] luck; (Zufriedenheit)
happiness; G~ bringend lucky;
G~/kein G~ haben be lucky/unlucky;
zum G~ luckily, fortunately; auf gut G~
on the off chance; (wahllos) at random.
g~bringend a (NEW) G~ bringend, s.
Glück. g~en vi (sein) succeed; es ist mir
geglückt I succeeded

gluckern vi (haben) gurgle

glücklich a lucky, fortunate; (zufrieden)
happy; (sicher) safe □ adv happily; safely;
(fam: endlich) finally. g~erweise adv
luckily, fortunately

glückselig a blissfully happy. G~keit f
bliss

glucksen vi (haben) gurgle

Glücksspiel nt game of chance; (Spielen)
gambling

Glückwunsch m good wishes pl; (Gratu-
lation) congratulations pl; herzlichen
G~! congratulations! (zum Geburtstag)
happy birthday! G~karte f greetings
card

Glüh|birne f light-bulb. g~en vi (haben) glow. g~end a glowing; (rot-) red-hot; ⟨Hitze⟩ scorching; (leidenschaftlich) fervent, adv -ly. G~faden m filament. G~wein m mulled wine. G~würmchen nt -s,- glow-worm

Glukose f - glucose

Glut f - embers pl; (Röte) glow; (Hitze) heat; (fig) ardour

Glyzinie /-jə/ f -,-n wisteria

GmbH abbr (Gesellschaft mit beschränkter Haftung) ≈ plc

Gnade f - mercy; (Gunst) favour; (Relig) grace. G~nfrist f reprieve. g~nlos a merciless, adv -ly

gnädig a gracious, adv -ly; (mild) lenient, adv -ly; g~e Frau Madam

Gnom m -en,-en gnome

Gobelin /gobə'lɛ̃:/ m -s,-s tapestry

Gold nt -[e]s gold. g~en a gold …; (g~farben) golden; g~ene Hochzeit golden wedding. G~fisch m goldfish. G~grube f gold-mine. g~ig a sweet, lovely. G~lack m wallflower. G~regen m laburnum. G~schmied m goldsmith

Golf¹ m -[e]s,-e (Geog) gulf

Golf² nt -s golf. G~platz m golf-course. G~schläger m golf-club. G~spieler(in) m(f) golfer

Gondel f -,-n gondola; (Kabine) cabin

Gong m -s,-s gong

gönnen vt jdm etw g~ not begrudge s.o. sth; jdm etw nicht g~ begrudge s.o. sth; sie gönnte sich (dat) keine Ruhe she allowed herself no rest

Gönner m -s,- patron. g~haft a patronizing, adv -ly

Gör nt -s,-en, **Göre** f -,-n (fam) kid

Gorilla m -s,-s gorilla

Gosse f -,-n gutter

Got|ik f - Gothic. g~isch a Gothic

Gott m -[e]s,-er God; (Myth) god

Götterspeise f jelly

Gottes|dienst m service. g~lästerlich a blasphemous, adv -ly. G~lästerung f blasphemy

Gottheit f -,-en deity

Göttin f -,-nen goddess

göttlich a divine, adv -ly

gott|los a ungodly; (atheistisch) godless; g~ verlassen a God-forsaken

Götze m -n,-n, G~nbild nt idol

Gouver|nante /guvɛr'nantə/ f -,-n governess. G~neur /-'nø:ɐ/ m -s,-e governor

Grab nt -[e]s,-er grave

graben† vt (haben) dig

Graben m -s,- ditch; (Mil) trench

Grab|mal nt tomb. G~stein m gravestone, tombstone

Grad m -[e]s,-e degree

Graf m -en,-en count

Grafik f -,-en graphics sg; (Kunst) graphic arts pl; (Druck) print

Gräfin f -,-nen countess

grafisch a graphic; g~e Darstellung diagram

Grafschaft f -,-en county

Gram m -s grief

grämen (sich) vr grieve

grämlich a morose, adv -ly

Gramm nt -s,-e gram

Gram|matik f -,-en grammar. g~matikalisch, g~matisch a grammatical, adv -ly

Granat m -[e]s,-e (Miner) garnet. G~apfel m pomegranate. G~e f -,-n shell; (Hand-) grenade

Granit m -s,-e granite

Graph|ik f, g~isch a = Grafik, grafisch

Gras nt -es,-er grass. g~en vi (haben) graze. G~hüpfer m -s,- grasshopper

grassieren vi (haben) be rife

grässlich (gräßlich) a dreadful, adv -ly

Grat m -[e]s,-e [mountain] ridge

Gräte f -,-n fishbone

Gratifikation /-'tsio:n/ f -,-en bonus

gratis adv free [of charge]. G~probe f free sample

Gratu|lant(in) m -en,-en (f -,-nen) wellwisher. G~lation /-'tsio:n/ f -,-en congratulations pl; (Glückwünsche) best wishes pl. g~lieren vi (haben) jdm g~lieren congratulate s.o. (zu on); (zum Geburtstag) wish s.o. happy birthday; [ich] g~liere! congratulations!

grau a, G~ nt -s,- grey. G~brot nt mixed rye and wheat bread

Gräuel m -s,- horror. G~tat f atrocity

grauen¹ vi (haben) der Morgen od es graut dawn is breaking

grauen² v impers mir graut [es] davor I dread it. G~ nt -s dread. g~haft, g~voll a gruesome; (grässlich) horrible, adv -bly

gräulich¹ a greyish

gräulich² a horrible, adv -bly

Graupeln fpl soft hail sg

grausam a cruel, adv -ly. G~keit f -,-en cruelty

grausen v impers mir graust davor I dread it. G~en nt -s horror, dread. g~ig a gruesome

gravieren vt engrave. g~d a (fig) serious

Grazie /'gra:tsiə/ f - grace

graziös a graceful, adv -ly

greifbar *a* tangible; in g∼er Nähe within reach

greifen† *vt* take hold of; (*fangen*) catch □ *vi* (*haben*) reach (nach for); g∼ zu (*fig*) turn to; um sich g∼ (*fig*) spread. G∼ *nt* G∼ spielen play tag

Greis *m* -es,-e old man. G∼enalter *nt* extreme old age. g∼enhaft *a* old. G∼in *f* -,-nen old woman

grell *a* glaring; (*Farbe*) garish; (*schrill*) shrill, *adv* -y

Gremium *nt* -s,-ien committee

Grenze *f* -,-n border; (*Staats-*) frontier; (*Grundstücks-*) boundary; (*fig*) limit. g∼en *vi* (*haben*) border (an + *acc* on). g∼enlos *a* boundless; (*maßlos*) infinite, *adv* -ly. G∼fall *m* borderline case

Greuel *el* *m* -s, ⟨NEW⟩ Gräuel. g∼lich *a* ⟨NEW⟩gräulich²

Griech|e *m* -n,-n Greek. G∼enland *nt* -s Greece. G∼in *f* -,-nen Greek woman. g∼isch *a* Greek. G∼isch *nt* -[s] (*Lang*) Greek

griesgrämig *a* (*fam*) grumpy

Grieß *m* -es semolina

Griff *m* -[e]s,-e grasp, hold; (*Hand-*) movement of the hand; (*Tür-, Messer-*) handle; (*Schwert-*) hilt. g∼bereit *a* handy

Grill *m* -s,-s grill; (*Garten-*) barbecue

Grille *f* -,-n (*Zool*) cricket; (*fig: Laune*) whim

grill|en *vt* grill; (*im Freien*) barbecue □ *vi* (*haben*) have a barbecue. G∼fest *nt* barbecue. G∼gericht *nt* grill

Grimasse *f* -,-n grimace; G∼n schneiden pull faces

grimmig *a* furious; (*Kälte*) bitter

grinsen *vi* (*haben*) grin. G∼ *nt* -s grin

Grippe *f* -,-n influenza, (*fam*) flu

grob *a* (gröber, gröbst) coarse, *adv* -ly; (*unsanft, ungefähr*) rough, *adv* -ly; (*unhöflich*) rude, *adv* -ly; (*schwer*) gross, *adv* -ly; (*Fehler*) bad; g∼e Arbeit rough work; g∼ geschätzt roughly. G∼ian *m* -s,-e brute

gröblich *a* gross, *adv* -ly

grölen *vt/i* (*haben*) bawl

Groll *m* -[e]s resentment; einen G∼ gegen jdn hegen bear s.o. a grudge. g∼en *vi* (*haben*) be angry (*dat* with); (*Donner:*) rumble

Grönland *nt* -s Greenland

Gros¹ *nt* -ses,- (*Maß*) gross

Gros² /gro:/ *nt* - majority, bulk

Groschen *m* -s,- (*Aust*) groschen; (*fam*) ten-pfennig piece; der G∼ ist gefallen (*fam*) the penny's dropped

groß *a* (größer, größt) big; (*Anzahl, Summe*) large; (*bedeutend, stark*) great; (*g∼artig*) grand; (*Buchstabe*) capital; g∼e Ferien summer holidays; g∼e Angst haben be very frightened; der größte Teil the majority *or* bulk; g∼ werden (*Person:*) grow up; g∼ in etw (*dat*) sein be good at sth; g∼ geschrieben werden (*fig*) be very important (bei jdm to s.o.); G∼ und Klein (g∼ und klein) young and old; im G∼en und Ganzen (im g∼en und ganzen) on the whole □ *adv* (*feiern*) in style; (*fam: viel*) much; jdn g∼ ansehen look at s.o. in amazement

groß|artig *a* magnificent, *adv* -ly. G∼aufnahme *f* close-up. G∼britannien *nt* -s Great Britain. G∼buchstabe *m* capital letter. G∼e(r) *m/f* unser G∼er our eldest; die G∼en the grown-ups; (*fig*) the great *pl*

Größe *f* -,-n size; (*Ausmaß*) extent; (*Körper-*) height; (*Bedeutsamkeit*) greatness; (*Math*) quantity; (*Person*) great figure

Groß|eltern *pl* grandparents. g∼enteils *adv* largely

Größenwahnsinn *m* megalomania

Groß|handel *m* wholesale trade. G∼händler *m* wholesaler. g∼herzig *a* magnanimous, *adv* -ly. G∼macht *f* superpower. G∼mut *f* magnanimity. g∼mütig *a* magnanimous, *adv* -ly. G∼mutter *f* grandmother. G∼onkel *m* great-uncle. G∼reinemachen *nt* -s spring-clean. g∼schreiben† *vt sep* write with a capital [initial] letter; g∼geschrieben werden (*fig*) ⟨NEW⟩ g∼ geschrieben werden, s. groß. G∼schreibung *f* capitalization. g∼sprecherisch *a* boastful. g∼spurig *a* pompous, *adv* -ly; (*überheblich*) arrogant, *adv* -ly. G∼stadt *f* [large] city. g∼städtisch *a* city ... G∼tante *f* great-aunt. G∼teil *m* large proportion; (*Hauptteil*) bulk

größtenteils *adv* for the most part

groß|tun† (sich) *vr sep* brag. G∼vater *m* grandfather. g∼ziehen† *vt sep* bring up; rear (*Tier*). g∼zügig *a* generous, *adv* -ly; (*weiträumig*) spacious. G∼zügigkeit *f* - generosity

grotesk *a* grotesque, *adv* -ly

Grotte *f* -,-n grotto

Grübchen *nt* -s,- dimple

Grube *f* -,-n pit

grübeln *vi* (*haben*) brood

Gruft *f* -,-e [burial] vault

grün *a* green; im G∼en out in the country; die G∼en the Greens. G∼ *nt* -s,- green; (*Laub, Zweige*) greenery

Grund *m* -[e]s,-e ground; (*Boden*) bottom; (*Hinter-*) background; (*Ursache*) reason; aus diesem G∼e for this reason; von G∼

auf(*fig*) radically; im G~e [genommen] basically; auf G~ laufen (*Naut*) run aground; auf G~ (+ *gen*) = aufgrund; zu G~e richten/gehen/liegen = zugrunde richten/gehen/liegen, *s.* zugrunde. G~begriffe *mpl* basics. G~besitz *m* landed property. G~besitzer *m* landowner

gründ|en *vt* found, set up; start ⟨*Familie*⟩. (*fig*) base (auf + *acc* on); sich g~en be based (auf + *acc* on). G~er(in) *m* -s,- (*f* -,-nen) founder

Grund|farbe *f* primary colour. G~form *f* (*Gram*) infinitive. G~gesetz *nt* (*Pol*) constitution. G~lage *f* basis, foundation. g~legend *a* fundamental, *adv* -ly

gründlich *a* thorough, *adv* -ly. G~keit *f* - thoroughness

grund|los *a* bottomless; (*fig*) groundless □ *adv* without reason. G~mauern *fpl* foundations

Gründonnerstag *m* Maundy Thursday

Grund|regel *f* basic rule. G~riss (G~riß) *m* ground-plan; (*fig*) outline. G~satz *m* principle. G~sätzlich *a* fundamental, *adv* -ly; (*im Allgemeinen*) in principle; (*prinzipiell*) on principle; G~schule *f* primary school. G~stein *m* foundation-stone. G~stück *nt* plot [of land]

Gründung *f* -,-en foundation

grün|en *vi* (*haben*) become green. G~gürtel *m* green belt. G~span *m* verdigris. G~streifen *m* grass verge; (*Mittel-*) central reservation, (*Amer*) median strip

grunzen *vi* (*haben*) grunt

Gruppe *f* -,-n group; (*Reise-*) party

gruppieren *vt* group; sich g~ form a group/groups

Grusel|geschichte *f* horror story. g~ig *a* creepy

Gruß *m* -es,ᵉe greeting; (*Mil*) salute; einen schönen G~ an X give my regards to X; viele/herzliche G~e regards; Mit freundlichen G~en Yours sincerely/(*Comm*) faithfully

grüßen *vt/i* (*haben*) say hallo (jdn to s.o.); (*Mil*) salute; g~ Sie X von mir give my regards to X; jdn g~ lassen send one's regards to s.o.; grüß Gott! (*SGer, Aust*) good morning/afternoon/evening!

guck|en *vi* (*haben*) (*fam*) look. G~loch *nt* peep-hole

Guerilla /ge'rɪlja/ *f* - guerrilla warfare. G~kämpfer *m* guerrilla

Gulasch *nt & m* -[e]s goulash

gültig *a* valid, *adv* -ly. G~keit *f* - validity

Gummi *m & nt* -s,-[s] rubber; (*Harz*) gum. G~band *nt* (*pl* -bänder) elastic *or* rubber band; (*G~zug*) elastic

gummiert *a* gummed

Gummi|knüppel *m* truncheon. G~stiefel *m* gumboot, wellington. G~zug *m* elastic

Gunst *f* - favour; zu jds G~en in s.o.'s favour; zu G~ (+ *gen*) = zugunsten

günstig *a* favourable, *adv* -bly; (*passend*) convenient, *adv* -ly

Günstling *m* -s,-e favourite

Gurgel *f* -,-n throat. g~n *vi* (*haben*) gargle. G~wasser *nt* gargle

Gurke *f* -,-n cucumber; (*Essig-*) gherkin

gurren *vi* (*haben*) coo

Gurt *m* -[e]s,-e strap; (*Gürtel*) belt; (*Auto*) safety-belt. G~band *nt* (*pl* -bänder) waistband

Gürtel *m* -s,- belt. G~linie *f* waistline. G~rose *f* shingles *sg*

GUS *abbr* (Gemeinschaft Unabhängiger Staaten) CIS

Guss *m* -es,ᵉe (Guß *m* -sses,ᵉsse) (*Techn*) casting; (*Strom*) stream; (*Regen-*) downpour; (*Torten-*) icing. G~eisen *nt* cast iron. g~eisern *a* cast-iron

gut *a* (besser, best) good; ⟨*Gewissen*⟩ clear; (*gütig*) kind (zu to); jdm gut sein be fond of s.o.; im G~en (g~en) amicably; zu g~er Letzt in the end; schon gut that's all right □ *adv* well; ⟨*schmecken, riechen*⟩ good; (*leicht*) easily; es gut haben be well off; (*Glück haben*) be lucky; gut zu sehen clearly visible; gut drei Stunden a good three hours; du hast gut reden it's easy for you to talk

Gut *nt* -[e]s,ᵉer possession, property; (*Land-*) estate; Gut und Böse good and evil; Güter (*Comm*) goods

Gutachten *nt* -s,- expert's report. G~er *m* -s,- expert

gut|artig *a* good-natured; (*Med*) benign. g~aussehend *a* (NEW) gut aussehend, *s.* aussehen. g~bezahlt *a* (NEW) gut bezahlt, *s.* bezahlen. G~dünken *nt* -s nach eigenem G~dünken at one's own discretion

Gute(s) *nt* etwas/nichts G~s something/nothing good; G~s tun do good; das G~ daran the good thing about it all; alles G~! all the best!

Güte *f* -,-n goodness, kindness; (*Qualität*) quality; du meine G~! my goodness!

Güterzug *m* goods/(*Amer*) freight train

gut|gehen† *vi sep* (*sein*) (NEW) gut gehen, *s.* gehen. g~gehend *a* (NEW) gut gehend, *s.* gehen. g~gemeint *a* (NEW) gut gemeint, *s.* meinen. g~gläubig *a* (NEW) gut gläubig *a* trusting. g~haben† *vt sep* fünfzig Mark g~haben have fifty marks credit (bei with). G~haben *nt* -s,- [credit] balance;

(*Kredit*) credit. g~heißen† *vt sep* approve of

gütig *a* kind, *adv* -ly

gütlich *a* amicable, *adv* -bly

gut|machen *vt sep* make up for; make good (*Schaden*). g~mütig *a* good-natured, *adv* -ly. G~mütigkeit *f* - good nature. G~schein *m* credit note; (*Bon*) voucher; (*Geschenk*-) gift token. g~schreiben† *vt sep* credit. G~schrift *f* credit

Guts|haus *nt* manor house. G~hof *m* manor

gut|situiert *a* NEW gut situiert, *s.* situiert. g~tun† *vi sep* (*haben*) NEW gut tun, *s.* tun. g~willig *a* willing, *adv* -ly

Gymnasium *nt* -s,-ien ≈ grammar school

Gymnast|ik *f* - [keep-fit] exercises *pl*; (*Turnen*) gymnastics *sg*. g~isch *a* g~ische Übung exercise

Gynäko|loge *m* -n,-n gynaecologist. G~logie *f* - gynaecology. g~logisch *a* gynaecological

H

H, h /ha:/ *nt*, -,- (*Mus*) B, b

Haar *nt* -[e]s,-e hair; sich (*dat*) die Haare *od* das H~ waschen wash one's hair; um ein H~ (*fam*) very nearly. H~bürste *f* hairbrush. h~en *vi* (*haben*) shed hairs; (*Tier:*) moult □ *vr* sich h~en moult. h~ig *a* hairy; (*fam*) tricky. H~klammer, H~klemme *f* hair-grip. H~nadel *f* hairpin. H~nadelkurve *f* hairpin bend. H~schleife *f* bow. H~schnitt *m* haircut. H~spange *f* slide. h~sträubend *a* hairraising; (*empörend*) shocking. H~trockner *m* -s,- hair-drier. H~waschmittel *nt* shampoo

Habe *f* - possessions *pl*

haben† *vt* have; Angst/Hunger/Durst h~ be frightened/hungry/thirsty; ich hätte gern I'd like; sich h~ (*fam*) make a fuss; es gut/schlecht h~ be well/badly off; etw gegen jdn h~ have sth against s.o.; was hat er? what's the matter with him? □ *v aux* have; ich habe/hatte geschrieben I have/had written; er hätte ihr geholfen he would have helped her

Habgier *f* greed. h~ig *a* greedy

Habicht *m* -[e]s,-e hawk

Hab|seligkeiten *fpl* belongings. H~sucht *f* = Habgier

Hachse *f* -,-n (*Culin*) knuckle

Hack|beil *nt* chopper. H~braten *m* meat loaf

Hacke¹ *f* -,-n hoe; (*Spitz*-) pick

Hacke² *f* -,-n, Hacken *m* -s,- heel

hack|en *vt* hoe; (*schlagen, zerkleinern*) chop; (*Vogel:*) peck; gehacktes Rindfleisch minced/ (*Amer*) ground beef. H~fleisch *nt* mince; (*Amer*) ground meat

Hafen *m* -s,- harbour; (*See-*) port. H~arbeiter *m* docker. H~damm *m* mole. H~stadt *f* port

Hafer *m* -s oats *pl*. H~flocken *fpl* [rolled] oats. H~mehl *nt* oatmeal

Haft *f* - custody; (*H~strafe*) imprisonment. h~bar *a* (*Jur*) liable. H~befehl *m* warrant [of arrest]

haften *vi* (*haben*) cling, stick; (*bürgen*) vouch/ (*Jur*) be liable (für for)

Häftling *m* -s,-e detainee

Haftpflicht *f* (*Jur*) liability. H~versicherung *f* (*Auto*) third-party insurance

Haftstrafe *f* imprisonment

Haftung *f* - (*Jur*) liability

Hagebutte *f* -,-n rose-hip

Hagel *m* -s hail. H~korn *nt* hailstone. h~n *vi* (*haben*) hail

hager *a* gaunt

Hahn *m* -[e]s,-ˉe cock; (*Techn*) tap, (*Amer*) faucet

Hähnchen *nt* -s,- (*Culin*) chicken

Hai|fisch *m* -[e]s,-e shark

Häkchen *nt* -s,- tick

häkel|n *vt/i* (*haben*) crochet. H~nadel *f* crochet-hook

Haken *m* -s,- hook; (*Häkchen*) tick; (*fam: Schwierigkeit*) snag. h~ *vt* hook (an + *acc* to). H~kreuz *nt* swastika. H~nase *f* hooked nose

halb *a* half; eine h~e Stunde half an hour; zum h~en Preis at half price; auf h~em Weg half-way □ *adv* half; h~ drei half past two; fünf [Minuten] vor/nach h~ vier twenty-five [minutes] past three/to four; h~ und h~ half and half; (*fast ganz*) more or less. H~blut *nt* halfbreed. H~dunkel *nt* semi-darkness. H~e(r,s) *f/m/nt* half [a litre]

halber *prep* (+ *gen*) for the sake of; Geschäfte h~ on business

Halb|finale *nt* semifinal. H~heit *f* -,-en (*fig*) half-measure

halbieren *vt* halve, divide in half; (*Geom*) bisect

Halb|insel *f* peninsula. H~kreis *m* semicircle. H~kugel *f* hemisphere. h~laut *a* low □ *adv* in an undertone. H~mast *adv* at half-mast. H~messer *m* -s,- radius. H~mond *m* half moon. H~pension *f* half-board. h~rund *a* semicircular.

H~schuh *m* [flat] shoe. h~stündlich *a*
& *adv* half-hourly. h~tags *adv* [for] half a
day; h~tags arbeiten ≈ work part-time.
H~ton *m* semitone. h~wegs *adv* half-
way; (*ziemlich*) more or less. h~wüchsig
a adolescent. H~zeit *f* (*Sport*) half-time;
(*Spielzeit*) half

Halde *f* -,-n dump, tip

Hälfte *f* -,-n half; zur H~ half

Halfter[1] *m* & *nt* -s,- halter

Halfter[2] *f* -,-n & *nt* -s,- holster

Hall *m* -[e]s,-e sound

Halle *f* -,-n hall; (*Hotel-*) lobby; (*Bahnhofs-*)
station concourse

hallen *vi* (*haben*) resound; (*wider-*) echo

Hallen- *pref* indoor

hallo *int* hallo

Halluzination /-'tsjo:n/ *f* -,-en hallucination

Halm *m* -[e]s,-e stalk; (*Gras-*) blade

Hals *m* -es,-e neck; (*Kehle*) throat; aus vollem H~e at the top of one's voice; (*lachen*)
out loud. H~ausschnitt *m* neckline.
H~band *nt* (*pl -bänder*) collar. H~kette
f necklace. H~schmerzen *mpl* sore
throat *sg*. h~starrig *a* stubborn. H~tuch
nt scarf

halt[1] *adv* (*SGer*) just; es geht h~ nicht it's
just not possible

halt[2] *int* stop! (*Mil*) halt! (*fam*) wait a
minute!

Halt *m* -[e]s,-e hold; (*Stütze*) support; (*in-
nerer*) stability; (*Anhalten*) stop; H~
machen stop. h~bar *a* durable; (*Tex*)
hard-wearing; (*fig*) tenable; h~bar bis ...
(*Comm*) use by ...

halten† *vt* hold; make (*Rede*); give (*Vortrag*); (*einhalten, bewahren*) keep; [sich
(*dat*)] keep (*Hund*); take (*Zeitung*);
run (*Auto*); warm h~ keep warm; h~ für
regard as; viel/nicht viel h~ von think
highly/little of; sich h~ hold on (an + *dat*
to); (*fig*) hold out; (*Geschäft:*) keep going;
(*haltbar sein*) keep; (*Wetter:*) hold; (*Blumen:*) last; sich links h~ keep left; sich
gerade h~ hold oneself upright; sich h~
an (+ *acc*) (*fig*) keep to □ *vi* (*haben*) hold;
(*haltbar sein, bestehen bleiben*) keep;
(*Freundschaft, Blumen:*) last; (*Halt
machen*) stop; h~ auf (+ *acc*) (*fig*) set
great store by; auf sich (*acc*) h~ take
pride in oneself; an sich (*acc*) h~ contain
oneself; zu jdm h~ be loyal to s.o.

Halter *m* -s,- holder

Halte|**stelle** *f* H~verbot *nt* waiting
restriction; 'H~verbot' 'no waiting'

halt|**los** *a* (*fig*) unstable; (*unbegründet*)
unfounded. h~machen *vi sep* (*haben*)
(NEW)H~ machen, *s.* Halt

Haltung *f* -,-en (*Körper-*) posture; (*Ver-
halten*) manner; (*Einstellung*) attitude;
(*Fassung*) composure; (*Halten*) keeping;
H~ annehmen (*Mil*) stand to attention

Halunke *m* -n,-n scoundrel

Hamburger *m* -s,- hamburger

hämisch *a* malicious, *adv* -ly

Hammel *m* -s,- ram; (*Culin*) mutton.
H~fleisch *nt* mutton

Hammer *m* -s,- hammer

hämmern *vt/i* (*haben*) hammer; (*Herz:*)
pound

Hämorrhoiden /hɛmɔroˈiːdən/, Hä-
morriden /hɛmɔˈriːdən/ *fpl* haemorrhoids

Hamster *m* -s,- hamster. h~n *vt/i* (*fam*)
hoard

Hand *f* -,-e hand; eine H~ voll Kirschen
a handful of cherries; jdm die H~ geben
shake hands with s.o.; rechter/linker
H~ on the right/left; [aus] zweiter H~
second-hand; unter der H~ unofficially;
(*geheim*) secretly; an H~ (+ *gen*) = anhand; H~ und Fuß haben (*fig*) be sound.
H~arbeit *f* manual work; (*handwerk-
lich*) handicraft; (*Nadelarbeit*) needlework; (*Gegenstand*) hand-made article.
H~ball *m* [German] handball. H~besen
m brush. H~bewegung *f* gesture.
H~bremse *f* handbrake. H~buch *nt*
handbook, manual

Händedruck *m* handshake

Handel *m* -s trade, commerce; (*Unternehmen*) business; (*Geschäft*) deal; H~ treiben trade. h~n *vi* (*haben*) act; (*Handel
treiben*) trade (mit in); von etw od über
etw (*acc*) h~n deal with sth; sich h~n
um be about, concern. H~smarine *f* merchant navy. H~sschiff *nt* merchant vessel. H~sschule *f* commercial college.
h~süblich *a* customary. H~sware *f*
merchandise

Hand|**feger** *m* -s,- brush. H~fertigkeit
f dexterity. h~fest *a* sturdy; (*fig*) solid.
H~fläche *f* palm. h~gearbeitet *a* hand-
made. H~gelenk *nt* wrist. h~gemacht
a handmade. H~gemenge *nt* -s,- scuffle.
H~gepäck *nt* hand-luggage. h~ge-
schrieben *a* hand-written. H~granate *f*
hand-grenade. h~greiflich *a* tangible;
h~greiflich werden become violent.
H~griff *m* handle; mit einem H~griff
with a flick of the wrist

handhaben *vt insep* (*reg*) handle

Handikap /'hɛndikɛp/ *nt* -s,-s handicap

Hand|**kuss** (Handkuß) *m* kiss on the
hand. H~lauf *m* handrail

Händler *m* -s,- dealer, trader

handlich *a* handy

Handlung f -,-en act; (*Handeln*) action; (*Roman-*) plot; (*Geschäft*) shop. H~sweise f conduct

Hand|schellen fpl handcuffs. H~schlag m handshake. H~schrift f handwriting; (*Text*) manuscript. H~schuh m glove. H~schuhfach nt glove compartment. H~stand m handstand. H~tasche f handbag. H~tuch nt towel. H~voll f -,-, eine H~voll ⟨NEW⟩ eine H~ voll, s. Hand

Handwerk nt craft, trade; sein H~ verstehen know one's job. H~er m -s,- craftsman; (*Arbeiter*) workman

Handy /'hɛndi/ nt -s,-s mobile phone

Hanf m -[e]s hemp

Hang m -[e]s,-e slope; (*fig*) inclination, tendency

Hänge|brücke f suspension bridge. H~lampe f [light] pendant. H~matte f hammock

hängen¹ vt (*reg*) hang

hängen†² vi (*haben*) hang; h~ an (+ *dat*) (*fig*) be attached to; h~ bleiben stick (an + *dat* to); ⟨*Kleid:*⟩ catch (an + *dat* on); h~ lassen leave; den Kopf h~ lassen be downcast. h~bleiben† vi sep (*sein*) ⟨NEW⟩ h~ bleiben, s. hängen. h~lassen† vt sep ⟨NEW⟩ h~ lassen, s. hängen

Hannover nt -s Hanover

hänseln vt tease

hantieren vi (*haben*) busy oneself

hapern vi (*haben*) es hapert there's a lack (an + *dat* of)

Happen m -s,- mouthful; einen H~ essen have a bite to eat

Harfe f -,-n harp

Harke f -,-n rake. h~n vt/i (*haben*) rake

harmlos a harmless; (*arglos*) innocent, adv -ly. H~igkeit f - harmlessness; innocence

Harmonie f -,-n harmony. h~ren vi (*haben*) harmonize; (*gut auskommen*) get on well

Harmonika f -,-s accordion; (*Mund-*) mouth-organ

harmonisch a harmonious, adv -ly

Harn m -[e]s urine. H~blase f bladder

Harpune f -,-n harpoon

hart (härter, härtest) a hard; (*heftig*) violent; (*streng*) harsh □ adv hard; (*streng*) harshly

Härte f -,-n hardness; (*Strenge*) harshness; (*Not*) hardship. h~n vt harden

Hart|faserplatte f hardboard. h~gekocht a ⟨NEW⟩ h~ gekocht, s. kochen. h~herzig a hard-hearted. h~näckig a

stubborn, adv -ly; (*ausdauernd*) persistent, adv -ly. H~näckigkeit f - stubbornness; persistence

Harz nt -es,-e resin

Haschee nt -s,-s (*Culin*) hash

haschen vi (*haben*) h~ nach try to catch

Haschisch nt & m -[s] hashish

Hase m -n,-n hare; falscher H~ meat loaf

Hasel f -,-n hazel. H~maus f dormouse. H~nuss (H~nuß) f hazel-nut

Hasenfuß m (*fam*) coward

Hass m -es (Haß m -sses) hatred

hassen vt hate

hässlich (häßlich) a ugly; (*unfreundlich*) nasty, adv -ily. H~keit f - ugliness; nastiness

Hast f - haste. h~en vi (*sein*) hasten, hurry. h~ig a hasty, adv -ily, hurried, adv -ly

hast, hat, hatte, hätte s. haben

Haube f -,-n cap; (*Trocken-*) drier; (*Kühler-*) bonnet, (*Amer*) hood

Hauch m -[e]s breath; (*Luft-*) breeze; (*Duft*) whiff; (*Spur*) tinge. h~dünn a very thin; ⟨*Strümpfe*⟩ sheer. h~en vt/i (*haben*) breathe

Haue f -,-n pick; (*fam: Prügel*) beating. h~nt vt beat; (*hämmern*) knock; (*meißeln*) hew; sich h~n fight; übers Ohr h~n (*fam*) cheat □ vi (*haben*) bang (auf + *acc* on); jdm ins Gesicht h~n hit s.o. in the face

Haufen m -s,- heap, pile; (*Leute*) crowd

häufen vt heap or pile [up]; sich h~ pile up; (*zunehmen*) increase

haufenweise adv in large numbers; h~ Geld pots of money

häufig a frequent, adv -ly. H~keit f - frequency

Haupt nt -[e]s, Häupter head. H~bahnhof m main station. H~darsteller m, H~darstellerin f male/female lead. H~fach nt main subject. H~gericht nt main course. H~hahn m mains tap; (*Wasser-*) stopcock

Häuptling m -s,-e chief

Haupt|mahlzeit f main meal. H~mann m (*pl* -leute) captain. H~person f most important person; (*Theat*) principal character. H~post f main post office. H~quartier nt headquarters pl. H~rolle f lead; (*fig*) leading role. H~sache f main thing; in der H~sache in the main. h~sächlich a main, adv -ly. H~satz m main clause. H~schlüssel m master key. H~stadt f capital. H~straße f main street. H~verkehrsstraße f main road. H~verkehrszeit f rush-hour. H~wort nt (*pl* -wörter) noun

Haus nt -es, Häuser house; (Gebäude) building; (Schnecken-) shell; zu H∼e at home; nach H∼e home; H∼ halten = haushalten. H∼angestellte(r) m/f domestic servant. H∼arbeit f housework; (Sch) homework. H∼arzt m family doctor. H∼aufgaben fpl homework sg. H∼besetzer m -s,- squatter. H∼besuch m house-call

hausen vi (haben) live; (wüten) wreak havoc

Haus|frau f housewife. H∼gehilfin f domestic help. h∼gemacht a homemade. H∼halt m -[e]s,-e household; (Pol) budget. h∼halten† vi sep (haben) h∼halten mit manage carefully; conserve (Kraft). H∼hälterin f -,-nen housekeeper. H∼haltsgeld nt housekeeping [money]. H∼haltsplan m budget. H∼herr m head of the household; (Gastgeber) host. h∼hoch a huge; (fam) big □ adv (fam) vastly; (verlieren) by a wide margin

hausier|en vi (haben) h∼en mit hawk. H∼er m -s,- hawker

Hauslehrer m [private] tutor. H∼in f governess

häuslich a domestic, (Person) domesticated

Haus|meister m caretaker. H∼nummer f house number. H∼ordnung f house rules pl. H∼putz m cleaning. H∼rat m -[e]s household effects pl. H∼schlüssel m front-door key. H∼schuh m slipper. H∼stand m household. H∼suchung f [police] search. H∼suchungsbefehl m search-warrant. H∼tier nt domestic animal; (Hund, Katze) pet. H∼tür f front door. H∼wart m -[e]s,-e caretaker. H∼wirt m landlord. H∼wirtin f landlady

Haut f -,Häute skin; (Tier-) hide; aus der H∼ fahren (fam) fly off the handle. H∼arzt m dermatologist

häuten vt skin; sich h∼ moult

haut|eng a skin-tight. H∼farbe f colour; (Teint) complexion

Haxe f -,-n = Hachse

Hbf. abbr s. Hauptbahnhof

Hebamme f -,-n midwife

Hebel m -s,- lever. H∼kraft, H∼wirkung f leverage

heben† vt lift; (hoch-, steigern) raise; sich h∼ rise; (Nebel:) lift; (sich verbessern) improve

hebräisch a Hebrew

hecheln vi (haben) pant

Hecht m -[e]s,-e pike

Heck nt -s,-s (Naut) stern; (Aviat) tail; (Auto) rear

Hecke f -,-n hedge. H∼nschütze m sniper

Heck|fenster nt rear window. H∼motor m rear engine. H∼tür f hatchback

Heer nt -[e]s,-e army

Hefe f - yeast. H∼teig m yeast dough. H∼teilchen nt Danish pastry

Heft¹ nt -[e]s,-e haft, handle

Heft² nt -[e]s,-e booklet; (Sch) exercise book; (Zeitschrift) issue. h∼en vt (nähen) tack; (stecken) pin/(klammern) clip/(mit Heftmaschine) staple (an + acc to). H∼er m -s,- file

heftig a fierce, adv -ly, violent, adv -ly; (Schlag, Regen) heavy, adv -ily; (Schmerz, Gefühl) intense, adv -ly; (Person) quick-tempered. H∼keit f - fierceness, violence; intensity

Heft|klammer f staple; (Büro-) paper-clip. H∼maschine f stapler. H∼pflaster nt sticking plaster. H∼zwecke f -,-n drawing-pin

hegen vt care for; (fig) cherish (Hoffnung); harbour (Verdacht)

Hehl nt & m kein[en] H∼ machen aus make no secret of. H∼er m -s,- receiver, fence

Heide¹ m -n,-n heathen

Heide² f -,-n heath; (Bot) heather. H∼kraut nt heather

Heidelbeere f bilberry, (Amer) blueberry

Heid|in f -,-nen heathen. h∼nisch a heathen

heikel a difficult, tricky; (delikat) delicate; (dial) (Person) fussy

heil a undamaged, intact; (Person) unhurt; (gesund) well; mit h∼er Haut (fam) unscathed

Heil nt -s salvation; sein H∼ versuchen try one's luck

Heiland m -s (Relig) Saviour

Heil|anstalt f sanatorium; (Nerven-) mental hospital. H∼bad nt spa. h∼bar a curable

Heilbutt m -[e]s,-e halibut

heilen vt cure; heal (Wunde) □ vi (sein) heal

heilfroh a (fam) very relieved

Heilgymnastik f physiotherapy

heilig a holy; (geweiht) sacred; der H∼e Abend Christmas Eve; die h∼e Anna Saint Anne; h∼ halten hold sacred; keep (Feiertag); h∼ sprechen canonize. H∼abend m Christmas Eve. H∼e(r) m/f saint. h∼en vt keep, observe. H∼enschein m halo. h∼halten† vt sep (NEW) h∼ halten, s. halten. H∼keit f - sanctity, holiness. h∼sprechen† vt sep (NEW) h∼ sprechen, s. heilig. H∼tum nt -s,-er shrine

heil|kräftig a medicinal. H∼kräuter ntpl medicinal herbs. h∼los a unholy.

H∼mittel *nt* remedy. H∼praktiker *m* -s,- practitioner of alternative medicine. h∼sam *a* (*fig*) salutary. H∼sarmee *f* Salvation Army. H∼ung *f* - cure

Heim *nt* -[e]s,-e home; (*Studenten*∼) hostel. h∼ *adv* home

Heimat *f* -,-en home; (*Land*) native land. H∼abend *m* folk evening. h∼los *a* homeless. H∼stadt *f* home town

heim|begleiten *vt sep* see home. h∼bringen† *vt sep* bring home; (*begleiten*) see home. H∼computer *m* home computer. h∼fahren† *v sep* □ *vi* (*sein*) go/drive home □ *vt* take/drive home. H∼fahrt *f* way home. h∼gehen† *vi* (*sein*) go home; (*sterben*) die

heimisch *a* native, indigenous; (*Pol*) domestic; h∼ sein/sich h∼fühlen be/feel at home

Heim|kehr *f* - return [home]. h∼kehren *vi sep* (*sein*) return home. h∼kommen† *vi sep* (*sein*) come home

heimlich *f* a secret, (*Relig*) h∼ tun be secretive; etw h∼ tun do sth secretly *or* in secret. H∼keit *f* -,-en secrecy; H∼keiten secrets. H∼tuerei *f* - secretiveness

Heim|reise *f* journey home. h∼reisen *vi sep* (*sein*) go home. H∼spiel *nt* home game. h∼suchen *vt sep* afflict. h∼tückisch *a* treacherous; (*Krankheit*) insidious. h∼wärts *adv* home. H∼weg *m* way home. H∼weh *nt* -s homesickness; H∼weh haben be homesick. H∼werker *m* -s,- [home] handyman. h∼zahlen *vt sep* jdm etw h∼zahlen (*fig*) pay s.o. back for sth

Heirat *f* -,-en marriage. h∼en *vt/i* (*haben*) marry. H∼santrag *m* proposal; jdm einen H∼santrag machen propose to s.o. h∼sfähig *a* marriageable

heiser *a* hoarse, *adv* -ly. H∼keit *f* - hoarseness

heiß *a* hot, *adv* -ly; (*hitzig*) heated; (*leidenschaftlich*) fervent, *adv* -ly; mein h∼ geliebter Sohn my beloved son; mir ist h∼ I am hot

heißen† *vi* (*haben*) be called; (*bedeuten*) mean; ich heiße ... my name is ...; wie h∼ Sie? what is your name? wie heißt ... auf Englisch? what's the English for ...? es heißt it says; (*man sagt*) it is said; das heißt that is [to say]; was soll das h∼? what does it mean? (*empört*) what is the meaning of this? □ *vt* call; jdn etw tun h∼ tell s.o. to do sth

heißgeliebt *a* (NEW) h∼ geliebt, s. heiß. h∼hungrig *a* ravenous. H∼wasserbereiter *m* -s,- water heater

heiter *a* cheerful, *adv* -ly; (*Wetter*) bright; (*amüsant*) amusing; aus h∼em Himmel (*fig*) out of the blue. H∼keit *f* - cheerfulness; (*Gelächter*) mirth

Heiz|anlage *f* heating; (*Auto*) heater. H∼decke *f* electric blanket. h∼en *vt* heat; light (*Ofen*) □ *vi* (*haben*) put the heating on; (*Ofen*) give out heat. H∼gerät *nt* heater. H∼kessel *m* boiler. H∼körper *m* radiator. H∼lüfter *m* -s,- fan heater. H∼material *nt* fuel. H∼ofen *m* heater. H∼ung *f* -,-en heating; (*Heizkörper*) radiator

Hektar *nt* & *m* -s,- hectare

hektisch *a* hectic

Held *m* -en,-en hero. h∼enhaft *a* heroic, *adv* -ally. H∼enmut *m* heroism. h∼enmütig *a* heroic, *adv* -ally. H∼entum *nt* -s heroism. H∼in *f* -,-nen heroine

helf|en† *vi* (*haben*) help (jdm s.o.); (*nützen*) be effective; sich (*dat*) nicht zu h∼en wissen not know what to do; es hilft nichts it's no use. H∼er(in) *m* -s,- (*f* -,-nen) helper, assistant. H∼ershelfer *m* accomplice

hell *a* light; (*Licht ausstrahlend, klug*) bright; (*Stimme*) clear; (*fam: völlig*) utter; h∼es Bier ≈ lager □ *adv* brightly; h∼ begeistert absolutely delighted. h∼hörig *a* poorly soundproofed; h∼hörig werden (*fig*) sit up and take notice

hellicht *a* (NEW) helllicht

Hell|igkeit *f* - brightness. h∼licht *a* h∼lichter Tag broad daylight. h∼seher(in) *m* -s,- (*f* -,-nen) clairvoyant. h∼wach *a* wide awake

Helm *m* -[e]s,-e helmet

Hemd *nt* -[e]s,-en vest, (*Amer*) undershirt; (*Ober*-) shirt. H∼bluse *f* shirt

Hemisphäre *f* -,-n hemisphere

hemm|en *vt* check; (*verzögern*) impede; (*fig*) inhibit. H∼ung *f* -,-en (*fig*) inhibition; (*Skrupel*) scruple; h∼ungen haben be inhibited. h∼ungslos *a* unrestrained, *adv* -ly

Hendl *nt* -s,-[n] (*Aust*) chicken

Hengst *m* -[e]s,-e stallion. H∼fohlen *nt* colt

Henkel *m* -s,- handle

henken *vt* hang

Henne *f* -,-n hen

her *adv* here; (*zeitlich*) ago; her mit ...! give me ...! von oben unten/Norden/weit her from above/below/the north/far away; von der Farbe/vom Thema her as far as the colour/subject is concerned; vor/hinter jdm/etw her in front of/behind s.o./sth; hinter jdm/etw her sein be after s.o./sth; her sein come (von from); es ist schon lange/drei Tage her it was a long time/three days ago

herab *adv* down [here]; von oben h~ from above; ⟨*fig*⟩ condescending, *adv* -ly. h~blicken *vi sep* (*haben*) = h~sehen

herablass|en† *vt sep* let down; sich h~en condescend (zu to). h~end *a* condescending, *adv* -ly. H~ung *f* - condescension

herab|sehen† *vi sep* (*haben*) look down (auf + *acc* on). h~setzen *vt sep* reduce, cut; ⟨*fig*⟩ belittle. h~setzend *a* disparaging, *adv* -ly. h~würdigen *vt sep* belittle, disparage

Heraldik *f* - heraldry

heran *adv* near; [bis] h~ an (+ *acc*) up to. h~bilden *vt sep* train. h~gehen† *vi sep* (*sein*) h~gehen an (+ *acc*) go up to; get down to ⟨*Arbeit*⟩. h~kommen *vi sep* (*sein*) approach; h~kommen an (+ *acc*) come up to; ⟨*erreichen*⟩ get at; ⟨*fig*⟩ measure up to. h~machen (sich) *vr sep* sich h~machen an (+ *acc*) approach; get down to ⟨*Arbeit*⟩. h~reichen *vi sep* (*haben*) h~reichen an (+ *acc*) reach; ⟨*fig*⟩ measure up to. h~wachsen† *vi sep* (*sein*) grow up. h~ziehen† *v sep* □ *vt* pull up (an + *acc* to); ⟨*züchten*⟩ raise; ⟨h~bilden⟩ train; ⟨*hinzuziehen*⟩ call in □ *vi* (*sein*) approach

herauf *adv* up [here]; die Treppe h~ up the stairs. h~beschwören *vt sep* evoke; ⟨*verursachen*⟩ cause. h~kommen *vi sep* (*sein*) come up. h~setzen *vt sep* raise, increase

heraus *adv* out (aus of); h~ damit *od* mit der Sprache! out with it! h~ sein be out; aus dem Gröbsten h~ sein be over the worst; fein h~ sein be sitting pretty. h~bekommen† *vt sep* get out; ⟨*ausfindig machen*⟩ find out; ⟨*lösen*⟩ solve; Geld h~bekommen get change. h~bringen† *vt sep* bring out; ⟨*fam*⟩ get out. h~finden† *v sep* □ *vt* find out □ *vi* (*haben*) find one's way out. H~forderer *m* -s, - challenger. h~fordern *vt sep* provoke; challenge ⟨*Person*⟩. H~forderung *f* provocation; challenge. H~gabe *f* handing over; ⟨*Admin*⟩ issue; ⟨*Veröffentlichung*⟩ publication. h~geben† *vt sep* hand over; ⟨*Admin*⟩ issue; ⟨*veröffentlichen*⟩ publish; edit ⟨*Zeitschrift*⟩; jdm Geld h~geben give s.o. change □ *vi* (*haben*) give change (auf + *acc* for). H~geber *m* -s,- publisher; editor. h~gehen† *vi sep* (*sein*) ⟨*Fleck:*⟩ come out; aus sich h~gehen ⟨*fig*⟩ come out of one's shell. h~halten† (sich) *vr sep* ⟨*fig*⟩ keep out (aus of). h~holen *vt sep* get out. h~kommen† *vi sep* (*sein*) come out; ⟨*aus Schwierigkeit, Takt*⟩ get out; auf eins *od* dasselbe h~kommen come to the same thing. h~lassen† *vt sep* let out. h~machen *vt sep* get out; sich gut

h~machen ⟨*fig*⟩ do well. h~nehmen† *vt sep* take out; sich zu viel h~nehmen ⟨*fig*⟩ take liberties. h~platzen *vi sep* (*haben*) ⟨*fam*⟩ burst out laughing. h~putzen (sich) *vr sep* doll oneself up. h~ragen *vi sep* (*haben*) jut out; ⟨*fig*⟩ stand out. h~reden (sich) *vr sep* make excuses. h~rücken *v sep* □ *vt* move out; ⟨*hergeben*⟩ hand over □ *vi* (*sein*) h~rücken mit hand over; ⟨*fig: sagen*⟩ come out with. h~rutschen *vi sep* (*sein*) slip out. h~schlagen† *vt sep* knock out; ⟨*fig*⟩ gain. h~stellen *vt sep* put out; sich h~stellen turn out (als to be; daß that). h~suchen *vt sep* pick out. h~wollen† *vi sep* (*haben*) nicht mit der Sprache h~wollen hum and haw. h~ziehen† *vt sep* pull out

herb *a* sharp; ⟨*Wein*⟩ dry; ⟨*Landschaft*⟩ austere; ⟨*fig*⟩ harsh

herbei *adv* here. h~führen *vt sep* ⟨*fig*⟩ bring about. h~lassen (sich) *vr sep* condescend (zu to). h~schaffen *vt sep* get. h~sehnen *vt sep* long for

Herberg|e *f* -,-n [youth] hostel; ⟨*Unterkunft*⟩ lodging. H~svater *m* warden

herbestellen *vt sep* summon

herbitten† *vt sep* ask to come

herbringen† *vt sep* bring [here]

Herbst *m* -[e]s,-e autumn. h~lich *a* autumnal

Herd *m* -[e]s,-e stove, cooker; ⟨*fig*⟩ focus

Herde *f* -,-n herd; ⟨*Schaf:*⟩ flock

herein *adv* in [here]; h~! come in! h~bitten† *vt sep* ask in. h~brechen† *vi sep* (*sein*) burst in; ⟨*fig*⟩ set in; ⟨*Nacht:*⟩ fall; h~brechen über (+ *acc*) ⟨*fig*⟩ overtake. h~fallen† *vi sep* (*sein*) ⟨*fam*⟩ be taken in (auf + *acc* by). h~kommen *vi sep* (*sein*) come in. h~lassen† *vt sep* let in. h~legen *vt sep* ⟨*fam*⟩ take for a ride. h~rufen† *vt sep* call in

Herfahrt *f* journey/drive here

herfallen† *vi sep* (*sein*) h~ über (+ *acc*) attack; fall upon ⟨*Essen*⟩

hergeben† *vt sep* hand over; ⟨*fig*⟩ give up; sich h~ zu ⟨*fig*⟩ be a party to

hergebracht *a* traditional

hergehen† *vi sep* (*sein*) h~ vor/neben/hinter (+ *dat*) walk along in front of/beside/behind; es ging lustig her ⟨*fam*⟩ there was a lot of merriment

herhalten† *vi sep* (*haben*) hold out; h~ müssen be the one to suffer

herholen *vt sep* fetch; weit hergeholt ⟨*fig*⟩ far-fetched

Hering *m* -s,-e herring; ⟨*Zeltpflock*⟩ tent-peg

her|kommen† *vi sep* (*sein*) come here; wo kommt das her? where does it come

from? h∼kömmlich *a* traditional.
H∼kunft *f* -origin

herlaufen† *vi sep* (*sein*) h∼ vor/neben/hinter (+ *dat*) run/(*gehen*) walk along in front of/beside/behind

herleiten *vt sep* derive

hermachen *vt sep* viel/wenig h∼ be impressive/unimpressive; (*wichtig nehmen*) make a lot of/little fuss (von of); sich h∼ über (+ *acc*) fall upon; tackle (*Arbeit*)

Hermelin[1] *nt* -s,-e (*Zool*) stoat

Hermelin[2] *m* -s,-e (*Pelz*) ermine

hermetisch *a* hermetic, *adv* -ally

Hernie /'hɛrnjə/ *f* -,-n hernia

Heroin *nt* -s heroin

heroisch *a* heroic, *adv* -ally

Herr *m* -n,-en gentleman; (*Gebieter*) master (über + *acc* of); [Gott,] der H∼ the Lord [God]; H∼ Meier Mr Meier; Sehr geehrte H∼en Dear Sirs. H∼chen *nt* -s,- master. H∼enhaus *nt* manor [house]. h∼enlos *a* ownerless; (*Tier*) stray. H∼ensitz *m* manor

Herrgott *m* der H∼ the Lord; H∼ [noch mal]! damn it!

herrichten *vt sep* prepare; wieder h∼ renovate

Herrin *f* -,-nen mistress

herrisch *a* imperious, *adv* -ly; (*Ton*) peremptory; (*herrschsüchtig*) overbearing

herrlich *a* marvellous, *adv* -ly; (*großartig*) magnificent, *adv* -ly. H∼keit *f* -,-en splendour

Herrschaft *f* -,-en rule; (*Macht*) power; (*Kontrolle*) control; meine H∼en! ladies and gentlemen!

herrsch|en *vi* (*haben*) rule; (*verbreitet sein*) prevail; es h∼te Stille/große Aufregung there was silence/great excitement. H∼er(in) *m* -s,- (*f* -,-nen) ruler. h∼süchtig *a* domineering

herrühren *vi sep* (*haben*) stem (von from)

hersein† *vi sep* (*sein*) [NEW] her sein, *s.* her

herstammen *vi sep* (*haben*) come (aus/ von from)

herstell|en *vt sep* establish; (*Comm*) manufacture, make. H∼er *m* -s,- manufacturer, maker. H∼ung *f* - establishment; manufacture

herüber *adv* over [here]. h∼kommen† *vi sep* (*sein*) come over [here]

herum *adv* im Kreis h∼ [round] in a circle; falsch h∼ the wrong way round; um ... h∼ round ...; (*ungefähr*) [round] about ...; h∼ sein be over. h∼albern *vi sep* (*haben*) fool around. h∼drehen *vt sep* turn round/(*wenden*) turn; turn (*Schlüssel*); sich h∼drehen turn round/over. h∼gehen† *vi sep* (*sein*) walk around;

(*Zeit:*) pass; h∼gehen um go round. h∼kommen† *vi sep* (*sein*) get about; h∼kommen um get round; come round (*Ecke*); um etw [nicht] h∼kommen (*fig*) [not] get out of sth. h∼kriegen *vt sep* jdn h∼kriegen (*fam*) talk s.o. round. h∼liegen† *vi sep* (*sein*) lie around. h∼lungern *vi sep* (*haben*) loiter. h∼schnüffeln *vi sep* (*haben*) (*fam*) nose about. h∼sitzen† *vi sep* (*haben*) sit around; h∼sitzen um sit round. h∼sprechen† (sich) *vr sep* (*Gerücht:*) get about. h∼stehen† *vi sep* (*haben*) stand around; h∼stehen um stand round. h∼treiben (sich) *vr sep* hang around. h∼ziehen† *vi sep* (*sein*) move around; (*ziellos*) wander about

herunter *adv* down [here]; die Treppe h∼ down the stairs; h∼ sein be down; (*körperlich*) be run down; (*Person*) be run down. h∼fallen† *vi sep* (*sein*) fall off. h∼gehen† *vi sep* (*sein*) come down; (*sinken*) go/come down. h∼gekommen *a* (*fig*) run-down; (*Gebäude*) dilapidated; (*Person*) down-at-heel. h∼kommen† *vi sep* (*sein*) come down; (*fig*) go to rack and ruin; (*Firma, Person:*) go downhill; (*gesundheitlich*) get run down. h∼lassen† *vt sep* let down, lower. h∼machen *vt sep* (*fam*) reprimand; (*herabsetzen*) run down. h∼spielen *vt sep* (*fig*) play down. h∼ziehen† *vt sep* pull down

hervor *adv* out (aus of). h∼bringen† *vt sep* produce; utter (*Wort*). h∼gehen† *vi sep* (*sein*) come/(sich ergeben) emerge/(*folgen*) follow (aus from). h∼heben† *vt sep* (*fig*) stress, emphasize. h∼quellen† *vi sep* (*sein*) stream out; (*h∼treten*) bulge. h∼ragen *vi sep* (*sein*) jut out; (*fig*) stand out. h∼ragend *a* (*fig*) outstanding. h∼rufen† *vt sep* (*fig*) cause. h∼stehen† *vi sep* (*haben*) protrude. h∼treten† *vi sep* (*sein*) protrude, bulge; (*fig*) stand out. h∼tun† (sich) *vr sep* (*fig*) distinguish oneself; (*angeben*) show off

Herweg *m* way here

Herz *nt* -ens,-en heart; (*Kartenspiel*) hearts *pl*; (*dat*) ein H∼ fassen pluck up courage. H∼anfall *m* heart attack

herzeigen *vt sep* show

herz|en *vt* hug. H∼enslust *f* nach H∼enslust to one's heart's content. h∼haft *a* hearty, *adv* -ily; (*würzig*) savoury

herziehen† *v sep* □ *vt* hinter sich (*dat*) h∼ pull along [behind one] □ *vi* (*sein*) hinter jdm h∼ follow along behind s.o.; über jdn h∼ (*fam*) run s.o. down

herz|ig *a* sweet, adorable. H∼infarkt *m* heart attack. H∼klopfen *nt* -s palpitations *pl*; ich hatte H∼klopfen my heart was pounding

herzlich a cordial, adv -ly; (warm) warm, adv -ly; (aufrichtig) sincere, adv -ly; h~en Dank! many thanks! h~e Grüße kind regards; h~ wenig precious little. H~keit f - cordiality; warmth; sincerity

herzlos a heartless

Herzog m -s,ˆe duke. H~in f -,-nen duchess. H~tum nt -s,ˆer duchy

Herz|schlag m heartbeat; (Med) heart failure. h~zerreißend a heart-breaking

Hessen nt -s Hesse

heterosexuell a heterosexual

Hetze f - rush; (Kampagne) virulent campaign (gegen against). h~n vt chase; sich h~n hurry □ vi (haben) agitate; (sich beeilen) hurry □ vi (sein) rush

Heu nt -s hay; Geld wie Heu haben (fam) have pots of money

Heuchelei f - hypocrisy

heuch|eln vt feign □ vi (haben) pretend. H~ler(in) m -s,- (f -,-nen) hypocrite. h~lerisch a hypocritical, adv -ly

heuer adv (Aust) this year

Heuer f -,-n (Naut) pay. h~n vt hire; sign on ⟨Matrosen⟩

heulen vi (haben) howl; (fam: weinen) cry; ⟨Sirene:⟩ wail

Heurige(r) m (Aust) new wine

Heu|schnupfen m hay fever. H~schober m -s,- haystack. H~schrecke f -,-n grasshopper; (Wander-) locust

heut|e adv today; (heutzutage) nowadays; h~e früh od Morgen (morgen) this morning; von h~e auf morgen from one day to the next. h~ig a today's . . . ; (gegenwärtig) present; der h~ige Tag today. h~zutage adv nowadays

Hexe f -,-n witch. h~n vi (haben) work magic; ich kann nicht h~n (fam) I can't perform miracles. H~njagd f witchhunt. H~nschuss (H~nschuß) m lumbago. H~rei f - witchcraft

Hieb m -[e]s,-e blow; (Peitschen-) lash; H~e hiding sg

hier adv here; h~ sein/bleiben/lassen/behalten be/stay/leave/keep here; h~ und da here and there; (zeitlich) now and again

Hierarchie /hjerar'çi:/ f -,-n hierarchy

hier|auf adv on this/these; (antworten) to this; (zeitlich) after this. h~aus adv out of or from this/these. h~behalten† vt sep h~ behalten, s. hier. h~bleiben† vi sep (sein) NEW h~ bleiben, s. hier. h~durch adv through this/these; (Ursache) as a result of this. h~für adv for this/these. h~her adv here. h~hin adv here. h~in adv in this/these. h~lassen† vt sep NEW h~ lassen, s. hier.

h~mit adv with this/these; (Admin) hereby. h~nach adv after this/these; (demgemäß) according to this/these. h~sein† vi sep (sein) NEW h~ sein, s. hier. h~über adv over/(höher) above this/these; ⟨sprechen, streiten⟩ about this/these. h~unter adv under/(tiefer) below this/these; (dazwischen) among these. h~von adv from this/these; (h~über) about this/these; (Menge) of this/these. h~zu adv to this/these; (h~für) for this/these. h~zulande adv here

hiesig a local. H~e(r) m/f local

Hilfe f -,-n help, aid; um H~e rufen call for help; jdm zu H~e kommen come to s.o.'s aid; mit H~e (+ gen) NEW mithilfe. h~los a helpless, adv -ly. H~losigkeit f - helplessness. h~reich a helpful

Hilfs|arbeiter m unskilled labourer. h~bedürftig a needy; h~bedürftig sein be in need of help. h~bereit a helpful, adv -ly. H~kraft f helper. H~mittel nt aid. H~verb, H~zeitwort nt auxiliary verb

Himbeere f raspberry

Himmel m -s,- sky; (Relig & fig) heaven; (Bett-) canopy; am H~ in the sky; unter freiem H~ in the open air. H~bett nt four-poster [bed]. H~fahrt f Ascension; Mariä H~fahrt Assumption. h~schreiend a scandalous. H~srichtung f compass point; in alle H~srichtungen in all directions. h~weit a (fam) vast

himmlisch a heavenly

hin adv there; hin und her to and fro; hin und zurück there and back; (Rail) return; hin und wieder now and again; an (+ dat) . . . hin along; auf (+ acc) . . . hin in reply to (Brief, Anzeige); on (jds Rat); zu od nach . . . hin towards; vor sich hin reden talk to oneself; hin sein (fam) be gone; (kaputt, tot) have had it; [ganz] hin sein vor be overwhelmed by; es ist noch/nicht mehr lange hin it's a long time yet/not long to go

hinab adv down [there]

hinauf adv up [there]; die Treppe/Straße h~ up the stairs/road. h~gehen† vi sep (sein) go up. h~setzen vt sep raise

hinaus adv out [there]; (nach draußen) outside; zur Tür h~ out of the door; auf Jahre h~ for years to come; über etw (acc) h~ beyond sth; (Menge) [over and] above sth; über etw (acc) h~ sein (fig) be past sth. h~fliegen† vi sep (sein) fly out; (fam) get the sack □ vt out fly out. h~gehen† vi sep (sein) go out; (Zimmer:) face (nach Norden north); h~gehen über (+ acc) go beyond, exceed. h~kommen† vi sep (sein) get out; h~kommen über (+ acc) get beyond. h~laufen† vi *sep* (*sein*) run out; h~laufen auf (+ *acc*) (*fig*) amount to. h~lehnen (sich) *vr sep* lean out. h~ragen *vi sep* (*haben*) h~ragen über (+ *acc*) project beyond; (*in der Höhe*) rise above; (*fig*) stand out above. h~schieben† *vt sep* push out; (*fig*) put off. h~schicken *vt sep* send out. h~sein† *vi sep* (*sein*) NEW h~ sein, s. hinaus. h~werfen† *vt sep* throw out; (*fam: entlassen*) fire. h~wollen† *vi sep* (*haben*) want to go out; h~wollen auf (+ *acc*) (*fig*) aim at; hoch h~wollen (*fig*) be ambitious. h~ziehen† *v sep* □ *vt* pull out; (*in die Länge ziehen*) drag out; (*verzögern*) delay; sich h~ziehen drag on; be delayed □ *vi* (*sein*) move out. h~zögern *vt* delay; sich h~zögern be delayed

Hinblick *m* im H~ auf (+ *acc*) in view of; (*hinsichtlich*) regarding

hinbringen† *vt sep* take there; (*verbringen*) spend

hinder|lich *a* awkward; jdm h~lich sein hamper s.o. h~n *vt* hamper; (*verhindern*) prevent. H~nis *nt* -ses,-se obstacle. H~nisrennen *nt* steeplechase

hindeuten *vi sep* (*haben*) point (auf + *acc* to)

Hindu *m* -s,-s Hindu. H~ismus *m* - Hinduism

hindurch *adv* through it/them; den Sommer h~ throughout the summer

hinein *adv* in [there]; (*nach drinnen*) inside; h~ in (+ *acc*) into. h~fallen† *vi sep* (*sein*) fall in. h~gehen† *vi sep* (*sein*) go in; h~gehen in (+ *acc*) go into. h~laufen† *vi sep* (*sein*) run in; h~laufen in (+ *acc*) run into. h~reden *vi sep* (*haben*) jdm h~reden interrupt s.o.; (*sich einmischen*) interfere in s.o.'s affairs. h~versetzen (sich) *vr sep* sich in jds Lage h~versetzen put oneself in s.o.'s position. h~ziehen† *vt sep* pull in; h~ziehen in (+ *acc*) pull into; in etw (*acc*) h~gezogen werden (*fig*) become involved in sth

hin|fahren† *v sep* □ *vi* (*sein*) go/drive there □ *vt* take/drive there. H~fahrt *f* journey/drive there; (*Rail*) outward journey. h~fallen† *vi sep* (*sein*) fall. h~fällig *a* (*gebrechlich*) frail; (*ungültig*) invalid. h~fliegen† *v sep* □ *vi* (*sein*) fly there; (*fam*) fall □ *vt* fly there. H~flug *m* flight there; (*Admin*) outward flight. H~gabe *f* - devotion; (*Eifer*) dedication

hingeb|en† *vt sep* give up; sich h~en (*fig*) devote oneself (einer Aufgabe to a task); abandon oneself (dem Vergnügen to pleasure). H~ung *f* - devotion. h~ungsvoll *a* devoted, *adv* -ly

hingegen *adv* on the other hand

hingehen† *vi sep* (*sein*) go/(*zu Fuß*) walk there; (*vergehen*) pass; h~ zu go up to; wo gehst du hin? where are you going? etw h~ lassen (*fig*) let sth pass

hingerissen *a* rapt, *adv* -ly; h~ sein be carried away (von by)

hin|halten† *vt sep* hold out; (*warten lassen*) keep waiting. h~hocken (sich) *vr sep* squat down. h~kauern (sich) *vr sep* crouch down

hinken *vi* (*haben*/*sein*) limp

hin|knien (sich) *vr sep* kneel down. h~kommen† *vi sep* (*sein*) get there; (h~gehören) belong, go; (*fam: auskommen*) manage (mit with); (*fam: stimmen*) be right. h~länglich *a* adequate, *adv* -ly. h~laufen† *vi sep* (*sein*) run/(*gehen*) walk there. h~legen *vt sep* lay or put down; sich h~legen lie down. h~nehmen† *vt sep* (*fig*) accept

hinreichen *v sep* □ *vt* hand (*dat* to) □ *vi* (*haben*) extend (bis to); (*ausreichen*) be adequate. h~d *a* adequate, *adv* -ly

Hinreise *f* journey there; (*Rail*) outward journey

hinreißen† *vt sep* (*fig*) carry away; sich h~ lassen get carried away. h~d *a* ravishing, *adv* -ly

hinricht|en *vt sep* execute. H~ung *f* execution

hinschicken *vt sep* send there

hinschleppen *vt sep* drag there; (*fig*) drag out; sich h~ drag oneself along; (*fig*) drag on

hinschreiben† *vt sep* write there; (*aufschreiben*) write down

hinsehen† *vi sep* (*haben*) look

hinsein† *vi sep* (*sein*) (*fam*) NEW hin sein, s. hin

hinsetzen *vt sep* put down; sich h~ sit down

Hinsicht *f* - in dieser/gewisser H~ in this respect/in a certain sense; in finanzieller H~ financially. h~lich *prep* (+ *gen*) regarding

hinstellen *vt sep* put or set down; park ⟨*Auto*⟩; (*fig*) make out (als to be); sich h~ stand

hinstrecken *vt sep* hold out; sich h~ extend

hintan|setzen, h~stellen *vt sep* ignore; (*vernachlässigen*) neglect

hinten *adv* at the back; dort h~ back there; nach/von h~ to the back/from behind. h~herum *adv* round the back; (*fam*) by devious means; (*erfahren*) in a roundabout way

hinter *prep* (+ *dat*/*acc*) behind; (*nach*) after; h~ jdm/etw herlaufen run after s.o./sth; h~ etw (*dat*) stecken (*fig*) be

behind sth; h~ etw (acc) kommen (fig)
get to the bottom of sth; etw h~ sich (acc)
bringen get sth over [and done] with.
H~bein nt hind leg

Hinterbliebene pl (Admin) surviving
dependants; die H~n the bereaved family
sg

hinterbringen† vt tell (jdm s.o.)

hintere|(r,s) a back, rear; h~s Ende far
end

hintereinander adv one behind/(zeitlich) after the other; dreimal h~ three
times in succession or (fam) in a row

Hintergedanke m ulterior motive

hintergehen† vt deceive

Hinter|grund m background. H~halt m
-[e]s,-e ambush; aus dem H~halt überfallen ambush. h~hältig a underhand

hinterher adv behind, after; (zeitlich)
afterwards. h~gehen† vi sep (sein) follow
(jdm s.o.). h~kommen† vi sep (sein) follow [behind]. h~laufen† vi sep (sein) run
after (jdm s.o.)

Hinter|hof m back yard. H~kopf m back
of the head

hinterlassen† vt leave [behind]; (Jur)
leave, bequeath (dat to). H~schaft f -,-en
(Jur) estate

hinterlegen vt deposit

Hinter|leib m (Zool) abdomen. H~list f
deceit. h~listig a deceitful, adv -ly. h~m
prep = hinter dem. H~mann m (pl
-männer) person behind. h~n prep =
hinter den. H~n m -s,- (fam) bottom,
backside. H~rad nt rear or back wheel.
h~rücks adv from behind. h~s prep =
hinter das. h~ste(r,s) a last; h~ste
Reihe back row. H~teil nt (fam) behind

hintertreiben† vt (fig) block

Hinter|treppe f back stairs pl. H~tür f
back door; (fig) loophole

hinterziehen† vt (Admin) evade

Hinterzimmer nt back room

hinüber adv over or across [there]; h~
sein (fam: unbrauchbar, tot) have had it;
(betrunken) be gone. h~gehen† vi sep
(sein) go over or across; h~gehen über
(+ acc) cross

hinunter adv down [there]; die Treppe/
Straße h~ down the stairs/road.
h~gehen† vi sep (sein) go down.
h~schlucken vt sep swallow

Hinweg m way there

hinweg adv away, off; h~ über (+ acc)
over; über eine Zeit h~ over a period.
h~gehen† vi sep (sein) h~gehen über
(+ acc) (fig) pass over. h~kommen† vi
sep (sein) h~kommen über (+ acc) (fig)
get over. h~sehen† vi sep (haben)
h~sehen über (+ acc) see over; (fig)

overlook. h~setzen vr sep sich
h~setzen über (+ acc) ignore

Hinweis m -es,-e reference; (Andeutung)
hint; (Anzeichen) indication; unter H~
auf (+ acc) with reference to. h~en† v
sep □ vi (haben) point (auf + acc to) □ vt
jdn auf etw (acc) h~en point sth out to
s.o. h~end a (Gram) demonstrative

hin|wenden vt sep turn; sich
h~wenden turn (zu to). h~werfen† vt
sep throw down; drop (Bemerkung);
(schreiben) jot down; (zeichnen) sketch;
(fam: aufgeben) pack in

hinwieder adv on the other hand

hin|zeigen vi sep (haben) point (auf +
acc to). h~ziehen† vt sep pull; (fig: in die
Länge ziehen) drag out; (verzögern) delay;
sich h~ziehen drag on; be delayed; sich
h~gezogen fühlen zu (fig) feel drawn to

hinzu adv in addition. h~fügen vt sep add.
h~kommen† vt sep (sein) be added; (ankommen) arrive (on the scene); join (zu
jdm s.o.). h~rechnen vt sep add. h~ziehen† vt sep call in

Hiobsbotschaft f bad news sg

Hirn nt -s brain; (Culin) brains pl. H~gespinst nt -[e]s,-e figment of the imagination. H~hautentzündung f meningitis. h~verbrannt a (fam) crazy

Hirsch m -[e]s,-e deer; (männlich) stag;
(Culin) venison

Hirse f - millet

Hirt m -en,-en, **Hirte** m -n,-n shepherd

hissen vt hoist

Histor|iker m -s,- historian. h~isch a
historical; (bedeutend) historic

Hit m -s (Mus) hit

Hitz|e f - heat. H~ewelle f heatwave.
h~ig a (fig) heated, adv -ly; (Person) hotheaded; (jähzornig) hot-tempered.
H~kopf m hothead. H~schlag m heatstroke

H-Milch /'ha:-/ f long-life milk

Hobby nt -s,-s hobby

Hobel m -s,- (Techn) plane; (Culin) slicer.
h~n vt/i (haben) plane; (Culin) slice.
H~späne mpl shavings

hoch a (höher, höchst; attrib hohe(r,s))
high; (Baum, Mast) tall; (Offizier) highranking; (Alter) great; (Summe) large;
(Strafe) heavy; hohe Schuhe ankle boots
□ adv high; (sehr) highly; h~ gewachsen
tall; h~ begabt highly gifted; h~ gestellte Persönlichkeit important person; die Treppe/den Berg h~ up the
stairs/hill; sechs Mann h~ six of us/
them. H~ nt -s,-s cheer; (Meteorol) high

Hoch|achtung f high esteem. H~achtungsvoll adv Yours faithfully. H~amt
nt High Mass. h~arbeiten (sich) vr sep

work one's way up. h~begabt *attrib a* NEW h~ begabt, *s.* hoch. H~betrieb *m* great activity; in den Geschäften herrscht H~betrieb the shops are terribly busy. H~burg *f* (*fig*) stronghold. H~deutsch *nt* High German. H~druck *m* high pressure. H~ebene *f* plateau. h~fahren† *vi sep* (*sein*) go up; (*auffahren*) start up; (*aufbrausen*) flare up. h~fliegend *a* (*fig*) ambitious. h~gehen† *vi sep* (*sein*) go up; (*explodieren*) blow up; (*aufbrausen*) flare up. h~gestellt *attrib a* (*Zahl*) superior; (*fig*) NEW h~ gestellt, *s.* hoch. h~gewachsen *a* NEW h~ gewachsen, *s.* hoch. h~glanz *m* high gloss. h~gradig *a* extreme, *adv* -ly. h~hackig *a* high-heeled. h~halten† *vt sep* up; (*fig*) uphold. h~haus *nt* high-rise building. H~heben† *vt sep* lift up; raise ⟨*Kopf, Hand*⟩. h~herzig *a* magnanimous, *adv* -ly. h~kommen† *vi sep* (*sein*) come up; (*aufstehen*) get up; (*fig*) get on [in the world]. H~konjunktur *f* boom. h~krempeln *vt sep* roll up. h~leben *vi sep* (*haben*) h~leben lassen give three cheers for; … lebe hoch! three cheers for …! H~mut *m* pride, arrogance. h~mütig *a* arrogant, *adv* -ly. h~näsig *a* (*fam*) snooty. h~nehmen† *vt sep* pick up; (*fam*) tease. H~ofen *m* blast-furnace. h~ragen *vi sep* rise [up]; ⟨*Turm:*⟩ soar. H~ruf *m* cheer. H~saison *f* high season. H~schätzung *f* high esteem. h~schlagen† *vt sep* turn up ⟨*Kragen*⟩. h~schrecken† *vi sep* (*sein*) start up. H~schule *f* university; (*Musik-, Kunst*) academy. h~sehen† *vi sep* (*haben*) look up. H~sommer *m* midsummer. H~spannung *f* high/(*fig*) great tension. h~spielen *vt sep* (*fig*) magnify. H~sprache *f* standard language. H~sprung *m* high jump

höchst *adv* extremely, most

Hochstapler *m* -s,- confidence trickster

höchst|**e(r,s)** *a* highest; ⟨*Baum, Turm*⟩ tallest; (*oberste, größte*) top; es ist h~e Zeit it is high time. h~ens *adv* at most; (*es sei denn*) except perhaps. H~fall *m* im H~fall at most. H~geschwindigkeit *f* top *or* maximum speed. H~maß *nt* maximum. h~persönlich *adv* in person. H~preis *m* top price. H~temperatur *f* maximum temperature. h~wahrscheinlich *adv* most probably

hoch|**trabend** *a* pompous, *adv* -ly. h~treiben† *vt sep* push up ⟨*Preis*⟩. H~verrat *m* high treason. H~wasser *nt* high tide; (*Überschwemmung*) floods *pl*. H~würden *m* -s Reverend; (*Anrede*) Father

Hochzeit *f* -,-en wedding; H~ feiern get married. H~skleid *nt* wedding dress.

H~sreise *f* honeymoon [trip]. H~stag *m* wedding day/(*Jahrestag*) anniversary

hochziehen† *vt sep* pull up; (*hissen*) hoist; raise ⟨*Augenbrauen*⟩

Hocke *f* - in der H~ sitzen squat; in die H~ gehen squat down. h~n *vi* (*haben*) squat □ *vr* sich h~n squat down

Hocker *m* -s,- stool

Höcker *m* -s,- bump; (*Kamel-*) hump

Hockey /hɔki/ *nt* -s hockey

Hode *f* -,-n, **Hoden** *m* -s,- testicle

Hof *m* -[e]s,ⁱe [court]yard; (*Bauern-*) farm; (*Königs-*) court; (*Schul-*) playground; (*Astr*) halo; Hof halten hold court

hoffen *vt/i* (*haben*) hope (auf + *acc* for). h~tlich *adv* I hope, let us hope; (*als Antwort*) h~tlich/h~tlich nicht let's hope so/not

Hoffnung *f* -,-en hope. h~slos *a* hopeless, *adv* -ly. h~svoll *a* hopeful, *adv* -ly

höflich *a* polite, *adv* -ly, courteous, *adv* -ly. H~keit *f* -,-en politeness, courtesy; (*Äußerung*) civility

hohe(r,s) *a s.* hoch

Höhe *f* -,-n height; (*Aviat, Geog*) altitude; (*Niveau*) level; (*einer Summe*) size; (*An-*) hill; in die H~ gehen rise, go up; nicht auf der H~ (*fam*) under the weather; das ist die H~! (*fam*) that's the limit!

Hoheit *f* -,-en (*Staats-*) sovereignty; (*Titel*) Highness. H~sgebiet *nt* [sovereign] territory. H~szeichen *nt* national emblem

Höhe|**nlinie** *f* contour line. H~nsonne *f* sun-lamp. H~nzug *m* mountain range. H~punkt *m* (*fig*) climax, peak; (*einer Vorstellung*) highlight. h~r *a* & *adv* higher; h~re Schule secondary school

hohl *a* hollow; (*leer*) empty

Höhle *f* -,-n cave; (*Tier-*) den; (*Hohlraum*) cavity; (*Augen-*) socket

Hohl|**maß** *nt* measure of capacity. H~raum *m* cavity

Hohn *m* -s scorn, derision

höhn|**en** *vt* deride □ *vi* (*haben*) jeer. h~isch *a* scornful, *adv* -ly

holen *vt* fetch, get; (*kaufen*) buy; (*nehmen*) take (aus from); h~ lassen send for; [tief] Atem *od* Luft h~ take a [deep] breath; sich (*dat*) etw h~ get sth; catch ⟨*Erkältung*⟩

Holland *nt* -s Holland

Holländ|**er** *m* -s,- Dutchman; die H~er the Dutch *pl*. H~erin *f* -,-nen Dutchwoman. h~isch *a* Dutch

Höll|**e** *f* -hell. h~isch *a* infernal; (*schrecklich*) terrible, *adv* -bly

holpern *vi* (*sein*) jolt *or* bump along □ *vi* (*haben*) be bumpy

holp[**e**]**rig** *a* bumpy

Holunder m -s (Bot) elder

Holz nt -es,-ᵉer wood; (Nutz-) timber. H~blasinstrument nt woodwind instrument

hölzern a wooden

Holz|hammer m mallet. h~ig a woody. H~kohle f charcoal. H~schnitt m woodcut. H~schuh m [wooden] clog. H~wolle f wood shavings pl. H~wurm m woodworm

homogen a homogeneous

Homöopathie f- homoeopathy

homosexuell a homosexual. H~e(r) m/f homosexual

Honig m -s honey. H~wabe f honeycomb

Hono|rar nt -s,-e fee. h~rieren vt remunerate; (fig) reward

Hopfen m -s hops pl; (Bot) hop

hopsen vi (sein) jump

Hör|apparat m hearing-aid. h~bar a audible, adv -bly

horchen vt (haben) listen (auf + acc to); (heimlich) eavesdrop

Horde f -,-n horde; (Gestell) rack

hören vt hear; (an-) listen to □ vi (haben) hear; (horchen) listen; (gehorchen) obey; h~auf (+ acc) listen to. H~sagen nt vom H~sagen from hearsay

Hör|er m -s,- listener; (Teleph) receiver. H~funk m radio. H~gerät nt hearing-aid

Horizon|t m -[e]s,-e horizon. h~tal a horizontal, adv -ly

Hormon nt -s,-e hormone

Horn nt -s,-ᵉer horn. H~haut f hard skin; (Augen-) cornea

Hornisse f -,-n hornet

Horoskop nt -[e]s,-e horoscope

Hörrohr nt stethoscope

Horrorfilm m horror film

Hör|saal m (Univ) lecture hall. H~spiel nt radio play

Hort m -[e]s,-e (Schatz) hoard; (fig) refuge. h~en vt hoard

Hortensie /-iə/ f -,-n hydrangea

Hörweite f in/außer H~ within/out of earshot

Hose f -,-n, **Hosen** pl trousers pl. H~nrock m culottes pl. H~nschlitz m fly, flies pl. H~nträger mpl braces, (Amer) suspenders

Hostess (Hosteß) f -,-tessen hostess; (Aviat) air hostess

Hostie /ˈhɔstiə/ f -,-n (Relig) host

Hotel nt -s,-s hotel; H~ garni / ~ garˈniː/ bed-and-breakfast hotel. H~ier /-ˈlje:/ m -s,-s hotelier

hübsch a pretty, adv -ily; (nett) nice, adv -ly; (Summe) tidy

Hubschrauber m -s,- helicopter

huckepack adv jdn h~ tragen give s.o. a piggyback

Huf m -[e]s,-e hoof. H~eisen nt horseshoe

Hüft|e f -,-n hip. H~gürtel, H~halter m -s,- girdle

Hügel m -s,- hill. h~ig a hilly

Huhn nt -s,-ᵉer chicken; (Henne) hen

Hühn|chen nt -s,- chicken. H~erauge nt corn. H~erbrühe f chicken broth. H~erstall m henhouse, chicken-coop

huldig|en vi (haben) pay homage (dat to). H~ung f- homage

Hülle f -,-n cover; (Verpackung) wrapping; (Platten-) sleeve; in H~ und Fülle in abundance. h~n vt wrap

Hülse f -,-n (Bot) pod; (Etui) case. H~nfrüchte fpl pulses

human a humane, adv -ly. h~itär a humanitarian. H~ität f- humanity

Hummel f -,-n bumble-bee

Hummer m -s,- lobster

Humor m -s humour; H~or haben have a sense of humour. H~oristisch a humorous. h~orvoll a humorous, adv -ly

humpeln vi (sein/haben) hobble

Humpen m -s,- tankard

Hund m -[e]s,-e dog; (Jagd-) hound. H~ehalsband nt dog-collar. H~ehütte f kennel. H~eleine f dog lead

hundert inv a one/a hundred. H~ nt -s,-e hundred; H~e od h~e von hundreds of. H~jahrfeier f centenary, (Amer) centennial. h~prozentig a & adv one hundred per cent. h~ste(r,s) a hundredth. H~stel nt -s,- hundredth

Hündin f -,-nen bitch

Hüne m -n,-n giant

Hunger m -s hunger; H~ haben be hungry. h~n vi (haben) starve; h~n nach (fig) hunger for. H~snot f famine

hungrig a hungry, adv -ily

Hupe f -,-n (Auto) horn. h~n vi (haben) sound one's horn

hüpf|en vi (sein) skip; (Vogel, Frosch:) hop; (Grashüpfer:) jump. H~er m -s,- skip, hop

Hürde f -,-n (Sport & fig) hurdle; (Schaf-) pen, fold

Hure f -,-n whore

hurra int hurray. H~ nt -s,-s hurray; (Beifallsruf) cheer

Husche f -,-n [short] shower. h~n vi (sein) slip; (Eidechse:) dart; (Maus:) scurry; (Lächeln:) flit

hüsteln vi (haben) give a slight cough

husten vi (haben) cough. H~ m -s cough. H~saft m cough mixture

Hut¹ m -[e]s,-e hat; (Pilz-) cap

Hut² f - auf der H~ sein be on one's guard (vor + dat against)

hüten vt watch over; tend ⟨Tiere⟩; (aufpassen) look after; das Bett h~ müssen be confined to bed; sich h~ be on one's guard (vor + dat against); sich h~, etw zu tun take care not to do sth

Hütte f -,-n hut; (Hunde-) kennel; (Techn) iron and steel works. H~nkäse m cottage cheese. H~nkunde f metallurgy

Hyäne f -,-n hyena

Hybride f -,-n hybrid

Hydrant m -en,-en hydrant

hydraulisch a hydraulic, adv -ally

hydroelektrisch /hydroˀeˈlɛktrɪʃ/ a hydroelectric

Hygien|e /hyˈgieːnə/ f - hygiene. h~isch a hygienic, adv -ally

hypermodern a ultra-modern

Hypno|se f - hypnosis. h~tisch a hypnotic. H~tiseur /-ˈzøːɐ̯/ m -s,-e hypnotist. h~tisieren vt hypnotize

Hypochonder /hypoˈxɔndɐ/ m -s,- hypochondriac

Hypothek f -,-en mortgage

Hypothe|se f -,-n hypothesis. h~tisch a hypothetical, adv -ly

Hys|terie f - hysteria. h~terisch a hysterical, adv -ly

I

ich pron I; ich bin's it's me. Ich nt -[s],-[s] self; (Psych) ego

IC-Zug /iˈtseː-/ m inter-city train

ideal a ideal. I~ nt -s,-e ideal. i~isieren vt idealize. I~ismus m - idealism. I~ist(in) m -en,-en (f -,-nen) idealist. i~istisch a idealistic

Idee f -,-n idea; fixe I~ obsession; eine I~ (fam: wenig) a tiny bit

identifizieren vt identify

identi|sch a identical. I~tät f -,-en identity

Ideo|logie f -,-n ideology. i~logisch a ideological

idiomatisch a idiomatic

Idiot m -en,-en idiot. i~isch a idiotic, adv -ally

Idol nt -s,-e idol

idyllisch /iˈdʏlɪʃ/ a idyllic

Igel m -s,- hedgehog

ignorieren vt ignore

ihm pron (dat of er, es) [to] him; (Ding, Tier) [to] it; Freunde von ihm friends of his

ihn pron (acc of er) him; (Ding, Tier) it. i~en pron (dat of sie pl) [to] them; Freunde von i~en friends of theirs. I~en pron (dat of Sie) [to] you; Freunde von I~en friends of yours

ihr pron (2nd pers pl) you □ (dat of sie sg) [to] her; (Ding, Tier) [to] it; Freunde von ihr friends of hers □ poss pron her; (Ding, Tier) its; (pl) their. Ihr poss pron your. i~e(r,s) poss pron hers; (pl) theirs. I~e(r,s) poss pron yours. i~erseits adv for her/(pl) their part. I~erseits adv on your part. i~etwegen adv for her/(Ding, Tier) its/(pl) their sake; (wegen) because of her/it/them, on her/its/their account. I~etwegen adv for your sake. (wegen) because of you, on your account. i~etwillen adv um i~etwillen for her/(Ding, Tier) its/(pl) their sake. I~etwillen adv um I~etwillen for your sake. i~ige poss pron der/die/das i~ige hers; (pl) theirs. I~ige poss pron der/die/das I~ige yours. i~s poss pron hers; (pl) theirs. I~s poss pron yours

Ikone f -,-n icon

illegal a illegal, adv -ly

Illus|ion f -,-en illusion; sich (dat) I~ionen machen delude oneself. i~o-risch a illusory

Illustr|ation /-ˈtsjoːn/ f -,-en illustration. i~ieren vt illustrate. I~ierte f -n,-[n] [illustrated] magazine

Iltis m -ses,-se polecat

im prep = in dem; im Mai in May; im Kino at the cinema

Image /ˈɪmɪdʒ/ nt -[s],-s /-ɪs/ [public] image

Imbiss (Imbiß) m snack. I~halle, I~-stube f snack-bar

Imitation /-ˈtsjoːn/ f -,-en imitation. i~ieren vt imitate

Imker m -s,- bee-keeper

Immatrikul|ation /-ˈtsjoːn/ f - (Univ) enrolment. i~ieren vt (Univ) enrol; sich i~ieren enrol

immer adv always; für i~ for ever; (endgültig) for good; i~ noch still; i~ mehr/weniger/wieder more and more/less and less/again and again; wer/was [auch] i~ whoever/whatever. i~fort adv = i~zu. i~grün a evergreen. i~hin adv (wenigstens) at least; (trotzdem) all the same; (schließlich) after all. i~zu adv all the time

Immobilien /-jən/ pl real estate sg. I~händler, I~makler m estate agent, (Amer) realtor

immun a immune (gegen to). i~isieren vt immunize. I~ität f - immunity

Imperativ m -s,-e imperative

Imperfekt nt -s,-e imperfect

Imperialismus m - imperialism

impf|en vt vaccinate, inoculate. I~stoff m vaccine. I~ung f -,-en vaccination, inoculation

Implantat nt -[e]s,-e implant

imponieren vi (haben) impress (jdm s.o.)

Impor|t m -[e]s,-e import. I~teur /-'tø:ɐ/ m -s,-e importer. i~tieren vt import

imposant a imposing

impoten|t a (Med) impotent. I~z f - (Med) impotence

imprägnieren vt waterproof

Impressionismus m - impressionism

improvisieren vt/i (haben) improvise

Impuls m -es,-e impulse. i~iv a impulsive, adv -ly

instande pred a able (zu to); capable (etw zu tun of doing sth)

in prep (+ dat) in; (+ acc) into, in; (bei Bus, Zug) on; in der Schule/Oper at school/ the opera; in die Schule to school □ a in sein be in

Inbegriff m embodiment. i~en pred a included

Inbrunst f - fervour

inbrünstig a fervent, adv -ly

indem conj (während) while; (dadurch) by (+ -ing)

Inder(in) m -s,- (f -,-nen) Indian

indessen conj while □ adv (unterdessen) meanwhile; (jedoch) however

Indian m -s,-e (Aust) turkey

Indian|er(in) m -s,- (f -,-nen) (American) Indian. i~isch a Indian

Indien /'ɪndjən/ nt -s India

indigniert a indignant, adv -ly

Indikativ m -s,-e indicative

indirekt a indirect, adv -ly

indisch a Indian

indiskre|t a indiscreet. I~tion /-'tsjo:n/ f -,-en indiscretion

indiskutabel a out of the question

indisponiert a indisposed

Individu|alist m -en,-en individualist. I~alität f - individuality. i~ell a individual, adv -ly. I~um /-'vi:duum/ nt -s,-duen individual

Indizienbeweis /ɪn'di:tsjən-/ m circumstantial evidence

indoktrinieren vt indoctrinate

industr|ialisiert a industrialized. I~ie f -,-n industry. i~iell a industrial. I~ielle(r) m industrialist

ineinander adv in/into one another

Infanterie f - infantry

Infektion /-'tsjo:n/ f -,-en infection. I~skrankheit f infectious disease

Infinitiv m -s,-e infinitive

infizieren vt infect; sich i~ become/⟨Person:⟩ be infected

Inflation /-'tsjo:n/ f - inflation. i~är a inflationary

infolge prep (+ gen) as a result of. i~dessen adv consequently

Inform|atik f - information science. I~ation /-'tsjo:n/ f -,-en information; I~ationen information sg. i~ieren vt inform; sich i~ieren find out (über + acc about)

infrage adv etw i~ stellen question sth; (ungewiss machen) make sth doubtful; nicht i~ kommen be out of the question

infrarot a infra-red

Ingenieur /ɪnʒe'njø:ɐ/ m -s,-e engineer

Ingwer m -s ginger

Inhaber(in) m -s,- (f -,-nen) holder; (Besitzer) proprietor; (Scheck-) bearer

inhaftieren vt take into custody

inhalieren vt/i (haben) inhale

Inhalt m -[e]s,-e contents pl; (Bedeutung, Gehalt) content; (Geschichte) story. I~sangabe f summary. I~sverzeichnis nt list/(in Buch) table of contents

Initiale /-'tsja:lə/ f -,-n initial

Initiative /initsja'ti:və/ f -,-n initiative

Injektion /-'tsjo:n/ f -,-en injection.

injizieren vt inject

inklusive prep (+ gen) including □ adv inclusive

inkognito adv incognito

inkonsequen|t a inconsistent, adv -ly. I~z f -,-en inconsistency

inkorrekt a incorrect, adv -ly

Inkubationszeit /-'tsjo:ns-/ f (Med) incubation period

Inland nt -[e]s home country; (Binnenland) interior. I~sgespräch nt inland call

inmitten prep (+ gen) in the middle of; (unter) amongst □ adv i~ von amongst, amidst

inne|haben† vt sep hold, have. i~halten† vi sep (haben) pause

innen adv inside; nach i~ inwards. I~architekt(in) m(f) interior designer. I~minister m Minister of the Interior; (in UK) Home Secretary. I~politik f domestic policy. I~stadt f town centre

inner|e(r,s) *a* inner; (*Med, Pol*) internal. I~e(s) *nt* interior; (*Mitte*) centre; (*fig: Seele*) inner being. I~eien *fpl* (*Culin*) offal *sg*. i~halb *prep* (+ *gen*) inside; (*zeitlich & fig*) within; (*während*) during □ *adv* i~halb von within; (*im Inneren*) inwardly. i~ste(r,s) *a* innermost; im I~sten (*fig*) deep down

innig *a* sincere, *adv* -ly; (*tief*) deep, *adv* -ly; (*eng*) intimate, *adv* -ly

Innung *f* -,-en guild

inoffiziell *a* unofficial, *adv* -ly

ins *prep* = in das; ins Kino/Büro to the cinema/office

Insasse *m* -n,-n inmate; (*im Auto*) occupant; (*Passagier*) passenger

insbesondere *adv* especially

Inschrift *f* inscription

Insekt *nt* -[e]s,-en insect. I~envertilgungsmittel *nt* insecticide

Insel *f* -,-n island

Inser|at *nt* -[e]s,-e [newspaper] advertisement. I~ent *m* -en,-en advertiser. i~ieren *vt/i* (*haben*) advertise

insge|heim *adv* secretly. i~samt *adv* [all] in all

Insignien /-jən/ *pl* insignia

insofern, insoweit *adv* /-'zo:-/ in this respect; i~ als in as much as □ *conj* /-zo-'fern, -'vajt/ i~ als in so far as

Insp|ektion /ɪnspɛk'tsjo:n/ *f* -,-en inspection. I~ektor *m* -en,-en /-'to:rən/ inspector

Inspir|ation /ɪnspira'tsjo:n/ *f* -,-en inspiration. i~ieren *vt* inspire

inspizieren /-sp-/ *vt* inspect

Install|ateur /ɪnstala'tø:ɐ̯/ *m* -s,-e fitter; (*Klempner*) plumber. i~ieren *vt* install

instand *adv* i~ halten maintain; (*pflegen*) look after; i~ setzen restore; (*reparieren*) repair. I~haltung *f* - maintenance, upkeep

inständig *a* urgent, *adv* -ly

Instandsetzung *f* - repair

Instant- /'ɪnstənt-/ *pref* instant

Instanz /-st-/ *f* -,-en authority

Instinkt /-st-/ *m* -[e]s,-e instinct. i~iv *a* instinctive, *adv* -ly

Institu|t /-st-/ *nt* -[e]s,-e institute. I~tion /-'tsjo:n/ *f* -,-en institution

Instrument /-st-/ *nt* -[e]s,-e instrument. I~almusik *f* instrumental music

Insulin *nt* -s insulin

inszenier|en *vt* (*Theat*) produce. I~ung *f* -,-en production

Integr|ation /-'tsjo:n/ *f* - integration. i~ieren *vt* integrate; sich i~ieren integrate. I~ität *f* - integrity

Intellekt *m* -[e]s intellect. i~uell *a* intellectual

intelligen|t *a* intelligent, *adv* -ly. I~z *f* - intelligence; (*Leute*) intelligentsia

Intendant *m* -en,-en director

Intens|ität *f* - intensity. i~iv *a* intensive, *adv* -ly. i~ivieren *vt* intensify. I~ivstation *f* intensive-care unit

inter|essant *a* interesting. I~esse *nt* -s,-n interest; I~esse haben be interested (an + *dat* in). I~essengruppe *f* pressure group. I~essent *m* -en,-en interested party; (*Käufer*) prospective buyer. i~essieren *vt* interest; sich i~essieren be interested (für in)

intern *a* (*fig*) internal, *adv* -ly

Inter|nat *nt* -[e]s,-e boarding school. i~national *a* international, *adv* -ly. i~nieren *vt* intern. I~nierung *f* - internment. I~nist *m* -en,-en specialist in internal diseases. I~pretation /-'tsjo:n/ *f* -,-en interpretation. i~pretieren *vt* interpret. I~punktion /-'tsjo:n/ *f* - punctuation. I~rogativpronomen *nt* interrogative pronoun. I~vall *nt* -s,-e interval. I~vention /-'tsjo:n/ *f* -,-en intervention

Interview /'ɪntɐvju:/ *nt* -s,-s interview. i~en /-'vju:ən/ *vt* interview

intim *a* intimate, *adv* -ly. I~ität *f* -,-en intimacy

intoleran|t *a* intolerant. I~z *f* - intolerance

intransitiv *a* intransitive, *adv* -ly

intravenös *a* intravenous, *adv* -ly

Intrig|e *f* -,-n intrigue. i~ieren *vi* (*haben*) plot

introvertiert *a* introverted

Intui|tion /-'tsjo:n/ *f* -,-en intuition. i~tiv *a* intuitive, *adv* -ly

Invalidenrente *f* disability pension

Invasion *f* -,-en invasion

Inven|tar *nt* -s,-e furnishings and fittings *pl*; (*Techn*) equipment; (*Bestand*) stock; (*Liste*) inventory. I~tur *f* -,-en stock-taking

investieren *vt* invest

inwendig *a* & *adv* inside

inwiefern *adv* in what way. i~weit *adv* how far, to what extent

Inzest *m* -[e]s incest

inzwischen *adv* in the meantime

Irak (der) -[s] Iraq. i~isch *a* Iraqi

Iran (der) -[s] Iran. i~isch *a* Iranian

irdisch *a* earthly

Ire *m* -n,-n Irishman; die I~n the Irish *pl*

irgend *adv* wer/was/wann i∼ whoever/whatever/whenever; wenn i∼ möglich if at all possible; i∼ etwas (NEW) i∼etwas; i∼ jemand (NEW) i∼jemand. i∼ein *indef art* some/any; i∼ein anderer someone/anyone else. i∼eine(r,s) *pron* any one; (*jemand*) someone. i∼etwas *pron* something; (*fragend, verneint*) anything. i∼jemand *pron* someone; (*fragend, verneint*) anyone. i∼wann *pron* at some time [or other]/at any time. i∼was *pron* (*fam*) something [or other]/anything. i∼welche(r,s) *pron* any. i∼wer *pron* someone/anyone.i∼wie *adv* somehow [or other]. i∼wo *adv* somewhere/anywhere; i∼wo anders somewhere else

Irin *f* -,-nen Irishwoman

Iris *f* -,- (*Anat, Bot*) iris

irisch *a* Irish

Irland *nt* -s Ireland

Ironie *f* - irony

ironisch *a* ironic, *adv* -ally

irr *a* = irre

irrational *a* irrational

irre *a* mad, crazy; (*fam: gewaltig*) incredible, *adv* -bly; i∼ werden (NEW) i∼werden. I∼(r) *m/f* lunatic. i∼führen *vt sep* (*fig*) mislead. i∼gehen† *vt sep* (*sein*) lose one's way; (*sich täuschen*) be wrong

irrelevant *a* irrelevant

irre|machen *vt sep* confuse. i∼n *vi/r* (*haben*) [sich] i∼n be mistaken; wenn ich mich nicht i∼ if I am not mistaken □ *vi* (*sein*) wander. I∼nanstalt *f*, I∼nhaus *nt* lunatic asylum. i∼reden *vi sep* (*haben*) ramble. i∼werden† *vi sep* (*sein*) get confused

Irr|garten *m* maze. i∼ig *a* erroneous

irritieren *vt* irritate

Irr|sinn *m* madness, lunacy. i∼sinnig *a* mad; (*fam: gewaltig*) incredible, *adv* -bly. I∼tum *m* -s,-er mistake. i∼tümlich *a* mistaken, *adv* -ly

Ischias *m & nt*- sciatica

Islam (der) -[s] Islam. islamisch *a* Islamic

Island *nt* -s Iceland

Isolier|band *nt* insulating tape. i∼en *vt* isolate; (*Phys, Electr*) insulate; (*gegen Schall*) soundproof. I∼ung *f* - isolation; insulation; soundproofing

Israel /'israe:l/ *nt* -s Israel. I∼eli *m* -[s], -s & *f* -,-[s] Israeli. i∼elisch *a* Israeli

ist *s.* sein; er ist he is

Italien /-jən/ *nt* -s Italy. I∼iener(in) *m* -s,- (*f* -,-nen) Italian. i∼ienisch *a* Italian. I∼ienisch *nt* -[s] (*Lang*) Italian

J

ja *adv*, Ja *nt* -[s] yes; ich glaube ja I think so; ja nicht! not on any account! seid ja vorsichtig! whatever you do, be careful! da seid ihr ja! there you are! das ist es ja that's just it; das mag ja wahr sein that may well be true

Jacht *f* -,-en yacht

Jacke *f* -,-n jacket; (*Strick*-) cardigan

Jackett /ʒa'kɛt/ *nt* -s,-s jacket

Jade *m* -[s] & *f*- jade

Jagd *f* -,-en hunt; (*Schießen*) shoot; (*Jagen*) hunting; shooting; (*fig*) pursuit (nach of); auf die J∼ gehen go hunting/shooting. J∼flugzeug *nt* aircraft. J∼gewehr *nt* sporting gun. J∼hund *m* gun-dog; (*Hetzhund*) hound

jagen *vt* hunt; (*schießen*) shoot; (*verfolgen, wegjagen*) chase; (*treiben*) drive; sich j∼ chase each other; in die Luft j∼ blow up □ *vi* (*haben*) hunt, go hunting/shooting; (*fig*) chase (nach after) □ *vi* (*sein*) race, dash

Jäger *m* -s,- hunter

jäh *a* sudden, *adv* -ly; (*steil*) steep, *adv* -ly

Jahr *nt* -[e]s,-e year. J∼buch *nt* year-book. j∼elang *adv* for years. J∼estag *m* anniversary. J∼eszahl *f* year. J∼eszeit *f* season. J∼gang *m* year; (*Wein*) vintage. J∼hundert *nt* century. J∼hundertfeier *f* centenary, (*Amer*) centennial

jährlich *a* annual, yearly □ *adv* annually, yearly

Jahr|markt *m* fair. J∼tausend *nt* millenium. J∼zehnt *nt* -[e]s,-e decade

Jähzorn *m* violent temper. j∼ig *a* hot-tempered

Jalousie /ʒalu'zi:/ *f* -,-n venetian blind

Jammer *m* -s misery; (*Klagen*) lamenting; es ist ein J∼ it is a shame

jämmerlich *a* miserable, *adv* -bly; (*Mitleid erregend*) pitiful, *adv* -ly

jammer|n *vi* (*haben*) lament □ *vt* jdn j∼n arouse s.o.'s pity. j∼schade j∼schade sein (*fam*) be a terrible shame

Jänner *m* -s,- (*Aust*) January

Januar *m* -s,-e January

Jap|an *nt* -s Japan. J∼aner(in) *m* -s,- (*f* -,-nen) Japanese. j∼anisch *a* Japanese. J∼anisch *nt* -[s] (*Lang*) Japanese

Jargon /ʒar'gõ:/ *m* -s jargon

jäten *vt/i* (*haben*) weed

jauchzen *vi* (*haben*) (*liter*) exult

jaulen *vi* (*haben*) yelp

Jause *f* -,-n (*Aust*) snack

jaw̲o̲hl adv yes

Jaw̲o̲rt nt jdm ein J∼ geben accept s.o.'s proposal [of marriage]

Jazz /jats, dʒɛs/ m - jazz

je adv (jemals) ever; (jeweils) each; (pro) per; je nach according to; seit eh und je always; besser denn je better than ever □ conj je mehr, desto od umso besser the more the better □ prep (+ acc) per

Jeans /dʒiːns/ pl jeans

jed̲e̲(r,s) pron every; (j∼er Einzelne) each; (j∼er Beliebige) any; (substantivisch) everyone; each one; anyone; ohne j∼en Grund without any reason; j∼enfalls adv in any case; (wenigstens) at least; j∼ermann pron everyone; j∼erzeit adv at any time; j∼esmal adv (NEW) jedes Mal, s. Mal¹

jed̲o̲ch adv & conj however

je̲her adv von od seit j∼ always

jem̲a̲ls adv ever

jem̲a̲nd pron someone, somebody; (fragend, verneint) anyone, anybody

jen̲e̲(r,s) pron that; (pl) those; (substantivisch) that one; (pl) those. j∼seits prep (+ gen) on the other side of

jetzig a present; (Preis) current

jetzt adv now. J∼zeit f present

jew̲e̲il|ig a respective. J∼s adv at a time

jiddisch a, J∼ nt -[s] Yiddish

Job /dʒɔp/ m -s,-s job. j∼ben vi (haben) (fam) work

Joch nt -[e]s,-e yoke

Jockei, **Jockey** /'dʒɔki/ m -s,-s jockey

J̲o̲d nt -[s] iodine

j̲o̲deln vi (haben) yodel

J̲o̲ga m & nt -[s] yoga

j̲o̲gg|en /'dʒɔgən/ vi (haben/sein) jog. J∼ing nt -[s] jogging

J̲o̲ghurt, **Jogurt** m & nt -[s] yoghurt

Joh̲a̲nnisbeere f redcurrant; schwarze J∼ blackcurrant

j̲o̲hlen vi (haben) yell; (empört) jeer

J̲o̲ker m -s,- (Karte) joker

J̲o̲lle f -,-n dinghy

Jongl|eur /ʒõˈgløːɐ̯/ m -s,-e juggler. j∼ieren vi (haben) juggle

Joppe f -,-n [thick] jacket

Jord̲a̲nien /-jən/ nt -s Jordan

Journalis|mus /ʒʊrnaˈlɪsmʊs/ m -journalism. J∼t(in) m -en,-en (f -,-nen) journalist

J̲u̲bel m -s rejoicing, jubilation. j∼n vi (haben) rejoice

Jubil|̲a̲r(in) m -s,-e (f -,-nen) person celebrating an anniversary. J∼äum nt -s,-äen jubilee; (Jahrestag) anniversary

juck|en vi (haben) itch; sich j∼en scratch; es j∼t mich I have an itch; (fam: möchte) I'm itching (zu to). J∼reiz m itch[ing]

J̲u̲de m -n,-n Jew. J∼ntum nt -s Judaism; (Juden) Jewry

J̲ü̲d|in f -,-nen Jewess. j∼isch a Jewish

J̲u̲do nt -[s] judo

J̲u̲gend f - youth; (junge Leute) young people pl. J∼herberge f youth hostel. J∼klub m youth club. J∼kriminalität f juvenile delinquency. j∼lich a youthful. J∼liche(r) m/f young man/woman; (Admin) juvenile. J∼liche pl young people. J∼stil m art nouveau. J∼zeit f youth

Jugosl̲a̲w|ien /-jən/ nt -s Yugoslavia. j∼isch a Yugoslav

J̲u̲li m -[s],-s July

jung a (jünger, jüngst) young; (Wein) new □ pron J∼ und Alt (j∼ und alt) young and old. J∼e m -n,-n boy. J∼e(s) nt young animal/bird; (Katzen-) kitten; (Bären-, Löwen-) cub; (Hunde-, Seehund-) pup; die J∼en the young pl. j∼enhaft a boyish

Jünger m -s,- disciple

Jungfer f -,-n alte J∼ old maid. J∼nfahrt f maiden voyage

Jung|frau f virgin; (Astr) Virgo. j∼fräulich a virginal. J∼geselle m bachelor

Jüngling m -s,-e youth

jüngst|e(r,s) a youngest; (neueste) latest; in j∼er Zeit recently

J̲u̲ni m -[s],-s June

J̲u̲nior m -s,-en /-'oːrən/ junior

J̲u̲ra pl law sg

Jur̲i̲st|(in) m -en,-en (f -,-nen) lawyer. j∼isch a legal, adv -ly

Jury /ʒyˈriː/ f -,-s jury; (Sport) judges pl

just̲ie̲ren vt adjust

Just̲i̲z f - die J∼ justice. J∼irrtum m miscarriage of justice. J∼minister m Minister of Justice

Juw̲e̲l nt -s,-en & (fig) -e jewel. J∼ier m -s,-e jeweller

Jux m -es,-e (fam) joke; aus Jux for fun

K

Kabar̲e̲tt nt -s,-s & -e cabaret

kabbelig a choppy

K̲a̲bel nt -s,- cable. K∼fernsehen nt cable television

Kabeljau m -s,-e & -s cod

Kab̲i̲ne f -,-n cabin; (Umkleide-) cubicle; (Telefon-) booth; (einer K∼nbahn) car. K∼nbahn f cable-car

Kabinett nt -s,-e (Pol) Cabinet

Kabriolett nt -s,-s convertible

Kachel f -,-n tile. k~n vt tile

Kadaver m -s,- carcass

Kadenz f -,-en (Mus) cadence; (für Solisten) cadenza

Kadett m -en,-en cadet

Käfer m -s,- beetle

Kaff nt -s,-s (fam) dump

Kaffee /ˈkafeː, kaˈfeː/ m -s,-s coffee; (Mahlzeit) afternoon coffee. K~grund m = K~satz. K~kanne f coffee-pot. K~maschine f coffee-maker. K~mühle f coffee-grinder. K~satz m coffee-grounds pl

Käfig m -s,-e cage

kahl a bare; (haarlos) bald; k~ geschoren shaven. k~geschoren a (NEW) k~ geschoren, s. kahl. k~köpfig a bald-headed

Kahn m -s,-̈e boat; (Last-) barge

Kai m -s,-s quay

Kaiser m -s,- emperor. K~in f -,-nen empress. k~lich a imperial. K~reich nt empire. K~schnitt m Caesarean [section]

Kajüte f -,-n (Naut) cabin

Kakao /kaˈkaʊ/ m -s cocoa

Kakerlak m -s & -en,-en cockroach

Kaktee /kakˈteːə/ f -,-n, **Kaktus** m -,-teen /-ˈteːən/ cactus

Kalb nt -[e]s,-̈er calf. K~fleisch nt veal

Kalender m -s,- calendar; (Taschen-, Termin-) diary

Kaliber nt -s,- calibre; (Gewehr-) bore

Kalium nt -s potassium

Kalk m -[e]s,-e lime; (Kalzium) calcium. k~en vt whitewash. K~stein m limestone

Kalkul|ation /-ˈtsi̯oːn/ f -,-en calculation. k~ieren vt/i (haben) calculate

Kalorie f -,-n calorie

kalt a (kälter, kältest) cold; es ist k~ it is cold; mir ist k~ I am cold. k~blütig a cold-blooded, adv -ly; (ruhig) cool, adv -ly

Kälte f -cold; (Gefühls-) coldness; 10 Grad K~ 10 degrees below zero. K~welle f cold spell

kalt|herzig a cold-hearted. k~schnäuzig a (fam) cold, adv -ly

Kalzium nt -s calcium

Kamel nt -s,-e camel; (fam: Idiot) fool

Kamera f -,-s camera

Kamerad (in) m -en,-en (f -,-nen) companion; (Freund) mate; (Mil, Pol) comrade. K~schaft f - comradeship

Kameramann m (pl -männer & -leute) cameraman

Kamille f - camomile

Kamin m -s,-e fireplace; (SGer: Schornstein) chimney. K~feger m -s,- (SGer) chimney-sweep

Kamm m -[e]s,-̈e comb; (Berg-) ridge; (Zool, Wellen-) crest

kämmen vt comb; jdn/sich k~ comb s.o.'s/one's hair

Kammer f -,-n small room; (Techn, Biol, Pol) chamber. K~diener m valet. K~musik f chamber music

Kammgarn nt (Tex) worsted

Kampagne /kamˈpanjə/ f -,-n (Pol, Comm) campaign

Kampf m -es,-̈e fight; (Schlacht) battle; (Wett-) contest; (fig) struggle; schwere K~e heavy fighting sg; den K~ ansagen (+ dat) (fig) declare war on

kämpf|en vi (haben) fight; sich k~en durch fight one's way through. K~er(in) m -s,- (f -,-nen) fighter

kampf|los adv without a fight. K~richter m (Sport) judge

kampieren vi (haben) camp

Kanada nt -s Canada

Kanad|ier(in) /-i̯ɐ, -i̯ərɪn/ m -s,- (f -,-nen) Canadian. k~isch a Canadian

Kanal m -s,-̈e canal; (Abfluss-) drain, sewer; (Radio, TV) channel; der K~ the [English] Channel

Kanalis|ation /-ˈtsi̯oːn/ f - sewerage system, drains pl. k~ieren vt canalize; (fig: lenken) channel

Kanarienvogel /-i̯ən-/ m canary

Kanarisch a K~e Inseln Canaries

Kandi|dat(in) m -en,-en (f -,-nen) candidate. k~dieren vi (haben) stand (für for)

kandiert a candied

Känguru (Känguruh) nt -s,-s kangaroo

Kaninchen nt -s,- rabbit

Kanister m -s,- canister; (Benzin-) can

Kännchen nt -s,- [small] jug; (Kaffee-) pot

Kanne f -,-n jug; (Kaffee-, Tee-) pot; (Öl-) can; (große Milch-) churn; (Gieß-) watering-can

Kannibal|e m -n,-n cannibal. K~ismus m - cannibalism

Kanon m -s,-s canon; (Lied) round

Kanone f -,-n cannon, gun; (fig: Könner) ace

kanonisieren vt canonize

Kantate f -,-n cantata

Kante f -,-n edge; auf die hohe K~ legen (fam) put by

Kanten m -s,- crust [of bread]

Kanter m -s,- canter

kantig a angular

Kantine f -,-n canteen

Kanton m -s,-e (*Swiss*) canton

Kantor m -s,-en /-'to:rən/ choir-master and organist

Kanu nt -s,-s canoe

Kanzel f -,-n pulpit; (*Aviat*) cockpit

Kanzleistil m officialese

Kanzler m -s,- chancellor

Kap nt -s,-s (*Geog*) cape

Kapazität f -,-en capacity; (*Experte*) authority

Kapelle f -,-n chapel; (*Mus*) band

Kaper f -,-n (*Culin*) caper

kapern vt (*Naut*) seize

kapieren vt (*fam*) understand, (*fam*) get

Kapital nt -s capital; K~ schlagen aus (*fig*) capitalize on. K~ismus m - capitalism. K~ist m -en,-en capitalist. k~istisch a capitalist

Kapitän m -s,-e captain

Kapitel nt -s,- chapter

Kapitul|ation /-'tsjo:n/ f - capitulation. k~ieren vi (*haben*) capitulate

Kaplan m -s,-e curate

Kappe f -,-n cap. k~n vt cut

Kapsel f -,-n capsule; (*Flaschen-*) top

kaputt a (*fam*) broken; (*zerrissen*) torn; (*defekt*) out of order; (*ruiniert*) ruined; (*erschöpft*) worn out. k~gehen† vi sep (*sein*) (*fam*) break; (*zerreißen*) tear; (*defekt werden*) pack up; (*Ehe, Freundschaft*): break up. k~lachen (sich) vr sep (*fam*) be in stitches. k~machen vt sep (*fam*) break; (*zerreißen*) tear; (*defekt machen*) put out of order; (*erschöpfen*) wear out; sich k~machen wear oneself out

Kapuze f -,-n hood

Kapuzinerkresse f nasturtium

Karaffe f -,-n carafe; (*mit Stöpsel*) decanter

Karambolage /karambo'la:ʒə/ f -,-n collision

Karamell (**Karamel**) m -s caramel. K~bonbon m & nt ≈ toffee

Karat nt -[e]s,-e carat

Karawane f -,-n caravan

Kardinal m -s,-e cardinal. K~zahl f cardinal number

Karfiol m -s (*Aust*) cauliflower

Karfreitag m Good Friday

karg a (kärger, kärgst) meagre; (*frugal*) frugal; (*spärlich*) sparse; (*unfruchtbar*) barren; (*gering*) scant. k~en vi (*haben*) be sparing (mit with)

kärglich a poor, meagre; (*gering*) scant

Karibik f - Caribbean

kariert a check[ed]; (*Papier*) squared; schottisch k~ tartan

Karik|atur f -,-en caricature; (*Journ*) cartoon. k~ieren vt caricature

karitativ a charitable

Karneval m -s,-e & -s carnival

Karnickel nt -s,- (*dial*) rabbit

Kärnten nt -s Carinthia

Karo nt -s,-s diamond; (*Viereck*) square; (*Muster*) check; (*Kartenspiel*) diamonds pl. K~muster nt check

Karosserie f -,-n bodywork

Karotte f -,-n carrot

Karpfen m -s,- carp

Karre f -,-n = Karren

Karree nt -s,-s square; ums K~ round the block

Karren m -s,- cart; (*Hand-*) barrow. k~ vt cart

Karriere /ka'rjɛ:rə/ f -,-n career; K~ machen get to the top

Karte f -,-n card; (*Eintritts-, Fahr-*) ticket; (*Speise-*) menu; (*Land-*) map

Kartei f -,-en card index. K~karte f index card

Karten|spiel nt card-game; (*Spielkarten*) pack/(*Amer*) deck of cards. K~vorverkauf m advance booking

Kartoffel f -,-n potato. K~brei m, K~püree nt mashed potatoes pl. K~salat m potato salad

Karton /kar'tɔŋ/ m -s,-s cardboard; (*Schachtel*) carton, cardboard box

Karussell nt -s,-s & -e roundabout

Karwoche f Holy Week

Käse m -s,- cheese. K~kuchen m cheesecake

Kaserne f -,-n barracks pl

Kasino nt -s,-s casino

Kasperle nt & m -s,- Punch. K~theater nt Punch and Judy show

Kasse f -,-n till; (*Registrier-*) cash register; (*Zahlstelle*) cash desk; (*im Supermarkt*) check-out; (*Theater-*) box-office; (*Geld*) pool [of money], (*fam*) kitty; (*Kranken-*) health insurance scheme; (*Spar-*) savings bank; knapp/gut bei K~ sein (*fam*) be short of cash/be flush. K~npatient m ≈ NHS patient. K~nschlager m box-office hit. K~nwart m -[e]s,-e treasurer. K~nzettel m receipt

Kasserolle f -,-n saucepan [with one handle]

Kassette f -,-n cassette; (*Film-, Farbband-*) cartridge; (*Geld-*) money-box; (*Schmuck-*) case. K~nrecorder /-rəkɔrdɐ/ m -s,- cassette recorder

kassier|en vi (*haben*) collect the money/(*im Bus*) the fares □ vt collect. K~er(in) m -s,- (f -,-nen) cashier

Kastagnetten /kastan'jɛtən/ *pl* castanets

Kastanie /kas'ta:njə/ *f* -,-n [horse] chestnut, (*fam*) conker. **k∼nbraun** *a* chestnut

Kaste *f* -,-n caste

Kasten *m* -s,- box; (*Brot-*) bin; (*Flaschen-*) crate; (*Brief-*) letter-box; (*Aust: Schrank*) cupboard; (*Kleider-*) wardrobe

kastrieren *vt* castrate; neuter (*Tier*)

Kasus *m* -,- /-u:s/ (*Gram*) case

Katalog *m* -[e]s,-e catalogue. **k∼isieren** *vt* catalogue

Katalysator *m* -s,-en /-'to:rən/ catalyst; (*Auto*) catalytic converter

Katapult *nt* -[e]s,-e catapult. **k∼ieren** *vt* catapult

Katarrh, **Katarr** *m* -s,-e catarrh

katastr|ophal *a* catastrophic. **K∼ophe** *f* -,-n catastrophe

Katechismus *m* - catechism

Kateg|orie *f* -,-n category. **k∼orisch** *a* categorical, *adv* -ly

Kater *m* -s,- tom-cat; (*fam: Katzenjammer*) hangover

Katheder *nt* -s,- [teacher's] desk

Kathedrale *f* -,-n cathedral

Kath|olik(in) *m* -en,-en (*f* -,-nen) Catholic. **k∼olisch** *a* Catholic. **K∼olizismus** *m* - Catholicism

Kätzchen *nt* -s,- kitten; (*Bot*) catkin

Katze *f* -,-n cat. **K∼njammer** *m* (*fam*) hangover. **K∼nsprung** *m* ein **K∼nsprung** (*fam*) a stone's throw

Kauderwelsch *nt* -[s] gibberish

kauen *vt/i* (*haben*) chew; bite (*Nägel*)

kauern *vi* (*haben*) crouch; **sich k∼** crouch down

Kauf *m* -[e]s, Käufe purchase; guter **K∼** bargain; in **K∼ nehmen** (*fig*) put up with. **k∼en** *vt/i* (*haben*) buy; **k∼en bei** shop at

Käufer(in) *m* -s,- (*f* -,-nen) buyer; (*im Geschäft*) shopper

Kauf|haus *nt* department store. **K∼kraft** *f* purchasing power. **K∼laden** *m* shop

käuflich *a* saleable; (*bestechlich*) corruptible; **k∼ sein** be for sale; **k∼ erwerben** buy

Kauf|mann *m* (*pl* -leute) businessman; (*Händler*) dealer; (*dial*) grocer. **k∼männisch** *a* commercial. **K∼preis** *m* purchase price

Kaugummi *m* chewing-gum

Kaulquappe *f* -,-n tadpole

kaum *adv* hardly; **k∼ glaublich** *od* zu **glauben** hard to believe

kauterisieren *vt* cauterize

Kaution /-'tsio:n/ *f* -,-en surety; (*Jur*) bail; (*Miet-*) deposit

Kautschuk *m* -s rubber

Kauz *m* -es, Käuze owl; komischer **K∼** (*fam*) odd fellow

Kavalier *m* -s,-e gentleman

Kavallerie *f* - cavalry

Kaviar *m* -s caviare

keck *a* bold; (*frech*) cheeky

Kegel *m* -s,- skittle; (*Geom*) cone; mit Kind und **K∼** (*fam*) with all the family. **K∼bahn** *f* skittle-alley. **k∼förmig** *a* conical. **k∼n** *vi* (*haben*) play skittles

Kehl|e *f* -,-n throat; aus voller **K∼e** at the top of one's voice; etw in die falsche **K∼e** bekommen (*fam*) take sth the wrong way. **K∼kopf** *m* larynx. **K∼kopfentzündung** *f* laryngitis

Kehr|e *f* -,-n [hairpin] bend. **k∼en** *vi* (*haben*) (*fegen*) sweep □ *vt* sweep; (*wenden*) turn; den Rücken **k∼en** turn one's back (*dat* on); sich **k∼en** turn; sich nicht **k∼en an** (+ *acc*) not care about. **K∼icht** *m* -[e]s sweepings *pl*. **K∼reim** *m* refrain. **K∼seite** *f* (*fig*) drawback; die **K∼seite der Medaille** the other side of the coin. **k∼tmachen** *vi sep* (*haben*) turn back; (*sich umdrehen*) turn round. **K∼twendung** *f* about-turn; (*fig*) U-turn

keifen *vi* (*haben*) scold

Keil *m* -[e]s,-e wedge

Keil|e *f* - (*fam*) hiding. **k∼n** (sich) *vr* (*fam*) fight. **K∼rei** *f* -,-en (*fam*) punch-up

Keil|kissen *nt* [wedge-shaped] bolster. **K∼riemen** *m* fan belt

Keim *m* -[e]s,-e (*Bot*) sprout; (*Med*) germ; im **K∼ ersticken** (*fig*) nip in the bud. **k∼en** *vi* (*haben*) germinate; (*austreiben*) sprout. **k∼frei** *a* sterile

kein *pron* no; not a; auf **k∼en Fall** on no account; **k∼e fünf Minuten** less than five minutes. **k∼e(r,s)** *pron* no one, nobody; (*Ding*) none, not one. **k∼esfalls** *adv* on no account. **k∼eswegs** *adv* by no means. **k∼mal** *adv* not once. **k∼s** *pron* none, not one

Keks *m* -[es],-[e] biscuit, (*Amer*) cookie

Kelch *m* -[e]s,-e goblet, cup; (*Relig*) chalice; (*Bot*) calyx

Kelle *f* -,-n ladle; (*Maurer-*, *Pflanz-*) trowel

Keller *m* -s,- cellar. **K∼ei** *f* -,-en winery. **K∼geschoss** (**K∼geschoß**) *nt* cellar; (*bewohnbar*) basement. **K∼wohnung** *f* basement flat

Kellner *m* -s,- waiter. **K∼in** *f* -,-nen waitress

keltern *vt* press

keltisch *a* Celtic

Kenia *nt* -s Kenya

kenn|en† *vt* know; **k∼en lernen** get to know; (*treffen*) meet; **sich k∼en lernen**

meet; *(näher)* get to know one another. k∼enlernen *vt sep* NEW k∼en lernen, *s.* kennen. K∼er *m* -s,-, K∼erin *f* -,-nen connoisseur; *(Experte)* expert. K∼melodie *f* signature tune. k∼tlich a recognizable; k∼tlich machen mark. K∼tnis *f* -,-se knowledge; zur K∼tnis nehmen take note of; in K∼tnis setzen inform (von of). K∼wort *nt* (*pl* -wörter) reference; *(geheimes)* password. K∼zeichen *nt* distinguishing mark *or* feature; *(Merkmal)* characteristic, *(Markierung)* mark, marking; *(Abzeichen)* badge; *(Auto)* registration. k∼zeichnen *vt* distinguish; *(markieren)* mark. k∼zeichnend *a* typical (für of). K∼ziffer *f* reference number

kentern *vi (sein)* capsize

Keramik *f* -,-en pottery, ceramics *sg*; *(Gegenstand)* piece of pottery

Kerbe *f* -,-n notch

Kerbholz *nt* etwas auf dem K∼ haben *(fam)* have a record

Kerker *m* -s,- dungeon; *(Gefängnis)* prison

Kerl *m* -s,-e & -s *(fam)* fellow, bloke

Kern *m* -s,-e pip; *(Kirsch-)* stone; *(Nuss-)* kernel; *(Techn)* core; *(Atom-, Zell- & fig)* nucleus; *(Stadt-)* centre; *(einer Sache)* heart. K∼energie *f* nuclear energy. K∼gehäuse *nt* core. k∼gesund a perfectly healthy. k∼ig a robust; *(Ausspruch)* pithy. k∼los a seedless. K∼physik *f* nuclear physics *sg*

Kerze *f* -,-n candle. k∼ngerade a & adv straight. K∼nhalter *m* -s,- candlestick

kess (keß) a (kesser, kessest) pert

Kessel *m* -s,- kettle; *(Heiz-)* boiler. K∼stein *m* fur

Ketchup (Ketchup) /ˈkɛtʃap/ *m* -[s],-s ketchup

Kette *f* -,-n chain; *(Hals-)* necklace. k∼n *vt* chain (an + *acc* to). K∼nladen *m* chain store. K∼nraucher *m* chain-smoker. K∼nreaktion *f* chain reaction

Ketze|r(in) *m* -s,- (*f* -,-nen) heretic. K∼rei *f* - heresy

keuch|en *vi (haben)* pant. K∼husten *m* whooping cough

Keule *f* -,-n club; *(Culin)* leg; *(Hühner-)* drumstick

keusch a chaste. K∼heit *f* - chastity

Kfz *abbr s.* Kraftfahrzeug

Khaki *nt* - khaki. k∼farben a khaki

kichern *vi (haben)* giggle

Kiefer[1] *m* -s,- pine[-tree]

Kiefer[2] *m* -s,- jaw

Kiel *m* -s,-e *(Naut)* keel. K∼wasser *nt* wake

Kiemen *fpl* gills

Kies *m* -es gravel. K∼el *m* -s,-, K∼elstein *m* pebble. K∼grube *f* gravel pit

Kilo *nt* -s,-[s] kilo. K∼gramm *nt* kilogram. K∼hertz *nt* kilohertz. K∼meter *m* kilometre. K∼meterstand *m* ≈ mileage. K∼watt *nt* kilowatt

Kind *nt* -es,-er child; von K∼ auf from childhood

Kinder|arzt *m*, K∼ärztin *f* paediatrician. K∼bett *nt* child's cot. K∼ei *f* -,-en childish prank. K∼garten *m* nursery school. K∼gärtnerin *f* nursery-school teacher. K∼geld *nt* child benefit. K∼gottesdienst *m* Sunday school. K∼lähmung *f* polio. k∼leicht a very easy. k∼los a childless. K∼mädchen *nt* nanny. k∼reich a k∼reiche Familie large family. K∼reim *m* nursery rhyme. K∼spiel *nt* children's game; das ist ein/kein K∼spiel that is dead easy/not easy. K∼tagesstätte *f* day nursery. K∼teller *m* children's menu. K∼wagen *m* pram, *(Amer)* baby carriage. K∼zimmer *nt* child's/children's room; *(für Baby)* nursery

Kind|heit *f* - childhood. k∼isch a childish, puerile. k∼lich a childlike

kinetisch a kinetic

Kinn *nt* -[e]s,-e chin. K∼lade *f* jaw

Kino *nt* -s,-s cinema

Kiosk *m* -[e]s,-e kiosk

Kippe *f* -,-n *(Müll-)* dump; *(fam: Zigaretten-)* fag-end; auf der K∼ stehen *(fam)* be in a precarious position; *(unsicher sein)* hang in the balance. k∼lig a wobbly. k∼ln *vi (haben)* wobble. k∼n *vt* tilt; *(schütten)* tip (in + *acc* into) □ *vi (sein)* topple

Kirch|e *f* -,-n church. K∼enbank *f* pew. K∼endiener *m* verger. K∼enlied *nt* hymn. K∼enschiff *nt* nave. K∼hof *m* churchyard. k∼lich a church … □ adv k∼lich getraut werden be married in church. K∼turm *m* church tower, steeple. K∼weih *f* -,-en [village] fair

Kirmes *f* -,-sen = Kirchweih

Kirsch|e *f* -,-n cherry. K∼wasser *nt* kirsch

Kissen *nt* -s,- cushion; *(Kopf-)* pillow

Kiste *f* -,-n crate; *(Zigarren-)* box

Kitsch *m* -es sentimental rubbish; *(Kunst)* kitsch. k∼ig a slushy; *(Kunst)* kitschy

Kitt *m* -s [adhesive] cement; *(Fenster-)* putty

Kittel *m* -s,- overall, smock; *(Arzt-, Labor-)* white coat

kitten *vt* stick; *(fig)* cement

Kitz *nt* -es,-e *(Zool)* kid

Kitz|el *m* -s,- tickle; *(Nerven-)* thrill. k∼eln *vt/i (haben)* tickle. k∼lig a ticklish

Kladde f -,-n notebook

klaffen vi (haben) gape

kläffen vi (haben) yap

Klage f -,-n lament; (Beschwerde) complaint; (Jur) action. k~n vi (haben) lament; (sich beklagen) complain; (Jur) sue

Kläger(in) m -s,- (f -,-nen) (Jur) plaintiff

kläglich a pitiful, adv -ly; (erbärmlich) miserable, adv -bly

klamm a cold and damp; (steif) stiff. K~ f -,-en (Geog) gorge

Klammer f -,-n (Wäsche-) peg; (Büro-) paper-clip; (Heft-) staple; (Haar-) grip; (für Zähne) brace; (Techn) clamp; (Typ) bracket. k~n (sich) vr cling (an + acc to)

Klang m -[e]s,-e sound; (K~farbe) tone. k~voll a resonant; (Stimme) sonorous

Klapp|bett nt folding bed. K~e f -,-n flap; (fam: Mund) trap. k~en vt fold; (hoch-) tip up □ vi (haben) (fam) work out. K~entext m blurb

Klapper f -,-n rattle. k~n vi (haben) rattle. K~schlange f rattlesnake

klapprig a rickety; (schwach) decrepit. K~stuhl m folding chair. K~tisch m folding table

Klaps m -es,-e pat; (strafend) smack. k~en vt smack

klar a clear; k~ werden clear; (fig) become clear (dat to); sich (dat) k~ werden make up one's mind; (erkennen) realize (dass that); sich (dat) k~ od im K~en (k~en) sein realize (dass that) □ adv clearly; (fam: natürlich) of course. K~e(r) m (fam) schnapps

klären vt clarify; sich k~ clear; (fig: sich lösen) resolve itself

Klarheit f - clarity

Klarinette f -,-n clarinet

klar|machen vt sep make clear (dat to); sich (dat) etw k~machen understand sth. K~sichtfolie f transparent/(haftend) cling film. k~stellen vt sep clarify

Klärung f - clarification

klarwerden† vi sep (sein) (NEW) klar werden, s. klar

Klasse f -,-n class; (Sch) class, form, (Amer) grade; (Zimmer) classroom; erster/zweiter K~ reisen travel first/second class. k~ inv a (fam) super. K~narbeit f [written] test. K~nbuch nt ≈ register. K~nkamerad(in) m(f) classmate. K~nkampf m class struggle. K~nzimmer nt classroom

klassifizier|en vt classify. K~ung f -,-en classification

Klass|ik f - classicism; (Epoche) classical period. K~iker m -s,- classical author/(Mus) composer. k~isch a classical; (mustergültig, typisch) classic

Klatsch m -[e]s gossip. K~base f (fam) gossip. k~en vt slap; Beifall k~en applaud □ vi (haben) make a slapping sound; (im Wasser) splash; (tratschen) gossip; (applaudieren) clap; [in die Hände] k~en clap one's hands □ vi (haben/sein) slap (gegen against). K~maul nt gossip. k~nass (k~naß) a (fam) soaking wet

klauben vt pick

Klaue f -,-n claw; (fam: Schrift) scrawl. k~n vt/i (haben) (fam) steal

Klausel f -,-n clause

Klaustrophobie f - claustrophobia

Klausur f -,-en (Univ) [examination] paper; (Sch) written test

Klaviatur f -,-en keyboard

Klavier nt -s,-e piano. K~spieler(in) m(f) pianist

kleb|en vt stick (mit Klebstoff) glue (an + acc to) □ vi (haben) stick (an + dat to). k~rig a sticky. K~stoff m adhesive, glue. K~streifen m adhesive tape

kleckern vi (haben) (fam) = klecksen

Klecks m -es,-e stain; (Tinten-) blot; (kleine Menge) dab. k~en vi (haben) make a mess

Klee m -s clover. K~blatt nt clover leaf

Kleid nt -[e]s,-er dress; K~er dresses; (Kleidung) clothes. k~en vt dress; (gut stehen) suit; sich k~en dress. K~erbügel m coat-hanger. K~erbürste f clothesbrush. K~erhaken m coat-hook. K~errock m pinafore dress. K~erschrank m wardrobe, (Amer) clothes closet. k~sam a becoming. K~ung f - clothes pl, clothing. K~ungsstück nt garment

Kleie f - bran

klein a small, little; (von kleinem Wuchs) short; k~ hacken/schneiden chop/cut up small or into small pieces; k~ geschrieben werden (fig) count for very little (bei jdm with s.o.); von k~ auf from childhood. K~arbeit f painstaking work. K~bus m minibus. K~e(r,s) m/f/nt little one. K~geld nt [small] change. k~hacken vt sep (NEW) k~ hacken, s. klein. K~handel m retail trade. K~heit f - smallness; (Wuchs) short stature. K~holz nt firewood. K~igkeit f -,-en trifle; (Mahl) snack. K~kind nt infant. K~kram m (fam) odds and ends pl; (Angelegenheiten) trivia pl. k~laut a subdued. k~lich a petty. K~lichkeit f - pettiness. k~mütig a faint-hearted

Kleinod nt -[e]s,-e jewel

klein|schneiden† vt sep (NEW) k~ schneiden, s. klein. k~schreiben† vt sep write with a small [initial] letter; k~geschrieben werden (fig) (NEW) k~ geschrieben werden, s. klein. K~stadt f small town. k~städtisch a provincial. K~wagen m small car

Kleister m -s paste. k~n vt paste

Klemme f -,-n [hair-]grip; in der K~sitzen (fam) be in a fix. k~n vt jam; sich (dat) den Finger k~n get one's finger caught □ vi (haben) jam, stick

Klempner m -s,- plumber

Klerus (der) - the clergy

Klette f -,-n burr; wie eine K~ (fig) like a limpet

klettern vi (sein) climb. K~pflanze f climber. K~rose f climbing rose

Klettverschluss (Klettverschluß) m Velcro (P) fastening

klicken vi (haben) click

Klient(in) /kli'ɛnt(ɪn)/ m -en,-en (f -,-nen) (Jur) client

Kliff nt -[e]s,-e cliff

Klima nt -s climate. K~anlage f air-conditioning

klimatisch a climatic. k~isiert a air-conditioned

klimpern vi (haben) jingle; k~ auf (+ dat) tinkle on (Klavier); strum (Gitarre)

Klinge f -,-n blade

Klingel f -,-n bell. k~n vi (haben) ring; es k~t there's a ring at the door

klingen† vi (haben) sound

Klinik f -,-en clinic. k~sch a clinical, adv -ly

Klinke f -,-n [door] handle

klipp pred a k~ und klar quite plain, adv -ly

Klipp m -s,-s = Klips

Klippe f -,-n [submerged] rock

Klips m -es,-e clip; (Ohr-) clip-on ear-ring

klirren vi (haben) rattle; (Geschirr, Glas:) chink

Klischee nt -s,-s cliché

Klo nt -s,-s (fam) loo, (Amer) john

klobig a clumsy

klönen vi (haben) (NGer fam) chat

klopf|en vi (haben) knock; (leicht) tap; (Herz:) pound; es k~te there was a knock at the door □ vt beat; (ein-) knock

Klops m -es,-e meatball; (Brat-) rissole

Klosett nt -s,-s lavatory

Kloß m -es,¨e dumpling; ein K~ im Hals (fam) a lump in one's throat

Kloster nt -s,¨ monastery; (Nonnen-) convent

klösterlich a monastic

Klotz m -es,¨e block

Klub m -s,-s club

Kluft¹ f -,¨e cleft; (fig: Gegensatz) gulf

Kluft² f -,-en outfit; (Uniform) uniform

klug a (klüger, klügst) intelligent, adv -ly; (schlau) clever, adv -ly; nicht k~ werden aus nt understand. K~heit f - cleverness

Klump|en m -s,- lump. k~en vi (haben) go lumpy

knabbern vt/i (haben) nibble

Knabe m -n,-n boy. k~nhaft a boyish

Knäckebrot nt crispbread

knack|en vt/i (haben) crack. K~s m -es,-e crack; einen K~s haben be cracked/(fam: verrückt sein) crackers

Knall m -[e]s,-e bang. K~bonbon m cracker. k~en vi (haben) go bang; (Peitsche:) crack □ vt (fam: werfen) chuck; jdm eine k~en (fam) clout s.o. k~ig a (fam) gaudy. k~rot a bright red

knapp a (gering) scant; (kurz) short; (mangelnd) scarce; (gerade ausreichend) bare; (eng) tight; ein k~es Pfund just under a pound; jdn k~ halten (fam) keep s.o. short (mit of). k~halten† vt sep (NEW) k~ halten, s. knapp. K~heit f - scarcity

Knarre f -,-n rattle. k~n vi (haben) creak

Knast m -[e]s (fam) prison

knattern vi (haben) crackle; (Gewehr:) stutter

Knäuel m & nt -s,- ball

Knauf m -[e]s,Knäufe knob

knauser|ig a (fam) stingy. k~n vi (haben) (fam) be stingy

knautschen vt (fam) crumple □ vi (haben) crease

Knebel m -s,- gag. k~n vt gag

Knecht m -[e]s,-e farm-hand; (fig) slave. k~en vt (fig) enslave. K~schaft f - (fig) slavery

kneif|en† vt pinch □ vi (haben) pinch; (fam: sich drücken) chicken out. K~zange f pincers pl

Kneipe f -,-n (fam) pub, (Amer) bar

knet|en vt knead; (formen) mould. K~masse f Plasticine (P)

Knick m -[e]s,-e bend; (im Draht) kink; (Kniff) crease. k~en vt bend; (kniffen) fold; geknickt sein (fam) be dejected. k~[e]rig a stingy

Knicks m -es,-e curtsy. k~en vi (haben) curtsy

Knie nt -s,- /'kni:ə/ knee. K~bundhose f knee-breeches pl. K~kehle f hollow of the knee

knien /'kni:ən/ vi (haben) kneel □ vr sich k~ kneel [down]

Knie|scheibe f kneecap. K~strumpf m knee-length sock

Kniff m -[e]s,-e pinch; (Falte) crease; (fam: Trick) trick. k~en vt fold. k~[e]lig a (fam) tricky

knipsen vt (lochen) punch; (Phot) photograph □ vi (haben) take a photograph/photographs

Knirps m -es,-e (fam) little chap; (P) (Schirm) telescopic umbrella

knirschen vi (haben) grate; (Schnee, Kies:) crunch; mit den Zähnen k~ grind one's teeth

knistern vi (haben) crackle; (Papier:) rustle

Knitter|falte f crease. k~frei a crease-resistant. k~n vi (haben) crease

knobeln vi (haben) toss (um for); (fam: überlegen) puzzle

Knoblauch m -s garlic

Knöchel m -s,- ankle; (Finger-) knuckle

Knochen m -s,- bone. K~mark nt bone marrow. k~trocken a bone-dry

knochig a bony

Knödel m -s,- (SGer) dumpling

Knolle f -,-n tuber. k~ig a bulbous

Knopf m -[e]s,-e button; (Kragen-) stud; (Griff) knob

knöpfen vt button

Knopfloch nt buttonhole

Knorpel m -s gristle; (Anat) cartilage

knorrig a gnarled

Knospe f bud

Knötchen nt -s,- nodule

Knoten m -s,- knot; (Med) lump; (Haar-) bun, chignon. k~ vt knot. K~punkt m junction

knotig a knotty; (Hände) gnarled

knuffen vt poke

knüll|en vt crumple □ vi (haben) crease. K~er m -s,- (fam) sensation

knüpfen vt knot; (verbinden) attach (an + acc to)

Knüppel m -s,- club; (Gummi-) truncheon

knurr|en vi (haben) growl; (Magen:) rumble; (fam: schimpfen) grumble. k~ig a grumpy

knusprig a crunchy, crisp

knutschen vi (haben) (fam) smooch

k.o. /ka'?o:/ a k.o. schlagen knock out; k.o. sein (fam) be worn out. K.o. m -s,-s knock-out

Koalition /koali'tsjo:n/ f -,-en coalition

Kobold m -[e]s,-e goblin, imp

Koch m -[e]s,-e cook; (im Restaurant) chef. K~buch nt cookery book, (Amer) cookbook. k~en vt cook; (sieden) boil; (Kaffee, Tee) make □ vi (haben) cook; (sieden) boil; (fam) seethe (vor + dat with). K~en nt -s cooking; (Sieden) boiling; zum K~en bringen/kommen bring/come to the boil. k~end a boiling □ adv k~end heiß boiling hot. K~er m -s,- cooker. K~gelegenheit f cooking facilities pl. K~herd m cooker, stove

Köchin f -,-nen [woman] cook

Koch|kunst f cookery. K~löffel m wooden spoon. K~nische f kitchenette. K~platte f hotplate. K~topf m saucepan

Kode /ko:t/ m -s,-s code

Köder m -s,- bait

Koexist|enz /'ko:?eksistɛnts/ f coexistence. k~ieren vi (haben) coexist

Koffein /kɔfe'i:n/ nt -s caffeine. k~frei a decaffeinated

Koffer m -s,- suitcase. K~kuli m luggage trolley. K~radio nt portable radio. K~raum m (Auto) boot, (Amer) trunk

Kognak /'kɔnjak/ m -s,-s brandy

Kohl m -[e]s cabbage

Kohle f -,-n coal. K~[n]hydrat nt -[e]s,-e carbohydrate. K~nbergwerk nt coalmine, colliery. K~ndioxid nt carbon dioxide. K~ngrube f = K~nbergwerk. K~nherd m [kitchen] range. K~nsäure f carbon dioxide. K~nstoff m carbon. K~papier nt carbon paper

Kohl|kopf m cabbage. K~rabi m -[s],-[s] kohlrabi. K~rübe f swede

Koje f -,-n (Naut) bunk

Kokain /koka'i:n/ nt -s cocaine

kokett a flirtatious. k~ieren vi (haben) flirt

Kokon /ko'kõ:/ m -s,-s cocoon

Kokosnuss (Kokosnuß) f coconut

Koks m -es coke

Kolben m -s,- (Gewehr-) butt; (Mais-) cob; (Techn) piston; (Chem) flask

Kolibri m -s,-s humming-bird

Kolik f -,-en colic

Kollabora|teur /-'tø:ɐ̯/ m -s,-e collaborator. K~tion /-'tsjo:n/ f collaboration

Kolleg nt -s,-s & -ien /-jən/ (Univ) course of lectures

Kolleg|e m -n,-n, K~in f -,-nen colleague. K~ium nt -s,-ien staff

Kollekt|e f -,-n (Relig) collection. K~ion /-'tsjo:n/ f -,-en collection. k~iv a collective. K~ivum nt -s,-va collective noun

kolli|dieren vi (sein) collide. K~sion f -,-en collision

Köln nt -s Cologne. K~ischwasser, K~isch Wasser nt eau-de-Cologne

Kolonialwaren fpl groceries

Kolon|ie f -,-n colony. k~isieren vt colonize

Kolonne f -,-n column; (Mil) convoy

Koloss m -es,-e (Koloß m -sses,-sse) giant

kolossal a enormous, adv -ly

Kolumne f -,-n (Journ) column

Koma nt -s,-s coma

Kombi m -s,-s = K~wagen. K~nation /-'tsio:n/ f -,-en combination; (Folgerung) deduction; (Kleidung) co-ordinating outfit. k~nieren vt combine; (fig) reason; (folgern) deduce. K~wagen m estate car, (Amer) station-wagon

Kombüse f -,-n (Naut) galley

Komet m -en,-en comet. k~enhaft a (fig) meteoric

Komfort /kɔm'foːɐ̯/ m -s comfort; (Luxus) luxury. k~abel /-'taːbəl/ a comfortable, adv -bly; (luxuriös) luxurious, adv -ly

Komik f - humour. K~er m -s,- comic, comedian

komisch a funny; ⟨Oper⟩ comic; (sonderbar) odd, funny □ adv funnily; oddly. k~erweise adv funnily enough

Komitee nt -s,-s committee

Komma nt -s,-s & -ta comma; (Dezimal-) decimal point; drei K~ fünf three point five

Komman|dant m -en,-en commanding officer. K~deur /-'døːɐ̯/ m -s,-e commander. k~dieren vt command; (befehlen) order; (fam: herum-) order about □ vi (haben) give the orders

Kommando nt -s,-s order; (Befehlsgewalt) command; (Einheit) detachment. K~brücke f bridge

kommen† vi (sein) come; (eintreffen) arrive; (gelangen) get (nach to); k~ lassen send for; auf/hinter etw (acc) k~ think of/find out about sth; um/zu etw k~ lose/acquire sth; wieder zu sich k~ come round; wie kommt das? why is that? K~ nt -s coming; K~ und Gehen coming and going. k~d a coming; k~den Montag next Monday

Kommen|tar m -s,-e commentary; (Bemerkung) comment. K~tator m -s,-en /-'toːrən/ commentator. k~tieren vt comment on

kommer|zialisieren vt commercialize. k~ziell a commercial, adv -ly

Kommili|tone m -n,-n, K~tonin f -,-nen fellow student

Kommiss m -es (Kommiß m -sses) (fam) army

Kommissar m -s,-e commissioner; (Polizei-) superintendent

Kommission f -,-en commission; (Gremium) committee

Kommode f -,-n chest of drawers

Kommunalwahlen fpl local elections

Kommunikation /-'tsio:n/ f -,-en communication

Kommunikee /kɔmyni'keː/ nt -s,-s = Kommuniqué

Kommunion f -,-en [Holy] Communion

Kommuniqué /kɔmyni'keː/ nt -s,-s communiqué

Kommun|ismus m - Communism. K~ist(in) m -en,-en (f -,-nen) Communist. k~istisch a Communist

kommunizieren vi (haben) receive [Holy] Communion

Komödie /ko'møːdjə/ f -,-n comedy

Kompagnon /'kɔmpanjoː/ m -s,-s (Comm) partner

kompakt a compact. K~schallplatte f compact disc

Kompanie f -,-n (Mil) company

Komparativ m -s,-e comparative

Komparse m -n,-n (Theat) extra

Kompass m -es,-e (Kompaß m -sses,-sse) compass

kompatibel a compatible

kompeten|t a competent. K~z f -,-en competence

komplett a complete, adv -ly

Komplex m -es,-e complex. k~ a complex

Komplikation /-'tsio:n/ f -,-en complication

Kompliment nt -[e]s,-e compliment

Komplize m -n,-n accomplice

komplizier|en vt complicate. k~t a complicated

Komplott nt -[e]s,-e plot

kompo|nieren vt/i (haben) compose. K~nist m -en,-en composer. K~sition /-'tsio:n/ f -,-en composition

Kompositum nt -s,-ta compound

Kompost m -[e]s compost

Kompott nt -[e]s,-e stewed fruit

Kompresse f -,-n compress

komprimieren vt compress

Kompromiss m -es,-e (Kompromiß m -sses,-sse) compromise; einen K~ schließen compromise. k~los a uncompromising

kompromittieren vt compromise

Konden|sation /-'tsio:n/ f - condensation. k~sieren vt condense

Kondensmilch f evaporated/(gesüßt) condensed milk

Kondition /-'tsio:n/ f - (Sport) fitness; in K~ in form. K~al m -s,-e (Gram) conditional

Konditor m -s,-en /-'to:rən/ confectioner. K~ei f -,-en patisserie

Kondolenzbrief m letter of condolence. k~lieren vi (haben) express one's condolences

Kondom nt & m -s,-e condom

Konfekt nt -[e]s confectionery; (Pralinen) chocolates pl

Konfektion /-'tsjo:n/ f - ready-to-wear clothes pl

Konferenz f -,-en conference; (Besprechung) meeting

Konfession f -,-en [religious] denomination. k~ell a denominational. k~slos a non-denominational

Konfetti nt -s confetti

Konfirm|and(in) m -en,-en (f -,-nen) candidate for confirmation. K~ation /-'tsjo:n/ f -,-en (Relig) confirmation. k~ieren vt (Relig) confirm

Konfitüre f -,-n jam

Konflikt m -[e]s,-e conflict

Konföderation /-'tsjo:n/ f confederation

Konfront|ation /-'tsjo:n/ f -,-en confrontation. k~ieren vt confront

konfus a confused

Kongress m -es,-e (Kongreß m -sses,-sse) congress

König m -s,-e king. K~in f -,-nen queen. k~lich a royal, adv -ly; (hoheitsvoll) regal, adv -ly; (großzügig) handsome, adv -ly; (fam: groß) tremendous, adv -ly. K~reich nt kingdom

konisch a conical

Konjug|ation /-'tsjo:n/ f -,-en conjugation. k~ieren vt conjugate

Konjunktion /-'tsjo:n/ f -,-en (Gram) conjunction

Konjunktiv m -s,-e subjunctive

Konjunktur f - economic situation; (Hoch-) boom

konkav a concave

konkret a concrete

Konkurren|t(in) m -en,-en (f -,-nen) competitor, rival. K~z f - competition; jdm K~z machen compete with s.o. k~zfähig a (Comm) competitive. K~zkampf m competition, rivalry

konkurrieren vi (haben) compete

Konkurs m -es,-e bankruptcy; K~ machen go bankrupt

können† vt/i (haben) etw k~ be able to do sth; (beherrschen) know sth; k~ Sie Deutsch? do you know any German? das kann ich nicht I can't do that; der kann nicht mehr he can't go on; für etw nichts k~ not be to blame for sth □ v aux lesen/schwimmen k~ be able to read/ swim; er kann/konnte es tun he can/ could do it; das kann od könnte [gut] sein that may [well] be. K~ nt -s ability; (Wissen) knowledge.

Könner(in) m -s,- (f -,-nen) expert

konsequen|t a consistent, adv -ly; (logisch) logical, adv -ly. K~z f -,-en consequence

konservativ a conservative

Konserv|en fpl tinned or canned food sg. K~enbüchse, K~endose f tin, can. k~ieren vt preserve; (in Dosen) tin, can. K~ierungsmittel nt preservative

Konsistenz f - consistency

konsolidieren vt consolidate

Konsonant m -en,-en consonant

konsterniert a dismayed

Konstitution /-'tsjo:n/ f -,-en constitution. k~ell a constitutional

konstruieren vt construct; (entwerfen) design

Konstruk|tion /-'tsjo:n/ f -,-en construction; (Entwurf) design. k~tiv a constructive

Konsul m -s,-n consul. K~at nt -[e]s,-e consulate

Konsult|ation /-'tsjo:n/ f -,-en consultation. k~ieren vt consult

Konsum m -s consumption. K~ent m -en,-en consumer. K~güter ntpl consumer goods

Kontakt m -[e]s,-e contact. K~linsen fpl contact lenses. K~person f contact

kontern vt/i (haben) counter

Kontinent /'kon-, konti'nɛnt/ m -[e]s,-e continent

Kontingent nt -[e]s,-e (Comm) quota; (Mil) contingent

Kontinuität f - continuity

Konto nt -s,-s account. K~auszug m [bank] statement. K~nummer f account number. K~stand m [bank] balance

Kontrabass (Kontrabaß) m double-bass

Kontrast m -[e]s,-e contrast

Kontroll|abschnitt m counterfoil. K~e f -,-n control; (Prüfung) check. K~eur /-'løːɐ/ m -s,-e [ticket] inspector. k~ieren vt check; inspect (Fahrkarten); (beherrschen) control

Kontroverse f -,-n controversy

Kontur f -,-en contour

Konvention /-'tsjo:n/ f -,-en convention. k~ell a conventional, adv -ly

Konversation /-'tsjo:n/ f -,-en conversation. K~slexikon nt encyclopaedia

konvert|ieren vi (haben) (Relig) convert. K~it m -en,-en convert

konvex a convex

Konvoi /kɔn'vɔy/ m -s,-s convoy

Konzentr|ation /-'tsjo:n/ f -,-en concentration. K~slager nt concentration camp

konzentrieren vt concentrate; sich k~ concentrate (auf + acc on)

Konzept nt -[e]s,-e [rough] draft; jdn aus dem K~ bringen put s.o. off his stroke. K~papier nt rough paper

Konzern m -s,-e (Comm) group [of companies]

Konzert nt -[e]s,-e concert; (Klavier-, Geigen-) concerto. K~meister m leader, (Amer) concertmaster

Konzession f -,-en licence; (Zugeständnis) concession

Konzil nt -s,-e (Relig) council

Kooperation /koˀopəraˈtsjoːn/ f cooperation

Koordin|ation /koˀˀordinaˈtsjoːn/ f - coordination. k~ieren vt co-ordinate

Kopf m -[e]s,ˉe head; ein K~ Kohl/Salat a cabbage/lettuce; aus dem K~ from memory; (auswendig) by heart; auf dem K~ (verkehrt) upside down; K~ an K~ neck and neck; (stehen) shoulder to shoulder; K~ stehen stand on one's head; sich (dat) den K~ waschen wash one's hair; sich (dat) den K~ zerbrechen rack one's brains. K~ball m header. K~bedeckung f head-covering

Köpf|chen nt -s,- little head; K~chen haben (fam) be clever. k~en vt behead; (Fußball) head

Kopf|ende nt head. K~haut f scalp. K~hörer m headphones pl. K~kissen nt pillow. K~kissenbezug m pillow-case. k~los a panic-stricken. K~nicken nt -s nod. K~rechnen nt mental arithmetic. K~salat m lettuce. K~schmerzen mpl headache sg. K~schütteln nt -s shake of the head. K~sprung m header, dive. K~stand m headstand. K~steinpflaster nt cobble-stones pl. K~stütze f head-rest. K~tuch nt headscarf. k~über adv head first; (fig) headlong. K~wäsche f shampoo. K~weh nt headache. K~zerbrechen nt -s sich (dat) K~zerbrechen machen rack one's brains; (sich sorgen) worry

Kopie f -,-n copy. k~ren vt copy

Koppel[1] f -,-n enclosure; (Pferde-) paddock

Koppel[2] nt -s,- (Mil) belt. k~n vt couple

Koralle f -,-n coral

Korb m -[e]s,ˉe basket; jdm einen K~ geben (fig) turn s.o. down. K~ball m [kind of] netball. K~stuhl m wicker chair

Kord m -s (Tex) corduroy

Kordel f -,-n cord

Korinthe f -,-n currant

Kork m -s,- cork. K~en m -s,- cork. K~enzieher m -s,- corkscrew

Korn[1] nt -[e]s,ˉer grain, (Samen-) seed; (coll: Getreide) grain, corn; (am Visier) front sight

Korn[2] m -[e]s,- (fam) grain schnapps

Körn|chen nt -s,- granule. k~ig a granular

Körper m -s,- body; (Geom) solid. K~bau m build, physique. k~behindert a physically disabled. k~lich a physical, adv -ly; (Strafe) corporal. K~pflege f personal hygiene. K~puder m talcum powder. K~schaft f -,-en corporation, body. K~strafe f corporal punishment. K~teil m part of the body

Korps /koːɐ̯/ nt -,- /-[s],-s/ corps

korpulent a corpulent

korrekt a correct, adv -ly. K~or m -s,-en /-ˈtoːrən/ proof-reader. K~ur f -,-en correction. K~urabzug, K~urbogen m proof

Korrespon|dent(in) m -en,-en (f -,-nen) correspondent. K~denz f -,-en correspondence. k~dieren vi (haben) correspond

Korridor m -s,-e corridor

korrigieren vt correct

Korrosion f - corrosion

korrumpieren vt corrupt

korrup|t a corrupt. K~tion /-ˈtsjoːn/ f - corruption

Korsett nt -[e]s,-e corset

koscher a kosher

Kose|name m pet name. K~wort nt (pl -wörter) term of endearment

Kosmet|ik f - beauty culture. K~ika ntpl cosmetics. K~ikerin f -,-nen beautician. k~isch a cosmetic; (Chirurgie) plastic

kosm|isch a cosmic. K~onaut(in) m -en,-en (f -,-nen) cosmonaut. k~opolitisch a cosmopolitan

Kosmos m - cosmos

Kost f - food; (Ernährung) diet; (Verpflegung) board

kostbar a precious. K~keit f -,-en treasure

kosten[1] vt/i (haben) [von] etw k~ taste sth

kosten[2] vt cost; (brauchen) take; wie viel kostet es? how much is it? K~ pl expense sg, cost sg; (Jur) costs; auf meine K~ at my expense. K~[vor]anschlag m estimate. k~los a free a adv free (of charge)

Kosthappen m taste

köstlich a delicious; (entzückend) delightful. K~keit f -,-en (fig) gem; (Culin) delicacy

Kost|probe f taste; (fig) sample. k~spielig a expensive, costly

Kostüm nt -s,-e (Theat) costume; (Verkleidung) fancy dress; (Schneider-) suit. K~fest nt fancy-dress party. k~iert a k~iert sein be in fancy dress

Kot m -[e]s excrement; (*Schmutz*) dirt

Kotelett /kɔt'lɛt/ nt -s,-s chop, cutlet. **K~en** pl sideburns

Köter m -s,- (*pej*) dog

Kotflügel m (*Auto*) wing, (*Amer*) fender

kotzen vi (*haben*) (*sl*) throw up; **es ist zum K~** it makes you sick

Krabbe f -,-n crab; (*Garnele*) shrimp; (*rote*) prawn

krabbeln vi (*sein*) crawl

Krach m -[e]s,-̈e (*Knall*) crash; (*fam: Streit*) row; (*fam: Ruin*) crash. **k~en** vi (*haben*) crash; **es hat gekracht** there was a bang/(*fam: Unfall*) a crash □ (*sein*) break, crack; (*auftreffen*) crash (*gegen* into)

krächzen vi (*haben*) croak

Kraft f -,-̈e strength; (*Gewalt*) force; (*Arbeits-*) worker; **in/außer K~** in/no longer in force; **in K~ treten** come into force. **k~** prep (+ gen) by virtue of. **K~ausdruck** m swear-word. **K~fahrer** m driver. **K~fahrzeug** nt motor vehicle. **K~fahrzeugbrief** m [vehicle] registration document

kräftig a strong; (*gut entwickelt*) sturdy; (*nahrhaft*) nutritious; (*heftig*) hard □ adv strongly; (*heftig*) hard. **k~en** vt strengthen

kraft|los a weak. **K~post** f post bus service. **K~probe** f trial of strength. **K~rad** nt motorcycle. **K~stoff** m (*Auto*) fuel. **k~voll** a strong, powerful. **K~wagen** m motor car. **K~werk** nt power station

Kragen m -s,- collar

Krähe f -,-n crow

krähen vi (*haben*) crow

krakeln vt/i (*haben*) scrawl

Kralle f -,-nclaw. **k~n (sich)** vr clutch (an jdn/etws.o./sth); ⟨*Katze:*⟩ dig its claws (in + acc into)

Kram m -s (*fam*) things pl, (*fam*) stuff; (*Angelegenheiten*) business; **wertloser K~** junk. **k~en** vi (*haben*) rummage about (in + dat in; nach for). **K~laden** m [small] general store

Krampf m -[e]s,-̈e cramp. **K~adern** fpl varicose veins. **k~haft** a convulsive, adv -ly; (*verbissen*) desperate, adv -ly

Kran m -[e]s,-̈e (*Techn*) crane

Kranich m -s,-e (*Zool*) crane

krank a (kränker, kränkst) sick; ⟨*Knie, Herz*⟩ bad; **k~ sein/werden/machen be/fall/make ill**; **jdn k~ melden/schreiben** ⟨NEW⟩ **jdn k~melden/krankschreiben, s. krankmelden, krankschreiben**. **K~e(r)** m/f sick man/woman, invalid; **die K~en** the sick pl

kränkeln vi (*haben*) be in poor health. **k~d** a ailing

kranken vi (*haben*) (*fig*) suffer (an + dat from)

kränken vt offend, hurt

Kranken|bett nt sick-bed. **K~geld** nt sickness benefit. **K~gymnast(in)** m -en,-en (f -,-nen) physiotherapist. **K~gymnastik** f physiotherapy. **K~haus** nt hospital. **K~kasse** f health insurance scheme/(*Amt*) office. **K~pflege** f nursing. **K~pfleger(in)** m(f) nurse. **K~saal** m [hospital] ward. **K~schein** m certificate of entitlement to medical treatment. **K~schwester** f nurse. **K~urlaub** m sick-leave. **K~versicherung** f health insurance. **K~wagen** m ambulance. **K~zimmer** nt sick-room

krank|haft a morbid; (*pathologisch*) pathological. **K~heit** f -,-en illness, disease

kränklich a sickly

krank|melden vt sep jdn **k~melden** report s.o. sick; **sich k~melden** report sick. **k~schreiben†** vt sep jdn **k~schreiben** give s.o. a medical certificate; **sich k~schreiben lassen** get a medical certificate

Kränkung f -,-en slight

Kranz m -es,-̈e wreath; (*Ring*) ring

Krapfen m -s,- doughnut

krass (kraß) a (krasser, krassest) glaring; (*offensichtlich*) blatant; (*stark*) gross; rank ⟨*Außenseiter*⟩

Krater m -s,- crater

kratz|bürstig a (*fam*) prickly. **k~en** vt/i (*haben*) scratch; **sich k~en** scratch oneself/⟨*Tier:*⟩ itself. **K~er** m -s,- scratch; (*Werkzeug*) scraper

Kraul nt -s (*Sport*) crawl. **k~en**[1] vi (*haben/sein*) (*Sport*) do the crawl

kraulen vt tickle; **sich am Kopf k~** scratch one's head

kraus a wrinkled; ⟨*Haar*⟩ frizzy; (*verworren*) muddled; **k~ ziehen** wrinkle. **K~e** f -,-n frill, ruffle; (*Haar-*) frizziness

kräuseln vt wrinkle; frizz ⟨*Haar*⟩; gather ⟨*Stoff*⟩; ripple ⟨*Wasser*⟩; **sich k~** wrinkle; (*sich kringeln*) curl; ⟨*Haar:*⟩ go frizzy; ⟨*Wasser:*⟩ ripple

krausen vt wrinkle; frizz ⟨*Haar*⟩; gather ⟨*Stoff*⟩; **sich k~** wrinkle; ⟨*Haar:*⟩ go frizzy

Kraut nt -[e]s, Kräuter herb; (*SGer*) cabbage; (*Sauer-*) sauerkraut; **wie K~ und Rüben** higgledy-piggledy

Krawall m -s,-e riot; (*Lärm*) row

Krawatte f -,-n [neck]tie

kraxeln vi (*sein*) (*fam*) clamber

krea|tiv /krea'ti:f/ a creative. K~tur f -,-en creature

Krebs m -es,-e crayfish; (Med) cancer; (Astr) Cancer. k~ig a cancerous

Kredit m -s,-e credit; (Darlehen) loan; auf K~ on credit. K~karte f credit card

Kreid|e f - chalk. k~ebleich a deathly pale. k~ig a chalky

kreieren /kre'i:rən/ vt create

Kreis m -es,-e circle; (Admin) district

kreischen vt/i (haben) screech; (schreien) shriek

Kreisel m -s,- [spinning] top; (fam: Kreisverkehr) roundabout

kreis|en vi (haben) circle; revolve (um around). k~förmig a circular. K~lauf m cycle; (Med) circulation. k~rund a circular. K~säge f circular saw. K~verkehr m [traffic] roundabout, (Amer) traffic circle

Krem f -,-s & m -s,-e cream

Krematorium nt -s,-ien crematorium

Krempe f -,-n [hat] brim

Krempel m -s (fam) junk

krempeln vt turn (nach oben up)

Kren m -[e]s (Aust) horseradish

krepieren vi (sein) explode; (sl: sterben) die

Krepp m -s,-s & -e crêpe

Krepppapier (Kreppapier) nt crêpe paper

Kresse f -,-n cress; (Kapuziner-) nasturtium

Kreta nt -s Crete

Kreuz nt -es,-e cross; (Kreuzung) intersection; (Mus) sharp; (Kartenspiel) clubs pl; (Anat) small of the back; über K~ crosswise; das K~ schlagen cross oneself. k~ adv k~ und quer in all directions. k~en vt/cross; sich k~en cross; (Straßen:) intersect; (Meinungen:) clash □ vi (haben/sein) cruise; (Segelschiff:) tack. K~er m -s,- cruiser. K~fahrt f (Naut) cruise; (K~zug) crusade. K~feuer nt crossfire. K~gang m cloister

kreuzig|en vt crucify. K~ung f -,-en crucifixion

Kreuz|otter f adder, common viper. K~ung f -,-en intersection; (Straßen-) crossroads sg; (Hybride) cross. K~verhör nt cross-examination; ins K~verhör nehmen cross-examine. K~weg m crossroads sg; (Relig) Way of the Cross. k~weise adv crosswise. K~worträtsel nt crossword [puzzle]. K~zug m crusade

kribbel|ig a (fam) edgy. k~n vi (haben) tingle; (kitzeln) tickle

kriech|en† vi (sein) crawl; (fig) grovel (vor + dat to). k~erisch a grovelling. K~spur f (Auto) crawler lane. K~tier nt reptile

Krieg m -[e]s,-e war; K~ führen wage war (gegen on)

kriegen vt (fam) get; ein Kind k~ have a baby

Krieger|denkmal nt war memorial. k~isch a warlike; (militärisch) military

kriegs|beschädigt a war-disabled. K~dienstverweigerer m -s,- conscientious objector. K~gefangene(r) m prisoner of war. K~gefangenschaft f captivity. K~gericht nt court martial. K~list f stratagem. K~rat m council of war. K~recht nt martial law. K~schiff nt warship. K~verbrechen nt war crime

Krimi m -s,-s (fam) crime story/film. K~nalität f - crime; (Vorkommen) crime rate. K~nalpolizei f criminal investigation department. K~nalroman m crime novel. k~nell a criminal. K~nelle(r) m criminal

kringeln (sich) vr curl [up]; (vor Lachen) fall about

Kripo f - = Kriminalpolizei

Krippe f -,-n manger; (Weihnachts-) crib; (Kinder-) crèche. K~nspiel nt Nativity play

Krise f -,-n crisis

Kristall¹ nt -s (Glas) crystal; (geschliffen) cut glass

Kristall² m -s,-e crystal. k~isieren vi/r (haben) [sich] k~isieren crystallize

Kriterium nt -s,-ien criterion

Kritik f -,-en criticism; (Rezension) review; unter aller K~ (fam) abysmal

Kriti|ker m -s,- critic; (Rezensent) reviewer. k~sch a critical, adv -ly. k~sieren vt criticize; review

krittel|n vi (haben) find fault (an + acc with)

kritzeln vt/i (haben) scribble

Krokette f -,-n (Culin) croquette

Krokodil nt -s,-e crocodile

Krokus m -,-[se] crocus

Krone f -,-n crown; (Baum-) top

krönen vt crown

Kron|leuchter m chandelier. K~prinz m crown prince

Krönung f -,-en coronation; (fig: Höhepunkt) crowning event/(Leistung) achievement

Kropf m -[e]s,-e (Zool) crop; (Med) goitre

Kröte f -,-n toad

Krücke f -,-n crutch; (Stock-) handle; an K~n on crutches

Krug m -[e]s,-e jug; (Bier-) tankard

Krume f -,-n soft part [of loaf]; (*Krümel*) crumb; (*Acker-*) topsoil

Krümel m -s,- crumb. **k~ig** a crumbly. **k~n** vt crumble □ vi (haben) be crumbly; (*Person:*) drop crumbs

krumm a crooked; (*gebogen*) curved; (*verbogen*) bent; etw **k~ nehmen** (fam) take sth amiss. **k~beinig** a bow-legged

krümmen vt bend; crook (*Finger*); sich **k~** bend; (*sich winden*) writhe; (*vor Schmerzen/Lachen*) double up

krummnehmen† vt sep (NEW) krumm nehmen, s. krumm

Krümmung f -,-en bend; (*Kurve*) curve

Krüppel m -s,- cripple

Kruste f -,-n crust; (*Schorf*) scab

Kruzifix nt -es,-e crucifix

Krypta /'krypta/ f -,-ten crypt

Kub|a nt -s Cuba. **k~anisch** a Cuban

Kübel m -s,- tub; (*Eimer*) bucket; (*Techn*) skip

Kubik- pref cubic. **K~meter** m & nt cubic metre

Küche f -,-n kitchen; (*Kochkunst*) cooking; kalte/warme **K~** cold/hot food; französische **K~** French cuisine

Kuchen m -s,- cake

Küchen|herd m cooker, stove. **K~maschine** f food processor, mixer. **K~schabe** f -,-n cockroach. **K~zettel** m menu

Kuckuck m -s,-e cuckoo; zum **K~**! (fam) hang it! **K~suhr** f cuckoo clock

Kufe f -,-n [sledge] runner

Kugel f -,-n ball; (*Geom*) sphere; (*Gewehr-*) bullet; (*Sport*) shot. **k~förmig** a spherical. **K~lager** nt ball-bearing. **k~n** vt/i (haben) roll; sich **k~n** roll/(vor Lachen) fall about. **k~rund** a spherical; (fam: dick) tubby. **K~schreiber** m -s,- ballpoint [pen]. **k~sicher** a bullet-proof. **K~stoßen** nt -s shot-putting

Kuh f -,-e cow

kühl a cool, adv -ly; (kalt) chilly. **K~box** f -,-en cool-box. **K~e** f - coolness; chilliness. **k~en** vt cool; refrigerate (*Lebensmittel*); chill (*Wein*). **K~er** m -s,- icebucket; (*Auto*) radiator. **K~erhaube** f bonnet, (*Amer*) hood. **K~fach** nt frozen-food compartment. **K~raum** m cold store. **K~schrank** m refrigerator. **K~truhe** f freezer. **K~ung** f - cooling; (*Frische*) coolness. **K~wasser** nt [radiator] water

Kuhmilch f cow's milk

kühn a bold, adv -ly; (wagemutig) daring. **K~heit** f - boldness

Kuhstall m cowshed

Küken nt -s,- chick; (*Enten-*) duckling

Kukuruz m -[es] (Aust) maize

kulant a obliging

Kuli m -s,- (fam: Kugelschreiber) ballpoint [pen], Biro (P)

kulinarisch a culinary

Kulissen fpl (Theat) scenery sg; (seitlich) wings; hinter den **K~** (fig) behind the scenes

kullern vt/i (sein) (fam) roll

Kult m -[e]s,-e cult

kultivier|en vt cultivate. **k~t** a cultured

Kultur f -,-en culture; **K~en** plantations. **K~beutel** m toiletbag. **k~ell** a cultural. **K~film** m documentary film

Kultusminister m Minister of Education and Arts

Kümmel m -s caraway; (*Getränk*) kümmel

Kummer m -s sorrow, grief; (*Sorge*) worry; (*Ärger*) trouble

kümmer|lich a puny; (dürftig) meagre; (armselig) wretched. **k~n** vt concern; sich **k~n** um look after; (sich befassen) concern oneself with; (beachten) take notice of; ich werde mich darum **k~n** I shall see to it; **k~e** dich um deine eigenen Angelegenheiten! mind your own business!

kummervoll a sorrowful

Kumpel m -s,- (fam) mate

Kunde m -n,-n customer. **K~ndienst** m [after-sales] service

Kund|gebung f -,-en (Pol) rally. **k~ig** a knowledgeable; (sach-) expert

kündig|en vt cancel (*Vertrag*); give notice of withdrawal for (*Geld*); give notice to quit (*Wohnung*); seine Stellung **k~en** give [in one's] notice □ vi (haben) give [in one's] notice; jdm **k~en** give s.o. notice [of dismissal/(*Vermieter:*) to quit]. **K~ung** f -,-en cancellation; notice [of withdrawal/dismissal/to quit]; (*Entlassung*) dismissal. **K~ungsfrist** f period of notice

Kund|in f -,-nen [woman] customer. **K~machung** f -,-en (Aust) [public] notice. **K~schaft** f - clientele, customers pl

künftig a future □ adv in future

Kunst f -,-e art; (*Können*) skill. **K~dünger** m artificial fertilizer. **K~faser** f synthetic fibre. **k~fertig** a skilful. **K~fertigkeit** f skill. **K~galerie** f art gallery. **k~gerecht** a expert, adv -ly. **K~geschichte** f history of art. **K~gewerbe** nt arts and crafts pl. **K~griff** m trick. **K~händler** m art dealer

Künstler m -s,- artist; (*Könner*) master. **K~in** f -,-nen [woman] artist. **k~isch** a artistic, adv -ally. **K~name** m pseudonym; (*Theat*) stage name

künstlich a artificial, adv -ly

kunst|los a simple. K~maler m painter. K~stoff m plastic. K~stopfen nt invisible mending. K~stück nt trick; (große Leistung) feat. k~voll a artistic; (geschickt) skilful, adv -ly; (kompliziert) elaborate, adv -ly. K~werk nt work of art

kunterbunt a multicoloured; (gemischt) mixed □ adv k~ durcheinander higgledy-piggledy

Kupfer nt -s copper. K~n a copper

kupieren vt crop

Kupon /ku'põ:/ m -s,-s voucher; (Zins-) coupon; (Stoff-) length

Kuppe f -,-n [rounded] top; (Finger-) end, tip

Kuppel f -,-n dome

kupp|eln vt couple (an + acc to) □ vi (haben) (Auto) operate the clutch. K~lung f -,-en coupling; (Auto) clutch

Kur f -,-en course of treatment; (im Kurort) cure

Kür f -,-en (Sport) free exercise; (Eislauf) free programme

Kurbel f -,-n crank. k~n vt wind (nach oben/unten up/down). K~welle f crankshaft

Kürbis m -ses,-se pumpkin; (Flaschen-) marrow

Kurgast m health-resort visitor

Kurier m -s,-e courier

kurieren vt cure

kurios a curious, odd. K~ität f -,-en oddness; (Objekt) curiosity; (Kunst) curio

Kur|ort m health resort; (Badeort) spa. K~pfuscher m quack

Kurs m -es,-e course; (Aktien-) price. K~buch nt timetable

kursieren vi (haben) circulate

kursiv a italic □ adv in italics. K~schrift f italics pl

Kursus m -,Kurse course

Kurswagen m through carriage

Kurtaxe f visitors' tax

Kurve f -,-n curve; (Straßen-) bend

kurz a (kürzer, kürzest) short; (knapp) brief; (rasch) quick; (schroff) curt; k~e Hosen shorts; vor k~em a short time ago; seit k~em lately; binnen k~em shortly; den Kürzeren (kürzeren) ziehen get the worst of it □ adv briefly; quickly; curtly; k~ vor/nach a little way/ (zeitlich) shortly before/after; sich k~ fassen be brief; k~ und gut in short; über k~ oder lang sooner or later; zu k~ kommen get less than one's fair share. K~arbeit f short-time working. K~ärmelig a short-sleeved. k~atmig a k~atmig sein be short of breath

Kürze f - shortness; (Knappheit) brevity; in K~ shortly. k~n vt shorten; (verringern) cut

kurz|erhand adv without further ado. k~fristig a short-term □ adv at short notice. K~geschichte f short story. k~lebig a short-lived

kürzlich adv recently

Kurz|meldung f newsflash. K~nachrichten fpl news headlines. K~schluss (K~schluß) m short circuit; (fig) brainstorm. K~schrift f shorthand. k~sichtig a short-sighted. K~sichtigkeit f - short-sightedness. K~streckenrakete f short-range missile. k~um adv in short

Kürzung f -,-en shortening; (Verringerung) cut (gen in)

Kurz|waren fpl haberdashery sg, (Amer) notions. k~weilig a amusing. K~welle f short wave

kuscheln (sich) vr snuggle (an + acc up to)

Kusine f -,-n [female] cousin

Kuss m -es,ꞌe (Kuß m -sses,ꞌsse) kiss

küssen vt/i (haben) kiss; sich k~ kiss

Küste f -,-n coast. K~nwache, K~nwacht f coastguard

Küster m -s,- verger

Kustos m -,-toden /-ꞌto:-/ curator

Kutsch|e f -,-n [horse-drawn] carriage/ (geschlossen) coach. K~er m -s,- coachman, driver. k~ieren vt/i (haben) drive

Kutte f -,-n (Relig) habit

Kutter m -s,- (Naut) cutter

Kuvert /ku'veːɐ̯/ nt -s,-s envelope

KZ /ka:ꞌtsɛt/ nt -[s],-[s] concentration camp

L

labil a unstable

Labor nt -s,-s & -e laboratory. L~ant(in) m -en,-en (f -,-nen) laboratory assistant. L~atorium nt -s,-ien laboratory

Labyrinth nt -[e]s,-e maze, labyrinth

Lache f -,-n puddle; (Blut-) pool

lächeln vi (haben) smile. L~ nt -s smile. l~d a smiling

lachen vi (haben) laugh. L~ nt -s laugh; (Gelächter) laughter

lächerlich a ridiculous, adv -ly; sich l~ machen make a fool of oneself. L~keit f -,-en ridiculousness; (Kleinigkeit) triviality

lachhaft a laughable

Lachs m -es,-e salmon. l~farben, l~rosa a salmon-pink

Lack m -[e]s,-e varnish; (Japan-) lacquer; (Auto) paint. l~en vt varnish. l~ieren vt varnish; (spritzen) spray. L~schuhe mpl patent-leather shoes

Lade f -,-n drawer

laden† vt load; (Electr) charge; (Jur: vor-) summons

Laden m -s,- shop, (Amer) store; (Fenster-) shutter. L~dieb m shop-lifter. L~diebstahl m shop-lifting. L~schluss (L~schluß) m [shop] closing-time. L~tisch m counter

Laderaum m (Naut) hold

lädieren vt damage

Ladung f -,-en load; (Naut, Aviat) cargo; (elektrische, Spreng-) charge; (Jur: Vor-) summons

Lage f -,-n position; (Situation) situation; (Schicht) layer; (fam: Runde) round; nicht in der L~ sein not be in a position (zu to)

Lager nt -s,- camp; (L~haus) warehouse; (Vorrat) stock; (Techn) bearing; (Erz-, Ruhe-) bed; (eines Tieres) lair; [nicht] auf L~[not] in stock. L~haus nt warehouse. l~n vt store; (legen) lay; sich l~n settle; (sich legen) lie down □ vi (haben) camp; (liegen) lie; (Waren:) be stored. L~raum m store-room. L~stätte f (Geol) deposit. L~ung f -storage

Lagune f -,-n lagoon

lahm a lame; l~ legen (fig) paralyse. l~en vi (haben) be lame

lähmen vt paralyse

lahmlegen vt sep (NEW) lahm legen, s. lahm

Lähmung f -,-en paralysis

Laib m -[e]s,-e loaf

Laich m -[e]s (Zool) spawn. l~en vi (haben) spawn

Laie m -n,-n layman; (Theat) amateur. l~nhaft a amateurish. L~nprediger m lay preacher

Lake f -,-n brine

Laken nt -s,- sheet

lakonisch a laconic, adv -ally

Lakritze f -liquorice

lallen vt/i (haben) mumble; (Baby:) babble

Lametta nt -s tinsel

Lamm nt -[e]s,-er lamb

Lampe f -,-n lamp; (Decken-, Wand-) light; (Glüh-) bulb. L~nfieber nt stage fright. L~nschirm m lampshade

Lampion /lam'pjoŋ/ m -s,-s Chinese lantern

lancieren /lã'si:rən/ vt (Comm) launch

Land nt -[e]s,-er country; (Fest-) land; (Bundes-) state, Land; (Aust) province; Stück L~ piece of land; auf dem L~e in the country; an L~ gehen (Naut) go ashore; hier zu L~e = hierzulande. L~arbeiter m agricultural worker. L~ebahn f runway. l~einwärts adv inland. l~en vt/i (sein) land; (fam: gelangen) end up

Ländereien pl estates

Länderspiel nt international

Landesteg m landing-stage

Landesverrat m treason

Land|karte f map. l~läufig a popular

ländlich a rural

Land|maschinen fpl agricultural machinery sg. L~schaft f -,-en scenery; (Geog, Kunst) landscape; (Gegend) countrylside]. l~schaftlich a scenic; (regional) regional. L~smann m (pl -leute) fellow countryman, compatriot. L~smännin f -,-nen fellow countrywoman. L~straße f country road; (Admin) ≈ B road. L~streicher m -s,- tramp. L~tag m state/(Aust) provincial parliament

Landung f -,-en landing. L~sbrücke f landing-stage

Land|vermesser m -s,- surveyor. L~weg m country lane; auf dem L~weg overland. L~wirt m farmer. L~wirtschaft f agriculture; (Hof) farm. l~wirtschaftlich a agricultural

lang[1] adv & prep (+ preceding acc or preceding an + dat) along; den od am Fluss l~ along the river

lang[2] a (länger, längst) long; (groß) tall; seit l~em for a long time □ adv eine Stunde/Woche l~ for an hour/a week; mein Leben l~ all my life. l~ärmelig a long-sleeved. l~andauernd late; l~e adv a long time; (schlafen) late; wie/zu l~e how/too long; schon l~e [for] a long time; (zurückliegend) a long time ago; so l~e wie möglich as long as possible; l~e nicht not for a long time; (bei weitem nicht) nowhere near

Länge f -,-n length; (Geog) longitude; der L~ nach lengthways; (liegen, fallen) full length

langen vt hand (dat to) □ vi (haben) reach (an etw acc sth; nach for); (genügen) be enough

Läng|engrad m degree of longitude. L~enmaß nt linear measure. l~er a & adv longer; (längere Zeit) [for] some time

Langeweile f - boredom; L~ haben be bored

lang|fristig a long-term; *(Vorhersage)* long-range. l~jährig a long-standing; *(Erfahrung)* long. l~lebig a long-lived

länglich a oblong; l~ rund oval

langmütig a long-suffering

längs adv & prep (+ gen/dat) along; *(der Länge nach)* lengthways

lang|sam a slow, adv -ly. L~samkeit f - slowness. L~schläfer(in) m(f) *(fam)* late riser. L~schrift f longhand

längst adv *[schon]* l~ for a long time; *(zurückliegend)* a long time ago; l~ nicht nowhere near

Lang|strecken- pref long-distance; *(Mil, Aviat)* long-range. l~weilen vt bore; sich l~weilen be bored. l~weilig a boring, adv -ly. L~welle f long wave. l~wierig a lengthy

Lanze f -,-n lance

Lappalie /la'pa:liə/ f -,-n trifle

Lappen m -s,- cloth; *(Anat)* lobe

läppisch a silly

Lapsus m -,- slip

Lärche f -,-n larch

Lärm m -s noise. l~en vi *(haben)* make a noise. l~end a noisy

Larve /'larfə/ f -,-n larva; *(Maske)* mask

lasch a listless; *(schlaff)* limp; *(fade)* insipid

Lasche f -,-n tab; *(Verschluss-)* flap; *(Zunge)* tongue

Laser /'le:-, 'la:zɐ/ m -s,- laser

lassen† vt leave; *(zulassen)* let; jdm etw l~ let s.o. keep sth; sein Leben l~ lose one's life; etw *[sein od bleiben]* l~ not do sth; *(aufhören)* stop *[doing]* sth; lass das! stop it! jdn schlafen/gewinnen l~ let s.o. sleep/win; jdn warten l~ keep s.o. waiting; etw machen/reparieren l~ have sth done/repaired; etw verschwinden l~ make sth disappear; sich *[leicht]* biegen/öffnen l~ bend/open *[easily]*; sich gut waschen l~ wash well; es lässt sich nicht leugnen it is undeniable; lasst uns gehen! let's go!

lässig a casual, adv -ly. L~keit f - casualness

Lasso nt -s,-s lasso

Last f -,-en load; *(Gewicht)* weight; *(fig)* burden; L~en charges; *(Steuern)* taxes; jdm zur L~ fallen be a burden on s.o. L~auto nt lorry. l~en vi *(haben)* weigh heavily/(liegen) rest (auf + dat on). L~enaufzug m goods lift

Laster¹ m -s,- *(fam)* lorry, *(Amer)* truck

Laster² nt -s,- vice. l~haft a depraved; *(zügellos)* dissolute

läster|lich a blasphemous. l~n vt blaspheme □ vi *(haben)* make disparaging remarks (über + acc about). L~ung f -,-en blasphemy

lästig a troublesome; l~ sein/werden be/become a nuisance

Last|kahn m barge. L~[kraft]wagen m lorry, *(Amer)* truck. L~zug m lorry with trailer[s]

Latein nt -[s] Latin. L~amerika nt Latin America. l~isch a Latin

latent a latent

Laterne f -,-n lantern; *(Straßen-)* street lamp. L~npfahl m lamp-post

latschen vi *(sein)* *(fam)* traipse; *(schlurfen)* shuffle

Latte f -,-n slat; *(Tor-, Hoch- sprung-)* bar

Latz m -es,-̈e bib

Lätzchen nt -s,- *[baby's]* bib

Latzhose f dungarees pl

lau a lukewarm; *(mild)* mild

Laub nt -[e]s leaves pl; *(L~werk)* foliage. L~baum m deciduous tree

Laube f -,-n summer-house; *(gewachsen)* arbour. L~ngang m pergola; *(Archit)* arcades pl

Laub|säge f fretsaw. L~wald m deciduous forest

Lauch m -[e]s leeks pl

Lauer f auf der L~ liegen lie in wait. l~n vi *(haben)* lurk; l~n auf (+ acc) lie in wait for

Lauf m -[e]s, Läufe run; *(Laufen)* running; *(Verlauf)* course; *(Wett-)* race; *(Sport: Durchgang)* heat; *(Gewehr-)* barrel; im L~[e] (+ gen) in the course of. L~bahn f career. l~en† vi *(sein)* run; *(zu Fuß gehen)* walk; *(gelten)* be valid; Ski/Schlittschuh l~en ski/skate; jdn l~en lassen *(fam)* let s.o. go. l~end a running; *(gegenwärtig)* current; *(regelmäßig)* regular; l~ende Nummer serial number; auf dem L~enden (l~enden) sein/jdn auf dem L~enden (l~enden) halten be/keep s.o. up to date □ adv continually. l~enlassen† vt sep (NEW) l~en lassen, s. laufen

Läufer m -s,- *(Person, Teppich)* runner; *(Schach)* bishop

Lauf|gitter nt play-pen. L~masche f ladder. L~rolle f castor. L~schritt m im L~schritt at a run; *(Mil)* at the double. L~stall m play-pen. L~zettel m circular

Lauge f -,-n soapy water

Laun|e f -,-n mood; *(Einfall)* whim; guter L~e sein, gute L~e haben be in a good mood. l~enhaft a capricious. l~isch a moody

Laus f -,Läuse louse; (Blatt-) greenfly. L~bub m (fam) rascal

lauschen vi (haben) listen; (heimlich) eavesdrop

lausig a (fam) lousy □ adv terribly

laut a loud, adv -ly; (geräuschvoll) noisy, adv -ily; l~ lesen read aloud; l~er stellen turn up □ prep (+ gen/dat) according to. L~ m -es,-e sound

Laute f -,-n (Mus) lute

lauten vi (haben) ⟨Text:⟩ run, read; auf jds Namen l~ be in s.o.'s name

läuten vt/i (haben) ring

lauter a pure; (ehrlich) honest; (Wahrheit) plain □ a inv sheer; (nichts als) nothing but. L~keit f - integrity

läutern vt purify

laut|hals adv at the top of one's voice; ⟨lachen⟩ out loud. l~los a silent, adv -ly; ⟨Stille⟩ hushed. L~schrift f phonetics pl. L~sprecher m loudspeaker. l~stark a vociferous, adv -ly. L~stärke f volume

lauwarm a lukewarm

Lava f -,-ven lava

Lavendel m -s lavender

lavieren vi (haben) manœuvre

Lawine f -,-n avalanche

lax a lax. L~heit f - laxity

Lazarett nt -[e]s,-e military hospital

leasen /'li:sən/ vt rent

Lebehoch nt cheer

leben vt/i (haben) live (von on); leb wohl! farewell! L~ nt -s,- life, (Treiben) bustle; am L~ alive. l~d a living

lebendig a live; (lebhaft) lively; (anschaulich) vivid, adv -ly; l~ sein be alive. L~keit f - liveliness; vividness

Lebens|abend m old age. L~alter nt age. L~art f manners pl. l~fähig a viable. L~gefahr f mortal danger; in L~gefahr in mortal danger; ⟨Patient⟩ critically ill. l~gefährlich a extremely dangerous; ⟨Verletzung⟩ critical □ adv critically. L~größe f in L~größe life-sized. L~haltungskosten pl cost of living sg. l~lang a lifelong. l~länglich a life ... □ adv for life. L~lauf m curriculum vitae. L~mittel ntpl food sg. L~mittelgeschäft nt food shop. L~mittelhändler m grocer. l~notwendig a vital. L~retter m rescuer; (beim Schwimmen) life-guard. L~standard m standard of living. L~unterhalt m livelihood; seinen L~unterhalt verdienen earn one's living. L~versicherung f life assurance. L~wandel m conduct. l~wichtig a vital. L~zeichen nt sign of life. L~zeit f auf L~zeit for life

Leber f -,-n liver. L~fleck m mole. L~wurst f liver sausage

Lebe|wesen nt living being. L~wohl nt -s,-s & -e farewell

leb|haft a lively; ⟨Farbe⟩ vivid. L~haftigkeit f - liveliness. L~kuchen m gingerbread. l~los a lifeless. L~tag m mein/dein L~tag all my/your life. L~zeiten fpl zu jds L~zeiten in s.o.'s lifetime

leck a leaking. L~ nt -s,-s leak. l~en¹ vi (haben) leak

lecken² vi (haben) lick

lecker a tasty. L~bissen m delicacy. L~ei f -,-en sweet

Leder nt -s,- leather. l~n a leather; (wie Leder) leathery

ledig a single. l~lich adv merely

Lee f & nt - nach Lee (Naut) to leeward

leer a empty; (unbesetzt) vacant; l~ laufen (Auto) idle. L~e f - emptiness; (leerer Raum) void. l~en vt empty; sich l~en empty. L~lauf m (Auto) neutral. L~ung f -,-en (Post) collection

legal a legal, adv -ly. l~isieren vt legalize. L~ität f - legality

Legas|thenie f - dyslexia. L~theniker m -s,- dyslexic

legen vt put; (hin-, ver-) lay; set ⟨Haare⟩; Eier l~ lay eggs; sich l~ lie down; ⟨Staub:⟩ settle; (nachlassen) subside

legendär a legendary

Legende f -,-n legend

leger /le'ʒɛːr/ a casual, adv -ly

legier|en vt alloy; (Culin) thicken. L~ung f -,-en alloy

Legion f -,-en legion

Legislative f - legislature

legitim a legitimate, adv -ly. l~ieren (sich) vr prove one's identity. L~ität f - legitimacy

Lehm m -s clay. l~ig a clayey

Lehne f -,-n (Rücken-) back; (Arm-) arm. l~en vt lean (an + acc against); sich l~en lean (an + acc against) □ vi (haben) be leaning (an + dat against). L~sessel, L~stuhl m armchair

Lehr|buch nt textbook. L~e f -,-n apprenticeship; (Anschauung) doctrine; (Theorie) theory; (Wissenschaft) science; (Ratschlag) advice; (Erfahrung) lesson; jdm eine L~e erteilen (fig) teach s.o. a lesson. l~en vt/i (haben) teach. L~er m -s,- teacher; (Fahr-, Ski-) instructor. L~erin f -,-nen teacher. L~erzimmer nt staff-room. L~fach nt (Sch) subject. L~gang m course. L~kraft f teacher. L~ling m -s,-e apprentice; (Auszubildender) trainee. L~plan m syllabus. l~

reich a instructive. L~stelle f apprenticeship. L~stuhl m (Univ) chair. L~zeit f apprenticeship

Leib m -es,-er body; (Bauch) belly. L~eserziehung f (Sch) physical education. L~eskraft f aus L~eskräften as hard/(schreien) loud as one can. L~gericht nt favourite dish. l~haftig a der l~haftige Satan the devil incarnate □ adv in the flesh. l~lich a physical; (blutsverwandt) real, natural. L~speise f = L~gericht. L~wache f (coll) bodyguard. L~wächter m bodyguard. L~wäsche f underwear

Leiche f -,-n [dead] body; corpse. L~nbegängnis nt -ses,-se funeral. L~nbestatter m -s,- undertaker. l~nblass a deathly pale. L~nhalle f mortuary. L~nwagen m hearse. L~nzug m funeral procession, cortège

Leichnam m -s,-e [dead] body

leicht a light, adv -ly; (Stoff, Anzug) lightweight; (gering) slight, adv -ly; (mühelos) easy, adv -ily; jdm l~ fallen be easy for s.o.; etw l~ machen make sth easy (dat for); es sich (dat) l~ machen take the easy way out; etw l~ nehmen (fig) take sth lightly. L~athletik f [track and field] athletics sg. l~fallen† vi sep (sein) NEW l~ fallen, s. leicht. l~fertig a thoughtless, adv -ly; (vorschnell) rash, adv -ly; (frivol) frivolous, adv -ly. L~gewicht nt (Boxen) lightweight. l~gläubig a gullible. l~hin adv casually. L~igkeit f - lightness; (Mühelosigkeit) ease; (L~sein) easiness; mit L~igkeit with ease. l~lebig a happy-go-lucky. l~machen vt sep NEW l~ machen, s. leicht. l~nehmen† vt sep NEW l~ nehmen, s. leicht. L~sinn m carelessness; recklessness; (Frivolität) frivolity. l~sinnig a careless, adv -ly; (unvorsichtig) reckless, adv -ly; (frivol) frivolous, adv -ly

Leid nt -[e]s sorrow, grief; (Böses) harm; es tut mir L~ I am sorry; er tut mir L~ I feel sorry for him; jdm etw zu L~e tun = jdm etw zuleide tun, s. zuleide. l~ a jdn/etw l~ sein/werden be/get tired of s.o./sth; jdm l~ tun NEW jdm L~ tun, s. Leid

Leide|form f passive. l~n† vt/i (haben) suffer (an + dat from); jdn [gut] l~n können like s.o.; jdn/etw nicht l~n können dislike s.o./sth. L~n nt -s,- suffering; (Med) complaint; (Krankheit) disease. l~nd a suffering; l~nd sein be in poor health. L~nschaft f -,-en passion. l~nschaftlich a passionate, adv -ly

leid|er adv unfortunately; l~er ja/nicht I'm afraid so/not. l~ig a wretched.

l~lich a tolerable, adv -bly. L~tragende(r) m/f person who suffers; (Trauernde) mourner. L~wesen nt zu meinem L~wesen to my regret

Leier f -,-n die alte L~ (fam) the same old story. L~kasten m barrel-organ. l~n vt/i (haben) wind; (herunter-) drone out

Leih|bibliothek, L~bücherei f lending library. L~e f -,-n loan. l~en† vt lend; sich (dat) etw l~en borrow sth. L~gabe f loan. L~gebühr f rental; (für Bücher) lending charge. L~haus nt pawnshop. L~wagen m hire-car. l~weise adv on loan

Leim m -s glue. l~en vt glue

Leine f -,-n rope; (Wäsche-) line; (Hunde-) lead, leash

Lein|en nt -s linen. l~ena linen. L~tuch nt sheet. L~wand f linen; (Kunst) canvas; (Film-) screen

leise a quiet, adv -ly; (Stimme, Musik, Berührung) soft, adv -ly; (schwach) faint, adv -ly; (leicht) light, adv -ly; l~r stellen turn down

Leiste f -,-n strip; (Holz-) batten; (Zier-) moulding; (Anat) groin

Leisten m -s,- [shoemaker's] last

leist|en vt achieve, accomplish; sich (dat) etw l~en treat oneself to sth; (fam: anstellen) get up to sth; ich kann es mir nicht l~en I can't afford it. L~ung f -,-en achievement; (Sport, Techn) performance; (Produktion) output; (Zahlung) payment. l~ungsfähig a efficient. L~ungsfähigkeit f efficiency

Leit|artikel m leader, editorial. L~bild nt (fig) model. l~en vt run, manage; (anl/hinführen) lead; (Mus, Techn, Phys) conduct; (lenken, schicken) direct. l~end a leading; (Posten) executive

Leiter[1] f -,-n ladder

Leit|er[2] m -s,- director; (Comm) manager; (Führer) leader; (Sch) head; (Mus, Phys) conductor. L~erin f -,-nen director; manageress; leader; head. L~faden m manual. L~kegel m [traffic] cone. L~planke f crash barrier. L~spruch m motto. L~ung f -,-en (Führung) direction; (Comm) management; (Aufsicht) control; (Electr: Schnur) lead, flex; (Kabel) cable; (Telefon-) line; (Rohr-) pipe; (Haupt-) main. L~ungswasser nt tap water

Lektion /-'tsjo:n/ f -,-en lesson

Lekt|or m -s,-en /-'to:ran/, L~orin f -,-nen (Univ) assistant lecturer; (Verlags-) editor. L~üre f -,-n reading matter; (Lesen) reading

Lende f -,-n loin

lenk|bar a steerable; (fügsam) tractable. l~en vt guide; (steuern) steer; (Aust) drive; (*regeln*) control; jds Aufmerksamkeit auf sich (*acc*) l~en attract s.o.'s attention. L~er *m* -s,- driver; (*L~stange*) handlebars *pl*. L~rad *nt* steering-wheel. L~stange *f* handlebars *pl*. L~ung *f* - steering

Leopard *m* -en,-en leopard

Lepra *f* - leprosy

Lerche *f* -,-n lark

lernen *vt/i* (*haben*) learn; (*für die Schule*) study; schwimmen l~ learn to swim

lesbar *a* readable; (*leserlich*) legible

Lesb|ierin /'lɛsbjərɪn/ *f* -,-nen lesbian. l~isch *a* lesbian

Lese *f* -,-n harvest. L~buch *nt* reader. l~n† *vt/i* (*haben*) read; (*Univ*) lecture □ *vt* pick, gather. L~n *nt* -s reading. L~r(in) *m* -s,- (*f* -,-nen) reader. L~ratte *f* (*fam*) bookworm. l~rlich *a* legible, *adv* -bly. L~zeichen *nt* bookmark

Lesung *f* -,-en reading

lethargisch *a* lethargic, *adv* -ally

Lettland *nt* -s Latvia

letzt|e(r,s) *a* last; (*neueste*) latest; in l~er Zeit recently; l~en Endes in the end; er kam als L~er (l~er) he arrived last. l~emal *adv* das l~emal/zum l~enmal (l~e)Mal/zum l~en Mal, *s.* Mal¹. l~ens *adv* recently; (*zuletzt*) lastly. l~ere(r,s) *a* the latter; der/die/das L~ere (l~ere) the latter

Leucht|e *f* -,-n light. l~en *vi* (*haben*) shine. l~end *a* shining. L~er *m* -s,- candlestick. L~feuer *nt* beacon. L~kugel, l~rakete *f* flare. L~reklame *f* neon sign. L~[stoff]röhre *f* fluorescent tube. L~turm *m* lighthouse. L~zifferblatt *nt* luminous dial

leugnen *vt* deny

Leukämie *f* - leukaemia

Leumund *m* -s reputation

Leute *pl* people; (*Mil*) men; (*Arbeiter*) workers

Leutnant *m* -s,-s second lieutenant

leutselig *a* affable, *adv* -bly

Levkoje /lɛfˈkoːjə/ *f* -,-n stock

Lexikon *nt* -s,-ka encyclopaedia; (*Wörterbuch*) dictionary

Libanon (der) -s Lebanon

Libelle *f* -,-n dragonfly; (*Techn*) spirit-level; (*Haarspange*) slide

liberal *a* (*Pol*) Liberal

Libyen *nt* -s Libya

Licht *nt* -[e]s,-er light; (*Kerze*) candle; L~ machen turn on the light; hinters L~ führen (*fam*) dupe. l~ *a* bright; (*Med*) lucid; (*spärlich*) sparse. L~bild *nt* [passport] photograph; (*Dia*) slide. L~bildervortrag *m* slide lecture. L~blick *m* (*fig*)

ray of hope. l~en *vt* thin out; den Anker l~en (*Naut*) weigh anchor; sich l~en become less dense; (*Haare:*) thin. L~hupe *f* headlight flasher; die L~hupe betätigen flash one's headlights. L~maschine *f* dynamo. L~schalter *m* light-switch. L~ung *f* -,-en clearing

Lid *nt* -[e]s,-er [eye]lid. L~schatten *m* eye-shadow

lieb *a* dear; (*nett*) nice; (*artig*) good; jdn l~ haben be fond of s.o.; (*lieben*) love s.o.; jdn l~ gewinnen grow fond of s.o.; es ist mir l~ I'm glad (dass that); es wäre mir l~er I should prefer it (wenn if). l~äugeln *vi* (*haben*) l~äugeln mit fancy; toy with (*Gedanken*)

Liebe *f* -,-n love. L~lei *f* -,-en flirtation. l~n *vt* love; (*mögen*) like; sich l~n love each other; (*körperlich*) make love. l~nd *a* loving □ *adv* etw l~nd gern love to do sth. l~nswert *a* lovable. l~nswürdig *a* kind. l~nswürdigerweise *adv* very kindly. L~nswürdigkeit *f* -,-en kindness

lieber *adv* rather; (*besser*) better; l~ mögen like better; ich trinke l~ Tee I prefer tea

Liebes|brief *m* love letter. L~dienst *m* favour. L~geschichte *f* love story. L~kummer *m* heartache; L~kummer haben be depressed over an unhappy love-affair. L~paar *nt* [pair of] lovers *pl*

lieb|evoll *a* loving, *adv* -ly, (*zärtlich*) affectionate, *adv* -ly. l~gewinnen† *vt sep* (NEW) l~ gewinnen, *s.* lieb. l~haben† *vt sep* (NEW) l~ haben, *s.* lieb. L~haber *m* -s,- lover; (*Sammler*) collector. L~haberei *f* -,-en hobby. l~kosen *vt* caress. L~kosung *f* -,-en caress. l~lich *a* lovely; (*sanft*) gentle; (*süß*) sweet. L~ling *m* -s,-e darling; (*Bevorzugte*) favourite. L~lings-*pref* favourite. l~los *a* loveless; (*Eltern*) uncaring; (*unfreundlich*) unkind □ *adv* unkindly; (*ohne Sorgfalt*) without care. L~schaft *f* -,-en [love] affair. l~ste(r,s) *a* dearest; (*bevorzugt*) favourite □ *adv* am l~sten best [of all]; jdn/etw am l~sten mögen like s.o./sth best [of all]; ich hätte am l~sten geweint I felt like crying. L~ste(r) *m/f* beloved; (*Schatz*) sweetheart

Lied *nt* -[e]s,-er song

liederlich *a* slovenly; (*unordentlich*) untidy; (*ausschweifend*) dissolute. L~keit *f* - slovenliness; untidiness; dissoluteness

Lieferant *m* -en,-en supplier

liefer|bar *a* (*Comm*) available. l~n *vt* supply; (*zustellen*) deliver; (*hervorbringen*) yield. L~ung *f* -,-en delivery; (*Sendung*) consignment; (*per Schiff*) shipment. L~wagen *m* delivery van

Liege f -,-n couch. l~n† vi (haben) lie; (gelegen sein) be situated; l~n bleiben remain lying [there]; (im Bett) stay in bed;
⟨Ding:⟩ be left; ⟨Schnee:⟩ settle; ⟨Arbeit:⟩ remain undone; (zurückgelassen werden) be
left behind; (Panne haben) break down;
l~n lassen leave [lying there]; (zurücklassen) leave behind; (nicht fortführen)
leave undone; l~n an (+ dat) ⟨fig⟩ be due
to; (abhängen) depend on; jdm [nicht]
l~n [not] suit s.o.; (ansprechen) [not] appeal to s.o.; mir liegt viel/nicht daran it
is very/ not important to me. l~nblei-
ben† vi sep (sein) NEW l~n bleiben, s.
liegen. l~nlassen† vt sep NEW l~n
lassen, s. liegen. L~sitz m reclining seat.
L~stuhl m deck-chair. L~stütz m -es,-e
press-up, (Amer) push-up. L~wagen m
couchette car. L~wiese f lawn for sun-
bathing

Lift m -[e]s,-e & -s lift, (Amer) elevator

Liga f -,-gen league

Likör m -s,-e liqueur

lila inv a mauve; (dunkel) purple

Lilie /'li:ljə/ f -,-n lily

Liliputaner(in) m -s,- (f -,-nen) dwarf

Limo f -,-[s] (fam), L~nade f -,-n fizzy
drink, (Amer) soda; (Zitronen-) lemonade

Limousine /limu'zi:nə/ f -,-n saloon,
(Amer) sedan; (mit Trennscheibe) limousine

lind a mild; (sanft) gentle

Linde f -,-n lime tree

linder|n vt relieve, ease. L~ung f - relief

Lineal nt -s,-e ruler. l~ar a linear

Linguistik f - linguistics sg

Linie /-jə/ f -,-n line; (Zweig) branch;
(Bus-) route; l~ 4 number 4 [bus/tram];
in erster L~ primarily. L~nflug m
scheduled flight.L~nrichter m linesman

lin[i]iert a lined, ruled

Link|e f -n,-n left side; (Hand) left hand;
(Boxen) left; die L~e (Pol) the left; zu
meiner L~en on my left. l~e(r,s) a left;
(Pol) left-wing; l~e Seite left[-hand] side;
(von Stoff) wrong side; l~e Masche purl.
l~isch a awkward, adv -ly

links adv on the left; (bei Stoff) on the
wrong side; (verkehrt) inside out; von/
nach l~ from/to the left; l~ stricken
purl. L~händer(in) m -s,- (f -,-nen) left-
hander. l~händig a & adv left-handed.
L~verkehr m driving on the left

Linoleum /-leʊm/ nt -s lino, linoleum

Linse f -,-n lens; (Bot) lentil

Lippe f -,-n lip. L~nstift m lipstick

Liquid|ation /-'tsjo:n/ f -,-en
liquidation. l~ieren vt liquidate

lispeln vt/i (haben) lisp

List f -,-en trick, ruse; (Listigkeit) cunning

Liste f -,-n list

listig a cunning, adv -ly, crafty, adv -ily

Litanei f -,-en litany

Litauen nt -s Lithuania

Liter m & nt -s,- litre

liter|arisch a literary. L~atur f - litera-
ture

Litfaßsäule f advertising pillar

Liturgie f -,-n liturgy

Litze f -,-n braid; (Electr) flex

live /laif/ adv (Radio, TV) live

Lizenz f -,-en licence

Lkw /ɛlka've:/ m -[s],-s = Lastkraftwa-
gen

Lob nt -[e]s praise

Lobby /'lɔbi/ f - (Pol) lobby

loben vt praise. l~swert a praiseworthy,
laudable

löblich a praiseworthy

Lobrede f eulogy

Loch nt -[e]s,-er hole. l~en vt punch a
hole/holes in; punch ⟨Fahrkarte⟩. L~er
m -s,- punch

löcher|ig a full of holes. l~n vt (fam) pes-
ter

Locke f -,-n curl. l~n¹ vt curl; sich l~n
curl

locken² vt lure, entice; (reizen) tempt. l~d
a tempting

Lockenwickler m -s,- curler; (Rolle)
roller

locker a loose, adv -ly; ⟨Seil⟩ slack; ⟨Erde,
Kuchen⟩ light; (zwanglos) casual; (zu frei)
lax; (unmoralisch) loose. l~n vt loosen;
slacken ⟨Seil, Zügel⟩; break up ⟨Boden⟩; relax ⟨Griff⟩; sich l~n become loose; ⟨Seil:⟩
slacken; (sich entspannen) relax. L~ungs-
übungen fpl limbering-up exercises

lockig a curly

Lock|mittel nt bait. L~ung f -,-en lure;
(Versuchung) temptation. L~vogel m de-
coy

Loden m -s (Tex) loden

lodern vi (haben) blaze

Löffel m -s,- spoon; (L~ voll) spoonful.
l~n vt spoon up

Logarithmus m -,-men logarithm

Logbuch nt (Naut) log-book

Loge /'lo:ʒə/ f -,-n lodge; (Theat) box

Logierbesuch /lo'ʒi:ɐ̯-/ m house
guest/guests pl

Log|ik f - logic. l~isch a logical, adv -ly

Logo nt -s,-s logo

Lohn m -[e]s,-e wages pl, pay; (fig) reward.
L~empfänger m wage-earner. l~en vi/r
(haben) [sich] l~en be worth it or worth

while □ *vt* be worth; jdm etw l∼en reward s.o. for sth. l∼end *a* worthwhile; (*befriedigend*) rewarding. L∼erhöhung *f* [pay] rise; (*Amer*) raise. L∼steuer *f* income tax

Lok *f* -,-s (*fam*) = Lokomotive

Lokal *nt* -s,-e restaurant; (*Trink-*) bar. l∼ *a* local. l∼sieren *vt* locate; (*begrenzen*) localize

Lokomotiv|e *f* -,-n engine, locomotive. L∼führer *m* engine driver

London *nt* -s London. L∼er *a* London ... □ *m* -s,- Londoner

Lorbeer *m* -s,-en laurel; echter L∼ bay. L∼blatt *nt* (*Culin*) bay-leaf

Lore *f* -,-n (*Rail*) truck

Los *nt* -es,-e lot; (*Lotterie-*) ticket; (*Schicksal*) fate; das große Los ziehen hit the jackpot

los *pred a* los sein be loose; jdn/etw los sein be rid of s.o./sth; was ist [mit ihm] los? what's the matter [with him]? □ *adv* los! go on! Achtung, fertig, los! ready, steady, go!

lösbar *a* soluble

losbinden† *vt sep* untie

Lösch|blatt *nt* sheet of blotting-paper. l∼¹ *vt* put out, extinguish; quench (*Durst*); blot (*Tinte*); (*tilgen*) cancel; (*streichen*) delete; erase (*Aufnahme*)

löschen² *vt* (*Naut*) unload

Lösch|fahrzeug *nt* fire-engine. L∼gerät *nt* fire extinguisher. L∼papier *nt* blotting-paper

lose *a* loose, *adv* -ly

Lösegeld *nt* ransom

losen *vt* (*haben*) draw lots (um for)

lösen *vt* undo; (*lockern*) loosen; (*entfernen*) detach; (*klären*) solve; (*auflösen*) dissolve; cancel (*Vertrag*); break off (*Beziehung, Verlobung*); (*kaufen*) buy; sich l∼ come off; (*sich trennen*) detach oneself/itself; (*lose werden*) come undone; (*sich entspannen*) relax; (*sich klären*) resolve itself; (*sich auflösen*) dissolve

los|fahren† *vi sep* (*sein*) start; (*Auto:*) drive off; l∼fahren auf (+ *acc*) head for; (*fig: angreifen*) go for. l∼gehen† *vi sep* (*sein*) set off; (*fam: anfangen*) start; (*fam: abgehen*) come off; (*Bombe, Gewehr:*) go off; l∼gehen auf (+ *acc*) head for; (*fig: angreifen*) go for. l∼kommen† *vi sep* (*sein*) get away (von from); l∼kommen auf (+ *acc*) come towards. l∼lachen *vi sep* (*haben*) burst out laughing. l∼lassen† *vt sep* let go of; (*freilassen*) release

löslich *a* soluble

los|lösen *vt sep* detach; sich l∼lösen become detached; (*fig*) break away (von

from). l∼machen *vt sep* detach; (*losbinden*) untie; sich l∼machen free oneself/itself. l∼platzen *vi sep* (*sein*) (*fam*) burst out laughing. l∼reißen† *vt sep* tear off; sich l∼reißen break free; (*fig*) tear oneself away. l∼sagen (sich) *vr sep* renounce (von etw sth). l∼schicken *vt sep* send off. l∼sprechen† *vt sep* absolve (von from). l∼steuern *vi sep* (*sein*) head (auf + *acc* for)

Losung *f* -,-en (*Pol*) slogan; (*Mil*) password

Lösung *f* -,-en solution. L∼smittel *nt* solvent

los|werden† *vt sep* get rid of. l∼ziehen† *vi sep* (*sein*) set off; l∼ziehen gegen *od* über (+ *acc*) (*beschimpfen*) run down

Lot *nt* -[e]s,-e perpendicular; (*Blei-*) plumb[-bob]; im Lot sein (*fig*) be all right. l∼en *vt* plumb

löt|en *vt* solder. L∼lampe *f* blow-lamp, (*Amer*) blowtorch. L∼metall *nt* solder

lotrecht *a* perpendicular, *adv* -ly

Lotse *m* -n,-n (*Naut*) pilot. l∼n *vt* (*Naut*) pilot; (*fig*) guide

Lotterie *f* -,-n lottery

Lotto *nt* -s,-s lotto; (*Lotterie*) lottery

Löw|e *m* -n,-n lion; (*Astr*) Leo. L∼enanteil *m* (*fig*) lion's share. L∼enzahn *m* (*Bot*) dandelion. L∼in *f* -,-nen lioness

loyal /lɔa'jaːl/ *a* loyal. L∼ität *f* - loyalty

Luchs *m* -es,-e lynx

Lücke *f* -,-n gap. L∼nbüßer *m* -s,- stop-gap. l∼nhaft *a* incomplete; (*Wissen*) patchy. l∼nlos *a* complete; (*Folge*) unbroken

Luder *nt* -s,- (*sl*) (*Frau*) bitch; armes L∼ poor wretch

Luft *f* -,*̈*e air; tief L∼ holen take a deep breath; in die L∼ gehen explode. L∼angriff *m* air raid. L∼aufnahme *f* aerial photograph. L∼ballon *m* balloon. L∼bild *nt* aerial photograph. L∼blase *f* air bubble

Lüftchen *nt* -s,- breeze

luft|dicht *a* airtight. L∼druck *m* atmospheric pressure

lüften *vt* air; raise (*Hut*); reveal (*Geheimnis*)

Luft|fahrt *f* aviation. L∼fahrtgesellschaft *f* airline. L∼gewehr *nt* air-gun. L∼hauch *m* breath of air. l∼ig *a* airy; (*Kleid*) light. L∼kissenfahrzeug *nt* hovercraft. L∼krieg *m* aerial warfare. L∼kurort *m* climatic health resort. l∼leer *a* l∼leerer Raum vacuum. L∼linie *f* 100 km l∼linie 100 km as the crow flies. L∼loch *nt* air-hole; (*Aviat*) air pocket. L∼matratze *f* air-bed, inflatable mattress. L∼pirat *m* [aircraft] hijacker. L∼post *f* airmail. L∼pumpe *f* air pump;

(*Fahrrad-*) bicycle-pump. L~röhre *f* windpipe. L~schiff *nt* airship. L~schlange *f* [paper] streamer. L~schlösser *ntpl* castles in the air. L~schutzbunker *m* air-raid shelter

Lüftung *f* ventilation

Luft|veränderung *f* change of air. L~waffe *f* air force. L~weg *m* auf dem L~weg by air. L~zug *m* draught

Lüg|e *f* -,-n lie. l~en† *vt/i* (haben) lie. L~ner(in) *m* -s,- (*f* -,-nen) liar. l~nerisch *a* untrue; (*Person*) untruthful

Luke *f* -,-n hatch; (*Dach-*) skylight

Lümmel *m* -s,- lout; (*fam: Schelm*) rascal. l~n (sich) *vr* loll

Lump *m* -en,-en scoundrel. L~en *m* -s,- rag; in L~en in rags. l~en *vt* sich nicht l~en lassen be generous. L~engesindel, L~enpack *nt* riff-raff. L~ensammler *m* rag-and-bone man. l~ig *a* mean, shabby; (*gering*) measly

Lunchpacket /'lan[t]ʃ-/ *nt* packed lunch

Lunge *f* -,-n lungs *pl*; (L~nflügel) lung. L~nentzündung *f* pneumonia

lungern *vi* (haben) loiter

Lunte *f* L~ riechen (*fam*) smell a rat

Lupe *f* -,-n magnifying glass

Lurch *m* -[e]s,-e amphibian

Lust *f* -,-e pleasure; (*Verlangen*) desire; (*sinnliche Begierde*) lust; L~ haben feel like (auf etw acc sth); ich habe keine L~ I don't feel like it; (*will nicht*) I don't want to

Lüster *m* -s,- lustre; (*Kronleuchter*) chandelier

lüstern *a* greedy (auf + acc for); (*sinnlich*) lascivious; (*geil*) lecherous

lustig *a* jolly; (*komisch*) funny; sich l~ machen über (+ acc) make fun of

Lüstling *m* -s,-e sex maniac

lust|los *a* listless, *adv* -ly. L~mörder *m* sex killer. L~spiel *nt* comedy

lutherisch *a* Lutheran

lutsch|en *vt/i* (haben) suck. L~er *m* -s,- lollipop; (*Schnuller*) dummy, (*Amer*) pacifier

lütt *a* (*NGer*) little

Lüttich *nt* -s Liège

Luv *f* & *nt*- nach Luv (*Naut*) to windward

luxuriös *a* luxurious, *adv* -ly

Luxus *m* - luxury. L~artikel *m* luxury article. L~ausgabe *f* de luxe edition. L~hotel *nt* luxury hotel

Lymph|drüse /'lymf-/ *f*, L~knoten *m* lymph gland

lynchen /'lynçən/ *vt* lynch

Lyr|ik *f* - lyric poetry. L~iker *m* -s,- lyric poet. l~isch *a* lyrical; (*Dichtung*) lyric

M

Mach|art *f* style. m~bar *a* feasible. m~en *vt* make; get (*Mahlzeit*); take (*Foto*); (*ausführen, tun, in Ordnung bringen*) do; (*Math: ergeben*) be; (*kosten*) come to; sich (*dat*) etw m~en lassen have sth made; was m~st du da? what are you doing? was m~t die Arbeit? how is work? das m~t 6 Mark [zusammen] that's 6 marks [altogether]; das m~t nichts it doesn't matter; sich (*dat*) wenig/nichts m~en aus care little/ nothing for □ *vr* sich m~en do well; sich an die Arbeit m~en get down to work □ *vi* (haben) ins Bett m~en (*fam*) wet the bed; schnell m~en! hurry. M~enschaften *fpl* machinations

Macht *f* -,-e power; mit aller M~ with all one's might. M~haber *m* -s,- ruler

mächtig *a* powerful; (*groß*) enormous □ *adv* (*fam*) terribly

macht|los *a* powerless. M~wort *nt* ein M~wort sprechen put one's foot down

Mädchen *nt* -s,- girl; (*Dienst-*) maid. m~haft *a* girlish. M~name *m* girl's name; (*vor der Ehe*) maiden name

Made *f* -,-n maggot

Mädel *nt* -s,- girl

madig *a* maggoty; jdn m~ machen (*fam*) run s.o. down

Madonna *f* -,-nen madonna

Magazin *nt* -s,-e magazine; (*Lager*) warehouse; (*Raum*) store-room

Magd *f* -,-e maid

Magen *m* -s,- stomach. M~schmerzen *mpl* stomachache *sg*. M~verstimmung *f* stomach upset

mager *a* thin; (*Fleisch*) lean; (*Boden*) poor; (*dürftig*) meagre. M~keit *f* - thinness; leanness. M~sucht *f* anorexia

Magie *f* - magic

Magier /'ma:giɐ/ *m* -s,- magician. m~isch *a* magic; (*geheimnisvoll*) magical

Magistrat *m* -s,-e city council

Magnesia *f* - magnesia

Magnet *m* -en & -[e]s,-e magnet. m~isch *a* magnetic. m~isieren *vt* magnetize. M~ismus *m* - magnetism

Mahagoni *nt* -s mahogany

Mäh|drescher *m* -s,- combine harvester. m~en *vt/i* (haben) mow

Mahl *nt* -[e]s,-er & -e meal

mahlen† *vt* grind

Mahlzeit *f* meal; M~! enjoy your meal!

Mähne *f* -,-n mane

mahn|en vt/i (haben) remind (wegen about); (ermahnen) admonish; (auffordern) urge (zu to); zur Vorsicht/Eile m~en urge caution/haste. M~ung f -,-en reminder; admonition; (Aufforderung) exhortation

Mai m -[e]s,-e May; der Erste Mai May Day. M~glöckchen nt -s,- lily of the valley. M~käfer m cockchafer

Mailand nt -s Milan

Mais m -es maize, (Amer) corn; (Culin) sweet corn. M~kolben m corn-cob

Majestät f -,-en majesty. m~isch a majestic, adv -ally

Major m -s,-e major

Majoran m -s marjoram

Majorität f -,-en majority

makaber a macabre

Makel m -s,- blemish; (Defekt) flaw; (fig) stain. m~los a flawless; (fig) unblemished

mäkeln vi (haben) grumble

Makkaroni pl macaroni sg

Makler m -s,- (Comm) broker

Makrele f -,-n mackerel

Makrone f -,-n macaroon

mal adv (Math) times; (bei Maßen) by; (fam: einmal) once; (eines Tages) one day; schon mal once before; (jemals) ever; nicht mal not even; hört/seht mal! listen!/look!

Mal[1] nt -[e]s,-e time; das erste/zweite/letzte/nächste Mal the first/second/last/next time; zum ersten/letzten Mal for the first/last time; mit einem Mal all at once; ein für alle Mal once and for all; jedes Mal every time; jedes Mal, wenn whenever; einige/mehrere Mal a few/several times

Mal[2] nt -[e]s,-e mark; (auf der Haut) mole; (Mutter-) birthmark

Mal|buch nt colouring book. m~en vt/i (haben) paint. M~er m -s,- painter. M~erei f -,-en painting. M~erin f -,-nen painter. m~erisch a picturesque

Malheur /ma'lø:ɐ/ nt -s,-e& -s (fam) mishap; (Ärger) trouble

Mallorca /ma'lɔrka, -'jɔrka/ nt -s Majorca

malnehmen† vt sep multiply (mit by)

Malz nt -es malt. M~bier nt malt beer

Mama /'mama, ma'ma:/ f -s,-s mummy

Mammut nt -s,-e & -s mammoth

mampfen vt (fam) munch

man pron one, you; (die Leute) people, they; man sagt they say, it is said

Manager /'mɛnidʒɐ/ m -s,- manager

manch inv pron m~ ein(e) many a; m~ einer/eine many a man/woman. m~e(r,s) pron many a; [so] m~es Mal

many a time; m~e Leute some people □ (substantivisch) m~er/m~e many a man/woman; m~e pl some; (Leute) some people; (viele) many [people]; m~e some things; (vieles) many things. m~erlei inv a various □ pron various things

manchmal adv sometimes

Mandant(in) m -en,-en (f -,-nen) (Jur) client

Mandarine f -,-n mandarin

Mandat nt -[e]s,-e mandate; (Jur) brief; (Pol) seat

Mandel f -,-n almond; (Anat) tonsil. M~entzündung f tonsillitis

Manege /ma'ne:ʒə/ f -,-n ring; (Reit-) arena

Mangel[1] m -s,- lack; (Knappheit) shortage; (Med) deficiency; (Fehler) defect; M~ leiden go short

Mangel[2] f -,-n mangle

mangel|haft a faulty, defective; (Sch) unsatisfactory. m~n† vi (haben) es m~t an (+ dat) there is a lack/(Knappheit) shortage of

mangeln[2] vt put through the mangle

mangels prep (+ gen) for lack of

Mango f -,-s mango

Manie f -,-n mania; (Sucht) obsession

Manier f -,-en manner; M~en manners. m~lich a well-mannered □ adv politely

Manifest nt -[e]s,-e manifesto. m~ieren (sich) vr manifest itself

Maniküre f -,-n manicure; (Person) manicurist. m~n† vt manicure

Manipul|ation/-'tsjo:n/ f -,-en manipulation. m~ieren vt manipulate

Manko nt -s,-s disadvantage; (Fehlbetrag) deficit

Mann m -[e]s,ˉer man; (Ehe-) husband

Männchen nt -s,- (Zool) male; M~ machen (Hund:) sit up

Mannequin /'manəkɛ̃/ nt -s,-s model

Männerchor m male voice choir

Mannes|alter nt manhood. M~kraft f virility

mannhaft a manful, adv -ly

mannigfaltig a manifold; (verschieden) diverse

männlich a male; (Gram & fig) masculine; (mannhaft) manly; (Frau) mannish. M~keit f -masculinity; (fig) manhood

Mannschaft f -,-en team; (Naut) crew. M~sgeist m team spirit

Manöv|er nt -s,- manœuvre (Winkelzug) trick. m~rieren vt/i (haben) manœuvre

Mansarde f -,-n attic room; (Wohnung) attic flat

Manschette f -,-n cuff; (*Blumentopf-*) paper frill. M∼knopf m cuff-link

Mantel m -s,⸚ coat; (*dick*) overcoat; (*Reifen-*) outer tyre

Manuskript nt -[e]s,-e manuscript

Mappe f -,-n folder; (*Akten-*) briefcase; (*Schul-*) bag

Marathon m -s,-s marathon

Märchen nt -s,- fairy-tale. m∼haft a fairy-tale …; (*phantastisch*) fabulous

Margarine f - margarine

Marienkäfer /maˈriːən-/ m lady-bird, (*Amer*) ladybug

Marihuana nt -s marijuana

Marille f -,-n (*Aust*) apricot

Marinade f -,-n marinade

Marine f marine; (*Kriegs-*) navy. m∼blau a navy [blue]. M∼infanterist m marine

marinieren vt marinade

Marionette f -,-n puppet, marionette

Mark[1] f -,- mark; drei M∼ three marks

Mark[2] nt -[e]s (*Knochen-*) marrow; (*Bot*) pith; (*Frucht-*) pulp; bis ins M∼ getroffen (*fig*) cut to the quick

markant a striking

Marke f -,-n token; (*rund*) disc; (*Erkennungs-*) tag; (*Brief-*) stamp; (*Lebensmittel-*) coupon; (*Spiel-*) counter; (*Markierung*) mark; (*Fabrikat*) make; (*Tabak-*) brand. M∼nartikel m branded article

markier|en vt mark; (*fam: vortäuschen*) fake. M∼ung f -,-en marking

Markise f -,-n awning

Markstück nt one-mark piece

Markt m -[e]s,⸚e market; (*M∼platz*) market-place. M∼forschung f market research. M∼platz m market-place

Marmelade f -,-n jam; (*Orangen-*) marmalade

Marmor m -s marble

Marokko nt -s Morocco

Marone f -,-n [sweet] chestnut

Marotte f -,-n whim

Marsch[1] f -,-en marsh

Marsch[2] m -[e]s,⸚e march. m∼ int (*Mil*) march! m∼ ins Bett! off to bed!

Marschall m -s,⸚e marshal

marschieren vi (*sein*) march

Marter f -,-n torture. m∼n vt torture

Martinshorn nt [police] siren

Märtyrer(in) m -s,- (f -,-nen) martyr

Martyrium nt -s martyrdom

Mar|xismus m - Marxism. m∼xistisch a Marxist

März m -,-e March

Marzipan nt -s marzipan

Masche f -,-n stitch; (*im Netz*) mesh; (*fam: Trick*) dodge. M∼ndraht m wire netting

Maschin|e f -,-n machine; (*Flugzeug*) plane; (*Schreib-*) typewriter; M∼e schreiben type. m∼egeschrieben a typewritten, typed. m∼ell a machine … ⸿ adv by machine. M∼enbau m mechanical engineering. M∼engewehr nt machine-gun. M∼enpistole f submachine-gun. M∼erie f - machinery. M∼eschreiben nt typing. M∼ist m -en,-en machinist; (*Naut*) engineer

Masern pl measles sg

Maserung f -,-en [wood] grain

Maske f -,-n mask; (*Theat*) make-up. M∼rade f -,-n disguise; (*fig: Heuchelei*) masquerade

maskieren vt mask; sich m∼ dress up (als a)

Maskottchen nt -s,- mascot

maskulin a masculine

Maskulinum nt -s,-na (*Gram*) masculine

Masochis|mus /mazoˈxɪsmʊs/ m - masochism. M∼t m -en,-en masochist

Maß[1] nt -es,-e measure; (*Abmessung*) measurement; (*Grad*) degree; (*Mäßigung*) moderation; Maß halten exercise moderation; in od mit Maß[en] in moderation; in hohem Maße to a high degree

Maß[2] f -,- (*SGer*) litre [of beer]

Massage /maˈsaːʒə/ f -,-n massage

Massaker nt -s,- massacre

Maß|anzug m made-to-measure suit. M∼band nt (*pl -bänder*) tape-measure

Masse f -,-n mass; (*Culin*) mixture; (*Menschen-*) crowd; eine M∼ Arbeit (*fam*) masses of work. M∼nartikel m mass-produced article. m∼nhaft adv in huge quantities. M∼nmedien pl mass media. M∼nproduktion f mass production. M∼nweise adv in huge numbers

Masseu|r /maˈsøːɐ̯/ m -s,-e masseur. M∼rin f -,-nen, M∼se /-ˈsøːzə/ f -,-n masseuse

maß|gebend a authoritative; (*einflussreich*) influential. m∼geblich a decisive, adv -ly. m∼geschneidert a made-to-measure. m∼halten† vi sep (*haben*) (NEW) Maß halten, s. Maß[1]

massieren[1] vt massage

massieren[2] (sich) vr mass

massig a massive

mäßig a moderate, adv -ly; (*mittelmäßig*) indifferent. m∼en vt moderate; sich m∼en moderate; (*sich beherrschen*) restrain oneself. M∼keit f - moderation. M∼ung f - moderation

massiv a solid; (*stark*) heavy

Maß|krug *m* beer mug. m~los *a* excessive; (*grenzenlos*) boundless; (*äußerst*) extreme, *adv* -ly. M~nahme *f* -,-n measure. m~regeln *vt* reprimand

Maßstab *m* scale; (*Norm & fig*) standard. m~sgerecht, m~sgetreu *a* scale ... ◻ *adv* to scale

maßvoll *a* moderate

Mast¹ *m* -[e]s,-en pole; (*Überland-*) pylon; (*Naut*) mast

Mast² *f* -fattening. M~darm *m* rectum

mästen *vt* fatten

Masturb|ation /-'tsjo:n/ *f* - masturbation. m~ieren *vi* (*haben*) masturbate

Material *nt* -s,-ien /-jən/ material; (*coll*) materials *pl*. M~ismus *m* - materialism. m~istisch *a* materialistic

Mater|ie /ma'te:rjə/ *f* -,-n matter; (*Thema*) subject. m~iell *a* material

Mathe *f* - (*fam*) maths *sg*

Mathe|matik *f* - mathematics *sg*. M~matiker *m* -s,- mathematician. m~matisch *a* mathematical

Matinee *f* -,-n (*Theat*) morning performance

Matratze *f* -,-n mattress

Mätresse *f* -,-n mistress

Matrose *m* -n,-n sailor

Matsch *m* -[e]s mud; (*Schnee-*) slush. m~ig *a* muddy; slushy; (*weich*) mushy

matt *a* weak; (*gedämpft*) dim; (*glanzlos*) dull; (*Politur, Farbe*) matt; jdn m~ setzen checkmate s.o. M~ *nt* -s (*Schach*) mate

Matte *f* -,-n mat

Mattglas *nt* frosted glass

Matt|igkeit *f* - weakness; (*Müdigkeit*) weariness. M~scheibe *f* (*fam*) television screen

Matura *f* - (*Aust*) ≈ A levels *pl*

Mauer *f* -,-n wall. m~n *vt* build ◻ *vi* (*haben*) lay bricks. M~werk *nt* masonry

Maul *nt* -[e]s, Mäuler (*Zool*) mouth; halt's M~! (*fam*) shut up! m~en *vi* (*haben*) (*fam*) grumble. M~korb *m* muzzle. M~tier *nt* mule. M~wurf *m* mole. M~wurfshaufen, M~wurfshügel *m* molehill

Maurer *m* -s,- bricklayer

Maus *f* -,Mäuse mouse. M~efalle *f* mousetrap

mausern (sich) *vr* moult; (*fam*) turn (zu into)

Maut *f* -,-en (*Aust*) toll. M~straße *f* toll road

maximal *a* maximum

Maximum *nt* -s,-ma maximum

Mayonnaise /majɔ'nɛ:zə/ *f* -,-n mayonnaise

Mäzen *m* -s,-e patron

Mechan|ik /me'ça:nɪk/ *f* - mechanics *sg*; (*Mechanismus*) mechanism. M~iker *m* -s,- mechanic. m~isch *a* mechanical, *adv* -ly. M~isieren *vt* mechanize. M~ismus *m* -,-men mechanism

meckern *vi* (*haben*) bleat; (*fam: nörgeln*) grumble

Medaill|e /me'daljə/ *f* -,-n medal. M~on /-'jõ:/ *nt* -s,-s medallion; (*Schmuck*) locket

Medikament *nt* -[e]s,-e medicine

Medit|ation /-'tsjo:n/ *f* -,-en meditation. m~ieren *vi* (*haben*) meditate

Medium *nt* -s,-ien medium; die Medien the media

Medizin *f* -,-en medicine. M~er *m* -s,- doctor; (*Student*) medical student. m~isch *a* medical; (*heilkräftig*) medicinal

Meer *nt* -[e]s,-e sea. M~busen *m* gulf. M~enge *f* strait. M~esspiegel *m* sea-level. M~jungfrau *f* mermaid. M~rettich *m* horseradish. M~schweinchen *nt* -s,- guinea-pig

Megaphon, Megafon *nt* -s,-e megaphone

Mehl *nt* -[e]s flour. m~ig *a* floury. M~schwitze *f* (*Culin*) roux. M~speise *f* (*Aust*) dessert; (*Kuchen*) pastry. M~tau *m* (*Bot*) mildew

mehr *pron & adv* more; nicht m~ no more; (*zeitlich*) no longer; nichts m~ no more; (*nichts weiter*) nothing else; nie m~ never again. m~deutig *a* ambiguous. m~en *vt* increase; sich m~en increase. m~ere *pron* several. m~eremal *adv* ⟨NEW⟩ m~ere Mal, *s.* Mal¹. m~eres *pron* several things *pl*. m~fach *a* multiple; (*mehrmalig*) repeated ◻ *adv* several times. M~fahrtenkarte *f* book of tickets. m~farbig *a* [multi]coloured. M~heit *f* -,-en majority. m~malig *a* repeated. m~mals *adv* several times. m~sprachig *a* multilingual. m~stimmig *a* (*Mus*) for several voices ◻ *adv* m~stimmig singen sing in harmony. M~wertsteuer *f* value-added tax, VAT. M~zahl *f* majority; (*Gram*) plural. M~zweck- *pref* multi-purpose

meiden† *vt* avoid, shun

Meierei *f* -,-en (*dial*) dairy

Meile *f* -,-n mile. M~nstein *m* milestone. m~nweit *adv* [for] miles

mein *poss pron* my. m~e(r,s) *poss pron* mine; die M~en *od* m~en *pl* my family *sg*

Meineid *m* perjury; einen M~ leisten perjure oneself

meinen *vt* mean; (*glauben*) think; (*sagen*) say; gut gemeinter Rat wel-meant advice; es gut m~ mean well

me̱in|erseits *adv* for my part.
m∼etwegen*adv* for my sake; (*wegen mir*)
because of me, on my account; (*fam: von
mir aus*) as far as I'm concerned. m∼et‐
willen*adv* um m∼etwillen for my sake.
m∼ige *poss pron* der/die/das m∼ige
mine. m∼s *poss pron* mine

Me̱inung *f* -,-en opinion; jdm die M∼
sagen give s.o. a piece of one's mind.
M∼sumfrage *f* opinion poll

Me̱ise *f* -,-n (*Zool*) tit

Me̱ißel *m* -s,- chisel. m∼n *vt/i* (*haben*)
chisel

me̱ist *adv* mostly; (*gewöhnlich*) usually.
m∼e *a* der/die/das m∼e most; die
m∼en Leute most people; die m∼e Zeit
most of the time; am m∼en [the] most
□ *pron* das m∼e most [of it]; die m∼en
most. m∼ens *adv* mostly; (*gewöhnlich*)
usually

Me̱ister *m* -s,- master craftsman; (*Könner*)
master; (*Sport*) champion. m∼haft *a* mas‐
terly □ *adv* in masterly fashion. m∼n *vt*
master. M∼schaft *f* -,-en mastery;
(*Sport*) championship. M∼stück,
M∼werk *nt* masterpiece

Melanch|olie /melaŋko'li:/ *f* - melan‐
choly. m∼olisch *a* melancholy

me̱ld|en *vt* report; (*anmelden*) register;
(*ankündigen*) announce; sich m∼en re‐
port (bei to); (*zum Militär*) enlist;
(*freiwillig*) volunteer; (*Teleph*) answer;
(*Sch*) put up one's hand; (*von sich hören
lassen*) get in touch (bei with); sich krank
m∼en (NEW) sich krankmelden M∼ung
f -,-en report; (*Anmeldung*) registration

meli̱ert *a* mottled; grau m∼es Haar hair
flecked with grey

me̱lken *vt* milk

Melod|ie *f* -,-n tune, melody. m∼iös *a*
melodious

melo̱disch *a* melodic; (*melodiös*) melodi‐
ous, tuneful

melodrama̱tisch *a* melodramatic, *adv*
-ally

Melo̱ne *f* -,-n melon; [schwarze] M∼
(*fam*) bowler [hat]

Membra̱n *f* -,-en membrane

Memo̱iren /me'mɔa:rən/ *pl* memoirs

Me̱nge *f* -,-n amount, quantity; (*Men‐
schen-*) crowd; (*Math*) set; eine M∼ Geld
a lot of money. m∼n *vt* mix

Me̱nsa *f* -,-sen (*Univ*) refectory

Me̱nsch *m* -en,-en human being; der M∼
man; die M∼en people; jeder/kein M∼
everybody/nobody. M∼enaffe *m* ape.
M∼enfeind *m* misanthropist. m∼en‐
feindlich *a* antisocial. M∼enfresser *m*
-s,- cannibal; (*Zool*) man-eater; (*fam*) ogre.
m∼enfreundlich *a* philanthropic.

M∼enleben *nt* human life; (*Lebenszeit*)
lifetime. m∼enleer *a* deserted. M∼en‐
menge *f* crowd. M∼enraub *m* kidnap‐
ping. M∼enrechte *ntpl* human rights.
m∼enscheu *a* unsociable. M∼enskind
int (*fam*) good heavens! M∼enverstand
m gesunder M∼enverstand common
sense. m∼enwürdig *a* humane, *adv* -ly.
M∼heit *f* - die M∼heit mankind, hu‐
manity. m∼lich *a* human; (*human*) hu‐
mane, *adv* -ly. M∼lichkeit *f* -humanity

Menstru|ation /-'tsjo:n/ *f* - menstru‐
ation. m∼ieren *vi* (*haben*) menstruate

Mentalitä̱t *f* -,-en mentality

Menü̱ *nt* -s,-s menu; (*festes M∼*) set meal

Menue̱tt *nt* -[e]s,-e minuet

Meridia̱n *m* -s,-e meridian

me̱rk|bar *a* noticeable. M∼blatt *nt* [ex‐
planatory] leaflet. m∼en *vt* notice; sich
(*dat*) etw m∼en remember sth. m∼lich
a noticeable, *adv* -bly. M∼mal *nt* feature

me̱rkwürdig *a* odd, *adv* -ly, strange, *adv*
-ly. m∼erweise *adv* oddly enough

me̱ss|bar (meßbar) *a* measurable.
M∼becher *m* (*Culin*) measure

Me̱sse[1] *f* -,-n (*Relig*) mass; (*Comm*) [trade]
fair

Me̱sse[2] *f* -,-n (*Mil*) mess

me̱ssen *vt/i* (*haben*) measure; (*ansehen*)
look at; [bei jdm] Fieber m∼en take s.o.'s
temperature; sich m∼en compete (mit
with); sich mit jdm m∼en/nicht m∼en
können be a/no match for s.o.

Me̱sser *nt* -s,- knife

Messi̱as *m* - Messiah

Me̱ssing *nt* -s brass

Me̱ssung *f* -,-en measurement

Metabolismus *m* - metabolism

Meta̱ll *nt* -s,-e metal. m∼en *a* metal;
(*metallisch*) metallic. m∼isch *a* metallic

Metallurgie̱ *f* - metallurgy

Metamorpho̱se *f* -,-n metamorphosis

Meta̱ph|er *f* -,-n metaphor. m∼orisch *a*
metaphorical, *adv* -ly

Mete̱or *m* -s,-e meteor. M∼ologe *m* -n,-n
meteorologist. M∼ologie̱ *f* -meteorology.
m∼ologisch *a* meteorological

Me̱ter *m* & *nt* -s,- metre, (*Amer*) meter.
M∼maß *nt* tape-measure

Metho̱d|e *f* -,-n method. m∼isch *a* meth‐
odical

me̱trisch *a* metric

Metropo̱le *f* -,-n metropolis

me̱tzeln *vt* (*fig*) massacre

Me̱tzger *m* -s,- butcher. M∼ei̱ *f* -,-en but‐
cher's shop

Me̱ute *f* -,-n pack [of hounds]; (*fig: Menge*)
mob

Meuterei f -,-en mutiny

meutern vi (haben) mutiny; (fam: schimpfen) grumble

Mexikan|er(in) m -s,- (f -,-nen) Mexican. **m∼isch** a Mexican

Mexiko nt -s Mexico

miauen vi (haben) mew, miaow

mich pron (acc of ich) me; (refl) myself

Mieder nt -s,- bodice; (Korsett) corset

Miene f -,-n expression; **M∼** machen make as if (zu to)

mies a (fam) lousy; mir ist m∼ I feel rotten

Miet|e f -,-n rent; (Mietgebühr) hire charge; zur M∼e wohnen live in rented accommodation. **m∼en** vt rent (Haus, Zimmer); hire (Auto, Boot, Fernseher). **M∼er(in)** m-s,- (f-,-nen) tenant. **m∼frei** a & adv rent-free. **M∼shaus** nt block of rented flats. **M∼vertrag** m lease. **M∼wagen** m hire-car. **M∼wohnung** f rented flat; (zu vermieten) flat to let

Mieze f -,-n (fam) puss[y]

Migräne f -,-n migraine

Mikrobe f -,-n microbe

Mikro|chip m microchip. **M∼computer** m microcomputer. **M∼film** m microfilm

Mikro|fon, M∼phon nt -s,-e microphone. **M∼prozessor** m -s,-en /-'so:rən/ microprocessor. **M∼skop** nt -s,-e microscope. **m∼skopisch** a microscopic

Mikrowelle f microwave. **M∼ngerät** nt, **M∼nherd** m microwave oven

Milbe f -,-n mite

Milch f - milk. **M∼bar** f milk bar. **M∼geschäft** nt dairy. **M∼glas** nt opal glass. **m∼ig** a milky. **M∼kuh** f dairy cow. **M∼mann** m (pl -männer) milkman. **M∼mixgetränk** nt milk shake. **M∼straße** f Milky Way. **M∼zahn** m milk tooth

mild a mild; (nachsichtig) lenient; m∼e Gaben alms. **M∼e** f - mildness; leniency. **m∼ern** vt make milder; (mäßigen) moderate; (lindern) alleviate, ease; sich m∼ern become milder; (sich mäßigen) abate; (nachlassen) abate; (Schmerz:) ease; m∼ernde Umstände mitigating circumstances. **m∼tätig** a charitable

Milieu /mi'ljø:/ nt -s,-s [social] environment

militant a militant

Militär nt -s army; (Soldaten) troops pl; beim M∼ in the army. **m∼isch** a military

Miliz f -,-en militia

Milliarde /mɪl'ljardə/ f -,-n thousand million, billion

Milli|gramm nt milligram. **M∼meter** m & nt millimetre. **M∼meterpapier** nt graph paper

Million /mi'ljo:n/ f -,-en million. **M∼är** m -s,-e millionaire. **M∼ärin** f -,-nen millionairess

Milz f - (Anat) spleen

mim|en vt (fam: vortäuschen) act. **M∼ik** f - [expressive] gestures and facial expressions pl

Mimose f -,-n mimosa

minder a lesser □ adv less; mehr oder m∼ more or less. **M∼heit** f-,-en minority

minderjährig a (Jur) under-age; m∼ sein be under age. **M∼e(r)** m/f (Jur) minor. **M∼keit** f - (Jur) minority

minder|n vt diminish; decrease (Tempo). **M∼ung** f- decrease

minderwertig a inferior. **M∼keit** f- inferiority. **M∼keitskomplex** m inferiority complex

Mindest- pref minimum. **m∼e** a & pron der/die/das M∼e od m∼e the least; zum M∼en od m∼en at least; nicht im M∼en od m∼en in the least. **m∼ens** adv at least. **M∼lohn** m minimum wage. **M∼maß** nt minimum

Mine f -,-n mine; (Bleistift-) lead; (Kugelschreiber-) refill. **M∼nfeld** nt minefield. **M∼nräumboot** nt minesweeper

Mineral nt -s,-e & -ien /-jən/ mineral. **m∼isch** a mineral. **M∼ogie** f - mineralogy. **M∼wasser** nt mineral water

Miniatur f -,-en miniature

Minigolf nt miniature golf

minimal a minimal

Minimum nt -s,-ma minimum

Minirock m miniskirt

Mini|ster m -s,- minister. **m∼steriell** a ministerial. **M∼sterium** nt -s,-ien ministry

Minorität f -,-en minority

minus conj, adv & prep (+ gen) minus. **M∼** nt - deficit; (Nachteil) disadvantage. **M∼zeichen** nt minus [sign]

Minute f -,-n minute

mir pron (dat of ich) [to] me; (refl) myself; mir nichts, dir nichts without so much as a 'by your leave'

Misch|ehe f mixed marriage. **m∼en** vt mix; blend (Tee, Kaffee); toss (Salat); shuffle (Karten); sich m∼en mix; (Person:) mingle (unter + acc with); sich m∼en in (+ acc) join in (Gespräch); meddle in (Angelegenheit) □ vi (haben) shuffle the cards. **M∼ling** m -s,-e halfcaste; (Hund) cross. **M∼masch** m -[e]s,-e (fam) hotchpotch. **M∼ung** f-,-en mixture; blend

miserabel a abominable; (erbärmlich) wretched

missachten (mißachten) vt disregard

Miss|achtung (Miß|achtung) f disregard. M~behagen nt [feeling of] unease. M~bildung f deformity

missbilligen (mißbilligen) vt disapprove of

Miss|billigung (Miß|billigung) f disapproval. M~brauch m abuse; M~brauch treiben mit abuse

miss|brauchen (miß|brauchen) vt abuse; (vergewaltigen) rape. m~deuten vt misinterpret

missen vt do without; ich möchte es nicht m~ I should not like to be without it

Miss|erfolg (Miß|erfolg) m failure. M~ernte f crop failure

Misse|tat f misdeed. M~täter m (fam) culprit

missfallen† (mißfallen†) vi (haben) displease (jdm s.o.)

Miss|fallen (Miß|fallen) nt -s displeasure; (Missbilligung) disapproval. m~gebildet a deformed. M~geburt f freak; (fig) monstrosity. M~geschick nt mishap; (Unglück) misfortune. m~gestimmt a m~gestimmt sein to be in a bad mood

miss|glücken (miß|glücken) vi (sein) fail. m~gönnen vt begrudge

Miss|griff (Miß|griff) m mistake. M~gunst f resentment. m~günstig a resentful

misshandeln (mißhandeln) vt ill-treat

Miss|handlung (Miß|handlung) f ill-treatment. M~helligkeit f -,-en disagreement

Mission f -,-en mission

Missionar(in) m -s,-e (f -,-nen) missionary

Miss|klang (Miß|klang) m discord. M~kredit m discredit; in M~kredit bringen discredit. m~lich a awkward. m~liebig a unpopular

misslingen† (mißlingen†) vi (sein) fail; es misslang ihr she failed. M~ nt -s failure

Missmut (Mißmut) m ill humour. m~ig a morose, adv -ly

missraten† (mißraten†) vi (sein) turn out badly

Miss|stand (Miß|stand) m abuse; (Zustand) undesirable state of affairs. M~stimmung f discord; (Laune) bad mood. M~ton m discordant note

misstrauen (mißtrauen) vi (haben) jdm/etw m~ mistrust s.o./sth; (Argwohn hegen) distrust s.o./sth

Misstrau|en (Mißtrau|en) nt -s mistrust; (Argwohn) distrust. M~ensvotum nt

vote of no confidence. m~isch a distrustful; (argwöhnisch) suspicious

Miss|verhältnis (Miß|verhältnis) nt disproportion. M~verständnis nt misunderstanding. m~verstehen† vt misunderstand. M~wirtschaft f mismanagement

Mist m -[e]s manure; (fam) rubbish

Mistel f -,-n mistletoe

Misthaufen m dungheap

mit prep (+ dat) with; (sprechen) to; (mittels) by; (inklusive) including; (bei) at; mit Bleistift in pencil; mit lauter Stimme in a loud voice; mit drei Jahren at the age of three □ adv (auch) as well; mit anfassen (fig) lend a hand; es ist mit das ärmste Land der Welt it is among the poorest countries in the world

Mitarbeit f collaboration. m~en vi sep collaborate (an + dat on). M~er(in) m(f) collaborator; (Kollege) colleague; (Betriebsangehörige) employee

Mitbestimmung f co-determination

mitbringen† vt sep bring [along]; jdm Blumen m~en bring/(hinbringen) take s.o. flowers. M~sel nt -s,- present (brought back from holiday etc)

Mitbürger m fellow citizen

miteinander adv with each other

miterleben vt sep witness

Mitesser m (Med) blackhead

mitfahren† vi sep (sein) go/come along; mit jdm m~ go with s.o.; (mitgenommen werden) be given a lift by s.o.

mitfühlen vi sep (haben) sympathize. m~d a sympathetic; (mitleidig) compassionate

mitgeben† vt sep jdm etw m~ give s.o. sth to take with him

Mitgefühl nt sympathy

mitgehen† vi sep (sein) mit jdm m~ go with s.o.; etw m~ lassen (fam) pinch sth

mitgenommen a worn; m~ sein be in a sorry state; (erschöpft) be exhausted

Mitgift f -,-en dowry

Mitglied nt member. M~schaft f - membership

mithalten† vi sep (haben) join in; mit jdm nicht m~ können not be able to keep up with s.o.

Mithilfe f assistance

mithilfe prep (+ gen) with the aid of

mitkommen† vi sep (sein) come [along] too; (fig: folgen können) keep up; (verstehen) follow

Mitlaut m consonant

Mitleid nt pity, compassion; M~ erregend pitiful. M~enschaft f in M~enschaft ziehen affect. m~erregend a =

M∼ erregend, s. Mitleid. m∼ig a pity-
ing; (mitfühlend) compassionate. m∼slos
a pitiless

mitmachen v sep □ vt take part in; (erleben) go through □ vi (haben) join in

Mitmensch m fellow man

mitnehmen† vt sep take along; (mitfahren lassen) give a lift to; (fig: schädigen)
affect badly; (erschöpfen) exhaust; 'zum
M∼' 'to take away', (Amer) 'to go'

mitnichten adv not at all

mitreden vi sep (haben) join in [the con-
versation]; (mit entscheiden) have a say
(bei in)

mitreißen† vt sep sweep along; (fig: be-
geistern) carry away; m∼d rousing

mitsamt prep (+ dat) together with

mitschneiden† vt sep record

mitschreiben† vt sep (haben) take down

Mitschuld f partial blame. m∼ig a m∼ig
sein be partly to blame

Mitschüler(in) m(f) fellow pupil

mitspiel|en vi sep (haben) join in; (Theat)
be in the cast; (beitragen) play a part; jdm
übel m∼en treat s.o. badly. M∼er m fellow player; (Mitwirkender) participant

Mittag m midday, noon; (Mahlzeit) lunch;
(Pause) lunch-break; heute/gestern M∼
at lunch-time today/yesterday; [zu] M∼
essen have lunch. m∼ adv heu-
te/gestern m∼ NEW heute/gestern
M∼, s. Mittag. M∼essen nt lunch. m∼s
adv at noon; (als Mahlzeit) for lunch; um
12 Uhr m∼s at noon. M∼spause f lunch-
hour; (Pause) lunch-break. M∼sschlaf m
after-lunch nap. M∼stisch m lunch table;
(Essen) lunch. M∼szeit f lunch-time

Mittäter|(in) m(f) accomplice.
M∼schaft f complicity

Mitte f -,-n middle; (Zentrum) centre; die
goldene M∼ the golden mean; M∼ Mai
in mid-May; in unserer M∼ in our midst

mitteil|en vt sep jdm etw m∼en tell s.o.
sth; (amtlich) inform s.o. of sth. m∼sam
a communicative. M∼ung f -,-en communication; (Nachricht) piece of news

Mittel nt -s,- means sg; (Heil)remedy; (Medikament) medicine; (M∼wert) mean;
(Durchschnitt) average; M∼ pl (Geld-)
funds, resources. m∼ pred a medium;
(m∼mäßig) middling. M∼alter nt Middle
Ages pl. m∼alterlich a medieval.
m∼bar a indirect, adv -ly. M∼ding nt
(fig) cross. m∼europäisch a Central
European. M∼finger m middle finger.
m∼groß a medium-sized; (Person) of medium height. M∼klasse f middle range.
m∼los a destitute. m∼mäßig a
middling; [nur] m∼mäßig mediocre.

M∼meer nt Mediterranean. **M∼punkt**
m centre; (fig) centre of attention

mittels prep (+ gen) by means of

Mittel|schule f = Realschule. M∼s-
mann m (pl -männer), M∼sperson f intermediary, go-between. M∼stand m
middle class. M∼ste(r,s) a middle.
M∼streifen m (Auto) central reservation, (Amer) median strip. M∼stürmer
m centre-forward. M∼weg m (fig) middle
course; goldener M∼weg happy medium. M∼welle f medium wave.
M∼wort nt (pl -wörter) participle

mitten adv m∼ in/auf (dat/acc) in the
middle of; m∼ unter (dat/acc) amidst.
m∼durch adv [right] through the middle

Mitternacht f midnight

mittler|e(r,s) a middle; (Größe, Qualität)
medium; (durchschnittlich) mean, average. m∼weile adv meanwhile; (seitdem)
by now

Mittwoch m -s,-e Wednesday. m∼s adv
on Wednesdays

mitunter adv now and again

mitwirk|en vi sep (haben) take part;
(helfen) contribute. M∼ung f participa-
tion

mix|en vt mix. M∼er m -s,- (Culin)
liquidizer, blender. M∼tur f -,-en (Med)
mixture

Möbel pl furniture sg. M∼stück nt piece
of furniture. M∼tischler m cabinet-
maker. M∼wagen m removal van

mobil a mobile; (fam: munter) lively; (nach
Krankheit) fit [and well]; m∼ machen
mobilize

Mobile nt -s,-s mobile

Mobiliar nt -s furniture

mobilisier|en vt mobilize. M∼ung f -
mobilization

Mobil|machung f - mobilization.
M∼telefon nt mobile phone

möblier|en vt furnish; m∼tes Zimmer
furnished room

mochte, möchte s. mögen

Modalverb nt modal auxiliary

Mode f -,-n fashion; M∼ sein be fashionable

Modell nt -s,-e model; M∼ stehen pose
(jdm for s.o.). m∼ieren vt model

Modenschau f fashion show

Modera|tor m -s,-en /-'to:rən/, M∼torin
f -,-nen (TV) presenter

modern¹ vi (haben) decay

modern² a modern; (modisch) fashionable. m∼isieren vt modernize

Mode|schmuck m costume jewellery.
M∼schöpfer m fashion designer

Modifi|kation /-'tsjo:n/ f -,-en modification. m~zieren vt modify

modisch a fashionable

Modistin f -,-nen milliner

modrig a musty

modulieren vt modulate

Mofa nt -s,-s moped

mogeln vi (haben) (fam) cheat

mögen† vt like; lieber m~ prefer □ v aux ich möchte I'd like; möchtest du nach Hause? do you want to go home? ich mag nicht mehr I've had enough; ich hätte weinen m~ I could have cried; ich mag mich irren I may be wrong; wer/was mag das sein? whoever/whatever can it be? wie mag es ihm ergangen sein? I wonder how he got on; [das] mag sein that may well be; mag kommen, was da will come what may

möglich a possible; alle m~en all sorts of; über alles M~e (m~e) sprechen talk about all sorts of things; sein M~stes (m~stes) tun do one's utmost. m~erweise adv possibly. M~keit f -,-en possibility. M~keitsform f subjunctive. m~st adv if possible; m~st viel/früh as much/early as possible

Mohammedan|er(in) m -s,- (f -,-nen) Muslim. m~isch a Muslim

Mohn m -s poppy; (Culin) poppyseed. M~blume f poppy

Möhre, Mohrrübe f -,-n carrot

mokieren (sich) vr make fun (über + acc of)

Mokka m -s mocha; (Geschmack) coffee

Molch m -[e]s,-e newt

Mole f -,-n (Naut) mole

Molekül nt -s,-e molecule

Molkerei f -,-en dairy

Moll nt - (Mus) minor

mollig a cosy; (warm) warm; (rundlich) plump

Moment m -s,-e moment; im/jeden M~ at the/any moment; M~ [mal]! just a moment! m~an a momentary, adv -ily; (gegenwärtig) at the moment

Momentaufnahme f snapshot

Monarch m -en,-en monarch. M~ie f -,-n monarchy

Monat m -s,-e month. m~elang adv for months. m~lich a & adv monthly. M~skarte f monthly season ticket

Mönch m -[e]s,-e monk

Mond m -[e]s,-e moon

mondän a fashionable, adv -bly

Mond|finsternis f lunar eclipse. m~hell a moonlit. M~sichel f crescent moon. M~schein m moonlight

monieren vt criticize

Monitor m -s,-en /-'to:rən/ (Techn) monitor

Monogramm nt -s,-e monogram

Mono|log m -s,-e monologue. M~pol nt -s,-e monopoly. m~polisieren vt monopolize. m~ton a monotonous, adv -ly. M~tonie f -monotony

Monster nt -s,- monster

monstr|ös a monstrous M~osität f -,-en monstrosity

Monstrum nt -s,-stren monster

Monsun m -s,-e monsoon

Montag m Monday

Montage /mɔn'ta:ʒə/ f -,-n fitting; (Zusammenbau) assembly; (Film-) editing; (Kunst) montage

montags adv on Mondays

Montanindustrie f coal and steel industry

Monteur /mɔn'tø:ɐ̯/ m -s,-e fitter. M~anzug m overalls pl

montieren vt fit; (zusammenbauen) assemble

Monument nt -[e]s,-e monument. m~al a monumental

Moor nt -[e]s,-e bog; (Heide-) moor

Moos nt es,-e moss. m~ig a mossy

Mop m -s,-s (NEW) Mopp

Moped nt -s,-s moped

Mopp m -s,-s mop

Mops m -s,ˑe pug [dog]

Moral f -morals pl; (Selbstvertrauen) morale; (Lehre) moral. m~isch a moral, adv -ly. m~isieren vi (haben) moralize

Morast m -[e]s,-emorass; (Schlamm) mud

Mord m -[e]s,-e murder, (Pol) assassination. M~anschlag m murder/assassination attempt. m~en vt/i (haben) murder, kill

Mörder m -s,- murderer, (Pol) assassin. M~in f -,-nen murderess. m~isch a murderous; (fam: schlimm) dreadful

Mords- pref (fam) terrific. m~mäßig a (fam) frightful, adv -ly

morgen adv tomorrow; m~ Abend (abend)/Nachmittag (nachmittag) tomorrow evening/afternoon; heute/gestern/Montag m~ (NEW) heute/gestern/Montag M~, s. Morgen

Morgen m -s,-morning; (Maß) ≈ acre; am M~ in the morning; heute/gestern/Montag M~ this/yesterday/Monday morning. M~dämmerung f dawn. m~dlich a morning ... M~grauen nt -s dawn; im M~grauen at dawn. m~mantel, M~rock m dressing-gown. M~rot nt red sky in the morning. m~s a in the morning

morgig a tomorrow's; der m~e Tag tomorrow

Morphium nt -s morphine

morsch a rotten

Morsealphabet nt Morse code

Mörtel m -s mortar

Mosaik /moza'i:k/ nt -s,-e[n] mosaic

Moschee f -,-n mosque

Mosel f - Moselle. M~wein m Moselle [wine]

Moskau nt -s Moscow

Moskito m -s,-s mosquito

Mos|lem m -s,-s Muslim. m~lemisch a Muslim

Most m -[e]s must; (Apfel-) ≈ cider

Mostrich m -s (NGer) mustard

Motel nt -s,-s motel

Motiv nt -s,-e motive; (Kunst) motif. M~ation /-'tsio:n/ f - motivation. m~ieren vt motivate

Motor /'mo:tor, mo'to:g/ m -s,-en /-'to:rən/ engine; (Elektro-) motor. M~boot nt motor boat

motorisieren vt motorize

Motor|rad nt motor cycle. M~radfahrer m motor-cyclist. M~roller m motor scooter

Motte f -,-n moth. M~nkugel f mothball

Motto nt -s,-s motto

Möwe f -,-n gull

Mücke f -,-n gnat; (kleine) midge; (Stech-) mosquito

mucksen (sich) vr sich nicht m~ (fam) keep quiet

müd|e a tired; nicht m~e werden/es m~e sein not tire/be tired (etw zu tun of doing sth). M~igkeit f - tiredness

Muff m -s,-e muff

muffig a musty; (fam: mürrisch) grumpy

Mühe f -,-n effort; (Aufwand) trouble;sich (dat) M~ geben make an effort; (sich bemühen) try; nicht der M~ wert not worth while; mitM~ und Not with great difficulty; (gerade noch) only just. m~los a effortless, adv -ly

muhen vi (haben) moo

mühe|n (sich) vr struggle. m~voll a laborious; (anstrengend) arduous

Mühl|e f -,-n mill; (Kaffee-) grinder. M~stein m millstone

Müh|sal f -,-e (liter) toil; (Mühe) trouble. m~sam a laborious, adv -ly; (beschwerlich) difficult, adv with difficulty. m~selig a laborious, adv -ly

Mulde f -,-n hollow

Müll m -s refuse, (Amer) garbage. M~abfuhr f refuse collection

Mullbinde f gauze bandage

Mülleimer m waste bin; (Mülltonne) dustbin, (Amer) garbage can

Müller m -s,- miller

Müll|halde f [rubbish] dump.M~schlucker m refuse chute.M~tonne f dustbin, (Amer) garbage can. M~wagen m dustcart, (Amer) garbage truck

mulmig a (fam) dodgy; (Gefühl) uneasy; ihm war m~ zumute he felt uneasy/ (übel) queasy

multi|national a multinational. M~plikation /-'tsio:n/ f -,-en multiplication.m~plizieren vt multiply

Mumie /'mu:mjə/ f -,-n mummy

mumifiziert a mummified

Mumm m -s (fam) energy

Mumps m - mumps

Mund m -[e]s,-er mouth; ein M~ voll Suppe a mouthful of soup; halt den M~! be quiet! (sl) shut up! M~art f dialect. m~artlich a dialect

Mündel nt & m -s,- (Jur) ward.m~sicher a gilt-edged

münden vi (sein) flow/(Straße:) lead (in + acc into)

mund|faul a taciturn. M~geruch m bad breath. M~harmonika f mouth-organ

mündig a m~ sein/werden (Jur) be/come of age. M~keit f - (Jur) majority

mündlich a verbal, adv -ly; m~e Prüfung oral

Mund|stück nt mouthpiece; (Zigaretten-) tip.m~tot am~tot machen (fig) gag

Mündung f -,-en (Fluss-) mouth; (Gewehr-) muzzle

Mund|voll m -,- ein M~voll (NEW)ein M~ voll, s. Mund. M~wasser nt mouthwash. M~werk nt ein gutes M~werk haben (fam) be very talkative. M~winkel m corner of the mouth

Munition /-'tsio:n/ f - ammunition

munkeln vt/i (haben) talk (von of); es wird gemunkelt rumour has it (dass that)

Münster nt -s,- cathedral

munter a lively; (heiter) merry; m~ sein (wach) be wide awake/(aufgestanden, gesund) up and about; gesund und m~ fit and well ☐ adv [immer] m~ merrily

Münz|e f -,-n coin; (M~stätte) mint. m~en vt mint; das war auf dich gemünzt (fam) that was aimed at you. M~fernsprecher m coin-box telephone, payphone. M~wäscherei f launderette

mürbe a crumbly; (Obst) mellow; (Fleisch) tender; jdn m~ machen (fig) wear s.o. down.M~teig m short pastry

Murmel f -,-n marble

murmeln *vt/i (haben)* murmur; *(undeutlich)* mumble, mutter. M~ *nt* -s murmur

Murmeltier *nt* marmot

murren *vt/i (haben)* grumble

mürrisch *a* surly

Mus *nt* -es purée

Muschel *f* -,-n mussel; *(Schale)* [sea] shell

Museum /mu'ze:ʊm/ *nt* -s,-seen /-'ze:ən/ museum

Musik *f* - music. M~alien /-jən/ *pl* [printed] music *sg.* m~alisch *a* musical

Musikbox *f* juke-box

Musiker(in) *m* -s,- *(f* -,-nen) musician

Musik|instrument *nt* musical instrument. M~kapelle *f* band. M~pavillon *m* bandstand

musisch *a* artistic

musizieren *vi (haben)* make music

Muskat *m* -[e]s nutmeg

Muskel *m* -s,-n muscle. M~kater *m* stiff and aching muscles *pl*

Muskullatur *f* - muscles *pl.* m~lös *a* muscular

Müsli *nt* -s muesli

muss (muß) *s.* müssen. Muss (Muß) *nt* - ein M~ a must

Muße *f* - leisure; mit M~ at leisure

müssen† *v aux* etw tun m~ have to/*(fam)* have got to do sth; ich muss jetzt gehen I have to *or* must go now; ich musste lachen I had to laugh; ich muss es wissen I need to know; du müsstest es mal versuchen you ought to *or* should try it; muss das sein? is that necessary?

müßig *a* idle; *(unnütz)* futile. M~gang *m* - idleness

musste (mußte), müsste (müßte) *s.* müssen

Muster *nt* -s,- pattern; *(Probe)* sample; *(Vorbild)* model. M~beispiel *nt* typical example; *(Vorbild)* perfect example. M~betrieb *m* model factory. m~gültig, m~haft *a* exemplary. m~n *vt* eye; *(inspizieren)* inspect. M~schüler(in) *m(f)* model pupil. M~ung *f* -,-en inspection; *(Mil)* medical; *(Muster)* pattern

Mut *m* -[e]s courage; jdm Mut machen encourage s.o.; zu M~e sein = zumute sein, *s.* zumute

Mutation /-'tsjo:n/ *f* -,-en *(Biol)* mutation

mut|ig *a* courageous, *adv* -ly. m~los *a* despondent; *(entmutigt)* disheartened

mutmaß|en *vt* presume; *(Vermutungen anstellen)* speculate. m~lich *a* probable, *adv* -bly; der m~liche Täter the suspect. M~ung *f* -,-en speculation, conjecture

Mutprobe *f* test of courage

Mutter¹ *f* -,*¨* mother; werdende M~ mother-to-be

Mutter² *f* -,-n *(Techn)* nut

Muttergottes *f* -,- madonna

Mutter|land *nt* motherland. M~leib *m* womb

mütterlich *a* maternal; *(fürsorglich)* motherly. m~erseits *adv* on one's/the mother's side

Mutter|mal *nt* birthmark; *(dunkel)* mole. M~schaft *f* - motherhood. m~seelenallein *a & adv* all alone. M~sprache *f* mother tongue. M~tag *m* Mother's Day

Mutti *f* -,-s *(fam)* mummy

Mutwill|e *m* wantonness. m~ig *a* wanton, *adv* -ly

Mütze *f* -,-n cap; wollene M~ woolly hat

MwSt. *abbr* (Mehrwertsteuer) VAT

mysteriös *a* mysterious, *adv* -ly

Myst|ik /'mʏstɪk/ *f* - mysticism. m~isch *a* mystical

myth|isch *a* mythical. M~ologie *f* - mythology. M~os *m* -,-then myth

N

na *int* well; na gut all right then; na ja oh well; na und? so what?

Nabe *f* -,-n hub

Nabel *m* -s,- navel. N~schnur *f* umbilical cord

nach *prep* (+ *dat*) after; *(Uhrzeit)* past; *(Richtung)* to; *(greifen, rufen, sich sehnen)* for; *(gemäß)* according to; meiner Meinung n~ in my opinion; n~ oben upwards □ *adv* n~ und n~ gradually, bit by bit; n~ wie vor still

nachäffen *vt sep* mimic

nachahm|en *vt sep* imitate. N~ung *f* -,-en imitation

nacharbeiten *vt sep* make up for

nacharten *vi sep (sein)* jdm n~ take after s.o.

Nachbar|(in) *m* -n,-n *(f* -,-nen) neighbour. N~haus *nt* house next door. N~land *nt* neighbouring country. n~lich *a* neighbourly; *(Nachbar-)* neighbouring. N~schaft *f* - neighbourhood; gute N~schaft neighbourliness

nachbestell|en *vt sep* reorder. N~ung *f* repeat order

nachbild|en *vt sep* copy, reproduce. N~ung *f* copy, reproduction

nachdatieren *vt sep* backdate

nachdem *conj* after; je n~ it depends

nachdenk|en† vi sep (haben) think (über + acc about). N~en nt -s reflection, thought. n~lich a thoughtful, adv -ly

Nachdruck m (pl -e) reproduction; (unveränderter) reprint; (Betonung) emphasis

nachdrücklich a emphatic, adv -ally

nacheifern vi sep (haben) jdm n~ emulate s.o.

nacheilen vi sep (sein) (+ dat) hurry after

nacheinander adv one after the other

Nachfahre m -n,-n descendant

Nachfolg|e f succession. n~en vi sep (sein) (+ dat) follow; (im Amt) succeed. N~er(in) m -s,- (f -,-nen) successor

nachforsch|en vi sep (haben) make enquiries. N~ung f enquiry; N~ungen anstellen make enquiries

Nachfrage f (Comm) demand. n~n vi sep (haben) enquire

nachfüllen vt sep refill (Behälter); Wasser n~ fill up with water

nachgeben† v sep □ vi (haben) give way; (sich fügen) give in, yield □ vt jdm Suppe n~ give s.o. more soup

Nachgebühr f surcharge

nachgehen† vi sep (sein) (Uhr:) be slow; jdm/etw n~ follow s.o./sth; follow up (Spur, Angelegenheit); pursue (Angelegenheit, Tätigkeit); go about (Arbeit)

nachgeraten† vi sep (sein) jdm n~ take after s.o.

Nachgeschmack m after-taste

nachgiebig a indulgent; (gefällig) compliant. N~keit f · indulgence; compliance

nachgrübeln vi sep (haben) ponder (über + acc on)

nachhallen vi sep (haben) reverberate

nachhaltig a lasting

nachhause adv = nach Hause, s. Haus

nachhelfen† vi sep (haben) help

nachher adv later; (danach) afterwards; bis n~! see you later!

Nachhilfeunterricht m coaching

Nachhinein (nachhinein) adv im N~ (n~) afterwards

nachhinken vi sep (sein) (fig) lag behind

nachholen vi sep (später holen) fetch later; (mehr holen) get more; (später machen) do later; (aufholen) catch up on; make up for (Zeit)

nachjagen vi sep (haben) (+ dat) chase after

Nachkomme m -n,-n descendant. n~n† vi sep (sein) follow [later], come later; (Schritt halten) keep up; etw (dat) n~n (fig) comply with (Bitte, Wunsch); carry out (Versprechen, Pflicht). N~nschaft f · descendants pl, progeny

Nachkriegszeit f post-war period

Nachlass m -es,-e (Nachlaß m -sses,-sse) discount; (Jur) [deceased's] estate

nachlassen† v sep □ vi (haben) decrease; (Regen, Hitze:) let up; (Schmerz:) ease; (Sturm:) abate; (Augen, Kräfte, Leistungen:) deteriorate; er ließ nicht nach [mit Fragen] he persisted [with his questions] □ vt etw vom Preis n~ take sth off the price

nachlässig a careless, adv -ly; (leger) casual, adv -ly; (unordentlich) sloppy, adv -ily. N~keit f · carelessness; sloppiness

nachlaufen† vi sep (sein) (+ dat) run after

nachlegen vt sep Holz/Kohlen n~ put more wood/coal on the fire

nachlesen† vt sep look up

nachlöse|n vi sep (haben) pay one's fare on the train/on arrival. N~schalter m excess-fare office

nachmachen vt sep (später machen) do later; (imitieren) imitate, copy; (fälschen) forge; jdm etw n~ copy sth from s.o.; repeat (Übung) after s.o.

Nachmittag m afternoon; heute/gestern N~ this/yesterday afternoon. n~ adv heute/gestern n~ (NEW) heute/gestern N~, s. Nachmittag. n~s adv in the afternoon

Nachnahme f etw per N~ schicken send sth cash on delivery or COD

Nachname m surname

Nachporto nt excess postage

nachprüfen vt sep check, verify

nachrechnen vt sep work out; (prüfen) check

Nachrede f üble N~ defamation

Nachricht f -,-en [piece of] news sg; N~en news sg; eine N~ hinterlassen leave a message; jdm N~ geben inform, notify s.o. N~endienst m (Mil) intelligence service. N~ensendung f news bulletin. N~enwesen nt communications pl

nachrücken vi sep (sein) move up

Nachruf m obituary

nachsagen vt sep repeat (jdm after s.o.); jdm Schlechtes/Gutes n~ speak ill/well of s.o.; man sagt ihm nach, dass er geizig ist he is said to be stingy

Nachsaison f late season

Nachsatz m postscript

nachschicken vt sep (später schicken) send later; (hinterher-) send after (jdm s.o.); send on (Post) (jdm to s.o.)

nachschlag|en† v sep □ vt look up □ vi (haben) in einem Wörterbuch n~en consult a dictionary; jdm n~en take after s.o. N~ewerk nt reference book

Nachschlüssel m duplicate key

Nachschrift f transcript; (*Nachsatz*) postscript

Nachschub m (*Mil*) supplies pl

nachsehen† v sep □ vt (*prüfen*) check; (*nachschlagen*) look up; (*hinwegsehen über*) overlook □ vi (*haben*) have a look; (*prüfen*) check; im Wörterbuch n~ consult a dictionary; jdm/etw n~ gaze after s.o./sth. N~ nt das N~ haben (*fam*) go empty-handed

nachsenden† vt sep forward; (*Post*) (jdm to s.o.); bitte n~' 'please forward'

Nachsicht f forbearance; (*Milde*) leniency; (*Nachgiebigkeit*) indulgence. n~ig a forbearing; lenient; indulgent

Nachsilbe f suffix

nachsitzen† vi sep (*haben*) n~ müssen be kept in [after school]; jdn n~ lassen give s.o. detention. N~ nt -s (*Sch*) detention

Nachspeise f dessert, sweet

Nachspiel nt (*fig*) sequel

nachspionieren vi sep (*haben*) jdm n~ spy on s.o.

nachsprechen† vt sep repeat (jdm after s.o.)

nachspülen vt sep rinse

nächst /-çst/ prep (+ dat) next to. n~beste(r,s) a first [available]; (*zweitbeste*) next best. n~e(r,s) a next; (*nächstgelegene*) nearest; (*Verwandte*) closest; n~e Woche next week; in n~er Nähe close by; am n~en sein be nearest or closest □ pron der/die/das N~e (n~e) the next; der N~e (n~e) bitte next please; als N~es (n~es) next;fürs N~e (n~e) for the time being. N~e(r) m fellow man

nachstehend a following □ adv below

nachstellen v sep □ vt readjust; put back (*Uhr*) □ vi (*haben*) (+ dat) pursue

nächst|emal adv das n~emal (NEW) das nächste Mal, s. Mal[1]. N~enliebe f charity. N~ens adv shortly. n~gelegen a nearest. n~liegend a most obvious

nachstreben vi sep (*haben*) jdm n~ emulate s.o.

nachsuchen vi sep (*haben*) search; n~ um request

Nacht f -,⁻e night; über/bei N~ overnight/at night; Montag/morgen N~ Monday/tomorrow night; heute N~ tonight; (*letzte Nacht*) last night; gestern N~ last night; (*vorletzte Nacht*) the night before last. n~ adv morgen/heute/ gestern n~ (NEW) morgen/heute/ gestern N~, s. Nacht. N~dienst m night duty

Nachteil m disadvantage; zum N~ to the detriment (*gen* of). n~ig a adverse, adv -ly

Nacht|essen nt (*SGer*) supper. N~falter m moth. N~hemd nt night-dress; (*Männer-*) night-shirt

Nachtigall f -,-en nightingale

Nachtisch m dessert

Nacht|klub m night-club. N~leben nt night-life

nächtlich a nocturnal, night . . .

Nacht|lokal nt night-club. N~mahl nt (*Aust*) supper

Nachtrag m postscript; (*Ergänzung*) supplement. n~en† vt sep add; jdm etw n~en walk behind s.o. carrying sth; (*fig*) bear a grudge against s.o. for sth. n~end a vindictive; n~end sein bear grudges

nachträglich a subsequent, later; (*verspätet*) belated □ adv later; (*nachher*) afterwards; (*verspätet*) belatedly

nachtrauern vi sep (*haben*) (+ dat) mourn the loss of

Nacht|ruhe f night's rest; angenehme N~ruhe! sleep well! n~s adv at night; 2 Uhr n~s 2 o'clock in the morning. N~schicht f night-shift. N~tisch m bedside table. N~tischlampe f bedside lamp. N~topf m chamber-pot. N~wächter m night-watchman. N~zeit f night-time

Nachuntersuchung f check-up

nachwachsen† vi sep (*sein*) grow again

Nachwahl f by-election

Nachweis m -es,-e proof. n~bar a demonstrable. n~en† vt sep prove; (*aufzeigen*) show; (*vermitteln*) give details of; jdm nichts n~en können have no proof against s.o. n~lich a demonstrable, adv -bly

Nachwelt f posterity

Nachwirkung f after-effect

Nachwort nt (pl -e) epilogue

Nachwuchs m new generation; (*fam: Kinder*) offspring. N~spieler m young player

nachzahlen vt/i sep (*haben*) pay extra; (*später zahlen*) pay later; Steuern n~ pay tax arrears

nachzählen vt/i sep (*haben*) count again; (*prüfen*) check

Nachzahlung f extra/later payment; (*Gehalts-*) back-payment

nachzeichnen vt sep copy

Nachzügler m -s,- late-comer; (*Zurückgebliebener*) straggler

Nacken m -s,- nape or back of the neck

nackt a naked; (*bloß, kahl*) bare; (*Wahrheit*) plain. N~baden nt nude bathing. N~heit f - nakedness, nudity. N~kultur f nudism. N~schnecke f slug

Nadel f -,-n needle; (*Häkel-*) hook; (*Schmuck-, Hut-*) pin. N~arbeit f needlework. N~baum m conifer. N~kissen nt pincushion. N~stich m stitch; (*fig*) pinprick. N~wald m coniferous forest

Nagel m -s,-: nail. N~bürste f nail-brush. N~feile f nail-file. N~haut f cuticle. N~lack m nail varnish. n~n vt nail. n~neu a brand-new. N~schere f nail scissors pl

nagen vt/i (haben) gnaw (an + dat at); n~d (*fig*) nagging

Nagetier nt rodent

nah a, adv & prep = nahe; von nah und fern from far and wide

Näharbeit f sewing; eine N~ a piece of sewing

Nahaufnahme f close-up

nahe a (näher, nächst) nearby; (*zeitlich*) imminent; (*eng*) close; der N~ Osten the Middle East; in n~r Zukunft in the near future; von n~m [from] close to; n~ sein be close (*dat* to); den Tränen n~ close to tears □ adv near, close; (*verwandt*) closely; n~ an (+ acc/dat) near [to], close to; n~ daran sein, etw zu tun nearly do sth; n~ liegen be close; (*fig*) be highly likely; n~ liegende Lösung obvious solution; n~ legen (*fig*) recommend (*dat* to); jdm n~ legen, etw zu tun urge s.o. to do sth; n~ stehen (*fig*) be close to s.o.; etw (*dat*) n~ kommen (*fig*) come close to sth; jdm n~ kommen (*fig*) get close to s.o.; jdm n~ gehen (*fig*) affect s.o. deeply; jdm zu n~ treten (*fig*) offend s.o. □ prep (+ dat) near [to], close to

Nähe f -nearness, proximity; aus der N~ [from] close to; in der N~ near or close by; in der N~ der Kirche near the church

nahebei adv near or close by

nahe|gehen† vi sep (sein) (NEW) n~ gehen, s. nahe. n~kommen† vi sep (sein) (NEW) n~ kommen, s. nahe. n~legen vt sep (NEW) n~ legen, s. nahe. n~liegen† vi sep (haben) (NEW) n~ liegen, s. nahe. n~liegend a (NEW) n~ liegend, s. nahe

nahen vi (sein) (liter) approach

nähen vt/i (haben) sew; (anfertigen) make; (*Med*) stitch [up]

näher a closer; (*Weg*) shorter; (*Einzelheiten*) further □ adv closer; (*genauer*) more closely; n~ kommen come closer, approach; (*fig*) get closer (*dat* to); sich n~ erkundigen make further enquiries; n~an (+ acc/dat) nearer [to], closer to □ prep (+ dat) nearer [to], closer to. N~e[s] nt [further] details pl. n~kommen† vi sep (sein) (NEW) n~ kommen, s. näher. n~n (sich) vr approach

nahestehen† vi sep (haben) (NEW) nahe stehen, s. nahe

nahezu adv almost

Nähgarn nt [sewing] cotton

Nahkampf m close combat

Näh|maschine f sewing machine. N~nadel f sewing-needle

nähren vt feed; (*fig*) nurture; sich n~ von live on □ vi (haben) be nutritious

nahrhaft a nutritious

Nährstoff m nutrient

Nahrung f - food, nourishment. N~smittel nt food

Nährwert m nutritional value

Naht f -,-:e seam; (*Med*) suture. n~los a seamless

Nahverkehr m local service. N~szug m local train

Nähzeug nt sewing; (*Zubehör*) sewing kit

naiv /na'i:f/ a naïve, adv -ly. N~ität /-'vi:tɛ:t/ f - naïvety

Name m -ns,-n name; im N~n (+ gen) in the name of; (*handeln*) on behalf of; das Kind beim rechten N~n nennen (*fam*) call a spade a spade. n~nlos a nameless; (*unbekannt*) unknown, anonymous. n~ns adv by the name of □ prep (+ gen) on behalf of. N~nstag m name-day. N~nsvetter m namesake. N~nszug m signature. n~ntlich adv by name; (*besonders*) especially

namhaft a noted; (*ansehnlich*) considerable; n~ machen name

nämlich adv (und zwar) namely; (*denn*) because

nanu int hallo

Napf m -[e]s,-:e bowl

Narbe f -,-n scar

Narkose f -,-n general anaesthetic. N~arzt m anaesthetist. N~mittel nt anaesthetic

Narkot|ikum nt -s,-ka narcotic; (*Narkosemittel*) anaesthetic. n~isieren vt anaesthetize

Narr m -en,-en fool; zum N~en haben od halten make a fool of. n~en vt fool. n~ensicher a foolproof. N~heit f -,-en folly

Närr|in f -,-nen fool. n~isch a foolish; (*fam: verrückt*) crazy (auf + acc about)

Narzisse f -,-n narcissus; gelbe N~ daffodil

nasal a nasal

nasch|en vt/i (haben) nibble (an + dat at); wer hat vom Kuchen genascht? who's been at the cake? n~haft a sweet-toothed

Nase f -,-n nose; an der N~ herumführen (*fam*) dupe

näseln vi (haben) speak through one's nose; n~d nasal

Nasen|bluten nt -s nosebleed. N~loch nt nostril. N~rücken m bridge of the nose

Naseweis m -es,-e (fam) know-all

Nashorn nt rhinoceros

nass (naß) a (nasser, nassest) wet

Nässe f - wet; (Nasssein) wetness. n~n vt wet

nasskalt (naßkalt) a cold and wet

Nation /na'tsio:n/ f -,-en nation. n~al a national. N~alhymne f national anthem. N~alismus m - nationalism. N~alität f -,-en nationality. N~alsozialismus m National Socialism. N~alspieler m international

Natrium nt -s sodium

Natron -s doppeltkohlensaures N~ bicarbonate of soda

Natter f -,-n snake; (Gift-) viper

Natur f -,-en nature; von N~ aus by nature. N~alien /-jən/ pl natural produce sg. n~alisieren vt naturalize. N~alisierung f -,-en naturalization

Naturell nt -s,-e disposition

Natur|erscheinung f natural phenomenon. n~farben a natural[-coloured]. N~forscher m naturalist. N~kunde f natural history. N~lehrpfad m nature trail

natürlich a natural ● adv naturally; (selbstverständlich) of course. N~keit f - naturalness

natur|rein a pure. N~schutz m nature conservation; unter N~schutz stehen be protected. N~schutzgebiet nt nature reserve. N~wissenschaft f [natural] science. N~wissenschaftler m scientist. n~wissenschaftlich a scientific; (Sch) science ...

nautisch a nautical

Navigation /-'tsio:n/ f - navigation

Nazi m -s,-s Nazi

n.Chr. abbr (nach Christus) AD

Nebel m -s,- fog; (leicht) mist. n~haft a hazy. N~horn nt foghorn. n~ig a = neblig

neben prep (+ dat/acc) next to, beside; (+ dat) (außer) apart from; n~ mir next to me. n~an adv next door

Neben|anschluss (N~anschluß) m (Teleph) extension. N~ausgaben fpl incidental expenses

nebenbei adv in addition; (beiläufig) casually; n~ bemerkt incidentally

Neben|bemerkung f passing remark. N~beruf m second job. N~beschäftigung f spare-time occupation. N~buhler(in) m -s,- (f -,-nen) rival

nebeneinander adv next to each other, side by side

Neben|eingang m side entrance. N~fach nt (Univ) subsidiary subject. N~fluss (N~fluß) m tributary. N~gleis nt siding. N~haus nt house next door

nebenher adv in addition. n~gehen† vi sep (sein) walk alongside

nebenhin adv casually

Neben|höhle f sinus. N~kosten pl additional costs. N~mann m (pl -männer) person next to one. N~produkt nt byproduct. N~rolle f supporting role; (kleine) minor role; eine N~rolle spielen (fig) be unimportant. N~sache f unimportant matter. n~sächlich a unimportant. N~satz m subordinate clause. N~straße f minor road; (Seiten-) side street. N~verdienst m additional earnings pl. N~wirkung f side-effect. N~zimmer nt room next door

neblig a foggy; (leicht) misty

nebst prep (+ dat) [together] with

Necessaire /nesε'sε:g/ nt -s,-s toilet bag; (Näh-, Nagel-) set

neck|en vt tease. N~erei f - teasing. n~isch a teasing; (kess) saucy

nee adv (fam) no

Neffe m -n,-n nephew

negativ a negative. N~ nt -s,-e (Phot) negative

Neger m -s,- Negro

nehmen† vt take (dat from); sich (dat) etw n~ take sth; help oneself to (Essen); jdn zu sich n~ have s.o. to live with one

Neid m -[e]s envy, jealousy. n~en vt jdm den Erfolg n~en be jealous of s.o.'s success. n~isch a envious, jealous (auf + acc of); auf jdn n~isch sein envy s.o.

neig|en vt incline; (zur Seite) tilt; (beugen) bend; sich n~en incline; (Boden:) slope; (Person:) bend (über + acc over) ● vi (haben) n~en zu (fig) have a tendency towards; be prone to (Krankheit); incline towards (Ansicht); dazu n~en, etw zu tun tend to do sth. N~ung f -,-en inclination; (Gefälle) slope; (fig) tendency; (Hang) leaning; (Herzens-) affection

nein adv, N~ nt -s no

Nektar m -s nectar

Nelke f -,-n carnation; (Feder-) pink; (Culin) clove

nenn|en† vt call; (taufen) name; (angeben) give; (erwähnen) mention; sich n~en call oneself. n~enswert a significant. N~ung f -,-en mention; (Sport) entry. N~wert m face value

Neofaschismus m neofascism

Neon nt -s neon. N~beleuchtung f fluorescent lighting

neppen *vt* (*fam*) rip off

Nerv *m* -s,-en /-fən/ nerve; die N~en verlieren lose control of oneself. n~en *vt* jdn n~en (*sl*) get on s.o.'s nerves. N~enarzt *m* neurologist. n~enaufreibend *a* nerveracking. N~enbündel *nt* (*fam*) bundle of nerves. N~enkitzel *m* (*fam*) thrill. N~ensystem *nt* nervous system. N~enzusammenbruch *m* nervous breakdown

nervös *a* nervy, edgy; (*Med*) nervous; n~ sein be on edge

Nervosität *f* - nerviness, edginess

Nerz *m* -es,-e mink

Nessel *f* -,-n nettle

Nessessär *nt* -s,-s = Necessaire

Nest *nt* -[e]s,-er nest; (*fam:Ort*) small place

nesteln *vi* (*haben*) fumble (an + *dat* with)

Nesthäkchen *nt* -s,- (*fam*) baby of the family

nett *a* nice, *adv* -ly; (*freundlich*) kind, *adv* -ly

netto *adv* net. N~gewicht *nt* net weight

Netz *nt* -es,-e net; (*Einkaufs-*) string bag; (*Spinnen-*) web; (*auf Landkarte*) grid; (*System*) network; (*Electr*) mains *pl*. N~haut *f* retina. N~karte *f* area season ticket. N~werk *nt* network

neu *a* new; (*modern*) modern; wie neu as good as new; das ist mir neu it's news to me; aufs N~e (n~e) [once] again; von n~em all over again □ *adv* newly; (*gerade erst*) only just; (*erneut*) again; etw neu schreiben/streichen rewrite/repaint sth; neu vermähltes Paar newly-weds *pl*. N~ankömmling *m* -s,-e newcomer. N~anschaffung *f* recent acquisition. n~artig *a* a new [kind of]. N~auflage *f* new edition; (*unverändert*) reprint. N~bau *m* (*pl* -ten) new house/building

Neu|e(r) *m/f* new person, newcomer; (*Schüler*) new boy/girl. N~e(s) *nt* das N~e the new; etwas N~es something new; (*Neuigkeit*) a piece of news; was gibt's N~es? what's the news?

neuer|dings *adv* [just] recently. n~lich *a* renewed, new □ *adv* again. N~ung *f* -,-en innovation

neuest|e(r,s) *a* newest; (*letzte*) latest; seit n~em just recently. N~e *nt* das N~e the latest thing; (*Neuigkeit*) the latest news *sg*

neugeboren *a* newborn

Neugier, Neugierde *f* - curiosity; (*Wissbegierde*) inquisitiveness

neugierig *a* curious (auf + *acc* about), *adv* -ly; (*wissbegierig*) inquisitive, *adv* -ly

Neuheit *f* -,-en novelty; (*Neusein*) newness; die letzte N~ the latest thing

Neuigkeit *f* -,-en piece of news; N~en news *sg*

Neujahr *nt* New Year's Day; über N~ over the New Year

neulich *adv* the other day

Neu|ling *m* -s,-e novice. n~modisch *a* newfangled. N~mond *m* new moon

neun *inv a*, N~ *f* -,-en nine. N~malkluge(r) *m* (*fam*) clever Dick. n~te(r,s) *a* ninth. n~zehn *inv a* nineteen. n~zehnte(r,s) *a* nineteenth. n~zig *inv a* ninety. n~zigste(r,s) *a* ninetieth

Neuralgie *f* -,-n neuralgia

neureich *a* nouveau riche

Neurologe *m* -n,-n neurologist

Neuro|se *f* -,-n neurosis. n~tisch *a* neurotic

Neuschnee *m* fresh snow

Neuseeland *nt* -s New Zealand

neuste(r,s) *a* = neueste(r,s)

neutral *a* neutral. n~isieren *vt* neutralize. N~ität *f* - neutrality

Neutrum *nt* -s,-tra neuter noun

neu|vermählt *a* NEW n~ vermählt, *s.* neu. N~zeit *f* modern times *pl*

nicht *adv* not; ich kann n~ I cannot *or* can't; er ist n~ gekommen he hasn't come; n~ mehr/besser als no more/better than; bitte n~! please don't! n~ berühren! do not touch! du kommst doch auch, ~ [wahr]? you are coming too, aren't you? du kennst ihn doch, n~? you know him, don't you?

Nichtachtung *f* disregard; (*Geringschätzung*) disdain

Nichte *f* -,-n niece

nichtig *a* trivial; (*Jur*) [null and] void

Nichtraucher *m* non-smoker. N~abteil *nt* non-smoking compartment

nichts *pron a* nothing; n~ anderes/Besseres nothing else/better; n~ mehr no more; ich weiß n~ I know nothing *or* don't know anything; n~ ahnend unsuspecting; n~ sagend meaningless; (*uninteressant*) nondescript. N~ *nt* - nothingness; (*fig: Leere*) void; (*Person*) nonentity. n~ahnend *a* NEW n~ ahnend, *s.* nichts

Nichtschwimmer *m* non-swimmer

nichtsdesto|trotz *adv* all the same. n~weniger *adv* nevertheless

nichts|nutzig *a* good-for-nothing; (*fam: unartig*) naughty. n~sagend *a* NEW n~ sagend, *s.* nichts. n~tun *nt* -s idleness

Nickel *nt* -s nickel

nicken *vi* (*haben*) nod. N~ *nt* -s nod

Nickerchen *nt* -s,- (*fam*) nap; ein N~ machen have forty winks

nie *adv* never

nieder *a* low □ *adv* down. n~brennen† *vt/i sep* (*sein*) burn down. N~deutsch *nt*

Low German. N~gang *m* (*fig*) decline. n~gedrückt *a* (*fig*) depressed. n~gehen† *vi sep* (*sein*) come down. n~geschlagen *a* dejected, despondent. N~geschlagenheit *f* -,-e dejection, despondency. N~kunft *f* -,-e confinement. N~lage *f* defeat

Niederlande (die) *pl* the Netherlands

Niederländ|er *m* -s,- Dutchman; die N~er the Dutch *pl*. N~erin *f* -,-nen Dutchwoman. n~isch *a* Dutch

nieder|lassen† *vt sep* let down; sich n~lassen settle; (*sich setzen*) sit down. N~lassung *f* -,-en settlement; (*Zweigstelle*) branch. n~legen *vt sep* put or lay down; resign (*Amt*); die Arbeit n~legen go on strike; sich n~legen lie down. n~machen, n~metzeln *vt sep* massacre. n~reißen† *vt sep* tear down. N~sachsen *nt* Lower Saxony. N~schlag *m* precipitation; (*Regen*) rainfall; (*radioaktiver*) fallout; (*Boxen*) knock-down; n~schlagen† *vt sep* knock down; lower (*Augen*); (*unterdrücken*) crush. n~schmettern *vt sep* (*fig*) shatter. n~schreiben† *vt sep* write down. n~schreien† *vt sep* shout down. n~setzen *vt sep* put or set down; sich n~setzen sit down. n~strecken *vt sep* fell; (*durch Schuss*) gun down

niederträchtig *a* base, vile

Niederung *f* -,-en low ground

nieder|walzen *vt sep* flatten. N~werfen† *vt sep* throw down; (*unterdrücken*) crush; sich n~werfen prostrate oneself

niedlich *a* pretty; (*goldig*) sweet; (*Amer*) cute

niedrig *a* low; (*fig: gemein*) base □ *adv* low

niemals *adv* never

niemand *pron* nobody, no one

Niere *f* -,-n kidney; künstliche N~ kidney machine

nieseln *vi* (*haben*) drizzle; es n~t it is drizzling. N~regen *m* drizzle

niesen *vi* (*haben*) sneeze. N~ *nt* -s sneezing; (*Nieser*) sneeze

Niet *m* & *nt* -[e]s,-e, Niete¹ *f* -,-n rivet; (*an Jeans*) stud

Niete² *f* -,-n blank; (*fam*) failure

nieten *vt* rivet

Nikotin *nt* -s nicotine

Nil *m* -[s] Nile. N~pferd *nt* hippopotamus

nimmer *adv* (*SGer*) not any more; nie und n~ never. n~müde *a* tireless. n~satt *a* insatiable. N~wiedersehen *nt* auf N~wiedersehen (*fam*) for good

nippen *vi* (*haben*) take a sip (an + *dat* of)

nirgends, nirgendwo *adv* nowhere

Nische *f* -,-n recess, niche

nisten *vi* (*haben*) nest

Nitrat *nt* -[e]s,-e nitrate

Niveau /ni'vo:/ *nt* -s,-s level; (*geistig, künstlerisch*) standard

nix *adv* (*fam*) nothing

Nixe *f* -,-n mermaid

nobel *a* noble; (*fam: luxuriös*) luxurious; (*fam: großzügig*) generous

noch *adv* still; (*zusätzlich*) as well; (*mit Komparativ*) even; n~ nicht not yet; gerade n~ only just; n~ immer *od* immer n~ still; n~ letzte Woche only last week; es ist n~ viel Zeit there's plenty of time yet; wer/was/wo n~? who/what/where else? n~ jemand/etwas someone/something else; (*Frage*) anyone/anything else? n~ einmal again; n~ einmal so viel as much again; n~ ein Bier another beer; n~ größer even bigger; n~ so sehr/schön however much/beautiful □ *conj* weder … n~ neither … nor

nochmal|ig *a* further. n~s *adv* again

Nomad|e *m* -n,-n nomad. n~isch *a* nomadic

Nominativ *m* -s,-e nominative

nominell *a* nominal, *adv* -ly

nominier|en *vt* nominate. N~ung *f* -,-en nomination

nonchalant /nõʃa'lã:/ *a* nonchalant, *adv* -ly

Nonne *f* -,-n nun. N~nkloster *nt* convent

Nonstopflug *m* direct flight

Nord *m* -[e]s north. N~amerika *nt* North America. n~deutsch *a* North German

Norden *m* -s north; nach N~ north

nordisch *a* Nordic

nördlich *a* northern; (*Richtung*) northerly □ *adv* & *prep* (+ *gen*) n~ [von] der Stadt [to the] north of the town

Nordosten *m* north-east

Nord|pol *m* North Pole. N~see *f* - North Sea. n~wärts *adv* northwards. N~westen *m* north-west

Nörgelei *f* -,-en grumbling

nörgeln *vi* (*haben*) grumble

Norm *f* -,-en norm; (*Techn*) standard; (*Soll*) quota

normal *a* normal, *adv* -ly. n~erweise *adv* normally. n~isieren *vt* normalize; sich n~isieren return to normal

normen, normieren *vt* standardize

Norwe|gen *nt* -s Norway. N~ger(in) *m* -s,- (*f* -,-nen) Norwegian. n~gisch *a* Norwegian

Nost|algie *f* -nostalgia. n~algisch *a* nostalgic

Not f -,⸚e need; (*Notwendigkeit*) necessity; (*Entbehrung*) hardship; (*seelisch*) trouble; Not leiden be in need, suffer hardship; Not leidende Menschen needy people; mit knapper Not only just; zur Not if need be; (*äußerstenfalls*) at a pinch

Notar m -s,-e notary public

Not|arzt m emergency doctor. N~ausgang m emergency exit. N~behelf m -[e]s,-e makeshift. N~bremse f emergency brake. N~dienst m N~dienst haben be on call. n~dürftig a scant; (*behelfsmäßig*) makeshift

Note f -,-n note; (*Zensur*) mark; ganze/halbe N~ (*Mus*) semi-breve/minim; (*Amer*) whole/half note; N~n lesen read music; persönliche N~ personal touch. N~nblatt nt sheet of music. N~nschlüssel m clef. N~nständer m music-stand

Notfall m emergency; im N~ in an emergency; (*notfalls*) if need be; für den N~ just in case. n~s adv if need be

not|gedrungen adv of necessity. N~groschen m nest-egg

notieren vt note down; (*Comm*) quote; sich (*dat*) etw n~ make a note of sth

nötig a necessary; n~ haben need; das N~ste the essentials pl □ adv urgently. n~en vt force; (*auffordern*) press; laßt euch nicht n~en help yourselves. n~enfalls adv if need be. N~ung f - coercion

Notiz f -,-en note; (*Zeitungs-*) item; [keine] N~ nehmen von take [no] notice of. N~buch nt notebook. N~kalender m diary

Not|lage f plight. n~landen vi (*sein*) make a forced landing. N~landung f forced landing. n~leidend a ⟨NEW⟩Not leidend, s. Not. N~lösung f stopgap. N~lüge f white lie

notorisch a notorious

Not|ruf m emergency call; (*Naut, Aviat*) distress call; (*Nummer*) emergency services number. N~signal nt distress signal. N~stand m state of emergency. N~unterkunft f emergency accommodation. N~wehr f - (*Jur*) self-defence

notwendig a necessary; (*unerlässlich*) essential □ adv urgently. N~keit f -,-en necessity

Notzucht f - (*Jur*) rape

Nougat /'nu:gat/ m & nt -s nougat

Novelle f -,-n novella; (*Pol*) amendment

November m -s,- November

Novität f -,-en novelty

Novize m -n,-n, **Novizin** f -,-nen (*Relig*) novice

Nu m im Nu (*fam*) in a flash

Nuance /'nŷã:sə/ f -,-n nuance; (*Spur*) shade

nüchtern a sober; (*sachlich*) matter-of-fact; (*schmucklos*) bare; (*ohne Würze*) bland; auf n~en Magen on an empty stomach □ adv soberly

Nudel f -,-n piece of pasta; N~n pasta sg; (*Band-*) noodles. N~holz nt rolling-pin

Nudist m -en,-en nudist

nuklear a nuclear

null inv a zero, nought; (*Teleph*) O; (*Sport*) nil; (*Tennis*) love;n~ Fehler no mistakes; n~ und nichtig (*Jur*) null and void. N~ f -,-en nought, zero; (*fig: Person*) nonentity; drei Grad unter N~ three degrees below zero. N~punkt m zero

numerieren vt ⟨NEW⟩nummerieren

numerisch a numerical

Nummer f -,-n number; (*Ausgabe*) issue; (*Darbietung*) item; (*Zirkus-*) act; (*Größe*) size. n~ieren vt number. N~nschild nt number-/(*Amer*) license-plate

nun adv now; (*na*) well; (*halt*) just; von nun an from now on; nun gut! very well then! das Leben ist nun mal so life's like that

nur adv only, just; wo kann sie nur sein? wherever can she be? alles, was ich nur will everything I could possibly want; er soll es nur versuchen! (*drohend*) just let him try! hätte ich nur ...! if only I could/had ...! nur Geduld! just be patient!

Nürnberg nt -s Nuremberg

nuscheln vt/i (*haben*) mumble

Nuss f -,⸚e (Nuß f -; ⸚sse) nut. N~baum m walnut tree. N~knacker m -s,- nutcrackers pl. N~schale f nutshell

Nüstern fpl nostrils

Nut f -,-en, **Nute** f -,-n groove

Nutte f -,-n (*sl*) tart (*sl*)

Nutz zu N~e machen = zunutze machen, s. zunutze. n~bar a usable; n~bar machen utilize; cultivate ⟨*Boden*⟩. n~bringend a profitable, adv -bly

nütze a zu etwas/nichts n~ sein be useful/useless

nutzen vt use, utilize; (*aus-*) take advantage of □ vi (*haben*) = nützen. N~ m -s benefit; (*Comm*) profit; N~ ziehen aus benefit from; von N~ sein be useful

nützen vi (*haben*) be useful or of use (dat to); (*Mittel:*) be effective; nichts n~ be useless or no use; was nützt mir das? what good is that to me? □ vt = nutzen

Nutzholz nt timber

nützlich a useful; sich n~ machen make oneself useful. N~keit f - usefulness

nutz|los a useless; (*vergeblich*) vain. N~losigkeit f - uselessness. N~nießer m -s,- beneficiary. N~ung f - use, utilization

Nylon /'naɪlɔn/ nt -s nylon

Nymphe /'nʏmfə/ f -,-n nymph

O

o int o ja/nein! oh yes/no! o weh! oh dear!

Oase f -,-n oasis

ob conj whether; ob reich, ob arm rich or poor; ob sie wohl krank ist? I wonder whether she is ill; und ob! (*fam*) you bet!

Obacht f O~ geben pay attention; O~ geben auf (+ acc) look after; O~! look out!

Obdach nt -[e]s shelter. o~los a homeless. O~lose(r) m/f homeless person; die O~losen the homeless pl

Obduktion /-'tsjo:n/ f -,-en post-mortem

O-Beine ntpl (*fam*) bow-legs, bandy legs. **o-beinig, o-beinig** a bandy-legged

oben adv at the top; (*auf der Oberseite*) on top; (*eine Treppe hoch*) upstairs; (*im Text*) above; da o~ up there; o~ im Norden up in the north; siehe o~ see above; o~ auf (+ acc/dat) on top of; nach o~ up[wards]; (*die Treppe hinauf*) upstairs; von o~ from above/upstairs; von o~ bis unten from top to bottom/⟨Person⟩ to toe; jdn von o~ bis unten mustern look s.o. up and down; o~ erwähnt od genannt above-mentioned. o~an adv at the top. o~auf adv on top; o~auf sein (*fig*) be cheerful. o~drein adv on top of that. o~erwähnt, o~genannt a ⟨NEW⟩ o~ erwähnt od genannt, s. oben. o~hin adv casually

Ober m -s,- waiter

Ober|arm m upper arm. O~arzt m ≈ senior registrar. O~befehlshaber m commander-in-chief. O~begriff m generic term. O~deck nt upper deck. o~e(r,s) a upper; (*höhere*) higher. O~fläche f surface. o~flächlich a superficial, adv -ly. O~geschoss (O~geschoß) nt upper storey. o~halb adv & prep (+ gen) above; o~halb vom Dorf od des Dorfes above the village. O~hand f die O~hand gewinnen gain the upper hand. O~haupt nt (*fig*) head. O~haus nt (*Pol*) upper house; (*in UK*) House of Lords. O~hemd nt [man's] shirt

Oberin f -,-nen matron; (*Relig*) mother superior

ober|irdisch a surface … □ adv above ground. O~kellner m head waiter. O~kiefer m upper jaw. O~körper m upper part of the body. O~leutnant m lieutenant. O~licht nt overhead light; (*Fenster*) skylight; (*über Tür*) fanlight. O~lippe f upper lip

Obers nt - (*Aust*) cream

Ober|schenkel m thigh. O~schicht f upper class. O~schule f grammar school. O~schwester f (*Med*) sister. O~seite f upper/(*rechte Seite*) right side

Oberst m -en & -s,-en colonel

oberste(r,s) a top; (*höchste*) highest; ⟨Befehlshaber, Gerichtshof⟩ supreme; (*wichtigste*) first

Ober|stimme f treble. O~stufe f upper school. O~teil nt top. O~weite f chest/(*der Frau*) bust size

obgleich conj although

Obhut f - care; in guter O~ sein be well looked after

obig a above

Objekt nt -[e]s,-e object; (*Haus, Grundstück*) property; O~ der Forschung subject of research

Objektiv nt -s,-e lens. o~ a objective, adv -ly. O~ität f - objectivity

Oblate f -,-n (*Relig*) wafer

obliga|t a (*fam*) inevitable. O~tion /-'tsjo:n/ f -,-en obligation; (*Comm*) bond. o~torisch a obligatory

Obmann m (pl -männer) [jury] foreman; (*Sport*) referee

Oboe /o'bo:ə/ f -,-n oboe

Obrigkeit f - authorities pl

obschon conj although

Observatorium nt -s,-ien observatory

obskur a obscure; (*zweifelhaft*) dubious

Obst nt -es (*coll*) fruit. O~baum m fruit-tree. O~garten m orchard. O~händler m fruiterer. O~kuchen m fruit flan. O~salat m fruit salad

obszön a obscene. O~ität f -,-en obscenity

O-Bus m trolley bus

obwohl conj although

Ochse m -n,-n ox. o~n vi (*haben*) (*fam*) swot. O~nschwanzsuppe f oxtail soup

öde a desolate; (*unfruchtbar*) barren; (*langweilig*) dull. Öde f - desolation; barrenness; dullness; (*Gegend*) waste

oder conj or; du kennst ihn doch, o~? you know him, don't you?

Ofen m -s,- ⁻ stove; (*Heiz-*) heater; (*Back-*) oven; (*Techn*) furnace

offen a open, adv -ly; ⟨Haar⟩ loose; ⟨Flamme⟩ naked; (o~herzig) frank, adv

-ly; (o~ *gezeigt*) overt, *adv* -ly; (*unent-schieden*) unsettled; o~e Stelle vacancy; Tag der o~en Tür open day; Wein o~ verkaufen sell wine by the glass; o~ bleiben remain open; o~ halten hold open ⟨*Tür*⟩; keep open ⟨*Mund, Augen*⟩; o~ lassen leave open; leave vacant ⟨*Stelle*⟩; o~ stehen be open; ⟨*Rechnung:*⟩ be outstanding; jdm o~ stehen (*fig*) be open to s.o.; *adv* ~ gesagt *od* gestanden to be honest. o~bar *a* obvious ▫ *adv* apparently. o~baren *vt* reveal. O~barung *f* -,-en revelation. o~bleiben† *vi sep* (*sein*) NEW o~ bleiben, s. offen. o~ halten† *vt sep* NEW o~ halten, s. offen. O~heit *f* - frankness, openness. o~herzig *a* frank, *adv* -ly. O~herzigkeit *f* - frankness. o~kundig *a* manifest, *adv* -ly. o~lassen† *vt sep* NEW o~ lassen, s. offen. o~sichtlich *a* obvious, *adv* -ly

offensiv *a* offensive. O~e *f* -,-n offensive

offenstehen† *vi sep* (*haben*) NEW offen stehen, s. offen

öffentlich *a* public, *adv* -ly. O~keit *f* - public; an die Ö~keit gelangen become public; in aller Ö~keit in public, publicly

Offerte *f* -,-n (*Comm*) offer

offiziell *a* official, *adv* -ly

Offizier *m* -s,-e (*Mil*) officer

öffn|en *vt/i* (*haben*) open; sich ö~en open. Ö~er *m* -s,- opener. Ö~ung *f* -,-en opening. Ö~ungszeiten *fpl* opening hours

oft *adv* often

öfter *adv* quite often. ö~e(r,s) *a* frequent; des Ö~en (ö~en) frequently. ö~s *adv* (*fam*) quite often

oftmals *adv* often

oh *int* oh!

ohne *prep* (+ *acc*) without; o~ mich! count me out! oben o~ topless; nicht o~ sein (*fam*) be not bad; (*nicht harmlos*) be quite nasty ▫ *conj* o~ zu überlegen without thinking; o~ dass ich es merkte without my noticing it. o~dies *adv* anyway. o~gleichen *pred* *a* unparalleled; eine Frechheit o~gleichen a piece of unprecedented insolence. o~hin *adv* anyway

Ohn|macht *f* -,-en faint; (*fig*) powerlessness; in O~macht fallen faint. o~mächtig *a* unconscious; (*fig*) powerless; o~mächtig werden faint

Ohr *nt* -[e]s,-en ear; übers Ohr hauen (*fam*) cheat

Öhr *nt* -[e]s,-e eye

ohren|betäubend *a* deafening. O~schmalz *nt* ear-wax. O~schmerzen *mpl* earache *sg*. O~sessel *m* wing-chair. O~tropfen *mpl* ear drops

Ohrfeige *f* slap in the face; jdm eine O~ geben slap s.o.'s face. o~n *vt* jdn o~n slap s.o.'s face

Ohr|läppchen *nt* -s,- ear-lobe. O~ring *m* ear-ring. O~wurm *m* earwig

oje *int* oh dear!

okay /o'ke:/ *a* & *adv* (*fam*) OK

okkult *a* occult

Öko|logie *f* - ecology. ö~logisch *a* ecological. O~nomie *f* - economy; (*Wissenschaft*) economics *sg*. ö~nomisch *a* economic; (*sparsam*) economical

Oktave *f* -,-n octave

Oktober *m* -s,- October

Okular *nt* -s,-e eyepiece

okulieren *vt* graft

ökumenisch *a* ecumenical

Öl *nt* -[e]s,-e oil; in Öl malen paint in oils. Ölbaum *m* olivetree. ölen *vt* oil; wie ein geölter Blitz (*fam*) like greased lightning. Ölfarbe *f* oil-paint. Ölfeld *nt* oil-field. Ölgemälde *nt* oil-painting. ölig *a* oily

Oliv|e *f* -,-n olive. O~enöl *nt* olive oil. o~grün *a* olive[-green]

oll *a* (*fam*) old; (*fam: hässlich*) nasty

Ölmessstab (Ölmeßstab) *m* dip-stick. Ölsardinen *fpl* sardines in oil. Ölstand *m* oil-level. Öltanker *m* oil-tanker. Ölteppich *m* oil-slick

Olympiade *f* -,-n Olympic Games *pl*, Olympics *pl*

Olymp|iasieger(in) /o'lympja-/ *m(f)* Olympic champion. o~isch *a* Olympic; O~ische Spiele Olympic Games

Ölzeug *nt* oilskins *pl*

Oma *f* -,-s (*fam*) granny

Omelett *nt* -[e]s,-e & -s omelette

Omen *nt* -s,- omen

ominös *a* ominous

Omnibus *m* bus; (*Reise-*) coach

onanieren *vi* (*haben*) masturbate

Onkel *m* -s,- uncle

Opa *m* -s,-s (*fam*) grandad

Opal *m* -s,-e opal

Oper *f* -,-n opera

Operation /-'tsjo:n/ *f* -,-en operation. O~ssaal *m* operating theatre

Operette *f* -,-n operetta

operieren *vt* operate on ⟨*Patient, Herz*⟩; sich o~ lassen have an operation ▫ *vi* (*haben*) operate

Opern|glas *nt* opera-glasses *pl*. O~haus *nt* opera-house. O~sänger(in) *m(f)* opera-singer

Opfer *nt* -s,- sacrifice; (*eines Unglücks*) victim; ein O~ bringen make a sacrifice; jdm/etw zum O~ fallen fall victim to s.o./sth. o~n *vt* sacrifice. O~ung *f* -,-en sacrifice

Opium *nt* -s opium

opponieren *vi* (*haben*) o~ gegen oppose

Opportunist *m* -en,-en opportunist. o~isch *a* opportunist

Opposition /-'tsio:n/ *f* - opposition. O~spartei *f* opposition party

Optik *f* - optics *sg* (*fam: Objektiv*) lens. O~er *m* -s,- optician

optimal *a* optimum

Optimis|mus *m* - optimism. O~t *m* -en, -en optimist. o~tisch *a* optimistic, *adv* -ally

Optimum *nt* -s,-ma optimum

Option /ɔp'tsio:n/ *f* -,-en option

optisch *a* optical; ⟨*Eindruck*⟩ visual

Orakel *nt* -s,- oracle

Orange /o'rãːʒə/ *f* -,-n orange. o~ *inv a* orange. O~ade /orãˈʒaːdə/ *f* -,-n orangeade. O~nmarmelade *f* [orange] marmalade. O~nsaft *m* orange juice

Oratorium *nt* -s,-ien oratorio

Orchest|er /ɔr'kɛstə/ *nt* -s,- orchestra. o~rieren *vt* orchestrate

Orchidee /ɔrçi'deːə/ *f* -,-n orchid

Orden *m* -s,- (*Ritter-, Kloster-*) order; (*Auszeichnung*) medal, decoration; jdm einen O~ verleihen decorate s.o. O~stracht *f* (*Relig*) habit

ordentlich *a* neat. tidy; (*anständig*) respectable; (*ordnungsgemäß, fam: richtig*) proper; (*Mitglied, Versammlung*) ordinary; (*fam: gut*) decent; (*fam: gehörig*) good □ *adv* neatly, tidily; respectably; properly; (*fam: gut, gehörig*) well; (*sehr*) very; (*regelrecht*) really

Order *f* -,-s & -n order

ordinär *a* common

Ordin|ation /-'tsio:n/ *f* -,-en (*Relig*) ordination; (*Aust*) surgery. o~ieren *vt* (*Relig*) ordain

ordn|en *vt* put in order; (*aufräumen*) tidy; (*an-*) arrange; sich zum Zug o~en form a procession. O~er *m* -s,- steward; (*Akten-*) file

Ordnung *f* order; O~ halten keep order; O~ machen tidy up; in O~ bringen put in order; (*aufräumen*) tidy; (*reparieren*) mend; (*fig*) put right; in O~ sein be in order; (*ordentlich sein*) be tidy; (*fig*) be all right; ich bin mit dem Magen *od* mein Magen ist nicht ganz in O~ I have a slight stomach upset; [geht] in O~! OK! o~sgemäß *a* proper, *adv* -ly. O~sstrafe *f* (*Jur*) fine. o~swidrig *a* improper, *adv* -ly

Ordonnanz Ordonanz *f* -,-en (*Mil*) orderly

Organ *nt* -s,-e organ; (*fam: Stimme*) voice

Organi|sation /-'tsio:n/ *f* -,-en organization. O~sator *m* -s,-en /-'to:ran/ organizer

organisch *a* organic, *adv* -ally

organisieren *vt* organize; (*fam: beschaffen*) get [hold of]

Organis|mus *m* -,-men organism; (*System*) system. O~t *m* -en,-en organist

Organspenderkarte *f* donor card

Orgasmus *m* -,-men orgasm

Orgel *f* -,-n (*Mus*) organ. O~pfeife *f* organ-pipe

Orgie /'ɔrgiə/ *f* -,-n orgy

Orien|t /'o:riɛnt/ *m* -s Orient. o~talisch *a* Oriental

orientier|en /oriɛn'tiːrən/ *vt* inform (*über + acc* about); sich o~en get one's bearings, orientate oneself; (*unterrichten*) inform oneself (*über + acc* about). O~ung *f* - orientation; die O~ung verlieren lose one's bearings

original *a* original. O~ *nt* -s,-e original; (*Person*) character. O~ität *f* - originality. O~übertragung *f* live transmission

originell *a* original; (*eigenartig*) unusual

Orkan *m* -s,-e hurricane

Ornament *nt* -[e]s,-e ornament

Ornat *m* -[e]s,-e robes *pl*

Ornithologie *f* - ornithology

Ort *m* -[e]s,-e place; (*Ortschaft*) [small] town; am Ort locally; am Ort des Verbrechens at the scene of the crime; an Ort und Stelle in the right place; (*sofort*) on the spot. o~en *vt* locate

ortho|dox *a* orthodox. O~graphie, O~grafie *f* - spelling. O~graphisch, o~grafisch *a* spelling ... O~päde *m* -n,-n orthopaedic specialist. o~pädisch *a* orthopaedic

örtlich *a* local, *adv* -ly. Ö~keit *f* -,-en locality

Ortschaft *f* -,-en [small] town; (*Dorf*) village; geschlossene O~ (*Auto*) built-up area

orts|fremd *a* o~fremd sein be a stranger. O~gespräch *nt* (*Teleph*) local call. O~name *m* place-name. o~sinn *m* sense of direction. O~verkehr *m* local traffic. O~zeit *f* local time

Öse *f* -,-n eyelet; (*Schlinge*) loop; Haken und Öse hook and eye

Ost *m* -[e]s east. o~deutsch *a* Eastern/(*Pol*) East German

Osten *m* -s east; nach O~ east

ostentativ *a* pointed, *adv* -ly

Osteopath *m* -en,-en osteopath

Oster|ei /ˈʔoːstɐˈʔai/ nt Easter egg. O∼fest nt Easter. O∼glocke f daffodil. O∼montag m Easter Monday. O∼n nt -,- Easter; frohe O∼n! happy Easter!

Österreich nt -s Austria. Ö∼er m, -s,-, Ö∼erin f -,-nen Austrian. ö∼isch a Austrian

östlich a eastern; (Richtung) easterly □ adv & prep (+ gen) ö∼ [von] der Stadt [to the] east of the town

Ost|see f Baltic [Sea]. o∼wärts adv eastwards

oszillieren vi (haben) oscillate

Otter[1] m -s,- otter

Otter[2] f -,-n adder

Ouverture /uvɛrˈtyːrə/ f -,-n overture

oval a oval. O∼ nt -s,-e oval

Ovation /-ˈtsi̯oːn/ f -,-en ovation

Ovulation /-ˈtsi̯oːn/ f -,-en ovulation

Oxid, **Oxyd** nt -[e]s,-e oxide

Ozean m -s,-e ocean

Ozon nt -s ozone. O∼loch nt hole in the ozone layer. O∼schicht f ozone layer

P

paar pron inv ein p∼ a few; ein p∼ Mal a few times; alle p∼ Tage every few days. P∼ nt -[e]s,-e pair; (Ehe-, Liebes-, Tanz-) couple. p∼en vt mate; (verbinden) combine; sich p∼en mate. p∼mal adv ein p∼mal NEW ein p∼ Mal, s. paar. P∼ung f -,-en mating. p∼weise adv in pairs, in twos

Pacht f -,-en lease; (P∼summe) rent. p∼en vt lease

Pächter m -s,- lessee; (eines Hofes) tenant

Pachtvertrag m lease

Pack[1] m -[e]s,-e bundle

Pack[2] nt -[e]s (sl) rabble

Päckchen nt -s,- package, small packet

pack|en vt/i (haben) pack; (ergreifen) seize; (fig: fesseln) grip; p∼ dich! (sl) beat it! P∼en m -s,- bundle. p∼end a (fig) gripping. P∼papier nt [strong] wrapping paper. P∼ung f -,-en packet; (Med) pack

Pädagog|e m -n,-n educationalist; (Lehrer) teacher. P∼ik f - educational science. p∼isch a educational

Paddel nt -s,- paddle. P∼boot nt canoe. p∼n vt/i (haben/sein) paddle. P∼sport m canoeing

Page /ˈpaːʒə/ m -n,-n page

Paillette /paiˈjɛtə/ f -,-n sequin

Paket nt -[e]s,-e packet; (Post-) parcel

Pakist|an nt -s Pakistan. P∼aner(in) m -s,-(f -,-nen) Pakistani. p∼anisch a Pakistani

Pakt m -[e]s,-e pact

Palast m -[e]s,-e palace

Palästina nt -s Palestine. P∼inenser(in) m -s,-(f -,-nen) Palestinian. p∼inensisch a Palestinian

Palette f -,-n palette

Palm|e f -,-n palm[-tree]; jdn auf die P∼e bringen (fam) drive s.o. up the wall. P∼sonntag m Palm Sunday

Pampelmuse f -,-n grapefruit

Panier|mehl nt (Culin) breadcrumbs pl. p∼t a (Culin) breaded

Panik f - panic; in P∼ geraten panic

panisch a p∼e Angst panic

Panne f -,-n breakdown; (Reifen-) flat tyre; (Missgeschick) mishap. P∼ndienst m breakdown service

Panorama nt -s panorama

panschen vt adulterate □ vi (haben) splash about

Panther, **Panter** m -s,- panther

Pantine f -,-n [wooden] clog

Pantoffel m -s,-n slipper; (ohne Ferse) mule. P∼held m (fam) henpecked husband

Pantomime[1] f -,-n mime

Pantomime[2] m -n,-n mime artist

pantschen vt/i = panschen

Panzer m -s,- armour; (Mil) tank; (Zool) shell. p∼n vt armourplate. P∼schrank m safe

Papa /ˈpapa, paˈpaː/ m -s,-s daddy

Papagei m -s & -en,-en parrot

Papier nt -[e]s,-e paper. P∼korb m waste-paper basket. P∼schlange f streamer. P∼waren fpl stationery sg

Pappe f - cardboard; (dial: Kleister) glue

Pappel f -,-n poplar

pappen vt/i (haben) (fam) stick

pappig a (fam) sticky

Papp|karton m, P∼schachtel f cardboard box

Paprika m -s,-[s] [sweet] pepper; (Gewürz) paprika □ f -,-[s] (P∼schote) pepper

Papst m -[e]s,-e pope

päpstlich a papal

Parade f -,-n parade

Paradeiser m -s,- (Aust) tomato

Paradies nt -es,-e paradise. p∼isch a heavenly

Paradox nt -es,-e paradox. p∼ a paradoxical

Paraffin nt -s paraffin

Paragraph, **Paragraf** m -en,-en section

parallel *a & adv* parallel. P~e *f* -,-n parallel

Paranuss (Paranuß) *f* Brazil nut

Parasit *m* -en,-en parasite

parat *a* ready

Pärchen *nt* -s,- pair; (*Liebes*-) couple

Parcours /par'ku:ɐ̯/ *m* -,- /-[s],-s/ (*Sport*) course

Pardon /par'dõ:/ *int* sorry!

Parfüm *nt* -s,-e & -s perfume, scent. p~iert *a* perfumed, scented

parieren[1] *vt* parry

parieren[2] *vi* (*haben*) (*fam*) obey

Parität *f* - parity; (*in Ausschuss*) equal representation

Park *m* -s,-s park. P~en *vt/i* (*haben*) park. P~en *nt* -s parking; 'P~en verboten' 'no parking'

Parkett *nt* -[e]s,-e parquet floor; (*Theat*) stalls *pl*

Park|haus *nt* multi-storey car park. P~lücke *f* parking space. P~platz *m* car park, (*Amer*) parking-lot; (*für ein Auto*) parking space; (*Autobahn*-) lay-by. P~scheibe *f* parking-disc. P~schein *m* car-park ticket. P~uhr *f* parking-meter. P~verbot *nt* parking ban; 'P~verbot' 'no parking'

Parlament *nt* -[e]s,-e parliament. p~arisch *a* parliamentary

Parodie *f* -,-n parody. p~ren *vt* parody

Parole *f* -,-n slogan; (*Mil*) password

Part *m* -s,-s (*Theat, Mus*) part

Partei *f* -,-en (*Pol, Jur*) party; (*Miet*-) tenant; für jdn P~ ergreifen take s.o.'s part. p~isch *a* biased. p~los *a* independent

Parterre /par'tɛr/ *nt* -s,-s ground floor, (*Amer*) first floor; (*Theat*) rear stalls *pl*. p~ *adv* on the ground floor

Partie *f* -,-n part; (*Tennis, Schach*) game; (*Golf*) round; (*Comm*) batch; eine gute P~ machen marry well

Partikel[1] *nt* -s,- particle

Partikel[2] *f* -,-n (*Gram*) particle

Partitur *f* -,-en (*Mus*) full score

Partizip *nt* -s,-ien /-jən/ participle; erstes/zweites P~ present/past participle

Partner|(in) *m* -s,- (*f* -,-nen) partner. P~schaft *f* -,-en partnership. P~stadt *f* twin town

Party /'pa:ɐ̯ti/ *f* -,-s party

Parzelle *f* -,-n plot [of ground]

Pass *m* -es,ˉe (Paß *m* -sses,ˉsse) passport; (*Geog, Sport*) pass

passabel *a* passable

Passage /pa'sa:ʒə/ *f* -,-n passage; (*Einkaufs*-) shopping arcade

Passagier /pasa'ʒi:ɐ̯/ *m* -s,-e passenger

Passamt (Paßamt) *nt* passport office

Passant(in) *m* -en,-en (*f* -,-nen) passerby

Passbild (Paßbild) *nt* passport photograph

Passe *f* -,-n yoke

passen *vi* (*haben*) fit; (*geeignet sein*) be right (für for); (*Sport*) pass the ball; (*aufgeben*) pass; p~ zu go [well] with; (*übereinstimmen*) match; jdm p~ fit s.o.; (*gelegen sein*) suit s.o.; seine Art passt mir nicht I don't like his manner; [ich] passe pass. p~d *a* suitable; (*angemessen*) appropriate; (*günstig*) convenient; (*übereinstimmend*) matching

passier|bar *a* passable. p~en *vt* pass; cross (*Grenze*); (*Culin*) rub through a sieve □ *vi* (*sein*) happen (jdm to s.o.); ist ein Unglück p~t there has been an accident. P~schein *m* pass

Passion *f* -,-en passion. p~iert *a* very keen (*Jäger, Angler*)

passiv *a* passive. P~ *nt* -s,-e (*Gram*) passive

Pass|kontrolle (Paßkontrolle) *f* passport control. P~straße *f* pass

Paste *f* -,-n paste

Pastell *nt* -[e]s,-e pastel. P~farbe *f* pastel colour

Pastet|chen *nt* -s,- [individual] pie; (*Königin*-) vol-au-vent. P~e *f* -,-n pie; (*Gänseleber*-) pâté

pasteurisieren /pastøri'zi:rən/ *vt* pasteurize

Pastille *f* -,-n pastille

Pastinake *f* -,-n parsnip

Pastor *m* -s,-en /-'to:rən/ pastor

Pate *m* -n,-n godfather; (*fig*) sponsor; P~n godparents. P~nkind *nt* godchild. P~nschaft *f* - sponsorship. P~nsohn *m* godson

Patent *nt* -[e]s,-e patent; (*Offiziers*-) commission. p~ *a* (*fam*) clever, able -ly; (*Person*) resourceful. p~ieren *vt* patent

Patentochter *f* god-daughter

Pater *m* -s,- (*Relig*) Father

pathetisch *a* emotional □ *adv* with emotion

Patholog|e *m* -n,-n pathologist. p~isch *a* pathological, *adv* -ly

Pathos *nt* - emotion, feeling

Patience /pa'sjã:s/ *f* -,-n patience

Patient(in) /pa'tsjɛnt(ɪn)/ *m* -en, -en (*f* -,-nen) patient

Patin *f* -,-nen godmother

Patriot(in) *m* -en,-en (*f* -,-nen) patriot. p~isch *a* patriotic. P~ismus *m* - patriotism

Patrone *f* -,-n cartridge

Patrouill|e /pa'truljə/ f -,-n patrol.
p~ieren /-'ji:rən/ vi (haben/sein) patrol

Patsch|e f in der P~e sitzen (fam) be in
a jam. p~en vi (haben/sein) splash □ vt
slap. p~nass (p~naß) a (fam) soaking
wet

Patt nt -s stalemate

Patz|er m -s,- (fam) slip. p~ig a (fam)
insolent

Pauk|e f -,-n kettledrum; auf die P~e
hauen (fam) have a good time; (prahlen)
boast. p~en vt/i (haben) (fam) swot.
P~er m -s,- (fam: Lehrer) teacher

pausbäckig a chubby-cheeked

pauschal a all-inclusive; (einheitlich) flat-
rate; (fig) sweeping ⟨Urteil⟩; p~e Summe
lump sum □ adv in a lump sum; (fig)
wholesale. P~e f -,-n lump sum. P~reise
f package tour. P~summe f lump sum

Pause¹ f -,-n break; (beim Sprechen) pause;
(Theat) interval; (im Kino) intermission;
(Mus) rest; P~ machen have a break

Pause² f -,-n tracing. p~n vt trace

pausenlos a incessant, adv -ly

pausieren vi (haben) have a break; (ausruhen) rest

Pauspapier nt tracing-paper

Pavian m -s,-e baboon

Pavillon /'paviljo/ m -s,-s pavilion

Pazifi|k m -s Pacific [Ocean]. p~sch a Pac-
ific

Pazifist m -en,-en pacifist

Pech nt -s pitch; (Unglück) bad luck; P~
haben be unlucky. p~schwarz a pitch-
black; ⟨Haare, Augen⟩ jet-black.
P~strähne f run of bad luck. P~vogel
m (fam) unlucky devil

Pedal nt -s,-e pedal

Pedant m -en,-en pedant. p~isch a pedantic, adv -ally

Pediküre f -,-n pedicure

Pegel m -s,- level; (Gerät) water-level indicator. P~stand m [water] level

peilen vt take a bearing on; über den Daumen gepeilt (fam) at a rough guess

Pein f - (liter) torment. p~igen vt torment

peinlich a embarrassing, awkward;
(genau) scrupulous, adv -ly; es war mir
sehr p~ I was very embarrassed

Peitsche f -,-n whip. p~n vt whip; (fig)
lash □ vi (sein) lash (an + acc against).
P~nhieb m lash

pekuniär a financial, adv -ly

Pelikan m -s,-e pelican

Pell|e f -,-n skin. p~en vt peel; shell ⟨Ei⟩;
sich p~en peel. P~kartoffeln fpl potatoes boiled in their skins

Pelz m -es,-e fur. P~mantel m fur coat

Pendel nt -s,- pendulum. p~n vi (haben)
swing □ vi (sein) commute. P~verkehr m
shuttle-service; (für Pendler) commuter
traffic

Pendler m -s,- commuter

penetrant a penetrating; (fig) obtrusive,
adv -ly

penibel a fastidious, fussy; (pedantisch)
pedantic

Penis m -,-se penis

Penne f -,-n (fam) school. p~n vi (haben)
(fam) sleep. P~r m -s,- (sl) tramp

Pension /pã'zjo:n/ f -,-en pension; (Hotel)
guest-house; bei voller/halber P~ with
full/half board. P~är(in) m -s,-e (f -,-nen)
pensioner. P~at nt -[e]s,-e boarding-
school. p~ieren vt retire. p~iert a retired. P~ierung f - retirement

Pensum nt -s [allotted] work

Peperoni f -,- chilli

per prep (+ acc) by; per Luftpost by air-
mail

perfekt a perfect, adv -ly; p~ sein ⟨Ver-
trag:⟩ be settled

Perfekt nt -s (Gram) perfect

Perfektion /-'tsjo:n/ f - perfection

perforiert a perforated

Pergament nt -[e]s,-e parchment.
P~papier nt grease-proof paper

Period|e f -,-n period. p~isch a periodic,
adv -ally

Perl|e f -,-n pearl; (Glas-, Holz-) bead;
(Sekt-) bubble; (fam: Hilfe) treasure.
p~en vi (haben) bubble. P~mutt nt -s,
P~mutter f - & nt -s mother-of-pearl

perplex a (fam) perplexed

Perserkatze f Persian cat

Pers|ien /-jən/ nt -s Persia. p~isch a Per-
sian

Person f -,-en person; (Theat) character;
ich für meine P~ [I] for my part; für
vier P~en for four people

Personal nt -s personnel, staff. P~aus-
weis m identity card. P~chef m personnel manager. P~ien /-jən/ pl personal
particulars. P~mangel m staff shortage.
P~pronomen nt personal pronoun

Personen|kraftwagen m private car.
P~zug m stopping train

personifizieren vt personify

persönlich a personal □ adv personally,
in person. P~keit f -,-en personality

Perspektive f -,-n perspective;
(Zukunfts-) prospect

Perücke f -,-n wig

pervers a [sexually] perverted. P~ion f
-,-en perversion

Pessimis|mus m - pessimism. P~t m -en,-en pessimist. p~tisch a pessimistic, adv -ally

Pest f - plague

Petersilie /-jə/ f - parsley

Petroleum /-leum/ nt -s paraffin, (Amer) kerosene

Petze f -,-n (fam) sneak. p~n vi (haben) (fam) sneak

Pfad m -[e]s,-e path. P~finder m -s,- [Boy] Scout. P~finderin f -,-nen [Girl] Guide

Pfahl m -[e]s,ːe stake, post

Pfalz (die) - the Palatinate

Pfand nt -[e]s,ːer pledge; (beim Spiel) forfeit; (Flaschen-) deposit

pfänd|en vt (Jur) seize. P~erspiel nt game of forfeits

Pfand|haus nt pawnshop. P~leiher m -s,- pawnbroker

Pfändung f -,-en (Jur) seizure

Pfann|e f -,-n (frying-]pan. P~kuchen m pancake; Berliner P~kuchen doughnut

Pfarr|er m -s,- vicar, parson; (katholischer) priest. P~haus nt vicarage

Pfau m -s,-en peacock

Pfeffer m -s pepper. P~kuchen m gingerbread. P~minzbonbon m & nt [pepper-]mint. P~minze f - (Bot) peppermint. P~minztee m [pepper]mint tea. p~n vt pepper; (fam: schmeißen) chuck. P~streuer m -s,- pepperpot

Pfeif|e f -,-n whistle; (Tabak-, Orgel-) pipe. p~en† vt/i (haben) whistle; (als Signal) blow the whistle; ich p~e darauf! (fam) I couldn't care less [about it]!

Pfeil m -[e]s,-e arrow

Pfeiler m -s,- pillar; (Brücken-) pier

Pfennig m -s,-e pfennig; 10 P~ 10 pfennigs

Pferch m -[e]s,-e [sheep] pen. p~en vt (fam) cram (in + acc into)

Pferd nt -[e]s,-e horse; zu P~e on horseback; das P~ beim Schwanz aufzäumen put the cart before the horse. P~erennen nt horse-race; (als Sport) [horse-]racing. P~eschwanz m horse's tail; (Frisur) pony-tail. P~estall m stable. P~estärke f horsepower. P~ewagen m horse-drawn cart

Pfiff m -[e]s,-e whistle; P~ haben (fam) have style

Pfifferling m -s,-e chanterelle

pfiffig a smart

Pfingst|en nt -s Whitsun. P~montag m Whit Monday. P~rose f peony

Pfirsich m -s,-e peach. p~farben a peach[-coloured]

Pflanz|e f -,-n plant. p~en vt plant. P~enfett nt vegetable fat. p~lich a vegetable; (Mittel) herbal. P~ung f -,-en plantation

Pflaster nt -s,- pavement; (Heft-) plaster. p~n vt pave. P~stein m paving-stone

Pflaume f -,-n plum

Pflege f - care; (Kranken-) nursing; in P~ nehmen look after; (Admin) foster (Kind). p~bedürftig a in need of care. P~eltern pl foster-parents. P~kind nt foster-child. p~leicht a easy-care. P~mutter f foster-mother. p~n vt look after, care for; nurse (Kranke); cultivate (Künste, Freundschaft). P~r(in) m -s,- (f -,-nen) nurse; (Tier-) keeper

Pflicht f -,-en duty; (Sport) compulsory exercise/routine. p~bewusst (p~bewußt) a conscientious, adv -ly. p~eifrig a zealous, adv -ly. P~fach nt (Sch) compulsory subject. P~gefühl nt sense of duty. p~gemäß a due □ adv duly

Pflock m -[e]s,ːe peg

pflücken vt pick

Pflug m -[e]s,ːe plough

pflügen vt/i (haben) plough

Pforte f -,-n gate

Pförtner m -s,- porter

Pfosten m -s,- post

Pfote f -,-n paw

Pfropfen m -s,- stopper; (Korken) cork. p~ vt graft (auf + acc on [to]); (fam: pressen) cram (in + acc into)

pfui int ugh; p~ schäm dich! you should be ashamed of yourself!

Pfund nt -[e]s,-e & - pound

Pfusch|arbeit f (fam) shoddy work. p~en vi (haben) botch one's work. P~er m -s,- (fam) shoddy worker. P~erei f -,-en (fam) botch-up

Pfütze f -,-n puddle

Phänomen nt -s,-e phenomenon. p~al a phenomenal

Phantasie f -,-n imagination; P~n fantasies; (Fieber-) hallucinations. p~los a unimaginative. p~ren vi (haben) fantasize; (im Fieber) be delirious. p~voll a imaginative, adv -ly

phantastisch a fantastic, adv -ally. P~om nt -s,-e phantom

pharma|zeutisch a pharmaceutical. P~zie f - pharmacy

Phase f -,-n phase

Philanthrop m -en,-en philanthropist. p~isch a philanthropic

Philolo|ge m -n,-n teacher/student of language and literature. P~gie f - [study of] language and literature

Philosoph m -en,-en philosopher. P~ie f -,-n philosophy. p~ieren vi (haben) philosophize

philosophisch a philosophical, adv -ly

phlegmatisch a phlegmatic

Phobie f -,-n phobia

Phonet|ik f - phonetics sg. p~isch a phonetic, adv -ally

Phonotypistin f -,-nen audio typist

Phosphor m -s phosphorus

Photo nt, Photo- = Foto, Foto-

Phrase f -,-n empty phrase

Physik f - physics sg. p~alisch a physical; ⟨Experiment, Forschung⟩ physics . . .

Physiker(in) m -s,- (f -,-nen) physicist

Physio|logie f - physiology. P~therapie f physiotherapy

physisch a physical, adv -ly

Pianist(in) m -en,-en (f -,-nen) pianist

Pickel m -s,- pimple, spot; ⟨Spitzhacke⟩ pick. p~ig a spotty

picken vt/i (haben) peck (nach at); ⟨fam: nehmen⟩ pick (aus out of); ⟨Aust fam: kleben⟩ stick

Picknick nt -s,-s picnic. p~en vi (haben) picnic

piep[s]|en vi (haben) ⟨Vogel:⟩ cheep; ⟨Maus:⟩ squeak; ⟨Techn⟩ bleep. P~er m -s,- bleeper

Pier m -s,-e [harbour] pier

Pietät /piɛ'tɛ:t/ f - reverence. p~los a irreverent, adv -ly

Pigment nt -[e]s,-e pigment. P~ierung f - pigmentation

Pik nt -s,-s ⟨Karten⟩ spades pl

pikant a piquant; ⟨gewagt⟩ racy

piken vt (fam) prick

pikiert a offended, hurt

piksen vt (fam) prick

Pilger|(in) m -s,- (f -,-nen) pilgrim. P~fahrt f pilgrimage. p~n vi (sein) make a pilgrimage

Pille f -,-n pill

Pilot m -en,-en pilot

Pilz m -es,-e fungus; ⟨essbarer⟩ mushroom; wie P~e aus dem Boden schießen ⟨fig⟩ mushroom

pingelig a (fam) fussy

Pinguin m -s,-e penguin

Pinie /-jə/ f -,-n stone-pine

pink pred a shocking pink

pinkeln vi (haben) (fam) pee

Pinsel m -s,- [paint]brush

Pinzette f -,-n tweezers pl

Pionier m -s,-e ⟨Mil⟩ sapper; ⟨fig⟩ pioneer. P~arbeit f pioneering work

Pirat m -en,-en pirate

pirschen vi (haben) p~ auf(+ acc) stalk □ vr sich p~ creep (an + acc up to)

pissen vi (haben) (sl) piss

Piste f -,-n ⟨Ski⟩ run, piste; ⟨Renn-⟩ track; ⟨Aviat⟩ runway

Pistole f -,-n pistol

pitschnass (pitschnaß) a (fam) soaking wet

pittoresk a picturesque

Pizza f -,-s pizza

Pkw /'pe:ka:ve:/ m -s,-s (= Personenkraftwagen) [private] car

placieren /-'tsi:rən/ vt = platzieren

Plackerei f - (fam) drudgery

plädieren vi (haben) plead (für for); auf Freispruch p~ ⟨Jur⟩ ask for an acquittal

Plädoyer /plɛdoa'je:/ nt -s,-s ⟨Jur⟩ closing speech; ⟨fig⟩ plea

Plage f -,-n [hard] labour; ⟨Mühe⟩ trouble; ⟨Belästigung⟩ nuisance. p~n vt torment, plague; ⟨bedrängen⟩ pester; sich p~n struggle; ⟨arbeiten⟩ work hard

Plagi|at nt -[e]s,-e plagiarism. p~ieren vt plagiarize

Plakat nt -[e]s,-e poster

Plakette f -,-n badge

Plan m -[e]s,-e plan

Plane f -,-n tarpaulin; ⟨Boden-⟩ groundsheet

planen vt/i (haben) plan

Planet m -en,-en planet

planier|en vt level. P~raupe f bulldozer

Planke f -,-n plank

plan|los a unsystematic, adv -ally. p~mäßig a systematic; ⟨Ankunft⟩ scheduled □ adv systematically; ⟨nach Plan⟩ according to plan; ⟨ankommen⟩ on schedule

Plansch|becken nt paddling pool. p~en vi (haben) splash about

Plantage /plan'ta:ʒə/ f -,-n plantation

Planung f - planning

Plapper|maul nt (fam) chatter-box. p~n vi (haben) chatter □ vt talk ⟨Unsinn⟩

plärren vi (haben) bawl; ⟨Radio:⟩ blare

Plasma nt -s plasma

Plastik¹ f -,-en sculpture

Plastik² nt -s plastic. p~isch a three-dimensional; ⟨formbar⟩ plastic; ⟨anschaulich⟩ graphic, adv -ally; p~ische Chirurgie plastic surgery

Platane f -,-n plane [tree]

Plateau /pla'to:/ nt -s,-s plateau

Platin nt -s platinum

Platitüde f -,-n ⟨NEW⟩ Plattitüde

platonisch a platonic

platschen vi (sein) splash

plätschern vi (haben) splash; ⟨Bach:⟩ babble □ vi (sein) ⟨Bach:⟩ babble along

platt a & adv flat; p~ sein (fam) be flabbergasted. P~ nt -[s] ⟨Lang⟩ Low German

Plättbrett nt ironing-board

Platte f -,-n slab; (Druck-) plate; (Metall-, Glas-) sheet; (Fliese) tile; (Koch-) hotplate; (Tisch-) top; (Auszieh-) leaf; (Schall-) record, disc; (zum Servieren) [flat] dish, platter; kalte P∼ assorted cold meats and cheeses pl

Plätt|eisen nt iron. p∼en vt/i (haben) iron

Plattenspieler m record-player

Platt|form f -,-en platform. P∼füße mpl flat feet. P∼heit f -,-en platitude

Plattitüde f -,-n platitude

Platz m -es,-̈e place; (von Häusern umgeben) square; (Sitz-) seat; (Sport-) ground; (Fußball-) pitch; (Tennis-) court; (Golf-) course; (freier Raum) room, space; P∼ nehmen take a seat; P∼ machen/lassen make/leave room; vom P∼ stellen (Sport) send off. P∼angst f agoraphobia; (Klaustrophobie) claustrophobia. P∼anweiserin f -,-nen usherette

Plätzchen nt -s,- spot; (Culin) biscuit

platzen vi (sein) burst; (auf-) split; (fam: scheitern) fall through; (Verlobung:) be off; vor Neugier p∼ be bursting with curiosity

platzieren vt place, put; sich p∼ (Sport) be placed

Platz|karte f seat reservation ticket. P∼konzert nt open-air concert. P∼mangel m lack of space. P∼patrone f blank. P∼regen m downpour. P∼verweis m (Sport) sending off. P∼wunde f laceration

Plauderei f -,-en chat

plaudern vi (haben) chat

Plausch m -[e]s,-e (SGer) chat. p∼en vi (haben) (SGer) chat

plausibel a plausible

plazieren vt NEW platzieren

pleite a (fam) p∼ sein be broke: (Firma:) be bankrupt; p∼ gehen NEW be bankrupt, s. Pleite. P∼ f -,-n (fam) bankruptcy; (Misserfolg) flop; P∼ gehen od machen go bankrupt

plissiert a [finely] pleated

Plombe f -,-n seal; (Zahn-) filling. p∼ieren vt seal; fill (Zahn)

plötzlich a sudden, adv -ly

plump a plump; (ungeschickt) clumsy, adv -ily

plumpsen vi (sein) (fam) fall

Plunder m -s (fam) junk, rubbish

plündern vt/i (haben) loot

Plunderstück nt Danish pastry

Plural m -s,-e plural

plus adv, conj & prep (+ dat) plus. P∼ nt - surplus; (Gewinn) profit; (Vorteil) advantage, plus. P∼punkt m (Sport) point; (fig)

plus. P∼quamperfekt nt pluperfect. P∼zeichen nt plus sign

Po m -s,-s (fam) bottom

Pöbel m -s mob, rabble. p∼haft a loutish

pochen vi (haben) knock; (Herz:) pound; p∼ auf (+ acc) (fig) insist on

pochieren /pɔ'ʃiːrən/ vt (Culin) poach

Pocken pl smallpox sg

Podest nt -[e]s,-e rostrum

Podium nt -s,-ien /-jən/ platform; (Podest) rostrum

Poesie /poe'ziː/ f - poetry

poetisch a poetic

Pointe /'pɔ̃ːtə/ f -,-n point (of a joke)

Pokal m -s,-e goblet; (Sport) cup

pökeln vt (Culin) salt

Poker nt -s poker

Pol m -s,-e pole. p∼ar a polar

polarisieren vt polarize

Polarstern m pole-star

Pole m, -n,-n Pole. P∼n nt -s Poland

Police /po'liːsə/ f -,-n policy

Polier m -s,-e foreman

polieren vt polish

Polin f -,-nen Pole

Politesse f -,-n [woman] traffic warden

Politik f - politics sg; (Vorgehen, Maßnahme) policy

Polit|iker(in) m -s,- (f, -,-nen) politician. p∼isch a political, adv -ly

Politur f -,-en polish

Polizei f - police pl. P∼beamte(r) m police officer. p∼lich a police . . . □ adv by the police; (sich anmelden) with the police. P∼streife f police patrol. P∼stunde f closing time. P∼wache f police station

Polizist m -en,-en policeman. P∼in f -,-nen policewoman

Pollen m -s pollen

polnisch a Polish

Polohemd nt polo shirt

Polster nt -s,- pad; (Kissen) cushion; (Möbel-) upholstery; (fam: Rücklage) reserves pl. P∼er m -s,- upholsterer. P∼möbel pl upholstered furniture sg. p∼n vt pad; upholster (Möbel). P∼ung f -,-en padding; upholstery

Polter|abend m wedding-eve party. p∼n vi (haben) thump, bang; (schelten) bawl □ vi (sein) crash down; (gehen) clump [along]; (fahren) rumble [along]

Polyäthylen nt -s polythene

Polyester m -s polyester

Polyp m -en,-en polyp; (sl: Polizist) copper; P∼en adenoids pl

Pomeranze f -,-n Seville orange

Pommes pl (fam) French fries

Pommes frites /pɔm'fri:t/ pl chips; (dünner) French fries

Pomp m -s pomp

Pompon /põ'põ:/ m -s,-s pompon

pompös a ostentatious, adv -ly

Pony¹ nt -s,-s pony

Pony² m -s,-s fringe

Pop m -[s] pop. P~musik f pop music

Popo m -s,-s (fam) bottom

populär a popular. P~arität f - popularity

Pore f -,-n pore

Porno|graphie, Pornografie f - pornography. p~graphisch, p~grafisch a pornographic

porös a porous

Porree m -s leeks pl; eine Stange P~ a leek

Portal nt -s,-e portal

Portemonnaie /pɔrtmɔ'ne:/ nt -s,-s purse

Portier /pɔr'tje:/ m -s,-s doorman, porter

Portion /-'tsjo:n/ f -,-en helping, portion

Portmonee nt -s,-s = Portemonnaie

Porto nt -s postage. p~frei adv post free, post paid

Porträt /pɔr'trɛ:/ nt -s,-s portrait. p~tieren vt paint a portrait of

Portugal nt -s Portugal

Portugies|e m -n,-n, P~in f -,-nen Portuguese. p~isch a Portuguese

Portwein m port

Porzellan nt -s china, porcelain

Posaune f -,-n trombone

Pose f -,-n pose

posieren vi (haben) pose

Position /-'tsjo:n/ f -,-en position

positiv a positive, adv -ly. P~ nt -s,-e (Phot) positive

Posse f -,-n (Theat) farce. P~n m -s,- prank; P~n pl tomfoolery sg

Possessivpronomen nt possessive pronoun

possierlich a cute

Post f - post office; (Briefe) mail, post; mit der P~ by post

postalisch a postal

Post|amt nt post office. P~anweisung f postal money order. P~bote m postman

Posten m -s,- post; (Wache) sentry; (Waren-) batch; (Rechnungs-) item, entry; P~ stehen stand guard; nicht auf dem P~ (fam) under the weather

Poster nt & m -s,- poster

Postfach nt post-office or PO box

postieren vt post, station; sich p~ station oneself

Post|karte f postcard. P~lagernd adv poste restante. P~leitzahl f postcode, (Amer) Zip code. P~scheckkonto nt ≈ National Girobank account. P~stempel m postmark

postum a posthumous, adv -ly

post|wendend adv by return of post. P~wertzeichen nt [postage] stamp

Poten|tial /-'tsja:l/ nt -s,-e = Potenzial. p~tiell /-'tsjɛl/ a = potenziell

Potenz f -,-en potency; (Math & fig) power. P~ial nt -s,-e potential. p~iell a potential, adv -ly

Pracht f - magnificence, splendour. P~exemplar nt magnificent specimen

prächtig a magnificent, adv -ly; (prima) splendid, adv -ly

prachtvoll a magnificent, adv -ly

Prädikat nt -[e]s,-e rating; (Comm) grade; (Gram) predicate. p~iv a (Gram) predicative, adv -ly. P~swein m high-quality wine

präge|n vt stamp (auf + acc on); emboss (Leder, Papier); mint (Münze); coin (Wort, Ausdruck); (fig) shape. P~stempel m die

pragmatisch a pragmatic, adv -ally

prägnant a succinct, adv -ly

prähistorisch a prehistoric

prahl|en vi (haben) boast, brag (mit about). p~erisch a boastful, adv -ly

Prakti|k f -,-en practice. P~kant(in) m -en,-en (f -,-nen) trainee

Prakti|kum nt -s,-ka practical training. p~sch a practical; (nützlich) handy; (tatsächlich) virtual; p~scher Arzt general practitioner □ adv practically; virtually; (in der Praxis) in practice; p~sch arbeiten do practical work. p~zieren vt/i (haben) practise; (anwenden) put into practice; (fam: bekommen) get

Praline f -,-n chocolate; Schachtel P~n box of chocolates

prall a bulging; (dick) plump; (Sonne) blazing □ adv p~ gefüllt full to bursting. p~en vi (sein) p~ auf (+ acc)/gegen collide with, hit; (Sonne:) blaze down on

Prämie /-jə/ f -,-n premium; (Preis) award

präm|iieren vt award a prize to

Pranger m -s,- pillory

Pranke f -,-n paw

Präparat nt -[e]s,-e preparation. p~ieren vt prepare; (zerlegen) dissect; (ausstopfen) stuff

Präposition /-'tsjo:n/ f -,-en preposition

Präsens nt - (Gram) present

präsentieren vt present; sich p~ present itself/(Person:) oneself

Präsenz f - presence

Präservativ nt -s,-e condom

Präsident|(in) m -en,-en (f -,-nen) president. **P~schaft** f - presidency

Präsidium nt -s presidency; (Gremium) executive committee; (Polizei-) headquarters pl

prasseln vi (haben) ⟨Regen:⟩ beat down; ⟨Feuer:⟩ crackle □ vi (sein) **p~** auf (+ acc)/gegen beat down on/beat against

prassen vi (haben) live extravagantly; (schmausen) feast

Präteritum nt -s imperfect

präventiv a preventive

Praxis f -,-xen practice; (Erfahrung) practical experience; (Arzt-) surgery; **in der P~** in practice

Präzedenzfall m precedent

präzis[e] a precise, adv -ly

Präzision f - precision

predig|en vt/i (haben) preach. **P~er** m -s,- preacher. **P~t** f -,-en sermon

Preis m -es,-e price; (Belohnung) prize; **um jeden/keinen P~** at any/not at any price. **P~ausschreiben** nt competition

Preiselbeere f -,-n (Bot) cowberry; (Culin) ≈ cranberry

preisen vt praise; **sich glücklich p~** count oneself lucky

preisgeben vt sep abandon (dat to); reveal (Geheimnis)

preis|gekrönt a award-winning. **P~gericht** nt jury. **p~günstig** a reasonably priced □ adv at a reasonable price. **P~lage** f price range. **p~lich** a price ... □ adv in price. **P~richter** m judge. **P~schild** nt price-tag. **P~träger(in)** m(f) prize-winner. **p~wert** a reasonable, adv -bly; (billig) inexpensive, adv -ly

prekär a difficult; (heikel) delicate

Prell|bock m buffers pl. **p~en** vt bounce; (verletzen) bruise; (fam: betrügen) cheat. **P~ung** f -,-en bruise

Premiere /prəˈmjeːrə/ f -,-n première

Premierminister(in) /prəˈmjeː-/ m(f) Prime Minister

Presse f -,-n press. **p~n** vt press; sich **p~n** press (an + acc against)

pressieren vi (haben) (SGer) be urgent

Pressluft (Preßluft) f compressed air. **P~bohrer** m pneumatic drill

Prestige /presˈtiːʒə/ nt -s prestige

Preuß|en nt -s Prussia. **p~isch** a Prussian

prickeln vi (haben) tingle

Priester m -s,- priest

prima inv a first-class, first-rate; (fam: toll) fantastic, adv fantastically well

primär a primary, adv -ily

Primel f -,-n primula; (Garten-) polyanthus

primitiv a primitive

Prinz m -en,-en prince. **P~essin** f -,-nen princess

Prinzip nt -s,-ien /-jən/ principle; **im/aus P~** in/on principle. **p~iell** a (Frage) of principle □ adv on principle; (im Prinzip) in principle

Priorität f -,-en priority

Prise f -,-n **P~ Salz** pinch of salt

Prisma nt -s,-men prism

privat a private, adv -ly; (persönlich) personal. **P~adresse** f home address. **p~isieren** vt privatize

Privat|leben nt private life. **P~lehrer** m private tutor. **P~lehrerin** f governess. **P~patient(in)** m(f) private patient

Privileg nt -[e]s,-ien /-jən/ privilege. **p~iert** a privileged

pro prep (+ dat) per. **Pro** nt - das Pro und Kontra the pros and cons pl

Probe f -,-n test, trial; (Menge, Muster) sample; (Theat) rehearsal; **auf die P~ stellen** put to the test; **ein Auto P~ fahren** test-drive a car. **P~fahrt** f test drive. **p~n** vt/i (haben) (Theat) rehearse. **p~weise** adv on a trial basis. **P~zeit** f probationary period

probieren vt/i (haben) try; (kosten) taste; (proben) rehearse

Problem nt -s,-e problem. **p~atisch** a problematic

problemlos a problem-free □ adv without any problems

Produkt nt -[e]s,-e product

Produk|tion /-ˈtsjoːn/ f -,-en production. **p~tiv** a productive. **P~tivität** f - productivity

Produ|zent m -en,-en producer. **p~zieren** vt produce; **sich p~zieren** (fam) show off

professionell a professional, adv -ly

Professor m -s,-en /-ˈsoːrən/ professor

Profi m -s,-s (Sport) professional

Profil nt -s,-e profile; (Reifen-) tread; (fig) image. **p~iert** a (fig) distinguished

Profit m -[e]s,-e profit. **p~ieren** vi (haben) profit (von from)

Prognose f -,-n forecast; (Med) prognosis

Programm nt -s,-e programme; (Computer-) program; (TV) channel; (Comm: Sortiment) range. **p~ieren** vt/i (haben) (Computer) program. **P~ierer(in)** m -s,- (f -,-nen) [computer] programmer

progressiv a progressive

Projekt nt -[e]s,-e project

Projektor *m* -s,-en /-'to:rən/ projector

projizieren *vt* project

Proklam|ation /-'tsjo:n/ *f* -,-en proclamation. p~ieren *vt* proclaim

Prolet *m* -en,-en boor. P~ariat *nt* -[e]s proletariat. P~arier /-jɐ/ *m* -s,- proletarian

Prolog *m* -s,-e prologue

Promenade *f* -,-n promenade. P~nmischung *f* (*fam*) mongrel

Promille *pl* (*fam*) alcohol level *sg* in the blood; zu viel P~ haben (*fam*) be over the limit

prominen|t *a* prominent. P~z *f* -prominent figures *pl*

Promiskuität *f* - promiscuity

promovieren *vi* (*haben*) obtain one's doctorate

prompt *a* prompt, *adv* -ly; (*fam: natürlich*) of course

Pronomen *nt* -s,- pronoun

Propag|anda *f* - propaganda; (*Reklame*) publicity. p~ieren *vt* propagate

Propeller *m* -s,- propeller

Prophet *m* -en,-en prophet. p~isch *a* prophetic

prophezei|en *vt* prophesy. P~ung *f* -,-en prophecy

Proportion /-'tsjo:n/ *f* -,-en proportion. p~al *a* proportional. p~iert *a* gut p~iert well proportioned

Prosa *f* - prose

prosaisch *a* prosaic, *adv* -ally

prosit *int* cheers!

Prospekt *m* -[e]s,-e brochure; (*Comm*) prospectus

prost *int* cheers!

Prostitu|ierte *f* -n,-n prostitute. P~tion /-'tsjo:n/ *f* - prostitution

Protest *m* -[e]s,-e protest

Protestant|(in) *m* -en,-en (*f* -,-nen) (*Relig*) Protestant. p~isch *a* (*Relig*) Protestant

protestieren *vi* (*haben*) protest

Prothese *f* -,-n artificial limb; (*Zahn-*) denture

Protokoll *nt* -s,-e record; (*Sitzungs-*) minutes *pl*; (*diplomatisches*) protocol; (*Strafzettel*) ticket

Prototyp *m* -s,-en prototype

protz|en *vi* (*haben*) show off (mit etw sth). p~ig *a* ostentatious

Proviant *m* -s provisions *pl*

Provinz *f* -,-en province. p~iell *a* provincial

Provision *f* -,-en (*Comm*) commission

provisorisch *a* provisional, *adv* -ly, temporary, *adv* -ily

Provokation /-'tsjo:n/ *f* -,-en provocation

provozieren *vt* provoke. p~d *a* provocative, *adv* -ly

Prozedur *f* -,-en [lengthy] business

Prozent *nt* -[e]s,-e & - per cent; 5 P~ 5 per cent. P~satz *m* percentage. p~ual *a* percentage ...

Prozeß *m* -es,-e (Prozeß *m* -sses,-sse) process; (*Jur*) lawsuit; (*Kriminal-*) trial

Prozession *f* -,-en procession

prüde *a* prudish

prüf|en *vt* test/(*über-*) check (auf + *acc* for); audit (*Bücher*); (*Sch*) examine; p~ender Blick searching look. P~er *m* -s,- inspector; (*Buch-*) auditor; (*Sch*) examiner. P~ling *m* -s,-e examination candidate. P~ung *f* -,-en examination; (*Test*) test; (*Bücher-*) audit; (*fig*) trial

Prügel *m* -s,- cudgel; P~ *pl* hiding *sg*, beating *sg*. P~ei *f* -,-en brawl, fight. p~n *vt* beat, thrash; sich p~n fight, brawl

Prunk *m* -[e]s magnificence, splendour. p~en *vi* (*haben*) show off (mit etw sth). p~voll *a* magnificent, *adv* -ly

prusten *vi* (*haben*) splutter; (*schnauben*) snort

Psalm *m* -s,-en psalm

Pseudonym *nt* -s,-e pseudonym

pst *int* shush!

Psychi|ater *m* -s,- psychiatrist. P~atrie *f* - psychiatry. p~atrisch *a* psychiatric

psychisch *a* psychological, *adv* -ly; (*Med*) mental, *adv* -ly

Psycho|analyse *f* psychoanalysis. P~loge *m* -n,-n psychologist. P~logie *f* - psychology. p~logisch *a* psychological, *adv* -ly

Pubertät *f* - puberty

publik *a* p~ werden/machen become/make public

Publi|kum *nt* -s public; (*Zuhörer*) audience; (*Zuschauer*) spectators *pl*. p~zieren *vt* publish

Pudding *m* -s,-s blancmange; (*im Wasserbad gekocht*) pudding

Pudel *m* -s,- poodle

Puder *m* & (*fam*) *nt* -s,- powder; (*Körper-*) talcum [powder]. P~dose *f* [powder] compact. p~n *vt* powder. P~zucker *m* icing sugar

Puff[1] *m* -[e]s,-e push, poke

Puff[2] *m* & *nt* -s,-s (*sl*) brothel

puffen *vt* (*haben*) poke ⊡ *vi* (*sein*) puff along

Puffer *m* -s,- (*Rail*) buffer; (*Culin*) pancake. P~zone *f* buffer zone

Pull|i *m* -s,-s jumper. P~over *m* -s,- jumper; (*Herren-*) pullover

Puls *m* -es pulse. P~ader *f* artery. p~ieren *vi* (*haben*) pulsate

Pult *nt* -[e]s,-e desk; (*Lese-*) lectern

Pulver *nt* -s,- powder. p~ig *a* powdery. p~isieren *vt* pulverize

Pulver|kaffee *m* instant coffee. P~schnee *m* powder snow

pummelig *a* (*fam*) chubby

Pump *m* auf P~ (*fam*) on tick

Pumpe *f* -,-n pump. p~n *vt/i* (*haben*) pump; (*fam: leihen*) lend; [sich (*dat*)] etw p~n (*fam: borgen*) borrow sth

Pumps /pœmps/ *pl* court shoes

Punkt *m* -[e]s,-e dot; (*Tex*) spot; (*Geom, Sport & fig*) point; (*Gram*) full stop, period; P~ sechs Uhr at six o'clock sharp; nach P~en siegen win on points. p~iert *a* (*Linie, Note*) dotted

pünktlich *a* punctual, *adv* -ly. P~keit *f* - punctuality

Punsch *m* -[e]s,-e [hot] punch

Pupille *f* -,-n (*Anat*) pupil

Puppe *f* -,-n doll; (*Marionette*) puppet; (*Schaufenster-, Schneider-*) dummy; (*Zool*) chrysalis

pur *a* pure; (*fam: bloß*) sheer; Whisky p~ neat whisky

Püree *nt* -s,-s purée; (*Kartoffel-*) mashed potatoes *pl*

puritanisch *a* puritanical

purpurrot *a* crimson

Purzel|baum *m* (*fam*) somersault. p~n *vi* (*sein*) (*fam*) tumble

pusseln *vi* (*haben*) (*fam*) potter

Puste *f* - (*fam*) breath; aus der P~ out of breath. p~n *vt/i* (*haben*) (*fam*) blow

Pute *f* -,-n turkey; (*Henne*) turkey hen. P~r *m* -s,- turkey cock

Putsch *m* -[e]s,-e coup

Putz *m* -es plaster; (*Staat*) finery. p~en *vt* clean; (*Aust*) dry-clean; (*zieren*) adorn; sich p~en dress up; sich (*dat*) die Zähne/Nase p~en clean one's teeth/blow one's nose. P~frau *f* cleaner, charwoman. p~ig *a* (*fam*) amusing, cute; (*seltsam*) odd. P~macherin *f* -,-nen milliner

Puzzlespiel /'pazl-/ *nt* jigsaw

Pyramide *f* -,-n pyramid

Q

Quacksalber *m* -s,- quack

Quadrat *nt* -[e]s,-e square. q~isch *a* square. Q~meter *m & nt* square metre

quaken *vi* (*haben*) quack; (*Frosch:*) croak

quäken *vi* (*haben*) screech; (*Baby:*) whine

Quäker(in) *m* -s,- (*f* -,-nen) Quaker

Qual *f* -,-en torment; (*Schmerz*) agony

quälen *vt* torment; (*foltern*) torture; (*bedrängen*) pester; sich q~ torment oneself; (*leiden*) suffer; (*sich mühen*) struggle. q~d *a* agonizing

Quälerei *f* -,-en torture; (*Qual*) agony

Quälgeist *m* (*fam*) pest

Qualifi|kation /-'tsio:n/ *f* -,-en qualification. q~zieren *vt* qualify; sich q~zieren qualify. q~ziert *a* qualified; (*fähig*) competent; (*Arbeit*) skilled

Qualität *f* -,-en quality

Qualle *f* -,-n jellyfish

Qualm *m* -s [thick] smoke. q~en *vi* (*haben*) smoke

qualvoll *a* agonizing

Quantität *f* -,-en quantity

Quantum *nt* -s,-ten quantity; (*Anteil*) share, quota

Quarantäne *f* - quarantine

Quark *m* -s quark, ≈ curd cheese; (*fam: Unsinn*) rubbish

Quartal *nt* -s,-e quarter

Quartett *nt* -[e]s,-e quartet

Quartier *nt* -s,-e accommodation; (*Mil*) quarters *pl*; ein Q~ suchen look for accommodation

Quarz *m* -es quartz

quasseln *vi* (*haben*) (*fam*) jabber

Quaste *f* -,-n tassel

Quatsch *m* -[e]s nonsense, rubbish; Q~ machen (*Unfug machen*) fool around; (*etw falsch machen*) do a silly thing. q~en *vi* (*fam*) *vi* (*haben*) talk; (*schwatzen*) natter; (*Wasser, Schlamm:*) squelch □ *vt* talk. q~nass (q~naß) *a* (*fam*) soaking wet

Quecksilber *nt* mercury

Quelle *f* -,-n spring; (*Fluss- & fig*) source. q~n† *vi* (*sein*) well [up]/(*fließen*) pour (aus from); (*aufquellen*) swell; (*hervortreten*) bulge

quengeln *vi* (*fam*) whine; (*Baby:*) grizzle

quer *adv* across, crosswise; (*schräg*) diagonally; q~ gestreift horizontally striped

Quere *f* - der Q~ nach across, crosswise; jdm in die Q~ kommen get in s.o.'s way

querfeldein *adv* across country

quer|gestreift *a* NEW q~ gestreift, *s.* quer. q~köpfig *a* (*fam*) awkward. Q~latte *f* crossbar. Q~schiff *nt* transept. Q~schnitt *m* cross-section. q~schnittsgelähmt *a* paraplegic. Q~straße *f* side-street; die erste Q~straße links the first turning on the left. Q~verweis *m* cross-reference

quetsch|en *vt* squash; *(drücken)* squeeze; *(zerdrücken)* crush; *(Culin)* mash; sich q~en in (+ *acc*) squeeze into; sich *(dat)* den Arm q~en bruise one's arm. Q~ung *f* -,-en, Q~wunde *f* bruise

Queue /køː/ *nt* -s,-s cue

quicklebendig *a* very lively

quieken *vi (haben)* squeal; *(Maus:)* squeak

quietschen *vi (haben)* squeal; *(Tür, Dielen:)* creak

Quintett *nt* -[e]s,-e quintet

Quirl *m* -[e]s,-e blender with a star-shaped head. q~en *vt* mix

quitt *a* q~ sein *(fam)* be quits

Quitte *f* -,-n quince

quittier|en *vt* receipt *(Rechnung)*; sign for *(Geldsumme, Sendung)*; *(reagieren auf)* greet (mit with); den Dienst q~ resign

Quittung *f* -,-en receipt

Quiz /kvis/ *nt* -,- quiz

Quote *f* -,-n proportion

R

Rabatt *m* -[e]s,-e discount

Rabatte *f* -,-n *(Hort)* border

Rabattmarke *f* trading stamp

Rabbiner *m* -s,- rabbi

Rabe *m* -n,-n raven. r~nschwarz *a* pitch-black

rabiat *a* violent, *adv* -ly; *(wütend)* furious, *adv* -ly

Rache *f* - revenge, vengeance

Rachen *m* -s,- pharynx; *(Maul)* jaws *pl*

rächen *vt* avenge; sich r~ take revenge (an + *dat* on); *(Fehler, Leichtsinn:)* cost s.o. dear

Racker *m* -s,- *(fam)* rascal

Rad *nt* -[e]s,-er wheel; *(Fahr-)* bicycle, *(fam)* bike; Rad fahren cycle

Radar *m & nt* -s radar

Radau *m* -s *(fam)* din, racket

radebrechen *vt/i (haben)* [Deutsch/ Englisch] r~ speak broken German/ English

radeln *vi (sein) (fam)* cycle

Rädelsführer *m* ringleader

radfahr|en† *vi sep (sein)* (NEW) Rad fahren, *s.* Rad. R~er(in) *m(f)* -s,- *(f* -,-nen) cyclist

radier|en *vt/i (haben)* rub out; *(Kunst)* etch. R~gummi *m* eraser, rubber. R~ung *f* -,-en etching

Radieschen /-'diːsçən/ *nt* -s,- radish

radikal *a* radical, *adv* -ly; *(drastisch)* drastic, *adv* -ally. R~e(r) *m/f (Pol)* radical

Radio *nt* -s,-s radio

radioaktiv *a* radioactive. R~ität *f* - radioactivity

Radioapparat *m* radio [set]

Radius *m* -,-ien /-jən/ radius

Rad|kappe *f* hub-cap. R~ler *m* -s,- cyclist; *(Getränk)* shandy. R~weg *m* cycle track

raffen *vt* grab; *(kräuseln)* gather; *(kürzen)* condense. r~gierig *a* avaricious

Raffin|ade *f* - refined sugar. R~erie *f* -,-n refinery. R~esse *f* -,-n refinement; *(Schlauheit)* cunning. r~ieren *vt* refine. r~iert *a* ingenious, *adv* -ly; *(durchtrieben)* crafty, *adv* -ily

Rage /'raːʒə/ *f* - *(fam)* fury

ragen *vi (haben)* rise [up]

Rahm *m* -s *(SGer)* cream

rahmen *vt* frame. R~ *m* -s,- frame; *(fig)* framework; *(Grenze)* limits *pl*; *(einer Feier)* setting

Rain *m* -[e]s,-e grass verge

räkeln *v* = rekeln

Rakete *f* -,-n rocket; *(Mil)* missile

Rallye /'rali/ *nt* -s,-s rally

rammen *vt* ram

Rampe *f* -,-n ramp; *(Theat)* front of the stage. R~nlicht *nt* im R~nlicht stehen *(fig)* be in the limelight

ramponier|en *vt (fam)* damage; *(ruinieren)* ruin; r~t battered

Ramsch *m* -[e]s junk. R~laden *m* junk-shop

ran *adv* = heran

Rand *m* -[e]s,-er edge; *(Teller-, Gläser-, Brillen-)* rim; *(Zier-)* border, edging; *(Buch-, Brief-)* margin; *(Stadt-)* outskirts *pl*; *(Ring)* ring; am R~e des Ruins on the brink of ruin; am R~e erwähnen mention in passing; zu R~e kommen mit = zurande kommen mit, *s.* zurande; außer R~ und Band *(fam: ausgelassen)* very boisterous

randalieren *vi (haben)* rampage

Rand|bemerkung *f* marginal note. R~streifen *m (Auto)* hard shoulder

Rang *m* -[e]s,-e rank; *(Theat)* tier; erster/zweiter R~ *(Theat)* dress/upper circle; ersten R~es first-class

rangieren /raŋ'ʒiːrən/ *vt* shunt □ *vi (haben)* rank (vor + *dat* before); an erster Stelle r~ come first

Rangordnung *f* order of importance; *(Hierarchie)* hierarchy

Ranke *f* -,-n tendril; *(Trieb)* shoot

ranken (sich) *vr (Bot)* trail; *(in die Höhe)* climb; sich r~ um twine around

Ranzen *m* -s,- ⟨*Sch*⟩ satchel

ranzig *a* rancid

Rappe *m* -n,-n black horse

rappeln *v* ⟨*fam*⟩ ◻ *vi* (*haben*) rattle ◻ *vr* sich r∼ pick oneself up; ⟨*fig*⟩ rally

Raps *m* -es ⟨*Bot*⟩ rape

rar *a* rare; **er macht sich rar** ⟨*fam*⟩ we don't see much of him. **R∼ität** *f* -,-en rarity

rasant *a* fast; ⟨*schnittig, schick*⟩ stylish ◻ *adv* fast; stylishly

rasch *a* quick, *adv* -ly

rascheln *vi* (*haben*) rustle

Rasen *m* -s,- lawn

rasen *vi* (*sein*) tear [along]; ⟨*Puls:*⟩ race; ⟨*Zeit:*⟩ fly; **gegen eine Mauer r∼** career into a wall ⟨*Sturm:*⟩ rage; **vor Begeisterung r∼** go wild with enthusiasm. **r∼d** *a* furious; ⟨*tobend*⟩ raving; ⟨*Sturm, Durst*⟩ raging; ⟨*Schmerz*⟩ excruciating; ⟨*Beifall*⟩ tumultuous ◻ *adv* terribly

Rasenmäher *m* lawn-mower

Raserei *f* - speeding; ⟨*Toben*⟩ frenzy

Rasier|apparat *m* razor. **r∼en** *vt* shave; **sich r∼en** shave. **R∼klinge** *f* razor blade. **R∼pinsel** *m* shaving-brush. **R∼wasser** *nt* aftershave [lotion]

Raspel *f* -,-n rasp; ⟨*Culin*⟩ grater. **r∼n** *vt* grate

Rasse *f* -,-n race. **R∼hund** *m* pedigree dog

Rassel *f* -,-n rattle. **r∼n** *vi* (*haben*) rattle; ⟨*Schlüssel:*⟩ jangle; ⟨*Kette:*⟩ clank ◻ *vi* (*sein*) rattle [along]

Rassen|diskriminierung *f* racial discrimination. **R∼trennung** *f* racial segregation

Rassepferd *nt* thoroughbred

rassisch *a* racial

Rassis|mus *m* - racism. **r∼tisch** *a* racist

Rast *f* -,-en rest. **r∼en** *vi* (*haben*) rest. **R∼haus** *nt* motorway restaurant. **r∼los** *a* restless, *adv* -ly; ⟨*ununterbrochen*⟩ ceaseless, *adv* -ly. **R∼platz** *m* picnic area. **R∼stätte** *f* motorway restaurant [and services]

Rasur *f* -,-en shave

Rat[1] *m* -[e]s ⟨*piece of*⟩ advice; **guter Rat** good advice; **sich** ⟨*dat*⟩ **keinen Rat wissen** not know what to do; **zu Rat[e] ziehen** = zurate ziehen, s. zurate

Rat[2] *m* -[e]s,-̈e ⟨*Admin*⟩ council; ⟨*Person*⟩ councillor

Rate *f* -,-n instalment

raten† *vt* guess; ⟨*empfehlen*⟩ advise ◻ *vi* (*haben*) guess; **jdm r∼** advise s.o.

Ratenzahlung *f* payment by instalments

Rat|geber *m* -s,- adviser; ⟨*Buch*⟩ guide. **R∼haus** *nt* town hall

ratifizier|en *vt* ratify. **R∼ung** *f* -,-en ratification

Ration /ra'tsɪo:n/ *f* -,-en ration; **eiserne R∼** iron rations *pl*. **r∼al** *a* rational, *adv* -ly. **r∼alisieren** *vt/i* (*haben*) rationalize. **r∼ell** *a* efficient, *adv* -ly. **r∼ieren** *vt* ration

rat|los *a* helpless, *adv* -ly; **r∼los sein** not know what to do. **r∼sam** *pred a* advisable; ⟨*klug*⟩ prudent. **R∼schlag** *m* piece of advice; **R∼schläge** advice *sg*

Rätsel *nt* -s,- riddle; ⟨*Kreuzwort-*⟩ puzzle; ⟨*Geheimnis*⟩ mystery. **r∼haft** *a* puzzling, mysterious. **r∼n** *vi* (*haben*) puzzle

Ratte *f* -,-n rat

rattern *vi* (*haben*) rattle ◻ *vi* (*sein*) rattle [along]

rau *a* rough, *adv* -ly; ⟨*unfreundlich*⟩ gruff, *adv* -ly; ⟨*Klima, Wind*⟩ harsh, raw; ⟨*Landschaft*⟩ rugged; ⟨*heiser*⟩ husky; ⟨*Hals*⟩ sore

Raub *m* -[e]s robbery; ⟨*Menschen-*⟩ abduction; ⟨*Beute*⟩ loot, booty. **r∼en** *vt* steal; abduct ⟨*Menschen*⟩; **jdm etw r∼en** rob s.o. of sth

Räuber *m* -s,- robber

Raub|mord *m* robbery with murder. **R∼tier** *nt* predator. **R∼überfall** *m* robbery. **R∼vogel** *m* bird of prey

Rauch *m* -[e]s smoke. **r∼en** *vt/i* (*haben*) smoke. **R∼en** *nt* -s smoking; '**R∼en verboten**' 'no smoking'. **R∼er** *m* -s,-smoker. **R∼erabteil** *nt* smoking compartment

Räucher|lachs *m* smoked salmon. **r∼n** *vt* ⟨*Culin*⟩ smoke

Rauch|fang *m* ⟨*Aust*⟩ chimney. **r∼ig** *a* smoky. **R∼verbot** *nt* smoking ban

räudig *a* mangy

rauf *adv* = herauf, hinauf

raufen *vt* pull; **sich** ⟨*dat*⟩ **die Haare r∼en** ⟨*fig*⟩ tear one's hair ◻ *vr/i* (*haben*) [sich] **r∼en** fight. **R∼erei** *f* -,-en fight

rauh *a* NEW rau

rau|haarig *a* wire-haired. **R∼heit** *f* - (*s.* rau) roughness; gruffness; harshness; ruggedness

rauh|haarig *a* NEW rauhaarig. **R∼reif** *m* NEW Raureif

Raum *m* -[e]s, Räume room; ⟨*Gebiet*⟩ area; ⟨*Welt-*⟩ space

räumen *vt* clear; vacate ⟨*Wohnung*⟩; evacuate ⟨*Gebäude, Gebiet, Mil Stellung*⟩; ⟨*bringen*⟩ put (in/auf + *acc* into/on); ⟨*holen*⟩ get (aus out of); **beiseite r∼** move/put to one side; **aus dem Weg r∼** ⟨*fam*⟩ get rid of

Raum|fahrer *m* astronaut. **R∼fahrt** *f* space travel. **R∼fahrzeug** *nt* spacecraft.

R~flug *m* space flight. R~inhalt *m* volume

räumlich *a* spatial. R~keiten *fpl* rooms

Raum|pflegerin *f* cleaner. R~schiff *nt* spaceship

Räumung *f* -(*s.* räumen) clearing; vacating; evacuation. R~sverkauf *m* clearance/closing-down sale

raunen *vt/i* (*haben*) whisper

Raupe *f* -,-n caterpillar

Raureif *m* hoar-frost

raus *adv* = heraus, hinaus

Rausch *m* -[e]s, Räusche intoxication; (*fig*) exhilaration; einen R~ haben be drunk

rauschen *vi* (*haben*) (*Wasser, Wind:*) rush; (*Bäume Blätter:*) rustle □ *vi* (*sein*) rush [along]; aus dem Zimmer r~ sweep out of the room. r~d *a* rushing; rustling; (*Applaus*) tumultuous

Rauschgift *nt* [narcotic] drug; (*coll*) drugs *pl*. R~süchtige(r) *m/f* drug addict

räuspern (sich) *vr* clear one's throat

rausschmeiß|en† *vt sep* (*fam*) throw out; (*entlassen*) sack. R~er *m* -s,- (*fam*) bouncer

Raute *f* -,-n diamond

Razzia *f* -,-ien /-jən/ [police] raid

Reagenzglas *nt* test-tube

reagieren *vi* (*haben*) react (auf + *acc* to)

Reaktion /-'tsjo:n/ *f* -,-en reaction. r~är *a* reactionary

Reaktor *m* -s,-en /-'to:rən/ reactor

real *a* real; (*gegenständlich*) tangible; (*realistisch*) realistic, *adv* -ally. r~isieren *vt* realize

Realis|mus *m* - realism. R~t *m* -en,-en realist. r~tisch *a* realistic, *adv* -ally

Realität *f* -,-en reality

Realschule *f* ≈ secondary modern school

Rebe *f* -,-n vine

Rebell *m* -en,-en rebel. r~ieren *vi* (*haben*) rebel. R~ion *f* -,-en rebellion

rebellisch *a* rebellious

Rebhuhn *nt* partridge

Rebstock *m* vine

Rechen *m* -s- rake. r~ *vt/i* (*haben*) rake

Rechen|aufgabe *f* arithmetical problem; (*Sch*) sum. R~fehler *m* arithmetical error. R~maschine *f* calculator

Rechenschaft *f* - R~ ablegen give account (über + *acc* of); jdn zur R~ ziehen call s.o. to account

recherchieren /refɛr'ʃi:rən/ *vt/i* (*haben*) investigate; (*Journ*) research

rechnen *vi* (*haben*) do arithmetic; (*schätzen*) reckon; (*zählen*) count (zu among; auf + *acc* on); r~ mit reckon with; (*erwarten*) expect; gut r~ können be good at figures □ *vt* calculate, work out; do (*Aufgabe*); (*dazu*) add (zu to); (*fig*) count (zu among). R~ *nt* -s arithmetic

Rechner *m* -s,- calculator; (*Computer*) computer; ein guter R~ sein be good at figures

Rechnung *f* -,-en bill, (*Amer*) check; (*Comm*) invoice; (*Berechnung*) calculation; R~ führen über (+ *acc*) keep account of; etw (*dat*) R~ tragen (*fig*) take sth into account. R~sjahr *nt* financial year. R~sprüfer *m* auditor

Recht *nt* -[e]s,-e law; (*Berechtigung*) right (auf + *acc* to); im R~ sein be in the right; R~ haben/behalten be right; R~ bekommen be proved right; jdm R~ geben agree with s.o.; mit *od* zu R~ rightly; von R~s wegen by right; (*eigentlich*) by rights

recht *a* right; (*wirklich*) real; ich habe keine r~e Lust I don't really feel like it; es jdm r~ machen please s.o.; jdm r~ sein be all right with s.o.; r~ haben/behalten/bekommen ⟨NEW⟩ Recht haben/behalten/bekommen, s. Recht; jdm r~ geben ⟨NEW⟩ jdm Recht geben, s. Recht □ *adv* correctly; (*ziemlich*) quite; (*sehr*) very; r~ vielen Dank many thanks

Recht|e *f* -n,-[n] right side; (*Hand*) right hand; (*Boxen*) right; die R~e (*Pol*) the right; zu meiner R~en on my right. r~e(r,s) *a* right; (*Pol*) right-wing; r~e Masche plain stitch. R~e(r) *m/f* der/die R~e the right man/woman; du bist mir der/die R~e! you're a fine one! R~e(s) *nt* das R~e the right thing; etwas R~es lernen learn something useful; nach dem R~en sehen see that everything is all right

Rechteck *nt* -[e]s,-e rectangle. r~ig *a* rectangular

rechtfertig|en *vt* justify; sich r~en justify oneself. R~ung *f* - justification

recht|haberisch *a* opinionated. r~lich *a* legal, *adv* -ly. r~mäßig *a* legitimate, *adv* -ly.

rechts *adv* on the right; (*bei Stoff*) on the right side; von/nach r~ from/to the right; zwei r~, zwei links stricken knit two, purl two. R~anwalt *m*, R~anwältin *f* lawyer

rechtschaffen *a* upright; (*ehrlich*) honest, *adv* -ly; r~ müde thoroughly tired

rechtschreib|en† *vi* (*inf only*) spell correctly. R~fehler *m* spelling mistake. R~ung *f* - spelling

Rechts|händer(in) *m* -s,- (*f* -,-nen) right-hander. r~händig *a* & *adv* right-handed. r~kräftig *a* legal, *adv* -ly.

R∼streit *m* law suit. R∼verkehr *m* driving on the right. r∼widrig *a* illegal, *adv* -ly. R∼wissenschaft *f* jurisprudence

recht|winklig *a* right-angled. R∼zeitig *a & adv* in time

Reck *nt* -[e]s,-e horizontal bar

recken *vt* stretch; sich r∼ stretch; den Hals r∼ crane one's neck

Redakteur /redak'tø:ɐ̯/ *m* -s,-e editor; (*Radio, TV*) producer

Redaktion /-'tsjo:n/ *f* -,-en editing; (*Radio, TV*) production; (*Abteilung*) editorial/production department. r∼ell *a* editorial

Rede *f* -,-n speech; zur R∼ stellen demand an explanation from; davon ist keine R∼ there's no question of it; nicht der R∼ wert not worth mentioning. r∼gewandt *a* eloquent, *adv* -ly

reden *vi/i* (*haben*) talk (von about; mit to); (*eine Rede halten*) speak □ *vt* talk; speak ⟨*Wahrheit*⟩; kein Wort r∼ not say a word. R∼sart *f* saying; ⟨*Phrase*⟩ phrase

Redewendung *f* idiom

redigieren *vt* edit

redlich *a* honest, *adv* -ly

Red|ner *m* -s,- speaker. r∼selig *a* talkative

reduzieren *vt* reduce

Reeder *m* -s,- shipowner. R∼ei *f* -,-en shipping company

reell *a* real; (*ehrlich*) honest, *adv* -ly; (*Preis, Angebot*) fair

Refer|at *nt* -[e]s,-e report; (*Abhandlung*) paper; (*Abteilung*) section. R∼ent(in) *m* -en,-en (*f* -,-nen) speaker; (*Sachbearbeiter*) expert. R∼enz *f* -,-en reference. r∼ieren *vi* (*haben*) deliver a paper; (*berichten*) report (über + *acc* on)

reflektieren *vt/i* (*haben*) reflect (über + *acc* on)

Reflex *m* -es,-e reflex; (*Widerschein*) reflection. R∼ion *f* -,-en reflection. r∼iv *a* reflexive. R∼ivpronomen *nt* reflexive pronoun

Reform *f* -,-en reform. R∼ation /-'tsjo:n/ *f* - (*Relig*) Reformation

Reform|haus *nt* health-food shop. r∼ieren *vt* reform

Refrain /rə'frɛ̃:/ *m* -s,-s refrain

Regal *nt* -s,-e [set of] shelves *pl*

Regatta *f* -,-ten regatta

rege *a* active; (*lebhaft*) lively; (*geistig*) alert; ⟨*Handel*⟩ brisk □ *adv* actively

Regel *f* -,-n rule; (*Monats-*) period; in der R∼ as a rule. r∼mäßig *a* regular, *adv* -ly. r∼n *vt* regulate; direct (*Verkehr*); (*erledigen*) settle. r∼recht *a* real, proper □ *adv*

really. R∼ung *f* -,-en regulation; settlement. r∼widrig *a* irregular, *adv* -ly

regen *vt* move; sich r∼ move; (*wach werden*) stir

Regen *m* -s,-. rain. R∼bogen *m* rainbow. R∼bogenhaut *f* iris

Regener|ation /-'tsjo:n/ *f* - regeneration. r∼ieren *vt* regenerate; sich r∼ieren regenerate

Regen|mantel *m* raincoat. R∼schirm *m* umbrella. R∼tag *m* rainy day. R∼tropfen *m* raindrop. R∼wetter *nt* wet weather. R∼wurm *m* earthworm

Regie /re'ʒi:/ *f* - direction; R∼ führen direct

regier|en *vt/i* (*haben*) govern, rule; ⟨*Monarch:*⟩ reign [over]; (*Gram*) take. r∼end *a* ruling; reigning. R∼ung *f* -,-en government; (*Herrschaft*) rule; (*eines Monarchen*) reign

Regime /re'ʒi:m/ *nt* -s,- /-mə/ regime

Regiment[1] *nt* -[e]s,-er regiment

Regiment[2] *nt* -[e]s,-e rule

Region *f* -,-en region. r∼al *a* regional, *adv* -ly

Regisseur /reʒɪ'sø:ɐ̯/ *m* -s,-e director

Register *nt* -s,- register; (*Inhaltsverzeichnis*) index; (*Orgel-*) stop

registrier|en *vt* register; (*Techn*) record. R∼kasse *f* cash register

Regler *m* -s,- regulator

reglos *a & adv* motionless

regn|en *vi* (*haben*) rain; es r∼et it is raining. r∼erisch *a* rainy

regul|är *a* normal, *adv* -ly; (*rechtmäßig*) legitimate, *adv* -ly. r∼ieren *vt* regulate

Regung *f* -,-en movement; (*Gefühls-*) emotion. r∼slos *a & adv* motionless

Reh *nt* -[e]s,-e roe-deer; (*Culin*) venison

Rehabilit|ation /-'tsjo:n/ *f* rehabilitation. r∼ieren *vt* rehabilitate

Rehbock *m* roebuck

Reib|e *f* -,-n grater. r∼en† *vt* rub; (*Culin*) grate; blank r∼en polish □ *vi* (*haben*) rub. R∼ereien *fpl* (*fam*) friction *sg*. R∼ung *f* - friction. r∼ungslos *a* (*fig*) smooth, *adv* -ly

reich *a* rich (an + *dat* in), *adv* -ly; (*r∼haltig*) abundant, *adv* -ly; Arm und R∼ (arm und r∼) rich and poor

Reich *nt* -[e]s,-e empire; (*König-*) kingdom; (*Bereich*) realm

Reich|e(r) *m/f* rich man/woman; die R∼en the rich *pl*

reichen *vt* hand; (*anbieten*) offer □ *vi* (*haben*) be enough; (*in der Länge*) be long enough; r∼ bis zu reach [up to]; (*sich erstrecken*) extend to; mit dem Geld r∼

have enough money; **mir reicht's! I've had enough!**

reich|haltig a extensive, large; ⟨Mahlzeit⟩ substantial. **r~lich** a ample; ⟨Vorrat⟩ abundant, plentiful; **eine r~liche Stunde a good hour □** adv amply; abundantly; ⟨fam: sehr⟩ very. **R~tum** m -s,-tümer wealth (an + dat of); **R~tümer** riches. **R~weite** f reach; ⟨Techn, Mil⟩ range

Reif m -[e]s [hoar-]frost

reif a ripe; ⟨fig⟩ mature; **r~ für** ready for. **R~e** f - ripeness; ⟨fig⟩ maturity. **r~en** vi (sein) ripen; ⟨Wein, Käse & fig⟩ mature

Reifen m -s,- hoop; ⟨Arm-⟩ bangle; ⟨Auto-⟩ tyre. **R~druck** m tyre pressure. **R~panne** f puncture, flat tyre

Reifeprüfung f ≈ A levels pl

reiflich a careful, adv -ly

Reihe f -,-n row; ⟨Anzahl & Math⟩ series; **der R~ nach in turn; außer der R~ out of turn; wer ist an der od kommt an die R~?** whose turn is it? **r~n** (sich) vr sich **r~n an** (+ acc) follow. **R~nfolge** f order. **R~nhaus** nt terraced house. **r~nweise** adv in rows; ⟨fam⟩ in large numbers

Reiher m -s,- heron

Reim m -[e]s,-e rhyme. **r~en** vt rhyme; **sich r~en** rhyme

rein[1] a pure; ⟨sauber⟩ clean; ⟨Unsinn, Dummheit⟩ sheer; **ins R~e (r~e) schreiben make a fair copy of; ins R~e (r~e) bringen** ⟨fig⟩ sort out **□** adv purely; ⟨fam⟩ absolutely

rein[2] adv = herein, hinein

Reineclaude /rɛːnəˈkloːdə/ f -,-n greengage

Reinfall m ⟨fam⟩ let-down; ⟨Misserfolg⟩ flop. **r~en†** vi sep (sein) fall in; ⟨fam⟩ be taken in (auf + acc by)

Rein|gewinn m net profit. **R~heit** f - purity

reinig|en vt clean; ⟨chemisch⟩ dry-clean. **R~ung** f -,-en cleaning; ⟨chemische⟩ drycleaning; ⟨Geschäft⟩ dry cleaner's

Reinkarnation /reˈɪnkarnaˈtsjoːn/ f -,-en reincarnation

reinlegen vt sep put in; ⟨fam⟩ dupe; ⟨betrügen⟩ take for a ride

reinlich a clean. **R~keit** f - cleanliness

Rein|machefrau f cleaner. **R~schrift** f fair copy. **r~seiden** a pure silk

Reis m -es rice

Reise f -,-n journey; ⟨See-⟩ voyage; ⟨Urlaubs-, Geschäfts-⟩ trip. **R~andenken** nt souvenir. **R~büro** nt travel agency. **R~bus** m coach. **R~führer** m tourist guide; ⟨Buch⟩ guide. **R~gesellschaft** f tourist group. **R~leiter(in)** m(f) courier.

r~n vi (sein) travel. **R~nde(r)** m/f traveller. **R~pass (R~paß)** m passport. **R~scheck** m traveller's cheque. **R~unternehmer, R~veranstalter** m -s,- tour operator. **R~ziel** nt destination

Reisig nt -s brushwood

Reißaus m **R~ nehmen** ⟨fam⟩ run away

Reißbrett nt drawing-board

reißen† vt tear; ⟨weg-⟩ snatch; ⟨töten⟩ kill; **Witze r~** crack jokes; **aus dem Schlaf r~** awaken rudely; **an sich (acc) r~** snatch; seize ⟨Macht⟩; **mit sich r~** sweep away; **sich r~ um** ⟨fam⟩ fight for; ⟨gern mögen⟩ be keen on; **hin und her gerissen sein** ⟨fig⟩ be torn **□** vi (sein) tear; ⟨Seil, Faden:⟩ break **□** vi (haben) **r~ an** (+ dat) pull at. **r~d** a raging; ⟨Tier⟩ ferocious; ⟨Schmerz⟩ violent

Reißer m -s,- ⟨fam⟩ thriller; ⟨Erfolg⟩ big hit. **r~isch** a ⟨fam⟩ sensational

Reiß|nagel m = **R~zwecke. R~verschluss (R~verschluß)** m zip [fastener]. **R~wolf** m shredder. **R~zwecke** f -,-n drawing-pin, ⟨Amer⟩ thumbtack

reit|en† vt/i (sein) ride. **R~er(in)** m -s,- ⟨f -,-nen⟩ rider. **R~hose** f riding breeches pl. **R~pferd** nt saddle-horse. **R~schule** f riding-school. **R~weg** m bridle-path

Reiz m -es,-e stimulus; ⟨Anziehungskraft⟩ attraction, appeal; ⟨Charme⟩ charm. **r~bar** a irritable. **R~barkeit** f - irritability. **r~en** vt provoke; ⟨Med⟩ irritate; ⟨interessieren, locken⟩ appeal to, attract; arouse ⟨Neugier⟩; ⟨beim Kartenspiel⟩ bid. **r~end** a charming, adv -ly; ⟨entzückend⟩ delightful. **R~ung** f -,-en ⟨Med⟩ irritation. **r~voll** a attractive

rekapitulieren vt/i (haben) recapitulate

rekeln (sich) vr stretch; ⟨lümmeln⟩ sprawl

Reklamation /-'tsjoːn/ f -,-en ⟨Comm⟩ complaint

Reklame f -,-n advertising, publicity; ⟨Anzeige⟩ advertisement; ⟨TV, Radio⟩ commercial; **R~e machen advertise** (für etw with). **r~ieren** vi complain about; ⟨fordern⟩ claim **□** vi (haben) complain

rekonstruieren vt reconstruct. **R~ktion** /-'tsjoːn/ f -,-en reconstruction

Rekonvaleszenz f - convalescence

Rekord m -[e]s,-e record

Rekrut m -en,-en recruit. **r~ieren** vt recruit

Rektor m -s,-en /-'toːrən/ ⟨Sch⟩ head[master]; ⟨Univ⟩ vice-chancellor. **R~torin** f -,-nen head[mistress]; vice-chancellor

Relais /rə'lɛː/ nt -,- /-s,s/ ⟨Electr⟩ relay

relativ a relative, adv -ly. **R~pronomen** nt relative pronoun

relevan|t a relevant (für to). **R~z** f - relevance

Relief /rə'ljɛf/ nt -s,-s relief

Religi|on f -,-en religion; (Sch) religious education. r~**ös** a religious

Reling f -,-s (Naut) rail

Reliquie /re'li:kvjə/ f -,-n relic

Remouladensoße /remu'la:dən-/ f ≈ tartar sauce

rempeln vt jostle; (stoßen) push

Ren nt -s,-s reindeer

Reneklode f -,-n greengage

Renn|auto nt racing car. R~**bahn** f racetrack; (Pferde-) racecourse. R~**boot** nt speed-boat. r~**en** vt/i (sein) run; um die Wette r~en have a race. R~en nt -s,- race. R~**pferd** nt racehorse. R~**sport** m racing. R~**wagen** m racing car

renommiert a renowned; (Hotel, Firma) of repute

renovier|en vt renovate; redecorate (Zimmer). R~**ung** f - renovation; redecoration

rentabel a profitable, adv -bly

Rente f -,-n pension; in R~ gehen (fam) retire. R~**nversicherung** f pension scheme

Rentier nt reindeer

rentieren (sich) vr be profitable; (sich lohnen) be worth while

Rentner(in) m -s,- (f -,-nen) [old-age] pensioner

Reparatur f -,-en repair. R~**werkstatt** f repair workshop; (Auto) garage

reparieren vt repair, mend

repatriieren vt repatriate

Repertoire /reper'toa:ɐ/ nt -s,-s repertoire

Reportage /-'ta:ʒə/ f -,-n report

Reporter(in) m -s,- (f -,-nen) reporter

repräsent|ativ a representative (für of); (eindrucksvoll) imposing; (Prestige verleihend) prestigious. r~**ieren** vt represent □ vi (haben) perform official/social duties

Repress|alie /-ljə/ f -,-n reprisal. r~**iv** a repressive

Reprodu|ktion /-'tsjo:n/ f -,-en reproduction. r~**zieren** vt reproduce

Reptil nt -s,-ien /-jən/ reptile

Republik f -,-en republic. r~**anisch** a republican

requirieren vt (Mil) requisition

Requisiten pl (Theat) properties, (fam) props

Reservat nt -[e]s,-e reservation

Reserve f -,-n reserve; (Mil, Sport) reserves pl. R~**rad** nt spare wheel. R~**spieler** m reserve. R~**tank** m reserve tank

reservier|en vt reserve; r~en lassen book. r~**t** a reserved. R~**ung** f -,-en reservation

Reservoir /rezɛr'voa:ɐ/ nt -s,-s reservoir

Resid|enz f -,-en residence. r~**ieren** vi (haben) reside

Resign|ation /-'tsjo:n/ f - resignation. r~**ieren** vi (haben) (fig) give up. r~**iert** a resigned, adv -ly

resolut a resolute, adv -ly

Resolution /-'tsjo:n/ f -,-en resolution

Resonanz f -,-en resonance; (fig: Widerhall) response

Respekt /-sp-,-ʃp-/ m -[e]s respect (vor + dat for). r~**abel** a respectable. r~**ieren** vt respect

respekt|los a disrespectful, adv -ly. r~**voll** a respectful, adv -ly

Ressort /rɛ'so:ɐ/ nt -s,-s department

Rest m -[e]s,-e remainder, rest; R~**e** remains; (Essens-) leftovers

Restaurant /rɛsto'rã:/ nt -s,-s restaurant

Restaur|ation /rɛstaura'tsjo:n/ f - restoration. r~**ieren** vt restore

Rest|betrag m balance. r~**lich** a remaining. r~**los** a utter, adv -ly

Resultat nt -[e]s,-e result

Retorte f -,-n (Chem) retort. R~**nbaby** nt (fam) test-tube baby

rett|en vt save (vor + dat from); (aus Gefahr befreien) rescue; sich r~en save oneself; (flüchten) escape. R~**er** m -s,- rescuer; (fig) saviour

Rettich m -s,-e white radish

Rettung f -,-en rescue; (fig) salvation; jds letzte R~ s.o.'s last hope. R~**sboot** nt lifeboat. R~**sdienst** m rescue service. R~**sgürtel** m lifebelt. r~**slos** adv hopelessly. R~**sring** m lifebelt. R~**swagen** m ambulance

retuschieren vt (Phot) retouch

Reu|e f - remorse; (Relig) repentance. r~**en** vt fill with remorse; es reut mich nicht I don't regret it. r~**ig** a penitent. r~**mütig** a contrite, adv -ly

Revanche /re'vã:ʃə/ f -,-n revenge; R~**e** fordern (Sport) ask for a return match. r~**ieren** (sich) vr take revenge; (sich erkenntlich zeigen) reciprocate (mit with); sich für eine Einladung r~**ieren** return an invitation

Revers /re've:ɐ/ nt -,- /-[s],-s/ lapel

revidieren vt revise; (prüfen) check

Revier nt -s,-e district; (Zool & fig) territory; (Polizei-) [police] station

Revision f -,-en revision; (Prüfung) check; (Bücher-) audit; (Jur) appeal

Revolte f -,-n revolt

Revolution /-'tsjo:n/ f -,-en revolution. r~är a revolutionary. r~ieren vt revolutionize

Revolver m -s,- revolver

Revue /rə'vy:/ f -,-n revue

Rezen|sent m -en,-en reviewer. r~sieren vt review. R~sion f -,-en review

Rezept nt -[e]s,-e prescription; (Culin) recipe

Rezeption /-'tsjo:n/ f -,-en reception

Rezession f -,-en recession

rezitieren vt recite

R-Gespräch nt reverse-charge call, (Amer) collect call

Rhabarber m -s rhubarb

Rhapsodie f -,-n rhapsody

Rhein m -s Rhine. R~land nt -s Rhineland. R~wein m hock

Rhetori|k f rhetoric. r~sch a rhetorical

Rheum|a nt -s rheumatism. r~atisch a rheumatic. R~atismus m - rheumatism

Rhinozeros nt -[ses],-se rhinoceros

rhyth|misch /'rɪt-/ a rhythmic[al], adv -ally. R~mus m -,-men rhythm

Ribisel f -,-n (Aust) redcurrant

richten vt direct (auf + acc at); address 〈Frage, Briefe〉 (an + acc to); aim, train 〈Waffe〉 (auf + acc at); (einstellen) set; (vorbereiten) prepare; (reparieren) mend; (hinrichten) execute; (SGer: ordentlich machen) tidy; in die Höhe r~ raise [up]; das Wort an jdn r~ address s.o.; sich r~ be directed (auf + acc at; gegen against); 〈Blick:〉 turn (auf + acc on); sich r~ nach comply with 〈Vorschrift, jds Wünschen〉; fit in with 〈jds Plänen〉; (befolgen) go by; (abhängen) depend on □ vi (haben) r~ über (+ acc) judge

Richter m -s,- judge

Richtfest nt topping-out ceremony

richtig a right, correct; (wirklich, echt) real; das R~e (r~e) the right thing □ adv correctly; really; r~ stellen put right 〈Uhr〉; (fig) correct 〈Irrtum〉; die Uhr geht r~ the clock is right. R~keit f - correctness. r~stellen vt sep (NEW) r~ stellen, s. richtig

Richtlinien fpl guidelines

Richtung f -,-en direction; (fig) trend

riechen† vt/i (haben) smell (nach of; an etw dat sth)

Riegel m -s,- bolt; (Seife) bar

Riemen m -s,- strap; (Ruder) oar

Riese m -n,-n giant

rieseln vi (sein) trickle; 〈Schnee:〉 fall lightly

Riesen|erfolg m huge success. r~groß a huge, enormous

riesig a huge; (gewaltig) enormous □ adv (fam) terribly

Riff nt -[e]s,-e reef

rigoros a rigorous, adv -ly

Rille f -,-n groove

Rind nt -es,-er ox; (Kuh) cow; (Stier) bull; (R~fleisch) beef; R~er cattle pl

Rinde f -,-n bark; (Käse-) rind; (Brot-) crust

Rinderbraten m roast beef

Rind|fleisch nt beef. R~vieh nt cattle pl; (fam: Idiot) idiot

Ring m -[e]s,-e ring

ringeln (sich) vr curl; 〈Schlange:〉 coil itself (um round)

ring|en† vi (haben) wrestle; (fig) struggle (um/nach for) □ vt wring 〈Hände〉. R~en nt -s wrestling. R~er m -s,- wrestler. R~kampf m wrestling match; (als Sport) wrestling. R~richter m referee

rings adv r~ im Kreis in a circle; r~ um jdn/etw all around s.o./sth. R~herum, r~um adv all around

Rinn|e f -,-n channel; (Dach-) gutter. r~en† vi (sein) run; 〈Sand:〉 trickle. R~stein m gutter

Rippe f -,-n rib. R~nfellentzündung f pleurisy. R~nstoß m dig in the ribs

Risiko nt -s,-s & -ken risk; ein R~ eingehen take a risk

risk|ant a risky. r~ieren vt risk

Riss m -es,-e (Riß m -sses,-sse) tear; (Mauer-) crack; (fig) rift

rissig a cracked; (Haut) chapped

Rist m -[e]s,-e instep

Ritt m -[e]s,-e ride

Ritter m -s,- knight. r~lich a chivalrous, adv -ly. R~lichkeit f - chivalry

rittlings adv astride

Ritu|al nt -s,-e ritual. r~ell a ritual

Ritz m -es,-e scratch. R~e f -,-n crack; (Fels-) cleft; (zwischen Betten, Vorhängen) gap. r~en vt scratch

Rival|e m -n,-n, R~in f -,-nen rival. r~isieren vi (haben) compete (mit with). r~isierend a rival ... R~ität f -,-en rivalry

Robbe f -,-n seal. r~n vi (sein) crawl

Robe f -,-n gown; (Talar) robe

Roboter m -s,- robot

robust a robust

röcheln vi (haben) breathe stertorously

Rochen m -s,- (Zool) ray

Rock¹ m -[e]s,-̈e skirt; (Jacke) jacket

Rock² m -[s] (Mus) rock

Rodel|bahn f toboggan run. r~n vi (sein/haben) toboggan. R~schlitten m toboggan

roden vt clear 〈Land〉; grub up 〈Stumpf〉

Rogen *m* -s,- [hard] roe

Roggen *m* -s rye

roh *a* rough; (*ungekocht*) raw; (*Holz*) bare; (*brutal*) brutal; r∼e Gewalt brute force □ *adv* roughly; brutally. R∼bau *m* -[e]s, -ten shell. R∼heit *f* -,-en brutality. R∼kost *f* raw [vegetarian] food. R∼ling *m* -s,-e brute. R∼material *nt* raw material. R∼öl *nt* crude oil

Rohr *nt* -[e]s,-e pipe; (*Geschütz-*) barrel; (*Bot*) reed; (*Zucker-, Bambus-*) cane

Röhr|chen *nt* -s,- [drinking] straw; (*Auto, fam*) breathalyser (P). R∼e *f* -,-n tube; (*Radio-*) valve; (*Back-*) oven

Rohstoff *m* raw material

Rokoko *nt* -s rococo

Rolladen *m* (NEW) Rollladen

Rollbahn *f* taxiway; (*Start-/Landebahn*) runway

Rolle *f* -,-n roll; (*Garn-*) reel; (*Draht-*) coil; (*Techn*) roller; (*Seil-*) pulley; (*Wäsche-*) mangle; (*Lauf-*) castor; (*Schrift-*) scroll; (*Theat*) part, role; das spielt keine R∼e (*fig*) that doesn't matter. r∼n *vt* roll; (*auf-*) roll up; roll out (*Teig*); put through the mangle (*Wäsche*); sich r∼n roll; (*sich ein-*) curl up □ *vi* (*sein*) roll; (*Flugzeug:*) taxi □ *vi* (*haben*) (*Donner:*) rumble. R∼r *m* -s,-scooter

Roll|feld *nt* airfield. R∼kragen *m* poloneck. R∼laden *m* roller shutter. R∼mops *m* rollmop[s] *sg*

Rollo *nt* -s,-s [roller] blind

Roll|schuh *m* roller-skate; R∼schuh laufen roller-skate. R∼splitt *m* -s loose chippings *pl*. R∼stuhl *m* wheelchair. R∼treppe *f* escalator

Rom *nt* -s Rome

Roman *m* -s,-e novel. r∼isch *a* Romanesque; (*Sprache*) Romance. R∼schriftsteller(in) *m(f)* novelist

Romant|ik *f* -romanticism. r∼isch *a* romantic, *adv* -ally

Romanze *f* -,-n romance

Röm|er(in) *m* -s,- (*f* -,-nen) Roman. r∼isch *a* Roman

Rommé, Rommee *f* 'rɔme:/ *nt* -s rummy

röntgen *vt* X-ray. R∼aufnahme *f*, R∼bild *nt* X-ray. R∼strahlen *mpl* X-rays

rosa *inv a*, R∼ *nt* -[s],- pink

Rose *f* -,-n rose. R∼nkohl *m* [Brussels] sprouts *pl*. R∼n-kranz *m* (*Relig*) rosary. R∼nmontag *m* Monday before Shrove Tuesday

Rosette *f* -,-n rosette

rosig *a* rosy

Rosine *f* -,-n raisin

Rosmarin *m* -s rosemary

Ross *nt* -es,ˉer (Roß *nt* -sses,ˉsser) horse. R∼kastanie *f* horse-chestnut

Rost[1] *m* -[e]s,-e grating; (*Kamin-*) grate; (*Brat-*) grill

Rost[2] *m* -[e]s rust. r∼en *vi* (*haben*) rust; nicht r∼end stainless

röst|en *vt* roast; toast (*Brot*). R∼er *m* -s,-toaster

rostfrei *a* stainless

rostig *a* rusty

rot *a* (röter, rötest), R∼ *nt* -s,- red; rot werden turn red; (*erröten*) go red, blush

Rotation /-'tsio:n/ *f* -,-en rotation

Röte *f* - redness; (*Scham-*) blush

Röteln *pl* German measles *sg*

röten *vt* redden; sich r∼ turn red

rothaarig *a* red-haired

rotieren *vi* (*haben*) rotate

Rot|kehlchen *nt* -s,- robin. R∼kohl *m* red cabbage

rötlich *a* reddish

Rot|licht *nt* red light. R∼wein *m* red wine

Roulade /ru'la:də/ *f* -,-n beef olive. R∼leau /-'lo:/ *nt* -s,-s [roller] blind

Route /'ru:tə/ *f* -,-n route

Routin|e /ru'ti:nə/ *f* -,-n routine; (*Erfahrung*) experience. r∼emäßig a routine . . . □ *adv* routinely. r∼iert *a* experienced

Rowdy /'raʊdi/ *m* -s,-s hooligan

Rübe *f* -,-n beet; rote R∼ beetroot; gelbe R∼ (*SGer*) carrot

rüber *adv* = herüber, hinüber

Rubin *m* -s,-e ruby

Rubrik *f* -,-en column; (*Kategorie*) category

Ruck *m* -[e]s,-e jerk

ruckartig *a* jerky, *adv* -ily

rück|bezüglich *a* (*Gram*) reflexive. R∼blende *f* flashback. R∼blick *m* (*fig*) review (auf + *acc* of). R∼blickend *a* in retrospect. r∼datieren *vt* (*inf & pp only*) backdate

rücken *vt/i* (*sein/haben*) move; an etw (*dat*) r∼ move sth

Rücken *m* -s,- back; (*Buch-*) spine; (*Berg-*) ridge. R∼lehne *f* back. R∼mark *nt* spinal cord. R∼schwimmen *nt* backstroke. R∼wind *m* following wind; (*Aviat*) tail wind

rückerstatten *vt* (*inf & pp only*) refund

Rückfahr|karte *f* return ticket. R∼t *f* return journey

Rück|fall *m* relapse. r∼fällig *a* r∼fällig werden (*Jur*) re-offend. R∼flug *m* return flight. R∼frage *f* [further] query. r∼fragen *vi* (*haben*) (*inf & pp only*) check (bei with). R∼gabe *f* return. R∼gang *m* decline; (*Preis-*) drop, fall. r∼gängig *a* r~gängig machen cancel; break off ⟨Verlobung⟩. R~grat nt -[e]s, -e spine, backbone. R~halt m (fig) support. R~hand f backhand. R~kehr return. R~lagen fpl reserves. R~licht nt rear-light. r~lings adv backwards; (von hinten) from behind. R~reise f return journey

Rucksack m rucksack

Rück|schau f review. R~schlag m (Sport) return; (fig) set-back. R~schluss (R~schluß) m conclusion. R~schritt m (fig) retrograde step. r~schrittlich a retrograde. R~seite f back; (einer Münze) reverse

Rücksicht f -,-en consideration; R~ nehmen auf (+ acc) show consideration for; (berücksichtigen) take into consideration. R~nahme f - consideration. r~slos a inconsiderate, adv -ly; (schonungslos) ruthless, adv -ly. r~svoll a considerate, adv -ly

Rück|sitz m back seat; (Sozius) pillion. R~spiegel m rear-view mirror. R~spiel nt return match. R~sprache f consultation; R~sprache nehmen mit consult. R~stand m (Chem) residue; (Arbeits-) backlog; R~stände arrears; im R~stand sein be behind. r~ständig a (fig) backward. R~stau m (Auto) tailback. R~strahler m -s,- reflector. R~tritt m resignation; (Fahrrad) back pedalling. r~vergüten vt (inf & pp only) refund. R~wanderer m repatriate

rückwärt|ig a back ..., rear ..., r~s adv backwards. R~sgang m reverse [gear]

Rückweg m way back

ruckweise adv jerkily

rück|wirkend a retrospective, adv -ly. R~wirkung f retrospective force; mit R~wirkung vom backdated to. R~zahlung f repayment. R~zug m retreat

Rüde m -n,-n [male] dog

Rudel nt -s,- herd; (Wolfs-) pack; (Löwen-) pride

Ruder nt -s,- oar; (Steuer-) rudder; am R~ (Naut & fig) at the helm. R~boot nt rowing boat. R~er m -s,- oarsman. r~n vt/i (haben/sein) row

Ruf m -[e]s,-e call; (laut) shout; (Telefon) telephone number; (Ansehen) reputation; Künstler von Ruf artist of repute. r~en† vt/i (haben) call (nach for); r~en lassen send for

Rüffel m -s,- (fam) telling-off. r~n vt (fam) tell off

Ruf|name m forename by which one is known. R~nummer f telephone number. R~zeichen nt dialling tone

Rüge f -,-n reprimand. r~n vt reprimand; (kritisieren) criticize

Ruhe f - rest; (Stille) quiet; (Frieden) peace; (innere) calm; (Gelassenheit) composure; die R~ bewahren keep calm; in R~ lassen leave in peace; sich zur R~ setzen retire; R~ [da]! quiet! R~gehalt nt [retirement] pension. r~los a restless, adv -ly. r~n vi (haben) rest (auf + dat on); (Arbeit, Verkehr:) have stopped; hier ruht ... here lies ... R~pause f rest, break. R~stand m retirement; in den R~stand treten retire; im R~stand retired. R~störung f disturbance of the peace. R~tag m day of rest; 'Montag R~tag' 'closed on Mondays'

ruhig a quiet, adv -ly; (erholsam) restful; (friedlich) peaceful, adv -ly; (unbewegt, gelassen) calm, adv -ly; r~ bleiben remain calm; sehen Sie sich r~ um you're welcome to look round; man kann r~ darüber sprechen there's no harm in talking about it

Ruhm m -[e]s fame; (Ehre) glory

rühmen vt praise; sich r~ boast (gen about)

ruhmreich a glorious

Ruhr f - (Med) dysentery

Rühr|ei nt scrambled eggs pl. r~en vt move; (Culin) stir; sich r~en move; zu Tränen r~en move to tears; r~t euch! (Mil) at ease! □ vi (haben) stir; r~en an (+ acc) touch; (fig) touch on; r~en von (fig) come from. r~end a touching, adv -ly

rühr|ig a active. r~selig a sentimental. R~ung f - emotion

Ruin m -s ruin. R~e f -,-n ruin; ruins pl (gen of). r~ieren vt ruin

rülpsen vi (haben) (fam) belch

Rum m -s rum

rum adv = herum

Rumän|ien /-jǝn/ nt -s Romania. r~isch a Romanian

Rummel m -s (fam) hustle and bustle; (Jahrmarkt) funfair. R~platz m fairground

rumoren vi (haben) make a noise; (Magen:) rumble

Rumpel|kammer f junk-room. r~n vi (haben/sein) rumble

Rumpf m -[e]s,-e body, trunk; (Schiffs-) hull; (Aviat) fuselage

rümpfen vt die Nase r~ turn up one's nose (über + acc at)

rund a round □ adv approximately; r~ um [a]round. R~blick m panoramic view. R~brief m circular [letter]

Runde f -,-n round; (Kreis) circle; (eines Polizisten) beat; (beim Rennen) lap; eine R~ Bier a round of beer. r~n vt round; sich r~n become round; (Backen:) fill out

Rund|fahrt f tour. R~frage f poll

Rundfunk m radio; im R~ on the radio. R~gerät nt radio [set]

Rund|gang m round; (Spaziergang) walk (durch round). r~heraus adv straight out. r~herum adv all around. r~lich a rounded; (mollig) plump. R~reise f [circular] tour. R~schreiben nt circular. r~um adv all round. R~ung f -,-en curve. r~weg adv ⟨ablehnen⟩ flatly

runter adv = herunter, hinunter

Runzel f -,-n wrinkle. r~n vt die Stirn r~n frown

runzlig a wrinkled

Rüpel m -s,- ⟨fam⟩ lout. r~haft a ⟨fam⟩ loutish

rupfen vt pull out; pluck ⟨Geflügel⟩; ⟨fam: schröpfen⟩ fleece

ruppig a rude, adv -ly

Rüsche f -,-n frill

Ruß m -es soot

Russe m -n,-n Russian

Rüssel m -s,- ⟨Zool⟩ trunk

ruß|en vi ⟨haben⟩ smoke. r~ig a sooty

Russ|in f -,-nen Russian. r~isch a Russian. R~isch nt -[s] ⟨Lang⟩ Russian

Russland (Rußland) nt -s Russia

rüsten vi ⟨haben⟩ prepare (zu/für for) □ vr sich r~ get ready; gerüstet sein be ready

rüstig a sprightly

rustikal a rustic

Rüstung f -,-en armament; (Harnisch) armour. R~skontrolle f arms control

Rute f -,-n twig; ⟨Angel-, Wünschel-⟩ rod; ⟨zur Züchtigung⟩ birch; ⟨Schwanz⟩ tail

Rutsch m -[e]s,-e slide. R~bahn f slide. R~e f -,-n chute. r~en vt slide ⟨rücken⟩ move □ vi ⟨sein⟩ slide; ⟨aus-, ab-⟩ slip; ⟨Auto⟩ skid; ⟨rücken⟩ move [along]. r~ig a slippery

rütteln vt shake □ vi ⟨haben⟩ r~ an (+ dat) rattle

S

Saal m -[e]s,Säle hall; (Theat) auditorium; (Kranken-) ward

Saat f -,-en seed; (Säen) sowing; (Gesätes) crop. S~gut nt seed

sabbern vi ⟨haben⟩ ⟨fam⟩ slobber; ⟨Baby:⟩ dribble; ⟨reden⟩ jabber

Säbel m -s,- sabre

Sabo|tage /zabo'ta:ʒə/ f - sabotage. S~teur /-'tø:ɐ/ m -s,-e saboteur. s~tieren vt sabotage

Sach|bearbeiter m expert. S~buch nt non-fiction book. s~dienlich a relevant

Sache f -,-n matter, business; (Ding) thing; (fig) cause; zur S~ kommen come to the point

Sach|gebiet nt ⟨fig⟩ area, field. s~gemäß a proper, adv -ly. S~kenntnis f expertise. s~kundig a expert, adv -ly. s~lich a factual, adv -ly; (nüchtern) matter-of-fact, adv -ly; (objektiv) objective, adv -ly; (schmucklos) functional

sächlich a ⟨Gram⟩ neuter

Sachse m -n,-n Saxon. S~n nt -s Saxony

sächsisch a Saxon

sacht a gentle, adv -ly

Sach|verhalt m -[e]s facts pl. s~verständig a expert, adv -ly. S~verständige(r) mf expert

Sack m -[e]s,¨e sack; mit S~ und Pack with all one's belongings

sacken vi ⟨sein⟩ sink; (zusammen-) go down; ⟨Person:⟩ slump

Sack|gasse f cul-de-sac; ⟨fig⟩ impasse. S~leinen nt sacking

Sadis|mus m - sadism. S~t m -en,-en sadist. s~tisch a sadistic, adv -ally

säen vt/i ⟨haben⟩ sow

Safe /ze:f/ m -s,-s safe

Saft m -[e]s,¨e juice; ⟨Bot⟩ sap. s~ig a juicy; ⟨Wiese⟩ lush; ⟨Preis, Rechnung⟩ hefty; ⟨Witz⟩ coarse. s~los a dry

Sage f -,-n legend

Säge f -,-n saw. S~mehl nt sawdust

sagen vt say; (mitteilen) tell; (bedeuten) mean; das hat nichts zu s~ it doesn't mean anything; ein viel s~der Blick a meaningful look

sägen vt/i ⟨haben⟩ saw

sagenhaft a legendary; ⟨fam: unglaublich⟩ fantastic, adv -ally

Säge|späne mpl wood shavings. S~werk nt sawmill

Sahn|e f - cream. S~ebonbon m & nt ≈ toffee. s~ig a creamy

Saison /zɛ'zõ:/ f -,-s season

Saite f -,-n ⟨Mus, Sport⟩ string. S~ninstrument nt stringed instrument

Sakko m & nt -s,-s sports jacket

Sakrament nt -[e]s,-e sacrament

Sakrileg nt -s,-e sacrilege

Sakrist|an m -s,-e verger. S~ei f -,-en vestry

Salat m -[e]s,-e salad; ein Kopf S~ a lettuce. S~soße f salad-dressing

Salbe f -,-n ointment

Salbei m -s & f - sage

salben vt anoint

Saldo m -s,-dos & -den balance

Salon /za'lõ:/ m -s,-s salon; ⟨Naut⟩ saloon

salopp a casual, adv -ly; ⟨Benehmen⟩ informal, adv -ly; ⟨Ausdruck⟩ slangy

Salto m -s,-s somersault

Salut m -[e]s,-e salute. s~ieren vi (haben) salute

Salve f -,-n volley; ⟨Geschütz-⟩ salvo; ⟨von Gelächter⟩ burst

Salz nt -es,-e salt. s~en† vt salt. S~fass (S~faß) nt salt-cellar. s~ig a salty. S~kartoffeln fpl boiled potatoes. S~säure f hydrochloric acid

Samen m -s,- seed; ⟨Anat⟩ semen, sperm

sämig a ⟨Culin⟩ thick

Sämling m -s,-e seedling

Sammel|becken nt reservoir. S~begriff m collective term. s~n vt/i (haben) collect; ⟨suchen, versammeln⟩ gather; sich s~n collect; ⟨sich versammeln⟩ gather; ⟨sich fassen⟩ collect oneself. S~name m collective noun

Samm|ler(in) m -s,- (f -,-nen) collector. S~lung f -,-en collection; ⟨innere⟩ composure

Samstag m -s,-e Saturday. s~s adv on Saturdays

samt prep (+ dat) together with □ adv s~ und sonders without exception

Samt m -[e]s velvet. s~ig a velvety

sämtlich indef pron inv all. s~e(r,s) indef pron all the; s~e Werke complete works; meine s~en Bücher all my books

Sanatorium nt -s,-ien sanatorium

Sand m -[e]s sand

Sandal|e f -,-n sandal. S~ette f -,-n high-heeled sandal

Sand|bank f sandbank. S~burg f sandcastle. s~ig a sandy. S~kasten m sandpit. S~kuchen m Madeira cake. S~papier nt sandpaper. S~stein m sandstone

sanft a gentle, adv -ly. s~mütig a meek

Sänger(in) m -s,- (f -,-nen) singer

sanieren vt clean up; redevelop ⟨Gebiet⟩; ⟨modernisieren⟩ modernize; make profitable ⟨Industrie, Firma⟩; sich s~ become profitable

sanitär a sanitary

Sanität|er m -s,- first-aid man; ⟨Fahrer⟩ ambulance man; ⟨Mil⟩ medical orderly. S~swagen m ambulance

Sanktion /zaŋkˈtsjoːn/ f -,-en sanction. s~ieren vt sanction

Saphir m -s,-e sapphire

Sardelle f -,-n anchovy

Sardine f -,-n sardine

Sarg m -[e]s,-e coffin

Sarkas|mus m - sarcasm. s~tisch a sarcastic, adv -ally

Sat|an m -s Satan; ⟨fam: Teufel⟩ devil. s~anisch a satanic

Satellit m -en,-en satellite. S~enfernsehen nt satellite television

Satin /zaˈtɛ̃ː/ m -s satin

Satir|e f -,-n satire. s~isch a satirical, adv -ly

satt a full; ⟨Farbe⟩ rich; s~ sein have had enough [to eat]; sich s~ essen eat as much as one wants; s~ machen feed; ⟨Speise:⟩ be filling; etw s~ haben ⟨fam⟩ be fed up with sth

Sattel m -s,- saddle. s~n vt saddle. S~schlepper m tractor unit. S~zug m articulated lorry

sättigen vt satisfy; ⟨Chem & fig⟩ saturate □ vi (haben) be filling. s~d a filling

Satz m -es,-e sentence; ⟨Teil-⟩ clause; ⟨These⟩ proposition; ⟨Math⟩ theorem; ⟨Mus⟩ movement; ⟨Tennis, Zusammengehöriges⟩ set; ⟨Boden-⟩ sediment; ⟨Kaffee-⟩ grounds pl; ⟨Steuer-, Zins-⟩ rate; ⟨Druck-⟩ setting; ⟨Schrift-⟩ type; ⟨Sprung⟩ leap, bound. S~aussage f predicate. S~gegenstand m subject. S~zeichen nt punctuation mark

Sau f -,-Säue sow; ⟨sl: schmutziger Mensch⟩ dirty pig

sauber a clean; ⟨ordentlich⟩ neat, adv -ly; ⟨anständig⟩ decent, adv -ly; ⟨fam: nicht anständig⟩ fine; s~ halten keep clean; s~ machen clean. s~halten† vt sep (NEW) s~ halten, s. sauber. S~keit f - cleanliness; neatness; decency

säuberlich a neat, adv -ly

saubermachen vt/i sep (haben) (NEW) sauber machen, s. sauber

säuber|n vt clean; ⟨befreien⟩ rid/ ⟨Pol⟩ purge ⟨von of⟩. S~ungsaktion f ⟨Pol⟩ purge

Sauce /ˈzoːsə/ f -,-n sauce; ⟨Braten-⟩ gravy

Saudi-Arabien /-jən/ nt -s Saudi Arabia

sauer a sour; ⟨Chem⟩ acid; ⟨eingelegt⟩ pickled; ⟨schwer⟩ hard; saurer Regen acid rain; s~ sein ⟨fam⟩ be annoyed

Sauerei f -,-en = Schweinerei

Sauerkraut nt sauerkraut

säuerlich a slightly sour

Sauer|stoff m oxygen

saufen† vt/i (haben) drink; ⟨sl⟩ booze

Säufer m -s,- ⟨sl⟩ boozer

saugen† vt/i (haben) suck; ⟨staub-⟩ vacuum, hoover; sich voll Wasser s~ soak up water

säugen vt suckle

Sauger m -s,- [baby's] dummy, ⟨Amer⟩ pacifier; ⟨Flaschen-⟩ teat

Säugetier nt mammal

saugfähig a absorbent

Säugling *m* -s,-e infant

Säule *f* -,-n column

Saum *m* -[e]s,Säume hem; (*Rand*) edge

säumen¹ *vt* hem; (*fig*) line

säum|en² *vi* (*haben*) delay. s∼ig *a* dilatory

Sauna *f* -,-nas & -nen sauna

Säure *f* -,-n acidity; (*Chem*) acid

säuseln *vi* (*haben*) rustle [softly]

sausen *vi* (*haben*) rush; (*Ohren:*) buzz □ *vi* (*sein*) rush [along]

Sauwetter *nt* (*sl*) lousy weather

Saxophon, Saxofon *nt* -s,-e saxophone

SB- /ɛs'be:-/ *pref* (= Selbstbedienung) self-service ...

S-Bahn *f* city and suburban railway

sch *int* shush! (*fort*) shoo!

Schabe *f* -,-n cockroach

schaben *vt/i* (*haben*) scrape

schäbig *a* shabby, *adv* -ily

Schablone *f* -,-n stencil; (*Muster*) pattern; (*fig*) stereotype

Schach *nt* -s chess; S∼! check! in S∼ halten (*fig*) keep in check. S∼brett *nt* chessboard

schachern *vi* (*haben*) haggle

Schachfigur *f* chess-man

schachmatt *a* s∼ setzen checkmate; s∼! checkmate!

Schachspiel *nt* game of chess

Schacht *m* -[e]s,-e shaft

Schachtel *f* -,-n box; (*Zigaretten-*) packet

Schachzug *m* move

schade *a* s∼ sein be a pity *or* shame: zu s∼ für too good for; [wie] s∼! [what a] pity *or* shame!

Schädel *m* -s, skull. S∼bruch *m* fractured skull

schaden *vi* (*haben*) (+ *dat*) damage; (*nachteilig sein*) hurt; das schadet nichts that doesn't matter. S∼ *m* -s,- damage; (*Defekt*) defect; (*Nachteil*) disadvantage; zu S∼ kommen be hurt. S∼ersatz *m* damages *pl*. S∼freude *f* malicious glee. s∼froh *a* gloating

schadhaft *a* defective

schädig|en *vt* damage, harm. S∼ung *f* -,-en damage

schädlich *a* harmful

Schädling *m* -s,-e pest. S∼sbe-kämpfungsmittel *nt* pesticide

Schaf *nt* -[e]s,-e sheep; (*fam: Idiot*) idiot. S∼bock *m* ram

Schäfchen *nt* -s,- lamb

Schäfer *m* -s,- shepherd. S∼hund *m* sheepdog; Deutscher S∼hund German shepherd, alsatian

Schaffell *nt* sheepskin

schaffen†¹ *vt* create; (*herstellen*) establish; make (*Platz*); wie geschaffen für made for

schaffen² *v* (*reg*) □ *vt* manage [to do]; pass (*Prüfung*); catch (*Zug*); (*bringen*) take; jdm zu s∼ machen trouble s.o.; sich (*dat*) zu s∼ machen busy oneself (an + *dat* with) □ *vi* (*haben*) (*SGer: arbeiten*) work. S∼ *nt* -s work

Schaffner *m* -s,- conductor; (*Zug-*) ticket-inspector

Schaffung *f* - creation

Schaft *m* -[e]s,-e shaft; (*Gewehr-*) stock; (*Stiefel-*) leg. S∼stiefel *m* high boot

Schal *m* -s,-s scarf

schal *a* insipid; (*abgestanden*) flat; (*fig*) stale

Schale *f* -,-n skin; (*abgeschält*) peel; (*Eier-, Nuss-, Muschel-*) shell; (*Schüssel*) dish

schälen *vt* peel; sich s∼ peel

schalkhaft *a* mischievous, *adv* -ly

Schall *m* -[e]s sound. S∼dämpfer *m* silencer. s∼dicht *a* soundproof. s∼en *vi* (*haben*) ring out; (*nachhallen*) resound; s∼end lachen roar with laughter. S∼mauer *f* sound barrier. S∼platte *f* record, disc

schalt|en *vt* switch □ *vi* (*haben*) switch/ (*Ampel:*) turn (auf + *acc* to); (*Auto*) change gear; (*fam: begreifen*) catch on. S∼er *m* -s,- switch; (*Post-, Bank-*) counter; (*Fahrkarten-*) ticket window. S∼hebel *m* switch; (*Auto*) gear lever. S∼jahr *nt* leap year. S∼kreis *m* circuit. S∼ung *f* -,-en circuit; (*Auto*) gear change

Scham *f* - shame; (*Anat*) private parts *pl*; falsche S∼ false modesty

schämen (sich) *vr* be ashamed; schämt euch! you should be ashamed of yourselves!

scham|haft *a* modest, *adv* -ly; (*schüchtern*) bashful, *adv* -ly. s∼los *a* shameless, *adv* -ly

Schampon *nt* -s shampoo. s∼ieren *vt* shampoo

Schande *f* - disgrace, shame; S∼ machen (+ *dat*) bring shame on; zu S∼n machen/werden = zuschanden machen/werden, s. zuschanden

schänd|en *vt* dishonour; (*fig*) defile; (*Relig*) desecrate; (*sexuell*) violate. s∼lich *a* disgraceful, *adv* -ly. S∼ung *f* -,-en defilement, desecration; violation

Schänke *f* -,-n = Schenke

Schanktisch *m* bar

Schanze *f* -,-n [ski-]jump

Schar *f* -,-en crowd; (*Vogel-*) flock; in [hellen] S∼en in droves

Scharade *f* -,-n charade

scharen vt um sich s~ gather round one; sich s~ um flock round. s~weise adv in droves

scharf a (schärfer, schärfst) sharp; (stark) strong; (stark gewürzt) hot; (Geruch) pungent; (Frost, Wind, Augen, Verstand) keen; (streng) harsh; (Galopp, Ritt) hard; (Munition) live; (Hund) fierce; s~ einstellen (Phot) focus; s~ sein (Phot) be in focus; s~ sein auf (+ acc) (fam) be keen on □ adv sharply; (hinsehen, nachdenken, bremsen, reiten) hard; (streng) harshly; s~ schießen fire live ammunition

Scharfblick m perspicacity

Schärfe f - (s. scharf) sharpness; strength; hotness; pungency; keenness; harshness. s~n vt sharpen

scharf|machen vt sep (fam) incite. S~richter m executioner. S~schütze m marksman. S~sichtig a perspicacious. S~sinn m astuteness. s~sinnig a astute, adv -ly

Scharlach m -s scarlet fever

Scharlatan m -s,-e charlatan

Scharnier nt -s,-e hinge

Schärpe f -,-n sash

scharren vi (haben) scrape; (Huhn) scratch; (Pferd) paw the ground □ vt scrape

Schart|e f -,-n nick. s~ig a jagged

Schaschlik m & nt -s,-s kebab

Schatten m -s,- shadow; (schattige Stelle) shade; im S~ in the shade. s~haft a shadowy. S~riss (S~riß) m silhouette. S~seite f shady side; (fig) disadvantage

schattier|en vt shade. S~ung f -,-en shading; (fig: Variante) shade

schattig a shady

Schatz m -es,-e treasure; (Freund, Freundin) sweetheart; (Anrede) darling

Schätzchen nt -s,- darling

schätzen vt estimate; (taxieren) value; (achten) esteem; (würdigen) appreciate; (fam: vermuten) reckon; sich glücklich s~ consider oneself lucky

Schätzung f -,-en estimate; (Taxierung) valuation. s~sweise adv approximately

Schau f -,-en show; zur S~ stellen display. S~bild nt diagram

Schauder m -s shiver; (vor Abscheu) shudder. s~haft a dreadful, adv -ly. s~n vi (haben) shiver; (vor Abscheu) shudder; mich s~te I shivered/shuddered

schauen vi (haben) (SGer, Aust) look; s~, dass make sure that

Schauer m -s,- shower; (Schauder) shiver. s~geschichte f horror story. s~lich a

ghastly. s~n vi (haben) shiver; mich s~te I shivered

Schaufel f -,-n shovel; (Kehr-) dustpan. s~n vt shovel; (graben) dig

Schaufenster nt shop-window. S~bummel m window-shopping. S~puppe f dummy

Schaukasten m display case

Schaukel f -,-n swing. s~n vt rock □ vi (haben) rock; (auf einer Schaukel) swing; (schwanken) sway. S~pferd nt rocking-horse. S~stuhl m rocking-chair

schaulustig a curious

Schaum m -[e]s foam; (Seifen-) lather; (auf Bier) froth; (als Frisier-, Rasiermittel) mousse

schäumen vi (haben) foam, froth; (Seife:) lather

Schaum|gummi m foam rubber. s~ig a frothy; s~ig rühren (Culin) cream. S~krone f white crest; (auf Bier) head. S~speise f mousse. S~stoff m [synthetic] foam. S~wein m sparkling wine

Schauplatz m scene

schaurig a dreadful, adv -ly; (unheimlich) eerie, adv eerily

Schauspiel nt play; (Anblick) spectacle. S~er m actor. S~erin f actress. s~ern vi (haben) act; (sich verstellen) play-act

Scheck m -s,-s cheque; (Amer) check. S~buch, S~heft nt cheque-book. S~karte f cheque card

Scheibe f -,-n disc; (Schieß-) target; (Glas-) pane; (Brot-, Wurst-) slice. S~nwaschanlage f windscreen washer. S~nwischer m -s,- windscreen-wiper

Scheich m -s,-e & -s sheikh

Scheide f -,-n sheath; (Anat) vagina

scheid|en† vt separate; (unterscheiden) distinguish; dissolve (Ehe); sich s~en lassen get divorced; sich s~en diverge; (Meinungen:) differ □ vi (sein) leave; (voneinander) part. S~ung f -,-en divorce

Schein m -[e]s,-e light; (Anschein) appearance; (Bescheinigung) certificate; (Geld-) note; etw nur zum S~ tun only pretend to do sth. s~bar a apparent, adv -ly. s~en† vi (haben) shine; (den Anschein haben) seem, appear; mir s~t it seems to me

scheinheilig a hypocritical, adv -ly. S~keit f hypocrisy

Scheinwerfer m -s,- floodlight; (Such-) searchlight; (Auto) headlight; (Theat) spotlight

Scheiß-, scheiß- pref (vulg) bloody. S~e f - (vulg) shit. s~en† vi (haben) (vulg) shit

Scheit nt -[e]s,-e log

Scheitel m -s,- parting. s~n vt part (Haar)

scheitern vi (sein) fail

Schelle f -,-n bell. s~n vi (haben) ring

Schellfisch m haddock

Schelm m -s,-e rogue. s~isch a mischievous, adv -ly

Schelte f- scolding. s~n† vi (haben) grumble (über + acc about); mit jdm s~n scold s.o. □ vt scold; (bezeichnen) call

Schema nt -s,-mata model, pattern; (Skizze) diagram

Schemel m -s,- stool

Schenke f -,-n tavern

Schenkel m -s,- thigh; (Geom) side

schenken vt give [as a present]; jdm Vertrauen/Glauben s~ trust/believe s.o.; sich (dat) etw s~ give sth a miss

scheppern vi (haben) clank

Scherbe f -,-n [broken] piece

Schere f -,-n scissors pl; (Techn) shears pl; (Hummer-) claw. s~n¹† vt shear; crop (Haar); clip (Hund)

scheren² vt (reg) (fam) bother; sich nicht s~ um not care about; scher dich zum Teufel! go to hell!

Scherenschnitt m silhouette

Schererreien fpl (fam) trouble sg

Scherz m -es,-e joke; im/zum S~ as a joke. s~en vi (haben) joke. S~frage f riddle. s~haft a humorous

scheu a shy, adv -ly; (Tier) timid; s~ werden (Pferd:) shy; s~ machen startle. S~ f - shyness; timidity; (Ehrfurcht) awe

scheuchen vt shoo

scheuen vt be afraid of; (meiden) shun; keine Mühe/Kosten s~ spare no effort/expense; sich s~ be afraid (vor + dat of); shrink (vor from doing sth) □ vi (haben) (Pferd:) shy

Scheuerllappen m floor-cloth. s~n vt scrub; (mit Scheuerpulver) scour; (reiben) rub; [wund] s~n chafe □ vi (haben) rub, chafe. S~tuch nt floor-cloth

Scheuklappen fpl blinkers

Scheune f -,-n barn

Scheusal nt -s,-e monster

scheußlich a horrible, adv -bly

Schi m -s,-er ski; S~ fahren od laufen ski

Schicht f -,-en layer; (Geol) stratum; (Gesellschafts-) class; (Arbeits-) shift. S~arbeit f shift work. s~en vt stack [up]

schick a stylish, adv -ly; (Frau) chic; (fam: prima) great. S~ m -[e]s style

schicken vt/i (haben) send; s~ nach send for; sich s~ in (+ acc) resign oneself to

schicklich a fitting, proper

Schicksal nt -s,-e fate. s~haft a fateful. S~sschlag m misfortune

Schiebldach nt (Auto) sun-roof. s~en† vt push; (gleitend) slide; (fam: handeln mit) traffic in; etw s~en auf (+ acc) (fig) put sth down to; shift (Schuld, Verantwortung) on to □ vi (haben) push. S~er m -s,- slide; (Person) black marketeer. S~etür f sliding door. S~ung f -,-en (fam) illicit deal; (Betrug) rigging, fixing

Schieds|gericht nt panel of judges; (Jur) arbitration tribunal. S~richter m referee; (Tennis) umpire; (Jur) arbitrator

schief a crooked; (unsymmetrisch) lopsided; (geneigt) slanting, sloping; (nicht senkrecht) leaning; (Winkel) oblique; (fig) false; (misstrauisch) suspicious □ adv not straight; jdn s~ ansehen look at s.o. askance; s~ gehen (fam) go wrong

Schiefer m -s slate

schief|gehen† vi sep (sein) ⟨NEW⟩ s~ gehen, s. schief. s~lachen (sich) vr sep double up with laughter

schielen vi (haben) squint

Schienbein nt shin; (Knochen) shinbone

Schiene f -,-n rail; (Gleit-) runner; (Med) splint. s~n vt (Med) put in a splint

schier¹ adv almost

schier² a pure; (Fleisch) lean

Schießlbude f shooting-gallery. s~en† vt shoot; fire (Kugel); score (Tor) □ vi (haben) shoot, fire (auf + acc at) □ vi (sein) shoot [along]; (strömen) gush; in die Höhe s~en shoot up. S~erei f -,-en shooting. S~scheibe f target. S~stand m shooting-range

Schifahrlen nt skiing. S~er(in) m(f) skier

Schiff nt -[e]s,-e ship; (Kirchen-) nave; (Seiten-) aisle

Schiffahrt f ⟨NEW⟩ Schifffahrt

schiff|bar a navigable. S~bau m shipbuilding. S~bruch m shipwreck. s~brüchig a shipwrecked. S~chen nt -s,- small boat; (Tex) shuttle. S~er m -s,- skipper. S~fahrt f shipping

Schikan|e f -,-n harassment; mit allen S~en (fam) with every refinement. s~ieren vt harass; (tyrannisieren) bully

Schillaufen nt -s skiing. S~läufer(in) m(f) -s,- (f -,-nen) skier

Schild¹ m -[e]s,-e shield; etw im S~e führen (fam) be up to sth

Schild² nt -[e]s,-er sign; (Namens-, Nummern-) plate; (Mützen-) badge; (Etikett) label

Schilddrüse f thyroid [gland]

schilder|n vt describe. S~ung f -,-en description

Schild|kröte f tortoise; (See-) turtle. S~patt nt -[e]s tortoiseshell

Schilf *nt* -[e]s reeds *pl*

schillern *vi* (haben) shimmer

Schimmel *m* -s,- mould; (*Pferd*) white horse. s~ig *a* mouldy. S~n *vi* (haben/ sein) go mouldy

Schimmer *m* -s gleam; (*Spur*) glimmer. s~n *vi* (haben) gleam

Schimpanse *m* -n,-n chimpanzee

schimpf|en *vt/i* grumble (mit at; über + *acc* about); scold (mit jdm s.o.) □ *vt* call. S~name *m* term of abuse. S~wort *nt* (*pl* -wörter) swear-word; (*Beleidigung*) insult

schind|en† *vt* work or drive hard; (*quälen*) ill-treat; sich s~en slave [away]; Eindruck s~en (*fam*) try to impress. S~er *m* -s,- slave-driver. S~erei *f* - slave-driving; (*Plackerei*) hard slog

Schinken *m* -s,- ham. S~speck *m* bacon

Schippe *f* -,-n shovel. s~n *vt* shovel

Schirm *m* -[e]s,-e umbrella; (*Sonnen-*) sunshade; (*Lampen-*) shade; (*Augen-*) visor; (*Mützen-*) peak; (*Ofen-, Bild-*) screen; (*fig: Schutz*) shield. S~herr *m* patron. S~herrschaft *f* patronage. S~mütze *f* peaked cap

schizophren *a* schizophrenic. S~ie *f* - schizophrenia

Schlacht *f* -,-en battle

schlachten *vt* slaughter, kill

Schlachter, Schlächter *m* -s,-(*NGer*) butcher

Schlacht|feld *nt* battlefield. S~haus *nt*, S~hof *m* abattoir. S~platte *f* plate of assorted cooked meats and sausages. S~schiff *nt* battleship

Schlacke *f* -,-n slag

Schlaf *m* -[e]s sleep; im S~ in one's sleep. S~anzug *m* pyjamas *pl*, (*Amer*) pajamas *pl*. S~couch *f* sofa bed

Schläfe *f* -,-n (*Anat*) temple

schlafen† *vi* (haben) sleep; (*fam: nicht aufpassen*) be asleep; s~ gehen go to bed; er schläft noch he is still asleep. S~szeit *f* bedtime

Schläfer(in) *m* -s,- (*f* -,-nen) sleeper

schlaff *a* limp, *adv* -ly; (*Seil*) slack; (*Muskel*) flabby

Schlaflied *nt* lullaby. S~los *a* sleepless. S~losigkeit *f* - insomnia. S~mittel *nt* sleeping drug

schläfrig *a* sleepy, *adv* -ily

Schlaf|saal *m* dormitory. S~sack *m* sleeping-bag. S~tablette *f* sleeping-pill. s~trunken *a* [still] half asleep. S~wagen *m* sleeping-car, sleeper. S~wandeln *vi* (haben/sein) sleep-walk. S~zimmer *nt* bedroom

Schlag *m* -[e]s,ِ-e blow; (*Faust-*) punch; (*Herz-, Puls-, Trommel-*) beat; (*einer Uhr*) chime; (*Glocken-, Gong- & Med*) stroke; (*elektrischer*) shock; (*Portion*) helping; (*Art*) type; (*Aust*) whipped cream; S~e bekommen get a beating; S~ auf S~ in rapid succession. S~ader *f* artery. S~anfall *m* stroke. s~artig *a* sudden, *adv* -ly. S~baum *m* barrier

Schlägel *m* -s,- mallet; (*Trommel-*) stick

schlagen† *vt* hit, strike; (*fällen*) fell; knock (*Loch, Nagel*) (in + *acc* into); (*prügeln, besiegen*) beat; (*Culin*) whisk (*Eiweiß*); whip (*Sahne*); (*legen*) throw; (*wickeln*) wrap; (*hinzufügen*) add (zu to); sich s~ fight; sich geschlagen geben admit defeat □ *vi* (haben) beat; (*Tür:*) bang; (*Uhr:*) strike; (*melodisch*) chime; mit den Flügeln s~ flap its wings; um sich s~ lash out; es schlug sechs the clock struck six □ *vi* (sein) in etw (*acc*) s~ (*Blitz, Kugel:*) strike sth; s~ an (+ *acc*) knock against; nach jdm s~ (*fig*) take after s.o. s~d *a* (*fig*) conclusive, *adv* -ly

Schlager *m* -s,- popular song; (*Erfolg*) hit

Schläger *m* -s,- racket; (*Tischtennis-*) bat; (*Golf-*) club; (*Hockey-*) stick; (*fam: Raufbold*) thug. S~ei *f* -,-en fight, brawl

schlag|fertig *a* quick-witted. S~instrument *nt* percussion instrument. S~loch *nt* pothole. S~sahne *f* whipped cream; (*ungeschlagen*) whipping cream. S~seite *f* (*Naut*) list. S~stock *m* truncheon. S~wort *nt* (*pl* -worte) slogan. S~zeile *f* headline. S~zeug *nt* (*Mus*) percussion. S~zeuger *m* -s,- percussionist; (*in Band*) drummer

schlaksig *a* gangling

Schlamassel *m* & *nt* -s (*fam*) mess

Schlamm *m* -[e]s mud. s~ig *a* muddy

Schlamp|e *f* -,-n (*fam*) slut. s~en *vi* (haben) (*fam*) be sloppy (bei in). S~erei *f* -,-en sloppiness; (*Unordnung*) mess. s~ig *a* slovenly; (*Arbeit*) sloppy □ *adv* in a slovenly way; sloppily

Schlange *f* -,-n snake; (*Menschen-, Auto-*) queue; S~ stehen queue, (*Amer*) stand in line

schlängeln (sich) *vr* wind; (*Person:*) weave (durch through)

Schlangen|biss (Schlangenbiß) *m* snakebite. S~linie *f* wavy line

schlank *a* slim. S~heit *f* - slimness. S~heitskur *f* slimming diet

schlapp *a* (*schlaff*) limp, *adv* -ly. S~e *f* -,-n (*fam*) setback

schlau *a* clever, *adv* -ly; (*gerissen*) crafty, *adv* -ily; ich werde nicht s~ daraus I can't make head or tail of it

Schlauch m -[e]s,Schläuche tube; (Wasser-) hose[pipe]. S∼boot nt rubber dinghy. s∼en vt (fam) exhaust

Schlaufe f -,-n loop

schlecht a bad; (böse) wicked; (unzulänglich) poor; s∼ werden go bad; (Wetter:) turn bad; s∼er werden get worse; s∼ aussehen look bad/(Person:) unwell; mir ist s∼ I feel sick; s∼ machen (fam) run down □ adv badly; poorly; (kaum) not really. s∼gehen† vi sep (sein) NEW≻ s∼ gehen, s. gehen. s∼gelaunt a NEW≻ s∼ gelaunt, s. gelaunt. s∼hin adv quite simply. S∼igkeit f -, wickedness. s∼machen vt sep NEW≻ s∼ machen, s. schlecht

schlecken vt/i (haben) lick (an etw dat sth); (auf-) lap up

Schlegel m -s,- (SGer:Keule) leg; (Hühner-) drumstick; (Techn, Mus) NEW≻ Schlägel

schleichen† vi (sein) creep; (langsam gehen/fahren) crawl □ vr sich s∼ creep. s∼d a creeping; (Krankheit) insidious

Schleier m -s,- veil; (fig) haze. s∼haft a es ist mir s∼haft (fam) it's a mystery to me

Schleife f -,-n bow; (Fliege) bow-tie; (Biegung) loop

schleifen¹ v (reg) □ vt drag; (zerstören) raze to the ground □ vi (haben) trail, drag

schleifen² vt grind; (schärfen) sharpen; cut (Edelstein, Glas); (drillen) drill

Schleim m -[e]s slime; (Anat) mucus; (Med) phlegm. s∼ig a slimy

schlemm|en vi (haben) feast □ vt feast on. S∼er m -s,- gourmet

schlendern vi (sein) stroll

schlenkern vt/i (haben) swing; s∼ mit swing; dangle (Beine)

Schlepp|dampfer m tug. S∼e f -,-n train. s∼en vt drag; (tragen) carry; (ziehen) tow; sich s∼en drag oneself; (sich hinziehen) drag on; sich s∼en mit carry. s∼end a slow, adv -ly. S∼er m -s,- tug; (Traktor) tractor. S∼kahn m barge. S∼lift m T-bar lift. S∼tau nt tow-rope; ins S∼tau nehmen take in tow

Schleuder f -,-n catapult; (Wäsche-) spindrier. s∼n vt hurl; spin (Wäsche); extract (Honig) □ vi (sein) skid; ins S∼n geraten skid. S∼preise mpl knock-down prices. S∼sitz m ejector seat

schleunigst adv hurriedly; (sofort) at once

Schleuse f -,-n lock; (Sperre) sluice[-gate]. s∼n vt steer

Schliche pl tricks; jdm auf die S∼ kommen (fam) get on to s.o.

schlicht a plain, adv -ly; (einfach) simple, adv -ply

schlicht|en vt settle □ vi (haben) arbitrate. S∼ung f -settlement; (Jur) arbitration

Schlick m -[e]s silt

Schließe f -,-n clasp; (Schnalle) buckle

schließen† vt close (ab-) lock; fasten (Kleid, Verschluss); (stilllegen) close down; (beenden, folgern) conclude; enter into (Vertrag); sich s∼ close; in die Arme s∼ embrace; etw s∼ an (+ acc) connect sth to; sich s∼ an (+ acc) follow □ vi (haben) close, (den Betrieb einstellen) close down; (den Schlüssel drehen) turn the key; (enden, folgern) conclude; s∼ lassen auf (+ acc) suggest

Schließ|fach nt locker. s∼lich adv finally, in the end; (immerhin) after all. S∼ung f -,-en closure

Schliff m -[e]s cut; (Schleifen) cutting; (fig) polish; der letzte S∼ the finishing touches pl

schlimm a bad, adv -ly; s∼er werden get worse; nicht so s∼! it doesn't matter! s∼stenfalls adv if the worst comes to the worst

Schlinge f -,-n loop; (Henkers-) noose; (Med) sling; (Falle) snare

Schlingel m -s,- (fam) rascal

schling|en† vt wind, wrap; tie (Knoten); sich s∼en um coil around □ vi (haben) bolt one's food. S∼pflanze f climber

Schlips m -es,-e tie

Schlitten m -s,- sledge; (Rodel-) toboggan; (Pferde-) sleigh; S∼ fahren toboggan

schlittern vi (haben/ sein) slide

Schlittschuh m skate; S∼ laufen skate. S∼läufer(in) m(f) -s,- (f -,-nen) skater

Schlitz m -es,-e slit; (für Münze) slot; (Jacken-) vent; (Hosen-) flies pl. s∼en vt slit

Schloss nt -es,̈er (Schloß nt -sses,̈sser) lock; (Vorhänge-) padlock; (Verschluss) clasp; (Gebäude) castle; (Palast) palace

Schlosser m -s,- locksmith; (Auto-) mechanic; (Maschinen-) fitter

Schlot m -[e]s,-e chimney

schlottern vi (haben) shake, tremble; (Kleider:) hang loose

Schlucht f -,-en ravine, gorge

schluchz|en vi (haben) sob. S∼er m -s,- sob

Schluck m -[e]s,-e mouthful; (klein) sip

Schluckauf m -s hiccups pl

schlucken vt/i (haben) swallow. S∼ m -s hiccups pl

schlud|ern vi (haben) be sloppy (bei in). s∼rig a sloppy, adv -ily; (Arbeit) slipshod

Schlummer m -s slumber. s∼n vi (haben) slumber

Schlund m -[e]s [back of the] throat; (fig) mouth

schlüpf|en vi (sein) slip; [aus dem Ei] s~en hatch. S~er m -s,- knickers pl. s~rig a slippery; (anstößig) smutty

schlurfen vi (sein) shuffle

schlürfen vt/i (haben) slurp

Schluss m -es,-̈e (Schluß m -sses,-̈sse) end; (S~folgerung) conclusion; zum S~ finally; S~ machen stop (mit etw sth); finish (mit jdm with s.o.)

Schlüssel m -s,- key; (Schrauben-) spanner; (Geheim-) code; (Mus) clef. S~bein nt collar-bone. S~bund m & nt bunch of keys. S~loch nt keyhole. S~ring m keyring

Schlussfolgerung (Schlußfolgerung) f conclusion

schlüssig a conclusive, adv -ly; sich (dat) s~ werden make up one's mind

Schluss|licht (Schluß|licht) nt rearlight. S~verkauf m [end of season] sale

Schmach f - disgrace

schmachten vi (haben) languish

schmächtig a slight

schmackhaft a tasty

schmal a narrow; (dünn) thin; (schlank) slender; (karg) meagre

schmälern vt diminish; (herabsetzen) belittle

Schmalz[1] nt -es lard; (Ohren-) wax

Schmalz[2] m -es (fam) schmaltz. s~ig a (fam) schmaltzy, slushy

schmarotz|en vi (haben) be parasitic (auf + acc on); (Person:) sponge (bei on). S~er m -s,- parasite; (Person) sponger

Schmarren m -s,- (Aust) pancake [torn into strips]; (fam: Unsinn) rubbish

schmatzen vi (haben) eat noisily

schmausen vi (haben) feast

schmecken vi (haben) taste (nach of); [gut] s~ taste good; hat es dir geschmeckt? did you enjoy it? ▫ vt taste

Schmeichelei f -,-en flattery; (Kompliment) compliment

schmeichel|haft a complimentary, flattering. s~n vi (haben) (+ dat) flatter

schmeißen† vt/i (haben) s~ [mit] (fam) chuck

Schmeißfliege f bluebottle

schmelz|en† vt/i (sein) melt; smelt (Erze). S~wasser nt melted snow and ice

Schmerbauch m (fam) paunch

Schmerz m -es,-en pain; (Kummer) grief; S~en haben be in pain. s~en vt hurt; (fig) grieve ▫ vi (haben) hurt, be painful. S~ensgeld nt compensation for pain and suffering. s~haft a painful. s~lich a (fig)

painful; (traurig) sad, adv -ly. s~los a painless, adv -ly. s~stillend a pain-killing; s~stillendes Mittel analgesic, painkiller. S~tablette f pain-killer

Schmetterball m (Tennis) smash

Schmetterling m -s,-e butterfly

schmettern vt hurl; (Tennis) smash; (singen) sing; (spielen) blare out ▫ vi (haben) sound; (Trompeten:) blare

Schmied m -[e]s,-e blacksmith

Schmiede f -,-n forge. S~eisen nt wrought iron. s~n vt forge; (fig) hatch; Pläne s~n make plans

schmieg|en vt press; sich s~en an (+ acc) nestle or snuggle up to; (Kleid:) cling to. s~sam a supple

Schmier|e f -,-n grease; (Schmutz) mess. s~en vt lubricate; (streichen) spread; (schlecht schreiben) scrawl; (sl: bestechen) bribe ▫ vi (haben) smudge; (schreiben) scrawl. S~fett nt grease. S~geld nt (fam) bribe. s~ig a greasy; (schmutzig) grubby; (anstößig) smutty; (Person) slimy. S~mittel nt lubricant

Schminke f -,-n make-up. s~n vt make up; sich s~n put on make-up; sich (dat) die Lippen s~n put on lipstick

schmirgel|n vt sand down. S~papier nt emery-paper

schmökern vt/i (haben) (fam) read

schmollen vi (haben) sulk; (s~d den Mund verziehen) pout

schmor|en vt/i (haben) braise; (fam: schwitzen) roast. S~topf m casserole

Schmuck m -[e]s jewellery; (Verzierung) ornament, decoration

schmücken vt decorate, adorn; sich s~ adorn oneself

schmuck|los a plain. S~stück nt piece of jewellery; (fig) jewel

schmuddelig a grubby

Schmuggel m -s smuggling. s~n vt smuggle. S~ware f contraband

Schmuggler m -s,- smuggler

schmunzeln vi (haben) smile

schmusen vi (haben) cuddle

Schmutz m -es dirt; in den S~ziehen (fig) denigrate. s~en vi (haben) get dirty. S~fleck m dirty mark. s~ig a dirty

Schnabel m -s,-̈ beak, bill; (eines Kruges) lip; (Tülle) spout

Schnake f -,-n mosquito; (Kohl-) daddy-long-legs

Schnalle f -,-n buckle. s~n vt strap; (zu-) buckle; den Gürtel enger s~n tighten one's belt

schnalzen vi (haben) mit der Zunge/den Fingern s~ click one's tongue/snap one's fingers

schnapp|en vi (haben) s~en nach snap at; gasp for (Luft; □ vt snatch, grab; (fam: festnehmen) nab. **S~schloss** (S~schloß) nt spring lock. **S~schuss** (S~schuß) m snapshot

Schnaps m -es, ⁓e schnapps

schnarchen vi (haben) snore

schnarren vi (haben) rattle; (Klingel:) buzz

schnattern vi (haben) cackle

schnauben vi (haben) snort □ vt sich (dat) die Nase s~ blow one's nose

schnaufen vi (haben) puff, pant

Schnauze f -,-n muzzle; (eines Kruges) lip; (Tülle) spout

schnäuzen (sich) vr blow one's nose

Schnecke f -,-n snail; (Nackt-) slug; (Spirale) scroll; (Gebäck) ≈ Chelsea bun. **S~nhaus** nt snail-shell

Schnee m -s snow; (Eier-) beaten egg-white. **S~ball** m snowball. **S~besen** m whisk. **S~brille** f snow-goggles pl. **S~fall** m snow-fall. **S~flocke** f snowflake. **S~glöckchen** nt -s,- snowdrop. **S~kette** f snow chain. **S~mann** m (pl -männer) snowman. **S~pflug** m snowplough. **S~schläger** m whisk. **S~sturm** m snowstorm, blizzard. **S~wehe** f -,-n snowdrift

Schneid m -[e]s (SGer) courage

Schneide f -,-n [cutting] edge; (Klinge) blade

schneiden† vt cut; (in Scheiben) slice; (kreuzen) cross; (nicht beachten) cut; Gesichter s~ pull faces; sich s~ cut oneself; (über-) intersect; sich (dat/acc) in den Finger s~ cut one's finger. **s~d** a cutting; (kalt) biting

Schneider m -s,- tailor. **S~in** f -,-nen dressmaker. **s~n** vt make (Anzug, Kostüm)

Schneidezahn m incisor

schneidig a dashing, adv -ly

schneien vi (haben) snow; es schneit it is snowing

Schneise f -,-n path; (Feuer-) firebreak

schnell a quick; (Auto, Tempo) fast □ adv quickly; (in s~em Tempo) fast; (bald) soon; mach s~! hurry up! s~en vi (sein) in die Höhe s~en shoot up. **S~igkeit** f - rapidity; (Tempo) speed. **S~imbiss** (S~imbiß) m snack-bar. **S~kochtopf** m pressure-cooker. **S~reinigung** f express cleaners. **s~stens** adv as quickly as possible. **S~zug** m express [train]

schnetzeln vt cut into thin strips

schneuzen (sich) vr (NEW) schnäuzen (sich)

schnippen vt flick

schnippisch a pert, adv -ly

Schnipsel m & nt -s,- scrap

Schnitt m -[e]s,-e cut; (Film-) cutting; (S~muster) [paper] pattern; im S~ (durchschnittlich) on average

Schnitte f -,-n slice [of bread]; (belegt) open sandwich

schnittig a stylish; (stromlinienförmig) streamlined

Schnitt|käse m hard cheese. **S~lauch** m chives pl. **S~muster** nt [paper] pattern. **S~punkt** m [point of] intersection. **S~wunde** f cut

Schnitzel nt -s,- scrap; (Culin) escalope. **s~n** vt shred

schnitz|en vt/i (haben) carve. **S~er** m -s,- carver; (fam: Fehler) blunder. **S~erei** f -,-en carving

schnodderig a (fam) brash

schnöde a despicable, adv -bly; (verächtlich) contemptuous, adv -ly

Schnorchel m -s,- snorkel

Schnörkel m -s,- flourish; (Kunst) scroll. **s~ig** a ornate

schnorren vt/i (haben) (fam) scrounge

schnüffeln vi (haben) sniff (an etw dat sth); (fam: spionieren) snoop [around]

Schnuller m -s,- [baby's] dummy, (Amer) pacifier

Schnupfen m -s,- [head] cold. **S~tabak** m snuff

schnupf|en vt sniff; Tabak s~en take snuff. **S~en** m -s,- [head] cold. **S~tabak** m snuff

schnuppern vt/i (haben) sniff (an etw dat sth)

Schnur f -,⁓e string; (Kordel) cord; (Besatz-) braid; (Electr) flex; eine S~ a piece of string

Schnür|chen nt -s,- wie am S~chen (fam) like clockwork. **s~en** vt tie; lace [up] (Schuhe)

schnurgerade a & adv dead straight

Schnurr|bart m moustache. **s~en** vi (haben) hum; (Katze:) purr

Schnür|schuh m lace-up shoe. **S~senkel** m [shoe-]lace

schnurstracks adv straight

Schock m -[e]s,-s shock. **s~en** vt (fam) shock; geschockt sein be shocked. **s~ieren** vt shock. **s~ierend** a shocking

Schöffe m -n,-n lay judge

Schokolade f - chocolate

Scholle f -,-n clod [of earth]; (Eis-) [ice-] floe; (Fisch) plaice

schon adv already; (allein) just; (sogar) even; (ohnehin) anyway; s~ einmal before; (jemals) ever; s~ immer/oft/wieder always/often/again; hast du ihn s~ gesehen? have you seen him yet? s~ der Gedanke daran the mere thought of it;

s~ deshalb for that reason alone; das ist s~ möglich that's quite possible; ja s~, aber well yes, but; nun geh/komm s~! go/come on then!

schön a beautiful; (Wetter) fine; (angenehm, nett) nice; (gut) good; (fam: beträchtlich) pretty; s~en Dank! thank you very much! na s~ all right then □ adv beautifully; nicely; (gut) well; s~ langsam nice and slowly

schonen vt spare; (gut behandeln) look after; sich s~ take things easy. s~d a gentle, adv -tly

Schönheit f -,-en beauty. S~sfehler m blemish. S~skonkurrenz f, S~swettbewerb m beauty contest

schönmachen vt sep smarten up; sich s~ make oneself look nice

Schonung f -,-en gentle care; (nach Krankheit) rest; (Baum-) plantation. s~slos a ruthless, adv -ly

Schonzeit f close season

schöpf|en vt scoop [up]; ladle (Suppe); Mut s~en take heart; frische Luft s~en get some fresh air. S~er m -s,- creator; (Kelle) ladle. s~erisch a creative. S~kelle f, S~löffel m ladle. S~ung f -,-en creation

Schoppen m -s,- (SGer) ≈ pint

Schorf m -[e]s scab

Schornstein m chimney. S~feger m -s,- chimney-sweep

Schoß m -es,-e lap; (Frack-) tail

Schößling (Schößling) m -s,-e (Bot) shoot

Schote f -,-n pod; (Erbse) pea

Schotte m -n,-n Scot, Scotsman

Schotter m -s gravel; (für Gleise) ballast

schott|isch a Scottish, Scots. S~land nt -s Scotland

schraffieren vt hatch

schräg a diagonal, adv -ly; (geneigt) sloping; s~ halten tilt. S~e f -,-n slope. S~strich m oblique stroke

Schramme f -,-n scratch. s~n vt scrape, scratch

Schrank m -[e]s,-e cupboard; (Kleider-) wardrobe; (Akten-, Glas-) cabinet

Schranke f -,-n barrier

Schraube f -,-n screw; (Schiffs-) propeller. s~n vt screw; (ab-) unscrew; (drehen) turn; sich in die Höhe s~n spiral upwards. S~nmutter f nut. S~nschlüssel m spanner. S~nzieher m -s,- screwdriver

Schraubstock m vice

Schrebergarten m ≈ allotment

Schreck m -[e]s,-e fright; jdm einen S~ einjagen give s.o. a fright. S~en m -s,- fright; (Entsetzen) horror. s~en vt (reg)

frighten; (auf-) startle □ vi† (sein) in die Höhe s~en start up

Schreck|gespenst nt spectre. s~haft a easily frightened; (nervös) jumpy. s~lich a terrible, adv -bly. S~schuss (S~schuß) m warning shot

Schrei m -[e]s,-e cry, shout; (gellend) scream; der letzte S~ (fam) the latest thing

Schreib|block m writing-pad. s~en† vt/i (haben) write; (auf der Maschine) type; richtig/falsch s~en spell right/wrong; sich s~en (Wort:) be spelt; (korrespondieren) correspond; krank s~en (NEW) krankschreiben. S~en nt -s,- writing; (Brief) letter. S~fehler m spelling mistake. S~heft nt exercise book. S~kraft f clerical assistant; (für Maschineschreiben) typist. S~maschine f typewriter. S~papier nt writing-paper. S~schrift f script. S~tisch m desk. S~ung f -,-en spelling. S~waren fpl stationery sg. S~weise f spelling

schrei|en† vt/i (haben) cry; (gellend) scream; (rufen, laut sprechen) shout; zum S~ sein (fam) be a scream. s~d a (fig) glaring; (grell) garish

Schreiner m -s,- joiner

schreiten† vi (sein) walk

Schrift f -,-en writing; (Druck-) type; (Abhandlung) paper; die Heilige S~ the Scriptures pl. S~führer m secretary. s~lich a written □ adv in writing. S~sprache f written language. S~steller(in) m -s,- (f -,-nen) writer. S~stück nt document. S~zeichen nt character

schrill a shrill, adv -y

Schritt m -[e]s,-e step; (Entfernung) pace; (Gangart) walk; (der Hose) crotch; im S~ in step; (langsam) at walking pace; S~ halten mit (fig) keep pace with. S~macher m -s,- pace-maker. s~weise adv step by step

schroff a precipitous, adv -ly; (abweisend) brusque, adv -ly; (unvermittelt) abrupt, adv -ly; (Gegensatz) stark

schröpfen vt (fam) fleece

Schrot m & nt -[e]s coarse meal; (Blei-) small shot. s~en vt grind coarsely. S~flinte f shotgun

Schrott m -[e]s scrap[-metal]; zu S~ fahren (fam) write off. S~platz m scrapyard. s~reif a ready for the scrap-heap

schrubb|en vt/i (haben) scrub. S~er m -s,- [long-handled] scrubbing-brush

Schrulle f -,-n whim; alte S~e (fam) old crone. s~ig a cranky

schrumpfen vi (sein) shrink; (Obst:) shrivel

schrump[e]lig a wrinkled

Schrunde f -,-n crack; (*Spalte*) crevasse

Schub m -[e]s,-e (*Phys*) thrust; (*S~fach*) drawer; (*Menge*) batch. S~fach nt drawer. S~karre f, S~karren m wheelbarrow. S~lade f drawer

Schubs m -es,-e push, shove. s~en vt push, shove

schüchtern a shy, adv -ly; (*zaghaft*) tentative, adv -ly. S~heit f - shyness

Schuft m -[e]s,-e (*pej*) swine. s~en vi (*haben*) (*fam*) slave away

Schuh m -[e]s,-e shoe. S~anzieher m -s,- shoehorn. S~band nt (pl -bänder) shoelace. S~creme f shoe-polish. S~löffel m shoehorn. S~macher m -s,- shoemaker; (*zum Flicken*) [shoe] mender. S~werk nt shoes pl

Schul|abgänger m -s,- schoolleaver. S~arbeiten, S~aufgaben fpl homework sg. S~buch nt school-book

Schuld f -,-en guilt; (*Verantwortung*) blame; (*Geld-*) debt; S~en machen get into debt; S~ haben be to blame (an + dat for); jdm S~ geben blame s.o.; sich (*dat*) etwas zu S~en kommen lassen = sich etwas zuschulden kommen lassen, s. zuschulden □ s~ sein be to blame (an + dat for); s~ haben/jdm s~ geben (NEW) S~ haben/jdm S~ geben, s. Schuld. s~ haben/jdm s~ owe

schuldig a guilty (gen of); (*gebührend*) due; jdm etw s~ sein owe s.o. sth. S~keit f - duty

schuld|los a innocent. S~ner m -s,- debtor. S~spruch m guilty verdict

Schule f -,-n school; in der/die S~ at/to school. s~n vt train

Schüler|(in) m -s,- (f -,-nen) pupil. S~lotse m pupil acting as crossing warden

schul|frei a s~freier Tag day without school; wir haben morgen s~frei there's no school tomorrow. S~hof m [school] playground. S~jahr nt school year; (*Klasse*) form. S~junge m schoolboy. S~kind nt schoolchild. S~leiter(in) m(f) head [teacher]. S~mädchen nt schoolgirl. S~stunde f lesson

Schulter f -,-n shoulder. S~blatt nt shoulder-blade. s~n vt shoulder. S~tuch nt shawl

Schulung f - training

schummeln vi (*haben*) (*fam*) cheat

Schund m -[e]s trash. S~roman m trashy novel

Schuppe f -,-n scale; S~n pl dandruff sg. s~n (sich) vr flake [off]

Schuppen m -s,- shed

Schur f - shearing

Schür|eisen nt poker. s~en vt poke; (*fig*) stir up

schürf|en vt mine; sich (*dat*) das Knie s~en graze one's knee □ vi (*haben*) s~en nach prospect for. S~wunde f abrasion, graze

Schürhaken m poker

Schurke m -n,-n villain

Schürze f -,-n apron. s~n vt (*raffen*) gather [up]; tie (*Knoten*); purse (*Lippen*). S~njäger m (*fam*) womanizer

Schuss m -es,-ë (Schuß m -sses,-sse) shot; (*kleine Menge*) dash

Schüssel f -,-n bowl; (*TV*) dish

schusselig a (*fam*) scatter-brained

Schuss|fahrt (Schußfahrt) f (*Ski*) schuss. S~waffe f firearm

Schuster m -s,- = Schuhmacher

Schutt m -[e]s rubble. S~abladeplatz m rubbish dump

Schüttel|frost m shivering fit. s~n vt shake; sich s~n shake oneself/itself; (*vor Ekel*) shudder; jdm die Hand s~n shake s.o.'s hand

schütten vt pour; (*kippen*) tip; (*ver-*) spill □ vi (*haben*) es schüttet it is pouring [with rain]

Schutthaufen m pile of rubble

Schutz m -es protection; (*Zuflucht*) shelter; (*Techn*) guard; S~ suchen take refuge; unter dem S~ der Dunkelheit under cover of darkness. S~anzug m protective suit. S~blech nt mudguard. S~brille goggles pl

Schütze m -n,-n marksman; (*Tor-*) scorer; (*Astr*) Sagittarius; guter S~ good shot

schützen vt protect/(*Zuflucht gewähren*) shelter (vor + dat from) □ vi (*haben*) give protection/shelter (vor + dat from). s~d a protective, adv -ly

Schützenfest nt fair with shooting competition

Schutz|engel m guardian angel. S~heilige(r) m/f patron saint

Schützling m -s,-e charge; (*Protégé*) protégé

schutz|los a defenceless, helpless. S~mann m (pl -männer & -leute) policeman. S~umschlag m dust-jacket

Schwaben nt -s Swabia

schwäbisch a Swabian

schwach a (schwächer, schwächst) weak, adv -ly; (*nicht gut; gering*) poor, adv -ly; (*leicht*) faint, adv -ly

Schwäche f -,-n weakness. s~n vt weaken

Schwach|heit f - weakness. S~kopf m (*fam*) idiot

schwäch|lich *a* delicate. S~ling *m* -s,-e weakling

Schwachsinn *m* mental deficiency. s~ig *a* mentally deficient; (*fam*) idiotic

Schwächung *f* - weakening

schwafeln (*fam*) *vi* (*haben*) waffle □ *vt* talk

Schwager *m* -s,⸚ brother-in-law

Schwägerin *f* -,-nen sister-in-law

Schwalbe *f* -,-n swallow

Schwall *m* -[e]s torrent

Schwamm *m* -[e]s,⸚e sponge; (*SGer: Pilz*) fungus; (*essbar*) mushroom. s~ig *a* spongy; (*aufgedunsen*) bloated

Schwan *m* -[e]s,⸚e swan

schwanen *vi* (*haben*) (*fam*) mir schwante, dass I had a nasty feeling that

schwanger *a* pregnant

schwängern *vt* make pregnant

Schwangerschaft *f* -,-en pregnancy

Schwank *m* -[e]s,⸚e (*Theat*) farce

schwank|en *vi* (*haben*) sway; ⟨*Boot:*⟩ rock; (*schwanken*) fluctuate; (*unentschieden sein*) be undecided □ (*sein*) stagger. S~ung *f* -,-en fluctuation

Schwanz *m* -es,⸚e tail

schwänzen *vt* (*fam*) skip; die Schule s~ play truant

Schwarm *m* -[e]s,⸚e swarm; (*Fisch-*) shoal; (*fam: Liebe*) idol

schwärmen *vi* (*haben*) swarm; s~ für (*fam*) adore; (*verliebt sein*) have a crush on; s~ von (*fam*) rave about

Schwarte *f* -,-n (*Speck-*) rind; (*fam: Buch*) tome

schwarz *a* (schwärzer, schwärzest) black; (*fam: illegal*) illegal, *adv* -ly; s~er Markt black market; s~ gekleidet dressed in black; s~ auf weiß in black and white; s~ sehen (*fig*) be pessimistic; ins S~e treffen score a bull's-eye. S~ *nt* -[e]s,- black. S~arbeit *f* moonlighting. s~arbeiten *vi sep* (*haben*) moonlight. S~brot *nt* black bread. S~e(r) *m/f* black

Schwärze *f* - blackness. s~n *vt* blacken

Schwarz|fahrer *m* fare-dodger. S~handel *m* black market (mit in). S~händler *m* black marketeer. S~markt *m* black market. S~sehen† *vt sep* (*haben*) watch television without a licence; (*fig*) (NEW) s~ sehen, s. schwarz. S~wald *m* Black Forest. s~weiß *a* black and white

Schwatz *m* -es (*fam*) chat

schwatzen, (*SGer*) schwätzen *vi* (*haben*) chat; (*klatschen*) gossip; (*Sch*) talk [in class] □ *vt* talk

schwatzhaft *a* garrulous

Schwebe *f* - in der S~ (*fig*) undecided. S~bahn *f* cable railway. s~n *vi* (*haben*) float; (*fig*) be undecided; ⟨*Verfahren:*⟩ be pending; in Gefahr s~n be in danger □ (*sein*) float

Schwed|e *m* -n,-n Swede. S~en *nt* -s Sweden. S~in *f* -,-nen Swede. s~isch *a* Swedish

Schwefel *m* -s sulphur. S~säure *f* sulphuric acid

schweigen† *vi* (*haben*) be silent; ganz zu s~ von to say nothing of, let alone. S~ *nt* -s silence; zum S~ bringen silence. s~d *a* silent, *adv* -ly

schweigsam *a* silent; (*wortkarg*) taciturn

Schwein *nt* -[e]s,-e pig; (*Culin*) pork; (*sl*) (*schmutziger Mensch*) dirty pig; (*Schuft*) swine; S~ haben (*fam*) be lucky. S~ebraten *m* roast pork. S~efleisch *nt* pork. S~ehund *m* (*sl*) swine. S~erei *f* -,-en (*sl*) [dirty] mess; (*Gemeinheit*) dirty trick. S~estall *m* pigsty. s~isch *a* lewd. S~sleder *nt* pigskin

Schweiß *m* -es sweat

schweiß|en *vt* weld. S~er *m* -s,- welder

Schweiz (die) - Switzerland. S~er *a* & *m* -s,-, S~erin *f* -,-nen Swiss. s~erisch *a* Swiss

schwelen *vi* (*haben*) smoulder

schwelgen *vi* (*haben*) feast; s~ in (+ *dat*) wallow in

Schwelle *f* -,-n threshold; (*Eisenbahn-*) sleeper

schwell|en† *vi* (*sein*) swell. S~ung *f* -,-en swelling

Schwemme *f* -,-n watering-place; (*fig: Überangebot*) glut. s~n *vt* wash; an Land s~n wash up

Schwenk *m* -[e]s swing. s~en *vt* swing; (*schwingen*) wave; (*spülen*) rinse; in Butter s~en toss in butter □ *vi* (*sein*) turn

schwer *a* heavy; (*schwierig*) difficult; (*mühsam, streng*) hard; (*ernst*) serious; (*schlimm*) bad; 3 Pfund s~ sein weigh 3 pounds □ *adv* heavily; with difficulty; (*mühsam, streng*) hard; (*schlimm, sehr*) badly, seriously; s~ krank/verletzt seriously ill/injured; s~ arbeiten work hard; s~ hören be hard of hearing; etw s~ nehmen take sth seriously; jdm s~ fallen be hard for s.o.; es jdm s~ machen make it or things difficult for s.o.; sich s~ tun have difficulty (mit with); s~ zu sagen difficult or hard to say

Schwere *f* - heaviness; (*Gewicht*) weight; (*Schwierigkeit*) difficulty; (*Ernst*) gravity. S~losigkeit *f* - weightlessness

schwer|fallen† *vi sep* (*sein*) (NEW) s~ fallen, s. schwer. s~fällig *a* ponderous, *adv* -ly; (*unbeholfen*) clumsy, *adv* -ily. S~gewicht *nt* heavyweight. s~hörig *a* s~hörig sein be hard of hearing.

S~kraft f (Phys) gravity. s~krank a (NEW)s~ krank, s. schwer. s~lich adv hardly. s~machen vt sep (NEW)s~ machen, s. schwer. s~mütig a melancholic. s~nehmen† vt sep (NEW)s~ nehmen, s. schwer. S~punkt m centre of gravity; (fig) emphasis

Schwert nt -[e]s,-er sword. S~lilie f iris

schwer|tun† (sich) vr sep (NEW)sich ~ tun (sich), s. schwer. s~verbrecher m serious offender. s~verdaulich a (NEW)s~ verdaulich, s. verdaulich. s~verletzt a (NEW)s~ verletzt, s. schwer. s~wiegend a weighty

Schwester f -,-n sister; (Kranken-) nurse. s~lich a sisterly

Schwieger|eltern pl parents-in-law. S~mutter f mother-in-law. S~sohn m son-in-law. S~tochter f daughter-in-law. S~vater m father-in-law

Schwiele f -,-n callus

schwierig a difficult. S~keit f -,-en difficulty

Schwimm|bad nt swimming-baths pl. S~becken nt swimming-pool. s~en† vi (sein/haben) swim; (auf dem Wasser treiben) float. S~er m -s,- swimmer; (Techn) float. S~weste f life-jacket

Schwindel m -s dizziness, vertigo; (fam: Betrug) fraud; (Lüge) lie. S~anfall m dizzy spell. s~frei a ~frei sein have a good head for heights. s~n vi (haben) (lügen) lie; mir od mich s~t I feel dizzy

schwinden† vi (sein) dwindle; (vergehen) fade; (nachlassen) fail

Schwindl|er m -s,- liar; (Betrüger) fraud, con-man. s~ig a dizzy; mir ist od wird s~ig I feel dizzy

schwingen|en† vi (haben) (Phys) oscillate; (vibrieren) vibrate □ vt swing; wave (Fahne); (drohend) brandish. S~tür f swing-door. S~ung f -,-en oscillation; vibration

Schwips m -es,-e einen S~ haben (fam) be tipsy

schwirren vi (haben/sein) buzz; (surren) whirr

Schwitz|e f -,-n (Culin) roux. s~en vi (haben) sweat; ich s~e od mich s~t I am hot □ vt (Culin) sweat

schwören† vt/i (haben) swear (auf + acc by); Rache ~ swear revenge

schwul a (fam: homosexuell) gay

schwül a close. S~e f - closeness

schwülstig a bombastic, adv -ally

Schwung m -[e]s,-e swing; (Bogen) sweep; (Schnelligkeit) momentum; (Kraft) vigour; (Feuer) verve; (fam: Anzahl) batch; in S~ kommen gather momentum; (fig) get going. s~haft a brisk, adv -ly. s~los

a dull. s~voll a vigorous, adv -ly; ⟨Bogen, Linie⟩ sweeping; (mitreißend) spirited, lively

Schwur m -[e]s,-e vow; (Eid) oath. S~gericht nt jury [court]

sechs inv a, S~ f -,-en six; (Sch) ≈ fail mark. s~eckig a hexagonal. s~te(r,s) a sixth

sech|zehn inv a sixteen. s~zehnte(r,s) a sixteenth. s~zig inv a sixty. s~zigste(r,s) a sixtieth

sedieren vt sedate

See¹ m -s,-n /'ze:ən/ lake

See² f - sea; an die/der See to/at the seaside; auf See at sea. S~bad nt seaside resort. S~fahrt f [sea] voyage; (Schifffahrt) navigation. S~gang m schwerer S~gang rough sea. S~hund m seal. s~krank a seasick

Seele f -,-n soul. s~nruhig a calm, adv -ly

seelisch a psychological, adv -ly; (geistig) mental, adv -ly

Seelsorger m -s,- pastor

See|luft f sea air. S~macht f maritime power. S~mann m (pl -leute) seaman, sailor. S~not f in S~not in distress. S~räuber m pirate. S~reise f [sea] voyage. S~rose f water-lily. S~sack m kitbag. S~stern m starfish. S~tang m seaweed. s~tüchtig a seaworthy. S~weg m sea route; auf dem S~weg by sea. S~zunge f sole

Segel nt -s,- sail. S~boot nt sailing-boat. S~fliegen nt gliding. S~flieger m glider pilot. S~flugzeug nt glider. s~n vt/i (sein/haben) sail. S~schiff nt sailing-ship. S~sport m sailing. S~tuch nt canvas

Segen m -s blessing. s~sreich a beneficial; (gesegnet) blessed

Segler m -s,- yachtsman

Segment nt -[e]s,-e segment

segnen vt bless; gesegnet mit blessed with

sehen† vt/i see; watch ⟨Fernsehsendung⟩; jdn/etw wieder s~ see s.o./sth again; sich s~ lassen show oneself □ vi (haben) see; (blicken) look (auf + acc at); (ragen) show (aus above); gut/schlecht s~ have good/bad eyesight; vom S~ kennen know by sight; s~ nach keep an eye on; (betreuen) look after; (suchen) look for; darauf s~, dass see [to it] that ... s~swert, s~swürdig a worth seeing. S~swürdigkeit f -,-en sight

Sehkraft f sight, vision

Sehne f -,-n tendon; (eines Bogens) string

sehnen (sich) vr long (nach for)

sehnig a sinewy; (zäh) stringy

sehn|lich|st a ⟨Wunsch⟩ dearest □ adv longingly. S~sucht f - longing (nach for).

s~süchtig *a* longing, *adv* -ly; ⟨*Wunsch*⟩ dearest

sehr *adv* very; (*mit Verb*) very much; so s~, dass so much that

seicht *a* shallow

seid *s.* sein[1]; ihr s~ you are

Seide *f* -,-n silk

Seidel *nt* -s,- beer-mug

seiden *a* silk ... S~papier *nt* tissue paper. S~raupe *f* silk-worm. s~weich *a* silky-soft

seidig *a* silky

Seife *f* -,-n soap. S~npulver *nt* soap powder. S~nschaum *m* lather

seifig *a* soapy

seihen *vt* strain

Seil *nt* -[e]s,-e rope; (*Draht-*) cable. S~bahn *f* cable railway. s~springen† *vi* (*sein*) (*inf & pp only*) skip. S~tänzer(in) *m(f)* tightrope walker

sein[1] *vi* (*sein*) be; er ist Lehrer he is a teacher; sei still! be quiet! mir ist kalt/schlecht I am cold/feel sick; wie dem auch sei be that as it may; etw s~ lassen leave sth; (*aufhören mit*) stop sth □ *v aux* have; angekommen/gestorben s~ have arrived/died; er war/wäre gefallen he had/would have fallen; es ist/war viel zu tun/nichts zu sehen there is/was a lot to be done/nothing to be seen

sein[2] *poss pron* his; (*Ding, Tier*) its; (*nach man*) one's; sein Glück versuchen try one's luck. s~e(r,s) *poss pron* his; (*nach man*) one's own; das S~e *od* seine tun do one's share. s~erseits *adv* for his part. s~erzeit *adv* in those days. s~etwegen *adv* for his sake; (*wegen ihm*) because of him, on his account. um s~etwillen for his sake. s~ige *poss pron* der/die/das s~ige his

seinlassen† *vt sep* (NEW) sein lassen, *s.* sein[1]

seins *poss pron* his; (*nach man*) one's own

seit *conj & prep* (+ *dat*) since; s~ wann? since when? s~ einiger Zeit for some time [past]; ich wohne s~ zehn Jahren hier I've lived here for ten years. s~dem *conj adv* □ *adv* since then

Seite *f* -,-n side; (*Buch-*) page; S~ an S~ side by side; zur S~ legen/treten put/step aside; jds starke S~ s.o.'s strong point; auf der einen/anderen S~ (*fig*) on the one/other hand; von S~n (s~n) (+ *gen*) = vonseiten

seitens *prep* (+ *gen*) on the part of

Seiten|schiff *nt* [side] aisle. S~sprung *m* infidelity; einen S~sprung machen be unfaithful. S~stechen *nt* -s (*Med*) stitch. S~straße *f* side-street. S~streifen *m* verge; (*Autobahn-*) hard shoulder

seither *adv* since then

seit|lich *a* side ... □ *adv* at/on the side; s~lich von to one side of □ *prep* (+ *gen*) to one side of. s~wärts *adv* on/to one side; (*zur Seite*) sideways

Sekret *nt* -[e]s,-e secretion

Sekret|är *m* -s,-e secretary; (*Schrank*) bureau. S~ariat *nt* -[e]s,-e secretary's office. S~ärin *f* -,-nen secretary

Sekt *m* -[e]s [German] sparkling wine

Sekte *f* -,-n sect

Sektion /'tsi̯oːn/ *f* -,-en section; (*Sezierung*) autopsy

Sektor *m* -s,-en /-'toːrən/ sector

Sekundant *m* -en,-en (*Sport*) second

sekundär *a* secondary

Sekunde *f* -,-n second

selber *pron* (*fam*) = selbst

selbst *pron* oneself; ich/du/er/sie s~ I myself /you yourself/he himself/she herself; wir/ihr/sie s~ we ourselves/you yourselves/they themselves; ich schneide mein Haar s~ I cut my own hair; von s~ of one's own accord; (*automatisch*) automatically; s~ gemacht home-made □ *adv* even. S~achtung *f* self-esteem, self-respect

selbständig *a* = selbstständig. S~keit *f* - = Selbstständigkeit

Selbstaufopferung *f* self-sacrifice

Selbstbedienung *f* self-service. S~s-restaurant *nt* self-service restaurant, cafeteria

Selbst|befriedigung *f* masturbation. S~beherrschung *f* self-control. S~bestimmung *f* self-determination. S~bewusst (S~bewußt) *a* self-confident. S~bewusstsein (S~bewußtsein) *nt* self-confidence. S~bildnis *nt* self-portrait. S~erhaltung *f* self-preservation. s~gefällig *a* self-satisfied, smug, *adv* -ly. s~gemacht *a* (NEW) s~ gemacht, *s.* selbst. s~gerecht *a* self-righteous. S~gespräch *nt* soliloquy; S~gespräche führen talk to oneself. s~haftend *a* self-adhesive. s~herrlich *a* autocratic, *adv* -ally. S~hilfe *f* self-help. s~klebend *a* self-adhesive. S~kostenpreis *m* cost price. s~los *a* selfless, *adv* -ly. S~mitleid *nt* self-pity. S~mord *m* suicide. S~mörder(in) *m(f)* suicide. s~mörderisch *a* suicidal. S~porträt *nt* self-portrait. s~sicher *a* self-assured. S~sicherheit *f* self-assurance. s~ständig *a* independent, *adv* -ly; self-employed ⟨*Handwerker*⟩; sich s~ständig machen set up on one's own. S~ständigkeit *f* - independence. s~süchtig *a* selfish, *adv*

-ly. S∼tanken *nt* self-service *(for petrol)*.
s∼tätig *a* automatic, *adv* -ally. S∼ver-
sorgung *f* self-catering

selbstverständlich *a* natural, *adv* -ly;
etw für s∼ halten take sth for granted;
das ist s∼ that goes without saying; s∼!
of course! S∼keit *f* - matter of course; das
ist eine S∼keit that goes without saying

Selbst|verteidigung *f* self-defence.
S∼vertrauen *nt* self-confidence. S∼ver-
waltung *f* self-government. s∼zufrie-
den *a* complacent, *adv* -ly

selig *a* blissfully happy; *(Relig)* blessed;
(verstorben) late. S∼keit *f* - bliss

Sellerie *m* -s,-s & *f* -,- celeriac; *(Stangen-)*
celery

selten *a* rare *a adv* rarely, seldom; *(besonders)* exceptionally. S∼heit *f* -,-en rarity

Selterswasser *nt* seltzer [water]

seltsam *a* odd, *adv* -ly, strange, *adv* -ly.
s∼erweise *adv* oddly/strangely enough

Semester *nt* -s,- *(Univ)* semester

Semikolon *nt* -s,-s semicolon

Seminar *nt* -s,-e seminar; *(Institut)* department; *(Priester-)* seminary

Semmel *f* -,-n [bread] roll. S∼brösel *pl*
breadcrumbs

Senat *m* -[e]s,-e senate. S∼or *m* -s,-en
/-'to:rən/ senator

senden[1] *vt* send

sende|n[2] *vt (reg)* broadcast; *(über Funk)*
transmit, send. S∼r *m* -s,- [broadcasting]
station; *(Anlage)* transmitter. S∼reihe *f*
series

Sendung *f* -,-en consignment, shipment;
(Auftrag) mission; *(Radio, TV)* programme

Senf *m* -s mustard

sengend *a* scorching

senil *a* senile. S∼ität *f* - senility

Senior *m* -s,-en /-'o:rən/ senior; S∼en
senior citizens. S∼enheim *nt* old people's
home. S∼enteller *m* senior citizen's
menu

Senke *f* -,-n dip, hollow

Senkel *m* -s,- [shoe-]lace

senken *vt* lower; bring down *(Fieber,
Preise)*; bow *(Kopf)*; sich s∼ come down,
fall; *(absinken)* subside; *(abfallen)* slope
down

senkrecht *a* vertical, *adv* -ly. S∼e *f* -n,-n
perpendicular

Sensation /-'tsio:n/ *f* -,-en sensation.
s∼ell *a* sensational, *adv* -ly

Sense *f* -,-n scythe

sensib|el *a* sensitive, *adv* -ly. S∼ilität *f* -
sensitivity

sentimental *a* sentimental. S∼ität *f* -
sentimentality

separat *a* separate, *adv* -ly

September *m* -s,- September

Serenade *f* -,-n serenade

Serie /'ze:rjə/ *f* -,-n series; *(Briefmarken)*
set; *(Comm)* range. S∼nnummer *f* serial
number

seriös *a* respectable, *adv* -bly; *(zuverlässig)*
reliable, *adv* -bly; *(ernst gemeint)* serious

Serpentine *f* -,-n winding road; *(Kehre)*
hairpin bend

Serum *nt* -s,Sera serum

Service[1] /zɛr'vi:s/ *nt* -[s],- /-'vi:s[əs], -'vi:-
sə/ service, set

Service[2] /'zø:ɐvis/ *m* & *nt* -s -vis[əs]/
(Comm, Tennis) service

servier|en *vt/i (haben)* serve. S∼erin *f*
-,-nen waitress. S∼wagen *m* trolley

Serviette *f* -,-n napkin, serviette

Servus *int (Aust)* cheerio; *(Begrüßung)*
hallo

Sessel *m* -s,- armchair. S∼bahn *f*, S∼lift
m chair-lift

sesshaft (seßhaft) *a* settled; s∼ werden
settle down

Set /zɛt/ *nt & m* -[s],-s set; *(Deckchen)* place-
mat

setz|en *vt* put; *(abstellen)* set down; *(hin-)*
sit down *(Kind)*; move *(Spielstein)*;
(pflanzen) plant; *(schreiben, wetten)* put;
sich s∼en sit down; *(sinken)* settle □ *vi
(sein)* leap □ *vi (haben)* s∼en auf (+ *acc)*
back. S∼ling *m* -s,-e seedling

Seuche *f* -,-n epidemic

seufz|en *vi (haben)* sigh. S∼er *m* -s,- sigh

Sex /zɛks/ *m* -[es] sex. s∼istisch *a* sexist

Sexu|alität *f* - sexuality. s∼ell *a* sexual,
adv -ly

sexy /'zɛksi/ *inv a* sexy

sezieren *vt* dissect

Shampoo /ʃam'pu:/, Shampoon /ʃam'po:
n/ *nt* -s shampoo

siamesisch *a* Siamese

sich *refl pron* oneself; *(mit er/sie/es)* him-
self/herself/itself; *(mit pl)* themselves;
(mit Sie) yourself; *(pl)* yourselves; *(einander)* each other; s∼ kennen know
oneself/*(einander)* each other; s∼
waschen have a wash; s∼ *(dat)* die
Zähne putzen/die Haare kämmen clean
one's teeth/comb one's hair; s∼ *(dat)* das
Bein brechen break a leg; s∼ wun-
dern/schämen be surprised/ashamed;
s∼ gut lesen/verkaufen read/sell well;
von s∼ aus of one's own accord

Sichel *f* -,-n sickle

sicher *a* safe; *(gesichert)* secure; *(gewiss)*
certain; *(zuverlässig)* reliable, sure *(Urteil, Geschmack)*; steady *(Hand)*;
(selbstbewusst) self-confident; sich *(dat)*

etw *(gen)* s~ sein be sure of sth; bist du s~? are you sure? □ *adv* safely; securely; certainly; reliably; self-confidently; *(wahrscheinlich)* most probably; er kommt s~ he is sure to come; s~! certainly! s~gehen† *vi sep (sein) (fig)* be sure

Sicherheit *f* - safety; *(Pol, Psych, Comm)* security; *(Gewissheit)* certainty; *(Zuverlässigkeit)* reliability; *(des Urteils, Geschmacks)* surety; *(Selbstbewusstsein)* self-confidence. S~sgurt *m* safety-belt; *(Auto)* seat-belt. s~shalber *adv* to be on the safe side. S~snadel *f* safety-pin

sicherlich *adv* certainly; *(wahrscheinlich)* most probably

sicher|n *vt* secure; *(garantieren)* safeguard; *(schützen)* protect; put the safety-catch on *(Pistole)*; sich *(dat)* etw s~n secure sth. s~stellen *vt sep* safeguard; *(beschlagnahmen)* seize. S~ung *f* -,-en safeguard, protection; *(Gewehr-)* safety-catch; *(Electr)* fuse

Sicht *f* - view; *(Aussicht)* visibility; in S~ kommen come into view; auf lange S~ in the long term. s~bar *a* visible, *adv*-bly. s~en *vt* sight; *(durchsehen)* sift through. s~lich *a* obvious, *adv*-ly. S~vermerk *m* visa. S~weite *f* visibility; in/außer S~weite within/out of sight

sickern *vi (sein)* seep

sie *pron (nom) (sg)* she; *(Ding, Tier)* it; *(pl)* they; *(acc) (sg)* her; *(Ding, Tier)* it; *(pl)* them

Sie *pron* you; gehen/warten Sie! go/wait!

Sieb *nt* -[e]s,-e sieve; *(Tee-)* strainer. s~en[1] *vt* sieve, sift

sieben[2] *inv a*, S~ *f* -,-en seven. S~sachen *fpl (fam)* belongings. S~te(r,s) *a* seventh

sieb|te(r,s) *a* seventh. s~zehn *inv a* seventeen. s~zehnte(r,s) *a* seventeenth. s~zig *inv a* seventy. s~zigste(r,s) *a* seventieth

siede|n† *vt/i (haben)* boil; s~nd heiß boiling hot. S~punkt *m* boiling point

Siedl|er *m* -s,- settler. S~ung *f* -,-en [housing] estate; *(Niederlassung)* settlement

Sieg *m* -[e]s,-e victory

Siegel *nt* -s,- seal. S~ring *m* signet-ring

sieg|en *vi (haben)* win. S~er(in) *m* -s,- *(f* -,-nen) winner. s~reich *a* victorious

siezen *vt* jdn s~ call s.o. 'Sie'

Signal *nt* -s,-e signal. s~isieren *vt* signal

signieren *vt* sign

Silbe *f* -,-n syllable. S~ntrennung *f* word-division

Silber *nt* -s silver. S~hochzeit *f* silver wedding. s~n *a* silver. S~papier *nt* silver paper

Silhouette /zɪˈluɛtə/ *f* -,-n silhouette

Silizium *nt* -s silicon

Silo *m & nt* -s,-s silo

Silvester *nt* -s New Year's Eve

simpel *a* simple, *adv*-ply; *(einfältig)* simple-minded

Simplex *nt* -,-e simplex

Sims *m & nt* -es,-e ledge; *(Kamin-)* mantelpiece

Simul|ant *m* -en,-en malingerer. s~ieren *vt* feign; *(Techn)* simulate □ *vi (haben)* pretend; *(sich krank stellen)* malinger

simultan *a* simultaneous, *adv*-ly

sind *s*. sein[1]; wir/sie s~ we/they are

Sinfonie *f* -,-n symphony

singen† *vt/i (haben)* sing

Singular *m* -s,-e singular

Singvogel *m* songbird

sinken† *vi (sein)* sink; *(nieder-)* drop; *(niedriger werden)* go down, fall; den Mut s~ lassen lose courage

Sinn *m* -[e]s,-e sense; *(Denken)* mind; *(Zweck)* point; im S~ haben have in mind; in gewissem S~e in a sense; es hat keinen S~ it is pointless; nicht bei S~en sein be out of one's mind. S~bild *nt* symbol. s~en† *vi (haben)* think; auf Rache s~en plot one's revenge

sinnlich *a* sensory; *(sexuell)* sensual; *(Genüsse)* sensuous. S~keit *f* - sensuality; sensuousness

sinn|los *a* senseless, *adv*-ly; *(zwecklos)* pointless, *adv*-ly. s~voll *a* meaningful; *(vernünftig)* sensible, *adv*-bly

Sintflut *f* flood

Siphon /ˈziːfɔ̃/ *m* -s,-s siphon

Sipp|e *f* -,-n clan. S~schaft *f* - clan; *(Pack)* crowd

Sirene *f* -,-n siren

Sirup *m* -s,-e syrup; *(schwarzer)* treacle

Sitte *f* -,-n custom; S~n manners. s~nlos *a* immoral

sittlich *a* moral, *adv*-ly. S~keit *f* - morality. S~keitsverbrecher *m* sex offender

sittsam *a* well-behaved; *(züchtig)* demure, *adv*-ly

Situation /-ˈtsjoːn/ *f* -,-en situation. s~iert *a* gut/schlecht s~iert well/badly off

Sitz *m* -es,-e seat; *(Passform)* fit

sitzen† *vi (haben)* sit; *(sich befinden)* be; *(passen)* fit; *(fam: treffen)* hit home; [im Gefängnis] s~ *(fam)* be in jail; s~ bleiben remain seated; *(fam) (Sch)* stay or be kept down; *(nicht heiraten)* be left on the shelf; s~ bleiben auf *(+ dat)* be left with; jdn s~ lassen let s.o. sit down; *(fam) (Sch)* keep s.o. down; *(nicht heiraten)* leave s.o.; *(im Stich lassen)* leave s.o. in the lurch. s~bleiben† *vi sep (sein)* ⟨NEW⟩ s~ bleiben, *s.* sitzen. s∼d *a* seated; *(Tätigkeit)* sedentary. s∼lassen† *vt sep* NEW s∼ lassen, *s.* sitzen

Sitz|gelegenheit *f* seat. S∼platz *m* seat. S∼ung *f* -,-en session

Sizilien /-jən/ *nt* -s Sicily

Skala *f* -,-len scale; *(Reihe)* range

Skalpell *nt* -s,-e scalpel

skalpieren *vt* scalp

Skandal *m* -s,-e scandal. s∼ös *a* scandalous

skandieren *vt* scan ⟨*Verse*⟩; chant ⟨*Parolen*⟩

Skandinav|ien /-jən/ *nt* -s Scandinavia. s∼isch *a* Scandinavian

Skat *m* -s skat

Skelett *nt* -[e]s,-e skeleton

Skep|sis *f* - scepticism. s∼tisch *a* sceptical, *adv* -ly; *(misstrauisch)* doubtful, *adv* -ly

Ski /ʃiː/ *m* -s,-er ski; Ski fahren od laufen ski. S∼fahrer(in), S∼läufer(in) *m(f)* -s,- *(f* -,-nen) skier. S∼sport *m* skiing

Skizze *f* -,-n sketch. s∼enhaft *a* sketchy, *adv* -ily. s∼ieren *vt* sketch

Sklav|e *m* -n,-n slave. S∼erei *f* - slavery. S∼in *f* -,-nen slave. s∼isch *a* slavish, *adv* -ly

Skorpion *m* -s,-e scorpion; *(Astr)* Scorpio

Skrupel *m* -s,- scruple. s∼los *a* unscrupulous

Skulptur *f* -,-en sculpture

skurril *a* absurd, *adv* -ly

Slalom *m* -s,-s slalom

Slang /slɛŋ/ *m* -s slang

Slaw|e *m* -n,-n, S∼in *f* -,-nen Slav. S∼isch *a* Slav; *(Lang)* Slavonic

Slip *m* -s,-s briefs *pl*

Smaragd *m* -[e]s,-e emerald

Smoking *m* -s,-s dinner jacket, *(Amer)* tuxedo

Snob *m* -s,-s snob. S∼ismus *m* - snobbery. s∼istisch *a* snobbish

so *adv* so; *(so sehr)* so much; *(auf diese Weise)* like this/that; *(solch)* such; *(fam: sowieso)* anyway; *(fam: umsonst)* free; *(fam: ungefähr)* about; nicht so schnell/viel not so fast/much; so gut/bald wie as good/soon as; so ein Mann a man like that; so ein Zufall! what a coincidence! so nicht not like that; mir ist so, als ob I feel as if; so oder so in any case; eine Stunde oder so an hour or so; so um zehn Mark *(fam)* about ten marks; [es ist] gut so that's fine; so, das ist geschafft there, that's done; so? really? so kommt doch! come on then! □ *conj (also)* so; *(dann)* then; so gern ich auch käme as much as I would like to come; so dass (daß) = sodass

sobald *conj* as soon as

Söckchen *nt* -s,- [ankle] sock

Socke *f* -,-n sock

Sockel *m* -s,- plinth, pedestal

Socken *m* -s,- sock

Soda *nt* -s soda

sodass *conj* so that

Sodawasser *nt* soda water

Sodbrennen *nt* -s heartburn

soeben *adv* just [now]

Sofa *nt* -s,-s settee, sofa

sofern *adv* provided [that]

sofort *adv* at once, immediately; *(auf der Stelle)* instantly. s∼ig *a* immediate

Software /'zɔftveːɐ̯/ *f* - software

sogar *adv* even

sogenannt *a* so-called

sogleich *adv* at once

Sohle *f* -,-n sole; *(Tal-)* bottom

Sohn *m* -[e]s,-e son

Sojabohne *f* soya bean

solange *conj* as long as

solch *inv pron* such; s∼ ein(e) such a; s∼ einer/eine/eins one/*(Person)* someone like that. s∼e(r,s) *pron* such; ein s∼er Mann/eine s∼e Frau a man/woman like that; ich habe s∼e Angst I am so afraid □ *(substantivisch)* ein s∼er/eine s∼e/ ein s∼es one/*(Person)* someone like that; s∼ *(pl)* those; *(Leute)* people like that

Sold *m* -[e]s *(Mil)* pay

Soldat *m* -en,-en soldier

Söldner *m* -s,- mercenary

solidarisch *a* s∼e Handlung act of solidarity; sich s∼ erklären declare one's solidarity

Solidarität *f* - solidarity

solid|e *a* solid, *adv* -ly; *(haltbar)* sturdy, *adv* -ily; *(sicher)* sound, *adv* -ly; *(anständig)* respectable, *adv* -bly

Solist(in) *m* -en,-en *(f* -,-nen) soloist

Soll *nt* -s *(Comm)* debit; *(Produktions-)* quota

sollen† *v aux* er soll warten he is to wait; *(möge)* let him wait; was soll ich machen? what shall I do? du sollst nicht lügen you shouldn't tell lies; du sollst nicht töten *(liter)* thou shalt not kill; ihr sollt jetzt still sein! will you be quiet now! du solltest dich schämen you ought to *or* should be ashamed of yourself; es hat nicht sein s∼ it was not to be; ich hätte es nicht tun s∼ I ought not to *or* should not have done it; er soll sehr nett/ reich sein he is supposed to be very nice/rich; sollte es regnen, so ... if it should rain then ...; das soll man nicht [tun] you're not supposed to [do that]; soll

ich [mal versuchen]? shall I [try]? soll
er doch! let him! was soll's! so what!

Solo nt -s,-los & -li solo. **s~** adv solo

somit adv therefore, so

Sommer m -s,-. summer. **S~ferien** pl
summer holidays. **s~lich** a summery;
(Sommer-) summer … □ adv **s~lich**
warm as warm as summer.
S~schlussverkauf (**S~schlußverkauf**)
m summer sale. **S~sprossen** fpl freckles.
s~sprossig a freckled

Sonate f -,-n sonata

Sonde f -,-n probe

Sonder|angebot nt special offer. **s~bar**
a odd, adv -ly. **S~fahrt** f special excursion. **S~fall** m special case. **s~gleichen**
adv eine Gemeinheit/Grausamkeit
s~gleichen unparalleled mean-
ness/cruelty. **s~lich** a particular, adv -ly;
(sonderbar) odd, adv -ly. **S~ling** m -s,-e
crank. **S~marke** f special stamp

sondern conj but; nicht nur … s~ auch
not only … but also

Sonder|preis m special price. **S~schule**
f special school. **S~zug** m special train

sondieren vt sound out

Sonett nt -[e]s,-e sonnet

Sonnabend m -s,-e Saturday. **s~s** adv on
Saturdays

Sonne f -,-n sun. **s~n** (sich) vr sun oneself;
(fig) bask (in + dat in)

Sonnen|aufgang m sunrise. **s~baden**
vi (haben) sunbathe. **S~bank** f sun-bed.
S~blume f sunflower. **S~brand** m sun-
burn. **S~brille** f sun-glasses pl. **S~ener-
gie** f solar energy. **S~finsternis** f solar
eclipse. **S~milch** f sun-tan lotion. **S~öl**
nt sun-tan oil. **S~schein** m sunshine.
S~schirm m sunshade. **S~stich** m sun-
stroke. **S~uhr** f sundial. **S~untergang**
m sunset. **S~wende** f solstice

sonnig a sunny

Sonntag m -s,-e Sunday. **s~s** adv on Sun-
days

sonst adv (gewöhnlich) usually; (im Übrigen) apart from that; (andernfalls)
otherwise, or [else]; wer/was/wie/wo
s~? who/what/how/where else? **s~ nie-
mand/nichts** no one/nothing else; **s~
noch jemand/etwas**? anyone/anything
else? **s~ noch Fragen**? any more questions? **s~ jemand** od wer
someone/(fragend, verneint) anyone else;
(irgendjemand) [just] anyone; **s~ wie**
some/(fragend, verneint) any other way;
s~ wo somewhere/(fragend, verneint)
anywhere else; (irgendwo) [just] anywhere. **s~ig** a other. **s~jemand**
pron NEW **s~ jemand**, s. sonst. **s~wer**
pron NEW **s~ wer**, s. sonst. **s~wie**

adv NEW **s~ wie**, s. sonst. **s~wo**
adv NEW **s~ wo**, s. sonst

sooft conj whenever

Sopran m -s,-e soprano

Sorge f -,-n worry (um about); (Fürsorge)
care; in **S~** sein be worried; sich (dat)
S~n machen worry; keine **S~**! don't
worry! **s~n** vi (haben) **s~n für** look after,
care for; (vorsorgen) provide for; (sich
kümmern) see to; dafür **s~n, dass** see [to
it] or make sure that o vr sich **s~n** worry.
s~nfrei a carefree. **s~nvoll** a worried,
adv -ly. **S~recht** nt (Jur) custody

Sorg|falt f - care. **s~fältig** a careful, adv
-ly. **s~los** a careless, adv -ly; (unbekümmert) carefree. **s~sam** a careful, adv -ly

Sorte f -,-n kind, sort; (Comm) brand

sort|ieren vt sort [out]; (Comm) grade.
S~iment nt -[e]s,-e range

sosehr conj however much

Soße f -,-n sauce; (Braten-) gravy; (Salat-)
dressing

Souffl|eur /zuˈfløːɐ̯/ m -s,-e, **S~euse**
/-øːzə/ f -,-n prompter. **s~ieren** vi (haben) prompt

Souvenir /zuvəˈniːɐ̯/ nt -s,-s souvenir

souverän /zuvəˈrɛːn/ a sovereign; (fig:
überlegen) expert, adv -ly. **S~ität** f - sovereignty

soviel conj however much; **s~ ich weiß**
as far as I know □ adv NEW **so viel**, s. viel

soweit conj as far as; (insoweit) [in] so far
as □ adv NEW **so weit**, s. weit

sowenig conj however little □ adv NEW
so wenig, s. wenig

sowie conj as well as; (sobald) as soon as

sowieso adv anyway, in any case

sowjet|isch a Soviet. **S~union** f - Soviet
Union

sowohl adv **s~ … als** od wie auch … …
as well as …; **s~ er als auch seine
Frau** both he and his wife

sozial a social, adv -ly; (Einstellung, Beruf)
caring. **S~arbeit** f social work. **S~arbei-
ter(in)** m(f) social worker. **S~demokrat**
m social democrat. **S~hilfe** f social security

Sozialis|mus m - socialism. **S~t** m -en,
-en socialist. **s~tisch** a socialist

Sozial|versicherung f National Insur-
ance. **S~wohnung** f ≈ council flat

Sozio|loge m -n,-n sociologist. **S~ogie** f
- sociology

Sozius m -,-se (Comm) partner; (Beifahrersitz) pillion

sozusagen adv so to speak

Spachtel m -s,- & f -,-n spatula

Spagat m -[e]s,-e (Aust) string; **s~
machen** do the splits pl

Spaghetti, Spagetti *pl* spaghetti *sg*

spähen *vi (haben)* peer

Spalier *nt* -s,-e trellis; S∼ stehen line the route

Spalt *m* -[e]s,-e crack; *(im Vorhang)* chink

Spalt|e *f* -,-n crack, crevice; *(Gletscher-)* crevasse; *(Druck-)* column; *(Orangen-)* segment. s∼en *vt* split; sich s∼en split. S∼ung *f* -,-en splitting; *(Kluft)* split; *(Phys)* fission

Span *m* -[e]s,-̈e [wood] chip; *(Hobel-)* shaving

Spange *f* -,-n clasp; *(Haar-)* slide; *(Zahn-)* brace; *(Arm-)* bangle

Span|ien /-jən/ *nt* -s Spain. S∼ier *m* -s,-, S∼ierin *f* -,-nen Spaniard. s∼isch *a* Spanish. S∼isch *nt* -[s] *(Lang)* Spanish

Spann *m* -[e]s instep

Spanne *f* -,-n span; *(Zeit-)* space; *(Comm)* margin

spann|en *vt* stretch; put up *(Leine)*; *(straffen)* tighten; *(an-)* harness (an + *acc* to); den Hahn s∼en cock the gun; sich s∼en tighten □ *vi (haben)* be too tight. s∼end *a* exciting. S∼er *m* -s,- *(fam)* Peeping Tom. S∼ung *f* -,-en tension; *(Erwartung)* suspense; *(Electr)* voltage

Spar|buch *nt* savings book. S∼büchse *f* money-box. s∼en *vt/i (haben)* save; *(sparsam sein)* economize (mit/an + *dat* on); sich *(dat)* die Mühe s∼en save oneself the trouble. S∼er *m* -s,- saver

Spargel *m* -s,- asparagus

Spar|kasse *f* savings bank. S∼konto *nt* deposit account

spärlich *a* sparse, *adv* -ly; *(dürftig)* meagre; *(knapp)* scanty, *adv* -ily

Sparren *m* -s,- rafter

sparsam *a* economical, *adv* -ly; *(Person)* thrifty. S∼keit *f* - economy; thrift

Sparschwein *nt* piggy bank

spartanisch *a* Spartan

Sparte *f* -,-n branch; *(Zeitungs-)* section; *(Rubrik)* column

Spaß *m* -es,-̈e fun; *(Scherz)* joke; im/aus/zum S∼ for fun; S∼ machen be fun; *(Person:)* be joking; es macht mir keinen S∼ I don't enjoy it; viel S∼! have a good time! s∼en *vi (haben)* joke. s∼ig *a* amusing, funny. S∼vogel *m* joker

Spast|iker *m* -s,- spastic. s∼isch *a* spastic

spät *a & adv* late; wie s∼ ist es? what time is it? zu s∼ too late; zu s∼ kommen be late. s∼abends *adv* late at night

Spatel *m* -s,- & *f* -,-n spatula

Spaten *m* -s,- spade

später *a* later; *(zukünftig)* future □ *adv* later

spätestens *adv* at the latest

Spatz *m* -en,-en sparrow

Spätzle *pl (Culin)* noodles

spazieren *vi (sein)* stroll; s∼ gehen go for a walk. s∼gehen† *vi sep (sein)* (NEW) s∼ gehen, s. spazieren

Spazier|gang *m* walk; einen S∼gang machen go for a walk. S∼gänger(in) *m* -s,-(*f* -,-nen) walker. S∼stock *m* walking-stick

Specht *m* -[e]s,-e woodpecker

Speck *m* -s bacon; *(fam: Fettpolster)* fat. s∼ig *a* greasy

Spedi|teur /ʃpedi'tøːɐ̯/ *m* -s,-e haulage/*(für Umzüge)* removals contractor. S∼tion /-'tsi̯oːn/ *f* -,-en carriage, haulage; *(Firma)* haulage/*(für Umzüge)* removals firm

Speer *m* -[e]s,-e spear; *(Sport)* javelin

Speiche *f* -,-n spoke

Speichel *m* -s saliva

Speicher *m* -s,- warehouse; *(dial: Dachboden)* attic; *(Computer)* memory. s∼n *vt* store

speien† *vt* spit; *(erbrechen)* vomit

Speise *f* -,-n food; *(Gericht)* dish; *(Pudding)* blancmange. S∼eis *nt* ice-cream. S∼kammer *f* larder. S∼karte *f* menu. s∼n *vt/i (haben)* eat; zu Abend s∼n have dinner □ *vt* feed. S∼röhre *f* oesophagus. S∼saal *m* dining-room. S∼wagen *m* dining-car

Spektakel *m* -s *(fam)* noise

spektakulär *a* spectacular

Spektrum *nt* -s,-tra spectrum

Spekul|ant *m* -en,-en speculator. S∼ation /-'tsi̯oːn/ *f* -,-en speculation. s∼ieren *vi (haben)* speculate; s∼ieren auf (+ *acc*) *(fam)* hope to get

Spelze *f* -,-n husk

spendabel *a* generous

Spende *f* -,-n donation. s∼n *vt* donate; give *(Blut, Schatten)*; Beifall s∼n applaud. S∼r *m* -s,- donor; *(Behälter)* dispenser

spendieren *vt* pay for; jdm etw/ein Bier s∼ treat s.o. to sth/stand s.o. a beer

Spengler *m* -s,- *(SGer)* plumber

Sperling *m* -s,-e sparrow

Sperre *f* -,-n barrier; *(Verbot)* ban; *(Comm)* embargo. s∼n *vt* close; *(ver-)* block; *(verbieten)* ban; cut off *(Strom, Telefon)*; stop *(Scheck, Kredit)*; s∼n in (+ *acc*) put in *(Gefängnis, Käfig)*; sich s∼n balk (gegen at); gesperrt gedruckt *(Typ)* spaced

Sperr|holz *nt* plywood. s∼ig *a* bulky. S∼müll *m* bulky refuse. S∼stunde *f* closing time

Spesen *pl* expenses

spezial|isieren (sich) vr specialize (auf + acc in). S~ist m -en,-en specialist. S~ität f -,-en speciality

speziell a special, adv -ly

spezifisch a specific, adv -ally

Sphäre /'sfɛ:rə/ f -,-n sphere

spicken vt (Culin) lard; gespickt mit (fig) full of □ vi (haben) (fam) crib (bei from)

Spiegel m -s,- mirror; (Wasser-, Alkohol-) level. S~bild nt reflection. S~ei nt fried egg. s~n vt reflect; sich s~n be reflected □ vi (haben) reflect [the light]; (glänzen) gleam. S~ung f -,-en reflection

Spiel nt -[e]s,-e game; (Spielen) playing; (Glücks-) gambling; (Schau-) play; (Satz) set; ein S~ Karten a pack/(Amer) deck of cards; auf dem S~ stehen be at stake; aufs S~ setzen risk. S~art f variety. S~automat m fruit machine. S~bank f casino. S~dose f musical box. s~en vt/i (haben) play; (im Glücksspiel) gamble; (vortäuschen) act; (Roman:) be set (in + dat in); s~en mit (fig) toy with. s~end a (mühelos) effortless, adv -ly

Spieler|(in) m -s,- (f -,-nen) player; (Glücks-) gambler. S~ei f -,-en amusement; (Kleinigkeit) trifle

Spiel|feld nt field, pitch. S~gefährte m, S~gefährtin f playmate. S~karte f playing-card. S~marke f chip. S~plan m programme. S~platz m playground. S~raum m (fig) scope; (Techn) clearance. S~regeln fpl rules [of the game]. S~sachen fpl toys. S~verderber m -s,- spoilsport. S~waren fpl toys. S~warengeschäft nt toyshop. S~zeug m toy; (S~sachen) toys pl

Spieß m -es,-e spear; (Brat-) spit; (für Schaschlik) skewer; (Fleisch-) kebab; den S~ umkehren turn the tables on s.o. S~bürger m [petit] bourgeois. s~bürgerlich a bourgeois. s~en vt etw auf etw (acc) s~en spear sth with sth. S~er m -s,- [petit] bourgeois. s~ig a bourgeois. S~ruten fpl S~ruten laufen run the gauntlet

Spike[s]reifen /'ʃpaɪk[s]-/ m studded tyre

Spinat m -s spinach

Spind m & nt -[e]s,-e locker

Spindel f -,-n spindle

Spinne f -,-n spider

spinn|en vt/i (haben) spin; er spinnt (fam) he's crazy. S~ennetz nt spider's web. S~[en]gewebe nt, S~webe f -,-n cobweb

Spion m -s,-e spy

Spionage /ʃpjo'na:ʒə/ f - espionage, spying; S~ treiben spy. S~abwehr f counter-espionage

spionieren vi (haben) spy

Spionin f -,-nen [woman] spy

Spiral|e f -,-n spiral. s~ig a spiral

Spiritis|mus m - spiritualism. s~tisch a spiritualist

Spirituosen pl spirits

Spiritus m - alcohol; (Brenn-) methylated spirits pl. S~kocher m spirit stove

Spital nt -s,-er (Aust) hospital

spitz a pointed; (scharf) sharp; (schrill) shrill; (Winkel) acute; s~e Bemerkung dig. S~bube m scoundrel; (Schlingel) rascal. s~bübisch a mischievous, adv -ly

Spitze f -,-n point; (oberer Teil) top; (vorderer Teil) front; (Pfeil-, Finger-, Nasen-) tip; (Schuh-, Strumpf-) toe; (Zigarren-, Zigaretten-) holder; (Höchstleistung) maximum; (Tex) lace; (fam: Anspielung) dig; an der S~ liegen be in the lead

Spitzel m -s,- informer

spitzen vt sharpen; purse (Lippen); prick up (Ohren); sich s~ auf (+ acc) (fam) look forward to. S~geschwindigkeit f top speed

spitz|findig a over-subtle. S~hacke f pickaxe. S~name m nickname

Spleen /ʃpli:n/ m -s,-e obsession; einen S~ haben be crazy. s~ig a eccentric

Splitter m -s,- splinter. s~n vi (sein) shatter. s~[faser]nackt a (fam) stark naked

sponsern vt sponsor

spontan a spontaneous, adv -ly

sporadisch a sporadic, adv -ally

Spore f -,-n (Biol) spore

Sporn m -[e]s, Sporen spur; einem Pferd die Sporen geben spur a horse

Sport m -[e]s sport; (Hobby) hobby. S~art f sport. S~fest nt sports day. S~ler m -s,- sportsman. S~lerin f -,-nen sportswoman. s~lich a sports ...; (fair) sporting, adv -ly; (flott, schlank) sporty. S~platz m sports ground. S~verein m sports club. S~wagen m sports car; (Kinder-) push-chair, (Amer) stroller

Spott m -[e]s mockery. s~billig a & adv dirt cheap

spötteln vi (haben) mock; s~ über (+ acc) poke fun at

spotten vi (haben) mock; s~ über (+ acc) make fun of; (höhnend) ridicule

spöttisch a mocking, adv -ly

Sprach|e f -,-n language; (Sprechfähigkeit) speech; zur S~e bringen bring up. S~fehler m speech defect. S~labor nt language laboratory. s~lich a linguistic, adv -ally. s~los a speechless

Spray /ʃpreː/ nt & m -s,-s spray. S~dose f aerosol [can]

Sprech|anlage f intercom. S~chor m chorus; im S~chor rufen chant

sprechen† vi (haben) speak/(sich unterhalten) talk (über + acc/von about/of); Deutsch/Englisch s~ speak German/English □ vt speak; (sagen, aufsagen) say; pronounce (Urteil); schuldig s~ find guilty; jdn s~ speak to s.o.; Herr X ist nicht zu s~ Mr X is not available

Sprecher(in) m -s,- (f -,-nen) speaker; (Radio, TV) announcer; (Wortführer) spokesman, f spokeswoman

Sprechstunde f consulting hours pl; (Med) surgery. S~nhilfe f (Med) receptionist

Sprechzimmer nt consulting room

spreizen vt spread

Sprengel m -s,- parish

spreng|en vt blow up; blast (Felsen); (fig) burst; (begießen) water; (mit Sprenger) sprinkle; dampen (Wäsche). S~er m -s,- sprinkler. S~kopf m warhead. S~körper m explosive device. S~stoff m explosive

Spreu f - chaff

Sprich|wort nt (pl -wörter) proverb. s~wörtlich a proverbial

sprießen† vi (sein) sprout

Springbrunnen m fountain

spring|en† vi (sein) jump; (Schwimmsport) dive; (Ball:) bounce; (spritzen) spurt; (zer-) break; (rissig werden) crack; (SGer: laufen) run. S~er m -s,- jumper; (Kunst-) diver; (Schach) knight. S~reiten nt show-jumping. S~seil nt skipping-rope

Sprint m -s,-s sprint

Sprit m -s (fam) petrol

Spritz|e f -,-n syringe; (Injektion) injection; (Feuer-) hose. s~en vt spray; (be-, ver-) splash; (Culin) pipe; (Med) inject □ vi (haben) splash; (Fett:) spit □ vi (sein) splash; (hervor-) spurt; (fam: laufen) dash. S~er m -s,- splash; (Schuss) dash. s~ig a lively; (Wein, Komödie) sparkling. S~tour f (fam) spin

spröde a brittle; (trocken) dry; (rissig) chapped; (Stimme) harsh; (abweisend) aloof

Spross m -es,-e (Sproß m -sses, -sse) shoot

Sprosse f -,-n rung. S~nkohl m (Aust) Brussels sprouts pl

Sprössling (Sprößling) m -s,-e (fam) offspring

Sprotte f -,-n sprat

Spruch m -[e]s,·e saying; (Denk-) motto; (Zitat) quotation. S~band nt (pl -bänder) banner

Sprudel m -s,- sparkling mineral water. s~n vi (haben/sein) bubble

Sprüh|dose f aerosol [can]. s~en vt spray □ vi (sein) (Funken:) fly; (fig) sparkle. S~regen m fine drizzle

Sprung m -[e]s,·e jump, leap; (Schwimmsport) dive; (fam: Katzen-) stone's throw; (Riss) crack; auf einen S~ (fam) for a moment. S~brett nt springboard. s~haft a erratic; (plötzlich) sudden, adv -ly. S~schanze f ski-jump. S~seil nt skipping-rope

Spucke f - spit. s~n vt/i (haben) spit; (sich übergeben) be sick

Spuk m -[e]s,-e [ghostly] apparition. s~en vi (haben) (Geist:) walk; in diesem Haus s~t es this house is haunted

Spülbecken nt sink

Spule f -,-n spool

Spüle f -,-n sink unit; (Becken) sink

spulen vt spool

spül|en vt rinse; (schwemmen) wash; Geschirr s~en wash up □ vi (haben) flush [the toilet]. S~kasten m cistern. S~mittel nt washing-up liquid. S~tuch nt dishcloth

Spur f -,-en track; (Fahr-) lane; (Fährte) trail; (Anzeichen) trace; (Hinweis) lead; keine od nicht die S~ (fam) not in the least

spürbar a noticeable, adv -bly

spuren vi (haben) (fam) toe the line

spür|en vt feel; (seelisch) sense. S~hund m tracker dog

spurlos adv without trace

spurten vi (sein) put on a spurt; (fam: laufen) sprint

sputen (sich) vr hurry

Staat m -[e]s,-en state; (Land) country; (Putz) finery. s~lich a state ... □ adv by the state

Staatsangehörig|e(r) m/f national. S~keit f - nationality

Staats|anwalt m state prosecutor. S~beamte(r) m civil servant. S~besuch m state visit. S~bürger(in) m(f) national. S~mann m (pl -männer) statesman. S~streich m coup

Stab m -[e]s,·e rod; (Gitter-) bar; (Sport) baton; (Mitarbeiter-) team; (Mil) staff

Stäbchen ntpl chopsticks

Stabhochsprung m pole-vault

stabil a stable; (gesund) robust; (solide) sturdy, adv -ily. s~isieren vt stabilize; sich s~isieren stabilize. S~ität f - stability

Stachel m -s,- spine; (Gift-) sting; (Spitze) spike. S~beere f goose-berry. S~draht *m* barbed wire. s~ig *a* prickly. S~schwein *nt* porcupine

Stadion *nt* -s,-ien stadium

Stadium *nt* -s,-ien stage

Stadt *f* -,-̈e town; (*Groß*-) city

Städt|chen *nt* -s,- small town. s~isch *a* urban; (*kommunal*) municipal

Stadt|mauer *f* city wall. S~mitte *f* town centre. S~plan *m* street map. S~teil *m* district. S~zentrum *nt* town centre

Staffel *f* -,-n team; (*S~lauf*) relay; (*Mil*) squadron

Staffelei *f* -,-en easel

Staffel|lauf *m* relay race. s~n *vt* stagger; (*abstufen*) grade

Stagnation /-'tsjo:n/ *f* - stagnation. s~ieren *vi* (*haben*) stagnate

Stahl *m* -s steel. S~beton *m* reinforced concrete

Stall *m* -[e]s,-̈e stable; (*Kuh*-) shed; (*Schweine*-) sty; (*Hühner*-) coop; (*Kaninchen*-) hutch ·

Stamm *m* -[e]s-̈e trunk; (*Sippe*) tribe; (*Kern*) core; (*Wort*-) stem. S~baum *m* family tree; (*eines Tieres*) pedigree

stammeln *vt/i* (*haben*) stammer

stammen *vi* (*haben*) come/(*zeitlich*) date (*von/aus* from); das Zitat stammt von Goethe the quotation is from Goethe

Stamm|gast *m* regular. S~halter *m* son and heir

stämmig *a* sturdy

Stamm|kundschaft *f* regulars *pl*. S~lokal *nt* favourite pub. S~tisch *m* table reserved for the regulars; (*Treffen*) meeting of the regulars

stampf|en *vi* (*haben*) stamp; (*Maschine:*) pound; mit den Füßen s~en stamp one's feet □ *vi* (*sein*) tramp □ *vt* pound; mash (*Kartoffeln*). S~kartoffeln *fpl* mashed potatoes

Stand *m* -[e]s,-̈e standing position; (*Zustand*) state; (*Spiel*-) score; (*Höhe*) level; (*gesellschaftlich*) class; (*Verkaufs*-) stall; (*Messe*-) stand; (*Taxi*-) rank; auf den neuesten S~ bringen update; in S~ halten/setzen = instand halten/setzen, s. instand; im/außer S~e sein = instande/außerstande sein, s. imstande, außerstande; zu S~e bringen/kommen = zustande bringen/kommen, s. zustande

Standard *m* -s,-s standard. s~isieren *vt* standardize

Standarte *f* -,-n standard

Standbild *nt* statue

Ständchen *nt* -s,- serenade; jdm ein S~ bringen serenade s.o.

Ständer *m* -s,- stand; (*Geschirr*-, *Platten*-) rack; (*Kerzen*-) holder

Standes|amt *nt* registry office. S~beamte(r) *m* registrar. S~unterschied *m* class distinction

stand|haft *a* steadfast, *adv* -ly. s~halten† *vi sep* (*haben*) stand firm; etw (*dat*) s~halten stand up to sth

ständig *a* constant, *adv* -ly; (*fest*) permanent, *adv* -ly

Stand|licht *nt* sidelights *pl*. S~ort *m* position; (*Firmen*-) location; (*Mil*) garrison. S~pauke *f* (*fam*) dressing-down. S~punkt *m* point of view. S~spur *f* hard shoulder. S~uhr *f* grandfather clock

Stange *f* -,-n bar; (*Holz*-) pole; (*Gardinen*-) rail; (*Hühner*-) perch; (*Zimt*-) stick; von der S~ (*fam*) off the peg

Stängel *m* -s,- stalk, stem

Stangen|bohne *f* runner bean. S~brot *nt* French bread

Stanniol *nt* -s tin foil. S~papier *nt* silver paper

stanzen *vt* stamp; (*aus*-) stamp out; punch 〈*Loch*〉

Stapel *m* -s,- stack, pile; vom S~ laufen be launched. S~lauf *m* launch[ing]. s~n *vt* stack *or* pile up; sich s~n pile up

stapfen *vi* (*sein*) tramp, trudge

Star[1] *m* -[e]s,-e starling

Star[2] *m* -[e]s 〈*Med*〉 [grauer] S~ cataract; grüner S~ glaucoma

Star[3] *m* -s,-s 〈*Theat, Sport*〉 star

stark *a* (stärker, stärkst) strong; (*Motor*) powerful; (*Verkehr, Regen*) heavy; (*Hitze, Kälte*) severe; (*groß*) big; (*schlimm*) bad; (*dick*) thick; (*korpulent*) stout □ *adv* strongly; heavily; badly; (*sehr*) very much

Stärk|e *f* -,-n (*s. stark*) strength; power; thickness; stoutness; (*Größe*) size; (*Mais*-, *Wäsche*-) starch. S~emehl *nt* cornflour. s~en *vt* strengthen; starch 〈*Wäsche*〉; sich s~en fortify oneself. S~ung *f* -,-en strengthening; (*Erfrischung*) refreshment

starr *a* rigid, *adv* -ly; (*steif*) stiff, *adv* -ly; 〈*Blick*〉 fixed; (*unbeugsam*) inflexible, *adv* -bly

starren *vi* (*haben*) stare; vor Schmutz s~ be filthy

starr|köpfig *a* stubborn. S~sinn *m* obstinacy. s~sinnig *a* obstinate, *adv* -ly

Start *m* -s,-s start; 〈*Aviat*〉 take-off. S~bahn *f* runway. s~en *vi* (*sein*) start; 〈*Aviat*〉 take off; (*aufbrechen*) set off; (*teilnehmen*) compete □ *vt* start; 〈*fig*〉 launch

Station /-'tsjo:n/ *f* -,-en station; (*Haltestelle*) stop; (*Abschnitt*) stage; (*Med*) ward; S~ machen break one's journey; bei freier S~ all found. s~är *adv* as an inpatient. s~ieren *vt* station

statisch *a* static

Statist(in) *m* -en,-en (*f* -,-nen) (*Theat*) extra

Statisti|k *f* -,-en statistics *sg*; (*Aufstellung*) statistics *pl*. s∼sch *a* statistical, *adv* -ly

Stativ *nt* -s,-e (*Phot*) tripod

statt *prep* (+ *gen*) instead of; an seiner s∼ in his place; an Kindes s∼ annehmen adopt; s∼ dessen NEW s∼dessen □ *conj* s∼ dessen; s∼ etw zu tun instead of doing sth. s∼dessen *adv* instead

Stätte *f* -,-n place

statt|finden† *vi sep* (*haben*) take place. s∼haft *a* permitted

stattlich *a* imposing; (*beträchtlich*) considerable

Statue */ˈʃtaːtuə/ f* -,-n statue

Statur *f* - build, stature

Status *m* - status. S∼symbol *nt* status symbol

Statut *nt* -[e]s,-en statute

Stau *m* -[e]s,-s congestion; (*Auto*) [traffic] jam; (*Rück-*) tailback

Staub *m* -[e]s dust; s∼ wischen dust; s∼ saugen vacuum, hoover

Staubecken *nt* reservoir

staub|en *vi* (*haben*) raise dust; es s∼t it's dusty. s∼ig *a* dusty. s∼saugen *vt/i* (*haben*) vacuum, hoover. S∼sauger *m* vacuum cleaner, Hoover (P). S∼tuch *nt* duster

Staudamm *m* dam

Staude *f* -,-n shrub

stauen *vt* dam up; sich s∼ accumulate; (*Autos*) form a tailback

staunen *vi* (*haben*) be amazed *or* astonished. S∼ *nt* -s amazement, astonishment

Stau|see *m* reservoir. S∼ung *f* -,-en congestion; (*Auto*) [traffic] jam

Steak */ʃteːk, stek/ nt* -s,-s steak

stechen† *vt* stick (in + *acc* in); (*verletzen*) prick; (*mit Messer*) stab; (*Insekt:*) sting; (*Mücke:*) bite; (*gravieren*) engrave □ *vi* (*haben*) prick; (*Insekt:*) sting; (*Mücke:*) bite; (*mit Stechuhr*) clock in/out; in See s∼ put to sea. s∼d *a* stabbing; (*Geruch*) pungent

Stech|ginster *m* gorse. S∼kahn *m* punt. S∼mücke *f* mosquito. S∼palme *f* holly. S∼uhr *f* time clock

Steck|brief *m* 'wanted' poster. S∼dose *f* socket. s∼en *vt* put; (*mit Nadel, Reißzwecke*) pin; (*pflanzen*) plant □ *vi* (*haben*) be; (*fest-*) be stuck; s∼ bleiben get stuck; den Schlüssel s∼ lassen leave the key in the lock; hinter etw (*dat*) s∼en (*fig*) be behind sth

Stecken *m* -s,- (*SGer*) stick

stecken|bleiben† *vi sep* (*sein*) NEW s∼ bleiben, s. stecken. s∼lassen† *vt sep* NEW s∼ lassen, s. stecken. S∼pferd *nt* hobby-horse

Steck|er *m* -s,- (*Electr*) plug. S∼ling *m* -s,-e cutting. S∼nadel *f* pin. S∼rübe *f* swede

Steg *m* -[e]s,-e foot-bridge; (*Boots-*) landing-stage; (*Brillen-*) bridge. S∼reif *m* aus dem S∼reif extempore

stehen† *vi* (*haben*) stand; (*sich befinden*) be; (*still-*) be stationary; (*Maschine, Uhr:*) have stopped; s∼ bleiben remain standing; (*Gebäude:*) be left standing; (*anhalten*) stop; (*Motor:*) stall; (*Zeit:*) stand still; s∼ lassen leave [standing]; sich (*dat*) einen Bart s∼ lassen grow a beard; vor dem Ruin s∼ face ruin; zu jdm/etw s∼ (*fig*) stand by s.o./sth; gut s∼ (*Getreide, Aktien:*) be doing well; (*Chancen:*) be good; jdm [gut] s∼ suit s.o.; sich gut s∼ be on good terms; es steht 3 zu 1 the score is 3–1; es steht schlecht um ihn he is in a bad way. S∼ *nt* -s standing; zum S∼ bringen/kommen bring/come to a standstill. s∼bleiben† *vi sep* (*sein*) NEW s∼ bleiben, s. stehen. s∼d *a* standing; (*sich nicht bewegend*) stationary; (*Gewässer*) stagnant. s∼lassen† *vt sep* NEW s∼ lassen, s. stehen

Steh|lampe *f* standard lamp. S∼leiter *f* step-ladder

stehlen† *vt/i* (*haben*) steal; sich s∼ steal, creep

Steh|platz *m* standing place. S∼vermögen *nt* stamina, staying-power

steif *a* stiff, *adv* -ly. S∼heit *f* - stiffness

Steig|bügel *m* stirrup. S∼eisen *nt* crampon

steigen† *vi* (*sein*) climb; (*hochgehen*) rise, go up; (*Schulden, Spannung:*) mount; s∼ auf (+ *acc*) climb on [to] (*Stuhl*); climb (*Berg, Leiter*); get on (*Pferd, Fahrrad*); s∼ in (+ *acc*) climb into; get in (*Auto*); get on (*Bus, Zug*); s∼ aus climb out of; get out of (*Bett, Auto*); get off (*Bus, Zug*); einen Drachen s∼ lassen fly a kite; s∼de Preise rising prices

steiger|n *vt* increase; sich s∼n increase; (*sich verbessern*) improve. S∼ung *f* -,-en increase; improvement; (*Gram*) comparison

Steigung *f* -,-en gradient; (*Hang*) slope

steil *a* steep, *adv* -ly. S∼küste *f* cliffs *pl*

Stein *m* -[e]s,-e stone; (*Ziegel-*) brick; (*Spiel-*) piece. s∼alt *a* ancient. S∼bock *m* ibex; (*Astr*) Capricorn. S∼bruch *m* quarry. S∼garten *m* rockery. S∼gut *nt* earthenware. s∼hart *a* rock-hard. s∼ig *a* stony. s∼igen *vt* stone. S∼kohle *f* [hard] coal. s~reich a (fam) very rich. S~schlag m rock fall

Stelle f -,-n place; (Fleck) spot; (Abschnitt) passage; (Stellung) job, post; (Büro) office; (Behörde) authority; kahle S~ bare patch; auf der S~ immediately; an deiner S~ in your place

stellen vt put; (aufrecht) stand; set (Wecker, Aufgabe); ask (Frage); make (Antrag, Forderung, Diagnose); zur Verfügung s~ provide; lauter/leiser s~ turn up/down; kalt/warm s~ chill/keep hot; sich s~ [go and] stand; give oneself up (der Polizei to the police); sich tot/schlafend s~ pretend to be dead/asleep; gut gestellt sein be well off

Stellen|anzeige f job advertisement. S~vermittlung f employment agency. s~weise adv in places

Stellung f -,-en position; (Arbeit) job; S~ nehmen make a statement (zu on). s~slos a jobless. S~suche f job-hunting

stellvertret|end a deputy ... □ adv as a deputy; s~end für jdn on s.o.'s behalf. S~er m deputy

Stellwerk nt signal-box

Stelzen fpl stilts. s~ vi (sein) stalk

stemmen vt press; lift (Gewicht); sich s~ gegen brace oneself against

Stempel m -s,- stamp; (Post-) post-mark; (Präge-) die; (Feingehalts-) hallmark. s~n vt stamp; hallmark (Silber); cancel (Marke)

Stengel m -s,- (NEW) Stängel

Steno f - (fam) shorthand

Steno|gramm nt -[e]s,-e shorthand text. S~graphie, S~grafie f - shorthand. s~graphieren, s~grafieren vt take down in shorthand □ vi (haben) do shorthand. S~typistin f -,-nen shorthand typist

Steppdecke f quilt

Steppe f -,-n steppe

Stepptanz (Steptanz) m tap-dance

sterben† vi (sein) die (an + dat of); im S~ liegen be dying

sterblich a mortal. S~e(r) m/f mortal. S~keit f - mortality

stereo adv in stereo. S~anlage f stereo [system]

stereotyp a stereotyped

steril a sterile. s~isieren vt sterilize. S~ität f - sterility

Stern m -[e]s,-e star. S~bild nt constellation. S~chen nt -s,- asterisk. S~kunde f astronomy. S~schnuppe f -,-n shooting star. S~warte f -,-n observatory

stetig a steady, adv -ily

stets adv always

Steuer¹ nt -s,- steering-wheel; (Naut) helm; am S~ at the wheel

Steuer² f -,-n tax

Steuer|bord nt -[e]s starboard [side]. S~erklärung f tax return. s~frei a & adv tax-free. S~mann m (pl -leute) helmsman; (beim Rudern) cox. s~n vt steer; (Aviat) pilot; (Techn) control □ vi (haben) be at the wheel/(Naut) helm □ (sein) head (nach for). s~pflichtig a taxable. S~rad nt steering-wheel. S~ruder nt helm. S~ung f - steering; (Techn) controls pl. S~zahler m -s,- taxpayer

Stewardess /'stju:ɐdɛs/ f -,-en (Stewardeß f -,-ssen) air hostess, stewardess

Stich m -[e]s,-e prick; (Messer-) stab; (S~wunde) stab wound; (Bienen-) sting; (Mücken-) bite; (Schmerz) stabbing pain; (Näh-) stitch; (Kupfer-) engraving; (Kartenspiel) trick; S~ ins Rötliche tinge of red; jdn im S~ lassen leave s.o. in the lurch; (Gedächtnis-) fail s.o. s~eln vi (haben) make snide remarks

Stich|flamme f jet of flame. s~haltig a valid. S~probe f spot check. S~wort nt (pl -wörter) headword; (pl -worte) (Theat) cue; S~worte notes

stick|en vt/i (haben) embroider. S~erei f - embroidery

stickig a stuffy

Stickstoff m nitrogen

Stiefbruder m stepbrother

Stiefel m -s,- boot

Stief|kind nt stepchild. S~mutter f stepmother. S~mütterchen nt -s,- pansy. S~schwester f stepsister. S~sohn m stepson. S~tochter f stepdaughter. S~vater m stepfather

Stiege f -,-n stairs pl

Stiel m -[e]s,-e handle; (Blumen-, Gläser-) stem; (Blatt-) stalk

Stier m -[e]s,-e bull; (Astr) Taurus

stieren vi (haben) stare

Stier|kampf m bullfight

Stift¹ m -[e]s,-e pin; (Nagel) tack; (Blei-) pencil; (Farb-) crayon

Stift² nt -[e]s,-e endowed] foundation. s~en vt endow; (spenden) donate; create (Unheil, Verwirrung); bring about (Frieden). S~er m -s,- founder; (Spender) donor. S~ung f -,-en foundation; (Spende) donation

Stigma nt -s (fig) stigma

Stil m -[e]s,-e style; in großem S~ in style. s~isiert a stylized. s~istisch a stylistic, adv -ally

still a quiet, adv -ly; (reglos; ohne Kohlensäure) still; (heimlich) secret, adv -ly; der

S∼e Ozean the Pacific; im S∼en (s∼en) secretly; (bei sich) inwardly. S∼e f - quiet; (Schweigen) silence

Stilleben nt (NEW) Stillleben

stillegen vt sep (NEW) stilllegen

stillen vt satisfy; quench ⟨Durst⟩; stop ⟨Schmerzen, Blutung⟩; breast-feed ⟨Kind⟩

still|**halten**† vi sep keep still. S∼leben nt still life. s∼legen vt sep close down. S∼legung f -,-en closure

Stillschweigen nt silence. s∼d a silent, adv -ly; (fig) tacit, adv -ly

still|**sitzen**† vi sep (haben) sit still. S∼stand m standstill; zum S∼stand bringen/kommen stop. s∼stehen† vi sep (haben) stand still; (anhalten) stop; (Verkehr:) be at a standstill

Stil|**möbel** pl reproduction furniture sg. s∼voll a stylish, adv -ly

Stimm|**bänder** ntpl vocal cords. s∼berechtigt a entitled to vote. S∼bruch m er ist im S∼bruch his voice is breaking

Stimme f -,-n voice; (Wahl-) vote

stimmen vi (haben) be right; (wählen) vote; stimmt das? is that right/(wahr) true? ⬜ vt tune; jdn traurig/fröhlich s∼ make s.o. feel sad/happy

Stimm|**enthaltung** f abstention. S∼recht nt right to vote

Stimmung f -,-en mood; (Atmosphäre) atmosphere. S∼svoll a full of atmosphere

Stimmzettel m ballot-paper

stimulieren vt stimulate

stink|**en**† vi (haben) smell/(stark) stink (nach di). S∼tier nt skunk

Stipendium nt -s,-ien scholarship; (Beihilfe) grant

Stirn f -,-en forehead; die S∼ bieten (+ dat) defy. S∼runzeln nt -s frown

stöbern vi (haben) rummage

stochern vi (haben) s∼ in (+ dat) poke ⟨Feuer⟩; pick at ⟨Essen⟩; pick ⟨Zähne⟩

Stock¹ m -[e]s,-e stick; (Ski-) pole; (Bienen-) hive; (Rosen-) bush; (Reb-) vine

Stock² m -[e]s,- storey, floor. S∼bett nt bunk-beds pl. s∼dunkel a (fam) pitch-dark

stock|**en** vi (haben) stop; (Verkehr:) come to a standstill; (Person:) falter. s∼end a hesitant, adv -ly. s∼taub a (fam) stone-deaf. S∼ung f -,-en hold-up

Stockwerk nt storey, floor

Stoff m -[e]s,-e substance; (Tex) fabric, material; (Thema) subject [matter]; (Gesprächs-) topic. S∼tier nt soft toy. S∼wechsel m metabolism

stöhnen vi (haben) groan, moan. S∼ nt -s groan, moan

stoisch a stoic, adv -ally

Stola f -,-len stole

Stollen m -s,- gallery; (Kuchen) stollen

stolpern vi (sein) stumble; s∼ über (+ acc) trip over

stolz a proud (auf + acc of), adv -ly. S∼ m -es pride

stolzieren vi (sein) strut

stopfen vt stuff; (stecken) put; (ausbessern) darn ⬜ vi (haben) be constipating; (fam: essen) guzzle

Stopp m -s,-s stop. s∼ int stop!

stoppel|**ig** a stubbly. S∼n fpl stubble sg

stopp|**en** vt stop; (Sport) time ⬜ vi (haben) stop. S∼schild nt stop sign. S∼uhr f stopwatch

Stöpsel m -s,- plug; (Flaschen-) stopper

Storch m -[e]s,-e stork

Store /ʃtoːɐ/ m -s,-s net curtain

stören vt disturb; disrupt ⟨Rede, Sitzung⟩; jam ⟨Sender⟩; (missfallen) bother; stört es Sie, wenn ich rauche? do you mind if I smoke? ⬜ vi (haben) be a nuisance; entschuldigen Sie, dass ich störe I'm sorry to bother you

stornieren vt cancel

störrisch a stubborn, adv -ly

Störung f -,-en (s. stören) disturbance; disruption; (Med) trouble; (Radio) interference; technische S∼ technical fault

Stoß m -es,-e push, knock; (mit Ellbogen) dig; (Hörner-) butt; (mit Waffe) thrust; (Schwimm-) stroke; (Ruck) jolt; (Erd-) shock; (Stapel) stack, pile. S∼dämpfer m -s,- shock absorber

stoßen† vt push, knock; (mit Füßen) kick; (mit Kopf, Hörnern) butt; (an-) poke, nudge; (treiben) thrust; sich s∼ knock oneself; sich (dat) den Kopf s∼ hit one's head ⬜ vi (haben) push; s∼ an (+ acc) knock against; (angrenzen) adjoin ⬜ vi (sein) s∼ gegen knock against; bump into ⟨Tür⟩; s∼ auf (+ acc) bump into; (entdecken) come across; strike ⟨Öl⟩; (fig) meet with ⟨Ablehnung⟩

Stoß|**stange** f bumper. S∼verkehr m rush-hour traffic. S∼zahn m tusk. S∼zeit f rush-hour

stottern vt/i (haben) stutter, stammer

Str. abbr (Straße) St

Straf|**anstalt** f prison. S∼arbeit f (Sch) imposition. s∼bar a punishable; sich s∼bar machen commit an offence

Strafe f -,-n punishment; (Jur & fig) penalty; (Geld-) fine; (Freiheits-) sentence. s∼n vt punish

straff a tight, taut. s∼en vt tighten; sich s∼en tighten

Strafgesetz nt criminal law

sträf|lich a criminal, adv -ly. S~ling m -s,-e prisoner

Straf|mandat nt (Auto) [parking/speeding] ticket. S~porto nt excess postage. S~predigt f (fam) lecture. S~raum m penalty area. S~stoss (S~stoß) m penalty. S~tat f crime. S~zettel m (fam) = S~mandat

Strahl m -[e]s,-en ray; (einer Taschenlampe) beam; (Wasser-) jet. S~en vi (haben) shine; (funkeln) sparkle; (lächeln) beam. S~enbehandlung f radiotherapy. s~end a shining; sparkling; beaming; radiant (Schönheit). S~entherapie f radiotherapy. S~ung f - radiation

Strähn|e f -,-n strand. s~ig a straggly

stramm a tight, adv -ly; (kräftig) sturdy; (gerade) upright

Strampel|höschen /-sç-/ nt -s,- rompers pl. s~n vi (haben) (Baby:) kick

Strand m -[e]s,-e beach. s~en vi (sein) run aground; (fig) fail. S~korb m wicker beach-chair. S~promenade f promenade

Strang m -[e]s,-e rope

Strapaz|e f -,-n strain. s~ieren vt be hard on; tax (Nerven, Geduld). s~ierfähig a hard-wearing. s~iös a exhausting

Strass m - & -es (Straß m - & -sses) paste

Straße f -,-n road; (in der Stadt auch) street; (Meeres-) strait; auf der S~ in the road/street. S~nbahn f tram, (Amer) streetcar. S~nkarte f road-map. S~nlaterne f street lamp. S~nsperre f roadblock

Strat|egie f -,-n strategy. s~egisch a strategic, adv -ally

sträuben vt ruffle up (Federn); sich s~ (Fell, Haar:) stand on end; (fig) resist

Strauch m -[e]s, Sträucher bush

straucheln vi (sein) stumble

Strauß¹ m -es, Sträuße bunch [of flowers]; (Bukett) bouquet

Strauß² m -es,-e ostrich

Strebe f -,-n brace, strut

streben vi (haben) strive (nach for) □ vi (sein) head (nach/zu for)

Streb|er m -s,- pushy person; (Sch) swot. s~sam a industrious

Strecke f -,-n stretch, section; (Entfernung) distance; (Rail) line; (Route) route

strecken vt stretch; (aus-) stretch out; (gerade machen) straighten; (Culin) thin down; sich s~ stretch; (sich aus-) stretch out; den Kopf aus dem Fenster s~ put one's head out of the window

Streich m -[e]s,-e prank, trick; jdm einen S~ spielen play a trick on s.o.

streicheln vt stroke

streichen† vt spread; (weg-) smooth; (an-) paint; (aus-) delete; (kürzen) cut □ vi (haben) s~ über (+ acc) stroke

Streicher m -s,- string-player; die S~ the strings

Streichholz nt match. S~schachtel f matchbox

Streich|instrument nt stringed instrument. S~käse m cheese spread. S~orchester nt string orchestra. S~ung f -,-en deletion; (Kürzung) cut

streifen vt brush against; (berühren) touch; (verletzen) graze; (fig) touch on (Thema); (ziehen) slip (über + acc over); mit dem Blick s~ glance at □ vi (sein) roam

Streifen m -s,- stripe; (Licht-) streak; (auf der Fahrbahn) line; (schmales Stück) strip

Streif|enwagen m patrol car. s~ig a streaky. S~schuss (S~schuß) m glancing shot; (Wunde) graze

Streik m -s,-s strike; in den S~ treten go on strike. S~brecher m strike-breaker, (pej) scab. s~en vi (haben) strike; (fam) refuse; (versagen) pack up. S~ende(r) m striker. S~posten m picket

Streit m -[e]s,-e quarrel; (Auseinandersetzung) dispute. s~en† vr/i (haben) [sich] s~en quarrel. s~ig a jdm etw s~ig machen dispute s.o.'s right to sth. S~igkeiten fpl quarrels. S~kräfte fpl armed forces. s~süchtig a quarrelsome

streng a strict, adv -ly; (Blick, Ton) stern, adv -ly; (rau, nüchtern) severe, adv -ly; (Geschmack) sharp; s~ genommen strictly speaking. S~e f - strictness; sternness; severity. s~genommen adv NEW s~ genommen, s. streng. s~gläubig a strict; (orthodox) orthodox. s~stens adv strictly

Stress m -es,-e (Streß m -sses,-sse) stress

stressig a (fam) stressful

streuen vt spread; (ver-) scatter; sprinkle (Zucker, Salz); die Straßen s~ grit the roads

streunen vi (sein) roam; s~der Hund stray dog

Strich m -[e]s,-e line; (Feder-, Pinsel-) stroke; (Morse-, Gedanken-) dash; gegen den S~ the wrong way; (fig) against the grain. S~kode m bar code. S~punkt m semicolon

Strick m -[e]s,-e cord; (Seil) rope; (fam: Schlingel) rascal

strick|en vt/i (haben) knit. S~jacke f cardigan. S~leiter f rope-ladder. S~nadel f knitting-needle. S~waren fpl knitwear sg. S~zeug nt knitting

striegeln *vt* groom

strikt *a* strict, *adv* -ly

strittig *a* contentious

Stroh *nt* -[e]s straw. S~blumen *fpl* everlasting flowers. S~dach *nt* thatched roof. s~gedeckt *a* thatched. S~halm *m* straw

Strolch *m* -[e]s,-e (*fam*) rascal

Strom *m* -[e]s,-̈e river; (*Menschen-, Auto-, Blut-*) stream; (*Tränen-*) flood; (*Schwall*) torrent; (*Electr*) current, power; gegen den S~ (*fig*) against the tide; es regnet in Strömen it is pouring with rain. s~abwärts *adv* downstream. s~aufwärts *adv* upstream

strömen *vi* (*sein*) flow; (*Menschen, Blut:*) stream, pour; s~der Regen pouring rain

Strom|kreis *m* circuit. s~linienförmig *a* streamlined. S~sperre *f* power cut

Strömung *f* -,-en current

Strophe *f* -,-n verse

strotzen *vi* (*haben*) be full (vor + *dat* of); vor Gesundheit s~d bursting with health

Strudel *m* -s,- whirlpool; (*SGer Culin*) strudel

Struktur *f* -,-en structure; (*Tex*) texture

Strumpf *m* -[e]s,-̈e stocking; (*Knie-*) sock. S~band *nt* (*pl* -bänder) suspender, (*Amer*) garter. S~bandgürtel *m* suspender/(*Amer*) garter belt. S~halter *m* = S~band. S~hose *f* tights *pl*, (*Amer*) pantyhose

Strunk *m* -[e]s,-̈e stalk; (*Baum-*) stump

struppig *a* shaggy

Stube *f* -,-n room. s~nrein *a* house-trained

Stuck *m* -s stucco

Stück *nt* -[e]s,-e piece; (*Zucker-*) lump; (*Seife*) tablet; (*Theater-*) play; (*Gegenstand*) item; (*Exemplar*) specimen; 20 S~ Vieh 20 head of cattle; ein S~ (*Entfernung*) some way; aus freien S~en voluntarily. S~chen *nt* -s,- [little] bit. s~weise *adv* bit by bit; (*einzeln*) singly

Student|(in) *m* -en,-en (*f* -,-nen) student. s~isch *a* student ...

Studie /-jə/ *f* -,-n study

studier|en *vt/i* (*haben*) study. S~zimmer *nt* study

Studio *nt* -s,-s studio

Studium *nt* -s,-ien studies *pl*

Stufe *f* -,-n step; (*Treppen-*) stair; (*Raketen-*) stage; (*Niveau*) level. s~n *vt* terrace; (*staffeln*) grade

Stuhl *m* -[e]s,-̈e chair; (*Med*) stools *pl*. S~gang *m* bowel movement

stülpen *vt* put (über + *acc* over)

stumm *a* dumb; (*schweigsam*) silent, *adv* -ly

Stummel *m* -s,- stump; (*Zigaretten-*) butt; (*Bleistift-*) stub

Stümper *m* -s,- bungler. s~haft *a* incompetent, *adv* -ly

stumpf *a* blunt; (*Winkel*) obtuse; (*glanzlos*) dull; (*fig*) apathetic, *adv* -ally. S~ *m* -[e]s, -̈e stump

Stumpfsinn *m* apathy; (*Langweiligkeit*) tedium. s~ig *a* apathetic, *adv* -ally; (*langweilig*) tedious

Stunde *f* -,-n hour; (*Sch*) lesson

stunden *vt* jdm eine Schuld s~ give s.o. time to pay a debt

Stunden|kilometer *mpl* kilometres per hour. s~lang *adv* for hours. S~lohn *m* hourly rate. S~plan *m* timetable. s~weise *adv* by the hour

stündlich *a* & *adv* hourly

Stups *m* -es,-e nudge; (*Schubs*) push. s~en *vt* nudge; (*schubsen*) push. S~nase *f* snub nose

stur *a* pigheaded; (*phlegmatisch*) stolid, *adv* -ly; (*unbeirrbar*) dogged, *adv* -ly

Sturm *m* -[e]s,-̈e gale; (*schwer*) storm; (*Mil*) assault

stürm|en *vi* (*haben*) (*Wind:*) blow hard; es s~t it's blowing a gale □ *vi* (*sein*) rush □ *vt* storm; (*bedrängen*) besiege. S~er *m* -s,- forward. s~isch *a* stormy; (*Überfahrt*) rough; (*fig*) tumultuous, *adv* -ly; (*ungestüm*) tempestuous, *adv* -ly

Sturz *m* -es,-̈e [heavy] fall; (*Preis-, Kurs-*) sharp drop; (*Pol*) overthrow

stürzen *vi* (*sein*) fall [heavily]; (*in die Tiefe*) plunge; (*Preise, Kurse:*) drop sharply; (*Regierung:*) fall; (*eilen*) rush □ *vt* throw; (*umkippen*) turn upside down; turn out (*Speise, Kuchen*); (*Pol*) overthrow, topple; sich s~ throw oneself (aus/in + *acc* out of/into); sich s~ auf (+ *acc*) pounce on

Sturz|flug *m* (*Aviat*) dive. S~helm *m* crash-helmet

Stute *f* -,-n mare

Stütze *f* -,-n support; (*Kopf-, Arm-*) rest

stutzen *vi* (*haben*) stop short □ *vt* trim; (*Hort*) cut back; (*kupieren*) crop

stützen *vt* support; (*auf-*) rest; sich s~ auf (+ *acc*) lean on; (*beruhen*) be based on

Stutzer *m* -s,- dandy

stutzig *a* puzzled; (*misstrauisch*) suspicious

Stützpunkt *m* (*Mil*) base

Subjekt *nt* -[e]s,-e subject. s~iv *a* subjective, *adv* -ly

Subskription /-'tsjo:n/ *f* -,-en subscription

Substantiv *nt* -s,-e noun

Substanz *f* -,-en substance

subtil a subtle, adv -tly

subtra|hieren vt subtract. S~ktion /-'tsio:n/ f -,-en subtraction

Subvention /-'tsio:n/ f -,-en subsidy. s~ieren vt subsidize

subversiv a subversive

Such|e f - search; auf der S~e nach looking for. s~en vt look for; (intensiv) search for; seek ⟨Hilfe, Rat⟩; 'Zimmer gesucht' 'room wanted' □ vi (haben) look, search ⟨nach dat⟩. S~er m -s,- (Phot) viewfinder

Sucht f -,-ë addiction; (fig) mania

süchtig a addicted. S~e(r) m/f addict

Süd m -[e]s south. S~afrika nt South Africa. S~amerika nt South America. s~deutsch a South German

Süden m -s south; nach S~ south

Süd|frucht f tropical fruit. s~lich a southern; ⟨Richtung⟩ southerly □ adv & prep (+ gen) s~lich [von] der Stadt [to the] south of the town. S~osten m southeast. S~pol m South Pole. s~wärts adv southwards. S~westen m south-west

süffisant a smug, adv -ly

suggerieren vt suggest ⟨dat to⟩

Suggest|ion /-'tio:n/ f -,-en suggestion. s~iv a suggestive

Sühne f -,-n atonement; (Strafe) penalty. s~n vt atone for

Sultanine f -,-n sultana

Sülze f -,-n [meat] jelly; (Schweinskopf-) brawn

Summe f -,-n sum

summ|en vi (haben) hum; ⟨Biene:⟩ buzz □ vt hum. S~er m -s,- buzzer

summieren (sich) vr add up; (sich häufen) increase

Sumpf m -[e]s,-ë marsh, swamp. s~ig a marshy

Sünd|e f -,-n sin. S~enbock m scapegoat. S~er(in) m -s,- (f -,-nen) sinner. s~haft a sinful. s~igen vi (haben) sin

super inv a (fam) great. S~lativ m -s,-e superlative. S~markt m supermarket

Suppe f -,-n soup. S~nlöffel m soupspoon. S~nteller m soup-plate. S~nwürfel m stock cube

Surf|brett /'sœ:ɐ̯f-/ nt surfboard. S~en nt -s surfing

surren vi (haben) whirr

süß a sweet, adv -ly. S~e f - sweetness. s~en vt sweeten. S~igkeit f -,-en sweet. s~lich a sweetish; (fig) sugary. S~speise f sweet. S~stoff m sweetener. S~waren fpl confectionery sg, sweets pl. S~wasser- pref freshwater ...

Sylvester nt -s = Silvester

Symbol nt -s,-e symbol. S~ik f - symbolism. s~isch a symbolic, adv -ally. s~isieren vt symbolize

Sym|metrie f - symmetry. s~metrisch a symmetrical, adv -ly

Sympathie f -,-n sympathy

sympath|isch a agreeable; ⟨Person⟩ likeable. s~isieren vi (haben) be sympathetic ⟨mit to⟩

Symphonie f -,-n = Sinfonie

Symptom nt -s,-e symptom. s~atisch a symptomatic

Synagoge f -,-n synagogue

synchronisieren /zynkroni'zi:rən/ vt synchronize; dub ⟨Film⟩

Syndikat nt -[e]s,-e syndicate

Syndrom nt -s,-e syndrome

synonym a synonymous, adv -ly. S~ nt -s,-e synonym

Syntax /'zyntaks/ f - syntax

Synthe|se f -,-n synthesis. S~tik nt -s synthetic material. s~tisch a synthetic, adv -ally

Syrien /-jən/ nt -s Syria

System nt -s,-e system. s~atisch a systematic, adv -ally

Szene f -,-n scene. S~rie f - scenery

T

Tabak m -s,-e tobacco

Tabelle f -,-n table; (Sport) league table

Tablett nt -[e]s,-s tray

Tablette f -,-n tablet

tabu a taboo. T~ nt -s,-s taboo

Tacho m -s,-s, **Tachometer** m & nt speedometer

Tadel m -s,- reprimand; (Kritik) censure; (Sch) black mark. t~los a impeccable, adv -bly. t~n vt reprimand; censure. t~nswert a reprehensible

Tafel f -,-n (Tisch, Tabelle) table; (Platte) slab; (Anschlag-, Hinweis-) board; (Gedenk-) plaque; (Schiefer-) slate; (Wand-) blackboard; (Bild-) plate; (Schokolade) bar. t~n vi (haben) feast

Täfelung f - panelling

Tag m -[e]s,-e day; Tag für Tag day by day; am T~e in the daytime; eines T~es one day; unter T~e underground; es wird Tag it is getting light; guten Tag! good morning/afternoon! zu T~e treten od kommen/bringen = zutage treten od kommen/bringen, s. zutage. t~aus adv t~aus, t~ein day in, day out

Tage|buch nt diary. t~lang adv for days

tagen vi (haben) meet; (Gericht:) sit; es tagt day is breaking

Tages|anbruch m daybreak. T~ausflug m day trip. T~decke f bedspread. T~karte f day ticket; (Speise-) menu of the day. T~licht nt daylight. T~mutter f child-minder. T~ordnung f agenda. T~rückfahrkarte f day return [ticket]. T~zeit f time of the day. T~zeitung f daily [news]paper

täglich a & adv daily; zweimal t~ twice a day

tags adv by day; t~ zuvor/darauf the day before/after

tagsüber adv during the day

tag|täglich a daily □ adv every single day. T~traum m day-dream. T~undnachtgleiche f ~-n equinox. T~ung f ~,-en meeting; (Konferenz) conference

Taille /'taljə/ f ~,-n waist. t~iert /ta'ji:ɐt/ a fitted

Takt m -[e]s,-e tact; (Mus) bar; (Tempo) time; (Rhythmus) rhythm; im T~ in time [to the music]. T~gefühl nt tact

Takt|ik f ~ tactics pl. t~isch a tactical, adv -ly

takt|los a tactless, adv -ly. T~losigkeit f ~ tactlessness. T~stock m baton. t~voll a tactful, adv -ly

Tal nt -[e]s,-e valley

Talar m -s,-e robe; (Univ) gown

Talent nt -[e]s,-e talent. t~iert a talented

Talg m -s tallow; (Culin) suet

Talsperre f dam

Tampon /'tampõ:/ m -s,-s tampon

Tang m -s seaweed

Tangente f ~,-n tangent; (Straße) bypass

Tank m -s,-s tank. t~en vi fill up with (Benzin) □ vi (haben) fill up with petrol; (Aviat) refuel; ich muss t~en I need petrol. T~er m -s,- tanker. T~stelle f petrol/(Amer) gas station. T~wart m -[e]s,-e petrol-pump attendant

Tanne f ~,-n fir [tree]. T~nbaum m fir tree; (Weihnachtsbaum) Christmas tree. T~nzapfen m fir cone

Tante f ~,-n aunt

Tantiemen /tan'tje:mən/ pl royalties

Tanz m -es,-e dance. t~en vt/i (haben) dance

Tänzer(in) m -s,- (f ~,-nen) dancer

Tanz|lokal nt dance-hall. T~musik f dance music

Tapete f ~,-n wallpaper. T~nwechsel m (fam) change of scene

tapezier|en vt paper. T~er m -s,- paperhanger, decorator

tapfer a brave, adv -ly. T~keit f bravery

tappen vi (sein) walk hesitantly; (greifen) grope (nach for)

Tarif m -s,-e rate; (Verzeichnis) tariff

tarn|en vt disguise; (Mil) camouflage; sich t~en disguise/camouflage oneself. T~ung f - disguise; camouflage

Tasche f ~,-n bag; (Hosen-, Mantel-) pocket. T~nbuch nt paperback. T~ndieb m pickpocket. T~ngeld nt pocket-money. T~nlampe f torch, (Amer) flashlight. T~nmesser nt penknife. T~ntuch nt handkerchief

Tasse f ~,-n cup

Tastatur f ~,-en keyboard

tast|bar a palpable. T~e f ~,-n key; (Druck-) push-button. t~en vi (haben) feel, grope (nach for) □ vt key in (Daten); sich t~en feel one's way (zu to). t~end a tentative, adv -ly

Tat f ~,-en action; (Helden-) deed; (Straf-) crime; in der Tat indeed; auf frischer Tat ertappt caught in the act. t~enlos adv passively

Täter(in) m -s,- (f ~,-nen) culprit; (Jur) offender

tätig a active, adv -ly; t~ sein work. T~keit f ~,-en activity; (Funktionieren) action; (Arbeit) work, job

Tatkraft f energy

tätlich a physical, adv -ly; t~ werden become violent. T~keiten fpl violence sg

Tatort m scene of the crime

tätowier|en vt tattoo. T~ung f ~,-en tattooing; (Bild) tattoo

Tatsache f fact. T~nbericht m documentary

tatsächlich a actual, adv -ly

tätscheln vt pat

Tatze f ~,-n paw

Tau[1] m -[e]s dew

Tau[2] nt -[e]s,-e rope

taub a deaf; (gefühllos) numb; (Nuss) empty; (Gestein) worthless

Taube f ~,-n pigeon; (Turtel- & fig) dove. T~nschlag m pigeon-loft

Taub|heit f - deafness; (Gefühllosigkeit) numbness. t~stumm a deaf and dumb

tauch|en vt dip, plunge; (unter-) duck □ vi (haben/sein) dive/(ein-) plunge (in + acc into); (auf-) appear (aus out of). T~er m -s,- diver. T~eranzug m diving-suit. T~sieder m -s,- [small, portable] immersion heater

tauen vi (sein) melt, thaw □ impers es taut it is thawing

Tauf|becken nt font. T~e f ~,-n christening, baptism. t~en vt christen, baptize. T~pate m godfather. T~stein m font

taugen vi (haben) etwas/nichts t∼n be good/no good; zu etw t∼n/nicht t∼n be good/no good for sth. T∼nichts m -es,-e good-for-nothing

tauglich a suitable; (Mil) fit. T∼keit f - suitability; fitness

Taumel m -s daze; wie im T∼ in a daze. t∼n vi (sein) stagger

Tausch m -[e]s,-e exchange, (fam) swap. t∼en vt exchange/(handeln) barter (gegen for); die Plätze t∼en change places □ vi (haben) swap (mit etw sth; mit jdm with s.o.)

täuschen vt deceive, fool; betray ⟨Vertrauen⟩; sich t∼ delude oneself; (sich irren) be mistaken □ vi (haben) be deceptive. t∼d a deceptive; ⟨Ähnlichkeit⟩ striking

Tausch|geschäft nt exchange. T∼handel m barter; (T∼geschäft) exchange

Täuschung f -,-en deception; (Irrtum) mistake; (Illusion) delusion

tausend inv a one/a thousand. T∼ nt -s, -e thousand; T∼e od t∼e von thousands of. T∼füßler m -s,- centipede. t∼ste(r,s) a thousandth. T∼stel nt -s,- thousandth

Tau|tropfen m dewdrop. T∼wetter nt thaw. T∼ziehen nt -s tug of war

Taxe f -,-n charge; (Kur-) tax; (Taxi) taxi

Taxi nt -s,-s taxi, cab

taxieren vt estimate/(im Wert) value (auf + acc at); (fam: mustern) size up

Taxi|fahrer m taxi driver. T∼stand m taxi rank

Teakholz /'ti:k-/ nt teak

Team /ti:m/ nt -s,-s team

Technik f -,-en technology; (Methode) technique. T∼ker m -s,- technician. t∼sch a technical, adv -ly; (technologisch) technological, adv -ly. T∼sche Hochschule Technical University

Techno|logie f -,-n technology. t∼logisch a technological

Teckel m -s,- dachshund

Teddybär m teddy bear

Tee m -s,-s tea. T∼beutel m tea-bag. T∼kanne f teapot. T∼kessel m kettle. T∼löffel m teaspoon

Teer m -s tar. t∼en vt tar

Tee|sieb nt tea-strainer. T∼tasse f teacup. T∼wagen m [tea] trolley

Teich m -[e]s,-e pond

Teig m -[e]s,-e pastry; (Knet-) dough; (Rühr-) mixture; (Pfannkuchen-) batter. T∼rolle f, T∼roller m rolling-pin. T∼waren fpl pasta sg

Teil m & nt -[e]s,-e part; (Bestand-) component; (Jur) party; der vordere T∼ the front part; zum T∼ partly; zum großen/

größten T∼ for the most part □ m & nt -[e]s (Anteil) share; sein[en] T∼ beitragen do one's share; für mein[en] T∼ for my part □ nt -[e]s,-e part; (Ersatz-) spare part; (Anbau-) unit

teil|bar a divisible. T∼chen nt -s,- particle. t∼en vt divide; (auf-) share out; (gemeinsam haben) share; (Pol) partition ⟨Land⟩; sich (dat) etw [mit jdm] share sth [with s.o.]; sich t∼en divide; (sich gabeln) fork; ⟨Vorhang:⟩ open; ⟨Meinungen:⟩ differ □ vi (haben) share

teilhab|en† vi sep (haben) share (an etw dat sth). T∼er m -s,- (Comm) partner

Teilnahm|e f - participation; (innere) interest; (Mitgefühl) sympathy. t∼slos a apathetic, adv -ly

teilnehm|en† vi sep (haben) t∼en an (+ dat) take part in; (mitfühlen) share [in]. T∼er(in) m -s,- (f-,-nen) participant; (an Wettbewerb) competitor

teil|s adv partly. T∼ung f -,-en division; (Pol) partition. t∼weise a partial □ adv partially, partly; (manchmal) in some cases. T∼zahlung f part-payment; (Rate) instalment. T∼zeitbeschäftigung f part-time job

Teint /tɛ̃:/ m -s,-s complexion

Telefax nt fax

Telefon nt -s,-e [tele]phone. T∼anruf m, T∼at nt -[e]s,-e [tele]phone call. T∼buch nt [tele]phone book. t∼ieren vi (haben) [tele]phone

telefon|isch a [tele]phone ... □ adv by [tele]phone. T∼ist(in) m -en,-en (f-,-nen) telephonist. T∼karte f phone card. T∼nummer f [tele]phone number. T∼zelle f [tele]phone box

Telegraf m -en,-en telegraph. T∼enmast m telegraph pole. t∼ieren vi (haben) send a telegram. t∼isch a telegraphic □ adv by telegram

Telegramm nt -s,-e telegram

Telegraph m -en,-en = Telegraf

Teleobjektiv nt telephoto lens

Telepathie f - telepathy

Telephon nt -s,-e = Telefon

Teleskop nt -s,-e telescope. t∼isch a telescopic

Telex nt -,-[e] telex. t∼en vt telex

Teller m -s,- plate

Tempel m -s,- temple

Temperament nt -s,-e temperament; (Lebhaftigkeit) vivacity. t∼los a dull. t∼voll a vivacious; ⟨Pferd⟩ spirited

Temperatur f -,-en temperature

Tempo nt -s,-s speed; (Mus: pl -pi) tempo; T∼ [T∼]! hurry up!

Tend|enz f -,-en trend; (*Neigung*) tendency. t~**ieren** vi (*haben*) tend (zu towards)

Tennis nt - tennis. T~**platz** m tenniscourt. T~**schläger** m tennis-racket

Tenor m -s,ˆe (*Mus*) tenor

Teppich m -s,e carpet. T~**boden** m fitted carpet

Termin m -s,-e date; (*Arzt-*) appointment; [letzter] T~ deadline. T~**kalender** m [appointments] diary

Terminologie f -,-n terminology

Terpentin nt -s turpentine

Terrain /tɛˈrɛ̃/ nt -s,-s terrain

Terrasse f -,-n terrace

Terrier /ˈtɛri̯ɐ/ m -s,- terrier

Terrine f -,-n tureen

Territorium nt -s,-ien territory

Terror m -s terror. t~**isieren** vt terrorize. T~**ismus** m - terrorism. T~**ist** m -en,-en terrorist

Terzett nt -[e]s,-e [vocal] trio

Tesafilm (P) m ≈ Sellotape (P)

Test m -[e]s,-s & -e test

Testament nt -[e]s,-e will; Altes/Neues T~ Old/New Testament. T~**svollstrecker** m -s,- executor

testen vt test

Tetanus m - tetanus

teuer a expensive, adv -ly; (*lieb*) dear; wie t~? how much? T~**ung** f -,-en rise in prices

Teufel m -s,- devil; zum T~! (*sl*) damn [it]! T~**skreis** m vicious circle

teuflisch a fiendish

Text m -[e]s,-e text; (*Passage*) passage; (*Bild-*) caption; (*Lied-*) lyrics pl, words pl; (*Opern-*) libretto. T~**er** m -s,- copy-writer; (*Schlager-*) lyricist

Textil|ien /-i̯ən/ pl textiles; (*Textilwaren*) textile goods. T~**industrie** f textile industry

Textverarbeitungssystem nt word processor

TH abbr = Technische Hochschule

Theater nt -s,- theatre; (*fam: Getue*) fuss, to-do; T~ spielen act; (*fam*) put on an act. T~**kasse** f box-office. T~**stück** nt play

theatralisch a theatrical, adv -ly

Theke f -,-n bar; (*Ladentisch*) counter

Thema nt -s,-men subject; (*Mus*) theme

Themse f - Thames

Theolo|ge m -n,-n theologian. T~**gie** f - theology

theor|etisch a theoretical, adv -ly. T~**ie** f -,-n theory

Therapeut|(in) m -en,-en (f -,-nen) therapist. t~**isch** a therapeutic

Therapie f -,-n therapy

Thermal|bad nt thermal bath; (*Ort*) thermal spa. T~**quelle** f thermal spring

Thermometer nt -s,- thermometer

Thermosflasche (P) f Thermos flask (P)

Thermostat m -[e]s,-e thermostat

These f -,-n thesis

Thrombose f -,-n thrombosis

Thron m -[e]s,-e throne. t~**en** vi (*haben*) sit [in state]. T~**folge** f succession. T~**folger** m -s,- heir to the throne

Thunfisch m tuna

Thymian m -s thyme

Tick m -s,-s (*fam*) quirk; einen T~ haben be crazy

ticken vi (*haben*) tick

tief a deep; (t~ *liegend, niedrig*) low; (t~*gründig*) profound; t~er Teller soupplate; im t~sten Winter in the depths of winter □ adv deep; low; (*sehr*) deeply, profoundly; (*schlafen*) soundly; t~**greifend** (*fig*) radical, adv -ly; t~**schürfend** (*fig*) profound. T~ nt -s,-s (*Meteorol*) depression. T~**bau** m civil engineering. T~**e** f -,-n depth

Tief|ebene f [lowland] plain. T~**garage** f underground car park. t~**gekühlt** a [deep-]frozen. t~**greifend** a NEW t~**greifend**, s. tief. t~**gründig** a (*fig*) profound

Tiefkühl|fach nt freezer compartment. T~**kost** f frozen food. T~**truhe** f deepfreeze

Tief|land nt lowlands pl. T~**punkt** m (*fig*) low. t~**schürfend** a NEW t~**schürfend**, s. tief. t~**sinnig** (*fig*) profound; (*trübsinnig*) melancholy. T~**stand** m (*fig*) low

Tiefsttemperatur f minimum temperature

Tier nt -[e]s,-e animal. T~**arzt** m, T~**ärztin** f vet, veterinary surgeon. T~**garten** m zoo. t~**isch** a animal ...; (*fig: roh*) bestial. T~**kreis** m zodiac. T~**kreiszeichen** nt sign of the zodiac. T~**kunde** f zoology. T~**quälerei** f cruelty to animals

Tiger m -s,- tiger

tilgen vt pay off (*Schuld*); (*streichen*) delete; (*fig: auslöschen*) wipe out

Tinte f -,-n ink. T~**nfisch** m squid

Tipp (Tip) m -s,-s (*fam*) tip

tipp|en vt (*fam*) type □ vi (*haben*) (*berühren*) touch (auf/an etw acc sth); (*fam: Maschine schreiben*) type; t~**en auf** (+ acc) (*fam: wetten*) bet on. T~**fehler** m (*fam*) typing error. T~**schein** m pools/lottery coupon

tipptopp a (*fam*) immaculate, adv -ly

Tirol nt -s [the] Tyrol

Tisch *m* -[e]s,-e table; (*Schreib-*) desk; nach T~ after the meal. T~decke *f* table-cloth. T~gebet *nt* grace. T~ler *m* -s,-, joiner; (*Möbel-*) cabinet-maker. T~rede *f* after-dinner speech. T~tennis *nt* table tennis. T~tuch *nt* table-cloth

Titel *m* -s,- title. T~rolle *f* title-role

Toast /to:st/ *m* -[e]s,-e toast; (*Scheibe*) piece of toast; einen T~ ausbringen propose a toast (auf + *acc* to). T~er *m* -s,- toaster

tob|en *vi* (*haben*) rave; (*Sturm:*) rage; (*Kinder:*) play boisterously □ *vi* (*sein*) rush. t~süchtig *a* raving mad

Tochter *f* -," daughter. T~gesellschaft *f* subsidiary

Tod *m* -es death. t~blass (t~blaß) *n* deathly pale. t~ernst *a* deadly serious, *adv* -ly

Todes|angst *f* mortal fear. T~anzeige *f* death announcement; (*Zeitungs-*) obituary. T~fall *m* death. T~opfer *nt* fatality, casualty. T~strafe *f* death penalty. T~urteil *nt* death sentence

tödlich *a* fatal, *adv* -ly; (*Gefahr*) mortal, *adv* -ly; (*groß*) deadly; t~ gelangweilt bored to death

tod|müde *a* dead tired. t~sicher *a* (*fam*) dead certain □ *adv* for sure. T~sünde *f* deadly sin. t~unglücklich *a* desperately unhappy

Toilette /tŏa'lɛtə/ *f* -,-n toilet. T~npapier *nt* toilet paper

toler|ant *a* tolerant. T~anz *f* - tolerance. t~ieren *vt* tolerate

toll *a* crazy, mad; (*fam: prima*) fantastic; (*schlimm*) awful □ *adv* beautifully; (*sehr*) very; (*schlimm*) badly. t~en *vi* (*haben/sein*) romp. t~kühn *a* foolhardy. t~patschig *a* clumsy, *adv* -ily. t~wut *f* rabies. t~wütig *a* rabid

tolpatschig *a* [NEW] tollpatschig

Tölpel *m* -s,- fool

Tomate *f* -,-n tomato. T~nmark *nt* tomato purée

Tombola *f* -,-s raffle

Ton[^1] *m* -[e]s clay

Ton[^2] *m* -[e]s,-e tone; (*Klang*) sound; (*Note*) note; (*Betonung*) stress; (*Farb-*) shade; der gute Ton (*fig*) good form. T~abnehmer *m* -s,- pick-up. t~angebend *a* (*fig*) leading. T~art *f* tone [of voice]; (*Mus*) key. T~band *nt* (*pl* -bänder) tape. T~bandgerät *nt* tape recorder

tönen *vi* (*haben*) sound □ *vt* tint

Ton|fall *m* tone [of voice]; (*Akzent*) intonation. T~leiter *f* scale. t~los *a* toneless, *adv* -ly

Tonne *f* -,-n barrel, cask; (*Müll-*) bin; (*Maß*) tonne, metric ton

Topf *m* -[e]s,-e pot; (*Koch-*) pan

Topfen *m* -s (Aust) ≈ curd cheese

Töpf|er *m* -s,- (*f* -,-nen) potter. T~ei *f* -,-en pottery

Töpferwaren *fpl* pottery *sg*

Topf|lappen *m* oven-cloth. T~pflanze *f* potted plant

Tor[^1] *m* -en,-en fool

Tor[^2] *nt* -[e]s,-e gate; (*Einfahrt*) gateway; (*Sport*) goal. T~bogen *m* archway

Torf *m* -s peat

Torheit *f* -,-en folly

Torhüter *m* -s,- goalkeeper

töricht *a* foolish, *adv* -ly

torkeln *vi* (*sein/habe*) stagger

Tornister *m* -s,- knapsack; (*Sch*) satchel

torp|edieren *vt* torpedo. T~edo *m* -s,-s torpedo

Torpfosten *m* goal-post

Torte *f* -,-n gateau; (*Obst-*) flan

Tortur *f* -,-en torture

Torwart *m* -s,-e goalkeeper

tosen *vi* (*haben*) roar; (*Sturm:*) rage

tot *a* dead; tot geboren stillborn; sich tot stellen pretend to be dead; einen t~en Punkt haben (*fig*) be at a low ebb

total *a* total, *adv* -ly. t~itär *a* totalitarian. T~schaden *m* ≈ write-off

Tote(r) *m/f* dead man/woman; (*Todesopfer*) fatality; die T~n the dead *pl*

töten *vt* kill

toten|blass (totenblaß) *a* deathly pale. T~gräber *m* -s,- grave-digger. T~kopf *m* skull. T~schein *m* death certificate. T~stille *f* deathly silence

tot|fahren† *vt sep* run over and kill. t~geboren *a* [NEW] tot geboren, *s*. tot. t~lachen (sich) *vt sep* (*fam*) be in stitches

Toto *nt & m* -s football pools *pl*. T~schein *m* pools coupon

tot|schießen† *vt sep* shoot dead. T~schlag *m* (*Jur*) manslaughter. t~schlagen† *vt sep* kill. t~schweigen† *vt sep* (*fig*) hush up. t~stellen (sich) *vr sep* [NEW] tot stellen (sich), *s*. tot

Tötung *f* -,-en killing; fahrlässige T~ (*Jur*) manslaughter

Toup|et /tu'pe:/ *nt* -s,-s toupee. t~ieren *vt* back-comb

Tour /tuːɐ/ *f* -,-en tour; (*Ausflug*) trip; (*Auto-*) drive; (*Rad-*) ride; (*Strecke*) distance; (*Techn*) revolution; (*fam: Weise*) way; auf vollen T~en at full speed; (*fam*) flat out

Touris|mus /tu'rɪsmʊs/ *m* - tourism. T~t *m* -en,-en tourist

[^1]: 1
[^2]: 2

Tournee /tur'ne:/ f -,-n tour

Trab m -[e]s trot

Trabant m -en,-en satellite

traben vi (haben/sein) trot

Tracht f -,-en [national] costume; eine T~ Prügel a good hiding

trachten vi (haben) strive (nach for); jdm nach dem Leben t~ be out to kill s.o

trächtig a pregnant

Tradition /-'tsio:n/ f -,-en tradition. t~ell a traditional, adv ·ly

Trafik f -,-en (Aust) tobacconist's

Trag|bahre f stretcher. t~bar a portable; ⟨Kleidung⟩ wearable; ⟨erträglich⟩ bearable

träge a sluggish, adv ·ly; ⟨faul⟩ lazy, adv ·ily; ⟨Phys⟩ inert

tragen† vt carry; ⟨an-/ aufhaben⟩ wear; ⟨fig⟩ bear □ vi (haben) carry; gut t~ ⟨Baum:⟩ produce a good crop; schwer t~ carry a heavy load; ⟨fig⟩ be deeply affected (an + dat by). t~d a ⟨Techn⟩ load-bearing; ⟨trächtig⟩ pregnant

Träger m -s,- porter; ⟨Inhaber⟩ bearer; ⟨eines Ordens⟩ holder; ⟨Bau-⟩ beam; ⟨Stahl-⟩ girder; ⟨Achsel-⟩ [shoulder] strap. T~kleid nt pinafore dress

Trag|etasche f carrier bag. T~fläche f ⟨Aviat⟩ wing; ⟨Naut⟩ hydrofoil. T~flächenboot, T~flügelboot nt hydrofoil

Trägheit f -sluggishness; ⟨Faulheit⟩ laziness; ⟨Phys⟩ inertia

Trag|ik f - tragedy. t~isch a tragic, adv ·ally

Tragödie /-jǝ/ f -,-n tragedy

Tragweite f range; ⟨fig⟩ consequence

Train|er /'trɛ:nɐ/ m -s,- trainer; ⟨Tennis-⟩ coach. t~ieren vt/i (haben) train

Training /'trɛ:nɪŋ/ nt -s training. T~anzug m tracksuit. T~s-schuhe mpl trainers

Trakt m -[e]s,-e section; ⟨Flügel⟩ wing

traktieren vt (haben) mit Schlägen/ Tritten t~ hit/kick

Traktor m -s,-en /-'to:rǝn/ tractor

trampeln vi (haben) stamp one's feet □ vi (sein) trample (auf + acc on) □ vt trample

trampen /'trɛmpǝn/ vi (sein) (fam) hitchhike

Trance /'trã:sǝ/ f -,-n trance

Tranchier|messer /trã'ʃiːɐ̯-/ nt carving-knife. t~en vt carve

Träne f -,-n tear. t~n vi (haben) water. T~ngas nt tear-gas

Tränke f -,-n watering-place; ⟨Trog⟩ drinking-trough. t~n vt water ⟨Pferd⟩; ⟨nässen⟩ soak (mit with)

Trans|aktion f transaction. T~fer m -s,-s transfer. T~formator m -s,-en

/-'to:rǝn/ transformer. T~fusion f -,-en [blood] transfusion

Transistor m -,-en /-'to:rǝn/ transistor

Transit /tran'zi:t/ m -s transit

transitiv a transitive, adv ·ly

Transparent nt -[e]s,-e banner; ⟨Bild⟩ transparency

transpirieren vi (haben) perspire

Transplantation /-'tsio:n/ f -,-en transplant

Transport m -[e]s,-e transport; ⟨Güter-⟩ consignment. t~ieren vt transport. T~mittel nt means of transport

Trapez nt -es,-e trapeze; ⟨Geom⟩ trapezium

Tratsch m -[e]s (fam) gossip. t~en vi (haben) (fam) gossip

Tratte f -,-n (Comm) draft

Traube f -,-n bunch of grapes; ⟨Beere⟩ grape; ⟨fig⟩ cluster. T~nzucker m glucose

trauen vi (haben) (+ dat) trust; ich traute kaum meinen Augen I could hardly believe my eyes □ vt marry; sich t~ dare (etw zu tun [to] do sth); venture (in + acc/ aus into/out of)

Trauer f -mourning; ⟨Schmerz⟩ grief (um for); T~ tragen be [dressed] in mourning. T~fall m bereavement. T~feier f funeral service. T~marsch m funeral march. t~n vi (haben) grieve; t~n um mourn [for]. T~spiel nt tragedy. T~weide f weeping willow

traulich a cosy, adv ·ily

Traum m -[e]s, Träume dream

Trau|ma nt -s,-men trauma. t~matisch a traumatic

träumen vt/i (haben) dream

traumhaft a dreamlike; ⟨schön⟩ fabulous, adv ·ly

traurig a sad, adv ·ly; ⟨erbärmlich⟩ sorry. T~keit f - sadness

Trau|ring m wedding-ring. T~schein m marriage certificate. T~ung f -,-en wedding [ceremony]

Treck m -s,-s trek

Trecker m -s,- tractor

Treff nt -s,-s ⟨Karten⟩ spades pl

treff|en† vt hit; ⟨Blitz:⟩ strike; ⟨fig: verletzen⟩ hurt; ⟨zusammenkommen mit⟩ meet; take ⟨Maßnahme⟩; sich t~en meet (mit jdm s.o.); sich gut t~en be convenient; es traf sich, dass it so happened that; es gut/schlecht t~en be lucky/unlucky □ vi (haben) hit the target; t~en auf (+ acc) meet; ⟨fig⟩ meet with. T~en nt -s,- meeting. t~end a apt, adv ·ly; ⟨Ähnlichkeit⟩ striking. T~er m -s,- hit; ⟨Los⟩ winner. T~punkt m meeting-place treiben† vt drive; (sich befassen mit) do; carry on ⟨Gewerbe⟩; indulge in ⟨Luxus⟩; get up to ⟨Unfug⟩; Handel t~ trade; Blüten/Blätter t~ come into flower/leaf; zur Eile t~ hurry [up]; was treibt ihr da? (fam) what are you up to? □ vi (sein) drift; (schwimmen) float □ vi (haben) (Bot) sprout. T~ nt -s activity; (Getriebe) bustle

Treib|haus nt hothouse. T~hauseffekt m greenhouse effect. T~holz nt driftwood. T~riemen m transmission belt. T~sand m quicksand. T~stoff m fuel

Trend m -s trend

trenn|bar a separable. t~en vt separate/(abmachen) detach (von from); divide, split ⟨Wort⟩; sich t~en separate; (auseinander gehen) part; sich t~en von leave; (fortgeben) part with. T~ung f -,-en separation; (Silben-) division. T~ungsstrich m hyphen. T~wand f partition

trepp|ab adv downstairs. t~auf adv upstairs

Treppe f -,-n stairs pl; (Außen-) steps pl; eine T~ a flight of stairs/steps. T~nflur m landing. T~ngeländer nt banisters pl. T~nhaus nt stairwell. T~nstufe f stair, step

Tresor m -s,-e safe

Tresse f -,-n braid

Treteimer m pedal bin

treten† vi (sein/haben) step; (versehentlich) tread; (ausschlagen) kick (nach at); in Verbindung t~ get in touch □ vt tread; (mit Füßen) kick

treu a faithful, adv -ly; (fest) loyal, adv -ly. T~e f - faithfulness; loyalty; (eheliche) fidelity. T~händer m -s,- trustee. t~herzig a trusting, adv -ly; (arglos) innocent, adv -ly. t~los a disloyal, adv -ly; (untreu) unfaithful

Tribüne f -,-n platform; (Zuschauer-) stand

Tribut m -[e]s,-e tribute; (Opfer) toll

Trichter m -s,- funnel; (Bomben-) crater

Trick m -s,-s trick. T~film m cartoon. t~reich a clever

Trieb m -[e]s,-e drive, urge; (Instinkt) instinct; (Bot) shoot. T~täter, T~verbrecher m sex offender. T~werk nt (Aviat) engine; (Uhr-) mechanism

trief|en† vi (haben) drip; (nass sein) be dripping (von/vor + dat with). t~nass (t~naß) a dripping wet

triftig a valid

Trigonometrie f - trigonometry

Trikot¹ /tri'ko:/ m -s (Tex) jersey

Trikot² nt -s,-s (Sport) jersey; (Fußball-) shirt

Trimester nt -s,- term

Trimm-dich nt -s keep-fit

trimmen vt trim; (fam) train; tune ⟨Motor⟩; sich t~ keep fit

trink|bar a drinkable. t~en† vt/i (haben) drink. T~er(in) m -s,- (f-,-nen) alcoholic. T~geld nt tip. T~halm m [drinking-] straw. T~spruch m toast. T~wasser nt drinking-water

Trio nt -s,-s trio

trippeln vi (sein) trip along

trist a dreary

Tritt m -[e]s,-e step; (Fuß-) kick. T~brett nt step. T~leiter f step-ladder

Triumph m -s,-e triumph. t~ieren vi (haben) rejoice; t~ieren über (+ acc) triumph over. t~ierend a triumphant, adv -ly

trocken a dry, adv drily. T~haube f drier. T~heit f -,-en dryness; (Dürre) drought. t~legen vt sep change ⟨Baby⟩; drain ⟨Sumpf⟩. T~milch f powdered milk

trockn|en vt/i (sein) dry. T~er m -s,- drier

Troddel f -,-n tassel

Trödel m -s (fam) junk. T~laden m (fam) junk-shop. T~markt m (fam) flea market. t~n vi (haben) dawdle

Trödler m -s,- (fam) slowcoach; (Händler) junk-dealer

Trog m -[e]s,-e trough

Trommel f -,-n drum. T~fell nt ear-drum. t~n vi (haben) drum

Trommler m -s,- drummer

Trompete f -,-n trumpet. T~r m -s,- trumpeter

Tropen pl tropics

Tropf m -[e]s,-e (Med) drip

tröpfeln vt/i (sein/haben) drip; es tröpfelt it's spitting with rain

tropfen vt/i (sein/haben) drip. T~ m -s,- drop; (fallend) drip. t~weise adv drop by drop

tropf|nass (tropfnaß) a dripping wet. T~stein m stalagmite; (hängend) stalactite

Trophäe /tro'fɛ:ə/ f -,-n trophy

tropisch a tropical

Trost m -[e]s consolation, comfort

tröst|en vt console, comfort; sich t~en console oneself. t~lich a comforting

trost|los a desolate; (elend) wretched; (reizlos) dreary. T~preis m consolation prize. t~reich a comforting

Trott m -s amble; (fig) routine

Trottel m -s,- (fam) idiot

trotten vi (sein) traipse; (Tier-) amble

Trottoir /trɔ'toaːɐ̯/ nt -s,-s pavement, (Amer) sidewalk

trotz *prep* (+ *gen*) despite, in spite of. T~ *m* -es defiance. t~dem *adv* nevertheless. t~en *vi* (*haben*) (+ *dat*) defy. t~ig *a* defiant, *adv* -ly; ⟨*Kind*⟩ stubborn

trübe *a* dull; ⟨*Licht*⟩ dim; ⟨*Flüssigkeit*⟩ cloudy; (*fig*) gloomy

Trubel *m* -s bustle

trüben *vt* dull; make cloudy (*Flüssigkeit*); (*fig*) spoil; strain ⟨*Verhältnis*⟩; sich t~ ⟨*Flüssigkeit*:⟩ become cloudy; ⟨*Himmel*:⟩ cloud over; ⟨*Augen*:⟩ dim; ⟨*Verhältnis, Erinnerung*:⟩ deteriorate

Trüb|sal *f* - misery; T~sal blasen (*fam*) mope. t~selig *a* miserable; ⟨*trübe*⟩ gloomy, *adv* -ily. T~sinn *m* melancholy. t~sinnig *a* melancholy

Trugbild *nt* illusion

trüg|en† *vt* deceive ▫ *vi* (*haben*) be deceptive. t~erisch *a* false; ⟨*täuschend*⟩ deceptive

Trugschluss (**Trugschluß**) *m* fallacy

Truhe *f* -,-n chest

Trümmer *pl* rubble *sg*; (T~teile) wreckage *sg*; (*fig*) ruins. T~haufen *m* pile of rubble

Trumpf *m* -[e]s,¨e trump [card]; T~ sein be trumps. t~en *vi* (*haben*) play trumps

Trunk *m* -[e]s drink. T~enbold *m* -[e]s, -e drunkard. T~enheit *f* - drunkenness; T~enheit am Steuer drink-driving. T~sucht *f* alcoholism

Trupp *m* -s,-s group; (*Mil*) squad. T~e *f* -,-n (*Mil*) unit; (*Theat*) troupe; T~en troops

Truthahn *m* turkey

Tschech|e *m* -n,-n, T~in *f* -,-nen Czech. t~isch *a* Czech. T~oslowak ei (die) - Czechoslovakia

tschüs, tschüss *int* bye, cheerio

Tuba *f* -,-ben (*Mus*) tuba

Tube *f* -,-n tube

Tuberkulose *f* - tuberculosis

Tuch[1] *nt* -[e]s,¨er cloth; (*Hals-, Kopf-*) scarf; (*Schulter-*) shawl

Tuch[2] *nt* -[e]s,-e (*Stoff*) cloth

tüchtig *a* competent; (*reichlich, beträchtlich*) good; (*groß*) ▫ *adv* competently; (*ausreichend*) well; ⟨*regnen, schneien*⟩ hard. T~keit *f* - competence

Tück|e *f* -,-n malice; T~en haben be temperamental; (*gefährlich sein*) be treacherous. t~isch *a* malicious, *adv* -ly; (*gefährlich*) treacherous

tüfteln *vi* (*haben*) (*fam*) fiddle (an + *dat* with); (*geistig*) puzzle (an + *dat* over)

Tugend *f* -,-en virtue. t~haft *a* virtuous

Tülle *f* -,-n spout

Tulpe *f* -,-n tulip

tummeln (sich) *vr* romp [about]; (*sich beeilen*) hurry [up]

Tümmler *m* -s,- porpoise

Tumor *m* -s,-en /-'mo:rən/ tumour

Tümpel *m* -[e]s,- pond

Tumult *m* -[e]s,-e commotion; (*Aufruhr*) riot

tun† *vt* do; take ⟨*Schritt, Blick*⟩; work ⟨*Wunder*⟩; (*bringen*) put (in + *acc* into); sich tun happen; jdm etwas tun hurt s.o.; viel zu tun haben have a lot to do; das tut man nicht it isn't done; das tut nichts it doesn't matter ▫ *vi* (*haben*) act (als ob as if); überrascht tun pretend to be surprised; er tut nur so he's just pretending; jdm/etw gut tun do s.o./sth good; zu tun haben have things/work to do; [es] zu tun haben mit have to deal with; [es] mit dem Herzen zu tun haben have heart trouble. **Tun** *nt* -s actions *pl*

Tünche *f* -,-n whitewash; (*fig*) veneer. t~n *vt* whitewash

Tunesien /-jən/ *nt* -s Tunisia

Tunfisch *m* = **Thunfisch**

Tunke *f* -,-n sauce. t~n *vt/i* (*haben*) (*fam*) dip (in + *acc* into)

Tunnel *m* -s,- tunnel

tupf|en *vt* dab ▫ *vi* (*haben*) t~en an/auf (+ *acc*) touch. T~en *m* -s,- spot. T~er *m* -s,- spot; (*Med*) swab

Tür *f* -,-en door

Turban *m* -s,-e turban

Turbine *f* -,-n turbine

turbulen|t *a* turbulent. T~z *f* -,-en turbulence

Türk|e *m* -n,-n Turk. T~ei (die) - Turkey. T~in *f* -,-nen Turk

türkis *inv a* turquoise. T~ *m* -es,-e turquoise

türkisch *a* Turkish

Turm *m* -[e]s,¨e tower; (*Schach*) rook, castle

Türm|chen *nt* -s,- turret. t~en *vt* pile [up]; sich t~en pile up ▫ *vi* (*sein*) (*fam*) escape

Turmspitze *f* spire

turn|en *vi* (*haben*) do gymnastics. T~en *nt* -s gymnastics *sg*; (*Sch*) physical education, (*fam*) gym. T~er(in *m* -s,-/-f-,-nen) gymnast. T~halle *f* gymnasium

Turnier *nt* -s,-e tournament; (*Reit-*) show

Turnschuhe *mpl* gym shoes; (*Trainingsschuhe*) trainers

Türschwelle *f* doorstep, threshold

Tusch *m* -[e]s,-e fanfare

Tusche *f* -,-n (*drawing*) ink; (*Wasserfarbe*) watercolour

tuscheln *vt/i* (*haben*) whisper

Tüte *f* -,-n bag; (*Comm*) packet; (*Eis-*) cornet; in die T~ blasen (*fam*) be breathalysed tuten *vi* (*haben*) hoot; ⟨*Schiff:*⟩ sound its hooter; ⟨*Sirene:*⟩ sound

TÜV *m* - ≈ MOT [test]

Typ *m* -s,-en type; (*fam: Kerl*) bloke. T~e *f* -,-n type; (*fam: Person*) character

Typhus *m* - typhoid

typisch *a* typical, *adv* -ly (für of)

Typographie, Typografie *f* - typography

Typus *m* -, Typen type

Tyrann *m* -en,-en tyrant. T~ei *f* - tyranny. t~isch *a* tyrannical. t~isieren *vt* tyrannize

U

u.a. *abbr* (unter anderem) amongst other things

U-Bahn *f* underground, (*Amer*) subway

übel *a* bad; (*hässlich*) nasty, *adv* -ily; mir ist/wird ü~ I feel sick; etw ü~ nehmen take sth amiss; jdm etw ü~ nehmen hold sth against s.o. Ü~ *nt* -s,- evil. Ü~keit *f* - nausea. ü~nehmen† *vt sep* NEW ü~ nehmen, s. übel. Ü~täter *m* culprit

üben *vt/i* (*haben*) practise; sich in etw (*dat*) ü~ practise sth

über *prep* (+ *dat/acc*) over; (*höher als*) above; (*betreffend*) about; ⟨*Buch, Vortrag*⟩ on; ⟨*Scheck, Rechnung*⟩ for; (*quer* ü~) across; ü~ Köln fahren go via Cologne; ü~ Ostern over Easter; die Woche ü~ during the week; heute ü~ eine Woche a week today; Fehler ü~ Fehler mistake after mistake ▫ *a* über ü~ und ü~ all over; jdm ü~ sein be better/(*stärker*) stronger than s.o. ▫ *a* (*fam*) ü~ sein be left over; etw ü~ sein be fed up with sth

überall *adv* everywhere

überanstrengen *vt insep* overtax; strain ⟨*Augen*⟩; sich ü~ overexert oneself

überarbeit|en *vt insep* revise; sich ü~en overwork. Ü~ung *f* - revision; overwork

überaus *adv* extremely

überbewerten *vt insep* overrate

überbieten† *vt insep* outbid; (*fig*) outdo; (*übertreffen*) surpass

Überblick *m* overall view; (*Abriss*) summary

überblicken *vt insep* overlook; (*abschätzen*) assess

überbringen† *vt insep* deliver

überbrücken *vt insep* (*fig*) bridge

überdauern *vt insep* survive

überdenken† *vt insep* think over

überdies *adv* moreover

überdimensional *a* oversized

Überdosis *f* overdose

Überdruss *m* -es (Überdruß *m* -sses) surfeit; bis zum Ü~ ad nauseam

überdrüssig *a* ü~ sein/werden be/grow tired (*gen* of)

übereignen *vt insep* transfer

übereilt *a* over-hasty, *adv* -ily

übereinander *adv* one on top of/above the other; (*sprechen*) about each other; die Arme/Beine ü~ schlagen fold one's arms/cross one's legs. ü~schlagen† *vt sep* NEW ü~ schlagen, s. übereinander

überein|kommen† *vi sep* (*sein*) agree. Ü~kunft *f* - agreement. ü~stimmen *vi sep* (*haben*) agree; ⟨*Zahlen:*⟩ tally; ⟨*Ansichten:*⟩ coincide; ⟨*Farben:*⟩ match. Ü~stimmung *f* agreement

überempfindlich *a* over-sensitive; (*Med*) hypersensitive

überfahren† *vt insep* run over

Überfahrt *f* crossing

Überfall *m* attack; (*Bank-*) raid

überfallen† *vt insep* attack; raid ⟨*Bank*⟩; (*bestürmen*) bombard (mit with); (*überkommen*) come over; (*fam: besuchen*) surprise

überfällig *a* overdue

überfliegen† *vt insep* fly over; (*lesen*) skim over

überflügeln *vt insep* outstrip

Überfluss *m* (Überfluß) *m* abundance; (*Wohlstand*) affluence

überflüssig *a* superfluous

überfluten *vt insep* flood

überfordern *vt insep* overtax

überführ|en *vt insep* transfer; (*Jur*) convict (*gen* of). Ü~ung *f* transfer; (*Straße*) flyover; (*Fußgänger-*) foot-bridge

überfüllt *a* overcrowded

Übergabe *f* (s. übergeben) handing over; transfer

Übergang *m* crossing; (*Wechsel*) transition. Ü~stadium *nt* transitional stage

übergeben† *vt insep* hand over; (*übereignen*) transfer; sich ü~ be sick

übergehen¹ *vi sep* (*sein*) transfer; (an + *acc* to); (*überwechseln*) go over (zu to); (*werden zu*) turn (in + *acc* into); zum Angriff ü~ start the attack

übergehen² *vt insep* (*fig*) pass over; (*nicht beachten*) ignore; (*auslassen*) leave out

Übergewicht *nt* excess weight; (*fig*) predominance; Ü~ haben be overweight

übergießen† *vt insep* mit Wasser ü~ pour water over

überglücklich *a* overjoyed

über|greifen† *vi sep* (haben) spread (auf + *acc* to). Ü~griff *m* infringement

über|groß *a* outsize; (*übertrieben*) exaggerated. Ü~größe *f* outsize

überhaben† *vt sep* have on; (*fam:* satthaben) be fed up with

überhand *adv* ü~ nehmen increase alarmingly. ü~nehmen† *vi sep* (haben) NEW ü~ nehmen, s. überhand

überhängen *v sep □ vi* (haben) overhang □ *vt* (*reg*) sich (*dat*) etw ü~ sling over one's shoulder (*Gewehr*); put round one's shoulders (*Jacke*)

überhäufen *vt insep* inundate (mit with)

überhaupt *adv* (*im Allgemeinen*) altogether; (*eigentlich*) anyway; (*überdies*) besides; ü~ nicht/nichts not/nothing at all

überheblich *a* arrogant, *adv* -ly. Ü~keit *f* - arrogance

überhol|en *vt insep* overtake; (*reparieren*) overhaul. ü~t *a* out-dated. Ü~ung *f* -,-en overhaul. Ü~verbot *nt* 'Ü~verbot' 'no overtaking'

überhören *vt insep* fail to hear; (*nicht beachten*) ignore

überirdisch *a* supernatural

überkochen *vi sep* (sein) boil over

überladen† *vt insep* overload □ *a* overornate

überlassen† *vt insep* jdm etw ü~ leave sth to s.o.; (*geben*) let s.o. have sth; sich seinem Schmerz ü~ abandon oneself to one's grief; sich (*dat*) selbst ü~ sein be left to one's own devices

überlasten *vt insep* overload; overtax (*Person*)

Überlauf *m* overflow

überlaufen†[1] *vi sep* (sein) overflow; (*Mil, Pol*) defect

überlaufen†[2] *vt insep* jdn ü~ (*Gefühl:*) come over s.o. □ *a* over-run; (*Kursus*) oversubscribed

Überläufer *m* defector

überleben *vt/i insep* (haben) survive. Ü~de(r) *m/f* survivor

überlegen[1] *vt sep* put over

überlegen[2] *v insep □ vt* [sich *dat*] ü~ think over, consider; es sich (*dat*) anders ü~ change one's mind □ *vi* (haben) think, reflect; ohne zu ü~ without thinking

überlegen[3] *a* superior; (*herablassend*) supercilious, *adv* -ly. Ü~heit *f* - superiority

Überlegung *f* -,-en reflection

überliefer|n *vt insep* hand down. Ü~ung *f* tradition

überlisten *vt insep* outwit

überm *prep* = über dem

Über|macht *f* superiority. ü~mächtig *a* superior; (*Gefühl*) overpowering

übermannen *vt insep* overcome

Über|maß *nt* excess. ü~mäßig *a* excessive, *adv* -ly

Übermensch *m* superman. ü~lich *a* superhuman

übermitteln *vt insep* convey; (*senden*) transmit

übermorgen *adv* the day after tomorrow

übermüdet *a* overtired

Über|mut *m* high spirits *pl*. ü~mütig *a* high-spirited □ *adv* in high spirits

übern *prep* = über den

übernächste(r,s) *a* next ... but one; ü~es Jahr the year after next

übernacht|en *vi insep* (haben) stay overnight. Ü~ung *f* -,-en overnight stay; Ü~ung und Frühstück bed and breakfast

Übernahme *f* - taking over; (*Comm*) takeover

übernatürlich *a* supernatural

übernehmen† *vt insep* take over; (*annehmen*) take on; sich ü~ overdo things; (*finanziell*) over-reach oneself

überprüf|en *vt insep* check. Ü~ung *f* check

überqueren *vt insep* cross

überragen *vt insep* tower above; (*fig*) surpass. ü~d *a* outstanding

überrasch|en *vt insep* surprise. ü~end *a* surprising, *adv* -ly; (*unerwartet*) unexpected, *adv* -ly. Ü~ung *f* -,-en surprise

überreden *vt insep* persuade

überreichen *vt insep* present

überreizt *a* overwrought

überrennen† *vt insep* overrun

Überreste *mpl* remains

überrumpeln *vt insep* take by surprise

übers *prep* = über das

Überschall- *pref* supersonic

überschatten *vt insep* overshadow

überschätzen *vt insep* overestimate

Überschlag *m* rough estimate; (*Sport*) somersault

überschlagen†[1] *vt sep* cross (*Beine*)

überschlagen†[2] *vt insep* estimate roughly; (*auslassen*) skip; sich ü~ somersault; (*Ereignisse:*) happen fast □ *a* tepid

überschnappen *vi sep* (sein) (*fam*) go crazy

überschneiden† (sich) *vr insep* intersect, cross; (*zusammenfallen*) overlap

überschreiben† *vt insep* entitle; (*übertragen*) transfer

überschreiten† *vt insep* cross; (*fig*) exceed

Überschrift f heading; (Zeitungs-) head-line

Über|schuss (Überschuß) m surplus. ü~schüssig a surplus

überschütten vt insep ü~ mit cover with; (fig) shower with

überschwänglich a effusive, adv -ly

überschwemm|en vt insep flood; (fig) inundate. Ü~ung f -,-en flood

überschwenglich a (NEW) über-schwänglich

Übersee in/nach Ü~ overseas; aus/von Ü~ from overseas. Ü~dampfer m ocean liner. ü~isch a overseas

übersehen† vt insep look out over; (ab-schätzen) assess; (nicht sehen) overlook, miss; (ignorieren) ignore

übersenden† vt insep send

übersetzen¹ vi sep (haben/sein) cross [over]

übersetz|en² vt insep translate. Ü~er(in) m -s,- (f -,-nen) translator. Ü~ung f -,-en translation

Übersicht f overall view; (Abriss) sum-mary; (Tabelle) table. ü~lich a clear, adv -ly

übersied|eln vi sep (sein), übersied|eln vi insep (sein) move (nach to). Ü~ung f move

übersinnlich a supernatural

überspannt a exaggerated; (verschroben) eccentric

überspielen vt insep (fig) cover up; auf Band ü~ tape

überspitzt a exaggerated

überspringen† vt insep jump [over]; (auslassen) skip

überstehen†¹ vt insep (haben), jut out

überstehen†² vt insep come through; get over (Krankheit); (überleben) survive

übersteigen† vt insep climb [over]; (fig) exceed

überstimmen vt insep outvote

überstreifen vt sep slip on

Überstunden fpl overtime sg; Ü~ machen work overtime

überstürz|en vt insep rush; sich ü~en (Ereignisse:) happen fast; (Worte:) tumble out. ü~t a hasty, adv -ily

übertölpeln vt insep dupe

übertönen vt insep drown [out]

übertrag|bar a transferable; (Med) infec-tious. ü~en† vt insep transfer; (über-geben) assign (dat to); (Techn, Med) transmit; (Radio, TV) broadcast; (über-setzen) translate; (anwenden) apply (auf + acc to). □ a transferred, figurative.

Ü~ung f -,-en transfer; transmission; broadcast; translation; application

übertreffen† vt insep surpass; (über-steigen) exceed; sich selbst ü~ excel one-self

übertreib|en† vt insep exaggerate; (zu weit treiben) overdo. Ü~ung f -,-en exag-geration

übertret|en†¹ vi sep (sein) step over the line; (Pol) go over/(Relig) convert (zu to)

übertret|en†² vt insep infringe; break (Gesetz). Ü~ung f -,-en infringement; breach

übertrieben a exaggerated; (übermäßig) excessive, adv -ly

übervölkert a overpopulated

übervorteilen vt insep cheat

überwachen vt insep supervise; (kon-trollieren) monitor; (bespitzeln) keep un-der surveillance

überwachsen a overgrown

überwältigen vt insep overpower; (fig) overwhelm. ü~d a overwhelming

überweis|en† vt insep transfer; refer (Patienten). Ü~ung f transfer; (ärztliche) referral

überwerfen†¹ vt sep throw on (Mantel)

überwerfen†² (sich) vr insep fall out (mit with)

überwiegen† v insep □ vi (haben) pre-dominate □ vt outweigh. ü~d a predomin-ant, adv -ly

überwind|en† vt insep overcome; sich ü~en force oneself. Ü~ung f effort

Überwurf m wrap; (Bett-) bedspread

Über|zahl f majority. ü~zählig a spare

überzeug|en vt insep convince; sich [selbst] ü~en satisfy oneself. ü~end a convincing, adv -ly. Ü~ung f -,-en convic-tion

überziehen†¹ vt sep put on

überziehen†² vt insep cover; overdraw (Konto)

Überzug m cover; (Schicht) coating

üblich a usual; (gebräuchlich) customary

U-Boot nt submarine

übrig a remaining; (andere) other; alles Ü~e (ü~e) [all] the rest; im Ü~en (ü~en) besides; (ansonsten) apart from that; ü~ sein od bleiben be left [over]; etw ü~ haben od behalten have sth left [over]; etw ü~ lassen leave sth left [over]; uns blieb nichts anderes ü~ we had no choice. ü~behalten† vt sep (NEW) ü~ be-halten, s. übrig. ü~bleiben† vi sep (sein) (NEW) ü~ bleiben, s. übrig. ü~ens adv by the way. ü~lassen† vt sep (NEW) ü~ lassen, s. übrig

Übung f -,-en exercise; (*Üben*) practice; außer od aus der Ü~ out of practice

UdSSR f - USSR

Ufer nt -s,- shore; (*Fluss-*) bank

Uhr f -,-en clock; (*Armband-*) watch; (*Zähler*) meter; um ein U~ at one o'clock; wie viel U~ ist es? what's the time? U~armband nt watch-strap. U~macher m -s,- watch and clockmaker. U~werk nt clock/watch mechanism. U~zeiger m [clock-/watch-]hand. U~zeigersinn m im/entgegen dem U~zeigersinn clockwise/anticlockwise. U~zeit f time

Uhu m -s,-s eagle owl

UKW abbr (*Ultrakurzwelle*) VHF

Ulk m -s fun; (*Streich*) trick. u~en vi (haben) joke. u~ig a funny; (*seltsam*) odd, adv -ly

Ulme f -,-n elm

Ultimatum nt -s,-ten ultimatum

Ultrakurzwelle f very high frequency

Ultraschall m ultrasound

ultraviolett a ultraviolet

um prep (+ acc) [a]round; (*Uhrzeit*) at; (*bitten, kämpfen*) for; (*streiten*) over; (*sich sorgen*) about; (*betrügen*) out of; (*bei Angabe einer Differenz*) by; um [... herum] around, [round] about; Tag um Tag day after day; einen Tag um den andern every other day; um seinetwillen for his sake □ adv (ungefähr) around, about; um sein (*Zeit*) be up □ conj um zu; (*Absicht*) [in order] to; zu müde, um zu ... too tired to ...; um so besser (NEW) umso besser, s. umso

umändern vt sep alter

umarbeiten vt sep alter; (*bearbeiten*) revise

umarmen† vt insep embrace, hug. U~ung f -,-en embrace, hug

Umbau m rebuilding; conversion (zu into). u~en vt sep rebuild; convert (zu into)

umbild|en vt sep change; (*umgestalten*) reorganize; reshuffle (Kabinett). U~ung f reorganization; (*Pol*) reshuffle

umbinden† vt sep put on

umblättern v sep □ vt turn [over] □ vi (haben) turn the page

umblicken (sich) vr sep look round; (*zurück*) look back

umbringen† vt sep kill; sich u~ kill oneself

Umbruch m (fig) radical change

umbuchen v sep □ vt change; (*Comm*) transfer □ vi (haben) change one's booking

umdrehen v sep □ vt turn round/(wenden) over; turn (Schlüssel);

(*umkrempeln*) turn inside out; sich u~ turn round; (*im Liegen*) turn over □ vi (haben/sein) turn back

Umdrehung f turn; (*Motor-*) revolution

umeinander adv around each other; sich u~ sorgen worry about each other

umfahren†[1] vt sep run over

umfahren†[2] vt insep go round; bypass (Ort)

umfallen† vi sep (sein) fall over; (*Person.*) fall down

Umfang m girth; (*Geom*) circumference; (*Größe*) size; (*Ausmaß*) extent; (*Mus*) range

umfangen† vt insep embrace; (fig) envelop

umfangreich a extensive; (*dick*) big

umfassen vt insep consist of, comprise; (*umgeben*) surround. u~d a comprehensive

Umfrage f survey, poll

umfüllen vt sep transfer

umfunktionieren vt sep convert

Umgang m [social] contact; (*Umgehen*) dealing (mit with); U~ haben mit associate with

umgänglich a sociable

Umgangs|formen fpl manners. U~sprache f colloquial language. u~sprachlich a colloquial, adv -ly

umgeb|en† vt/i insep (haben) surround □ a u~en von surrounded by. U~ung f -,-en surroundings pl

umgehen†[1] vi sep (sein) go round; u~ mit treat, handle; (*verkehren*) associate with; in dem Schloss geht ein Gespenst um the castle is haunted

umgehen†[2] vt insep avoid; (*nicht beachten*) evade; (*Straße-*) bypass

umgehend a immediate, adv -ly

Umgehungsstraße f bypass

umgekehrt a inverse; (*Reihenfolge*) reverse; es war u~ it was the other way round □ adv conversely; und u~ and vice versa

umgraben† vt sep dig [over]

umhaben† vt sep have on

Umhang m cloak

umhauen† vt sep knock down; (*fällen*) chop down

umher adv weit u~ all around. u~gehen† vi sep (sein) walk about

umhören (sich) vr sep ask around

Umkehr f - turning back. u~en v sep □ vi (sein) turn back □ vt turn round; turn inside out (Tasche); (fig) reverse. U~ung f - reversal umkippen *v sep* □ *vt* tip over; (*versehentlich*) knock over □ *vi* (*sein*) fall over; ⟨*Boot:*⟩ capsize; (*fam: ohnmächtig werden*) faint

Umkleide|kabine *f* changing-cubicle. u∼n (*sich*) *vr sep* change. U∼raum *m* changing-room

umknicken *v sep* □ *vt* bend; (*falten*) fold □ *vi* (*sein*) bend; (*mit dem Fuß*) go over on one's ankle

umkommen† *vi sep* (*sein*) perish; u∼ lassen waste (*Lebensmittel*)

Umkreis *m* surroundings *pl*; im U∼ von within a radius of

umkreisen *vt insep* circle; (*Astr*) revolve around; ⟨*Satellit:*⟩ orbit

umkrempeln *vt sep* turn up; (*von innen nach außen*) turn inside out; (*ändern*) change radically

Umlauf *m* circulation; (*Astr*) revolution. U∼bahn *f* orbit

Umlaut *m* umlaut

umlegen *vt sep* lay *or* put down; flatten (*Getreide*); turn down ⟨*Kragen*⟩; put on (*Schal*); throw (*Hebel*); (*verlegen*) transfer; (*fam: niederschlagen*) knock down; (*töten*) kill

umleit|en *vt sep* divert. U∼ung *f* diversion

umliegend *a* surrounding

umpflanzen *vt sep* transplant

umrahmen *vt insep* frame

umranden *vt insep* edge

umräumen *vt sep* rearrange

umrechn|en *vt sep* convert. U∼ung *f* conversion

umreißen†[1] *vt sep* tear down; knock down ⟨*Person*⟩

umreißen†[2] *vt insep* outline

umringen *vt insep* surround

Umriss (Umriß) *m* outline

umrühren *vt/i sep* (*haben*) stir

ums *pron* = um das; u∼ Leben kommen lose one's life

Umsatz *m* (*Comm*) turnover

umschalten *vt/i sep* (*haben*) switch over; auf Rot u∼ ⟨*Ampel:*⟩ change to red

Umschau *f* U∼ halten nach look out for. u∼en (*sich*) *vr sep* look round/(*zurück*) back

Umschlag *m* cover; (*Schutz-*) jacket; (*Brief-*) envelope; (*Med*) compress; (*Hosen-*) turn-up; (*Wechsel*) change. u∼en† *v sep* □ *vt* turn up; turn over (*Seite*); (*fällen*) chop down □ *vi* (*sein*) topple over; ⟨*Boot:*⟩ capsize; ⟨*Wetter:*⟩ change; ⟨*Wind:*⟩ veer

umschließen† *vt insep* enclose

umschnallen *vt sep* buckle on

umschreiben†[1] *vt sep* rewrite

umschreib|en[2] *vt insep* define; (*anders ausdrücken*) paraphrase. U∼ung *f* definition; paraphrase

umschulen *vt sep* retrain; (*Sch*) transfer to another school

Umschweife *pl* keine U∼ machen come straight out with it; ohne U∼ straight out

Umschwung *m* (*fig*) change; (*Pol*) U-turn

umsehen† (*sich*) *vr sep* (*zurück*) look back; sich u∼ nach look for

umsein† *vi sep* (*sein*) NEW um sein, s. um

umseitig *a* & *adv* overleaf

umsetzen *vt sep* move; (*umpflanzen*) transplant; (*Comm*) sell

Umsicht *f* circumspection. u∼ig *a* circumspect, *adv* -ly

umsied|eln *v sep* □ *vt* resettle □ *vi* (*sein*) move. U∼lung *f* resettlement

umso *conj* ∼ besser/mehr all the better/more; je mehr, ∼ besser the more the better

umsonst *adv* in vain; (*grundlos*) without reason; (*gratis*) free

umspringen† *vi sep* (*sein*) change; ⟨*Wind:*⟩ veer; übel u∼ mit treat badly

Umstand *m* circumstance; (*Tatsache*) fact; (*Aufwand*) fuss; (*Mühe*) trouble; unter U∼en possibly; U∼e machen make a fuss; jdm U∼e machen put s.o. to trouble; in andern U∼en pregnant

umständlich *a* laborious, *adv* -ly; (*kompliziert*) involved; (*Person*) fussy

Umstands|kleid *nt* maternity dress. U∼wort *nt* (*pl* -wörter) adverb

umstehen† *vi insep* surround

Umstehende *pl* bystanders

umsteigen† *vi sep* (*sein*) change

umstellen[1] *vt insep* surround

umstell|en[2] *vt sep* rearrange; transpose ⟨*Wörter*⟩; (*anders einstellen*) reset; (*Techn*) convert; (*ändern*) change; sich u∼en adjust. U∼ung *f* rearrangement; transposition; resetting; conversion; change; adjustment

umstimmen *vt sep* jdn u∼ change s.o.'s mind

umstoßen† *vt sep* knock over; (*fig*) overturn; upset ⟨*Plan*⟩

umstritten *a* controversial; (*ungeklärt*) disputed

umstülpen *vt sep* turn upside down; (*von innen nach außen*) turn inside out

Um|sturz *m* coup. u∼stürzen *v sep* □ *vt* overturn; (*Pol*) overthrow □ *vi* (*sein*) fall over

umtaufen *vt sep* rename

Umtausch m exchange. u~en vt sep change; exchange (gegen for)

umwälzend a revolutionary

umwandeln vt sep convert; (fig) transform

umwechseln vt sep change

Umweg m detour; auf U~en (fig) in a roundabout way

Umwelt f environment. u~freundlich a environmentally friendly. U~schutz m protection of the environment. U~schützer m environmentalist

umwenden† vt sep turn over; sich u~ turn round

umwerfen† vt sep knock over; (fig) upset ⟨Plan⟩; (fam) bowl over ⟨Person⟩

umziehen† v sep □ vi (sein) move □ vt change; sich u~ change

umzingeln vt insep surround

Umzug m move; (Prozession) procession

unabänderlich a irrevocable; ⟨Tatsache⟩ unalterable

unabhängig a independent, adv -ly; u~ davon, ob irrespective of whether. U~keit f - independence

unabkömmlich pred a busy

unablässig a incessant, adv -ly

unabsehbar a incalculable

unabsichtlich a unintentional, adv -ly

unachtsam a careless, adv -ly. U~keit f - carelessness

unangebracht a inappropriate

unangemeldet a unexpected, adv -ly

unangemessen a inappropriate, adv -ly

unangenehm a unpleasant, adv -ly; ⟨peinlich⟩ embarrassing

Unannehmlichkeiten fpl trouble sg

unansehnlich a shabby; ⟨Person⟩ plain

unanständig a indecent, adv -ly

unantastbar a inviolable

unappetitlich a unappetizing

Unart f -,-en bad habit. u~ig a naughty

unauffällig a inconspicuous, adv -ly, unobtrusive, adv -ly

unauffindbar a u~ sein be nowhere to be found

unaufgefordert adv without being asked

unaufhaltsam a inexorable, adv -bly. u~hörlich a incessant, adv -ly

unaufmerksam a inattentive

unaufrichtig a insincere

unausbleiblich a inevitable

unausgeglichen a unbalanced; ⟨Person⟩ unstable

unauslöschlich a (fig) indelible, adv -bly. u~sprechlich a indescribable, adv -bly. u~stehlich a insufferable

unbarmherzig a merciless, adv -ly

unbeabsichtigt a unintentional, adv -ly

unbedacht a rash, adv -ly

unbedenklich a harmless □ adv without hesitation

unbedeutend a insignificant; ⟨geringfügig⟩ slight, adv -ly

unbedingt a absolute, adv -ly; nicht u~ not necessarily

unbefangen a natural, adv -ly; ⟨unparteiisch⟩ impartial

unbefriedigend a unsatisfactory. u~t a dissatisfied

unbefugt a unauthorized □ adv without authorization

unbegreiflich a incomprehensible

unbegrenzt a unlimited □ adv indefinitely

unbegründet a unfounded

Unbehag|en nt unease; (körperlich) discomfort. u~lich a uncomfortable, adv -bly

unbeholfen a awkward, adv -ly

unbekannt a unknown; (nicht vertraut) unfamiliar. U~e(r) m/f stranger

unbekümmert a unconcerned; (unbeschwert) carefree

unbeliebt a unpopular. U~heit f unpopularity

unbemannt a unmanned

unbemerkt a & adv unnoticed

unbenutzt a unused

unbequem a uncomfortable, adv -bly; (lästig) awkward

unberechenbar a unpredictable

unberechtigt a unjustified; (unbefugt) unauthorized

unberufen int touch wood!

unberührt a untouched; (fig) virgin; ⟨Landschaft⟩ unspoilt

unbescheiden a presumptuous

unbeschrankt a unguarded

unbeschränkt a unlimited □ adv without limit

unbeschreiblich a indescribable, adv -bly

unbeschwert a carefree

unbesiegbar a invincible

unbesiegt a undefeated

unbesonnen a rash, adv -ly

unbespielt a blank

unbeständig a inconsistent; ⟨Wetter⟩ unsettled

unbestechlich a incorruptible

unbestimmt a indefinite; ⟨Alter⟩ indeterminate; (ungewiss) uncertain; (unklar) vague □ adv vaguely

unbestreitbar *a* indisputable, *adv* -bly
unbestritten *a* undisputed □ *adv* indisputably
unbeteiligt *a* indifferent; u~ an (+ *dat*) not involved in
unbetont *a* unstressed
unbewacht *a* unguarded
unbewaffnet *a* unarmed
unbeweglich *a* & *adv* motionless, still
unbewohnt *a* uninhabited
unbewusst (unbewußt) *a* unconscious, *adv* -ly
unbezahlbar *a* priceless
unbezahlt *a* unpaid
unbrauchbar *a* useless
und *conj* and; und so weiter and so on; nach und nach bit by bit
Undank *m* ingratitude. u~bar *a* ungrateful; (*nicht lohnend*) thankless. U~barkeit *f* ingratitude
undefinierbar *a* indefinable
undenk|bar *a* unthinkable. u~lich *a* seit u~lichen Zeiten from time immemorial
undeutlich *a* indistinct, *adv* -ly; (*vage*) vague, *adv* -ly
undicht *a* leaking; u~e Stelle leak
Unding *nt* absurdity
undiplomatisch *a* undiplomatic, *adv* -ally
unduldsam *a* intolerant
undurch|dringlich *a* impenetrable; (*Miene*) inscrutable. u~führbar *a* impracticable
undurch|lässig *a* impermeable. u~sichtig *a* opaque; (*fig*) doubtful
uneben *a* uneven, *adv* -ly. U~heit *f* -,-en unevenness; (*Buckel*) bump
unecht *a* false; u~er Schmuck/Pelz imitation jewellery/fur
unehelich *a* illegitimate
unehr|enhaft *a* dishonourable, *adv* -bly. u~lich *a* dishonest, *adv* -ly. U~lichkeit *f* dishonesty
uneinig *a* (*fig*) divided; [sich (*dat*)] u~ sein disagree. U~keit *f* disagreement; (*Streit*) discord
uneins *a* u~ sein be at odds
unempfindlich *a* insensitive (gegen to); (*widerstandsfähig*) tough; (*Med*) immune
unendlich *a* infinite, *adv* -ly; (*endlos*) endless, *adv* -ly. U~keit *f* - infinity
unentbehrlich *a* indispensable
unentgeltlich *a* free; (*Arbeit*) unpaid □ *adv* free of charge; (*arbeiten*) without pay
unentschieden *a* undecided; (*Sport*) drawn; u~ spielen draw. U~ *nt* -s,- draw

unentschlossen *a* indecisive; (*unentschieden*) undecided. U~heit *f* indecision
unentwegt *a* persistent *adv* -ly; (*unaufhörlich*) incessant, *adv* -ly
unerbittlich *a* implacable, *adv* -bly; (*Schicksal*) inexorable
unerfahren *a* inexperienced. U~heit *f* - inexperience
unerfreulich *a* unpleasant, *adv* -ly
unergründlich *a* unfathomable
unerhört *a* enormous, *adv* -ly; (*empörend*) outrageous, *adv* -ly
unerklärlich *a* inexplicable
unerlässlich (unerläßlich) *a* essential
unerlaubt *a* unauthorized □ *adv* without permission
unermesslich (unermeßlich) *a* immense, *adv* -ly
unermüdlich *a* tireless, *adv* -ly
unersättlich *a* insatiable
unerschöpflich *a* inexhaustible
unerschütterlich *a* unshakeable
unerschwinglich *a* prohibitive
unersetzlich *a* irreplaceable; (*Verlust*) irreparable
unerträglich *a* unbearable, *adv* -bly
unerwartet *a* unexpected, *adv* -ly
unerwünscht *a* unwanted; (*Besuch*) unwelcome
unfähig *a* incompetent; u~, etw zu tun incapable of doing sth; (*nicht in der Lage*) unable to do sth. U~keit *f* incompetence; inability (zu to)
unfair *a* unfair, *adv* -ly
Unfall *m* -s accident. U~flucht *f* failure to stop after an accident. U~station *f* casualty department
unfassbar (unfaßbar) *a* incomprehensible; (*unglaublich*) unimaginable
unfehlbar *a* infallible. U~keit *f* - infallibility
unfolgsam *a* disobedient
unförmig *a* shapeless
unfreiwillig *a* involuntary, *adv* -ily; (*unbeabsichtigt*) unintentional, *adv* -ly
unfreundlich *a* unfriendly; (*unangenehm*) unpleasant, *adv* -ly. U~keit *f* unfriendliness; unpleasantness
Unfriede[n] *m* discord
unfruchtbar *a* infertile; (*fig*) unproductive. U~keit *f* infertility
Unfug *m* -s mischief; (*Unsinn*) nonsense
Ungar|(in) *m* -n,-n (*f* -,-nen) Hungarian. u~isch *a* Hungarian. U~n *nt* -s Hungary
ungastlich *a* inhospitable

ungeachtet *prep* (+ *gen*) in spite of; dessen u~ notwithstanding [this]. **ungebärdig** *a* unruly. **ungebeugt** *a* (*Gram*) uninflected. **ungebraucht** *a* unused. **ungebührlich** *a* improper, *adv* -ly. **ungedeckt** *a* uncovered; (*Sport*) unmarked; (*Tisch*) unlaid

Ungeduld *f* impatience. u~ig *a* impatient, *adv* -ly

ungeeignet *a* unsuitable

ungefähr *a* approximate, *adv* -ly, rough, *adv* -ly

ungefährlich *a* harmless

ungehalten *a* angry, *adv* -ily

ungeheuer *a* enormous, *adv* -ly. U~ *nt* -s,- monster

ungeheuerlich *a* outrageous

ungehobelt *a* uncouth

ungehörig *a* improper, *adv* -ly; (*frech*) impertinent, *adv* -ly

ungehorsam *a* disobedient. U~ *m* disobedience

ungeklärt *a* unsolved; (*Frage*) unsettled; (*Ursache*) unknown

ungeladen *a* unloaded; (*Gast*) uninvited

ungelegen *a* inconvenient. U~heiten *fpl* trouble *sg*

ungelernt *a* unskilled. **ungemein** *a* tremendous, *adv* -ly

ungemütlich *a* uncomfortable, *adv* -bly; (*unangenehm*) unpleasant, *adv* -ly

ungenau *a* inaccurate, *adv* -ly; (*vage*) vague, *adv* -ly. U~igkeit *f* -,-en inaccuracy

ungeniert /ˈʊnʒeniːɐ̯t/ *a* uninhibited □ *adv* openly

ungenießbar *a* inedible; (*Getränk*) undrinkable. **ungenügend** *a* inadequate, *adv* -ly; (*Sch*) unsatisfactory. **ungepflegt** *a* neglected; (*Person*) unkempt. **ungerade** *a* (*Zahl*) odd

ungerecht *a* unjust, *adv* -ly. U~igkeit *f* -,-en injustice

ungern *adv* reluctantly

ungesalzen *a* unsalted

ungeschehen *a* u~ machen undo

Ungeschick|lichkeit *f* clumsiness. u~t *a* clumsy, *adv* -ily

ungeschminkt *a* without make-up; (*Wahrheit*) unvarnished. **ungeschrieben** *a* unwritten. **ungesehen** *a* & *adv* unseen. **ungesellig** *a* unsociable. **ungesetzlich** *a* illegal, *adv* -ly. **ungestört** *a* undisturbed. **ungestraft** *adv* with impunity. **ungestüm** *a* impetuous, *adv* -ly. **ungesund** *a* unhealthy. **ungesüßt** *a* unsweetened. **ungetrübt** *a* perfect

Ungetüm *nt* -s,-e monster

ungewiss (**ungewiß**) *a* uncertain; im Ungewissen (ungewissen) sein/lassen be/leave in the dark. U~heit *f* uncertainty

ungewöhnlich *a* unusual, *adv* -ly. **ungewohnt** *a* unaccustomed; (*nicht vertraut*) unfamiliar. **ungewollt** *a* unintentional, *adv* -ly; (*Schwangerschaft*) unwanted

Ungeziefer *nt* -s vermin

ungezogen *a* naughty, *adv* -ily

ungezwungen *a* informal, *adv* -ly; (*natürlich*) natural, *adv* -ly

ungläubig *a* incredulous

unglaublich *a* incredible, *adv* -bly, unbelievable, *adv* -bly

ungleich *a* unequal, *adv* -ly; (*verschieden*) different. U~heit *f* - inequality. u~mäßig *a* uneven, *adv* -ly

Unglück *nt* -s,-e misfortune; (*Pech*) bad luck; (*Missgeschick*) mishap; (*Unfall*) accident; U~ bringen be unlucky. u~lich *a* unhappy, *adv* -ily; (*ungünstig*) unfortunate, *adv* -ly. u~licherweise *adv* unfortunately. u~selig *a* unfortunate. U~sfall *m* accident

ungültig *a* invalid; (*Jur*) void

ungünstig *a* unfavourable, *adv* -bly; (*unpassend*) inconvenient, *adv* -ly

ungut *a* (*Gefühl*) uneasy; nichts für u~! no offence!

unhandlich *a* unwieldy

Unheil *nt* -s disaster; U~ anrichten cause havoc

unheilbar *a* incurable, *adv* -bly

unheimlich *a* eerie; (*gruselig*) creepy; (*fam: groß*) terrific □ *adv* eerily; (*fam: sehr*) terribly

unhöflich *a* rude, *adv* -ly. U~keit *f* rudeness

unhörbar *a* inaudible, *adv* -bly

unhygienisch *a* unhygienic

Uni *f* -,-s (*fam*) university

uni /yˈniː/ *inv a* plain

Uniform *f* -,-en uniform

uninteress|ant *a* uninteresting. u~iert *a* uninterested; (*unbeteiligt*) disinterested

Union *f* -,-en union

universal *a* universal

universell *a* universal, *adv* -ly

Universität *f* -,-en university

Universum *nt* -s universe

unkennt|lich *a* unrecognizable. U~nis *f* ignorance

unklar *a* unclear; (*ungewiss*) uncertain; (*vage*) vague, *adv* -ly; im U~en (u~en) sein/lassen be/leave in the dark. U~heit *f* -,-en uncertainty

unklug *a* unwise, *adv* -ly

unkompliziert *a* uncomplicated

Unkosten pl expenses

Unkraut nt weed; (coll) weeds pl; U~
jäten weed. U~vertilgungsmittel nt
weed-killer

unkultiviert a uncultured

unlängst adv recently

unlauter a dishonest; (unfair) unfair

unleserlich a illegible, adv -bly

unleugbar a undeniable, adv -bly

unlogisch a illogical, adv -ly

unlös|bar a (fig) insoluble. u~lich a
(Chem) insoluble

unlustig a listless, adv -ly

unmäßig a excessive, adv -ly; (äußerst)
extreme, adv -ly

Unmenge f enormous amount/(Anzahl)
number

Unmensch m (fam) brute. u~lich a in-
human; (entsetzlich) appalling, adv -ly

unmerklich a imperceptible, adv -bly

unmissverständlich (unmißver-
ständlich) a unambiguous, adv -ly; (offen)
unequivocal, adv -ly

unmittelbar a immediate, adv -ly; (direkt) direct, adv -ly

unmöbliert a unfurnished

unmodern a old-fashioned

unmöglich a impossible, adv -bly. U~-
keit f - impossibility

Unmoral f immorality. u~isch a immoral, adv -ly

unmündig a under-age

Unmut m displeasure

unnachahmlich a inimitable

unnachgiebig a intransigent

unnatürlich a unnatural, adv -ly

unnormal a abnormal, adv -ly

unnötig a unnecessary, adv -ily

unnütz a useless □ adv needlessly

unord|entlich a untidy, adv -ily; (nach-
lässig) sloppy, adv -ily. U~nung f dis-
order; (Durcheinander) muddle

unorganisiert a disorganized

unorthodox a unorthodox □ adv in an
unorthodox manner

unparteiisch a impartial, adv -ly

unpassend a inappropriate, adv -ly; (Moment) inopportune

unpässlich (unpäßlich) a indisposed

unpersönlich a impersonal

unpraktisch a impractical

unpünktlich a unpunctual □ adv late

unrasiert a unshaven

Unrast f restlessness

unrealistisch a unrealistic, adv -ally

unrecht a wrong, adv -ly □ n jdm u~ tun
do s.o. an injustice; u~ haben/ge-
ben (NEW)U~ haben/geben, s. Unrecht.
U~ nt wrong; zu U~ wrongly; U~ haben
be wrong; jdm U~ geben disagree with
s.o. u~mäßig a unlawful, adv -ly

unregelmäßig a irregular, adv -ly. U~-
keit f irregularity

unreif a unripe; (fig) immature

unrein a impure; (Luft) polluted; (Haut)
bad; ins U~e (u~e) schreiben make a
rough draft of

unrentabel a unprofitable, adv -bly

unrichtig a incorrect

Unruh|e f -,-n restlessness; (Erregung)
agitation; (Besorgnis) anxiety; U~en
(Pol) unrest sg. u~ig a restless, adv -ly;
(Meer) agitated; (laut) noisy, adv -ily; (besorgt) anxious, adv -ly

uns pron (acc/dat of wir) us; (refl) ourselves; (einander) each other; ein Freund
von uns a friend of ours

unsagbar, **unsäglich** a indescribable,
adv -bly

unsanft a rough, adv -ly

unsauber a dirty; (nachlässig) sloppy, adv
-ily; (unlauter) dishonest, adv -ly

unschädlich a harmless

unscharf a blurred

unschätzbar a inestimable

unscheinbar a inconspicuous

unschicklich a improper, adv -ly

unschlagbar a unbeatable

unschlüssig a undecided

Unschuld f - innocence; (Jungfräulich-
keit) virginity. u~ig a innocent, adv -ly

unselbstständig, unselbständig a dependent □ adv u~ denken not think for
oneself

unser poss pron our. u~e(r,s) poss pron
ours. u~erseits adv for our part.
u~twegen adv for our sake; (wegen uns)
because of us, on our account. u~twillen
adv um u~twillen for our sake

unsicher a unsafe; (ungewiss) uncertain;
(nicht zuverlässig) unreliable; (Schritte,
Hand) unsteady; (Person) insecure □ adv
unsteadily. U~heit f uncertainty; unreli-
ability; insecurity

unsichtbar a invisible

Unsinn m nonsense. u~ig a nonsensical,
absurd

Unsitt|e f bad habit. u~lich a indecent,
adv -ly

unsportlich a not sporty; (unfair) un-
sporting, adv -ly

uns|re(r,s) poss pron = unsere(r,s). u~-
rige poss pron der/die/das u~rige ours

unsterblich a immortal. U~keit f immortality

unstet a restless, adv -ly; (unbeständig) unstable

Unstimmigkeit f -,-en inconsistency; (Streit) difference

Unsumme f vast sum

unsymmetrisch a not symmetrical

unsympathisch a unpleasant; er ist mir u~ I don't like him

untätig a idle, adv idly. U~keit f - idleness

untauglich a unsuitable; (Mil) unfit

unteilbar a indivisible

unten adv at the bottom; (auf der Unterseite) underneath; (im Treppe tiefer) downstairs; (im Text) below; hier/da u~ down here/there; nach u~ down[wards]; (die Treppe hinunter) downstairs; siehe u~ see below

unter prep (+ dat/acc) under; (niedriger als) below; (inmitten, zwischen) among; u~ anderem among other things; u~ der Woche during the week; u~ sich by themselves; u~ uns gesagt between ourselves

Unter|arm m forearm. U~bewusstsein (U~bewußtsein) nt subconscious

unterbieten† vt insep undercut; beat (Rekord)

unterbinden† vt insep stop

unterbleiben† vi insep (sein) cease; es hat zu u~ it must stop

unterbrech|en† vt insep interrupt; break (Reise). U~ung f -,-en interruption; break

unterbreiten vt insep present

unterbringen† vt sep put; (beherbergen) put up

unterdessen adv in the meantime

unterdrück|en vt insep suppress; oppress (Volk). U~ung f - suppression; oppression

untere(r,s) a lower

untereinander adv one below the other; (miteinander) among ourselves/yourselves/themselves

unterernähr|t a undernourished. U~ung f malnutrition

Unterfangen nt -s,- venture

Unterführung f underpass; (Fußgänger-) subway

Untergang m (Astr) setting; (Naut) sinking; (Zugrundegehen) disappearance; (der Welt) end

Untergebene(r) m/f subordinate

untergehen† vi sep (sein) (Astr) set; (versinken) go under; (Schiff:) go down, sink; (zugrunde gehen) disappear; (Welt:) come to an end

untergeordnet a subordinate

Untergeschoss (Untergeschoß) nt basement

untergraben† vt insep (fig) undermine

Untergrund m foundation; (Hintergrund) background; (Pol) underground. U~bahn f underground [railway]; (Amer) subway

unterhaken vt sep jdn u~ take s.o.'s arm; untergehakt arm in arm

unterhalb adv & prep (+ gen) below

Unterhalt m maintenance

unterhalt|en† vt insep maintain; (ernähren) support; (betreiben) run; (erheitern) entertain; sich u~en talk; (sich vergnügen) enjoy oneself. u~sam a entertaining. U~ung f -,-en maintenance; (Gespräch) conversation; (Zeitvertreib) entertainment

unterhandeln vi insep (haben) negotiate

Unter|haus nt (Pol) lower house; (in UK) House of Commons. U~hemd nt vest. U~holz nt undergrowth. U~hose f underpants pl. u~irdisch a & adv underground

unterjochen vt insep subjugate

Unterkiefer m lower jaw

unter|kommen† vi sep (sein) find accommodation; (eine Stellung finden) get a job. u~kriegen vt sep (fam) get down

Unterkunft f -,-künfte accommodation

Unterlage f pad; U~n papers

Unterlass (Unterlaß) m ohne U~ incessantly

unterlass|en† vt insep etw u~en refrain from [doing] sth; es u~en, etw zu tun fail or omit to do sth. U~ung f -,-en omission

unterlaufen† vi insep (sein) occur; mir ist ein Fehler u~ I made a mistake

unterlegen¹ vt sep put underneath

unterlegen² a inferior; (Sport) losing; zahlenmäßig u~ out-numbered (dat by). U~e(r) m/f loser

Unterleib m abdomen

unterliegen† vi insep (sein) lose (dat to); (unterworfen sein) be subject (dat to)

Unterlippe f lower lip

unterm prep = unter dem

Untermiete f zur U~ wohnen be a lodger. U~r(in) m(f) lodger

unterminieren vt insep undermine

untern prep = unter den

unternehm|en† vt insep undertake; take (Schritte); etw/nichts u~en do sth/nothing. U~en nt -s,- undertaking, enterprise; (Betrieb) concern. u~end a enterprising. U~er m -s,- employer; (Bau-) contractor; (Industrieller) industrialist. U~ung f -,-en undertaking; (Comm) venture. u~ungslustig a enterprising; (abenteuerlustig) adventurous

Unteroffizier m non-commissioned officer

unterordnen vt sep subordinate; sich u~ accept a subordinate role

Unterredung f -,-en talk

Unterricht m -[e]s teaching; (Privat-) tuition; (U~sstunden) lessons pl; U~ geben/nehmen give/have lessons

unterrichten vt/i insep (haben) teach; (informieren) inform; sich u~ inform oneself

Unterrock m slip

unters prep = unter das

untersagen vt insep forbid

Untersatz m mat; (mit Füßen) stand; (Gläser-) coaster

unterschätzen vt insep underestimate

unterscheid|en vt/i insep (haben) distinguish; (auseinander halten) tell apart; sich u~en differ. U~ung f -,-en distinction

Unterschied m -[e]s,-e difference; (Unterscheidung) distinction; im U~ zu ihm unlike him. u~lich a different; (wechselnd) varying; das ist u~lich it varies. u~slos a equal, adv -ly

unterschlag|en vt insep embezzle; (verheimlichen) suppress. U~ung f -,-en embezzlement; suppression

Unterschlupf m -[e]s shelter; (Versteck) hiding-place

unterschreiben vt/i insep (haben) sign

Unter|schrift f signature; (Bild-) caption. U~seeboot nt submarine. U~setzer m -s,- = Untersatz

untersetzt a stocky

Unterstand m shelter

unterste(r,s) a lowest, bottom

unterstehen[1] vi sep (haben) shelter

unterstehen[2] v insep □ vi (haben) be answerable (dat to); (unterliegen) be subject (dat to) □ vr sich u~ dare; untersteh dich! don't you dare!

unterstellen[1] vt sep put underneath; (abstellen) store; sich u~ shelter

unterstellen[2] vt insep place under the control (dat of); (annehmen) assume; (fälschlich zuschreiben) impute (dat to)

unterstreichen† vt insep underline

unterstütz|en vt insep support; (helfen) aid. U~ung f -,-en support; (finanziell) aid; (regelmäßiger Betrag) allowance; (Arbeitslosen-) benefit

untersuch|en vt insep examine; (Jur) investigate; (prüfen) test; (überprüfen) check; (durchsuchen) search. U~ung f -,-en examination; investigation; test;

check; search. U~ungshaft f detention on remand; in U~ungshaft on remand. U~ungsrichter m examining magistrate

Untertan m -s & -en,-en subject

Untertasse f saucer

untertauchen v sep □ vt duck □ vi (sein) go under; (fig) disappear

Unterteil nt bottom (part)

unterteilen vt insep subdivide; (aufteilen) divide

Untertitel m subtitle

Unterton m undertone

untervermieten vt/i insep (haben) sublet

unterwandern vt insep infiltrate

Unterwäsche f underwear

Unterwasser- pref underwater

unterwegs adv on the way; (außer Haus) out; (verreist) away

unterweisen† vt insep instruct

Unterwelt f underworld

unterwerfen† vt insep subjugate; sich u~ submit (dat to); etw (dat) unterworfen sein be subject to sth

unterwürfig a obsequious, adv -ly

unterzeichnen vt insep sign

unterziehen[1]† vt sep put on underneath; (Culin) fold in

unterziehen[2]† vr insep etw einer Untersuchung/Überprüfung u~ examine/check sth; sich einer Operation/Prüfung u~ have an operation/take a test

Untier nt monster

untragbar a intolerable

untrennbar a inseparable

untreu a disloyal; (in der Ehe) unfaithful. U~e f disloyalty; infidelity

untröstlich a inconsolable

untrüglich a infallible

Untugend f bad habit

unüberlegt a rash, adv -ly

unüber|sehbar a obvious; (groß) immense. u~troffen a unsurpassed

unum|gänglich a absolutely necessary. u~schränkt a absolute. u~wunden adv frankly

ununterbrochen a incessant, adv -ly

unveränderlich a invariable; (gleich bleibend) unchanging

unverändert a unchanged

unverantwortlich a irresponsible, adv -bly

unverbesserlich a incorrigible

unverbindlich a non-committal; (Comm) not binding □ adv without obligation

unverblümt a blunt, adv -ly

unverdaulich *a* indigestible

unver|einbar *a* incompatible. u~gesslich (u~geßlich) *a* unforgettable. u~gleichlich *a* incomparable

unver|hältnismäßig *adv* disproportionately. u~heiratet *a* unmarried. u~hofft *a* unexpected, *adv* -ly. u~hohlen *a* undisguised □ *adv* openly. u~käuflich *a* not for sale; ⟨*Muster*⟩ free

unverkennbar *a* unmistakable, *adv* -bly

unverletzt *a* unhurt

unvermeidlich *a* inevitable

unver|mindert *a* & *adv* undiminished. u~mittelt *a* abrupt, *adv* -ly. u~mutet *a* unexpected, *adv* -ly

Unver|nunft *f* folly. u~nünftig *a* foolish, *adv* -ly

unverschämt *a* insolent, *adv* -ly; ⟨*fam: ungeheuer*⟩ outrageous, *adv* -ly. U~heit *f* -,-en insolence

unver|sehens *adv* suddenly. u~sehrt *a* unhurt; ⟨*unbeschädigt*⟩ intact. u~söhnlich *a* irreconcilable; ⟨*Gegner*⟩ implacable

unverständ|lich *a* incomprehensible; ⟨*undeutlich*⟩ indistinct. U~nis *nt* lack of understanding

unverträglich *a* incompatible; ⟨*Person*⟩ quarrelsome; ⟨*unbekömmlich*⟩ indigestible

unverwandt *a* fixed, *adv* -ly

unver|wundbar *a* invulnerable. u~wüstlich *a* indestructible; ⟨*Person, Humor*⟩ irrepressible; ⟨*Gesundheit*⟩ robust. u~zeihlich *a* unforgivable

unverzüglich *a* immediate, *adv* -ly

unvollendet *a* unfinished

unvollkommen *a* imperfect; ⟨*unvollständig*⟩ incomplete. U~heit *f* -,-en imperfection

unvollständig *a* incomplete

unvor|bereitet *a* unprepared. u~eingenommen *a* unbiased. u~hergesehen *a* unforeseen

unvorsichtig *a* careless, *adv* -ly. U~keit *f* - carelessness

unvorstellbar *a* unimaginable, *adv* -bly

unvorteilhaft *a* unfavourable; ⟨*nicht hübsch*⟩ unattractive; ⟨*Kleid, Frisur*⟩ unflattering

unwahr *a* untrue. U~heit *f* -,-en untruth. u~scheinlich *a* unlikely; ⟨*unglaublich*⟩ improbable; ⟨*fam: groß*⟩ incredible, *adv* -bly

unweigerlich *a* inevitable, *adv* -bly

unweit *adv* & *prep* (+ *gen*) not far; u~ vom Fluss *od* des Flusses not far from the river

unwesentlich *a* unimportant □ *adv* slightly

Unwetter *nt* -s,- storm

unwichtig *a* unimportant

unwider|legbar *a* irrefutable. u~ruflich *a* irrevocable, *adv* -bly. u~stehlich *a* irresistible

Unwill|e *m* displeasure. u~ig *a* angry, *adv* -ily; ⟨*widerwillig*⟩ reluctant, *adv* -ly. u~kürlich *a* involuntary, *adv* -ily; ⟨*instinktiv*⟩ instinctive, *adv* -ly

unwirklich *a* unreal

unwirksam *a* ineffective

unwirsch *a* irritable, *adv* -bly

unwirtlich *a* inhospitable

unwirtschaftlich *a* uneconomic, *adv* -ally

unwissen|d *a* ignorant. U~heit *f* - ignorance

unwohl *a* unwell; ⟨*unbehaglich*⟩ uneasy. U~sein *nt* -s indisposition

unwürdig *a* unworthy ⟨*gen* of⟩; ⟨*würdelos*⟩ undignified

Unzahl *f* vast number. unzählig *a* innumerable, countless

unzerbrechlich *a* unbreakable

unzerstörbar *a* indestructible

unzertrennlich *a* inseparable

Unzucht *f* sexual offence; gewerbsmäßige U~ prostitution

unzüchtig *a* indecent, *adv* -ly; ⟨*Schriften*⟩ obscene

unzufrieden *a* dissatisfied; ⟨*innerlich*⟩ discontented. U~heit *f* dissatisfaction; ⟨*Pol*⟩ discontent

unzulänglich *a* inadequate, *adv* -ly

unzulässig *a* inadmissible

unzumutbar *a* unreasonable

unzurechnungsfähig *a* insane. U~keit *f* insanity

unzusammenhängend *a* incoherent

unzutreffend *a* inapplicable; ⟨*falsch*⟩ incorrect

unzuverlässig *a* unreliable

unzweckmäßig *a* unsuitable, *adv* -bly

unzweideutig *a* unambiguous

unzweifelhaft *a* undoubted, *adv* -ly

üppig *a* luxuriant, *adv* -ly; ⟨*überreichlich*⟩ lavish, *adv* -ly; ⟨*Busen, Figur*⟩ voluptuous

uralt *a* ancient

Uran *nt* -s uranium

Uraufführung *f* first performance

urbar *a* u~ machen cultivate

Ureinwohner *mpl* native inhabitants

Urenkel *m* great-grandson; (*pl*) great-grandchildren

Urgroß|mutter *f* great-grandmother. U~vater *m* great-grandfather

Urheber *m* -s,- originator; (*Verfasser*) author. U~recht *nt* copyright

Urin *m* -s,-e urine

Urkunde *f* -,-n certificate; (*Dokument*) document

Urlaub *m* -s holiday; (*Mil, Admin*) leave; auf U~ on holiday/leave; U~ haben be on holiday/leave. U~er(in) *m* -s,- (*f* -,-nen) holiday-maker. U~sort *m* holiday resort

Urne *f* -,-n urn; (*Wahl-*) ballot-box

Ursache *f* cause; (*Grund*) reason; keine U~! don't mention it!

Ursprung *m* origin

ursprünglich *a* original, *adv* -ly; (*anfänglich*) initial, *adv* -ly; (*natürlich*) natural

Urteil *nt* -s,-e judgement; (*Meinung*) opinion; (*U~sspruch*) verdict; (*Strafe*) sentence. u~en *vi* (*haben*) judge. U~svermögen *nt* [power of] judgement

Urwald *m* primeval forest; (*tropischer*) jungle

urwüchsig *a* natural; (*derb*) earthy

Urzeit *f* primeval times *pl*; seit U~en from time immemorial

USA *pl* USA *sg*

usw. *abbr* (und so weiter) etc.

Utensilien /-jən/ *ntpl* utensils

utopisch *a* Utopian

V

vage /'va:gə/ *a* vague, *adv* -ly

Vakuum /'va:kuʊm/ *nt* -s vacuum. v~verpackt *a* vacuum-packed

Vanille /va'nıljə/ *f* - vanilla

vari|abel /va'rja:bəl/ *a* variable. V~ante *f* -,-n variant. V~ation /-'tsjo:n/ *f* -,-en variation. v~ieren *vt/i* (*haben*) vary

Vase /'va:zə/ *f* -,-n vase

Vater *m* -s,- father. V~land *nt* fatherland

väterlich *a* paternal; (*fürsorglich*) fatherly. v~erseits *adv* on one's/the father's side

Vater|schaft *f* - fatherhood; (*Jur*) paternity. V~unser *nt* -s,- Lord's Prayer

Vati *m* -s,-s (*fam*) daddy

v. Chr. *abbr* (vor Christus) BC

Vegetar|ier(in) /vege'ta:rjɐ, -jərın/ *m(f)* -s,- (*f*-,-nen) vegetarian. v~isch *a* vegetarian

Vegetation /vegeta'tsjo:n/ *f* -,-en vegetation

Veilchen *nt* -s,-n violet

Vene /'ve:nə/ *f* -,-n vein

Venedig /ve'ne:dıç/ *nt* -s Venice

Ventil /vɛn'ti:l/ *nt* -s,-e valve. V~ator *m* -s,-en /-'to:rən/ fan

verabred|en *vt* arrange; sich [mit jdm] v~en arrange to meet [s.o.]. V~ung *f* -,-en arrangement; (*Treffen*) appointment

verabreichen *vt* administer

verabscheuen *vt* detest, loathe

verabschieden *vt* say goodbye to; (*aus dem Dienst*) retire; pass (*Gesetz*); sich v~ say goodbye

verachten *vt* despise. v~swert *a* contemptible

verächtlich *a* contemptuous, *adv* -ly; (*unwürdig*) contemptible

Verachtung *f* - contempt

verallgemeiner|n *vt/i* (*haben*) generalize. V~ung *f* -,-en generalization

veralte|n *vi* (*sein*) become obsolete. v~t *a* obsolete

Veranda /ve'randa/ *f* -,-den veranda

veränder|lich *a* changeable; (*Math*) variable. v~n *vt* change; sich v~n change; (*beruflich*) change one's job. V~ung *f* change

verängstigt *a* frightened, scared

verankern *vt* anchor

veranlag|t *a* künstlerisch/musikalisch v~t sein have an artistic/a musical bent; praktisch v~t practically minded. V~ung *f* -,-en disposition; (*Neigung*) tendency; (*künstlerisch*) bent

veranlass|en *vt* (*reg*) arrange for; (*einleiten*) institute; jdn v~en prompt s.o. (zu to). V~ung *f* - reason; auf meine V~ung at my suggestion; (*Befehl*) on my orders

veranschaulichen *vt* illustrate

veranschlagen *vt* (*reg*) estimate

veranstalt|en *vt* organize; hold, give (*Party*); make (*Lärm*). V~er *m* -s,- organizer. V~ung *f* -,-en event

verantwort|en *vt* take responsibility for; sich v~en answer (für for). v~lich *a* responsible; v~lich machen hold responsible. V~ung *f* - responsibility. v~ungsbewusst (v~ungsbewußt) *a* responsible, *adv* -bly. v~ungslos *a* irresponsible, *adv* -bly. v~ungsvoll *a* responsible

verarbeiten *vt* use; (*Techn*) process; (*verdauen & fig*) digest; v~ zu make into

verärgern *vt* annoy

verarmt *a* impoverished

verästeln (sich) *vr* branch out

verausgaben (sich) *vr* spend all one's money; (*körperlich*) wear oneself out

veräußern vt sell

Verb /vɛrp/ nt -s,-en verb. **v~al**
/vɛr'ba:l/ a verbal, adv -ly

Verband m -[e]s,-e association; (Mil) unit;
(Med) bandage; (Wund-) dressing.
V~szeug nt first-aid kit

verbannen vt exile; (fig) banish. **V~ung**
f - exile

verbarrikadieren vt barricade

verbeißen† vt suppress; ich konnte mir
kaum das Lachen v~ I could hardly keep
a straight face

verbergen† vt hide; sich v~ hide

verbessern vt improve; (berichtigen) correct. **V~ung** f -,-en improvement; correction

verbeugen (sich) vr bow. **V~ung** f bow

verbeulen vt dent

verbiegen† vt bend; sich v~ bend

verbieten† vt forbid; (Admin) prohibit,
ban

verbilligen vt reduce [in price]. **v~t** a
reduced

verbinden† vt connect (mit to); (zusammenfügen) join; (verknüpfen) combine; (in
Verbindung bringen) associate; (Med)
bandage; dress (Wunde); sich v~ combine; (sich zusammentun) join together;
jdm die Augen v~ blindfold s.o.; jdm
verbunden sein (fig) be obliged to s.o.

verbindlich a friendly; (bindend)
binding. **V~keit** f -,-en friendliness;
V~keiten obligations; (Comm) liabilities

Verbindung f connection; (Ver-
knüpfung) combination; (Kontakt) contact; (Vereinigung) association;
chemische V~ chemical compound; in
V~ stehen/sich in V~ setzen be/get in
touch

verbissen a grim, adv -ly; (zäh) dogged,
adv -ly

verbitten† vt sich (dat) etw v~ not stand
for sth

verbittern vt make bitter. **v~t** a bitter.
V~ung f - bitterness

verblassen vi (sein) fade

verbläuen vt (fam) thrash

Verbleib m -s whereabouts pl. **v~en†** vi
(sein) remain

verbleichen† vi (sein) fade

verbleit a (Benzin) leaded

verbleuen vt (NEW) verbläuen

verblüffen vt amaze, astound. **V~ung** f
- amazement

verblühen vi (sein) wither, fade

verbluten vi (sein) bleed to death

verborgen¹ a hidden

verborgen² vt lend

Verbot nt -[e]s,-e ban. **v~en** a forbidden;
(Admin) prohibited; 'Rauchen v~en' 'no
smoking'

Verbrauch m -[e]s consumption. **v~en**
vt use; consume (Lebensmittel); (erschöpfen) use up, exhaust. **V~er** m -s,-
consumer. **v~t** a worn; (Luft) stale

verbrechen† vt (fam) perpetrate. **V~** nt
-s,- crime

Verbrecher m -s,- criminal. **v~isch** a
criminal

verbreiten vt spread; sich v~en spread.
v~ern vt widen; sich v~ern widen. **v~et**
a widespread. **V~ung** f - spread; (Verbreiten) spreading

verbrennen† vt/i (sein) burn; cremate
(Leiche). **V~ung** f -,-en burning; cremation; (Wunde) burn

verbringen† vt spend

verbrühen vt scald

verbuchen vt enter; (fig) notch up (Erfolg)

verbünden (sich) vr form an alliance.
V~ete(r) m/f ally

verbürgen vt guarantee; sich v~ für
vouch for

verbüßen vt serve (Strafe)

Verdacht m -[e]s suspicion; in or im V~
haben suspect

verdächtig a suspicious, adv -ly. **v~en** vt
suspect (gen of). **V~te(r)** m/f suspect

verdammen vt condemn; (Relig) damn.
V~nis f - damnation. **v~t** a & adv (sl)
damned; **v~t!** damn!

verdampfen vt/i (sein) evaporate

verdanken vt owe (dat to)

verdauen vt digest. **v~lich** a digestible;
schwer v~lich indigestible. **V~ung** f -
digestion

Verdeck nt -[e]s,-e hood; (Oberdeck) top
deck. **v~en** vt cover; (verbergen) hide,
conceal

verdenken† vt das kann man ihm nicht
v~ you can't blame him for it

verderben† vi (sein) spoil; (Lebensmittel:)
go bad □ vt spoil; (zerstören) ruin;
(moralisch) corrupt; ich habe mir den
Magen verdorben I have an upset
stomach. **V~en** nt -s ruin. **v~lich** a per-
ishable; (schädlich) pernicious

verdeutlichen vt make clear

verdichten vt compress; sich v~ (Nebel:)
thicken

verdienen vt/i (haben) earn; (fig) de-
serve. **V~er** m -s,- wage-earner

Verdienst¹ m -[e]s earnings pl

Verdienst² nt -[e]s,-e merit

verdient a well-deserved; ⟨Person⟩ of outstanding merit. **v∼ermaßen** adv deservedly

verdoppeln vt double; ⟨fig⟩ redouble; sich v∼ double

verdorben a spoilt, ruined; ⟨Magen⟩ upset; ⟨moralisch⟩ corrupt; ⟨verkommen⟩ depraved

verdorren vi (sein) wither

verdrängen vt force out; ⟨fig⟩ displace; ⟨psychisch⟩ repress

verdreh|en vt twist; roll ⟨Augen⟩; ⟨fig⟩ distort. **v∼t** a ⟨fam⟩ crazy

verdreifachen vt treble, triple

verdreschen† vt ⟨fam⟩ thrash

verdrießlich a morose, adv ·ly

verdrücken vt crumple; ⟨fam: essen⟩ polish off; sich v∼ ⟨fam⟩ slip away

Verdruss m -es (Verdruß m -sses) annoyance

verdunk|eln vt darken; black out ⟨Zimmer⟩; sich v∼eln darken. **V∼[e]lung** f · black-out

verdünnen vt dilute; sich v∼ taper off

verdunst|en vi (sein) evaporate. **V∼ung** f · evaporation

verdursten vi (sein) die of thirst

verdutzt a baffled

veredeln vt refine; ⟨Hort⟩ graft

verehr|en vt revere; ⟨Relig⟩ worship; ⟨bewundern⟩ admire; ⟨schenken⟩ give. **V∼er(in)** m -s,- (f -,-nen) admirer. **V∼ung** f · veneration; worship; admiration

vereidigen vt swear in

Verein m -s,-e society; ⟨Sport-⟩ club

vereinbar a compatible. **v∼en** vt arrange; nicht zu v∼en incompatible. **V∼ung** f -,-en agreement

vereinen vt unite; sich v∼ unite

vereinfachen vt simplify

vereinheitlichen vt standardize

vereinig|en vt unite; merge ⟨Firmen⟩; wieder v∼en reunite; reunify ⟨Land⟩; sich v∼en unite; **V∼te Staaten [von Amerika]** United States sg [of America]. **V∼ung** f -,-en union; ⟨Organisation⟩ organization

vereinsamt a lonely

vereinzelt a isolated □ adv occasionally

vereist a frozen; ⟨Straße⟩ icy

vereiteln vt foil, thwart

vereitert a septic

verenden vi (sein) die

verengen vt restrict; sich v∼ narrow; ⟨Pupille:⟩ contract

vererb|en vt leave (dat to); ⟨Biol & fig⟩ pass on (dat to). **V∼ung** f · heredity

verewigen vt immortalize; sich v∼ ⟨fam⟩ leave one's mark

verfahren† vi (sein) proceed; v∼ mit deal with □ vr sich v∼ lose one's way □ a muddled. **V∼** nt -s,- procedure; ⟨Techn⟩ process; ⟨Jur⟩ proceedings pl

Verfall m decay; ⟨eines Gebäudes⟩ dilapidation; ⟨körperlich & fig⟩ decline; ⟨Ablauf⟩ expiry. **v∼en†** vi (sein) decay; ⟨Person, Sitten:⟩ decline; ⟨ablaufen⟩ expire; v∼en in (+ acc) lapse into; v∼en auf (+ acc) hit on ⟨Idee⟩; jdm/etw v∼en sein be under the spell of s.o./sth; be addicted to ⟨Alkohol⟩

verfälschen vt falsify; adulterate ⟨Wein, Lebensmittel⟩

verfänglich a awkward

verfärben (sich) vr change colour; ⟨Stoff:⟩ discolour

verfass|en vt write; ⟨Jur⟩ draw up; ⟨entwerfen⟩ draft. **V∼er** m -s,- author. **V∼ung** f ⟨Pol⟩ constitution; ⟨Zustand⟩ state

verfaulen vi (sein) rot, decay

verfechten† vt advocate

verfehlen vt miss

verfeinde|n (sich) vr become enemies; **v∼t sein** be enemies

verfeinern vt refine; ⟨verbessern⟩ improve

verfilmen vt film

verfilzt a matted

verfliegen† vi (sein) evaporate; ⟨Zeit:⟩ fly

verflixt a ⟨fam⟩ awkward; ⟨verdammt⟩ blessed; v∼! damn!

verfluch|en vt curse. **v∼t** a & adv ⟨fam⟩ damned; v∼t! damn!

verflüchtigen (sich) vr evaporate

verflüssigen vt liquefy

verfolg|en vt pursue; ⟨folgen⟩ follow; ⟨bedrängen⟩ pester; ⟨Pol⟩ persecute; strafrechtlich v∼en prosecute. **V∼er** m -s,- pursuer. **V∼ung** f · pursuit; persecution

verfrachten vt ship

verfrüht a premature

verfügbar a available

verfüg|en vt order; ⟨Jur⟩ decree □ vi (haben) v∼en über (+ acc) have at one's disposal. **V∼ung** f order; ⟨Jur⟩ decree; jdm zur V∼ung stehen/stellen be/place at s.o.'s disposal

verführ|en vt seduce; ⟨verlocken⟩ tempt. **V∼er** m seducer. **v∼erisch** a seductive; tempting. **V∼ung** f seduction; temptation

vergammelt a rotten; ⟨Gebäude⟩ decayed; ⟨Person⟩ scruffy

vergangen a past; ⟨letzte⟩ last. **V∼heit** f · past; ⟨Gram⟩ past tense

vergänglich a transitory

vergas|en vt gas. V∼er m -s,- carburettor

vergeb|en† vt award (an + dat to); (weggeben) give away; (verzeihen) forgive. v∼ens adv in vain. v∼lich a futile, vain □ adv in vain. V∼ung f - forgiveness

vergehen† vi (sein) pass; v∼ vor (+ dat) nearly die of; sich v∼ violate (gegen etw sth); (sexuell) sexually assault (an jdm s.o.). V∼ nt -s, - offence

vergelt|en† vt repay. V∼ung f - retaliation; (Rache) revenge. V∼ungsmaßnahme f reprisal

vergessen† vt forget; (liegen lassen) leave behind. V∼heit f - oblivion; in V∼heit geraten be forgotten

vergesslich (vergeßlich) a forgetful. V∼keit f - forgetfulness

vergeuden vt waste, squander

vergewaltig|en vt rape. V∼ung f -,-en rape

vergewissern (sich) vr make sure (gen of)

vergießen† vt spill; shed ⟨Tränen, Blut⟩

vergift|en vt poison. V∼ung f -,-en poisoning

Vergissmeinnicht (Vergißmeinnicht) nt -[e]s,-[e] forget-me-not

vergittert a barred

verglasen vt glaze

Vergleich m -[e]s,-e comparison; (Jur) settlement. v∼bar a comparable. v∼en† vt compare (mit with/to). v∼sweise adv comparatively

vergnüg|en (sich) vr enjoy oneself. V∼en nt -s,- pleasure; (Spaß) fun; viel V∼en! have a good time! v∼lich a enjoyable. v∼t a cheerful, adv -ly; (zufrieden) happy, adv -ily; (vergnüglich) enjoyable. V∼ungen fpl entertainments

vergolden vt gild; (plattieren) gold-plate

vergönnen vt grant

vergöttern vt idolize

vergraben† vt bury

vergreifen† (sich) vr sich v∼an (+ dat) assault; (stehlen) steal

vergriffen a out of print

vergrößer|n vt enlarge; ⟨Linse:⟩ magnify; (vermehren) increase; (erweitern) extend; expand ⟨Geschäft⟩; sich v∼n grow bigger; ⟨Firma:⟩ expand; (zunehmen) increase. V∼ung f -,-en magnification; increase; expansion; (Phot) enlargement. V∼ungsglas nt magnifying glass

Vergünstigung f -,-en privilege

vergüt|en† vt pay for; jdm etw v∼en reimburse s.o. for sth. V∼ung f -,-en remuneration; (Erstattung) reimbursement

verhaft|en vt arrest. V∼ung f -,-en arrest

verhalten† (sich) vr behave; (handeln) act; (beschaffen sein) be; sich still v∼ keep quiet. V∼ nt -s behaviour, conduct

Verhältnis nt -ses,-se relationship; (Liebes-) affair; (Math) ratio; V∼se circumstances; (Bedingungen) conditions; über seine V∼se leben live beyond one's means. v∼mäßig adv comparatively, relatively

verhand|eln vt discuss; (Jur) try □ vi (haben) negotiate; v∼eln gegen (Jur) try. V∼lung f (Jur) trial; V∼lungen negotiations

verhängen vt cover; (fig) impose

Verhängnis nt -ses fate, doom. v∼voll a fatal, disastrous

verharmlosen vt play down

verharren vi (haben) remain

verhärten vt/i (sein) harden; sich v∼ harden

verhasst (verhaßt) a hated

verhätscheln vt spoil, pamper

verhauen† vt (fam) beat; make a mess of ⟨Prüfung⟩

verheerend a devastating; (fam) terrible

verhehlen vt conceal

verheilen vi (sein) heal

verheimlichen vt keep secret

verheirat|en (sich) vr get married (mit to); sich wieder v∼en remarry. v∼et a married

verhelfen† vi (haben) jdm zu etw v∼ help s.o. get sth

verherrlichen vt glorify

verhexen vt bewitch; es ist wie verhext (fam) there is a jinx on it

verhinder|n vt prevent; v∼t sein be unable to come. V∼ung f - prevention

verhöhnen vt deride

Verhör nt -s,-e interrogation; ins V∼ nehmen interrogate. v∼en vt interrogate; sich v∼en mishear

verhüllen vt cover; (fig) disguise. v∼d a euphemistic, adv -ally

verhungern vi (sein) starve

verhüt|en vt prevent. V∼ung f - prevention. V∼ungsmittel nt contraceptive

verhutzelt a wizened

verirren (sich) vr get lost

verjagen vt chase away

verjüngen vt rejuvenate; sich v∼ taper

verkalkt a (fam) senile

verkalkulieren (sich) vr miscalculate

Verkauf m sale; zum V∼ for sale. v∼en vt sell; zu v∼en for sale

Verkäufer(in) m(f) seller; (im Geschäft) shop assistant

Verkehr m -s traffic; (*Kontakt*) contact; (*Geschlechts-*) intercourse; aus dem V~ ziehen take out of circulation. v~en vi (*haben*) operate; (*Bus, Zug:*) run; (*Umgang haben*) associate, mix (mit with); (*Gast sein*) visit (bei jdm s.o.); frequent (in einem Lokal a restaurant); brieflich v~en correspond □ vt ins Gegenteil v~en turn round

Verkehrs|ampel f traffic lights pl. V~büro nt = V~verein. V~funk m [radio] traffic information. V~unfall m road accident. V~verein m tourist office. V~zeichen nt traffic sign

verkehrt a wrong, adv -ly; v~ herum the wrong way round; (*links*) inside out

verkennen† vt misjudge

verklagen vt sue (auf + acc for)

verkleid|en vt disguise; (*Techn*) line; sich v~en disguise oneself; (*für Kostümfest*) dress up. V~ung f -,-en disguise; (*Kostüm*) fancy dress; (*Techn*) lining

verkleiner|n vt reduce [in size]. V~ung f - reduction. V~ungsform f diminutive

verklemmt a jammed; (*psychisch*) inhibited

verkneifen† vt sich (*dat*) etw v~ do without sth; (*verbeißen*) suppress sth

verknittern vt/i (*sein*) crumple

verknüpfen vt knot together; (*verbinden*) connect, link; (*zugleich tun*) combine

verkommen vi (*sein*) be neglected; (*sittlich*) go to the bad; (*verfallen*) decay; (*Haus:*) fall into disrepair; (*Gegend:*) become run-down; (*Lebensmittel:*) go bad □ a neglected; (*sittlich*) depraved; (*Haus*) dilapidated; (*Gegend*) run-down

verkörper|n vt embody, personify. V~ung f -,-en embodiment, personification

verkraften vt cope with

verkrampft a (fig) tense

verkriechen† (sich) vr hide

verkrümmt a crooked, bent

verkrüppelt a crippled; (*Glied*) deformed

verkühl|en (sich) vr catch a chill. V~ung f -,-en chill

verkümmer|n vi (*sein*) waste/(*Pflanze:*) wither away. v~t a stunted

verkünd|en vt announce; pronounce (*Urteil*). v~igen vt announce; (*predigen*) preach

verkürzen vt shorten; (*verringern*) reduce; (*abbrechen*) cut short; while away (*Zeit*)

verladen† vt load

Verlag m -[e]s,-e publishing firm

verlangen vt ask for; (*fordern*) demand; (*berechnen*) charge; am Telefon verlangt

werden be wanted on the telephone. V~ nt -s desire; (*Bitte*) request; auf V~ on demand

verlänger|n vt extend; lengthen (*Kleid*); (*zeitlich*) prolong; renew (*Pass, Vertrag*); (*Culin*) thin down. V~ung f -,-en extension; renewal. V~ungsschnur f extension cable

verlangsamen vt slow down

Verlass (*Verläß*) m auf ihn ist kein V~ you cannot rely on him

verlassen† vt leave; (*im Stich lassen*) desert; sich v~ auf (+ acc) rely or depend on □ a deserted. V~heit f - desolation

verlässlich (*verläßlich*) a reliable

Verlauf m course; im V~ (+ gen) in the course of. v~en† vi (*sein*) run; (*ablaufen*) go; (*zerlaufen*) melt; gut v~en go [off] well □ vr sich v~en lose one's way; (*Menge:*) disperse; (*Wasser:*) drain away

verleben vt spend

verlegen vt move; (*verschieben*) postpone; (*vor-*) bring forward; (*verlieren*) mislay; (*versperren*) block; (*legen*) lay (*Teppich, Rohre*); (*veröffentlichen*) publish; sich v~ auf (+ acc) take up (*Beruf, Fach*); resort to (*Taktik, Bitten*) □ a embarrassed; nie v~ um never at a loss for. V~heit f - embarrassment

Verleger m -s,- publisher

verleihen† vt lend; (*gegen Gebühr*) hire out; (*überreichen*) award, confer; (*fig*) give

verleiten vt induce/(*verlocken*) tempt (zu to)

verlernen vt forget

verlesen†[1] vt read out; ich habe mich v~ I misread it

verlesen†[2] vt sort out

verletz|en vt injure; (*kränken*) hurt; (*verstoßen gegen*) infringe; violate (*Grenze*). v~end a hurtful, wounding. v~lich a vulnerable. V~te(r) m/f injured person; (*bei Unfall*) casualty. V~ung f -,-en injury; (*Verstoß*) infringement; violation

verleugnen vt deny; disown (*Freund*)

verleumd|en vt slander; (*schriftlich*) libel. v~erisch a slanderous; libellous. V~ung f -,-en slander; (*schriftlich*) libel

verlieben (sich) vr fall in love (in + acc with); verliebt sein be in love (in + acc with)

verlier|en† vt lose; shed (*Laub*); sich v~en disappear; (*Weg:*) peter out □ vi (*haben*) lose (an etw dat sth). V~er m -s,- loser

verlob|en (sich) vr get engaged (mit to); v~t sein be engaged. V~te f fiancée. V~te(r) m fiancé. V~ung f -,-en engagement verlock|en *vt* tempt; v∼end tempting. V∼ung *f* -,-en temptation

verlogen *a* lying

verloren *a* lost; v∼e Eier poached eggs; v∼ gehen get lost. v∼gehent *vi sep* (sein) NEW v∼ gehen, s. verloren

verlos|en *vt* raffle. V∼ung *f* -,-en raffle; (*Ziehung*) draw

verlottert *a* run-down; (*Person*) scruffy; (*sittlich*) dissolute

Verlust *m* -[e]s,-e loss

vermachen *vt* leave, bequeath

Vermächtnis *nt* -ses,-se legacy

vermähl|en (sich) *vr* marry. V∼ung *f* -,-en marriage

vermehren *vt* increase; propagate (*Pflanzen*); sich v∼ increase; (*sich fortpflanzen*) breed, multiply

vermeident *vt* avoid

vermeintlich *a* supposed, *adv* -ly

Vermerk *m* -[e]s,-e note. v∼en *vt* note [down]; übel v∼en take amiss

vermess|ent *vt* measure; survey (*Gelände*) □ *a* presumptuous. V∼enheit *f* - presumption. V∼ung *f* measurement; (*Land*-) survey

vermiet|en *vt* let, rent [out]; hire out (*Boot, Auto*); zu v∼en to let; (*Boot:*) for hire. V∼er *m* landlord. V∼erin *f* landlady

vermind|ern *vt* reduce, lessen. V∼ung *f* - reduction, decrease

vermischen *vt* mix; sich v∼ mix

vermissen *vt* miss

vermisst (vermißt) *a* missing. V∼e(r) *m* missing person/(*Mil*) soldier

vermittel|n *vi* (haben) mediate □ *vt* arrange; (*beschaffen*) find; place (*Arbeitskräfte*); impart (*Wissen*); convey (*Eindruck*). v∼s *prep* (+ *gen*) by means of

Vermittl|er *m* -s,- agent; (*Schlichter*) mediator. V∼ung *f* -,-en arrangement; (*Agentur*) agency; (*Teleph*) exchange; (*Schlichtung*) mediation

vermögent *vt* be able (zu) to. V∼ *nt* -s,- fortune. v∼d *a* wealthy

vermut|en *vt* suspect; (*glauben*) presume. v∼lich *a* probable □ *adv* presumably. V∼ung *f* -,-en supposition; (*Verdacht*) suspicion; (*Mutmaßung*) conjecture

vernachlässig|en *vt* neglect. V∼ung *f* - neglect

vernehm|ent *vt* hear; (*verhören*) question; (*Jur*) examine. V∼ung *f* -,-en questioning

verneig|en (sich) *vr* bow. V∼ung *f* -,-en bow

vernein|en *vt* answer in the negative; (*ablehnen*) reject. v∼end *a* negative. V∼ung *f* -,-en negative answer; (*Gram*) negative

vernicht|en *vt* destroy; (*ausrotten*) exterminate. v∼end *a* devastating; (*Niederlage*) crushing. V∼ung *f* - destruction; extermination

Vernunft *f* - reason; V∼ annehmen see reason

vernünftig *a* reasonable, sensible; (*fam: ordentlich*) decent □ *adv* sensibly; (*fam*) properly

veröffentlich|en *vt* publish. V∼ung *f* -,-en publication

verordn|en *vt* prescribe (*dat* for). V∼ung *f* -,-en prescription; (*Verfügung*) decree

verpachten *vt* lease [out]

verpack|en *vt* pack; (*einwickeln*) wrap. V∼ung *f* packaging; wrapping

verpassen *vt* miss; (*fam: geben*) give

verpfänden *vt* pawn

verpflanzen *vt* transplant

verpfleg|en *vt* feed; sich selbst v∼en cater for oneself. V∼ung *f* - board; (*Essen*) food; Unterkunft und V∼ung board and lodging

verpflicht|en *vt* oblige; (*einstellen*) engage; (*Sport*) sign; sich v∼en undertake/(*versprechen*) promise (zu to); (*vertraglich*) sign a contract; jdm v∼et sein be indebted to s.o. V∼ung *f* -,-en obligation, commitment

verpfuschen *vt* make a mess of

verpönt *a* v∼ sein be frowned upon

verprügeln *vt* beat up, thrash

Verputz *m* -es plaster. v∼en *vt* plaster; (*fam: essen*) polish off

Verrat *m* -[e]s betrayal, treachery. v∼ent *vt* betray; give away (*Geheimnis*); (*fam: sagen*) tell; sich v∼en give oneself away

Verräter *m* -s,- traitor. v∼isch *a* treacherous; (*fig*) revealing

verräuchert *a* smoky

verrechnen *vt* settle; clear (*Scheck*); sich v∼nen make a mistake; (*fig*) miscalculate. V∼nungsscheck *m* crossed cheque

verregnet *a* spoilt by rain; (*Tag*) rainy, wet

verreisen *vi* (sein) go away; verreist sein be away

verreißent *vt* (fam) pan, slate

verrenken *vt* dislocate; sich v∼ contort oneself

verricht|en *vt* perform, do; say (*Gebet*). V∼ung *f* -,-en task

verriegeln *vt* bolt

verring|ern *vt* reduce; sich v∼n decrease. V∼ung *f* - reduction; decrease

verrost|en *vi* (sein) rust. v∼et *a* rusty

verrücken *vt* move

verrückt *a* crazy, mad; v∼ werden/machen go/drive crazy. V∼e(r) *m*/*f* lunatic. V∼heit *f* -,-en madness; 〈*Torheit*〉 folly

Verruf *m* disrepute. v∼en *a* disreputable

verrühren *vt* mix

verrunzelt *a* wrinkled

verrutschen *vt* (*sein*) slip

Vers /fɛrs/ *m* -es,-e verse

versag|en *vi* (*haben*) fail □ *vt* jdm/sich etw v∼en deny s.o./oneself sth. V∼en *nt* -s,- failure. V∼er *m* -s,- failure

versalzen† *vt* put too much salt in/on; 〈*fig*〉 spoil

versamm|eln *vt* assemble; sich v∼eln assemble, meet. V∼lung *f* assembly, meeting

Versand *m* -[e]s dispatch. V∼haus *nt* mail-order firm

versäum|en *vt* miss; lose 〈*Zeit*〉; 〈*unterlassen*〉 neglect; [es] v∼en, etw zu tun fail or neglect to do sth. V∼nis *nt* -ses,-se omission

verschaffen *vt* get; sich (*dat*) v∼ obtain; gain 〈*Respekt*〉

verschämt *a* bashful, *adv* -ly

verschandeln *vt* spoil

verschärfen *vt* intensify; tighten 〈*Kontrolle*〉; increase 〈*Tempo*〉; aggravate 〈*Lage*〉; sich v∼ intensify; increase; 〈*Lage:*〉 worsen

verschätzen (sich) *vr* sich v∼ in (+ *dat*) misjudge

verschenken *vt* give away

verscheuchen *vt* shoo/〈*jagen*〉 chase away

verschicken *vt* send; 〈*Comm*〉 dispatch

verschieb|en† *vt* move; 〈*aufschieben*〉 put off, postpone; 〈*sl: handeln mit*〉 traffic in; sich v∼en move, shift; 〈*verrutschen*〉 〈*zeitlich*〉 be postponed. V∼ung *f* shift; postponement

verschieden *a* different; v∼e (*pl*) different; 〈*mehrere*〉 various; V∼es (v∼es) some things; 〈*dieses und jenes*〉 various things; die v∼sten Farben a whole variety of colours; das ist v∼ it varies □ *adv* differently; v∼ groß/lang of different sizes/lengths. v∼artig *a* diverse. V∼heit *f* - difference; 〈*Vielfalt*〉 diversity. v∼tlich *adv* several times

verschimmel|n *vi* (*sein*) go mouldy. v∼t *a* mouldy

verschlafen† *vi* (*haben*) oversleep □ *vt* sleep through 〈*Tag*〉; 〈*versäumen*〉 miss 〈*Zug, Termin*〉; sich v∼ oversleep □ *a* sleepy; noch v∼ still half asleep

Verschlag *m* -[e]s,⁻e shed

verschlagen† *vt* lose 〈*Seite*〉; jdm die Sprache/den Atem v∼ leave s.o. speechless/take s.o.'s breath away; nach X v∼ werden end up in X □ *a* sly, *adv* -ly

verschlechter|n *vt* make worse;. sich v∼n get worse, deteriorate. V∼ung *f* -,-en deterioration

verschleiern *vt* veil; 〈*fig*〉 hide

Verschleiß *m* -es wear and tear; 〈*Verbrauch*〉 consumption. v∼en† *vt*/*i* (*sein*) wear out

verschleppen *vt* carry off; 〈*entführen*〉 abduct; spread 〈*Seuche*〉; neglect 〈*Krankheit*〉; 〈*hinausziehen*〉 delay

verschleudern *vt* sell at a loss; 〈*verschwenden*〉 squander

verschließen† *vt* close; 〈*abschließen*〉 lock; 〈*einschließen*〉 lock up

verschlimmer|n *vt* make worse; aggravate 〈*Lage*〉; sich v∼n get worse, deteriorate. V∼ung *f* -,-en deterioration

verschlingen† *vt* intertwine; 〈*fressen*〉 devour; 〈*fig*〉 swallow

verschlissen *a* worn

verschlossen *a* reserved. V∼heit *f* - reserve

verschlucken *vt* swallow; sich v∼ choke (an + *dat* on)

Verschluss *m* -es,⁻e (Verschluß *m* -sses, ⁻sse) fastener, clasp; 〈*Fenster-, Koffer-*〉 catch; 〈*Flaschen-*〉 top; 〈*luftdicht*〉 seal; 〈*Phot*〉 shutter; unter V∼ under lock and key

verschlüsselt *a* coded

verschmähen *vt* spurn

verschmelzen† *vt*/*i* (*sein*) fuse

verschmerzen *vt* get over

verschmutz|en *vt* soil; pollute 〈*Luft*〉 □ *vi* (*sein*) get dirty. V∼ung *f* - pollution

verschnaufen *vi*/*r* (*haben*) [sich] v∼ get one's breath

verschneit *a* snow-covered

verschnörkelt *a* ornate

verschnüren *vt* tie up

verschollen *a* missing

verschonen *vt* spare

verschönern *vt* brighten up; 〈*verbessern*〉 improve

verschossen *a* faded

verschrammt *a* scratched

verschränken *vt* cross

verschreiben† *vt* prescribe; sich v∼ make a slip of the pen·

verschrie[e]n *a* notorious

verschroben *a* eccentric

verschrotten *vt* scrap

verschulden *vt* be to blame for; sich v∼ get into debt. V∼ *nt* -s fault

verschuldet *a* v~ sein be in debt

verschütten *vt* spill; ⟨*begraben*⟩ bury

verschweigen† *vt* conceal, hide

verschwend|en *vt* waste. v~erisch *a* extravagant, *adv* -ly; ⟨*üppig*⟩ lavish, *adv* -ly. V~ung *f* - extravagance; ⟨*Vergeudung*⟩ waste

verschwiegen *a* discreet; ⟨*Ort*⟩ secluded. V~heit *f* - discretion

verschwimmen† *vi* (sein) become blurred

verschwinden† *vi* (sein) disappear; [mal] v~ ⟨*fam*⟩ spend a penny. V~ *nt* -s disappearance

verschwommen *a* blurred

verschwör|en (sich) *vr* conspire. V~ung *f* -,-en conspiracy

versehen† *vt* perform; hold ⟨*Posten*⟩; keep ⟨*Haushalt*⟩; v~ mit provide with; sich v~ make a mistake; ehe man sich's versieht before you know where you are. V~ *nt* -s,- oversight; ⟨*Fehler*⟩ slip; aus V~ by mistake. v~tlich *adv* by mistake

Versehrte(r) *m* disabled person

versenden† *vt* send [out]

versengen *vt* singe; ⟨*stärker*⟩ scorch

versenken *vt* sink; sich v~ in (+ *acc*) immerse oneself in

versessen *a* keen (auf + *acc* on)

versetz|en *vt* move; transfer ⟨*Person*⟩; ⟨*Sch*⟩ move up; ⟨*verpfänden*⟩ pawn; ⟨*verkaufen*⟩ sell; ⟨*vermischen*⟩ blend; ⟨*antworten*⟩ reply; jdn v~en ⟨*fam:* warten lassen⟩ stand s.o. up; jdm einen Stoß/Schreck v~en give s.o. a push/fright; jdm in Angst/Erstaunen v~en frighten/astonish s.o.; sich in jds Lage v~en put oneself in s.o.'s place. V~ung *f* -,-en move; transfer; ⟨*Sch*⟩ move to a higher class

verseuch|en *vt* contaminate. V~ung *f* - contamination

versicher|n *vt* insure; ⟨*bekräftigen*⟩ affirm; jdm v~n assure s.o ⟨dass that⟩. V~ung *f* -,-en insurance; assurance

versiegeln *vt* seal

versiegen *vi* (sein) dry up

versiert /vɛrˈʒiːɐt/ *a* experienced

versilbert *a* silver-plated

versinken† (sein) sink; in Gedanken versunken lost in thought

Version /vɛrˈzjoːn/ *f* -,-en version

Versmaß /ˈfɛrs-/ *nt* metre

versöhn|en *vt* reconcile; sich v~en become reconciled. v~lich *a* conciliatory. V~ung *f* -,-en reconciliation

versorg|en *vt* provide, supply (mit with); provide for ⟨*Familie*⟩; ⟨*betreuen*⟩ look after; keep ⟨*Haushalt*⟩. V~ung *f* - provision, supply; ⟨*Betreuung*⟩ care

verspät|en (sich) *vr* be late. v~et *a* late; ⟨*Zug*⟩ delayed; ⟨*Dank, Glückwunsch*⟩ belated □ *adv* late; belatedly. V~ung *f* - lateness; V~ung haben be late

versperren *vt* block; bar ⟨*Weg*⟩

verspiel|en *vt* gamble away; sich v~en play a wrong note. v~t *a* playful, *adv* -ly

verspotten *vt* mock, ridicule

versprech|en *vt* promise; sich v~en make a slip of the tongue; sich ⟨*dat*⟩ viel v~en von have high hopes of; ein viel v~ender Anfang a promising start. V~en *nt* -s,- promise. V~ungen *fpl* promises

verspüren *vt* feel

verstaatlich|en *vt* nationalize. V~ung *f* - nationalization

Verstand *m* -[e]s mind; ⟨*Vernunft*⟩ reason; den V~ verlieren go out of one's mind. v~esmäßig *a* rational, *adv* -ly

verständig *a* sensible, *adv* -bly; ⟨*klug*⟩ intelligent, *adv* -ly. v~en *vt* notify, inform; sich v~en communicate; ⟨*sich verständlich machen*⟩ make oneself understood; ⟨*sich einigen*⟩ reach agreement. V~ung *f* - notification; communication; ⟨*Einigung*⟩ agreement

verständlich *a* comprehensible, *adv* -bly; ⟨*deutlich*⟩ clear, *adv* -ly; ⟨*begreiflich*⟩ understandable; leicht v~ easily understood; sich v~ machen make oneself understood. v~erweise *adv* understandably

Verständnis *nt* -ses understanding. v~los *a* uncomprehending, *adv* -ly. v~voll *a* understanding, *adv* -ly

verstärk|en *vt* strengthen, reinforce; ⟨*steigern*⟩ intensify, increase; amplify ⟨*Ton*⟩; sich v~en intensify. V~er *m* -s,- amplifier. V~ung *f* reinforcement; increase; amplification; ⟨*Truppen*⟩ reinforcements *pl*

verstaubt *a* dusty

verstauchen *vt* sprain

verstauen *vt* stow

Versteck *nt* -[e]s,-e hiding-place; V~ spielen play hide-and-seek. v~en *vt* hide; sich v~en hide. v~t *a* hidden; ⟨*heimlich*⟩ secret; ⟨*verstohlen*⟩ furtive, *adv* -ly

versteh|en† *vt* understand; ⟨*können*⟩ know; falsch v~en misunderstand; sich v~en understand one another; ⟨*auskommen*⟩ get on; das versteht sich von selbst that goes without saying

versteifen *vt* stiffen; sich v~ stiffen; ⟨*fig*⟩ insist (auf + *acc* on)

versteiger|n *vt* auction. V~ung *f* auction

versteinert a fossilized

verstellbar a adjustable. v~en vt adjust; (versperren) block; (verändern) disguise; sich v~en pretend. V~ung f - pretence

versteuern vt pay tax on

verstiegen a (fig) extravagant

verstimm|t a disgruntled; ⟨Magen⟩ upset; (Mus) out of tune. V~ung f - ill humour; ⟨Magen-⟩ upset

verstockt a stubborn, adv -ly

verstohlen a furtive, adv -ly

verstopf|en vt plug; (versperren) block; v~t blocked; ⟨Person⟩ constipated. V~ung f -,-en blockage; (Med) constipation

verstorben a late, deceased. V~e(r) m/f deceased

verstört a bewildered

Verstoß m -[e]s,ᵉe infringement. v~en† vt disown □ vi (haben) v~en gegen contravene, infringe; offend against ⟨Anstand⟩

verstreichen† vt spread □ vi (sein) pass

verstreuen vt scatter

verstümmeln vt mutilate; garble ⟨Text⟩

verstummen vi (sein) fall silent; ⟨Gespräch, Lärm:⟩ cease

Versuch m -[e]s,-e attempt; (Experiment) experiment. v~en vt/i (haben) try; sich v~en in (+ dat) try one's hand at; v~t sein be tempted (zu to). V~skaninchen nt (fig) guinea-pig. v~sweise adv as an experiment. V~ung f -,-en temptation

versündigen (sich) vr sin (an + dat against)

vertagen vt adjourn; (aufschieben) postpone; sich v~ adjourn

vertauschen vt exchange; (verwechseln) mix up

verteidig|en vt defend. V~er m -s,- defender; (Jur) defence counsel. V~ung f -,-en defence

verteil|en vt distribute; (zuteilen) allocate; (ausgeben) hand out; (verstreichen) spread; sich v~en spread out. V~ung f - distribution; allocation

vertief|en vt deepen; v~t sein in (+ acc) be engrossed in. V~ung f -,-en hollow, depression

vertikal /verti'ka:l/ a vertical, adv -ly

vertilgen vt exterminate; kill [off] ⟨Unkraut⟩; (fam: essen) demolish

vertippen (sich) vr make a typing mistake

vertonen vt set to music

Vertrag m -[e]s,ᵉe contract; (Pol) treaty

vertragen† vt tolerate, stand; take ⟨Kritik, Spaß⟩; sich v~ get on; (passen) go (mit with); sich wieder v~ make it up □ a worn

verträglich a contractual

verträglich a good-natured; (bekömmlich) digestible

vertrauen vi (haben) trust ⟨jdm/etw s.o./sth⟩; auf + acc in). V~ nt -s trust, confidence (zu in); im V~ in confidence. V~smann m (pl -leute) representative; (Sprecher) spokesman. v~svoll a trusting, adv -ly. v~swürdig a trustworthy

vertraulich a confidential, adv -ly; (intim) familiar, adv -ly

vertraut a intimate; (bekannt) familiar; sich v~ machen mit familiarize oneself with. V~heit f - intimacy; familiarity

vertreiben† vt drive away; drive out ⟨Feind⟩; (Comm) sell; sich (dat) die Zeit v~en pass the time. V~ung f -,-en expulsion

vertret|en† vt represent; (einspringen für) stand in or deputize for; (verfechten) support; hold ⟨Meinung⟩; sich (dat) den Fuß v~en twist one's ankle; sich (dat) die Beine v~en stretch one's legs. V~er m -s,- representative; deputy; ⟨Arzt-⟩ locum; (Verfechter) supporter, advocate. V~ung f -,-en representation; (Person) deputy; (eines Arztes) locum; (Handels-) agency

Vertrieb m -[e]s (Comm) sale. V~ene(r) m/f displaced person

vertrocknen vi (sein) dry up

vertrösten vt jdn auf später v~ put s.o. off until later

vertun† vt waste; sich v~ (fam) make a mistake

vertuschen vt hush up

verübeln vt jdm etw v~ hold sth against s.o.

verüben vt commit

verunglimpfen vt denigrate

verunglücken vi (sein) be involved in an accident; (fam: missglücken) go wrong; tödlich v~ be killed in an accident

verunreinigen vt pollute; (verseuchen) contaminate; (verschmutzen) soil

verunstalten vt disfigure

veruntreu|en vt embezzle. V~ung f - embezzlement

verursachen vt cause

verurteil|en vt condemn; (Jur) convict (wegen of); sentence (zum Tode to death). V~ung f - condemnation; (Jur) conviction

vervielfachen vt multiply

vervielfältigen vt duplicate

vervollkommnen vt perfect

vervollständigen vt complete

verwachsen a deformed

verwählen (sich) vr misdial

verwahren *vt* keep; (*verstauen*) put away; sich v~ (*fig*) protest

verwahrlost *a* neglected; (*Haus*) dilapidated; (*sittlich*) depraved

Verwahrung *f* - keeping; in V~ nehmen take into safe keeping

verwaist *a* orphaned

verwalt|en *vt* administer; (*leiten*) manage; govern (*Land*). V~er *m* -s,- administrator; manager. V~ung *f* -,-en administration; management; government

verwand|eln *vt* transform, change (in + *acc* into); sich v~eln change, turn (in + *acc* into). V~lung *f* transformation

verwandt *a* related (mit to). V~e(r) *m*/*f* relative. V~schaft *f* - relationship; (*Menschen*) relatives *pl*

verwarn|en *vt* warn, caution. V~ung *f* warning, caution

verwaschen *a* washed out, faded

verwechs|eln *vt* mix up, confuse; (*halten für*) mistake (mit for). V~lung *f* -,-en mix-up

verwegen *a* audacious, *adv* -ly

Verwehung *f* -,-en [snow-]drift

verweichlicht *a* (*fig*) soft

verweiger|n *vt*/*i* (*haben*) refuse (jdm etw s.o sth); den Gehorsam v~n refuse to obey. V~ung *f* refusal

verweilen *vi* (*sein*) stay

Verweis *m* -es,-e reference (auf + *acc* to); (*Tadel*) reprimand; v~en† *vt* refer (auf/ an + *acc* to); (*tadeln*) reprimand; von der Schule v~en expel

verwelken *vi* (*sein*) wilt

verwend|en† *vt* use; spend (*Zeit, Mühe*). V~ung *f* use

verwerf|en† *vt* reject; sich v~en warp. v~lich *a* reprehensible

verwert|en *vt* utilize, use; (*Comm*) exploit. V~ung *f* - utilization; exploitation

verwesen *vi* (*sein*) decompose

verwick|eln *vt* involve (in + *acc* in); sich v~eln get tangled up; in etw (*acc*) v~elt sein (*fig*) be involved *or* mixed up in sth. v~elt *a* complicated

verwildert *a* wild; (*Garten*) overgrown; (*Aussehen*) unkempt

verwinden† *vt* (*fig*) get over

verwirken *vt* forfeit

verwirklichen *vt* realize; sich v~ be realized

verwirr|en *vt* tangle up; (*fig*) confuse; sich v~en get tangled up; (*fig*) become confused. v~t *a* confused. V~ung *f* confusion

verwischen *vt* smudge

verwittert *a* weathered; (*Gesicht*) weather-beaten

verwitwet *a* widowed

verwöhn|en *vt* spoil. v~t *a* spoilt; (*anspruchsvoll*) discriminating

verworren *a* confused

verwund|bar *a* vulnerable. v~en *vt* wound

verwunder|lich *a* surprising. v~n *vt* surprise; sich v~n be surprised. V~ung *f* - surprise

Verwund|ete(r) *m* wounded soldier; die V~eten the wounded *pl*. V~ung *f* -,-en wound

verwünsch|en *vt* curse. v~t *a* confounded

verwüst|en *vt* devastate, ravage. V~ung *f* -,-en devastation

verzagen *vi* (*haben*) lose heart

verzählen (sich) *vr* miscount

verzärteln *vt* mollycoddle

verzaubern *vt* bewitch; (*fig*) enchant; v~ in (+ *acc*) turn into

Verzehr *m* -s consumption. v~en *vt* eat; (*aufbrauchen*) use up; sich v~en (*fig*) pine away

verzeich|nen *vt* list; (*registrieren*) register. V~nis *nt* -ses,-se list; (*Inhalts-*) index

verzeih|en† *vt* forgive; v~en Sie! excuse me! V~ung *f* - forgiveness; um V~ung bitten apologize; (*Gewitter*) disperse; V~ung! sorry! (*bei Frage*) excuse me!

verzerren *vt* distort; contort (*Gesicht*); pull (*Muskel*)

Verzicht *m* -[e]s renunciation (auf + *acc* of). v~en *vi* (*haben*) do without; v~en auf (+ *acc*) give up; renounce (*Recht, Erbe*)

verzieh|en† *vt* pull out of shape; (*verwöhnen*) spoil; sich v~ lose shape; (*Holz:*) warp; (*Gesicht:*) twist; (*verschwinden*) disappear; (*Nebel:*) disperse; (*Gewitter:*) pass; das Gesicht v~ pull a face □ *vi* (*sein*) move [away]

verzier|en *vt* decorate. V~ung *f* -,-en decoration

verzinsen *vt* pay interest on

verzöger|n *vt* delay; (*verlangsamen*) slow down; sich v~n be delayed. V~ung *f* -,-en delay

verzollen *vt* pay duty on; haben Sie etwas zu v~? have you anything to declare?

verzück|t *a* ecstatic, *adv* -ally. V~ung *f* - rapture, ecstasy

Verzug *m* delay; in V~ in arrears

verzweif|eln *vi* (*sein*) despair. v~elt *a* desperate, *adv* -ly; v~elt sein be in despair; (*ratlos*) be desperate. V~lung *f* - despair; (*Ratlosigkeit*) desperation verzw**ei**gen (sich) *vr* branch [out]

verzw**i**ckt *a* (*fam*) tricky

Veto /'ve:to/ *nt* -s,-s veto

V**e**tter *m* -s,-n cousin. V~nwirtschaft *f* nepotism

vgl. *abbr* (vergleiche) cf.

Viadukt /vja'dʊkt/ *nt* -[e]s,-e viaduct

vibr**ie**ren /vi'bri:rən/ *vi* (haben) vibrate

Video /'vi:deo/ *nt* -s,-s video. V~kassette *f* video cassette. V~recorder /-rəkɔrdɐ/ *m* -s,- video recorder

V**ie**h *nt* -[e]s livestock; (*Rinder*) cattle *pl*; (*fam: Tier*) creature. v~isch *a* brutal, *adv* -ly

v**ie**l *pron* a great deal/(*fam*) a lot of; (*pl*) many, (*fam*) a lot of; (*substantivisch*) v~[es] much, (*fam*) a lot; nicht/so/ wie/zu viel not/so/how/too much/ (*pl*) many; v~e *pl* many; das v~e Geld/ Lesen all that money/reading □ *adv* much, (*fam*) a lot; v~ mehr/weniger much more/less; v~ zu groß/klein/viel much *or* far too big/small/much; so v~ wie möglich as much as possible; so/zu v~ arbeiten work so/too much

v**ie**l|deutig *a* ambiguous. V~erlei *inv a* many kinds of □ *pron* many things. v~fach *a* multiple □ *adv* many times; (*fam: oft*) frequently. V~falt *f* -diversity, [great] variety. v~fältig *a* diverse, varied

viell**ei**cht *adv* perhaps, maybe; (*fam: wirklich*) really

v**ie**lmals *adv* very much; danke v~! thank you very much!

v**ie**l|mehr *adv* rather; (*im Gegenteil*) on the contrary. v~sagend *a* (NEW) v~ sa-gend, s. sagen

v**ie**lseitig *a* varied; (*Person*) versatile □ *adv* v~ begabt versatile. V~keit *f* -versatility

v**ie**lversprechend *a* (NEW) viel verspre-chend, s. versprechen

v**ie**r *inv a*, V~ *f* -,-en four; (*Sch*) ≈ fair. V~eck *nt* -[e]s,-e oblong, rectangle; (*Quadrat*) square. v~eckig *a* oblong, rectan-gular; square. v~fach *a* quadruple. V~linge *mpl* quadruplets

viertel /'fɪrtl/ *inv a* a quarter; eine v~ Million a quarter of a million; um v~ neun at [a] quarter past eight; um drei v~ neun at [a] quarter to nine; eine v~ Stunde = eine Viertelstunde. V~ *nt* -s,- quarter; (*Wein*) quarter litre; v~ vor/ nach sechs [a] quarter to/past six; um V~/drei v~ neun (NEW) um v~/drei v~ neun, s. viertel. V~finale *nt* quarter-fi-nal. V~jahr *nt* three months *pl*; (*Comm*) quarter. v~jährlich *a* & *adv* quarterly. v~n *vt* quarter. V~note *f* crotchet,

(*Amer*) quarter note. V~stunde *f* quarter of an hour

v**ie**r|zehn /'fɪr-/ *inv a* fourteen. v~zehnte(r,s) *a* fourteenth. v~zig *inv a* forty. v~zigste(r,s) *a* fortieth

Villa /'vɪla/ *f* -,-len villa

violett /vjo'lɛt/ *a* violet

Vio|line /vjo'li:nə/ *f* -,-n violin. V~linschlüssel *m* treble clef. V~lon-cello /-lɔn'tʃɛlo/ *nt* cello

Virtuose /vɪr'tʊo:zə/ *m* -n,-n virtuoso

Virus /'vi:rʊs/ *nt* -,-ren virus

Visier /vi'zi:ɐ/ *nt* -s,-e visor

Vision /vi'zjo:n/ *f* -,-en vision

Visite /vi'zi:tə/ *f* -,-n round; V~ machen do one's round

visuell /vi'zʊɛl/ *a* visual, *adv* -ly

Visum /'vi:zʊm/ *nt* -s,-sa visa

vital /vi'ta:l/ *a* vital; (*Person*) energetic. V~ität *f* - vitality

Vitamin /vita'mi:n/ *nt* -s,-e vitamin

Vitrine /vi'tri:nə/ *f* -,-n display cabinet; (*im Museum*) case

Vizepräsident /'fi:tsə-/ *m* vice president

Vogel *m* -s,- bird; einen V~ haben (*fam*) have a screw loose. V~scheuche *f* -,-n scarecrow

Vokab|eln /vo'ka:bəln/ *fpl* vocabulary *sg*. V~ular *nt* -s,-e vocabulary

Vokal /vo'ka:l/ *m* -s,-e vowel

Volant /vo'lã:/ *m* -s,-s flounce; (*Auto*) steering-wheel

Volk *nt* -[e]s,-er people *sg*; (*Bevölkerung*) people *pl*; (*Bienen-*) colony

Völker|kunde *f* ethnology. V~mord *m* genocide. V~recht *nt* international law

Volks|abstimmung *f* plebiscite. V~fest *nt* public festival. V~hoch-schule *f* adult education classes *pl*/ (*Gebäude*) centre. V~lied *nt* folk-song. V~tanz *m* folk-dance. v~tümlich *a* pop-ular. V~wirt *m* economist. V~wirt-schaft *f* economics *sg*. V~zählung *f* [national] census

voll *a* full (von *od* mit of); (*Haar*) thick; (*Erfolg, Ernst*) complete; (*Wahrheit*) whole; v~ machen fill up; v~ tanken fill up with petrol; die Uhr schlug v~ (*fam*) the clock struck the hour □ *adv* (*ganz*) completely; (*arbeiten*) full-time; (*auszahlen*) in full; v~ und ganz com-pletely

voll**au**f *adv* fully, completely

Voll|beschäftigung *f* full employment. V~blut *nt* thoroughbred

vollbringen† *vt insep* accomplish; work (*Wunder*)

vollende|n vt insep complete. v∼t a perfect, adv -ly; v∼te Gegenwart/Vergangenheit perfect/pluperfect

vollends adv completely

Vollendung f completion; (Vollkommenheit) perfection

voller inv a full of; v∼ Angst/Freude filled with fear/joy; v∼ Flecken covered with stains

Völlerei f - gluttony

Volleyball /'vɔli-/ m volleyball

vollführen vt insep perform

vollfüllen vt sep fill up

Vollgas nt V∼ geben put one's foot down; mit V∼ flat out

völlig a complete, adv -ly

volljährig a v∼ sein (Jur) be of age. V∼keit f - (Jur) majority

Vollkaskoversicherung f fully comprehensive insurance

vollkommen a perfect, adv -ly; (völlig) complete, adv -ly. V∼heit f - perfection

Voll|kornbrot nt wholemeal bread. V∼macht f -,-en authority; (Jur) power of attorney. V∼mond m full moon. V∼pension f full board. v∼schlank a with a fuller figure

vollständig a complete, adv -ly

vollstrecken vt insep execute; carry out ⟨Urteil⟩

volltanken vi sep (haben) (NEW) voll tanken, s. voll

Volltreffer m direct hit

vollzählig a complete; sind wir v∼? are we all here?

vollziehen† vt insep carry out; perform ⟨Handlung⟩; consummate ⟨Ehe⟩; sich v∼ take place

Volt /vɔlt/ nt -[s],- volt

Volumen /vo'luːmən/ nt -s,- volume

vom prep = von dem; vom Rauchen from smoking

von prep (+ dat) of; (über) about; (Ausgangspunkt, Ursache) from; (beim Passiv) by; Musik von Mozart music by Mozart; einer von euch one of you; von hier/heute an from here/today; von mir aus I don't mind

voneinander adv from each other; ⟨abhängig⟩ on each other

vonseiten prep (+ gen) on the part of

vonstatten adv v∼ gehen take place; gut v∼ gehen go [off] well

vor prep (+ dat/acc) in front of; (zeitlich, Reihenfolge) before; (+ dat) (bei Uhrzeit) to; ⟨warnen, sich fürchten/schämen⟩ of; ⟨schützen, davonlaufen⟩ from; ⟨Respekt haben⟩ for; vor Angst/Kälte zittern tremble with fear/cold; vor drei Tagen/ Jahren three days/years ago; vor sich (acc) hin murmeln mumble to oneself; vor allen Dingen above all □ adv forward; vor und zurück backwards and forwards

Vor|abend m eve. V∼ahnung f premonition

voran adv at the front; (voraus) ahead; (vorwärts) forward. v∼gehen† vi sep (sein) lead the way; (Fortschritte machen) make progress; jdm/etw v∼gehen precede s.o./sth. v∼kommen† vi sep (sein) make progress; (fig) get on

Vor|anschlag m estimate. V∼anzeige f advance notice. V∼arbeit f preliminary work. V∼arbeiter m foreman

voraus adv ahead (dat of); (vorn) at the front; (vorwärts) forward □ im Voraus (voraus) in advance. v∼bezahlen vt sep pay in advance. v∼gehen† vi sep (sein) go on ahead; jdm/etw v∼gehen precede s.o./sth. V∼sage f -,-n prediction. v∼sagen vt sep predict. v∼sehen† vt sep foresee

voraussetz|en vt sep take for granted; (erfordern) require; vorausgesetzt, dass provided that. V∼ung f -,-en assumption; (Erfordernis) prerequisite; unter der V∼ung, dass on condition that

Voraussicht f foresight; aller V∼ nach in all probability. v∼lich a anticipated, expected □ adv probably

Vorbehalt m -[e]s,-e reservation. s. v∼en† vt sep sich (dat) v∼en reserve ⟨Recht⟩; jdm v∼en sein/bleiben be left to s.o. v∼los a unreserved, adv -ly

vorbei adv past (an jdm/etw s.o./sth); (zu Ende) over. v∼fahren† vi sep (sein) drive/go past. v∼gehen† vi sep (sein) go past; (verfehlen) miss; ⟨verpassen⟩ pass; (fam: besuchen) drop in (bei on). v∼kommen† vi sep (sein) pass/(v∼können) get past (an jdm/etw s.o./sth); (fam: besuchen) drop in (bei on)

vorbereit|en vt sep prepare; prepare for ⟨Reise⟩; sich v∼en prepare [oneself] (auf + acc for). V∼ung f -,-en preparation

vorbestellen vt sep order/(im Theater, Hotel) book in advance

vorbestraft a v∼ sein have a [criminal] record

vorbeug|en v sep □ vt bend forward; sich v∼en bend or lean forward □ vi (haben) prevent (etw dat sth); v∼end preventive. V∼ung f - prevention

Vorbild nt model. v∼lich a exemplary, model □ adv in an exemplary manner

vorbringen† vt sep put forward; offer ⟨Entschuldigung⟩

vordatieren vt sep post-date

Vorder|bein nt foreleg. v∼e(r,s) a front.
V∼grund m foreground. V∼mann m (pl
-männer) person in front; auf V∼mann
bringen (fam) lick into shape; (aufräumen) tidy up. V∼rad nt front wheel.
V∼seite f front; (einer Münze) obverse.
v∼ste(r,s) a front, first. V∼teil nt front

vor|drängeln (sich) vr sep (fam) jump
the queue. v∼drängen (sich) vr sep push
forward. v∼dringen† vi sep (sein) advance

vor|ehelich a pre-marital. v∼eilig a
rash, adv -ly

voreingenommen a biased, prejudiced.
V∼heit f - bias

vorenthalten† vt sep withhold

vorerst adv for the time being

Vorfahr m -en,-en ancestor

vorfahren† vi sep (sein) drive up;
(vorwärts-) move forward; (voraus-) drive
on ahead

Vorfahrt f right of way; 'V∼ beachten'
'give way'. V∼sstraße f ≈ major road

Vorfall m incident. v∼en† vi sep (sein)
happen

vorfinden† vt sep find

Vorfreude f [happy] anticipation

vorführ|en vt sep present, show; (de-
monstrieren) demonstrate; (aufführen)
perform. V∼ung f presentation; demonstration; performance

Vor|gabe f (Sport) handicap. V∼gang m
occurrence; (Techn) process. V∼gän-
ger(in) m -s,- (f -,-nen) predecessor.
V∼garten m front garden

vorgeben† vt sep pretend

vor|gefasst (vor|gefaßt) a preconceived.
v∼gefertigt a prefabricated

vorgehen† vi sep (sein) go forward;
(voraus-) go on ahead; (Uhr:) be fast; (wichtig sein) take precedence; (verfahren) act,
proceed; (geschehen) happen, go on. V∼
nt -s action

vor|geschichtlich a prehistoric.
V∼geschmack m foretaste. V∼ge-
setzte(r) m/f superior. V∼gestern adv
the day before yesterday; v∼gestern
Abend/Nacht the evening/night before
last

vorhaben† vt sep propose, intend (zu to);
etw v∼ have sth planned; nichts v∼ have
no plans. V∼ nt -s,- plan; (Projekt) project

vorhalt|en† v sep □ vt hold up; jdm etw
v∼en reproach s.o. for sth □ vi (haben)
last. V∼ungen fpl jdm V∼ungen
machen reproach s.o. (wegen for)

Vorhand f (Sport) forehand

vorhanden a existing; v∼ sein exist;
(verfügbar sein) be available. V∼sein nt
-s existence

Vorhang m curtain

Vorhängeschloss (Vorhängeschloß)
nt padlock

vorher adv before[hand]

vorhergehend a previous

vorherig a prior; (vorhergehend) previous

Vorherrsch|aft f supremacy. v∼en vi
sep (haben) predominate. v∼end a pre-
dominant

Vorher|sage f -,-n prediction; (Wetter-)
forecast. v∼sagen vt sep predict; forecast
(Wetter). v∼sehen† vt sep foresee

vorhin adv just now

vorige(r,s) a last, previous

Vor|kämpfer m (fig) champion.
V∼kehrungen fpl precautions.
V∼kenntnisse fpl previous knowledge
sg

vorkommen† vi sep (sein) happen; (vorhanden sein) occur; (nach vorn kommen)
come forward; (hervorkommen) come out;
(zu sehen sein) show; jdm bekannt/ver-
dächtig v∼ seem familiar/suspicious to
s.o.; sich (dat) dumm/alt v∼ feel
stupid/old. V∼ nt -s,- occurrence; (Geol)
deposit

Vorkriegszeit f pre-war period

vorlad|en† vt sep (Jur) summons. V∼ung
f summons

Vorlage f model; (Muster) pattern;
(Gesetzes-) bill

vorlassen† vt sep admit; jdn v∼ (fam) let
s.o. pass; (den Vortritt lassen) let s.o. go
first

Vor|lauf m (Sport) heat. V∼läufer m fore-
runner. v∼läufig a provisional, adv -ly;
(zunächst) for the time being. v∼laut a
forward. V∼leben nt past

vorleg|en vt sep put on (Kette); (unter-
breiten) present; (vorzeigen) show; jdm
Fleisch v∼en serve s.o. with meat. V∼er
m -s,- mat; (Bett-) rug

vorles|en† vt sep read [out]; jdm v∼en
read to s.o. V∼ung f (Univ) lecture

vorletzt|e(r,s) a last ... but one; (Silbe)
penultimate; v∼es Jahr the year before
last

vorlieb adv v∼ nehmen make do (mit
with). v∼nehmen† vt sep (NEW) v∼ nehmen, s. vorlieb

Vorliebe f preference

vorliegen† vt sep (haben) be present/(verfügbar) available; (bestehen) exist, be; es
muss ein Irrtum v∼ there must be some
mistake. v∼d a present; (Frage) at issue

vorlügen† vt sep lie (dat to)

vorm prep = vor dem

vormachen vt sep put up; put on ⟨Kette⟩; push ⟨Riegel⟩; (zeigen) demonstrate; jdm etwas v∼ (fam: täuschen) kid s.o.

Vormacht f supremacy

vormals adv formerly

Vormarsch m (Mil & fig) advance

vormerken vt sep make a note of; (reservieren) reserve

Vormittag m morning; gestern/heute V∼ yesterday/this morning. v∼adv gestern/heute v∼ (NEW) gestern/heute V∼, s. Vormittag. v∼s adv in the morning

Vormund m -[e]s,-munde & -münder guardian

vorn adv at the front; nach v∼ to the front; von v∼ from the front/(vom Anfang) beginning; wieder von v∼ anfangen start afresh

Vorname m first name

vorne adv = vorn

vornehm a distinguished; (elegant) smart, adv -ly

vornehmen† vt sep carry out; sich ⟨dat⟩ v∼, etw zu tun plan/(beschließen) resolve to do sth

vorn/herein adv von v∼herein from the start. **v∼über** adv forward

Vor/ort m suburb. V∼rang m priority, precedence (vor + dat over). V∼rat m -[e]s,-e supply, stock (an + dat of). v∼rätig a available; v∼rätig haben have in stock. V∼ratskammer f larder. V∼raum m ante-room. V∼recht nt privilege. V∼richtung f device

vorrücken vt/i sep (sein) move forward; (Mil) advance

Vorrunde f qualifying round

vors prep = vor das

vorsagen vt/i sep (haben) recite; jdm [die Antwort] v∼ tell s.o. the answer

Vor/satz m resolution. v∼sätzlich a deliberate, adv -ly; (Jur) premeditated

Vorschau f preview; (Film-) trailer

Vorschein m zum V∼ kommen appear

vorschießen† vt sep advance ⟨Geld⟩

Vorschlag m suggestion, proposal. v∼en† vt sep suggest, propose

vorschnell a rash, adv -ly

vorschreiben† vt sep lay down; dictate (dat to); vorgeschriebene Dosis prescribed dose

Vorschrift f regulation; (Anweisung) instruction; jdm V∼en machen tell s.o. what to do; Dienst nach V∼ work to rule. v∼smäßig a correct, adv -ly

Vorschule f nursery school

Vorschuss (Vorschuß) m advance

vorschützen vt sep plead [as an excuse]; feign ⟨Krankheit⟩

vorseh|en† v sep ☐ vt intend (für/als for/as); (planen) plan; sich v∼en be careful (vor + dat of) ☐ vi (haben) peep out. V∼ung f - providence

vorsetzen vt sep move forward; jdm etw v∼ serve s.o. sth

Vorsicht f - care; (bei Gefahr) caution; V∼! careful! (auf Schild) 'caution'. v∼ig a careful, adv -ly; cautious, adv -ly. v∼shalber adv to be on the safe side. V∼smaßnahme f precaution

Vorsilbe f prefix

Vorsitz m chairmanship; den V∼ führen be in the chair. V∼en† vi sep (haben) preside (dat over). V∼ende(r) m/f chair[man]

Vorsorge f V∼ treffen take precautions; make provisions (für for). v∼n vi sep (haben) provide (für for). V∼untersuchung f check-up

vorsorglich adv as a precaution

Vorspeise f starter

Vorspiel nt prelude. v∼en v sep ☐ vt perform/ (Mus) play (dat to) ☐ vi (haben) audition

vorsprechen† v sep ☐ vt recite; (zum Nachsagen) say (dat to) ☐ vi (haben) (Theat) audition; bei jdm v∼ call on s.o.

vorspringen† vi sep (sein) jut out; v∼des Kinn prominent chin

Vor/sprung m projection; (Fels-) ledge; (Vorteil) lead (vor + dat over). V∼stadt f suburb. v∼städtisch a suburban. V∼stand m board [of directors]; (Vereins-) committee; (Partei-) executive

vorsteh|en† vi sep (haben) project, protrude; einer Abteilung v∼en be in charge of a department; v∼end protruding; ⟨Augen⟩ bulging. V∼er m -s,- head; (Gemeinde-) chairman

vorstell|bar a imaginable, conceivable. v∼en vt sep put forward ⟨Bein, Uhr⟩; (darstellen) represent; (bekannt machen) introduce; sich v∼en introduce oneself; (als Bewerber) go for an interview; sich ⟨dat⟩ etw v∼en imagine sth. V∼ung f introduction; (bei Bewerbung) interview; (Aufführung) performance; (Idee) idea; (Phantasie) imagination. V∼ungsgespräch nt interview. V∼ungskraft f imagination

Vorstoß m advance

Vorstrafe f previous conviction

Vortag m day before

vortäuschen vt sep feign, fake

Vorteil m advantage. v∼haft a advantageous, adv -ly; ⟨Kleidung, Farbe⟩ flattering

Vortrag m -[e]s,-e talk; (wissenschaftlich) lecture; ⟨Klavier-, Gedicht-⟩ recital. v∼en† vt sep perform; (aufsagen) recite; (singen)

sing; (darlegen) present (dat to); express ⟨Wunsch⟩

vortrefflich a excellent, adv -ly

vortreten† vi sep (sein) step forward; (hervor-) protrude

Vortritt m precedence; jdm den V~ lassen let s.o. go first

vorüber adv v~ sein be over; an etw (dat) v~ past sth. v~gehen† vi sep (sein) walk past; (vergehen) pass. v~gehend a temporary, adv -ily

Vor|urteil nt prejudice. V~verkauf m advance booking

Vor|wahl[nummer] f dialling code. V~wand m -[e]s,-̈e pretext; (Ausrede) excuse

vorwärts adv forward[s]; v~ kommen make progress; (fig) get on or ahead. v~kommen† vi sep (sein) (NEW) v~ kommen, s. vorwärts

vorweg adv beforehand; (vorn) in front; (voraus) ahead. v~nehmen† vt sep anticipate

vorweisen† vt sep show

vorwerfen† vt sep throw (dat to); jdm etw v~ reproach s.o. with sth; (beschuldigen) accuse s.o. of sth

vorwiegend adv predominantly

Vorwort nt (pl -worte) preface

Vorwurf m reproach; jdm Vorwürfe machen reproach s.o. v~svoll a reproachful, adv -ly

Vorzeichen nt sign; (fig) omen

vorzeigen vt sep show

vorzeitig a premature, adv -ly

vorziehen† vt sep pull forward; draw ⟨Vorhang⟩; (vorverlegen) bring forward; (lieber mögen) prefer; (bevorzugen) favour

Vor|zimmer nt ante-room; (Büro) outer office. V~zug m preference; (gute Eigenschaft) merit, virtue; (Vorteil) advantage

vorzüglich a excellent, adv -ly

vorzugsweise adv preferably

vulgär /vʊlˈgɛːɐ̯/ a vulgar □ adv in a vulgar way

Vulkan /vʊlˈkaːn/ m -s,-e volcano

W

Waage f -,-n scales pl; (Astr) Libra. w~recht a horizontal, adv -ly

Wabe f -,-n honeycomb

wach a awake; (aufgeweckt) alert; w~ werden wake up

Wach|e f -,-n guard; (Posten) sentry; (Dienst) guard duty; (Naut) watch; (Polizei-) station; W~e halten keep watch; W~e stehen stand guard. w~en vi (haben) be awake; w~en über (+ acc) watch over. W~hund m guard-dog

Wacholder m -s juniper

Wachposten m sentry

Wachs nt -es wax

wachsam a vigilant, adv -ly. W~keit f -vigilance

wachsen†¹ vi (sein) grow

wachs|en² vt (reg) wax. W~figur f waxwork. W~tuch nt oil-cloth

Wachstum nt -s growth

Wächter m -s,- guard; (Park-) keeper; (Parkplatz-) attendant

Wacht|meister m [police] constable. W~posten m sentry

Wachturm m watch-tower

wackel|ig a wobbly; ⟨Stuhl⟩ rickety; ⟨Person⟩ shaky. W~kontakt m loose connection. w~n vi (haben) wobble; (zittern) shake □ vi (sein) totter

wacklig a = wackelig

Wade f -,-n (Anat) calf

Waffe f -,-n weapon; W~n arms

Waffel f -,-n waffle; (Eis-) wafer

Waffen|ruhe f cease-fire. W~schein m firearms licence. W~stillstand m armistice

Wagemut m daring. w~ig a daring, adv -ly

wagen vt risk; es w~, etw zu tun dare [to] do sth; sich w~ (gehen) venture

Wagen m -s,- cart; (Eisenbahn-) carriage, coach; (Güter-) wagon; (Kinder-) pram; (Auto) car. W~heber m -s,- jack

Waggon /vaˈgõː/ m -s,-s wagon

waghalsig a daring, adv -ly

Wagnis nt -ses,-se risk

Wagon /vaˈgõː/ m -s,-s = Waggon

Wahl f -,-en choice; (Pol, Admin) election; (geheime) ballot; zweite W~ (Comm) seconds pl

wähl|en vt/i (haben) choose; (Pol, Admin) elect; (stimmen) vote; (Teleph) dial; jdn wieder w~en re-elect s.o. W~er(in) m -s,- (f -,-nen) voter. w~erisch a choosy, fussy

Wahl|fach nt optional subject. w~frei a optional. W~kampf m election campaign. W~kreis m constituency. W~lokal nt polling-station. w~los a indiscriminate, adv -ly. W~recht nt [right to] vote

Wählscheibe f (Teleph) dial

Wahl|spruch m motto. W~urne f ballot-box

Wahn m -[e]s delusion; (Manie) mania

wähnen vt believe

Wahnsinn m madness. w~ig a mad, insane; (fam: unsinnig) crazy; (fam: groß) terrible; w~ig werden go mad □ adv (fam) terribly. W~ige(r) m/f maniac

wahr a true; (echt) real; w~ werden come true; du kommst doch, nicht w~? you are coming, aren't you?

wahren vt keep; (verteidigen) safeguard; den Schein w~ keep up appearances

währen vi (haben) last

während prep (+ gen) during □ conj while; (wohingegen) whereas. w~dessen adv in the meantime

wahrhaben vt etw nicht w~ wollen refuse to admit sth

wahrhaftig adv really, truly

Wahrheit f -,-en truth. w~sgemäß a truthful, adv -ly

wahrnehm|bar a perceptible. w~en† vt sep notice; (nutzen) take advantage of; exploit (Vorteil); look after (Interessen). W~ung f -,-en perception

wahrsag|en v sep □ vt predict □ vi (haben) jdm w~en tell s.o.'s fortune. W~erin f -,-nen fortune-teller

wahrscheinlich a probable, adv -bly. W~keit f -,-en probability

Währung f -,-en currency

Wahrzeichen nt symbol

Waise f -,-n orphan. W~nhaus nt orphanage. W~nkind nt orphan

Wal m -[e]s whale

Wald m -[e]s,¨er wood; (groß) forest. w~ig a wooded

Wal|ser m -s,- Welshman. w~isch a Welsh

Wall m -[e]s,¨e mound; (Mil) rampart

Wallfahr|er|in m(f) pilgrim. W~t f pilgrimage

Walnuss (Walnuß) f walnut

Walze f -,-n roller. w~n vt roll

wälzen vt roll; pore over (Bücher); mull over (Probleme); sich w~ roll [about]; (schlaflos) toss and turn

Walzer m -s,- waltz

Wand f -,¨e wall; (Trenn-) partition; (Seite) side; (Fels-) face

Wandel m -s change. w~bar a changeable. w~n vi (sein) stroll □ vr sich w~n change

Wander|er m -s,-, ~in f -,-nen hiker, rambler. w~n vi (sein) hike, ramble; (ziehen) travel; (gemächlich gehen) wander; (ziellos) roam. W~schaft f travels pl. W~ung f -,-en hike, ramble; (länger) walking tour. W~weg m footpath

Wandgemälde nt mural

Wandlung f -,-en change, transformation

Wand|malerei f mural. W~tafel f blackboard. W~teppich m tapestry

Wange f -,-n cheek

wank|elmütig a fickle. w~en vi (haben) sway; (Person:) stagger; (fig) waver □ vi (sein) stagger

wann adv when

Wanne f -,-n tub

Wanze f -,-n bug

Wappen nt -s,- coat of arms. W~kunde f heraldry

war, wäre s. sein¹

Ware f -,-n article; (Comm) commodity; (coll) merchandise; W~n goods. W~nhaus nt department store. W~nprobe f sample. W~nzeichen nt trademark

warm a (wärmer, wärmst) warm; (Mahlzeit) hot; w~ machen heat □ adv warmly; w~ essen have a hot meal

Wärm|e f - warmth; (Phys) heat; 10 Grad W~e 10 degrees above zero. w~en vt warm; heat (Essen, Wasser). W~flasche f hot-water bottle

warmherzig a warm-hearted

Warn|blinkanlage f hazard [warning] lights pl. w~en vt/i (haben) warn (vor + dat of). W~ung f -,-en warning

Warteliste f waiting list

warten vi (haben) wait (auf + acc for); auf sich (acc) w~ lassen take one's/its time □ vt (Techn) service

Wärter(in) m -s,- (f -,-nen) keeper; (Museums-) attendant; (Gefängnis-) warder, (Amer) guard; (Kranken-) orderly

Warte|raum, W~saal m waiting-room. W~zimmer nt (Med) waiting-room

Wartung f - (Techn) service

warum adv why

Warze f -,-n wart

was pron what; was für [ein]? what kind of [a]? was für ein Pech! what bad luck! das gefällt dir, was? you like that, don't you? □ rel pron that; alles, was ich brauche all [that] I need □ indef pron (fam: etwas) something; (fragend, verneint) anything; was zu essen something to eat; so was Ärgerliches! what a nuisance! □ adv (fam) (warum) why; (wie) how

wasch|bar a washable. W~becken nt wash-basin. W~beutel m sponge-bag

Wäsche f - washing; (Unter-) underwear; in der W~ in the wash

waschecht a colour-fast; (fam) genuine

Wäsche|klammer f clothes-peg. W~leine f clothes-line

waschen† *vt* wash; sich w∼ have a wash; sich (*dat*) die Hände w∼ wash one's hands; W∼ und Legen shampoo and set □ *vi* (*haben*) do the washing

Wäscherei *f* -,-en laundry

Wäsche|schleuder *f* spin-drier. W∼trockner *m* tumble-drier

Wasch|küche *f* laundry-room. W∼lappen *m* face-flannel, (*Amer*) washcloth; (*fam: Feigling*) sissy. W∼maschine *f* washing machine. W∼mittel *nt* detergent. W∼pulver *nt* washing-powder. W∼raum *m* wash-room. W∼salon *m* launderette. W∼zettel *m* blurb

Wasser *nt* -s water; (*Haar-*) lotion; ins W∼ fallen (*fam*) fall through; mir lief das W∼ im Mund zusammen my mouth was watering. W∼ball *m* beach-ball; (*Spiel*) water polo. W∼dicht *a* watertight; (*Kleidung*) waterproof. W∼fall *m* waterfall. W∼farbe *f* water-colour. W∼hahn *m* tap, (*Amer*) faucet. W∼kasten *m* cistern. W∼kraft *f* water-power. W∼kraftwerk *nt* hydroelectric power-station. W∼leitung *f* water-main; aus der W∼leitung from the tap. W∼mann *m* (*Astr*) Aquarius

wässern *vt* soak; (*begießen*) water □ *vi* (*haben*) water

Wasser|scheide *f* watershed. W∼ski *m* -s water-skiing. W∼stoff *m* hydrogen. W∼straße *f* waterway. W∼waage *f* spirit-level. W∼werfer *m* -s,- water-cannon. W∼zeichen *nt* watermark

wässrig (*wäßrig*) *a* watery

waten *vi* (*sein*) wade

watscheln *vi* (*sein*) waddle

Watt¹ *nt* -[e]s mud-flats *pl*

Watt² *nt* -s,- (*Phys*) watt

Watt|e *f* - cotton wool. w∼iert *a* padded; (*gesteppt*) quilted

WC /ve'tse:/ *nt* -s,-s WC

web|en *vt/i* (*haben*) weave. W∼er *m* -s,- weaver. W∼stuhl *m* loom

Wechsel *m* -s,- change; (*Tausch*) exchange; (*Comm*) bill of exchange. W∼geld *nt* change. w∼haft *a* changeable. W∼jahre *npl* menopause *sg*. W∼kurs *m* exchange rate. w∼n *vt* change; (*tauschen*) exchange □ *vi* (*haben*) change; (*ab-*) alternate; (*verschieden sein*) vary. w∼nd *a* changing; (*verschieden*) varying. w∼seitig *a* mutual, *adv* -ly. W∼strom *m* alternating current. W∼stube *f* bureau de change. w∼weise *adv* alternately. W∼wirkung *f* interaction

weck|en *vt* wake [up]; (*fig*) awaken □ *vi* (*haben*) (*Wecker:*) go off. W∼er *m* -s,- alarm [clock]

wedeln *vi* (*haben*) wave; mit dem Schwanz w∼ wag its tail

weder *conj* w∼ ... noch neither ... nor

Weg *m* -[e]s,-e way; (*Fuß-*) path; (*Fahr-*) track; (*Gang*) errand; auf dem Weg on the way (nach to); sich auf den Weg machen set off; im Weg sein be in the way; zu W∼e bringen = zuwege bringen, *s.* zuwege

weg *adv* away, off; (*verschwunden*) gone; weg sein be away; (*gegangen/verschwunden*) have gone; (*fam: schlafen*) be asleep; Hände weg! hands off! w∼bleiben† *vi sep* (*sein*) stay away. w∼bringen† *vt sep* take away

wegen *prep* (+ *gen*) because of; (*um ... willen*) for the sake of; (*bezüglich*) about

weg|fahren† *vi sep* (*sein*) go away; (*abfahren*) leave. w∼fallen† *vi sep* (*sein*) be dropped/(*ausgelassen*) omitted; (*entfallen*) no longer apply; (*aufhören*) cease. w∼geben† *vt sep* give away; send to the laundry (*Wäsche*). w∼gehen† *vi sep* (*sein*) leave, go away; (*ausgehen*) go out; (*Fleck:*) come out. w∼jagen *vt sep* chase away. w∼kommen† *vi sep* (*sein*) get away; (*verloren gehen*) disappear; schlecht w∼kommen (*fam*) get a raw deal. w∼lassen† *vt sep* let go; (*auslassen*) omit. w∼laufen† *vi sep* (*sein*) run away. w∼machen *vt sep* remove. w∼nehmen† *vt sep* take away. w∼räumen *vt sep* put away; (*entfernen*) clear away. w∼schicken *vt sep* send away; (*abschicken*) send off. w∼tun† *vt sep* put away; (*wegwerfen*) throw away

Wegweiser *m* -s,- signpost

weg|werfen† *vt sep* throw away. w∼ziehen† *v sep* □ *vt* pull away □ *vi* (*sein*) move away

weh *a* sore; weh tun hurt; (*Kopf, Rücken:*) ache; jdm weh tun hurt s.o. □ *int* oh weh! oh dear!

wehe *int* alas; w∼ [dir/euch]! (*drohend*) don't you dare!

wehen *vi* (*haben*) blow; (*flattern*) flutter □ *vt* blow

Wehen *fpl* contractions; in den W∼ liegen be in labour

weh|leidig *a* soft; (*weinerlich*) whining. W∼mut *f* - wistfulness. w∼mütig *a* wistful, *adv* -ly

Wehr¹ *nt* -[e]s,-e weir

Wehr² *f* sich zur W∼ setzen resist. W∼dienst *m* military service. W∼dienstverweigerer *m* -s,- conscientious objector

wehren (sich) *vr* resist; (*gegen Anschuldigung*) protest; (*sich sträuben*) refuse

wehr|los *a* defenceless. **W~macht** *f* armed forces *pl*. **W~pflicht** *f* conscription

Weib *nt* -[e]s,-er woman; (*Ehe-*) wife. **W~chen** *nt* -s,- (*Zool*) female. **W~erheld** *m* womanizer. **w~isch** *a* effeminate. **w~lich** *a* feminine; (*Biol*) female. **W~lichkeit** *f* - femininity

weich *a* soft, *adv* -ly; (*Ei*) done; ⟨*Ei*⟩ soft-boiled; ⟨*Mensch*⟩ soft-hearted; **w~ werden** (*fig*) relent

Weiche *f* -,-n (*Rail*) points *pl*

weichen¹ *vi* (*sein*) (*reg*) soak

weichen†² *vi* (*sein*) give way (*dat* to); **nicht von jds Seite w~** not leave s.o.'s side

Weich|heit *f* - softness. **w~herzig** *a* soft-hearted. **w~lich** *a* soft; ⟨*Charakter*⟩ weak. **W~spüler** *m* -s,- (*Tex*) conditioner. **W~tier** *nt* mollusc

Weide¹ *f* -,-n (*Bot*) willow

Weide² *f* -,-n pasture. **w~n** *vt/i* (*haben*) graze; **sich w~n an** (+ *dat*) enjoy; (*schadenfroh*) gloat over

weiger|n (sich) *vr* refuse. **W~ung** *f* -,-en refusal

Weihe *f* -,-n consecration; (*Priester-*) ordination. **w~n** *vt* consecrate; (*zum Priester*) ordain; dedicate ⟨*Kirche*⟩ (*dat* to)

Weiher *m* -s,- pond

Weihnacht|en *nt* -s & *pl* Christmas. **w~lich** *a* Christmassy. **W~sbaum** *m* Christmas tree. **W~sfest** *nt* Christmas. **W~slied** *nt* Christmas carol. **W~smann** *m* (*pl* -männer) Father Christmas. **W~stag** *m* erster/zweiter **W~stag** Christmas Day/Boxing Day

Weih|rauch *m* incense. **W~wasser** *nt* holy water

weil *conj* because; (*da*) since

Weile *f* - while

Wein *m* -[e]s,-e wine; (*Bot*) vines *pl*; (*Trauben*) grapes *pl*. **W~bau** *m* wine-growing. **W~beere** *f* grape. **W~berg** *m* vineyard. **W~brand** *m* -[e]s brandy

wein|en *vt/i* (*haben*) cry, weep. **w~erlich** *a* tearful, *adv* -ly

Wein|glas *nt* wineglass. **W~karte** *f* wine-list. **W~keller** *m* wine-cellar. **W~lese** *f* grape harvest. **W~liste** *f* wine-list. **W~probe** *f* wine-tasting. **W~rebe** *f*, **W~stock** *m* vine. **W~stube** *f* wine-bar. **W~traube** *f* bunch of grapes; (*W~beere*) grape

weise *a* wise, *adv* -ly

Weise *f* -,-n way; (*Melodie*) tune; **auf diese W~** in this way

weisen† *vt* show; **von sich w~** (*fig*) reject ⊓ *vi* (*haben*) point (**auf** + *acc* at)

Weisheit *f* -,-en wisdom. **W~szahn** *m* wisdom tooth

weiß *a*, **W~** *nt* -,- white

weissag|en *vt/i insep* (*haben*) prophesy. **W~ung** *f* -,-en prophecy

Weiß|brot *nt* white bread. **W~e(r)** *m/f* white man/woman. **w~en** *vt* whitewash. **W~wein** *m* white wine

Weisung *f* -,-en instruction; (*Befehl*) order

weit *a* wide; (*ausgedehnt*) extensive; (*lang*) long ⊓ *adv* widely; (*offen, öffnen*) wide; (*lang*) far; **von w~em** from a distance; **bei w~em** by far; **w~** und breit far and wide; **ist es noch w~?** is it much further? **so w~ wie möglich** as far as possible; **ich bin so w~** I'm ready; **es ist so w~** the time has come; **zu w~ gehen** (*fig*) go too far; **w~ verbreitet** widespread; **w~blickend** (*fig*) far-sighted; **w~reichende Folgen** far-reaching consequences. **w~aus** *adv* far. **W~blick** *m* (*fig*) far-sightedness. **w~blickend** *a* = **w~ blickend, s. weit**

Weite *f* -,-n expanse; (*Entfernung*) distance; (*Größe*) width. **w~n** *vt* widen; stretch ⟨*Schuhe*⟩; **sich w~n** widen; stretch; ⟨*Pupille*⟩ dilate

weiter *a* further ⊓ *adv* further; (*außerdem*) in addition; (*anschließend*) then; **etw w~ tun** go on doing sth; **w~ nichts/niemand** nothing/no one else; **und so w~** and so on. **w~arbeiten** *vi sep* (*haben*) go on working

weiter|e(r,s) *a* further; **im w~en Sinne** in a wider sense; **ohne w~es** just like that; (*leicht*) easily; **bis auf w~es** until further notice; (*vorläufig*) for the time being

weiter|erzählen *vt sep* go on with; (*w~sagen*) repeat. **w~fahren†** *vi sep* (*sein*) go on. **w~geben†** *vt sep* pass on. **w~gehen†** *vi sep* (*sein*) go on. **w~hin** *adv* (*immer noch*) still; (*in Zukunft*) in future; (*außerdem*) furthermore; **etw w~hin tun** go on doing sth. **w~kommen†** *vi sep* (*sein*) get on. **w~machen** *vt/i sep* (*haben*) carry on. **w~sagen** *vt sep* pass on; (*verraten*) repeat

weit|gehend *a* extensive ⊓ *adv* to a large extent. **w~hin** *adv* a long way; (*fig*) widely. **w~läufig** *a* spacious; (*entfernt*) distant, *adv* -ly; (*ausführlich*) lengthy; **at length**. **w~reichend** *a* = **w~ reichend, s. weit**. **w~schweifig** *a* long-winded. **w~sichtig** *a* long-sighted; (*fig*) far-sighted. **W~sprung** *m* long jump. **w~verbreitet** *a* = **w~ verbreitet, s. weit**

Weizen *m* -s wheat

welch *inv pron* what; w∼ ein(e) what a. w∼e(r,s) *pron* which; um w∼e Zeit? at what time? □ *rel pron* which; (*Person*) who □ *indef pron* some; (*fragend*) any; was für w∼e? what sort of?

welk *a* wilted; (*Laub*) dead. w∼en *vi* (*haben*) wilt; (*fig*) fade

Wellblech *nt* corrugated iron

Well|e *f* -,-n wave; (*Techn*) shaft. W∼en-länge *f* wavelength. W∼enlinie *f* wavy line. W∼enreiten *nt* surfing. W∼ensittich *m* -s,-e budgerigar. w∼ig *a* wavy

Welt *f* -,-en world; auf der W∼ in the world; auf die od zur W∼ kommen be born. W∼all *nt* universe. w∼berühmt *a* world-famous. w∼fremd *a* unworldly. w∼gewandt *a* sophisticated. W∼kugel *f* globe. w∼lich *a* worldly; (*nicht geistlich*) secular

Weltmeister|(in) *m(f)* world champion. W∼schaft *f* world championship

Weltraum *m* space. W∼fahrer *m* astronaut

Welt|rekord *m* world record. w∼weit *a & adv* world-wide

wem *pron* (*dat of* wer) to whom

wen *pron* (*acc of* wer) whom

Wende *f* -,-n change. W∼kreis *m* (*Geog*) tropic

Wendeltreppe *f* spiral staircase

wenden¹ *vt* (*reg*) turn; sich zum Guten w∼ take a turn for the better □ *vi* (*haben*) turn [round]

wenden†² (*& reg*) *vt* turn; sich w∼ turn; sich an jdn w∼ turn/(*schriftlich*) write to s.o.

Wende|punkt *m* (*fig*) turning-point. w∼ig *a* nimble; (*Auto*) manœuvrable. W∼ung *f* -,-en turn; (*Biegung*) bend; (*Veränderung*) change; eine W∼ung zum Besseren/Schlechteren a turn for the better/worse

wenig *pron* little; (*pl*) few; so/zu w∼ so/too little/(*pl*) few; w∼e *pl* few □ *adv* little; (*kaum*) not much; so/zu w∼ verdienen earn so/too little; so w∼ wie möglich as little as possible. w∼er *pron* less; (*pl*) fewer; immer w∼er less and less □ *adv & conj* less □ *a* less; am w∼sten least [of all]. w∼stens *adv* at least

wenn *conj* if; (*sobald*) when; immer w∼ whenever; w∼ nicht *od* außer w∼ unless; w∼ auch even though

wer *pron* who; (*fam: jemand*) someone; (*fragend*) anyone; ist da wer? is anyone there?

Werbe|agentur *f* advertising agency. w∼n† *vt* recruit; attract (*Kunden, Besucher*) □ *vi* (*haben*) w∼n für advertise;

canvass for (*Partei*); w∼n um try to attract (*Besucher*); court (*Frau, Gunst*). W∼spot /-sp-/ *m* -s,-s commercial

Werbung *f* advertising

werden† *vi* (*sein*) become; (*müde, alt, länger*) get, grow; (*blind, wahnsinnig*) go; blass w∼ turn pale; krank w∼ fall ill; es wird warm/dunkel it is getting warm/dark; mir wurde schlecht/schwindlig I felt sick/dizzy; er will Lehrer w∼ he wants to be a teacher; was ist aus ihm geworden? what has become of him? □ *v aux* (*Zukunft*) shall; wir w∼ sehen we shall see; es wird bald regnen it's going to rain soon; würden Sie so nett sein? would you be so kind? □ (*Passiv*; *pp* worden) be; geliebt/geboren w∼ be loved/born; es wurde gemunkelt it was rumoured

werfen† *vt* throw; cast (*Blick, Schatten*); sich w∼ (*Holz:*) warp □ *vi* (*haben*) w∼ mit throw

Werft *f* -,-en shipyard

Werk *nt* -[e]s,-e work; (*Fabrik*) works *sg*, factory; (*Trieb-*) mechanism. W∼en *nt* -s (*Sch*) handicraft. W∼statt *f* -,-en workshop; (*Auto-*) garage; (*Künstler-*) studio. W∼tag *m* weekday. w∼tags *adv* on weekdays. w∼tätig *a* working. W∼unterricht *m* (*Sch*) handicraft

Werkzeug *nt* tool; (*coll*) tools *pl*. W∼maschine *f* machine tool

Wermut *m* -s vermouth

wert *a* viel/50 Mark w∼ worth a lot/50 marks; nichts w∼ sein be worthless; jds/etw (*gen*) w∼ sein be worthy of s.o./sth. W∼ *m* -[e]s,-e value; (*Nenn-*) denomination; im W∼ von worth; W∼ legen auf (+ *acc*) set great store by. w∼en *vt* rate

Wert|gegenstand *m* object of value; W∼gegenstände valuables. w∼los *a* worthless. W∼minderung *f* depreciation. W∼papier *nt* (*Comm*) security. W∼sachen *fpl* valuables. w∼voll *a* valuable

Wesen *nt* -s,- nature; (*Lebe-*) being; (*Mensch*) creature

wesentlich *a* essential; (*grundlegend*) fundamental; (*erheblich*) considerable; im W∼en (w∼en) essentially □ *adv* considerably, much

weshalb *adv* why

Wespe *f* -,-n wasp

wessen *pron* (*gen of* wer) whose

westdeutsch *a* West German

Weste *f* -,-n waistcoat, (*Amer*) vest

Westen *m* -s west; nach W∼ west

Western *m* -[s],- western

Westfalen *nt* -s Westphalia

Westindien nt West Indies pl

west|lich a western; ⟨Richtung⟩ westerly
□ adv & prep (+ gen) w∼lich [von] der
Stadt [to the] west of the town. w∼wärts
adv westwards

weswegen adv why

wett a w∼ sein be quits

Wett|bewerb m -s,-e competition.
W∼büro nt betting shop

Wette f -,-n bet; um die W∼ laufen race
(mit jdm s.o.)

wetteifern vi (haben) compete

wetten vt/i (haben) bet (auf + acc on); mit
jdm w∼ have a bet with s.o.

Wetter nt -s,- weather; ⟨Un-⟩ storm.
W∼bericht m weather report. W∼hahn
m weathercock. W∼lage f weather conditions f. W∼vorhersage f weather
forecast. W∼warte f -,-n meteorological
station

Wett|kampf m contest. W∼kämpfer(in)
m(f) competitor. W∼lauf m race.
w∼machen vt sep make up for.
W∼rennen nt race. W∼streit m contest

wetzen vt sharpen □ vi (sein) (fam) dash

Whisky m -s whisky

wichsen vt polish

wichtig a important; w∼ nehmen take
seriously. W∼keit f - importance.
w∼tuerisch a self-important

Wicke f -,-n sweet pea

Wickel m -s,- compress

wick|eln vt wind; ⟨ein-⟩ wrap; ⟨banda-
gieren⟩ bandage; ein Kind frisch w∼eln
change a baby. W∼ler m -s,- curler

Widder m -s,- ram; (Astr) Aries

wider prep (+ acc) against; (entgegen) contrary to; w∼ Willen against one's will

widerfahren† vi insep (sein) jdm w∼
happen to s.o.

widerhallen vi sep (haben) echo

widerlegen vt insep refute

wider|lich a repulsive; (unangenehm)
nasty, adv -ily. w∼rechtlich a unlawful,
adv -ly. W∼rede f contradiction; keine
W∼rede! don't argue!

widerrufen† vt/i insep (haben) retract;
revoke ⟨Befehl⟩

Widersacher m -s,- adversary

widersetzen (sich) vr insep resist
(jdm/etw s.o./sth)

wider|sinnig a absurd. w∼spenstig a
unruly; (störrisch) stubborn

widerspiegeln vt sep reflect; sich w∼ be
reflected

widersprechen† vi insep (haben) contradict (jdm/etw s.o./sth)

Wider|spruch m contradiction; (Protest)
protest. w∼sprüchlich a contradictory.
w∼spruchslos adv without protest

Widerstand m resistance; W∼ leisten
resist. w∼sfähig a resistant; (Bot) hardy

widerstehen† vi insep (haben) resist
(jdm/etw s.o./sth); (anwidern) be repugnant (jdm to s.o.)

widerstreben vi insep (haben) es wider-
strebt mir I am reluctant (zu to). W∼ nt
-s reluctance. w∼d a reluctant, adv -ly

widerwärtig a disagreeable, unpleasant;
(ungünstig) adverse

Widerwill|e m aversion, repugnance.
w∼ig a reluctant, adv -ly

widmen vt dedicate (dat to); (verwenden)
devote (dat to); sich w∼en (+ dat) devote
oneself to. W∼ung f -,-en dedication

widrig a adverse, unfavourable

wie adv how; wie viel how much/(pl)
many; um wie viel Uhr? at what time?
wie viele? how many? wie ist Ihr Name?
what is your name? wie ist das Wetter?
what is the weather like? □ conj as; (gleich
wie) like; (sowie) as well as; (als) when, as;
genau wie du just like you; so gut/reich
wie as good/rich as; nichts wie nothing
but; größer wie ich (fam) bigger than me

wieder adv again; er ist w∼ da he is back;
jdn/etw w∼ erkennen recognize
s.o./sth; eine Tätigkeit w∼ aufnehmen
resume an activity; etw w∼ verwenden/
verwerten reuse/recycle sth; etw w∼
gutmachen make up for ⟨Schaden⟩; redress ⟨Unrecht⟩; (bezahlen) pay for sth

Wiederaufbau m reconstruction. w∼en
vt sep NEW wieder aufbauen, s. aufbau-
en

wieder|aufnehmen† vt sep NEW w∼
aufnehmen, s. wieder. W∼aufrüstung
f rearmament

wieder|bekommen† vt sep get back.
w∼beleben vt sep NEW w∼ beleben, s.
beleben. W∼belebung f - resuscitation.
w∼bringen† vt sep bring back. w∼er-
kennen† vt sep NEW w∼ erkennen, s.
wieder. W∼gabe f (s. w∼geben) return;
portrayal; rendering; reproduction. w∼
geben† vt sep give back, return; (darstellen) portray; (ausdrücken, übersetzen)
render; (zitieren) quote; (Techn) reproduce. W∼geburt f reincarnation

wiedergutmach|en vt sep NEW w∼
gutmachen, s. wieder. W∼ung f - repar-
ation; (Entschädigung) compensation

wiederher|stellen vt sep NEW w∼
stellen, s. wieder. W∼ re-establish;
restore ⟨Gebäude⟩; restore to health
⟨Kranke⟩; w∼gestellt sein be fully re-
covered. W∼stellung f re-establishment;
restoration; (Genesung) recovery

wiederholen[1] *vt sep* get back

wiederhol|en[2] *vt insep* repeat; ⟨*Sch*⟩ revise; sich w∼en recur; ⟨*Person:*⟩ repeat oneself. w∼t *a* repeated, *adv* -ly. W∼ung *f* -,-en repetition; ⟨*Sch*⟩ revision

Wieder|hören *nt* auf W∼hören! goodbye! W∼käuer *m* -s,- ruminant. W∼kehr *f* - return; ⟨*W∼holung*⟩ recurrence. w∼kehren *vi sep* (sein) return; ⟨*sich wiederholen*⟩ recur. w∼kommen† *vi sep* (sein) come back

wiedersehen† *vt sep* (NEW) wieder sehen, *s.* sehen. W∼ *nt* -s,- reunion; auf W∼! goodbye!

wiederum *adv* again; ⟨*andererseits*⟩ on the other hand

wiedervereinig|en *vt sep* (NEW) wieder vereinigen, *s.* vereinigen. W∼ung *f* re-unification

wieder|verheiraten (sich) *vr sep* (NEW) w∼ verheiraten (sich), *s.* verheiraten. w∼verwenden† *vt sep* (NEW) w∼ verwenden, *s.* wieder. w∼verwerten *vt sep* (NEW) w∼ verwerten, *s.* wieder. w∼wählen *vt sep* (NEW) w∼ wählen, *s.* wählen

Wiege *f* -,-n cradle

wiegen†[1] *vt/i* (haben) weigh

wiegen[2] *vt* (reg) rock; sich w∼ sway; ⟨*schaukeln*⟩ rock. W∼lied *nt* lullaby

wiehern *vi* (haben) neigh

Wien *nt* -s Vienna. W∼er *a* Viennese; W∼er Schnitzel Wiener schnitzel □ *m* -s,- Viennese □ *f* -,- ≈ frankfurter. w∼erisch *a* Viennese

Wiese *f* -,-n meadow

Wiesel *nt* -s,- weasel

wieso *adv* why

wieviel *pron* (NEW) wie viel, *s.* wie. w∼te(r,s) *a* which; der W∼te ist heute? what is the date today?

wieweit *adv* how far

wild *a* wild, *adv* -ly; ⟨*Stamm*⟩ savage; w∼er Streik wildcat strike; w∼ wachsen grow wild. W∼ *nt* -[e]s game; ⟨*Rot-*⟩ deer; ⟨*Culin*⟩ venison. W∼dieb *m* poacher. W∼e(r) *m/f* savage

Wilder|er *m* -s,- poacher. w∼n *vt/i* (haben) poach

wildfremd *a* totally strange; w∼e Leute total strangers

Wild|heger, W∼hüter *m* -s,- gamekeeper. W∼leder *nt* suede. w∼ledern *a* suede. W∼nis *f* - wilderness. W∼schwein *nt* wild boar. W∼westfilm *m* western

Wille *m* -ns will; letzter W∼ will; seinen W∼n durchsetzen get one's [own] way; mit W∼n intentionally

willen *prep* (+ gen) um ... w∼ for the sake of ...

Willens|kraft *f* will-power. w∼stark *a* strong-willed

willig *a* willing, *adv* -ly

willkommen *a* welcome; w∼ heißen welcome. W∼ *nt* -s welcome

willkürlich *a* arbitrary, *adv* -ily

wimmeln *vi* (haben) swarm

wimmern *vi* (haben) whimper

Wimpel *m* -s,- pennant

Wimper *f* -,- [eye]lash; nicht mit der W∼ zucken (fam) not bat an eyelid. W∼ntusche *f* mascara

Wind *m* -[e]s,-e wind

Winde *f* -,-n ⟨*Techn*⟩ winch

Windel *f* -,-n nappy, (Amer) diaper

winden† *vt* wind; make ⟨*Kranz*⟩; in die Höhe w∼ winch up; sich w∼ wind (um round); ⟨*sich krümmen*⟩ writhe

Wind|hund *m* greyhound. w∼ig *a* windy. W∼mühle *f* windmill. W∼pocken *fpl* chickenpox *sg*. W∼schutzscheibe *f* windscreen, (Amer) windshield. w∼still *a* calm. W∼stille *f* calm. W∼stoß *m* gust of wind. W∼surfen *nt* windsurfing

Windung *f* -,-en bend; ⟨*Spirale*⟩ spiral

Wink *m* -[e]s,-e sign; ⟨*Hinweis*⟩ hint

Winkel *m* -s,- angle; ⟨*Ecke*⟩ corner. W∼messer *m* -s,- protractor

winken *vi* (haben) wave; jdm w∼ wave/⟨*herbei-*⟩ beckon to s.o.

winseln *vi* (haben) whine

Winter *m* -s,- winter. w∼lich *a* wintry; ⟨*Winter-*⟩ winter ... W∼schlaf *m* hibernation; W∼schlaf halten hibernate. W∼sport *m* winter sports *pl*

Winzer *m* -s,- winegrower

winzig *a* tiny, minute

Wipfel *m* -s,- [tree]top

Wippe *f* -,-n see-saw. w∼n *vi* (haben) bounce; ⟨*auf Wippe*⟩ play on the see-saw

wir *pron* we; wir sind es it's us

Wirbel *m* -s,- eddy; ⟨*Drehung*⟩ whirl; ⟨*Trommel-*⟩ roll; ⟨*Anat*⟩ vertebra; ⟨*Haar-*⟩ crown; ⟨*Aufsehen*⟩ fuss. w∼n *vt/i* (sein/haben) whirl. W∼säule *f* spine. W∼sturm *m* cyclone. W∼tier *nt* vertebrate. W∼wind *m* whirlwind

wird *s.* werden

wirken *vi* (haben) have an effect (auf + acc on); ⟨*zur Geltung kommen*⟩ be effective; ⟨*tätig sein*⟩ work; ⟨*scheinen*⟩ seem □ *vt* ⟨*Tex*⟩ knit; Wunder w∼ work miracles

wirklich *a* real, *adv* -ly. W∼keit *f* -,-en reality

wirksam *a* effective, *adv* -ly. W∼keit *f* - effectiveness

Wirkung f -,-en effect. w∼slos a ineffective, adv -ly. w∼svoll a effective, adv -ly

wirr a tangled; ⟨Haar⟩ tousled; ⟨verwirrt, verworren⟩ confused. W∼warr m -s tangle; ⟨fig⟩ confusion; ⟨von Stimmen⟩ hubbub

Wirt m -[e]s,-e landlord. W∼in f -,-nen landlady

Wirtschaft f -,-en economy; ⟨Gast-⟩ restaurant; ⟨Kneipe⟩ pub. w∼en vi ⟨haben⟩ manage one's finances; ⟨sich betätigen⟩ busy oneself; sie kann nicht w∼en she's a bad manager. W∼erin f -,-nen housekeeper. w∼lich a economic, adv -ally; ⟨sparsam⟩ economical, adv -ly. W∼sgeld nt housekeeping [money]. W∼sprüfer m auditor

Wirtshaus nt inn; ⟨Kneipe⟩ pub

Wisch m -[e]s,-e ⟨fam⟩ piece of paper

wisch|en vt/i ⟨haben⟩ wipe; wash ⟨Fußboden⟩ □ vi ⟨sein⟩ slip; ⟨Maus:⟩ scurry. W∼lappen m cloth; ⟨Aufwisch-⟩ floorcloth

wispern vt/i ⟨haben⟩ whisper

wissen vt/i ⟨haben⟩ know; weißt du noch? do you remember? ich wüsste gern... I should like to know...; nichts w∼ wollen von not want anything to do with. W∼ nt -s knowledge; meines W∼s to my knowledge

Wissenschaft f -,-en science. W∼ler m -s,- academic; ⟨Natur-⟩ scientist. w∼lich a academic, adv -ally; scientific, adv -ally

wissen|swert a worth knowing. w∼tlich a deliberate □ adv knowingly

witter|n vt scent; ⟨ahnen⟩ sense. W∼ung f - scent; ⟨Wetter⟩ weather

Witwe f -,-n widow. W∼r m -s,- widower

Witz m -es,-e joke; ⟨Geist⟩ wit. W∼bold m -[e]s,-e joker. w∼ig a funny; ⟨geistreich⟩ witty

wo adv where; ⟨als⟩ when; ⟨irgendwo⟩ somewhere; wo immer wherever □ conj seeing that; ⟨obwohl⟩ although; ⟨wenn⟩ if

woanders adv somewhere else

wobei adv how; ⟨relativ⟩ during the course of which

Woche f -,-n week. W∼nende nt weekend. W∼nkarte f weekly ticket. w∼nlang adv for weeks. W∼ntag m day of the week; ⟨Werktag⟩ weekday. w∼tags adv on weekdays

wöchentlich a & adv weekly

Wodka m -s vodka

wodurch adv how; ⟨relativ⟩ through/⟨Ursache⟩ by which; ⟨Folge⟩ as a result of which

wofür adv what ... for; ⟨relativ⟩ for which

Woge f -,-n wave

wogegen adv what ... against; ⟨relativ⟩ against which □ conj whereas. **woher** adv where from; **woher weißt du das?** how do you know that? **wohin** adv where [to]; **wohin gehst du?** where are you going? **wohingegen** conj whereas

wohl adv well; ⟨vermutlich⟩ probably; ⟨etwa⟩ about; ⟨zwar⟩ perhaps; w∼ kaum hardly; w∼ oder übel willy-nilly; sich w∼ fühlen feel well/⟨behaglich⟩ comfortable; jdm w∼ tun do s.o. good; der ist w∼ verrückt! he must be mad! W∼ nt -[e]s welfare, well-being; auf jds W∼ trinken drink s.o.'s health; zum W∼e (+ gen) for the good of; zum W∼! cheers!

wohlauf a w∼ sein be well

Wohl|befinden nt well-being. w∼behagen nt feeling of well-being. w∼behalten a safe, adv -ly. W∼ergehen nt -s welfare. w∼erzogen a well brought-up

Wohlfahrt f - welfare. W∼sstaat m Welfare State

Wohl|gefallen nt -s pleasure. W∼geruch m fragrance. w∼gesinnt a well disposed ⟨dat towards⟩. w∼habend a prosperous, well-to-do. w∼ig a comfortable, adv -bly. w∼klingend a melodious. w∼riechend a fragrant. w∼schmeckend a tasty

Wohlstand m prosperity. W∼sgesellschaft f affluent society

Wohltat f [act of] kindness; ⟨Annehmlichkeit⟩ treat; ⟨Genuss⟩ bliss

Wohltät|er m benefactor. w∼ig a charitable

wohl|tuend a agreeable, adv -bly. w∼tun† vi sep ⟨haben⟩ (NEW) w∼ tun, s. wohl. w∼verdient a well-deserved. w∼weislich adv deliberately

Wohlwollen nt -s goodwill; ⟨Gunst⟩ favour. w∼d a benevolent, adv -ly

Wohn|anhänger m = Wohnwagen. W∼block m block of flats. w∼en vi ⟨haben⟩ live; ⟨vorübergehend⟩ stay. W∼gegend f residential area. w∼haft a resident. W∼haus nt [dwelling-]house. W∼heim nt hostel; ⟨Alten-⟩ home. w∼lich a comfortable, adv -bly. W∼mobil nt -s,-e camper. W∼ort m place of residence. W∼raum m living space; ⟨Zimmer⟩ living-room. W∼sitz m place of residence

Wohnung f -,-en flat, ⟨Amer⟩ apartment; ⟨Unterkunft⟩ accommodation. W∼snot f housing shortage

Wohn|wagen m caravan, ⟨Amer⟩ trailer. W∼zimmer nt living-room

wölben vt curve; arch ⟨Rücken⟩. W∼ung f -,-en curve; ⟨Archit⟩ vault

Wolf *m* -[e]s,⸚e wolf; (*Fleisch-*) mincer; (*Reiß-*) shredder

Wolk|e *f* -,-n cloud. W∼enbruch *m* cloudburst. W∼enkratzer *m* skyscraper. w∼enlos *a* cloudless. w∼ig *a* cloudy

Woll|decke *f* blanket. W∼e *f* -,-n wool

wollen†¹ *vt/i* (*haben*) & *v aux* want; etw tun w∼ want to do sth; (*beabsichtigen*) be going to do sth; ich will nach Hause I want to go home; wir wollten gerade gehen we were just going; ich wollte, ich könnte dir helfen I wish I could help you; der Motor will nicht anspringen the engine won't start

woll|en² *a* woollen. w∼ig *a* woolly. W∼sachen *fpl* woollens

wollüstig *a* sensual, *adv* -ly

womit *adv* what ... with; (*relativ*) with which. womöglich *adv* possibly. wonach *adv* what ... after/(*suchen*) for/(*riechen*) of; (*relativ*) after/for/of which

Wonn|e *f* -,-n bliss; (*Freude*) joy. w∼ig *a* sweet

woran *adv* what ... on/(*denken, sterben*) of; (*relativ*) on/of which; woran hast du ihn erkannt? how did you recognize him? worauf *adv* what ... on/(*warten*) for; (*relativ*) on/for which; (*woraufhin*) whereupon. woraufhin *adv* whereupon. woraus *adv* what ... from; (*relativ*) from which. worin *adv* what ... in; (*relativ*) in which

Wort *nt* -[e]s,⸚er & -e word; jdm ins W∼ fallen interrupt s.o.; ein paar W∼e sagen say a few words. w∼brüchig *a* w∼brüchig werden break one's word

Wörterbuch *nt* dictionary

Wort|führer *m* spokesman. w∼getreu *a* & *adv* word-for-word. w∼gewandt *a* eloquent, *adv* -ly. w∼karg *a* taciturn. W∼laut *m* wording

wörtlich *a* literal, *adv* -ly; (*wortgetreu*) word-for-word

wort|los *a* silent □ *adv* without a word. W∼schatz *m* vocabulary. W∼spiel *nt* pun, play on words. W∼wechsel *m* exchange of words; (*Streit*) argument. w∼wörtlich *a* & *adv* = wörtlich

worüber *adv* what ... over/(*lachen, sprechen*) about; (*relativ*) over/about which. worum *adv* what ... round/(*bitten, kämpfen*) for; (*relativ*) round/for which; worum geht es? what is it about? worunter *adv* what ... under/(*wozwischen*) among; (*relativ*) under/among which. wovon *adv* what ... from/(*sprechen*) about; (*relativ*) from/about which. wovor *adv* what ... in front of; (*sich fürchten*) what ... of; (*relativ*) in front of which; of which. wozu *adv* what ...

to/(*brauchen, benutzen*) for; (*relativ*) to/for which; wozu? what for?

Wrack *nt* -s,-s wreck

wringen† *vt* wring

wucher|n *vi* (*haben/sein*) grow profusely. W∼preis *m* extortionate price. W∼ung *f* -,-en growth

Wuchs *m* -es growth; (*Gestalt*) stature

Wucht *f* - force. w∼en *vt* heave. w∼ig *a* massive

wühlen *vi* (*haben*) rummage; (*in der Erde*) burrow □ *vt* dig

Wulst *m* -[e]s,⸚e bulge; (*Fett-*) roll. w∼ig *a* bulging; (*Lippen*) thick

wund *a* sore; w∼ reiben chafe; sich w∼ liegen get bedsores. W∼brand *m* gangrene

Wunde *f* -,-n wound

Wunder *nt* -s,- wonder, marvel; (*übernatürliches*) miracle; kein W∼! no wonder! w∼bar *a* miraculous; (*herrlich*) wonderful, *adv* -ly, marvellous, *adv* -ly. W∼kind *nt* infant prodigy. w∼lich *a* odd, *adv* -ly. w∼n *vt* surprise; sich w∼n be surprised (über + *acc* at). w∼schön *a* beautiful, *adv* -ly. w∼voll *a* wonderful, *adv* -ly

Wundstarrkrampf *m* tetanus

Wunsch *m* -[e]s,⸚e wish; (*Verlangen*) desire; (*Bitte*) request

wünschen *vt* want; sich (*dat*) etw w∼ want sth; (*bitten um*) ask for sth; jdm Glück/gute Nacht w∼ wish s.o. luck/good night; ich wünschte, ich könnte ... I wish I could ...; Sie w∼? can I help you? zu w∼ übrig lassen leave something to be desired. w∼swert *a* desirable

Wunsch|konzert *nt* musical request programme. W∼traum *m* (*fig*) dream

wurde, würde *s.* werden

Würde *f* -,-n dignity; (*Ehrenrang*) honour. w∼los *a* undignified. W∼nträger *m* dignitary. w∼voll *a* dignified □ *adv* with dignity

würdig *a* dignified; (*wert*) worthy. w∼en *vt* recognize; (*schätzen*) appreciate; keines Blickes w∼en not deign to look at

Wurf *m* -[e]s,⸚e throw; (*Junge*) litter

Würfel *m* -s,- cube; (*Spiel-*) dice; (*Zucker-*) lump. w∼n *vi* (*haben*) throw the dice; w∼n um play dice for □ *vt* throw; (*in Würfel schneiden*) dice. W∼zucker *m* cube sugar

Wurfgeschoss (Wurfgeschoß) *nt* missile

würgen *vt* choke □ *vi* (*haben*) retch; choke (an + *dat* on)

Wurm *m* -[e]s,⸚er worm; (*Made*) maggot. w∼en *vi* (*haben*) jdn w∼en (*fam*) rankle [with s.o.]. w∼stichig *a* worm-eaten

Wurst f -,ˇe sausage; das ist mir W∼ (fam) I couldn't care less

Würstchen nt -s,- small sausage; Frankfurter W∼ frankfurter

Würze f -,-n spice; (Aroma) aroma

Wurzel f -,-n root; W∼n schlagen take root. w∼n vi (haben) root

würz|en vt season. w∼ig a tasty; (aromatisch) aromatic; (pikant) spicy

wüst a chaotic; (wirr) tangled; (öde) desolate; (wild) wild, adv -ly; (schlimm) terrible, adv -bly

Wüste f -,-n desert

Wut f - rage, fury. W∼anfall m fit of rage

wüten vi (haben) rage. w∼d a furious, adv -ly; w∼d machen infuriate

X

x /ɪks/ inv a (Math) x; (fam) umpteen. X-Beine ntpl knock-knees. x-beinig. X-beinig a knock-kneed. x-beliebig a (fam) any; eine x-beliebige Zahl any number [you like]. x-mal adv (fam) umpteen times; zum x-ten Mal for the umpteenth time

Y

Yoga /ˈjoːga/ m & nt -[s] yoga

Z

Zack|e f -,-n point; (Berg-) peak; (Gabel-) prong. z∼ig a jagged; (gezackt) serrated; (fam: schneidig) smart, adv -ly

zaghaft a timid, adv -ly; (zögernd) tentative, adv -ly

zäh a tough; (hartnäckig) tenacious, adv -ly; (zähflüssig) viscous; (schleppend) sluggish, adv -ly. z∼flüssig a viscous; (Verkehr) slow-moving. Z∼igkeit f - toughness; tenacity

Zahl f -,-en number; (Ziffer, Betrag) figure

zahl|bar a payable. z∼en vt/i (haben) pay; (bezahlen) pay for; bitte z∼en! the bill please!

zählen vi (haben) count; z∼ zu (fig) be one/(pl) some of; z∼ auf (+ acc) count on □ vt count; z∼ zu add to; (fig) count among; die Stadt zählt 5000 Einwohner the town has 5000 inhabitants

zahlenmäßig a numerical, adv -ly

Zähler m -s,- meter

Zahl|grenze f fare-stage. Z∼karte f paying-in slip. z∼los a countless. z∼reich a numerous; (Anzahl, Gruppe) large □ adv in large numbers. Z∼ung f -,-en payment; in Z∼ung nehmen take in part-exchange

Zählung f -,-en count

zahlungsunfähig a insolvent

Zahlwort nt (pl -wörter) numeral

zahm a tame

zähmen vt tame; (fig) restrain

Zahn m -[e]s,ˇe tooth; (am Zahnrad) cog. Z∼arzt m, Z∼ärztin f dentist. Z∼belag m plaque. Z∼bürste f toothbrush. z∼en vi (haben) be teething. Z∼fleisch nt gums pl. z∼los a toothless. Z∼pasta f -,-en toothpaste. Z∼rad nt cog-wheel. Z∼schmelz m enamel. Z∼schmerzen mpl toothache sg. Z∼spange f brace. Z∼stein m tartar. Z∼stocher m -s,- toothpick

Zange f -,-n pliers pl; (Kneif-) pincers pl; (Kohlen-, Zucker-) tongs pl; (Geburts-) forceps pl

Zank m -[e]s squabble. z∼en vr sich z∼en squabble □ vi (haben) scold (mit jdm s.o.)

zänkisch a quarrelsome

Zäpfchen nt -s,- (Anat) uvula; (Med) suppository

Zapfen m -s,- (Bot) cone; (Stöpsel) bung; (Eis-) icicle. z∼ vt tap, draw. Z∼streich m (Mil) tattoo

Zapf|hahn m tap. Z∼säule f petrol-pump

zappel|ig a fidgety; (nervös) jittery. z∼n vi (haben) wriggle; (Kind:) fidget

zart a delicate, adv -ly; (weich, zärtlich) tender, adv -ly; (sanft) gentle, adv -ly. Z∼gefühl nt tact. Z∼heit f - delicacy; tenderness; gentleness

zärtlich a tender, adv -ly; (liebevoll) loving, adv -ly. Z∼keit f -,-en tenderness; (Liebkosung) caress

Zauber m -s magic; (Bann) spell. Z∼er m -s,- magician. z∼haft a enchanting. Z∼künstler m conjuror. Z∼kunststück nt = Z∼trick. z∼n vi (haben) do magic; (Zaubertricks ausführen) do conjuring tricks □ vt produce as if by magic. Z∼stab m magic wand. Z∼trick m conjuring trick

zaudern vi (haben) delay; (zögern) hesitate

Zaum m -[e]s,Zäume bridle; im Z~ halten(fig) restrain

Zaun m -[e]s,Zäune fence. Z~könig m wren

z.B. abbr (zum Beispiel) e.g.

Zebra nt -s,-s zebra. Z~streifen m zebra crossing

Zeche f -,-n bill; (Bergwerk) pit

zechen vi (haben) (fam) drink

Zeder f -,-n cedar

Zeh m -[e]s,-en toe. Z~e f -,-n toe; (Knoblauch-) clove. Z~ennagel m toenail

zehn inv a, Z~ f -,-en ten. z~te(r,s) a tenth. Z~tel nt -s,-tenth

Zeichen nt -s,- sign; (Signal) signal. Z~setzung f -punctuation. Z~trickfilm m cartoon [film]

zeichn|en vt/i (haben) draw; (kenn-) mark; (unter-) sign. Z~er m -s,-draughts-man. Z~ung f -,-en drawing; (auf Fell) markings pl

Zeige|finger m index finger. z~n vt show; sich z~n appear; (sich herausstellen) be-come clear; das wird sich z~n we shall see □ vi (haben) point (auf + acc to). Z~r m -s,-pointer; (Uhr-) hand

Zeile f -,-n line; (Reihe) row

zeit prep (+ gen) z~ meines/seines Le-bens all my/his life

Zeit f -,-en time; sich(dat) Z~ lassen take one's time; es hat Z~ there's no hurry; mit der Z~ in time; in nächster Z~ in the near future; die erste Z~ at first; von Z~ zu Z~ from time to time; zur Z~ (rechtzeitig) in time; (derzeit) (NEW) zur-zeit; eine Z~ lang for a time or while; [ach] du liebe Z~! (fam) good heavens!

Zeit|alter nt age, era. Z~arbeit f temporary work. Z~bombe f time bomb. z~gemäß a modern, up-to-date. Z~genosse m, Z~genossin f contemporary. z~genössisch a contemporary. z~ig a & adv early. Z~lang f eine Z~lang eine Z~ lang s. Zeit. z~lebens adv all one's life

zeitlich a (Dauer) in time; (Folge) chronol-ogical □ adv z~ begrenzt for a limited time

zeit|los a timeless. Z~lupe f slow motion. Z~punkt m time. Z~raubend a time-consuming. Z~raum m period. Z~schrift f magazine, periodical

Zeitung f -,-en newspaper. Z~spapier nt newspaper

Zeit|verschwendung f waste of time. Z~vertreib m pastime; zum Z~vertreib to pass the time. z~weilig a temporary □ adv temporarily; (hin und wieder) at times. z~weise adv at times. Z~wort nt (pl -wörter) verb. Z~zünder m time fuse

Zelle f -,-n cell; (Telefon-) box

Zelt nt -[e]s,-e tent; (Fest-) marquee. z~en vi (haben) camp. Z~en nt -s camping. Z~plane f tarpaulin. Z~platz m camp-site

Zement m -[e]s cement. z~ieren vt ce-ment

zen|sieren vt (Sch) mark; censor (Presse, Film). Z~sur f -,-en (Sch) mark, (Amer) grade; (Presse-) censorship

Zentimeter m & nt centimetre. Z~maß nt tape-measure

Zentner m -s,- [metric] hundredweight (50 kg)

zentral a central, adv -ly. Z~e f -,-n cen-tral office; (Partei-) headquarters pl; (Te-leph) exchange. Z~heizung f central heating. z~isieren vt centralize

Zentrum nt -s,-tren centre

zerbrech|en vt/i (sein) break; sich(dat) den Kopf z~en rack one's brains. z~-lich a fragile

zerdrücken vt crush; mash (Kartoffeln)

Zeremonie f -,-n ceremony

Zeremoniell nt -s,-e ceremonial. z~ a ceremonial, adv -ly

Zerfall m disintegration; (Verfall) decay. z~en vt (sein) disintegrate; (verfallen) decay; in drei Teile z~en be divided into three parts

zerfetzen vt tear to pieces

zerfließen vi (sein) melt; (Tinte:) run

zergehen vi (sein) melt; (sich auflösen) dissolve

zergliedern vt dissect

zerkleinern vt chop/(schneiden) cut up; (mahlen) grind

zerknirscht a contrite

zerknüllen vt crumple [up]

zerkratzen vt scratch

zerlassen† vt melt

zerlegen vt take to pieces, dismantle; (zerschneiden) cut up; (tranchieren) carve

zerlumpt a ragged

zermalmen vt crush

zermürb|en vt (fig) wear down. Z~ungs-krieg m war of attrition

zerplatzen vi (sein) burst

zerquetschen vt squash, crush; mash (Kartoffeln)

Zerrbild nt caricature

zerreißen† vt tear; (in Stücke) tear up; break (Faden, Seil) □ vi (sein) tear; break

zerren vt drag; pull (Muskel) □ vi (haben) pull (an + dat at)

zerrinnen† vi (sein) melt

zerrissen a torn

zerrütten vt ruin, wreck; shatter ⟨Nerven⟩; zerrüttete Ehe broken marriage

zerschlagen† vt smash; smash up ⟨Möbel⟩; sich z~ ⟨fig⟩ fall through; ⟨Hoffnung:⟩ be dashed □ a ⟨erschöpft⟩ worn out

zerschmettern vt/i (sein) smash

zerschneiden† vt cut; ⟨in Stücke⟩ cut up

zersetzen vt corrode; undermine ⟨Moral⟩; sich z~ decompose

zersplittern vi (sein) splinter; ⟨Glas:⟩ shatter □ vt shatter

zerspringen† vi (sein) shatter; ⟨bersten⟩ burst

Zerstäuber m -s,- atomizer

zerstör|en vt destroy; ⟨zunichte machen⟩ wreck. Z~er m -s,- destroyer. Z~ung f destruction

zerstreu|en vt scatter; disperse ⟨Menge⟩; dispel ⟨Zweifel⟩; sich z~en disperse; ⟨sich unterhalten⟩ amuse oneself. z~t a absent-minded, adv -ly. Z~ung f -,-en ⟨Unterhaltung⟩ entertainment

zerstückeln vt cut up into pieces

zerteilen vt divide up

Zertifikat nt -[e]s,-e certificate

zertreten† vt stamp on; ⟨zerdrücken⟩ crush

zertrümmern vt smash [up]; wreck ⟨Gebäude, Stadt⟩

zerzaus|en vt tousle. z~t a dishevelled; ⟨Haar:⟩ tousled

Zettel m -s,- piece of paper; ⟨Notiz⟩ note; ⟨Bekanntmachung⟩ notice; ⟨Reklame-⟩ leaflet

Zeug nt -s (fam) stuff; ⟨Sachen⟩ things pl; ⟨Ausrüstung⟩ gear; dummes Z~ nonsense; das Z~ haben zu have the makings of

Zeuge m -n,-n witness. z~n vi (haben) testify; z~n von ⟨fig⟩ show □ vt father. Z~naussage f testimony. Z~nstand m witness box/(Amer) stand

Zeugin f -,-nen witness

Zeugnis nt -ses,-se certificate; ⟨Sch⟩ report; ⟨Referenz⟩ reference; ⟨fig: Beweis⟩ evidence

Zickzack m -[e]s,-e zigzag

Ziege f -,-n goat

Ziegel m -s,- brick; ⟨Dach-⟩ tile. Z~stein m brick

ziehen† vt pull; ⟨sanfter; zücken; zeichnen⟩ draw; ⟨heraus-⟩ pull out; extract ⟨Zahn⟩; raise ⟨Hut⟩; put on ⟨Bremse⟩; move ⟨Schachfigur⟩; put up ⟨Leine, Zaun⟩; ⟨dehnen⟩ stretch; make ⟨Grimasse, Scheitel⟩; ⟨züchten⟩ breed; grow ⟨Rosen, Gemüse⟩; nach sich z~ ⟨fig⟩ entail □ vr sich z~ ⟨sich erstrecken⟩ run; ⟨sich verziehen⟩

warp □ vi (haben) pull (an + dat on/at); ⟨Tee, Ofen:⟩ draw; ⟨Culin⟩ simmer; es zieht there is a draught; solche Filme z~ nicht mehr films like that are no longer popular □ vi (sein) ⟨um-⟩ move (nach to); ⟨Menge:⟩ march; ⟨Vögel:⟩ migrate; ⟨Wolken, Nebel:⟩ drift. Z~ nt -s ache

Ziehharmonika f accordion

Ziehung f -,-en draw

Ziel nt -[e]s,-e destination; ⟨Sport⟩ finish; ⟨Z~scheibe & Mil⟩ target; ⟨Zweck⟩ aim, goal. z~bewusst ⟨z~bewußt⟩ a purposeful, adv -ly. z~en vi (haben) aim (auf + acc at). z~end a ⟨Gram⟩ transitive. z~los a aimless, adv -ly. Z~scheibe f target; ⟨fig⟩ butt. z~strebig a single-minded, adv -ly

ziemen (sich) vr be seemly

ziemlich a ⟨fam⟩ fair □ adv rather, fairly; ⟨fast⟩ pretty well

Zier|de f -,-n ornament. z~en vt adorn; sich z~en make a fuss; ⟨sich bitten lassen⟩ need coaxing

zierlich a dainty, adv -ily; ⟨fein⟩ delicate, adv -ly; ⟨Frau⟩ petite

Ziffer f -,-n figure, digit; ⟨Zahlzeichen⟩ numeral. Z~blatt nt dial

zig inv a ⟨fam⟩ umpteen

Zigarette f -,-n cigarette

Zigarre f -,-n cigar

Zigeuner(in) m -s,- (f -,-nen) gypsy

Zimmer nt -s,- room. Z~mädchen nt chambermaid. Z~mann m (pl -leute) carpenter. Z~n vt make □ vi (haben) do carpentry. Z~nachweis m accommodation bureau. Z~pflanze f house plant

zimperlich a squeamish; ⟨wehleidig⟩ soft; ⟨prüde⟩ prudish

Zimt m -[e]s cinnamon

Zink nt -s zinc

Zinke f -,-n prong; ⟨Kamm-⟩ tooth

Zinn m -s tin; ⟨Gefäße⟩ pewter

Zins|en mpl interest sg; Z~en tragen earn interest. Z~eszins m -es,-en compound interest. Z~fuß, Z~satz m interest rate

Zipfel m -s,- corner; ⟨Spitze⟩ point; ⟨Wurst-⟩ [tail-]end

zirka adv circa

Zirkel m -s,- [pair of] compasses pl; ⟨Gruppe⟩ circle

Zirkul|ation /-'tsjo:n/ f - circulation. z~ieren vi (sein) circulate

Zirkus m -,-se circus

zirpen vi (haben) chirp

zischen vi (haben) hiss; ⟨Fett:⟩ sizzle □ vt hiss

Zit|at nt -[e]s,-e quotation. z~ieren vt/i (haben) quote; ⟨rufen⟩ summon

Zitr|onat nt -[e]s candied lemon-peel. Z~**one** f -,-n lemon. Z~**onenlimonade** f lemonade

zittern vi (haben) tremble; (vor Kälte) shiver; (beben) shake

zittrig a shaky, adv -ily

Zitze f -,-n teat

zivil a civilian; (Ehe, Recht, Luftfahrt) civil; (mäßig) reasonable. Z~ nt -s civilian clothes pl. Z~**courage** /-kura:ʒə/ f - courage of one's convictions. Z~**dienst** m community service

Zivili|sation /-'tsio:n/ f -,-en civilization. z~**sieren** vt civilize. z~**siert** a civilized □ adv in a civilized manner

Zivilist m -en,-en civilian

zögern vi (haben) hesitate. Z~ nt -s hesitation. z~d a hesitant, adv -ly

Zoll¹ m -[e]s,- inch

Zoll² m -[e]s,ˆe [customs] duty; (Behörde) customs pl. Z~**abfertigung** f customs clearance. z~**beamte(r)** m customs officer. z~**frei** a & adv duty-free. Z~**kontrolle** f customs check

Zone f -,-n zone

Zoo m -s,-s zoo

Zoo|loge /tsoo'lo:gə/ m -n,-n zoologist. Z~**logie** f -. zoology. z~**logisch** a zoological

Zopf m -[e]s,ˆe plait

Zorn m -[e]s anger. z~**ig** a angry, adv -ily

zotig a smutty, dirty

zottig a shaggy

z.T. abbr (zum Teil) partly

zu prep (+ dat) to; (dazu) with; (zeitlich; preislich) at; (Zweck) for; (über) about; to ... hin towards; zu Hause at home; zu Fuß/Pferde on foot/horseback; zu beiden Seiten on both sides; zu Ostern at Easter; zu diesem Zweck for this purpose; zu meinem Erstaunen/Entsetzen to my surprise/horror; zu Dutzenden by the dozen; eine Marke zu 60 Pfennig a 60-pfennig stamp; das Stück zu zwei Mark at two marks each; wir waren zu dritt/viert there were three/four of us; es steht 3zu 3 the score is 5–3; zu etw werden turn into sth □ adv (allzu) too; (Richtung) towards; (geschlossen) closed; (an Schalter, Hahn) off; zu sein be closed; zu groß/viel/weit too big/much/far; nach dem Fluss zu towards the river; Augen zu! close your eyes! Tür zu! shut the door! nur zu! go on! macht zu! (fam) hurry up! □ conj to; etwas zu essen something to eat; nicht zu glauben unbelievable; zu erörternde Probleme problems to be discussed

zuallererst adv first of all. z~**letzt** adv last of all

Zubehör nt -s accessories pl

zubereit|en vt sep prepare. Z~**ung** f - preparation; (in Rezept) method

zubilligen vt sep grant

zubinden† vt sep tie [up]

zubringen† vt sep spend. Z~**er** m -s,- access road; (Bus) shuttle

Zucchini /tsu'ki:ni/ pl courgettes

Zucht f -,-en breeding; (Pflanzen-) cultivation; (Art, Rasse) breed; (von Pflanzen) strain; (Z~farm) farm; (Pferde-) stud; (Disziplin) discipline

zücht|en vt breed; cultivate, grow (Rosen, Gemüse). Z~**er** m -s,- breeder; grower

Zuchthaus nt prison

züchtigen vt chastise

Züchtung f -,-en breeding; (Pflanzen-) cultivation; (Art, Rasse) breed; (von Pflanzen) strain

zucken vi (haben) twitch; (sich z~d bewegen) jerk; (Blitz:) flash; (Flamme:) flicker □ vt die Achseln z~ shrug one's shoulders

zücken vt draw (Messer)

Zucker m -s sugar. Z~**dose** f sugar basin. Z~**guß** (Z~guß) m icing. z~**krank** a diabetic. Z~**krankheit** f diabetes. z~**n** vt sugar. Z~**rohr** nt sugar cane. Z~**rübe** f sugar beet. z~**süß** a sweet; (fig) sugary. Z~**watte** f candyfloss. Z~**zange** f sugar tongs pl

zuckrig a sugary

zudecken vt sep cover up; (im Bett) tuck up; cover (Topf)

zudem adv moreover

zudrehen vt sep turn off; jdm den Rücken z~ turn one's back on s.o.

zudringlich a pushing, (fam) pushy

zudrücken vt sep press or push shut; close (Augen)

zueinander adv to one another; z~ passen go together; z~ halten (fig) stick together. z~**halten†** vi sep (haben) ⟨NEW⟩ z~ halten, s. zueinander

zuerkennen† vt sep award (dat to)

zuerst adv first; (anfangs) at first; mit dem Kopf z~ head first

zufahr|en† vi sep (sein) z~en auf (+ acc) drive towards. Z~t f access; (Einfahrt) drive

Zufall m chance; (Zusammentreffen) coincidence; durch Z~ by chance/coincidence. z~**en†** vi sep (sein) close, shut; jdm z~en ⟨Aufgabe:⟩ fall/⟨Erbe:⟩ go to s.o.

zufällig a chance, accidental □ adv by chance; ich war z~ da I happened to be there

Zuflucht f refuge; (Schutz) shelter. Z~**sort** m refuge

zufolge prep (+ dat) according to

zufrieden a contented, adv -ly; (befriedigt) satisfied; sich z~ geben be satisfied; jdn z~ lassen leave s.o. in peace; jdn z~ stellen satisfy s.o.; z~ stellend satisfactory. z~geben † (sich) vr sep NEW~ geben (sich), s. zufrieden. Z~heit f- contentment; satisfaction. z~lassen† vt sep NEW~ lassen, s. zufrieden. z~stellen vt sep NEW~ stellen, s. zufrieden, z~stellend a NEW~ stellend, s. zufrieden

zufrieren† vi sep (sein) freeze over

zufügen vt sep inflict (dat on); do (Unrecht) (dat to)

Zufuhr f- supply

zuführen vt sep □ vt supply □ vi (haben) z~ auf (+ acc) lead to

Zug m -[e]s,-̈e train; (Kolonne) column; (Um-) procession; (Mil) platoon; (Vogelschar) flock; (Ziehen, Zugkraft) pull; (Wandern, Ziehen) migration; (Schluck, Luft-) draught; (Atem-) breath; (beim Rauchen) puff; (Schach-) move; (beim Schwimmen, Rudern) stroke; (Gesichts-) feature; (Wesens-) trait; etw in vollen Zügen genießen enjoy sth to the full; in einem Zug[e] at one go

Zugabe f (Geschenk) [free] gift; (Mus) encore

Zugang m access

zugänglich a accessible; (Mensch:) approachable; (fig) amenable (dat/für to)

Zugbrücke f drawbridge

zugeben† vt sep add; (gestehen) admit; (erlauben) allow. zugegebenermaßen adv admittedly

zugegen a z~ sein be present

zugehen† vi sep (sein) close; jdm z~ be sent to s.o.; z~ auf (+ acc) go towards; dem Ende z~ draw to a close; (Vorräte:) run low; auf der Party ging es lebhaft zu the party was pretty lively

Zugehörigkeit f- membership

Zügel m -s,- rein

zugelassen a registered

zügel|los a unrestrained, adv -ly; (sittenlos) licentious. z~n vt rein in; (fig) curb

Zuge|ständnis nt concession. z~stehen† vt sep grant

zugetan a fond (dat of)

zugig a draughty

zügig a quick, adv -ly

Zug|kraft f pull; (fig) attraction. z~kräftig a effective; (anreizend) popular; (Titel:) catchy

zugleich adv at the same time

Zug|luft f draught. Z~pferd nt draught-horse; (fam) draw

zugreifen† vi sep (haben) grab it/them; (bei Tisch) help oneself; (bei Angebot) jump at it; (helfen) lend a hand

zugrunde adv z~ richten destroy; z~ gehen be destroyed; (Ehe:) founder; (sterben) die; z~ liegen form the basis (dat of)

zugucken vi sep (haben) = zusehen

zugunsten prep (+ gen) in favour of; (Sammlung) in aid of

zugute adv jdm/etw z~ kommen benefit s.o./sth; jdm seine Jugend z~ halten make allowances for s.o.'s youth

Zugvogel m migratory bird

zuhalten† v sep □ vt keep closed; (bedecken) cover; sich (dat) die Nase z~ hold one's nose □ vi (haben) z~ auf (+ acc) head for

Zuhälter m -s,- pimp

zuhause adv = zu Hause, s. Haus. Z~ nt -s,- home

zuhör|en vi sep (haben) listen (dat to). Z~er(in) m(f) listener

zujubeln vi sep (haben) jdm z~ cheer s.o.

zukehren vt sep turn (dat to)

zukleben vt sep seal

zuknallen vt/i sep (sein) slam

zuknöpfen vt sep button up

zukommen† vi sep (sein) z~ auf (+ acc) come towards; (sich nähern) approach; z~ lassen send (jdm s.o.); devote (Pflege) (dat to); jdm z~ be s.o.'s right

Zukunft f- future. zukünftig a future □ adv in future

Zulage f -,-n extra allowance

zulangen vi sep (haben) help oneself; tüchtig z~ tuck in

zulassen† vt sep allow, permit; (teilnehmen lassen) admit; (Admin) license, register; (geschlossen lassen) leave closed; leave unopened (Brief)

zulässig a permissible

Zulassung f -,-en admission; registration; (Lizenz) licence

zulaufen† vi sep (sein) z~en auf (+ acc) run towards; spitz z~en taper to a point

zulegen vt sep add; sich (dat) etw z~ get sth; grow (Bart)

zuleide adv jdm etwas z~ tun hurt s.o.

zuletzt adv last; (schließlich) in the end; nicht z~ not least

zuliebe adv jdm/etw z~ for the sake of s.o./sth

zum prep = zu dem; zum Spaß for fun; etw zum Lesen sth to read zu̱machen *v sep* ◻ *vt* close, shut; do up ⟨*Jacke*⟩; seal ⟨*Umschlag*⟩; turn off ⟨*Hahn*⟩; (*stillegen*) close down ◻ *vi* (*haben*) close, shut; (*stillgelegt werden*) close down

zumal *adv* especially ◻ *conj* especially since

zume̱ist *adv* for the most part

zumi̱ndest *adv* at least

zu̱mutbar *a* reasonable

zu̱mute *adv* mir ist traurig/elend z∼ I feel sad/wretched; mir ist nicht danach z∼ I don't feel like it

zu̱mut|en *vt sep* jdm etw z∼en ask *or* expect sth of s.o.; sich (*dat*) zu viel z∼en overdo things. Z∼ung *f*- imposition; eine Z∼ung sein be unreasonable

zunä̱chst *adv* first [of all]; (*anfangs*) at first; (*vorläufig*) for the moment ◻ *prep* (+ *dat*) nearest to

Zu̱nahme *f*-,-n increase

Zu̱name *m* surname

zünd|en *vt/i* (*haben*) ignite; z∼ende Rede rousing speech. Z∼er *m* -s,- detonator, fuse. Z∼holz *nt* match. Z∼kerze *f* sparking-plug. Z∼schlüssel *m* ignition key. Z∼schnur *f* fuse. Z∼ung *f*-,-en ignition

zu̱nehmen† *vi sep* (*haben*) increase (an + *dat* in); ⟨*Mond:*⟩ wax; (*an Gewicht*) put on weight. z∼d *a* increasing, *adv* -ly

Zu̱neigung *f*- affection

Zunft *f*-,¨e guild

zünftig *a* proper, *adv* -ly

Zu̱nge *f* -,-n tongue. Z∼nbrecher *m* tongue-twister

zu̱nichte *a* z∼ machen wreck; z∼ werden come to nothing

zu̱nicken *vi sep* (*haben*) nod (*dat* to)

zu̱nutze *a* sich (*dat*) etw z∼ machen make use of sth; (*ausnutzen*) take advantage of sth

zu̱oberst *adv* right at the top

zu̱ordnen *vt sep* assign (*dat* to)

zu̱pfen *vt/i* (*haben*) pluck (an + *dat* at); pull out ⟨*Unkraut*⟩

zu̱r *prep* = zu der; zur Schule/Arbeit to school/work

zurande *adv* z∼ kommen mit (*fam*) cope with

zu̱rate *adv* z∼ ziehen consult

zurechnungsfähig *a* of sound mind

zurecht|finden† (sich) *vr sep* find one's way. z∼kommen† *vi sep* (*sein*) cope (mit with); (*rechtzeitig kommen*) be in time. z∼legen *vt sep* put out ready; sich (*dat*) eine Ausrede z∼legen have an excuse all ready. z∼machen *vt sep* get ready; sich z∼machen get ready. z∼weisen† *vt sep* reprimand. z∼weisung *f* reprimand

zu̱reden *vi sep* (*haben*) jdm z∼ try to persuade s.o.

zu̱richten *vt sep* prepare; (*beschädigen*) damage; (*verletzen*) injure

zu̱riegeln *vt sep* bolt

zurück *adv* back; Berlin, hin und z∼ return to Berlin. z∼behalten† *vt sep* keep back; be left with ⟨*Narbe*⟩. z∼bekommen† *vt sep* get back; 20 Pfennig z∼bekommen get 20 pfennigs change. z∼bleiben† *vi sep* (*sein*) stay behind; (*nicht mithalten*) lag behind. z∼blicken *vi sep* (*haben*) look back. z∼bringen† *vt sep* bring back; (*wieder hinbringen*) take back. z∼erobern *vt sep* recapture; (*fig*) regain. z∼erstatten *vt sep* refund. z∼fahren† *vi sep* ◻ *vt* drive back ◻ *vi* (*sein*) return, go back; (*im Auto*) drive back; (*z∼weichen*) recoil. z∼finden† *vi sep* (*haben*) find one's way back. z∼führen *v sep* ◻ *vt* take back; (*fig*) attribute (auf + *acc* to) ◻ *vi* (*haben*) lead back. z∼geben† *vt sep* give back, return. z∼geblieben *a* retarded. z∼gehen† *vi sep* (*sein*) go back, return; (*abnehmen*) go down; z∼gehen auf (+ *acc*) (*fig*) go back to

zurückgezogen *a* secluded. Z∼heit *f*- seclusion

zurückhalt|en† *vt sep* hold back; (*abhalten*) stop; sich z∼en restrain oneself. z∼end *a* reserved. Z∼ung *f*- reserve

zurück|kehren *vi sep* (*sein*) return. z∼kommen† *vi sep* (*sein*) come back, return; (*ankommen*) get back; z∼kommen auf (+ *acc*) (*fig*) come back to. z∼lassen† *vt sep* leave behind; (*z∼kehren lassen*) allow back. z∼legen *vt sep* put back; (*reservieren*) keep; (*sparen*) put by; cover ⟨*Strecke*⟩. z∼lehnen (sich) *vr sep* lean back. z∼liegen† *vi sep* (*haben*) be in the past; (*Sport*) be behind; das liegt lange zurück that was long ago. z∼melden (sich) *vr sep* report back. z∼nehmen† *vt sep* take back. z∼rufen† *vt/i sep* (*haben*) call back. z∼scheuen *vi sep* (*sein*) shrink (vor + *dat* from). z∼schicken *vt sep* send back. z∼schlagen† *v sep* ◻ *vi* (*haben*) hit back ◻ *vt* hit back; (*abwehren*) beat back; (*umschlagen*) turn back. z∼schneiden† *vt sep* cut back. z∼schrecken† *vi sep* (*sein*) shrink back, recoil; (*fig*) shrink (vor + *dat* from). z∼setzen *v sep* ◻ *vt* put back; (*Auto*) reverse, back; (*herabsetzen*) reduce; (*fig*) neglect ◻ *vi* (*haben*) reverse, back. z∼stellen *vt sep* put back; (*reservieren*) keep; (*fig*) put aside; (*aufschieben*) postpone. z∼stoßen† *v sep* ◻ *vt* push back ◻ *vi* (*sein*) reverse, back. z∼treten† *vi sep* (*sein*) step back; (*vom Amt*) resign; (*verzichten*) withdraw. z∼weichen† *vi sep* (*sein*) draw back; (*z∼schrecken*) shrink back. z~weisen† *vt sep* turn away; *(fig)* reject. z~werfen† *vt sep* throw back; *(reflektieren)* reflect. z~zahlen *vt sep* pay back. z~ziehen† *vt sep* draw back; *(fig)* withdraw; sich z~ziehen withdraw; *(vom Beruf)* retire; *(Mil)* retreat

Zuruf *m* shout. z~en† *vt sep* shout *(dat* to)

zurzeit *adv* at present

Zusage *f* -,-n acceptance; *(Versprechen)* promise. z~n *v sep* □ *vt* promise □ *vi (haben)* accept; jdm z~n appeal to s.o.

zusammen *adv* together; *(insgesamt)* altogether. z~ sein be together. Z~arbeit *f* co-operation. z~arbeiten *vi sep (haben)* co-operate. z~bauen *vt sep* assemble. z~beißen† *vt sep* die Zähne z~beißen clench/*(fig)* grit one's teeth. z~bleiben† *vi sep (sein)* stay together. z~brechen† *vi sep (sein)* collapse. z~bringen† *vt sep* bring together; *(beschaffen)* raise. Z~bruch *m* collapse; *(Nerven- & fig)* breakdown. z~fahren† *vi sep (sein)* collide; *(z~zucken)* start. z~fallen† *vi sep (sein)* collapse; *(zeitlich)* coincide. z~falten *vt sep* fold up. z~fassen *vt sep* summarize, sum up. Z~fassung *f* summary. z~fügen *vt sep* fit together. z~führen *vt sep* bring together. z~gehören *vi sep (haben)* belong together; *(z~passen)* go together. z~gesetzt *a (Gram)* compound. z~halten† *v sep* □ *vt* hold together; *(beisammenhalten)* keep together □ *vi (haben) (fig)* stick together. Z~hang *m* connection; *(Kontext)* context. z~hängen† *vi sep (sein)* be connected. z~hanglos *a* incoherent, *adv* -ly. z~klappen *v sep* □ *vt* fold up □ *vi (sein)* collapse. z~kommen† *vi sep (sein)* meet; *(sich sammeln)* accumulate. Z~kunft *f* -, -e meeting. z~laufen† *vi sep (sein)* gather; *(Flüssigkeit:)* collect; *(Linien:)* converge. z~leben *vi sep (haben)* live together. z~legen *v sep* □ *vt* put together; *(z~falten)* fold up; *(vereinigen)* amalgamate; pool *(Geld)* □ *vi (haben)* club together. z~nehmen† *vt sep* gather up; summon up *(Mut)*; collect *(Gedanken)*; sich z~nehmen pull oneself together. z~passen *vi sep (haben)* go together, match; *(Personen:)* be well matched. Z~prall *m* collision. z~prallen *vi sep (sein)* collide. z~rechnen *vt sep* add up. z~reißen† *(sich) vr sep (fam)* pull oneself together. z~rollen *vt sep* roll up; sich z~rollen curl up. z~schlagen† *vt sep* smash up; *(prügeln)* beat up. z~schließen† *(sich) vr sep* join together; *(Firmen:)* merge. Z~schluss (Z~schluß) *m* union; *(Comm)* merger. z~schreiben† *vt sep* write as one word

zusammensein† *vi sep (sein)* (NEW) zusammen sein, s. zusammen. Z~ *nt* -s get-together

zusammensetz|en *vt sep* put together; *(Techn)* assemble; sich z~en sit [down] together; *(bestehen)* be made up *(aus* from). Z~ung *f* -,-en composition; *(Techn)* assembly; *(Wort)* compound

zusammen|stellen *vt sep* put together; *(gestalten)* compile. Z~stoß *m* collision; *(fig)* clash. z~stoßen† *vi sep (sein)* collide. z~treffen† *vi sep (sein)* meet; *(zeitlich)* coincide. Z~treffen *nt* meeting; coincidence. z~zählen *vt sep* add up. z~ziehen† *v sep* □ *vt* draw together; *(addieren)* add up; *(konzentrieren)* mass; sich z~ziehen contract; *(Gewitter:)* gather □ *vi (sein)* move in together; move in *(mit* with). z~zucken *vi sep (sein)* start; *(vor Schmerz)* wince

Zusatz *m* addition; *(Jur)* rider; *(Lebensmittel-)* additive. Z~gerät *nt* attachment. zusätzlich *a* additional □ *adv* in addition

zuschanden *adv* z~ machen ruin, wreck; z~ werden be wrecked *or* ruined; z~ fahren wreck

zuschau|en *vi sep (haben)* watch. Z~er(in) *m* -s,- (*f* -,-nen) spectator; *(TV)* viewer. Z~erraum *m* auditorium

zuschicken *vt sep* send *(dat* to)

Zuschlag *m* surcharge; *(D-Zug-)* supplement. z~en† *v sep* □ *vt* shut; *(heftig)* slam; *(bei Auktion)* knock down *(jdm* to s.o.) □ *vi (haben)* hit out; *(Feind:)* strike □ *vi (sein)* slam shut. z~pflichtig *a (Zug)* for which a supplement is payable

zuschließen† *v sep* □ *vt* lock □ *vi (haben)* lock up

zuschneiden† *vt sep* cut out; cut to size *(Holz)*

zuschreiben† *vt sep* attribute *(dat* to); jdm die Schuld z~ blame s.o.

Zuschrift *f* letter; *(auf Annonce)* reply

zuschulden *adv* sich *(dat)* etwas z~ kommen lassen do wrong

Zuschuss (**Zuschuß**) *m* contribution; *(staatlich)* subsidy

zusehen† *vi sep (haben)* watch; z~, dass see [to it] that

zusehends *adv* visibly

zusein† *vi sep (sein)* (NEW) zu sein, s. zu

zusenden† *vt sep* send *(dat* to)

zusetzen *v sep* □ *vt* add; *(einbüßen)* lose □ *vi (haben)* jdm z~ pester s.o.; *(Hitze:)* take it out of s.o.

zusicher|n *vt sep* promise. Z~ung *f* promise

Zuspätkommende(r) *m/f* late-comer

zuspielen *vt sep (Sport)* pass

zu|spitzen (sich) *vr sep* ⟨*fig*⟩ become critical

zu|sprechen† *v sep* □ *vt* award (jdm s.o.); jdm Trost/Mut z~ comfort/encourage s.o. □ *vi* (*haben*) dem Essen z~ eat heartily

Zustand *m* condition, state

zustande *adv* z~ bringen/kommen bring/come about

zuständig *a* competent; (*verantwortlich*) responsible. Z~keit *f* - competence; responsibility

zu|stehen† *vi sep* (*haben*) jdm z~ be s.o.'s right; (*Urlaub:*) be due to s.o.; es steht ihm nicht zu he is not entitled to it; (*gebührt*) it is not for him (zu to)

zu|steigen† *vi sep* (*sein*) get on; noch jemand zugestiegen? tickets please; (*im Bus*) any more fares please?

zu|stell|en *vt sep* block; (*bringen*) deliver. Z~ung *f* delivery

zu|steuern *v sep* □ *vi* (*sein*) head (auf + *acc* for) □ *vt* contribute

zu|stimm|en *vi sep* (*haben*) agree; (*billigen*) approve (*dat* of). Z~ung *f* consent; approval

zu|stoßen† *vi sep* (*sein*) happen (*dat* to)

Zustrom *m* influx

zutage *adv* z~ treten *od* kommen/bringen come/bring to light

Zutat *f* (*Culin*) ingredient

zu|teil|en *vt sep* allocate; assign ⟨*Aufgabe*⟩. Z~ung *f* allocation

zutiefst *adv* deeply

zu|tragen† *vt sep* carry/(*fig*) report (*dat* to); sich z~ happen

zu|trau|en *vt sep* jdm etw z~ believe s.o. capable of sth. Z~en *nt* -s confidence. z~lich *a* trusting, *adv* -ly; ⟨*Tier*⟩ friendly

zu|treffen† *vi sep* (*haben*) be correct; z~ auf (+ *acc*) apply to. z~d *a* applicable (auf + *acc* to); (*richtig*) correct, *adv* -ly

zu|trinken† *vi sep* (*haben*) jdm z~ drink to s.o.

Zutritt *m* admittance

zuunterst *adv* right at the bottom

zuverlässig *a* reliable, *adv* -bly. Z~keit *f* - reliability

Zuversicht *f* - confidence. z~lich *a* confident, *adv* -ly

zuviel *pron* & *adv* (NEW) zu viel, *s.* viel

zuvor *adv* before; (*erst*) first

zu|vorkommen† *vi sep* (*sein*) (+ *dat*) anticipate; jdm z~ beat s.o. to it. z~d *a* obliging, *adv* -ly

Zuwachs *m* -es increase

zuwege *adv* z~ bringen achieve

zuweilen *adv* now and then

zu|weisen† *vt sep* assign; (*zuteilen*) allocate

zu|wend|en† *vt sep* turn (*dat* to); sich z~en (+ *dat*) turn to; (*fig*) devote oneself to. Z~ung *f* donation; (*Fürsorge*) care

zuwenig *pron* & *adv* (NEW) zu wenig, *s.* wenig

zu|werfen† *vt sep* slam ⟨*Tür*⟩; jdm etw z~ throw s.o. sth; give s.o. ⟨*Blick, Lächeln*⟩

zuwider *adv* jdm z~ sein be repugnant to s.o. □ *prep* (+ *dat*) contrary to. z~handeln *vi sep* (*haben*) contravene (etw *dat* sth)

zu|zahlen *vt sep* pay extra

zu|ziehen† *v sep* □ *vt* pull tight; draw ⟨*Vorhänge*⟩; (*hinzu-*) call in; sich (*dat*) etw z~ contract ⟨*Krankheit*⟩; sustain ⟨*Verletzung*⟩; incur ⟨*Zorn*⟩ □ *vi* (*sein*) move into the area

zuzüglich *prep* (+ *gen*) plus

Zwang *m* -[e]s,ˑe compulsion; (*Gewalt*) force; (*Verpflichtung*) obligation

zwängen *vt* squeeze

zwanglos *a* informal, *adv* -ly; ⟨*Benehmen*⟩ free and easy. Z~igkeit *f* - informality

Zwangs|jacke *f* straitjacket. Z~lage *f* predicament. z~läufig *a* inevitable, *adv* -bly

zwanzig *inv a* twenty. z~ste(r,s) *a* twentieth

zwar *adv* admittedly; und z~ to be precise

Zweck *m* -[e]s,ˑe purpose; (*Sinn*) point; es hat keinen Z~ there is no point. z~dienlich *a* appropriate; (*Information*) relevant. Z~los *a* pointless. z~mäßig *a* suitable, *adv* -bly; (*praktisch*) functional, *adv* -ly. z~s *prep* (+ *gen*) for the purpose of

zwei *inv a*, Z~ *f* -,-en two; (*Sch*) ≈ B. Z~bettzimmer *nt* twin-bedded room

zweideutig *a* ambiguous, *adv* -ly; (*schlüpfrig*) suggestive, *adv* -ly. Z~keit *f* -,-en ambiguity

zwei|erlei *inv a* two kinds of □ *pron* two things. z~fach *a* double

Zweifel *m* -s,- doubt. z~haft *a* doubtful; (*fragwürdig*) dubious. z~los *adv* undoubtedly. z~n *vi* (*haben*) doubt (an etw *dat* sth)

Zweig *m* -[e]s,ˑe branch. Z~geschäft *nt* branch. Z~stelle *f* branch [office]

Zwei|kampf *m* duel. z~mal *adv* twice. z~reihig *a* ⟨*Anzug*⟩ double-breasted. z~sprachig *a* bilingual

zweit *adv* zu z~ in twos; wir waren zu z~ there were two of us. z~beste(r,s) *a* second-best. z~e(r,s) *a* second

zwei|teilig *a* two-piece; ⟨*Film, Programm*⟩ two-part. z~tens *adv* secondly

zweitklassig a second-class
Zwerchfell nt diaphragm
Zwerg m -[e]s,-e dwarf
Zwetsch[g]e f -,-n quetsche
Zwickel m -s,- gusset
zwicken vt/i (haben) pinch
Zwieback m -[e]s,-̈e rusk
Zwiebel f -,-n onion; (Blumen-) bulb
Zwielicht nt half-light; (Dämmerlicht)
   twilight. z~ig a shady
Zwie|spalt m conflict. z~spältig a con-
   flicting. Z~tracht f - discord
Zwilling m -s,-e twin; Z~e (Astr) Gemini
zwingen† vt force; sich z~ force oneself.
   z~d a compelling
Zwinger m -s,- run; (Zucht-) kennels pl
zwinkern vi (haben) blink; (als Zeichen)
   wink
Zwirn m -[e]s button thread
zwischen prep (+ dat/acc) between; (unter) among[st]. Z~bemerkung f interjection. Z~ding nt (fam) cross. z~durch

adv in between; (in der Z~zeit) in the
meantime; (ab und zu) now and again.
Z~fall m incident. Z~händler m middle-
man. Z~landung f stopover. Z~raum m
gap, space. Z~ruf m interjection. Z~ste-
cker m adaptor. Z~wand f partition.
Z~zeit f in der Z~zeit in the meantime
Zwist m -[e]s,-e discord; (Streit) feud.
   Z~igkeiten fpl quarrels
zwitschern vi (haben) chirp
zwo inv a two
zwölf inv a twelve. z~te(r,s) a twelfth
zwote(r,s) a second
Zylind|er m -s,- cylinder; (Hut) top hat.
   z~risch a cylindrical
Zyniker m -s,- cynic. z~isch a cynical,
   adv -ly. Z~ismus m - cynicism
Zypern nt -s Cyprus
Zypresse f -,-n cypress
Zyste /'tsystə/ f -,-n cyst

1. Join Up the Nouns

These German nouns are all made up of two separate words, but they have split apart. Draw a line between two pieces of paper that make up a noun. Watch out: one of the first words goes with two of the second words!

When you've made all the German words, do the same for the English translations and match them up with the German.

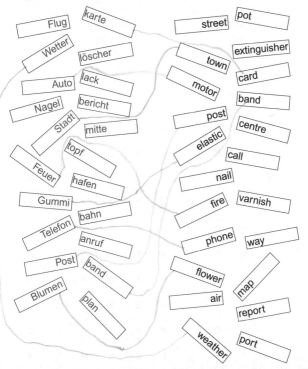

Flug — karte

Wetter — löscher

Auto — lack

Nagel — bericht

Stadt — mitte

Feuer — topf

Gummi — hafen

Telefon — bahn

Post — anruf

Blumen — band

                — plan

street — pot

town — extinguisher

motor — card

post — band

elastic — centre

                — call

nail — fire

                — varnish

phone — way

flower — map

air — report

weather — port

2. Wordsearch

Fifteen German words are hidden among the letters in the grid. Can you find them all? Watch out: six of the words read downwards, while all the others read across.

To help you, here are the English meanings of the German words. You can tick them off as you find the German.

ace	rough
almost	save
also	speak
better	ten
daughter	under
opera	village
powder	wide
quay	

M	W	N	B	U	N	T	E	R	V
Z	E	H	N	C	X	Z	L	K	J
H	I	G	F	P	U	L	V	E	R
D	T	O	C	H	T	E	R	S	A
D	S	P	R	E	C	H	E	N	P
O	B	E	S	S	E	R	A	O	I
R	U	R	K	U	F	A	S	T	A
F	Y	T	A	R	E	W	S	Q	U
Z	X	C	I	V	B	R	A	U	C
N	R	E	T	T	E	N	M	L	H

3. Odd Meaning Out

One word can have several different meanings. In the following exercise, only two of the three English translations given for each German word are correct. Use the dictionary to spot the odd one out, and then look up the right German translation for it:

fordern	demand challenge convince	**Pilz**	mushroom fungus beer
Schnee	snow icing beaten egg-white	**schwer**	swift difficult heavy
patent	obvious resourceful clever	**gerade**	straight grand even
Haken	tick hake hook	**drehen**	turn shoot catch
Brause	bruise fizzy drink shower	**Strom**	power storm stream
neben	next to apart from foggy	**Blase**	blanket blister bladder

4. Troubleshooting

Our computer has developed some annoying little problems. Can you help put them right?

First, when we type any three-letter word beginning with d, the computer shows three d's on the screen! The problem words are all highlighted in our "Recipe of the Week". Can you correct them in the box above each word?

Ddd Rezept ddd Woche

Für ddd Kuchenteig ddd Butter in Stückchen schneiden

und mit ddd Mehl vermischen. Ddd Gemisch mit ddd Honig

und ddd Milch zu einem festen Teig verarbeiten. Ddd

Äpfel waschen, halbieren und in ddd Pfanne mit ddd

Butter, ddd Zimt und ddd Zitronensaft aufkochen lassen.

Ddd Teig in ddd Form geben und mit ddd Obst belegen.

Ddd Kuchen in ddd Backofen schieben und 35 Minuten

backen.

5. Crossword

If you need to, you can use the dictionary to solve this crossword.
Just translate the clues into German, and write the translations
in capital letters.

Across
1 mature (4)
3 journeys (6)
8 advertisement, small ad (7)
9 pale (adjective) (5)
10 to hurry (5)
11 few (6)
13 a (male) industrialist (13)
15 to catch (6)
17 (male) Russian (5)
20 price or prize (5)
21 bags or pockets (7)
22 saddle (noun) (6)
23 stove (4)

Down
1 (female) rider (8)
2 island (5)
4 heiress (5)
5 asparagus (7)
6 nest (4)
7 crane (machine) (4)
11 goods, or (they) were (5)
12 to appoint (8)
14 dialect (7)
16 alley (5)
17 pink (4)
18 sheep (5)
19 epic (noun) (4)

6. Curly Words

One word is missing in each of the curly lists. Which day, month, number and capital city are missing?

Can you write out the four lists in the right order?

7. True or False?

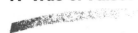

Can you crack the code to say whether these four statements are
true or false? First use the key to translate the symbols into
German.

Code key

a	♋	A		r	□	R	☼
b	♌	B		s	♦	S	◆
c	♍	C		t	◆	T	✳
d	♎	D		u	◆	U	✝
e	♏	E		v	❖	V	✟
f	♐	F		w	◆	W	✦
g	♑	G		x	⊠	X	✴
h	♒	H		y	☒	Y	✿
i	♓	I		z	⌘	Z	☾
j	er	J	☺	ä	⑩	Ä	⓪
k	&	K	☻	ö	✆	Ö	⑤
l	●	L	⊗	ü	•	Ü	⑥
m	○	M	◗	ß	▪	🗁	1
n	■	N	☇	,	🗈	🖹	2
o	□	O	ꝓ	.	🖉	🖺	3
p	□	P	ꝓ	?	✎	🖫	4
q	□	Q	➔				

🗁 ♏ ■ □ ● ♒ ♓ ■   ♓ ◆ ◆   ♎ ♓ ♏   ꝓ ♋ ◆ □ ◆ ◆ ♋ ♎ ◆
   ❖ □ ♏   ♍ ♏ ◆ ◆ ♍ ♒ ♋ ♋ ♎ 🖉

🖹 ☼ □ ◆ ♏ ■   ◆ ■ ♎   ꝓ ◆ ♏ □ ♑ ● □ ♍ & ♏ ■   ◆ ♓ ■ ♎
   ꝓ ◆ ◆ ♎ ♎ ♋ □ □ ◆ ♏ ■ 🖉

🖺 ◆ ♍ ♒ ■ ■ ♏ ♍ ♍ & ♏ ■   ◆ ♓ ■ ♎   ♎ ♓ ♏
   ◆ ♍ ♒ ♒ ♏ ● ● ◆ ♏ ■   ✴ ♓ ♏ □ ♏ 🖉

🖫 ◗ ◆ ♋ □ □ & & □   ♓ ◆ ◆   ♏ ♓ ■
   ♋ ♐ □ ♓ & & □ ■ ♓ ◆ ♒ ♍ ◆   ⓪ ♋ ■ ♎ 🖉

8. Sporting Links

Can you match each piece of sporting equipment to the right sport?
Can you translate the sports into German?

das Seil	archery
die Zielscheibe	tennis
der Schlittschuh	skittles
der Tennisschläger	surfing
der Kegel	mountaineering
der Ski	football
der Federball	swimming
das Segel	golf
die Kugel	skating
der Fußball	riding
die Flosse	cycling
der Zügel	gymnastics
das Sprungbrett	skiing
das Fahrrad	fencing
der Golfschläger	diving
die Turnschuhe	shot-putting
das Florett	sailing
das Surfbrett	badminton

Answers

1. Join Up the Nouns

Flughafen	airport
Wetterbericht	weather report
Autobahn	motorway
Nagellack	nail varnish
Stadtmitte	*town centre*
Stadtplan	*street map*
Feuerlöscher	fire extinguisher
Gummiband	elastic band
Telefonanruf	phone call
Postkarte	postcard
Blumentopf	flowerpot

2. Wordsearch

Ass	ace	rau	rough
fast	almost	retten	save
auch	also	sprechen	speak
besser	better	zehn	ten
Tochter	daughter	unter	under
Oper	opera	Dorf	village
Pulver	powder	weit	wide
Kai	quay		

3. Odd Meaning Out

convince	überzeugen
icing	Zuckerguss
obvious	offensichtlich
hake	Seehecht
bruise	blauer Fleck
foggy	neblig
beer	Bier
swift	schnell
grand	großartig
catch	fangen
storm	Sturm
blanket	Decke

4. Troubleshooting

Das Rezept *der* Woche
Für *den* Kuchenteig *die* Butter in Stückchen schneiden und mit *dem* Mehl vermischen. *Das* Gemisch mit *dem* Honig und *der* Milch zu einem festen Teig verarbeiten. *Die* Äpfel waschen, halbieren und in *der* Pfanne mit *der* Butter, *dem* Zimt und *dem* Zitronensaft aufkochen lassen. *Den* Teig in *die* Form geben und mit *dem* Obst belegen. *Den* Kuchen in *den* Backofen schieben und 35 Minuten backen.

5. Crossword

6. Curly Words

Freitag;Sonntag, Montag, Dienstag, Mittwoch, Donnerstag, Freitag,
  Samstag;
November; Januar, Februar, März, April, Mai, Juni, Juli, August,
  September, Oktober, November, Dezember;
Rom; Deutschland/Berlin, Österreich/Wien, die Schweiz/Bern,
  Frankreich/Paris, Italien/Rom
zehn; eins. zwei, drei, vier. fünf, sechs, sieben, acht, neun, zehn, elf, zwölf.

7. True or False?

1) Berlin ist die Hauptstadt von Deutschland.
   True: Berlin is the capital of Germany.
2) Rosen und Osterglocken sind Hundearten.
   False: Roses and daffodils are not kinds of dog.
3) Schnecken sind die schnellsten Tiere.
   False: Snails are not the fastest animals.
4) Marokko ist ein afrikanisches Land.
   True: Morocco is an African country.

8. Sporting Links

das Fahrrad	bicycle	cycling	das Radfahren
der Federball	shuttlecock	badminton	der Federball
das Florett	foil	fencing	das Fechten
die Flosse	flipper	swimming	das Schwimmen
der Fußball	football	football	der Fußball
der Golfschläger	golf-club	golf	das Golf
der Kegel	skittle	skittles	das Kegeln
die Kugel	shot	shot-putting	das Kugelstoßen
der Schlittschuh	ice-skate	skating	das Eislaufen
das Segel	sail	sailing	der Segelsport
das Seil	rope	mountaineering	das Bergsteigen
der Ski	ski	skiing	das Skilaufen
das Sprungbrett	springboard	diving	das Kunstspringen
das Surfbrett	surfboard	surfing	das Surfen
der Tennisschläger	tennis-racket	tennis	das Tennis
die Turnschuhe	gym-shoes	gymnastics	das Turnen
die Zielscheibe	target	archery	das Bogenschießen
der Zügel	rein	riding	das Reiten

A

a /ə, *betont* eɪ/ (*vor einem Vokal* an) *indef art* ein(e); (*each*) pro; not a kein(e)

aback /ə'bæk/ *adv* be taken ∼ verblüfft sein

abandon /ə'bændən/ *vt* verlassen; (*give up*) aufgeben □ *n* Hingabe *f*. ∼ed *a* verlassen; ⟨*behaviour*⟩ hemmungslos

abase /ə'beɪs/ *vt* demütigen

abashed /ə'bæʃt/ *a* beschämt, verlegen

abate /ə'beɪt/ *vi* nachlassen

abattoir /'æbətwɑ:(r)/ *n* Schlachthof *m*

abb|ey /'æbɪ/ *n* Abtei *f*. ∼ot /-ət/ *n* Abt *m*

abbreviat|e /ə'bri:vɪeɪt/ *vt* abkürzen. ∼ion /-'eɪʃn/ *n* Abkürzung *f*

abdicat|e /'æbdɪkeɪt/ *vi* abdanken. ∼ion /-'keɪʃn/ *n* Abdankung *f*

abdom|en /'æbdəmən/ *n* Unterleib *m*. ∼i-nal /-'dɒmɪnl/ *a* Unterleibs-

abduct /əb'dʌkt/ *vt* entführen. ∼ion /-ʌkʃn/ *n* Entführung *f*. ∼or *n* Entführer *m*

aberration /æbə'reɪʃn/ *n* Abweichung *f*; (*mental*) Verwirrung *f*

abet /ə'bet/ *vt* (*pt/pp* abetted) aid and ∼ (*Jur*) Beihilfe leisten (+ *dat*)

abeyance /ə'beɪəns/ *n* in ∼ [zeitweilig] außer Kraft; fall into ∼ außer Kraft kommen

abhor /əb'hɔ:(r)/ *vt* (*pt/pp* abhorred) verabscheuen. ∼rence /-'hɒrəns/ *n* Abscheu *m*. ∼rent /-'hɒrənt/ *a* abscheulich

abid|e /ə'baɪd/ *vt* (*pt/pp* abided) (*tolerate*) aushalten; ausstehen ⟨*person*⟩ □ *vi* ∼e by sich halten an (+ *acc*). ∼ing *a* bleibend

ability /ə'bɪlətɪ/ *n* Fähigkeit *f*; (*talent*) Begabung *f*

abject /'æbdʒekt/ *a* erbärmlich; (*humble*) demütig

ablaze /ə'bleɪz/ *a* in Flammen; be ∼ in Flammen stehen

able /'eɪbl/ *a* (-r, -st) fähig; be ∼ to do sth etw tun können. ∼-'bodied *a* körperlich gesund; (*Mil*) tauglich

ably /'eɪblɪ/ *adv* gekonnt

abnormal /æb'nɔ:ml/ *a* anormal; (*Med*) abnorm. ∼ity /-'mælətɪ/ *n* Abnormität *f*. ∼ly *adv* ungewöhnlich

aboard /ə'bɔ:d/ *adv & prep* an Bord (+ *gen*)

abode /ə'bəʊd/ *n* Wohnsitz *m*

abol|ish /ə'bɒlɪʃ/ *vt* abschaffen. ∼ition /æbə'lɪʃn/ *n* Abschaffung *f*

abominable /ə'bɒmɪnəbl/ *a*, -bly *adv* abscheulich

abominate /ə'bɒmɪneɪt/ *vt* verabscheuen

aborigines /æbə'rɪdʒəni:z/ *npl* Ureinwohner *pl*

abort /ə'bɔ:t/ *vt* abtreiben. ∼ion /-ɔ:ʃn/ *n* Abtreibung *f*; have an ∼ion eine Abtreibung vornehmen lassen. ∼ive /-tɪv/ *a* ⟨*attempt*⟩ vergeblich

abound /ə'baʊnd/ *vi* reichlich vorhanden sein; ∼ in reich sein an (+ *dat*)

about /ə'baʊt/ *adv* umher, herum; (*approximately*) ungefähr; be ∼ (*in circulation*) umgehen; (*in existence*) vorhanden sein; be up and ∼ auf den Beinen sein; be ∼ to do sth im Begriff sein, etw zu tun; there are a lot ∼ es gibt viele; there was no one ∼ es war kein Mensch da; run/play ∼ herumlaufen/-spielen □ *prep* um (+ *acc*) [. . . herum]; (*concerning*) über (+ *acc*); what is it ∼? worum geht es? ⟨*book:*⟩ wovon handelt es? I know nothing ∼ it ich weiß nichts davon; talk/know ∼ reden/wissen von

about: ∼-'face *n*, ∼-'turn *n* Kehrtwendung *f*

above /ə'bʌv/ *adv* oben □ *prep* über (+ *dat/acc*); ∼ all vor allem

above: ∼-'board *a* legal. ∼-mentioned *a* oben erwähnt

abrasion /ə'breɪʒn/ *n* Schürfwunde *f*

abrasive /ə'breɪsɪv/ *a* Scheuer-; ⟨*remark*⟩ verletzend □ *n* Scheuermittel *nt*; (*Techn*) Schleifmittel *nt*

abreast /ə'brest/ *adv* nebeneinander; keep ∼ of Schritt halten mit

abridge /ə'brɪdʒ/ *vt* kürzen

abroad /ə'brɔ:d/ *adv* im Ausland; go ∼ ins Ausland fahren

abrupt /ə'brʌpt/ *a*, -ly *adv* abrupt; (*sudden*) plötzlich; (*curt*) schroff

abscess /'æbsɪs/ *n* Abszess *m*

abscond /əb'skɒnd/ *vi* entfliehen

absence /'æbsəns/ *n* Abwesenheit *f*

absent[1] /'æbsənt/ *a*, -ly *adv* abwesend; be ∼ fehlen

absent[2] /æb'sent/ *vt* ∼ oneself fernbleiben

absentee /æbsən'ti:/ *n* Abwesende(r) *m/f*

absent-minded /æbsənt'maɪndɪd/ *a*, -ly *adv* geistesabwesend; (*forgetful*) zerstreut

absolute /'æbsəlu:t/ *a*, -ly *adv* absolut

absolution /æbsəˈluːʃn/ n Absolution f

absolve /əbˈzɒlv/ vt lossprechen

absorb /əbˈsɔːb/ vt absorbieren, aufsaugen; ~ed in vertieft in (+ acc). ~ent /-ənt/ a saugfähig

absorption /əbˈsɔːpʃn/ n Absorption f

abstain /əbˈsteɪn/ vi sich enthalten (from gen); ~ from voting sich der Stimme enthalten

abstemious /əbˈstiːmɪəs/ a enthaltsam

abstention /əbˈstenʃn/ n (Pol) [Stimm]enthaltung f

abstinence /ˈæbstɪnəns/ n Enthaltsamkeit f

abstract /ˈæbstrækt/ a abstrakt □ n (summary) Abriss m

absurd /əbˈsɜːd/ a, -ly adv absurd. ~ity n Absurdität f

abundan|ce /əˈbʌndəns/ n Fülle f (of an + dat). ~t a reichlich

abuse¹ /əˈbjuːz/ vt missbrauchen; (insult) beschimpfen

abus|e² /əˈbjuːs/ n Missbrauch m; (insults) Beschimpfungen pl. ~ive/-ɪv/ ausfallend

abut /əˈbʌt/ vi (pt/pp abutted) angrenzen (on to an + acc)

abysmal /əˈbɪzml/ a (fam) katastrophal

abyss /əˈbɪs/ n Abgrund m

academic /ækəˈdemɪk/ a, -ally adv akademisch □ n Akademiker(in) m(f)

academy /əˈkædəmɪ/ n Akademie f

accede /əkˈsiːd/ vi ~ to zustimmen (+ dat); besteigen ⟨throne⟩

accelerat|e /əkˈseləreɪt/ vt beschleunigen □ vi die Geschwindigkeit erhöhen. ~ion /-ˈreɪʃn/ n Beschleunigung f. ~or n (Auto) Gaspedal nt

accent¹ /ˈæksənt/ n Akzent m

accent² /ækˈsent/ vt betonen

accentuate /əkˈsentjʊeɪt/ vt betonen

accept /əkˈsept/ vt annehmen; (fig) akzeptieren □ vi zusagen. ~able /-əbl/ a annehmbar. ~ance n Annahme f; (of invitation) Zusage f

access /ˈækses/ n Zugang m; (road) Zufahrt f. ~ible /əkˈsesəbl/ a zugänglich

accession /əkˈseʃn/ n (to throne) Thronbesteigung f

accessor|y /əkˈsesərɪ/ n (Jur) Mitschuldige(r) m/f; ~ies pl ⟨fashion⟩ Accessoires pl; ⟨Techn⟩ Zubehör nt

accident /ˈæksɪdənt/ n Unfall m; (chance) Zufall m; by ~ zufällig; (unintentionally) versehentlich. ~al /-ˈdentl/ a, -ly adv zufällig; (unintentional) versehentlich

acclaim /əˈkleɪm/ n Beifall m □ vt feiern (as als)

acclimate /ˈæklɪmeɪt/ vt (Amer) = acclimatize

acclimatize /əˈklaɪmətaɪz/ vt become ~d sich akklimatisieren

accolade /ˈækəleɪd/ n Auszeichnung f

accommodat|e /əˈkɒmədeɪt/ vt unterbringen; (oblige) entgegenkommen (+ dat). ~ing a entgegenkommend. ~ion /-ˈdeɪʃn/ n (rooms) Unterkunft f

accompan|iment /əˈkʌmpənɪmənt/ n Begleitung f. ~ist n (Mus) Begleiter(in) m(f)

accompany /əˈkʌmpənɪ/ vt (pt/pp -ied) begleiten

accomplice /əˈkʌmplɪs/ n Komplize/-zin m/f

accomplish /əˈkʌmplɪʃ/ vt erfüllen ⟨task⟩; (achieve) erreichen. ~ed a fähig. ~ment n Fertigkeit f; (achievement) Leistung f

accord /əˈkɔːd/ n (treaty) Abkommen nt; of one ~ einmütig; of one's own ~ aus eigenem Antrieb □ vt gewähren. ~ance n in ~ance with entsprechend (+ dat)

according /əˈkɔːdɪŋ/ adv ~ to nach (+ dat). ~ly adv entsprechend

accordion /əˈkɔːdɪən/ n Akkordeon nt

accost /əˈkɒst/ vt ansprechen

account /əˈkaʊnt/ n Konto nt; (bill) Rechnung f; (description) Darstellung f; (report) Bericht m; ~s pl (Comm) Bücher pl; on ~ of wegen (+ gen); on no ~ auf keinen Fall; on this ~ deshalb; on my ~ meinetwegen; of no ~ ohne Bedeutung; take into ~ in Betracht ziehen, berücksichtigen □ vi ~ for Rechenschaft ablegen für; (explain) erklären

accountant /əˈkaʊntənt/ n Buchhalter(in) m(f); (chartered) Wirtschaftsprüfer m; (for tax) Steuerberater m

accoutrements /əˈkuːtrəmənts/ npl Ausrüstung f

accredited /əˈkredɪtɪd/ a akkreditiert

accrue /əˈkruː/ vi sich ansammeln

accumulat|e /əˈkjuːmjʊleɪt/ vt ansammeln, anhäufen □ vi sich ansammeln, sich anhäufen. ~ion /-ˈleɪʃn/ n Ansammlung f, Anhäufung f. ~or n (Electr) Akkumulator m

accura|cy /ˈækʊrəsɪ/ n Genauigkeit f. ~te /-rət/ a, -ly adv genau

accusation /ækjuːˈzeɪʃn/ n Anklage f

accusative /əˈkjuːzətɪv/ a & n ~ [case] (Gram) Akkusativ m

accuse /əˈkjuːz/ vt (Jur) anklagen (of gen); ~ s.o. of doing sth jdn beschuldigen, etw getan zu haben. ~d n the ~d der/die Angeklagte accustom /ə'kʌstəm/ vt gewöhnen (to an + dat); growor get ~ed tosich gewöhnen an (+ acc). ~ed a gewohnt

ace /eis/ n (Cards, Sport) Ass nt

ache /eik/ n Schmerzen pl □ vi weh tun, schmerzen

achieve /ə'tʃiːv/ vt leisten; (gain) erzielen; (reach) erreichen. ~ment n (feat) Leistung f

acid /'æsid/ a sauer; (fig) beißend □ n Säure f. ~ity /-'sidəti/ n Säure f. ~ 'rain n saurer Regen m

acknowledge /ək'nɒlidʒ/ vt anerkennen; (admit) zugeben; erwidern (greeting); ~ receipt of den Empfang bestätigen (+ gen). ~ment n Anerkennung f; (of letter) Empfangsbestätigung f

acne /'ækni/ n Akne f

acorn /'eikɔːn/ n Eichel f

acoustic /ə'kuːstik/ a, -ally adv akustisch. ~s npl Akustik f

acquaint /ə'kweint/ vt ~ s.o. with jdn bekannt machen mit; be ~ed with kennen; vertraut sein mit (fact). ~ance n Bekanntschaft f; (person) Bekannte(r) m/f; make s.o.'s ~ance jdn kennen lernen

acquiesce /ækwi'es/ vi einwilligen (to in + acc). ~nce n Einwilligung f

acquire /ə'kwaiə(r)/ vt erwerben

acquisit|ion /ækwi'ziʃn/ n Erwerb m; (thing) Erwerbung f. ~ive /æ'kwizətiv/ a habgierig

acquit /ə'kwit/ vt (pt/pp acquitted) freisprechen; ~ oneself well seiner Aufgabe gerecht werden. ~tal n Freispruch m

acre /'eikə(r)/ n ≈ Morgen m

acrid /'ækrid/ a scharf

acrimon|ious /ækri'məuniəs/ a bitter. ~y /'ækriməni/ n Bitterkeit f

acrobat /'ækrəbæt/ n Akrobat(in) m(f). ~ic /-'bætik/ a akrobatisch

across /ə'krɒs/ adv hinüber/herüber; (wide) breit; (not lengthwise) quer; (in crossword) waagerecht; come ~ sth auf etw (acc) stoßen; go ~ hinübergehen; bring ~ herüberbringen □ prep über (+ acc); (crosswise) quer über (+ acc/dat); (on the other side of) auf der anderen Seite (+ gen)

act /ækt/ n Tat f; (action) Handlung f; (law) Gesetz nt; (Theat) Akt m; (item) Nummer f; put on an ~ (fam) sich verstellen □ vi handeln; (behave) sich verhalten; (Theat) spielen; (pretend) sich verstellen; ~ as fungieren als □ vt spielen (role). ~ing a (deputy) stellvertretend □ n (Theat) Schauspielerei f. ~ing profession n Schauspielerberuf m

action /'ækʃn/ n Handlung f; (deed) Tat f; (Mil) Einsatz m; (Jur) Klage f; (effect) Wirkung f; (Techn) Mechanismus m; out of ~ (machine:) außer Betrieb; take ~ handeln; killed in ~ gefallen. ~ 'replay n (TV) Wiederholung f

activate /'æktiveit/ vt betätigen; (Chem, Phys) aktivieren

activ|e /'æktiv/ a, -ly adv aktiv; on ~e service im Einsatz. ~ity /-'tivəti/ n Aktivität f

act|or /'æktə(r)/ n Schauspieler m. ~ress n Schauspielerin f

actual /'æktʃuəl/ a, -ly adv eigentlich; (real) tatsächlich. ~ity /-'ælətɪ/ n Wirklichkeit f

acumen /'ækjʊmən/ n Scharfsinn m

acupuncture /'ækjʊ-/ n Akupunktur f

acute /ə'kjuːt/ a scharf; (angle) spitz; (illness) akut. ~ly adv sehr

ad /æd/ n (fam) = advertisement

AD abbr (Anno Domini) n.Chr.

adamant /'ædəmənt/ a be ~ that darauf bestehen, dass

adapt /ə'dæpt/ vt anpassen; bearbeiten (play) □ vi sich anpassen. ~ability /-ə'biləti/ n Anpassungsfähigkeit f. ~able /-əbl/ a anpassungsfähig

adaptation /ædæp'teiʃn/ n (Theat) Bearbeitung f

adapter, adaptor /ə'dæptə(r)/ n (Techn) Adapter m; (Electr) (two-way) Doppelstecker m

add /æd/ vt hinzufügen; (Math) addieren □ vi zusammenzählen, addieren; ~ to hinzufügen zu; (fig: increase) steigern; (compound) verschlimmern. ~ up vt zusammenzählen (figures) □ vi zusammenzählen, addieren; ~ up to machen; it doesn't ~ up (fig) da stimmt etwas nicht

adder /'ædə(r)/ n Kreuzotter f

addict /'ædikt/ n Süchtige(r) m/f

addict|ed /ə'diktid/ a süchtig; ~ed to drugs drogensüchtig. ~ion /-ikʃn/ n Sucht f. ~ive /-iv/ a be ~ive zur Süchtigkeit führen

addition /ə'diʃn/ n Hinzufügung f; (Math) Addition f; (thing added) Ergänzung f; in ~ zusätzlich. ~al a, -ly adv zusätzlich

additive /'ædɪtɪv/ n Zusatz m

address /ə'dres/ n Adresse f, Anschrift f; (speech) Ansprache f; form of ~ Anrede f □ vt adressieren (to an + acc); (speak to) anreden (person); sprechen vor (+ dat) (meeting). ~ee /ædre'siː/ n Empfänger m

adenoids /'ædənɔidz/ npl [Rachen]-polypen pl

adept /'ædept/ a geschickt (at in + dat)

adequate /'ædɪkwət/ a, -ly adv ausreichend

adhere /əd'hɪə(r)/ vi kleben/(fig) festhalten (to an + dat). ∼nce n Festhalten nt

adhesive /əd'hi:sɪv/ a klebend □ n Klebstoff m

adjacent /ə'dʒeɪsnt/ a angrenzend

adjective /'ædʒɪktɪv/ n Adjektiv nt

adjoin /ə'dʒɔɪn/ vt angrenzen an (+ acc). ∼ing a angrenzend

adjourn /ə'dʒɜ:n/ vt vertagen (until an + acc) □ vi sich vertagen. ∼ment n Vertagung f

adjudicate /ə'dʒu:dɪkeɪt/ vi entscheiden; (in competition) Preisrichter sein

adjust /ə'dʒʌst/ vt einstellen; (alter) verstellen □ vi sich anpassen (to dat). ∼able /-əbl/ a verstellbar. ∼ment n Einstellung f; Anpassung f

ad lib /æd'lɪb/ adv aus dem Stegreif □ vi (pt/pp ad libbed) (fam) improvisieren

administer /əd'mɪnɪstə(r)/ vt verwalten; verabreichen (medicine)

administrat|ion /ədmɪnɪ'streɪʃn/ n Verwaltung f; (Pol) Regierung f. ∼or /əd'mɪnɪstreɪtə(r)/ n Verwaltungsbeamte(r) m /-beamtin f

admirable /'ædmərəbl/ a bewundernswert

admiral /'ædmərəl/ n Admiral m

admiration /ædmə'reɪʃn/ n Bewunderung f

admire /əd'maɪə(r)/ vt bewundern. ∼r n Verehrer(in) m(f)

admissable /əd'mɪsəbl/ a zulässig

admission /əd'mɪʃn/ n Eingeständnis nt; (entry) Eintritt m

admit /əd'mɪt/ vt (pt/pp admitted) (let in) hereinlassen; (acknowledge) zugeben; ∼ to sth etw zugeben. ∼tance n Eintritt m. ∼tedly adv zugegebenermaßen

admoni|sh /əd'mɒnɪʃ/ vt ermahnen. ∼tion /ædmə'nɪʃn/ n Ermahnung f

ado /ə'du:/ n without more ∼ ohne weiteres

adolescen|ce /ædə'lesns/ n Jugend f, Pubertät f. ∼t a (young); (boy, girl) halbwüchsig □ n Jugendliche(r) m/f

adopt /ə'dɒpt/ vt adoptieren; ergreifen (measure); (Pol) annehmen (candidate). ∼ion /-ɒpʃn/ n Adoption. f. ∼ive /-ɪv/ a Adoptiv-

ador|able /ə'dɔ:rəbl/ a bezaubernd. ∼ation /ædə'reɪʃn/ n Anbetung f

adore /ə'dɔ:(r)/ vt (worship) anbeten; (fam: like) lieben

adorn /ə'dɔ:n/ vt schmücken. ∼ment n Schmuck m

adrenalin /ə'drenəlɪn/ n Adrenalin nt

Adriatic /eɪdrɪ'ætɪk/ a & n ∼ [Sea] Adria f

adrift /ə'drɪft/ a be ∼ treiben; come ∼ sich losreißen

adroit /ə'drɔɪt/ a, -ly adv gewandt, geschickt

adulation /ædjʊ'leɪʃn/ n Schwärmerei f

adult /'ædʌlt/ n Erwachsene(r) m/f

adulterate /ə'dʌltəreɪt/ vt verfälschen; panschen (wine)

adultery /ə'dʌltərɪ/ n Ehebruch m

advance /əd'vɑ:ns/ n Fortschritt m; (Mil) Vorrücken nt; (payment) Vorschuss m; in ∼ im Voraus □ vi vorankommen; (Mil) vorrücken; (make progress) Fortschritte machen □ vt fördern (cause); vorbringen (idea); vorschießen (money). ∼ booking n Kartenvorverkauf m. ∼d a fortgeschritten; (progressive) fortschrittlich. ∼ment n Förderung f; (promotion) Beförderung f

advantage /əd'vɑ:ntɪdʒ/ n Vorteil m; take ∼ of ausnutzen. ∼ous /ædvən'teɪdʒəs/ a vorteilhaft

advent /'ædvent/ n Ankunft f; A∼ (season) Advent m

adventur|e /əd'ventʃə(r)/ n Abenteuer nt. ∼er n Abenteurer m. ∼ous /-rəs/ a abenteuerlich; (person) abenteuerlustig

adverb /'ædvɜ:b/ n Adverb nt

adversary /'ædvəsərɪ/ n Widersacher m

advers|e /'ædvɜ:s/ a ungünstig. ∼ity /əd'vɜ:sətɪ/ n Not f

advert /'ædvɜ:t/ n (fam) = advertisement

advertise /'ædvətaɪz/ vt Reklame machen für; (by small ad) inserieren □ vi Reklame machen; inserieren; ∼ for per Anzeige suchen

advertisement /əd'vɜ:tɪsmənt/ n Anzeige f; (publicity) Reklame f; (small ad) Inserat nt

advertis|er /'ædvətaɪzə(r)/ n Inserent m. ∼ing n Werbung f □ attrib Werbe-

advice /əd'vaɪs/ n Rat m. ∼ note n Benachrichtigung f

advisable /əd'vaɪzəbl/ a ratsam

advis|e /əd'vaɪz/ vt raten (s.o. jdm); (counsel) beraten; (inform) benachrichtigen; ∼e s.o. against sth jdm von etw abraten □ vi raten. ∼er n Berater(in) m(f). ∼ory /-ərɪ/ a beratend

advocate¹ /'ædvəkət/ n [Rechts]anwalt m/-anwältin f; (supporter) Befürworter m

advocate² /'ædvəkeɪt/ vt befürworten

aerial /'eərɪəl/ a Luft- □ n Antenne f

aerobics /eə'rəʊbɪks/ n Aerobic nt

aero|drome /'eərədrəum/ n Flugplatz m. ~plane n Flugzeug nt

aerosol /'eərəsɒl/ n Spraydose f

aesthetic /i:s'θetɪk/ a ästhetisch

afar /ə'fɑ:(r)/ adv from ~ aus der Ferne

affable /'æfəbl/ a, -bly adv freundlich

affair /ə'feə(r)/ n Angelegenheit f, Sache f; (scandal) Affäre f; [love-]~ [Liebes-]verhältnis nt

affect /ə'fekt/ vt sich auswirken auf (+ acc); (concern) betreffen; (move) rühren; (pretend) vortäuschen. ~ation /æfek-'teɪʃn/ n Affektiertheit f. ~ed a affektiert

affection /ə'fekʃn/ n Liebe f. ~ate /-ət/ a, -ly adv liebevoll

affiliated /ə'fɪlɪeɪtɪd/ a angeschlossen (to dat)

affinity /ə'fɪnətɪ/ n Ähnlichkeit f; (attraction) gegenseitige Anziehung f

affirm /ə'fɜ:m/ vt behaupten; (Jur) eidesstattlich erklären

affirmative /ə'fɜ:mətɪv/ a bejahend □ n Bejahung f

affix /ə'fɪks/ vt anbringen (to dat); (stick) aufkleben (to auf + acc); setzen (signature) (to unter + acc)

afflict /ə'flɪkt/ vt be ~ed with behaftet sein mit. ~ion /-ɪkʃn/ n Leiden nt

affluen|ce /'æfluəns/ n Reichtum m. ~t a wohlhabend. ~t society n Wohlstandsgesellschaft f

afford /ə'fɔ:d/ vt (provide) gewähren; be able to ~ sth sich (dat) etw leisten können. ~able /-əbl/ a erschwinglich

affray /ə'freɪ/ n Schlägerei f

affront /ə'frʌnt/ n Beleidigung f □ vt beleidigen

afield /ə'fi:ld/ adv further ~ weiter weg

afloat /ə'fləʊt/ a be ~ (ship:) flott sein; keep ~ (person:) sich über Wasser halten

afoot /ə'fʊt/ a im Gange

aforesaid /ə'fɔ:sed/ a (Jur) oben erwähnt

afraid /ə'freɪd/ a be ~ Angst haben (of vor + dat); I'm ~ not leider nicht; I'm ~ so [ja] leider; I'm ~ I can't help you ich kann Ihnen leider nicht helfen

afresh /ə'freʃ/ adv von vorne

Africa /'æfrɪkə/ n Afrika nt. ~n a afrikanisch □ n Afrikaner(in) m(f)

after /'ɑ:ftə(r)/ adv danach □ prep nach (+ dat); ~ that danach; ~ all schließlich; the day ~ tomorrow übermorgen; be ~ aus sein auf (+ acc) □ conj nachdem

after: ~-effect n Nachwirkung f. ~math /-mɑ:θ/ n Auswirkungen pl. ~noon n Nachmittag m; good ~noon! guten Tag! ~-sales service n Kundendienst m. ~shave n Rasierwasser nt. ~thought

nachträglicher Einfall m. ~wards adv nachher

again /ə'gen/ adv wieder; (once more) noch einmal; (besides) außerdem; ~ and ~ immer wieder

against /ə'genst/ prep gegen (+ acc)

age /eɪdʒ/ n Alter nt; (era) Zeitalter nt; ~s (fam) ewig; under ~ minderjährig; of ~ volljährig; two years of ~ zwei Jahre alt □ v (pres p ageing) □ vt älter machen □ vi altern; (mature) reifen

aged[1] /eɪdʒd/ a ~ two zwei Jahre alt

aged[2] /'eɪdʒɪd/ a betagt □ n the ~ pl die Alten

ageless /'eɪdʒlɪs/ a ewig jung

agency /'eɪdʒənsɪ/ n Agentur f; (office) Büro nt; have the ~ for die Vertretung haben für

agenda /ə'dʒendə/ n Tagesordnung f; on the ~ auf dem Programm

agent /'eɪdʒənt/ n Agent(in) m(f); (Comm) Vertreter(in) m(f); (substance) Mittel nt

aggravat|e /'ægrəveɪt/ vt verschlimmern; (fam: annoy) ärgern. ~ion /-'veɪʃn/ n (fam) Ärger m

aggregate /'ægrɪgət/ a gesamt □ n Gesamtzahl f; (sum) Gesamtsumme f

aggress|ion /ə'greʃn/ n Aggression f. ~ive /-sɪv/ a, -ly adv aggressiv. ~iveness n Aggressivität f. ~or n Angreifer(in) m(f)

aggrieved /ə'gri:vd/ a verletzt

aggro /'ægrəʊ/ n (fam) Ärger m

aghast /ə'gɑ:st/ a entsetzt

agil|e /'ædʒaɪl/ a flink, behände; (mind) wendig. ~ity /ə'dʒɪlətɪ/ n Flinkheit f, Behändigkeit f

agitat|e /'ædʒɪteɪt/ vt bewegen; (shake) schütteln □ vi (fig) ~ for agitieren für. ~ed a, -ly adv erregt. ~ion /-'teɪʃn/ n Erregung f; (Pol) Agitation f. ~or n Agitator m

agnostic /æg'nɒstɪk/ n Agnostiker m

ago /ə'gəʊ/ adv vor (+ dat); a month ~ vor einem Monat; a long time ~ vor langer Zeit; how long ~ is it? wie lange ist es her?

agog /ə'gɒg/ a gespannt

agoniz|e /'ægənaɪz/ vi [innerlich] ringen. ~ing a qualvoll

agony /'ægənɪ/ n Qual f; be in ~ furchtbare Schmerzen haben

agree /ə'gri:/ vt vereinbaren; (admit) zugeben; ~ to do sth sich bereit erklären, etw zu tun □ vi (people, figures:) übereinstimmen; (reach agreement) sich einigen; (get on) gut miteinander auskommen; (consent) einwilligen (to in + acc); I ~ der Meinung bin ich auch; ~ with s.o. jdm zustimmen; ⟨food:⟩ jdm bekommen; ~ with sth ⟨approve of⟩ mit etw einverstanden sein

agreeable /əˈgriːəbl/ a angenehm; be ~ einverstanden sein (to mit)

agreed /əˈgriːd/ a vereinbart

agreement /əˈgriːmənt/ n Übereinstimmung f; ⟨consent⟩ Einwilligung f; ⟨contract⟩ Abkommen nt; reach ~ sich einigen

agricultur|al /ægrɪˈkʌltʃərəl/ a landwirtschaftlich. ~e /ˈægrɪkʌltʃə(r)/ n Landwirtschaft f

aground /əˈgraʊnd/ a gestrandet; run ~ ⟨ship:⟩ stranden

ahead /əˈhed/ adv straight ~ geradeaus; be ~ of s.o./sth vor jdm/etw sein; ⟨fig⟩ jdm/etw voraus sein; draw ~ nach vorne ziehen; go on ~ vorgehen; get ~ vorankommen; go on ~! ⟨fam⟩ bitte! look/plan ~ vorausblicken/-planen

aid /eɪd/ n Hilfe f; ⟨financial⟩ Unterstützung f; in ~ of zugunsten (+ gen) □ vt helfen (+ dat)

aide /eɪd/ n Berater m

Aids /eɪdz/ n Aids nt

ail|ing /ˈeɪlɪŋ/ a kränkelnd. ~ment n Leiden nt

aim /eɪm/ n Ziel nt; take ~ zielen □ vt richten (at auf + acc) □ vi zielen (at auf + acc); ~ to do sth beabsichtigen, etw zu tun. ~less a, -ly adv ziellos

air /eə(r)/ n Luft f; ⟨tune⟩ Melodie f; ⟨expression⟩ Miene f; ⟨appearance⟩ Anschein m; be on the ~ ⟨programme:⟩ gesendet werden; ⟨person:⟩ senden, auf Sendung sein; put on ~s vornehm tun; by ~ auf dem Luftweg; ⟨airmail⟩ mit Luftpost □ vt lüften; vorbringen ⟨views⟩

air: ~-bed n Luftmatratze f. ~-conditioned a klimatisiert. ~-conditioning n Klimaanlage f. ~craft n Flugzeug nt. ~fare n Flugpreis m. ~field n Flugplatz m. ~-force n Luftwaffe f. ~ freshener n Raumspray nt. ~gun n Luftgewehr nt. ~ hostess n Stewardess f. ~ letter n Aerogramm nt. ~line n Fluggesellschaft f. ~lock n Luftblase f. ~mail n Luftpost f. ~man n Flieger m. ~plane n ⟨Amer⟩ Flugzeug nt. ~ pocket n Luftloch nt. ~port n Flughafen m. ~-raid n Luftangriff m. ~-raid shelter n Luftschutzbunker m. ~ship n Luftschiff nt. ~ ticket n Flugschein m. ~tight a luftdicht. ~-traffic n Luftverkehr m. ~-traffic controller n Fluglotse m. ~worthy a flugtüchtig

airy /ˈeərɪ/ a ⟨ier,-iest⟩ luftig; ⟨manner⟩ nonchalant

aisle /aɪl/ n Gang m

ajar /əˈdʒɑː(r)/ a angelehnt

akin /əˈkɪn/ a ~ to verwandt mit; ⟨similar⟩ ähnlich ⟨to dat⟩

alabaster /ˈæləbɑːstə(r)/ n Alabaster m

alacrity /əˈlækrɪtɪ/ n Bereitfertigkeit f

alarm /əˈlɑːm/ n Alarm m; ⟨device⟩ Alarmanlage f; ⟨clock⟩ Wecker m; ⟨fear⟩ Unruhe f □ vt erschrecken; alarmieren. ~ clock n Wecker m

alas /əˈlæs/ int ach!

album /ˈælbəm/ n Album nt

alcohol /ˈælkəhɒl/ n Alkohol m. ~ic /-ˈhɒlɪk/ a alkoholisch □ n Alkoholiker(in) m(f). ~ism n Alkoholismus m

alcove /ˈælkəʊv/ n Nische f

alert /əˈlɜːt/ a aufmerksam □ n Alarm m; on the ~ auf der Hut □ vt alarmieren

algae /ˈældʒiː/ npl Algen pl

algebra /ˈældʒɪbrə/ n Algebra f

Algeria /ælˈdʒɪərɪə/ n Algerien nt

alias /ˈeɪlɪəs/ n Deckname m □ adv alias

alibi /ˈælɪbaɪ/ n Alibi nt

alien /ˈeɪlɪən/ a fremd □ n Ausländer(in) m(f)

alienat|e /ˈeɪlɪəneɪt/ vt entfremden. ~ion /-ˈneɪʃn/ n Entfremdung f

alight[1] /əˈlaɪt/ vi aussteigen (from aus); ⟨bird:⟩ sich niederlassen

alight[2] a be ~ brennen; set ~ anzünden

align /əˈlaɪn/ vt ausrichten. ~ment n Ausrichtung f; out of ~ment nicht richtig ausgerichtet

alike /əˈlaɪk/ a & adv ähnlich; ⟨same⟩ gleich; look ~ sich ⟨dat⟩ ähnlich sehen

alimony /ˈælɪmənɪ/ n Unterhalt m

alive /əˈlaɪv/ a lebendig; be ~ leben; be ~ with wimmeln von

alkali /ˈælkəlaɪ/ n Base f, Alkali nt

all /ɔːl/ a alle pl; ⟨whole⟩ ganz; ~ [the] children alle Kinder; ~ our children alle unsere Kinder; ~ the others alle anderen; ~ day den ganzen Tag; ~ the wine der ganze Wein; for ~ that ⟨nevertheless⟩ trotzdem; in ~ innocence in aller Unschuld □ pron alle pl; ⟨everything⟩ alles; ~ of you/them Sie/sie alle; ~ of the town die ganze Stadt; not at ~ gar nicht; in ~ insgesamt; ~ in ~ alles in allem; most of ~ am meisten; once and for ~ ein für alle Mal □ adv ganz; ~ but fast; ~ at once auf einmal; ~ too soon viel zu früh; ~ the same ⟨nevertheless⟩ trotzdem; ~ the better umso besser; be ~ in ⟨fam⟩ völlig erledigt sein; four ~ ⟨Sport⟩ vier zu vier

allay /əˈleɪ/ vt zerstreuen

allegation /ælɪˈgeɪʃn/ n Behauptung f

allege /əˈledʒ/ vt behaupten. ~d a -ly /-ɪdlɪ/ adv angeblich allegiance /əˈliːdʒəns/ n Treue f

allegor|ical /ælɪˈɡɒrɪkl/ a allegorisch.
~y /ˈælɪɡərɪ/ n Allegorie f

allerg|ic /əˈlɜːdʒɪk/ a allergisch (to
gegen). ~y /ˈælədʒɪ/ n Allergie f

alleviate /əˈliːvɪeɪt/ vt lindern

alley /ˈælɪ/ n Gasse f; (for bowling) Bahn
f

alliance /əˈlaɪəns/ n Verbindung f; (Pol)
Bündnis nt

allied /ˈælaɪd/ a alliiert; (fig: related) verwandt (to mit)

alligator /ˈælɪɡeɪtə(r)/ n Alligator m

allocat|e /ˈæləkeɪt/ vt zuteilen; (share out)
verteilen. ~ion /-ˈkeɪʃn/ n Zuteilung f

allot /əˈlɒt/ vt (pt/pp allotted) zuteilen
(s.o. jdm). ~ment n ≈ Schrebergarten m

allow /əˈlaʊ/ vt erlauben; (give) geben;
(grant) gewähren; (reckon) rechnen;
(agree, admit) zugeben; ~ for berücksichtigen; ~ s.o. to do sth jdm erlauben,
etw zu tun; be ~ed to do sth etw tun
dürfen

allowance /əˈlaʊəns/ n [finanzielle] Unterstützung f; ~ for petrol Benzingeld
nt; make ~s for berücksichtigen

alloy /ˈælɔɪ/ n Legierung f

allude /əˈluːd/ vi anspielen (to auf + acc)

allure /əˈljʊə(r)/ n Reiz m

allusion /əˈluːʒn/ n Anspielung f

ally[1] /ˈælaɪ/ n Verbündete(r) m/f; the Allies pl die Alliierten

ally[2] /əˈlaɪ/ vt (pt/pp -ied) verbinden; ~
oneself with sich verbünden mit

almighty /ɔːlˈmaɪtɪ/ a allmächtig; (fam:
big) Riesen-. □ n the A ~ der Allmächtige

almond /ˈɑːmənd/ n (Bot) Mandel f

almost /ˈɔːlməʊst/ adv fast, beinahe

alms /ɑːmz/ npl (liter) Almosen pl

alone /əˈləʊn/ a & adv allein; leave me ~
lass mich in Ruhe; leave that ~!lass die
Finger davon! let ~ ganz zu schweigen
von

along /əˈlɒŋ/ prep entlang (+ acc); ~ the
river den Fluss entlang □ adv ~ with zusammen mit; all ~ die ganze Zeit; come
~ komm doch; I'll bring it ~ ich bringe
es mit; move ~ weitergehen

along'side adv daneben □ prep neben (+
dat)

aloof /əˈluːf/ a distanziert

aloud /əˈlaʊd/ adv laut

alphabet /ˈælfəbet/ n Alphabet nt. ~ical
/-ˈbetɪkl/ a, -ly adv alphabetisch

alpine /ˈælpaɪn/ a alpin; A~ Alpen-

Alps /ælps/ npl Alpen pl

already /ɔːlˈredɪ/ adv schon

Alsace /ælˈsæs/ n Elsass nt

Alsatian /ælˈseɪʃn/ n (dog) [deutscher]
Schäferhund m

also /ˈɔːlsəʊ/ adv auch

altar /ˈɔːltə(r)/ n Altar m

alter /ˈɔːltə(r)/ vt ändern □ vi sich verändern. ~ation /-ˈreɪʃn/ n Änderung f

alternate[1] /ˈɔːltəneɪt/ vi [sich] abwechseln □ vt abwechseln

alternate[2] /ɔːlˈtɜːnət/ a, -ly adv abwech-
selnd; (Amer: alternative) andere(r,s); on
~ days jeden zweiten Tag

'alternating current n Wechselstrom
m

alternative /ɔːlˈtɜːnətɪv/ a andere(r,s)
□ n Alternative f. ~ly adv oder aber

although /ɔːlˈðəʊ/ conj obgleich, obwohl

altitude /ˈæltɪtjuːd/ n Höhe f

altogether /ɔːltəˈɡeðə(r)/ adv insgesamt;
(on the whole) alles in allem

altruistic /æltruˈɪstɪk/ a altruistisch

aluminium /æljʊˈmɪnɪəm/ n, (Amer) aluminum /əˈluːmɪnəm/ n Aluminium nt

always /ˈɔːlweɪz/ adv immer

am /æm/ see be

a.m. abbr (ante meridiem) vormittags

amalgamate /əˈmælɡəmeɪt/ vt vereinigen; (Chem) amalgamieren □ vi sich
vereinigen; (Chem) sich amalgamieren

amass /əˈmæs/ vt anhäufen

amateur /ˈæmətə(r)/ n Amateur m
□ attrib Amateur-; (Theat) Laien-. ~ish a
laienhaft

amaze /əˈmeɪz/ vt erstaunen. ~d a erstaunt. ~ment n Erstaunen nt

amazing /əˈmeɪzɪŋ/ a, -ly adv erstaunlich

ambassador /æmˈbæsədə(r)/ n Bot-
schafter m

amber /ˈæmbə(r)/ n Bernstein m □ a (colour) gelb

ambidextrous /æmbɪˈdekstrəs/ a be ~
mit beiden Händen gleich geschickt sein

ambience /ˈæmbɪəns/ n Atmosphäre f

ambigu|ity /æmbɪˈɡjuːətɪ/ n Zweideutig-
keit f. ~ous /-ˈbɪɡjʊəs/ a -ly adv zweideutig

ambiti|on /æmˈbɪʃn/ n Ehrgeiz m; (aim)
Ambition f. ~ous /-ʃəs/ a ehrgeizig

ambivalent /æmˈbɪvələnt/ a zwiespältig;
be/feel ~ im Zwiespalt sein

amble /ˈæmbl/ vi schlendern

ambulance /ˈæmbjʊləns/ n Kranken-
wagen m. ~ man n Sanitäter m

ambush /ˈæmbʊʃ/ n Hinterhalt m □ vt aus
dem Hinterhalt überfallen

amen /ɑːˈmen/ int amen

amenable /əˈmiːnəbl/ a ~ to zugänglich
(+ dat)

amend /ə'mɛnd/ vt ändern. ~ment n Änderung f. ~s npl make ~s for sth etw wieder gutmachen

amenities /ə'miːnətɪz/ npl Einrichtungen pl

America /ə'mɛrɪkə/ n Amerika nt. ~n a amerikanisch □ n Amerikaner(in) m(f). ~nism n Amerikanismus m

amiable /'eɪmɪəbl/ a nett

amicable /'æmɪkəbl/ a, -bly adv freundschaftlich; ⟨agreement⟩ gütlich

amid[st] /ə'mɪd[st]/ prep inmitten (+ gen)

amiss /ə'mɪs/ a be ~ nicht stimmen □ adv not come ~ nicht unangebracht sein; take sth ~ etw übel nehmen

ammonia /ə'məʊnɪə/ n Ammoniak nt

ammunition /æmjʊ'nɪʃn/ n Munition f

amnesia /æm'niːzɪə/ n Amnesie f

amnesty /'æmnəstɪ/ n Amnestie f

among[st] /ə'mʌŋ[st]/ prep unter (+ dat/acc); ~ yourselves untereinander

amoral /eɪ'mɒrəl/ a amoralisch

amorous /'æmərəs/ a zärtlich

amount /ə'maʊnt/ n Menge f; ⟨sum of money⟩ Betrag m; ⟨total⟩ Gesamtsumme f □ vi ~ to sich belaufen auf (+ acc); ⟨fig⟩ hinauslaufen auf (+ acc)

amp /æmp/ n Ampere nt

amphibi|an /æm'fɪbɪən/ n Amphibie f. ~ous /-ɪəs/ a amphibisch

amphitheatre /'æmfɪ-/ n Amphitheater nt

ample /'æmpl/ a (-r, -st), -ly adv reichlich; ⟨large⟩ füllig

amplif|ier /'æmplɪfaɪə(r)/ n Verstärker m. ~y /-faɪ/ vt (pt/pp -ied) weiter ausführen; verstärken ⟨sound⟩

amputat|e /'æmpjʊteɪt/ vt amputieren. ~ion /-'teɪʃn/ n Amputation f

amuse /ə'mjuːz/ vt amüsieren, belustigen; ⟨entertain⟩ unterhalten. ~ment n Belustigung f; Unterhaltung f. ~ment arcade n Spielhalle f

amusing /ə'mjuːzɪŋ/ a amüsant

an /ən/, betont æn/ see a

anaem|ia /ə'niːmɪə/ n Blutarmut f, Anämie f. ~ic a blutarm

anaesthesia /ænəs'θiːzɪə/ n Betäubung f

anaesthetic /ænəs'θɛtɪk/ n Narkosemittel nt, Betäubungsmittel nt; under [an] ~ in Narkose; give s.o. an ~ jdm eine Narkose geben

anaesthet|ist /ə'niːsθətɪst/ n Narkosearzt m. ~ize /-taɪz/ vt betäuben

analog[ue] /'ænəlɒg/ a Analog-

analogy /ə'nælədʒɪ/ n Analogie f

analyse /'ænəlaɪz/ vt analysieren

analysis /ə'næləsɪs/ n Analyse f

analyst /'ænəlɪst/ n Chemiker(in) m(f); ⟨Psych⟩ Analytiker m

analytical /ænə'lɪtɪkl/ a analytisch

anarch|ist /'ænəkɪst/ n Anarchist m. ~y n Anarchie f

anathema /ə'næθəmə/ n Gräuel m

anatom|ical /ænə'tɒmɪkl/ a, -ly adv anatomisch. ~y /ə'nætəmɪ/ n Anatomie f

ancest|or /'ænsɛstə(r)/ n Vorfahr m. ~ry n Abstammung f

anchor /'æŋkə(r)/ n Anker m □ vi ankern □ vt verankern

anchovy /'æntʃəvɪ/ n Sardelle f

ancient /'eɪnʃənt/ a alt

ancillary /æn'sɪlərɪ/ a Hilfs-

and /ənd, betont ænd/ conj und; ~ so on und so weiter; six hundred ~ two sechshundertzwei; more ~ more immer mehr; nice ~ warm schön warm; try ~ come versuche zu kommen

anecdote /'ænɪkdəʊt/ n Anekdote f

anew /ə'njuː/ adv von neuem

angel /'eɪndʒl/ n Engel m. ~ic /æn'dʒɛlɪk/ a engelhaft

anger /'æŋgə(r)/ n Zorn m □ vt zornig machen

angle¹ /'æŋgl/ n Winkel m; ⟨fig⟩ Standpunkt m; at an ~ schräg

angle² vi angeln; ~ for ⟨fig⟩ fischen nach. ~r n Angler m

Anglican /'æŋglɪkən/ a anglikanisch □ n Anglikaner(in) m(f)

Anglo-Saxon /æŋgləʊ'sæksn/ a angelsächsisch □ n Angelsächsisch nt

angry /'æŋgrɪ/ a (-ier, -iest), -ily adv zornig; be ~ with böse sein auf (+ acc)

anguish /'æŋgwɪʃ/ n Qual f

angular /'æŋgjʊlə(r)/ a eckig; ⟨features⟩ kantig

animal /'ænɪml/ n Tier nt □ a tierisch

animate¹ /'ænɪmət/ a lebendig

animat|e² /'ænɪmeɪt/ vt beleben. ~ed a lebhaft. ~ion /-'meɪʃn/ n Lebhaftigkeit f

animosity /ænɪ'mɒsətɪ/ n Feindseligkeit f

aniseed /'ænɪsiːd/ n Anis m

ankle /'æŋkl/ n [Fuß]knöchel m

annex /ə'nɛks/ vt annektieren

annex[e] /'ænɛks/ n Nebengebäude nt; ⟨extension⟩ Anbau m

annihilat|e /ə'naɪəleɪt/ vt vernichten. ~ion /-'leɪʃn/ n Vernichtung f

anniversary /ænɪ'vɜːsərɪ/ n Jahrestag m

annotate /'ænəteɪt/ vt kommentieren

announce /ə'naʊns/ vt bekannt geben; ⟨over loudspeaker⟩ durchsagen; ⟨at reception⟩ ankündigen; ⟨Radio, TV⟩ ansagen;

(*in newspaper*) anzeigen. ~ment *n* Bekanntgabe *f*, Bekanntmachung *f*; Durchsage *f*; Ansage *f*; Anzeige *f*. ~r *n* Ansager(in) *m(f)*

annoy /əˈnɔɪ/ *vt* ärgern; (*pester*) belästigen; get ~ed sich ärgern. ~ance *n* Ärger *m*. ~ing *a* ärgerlich

annual /ˈænjʊəl/ *a*, -ly *adv* jährlich □ *n* (*Bot*) einjährige Pflanze *f*; (*book*) Jahresalbum *nt*

annuity /əˈnjuːətɪ/ *n* [Leib]rente *f*

annul /əˈnʌl/ *vt* (*pt/pp* annulled) annullieren

anoint /əˈnɔɪnt/ *vt* salben

anomaly /əˈnɒmlɪ/ *n* Anomalie *f*

anonymous /əˈnɒnɪməs/ *a*, -ly *adv* anonym

anorak /ˈænəræk/ *n* Anorak *m*

anorexia /ænəˈreksɪə/ *n* Magersucht *f*

another /əˈnʌðə(r)/ *a & pron* ein anderer/ eine andere/ein anderes; (*additional*) noch ein(e); ~ [one] noch einer/eine/ eins; ~ day an einem anderen Tag; in ~ way auf andere Weise; ~ time ein andermal; one ~ einander

answer /ˈɑːnsə(r)/ *n* Antwort *f*; (*solution*) Lösung *f* □ *vt* antworten (s.o. jdm); beantworten (*question, letter*); ~ the door/ telephone an die Tür/ans Telefon gehen □ *vi* antworten; (*Teleph*) sich melden; ~ back eine freche Antwort geben; ~ for verantwortlich sein für. ~able /-əbl/ *a* verantwortlich. ~ing machine *n* (*Teleph*) Anrufbeantworter *m*

ant /ænt/ *n* Ameise *f*

antagonis|m /ænˈtægənɪzm/ *n* Antagonismus *m*. ~tic /-ˈnɪstɪk/ *a* feindselig

antagonize /ænˈtægənaɪz/ *vt* gegen sich aufbringen

Antarctic /ænˈtɑːktɪk/ *n* Antarktis *f*

antelope /ˈæntɪləʊp/ *n* Antilope *f*

antenatal /æntɪˈneɪtl/ *a* ~ care Schwangerschaftsfürsorge *f*

antenna /ænˈtenə/ *n* Fühler *m*; (*Amer: aerial*) Antenne *f*

ante-room /ˈæntɪ-/ *n* Vorraum *m*

anthem /ˈænθəm/ *n* Hymne *f*

anthology /ænˈθɒlədʒɪ/ *n* Anthologie *f*

anthropology /ænθrəˈpɒlədʒɪ/ *n* Anthropologie *f*

anti-'aircraft /æntɪ-/ *a* Flugabwehr-

antibiotic /æntɪbaɪˈɒtɪk/ *n* Antibiotikum *nt*

'antibody *n* Antikörper *m*

anticipat|e /ænˈtɪsɪpeɪt/ *vt* vorhersehen; (*forestall*) zuvorkommen (+ *dat*); (*expect*) erwarten. ~ion /-ˈpeɪʃn/ *n* Erwartung *f*

anti'climax *n* Enttäuschung *f*

anti'clockwise *a & adv* gegen den Uhrzeigersinn

antics /ˈæntɪks/ *npl* Mätzchen *pl*

anti'cyclone *n* Hochdruckgebiet *nt*

'antifreeze *n* Frostschutzmittel *nt*

antipathy /ænˈtɪpəθɪ/ *n* Abneigung *f*, Antipathie *f*

antiquarian /æntɪˈkweərɪən/ *a* antiquarisch. ~ bookshop *n* Antiquariat *nt*

antiquated /ˈæntɪkweɪtɪd/ *a* veraltet

antique /ænˈtiːk/ *a* antik □ *n* Antiquität *f*. ~ dealer *n* Antiquitätenhändler *m*

antiquity /ænˈtɪkwətɪ/ *n* Altertum *nt*

anti-Semitic /æntɪsɪˈmɪtɪk/ *a* antisemitisch

anti'septic *a* antiseptisch □ *n* Antiseptikum *nt*

anti'social *a* asozial; (*fam*) ungesellig

antithesis /ænˈtɪθəsɪs/ *n* Gegensatz *m*

antlers /ˈæntləz/ *npl* Geweih *nt*

anus /ˈeɪnəs/ *n* After *m*

anvil /ˈænvɪl/ *n* Amboss *m*

anxiety /æŋˈzaɪətɪ/ *n* Sorge *f*

anxious /ˈæŋkʃəs/ *a*, -ly *adv* ängstlich; (*worried*) besorgt; be ~ to do sth etw gerne machen wollen

any /ˈenɪ/ *a* irgendein(e); (*every*) jede(r,s); *pl* alle; (*after negative*) kein(e); *pl* keine; ~ colour/number you like eine beliebige Farbe/Zahl; have you ~ wine/apples? haben Sie Wein/Äpfel? for ~ reason aus irgendeinem Grund □ *pron* [irgend]einer/eine/eins; *pl* [irgend]welche; (*some*) welche(r,s); *pl* welche; (*all*) alle *pl*; (*negative*) keiner/keine/ keins; *pl* keine; I don't want ~ of it ich will nichts davon; there aren't ~ es gibt keine; I need some wine/apples/money— have we ~? ich brauche Wein/Äpfel/ Geld—haben wir welchen/welche/ welches? □ *adv* noch; (*quicker/slower*) noch schneller/langsamer; is it ~ better? geht es etwas besser? would you like ~ more? möchten Sie noch [etwas]? I can't eat ~ more ich kann nichts mehr essen; I can't go ~ further ich kann nicht mehr weiter

'anybody *pron* [irgend]jemand; (*after negative*) niemand; ~ can do that das kann jeder

'anyhow *adv* jedenfalls; (*nevertheless*) trotzdem; (*badly*) irgendwie

'anyone *pron* = anybody

'anything *pron* [irgend]etwas; (*after negative*) nichts; (*everything*) alles

'anyway *adv* jedenfalls; (*in any case*) sowieso

'**anywhere** adv irgendwo; (after negative) nirgendwo; (be, live) überall; I'd go ~ ich würde überallhin gehen

apart /ə'pɑ:t/ adv auseinander; live ~ getrennt leben; ~ from abgesehen von

apartment /ə'pɑːtmənt/ n Zimmer nt; (Amer: flat) Wohnung f

apathy /'æpəθɪ/ n Apathie f

ape /eɪp/ n [Menschen]affe m □ vt nachäffen

aperitif /ə'perəti:f/ n Aperitif m

aperture /'æpətʃə(r)/ n Öffnung f; (Phot) Blende f

apex /'eɪpeks/ n Spitze f; (fig) Gipfel m

apiece /ə'pi:s/ adv pro Person; (thing) pro Stück

apologetic /əpɒlə'dʒetɪk/ a, -ally adv entschuldigend; be ~ sich entschuldigen

apologize /ə'pɒlədʒaɪz/ vi sich entschuldigen (to bei)

apology /ə'pɒlədʒɪ/ n Entschuldigung f

apostle /ə'pɒsl/ n Apostel m

apostrophe /ə'pɒstrəfɪ/ n Apostroph m

appal /ə'pɔːl/ vt (pt/pp appalled) entsetzen. ~ling a entsetzlich

apparatus /æpə'reɪtəs/ n Apparatur f; (Sport) Geräte pl; (single piece) Gerät nt

apparel /ə'pærəl/ n Kleidung f

apparent /ə'pærənt/ a offenbar; (seeming) scheinbar. ~ly adv offenbar, anscheinend

apparition /æpə'rɪʃn/ n Erscheinung f

appeal /ə'pi:l/ n Appell m, Aufruf m; (request) Bitte f; (attraction) Reiz m; (Jur) Berufung f □ vi appellieren (to an + acc); (ask) bitten (for um); (be attractive) zusagen (to dat); (Jur) Berufung einlegen. ~ing a ansprechend

appear /ə'pɪə(r)/ vi erscheinen; (seem) scheinen; (Theat) auftreten. ~ance n Erscheinen nt; (look) Aussehen nt; to all ~ances allem Anschein nach

appease /ə'pi:z/ vt beschwichtigen

append /ə'pend/ vt nachtragen; setzen (signature) (to unter + acc). ~age /-ɪdʒ/ n Anhängsel nt

appendicitis /əpendɪ'saɪtɪs/ n Blinddarmentzündung f

appendix /ə'pendɪks/ n (pl -ices /-ɪsi:z/) (of book) Anhang m □ (pl-es) (Anat) Blinddarm m

appertain /æpə'teɪn/ vi ~ to betreffen

appetite /'æpɪtaɪt/ n Appetit m

appetizing /'æpɪtaɪzɪŋ/ a appetitlich

applau|d /ə'plɔːd/ vt/i Beifall klatschen (+ dat). ~se n Beifall m

apple /'æpl/ n Apfel m

appliance /ə'plaɪəns/ n Gerät nt

applicable /'æplɪkəbl/ a anwendbar (to auf + acc); (on form) not ~ nicht zutreffend

applicant /'æplɪkənt/ n Bewerber(in) m(f)

application /æplɪ'keɪʃn/ n Anwendung f; (request) Antrag m; (for job) Bewerbung f; (diligence) Fleiß m

applied /ə'plaɪd/ a angewandt

apply /ə'plaɪ/ vt (pt/pp -ied) auftragen (paint); anwenden (force, rule) □ vi zutreffen (to auf + acc); ~ for beantragen; sich bewerben um (job)

appoint /ə'pɔɪnt/ vt ernennen; (fix) festlegen; well ~ed gut ausgestattet. ~ment n Ernennung f; (meeting) Verabredung f; (at doctor's, hairdresser's) Termin m; (job) Posten m; make an ~ment sich anmelden

apposite /'æpəzɪt/ a treffend

appraise /ə'preɪz/ vt abschätzen

appreciable /ə'pri:ʃəbl/ a merklich; (considerable) beträchtlich

appreciat|e /ə'pri:ʃɪeɪt/ vt zu schätzen wissen; (be grateful for) dankbar sein für; (enjoy) schätzen; (understand) verstehen □ vi (increase in value) im Wert steigen. ~ion /-'eɪʃn/ n (gratitude) Dankbarkeit f; in ~ion als Dank (of für). ~ive /-ətɪv/ a dankbar

apprehend /æprɪ'hend/ vt festnehmen

apprehens|ion /æprɪ'henʃn/ n Festnahme f; (fear) Angst f. ~ive /-sɪv/ a ängstlich

apprentice /ə'prentɪs/ n Lehrling m. ~ship n Lehre f

approach /ə'prəʊtʃ/ n Näherkommen nt; (of time) Nahen nt; (access) Zugang m; (road) Zufahrt f □ vi sich nähern; (time:) nahen □ vt sich nähern (+ dat); (with request) herantreten an (+ acc); (set about) sich heranmachen an (+ acc). ~able /-əbl/ a zugänglich

approbation /æprə'beɪʃn/ n Billigung f

appropriate¹ /ə'prəʊprɪət/ a angebracht, angemessen

appropriate² /ə'prəʊprɪeɪt/ vt sich (dat) aneignen

approval /ə'pru:vl/ n Billigung f; on ~ zur Ansicht

approv|e /ə'pru:v/ vt billigen □ vi ~e of sth/s.o. mit etw/jdm einverstanden sein. ~ing a, -ly adv anerkennend

approximate¹ /ə'prɒksɪmeɪt/ vi ~ to nahe kommen (+ dat)

approximate² /ə'prɒksɪmət/ a ungefähr. ~ly adv ungefähr, etwa

approximation /əprɒksɪ'meɪʃn/ n Schätzung f

apricot /'eɪprɪkɒt/ n Aprikose f

April /'eɪprəl/ n April m; make an ~ fool of in den April schicken

apron /'eɪprən/ n Schürze f

apropos /'æprəpəʊ/ adv ~ [of] betreffs (+ gen)

apt /æpt/ a, -ly adv passend; ⟨pupil⟩ begabt; be ~ to do sth dazu neigen, etw zu tun

aptitude /'æptɪtjuːd/ n Begabung f

aqualung /'ækwəlʌŋ/ n Tauchgerät nt

aquarium /ə'kweərɪəm/ n Aquarium nt

Aquarius /ə'kweərɪəs/ n (Astr) Wassermann m

aquatic /ə'kwætɪk/ a Wasser-

Arab /'ærəb/ a arabisch □ n Araber(in) m(f). ~ian /ə'reɪbɪən/ a arabisch

Arabic /'ærəbɪk/ a arabisch

arable /'ærəbl/ a ~ land Ackerland nt

arbitrary /'ɑːbɪtrərɪ/ a, -ily adv willkürlich

arbitrat|e /'ɑːbɪtreɪt/ vi schlichten. ~ion /-'treɪʃn/ n Schlichtung f

arc /ɑːk/ n Bogen m

arcade /ɑː'keɪd/ n Laubengang m; ⟨shops⟩ Einkaufspassage f

arch /ɑːtʃ/ n Bogen m; (of foot) Gewölbe nt □ vt ~ its back ⟨cat:⟩ einen Buckel machen

archaeological /ɑːkɪə'lɒdʒɪkl/ a archäologisch

archaeolog|ist /ɑːkɪ'ɒlədʒɪst/ n Archäologe m/-login f. ~y n Archäologie f

archaic /ɑː'keɪɪk/ a veraltet

arch'bishop /ɑːtʃ-/ n Erzbischof m

arch-'enemy n Erzfeind m

archer /'ɑːtʃə(r)/ n Bogenschütze m. ~y n Bogenschießen nt

architect /'ɑːkɪtekt/ n Architekt(in) m(f). ~ural /ɑːkɪ'tektʃərəl/ a, -ly adv architektonisch

architecture /'ɑːkɪtektʃə(r)/ n Architektur f

archives /'ɑːkaɪvz/ npl Archiv nt

archway /'ɑːtʃweɪ/ n Torbogen m

Arctic /'ɑːktɪk/ a arktisch □ n the ~ die Arktis

ardent /'ɑːdənt/ a, -ly adv leidenschaftlich

ardour /'ɑːdə(r)/ n Leidenschaft f

arduous /'ɑːdjʊəs/ a mühsam

are /ɑː(r)/ see be

area /'eərɪə/ n (surface) Fläche f; (Geom) Flächeninhalt m; (region) Gegend f; (fig) Gebiet nt. ~ code n Vorwahlnummer f

arena /ə'riːnə/ n Arena f

aren't /ɑːnt/ = are not. See be

Argentina /ɑːdʒən'tiːnə/ n Argentinien nt

Argentin|e /'ɑːdʒəntaɪn/, ~ian /-'tɪnɪən/ a argentinisch

argue /'ɑːgjuː/ vi streiten (about über + acc); ⟨two people:⟩ sich streiten; (debate) diskutieren; don't ~! keine Widerrede! □ vt (debate) diskutieren; (reason) ~ that argumentieren, dass

argument /'ɑːgjʊmənt/ n Streit m, Auseinandersetzung f; (reasoning) Argument nt; have an ~ sich streiten. ~ative /-'mentətɪv/ a streitlustig

aria /'ɑːrɪə/ n Arie f

arid /'ærɪd/ a dürr

Aries /'eəriːz/ n (Astr) Widder m

arise /ə'raɪz/ vi (pt arose, pp arisen) sich ergeben (from aus)

aristocracy /ærɪ'stɒkrəsɪ/ n Aristokratie f

aristocrat /'ærɪstəkræt/ n Aristokrat(in) m(f). ~ic /-'krætɪk/ a aristokratisch

arithmetic /ə'rɪθmətɪk/ n Rechnen nt

ark /ɑːk/ n Noah's A ~ die Arche Noah

arm /ɑːm/ n Arm m; (of chair) Armlehne f; ~s pl (weapons) Waffen pl; (Heraldry) Wappen nt; up in ~s (fam) empört □ vt bewaffnen

armament /'ɑːməmənt/ n Bewaffnung f; ~s pl Waffen pl

'armchair n Sessel m

armed /ɑːmd/ a bewaffnet; ~ forces Streitkräfte pl

armistice /'ɑːmɪstɪs/ n Waffenstillstand m

armour /'ɑːmə(r)/ n Rüstung f. ~ed a Panzer-

'armpit n Achselhöhle f

army /'ɑːmɪ/ n Heer nt; (specific) Armee f; join the ~ zum Militär gehen

aroma /ə'rəʊmə/ n Aroma nt, Duft m. ~tic /ærə'mætɪk/ a aromatisch

arose /ə'rəʊz/ see arise

around /ə'raʊnd/ adv [all] ~ rings herum; he's not ~ er ist nicht da; look/ turn ~ sich umsehen/umdrehen; travel ~ herumreisen □ prep um (+ acc) ... herum; (approximately) gegen

arouse /ə'raʊz/ vt aufwecken; (excite) erregen

arrange /ə'reɪndʒ/ vt arrangieren; anordnen (furniture, books); (settle) abmachen; I have ~d to go there ich habe abgemacht, dass ich dahingehe. ~ment n Anordnung f; (agreement) Vereinbarung f; (of flowers) Gesteck nt; make ~ments Vorkehrungen treffen

arrears /ə'rɪəz/ npl Rückstände pl; in ~ im Rückstand

arrest /ə'rest/ n Verhaftung f; under ~ verhaftet □ vt verhaften

arrival /ə'raɪvl/ n Ankunft f; new ~s pl Neuankömmlinge pl

arrive /ə'raɪv/ vi ankommen; ~ at (fig) gelangen zu

arrogan|ce /'ærəgəns/ n Arroganz f. ~t a, -ly adv arrogant

arrow /'ærəʊ/ n Pfeil m

arse /ɑ:s/ n (vulg) Arsch m

arsenic /'ɑ:sənɪk/ n Arsen nt

arson /'ɑ:sn/ n Brandstiftung f. ~ist /-sənɪst/ n Brandstifter m

art /ɑ:t/ n Kunst f; work of ~ Kunstwerk nt; ~s and crafts pl Kunstgewerbe nt; A~s pl (Univ) Geisteswissenschaften pl

artery /'ɑ:tərɪ/ n Schlagader f, Arterie f

artful /'ɑ:tfl/ a gerissen

'art gallery n Kunstgalerie f

arthritis /ɑ:'θraɪtɪs/ n Arthritis f

artichoke /'ɑ:tɪtʃəʊk/ n Artischocke f

article /'ɑ:tɪkl/ n Artikel m; (object) Gegenstand m; ~ of clothing Kleidungsstück m

articulate[1] /ɑ:'tɪkjʊlət/ a deutlich; be ~ sich gut ausdrücken können

articulate[2] /ɑ:'tɪkjʊleɪt/ vt aussprechen. ~d lorry n Sattelzug m

artifice /'ɑ:tɪfɪs/ n Arglist f

artificial /ɑ:tɪ'fɪʃl/ a, -ly adv künstlich

artillery /ɑ:'tɪlərɪ/ n Artillerie f

artist /'ɑ:tɪst/ n Künstler m(f)

artiste /ɑ:'ti:st/ n (Theat) Artist(in) m(f)

artistic /ɑ:'tɪstɪk/ a, -ally adv künstlerisch

artless /'ɑ:tlɪs/ a unschuldig

as /æz/ conj (because) da; (when) als; (while) während □ prep als; as a child/foreigner als Kind/Ausländer □ adv as well auch; as soon as sobald; as much as so viel wie; as quick as you so schnell wie du; as you know wie Sie wissen; as far as I'm concerned was mich betrifft

asbestos /æz'bestɒs/ n Asbest m

ascend /ə'send/ vi [auf]steigen □ vt besteigen (throne)

Ascension /ə'senʃn/ n (Relig) [Christi] Himmelfahrt f

ascent /ə'sent/ n Aufstieg m

ascertain /æsə'teɪn/ vt ermitteln

ascribe /ə'skraɪb/ vt zuschreiben (to dat)

ash[1] /æʃ/ n (tree) Esche f

ash[2] n Asche f

ashamed /ə'ʃeɪmd/ a beschämt; be ~ sich schämen (of über + acc)

ashore /ə'ʃɔ:(r)/ adv an Land

ash: ~tray n Aschenbecher m. A ~ 'Wednesday n Aschermittwoch m

Asia /'eɪʃə/ n Asien nt. ~n a asiatisch □ n Asiat(in) m(f). ~tic /eɪʃɪ'ætɪk/ a asiatisch

aside /ə'saɪd/ adv beiseite; ~ from (Amer) außer (+ dat)

ask /ɑ:sk/ vt/i fragen; stellen (question); (invite) einladen; ~ for bitten um; verlangen (s.o.); ~ after sich erkundigen nach; ~ s.o. in jdn hereinbitten; ~ s.o. to do sth jdn bitten, etw zu tun

askance /ə'skɑ:ns/ adv look ~ at schief ansehen

askew /ə'skju:/ a & adv schief

asleep /ə'sli:p/ a be ~ schlafen; fall ~ einschlafen

asparagus /ə'spærəgəs/ n Spargel m

aspect /'æspekt/ n Aspekt m

aspersions /ə'spɜ:ʃnz/ npl cast ~ on schlecht machen

asphalt /'æsfælt/ n Asphalt m

asphyxia /æ'sfɪksɪə/ n Erstickung f. ~te /æ'sfɪksɪeɪt/ vt/i ersticken. ~tion /-'eɪʃn/ n Erstickung f

aspirations /æspə'reɪʃnz/ npl Streben nt

aspire /ə'spaɪə(r)/ vi ~ to streben nach

ass /æs/ n Esel m

assail /ə'seɪl/ vt bestürmen. ~ant n Angreifer(in) m(f)

assassin /ə'sæsɪn/ n Mörder(in) m(f). ~ate vt ermorden. ~ation /-'neɪʃn/ n [politischer] Mord m

assault /ə'sɔ:lt/ n (Mil) Angriff m; (Jur) Körperverletzung f □ vt [tätlich] angreifen

assemble /ə'sembl/ vi sich versammeln □ vt versammeln; (Techn) montieren

assembly /ə'semblɪ/ n Versammlung f; (Sch) Andacht f; (Techn) Montage f. ~ line n Fließband nt

assent /ə'sent/ n Zustimmung f □ vi zustimmen (to dat)

assert /ə'sɜ:t/ vt behaupten; ~ oneself sich durchsetzen. ~ion /-ʃn/ n Behauptung f. ~ive /-tɪv/ a be ~ive sich durchsetzen können

assess /ə'ses/ vt bewerten; (fig & for tax purposes) einschätzen: schätzen (value). ~ment n Einschätzung f, (of tax) Steuerbescheid m

asset /'æset/ n Vorteil m; ~s pl (money) Vermögen nt; (Comm) Aktiva pl

assiduous /ə'sɪdjʊəs/ a, -ly adv fleißig

assign /ə'saɪn/ vt zuweisen (to dat). ~ment n (task) Aufgabe f

assimilate /ə'sɪmɪleɪt/ vt aufnehmen; (integrate) assimilieren

assist /ə'sɪst/ vt/i helfen (+ dat). ~ance n Hilfe f. ~ant a Hilfs- □ n Assistent(in) m(f); (in shop) Verkäufer(in) m(f)

associat|e[1] /ə'səʊʃɪeɪt/ vt verbinden; (Psych) assoziieren □ vi ~ with verkehren mit. ~ion /-'eɪʃn/ n Verband m. A~ion 'football n Fußball m

associate[2] /ə'səʊʃɪət/ a assoziiert □ n Kollege m/-gin f

assort|ed /ə'sɔːtɪd/ a gemischt. ~ment n Mischung f

assum|e /ə'sjuːm/ vt annehmen; übernehmen ⟨office⟩; ~ing that angenommen, dass

assumption /ə'sʌmpʃn/ n Annahme f; on the ~ in der Annahme (that dass)

assurance /ə'ʃʊərəns/ n Versicherung f; (confidence) Selbstsicherheit f

assure /ə'ʃʊə(r)/ vt versichern (s.o. jdm); I ~ you [of that] das versichere ich Ihnen. ~d a sicher

asterisk /'æstərɪsk/ n Sternchen nt

astern /ə'stɜːn/ adv achtern

asthma /'æsmə/ n Asthma nt. ~tic /-'mætɪk/ a asthmatisch

astonish /ə'stɒnɪʃ/ vt erstaunen. ~ing a erstaunlich. ~ment n Erstaunen nt

astound /ə'staʊnd/ vt in Erstaunen setzen

astray /ə'streɪ/ adv go ~ verloren gehen; ⟨person:⟩ sich verlaufen; (fig) vom rechten Weg abkommen; lead ~ verleiten

astride /ə'straɪd/ adv rittlings □ prep rittlings auf (+ dat/acc)

astringent /ə'strɪndʒənt/ a adstringierend; (fig) beißend

astrolog|er /ə'strɒlədʒə(r)/ n Astrologe m/-gin f. ~y n Astrologie f

astronaut /'æstrənɔːt/ n Astronaut(in) m(f)

astronom|er /ə'strɒnəmə(r)/ n Astronom m. ~ical /æstrə'nɒmɪkl/ a astronomisch. ~y n Astronomie f

astute /ə'stjuːt/ a scharfsinnig. ~ness n Scharfsinn m

asylum /ə'saɪləm/ n Asyl nt; [lunatic] ~ Irrenanstalt f

at /ət, betont æt/ prep an (+ dat/acc); (with town) in; (price) zu; (speed) mit; at the station am Bahnhof; at the beginning/ end am Anfang/Ende; at home zu Hause; at John's bei John; at work/the hairdresser's bei der Arbeit/beim Friseur; at school/the office in der Schule/im Büro; at a party/wedding auf einer Party/Hochzeit; at one o'clock um ein Uhr; at Christmas/Easter zu Weihnachten/Ostern; at the age of im Alter von; not at all gar nicht; at times manchmal; two at a time zwei auf einmal; good/bad at languages gut/schlecht in Sprachen

ate /et/ see eat

atheist /'eɪθɪɪst/ n Atheist(in) m(f)

athlet|e /'æθliːt/ n Athlet(in) m(f). ~ic /-'letɪk/ a sportlich. ~ics /-'letɪks/ n Leichtathletik f

Atlantic /ət'læntɪk/ a & n the ~ [Ocean] der Atlantik

atlas /'ætləs/ n Atlas m

atmospher|e /'ætməsfɪə(r)/ n Atmosphäre f. ~ic /-'ferɪk/ a atmosphärisch

atom /'ætəm/ n Atom nt. ~ bomb n Atombombe f

atomic /ə'tɒmɪk/ a Atom-

atone /ə'təʊn/ vi büßen (for für). ~ment n Buße f

atrocious /ə'trəʊʃəs/ a abscheulich

atrocity /ə'trɒsəti/ n Gräueltat f

attach /ə'tætʃ/ vt befestigen (to an + dat); beimessen (importance) (to dat); be ~ed to (fig) hängen an (+ dat)

attaché /ə'tæʃeɪ/ n Attaché m. ~ case n Aktenkoffer m

attachment /ə'tætʃmənt/ n Bindung f; (tool) Zubehörteil nt; (additional) Zusatzgerät nt

attack /ə'tæk/ n Angriff m; (Med) Anfall m □ vt/i angreifen. ~er n Angreifer m

attain /ə'teɪn/ vt erreichen; (get) erlangen. ~able /-əbl/ a erreichbar

attempt /ə'tempt/ n Versuch m □ vt versuchen

attend /ə'tend/ vt anwesend sein bei; (go regularly to) besuchen; (take part in) teilnehmen an (+ dat); (accompany) begleiten; ⟨doctor:⟩ behandeln □ vi anwesend sein; (pay attention) aufpassen; ~ to sich kümmern um; (in shop) bedienen. ~ance n Anwesenheit f; (number) Besucherzahl f. ~ant n Wärter(in) m(f); (in car park) Wächter m

attention /ə'tenʃn/ n Aufmerksamkeit f; ~! (Mil) stillgestanden! pay ~ aufpassen; pay ~ to beachten, achten auf (+ acc); need ~ reparaturbedürftig sein; for the ~ of zu Händen von

attentive /ə'tentɪv/ a, -ly adv aufmerksam

attest /ə'test/ vt/i ~ [to] bezeugen

attic /'ætɪk/ n Dachboden m

attire /ə'taɪə(r)/ n Kleidung f □ vt kleiden

attitude /'ætɪtjuːd/ n Haltung f

attorney /ə'tɜːni/ n (Amer: lawyer) Rechtsanwalt m; power of ~ Vollmacht f

attract /ə'trækt/ vt anziehen; erregen (attention); ~ s.o.'s attention jds Aufmerksamkeit auf sich (acc) lenken. ~ion /-ækʃn/ n Anziehungskraft f; (charm) Reiz m; (thing) Attraktion f. ~ive /-tɪv/ a, -ly adv attraktiv

attribute[1] /'ætrɪbjuːt/ n Attribut nt

attribute|e² /əˈtrɪbjuːt/ vt zuschreiben (to dat). ~ive /-tɪv/ a, -ly adv attributiv

attrition /əˈtrɪʃn/ n war of ~ Zermürbungskrieg m

aubergine /ˈəʊbəʒiːn/ n Aubergine f

auburn /ˈɔːbən/ a kastanienbraun

auction /ˈɔːkʃn/ n Auktion f, Versteigerung f ▢ vt versteigern. ~eer /-ʃəˈnɪə(r)/ n Auktionator m

audaci|ous /ɔːˈdeɪʃəs/ a, -ly adv verwegen. ~ty /-ˈdæsəti/ n Verwegenheit f; (impudence) Dreistigkeit f

audible /ˈɔːdəbl/ a, -bly adv hörbar

audience /ˈɔːdɪəns/ n Publikum nt; (Theat, TV) Zuschauer pl; (Radio) Zuhörer pl; (meeting) Audienz f

audio /ˈɔːdɪəʊ/: ~ typist n Phonotypistin f. ~ visual a audiovisuell

audit /ˈɔːdɪt/ n Bücherrevision f ▢ vt (Comm) prüfen

audition /ɔːˈdɪʃn/ n (Theat) Vorsprechen nt; (Mus) Vorspielen nt; (for singer) Vorsingen nt ▢ vi vorsprechen; vorspielen; vorsingen

auditor /ˈɔːdɪtə(r)/ n Buchprüfer m

auditorium /ɔːdɪˈtɔːrɪəm/ n Zuschauerraum m

augment /ɔːɡˈment/ vt vergrößern

augur /ˈɔːɡə(r)/ vi ~ well/ill etwas/nichts Gutes verheißen

august /ɔːˈɡʌst/ a hoheitsvoll

August /ˈɔːɡəst/ n August m

aunt /ɑːnt/ n Tante f

au pair /əʊˈpeə(r)/ n ~ [girl] Aupairmädchen nt

aura /ˈɔːrə/ n Fluidum nt

auspices /ˈɔːspɪsɪz/ npl (protection) Schirmherrschaft f

auspicious /ɔːˈspɪʃəs/ a günstig; (occasion) freudig

auster|e/ɒˈstɪə(r)/ a streng; (simple) nüchtern. ~ity /-ˈsterəti/ n Strenge f; (hardship) Entbehrung f

Australia /ɒˈstreɪlɪə/ n Australien nt. ~n a australisch ▢ n Australier(in) m(f)

Austria /ˈɒstrɪə/ n Österreich nt. ~n a österreichisch ▢ n Österreicher(in) m(f)

authentic /ɔːˈθentɪk/ a echt, authentisch. ~ate vt beglaubigen. ~ity /-ˈtɪsəti/ n Echtheit f

author /ˈɔːθə(r)/ n Schriftsteller m, Autor m; (of document) Verfasser m

authoritarian /ɔːθɒrɪˈteərɪən/ a autoritär

authoritative /ɔːˈθɒrɪtətɪv/ a maßgebend; be ~ Autorität haben

authority /ɔːˈθɒrəti/ n Autorität f; (public) Behörde f; in ~ verantwortlich

authorization /ɔːθəraɪˈzeɪʃn/ n Ermächtigung f

authorize /ˈɔːθəraɪz/ vt ermächtigen ⟨s.o.⟩; genehmigen ⟨sth⟩

autobi'ography /ɔːtə-/ n Autobiographie f

autocratic /ɔːtəˈkrætɪk/ a autokratisch

autograph /ˈɔːtə-/ n Autogramm nt

automatic /ɔːtəˈmætɪk/ a, -ally adv automatisch ▢ n (car) Fahrzeug nt mit Automatikgetriebe; (washing machine) Waschautomat m

automation /ɔːtəˈmeɪʃn/ n Automation f

automobile /ˈɔːtəməbiːl/ n Auto nt

autonom|ous /ɔːˈtɒnəməs/ a autonom. ~y n Autonomie f

autopsy /ˈɔːtɒpsɪ/ n Autopsie f

autumn /ˈɔːtəm/ n Herbst m. ~al /-ˈtʌmnl/ a herbstlich

auxiliary /ɔːɡˈzɪlɪərɪ/ a Hilfs- ▢ n Helfer(in) m(f), Hilfskraft f

avail /əˈveɪl/ n to no ~ vergeblich ▢ vi ~ oneself of Gebrauch machen von

available /əˈveɪləbl/ a verfügbar; (obtainable) erhältlich

avalanche /ˈævəlɑːnʃ/ n Lawine f

avaric|e /ˈævərɪs/ n Habsucht f. ~ious /-ˈrɪʃəs/ a habgierig, habsüchtig

avenge /əˈvendʒ/ vt rächen

avenue /ˈævənjuː/ n Allee f

average /ˈævərɪdʒ/ a Durchschnitts-, durchschnittlich ▢ n Durchschnitt m; on ~ im Durchschnitt, durchschnittlich ▢ vt durchschnittlich schaffen ▢ vi ~ out at im Durchschnitt ergeben

avers|e /əˈvɜːs/ a not be ~e to sth etw (dat) nicht abgeneigt sein. ~ion /-ɜːʃn/ n Abneigung f (to gegen)

avert /əˈvɜːt/ vt abwenden

aviary /ˈeɪvɪərɪ/ n Vogelhaus nt

aviation /eɪvɪˈeɪʃn/ n Luftfahrt f

avid /ˈævɪd/ a gierig (for nach); (keen) eifrig

avocado /ævəˈkɑːdəʊ/ n Avocado f

avoid /əˈvɔɪd/ vt vermeiden; ~ s.o. jdm aus dem Weg gehen. ~able /-əbl/ a vermeidbar. ~ance n Vermeidung f

await /əˈweɪt/ vt warten auf (+ acc)

awake /əˈweɪk/ a wach; wide ~ hellwach ▢ vi (pt awoke, pp awoken) erwachen

awaken /əˈweɪkn/ vt wecken ▢ vi erwachen. ~ing n Erwachen nt

award /əˈwɔːd/ n Auszeichnung f; (prize) Preis m ▢ vt zuerkennen (to s.o. dat); verleihen ⟨prize⟩

aware /əˈweə(r)/ a become ~ gewahr werden (of gen); be ~ that wissen, dass. ~ness n Bewusstsein nt awash /ə'wɒʃ/ *a* be ~unter Wasser stehen

away /ə'weɪ/ *adv* weg, fort; (*absent*) abwesend; be ~nicht da sein; far ~weit weg; four kilometres ~vier Kilometer entfernt; play ~(*Sport*) auswärts spielen; go/stay ~weggehen/-bleiben. ~ game *n* Auswärtsspiel *nt*

awe /ɔ:/ *n* Ehrfurcht *f*

awful /'ɔ:fl/ *a*, ~ly *adv* furchtbar

awhile /ə'waɪl/ *adv* eine Weile

awkward /'ɔ:kwəd/ *a* schwierig; (*clumsy*) ungeschickt; (*embarrassing*) peinlich; (*inconvenient*) ungünstig. ~ly *adv* ungeschickt; (*embarrassedly*) verlegen

awning /'ɔ:nɪŋ/ *n* Markise *f*

awoke(n) /ə'wəʊk(n)/ *see* awake

awry /ə'raɪ/ *adv* schief

axe /æks/ *n* Axt *f* □ *vt* (*pres p* axing) streichen; (*dismiss*) entlassen

axis /'æksɪs/ *n* (*pl* axes /-si:z/) Achse *f*

axle /'æksl/ *n* (*Techn*) Achse *f*

ay[e] /aɪ/ *adv* ja □ *n* Jastimme *f*

B

B /bi:/ *n* (*Mus*) H *nt*

BA *abbr of* Bachelor of Arts

babble /'bæbl/ *vi* plappern; (*stream*:) plätschern

baboon /bə'bu:n/ *n* Pavian *m*

baby /'beɪbɪ/ *n* Baby *nt*; (*Amer, fam*) Schätzchen *nt*

baby: ~ carriage *n* (*Amer*) Kinderwagen *m*. ~ish *a* kindisch. ~minder *n* Tagesmutter *f*. ~sit *vi* babysitten. ~sitter *n* Babysitter *m*

bachelor /'bætʃələ(r)/ *n* Junggeselle *m*; B~ of Arts/Science Bakkalaureus Artium/Scientium

bacillus /bə'sɪləs/ *n* (*pl* -lli) Bazillus *m*

back /bæk/ *n* Rücken *m*; (*reverse*) Rückseite *f*; (*of chair*) Rückenlehne *f*; (*Sport*) Verteidiger *m*; at/(*Auto*) in the ~hinten; on the ~ auf der Rückseite; ~ to front verkehrt; at the ~ of beyond am Ende der Welt □ *a* Hinter- □ *adv* zurück; ~ here/ there hier/da hinten; ~ at home zu Hause; go/pay ~ zurückgehen/-zahlen □ *vt* (*support*) unterstützen; (*with money*) finanzieren; (*Auto*) zurücksetzen; (*Betting*) [Geld] setzen auf (+ *acc*); (*cover the back of*) mit einer Verstärkung versehen □ *vi* (*Auto*) zurücksetzen. ~ down *vi* klein beigeben. ~ in *vi* rückwärts hineinfahren. ~ out *vi* rückwärts hinaus-/

herausfahren; (*fig*) aussteigen (ofaus). ~ up *vt* unterstützen; (*confirm*) bestätigen □ *vi* (*Auto*) zurücksetzen

back: ~ache *n* Rückenschmerzen *pl*. ~biting *n* gehässiges Gerede *nt*. ~bone *n* Rückgrat *nt*. ~chat *n* Widerrede *f*. ~comb *vt* toupieren. ~date *vt* rückdatieren; ~dated torückwirkend von. ~'door *n* Hintertür *f*

backer /'bækə(r)/ *n* Geldgeber *m*

back: ~fire *vi* (*Auto*) fehlzünden; (*fig*) fehlschlagen. ~ground Hintergrund *m*; family ~ground Familienverhältnisse *pl*. ~hand *n* (*Sport*) Rückhand *f*. ~'handed *a* (*compliment*) zweifelhaft. ~'hander *n* (*Sport*) Rückhandschlag *m*; (*fam: bribe*) Schmiergeld *nt*

backing /'bækɪŋ/ *n* (*support*) Unterstützung *f*; (*material*) Verstärkung *f*

back: ~lash *n* (*fig*) Gegenschlag *m*. ~log *n* Rückstand *m* (of an + *dat*). ~'seat *n* Rücksitz *m*. ~side *n* (*fam*) Hintern *m*. ~stage *adv* hinter der Bühne. ~stroke *n* Rückenschwimmen *nt*. ~up *n* Unterstützung *f*; (*Amer: traffic jam*) Stau *m*

backward /'bækwəd/ *a* zurückgeblieben; (*country*) rückständig □ *adv* rückwärts. ~s rückwärts; ~s and forwards hin und her

back: ~water *n* (*fig*) unberührtes Fleckchen *nt*. ~'yard *n* Hinterhof *m*; not in my ~ yard (*fam*) nicht vor meiner Haustür

bacon /'beɪkn/ *n* [Schinken]speck *m*

bacteria /bæk'tɪərɪə/ *npl* Bakterien *pl*

bad /bæd/ *a* (worse, worst) schlecht; (*serious*) schwer, schlimm; (*naughty*) unartig; ~ language gemeine Ausdrucksweise *f*; feel ~ sich schlecht fühlen; (*feel guilty*) ein schlechtes Gewissen haben; go ~ schlecht werden

bade /bæd/ *see* bid²

badge /bædʒ/ *n* Abzeichen *nt*

badger /'bædʒə(r)/ *n* Dachs *m* □ *vt* plagen

badly /'bædlɪ/ *adv* schlecht; (*seriously*) schwer; ~ off schlecht gestellt; ~ behaved unerzogen; want ~ sich (*dat*) sehnsüchtig wünschen; need ~ dringend brauchen

bad-'mannered *a* mit schlechten Manieren

badminton /'bædmɪntən/ *n* Federball *m*

bad-'tempered *a* schlecht gelaunt

baffle /'bæfl/ *vt* verblüffen

bag /bæg/ *n* Tasche *f*; (*of paper*) Tüte *f*; (*pouch*) Beutel *m*; ~s of (*fam*) jede Menge □ *vt* (*fam: reserve*) in Beschlag nehmen

baggage /'bægɪdʒ/ *n* [Reise]gepäck *nt*

baggy /'bægɪ/ *a* (*clothes*) ausgebeult

'bagpipes *npl* Dudelsack *m*

bail /beɪl/ n Kaution f; on ~ gegen Kaution
□ vt ~ s.o. out jdn gegen Kaution freibekommen; (fig) jdm aus der Patsche helfen.
~ out vt (Naut) ausschöpfen □ vi (Aviat)
abspringen

bailiff /'beɪlɪf/ n Gerichtsvollzieher m; (of
estate) Gutsverwalter m

bait /beɪt/ n Köder m □ vt mit einem Köder
versehen; (fig: torment) reizen

bake /beɪk/ vt/i backen

baker /'beɪkə(r)/ n Bäcker m; ~'s [shop]
Bäckerei f. ~y n Bäckerei f

baking /'beɪkɪŋ/ n Backen nt. ~-powder
n Backpulver nt. ~-tin n Backform f

balance /'bæləns/ n (equilibrium) Gleichgewicht nt, Balance f; (scales) Waage f;
(Comm) Saldo m; (outstanding sum)
Restbetrag m; [bank] ~ Kontostand m; in
the ~ (fig) in der Schwebe □ vt balancieren; (equalize) ausgleichen; (Comm)
abschließen (books) □ vi balancieren; (fig
& Comm) sich ausgleichen. ~d a ausgewogen. ~ sheet n Bilanz f

balcony /'bælkənɪ/ n Balkon m

bald /bɔːld/ a (-er, -est) kahl; (person)
kahlköpfig; go ~ eine Glatze bekommen

balderdash /'bɔːldədæʃ/ n Unsinn m

bald|ing /'bɔːldɪŋ/ a be ~ing eine Glatze
bekommen. ~ly adv unverblümt. ~ness
n Kahlköpfigkeit f

bale /beɪl/ n Ballen m

baleful /'beɪlfl/ a, -ly adv böse

balk /bɔːlk/ vt vereiteln □ vi ~ at zurückschrecken vor (+ dat)

Balkans /'bɔːlkənz/ npl Balkan m

ball¹ /bɔːl/ n Ball m; (Billiards, Croquet)
Kugel f; (of yarn) Knäuel m & nt; on the
~ (fam) auf Draht

ball² n (dance) Ball m

ballad /'bæləd/ n Ballade f

ballast /'bæləst/ n Ballast m

ball-bearing n Kugellager nt

ballerina /bælə'riːnə/ n Ballerina f

ballet /'bæleɪ/ m Ballett nt. ~ dancer n
Balletttänzer(in) m(f)

ballistic /bə'lɪstɪk/ a ballistisch. ~s n Bal-
listik f

balloon /bə'luːn/ n Luftballon m; (Aviat)
Ballon m

ballot /'bælət/ n [geheime] Wahl f; (on
issue) [geheime] Abstimmung f. ~-box n
Wahlurne f. ~-paper n Stimmzettel m

ball: ~-point ['pen] n Kugelschreiber m.
~-room n Ballsaal m

balm /bɑːm/ n Balsam m

balmy /'bɑːmɪ/ a (-ier, -iest) a sanft; (fam:
crazy) verrückt

Baltic /'bɔːltɪk/ a & n the ~ [Sea] die
Ostsee

balustrade /bælə'streɪd/ n Balustrade f

bamboo /bæm'buː/ n Bambus m

bamboozle /bæm'buːzl/ vt (fam) übers
Ohr hauen

ban /bæn/ n Verbot nt □ vt (pt/pp banned)
verbieten

banal /bə'nɑːl/ a banal. ~ity /-'nælətɪ/
n Banalität f

banana /bə'nɑːnə/ n Banane f

band /bænd/ n Band nt; (stripe) Streifen
m; (group) Schar f; (Mus) Kapelle f □ vi
~ together sich zusammenschließen

bandage /'bændɪdʒ/ n Verband m; (for
support) Bandage f □ vt verbinden; ban-
dagieren (limb)

b. & b. abbr of bed and breakfast

bandit /'bændɪt/ n Bandit m

band: ~stand n Musikpavillon m. ~wa-
gon n jump on•the ~wagon (fig) sich
einer erfolgreichen Sache anschließen

bandy¹ /'bændɪ/ vt (pt/pp -ied) wechseln
(words)

bandy² a (-ier, -iest) be ~ O-Beine haben.
~-legged a O-beinig

bang /bæŋ/ n (noise) Knall m; (blow) Schlag
m □ adv go ~ knallen □ int bums! peng!
□ vt knallen; (shut noisily) zuknallen;
(strike) schlagen auf (+ acc); ~ one's
head sich (dat) den Kopf stoßen (on an +
acc) □ vi schlagen; (door:) zuknallen

banger /'bæŋə(r)/ n (firework) Knall-
frosch m; (fam: sausage) Wurst f; old ~
(fam: car) Klapperkiste f

bangle /'bæŋgl/ n Armreifen m

banish /'bænɪʃ/ vt verbannen

banisters /'bænɪstəz/ npl [Treppen]ge-
länder nt

banjo /'bændʒəʊ/ n Banjo nt

bank¹ /bæŋk/ n (of river) Ufer nt; (slope)
Hang m □ vi (Aviat) in die Kurve gehen

bank² n Bank f □ vt einzahlen; ~ with ein
Konto haben bei. ~ on vt sich verlassen
auf (+ acc)

bank account n Bankkonto nt

banker /'bæŋkə(r)/ n Bankier m

bank: ~ holiday n gesetzlicher Feiertag
m. ~ing n Bankwesen nt. ~note n Banknote f

bankrupt /'bæŋkrʌpt/ a bankrott; go ~
Bankrott machen □ n Bankrotteur m □ vt
Bankrott machen. ~cy n Bankrott m

banner /'bænə(r)/ n Banner nt; (carried
by demonstrators) Transparent nt,
Spruchband nt

banns /bænz/ npl (Relig) Aufgebot nt

banquet /'bæŋkwɪt/ n Bankett nt

banter /'bæntə(r)/ n Spötterei f

bap /bæp/ n weiches Brötchen nt

baptism /'bæptɪzm/ n Taufe f

Baptist /'bæptɪst/ n Baptist(in) m(f)

baptize /bæp'taɪz/ vt taufen

bar /bɑ:(r)/ n Stange f; (of cage) [Gitter]stab m; (of gold) Barren m; (of chocolate) Tafel f; (of soap) Stück nt; (long) Riegel m; (café) Bar f; (counter) Theke f; (Mus) Takt m; (fig: obstacle) Hindernis nt; parallel ~s (Sport) Barren m; **be called to the ~** (Jur) als plädierender Anwalt zugelassen werden; **behind ~s** (fam) hinter Gittern □ vt (pt/pp barred) versperren (way, door); ausschließen (person); prep außer; **~ none** ohne Ausnahme

barbarian /bɑ:'beərɪən/ n Barbar m

barbar|ic /bɑ:'bærɪk/ a barbarisch. ~ity n Barbarei f. ~ous /'bɑ:bərəs/ a barbarisch

barbecue /'bɑ:bɪkju:/ n Grill m; (party) Grillfest m □ vt inf [im Freien] grillen

barbed /'bɑ:bd/ a ~ **wire** Stacheldraht m

barber /'bɑ:bə(r)/ n [Herren]friseur m

barbiturate /bɑ:'bɪtjʊrət/ n Barbiturat nt

'bar code n Strichkode m

bare /beə(r)/ a (-r, -st) nackt, bloß; (tree) kahl; (empty) leer; (mere) bloß □ vt entblößen; fletschen (teeth)

bare: ~**back** adv ohne Sattel. ~**faced** a schamlos. ~**foot** adv barfuß. ~**'headed** a mit unbedecktem Kopf

barely /'beəlɪ/ adv kaum

bargain /'bɑ:gɪn/ n (agreement) Geschäft nt; (good buy) Gelegenheitskauf m; **into the** ~ noch dazu; **make a** ~ sich einigen □ vi handeln; (haggle) feilschen; ~ **for** (expect) rechnen mit

barge /bɑ:dʒ/ n Lastkahn m; (towed) Schleppkahn m □ vi ~ **in** (fam) hereinplatzen

baritone /'bærɪtəʊn/ n Bariton m

bark[1] /bɑ:k/ n (of tree) Rinde f

bark[2] n Bellen nt □ vi bellen

barley /'bɑ:lɪ/ n Gerste f

bar: ~**maid** n Schankmädchen nt. ~**man** Barmann m

barmy /'bɑ:mɪ/ a (fam) verrückt

barn /bɑ:n/ n Scheune f

barometer /bə'rɒmɪtə(r)/ n Barometer nt

baron /'bærn/ n Baron m. ~**ess** n Baronin f

baroque /bə'rɒk/ a barock □ n Barock nt

barracks /'bærəks/ npl Kaserne f

barrage /'bærɑ:ʒ/ n (in river) Wehr nt; (Mil) Sperrfeuer nt; (fig) Hagel m

barrel /'bærl/ n Fass nt; (of gun) Lauf m; (of cannon) Rohr nt. ~-**organ** n Drehorgel f

barren /'bærn/ a unfruchtbar; (landscape) öde

barricade /bærɪ'keɪd/ n Barrikade f □ vt verbarrikadieren

barrier /'bærɪə(r)/ n Barriere f; (across road) Schranke f; (Rail) Sperre f; (fig) Hindernis nt

barring /'bɑ:rɪŋ/ prep ~ **accidents** wenn alles gut geht

barrister /'bærɪstə(r)/ n [plädierender] Rechtsanwalt m

barrow /'bærəʊ/ n Karre f, Karren m. ~ **boy** n Straßenhändler m

barter /'bɑ:tə(r)/ vt tauschen (for gegen)

base /beɪs/ n Fuß m; (fig) Basis f; (Mil) Stützpunkt m □ a gemein; (metal) unedel □ vt stützen (on auf + acc); **be** ~**d on** basieren auf (+ dat)

base: ~**ball** n Baseball m. ~**less** a unbegründet. ~**ment** n Kellergeschoss nt. ~**ment flat** n Kellerwohnung f

bash /bæʃ/ n Schlag m; **have a** ~! (fam) probier es mal! □ vt hauen; (dent) einbeulen; ~**ed in** verbeult

bashful /'bæʃfl/ a, -**ly** adv schüchtern

basic /'beɪsɪk/ a Grund-; (fundamental) grundlegend; (essential) wesentlich; (unadorned) einfach; **the** ~**s** das Wesentliche. ~**ally** adv grundsätzlich

basil /'bæzɪl/ n Basilikum nt

basilica /bə'zɪlɪkə/ n Basilika f

basin /'beɪsn/ n Becken nt; (for washing) Waschbecken nt; (for food) Schüssel f

basis /'beɪsɪs/ n (pl -ses /-si:z/) Basis f

bask /bɑ:sk/ vi sich sonnen

basket /'bɑ:skɪt/ n Korb m. ~**ball** n Basketball m

Basle /bɑ:l/ n Basel nt

bass /beɪs/ a Bass-; ~ **voice** Bassstimme f □ n Bass m; (person) Bassist m

bassoon /bə'su:n/ n Fagott nt

baste[1] /beɪst/ vt (sew) heften

baste[2] vt (Culin) begießen

bastion /'bæstɪən/ n Bastion f

bat[1] /bæt/ n Schläger m; **off one's own** ~ (fam) auf eigene Faust □ vt (pt/pp batted) schlagen; **not** ~ **an eyelid** (fig) nicht mit der Wimper zucken

bat[2] n (Zool) Fledermaus f

batch /bætʃ/ n (of people) Gruppe f; (of papers) Stoß m; (of goods) Sendung f; (of bread) Schub m

bated /'beɪtɪd/ a **with** ~ **breath** mit angehaltenem Atem

bath /bɑ:θ/ n (pl ~s /bɑ:ðz/) Bad nt; (tub) Badewanne f; ~**s** pl Badeanstalt f; **have a** ~ baden □ vt/i baden

bathe /beɪð/ n Bad nt □ vt/i baden. ~r n Badende(r) m/f

bathing /'beɪðɪŋ/ n Baden nt. ~-cap n Bademütze f. ~-costume n Badeanzug m

bath: ~-mat n Badematte f. ~-robe n (Amer) Bademantel m. ~-room n Badezimmer nt. ~-towel n Badetuch nt

baton /'bætn/ n (Mus) Taktstock m; (Mil) Stab m

battalion /bə'tælɪən/ n Bataillon nt

batten /'bætn/ n Latte f

batter /'bætə(r)/ n (Culin) flüssiger Teig m □ vt schlagen. ~ed a ⟨car⟩ verbeult; ⟨wife⟩ misshandelt

battery /'bætərɪ/ n Batterie f

battle /'bætl/ n Schlacht f; (fig) Kampf m □ vi (fig) kämpfen (for um)

battle: ~-axe n (fam) Drachen m. ~-field n Schlachtfeld nt. ~-ship n Schlachtschiff nt

batty /'bætɪ/ a (fam) verrückt

Bavaria /bə'veərɪə/ n Bayern nt. ~n a bayrisch □ n Bayer(in) m(f)

bawdy /'bɔ:dɪ/ a (-ier, -iest) derb

bawl /bɔ:l/ vt/i brüllen

bay [1] /beɪ/ n (Geog) Bucht f; (Archit) Erker m

bay [2] n keep at ~ fern halten

bay [3] n ⟨horse⟩ Braune(r) m

bay [4] n (Bot) ⟨echter⟩ Lorbeer m. ~-leaf n Lorbeerblatt nt

bayonet /'beɪənet/ n Bajonett nt

bay 'window n Erkerfenster nt

bazaar /bə'zɑ:(r)/ n Basar m

BC abbr (before Christ's) v. Chr.

be /bi:/ vi (pres am, are, is, pl are; pt was, pl were; pp been) sein; (lie) liegen; (stand) stehen; (cost) kosten; he is a teacher er ist Lehrer; be quiet! sei still! I am cold/hot mir ist kalt/heiß; how are you? wie geht es Ihnen? I am well mir geht es gut; there is/are es gibt; what do you want to be? was willst du werden? I have been to Vienna ich bin in Wien gewesen; has the postman been? war der Briefträger schon da? it's hot, isn't it? es ist heiß, nicht ⟨wahr⟩? you are coming too, aren't you? du kommst mit, nicht ⟨wahr⟩? it's yours, is it? das gehört also Ihnen? yes he is/I am ja; (negating previous statement) doch; three and three are six drei und drei macht sechs □ v aux ~ reading/going lesen/gehen; I am coming/staying ich komme/bleibe; what is he doing? was macht er? I am being lazy ich faulenze; I was thinking of you ich dachte an dich; you were going to ... du wolltest ...; I am to stay ich soll bleiben; you are not to ... du

darfst nicht ...; you are to do that immediately das musst du sofort machen □ passive werden; be attacked/deceived überfallen/betrogen werden

beach /bi:tʃ/ n Strand m. ~-wear n Strandkleidung f

beacon /'bi:kn/ n Leuchtfeuer nt; (Naut, Aviat) Bake f

bead /bi:d/ n Perle f

beak /bi:k/ n Schnabel m

beaker /'bi:kə(r)/ n Becher m

beam /bi:m/ n Balken m; (of light) Strahl m □ vi strahlen. ~ing a [freude]strahlend

bean /bi:n/ n Bohne f; spill the ~s (fam) alles ausplaudern

bear [1] /beə(r)/ n Bär m

bear [2] vt/i (pt bore, pp borne) tragen; (endure) ertragen; gebären ⟨child⟩; ~ right sich rechts halten. ~able /-əbl/ a erträglich

beard /bɪəd/ n Bart m. ~ed a bärtig

bearer /'beərə(r)/ n Träger m; (of news, cheque) Überbringer m; (of passport) Inhaber(in) m(f)

bearing /'beərɪŋ/ n Haltung f; (Techn) Lager nt; have a ~ on von Belang sein für; get one's ~s sich orientieren; lose one's ~s die Orientierung verlieren

beast /bi:st/ n Tier nt; (fam: person) Biest nt

beastly /'bi:stlɪ/ a (-ier, -iest) (fam) scheußlich; ⟨person⟩ gemein

beat /bi:t/ n Schlag m; (of policeman) Runde f; (rhythm) Takt m □ vt/i (pt beat, pp beaten) schlagen; (thrash) verprügeln; klopfen ⟨carpet⟩; (hammer) hämmern (on an + acc); ~ a retreat (Mil) sich zurückziehen; ~ it! (fam) hau ab! it ~s me (fam) das begreife ich nicht. ~ up vt zusammenschlagen

beat|en /'bi:tn/ a off the ~en track abseits. ~ing n Prügel pl

beautician /bju:'tɪʃn/ n Kosmetikerin f

beauti|ful /'bju:tɪfl/ a, ~ly adv schön. ~fy /-faɪ/ vt (pt/pp -ied) verschönern

beauty /'bju:tɪ/ n Schönheit f. ~ parlour n Kosmetiksalon m. ~ spot n Schönheitsfleck m; (place) landschaftlich besonders reizvolles Fleckchen nt

beaver /'bi:və(r)/ n Biber m

became /bɪ'keɪm/ see become

because /bɪ'kɒz/ conj weil □ adv ~ of wegen (+ gen)

beckon /'bekn/ vt/i ~ [to] herbeiwinken

becom|e /bɪ'kʌm/ vt/i (pt became, pp become) werden. ~ing a ⟨clothes⟩ kleidsam

bed /bed/ n Bett nt; (layer) Schicht f; (of flowers) Beet nt; in ~ im Bett; go to ~ ins od zu Bett gehen; ~ and breakfast

Zimmer mit Frühstück. ~clothes npl, ~ding n Bettzeug nt

bedlam /'bedləm/ n Chaos nt

bedpan n Bettpfanne f

bedraggled /bɪ'drægld/ a nass und verschmutzt

bed: ~ridden a bettlägerig. ~room n Schlafzimmer nt

bedside n at his ~ an seinem Bett. ~ 'lamp n Nachttischlampe f. ~ 'rug n Bettvorleger m. ~ 'table n Nachttisch m

bed: ~'sitter n, ~'sitting-room n Wohnschlafzimmer nt. ~spread n Tagesdecke f. ~time n Schlafenszeit f; at ~time vor dem Schlafengehen

bee /biː/ n Biene f

beech /biːtʃ/ n Buche f

beef /biːf/ n Rindfleisch nt. ~burger n Hamburger m

bee: ~hive n Bienenstock m. ~keeper n Imker(in) m(f). ~keeping n Bienenzucht f. ~line n make a ~line for (fam) zusteuern auf (+ acc)

been /biːn/ see be

beer /bɪə(r)/ n Bier nt

beet /biːt/ n (Amer: beetroot) rote Bete f; [sugar] ~ Zuckerrübe f

beetle /'biːtl/ n Käfer m

beetroot n rote Bete f

before /bɪ'fɔː(r)/ prep vor (+ dat/acc); the day ~ yesterday vorgestern; ~ long bald □ adv vorher; (already) schon; never ~ noch nie; ~ that davor □ conj (time) ehe, bevor. ~hand adv vorher, im Voraus

befriend /bɪ'frend/ vt sich anfreunden mit

beg /beg/ v (pt/pp begged) □ vi betteln □ vt (entreat) anflehen; (ask) bitten (for um)

began /bɪ'gæn/ see begin

beggar /'begə(r)/ n Bettler(in) m(f); (fam) Kerl m

begin /bɪ'gɪn/ vt/i (pt began, pp begun, pres p beginning) anfangen, beginnen; to ~ with anfangs. ~ner n Anfänger(in) m(f). ~ning n Anfang m, Beginn m

begonia /bɪ'gəʊnɪə/ n Begonie f

begrudge /bɪ'grʌdʒ/ vt ~ s.o. sth jdm etw missgönnen

beguile /bɪ'gaɪl/ vt betören

begun /bɪ'gʌn/ see begin

behalf /bɪ'hɑːf/ n on ~ of im Namen von; on my ~ meinetwegen

behave /bɪ'heɪv/ vi sich verhalten; ~ one-self sich benehmen

behaviour /bɪ'heɪvjə(r)/ n Verhalten nt; good/bad ~ gutes/schlechtes Benehmen nt; ~ pattern Verhaltensweise f

behead /bɪ'hed/ vt enthaupten

beheld /bɪ'held/ see behold

behind /bɪ'haɪnd/ prep hinter (+ dat/ acc); be ~ sth hinter etw (dat) stecken □ adv hinten; (late) im Rückstand; a long way ~ weit zurück; in the car ~ im Wagen dahinter □ n (fam) Hintern m. ~hand adv im Rückstand

behold /bɪ'həʊld/ vt (pt/pp beheld) (liter) sehen

beholden /bɪ'həʊldn/ a verbunden (to dat)

beige /beɪʒ/ a beige

being /'biːɪŋ/ n Dasein nt; living ~ Lebewesen nt; come into ~ entstehen

belated /bɪ'leɪtɪd/ a, ~ly adv verspätet

belch /beltʃ/ vi rülpsen □ vt ~ out ausstoßen (smoke)

belfry /'belfrɪ/ n Glockenstube f; (tower) Glockenturm m

Belgian /'beldʒən/ a belgisch □ n Belgier(in) m(f)

Belgium /'beldʒəm/ n Belgien nt

belief /bɪ'liːf/ n Glaube m

believable /bɪ'liːvəbl/ a glaubhaft

believe /bɪ'liːv/ vt/i glauben (s.o. jdm; in an + acc). ~r n (Relig) Gläubige(r) m/f

belittle /bɪ'lɪtl/ vt herabsetzen

bell /bel/ n Glocke f; (on door) Klingel f

belligerent /bɪ'lɪdʒərənt/ a Krieg führend; (aggressive) streitlustig

bellow /'beləʊ/ vt/i brüllen

bellows /'beləʊz/ npl Blasebalg m

belly /'belɪ/ n Bauch m

belong /bɪ'lɒŋ/ vi gehören (to dat); (be member) angehören (to dat). ~ings npl Sachen pl

beloved /bɪ'lʌvɪd/ a geliebt □ n Geliebte(r) m/f

below /bɪ'ləʊ/ prep unter (+ dat/acc) □ adv unten; (Naut) unter Deck

belt /belt/ n Gürtel m; (area) Zone f; (Techn) [Treib]riemen m □ vi (fam: rush) rasen □ vt (fam: hit) hauen

bemused /bɪ'mjuːzd/ a verwirrt

bench /bentʃ/ n Bank f; (work-) Werkbank f; the B ~ (Jur) ≈ die Richter pl

bend /bend/ n Biegung f; (in road) Kurve f; round the ~ (fam) verrückt □ v (pt/pp bent) □ vt biegen; beugen (arm, leg) □ vi sich bücken; (thing:) sich biegen; (road:) eine Biegung machen. ~ down vi sich bücken. ~ over vi sich vornüberbeugen

beneath /bɪ'niːθ/ prep unter (+ dat/acc); ~ him (fig) unter seiner Würde; ~ contempt unter aller Würde □ adv darunter

benediction /benɪ'dɪkʃn/ n (Relig) Segen m

benefactor /ˈbenɪfæktə(r)/ n Wohltäter(in) m(f)

beneficial /benɪˈfɪʃl/ a nützlich

beneficiary /benɪˈfɪʃərɪ/ n Begünstigte(r) m/f

benefit /ˈbenɪfɪt/ n Vorteil m; (allowance) Unterstützung f; (insurance) Leistung f; sickness ~ Krankengeld nt □ v (pt/pp -fited, pres p -fiting) □ vt nützen (+ dat) □ vi profitieren (from von)

benevolen|ce /bɪˈnevələns/ n Wohlwollen nt. ~t a, -ly adv wohlwollend

benign /bɪˈnaɪn/ a, -ly adv gütig; (Med) gutartig

bent /bent/ see bend □ a (person) gebeugt; (distorted) verbogen; (fam: dishonest) korrupt; be ~ on doing sth darauf erpicht sein, etw zu tun □ n Hang m, Neigung f (for zu); artistic ~ künstlerische Ader f

be|queath /bɪˈkwiːð/ vt vermachen (to dat). ~quest /-ˈkwest/ n Vermächtnis nt

bereave|d /bɪˈriːvd/ n the ~d pl die Hinterbliebenen. ~ment n Trauerfall m; (state) Trauer f

bereft /bɪˈreft/ a ~ of beraubt (+ gen)

beret /ˈbereɪ/ n Baskenmütze f

Berne /bɜːn/ n Bern nt

berry /ˈberɪ/ n Beere f

berserk /bəˈsɜːk/ a go ~ wild werden

berth /bɜːθ/ n (on ship) [Schlaf]koje f; (ship's anchorage) Liegeplatz m; give a wide ~ to (fam) einen großen Bogen machen um □ vi anlegen

beseech /bɪˈsiːtʃ/ vt (pt/pp beseeched or besought) anflehen

beside /bɪˈsaɪd/ prep neben (+ dat/acc); ~ oneself außer sich (dat)

besides /bɪˈsaɪdz/ prep außer (+ dat) □ adv außerdem

besiege /bɪˈsiːdʒ/ vt belagern

besought /bɪˈsɔːt/ see beseech

bespoke /bɪˈspəʊk/ a (suit) maßgeschneidert

best /best/ a & n beste(r,s); the ~ der/die/das Beste; at ~ bestenfalls; all the ~! alles Gute! do one's ~ sein Bestes tun; the ~ part of a year fast ein Jahr; to the ~ of my knowledge so viel ich weiß; make the ~ of it das Beste daraus machen □ adv am besten; as ~ I could so gut ich konnte. ~ 'man n ≈ Trauzeuge m

bestow /bɪˈstəʊ/ vt schenken (on dat)

best'seller n Bestseller m

bet /bet/ n Wette f □ v (pt/pp bet or betted) □ vt ~ s.o. £5 mit jdm um £5 wetten □ vi wetten; ~ on [Geld] setzen auf (+ acc)

betray /bɪˈtreɪ/ vt verraten. ~al n Verrat m

better /ˈbetə(r)/ a besser; get ~ sich bessern; (after illness) sich erholen □ adv besser; ~ off besser dran; ~ not lieber nicht; all the ~ umso besser; the sooner the ~ je eher, desto besser; think ~ of sth sich eines Besseren besinnen; you'd ~ stay du bleibst am besten hier □ vt verbessern; (do better than) übertreffen; ~ oneself sich verbessern

'betting shop n Wettbüro nt

between /bɪˈtwiːn/ prep zwischen (+ dat/acc); ~ you and me unter uns; ~ us (together) zusammen □ adv [in] ~ dazwischen

beverage /ˈbevərɪdʒ/ n Getränk nt

bevy /ˈbevɪ/ n Schar f

beware /bɪˈweə(r)/ vi sich in Acht nehmen (of vor + dat); ~ of the dog! Vorsicht, bissiger Hund!

bewilder /bɪˈwɪldə(r)/ vt verwirren. ~ment n Verwirrung f

bewitch /bɪˈwɪtʃ/ vt verzaubern; (fig) bezaubern

beyond /bɪˈjɒnd/ prep über (+ acc) ... hinaus; (further) weiter als; ~ reach außer Reichweite; ~ doubt ohne jeden Zweifel; it's ~ me (fam) das geht über meinen Horizont □ adv darüber hinaus

bias /ˈbaɪəs/ n Voreingenommenheit f; (preference) Vorliebe f; (Jur) Befangenheit f; cut on the ~ schräg geschnitten □ vt (pt/pp biased) (influence) beeinflussen. ~ed a voreingenommen; (Jur) befangen

bib /bɪb/ n Lätzchen nt

Bible /ˈbaɪbl/ n Bibel f

biblical /ˈbɪblɪkl/ a biblisch

bibliography /bɪblɪˈɒɡrəfɪ/ n Bibliographie f

bicarbonate /baɪˈkɑːbəneɪt/ n ~ of soda doppeltkohlensaures Natron nt

bicker /ˈbɪkə(r)/ vi sich zanken

bicycle /ˈbaɪsɪkl/ n Fahrrad nt □ vi mit dem Rad fahren

bid[1] /bɪd/ n Gebot nt; (attempt) Versuch m □ vt/i (pt/pp bid, pres p bidding) bieten (for auf + acc); (Cards) reizen

bid[2] vt (pt bade or bid, pp bidden or bid, pres p bidding) (liter) heißen; ~ s.o. welcome jdn willkommen heißen

bidder /ˈbɪdə(r)/ n Bieter(in) m(f)

bide /baɪd/ vt ~ one's time den richtigen Moment abwarten

biennial /baɪˈenɪəl/ a zweijährlich; (lasting two years) zweijährig

bier /bɪə(r)/ n [Toten]bahre f

bifocals /baɪˈfəʊklz/ npl [pair of] ~ Bifokalbrille f

big /bɪɡ/ a (bigger, biggest) groß □ adv talk ~ (fam) angeben

bigam|ist /'bɪgəmɪst/ n Bigamist m. ~y n Bigamie f

big-'headed a (fam) eingebildet

bigot /'bɪgət/ n Eiferer m. ~ed a engstirnig

'bigwig n (fam) hohes Tier nt

bike /baɪk/ n (fam) [Fahr]rad nt

bikini /bɪ'kiːnɪ/ n Bikini m

bilberry /'bɪlbərɪ/ n Heidelbeere f

bile /baɪl/ n Galle f

bilingual /baɪ'lɪŋgwəl/ a zweisprachig

bilious /'bɪljəs/ a (Med) ~ attack verdorbener Magen m

bill[1] /bɪl/ n Rechnung f; (poster) Plakat nt; (Pol) Gesetzentwurf m; (Amer: note) Banknote f; ~ of exchange Wechsel m □ vt eine Rechnung schicken (+ dat)

bill[2] n (break) Schnabel m

billet /'bɪlɪt/ n (Mil) Quartier nt □ vt (pt/pp billeted) einquartieren (on bei)

'billfold n (Amer) Brieftasche f

billiards /'bɪljədz/ n Billard nt

billion /'bɪljən/ n (thousand million) Milliarde f; (million million) Billion f

billy-goat /'bɪlɪ-/ n Ziegenbock m

bin /bɪn/ n Mülleimer m; (for bread) Kasten m

bind /baɪnd/ vt (pt/pp bound) binden (to an + acc); (bandage) verbinden; (Jur) verpflichten; (cover the edge of) einfassen. ~ing a verbindlich □ n Einband m; (braid) Borte f; (on ski) Bindung f

binge /bɪndʒ/ n (fam) go on the ~ eine Sauftour machen

binoculars /bɪ'nɒkjʊləz/ npl [pair of] ~ Fernglas nt

bio|'chemistry /baɪəʊ-/ n Biochemie f. ~degradable /-dɪ'greɪdəbl/ a biologisch abbaubar

biograph|er /baɪ'ɒgrəfə(r)/ n Biograph(in) m(f). ~y n Biographie f

biological /baɪə'lɒdʒɪkl/ a biologisch

biolog|ist /baɪ'ɒlədʒɪst/ n Biologe m. ~y n Biologie f

birch /bɜːtʃ/ n Birke f; (whip) Rute f

bird /bɜːd/ n Vogel m; (fam: girl) Mädchen nt; kill two ~s with one stone zwei Fliegen mit einer Klappe schlagen

Biro (P) /'baɪrəʊ/ n Kugelschreiber m

birth /bɜːθ/ n Geburt f

birth[:] ~ certificate n Geburtsurkunde f. ~-control n Geburtenregelung f. ~day n Geburtstag m. ~mark n Muttermal nt. ~-rate n Geburtenziffer f. ~right n Geburtsrecht nt

biscuit /'bɪskɪt/ n Keks m

bisect /baɪ'sekt/ vt halbieren

bishop /'bɪʃəp/ n Bischof m; (Chess) Läufer m

bit[1] /bɪt/ n Stückchen nt; (for horse) Gebiss nt; (Techn) Bohreinsatz m; a ~ ein bisschen; ~ by ~ nach und nach; a ~ of bread ein bisschen Brot; do one's ~ sein Teil tun

bit[2] see bite

bitch /bɪtʃ/ n Hündin f; (sl) Luder nt. ~y a gehässig

bit|e /baɪt/ n Biss m; (mouthful) Bissen m; (insect) ~ Stich m □ v/i (pt bit, pp bitten) beißen; (insect:) stechen; kauen ⟨one's nails⟩. ~ing a beißend

bitten /'bɪtn/ see bite

bitter /'bɪtə(r)/ a, -ly adv bitter; cry ~ly bitterlich weinen; ~ly cold bitterkalt □ n bitteres Bier nt. ~ness n Bitterkeit f

bitty /'bɪtɪ/ a zusammengestoppelt

bizarre /bɪ'zɑː(r)/ a bizarr

blab /blæb/ vi (pt/pp blabbed) alles ausplaudern

black /blæk/ a (-er, -est) schwarz; be ~ and blue grün und blau sein □ n Schwarz nt; (person) Schwarze(r) m/f □ vt schwärzen; boykottieren (goods). ~ out vt verdunkeln □ vi (lose consciousness) das Bewusstsein verlieren

black[:] ~berry n Brombeere f. ~bird n Amsel f. ~board n (Sch) [Wand]tafel f. ~currant n schwarze Johannisbeere f

blacken vt/i schwärzen

black[:] ~ eye n blaues Auge nt. B~ 'Forest n Schwarzwald m. ~ 'ice n Glatteis nt. ~leg n Streikbrecher m. ~list vt auf die schwarze Liste setzen. ~mail n Erpressung f □ vt erpressen. ~mailer n Erpresser(in) m(f). ~ 'market n schwarzer Markt m. ~out n Verdunkelung f; have a ~out (Med) das Bewusstsein verlieren. ~ 'pudding n Blutwurst f. ~smith n [Huf]schmied m

bladder /'blædə(r)/ n (Anat) Blase f

blade /bleɪd/ n Klinge f; (of grass) Halm m

blame /bleɪm/ n Schuld f □ vt die Schuld geben (+ dat); no one is to ~ keiner ist schuld daran. ~less a schuldlos

blanch /blɑːntʃ/ vi blass werden □ vt (Culin) blanchieren

blancmange /blə'mɒnʒ/ n Pudding m

bland /blænd/ a (-er, -est) mild

blank /blæŋk/ a leer; (look) ausdruckslos □ n Lücke f; (cartridge) Platzpatrone f. ~ 'cheque n Blankoscheck m

blanket /'blæŋkɪt/ n Decke f; wet ~ (fam) Spielverderber(in) m(f)

blank 'verse n Blankvers m

blare /bleə(r)/ vt/i schmettern

blasé /ˈblɑːzeɪ/ a blasiert

blaspheme /blæsˈfiːm/ vi lästern

blasphem|ous /ˈblæsfəməs/ a [gottes]-lästerlich. ~y n [Gottes]lästerung f

blast /blɑːst/ n (gust) Luftstoß m; (sound) Schmettern nt; (of horn) Tuten nt □ vt sprengen □ int (sl) verdammt. ~ed a (sl) verdammt

blast: ~furnace n Hochofen m. ~-off n (of missile) Start m

blatant /ˈbleɪtənt/ a offensichtlich

blaze /bleɪz/ n Feuer nt □ vi brennen

blazer /ˈbleɪzə(r)/ n Blazer m

bleach /bliːtʃ/ n Bleichmittel nt □ vt/i bleichen

bleak /bliːk/ a (-er, -est) öde; (fig) trostlos

bleary-eyed /ˈblɪərɪ-/ a mit trüben/(on waking up) verschlafenen Augen

bleat /bliːt/ vi blöken; (goat:) meckern

bleed /bliːd/ v (pt/pp bled) □ vi bluten □ vt entlüften (radiator)

bleep /bliːp/ n Piepton m □ vi piepsen □ vt mit dem Piepser rufen. ~er n Piepser m

blemish /ˈblemɪʃ/ n Makel m

blend /blend/ n Mischung f □ vt mischen □ vi sich vermischen. ~er n (Culin) Mixer m

bless /bles/ vt segnen. ~ed /ˈblesɪd/ a heilig; (sl) verflixt. ~ing n Segen m

blew /bluː/ see blow²

blight /blaɪt/ n (Bot) Brand m □ vt (spoil) vereiteln

blind /blaɪnd/ a blind; (corner) unübersichtlich; ~ man/woman Blinde(r) m/f □ n [roller] ~ Rouleau nt □ vt blenden

blind: ~ alley n Sackgasse f. ~fold a & adv mit verbundenen Augen □ n Augenbinde f □ vt die Augen verbinden (+ dat). ~ly adv blindlings. ~ness n Blindheit f

blink /blɪŋk/ vi blinzeln; (light:) blinken

blinkers /ˈblɪŋkəz/ npl Scheuklappen pl

bliss /blɪs/ n Glückseligkeit f. ~ful a glücklich

blister /ˈblɪstə(r)/ n (Med) Blase f □ vi (paint:) Blasen werfen

blitz /blɪts/ n Luftangriff m; (fam) Großaktion f

blizzard /ˈblɪzəd/ n Schneesturm m

bloated /ˈbləʊtɪd/ a aufgedunsen

blob /blɒb/ n Klecks m

bloc /blɒk/ n (Pol) Block m

block /blɒk/ n Block m; (of wood) Klotz m; (of flats) [Wohn]block m □ vt blockieren. ~ up vt zustopfen

blockade /blɒˈkeɪd/ n Blockade f □ vt blockieren

blockage /ˈblɒkɪdʒ/ n Verstopfung f

block: ~head n (fam) Dummkopf m. ~ letters npl Blockschrift f

bloke /bləʊk/ n (fam) Kerl m

blonde /blɒnd/ a blond □ n Blondine f

blood /blʌd/ n Blut nt

blood: ~ count n Blutbild nt. ~-curdling a markerschütternd. ~ donor n Blutspender m. ~ group n Blutgruppe f. ~hound n Bluthund m. ~-poisoning n Blutvergiftung f. ~ pressure n Blutdruck m. ~ relative n Blutsverwandte(r) m/f. ~shed n Blutvergießen nt. ~shot a blutunterlaufen. ~ sports npl Jagdsport m. ~-stained a blutbefleckt. ~stream n Blutbahn f. ~ test n Blutprobe f. ~thirsty a blutdürstig. ~ transfusion n Blutübertragung f. ~-vessel n Blutgefäß nt

bloody /ˈblʌdɪ/ a (-ier, -iest) blutig; (sl) verdammt. ~-minded a (sl) stur

bloom /bluːm/ n Blüte f □ vi blühen

bloom|er /ˈbluːmə(r)/ n (fam) Schnitzer m. ~ing a (fam) verdammt

blossom /ˈblɒsəm/ n Blüte f □ vi blühen. ~ out vi (fig) aufblühen

blot /blɒt/ n [Tinten]klecks m; (fig) Fleck m □ vt (pt/pp blotted) löschen. ~ out vt (fig) auslöschen

blotch /blɒtʃ/ n Fleck m. ~y a fleckig

'blotting-paper n Löschpapier nt

blouse /blaʊz/ n Bluse f

blow¹ /bləʊ/ n Schlag m

blow² /bləʊ/ v (pt blew, pp blown) □ vt blasen; (fam: squander) verpulvern; ~ one's nose sich (dat) die Nase putzen □ vi blasen; (fuse:) durchbrennen. ~ away vt wegblasen □ vi wegfliegen. ~ down vt umwehen □ vi umfallen. ~ out vt (extinguish) ausblasen. ~ over vi umfallen; (fig: die down) vorübergehen. ~ up vt (inflate) aufblasen; (enlarge) vergrößern; (shatter by explosion) sprengen □ vi explodieren

blow: ~-dry vt föhnen. ~fly n Schmeißfliege f. ~lamp n Lötlampe f

blown /bləʊn/ see blow²

'blowtorch n (Amer) Lötlampe f

blowy /ˈbləʊɪ/ a windig

bludgeon /ˈblʌdʒn/ vt (fig) zwingen

blue /bluː/ a (-r, -st) blau; feel ~ deprimiert sein □ n Blau nt; have the ~s deprimiert sein; out of the ~ aus heiterem Himmel

blue: ~bell n Sternhyazinthe f. ~berry n Heidelbeere f. ~bottle n Schmeißfliege f. ~ film n Pornofilm m. ~print n (fig) Entwurf m

bluff /blʌf/ n Bluff m □ vi bluffen

blunder /ˈblʌndə(r)/ n Schnitzer m □ vi einen Schnitzer machen

blunt /blʌnt/ a stumpf; ⟨person⟩ geradeheraus. ~ly adv unverblümt, geradeheraus

blur /blɜ:(r)/ n it's all a ~ alles ist verschwommen ▢ vt ⟨pt/pp blurred⟩ verschwommen machen; ~red verschwommen

blurb /blɜ:b/ n Klappentext m

blurt /blɜ:t/ vt ~ out herausplatzen mit

blush /blʌʃ/ n Erröten nt ▢ vi erröten

bluster /'blʌstə(r)/ n Großtuerei f. ~y a windig

boar /bɔ:(r)/ n Eber m

board /bɔ:d/ n Brett nt; ⟨for notices⟩ schwarzes Brett nt; ⟨committee⟩ Ausschuss m; ⟨of directors⟩ Vorstand m; on ~ an Bord; full ~ Vollpension f; ~ and lodging Unterkunft und Verpflegung pl; go by the ~ ⟨fam⟩ unter den Tisch fallen ▢ vt einsteigen in (+ acc); ⟨Naut, Aviat⟩ besteigen ▢ vi an Bord gehen; ~ with in Pension wohnen bei. ~ up vt mit Brettern verschlagen

boarder /'bɔ:də(r)/ n Pensionsgast m; ⟨Sch⟩ Internatsschüler(in) m(f)

board: ~-game n Brettspiel nt. ~inghouse n Pension f. ~ing-school n Internat nt

boast /bəʊst/ vt sich rühmen (+ gen) ▢ vi prahlen (about mit). ~ful a, -ly adv prahlerisch

boat /bəʊt/ n Boot nt; ⟨ship⟩ Schiff nt. ~er n ⟨hat⟩ flacher Strohhut m

bob /bɒb/ n Bubikopf m ▢ vi ⟨pt/pp bobbed⟩ ⟨curtsy⟩ knicksen; ~ up and down sich auf und ab bewegen

bobbin /'bɒbɪn/ n Spule f

bob-sleigh n Bob m

bode /bəʊd/ vi ~ well/ill etwas/nichts Gutes verheißen

bodice /'bɒdɪs/ n Mieder nt

bodily /'bɒdɪlɪ/ a körperlich ▢ adv ⟨forcibly⟩ mit Gewalt

body /'bɒdɪ/ n Körper m; ⟨corpse⟩ Leiche f; ⟨corporation⟩ Körperschaft f; the main ~ der Hauptanteil. ~guard n Leibwächter m. ~work n ⟨Auto⟩ Karosserie f

bog /bɒg/ n Sumpf m ▢ vt ⟨pt/pp bogged⟩ get ~ged down stecken bleiben

boggle /'bɒgl/ vi the mind ~s es ist kaum vorstellbar

bogus /'bəʊgəs/ a falsch

boil¹ /bɔɪl/ n Furunkel m

boil² n bring/come to the ~ zum Kochen bringen/kommen ▢ vt/i kochen; ~ed potatoes Salzkartoffeln pl. ~ down vi ⟨fig⟩ hinauslaufen (to auf + acc). ~ over vi überkochen. ~ up vt aufkochen

boiler /'bɔɪlə(r)/ n Heizkessel m. ~ suit n Overall m

boiling point n Siedepunkt m

boisterous /'bɔɪstərəs/ a übermütig

bold /bəʊld/ a (-er, -est), -ly adv kühn; ⟨Typ⟩ fett. ~ness n Kühnheit f

bollard /'bɒlɑ:d/ n Poller m

bolster /'bəʊlstə(r)/ n Nackenrolle f ▢ vt ~ up Mut machen (+ dat)

bolt /bəʊlt/ n Riegel m; ⟨Techn⟩ Bolzen m; nuts and ~s Schrauben und Muttern pl ▢ vt schrauben (to an + acc); verriegeln ⟨door⟩; hinunterschlingen ⟨food⟩ ▢ vi abhauen; ⟨horse:⟩ durchgehen ▢ adv ~ upright kerzengerade

bomb /bɒm/ n Bombe f ▢ vt bombardieren

bombard /bɒm'bɑ:d/ vt beschießen; ⟨fig⟩ bombardieren

bombastic /bɒm'bæstɪk/ a bombastisch

bomb|er /'bɒmə(r)/ n ⟨Aviat⟩ Bomber m; ⟨person⟩ Bombenleger(in) m(f). ~shell n be a ~shell ⟨fig⟩ wie eine Bombe einschlagen

bond /bɒnd/ n ⟨fig⟩ Band nt; ⟨Comm⟩ Obligation f; be in ~ unter Zollverschluss stehen

bondage /'bɒndɪdʒ/ n ⟨fig⟩ Sklaverei f

bone /bəʊn/ n Knochen m; ⟨of fish⟩ Gräte f ▢ vt von den Knochen lösen ⟨meat⟩; entgräten ⟨fish⟩. ~-'dry a knochentrocken

bonfire /'bɒn-/ n Gartenfeuer nt; ⟨celebratory⟩ Freudenfeuer nt

bonnet /'bɒnɪt/ n Haube f

bonus /'bəʊnəs/ n Prämie f; ⟨gratuity⟩ Gratifikation f; ⟨fig⟩ Plus nt

bony /'bəʊnɪ/ a (-ier, -iest) knochig; ⟨fish⟩ grätig

boo /bu:/ int buh! ▢ vt ausbuhen ▢ vi buhen

boob /bu:b/ n ⟨fam: mistake⟩ Schnitzer m ▢ vi ⟨fam⟩ einen Schnitzer machen

book /bʊk/ n Buch nt; ⟨of tickets⟩ Heft nt; keep the ~s ⟨Comm⟩ die Bücher führen ▢ vt/i buchen; ⟨reserve⟩ [vor]bestellen; ⟨for offence⟩ aufschreiben. ~able /-əbl/ a im Vorverkauf erhältlich

book: ~case n Bücherregal nt. ~ends npl Buchstützen pl. ~ing-office in Fahrkartenschalter m. ~keeping n Buchführung f. ~let n Broschüre f. ~maker n Buchmacher m. ~mark n Lesezeichen nt. ~seller n Buchhändler(in) m(f). ~shop n Buchhandlung f. ~stall n Bücherstand m. ~worm n Bücherwurm m

boom /bu:m/ n ⟨Comm⟩ Hochkonjunktur f; ⟨upturn⟩ Aufschwung m ▢ vi dröhnen; ⟨fig⟩ blühen

boon /bu:n/ n Segen m

boor /bʊə(r)/ n Flegel m. ~ish a flegelhaft

boost /buːst/ n Auftrieb m □ vt Auftrieb geben (+ dat). ∼er n (Med) Nachimpfung f

boot /buːt/ n Stiefel m; (Auto) Kofferraum m

booth /buːð/ n Bude f; (cubicle) Kabine f

booty /'buːti/ n Beute f

booze /buːz/ n (fam) Alkohol m □ vi (fam) saufen

border /'bɔːdə(r)/ n Rand m; (frontier) Grenze f; (in garden) Rabatte f □ vi ∼ on grenzen an (+ acc). ∼line n Grenzlinie f. ∼line case n Grenzfall m

bore[1] /bɔː(r)/ see bear[2]

bore[2] vt/i (Techn) bohren

bor|e[3] n (of gun) Kaliber nt; (person) langweiliger Mensch m; (thing) langweilige Sache f □ vt langweilen; be ∼ed sich langweilen. ∼edom n Langeweile f. ∼ing a langweilig

born /bɔːn/ pp be ∼ geboren werden □ a geboren

borne /bɔːn/ see bear[2]

borough /'bʌrə/ n Stadtgemeinde f

borrow /'bɒrəʊ/ vt [sich (dat)] borgen od leihen (from von)

bosom /'bʊzm/ n Busen m

boss /bɒs/ n (fam) Chef m □ vt herumkommandieren. ∼y a herrschsüchtig

botanical /bə'tænɪkl/ a botanisch

botan|ist /'bɒtənɪst/ n Botaniker(in) m(f). ∼y n Botanik f

botch /bɒtʃ/ vt verpfuschen

both /bəʊθ/ a & pron beide; ∼ [of] the children beide Kinder; ∼ of them beide [von ihnen] □ adv ∼ men and women sowohl Männer als auch Frauen

bother /'bɒðə(r)/ n Mühe f; (minor trouble) Ärger m □ int (fam) verflixt! □ vt belästigen; (disturb) stören □ vi sich kümmern (about um); don't ∼ nicht nötig

bottle /'bɒtl/ n Flasche f □ vt auf Flaschen abfüllen; (preserve) einmachen. ∼ up vt (fig) in sich (dat) aufstauen

bottle: ∼neck n (fig) Engpass m. ∼opener n Flaschenöffner m

bottom /'bɒtəm/ a unterste(r,s) □ n (of container) Boden m; (of river) Grund m; (of page, hill) Fuß m; (buttocks) Hintern m; at the ∼ unten; get to the ∼ of sth (fig) hinter etw (acc) kommen. ∼less a bodenlos

bough /baʊ/ n Ast m

bought /bɔːt/ see buy

boulder /'bəʊldə(r)/ n Felsblock m

bounce /baʊns/ vi [auf]springen; (cheque:) (fam) nicht gedeckt sein □ vt aufspringen lassen (ball)

bouncer /'baʊnsə(r)/ n (fam) Rausschmeißer m

bouncing /'baʊnsɪŋ/ a ∼ baby strammer Säugling m

bound[1] /baʊnd/ n Sprung m □ vi springen

bound[2] see bind □ a ∼ for (ship) mit Kurs auf (+ acc); be ∼ to do sth etw bestimmt machen; (obliged) verpflichtet sein, etw zu machen

boundary /'baʊndərɪ/ n Grenze f

boundless a grenzenlos

bounds /baʊndz/ npl (fig) Grenzen pl; out of ∼ verboten

bouquet /bʊ'keɪ/ n [Blumen]strauß m; (of wine) Bukett nt

bourgeois /'bʊəʒwɑː/ a (pej) spießbürgerlich

bout /baʊt/ n (Med) Anfall m; (Sport) Kampf m

bow[1] /bəʊ/ n (weapon & Mus) Bogen m; (knot) Schleife f

bow[2] /baʊ/ n Verbeugung f □ vi sich verbeugen □ vt neigen (head)

bow[3] /baʊ/ n (Naut) Bug m

bowel /'baʊəl/ n Darm m; ∼s pl Eingeweide pl; (digestion) Verdauung f

bowl[1] /bəʊl/ n Schüssel f; (shallow) Schale f; (of pipe) Kopf m; (of spoon) Schöpfteil m

bowl[2] n (ball) Kugel f □ vt/i werfen. ∼ over vt umwerfen

bow-legged /bəʊ'legd/ a O-beinig

bowler[1] /'bəʊlə(r)/ n (Sport) Werfer m

bowler[2] ∼ [hat] Melone f

bowling /'bəʊlɪŋ/ n Kegeln nt. ∼-alley n Kegelbahn f

bowls /bəʊlz/ n Bowlsspiel nt

bow-'tie /bəʊ-/ n Fliege f

box[1] /bɒks/ n Schachtel f; (wooden) Kiste f; (cardboard) Karton m; (Theat) Loge f

box[2] vt/i (Sport) boxen; ∼ s.o.'s ears jdn ohrfeigen

box|er /'bɒksə(r)/ n Boxer m. ∼ing n Boxen nt. B∼ing Day n zweiter Weihnachtstag m

box: ∼-office n (Theat) Kasse f. ∼-room n Abstellraum m

boy /bɔɪ/ n Junge m

boycott /'bɔɪkɒt/ n Boykott m □ vt boykottieren

boy: ∼friend n Freund m. ∼ish a jungenhaft

bra /brɑː/ n BH m

brace /breɪs/ n Strebe f, Stütze f; (dental) Zahnspange f; ∼s npl Hosenträger mpl □ vt ∼ oneself sich stemmen (against gegen); (fig) sich gefasst machen (for auf + acc)

bracelet /'breɪslɪt/ n Armband nt

bracing /'breɪsɪŋ/ a stärkend

bracken /'brækn/ n Farnkraut nt

bracket /'brækɪt/ n Konsole f; (group) Gruppe f; round/square ~s (Typ) runde/eckige Klammern □ vt einklammern

brag /bræg/ vi (pt/pp bragged) prahlen (about mit)

braid /breɪd/ n Borte f

braille /breɪl/ n Blindenschrift f

brain /breɪn/ n Gehirn nt; ~s (fig) Intelligenz f

brain: ~child n geistiges Produkt nt. ~less a dumm. ~wash vt einer Gehirnwäsche unterziehen. ~wave n Geistesblitz m

brainy /'breɪnɪ/ a (-ier, -iest) klug

braise /breɪz/ vt schmoren

brake /breɪk/ n Bremse f □ vt/i bremsen. ~light n Bremslicht nt

bramble /'bræmbl/ n Brombeerstrauch m

bran /bræn/ n Kleie f

branch /brɑːntʃ/ n Ast m; (fig) Zweig m; (Comm) Zweigstelle f; (shop) Filiale f □ vi sich gabeln. ~ off vi abzweigen. ~ out vi ~ out into sich verlegen auf (+ acc)

brand /brænd/ n Marke f; (on animal) Brandzeichen nt □ vt mit dem Brandeisen zeichnen (animal); (fig) brandmarken

brandish /'brændɪʃ/ vt schwingen

brand-'new a nagelneu

brandy /'brændɪ/ n Weinbrand m

brash /bræʃ/ a nassforsch

brass /brɑːs/ n Messing nt; (Mus) Blech nt; get down to ~ tacks (fam) zur Sache kommen; top ~ (fam) hohe Tiere pl. ~ band n Blaskapelle f

brassiere /'bræzɪə(r)/ n Büstenhalter m

brassy /'brɑːsɪ/ a (-ier, -iest) (fam) ordinär

brat /bræt/ n (pej) Balg nt

bravado /brə'vɑːdəʊ/ n Forschheit f

brave /breɪv/ a (-r, -st), -ly adv tapfer □ vt die Stirn bieten (+ dat). ~ry /-ərɪ/ n Tapferkeit f

bravo /brɑː'vəʊ/ int bravo!

brawl /brɔːl/ n Schlägerei f □ vi sich schlagen

brawn /brɔːn/ n (Culin) Sülze f

brawny /'brɔːnɪ/ a muskulös

bray /breɪ/ vi iahen

brazen /'breɪzn/ a unverschämt

brazier /'breɪzɪə(r)/ n Kohlenbecken nt

Brazil /brə'zɪl/ n Brasilien nt. ~ian a brasilianisch. ~ nut n Paranuss f

breach /briːtʃ/ n Bruch m; (Mil & fig) Bresche f; ~ of contract Vertragsbruch m □ vt durchbrechen; brechen (contract)

bread /bred/ n Brot nt; slice of ~ and butter Butterbrot nt

bread: ~crumbs npl Brotkrümel pl; (Culin) Paniermehl nt. ~line n be on the ~line gerade genug zum Leben haben

breadth /bredθ/ n Breite f

'**bread-winner** n Brotverdiener m

break /breɪk/ n Bruch m; (interval) Pause f; (interruption) Unterbrechung f; (fam: chance) Chance f □ v (pt broke, pp broken) □ vt brechen; (smash) zerbrechen; (damage) kaputtmachen (fam); (interrupt) unterbrechen; ~ one's arm sich (dat) den Arm brechen □ vi brechen; (day:) anbrechen; (storm:) losbrechen; (thing:) kaputtgehen (fam); (rope, thread:) reißen; (news:) bekannt werden; his voice is ~ing er ist im Stimmbruch. ~ away vi sich losreißen; (fig) sich absetzen (from von). ~ down vi zusammenbrechen; (Techn) eine Panne haben; (negotiations:) scheitern □ vt aufbrechen (door); aufgliedern (figures). ~ in vi einbrechen. ~ off vt/i abbrechen; lösen (engagement). ~ out vi ausbrechen. ~ up vt zerbrechen □ vi zerbrechen; (crowd:) sich zerstreuen; (marriage, couple:) auseinander gehen; (Sch) Ferien bekommen

break|able /'breɪkəbl/ a zerbrechlich. ~age /-ɪdʒ/ n Bruch m. ~down n (Techn) Panne f; (Med) Zusammenbruch m; (of figures) Aufgliederung f. ~er n (wave) Brecher m

breakfast /'brekfəst/ n Frühstück nt

break: ~through n Durchbruch m. ~water n Buhne f

breast /brest/ n Brust f. ~bone n Brustbein nt. ~feed vt stillen. ~stroke n Brustschwimmen nt

breath /breθ/ n Atem m; out of ~ außer Atem; under one's ~ vor sich (acc) hin

breathalyse /'breθəlaɪz/ vt ins Röhrchen blasen lassen. ~r (P) n Röhrchen nt. ~r test n Alcotest (P) m

breathe /briːð/ vt/i atmen. ~ in vt/i einatmen. ~ out vt/i ausatmen

breath|er /'briːðə(r)/ n Atempause f. ~ing n Atmen nt

breath /'breθ-/: ~less a atemlos. ~-taking a atemberaubend. ~ test n Alcotest (P) m

bred /bred/ see breed

breeches /'brɪtʃɪz/ npl Kniehose f; (for riding) Reithose f

breed /briːd/ n Rasse f □ v (pt/pp bred) □ vt züchten; (give rise to) erzeugen □ vi sich vermehren. ~er n Züchter m. ~ing n Zucht f; ⟨fig⟩ [gute] Lebensart f

breez|e /briːz/ n Lüftchen nt; ⟨Naut⟩ Brise f. ~y a [leicht] windig

brevity /'brevəti/ n Kürze f

brew /bruː/ n Gebräu nt □ vt brauen; kochen ⟨tea⟩ □ vi ⟨fig⟩ sich zusammenbrauen. ~er n Brauer m. ~ery n Brauerei f

bribe /braɪb/ n ⟨money⟩ Bestechungsgeld nt □ vt bestechen. ~ry /-əri/ n Bestechung f

brick /brɪk/ n Ziegelstein m, Backstein m □ vt ~ up zumauern

'bricklayer n Maurer m

bridal /'braɪdl/ a Braut-

bride /braɪd/ n Braut f. ~groom n Bräutigam m. ~smaid n Brautjungfer f

bridge¹ /brɪdʒ/ n Brücke f; ⟨of nose⟩ Nasenrücken m; ⟨of spectacles⟩ Steg m □ vt ⟨fig⟩ überbrücken

bridge² n ⟨Cards⟩ Bridge nt

bridle /'braɪdl/ n Zaum m. ~-path n Reitweg m

brief¹ /briːf/ a (-er, -est) kurz; be ~ ⟨person:⟩ sich kurz fassen

brief² n Instruktionen pl; ⟨Jur: case⟩ Mandat nt □ vt Instruktionen geben (+ dat); ⟨Jur⟩ beauftragen. ~case n Aktentasche f

brief|ing /'briːfɪŋ/ n Informationsgespräch nt. ~ly adv kurz. ~ness n Kürze f

briefs /briːfs/ npl Slip m

brigad|e /brɪ'geɪd/ n Brigade f. ~ier /-ə'dɪə(r)/ n Brigadegeneral m

bright /braɪt/ a (-er, -est), -ly adv hell; ⟨day⟩ heiter; ~ red hellrot

bright|en /'braɪtn/ v ~en [up] □ vt aufheitern □ vi sich aufheitern. ~ness n Helligkeit f

brilliance /'brɪljəns/ n Glanz m; ⟨of person⟩ Genialität f

brilliant /'brɪljənt/ a, -ly adv glänzend; ⟨person⟩ genial

brim /brɪm/ n Rand m; ⟨of hat⟩ Krempe f □ vi (pt/pp brimmed) ~ over überfließen

brine /braɪn/ n Salzwasser nt; ⟨Culin⟩ [Salz]lake f

bring /brɪŋ/ vt (pt/pp brought) bringen; ~ them with you bring sie mit; I can't b~ myself to do it ich bringe es nicht fertig. ~ about vt verursachen. ~ along vt mitbringen. ~ back vt zurückbringen. ~ down vt herunterbringen; senken ⟨price⟩. ~ off vt vollbringen. ~ on vt ⟨cause⟩ verursachen. ~ out vt herausbringen. ~ round vt vorbeibringen; ⟨persuade⟩ überreden; wieder zum

Bewusstsein bringen ⟨unconscious person⟩. ~ up vt heraufbringen; ⟨vomit⟩ erbrechen; aufziehen ⟨children⟩; erwähnen ⟨question⟩

brink /brɪŋk/ n Rand m

brisk /brɪsk/ a (-er, -est,) -ly adv lebhaft; ⟨quick⟩ schnell

brist|le /'brɪsl/ n Borste f. ~ly a borstig

Brit|ain /'brɪtn/ n Großbritannien nt. ~ish a britisch; the ~ish die Briten pl. ~on n Brite m/Britin f

Brittany /'brɪtəni/ n die Bretagne

brittle /'brɪtl/ a brüchig, spröde

broach /brəʊtʃ/ vt anzapfen; anschneiden ⟨subject⟩

broad /brɔːd/ a (-er, -est) breit; ⟨hint⟩ deutlich; in ~ daylight am helllichten Tag. ~ beans npl dicke Bohnen pl

'broadcast n Sendung f □ vt/i (pt/pp -cast) senden. ~er n Rundfunk- und Fernsehpersönlichkeit f. ~ing n Funk und Fernsehen pl

broaden /'brɔːdn/ vt verbreitern; ⟨fig⟩ erweitern □ vi sich verbreitern

broadly /'brɔːdli/ adv breit; ~ speaking allgemein gesagt

broad'minded a tolerant

brocade /brə'keɪd/ n Brokat m

broccoli /'brɒkəli/ n inv Brokkoli pl

brochure /'brəʊʃə(r)/ n Broschüre f

brogue /brəʊg/ n ⟨shoe⟩ Wanderschuh m; Irish ~ irischer Akzent m

broke /brəʊk/ see break □ a ⟨fam⟩ pleite

broken /'brəʊkn/ see break □ a zerbrochen, ⟨fam⟩ kaputt; ~ English gebrochenes Englisch nt. ~-hearted a untröstlich

broker /'brəʊkə(r)/ n Makler m

brolly /'brɒli/ n ⟨fam⟩ Schirm m

bronchitis /brɒŋ'kaɪtɪs/ n Bronchitis f

bronze /brɒnz/ n Bronze f

brooch /brəʊtʃ/ n Brosche f

brood /bruːd/ n Brut f □ vi brüten; ⟨fig⟩ grübeln

brook¹ /brʊk/ n Bach m

brook² vt dulden

broom /bruːm/ n Besen m; ⟨Bot⟩ Ginster m. ~stick n Besenstiel m

broth /brɒθ/ n Brühe f

brothel /'brɒθl/ n Bordell nt

brother /'brʌðə(r)/ n Bruder m

brother: ~-in-law n (pl ~s-in-law) Schwager m. ~ly a brüderlich

brought /brɔːt/ see bring

brow /braʊ/ n Augenbraue f; ⟨forehead⟩ Stirn f; ⟨of hill⟩ [Berg]kuppe f

'browbeat vt (pt -beat, pp -beaten) einschüchtern

brown /braʊn/ a (-er, -est) braun; ~ 'paper Packpapier nt ☐ n Braun nt ☐ vt bräunen ☐ vi braun werden

Brownie /'braʊnɪ/ n Wichtel m

browse /braʊz/ vi (read) schmökern; (in shop) sich umsehen

bruise /bruːz/ n blauer Fleck m ☐ vt beschädigen (fruit); ~ one's arm sich (dat) den Arm quetschen

brunch /brʌntʃ/ n Brunch m

brunette /bruː'net/ n Brünette f

Brunswick /'brʌnzwɪk/ n Braunschweig nt

brunt /brʌnt/ n the ~ of die volle Wucht (+ gen)

brush /brʌʃ/ n Bürste f; (with handle) Handfeger m; (for paint, pastry) Pinsel m; (bushes) Unterholz nt; (fig: conflict) Zusammenstoß m ☐ vt bürsten putzen (teeth); ~ against streifen [gegen]; ~ aside (fig) abtun; ~ off vt abbürsten; (reject) zurückweisen; ~ up vt/i (fig) ~ up [on] auffrischen

brusque /brʊsk/ a, -ly adv brüsk

Brussels /'brʌslz/ n Brüssel nt. ~ sprouts npl Rosenkohl m

brutal /'bruːtl/ a, -ly adv brutal. ~ity /-'tælətɪ/ n Brutalität f

brute /bruːt/ n Unmensch m. ~ force n rohe Gewalt f

B.Sc. abbr of Bachelor of Science

bubble /'bʌbl/ n [Luft]blase f ☐ vi sprudeln

buck¹ /bʌk/ n (deer & Gym) Bock m; (rabbit) Rammler m ☐ vi (horse:) bocken. ~ up vi (fam) sich aufheitern; (hurry) sich beeilen

buck² n (Amer, fam) Dollar m

buck³ n pass the ~ die Verantwortung abschieben

bucket /'bʌkɪt/ n Eimer m

buckle /'bʌkl/ n Schnalle f ☐ vt zuschnallen ☐ vi sich verbiegen

bud /bʌd/ n Knospe f ☐ vi (pt/pp budded) knospen

Buddhis|m /'bʊdɪzm/ n Buddhismus m. ~t a buddhistisch ☐ n Buddhist(in) m(f)

buddy /'bʌdɪ/ n (fam) Freund m

budge /bʌdʒ/ vt bewegen ☐ vi sich [von der Stelle] rühren

budgerigar /'bʌdʒərɪɡɑː(r)/ n Wellensittich m

budget /'bʌdʒɪt/ n Budget nt; (Pol) Haushaltsplan m; (money available) Etat m ☐ vi (pt/pp budgeted) ~ for sth etw einkalkulieren

buff /bʌf/ a (colour) sandfarben ☐ n Sandfarbe f; (Amer, fam) Fan m ☐ vt polieren

buffalo /'bʌfələʊ/ n (inv or pl -es) Büffel m

buffer /'bʌfə(r)/ n (Rail) Puffer m; old ~ (fam) alter Knacker m; ~ zone Pufferzone f

buffet¹ /'bʊfeɪ/ n Büfett nt; (on station) Imbissstube f

buffet² /'bʌfɪt/ vt (pt/pp buffeted) hin und her werfen

buffoon /bə'fuːn/ n Narr m

bug /bʌɡ/ n Wanze f; (fam: virus) Bazillus m; (fam: device) Abhörgerät nt, (fam) Wanze f ☐ vt (pt/pp bugged) (fam) verwanzen (room); abhören (telephone); (Amer: annoy) ärgern

buggy /'bʌɡɪ/ n [Kinder]sportwagen m

bugle /'bjuːɡl/ n Signalhorn nt

build /bɪld/ n (of person) Körperbau m ☐ vt/i (pt/pp built) bauen. ~ on vt anbauen (to an + acc). ~ up vt aufbauen ☐ vi zunehmen; (traffic:) sich stauen

builder /'bɪldə(r)/ n Bauunternehmer m

building /'bɪldɪŋ/ n Gebäude nt. ~ site n Baustelle f. ~ society n Bausparkasse f

built /bɪlt/ see build. ~-in a eingebaut. ~-in 'cupboard n Einbauschrank m. ~-up area n bebautes Gebiet nt; (Auto) geschlossene Ortschaft f

bulb /bʌlb/ n [Blumen]zwiebel f; (Electr) [Glüh]birne f

bulbous /'bʌlbəs/ a bauchig

Bulgaria /bʌl'ɡeərɪə/ n Bulgarien nt

bulge /bʌldʒ/ n Ausbauchung f ☐ vi sich ausbauchen. ~ing a prall; (eyes) hervorquellend; ~ing with prall gefüllt mit

bulk /bʌlk/ n Masse f; (greater part) Hauptteil m; in ~ en gros; (loose) lose. ~y a sperrig; (large) massig

bull /bʊl/ n Bulle m, Stier m

'bulldog n Bulldogge f

bulldozer /'bʊldəʊzə(r)/ n Planierraupe f

bullet /'bʊlɪt/ n Kugel f

bulletin /'bʊlɪtɪn/ n Bulletin nt

'bullet-proof a kugelsicher

'bullfight n Stierkampf m. ~er n Stierkämpfer m

'bullfinch n Dompfaff m

bullion /'bʊlɪən/ n gold ~ Barrengold nt

bullock /'bʊlək/ n Ochse m

bull: ~ring n Stierkampfarena f. ~'s-eye n score a ~'s-eye ins Schwarze treffen

bully /'bʊlɪ/ n Tyrann m ☐ vt tyrannisieren

bum¹ /bʌm/ n (sl) Hintern m

bum² n (Amer, fam) Landstreicher m

bumble-bee /'bʌmbl-/ n Hummel f

bump /bʌmp/ n Bums m; (swelling) Beule f; (in road) holperige Stelle f ▢ vt stoßen; ~ into stoßen gegen; (meet) zufällig treffen. ~ off vt (fam) um die Ecke bringen

bumper /ˈbʌmpə(r)/ a Rekord- ▢ n (Auto) Stoßstange f

bumpkin /ˈbʌmpkɪn/ n country ~ Tölpel m

bumptious /ˈbʌmpʃəs/ a aufgeblasen

bumpy /ˈbʌmpɪ/ a holperig

bun /bʌn/ n Milchbrötchen nt; (hair) [Haar]knoten m

bunch /bʌntʃ/ n (of flowers) Strauß m; (of radishes, keys) Bund m; (of people) Gruppe f; ~ of grapes [ganze] Weintraube f

bundle /ˈbʌndl/ n Bündel nt ▢ vt ~ [up] bündeln

bung /bʌŋ/ vt (fam) (throw) schmeißen. ~ up vt (fam) verstopfen

bungalow /ˈbʌŋgələʊ/ n Bungalow m

bungle /ˈbʌŋgl/ vt verpfuschen

bunion /ˈbʌnjən/ n (Med) Ballen m

bunk /bʌŋk/ n [Schlaf]koje f. ~-beds npl Etagenbett nt

bunker /ˈbʌŋkə(r)/ n Bunker m

bunkum /ˈbʌŋkəm/ n Quatsch m

bunny /ˈbʌnɪ/ n (fam) Kaninchen nt

buoy /bɔɪ/ n Boje f. ~ up vt (fig) stärken

buoyan|cy /ˈbɔɪənsɪ/ n Auftrieb m. ~t a be ~t schwimmen; (water:) gut tragen

burden /ˈbɜːdn/ n Last f ▢ vt belasten. ~some /-səm/ a lästig

bureau /ˈbjʊərəʊ/ n (pl -x /-əʊz/ or ~s) (desk) Sekretär m; (office) Büro nt

bureaucracy /bjʊəˈrɒkrəsɪ/ n Bürokratie f

bureaucrat /ˈbjʊərəkræt/ n Bürokrat m. ~ic /-ˈkrætɪk/ a bürokratisch

burger /ˈbɜːgə(r)/ n Hamburger m

burglar /ˈbɜːglə(r)/ n Einbrecher m. ~ alarm n Alarmanlage f

burglar|ize /ˈbɜːgləraɪz/ vt (Amer) einbrechen in (+ acc). ~y n Einbruch m

burgle /ˈbɜːgl/ vt einbrechen in (+ acc); they have been ~d bei ihnen ist eingebrochen worden

Burgundy /ˈbɜːgəndɪ/ n Burgund nt; b~ (wine) Burgunder m

burial /ˈberɪəl/ n Begräbnis nt

burlesque /bɜːˈlesk/ n Burleske f

burly /ˈbɜːlɪ/ a (-ier, -iest) stämmig

Burm|a /ˈbɜːmə/ n Birma nt. ~ese /-ˈmiːz/ a birmanisch

burn /bɜːn/ n Verbrennung f; (on skin) Brandwunde f; (on material) Brandstelle f ▢ v (pt/pp burnt or burned) ▢ vt verbrennen ▢ vi brennen; (food:) anbrennen. ~ down vt/i niederbrennen

burnish /ˈbɜːnɪʃ/ vt polieren

burnt /bɜːnt/ see burn

burp /bɜːp/ vi (fam) aufstoßen

burrow /ˈbʌrəʊ/ n Bau m ▢ vi wühlen

bursar /ˈbɜːsə(r)/ n Rechnungsführer m. ~y n Stipendium nt

burst /bɜːst/ n Bruch m; (surge) Ausbruch m ▢ v (pt/pp burst) ▢ vt platzen machen ▢ vi platzen; (bud:) aufgehen; ~ into tears in Tränen ausbrechen

bury /ˈberɪ/ vt (pt/pp -ied) begraben; (hide) vergraben

bus /bʌs/ n [Auto]bus m ▢ vt/i (pt/pp bussed) mit dem Bus fahren

bush /bʊʃ/ n Strauch m; (land) Busch m. ~y a (-ier, -iest) buschig

busily /ˈbɪzɪlɪ/ adv eifrig

business /ˈbɪznɪs/ n Angelegenheit f; (Comm) Geschäft nt; on ~ geschäftlich; he has no ~ er hat kein Recht (to zu); mind one's own ~ sich um seine eigenen Angelegenheiten kümmern; that's none of your ~ das geht Sie nichts an. ~-like a geschäftsmäßig. ~man n Geschäftsmann m

busker /ˈbʌskə(r)/ n Straßenmusikant m

'bus-stop n Bushaltestelle f

bust¹ /bʌst/ n Büste f. ~ size n Oberweite f

bust² a (fam) kaputt; go ~ Pleite gehen ▢ v (pt/pp busted or bust) (fam) ▢ vt kaputtmachen ▢ vt kaputtgehen

bustl|e /ˈbʌsl/ n Betrieb m, Getriebe nt ▢ vi ~e about geschäftig hin und her laufen. ~ing a belebt

'bust-up n (fam) Streit m, Krach m

busy /ˈbɪzɪ/ a (-ier, -iest) beschäftigt; (day) voll; (street) belebt; (with traffic) stark befahren; (Amer Teleph) besetzt; be ~ zu tun haben ▢ vt ~ oneself sich beschäftigen (with mit)

'busybody n Wichtigtuer(in) m(f)

but /bʌt, unbetont bət/ conj aber; (after negative) sondern ▢ prep außer (+ dat); for (without) ohne (+ acc); the last ~ one der/die/das vorletzte; the next ~ one der/die/das übernächste ▢ adv nur

butcher /ˈbʊtʃə(r)/ n Fleischer m, Metzger m; ~'s [shop] Fleischerei f, Metzgerei f ▢ vt [ab]schlachten

butler /ˈbʌtlə(r)/ n Butler m

butt /bʌt/ n (of gun) [Gewehr]kolben m; (fig: target) Zielscheibe f; (of cigarette) Stummel m; (for water) Regentonne f ▢ vt mit dem Kopf stoßen ▢ vi ~ in unterbrechen

butter /'bʌtə(r)/ n Butter f ◻ vt mit Butter bestreichen. ~ **up** vt (fam) schmeicheln (+ dat)

butter: ~**cup** a Butterblume f, Hahnenfuß m. ~**fly** n Schmetterling m

buttocks /'bʌtəks/ npl Gesäß nt

button /'bʌtn/ n Knopf m ◻ vt ~ [up] zuknöpfen ◻ vi geknöpft werden. ~**hole** n Knopfloch nt

buttress /'bʌtrɪs/ n Strebepfeiler m; flying ~ Strebebogen m

buxom /'bʌksəm/ a drall

buy /baɪ/ n Kauf m ◻ vt (pt/pp bought) kaufen. ~**er** n Käufer(in) m(f)

buzz /bʌz/ n Summen nt ◻ vi summen. ~ **off** vi (fam) abhauen

buzzard /'bʌzəd/ n Bussard m

buzzer /'bʌzə(r)/ n Summer m

by /baɪ/ prep (close to) bei (+ dat); (next to) neben (+ dat/acc); (past) an (+ dat) ... vorbei; (to the extent of) um (+ acc); (at the latest) bis; (by means of) durch; by Mozart/Dickens von Mozart/Dickens; ~ oneself allein; ~ the sea am Meer; ~ car/bus mit dem Auto/Bus; ~ sea mit dem Schiff; ~ day/night bei Tag/Nacht; ~ the hour pro Stunde; ~ the metre meterweise; six metres ~ four sechs mal vier Meter; win ~ a length mit einer Länge Vorsprung gewinnen; miss the train ~ a minute den Zug um eine Minute verpassen ◻ adv ~ and ~ mit der Zeit; ~ and large im Großen und Ganzen; put ~ beiseite legen; go/pass ~ vorbeigehen

bye /baɪ/ int (fam) tschüs

by: ~-**election** n Nachwahl f. ~**gone** a vergangen. ~-**law** n Verordnung f. ~**pass** n Umgehungsstraße f; (Med) Bypass m ◻ vt umfahren. ~**product** n Nebenprodukt nt. ~-**road** n Nebenstraße f. ~**stander** n Zuschauer(in) m(f)

Byzantine /bɪ'zæntaɪn/ a byzantinisch

C

cab /kæb/ n Taxi nt; (of lorry, train) Führerhaus nt

cabaret /'kæbəreɪ/ n Kabarett nt

cabbage /'kæbɪdʒ/ n Kohl m

cabin /'kæbɪn/ n Kabine f; (hut) Hütte f

cabinet /'kæbɪnɪt/ n Schrank m; (TV, Radio) Gehäuse nt; C~ (Pol) Kabinett nt; [display] ~ Vitrine f; ~-**maker** n Möbeltischler m

cable /'keɪbl/ n Kabel nt; (rope) Tau nt. ~ '**railway** n Seilbahn f. ~ '**television** n Kabelfernsehen nt

cache /kæʃ/ n Versteck nt; ~ **of arms** Waffenlager nt

cackle /'kækl/ vi gackern

cactus /'kæktəs/ n (pl -ti /-taɪ/ or -tuses) Kaktus m

caddie /'kædɪ/ n Caddie m

caddy /'kædɪ/ n [tea-]~ Teedose f

cadet /kə'det/ n Kadett m

cadge /kædʒ/ vt/i (fam) schnorren

Caesarean /sɪ'zeərɪən/ a & n ~ [section] Kaiserschnitt m

café /'kæfeɪ/ n Café nt

cafeteria /kæfə'tɪərɪə/ n Selbstbedienungsrestaurant nt

caffeine /'kæfiːn/ n Koffein nt

cage /keɪdʒ/ n Käfig m

cagey /'keɪdʒɪ/ a (fam) **be** ~ mit der Sprache nicht herauswollen

cajole /kə'dʒəʊl/ vt gut zureden (+ dat)

cake /keɪk/ n Kuchen m; (of soap) Stück nt. ~**d** a verkrustet (with mit)

calamity /kə'læmətɪ/ n Katastrophe f

calcium /'kælsɪəm/ n Kalzium nt

calculat|e /'kælkjuleɪt/ vt berechnen; (estimate) kalkulieren. ~**ing** a (fig) berechnend. ~**ion** /-'leɪʃn/ n Rechnung f, Kalkulation f. ~**or** n Rechner m

calendar /'kælɪndə(r)/ n Kalender m

calf[1] /kɑːf/ n (pl calves) Kalb nt

calf[2] n (pl calves) (Anat) Wade f

calibre /'kælɪbə(r)/ n Kaliber nt

calico /'kælɪkəʊ/ n Kattun m

call /kɔːl/ n Ruf m; (Teleph) Anruf m; (visit) Besuch m; **be on** ~ (doctor:) Bereitschaftsdienst haben ◻ vt rufen; (Teleph) anrufen; (wake) wecken; ausrufen (strike); (name) nennen; **be** ~**ed** heißen ◻ vi rufen; ~ [in or round] vorbeikommen. ~ **back** vt zurückrufen ◻ vi noch einmal vorbeikommen. ~ **for** vt rufen nach; (demand) verlangen; (fetch) abholen. ~ **off** vt zurückrufen (dog); (cancel) absagen. ~ **on** vt bitten (for um); (appeal to) appellieren an (+ acc); (visit) besuchen. ~ **out** vt rufen; aufrufen (names) ◻ vi rufen. ~ **up** vt (Mil) einberufen; (Teleph) anrufen

call: ~-**box** n Telefonzelle f. ~**er** n Besucher m; (Teleph) Anrufer m. ~**ing** n Berufung f

callous /'kæləs/ a gefühllos

'**call-up** n (Mil) Einberufung f

calm /kɑːm/ a (-er, -est), -**ly** adv ruhig ◻ n Ruhe f ◻ vt ~ [**down**] beruhigen ◻ vi ~ **down** sich beruhigen. ~**ness** n Ruhe f; (of sea) Stille f

calorie /'kælərı/ n Kalorie f

calves /kɑ:vz/ npl see calf[1] & [2]

camber /'kæmbə(r)/ n Wölbung f

came /keım/ see come

camel /'kæml/ n Kamel nt

camera /'kæmərə/ n Kamera f. ~man n Kameramann m

camouflage /'kæməflɑ:ʒ/ n Tarnung f □ vt tarnen

camp /kæmp/ n Lager nt □ vi campen; (Mil) kampieren

campaign /kæm'peın/ n Feldzug m; (Comm, Pol) Kampagne f □ vi kämpfen; (pol) im Wahlkampf arbeiten

camp: ~-bed n Feldbett nt. ~er n Camper m; (Auto) Wohnmobil nt. ~ing n Camping nt. ~site n Campingplatz m

campus /'kæmpəs/ n (pl -puses) (Univ) Campus m

can[1] /kæn/ n (for petrol) Kanister m; (tin) Dose f, Büchse f; a ~ of beer eine Dose Bier □ vt in Dosen od Büchsen konservieren

can[2] /kæn, unbetont kən/ v aux (pres can; pt could) können; I cannot/can't go ich kann nicht gehen; he could not go er konnte nicht gehen; if I could go wenn ich gehen könnte

Canad|a /'kænədə/ n Kanada nt. ~ian /kə'neıdıən/ a kanadisch □ n Kanadier(in) m(f)

canal /kə'næl/ n Kanal m

Canaries /kə'neərız/ npl Kanarische Inseln pl

canary /kə'neərı/ n Kanarienvogel m

cancel /'kænsl/ vt/i (pt/pp cancelled) absagen; entwerten ⟨stamp⟩; (annul) rückgängig machen; (Comm) stornieren; abbestellen ⟨newspaper⟩; be ~led ausfallen. ~lation /-ə'leıʃn/ n Absage f

cancer /'kænsə(r)/ n, & (Astr) C~ Krebs m. ~ous /-rəs/ a krebsig

candelabra /kændə'lɑ:brə/ n Armleuchter m

candid /'kændıd/ a, -ly adv offen

candidate /'kændıdət/ n Kandidat(in) m(f)

candied /'kændıd/ a kandiert

candle /'kændl/ n Kerze f. ~stick n Kerzenständer m, Leuchter m

candour /'kændə(r)/ n Offenheit f

candy /'kændı/ n (Amer) Süßigkeiten pl; [piece of] ~ Bonbon m. ~floss /-flɒs/ n Zuckerwatte f

cane /keın/ n Rohr nt; (stick) Stock m □ vt mit dem Stock züchtigen

canine /'keınaın/ a Hunde-. ~ tooth n Eckzahn m

canister /'kænıstə(r)/ n Blechdose f

cannabis /'kænəbıs/ n Haschisch nt

canned /kænd/ a Dosen-, Büchsen-; ~ music (fam) Musik f aus der Konserve

cannibal /'kænıbl/ n Kannibale m. ~ism /-bəlızm/ n Kannibalismus m

cannon /'kænən/ n inv Kanone f. ~-ball n Kanonenkugel f

cannot /'kænɒt/ see can[2]

canny /'kænı/ a schlau

canoe /kə'nu:/ n Paddelboot nt; (Sport) Kanu nt □ vi paddeln; (Sport) Kanu fahren

canon /'kænən/ n Kanon m; (person) Kanonikus m. ~ize /-aız/ vt kanonisieren

'can-opener n Dosenöffner m, Büchsenöffner m

canopy /'kænəpı/ n Baldachin m

cant /kænt/ n Heuchelei f

can't /kɑ:nt/ = cannot. See can[2]

cantankerous /kæn'tæŋkərəs/ a zänkisch

canteen /kæn'ti:n/ n Kantine f; ~ of cutlery Besteckkasten m

canter /'kæntə(r)/ n Kanter m □ vi kantern

canvas /'kænvəs/ n Segeltuch nt; (Art) Leinwand f; (painting) Gemälde nt

canvass /'kænvəs/ vt/um Stimmen werben

canyon /'kænjən/ n Cañon m

cap /kæp/ n Kappe f, Mütze f; (nurse's) Haube f; (top, lid) Verschluss m □ vt (pt/pp capped) (fig) übertreffen

capability /keıpə'bılətı/ n Fähigkeit f

capable /'keıpəbl/ a, -bly adv fähig; be ~ of doing sth fähig sein, etw zu tun

capacity /kə'pæsətı/ n Fassungsvermögen nt; (ability) Fähigkeit f; in my ~ as in meiner Eigenschaft als

cape[1] /keıp/ n (cloak) Cape nt

cape[2] n (Geog) Kap nt

caper[1] /'keıpə(r)/ vi herumspringen

caper[2] n (Culin) Kaper f

capital /'kæpıtl/ a ⟨letter⟩ groß □ n (town) Hauptstadt f; (money) Kapital nt; (letter) Großbuchstabe m

capital|ism /'kæpıtəlızm/ n Kapitalismus m. ~ist /-ıst/ a kapitalistisch □ n Kapitalist m. ~ize /-aız/ vi ~ize on (fig) Kapital schlagen aus. ~ 'letter n Großbuchstabe m. ~ 'punishment n Todesstrafe f

capitulat|e /kə'pıtjʊleıt/ vi kapitulieren. ~ion /-'leıʃn/ n Kapitulation f

capricious /kə'prıʃəs/ a launisch

Capricorn /'kæprıkɔ:n/ n (Astr) Steinbock m

capsize /kæp'saız/ vi kentern □ vt zum Kentern bringen

capsule /'kæpsjʊl/ n Kapsel f

captain /'kæptɪn/ n Kapitän m; ⟨Mil⟩ Hauptmann m □ vt anführen ⟨team⟩

caption /'kæpʃn/ n Überschrift f; ⟨of illustration⟩ Bildtext m

captivate /'kæptɪveɪt/ vt bezaubern

captiv|e /'kæptɪv/ a hold/take ∼e gefangen halten/nehmen □ n Gefangene(r) m/f. ∼ity /-'tɪvətɪ/ n Gefangenschaft f

capture /'kæptʃə(r)/ n Gefangennahme f □ vt gefangen nehmen; [ein]fangen ⟨animal⟩; ⟨Mil⟩ einnehmen ⟨town⟩

car /kɑː(r)/ n Auto nt, Wagen m; by ∼ mit dem Auto od Wagen

carafe /kə'ræf/ n Karaffe f

caramel /'kærəmel/ n Karamell m

carat /'kærət/ n Karat nt

caravan /'kærəvæn/ n Wohnwagen m; ⟨procession⟩ Karawane f

carbohydrate /kɑːbə'haɪdreɪt/ n Kohlenhydrat nt

carbon /'kɑːbən/ n Kohlenstoff m; ⟨paper⟩ Kohlepapier nt; ⟨copy⟩ Durchschlag m

carbon: ∼ copy n Durchschlag m. ∼ di-'oxide n Kohlendioxid nt; ⟨in drink⟩ Kohlensäure f. ∼ paper n Kohlepapier nt

carburettor /kɑːbjʊ'retə(r)/ n Vergaser m

carcass /'kɑːkəs/ n Kadaver m

card /kɑːd/ n Karte f

'cardboard n Pappe f, Karton m. ∼ 'box n Pappschachtel f; ⟨large⟩ [Papp]karton m

'card-game n Kartenspiel nt

cardiac /'kɑːdɪæk/ a Herz-

cardigan /'kɑːdɪgən/ n Strickjacke f

cardinal /'kɑːdɪnl/ a Kardinal-; ∼ number Kardinalzahl f □ n ⟨Relig⟩ Kardinal m

card 'index n Kartei f

care /keə(r)/ n Sorgfalt f; ⟨caution⟩ Vorsicht f; ⟨protection⟩ Obhut f; ⟨looking after⟩ Pflege f; ⟨worry⟩ Sorge f; ∼ of ⟨on letter abbr c/o⟩ bei; take ∼ vorsichtig sein; take into ∼ in Pflege nehmen; take ∼ of sich kümmern um □ vi∼ about sich kümmern um; ∼ for ⟨like⟩ mögen; ⟨look after⟩ betreuen; I don't ∼ das ist mir gleich

career /kə'rɪə(r)/ n Laufbahn f; ⟨profession⟩ Beruf m □ vi rasen

care: ∼free a sorglos. ∼ful a, -ly adv sorgfältig; ⟨cautious⟩ vorsichtig. ∼less a, -ly adv nachlässig. ∼lessness n Nachlässigkeit f

caress /kə'res/ n Liebkosung f □ vt liebkosen

'caretaker n Hausmeister m

'car ferry n Autofähre f

cargo /'kɑːgəʊ/ n ⟨pl -es⟩ Ladung f

Caribbean /kærɪ'biːən/ n the ∼ die Karibik

caricature /'kærɪkətjʊə(r)/ n Karikatur f □ vt karikieren

caring /'keərɪŋ/ a ⟨parent⟩ liebevoll; ⟨profession, attitude⟩ sozial

carnage /'kɑːnɪdʒ/ n Gemetzel nt

carnal /'kɑːnl/ a fleischlich

carnation /kɑː'neɪʃn/ n Nelke f

carnival /'kɑːnɪvl/ n Karneval m

carnivorous /kɑː'nɪvərəs/ a Fleisch fressend

carol /'kærl/ n [Christmas] ∼ Weihnachtslied nt

carp¹ /kɑːp/ n inv Karpfen m

carp² vi nörgeln; ∼ at herumnörgeln an ⟨+ dat⟩

'car park n Parkplatz m; ⟨multi-storey⟩ Parkhaus nt; ⟨underground⟩ Tiefgarage f

carpent|er /'kɑːpɪntə(r)/ n Zimmermann m; ⟨joiner⟩ Tischler m. ∼ry n Tischlerei f

carpet /'kɑːpɪt/ n Teppich m □ vt mit Teppich auslegen

carriage /'kærɪdʒ/ n Kutsche f; ⟨Rail⟩ Wagen m; ⟨of goods⟩ Beförderung f; ⟨cost⟩ Frachtkosten pl; ⟨bearing⟩ Haltung f. ∼way n Fahrbahn f

carrier /'kærɪə(r)/ n Träger(in) m(f); ⟨Comm⟩ Spediteur m. ∼ [bag] Tragetasche f

carrot /'kærət/ n Möhre f, Karotte f

carry /'kærɪ/ vt/i ⟨pt/pp -ied⟩ tragen; be carried away ⟨fam⟩ hingerissen sein. ∼ off vt wegtragen; gewinnen ⟨prize⟩. ∼ on vi weitermachen; ∼ on at ⟨fam⟩ herumnörgeln an ⟨+ dat⟩; ∼ on with ⟨fam⟩ eine Affäre haben mit □ vt führen; ⟨continue⟩ fortführen. ∼ out vt hinaus-/heraustragen; ⟨perform⟩ ausführen

'carry-cot n Babytragetasche f

cart /kɑːt/ n Karren m; put the ∼ before the horse das Pferd beim Schwanz aufzäumen □ vt karren; ⟨fam: carry⟩ schleppen

cartilage /'kɑːtɪlɪdʒ/ n ⟨Anat⟩ Knorpel m

carton /'kɑːtn/ n [Papp]karton m; ⟨for drink⟩ Tüte f; ⟨of cream, yoghurt⟩ Becher m

cartoon /kɑː'tuːn/ n Karikatur f; ⟨joke⟩ Witzzeichnung f; ⟨strip⟩ Comic Strips pl; ⟨film⟩ Zeichentrickfilm m; ⟨Art⟩ Karton m. ∼ist n Karikaturist m

cartridge /'kɑːtrɪdʒ/ n Patrone f; ⟨for film, typewriter ribbon⟩ Kassette f; ⟨of record player⟩ Tonabnehmer m

carve /kɑːv/ vt schnitzen; ⟨in stone⟩ hauen; ⟨Culin⟩ aufschneiden

carving /'kɑːvɪŋ/ n Schnitzerei f. **~-knife** n Tranchiermesser nt

'**car wash** n Autowäsche f; (place) Autowaschanlage f

case¹ /keɪs/ n Fall m; in any ~ auf jeden Fall; just in ~ für alle Fälle; in ~ he comes falls er kommt

case² n Kasten m; (crate) Kiste f; (for spectacles) Etui nt; (suitcase) Koffer m; (for display) Vitrine f

cash /kæʃ/ n Bargeld nt; pay [in] ~ [in] bar bezahlen; ~ on delivery per Nachnahme □ vt einlösen (cheque). ~ **desk** n Kasse f

cashier /kæ'ʃɪə(r)/ n Kassierer(in) m(f)

'**cash register** n Registrierkasse f

casino /kə'siːnəʊ/ n Kasino nt

cask /kɑːsk/ n Fass nt

casket /'kɑːskɪt/ n Kasten m; (Amer: coffin) Sarg m

casserole /'kæsərəʊl/ n Schmortopf m; (stew) Eintopf m

cassette /kə'set/ n Kassette f. ~ **recorder** n Kassettenrecorder m

cast /kɑːst/ n (throw) Wurf m; (mould) Form f; (model) Abguss m; (Theat) Besetzung f; (plaster) ~ (Med) Gipsverband m □ vt (pt/pp cast) (throw) werfen; (shed) abwerfen; abgeben (vote); gießen (metal); (Theat) besetzen (role); ~ **a glance** at einen Blick werfen auf (+ acc). ~ **off** vi (Naut) ablegen □ vt (Knitting) abketten. ~ **on** vt (Knitting) anschlagen

castanets /kæstə'nets/ npl Kastagnetten pl

castaway /'kɑːstəweɪ/ n Schiffbrüchige(r) m/f

caste /kɑːst/ n Kaste f

cast 'iron n Gusseisen nt

cast-'iron a gusseisern

castle /'kɑːsl/ n Schloss nt; (fortified) Burg f; (Chess) Turm m

'**cast-offs** npl abgelegte Kleidung f

castor /'kɑːstə(r)/ n (wheel) [Lauf]rolle f

'**castor sugar** n Streuzucker m

castrate /kæ'streɪt/ vt kastrieren. ~**ion** /-eɪʃn/ n Kastration f

casual /'kæʒʊəl/ a, **-ly** adv (chance) zufällig; (offhand) lässig; (informal) zwanglos; (not permanent) Gelegenheits-; ~ **wear** Freizeitbekleidung f

casualty /'kæʒʊəltɪ/ n [Todes]opfer nt; (injured person) Verletzte(r) m/f; ~ [department] Unfallstation f

cat /kæt/ n Katze f

catalogue /'kætəlɒg/ n Katalog m □ vt katalogisieren

catalyst /'kætəlɪst/ n (Chem & fig) Katalysator m

catalytic /kætə'lɪtɪk/ a ~ **converter** (Auto) Katalysator m

catapult /'kætəpʌlt/ n Katapult nt □ vt katapultieren

cataract /'kætərækt/ n (Med) grauer Star m

catarrh /kə'tɑː(r)/ n Katarrh m

catastrophe /kə'tæstrəfɪ/ n Katastrophe f. ~**ic** /kætə'strɒfɪk/ a katastrophal

catch /kætʃ/ n (of fish) Fang m; (fastener) Verschluss m; (on door) Klinke f; (fam: snag) Haken m (fam) □ vt (pt/pp caught) □ vt fangen; (be in time for) erreichen; (travel by) fahren mit; bekommen (illness); ~ **a cold** sich erkälten; ~ **sight of** erblicken; ~ s.o. stealing jdn beim Stehlen erwischen; ~ **one's finger in the door** sich (dat) den Finger in der Tür [ein]klemmen □ vi (burn) anbrennen; (get stuck) klemmen. ~ **on** vi (fam) (understand) kapieren; (become popular) sich durchsetzen. ~ **up** vt einholen □ vi aufholen; ~ **up with** einholen (s.o.); nachholen (work)

catching /'kætʃɪŋ/ a ansteckend

catch: ~**-phrase** n, ~**word** n Schlagwort nt

catchy /'kætʃɪ/ a (-ier, -iest) einprägsam

catechism /'kætɪkɪzm/ n Katechismus m

categor|ical /kætə'gɒrɪkl/ a, **-ly** adv kategorisch. ~**y** /'kætɪgɒrɪ/ n Kategorie f

cater /'keɪtə(r)/ vi ~ **for** beköstigen; (firm:) das Essen liefern für (party); (fig) eingestellt sein auf (+ acc). ~**ing** n (trade) Gaststättengewerbe nt

caterpillar /'kætəpɪlə(r)/ n Raupe f

cathedral /kə'θiːdrl/ n Dom m, Kathedrale f

Catholic /'kæθəlɪk/ a katholisch □ n Katholik(in) m(f). **C~ism** /kə'θɒlɪsɪzm/ n Katholizismus m

catkin /'kætkɪn/ n (Bot) Kätzchen nt

cattle /'kætl/ npl Vieh nt

catty /'kætɪ/ a (-ier, -iest) boshaft

caught /kɔːt/ see catch

cauldron /'kɔːldrən/ n [großer] Kessel m

cauliflower /'kɒlɪ-/ n Blumenkohl m

cause /kɔːz/ n Ursache f; (reason) Grund m; good ~ gute Sache f □ vt verursachen; ~ s.o. to do sth jdn veranlassen, etw zu tun

'**causeway** n [Insel]damm m

caustic /'kɔːstɪk/ a ätzend; (fig) beißend

cauterize /'kɔːtəraɪz/ vt kauterisieren

caution /'kɔːʃn/ n Vorsicht f; (warning) Verwarnung f □ vt (Jur) verwarnen

cautious /'kɔːʃəs/ a, **-ly** adv vorsichtig

cavalry /'kævlrɪ/ n Kavallerie f

cave /keɪv/ n Höhle f □ vi ~ **in** einstürzen

cavern /'kævən/ n Höhle f

caviare /'kævɪɑː(r)/ n Kaviar m

caving /'keɪvɪŋ/ n Höhlenforschung f

cavity /'kævətɪ/ n Hohlraum m; (in tooth) Loch n

cavort /kə'vɔːt/ vi tollen nt

cease /siːs/ n without ~ unaufhörlich □ vt/i aufhören. ~fire n Waffenruhe f. ~less a, -ly adv unaufhörlich

cedar /'siːdə(r)/ n Zeder f

cede /siːd/ vt abtreten (to an + acc)

ceiling /'siːlɪŋ/ n [Zimmer]decke f; (fig) oberste Grenze f

celebrat|e /'selɪbreɪt/ vt/i feiern. ~ed a berühmt (for wegen). ~ion /-'breɪʃn/ n Feier f

celebrity /sɪ'lebrətɪ/ n Berühmtheit f

celery /'selərɪ/ n [Stangen]sellerie m & f

celiba|cy /'selɪbəsɪ/ n Zölibat nt. ~te a be ~te im Zölibat leben

cell /sel/ n Zelle f

cellar /'selə(r)/ n Keller m

cellist /'tʃelɪst/ n Cellist(in) m(f)

cello /'tʃeləʊ/ n Cello nt

Celsius /'selsɪəs/ a Celsius

Celt /kelt/ n Kelte m/ Keltin f. ~ic a keltisch

cement /sɪ'ment/ n Zement m; (adhesive) Kitt m □ vt zementieren; (stick) kitten

cemetery /'semətrɪ/ n Friedhof m

censor /'sensə(r)/ n Zensor m □ vt zensieren. ~ship n Zensur f

censure /'senʃə(r)/ n Tadel m □ vt tadeln

census /'sensəs/ n Volkszählung f

cent /sent/ n (coin) Cent m

centenary /sen'tiːnərɪ/ n, (Amer) centennial /sen'tenɪəl/ n Hundertjahrfeier f

center /'sentə(r)/ n (Amer) = centre

centi|grade /'sentɪ-/ a Celsius-; 5° ~ 5° Celsius. ~metre n Zentimeter m & nt. ~pede /-piːd/ n Tausendfüßler m

central /'sentrəl/ a, -ly adv zentral. ~ heating n Zentralheizung f. ~ize vt zentralisieren. ~ reser'vation n (Auto) Mittelstreifen m

centre /'sentə(r)/ n Zentrum nt; (middle) Mitte f □ v (pt/pp centred) □ vt zentrieren; ~ on (fig) sich drehen um. ~'forward n Mittelstürmer m

centrifugal /sentrɪ'fjuːgl/ a ~ force Fliehkraft f

century /'sentʃərɪ/ n Jahrhundert nt

ceramic /sɪ'ræmɪk/ a Keramik-. ~s n Keramik f

cereal /'sɪərɪəl/ n Getreide nt; (breakfast food) Frühstücksflocken pl

cerebral /'serɪbrl/ a Gehirn-

ceremon|ial /serɪ'məʊnɪəl/ a, -ly adv zeremoniell, feierlich □ n Zeremoniell nt. ~ious /-ɪəs/ a, -ly adv formell

ceremony /'serɪmənɪ/ n Zeremonie f, Feier f; without ~ ohne weitere Umstände

certain /'sɜːtn/ a sicher; (not named) gewiss; for ~ mit Bestimmtheit; make ~ (check) sich vergewissern (that dass); (ensure) dafür sorgen (that dass); he is ~ to win er wird ganz bestimmt siegen. ~ly adv bestimmt, sicher; ~ly not! auf keinen Fall! ~ty n Sicherheit f, Gewissheit f; it's a ~ty es ist sicher

certificate /sə'tɪfɪkət/ n Bescheinigung f; (Jur) Urkunde f; (Sch) Zeugnis nt

certify /'sɜːtɪfaɪ/ vt (pt/pp -ied) bescheinigen; (declare insane) für geisteskrank erklären

cessation /se'seɪʃn/ n Ende nt

cesspool /'ses-/ n Senkgrube f

cf. abbr (compare) vgl.

chafe /tʃeɪf/ vt wund reiben

chaff /tʃɑːf/ n Spreu f

chaffinch /'tʃæfɪntʃ/ n Buchfink m

chain /tʃeɪn/ n Kette f □ vt ketten (to an + acc). ~ up vt anketten

chain: ~ re'action n Kettenreaktion f. ~smoker n Kettenraucher m. ~ store n Kettenladen m

chair /tʃeə(r)/ n Stuhl m; (Univ) Lehrstuhl m; (Adm) Vorsitzende(r) m/f □ vt den Vorsitz führen bei. ~-lift n Sessellift m. ~man n Vorsitzende(r) m/f

chalet /'ʃæleɪ/ n Chalet nt

chalice /'tʃælɪs/ n (Relig) Kelch m

chalk /tʃɔːk/ n Kreide f. ~y a kreidig

challeng|e /'tʃælɪndʒ/ n Herausforderung f; (Mil) Anruf m □ vt herausfordern; (Mil) anrufen; (fig) anfechten (statement). ~er n Herausforderer m. ~ing a herausfordernd; (demanding) anspruchsvoll

chamber /'tʃeɪmbə(r)/ n Kammer f; ~s pl (Jur) [Anwalts]büro nt; C~ of Commerce Handelskammer f

chamber: ~maid n Zimmermädchen nt. ~ music n Kammermusik f. ~-pot n Nachttopf m

chamois[1] /'ʃæmwɑː/ n inv (animal) Gämse f

chamois[2] /'ʃæmɪ/ n ~[-leather] Ledertuch nt

champagne /ʃæm'peɪn/ n Champagner m

champion /'tʃæmpɪən/ n (Sport) Meister(in) m(f); (of cause) Verfechter m □ vt sich einsetzen für. ~ship n (Sport) Meisterschaft f

chance /tʃɑːns/ n Zufall m; (prospect) Chancen pl; (likelihood) Aussicht f; (opportunity) Gelegenheit f; by ~ zufällig; take a ~ein Risiko eingehen; give s.o. a ~jdm eine Chance geben □ attrib zufällig □ vt ~ it es riskieren

chancellor /'tʃɑːnsələ(r)/ n Kanzler m; (Univ) Rektor m; C~ of the Exchequer Schatzkanzler m

chancy /'tʃɑːnsɪ/ a riskant

chandelier /ʃændə'lɪə(r)/ n Kronleuchter m

change /tʃeɪndʒ/ n Veränderung f; (alteration) Änderung f; (money) Wechselgeld nt; for a ~ zur Abwechslung □ vt wechseln; (alter) ändern; (exchange) umtauschen (for gegen); (transform) verwandeln, trocken legen ⟨baby⟩; ~ one's clothes sich umziehen; ~ trains umsteigen □ vi sich verändern; ⟨~ clothes⟩ sich umziehen; ⟨~ trains⟩ umsteigen; all ~!alles aussteigen!

changeable /'tʃeɪndʒəbl/ a wechselhaft

'changing-room n Umkleideraum m

channel /'tʃænl/ n Rinne f; (Radio, TV) Kanal m; (fig) Weg m; the [English] C~ der Ärmelkanal; the C~ Islands die Kanalinseln □ vt (pt/pp channelled) leiten; (fig) lenken

chant /tʃɑːnt/ n liturgischer Gesang m □ vt singen; ⟨demonstrators:⟩ skandieren

chaos /'keɪɒs/ n Chaos nt. ~tic /-'ɒtɪk/ a chaotisch

chap /tʃæp/ n (fam) Kerl m

chapel /'tʃæpl/ n Kapelle f

chaperon /'ʃæpərəʊn/ n Anstandsdame f □ vt begleiten

chaplain /'tʃæplɪn/ n Geistliche(r) m

chapped /tʃæpt/ a ⟨skin⟩ aufgesprungen

chapter /'tʃæptə(r)/ n Kapitel nt

char¹ /tʃɑː(r)/ n (fam) Putzfrau f

char² vt (pt/pp charred) ⟨burn⟩ verkohlen

character /'kærɪktə(r)/ n Charakter m; (in novel, play) Gestalt f; (Typ) Schriftzeichen m; out of ~ uncharakteristisch; quite a ~ (fam) ein Original

characteristic /kærɪktə'rɪstɪk/ a, -ally adv charakteristisch (of für) □ n Merkmal nt

characterize /'kærɪktəraɪz/ vt charakterisieren

charade /ʃə'rɑːd/ n Scharade f

charcoal /'tʃɑː-/ n Holzkohle f

charge /tʃɑːdʒ/ n (price) Gebühr f; (Electr) Ladung f; (attack) Angriff m; (Jur) Anklage f; free of ~ kostenlos; be in ~ verantwortlich sein (of für); take ~ die Aufsicht übernehmen (ofüber + acc) □ vt berechnen ⟨fee⟩; (Electr) laden; (attack) angreifen; (Jur) anklagen (withgen); ~ s.o.

for sth jdm etw berechnen □ vi (attack) angreifen

chariot /'tʃærɪət/ n Wagen m

charisma /kə'rɪzmə/ n Charisma nt. ~tic /kærɪz'mætɪk/ a charismatisch

charitable /'tʃærɪtəbl/ a wohltätig; (kind) wohlwollend

charity /'tʃærɪtɪ/ n Nächstenliebe f; (organization) wohltätige Einrichtung f; for ~ für Wohltätigkeitszwecke; live on ~ von Almosen leben

charlatan /'ʃɑːlətən/ n Scharlatan m

charm /tʃɑːm/ n Reiz m; (of person) Charme f; (object) Amulett m □ vt bezaubern. ~ing a, -ly adv reizend; ⟨person, smile⟩ charmant

chart /tʃɑːt/ n Karte f; (table) Tabelle f

charter /'tʃɑːtə(r)/ n ~ [flight] Charterflug m □ vt chartern; ~ed accountant Wirtschaftsprüfer(in) m(f)

charwoman /'tʃɑː-/ n Putzfrau f

chase /tʃeɪs/ n Verfolgungsjagd f □ vt jagen, verfolgen. ~ away or offvt wegjagen

chasm /'kæzm/ n Kluft f

chassis /'ʃæsɪ/ n (pl chassis /-sɪz/) Chassis nt

chaste /tʃeɪst/ a keusch

chastise /tʃæ'staɪz/ vt züchtigen

chastity /'tʃæstɪtɪ/ n Keuschheit f

chat /tʃæt/ n Plauderei f; have a ~ with plaudern mit □ vi (pt/pp chatted) plaudern. ~ show n Talkshow f

chatter /'tʃætə(r)/ n Geschwätz nt □ vi schwatzen; ⟨child:⟩ plappern; ⟨teeth:⟩ klappern. ~box n (fam) Plappermaul nt

chatty /'tʃætɪ/ a (-ier, -iest) geschwätzig

chauffeur /'ʃəʊfə(r)/ n Chauffeur m

chauvin|ism /'ʃəʊvɪnɪzm/ n Chauvinismus m. ~ist n Chauvinist m; male ~ist (fam) Chauvi m

cheap /tʃiːp/ a & adv (-er, -est), -ly adv billig. ~en vt entwürdigen; ~en oneself sich erniedrigen

cheat /tʃiːt/ n Betrüger(in) m(f); (at games) Mogler m □ vt betrügen □ vi (at games) mogeln (fam)

check¹ /tʃek/ a (squared) kariert □ n Karo nt

check² n Überprüfung f; (inspection) Kontrolle f; (Chess) Schach nt; (Amer: bill) Rechnung f; (Amer: cheque) Scheck m; (Amer: tick) Haken m; keep a ~ on kontrollieren □ vt [über]prüfen; (inspect) kontrollieren; (restrain) hemmen; (stop) aufhalten □ vi [go and] ~ nachsehen. ~ in vi sich anmelden; (Aviat) einchecken □ vt abfertigen; einchecken. ~ out vi sich abmelden. ~ up *vi* prüfen, kontrollieren; ~ up on überprüfen

check|ed /tʃekt/ *a* kariert. ~ers *n* (*Amer*) Damespiel *nt*

check: ~mate *int* schachmatt! ~out *n* Kasse *f*. ~room *n* (*Amer*) Garderobe *f*. ~up *n* (*Med*) [Kontroll]untersuchung *f*

cheek /tʃiːk/ *n* Backe *f*; (*impudence*) Frechheit *f*. ~y *a*, -ily *adv* frech

cheep /tʃiːp/ *vi* piepen

cheer /tʃɪə(r)/ *n* Beifallsruf *m*; three ~s ein dreifaches Hoch (for auf + *acc*); ~s! prost! (*goodbye*) tschüs! □ *vt* zujubeln (+ *dat*) □ *vi* jubeln. ~ up *vt* aufmuntern; aufheitern □ *vi* munterer werden. ~ful *a*, -ly *adv* fröhlich. ~fulness *n* Fröhlichkeit *f*

cheerio /tʃɪərɪˈəʊ/ *int* (*fam*) tschüs!

'cheerless *a* trostlos

cheese /tʃiːz/ *n* Käse *m*. ~cake *n* Käsekuchen *m*

cheetah /ˈtʃiːtə/ *n* Gepard *m*

chef /ʃef/ *n* Koch *m*

chemical /ˈkemɪkl/ *a*, -ly *adv* chemisch □ *n* Chemikalie *f*

chemist /ˈkemɪst/ *n* (*pharmacist*) Apotheker(in) *m(f)*; (*scientist*) Chemiker(in) *m(f)*. ~'s [shop] Drogerie *f*; (*dispensing*) Apotheke *f*. ~ry *n* Chemie *f*

cheque /tʃek/ *n* Scheck *m*. ~book *n* Scheckbuch *nt*. ~ card *n* Scheckkarte *f*

cherish /ˈtʃerɪʃ/ *vt* lieben; (*fig*) hegen

cherry /ˈtʃerɪ/ *n* Kirsche *f* □ *attrib* Kirsch-

cherub /ˈtʃerəb/ *n* Engelchen *nt*

chess /tʃes/ *n* Schach *nt*

chess: ~board *n* Schachbrett *nt*. ~man *n* Schachfigur *f*

chest /tʃest/ *n* Brust *f*; (*box*) Truhe *f*

chestnut /ˈtʃesnʌt/ *n* Esskastanie *f*, Marone *f*; (*horse-*) [Ross]kastanie *f*

chest of 'drawers *n* Kommode *f*

chew /tʃuː/ *vt* kauen. ~ing-gum *n* Kaugummi *m*

chic /ʃiːk/ *a* schick

chick /tʃɪk/ *n* Küken *nt*

chicken /ˈtʃɪkɪn/ *n* Huhn *nt* □ *attrib* Hühner- *a* (*fam*) feige □ *vi* ~ out (*fam*) kneifen. ~pox *n* Windpocken *pl*

chicory /ˈtʃɪkərɪ/ *n* Chicorée *m*; (*in coffee*) Zichorie *f*

chief /tʃiːf/ *a* Haupt- □ *n* Chef *m*; (*of tribe*) Häuptling *m*. ~ly *adv* hauptsächlich

chilblain /ˈtʃɪlbleɪn/ *n* Frostbeule *f*

child /tʃaɪld/ *n* (*pl* ~ren) Kind *nt*

child: ~birth *n* Geburt *f*. ~hood *n* Kindheit *f*. ~ish *a* kindisch. ~less *a* kinderlos. ~like *a* kindlich. ~minder *n* Tagesmutter *f*

children /ˈtʃɪldrən/ *npl see* child

Chile /ˈtʃɪlɪ/ *n* Chile *nt*

chill /tʃɪl/ *n* Kälte *f*; (*illness*) Erkältung *f* □ *vt* kühlen

chilli /ˈtʃɪlɪ/ *n* (*pl* -es) Chili *m*

chilly /ˈtʃɪlɪ/ *a* kühl; I felt ~ mich fröstelte [es]

chime /tʃaɪm/ *vi* läuten; (*clock:*) schlagen

chimney /ˈtʃɪmnɪ/ *n* Schornstein *m*. ~pot *n* Schornsteinaufsatz *m*. ~sweep *n* Schornsteinfeger *m*

chimpanzee /tʃɪmpænˈziː/ *n* Schimpanse *m*

chin /tʃɪn/ *n* Kinn *nt*

china /ˈtʃaɪnə/ *n* Porzellan *nt*

Chin|a *n* China *nt*. ~ese /-ˈniːz/ *a* chinesisch □ *n* (*Lang*) Chinesisch *nt*; the ~ese *pl* die Chinesen. ~ese 'lantern *n* Lampion *m*

chink[1] /tʃɪŋk/ *n* (*slit*) Ritze *f*

chink[2] /tʃɪŋk/ *n* Geklirr *nt* □ *vi* klirren; (*coins:*) klimpern

chip /tʃɪp/ *n* (*fragment*) Span *m*; (*in china, paintwork*) angeschlagene Stelle *f*; (*Computing, Gambling*) Chip *m*; ~s *pl* (*Culin*) Pommes frites *pl*; (*Amer: crisps*) Chips *pl* □ *vt* (*pt/pp* chipped) (*damage*) anschlagen. ~ped *a* angeschlagen

chiropod|ist /kɪˈrɒpədɪst/ *n* Fußpfleger(in) *m(f)*. ~y *n* Fußpflege *f*

chirp /tʃɜːp/ *vi* zwitschern; (*cricket:*) zirpen. ~y *a* (*fam*) munter

chisel /ˈtʃɪzl/ *n* Meißel *m* □ *vt/i* (*pt/pp* chiselled) meißeln

chit /tʃɪt/ *n* Zettel *m*

chival|rous /ˈʃɪvlrəs/ *a*, -ly *adv* ritterlich. ~ry *n* Ritterlichkeit *f*

chives /tʃaɪvz/ *npl* Schnittlauch *m*

chlorine /ˈklɔːriːn/ *n* Chlor *nt*

chloroform /ˈklɒrəfɔːm/ *n* Chloroform *nt*

chocolate /ˈtʃɒkələt/ *n* Schokolade *f*; (*sweet*) Praline *f*

choice /tʃɔɪs/ *n* Wahl *f*; (*variety*) Auswahl *f* □ *a* auserlesen

choir /ˈkwaɪə(r)/ *n* Chor *m*. ~boy *n* Chorknabe *m*

choke /tʃəʊk/ *n* (*Auto*) Choke *m* □ *vt* würgen; (*to death*) erwürgen □ *vi* sich verschlucken; ~ on [fast] ersticken an (+ *dat*)

cholera /ˈkɒlərə/ *n* Cholera *f*

cholesterol /kəˈlestərɒl/ *n* Cholesterin *nt*

choose /tʃuːz/ *vt/i* (*pt* chose, *pp* chosen) wählen; (*select*) sich (*dat*) aussuchen; ~ to do/go [freiwillig] tun/gehen; as you ~ wie Sie wollen

choos[e]y /ˈtʃuːzɪ/ *a* (*fam*) wählerisch

chop /tʃɒp/ n (blow) Hieb m; (Culin) Kotelett nt ▫ vt (pt/pp chopped) hacken. ~ **down** vt abhacken; fällen ⟨tree⟩. ~ **off** vt abhacken

chop|per /'tʃɒpə(r)/ n Beil nt; (fam) Hubschrauber m. ~**py** a kabbelig

'chopsticks npl Essstäbchen pl

choral /'kɔːrəl/ a Chor-; ~ **society** Gesangverein m

chord /kɔːd/ n (Mus) Akkord m

chore /tʃɔː(r)/ n lästige Pflicht f; [household] ~s Hausarbeit f

choreography /kɒrɪ'ɒgrəfɪ/ n Choreographie f

chortle /'tʃɔːtl/ vi [vor Lachen] glucksen

chorus /'kɔːrəs/ n Chor m; (of song) Refrain m

chose, chosen /tʃəʊz, 'tʃəʊzn/ see **choose**

Christ /kraɪst/ n Christus m

christen /'krɪsn/ vt taufen. ~**ing** n Taufe f

Christian /'krɪstʃən/ a christlich ▫ n Christ(in) m(f). ~**ity** /-stɪ'ænətɪ/ n Christentum nt. ~ **name** n Vorname m

Christmas /'krɪsməs/ n Weihnachten nt. ~ **card** n Weihnachtskarte f. ~ **'Day** n erster Weihnachtstag m. ~ **'Eve** n Heiligabend m. ~ **tree** n Weihnachtsbaum m

chrome /krəʊm/ n, **chromium** /'krəʊmɪəm/ n Chrom nt

chromosome /'krəʊməsəʊm/ n Chromosom nt

chronic /'krɒnɪk/ a chronisch

chronicle /'krɒnɪkl/ n Chronik f

chronological /krɒnə'lɒdʒɪkl/ a, -ly adv chronologisch

chrysalis /'krɪsəlɪs/ n Puppe f

chrysanthemum /krɪ'sænθəməm/ n Chrysantheme f

chubby /'tʃʌbɪ/ a (-ier, -iest) mollig

chuck /tʃʌk/ vt (fam) schmeißen. ~ **out** vt (fam) rausschmeißen

chuckle /'tʃʌkl/ vi in sich (acc) hineinlachen

chum /tʃʌm/ n Freund(in) m(f)

chunk /tʃʌŋk/ n Stück nt

church /tʃɜːtʃ/ n Kirche f. ~**yard** n Friedhof m

churlish /'tʃɜːlɪʃ/ a unhöflich

churn /tʃɜːn/ n Butterfass nt; (for milk) Milchkanne f ▫ vt ~ **out** am laufenden Band produzieren

chute /ʃuːt/ n Rutsche f; (for rubbish) Müllschlucker m

CID abbr (Criminal Investigation Department) Kripo f

cider /'saɪdə(r)/ n Apfelwein m

cigar /sɪ'gɑː(r)/ n Zigarre f

cigarette /sɪgə'ret/ n Zigarette f

cine-camera /'sɪnɪ-/ n Filmkamera f

cinema /'sɪnɪmə/ n Kino nt

cinnamon /'sɪnəmən/ n Zimt m

cipher /'saɪfə(r)/ n (code) Chiffre f; (numeral) Ziffer f; (fig) Null f

circle /'sɜːkl/ n Kreis m; (Theat) Rang m ▫ vt umkreisen ▫ vi kreisen

circuit /'sɜːkɪt/ n Runde f; (racetrack) Rennbahn f; (Electr) Stromkreis m. ~**ous** /sə'kjuːɪtəs/ a ~ **route** Umweg m

circular /'sɜːkjʊlə(r)/ a kreisförmig ▫ n Rundschreiben nt. ~ **'saw** n Kreissäge f. ~ **'tour** n Rundfahrt f

circulat|e /'sɜːkjʊleɪt/ vt in Umlauf setzen ▫ vi zirkulieren. ~**ion** /-'leɪʃn/ n Kreislauf m; (of newspaper) Auflage f

circumcis|e /'sɜːkəmsaɪz/ vt beschneiden. ~**ion** /-'sɪʒn/ n Beschneidung f

circumference /sə'kʌmfərəns/ n Umfang m

circumspect /'sɜːkəmspekt/ a, -ly adv umsichtig

circumstance /'sɜːkəmstəns/ n Umstand m; ~**s** pl Umstände pl; (financial) Verhältnisse pl

circus /'sɜːkəs/ n Zirkus m

CIS abbr (Commonwealth of Independent States) GUS f

cistern /'sɪstən/ n (tank) Wasserbehälter m; (of WC) Spülkasten m

cite /saɪt/ vt zitieren

citizen /'sɪtɪzn/ n Bürger(in) m(f). ~**ship** n Staatsangehörigkeit f

citrus /'sɪtrəs/ n ~ **[fruit]** Zitrusfrucht f

city /'sɪtɪ/ n [Groß]stadt f

civic /'sɪvɪk/ a Bürger-

civil /'sɪvl/ a bürgerlich; ⟨aviation, defence⟩ zivil; (polite) höflich. ~ **engi'neering** n Hoch- und Tiefbau m

civilian /sɪ'vɪljən/ a Zivil-; in ~ **clothes** in Zivil ▫ n Zivilist m

civility /sɪ'vɪlətɪ/ n Höflichkeit f

civiliz|ation /sɪvəlaɪ'zeɪʃn/ n Zivilisation f. ~**e** /'sɪvəlaɪz/ vt zivilisieren

civil: ~ **'servant** n Beamte(r) m/Beamtin f. **C~ 'Service** n Staatsdienst m

clad /klæd/ a gekleidet (in **in** + acc)

claim /kleɪm/ n Anspruch m; (application) Antrag m; (demand) Forderung f; (assertion) Behauptung f ▫ vt beanspruchen; (apply for) beantragen; (demand) fordern; (assert) behaupten; (collect) abholen. ~**ant** n Antragsteller m

clairvoyant /kleə'vɔɪənt/ n Hellseher(in) m(f)

clam /klæm/ n Klaffmuschel f

clamber /'klæmbə(r)/ vi klettern

clammy /'klæmi/ a (-ier, -iest) feucht

clamour /'klæmə(r)/ n Geschrei nt □ vi ~ for schreien nach

clamp /klæmp/ n Klammer f □ vt [ein]-spannen □ vi (fam) ~ down durchgreifen; ~ down on vorgehen gegen

clan /klæn/ n Clan m

clandestine /klæn'destɪn/ a geheim

clang /klæŋ/ n Schmettern nt. ~er n (fam) Schnitzer m

clank /klæŋk/ vi klirren

clap /klæp/ n give s.o. a ~ jdm Beifall klatschen; ~ of thunder Donnerschlag m □ vt/i (pt/pp clapped) Beifall klatschen (+ dat); ~ one's hands [in die Hände] klatschen

claret /'klærət/ n roter Bordeaux m

clari|fication /klærɪfɪ'keɪʃn/ n Klärung f. ~fy /'klærɪfaɪ/ vt/i (pt/pp -ied) klären

clarinet /klærɪ'net/ n Klarinette f

clarity /'klærətɪ/ n Klarheit f

clash /klæʃ/ n Geklirr nt; (fig) Konflikt m □ vi klirren; ⟨colours:⟩ sich beißen; ⟨events:⟩ ungünstig zusammenfallen

clasp /klɑːsp/ n Verschluss m □ vt ergreifen; ⟨hold⟩ halten

class /klɑːs/ n Klasse f; travel first/se-cond ~ erster/zweiter Klasse reisen □ vt einordnen

classic /'klæsɪk/ a klassisch □ n Klassiker m; ~s pl (Univ) Altphilologie f. ~al a klassisch

classi|fication /klæsɪfɪ'keɪʃn/ n Klassi-fikation f. ~fy /'klæsɪfaɪ/ vt (pt/pp -ied) klassifizieren

'classroom n Klassenzimmer nt

classy /'klɑːsɪ/ a (-ier, -iest) (fam) schick

clatter /'klætə(r)/ n Geklapper nt □ vi klappern

clause /klɔːz/ n Klausel f; (Gram) Satzteil m

claustrophobia /klɔːstrə'fəʊbɪə/ n Klau-strophobie f. (fam) Platzangst f

claw /klɔː/ n Kralle f; ⟨of bird of prey & Techn⟩ Klaue f; ⟨of crab, lobster⟩ Schere f □ vt kratzen

clay /kleɪ/ n Lehm m; ⟨pottery⟩ Ton m

clean /kliːn/ a (-er, -est) sauber □ adv glatt □ vt sauber machen; putzen ⟨shoes, win-dows⟩; ~ one's teeth sich ⟨dat⟩ die Zähne putzen; have sth ~ed etw reinigen lassen. ~ up vt sauber machen

cleaner /'kliːnə(r)/ n Putzfrau f; ⟨sub-stance⟩ Reinigungsmittel nt; [dry] ~'s chemische Reinigung f

cleanliness /'klenlɪnɪs/ n Sauberkeit f

cleanse /klenz/ vt reinigen. ~r n Rei-nigungsmittel nt

clean-shaven a glatt rasiert

cleansing cream /'klenz-/ n Reinigungscreme f

clear /klɪə(r)/ a (-er, -est), -ly adv klar; ⟨obvious⟩ eindeutig; ⟨distinct⟩ deutlich; ⟨conscience⟩ rein; ⟨without obstacles⟩ frei; make sth ~ etw klarmachen (to dat) □ adv stand ~ zurücktreten; keep ~ of aus dem Wege gehen (+ dat) □ vt räumen; abräumen ⟨table⟩; ⟨acquit⟩ freisprechen; ⟨authorize⟩ genehmigen; ⟨jump over⟩ überspringen; ~ one's throat sich räus-pern □ vi ⟨fog:⟩ sich auflösen. ~ away vt wegräumen. ~ off vi (fam) abhauen. ~ out vt ausräumen □ vi (fam) abhauen. ~ up vt ⟨tidy⟩ aufräumen; ⟨solve⟩ aufklären □ vi ⟨weather:⟩ sich aufklären

clearance /'klɪərəns/ n Räumung f; ⟨au-thorization⟩ Genehmigung f; ⟨customs⟩ [Zoll]abfertigung f; ⟨Techn⟩ Spielraum m. ~ sale n Räumungsverkauf m

clear|ing /'klɪərɪŋ/ n Lichtung f. ~way n ⟨Auto⟩ Straße f mit Halteverbot

cleavage /'kliːvɪdʒ/ n Spaltung f; ⟨woman''s⟩ Dekolleté nt

clef /klef/ n Notenschlüssel m

cleft /kleft/ n Spalte f

clemen|cy /'klemənsɪ/ n Milde f. ~t a mild

clench /klentʃ/ vt ~ one's fist die Faust ballen; ~ one's teeth die Zähne zusam-menbeißen

clergy /'klɜːdʒɪ/ npl Geistlichkeit f. ~man n Geistliche(r) m

cleric /'klerɪk/ n Geistliche(r) m. ~al a Schreib-; ⟨Relig⟩ geistlich

clerk /klɑːk/, Amer: /klɜːk/ n Büroange-stellte(r) m/f; ⟨Amer: shop assistant⟩ Verkäufer(in) m(f)

clever /'klevə(r)/ a (-er, -est), -ly adv klug; ⟨skilful⟩ geschickt

cliché /'kliːʃeɪ/ n Klischee nt

click /klɪk/ vi klicken

client /'klaɪənt/ n Kunde m/ Kundin f; ⟨Jur⟩ Klient(in) m(f)

clientele /kliːɒn'tel/ n Kundschaft f

cliff /klɪf/ n Kliff nt

climat|e /'klaɪmət/ n Klima nt. ~ic /-'mætɪk/ a klimatisch

climax /'klaɪmæks/ n Höhepunkt m

climb /klaɪm/ n Aufstieg m □ vt besteigen ⟨mountain⟩; steigen auf (+ acc) ⟨ladder, tree⟩ □ vi klettern; ⟨rise⟩ steigen; ⟨road:⟩ ansteigen. ~ down vi hinunter-/herunterklettern; ⟨from ladder, tree⟩ he-runtersteigen; (fam) nachgeben

climber /'klaɪmə(r)/ n Bergsteiger m; ⟨plant⟩ Kletterpflanze f

clinch /klɪntʃ/ vt perfekt machen ⟨deal⟩ □ vi ⟨boxing⟩ clinchen

cling /klɪŋ/ vi (pt/pp clung) sich klammern ⟨to an + acc⟩; ⟨stick⟩ haften ⟨to an + dat⟩. ∼film n Sichtfolie f mit Hafteffekt

clinic /'klɪnɪk/ n Klinik f. ∼al a, -ly adv klinisch

clink /klɪŋk/ n Klirren nt; ⟨fam: prison⟩ Knast m □ vi klirren

clip[1] /klɪp/ n Klammer f; ⟨jewellery⟩ Klipp m □ vt (pt/pp clipped) anklammern ⟨to an + acc⟩

clip[2] n ⟨extract⟩ Ausschnitt m □ vt schneiden; knipsen ⟨ticket⟩. ∼board n Klemmbrett nt. ∼pers npl Schere f. ∼ping n ⟨extract⟩ Ausschnitt m

clique /kliːk/ n Clique f

cloak /kləʊk/ n Umhang m. ∼room n Garderobe f; ⟨toilet⟩ Toilette f

clobber /'klɒbə(r)/ n ⟨fam⟩ Zeug nt □ vt ⟨fam: hit, defeat⟩ schlagen

clock /klɒk/ n Uhr f; ⟨fam: speedometer⟩ Tacho m □ vi ∼ in/out stechen

clock-: ∼ tower n Uhrenturm m. ∼wise a & adv im Uhrzeigersinn. ∼work n Uhrwerk nt; ⟨of toy⟩ Aufziehmechanismus m; like ∼work ⟨fam⟩ wie am Schnürchen

clod /klɒd/ n Klumpen m

clog /klɒg/ n Holzschuh m □ vt/i (pt/pp clogged) ∼ (up) verstopfen

cloister /'klɔɪstə(r)/ n Kreuzgang m

close[1] /kləʊs/ a (-r, -st) nah[e] ⟨to dat⟩; ⟨friend⟩ eng; ⟨weather⟩ schwül; have a ∼ shave ⟨fam⟩ mit knapper Not davonkommen □ adv nahe; ∼ by nicht weit weg □ n ⟨street⟩ Sackgasse f

close[2] /kləʊz/ n Ende nt; draw to a ∼ sich dem Ende nähern □ vt zumachen, schließen; ⟨bring to an end⟩ beenden; sperren ⟨road⟩ □ vi sich schließen; ⟨shop:⟩ schließen, zumachen; ⟨end⟩ enden. ∼ down vt schließen; stilllegen ⟨factory⟩ □ vi schließen; ⟨factory:⟩ stillgelegt werden

closed '**shop** /kləʊzd-/ n ≈ Gewerkschaftszwang m

closely /'kləʊslɪ/ adv eng, nah[e]; ⟨with attention⟩ genau

close season /'kləʊs-/ n Schonzeit f

closet /'klɒzɪt/ n ⟨Amer⟩ Schrank m

close-up /'kləʊs-/ n Nahaufnahme f

closure /'kləʊʒə(r)/ n Schließung f; ⟨of factory⟩ Stilllegung f; ⟨of road⟩ Sperrung f

clot /klɒt/ n ⟨Blut⟩gerinnsel nt; ⟨fam: idiot⟩ Trottel m □ vi (pt/pp clotted) ⟨blood:⟩ gerinnen

cloth /klɒθ/ n Tuch nt

clothe /kləʊð/ vt kleiden

clothes /kləʊðz/ npl Kleider pl. ∼-brush n Kleiderbürste f. ∼-line n Wäscheleine f

clothing /'kləʊðɪŋ/ n Kleidung f

cloud /klaʊd/ n Wolke f □ vi ∼ over sich bewölken. ∼burst n Wolkenbruch m

cloudy /'klaʊdɪ/ a (-ier, -iest) wolkig, bewölkt; ⟨liquid⟩ trübe

clout /klaʊt/ n ⟨fam⟩ Schlag m; ⟨influence⟩ Einfluss m □ vt ⟨fam⟩ hauen

clove /kləʊv/ n ⟨Gewürz⟩nelke f; ∼ of garlic Knoblauchzehe f

clover /'kləʊvə(r)/ n Klee m. ∼-leaf n Kleeblatt nt

clown /klaʊn/ n Clown m □ vi ∼ [about] herumalbern

club /klʌb/ n Klub m; ⟨weapon⟩ Keule f; ⟨Sport⟩ Schläger m; ∼s pl ⟨Cards⟩ Kreuz nt, Treff nt □ v (pt/pp clubbed) vt ∼ knüppeln □ vi ∼ together zusammenlegen

cluck /klʌk/ vi glucken

clue /kluː/ n Anhaltspunkt m; ⟨in crossword⟩ Frage f; I haven't a ∼ ⟨fam⟩ ich habe keine Ahnung

clump /klʌmp/ n Gruppe f

clumsiness /'klʌmzɪnɪs/ n Ungeschicklichkeit f

clumsy /'klʌmzɪ/ a (-ier, -iest), -ily adv ungeschickt; ⟨unwieldy⟩ unförmig

clung /klʌŋ/ see cling

cluster /'klʌstə(r)/ n Gruppe f; ⟨of flowers⟩ Büschel nt □ vi sich scharen ⟨round um⟩

clutch /klʌtʃ/ n Griff m; ⟨Auto⟩ Kupplung f; be in s.o.'s ∼es ⟨fam⟩ in jds Klauen sein □ vt festhalten; ⟨grab⟩ ergreifen □ vi ∼ at greifen nach

clutter /'klʌtə(r)/ n Kram m □ vt ∼ [up] vollstopfen

c/o abbr ⟨care of⟩ bei

coach /kəʊtʃ/ n ⟨Reise⟩bus m; ⟨Rail⟩ Wagen m; ⟨horse-drawn⟩ Kutsche f; ⟨Sport⟩ Trainer m □ vt Nachhilfestunden geben ⟨+ dat⟩; ⟨Sport⟩ trainieren

coagulate /kəʊ'ægjʊleɪt/ vi gerinnen

coal /kəʊl/ n Kohle f

coalition /kəʊə'lɪʃn/ n Koalition f

'**coal-mine** n Kohlenbergwerk nt

coarse /kɔːs/ a (-r, -st), -ly adv grob

coast /kəʊst/ n Küste f □ vi ⟨freewheel⟩ im Freilauf fahren; ⟨Auto⟩ im Leerlauf fahren. ∼al a Küsten-. ∼er n ⟨mat⟩ Untersatz m

coast-: ∼guard n Küstenwache f. ∼line n Küste f

coat /kəʊt/ n Mantel m; ⟨of animal⟩ Fell nt; ⟨of paint⟩ Anstrich m; ∼ of arms Wappen nt □ vt überziehen; ⟨with paint⟩ streichen. ∼-hanger n Kleiderbügel m. ∼-hook n Kleiderhaken m

coating /'kəʊtɪŋ/ n Überzug m, Schicht f; (of paint) Anstrich m

coax /kəʊks/ vt gut zureden (+ dat)

cob /kɒb/ n (of corn) [Mais]kolben m

cobble[1] /'kɒbl/ n Kopfstein m; ∼s pl Kopfsteinpflaster nt

cobble[2] vt flicken. ∼r n Schuster m

'cobblestones npl = cobbles

cobweb /'kɒb-/ n Spinnengewebe nt

cocaine /kə'keɪn/ n Kokain nt

cock /kɒk/ n Hahn m; (any male bird) Männchen nt □ vt ⟨animal:⟩ ∼ its ears die Ohren spitzen; ∼ the gun den Hahn spannen. ∼-and-'bull story n (fam) Lügengeschichte f

cockerel /'kɒkərəl/ n [junger] Hahn m

cock-'eyed a (fam) schief; (absurd) verrückt

cockle /'kɒkl/ n Herzmuschel f

cockney /'kɒknɪ/ n (dialect) Cockney nt; (person) Cockney m

cock: ∼pit n (Aviat) Cockpit nt. ∼roach /-rəʊtʃ/ n Küchenschabe f. ∼tail n Cocktail m. ∼-up n (sl) make a ∼-up Mist bauen (of bei)

cocky /'kɒkɪ/ a (-ier, -iest) (fam) eingebildet

cocoa /'kəʊkəʊ/ n Kakao m

coconut /'kəʊkənʌt/ n Kokosnuß f

cocoon /kə'ku:n/ n Kokon m

cod /kɒd/ n inv Kabeljau m

COD abbr (cash on delivery) per Nachnahme

coddle /'kɒdl/ vt verhätscheln

code /kəʊd/ n Kode m; (Computing) Code m; (set of rules) Kodex m. ∼d a verschlüsselt

coedu'cational /kəʊ-/ a gemischt. ∼ school n Koedukationsschule f

coerc|e /kəʊ'ɜ:s/ vt zwingen. ∼ion /-'ɜ:ʃn/ n Zwang m

coe'xist vi koexistieren. ∼ence n Koexistenz f

coffee /'kɒfɪ/ n Kaffee m

coffee: ∼-grinder n Kaffeemühle f. ∼-pot n Kaffeekanne f. ∼-table n Couchtisch m

coffin /'kɒfɪn/ n Sarg m

cog /kɒg/ n (Techn) Zahn m

cogent /'kəʊdʒənt/ a überzeugend

cog-wheel n Zahnrad nt

cohabit /kəʊ'hæbɪt/ vi (Jur) zusammenleben

coherent /kəʊ'hɪərənt/ a zusammenhängend; (comprehensible) verständlich

coil /kɔɪl/ n Rolle f; (Electr) Spule f; (one ring) Windung f □ vt ∼ [up] zusammenrollen

coin /kɔɪn/ n Münze f □ vt prägen

coincide /kəʊɪn'saɪd/ vi zusammenfallen; (agree) übereinstimmen

coinciden|ce /kəʊ'ɪnsɪdəns/ n Zufall m. ∼tal /-'dentl/ a, -ly adv zufällig

coke /kəʊk/ n Koks m

Coke (P) n (drink) Cola f

colander /'kʌləndə(r)/ n (Culin) Durchschlag m

cold /kəʊld/ a (-er, -est) kalt; I am or feel ∼ mir ist kalt □ n Kälte f; (Med) Erkältung f

cold: ∼-'blooded a kaltblütig. ∼-'hearted a kaltherzig. ∼ly adv (fig) kalt, kühl. ∼ness n Kälte f

coleslaw /'kəʊlslɔː/ n Krautsalat m

colic /'kɒlɪk/ n Kolik f

collaborat|e /kə'læbəreɪt/ vi zusammenarbeiten (with mit); ∼e on sth mitarbeiten bei etw. ∼ion /-'reɪʃn/ n Zusammenarbeit f, Mitarbeit f; (with enemy) Kollaboration f. ∼or n Mitarbeiter(in) m(f); Kollaborateur m

collaps|e /kə'læps/ n Zusammenbruch m; Einsturz m □ vi zusammenbrechen; ⟨roof, building:⟩ einstürzen. ∼ible a zusammenklappbar

collar /'kɒlə(r)/ n Kragen m; (for animal) Halsband nt. ∼-bone n Schlüsselbein nt

colleague /'kɒliːg/ n Kollege m/Kollegin f

collect /kə'lekt/ vt sammeln; (fetch) abholen; einsammeln ⟨tickets⟩; einziehen ⟨taxes⟩ □ vi sich [an]sammeln □ adv call ∼ (Amer) ein R-Gespräch führen. ∼ed /-ɪd/ a gesammelt; (calm) gefasst

collection /kə'lekʃn/ n Sammlung f; (in church) Kollekte f; (of post) Leerung f; (designer's) Kollektion f

collective /kə'lektɪv/ a gemeinsam; (Pol) kollektiv. ∼ 'noun n Kollektivum nt

collector /kə'lektə(r)/ n Sammler(in) m(f)

college /'kɒlɪdʒ/ n College nt

collide /kə'laɪd/ vi zusammenstoßen

colliery /'kɒlɪərɪ/ n Kohlengrube f

collision /kə'lɪʒn/ n Zusammenstoß m

colloquial /kə'ləʊkwɪəl/ a, -ly adv umgangssprachlich. ∼ism n umgangssprachlicher Ausdruck m

Cologne /kə'ləʊn/ n Köln nt

colon /'kəʊlən/ n Doppelpunkt m; (Anat) Dickdarm m

colonel /'kɜːnl/ n Oberst m

colonial /kə'ləʊnɪəl/ a Kolonial-

colon|ize /'kɒlənaɪz/ vt kolonisieren. ∼y n Kolonie f

colossal /kə'lɒsl/ a riesig

colour /'kʌlə(r)/ n Farbe f; (complexion) Gesichtsfarbe f; (race) Hautfarbe f; ∼s pl *(flag)* Fahne *f*; off ~ *(fam)* nicht ganz auf der Höhe □ *vt* färben; ~ [in] ausmalen □ *vi (blush)* erröten

colour: ~ **bar** *n* Rassenschranke *f*. ~**blind** *a* farbenblind. ~**ed** *a* farbig *a* □ *n (person)* Farbige(r) *m/f*. ~**fast** *a* farbecht. ~**film** *n* Farbfilm *m*. ~**ful** *a* farbenfroh. ~**less** *a* farblos. ~ **photo[graph]** *n* Farbaufnahme *f*. ~ **television** *n* Farbfernsehen *nt*

colt /'kəʊlt/ *n* junger Hengst *m*

column /'kɒləm/ *n* Säule *f*; *(of soldiers, figures)* Kolonne *f*; *(Typ)* Spalte *f*; *(Journ)* Kolumne *f*. ~**ist** /-nɪst/ *n* Kolumnist *m*

coma /'kəʊmə/ *n* Koma *nt*

comb /kəʊm/ *n* Kamm *m* □ *vt* kämmen; *(search)* absuchen; ~ **one's hair** sich *(dat)* [die Haare] kämmen

combat /'kɒmbæt/ *n* Kampf *m* □ *vt (pt/pp* combated) bekämpfen

combination /kɒmbɪ'neɪʃn/ *n* Verbindung *f*; *(for lock)* Kombination *f*

combine¹ /kəm'baɪn/ *vt* verbinden □ *vi* sich verbinden; *(people:)* sich zusammenschließen

combine² /'kɒmbaɪn/ *n (Comm)* Konzern *m*; ~ **[harvester]** *n* Mähdrescher *m*

combustion /kəm'bʌstʃn/ *n* Verbrennung *f*

come /kʌm/ *vi (pt* came, *pp* come) kommen; *(reach)* reichen (to an + *acc)*; that ~**s to £10** das macht £10; ~ **into money** zu Geld kommen; ~ **true** wahr werden; ~ **in two sizes** in zwei Größen erhältlich sein; **the years to** ~ die kommenden Jahre; **how** ~? *(fam)* wie das? ~ **about** *vi* geschehen. ~ **across** *vi* herüberkommen; *(fam)* klar werden □ *vt* stoßen auf (+ *acc)*. ~ **apart** *vi* sich auseinander nehmen lassen; *(accidentally)* auseinander gehen. ~ **away** *vi* weggehen; *(thing:)* abgehen. ~ **back** *vi* zurückkommen. ~ **by** *vi* vorbeikommen □ *vt (obtain)* bekommen. ~ **in** *vi* hereinkommen. ~ **off** *vi* abgehen; *(take place)* stattfinden; *(succeed)* klappen *(fam)*. ~ **out** *vi* herauskommen; *(book:)* erscheinen; *(stain:)* herausgehen. ~ **round** *vi* vorbeikommen; *(after fainting)* [wieder] zu sich kommen; *(change one's mind)* sich umstimmen lassen. ~ **to** *vi* [wieder] zu sich kommen. ~ **up** *vi* heraufkommen; *(plant:)* aufgehen; *(reach)* reichen (to bis); ~ **up with** sich *(dat)* einfallen lassen

'**come-back** *n* Comeback *nt*

comedian /kə'miːdɪən/ *n* Komiker *m*

'**come-down** *n* Rückschritt *m*

comedy /'kɒmədɪ/ *n* Komödie *f*

comet /'kɒmɪt/ *n* Komet *m*

come-uppance /kʌm'ʌpəns/ *n* **get one's** ~ *(fam)* sein Fett abkriegen

comfort /'kʌmfət/ *n* Bequemlichkeit *f*; *(consolation)* Trost *m* □ *vt* trösten

comfortable /'kʌmfətəbl/ *a*, **-bly** *adv* bequem

'**comfort station** *n (Amer)* öffentliche Toilette *f*

comfy /'kʌmfɪ/ *a (fam)* bequem

comic /'kɒmɪk/ *a* komisch □ *n* Komiker *m*; *(periodical)* Comic-Heft *nt*. ~**al** *a*, **-ly** *adv* komisch. ~ **strip** *n* Comic Strips *pl*

coming /'kʌmɪŋ/ *a* kommend □ *n* Kommen *nt*; ~**s and goings** Kommen und Gehen *nt*

comma /'kɒmə/ *n* Komma *nt*

command /kə'mɑːnd/ *n* Befehl *m*; *(Mil)* Kommando *nt*; *(mastery)* Beherrschung *f* □ *vt* befehlen (+ *dat)*; kommandieren *(army)*

commandeer /kɒmən'dɪə(r)/ *vt* beschlagnahmen

command|er /kə'mɑːndə(r)/ *n* Befehlshaber *m*; *(of unit)* Kommandeur *m*; *(of ship)* Kommandant *m*. ~**ing** *a (view)* beherrschend. ~**ing officer** *n* Befehlshaber *m*. ~**ment** *n* Gebot *nt*

commemorat|e /kə'meməreɪt/ *vt* gedenken (+ *gen)*. ~**ion** /-'reɪʃn/ *n* Gedenken *nt*. ~**ive** /-ətɪv/ *a* Gedenk-

commence /kə'mens/ *vt/i* anfangen, beginnen. ~**ment** *n* Anfang *m*, Beginn *m*

commend /kə'mend/ *vt* loben; *(recommend)* empfehlen (to *dat)*. ~**able** /-əbl/ *a* lobenswert. ~**ation** /kɒmen'deɪʃn/ *n* Lob *nt*

commensurate /kə'menʃərət/ *a* angemessen; **be** ~ **with** entsprechen (+ *dat)*

comment /'kɒment/ *n* Bemerkung *f*; **no** ~! kein Kommentar! □ *vi* sich äußern (on zu); ~ **on** *(Journ)* kommentieren

commentary /'kɒmntrɪ/ *n* Kommentar *m*; *(running)* ~ *(Radio, TV)* Reportage *f*

commentator /'kɒmənteɪtə(r)/ *n* Kommentator *m*; *(Sport)* Reporter *m*

commerce /'kɒmɜːs/ *n* Handel *m*

commercial /kə'mɜːʃl/ *a*, **-ly** *adv* kommerziell □ *n (Radio, TV)* Werbespot *m*. ~**ize** *vt* kommerzialisieren

commiserate /kə'mɪzəreɪt/ *vi* sein Mitleid ausdrücken (with *dat)*

commission /kə'mɪʃn/ *n (order for work)* Auftrag *m*; *(body of people)* Kommission *f*; *(payment)* Provision *f*; *(Mil)* [Offiziers]patent *nt*; **out of** ~ außer Betrieb □ *vt* beauftragen *(s.o.)*; **in Auftrag geben** *(thing)*; *(Mil)* zum Offizier ernennen

commissionaire /kəmɪʃə'neə(r)/ *n* Portier *m*

commissioner /kə'mɪʃənə(r)/ n Kommissar m; ∼ for oaths Notar m

commit /kə'mɪt/ vt (pt/pp committed) begehen; (entrust) anvertrauen (to dat); (consign) einweisen (to in + acc); ∼ oneself sich festlegen; (involve oneself) sich engagieren; ∼ sth to memory sich (dat) etw einprägen. ∼ment n Verpflichtung f; (involvement) Engagement nt. ∼ted a engagiert

committee /kə'mɪtɪ/ n Ausschuss m, Komitee nt

commodity /kə'mɒdətɪ/ n Ware f

common /'kɒmən/ a (-er, -est) gemeinsam; (frequent) häufig; (ordinary) gewöhnlich; (vulgar) ordinär □ n Gemeindeland nt; have in ∼ gemeinsam haben; House of C∼s Unterhaus nt. ∼er n Bürgerliche(r) m/f

common: ∼ 'law n Gewohnheitsrecht nt. ∼ly adv allgemein. C∼ 'Market n Gemeinsamer Markt m. ∼place a häufig. ∼room n Aufenthaltsraum m. ∼ 'sense n gesunder Menschenverstand m

commotion /kə'məʊʃn/ n Tumult m

communal /'kɒmjʊnl/ a gemeinschaftlich

communicable /kə'mju:nɪkəbl/ a (disease) übertragbar

communicate /kə'mju:nɪkeɪt/ vt mitteilen (to dat); übertragen (disease) □ vi sich verständigen; (be in touch) in Verbindung stehen

communication /kəmju:nɪ'keɪʃn/ n Verständigung f; (contact) Verbindung f; (of disease) Übertragung f; (message) Mitteilung f; ∼s pl (technology) Nachrichtenwesen nt. ∼ cord n Notbremse f

communicative /kə'mju:nɪkətɪv/ a mitteilsam

Communion /kə'mju:nɪən/ n [Holy] ∼ das [heilige] Abendmahl; (Roman Catholic) die [heilige] Kommunion

communiqué /kə'mju:nɪkeɪ/ n Kommuniqué nt

Communis|m /'kɒmjʊnɪzm/ n Kommunismus m. ∼t /-ɪst/ a kommunistisch □ n Kommunist(in) m(f)

community /kə'mju:nətɪ/ n Gemeinschaft f; local ∼ Gemeinde f. ∼ centre n Gemeinschaftszentrum nt

commute /kə'mju:t/ vi pendeln □ vt (Jur) umwandeln. ∼r n Pendler(in) m(f)

compact¹ /kəm'pækt/ a kompakt

compact² /'kɒmpækt/ n Puderdose f. ∼ disc n CD f

companion /kəm'pænjən/ n Begleiter(in) m(f). ∼ship n Gesellschaft f

company /'kʌmpənɪ/ n Gesellschaft f; (firm) Firma f; (Mil) Kompanie f; (fam:

guests) Besuch m. ∼ car n Firmenwagen m

comparable /'kɒmpərəbl/ a vergleichbar

comparative /kəm'pærətɪv/ a vergleichend; (relative) relativ □ n (Gram) Komparativ m. ∼ly adv verhältnismäßig

compare /kəm'peə(r)/ vt vergleichen (with/to mit) □ vi sich vergleichen lassen

comparison /kəm'pærɪsn/ n Vergleich m

compartment /kəm'pɑ:tmənt/ n Fach nt; (Rail) Abteil nt

compass /'kʌmpəs/ n Kompass m. ∼es npl pair of ∼es Zirkel m

compassion /kəm'pæʃn/ n Mitleid nt. ∼ate /-ʃənət/ a mitfühlend

compatible /kəm'pætəbl/ a vereinbar; (drugs) verträglich; (Techn) kompatibel; be ∼ (people:) [gut] zueinander passen

compatriot /kəm'pætrɪət/ n Landsmann m /-männin f

compel /kəm'pel/ vt (pt/pp compelled) zwingen

compensat|e /'kɒmpənseɪt/ vt entschädigen □ vi ∼e for (fig) ausgleichen. ∼ion /-'seɪʃn/ n Entschädigung f; (fig) Ausgleich m

compère /'kɒmpeə(r)/ n Conférencier m

compete /kəm'pi:t/ vi konkurrieren; (take part) teilnehmen (in an + dat)

competen|ce /'kɒmpɪtəns/ n Tüchtigkeit f; (ability) Fähigkeit f; (Jur) Kompetenz f. ∼t a tüchtig; fähig; (Jur) kompetent

competition /kɒmpə'tɪʃn/ n Konkurrenz f; (contest) Wettbewerb m; (in newspaper) Preisausschreiben nt

competitive /kəm'petɪtɪv/ a (Comm) konkurrenzfähig

competitor /kəm'petɪtə(r)/ n Teilnehmer m; (Comm) Konkurrent m

compile /kəm'paɪl/ vt zusammenstellen; verfassen (dictionary)

complacen|cy /kəm'pleɪsənsɪ/ n Selbstzufriedenheit f. ∼t a, -ly adv selbstzufrieden

complain /kəm'pleɪn/ vi klagen (about/ of über + acc); (formally) sich beschweren. ∼t n Klage f; (formal) Beschwerde f; (Med) Leiden nt

complement¹ /'kɒmplɪmənt/ n Ergänzung f; full ∼ volle Anzahl f

complement² /'kɒmplɪment/ vt ergänzen; ∼ each other sich ergänzen. ∼ary /-'mentərɪ/ a sich ergänzend; be ∼ary sich ergänzen

complete /kəm'pli:t/ a vollständig; (finished) fertig; (utter) völlig □ vt vervollständigen; (finish) abschließen; (fill in) ausfüllen. ∼ly adv völlig completion /kəm'pli:ʃn/ n Vervollständigung f; (end) Abschluss m

complex /'kɒmpleks/ a komplex □ n Komplex m

complexion /kəm'plekʃn/ n Teint m; (colour) Gesichtsfarbe f; (fig) Aspekt m

complexity /kəm'pleksətɪ/ n Komplexität f

compliance /kəm'plaɪəns/ n Einverständnis nt; in ~ with gemäß (+ dat)

complicat|e /'kɒmplɪkeɪt/ vt komplizieren. ~ed a kompliziert. ~ion /-'keɪʃn/ n Komplikation f

complicity /kəm'plɪsətɪ/ n Mittäterschaft f

compliment /'kɒmplɪmənt/ n Kompliment nt; ~s pl Grüße pl □ vt ein Kompliment machen (+ dat). ~ary /-'mentərɪ/ a schmeichelhaft; (given free) Frei-

comply /kəm'plaɪ/ vi (pt/pp -ied) ~ with nachkommen (+ dat)

component /kəm'pəʊnənt/ a & n ~ [part] Bestandteil m, Teil nt

compose /kəm'pəʊz/ vt verfassen; (Mus) komponieren; ~ oneself sich fassen; be ~d of sich zusammensetzen aus. ~d a (calm) gefasst. ~r n Komponist m

composition /kɒmpə'zɪʃn/ n Komposition f; (essay) Aufsatz m

compost /'kɒmpɒst/ n Kompost m

composure /kəm'pəʊʒə(r)/ n Fassung f

compound¹ /kəm'paʊnd/ vt (make worse) verschlimmern

compound² /'kɒmpaʊnd/ a zusammengesetzt; (fracture) kompliziert □ n (Chem) Verbindung f; (Gram) Kompositum nt; (enclosure) Einfriedigung f. ~ 'interest n Zinseszins m

comprehen|d /kɒmprɪ'hend/ vt begreifen, verstehen; (include) umfassen. ~sible a, -bly adv verständlich. ~sion /-'henʃn/ n Verständnis nt

comprehensive /kɒmprɪ'hensɪv/ a & n umfassend; ~ [school] Gesamtschule f. ~ insurance n (Auto) Vollkaskoversicherung f

compress¹ /'kɒmpres/ n Kompresse f

compress² /kəm'pres/ vt zusammenpressen; ~ed air Druckluft f

comprise /kəm'praɪz/ vt umfassen, bestehen aus

compromise /'kɒmprəmaɪz/ n Kompromiss m □ vt kompromittieren (person) □ vi einen Kompromiss schließen

compuls|ion /kəm'pʌlʃn/ n Zwang m. ~ive /-sɪv/ a zwanghaft; ~ive eating Esszwang m. ~ory /-sərɪ/ a obligatorisch; ~ory subject Pflichtfach nt

compunction /kəm'pʌŋkʃn/ n Gewissensbisse pl

comput|er /kəm'pju:tə(r)/ n Computer m. ~erize vt computerisieren (data); auf Computer umstellen (firm). ~ing n Computertechnik f

comrade /'kɒmreɪd/ n Kamerad m; (Pol) Genosse m/Genossin f. ~ship n Kameradschaft f

con¹ /kɒn/ see pro

con² n (fam) Schwindel m □ vt (pt/pp conned) (fam) beschwindeln

concave /'kɒŋkeɪv/ a konkav

conceal /kən'si:l/ vt verstecken; (keep secret) verheimlichen

concede /kən'si:d/ vt zugeben; (give up) aufgeben

conceit /kən'si:t/ n Einbildung f. ~ed a eingebildet

conceivable /kən'si:vəbl/ a denkbar

conceive /kən'si:v/ vt (Biol) empfangen; (fig) sich (dat) ausdenken □ vi schwanger werden. ~ of (fig) sich (dat) vorstellen

concentrat|e /'kɒnsəntreɪt/ vt konzentrieren □ vi sich konzentrieren. ~ion /-'treɪʃn/ n Konzentration f. ~ion camp n Konzentrationslager nt

concept /'kɒnsept/ n Begriff m. ~ion /kən'sepʃn/ n Empfängnis f; (idea) Vorstellung f

concern /kən'sɜ:n/ n Angelegenheit f; (worry) Sorge f; (Comm) Unternehmen nt □ vt (be about, affect) betreffen; (worry) kümmern; be ~ed about besorgt sein um; ~ oneself with sich beschäftigen mit; as far as I am ~ed was mich angeht od betrifft. ~ing prep bezüglich (+ gen)

concert /'kɒnsət/ n Konzert nt; in ~ im Chor. ~ed /kən'sɜ:tɪd/ a gemeinsam

concertina /kɒnsə'ti:nə/ n Konzertina f

'concertmaster n (Amer) Konzertmeister m

concerto /kən'tʃeətəʊ/ n Konzert nt

concession /kən'seʃn/ n Zugeständnis nt; (Comm) Konzession f; (reduction) Ermäßigung f. ~ary a (reduced) ermäßigt

conciliation /kənsɪlɪ'eɪʃn/ n Schlichtung f

concise /kən'saɪs/ a, -ly adv kurz

conclude /kən'klu:d/ vt/i schließen

conclusion /kən'klu:ʒn/ n Schluss m; in ~ abschließend, zum Schluss

conclusive /kən'klu:sɪv/ a schlüssig

concoct /kən'kɒkt/ vt zusammenstellen; (fig) fabrizieren. ~ion /-ɒkʃn/ n Zusammenstellung f; (drink) Gebräu nt

concourse /'kɒŋkɔ:s/ a Halle f

concrete /'kɒŋkri:t/ a konkret □ n Beton m □ vt betonieren

concur /kən'kɜ:(r)/ vi (pt/pp concurred) übereinstimmen

concurrently /kən'kʌrəntlɪ/ adv gleichzeitig

concussion /kən'kʌʃn/ n Gehirnerschütterung f

condemn /kən'dem/ vt verurteilen; (declare unfit) für untauglich erklären. ~ation /kɒndem'neɪʃn/ n Verurteilung f

condensation /kɒnden'seɪʃn/ n Kondensation f

condense /kən'dens/ vt zusammenfassen; (Phys) kondensieren ▫ vi sich kondensieren. ~d milk n Kondensmilch f

condescend /kɒndɪ'send/ vi sich herablassen (to zu). ~ing a, -ly adv herablassend

condiment /'kɒndɪmənt/ n Gewürz nt

condition /kən'dɪʃn/ n Bedingung f; (state) Zustand m; ~s pl Verhältnisse pl; on ~ that unter der Bedingung, dass ▫ vt (Psych) konditionieren. ~al a bedingt; be ~al on abhängen von ▫ n (Gram) Konditional m. ~er n Haarkur f; (for fabrics) Weichspüler m

condolences /kən'dəʊlənsɪz/ npl Beileid nt

condom /'kɒndəm/ n Kondom nt

condominium /kɒndə'mɪnɪəm/ n (Amer) ≈ Eigentumswohnung f

condone /kən'dəʊn/ vt hinwegsehen über (+ acc)

conducive /kən'dju:sɪv/ a förderlich (to dat)

conduct[1] /'kɒndʌkt/ n Verhalten nt; (Sch) Betragen nt

conduct[2] /kən'dʌkt/ vt führen; (Phys) leiten; (Mus) dirigieren. ~or n Dirigent m; (of bus) Schaffner m; (Phys) Leiter m. ~ress n Schaffnerin f

cone /kəʊn/ n Kegel m; (Bot) Zapfen m; (for ice-cream) [Eis]tüte f; (Auto) Leitkegel m

confectioner /kən'fekʃənə(r)/ n Konditor m. ~y n Süßwaren pl

confederation /kənfedə'reɪʃn/ n Bund m; (Pol) Konföderation f

confer /kən'fɜ:(r)/ v (pt/pp conferred) ▫ vt verleihen (on dat) ▫ vi sich beraten

conference /'kɒnfərəns/ n Konferenz f

confess /kən'fes/ vt/i gestehen; (Relig) beichten. ~ion /-eʃn/ n Geständnis nt; (Relig) Beichte f. ~ional /-eʃənəl/ n Beichtstuhl m. ~or n Beichtvater m

confetti /kən'fetɪ/ n Konfetti nt

confide /kən'faɪd/ vt anvertrauen ▫ vi ~ in s.o. sich jdm anvertrauen

confidence /'kɒnfɪdəns/ n (trust) Vertrauen nt; (self-assurance) Selbstvertrauen nt; (secret) Geheimnis nt; in ~ im Vertrauen. ~ trick n Schwindel m

confident /'kɒnfɪdənt/ a, -ly adv zuversichtlich; (self-assured) selbstsicher

confidential /kɒnfɪ'denʃl/ a, -ly adv vertraulich

confine /kən'faɪn/ vt beschränken (to auf + acc); be ~d to bed das Bett hüten müssen. ~d a (narrow) eng. ~ment n Haft f

confines /'kɒnfaɪnz/ npl Grenzen pl

confirm /kən'fɜ:m/ vt bestätigen; (Relig) konfirmieren; (Roman Catholic) firmen. ~ation /kɒnfə'meɪʃn/ n Bestätigung f; Konfirmation f; Firmung f. ~ed a ~ed bachelor eingefleischter Junggeselle m

confiscat|e /'kɒnfɪskeɪt/ vt beschlagnahmen. ~ion /-'keɪʃn/ n Beschlagnahme f

conflict[1] /'kɒnflɪkt/ n Konflikt m

conflict[2] /kən'flɪkt/ vi im Widerspruch stehen (with zu). ~ing a widersprüchlich

conform /kən'fɔ:m/ vi (person:) sich anpassen; (thing:) entsprechen (to dat). ~ist n Konformist m

confounded /kən'faʊndɪd/ a (fam) verflixt

confront /kən'frʌnt/ vt konfrontieren. ~ation /kɒnfrən'teɪʃn/ n Konfrontation f

confus|e /kən'fju:z/ vt verwirren; (mistake for) verwechseln (with mit). ~ing a verwirrend. ~ion /-ju:ʒn/ n Verwirrung f; (muddle) Durcheinander nt

congeal /kən'dʒi:l/ vi fest werden; (blood:) gerinnen

congenial /kən'dʒi:nɪəl/ a angenehm

congenital /kən'dʒenɪtl/ a angeboren

congest|ed /kən'dʒestɪd/ a verstopft; (with people) überfüllt. ~ion /-estʃn/ n Verstopfung f; Überfüllung f

congratulat|e /kən'grætjʊleɪt/ vt gratulieren (+ dat) (on zu). ~ions /-'leɪʃnz/ npl Glückwünsche pl; ~ions! [ich] gratuliere!

congregat|e /'kɒŋgrɪgeɪt/ vi sich versammeln. ~ion /-'geɪʃn/ n (Relig) Gemeinde f

congress /'kɒŋgres/ n Kongress m. ~man n Kongressabgeordnete(r) m

conical /'kɒnɪkl/ a kegelförmig

conifer /'kɒnɪfə(r)/ n Nadelbaum m

conjecture /kən'dʒektʃə(r)/ n Mutmaßung f ▫ vt/i mutmaßen

conjugal /'kɒndʒʊgl/ a ehelich

conjugat|e /'kɒndʒʊgeɪt/ vt konjugieren. ~ion /-'geɪʃn/ n Konjugation f

conjunction /kən'dʒʌŋkʃn/ n Konjunktion f; in ~ with zusammen mit

conjunctivitis /kəndʒʌŋktɪ'vaɪtɪs/ n Bindehautentzündung f

conjur|e /'kʌndʒə(r)/ vi zaubern □ vt ~e up heraufbeschwören. ~or n Zauberkünstler m

conk /kɒŋk/ vi ~ out ⟨fam⟩ ⟨machine:⟩ kaputtgehen; ⟨person:⟩ zusammenklappen

conker /'kɒŋkə(r)/ n ⟨fam⟩ Kastanie f

'con-man n ⟨fam⟩ Schwindler m

connect /kə'nekt/ vt verbinden (to mit); ⟨Electr⟩ anschließen (to an + acc) □ vi verbunden sein; ⟨train.⟩ Anschluss haben (with an + acc); be ~ed with zu tun haben mit; ⟨be related to⟩ verwandt sein mit

connection /kə'nekʃn/ n Verbindung f; ⟨Rail, Electr⟩ Anschluss m; in ~ with in Zusammenhang mit. ~s npl Beziehungen pl

conniv|ance /kə'naɪvəns/ n stillschweigende Duldung f. ~e vi ~e at stillschweigend dulden

connoisseur /kɒnə'sɜ:(r)/ n Kenner m

connotation /kɒnə'teɪʃn/ n Assoziation f

conquer /'kɒŋkə(r)/ vt erobern; ⟨fig⟩ besiegen. ~or n Eroberer m

conquest /'kɒŋkwest/ n Eroberung f

conscience /'kɒnʃəns/ n Gewissen nt

conscientious /kɒnʃɪ'enʃəs/ a, -ly adv gewissenhaft. ~ ob'jector n Kriegsdienstverweigerer m

conscious /'kɒnʃəs/ a, -ly adv bewusst; [fully] ~ bei [vollem] Bewusstsein; be/ become ~ of sth sich ⟨dat⟩ etw ⟨gen⟩ bewusst sein/werden. ~ness n Bewusstsein nt

conscript[1] /'kɒnskrɪpt/ n Einberufene(r) m

conscript[2] /kən'skrɪpt/ vt einberufen. ~ion /-ɪpʃn/ n allgemeine Wehrpflicht f.

consecrat|e /'kɒnsɪkreɪt/ vt weihen; einweihen ⟨church⟩. ~ion /-'kreɪʃn/ n Weihe f; Einweihung f

consecutive /kən'sekjʊtɪv/ a aufeinanderfolgend. -ly adv fortlaufend

consensus /kən'sensəs/ n Übereinstimmung f

consent /kən'sent/ n Einwilligung f, Zustimmung f □ vi einwilligen (to in + acc), zustimmen (to dat)

consequen|ce /'kɒnsɪkwəns/ n Folge f; ⟨importance⟩ Bedeutung f. ~t a daraus folgend. ~tly adv folglich

conservation /kɒnsə'veɪʃn/ n Erhaltung f, Bewahrung f. ~ist n Umweltschützer m

conservative /kən'sɜ:vətɪv/ a konservativ; ⟨estimate⟩ vorsichtig. C~ ⟨Pol⟩ a konservativ □ n Konservative(r) m/f

conservatory /kən'sɜ:vətrɪ/ n Wintergarten m

conserve /kən'sɜ:v/ vt erhalten, bewahren; sparen ⟨energy⟩

consider /kən'sɪdə(r)/ vt erwägen; ⟨think over⟩ sich ⟨dat⟩ überlegen; ⟨take into account⟩ berücksichtigen; ⟨regard as⟩ betrachten als; ~ doing sth erwägen, etw zu tun. ~able /-əbl/ a, -bly adv erheblich

consider|ate /kən'sɪdərət/ a, -ly adv rücksichtsvoll. ~ation /-'reɪʃn/ n Erwägung f; ⟨thoughtfulness⟩ Rücksicht f; ⟨payment⟩ Entgelt nt; take into ~ation berücksichtigen. ~ing prep wenn man bedenkt (that dass); ~ing the circumstances unter den Umständen

consign /kən'saɪn/ vt übergeben (to dat). ~ment n Lieferung f

consist /kən'sɪst/ vi ~ of bestehen aus

consisten|cy /kən'sɪstənsɪ/ n Konsequenz f; ⟨density⟩ Konsistenz f. ~t a konsequent; ⟨unchanging⟩ gleichbleibend; be ~t with entsprechen (+ dat). ~tly adv konsequent; ⟨constantly⟩ ständig

consolation /kɒnsə'leɪʃn/ n Trost m. ~ prize n Trostpreis m

console /kən'səʊl/ vt trösten

consolidate /kən'sɒlɪdeɪt/ vt konsolidieren

consonant /'kɒnsənənt/ n Konsonant m

consort /'kɒnsɔ:t/ n Gemahl(in) m(f)

conspicuous /kən'spɪkjʊəs/ a auffällig

conspiracy /kən'spɪrəsɪ/ n Verschwörung f

conspire /kən'spaɪə(r)/ vi sich verschwören

constable /'kʌnstəbl/ n Polizist m

constant /'kɒnstənt/ a, -ly adv beständig; ⟨continuous⟩ ständig

constellation /kɒnstə'leɪʃn/ n Sternbild nt

consternation /kɒnstə'neɪʃn/ n Bestürzung f

constipat|ed /'kɒnstɪpeɪtɪd/ a verstopft. ~ion /-'peɪʃn/ n Verstopfung f

constituency /kən'stɪtjʊənsɪ/ n Wahlkreis m

constituent /kən'stɪtjʊənt/ n Bestandteil m; ⟨Pol⟩ Wähler(in) m(f)

constitut|e /'kɒnstɪtju:t/ vt bilden. ~ion /-'tju:ʃn/ n ⟨Pol⟩ Verfassung f; ⟨of person⟩ Konstitution f. ~ional /-'tju:ʃənl/ a Verfassungs- □ n Verdauungsspaziergang m

constrain /kən'streɪn/ vt zwingen. ~t n Zwang m; (restriction) Beschränkung f; (strained manner) Gezwungenheit f

constrict /kən'strɪkt/ vt einengen

construct /kən'strʌkt/ vt bauen. ~ion /-ʌkʃn/ n Bau m; (Gram) Konstruktion f; (interpretation) Deutung f; under ~ion im Bau. ~ive /-ɪv/ a konstruktiv

construe /kən'stru:/ vt deuten

consul /'kɒnsl/ n Konsul m. ~ate /'kɒnsjʊlət/ n Konsulat nt

consult /kən'sʌlt/ vt [um Rat] fragen; konsultieren (doctor); nachschlagen in (+ dat) (book). ~ant n Berater m; (Med) Chefarzt m. ~ation /kɒnsl'teɪʃn/ n Beratung f; (Med) Konsultation f

consume /kən'sju:m/ vt verzehren; (use) verbrauchen. ~r n Verbraucher m. ~r goods npl Konsumgüter pl

consummat|e /'kɒnsəmeɪt/ vt vollziehen. ~ion /-'meɪʃn/ n Vollzug m

consumption /kən'sʌmpʃn/ n Konsum m; (use) Verbrauch m

contact /'kɒntækt/ n Kontakt m; (person) Kontaktperson f □ vt sich in Verbindung setzen mit. ~ 'lenses npl Kontaktlinsen pl

contagious /kən'teɪdʒəs/ a direkt übertragbar

contain /kən'teɪn/ vt enthalten; (control) beherrschen. ~er n Behälter m; (Comm) Container m

contaminat|e /kən'tæmɪneɪt/ vt verseuchen. ~ion /-'neɪʃn/ n Verseuchung f

contemplat|e /'kɒntəmpleɪt/ vt betrachten; (meditate) nachdenken über (+ acc); ~e doing sth daran denken, etw zu tun. ~ion /-'pleɪʃn/ n Betrachtung f; Nachdenken nt

contemporary /kən'tempərərɪ/ a zeitgenössisch □ n Zeitgenosse m/ -genossin f

contempt /kən'tempt/ n Verachtung f; beneath ~ verabscheuungswürdig; ~ of court Missachtung f des Gerichts. ~ible /-əbl/ a verachtenswert. ~uous /-tjʊəs/ a, -ly adv verächtlich

contend /kən'tend/ vi kämpfen (with with) □ vt (assert) behaupten. ~er n Bewerber(in) m(f); (Sport) Wettkämpfer(in) m(f)

content¹ /'kɒntent/ n & contents pl Inhalt m

content² /kən'tent/ a zufrieden □ n to one's heart's ~ nach Herzenslust □ vt ~ oneself sich begnügen (with mit). ~ed a, -ly adv zufrieden

contention /kən'tenʃn/ n (assertion) Behauptung f

contentment /kən'tentmənt/ n Zufriedenheit f

contest¹ /'kɒntest/ n Kampf m; (competition) Wettbewerb m

contest² /kən'test/ vt (dispute) bestreiten; (Jur) anfechten; (Pol) kandidieren in (+ dat). ~ant n Teilnehmer m

context /'kɒntekst/ n Zusammenhang m

continent /'kɒntɪnənt/ n Kontinent m

continental /kɒntɪ'nentl/ a Kontinental-. ~ breakfast n kleines Frühstück nt. ~ quilt n Daunendecke f

contingen|cy /kən'tɪndʒənsɪ/ n Eventualität f. ~t a be ~t upon abhängen von □ n (Mil) Kontingent nt

continual /kən'tɪnjʊəl/ a, -ly adv dauernd

continuation /kəntɪnjʊ'eɪʃn/ n Fortsetzung f

continue /kən'tɪnju:/ vt fortsetzen; ~ doing or to do sth fortfahren, etw zu tun; to be ~d Fortsetzung folgt □ vi weitergehen; (doing sth) weitermachen; (speaking) fortfahren; (weather:) anhalten

continuity /kɒntɪ'nju:ətɪ/ n Kontinuität f

continuous /kən'tɪnjʊəs/ a, -ly adv anhaltend, ununterbrochen

contort /kən'tɔ:t/ vt verzerren. ~ion /-ɔ:ʃn/ n Verzerrung f

contour /'kɒntʊə(r)/ n Kontur f; (line) Höhenlinie f

contraband /'kɒntrəbænd/ n Schmuggelware f

contracep|tion /kɒntrə'sepʃn/ n Empfängnisverhütung f. ~tive /-tɪv/ a empfängnisverhütend □ n Empfängnisverhütungsmittel nt

contract¹ /'kɒntrækt/ n Vertrag m

contract² /kən'trækt/ vi sich zusammenziehen □ vt zusammenziehen; sich (dat) zuziehen (illness). ~ion /-ækʃn/ n Zusammenziehung f; (abbreviation) Abkürzung f; (in childbirth) Wehe f. ~or n Unternehmer m

contradict /kɒntrə'dɪkt/ vt widersprechen (+ dat). ~ion /-ɪkʃn/ n Widerspruch m. ~ory /-ərɪ/ a widersprüchlich

contra-flow /'kɒntrə-/ n Umleitung f [auf die entgegengesetzte Fahrbahn]

contralto /kən'træltəʊ/ n Alt m; (singer) Altistin f

contraption /kən'træpʃn/ n (fam) Apparat m

contrary¹ /'kɒntrərɪ/ a & adv entgegengesetzt; ~ to entgegen (+ dat) □ n Gegenteil nt; on the ~ im Gegenteil

contrary² /kən'treərɪ/ a widerspenstig

contrast¹ /'kɒntrɑ:st/ n Kontrast m

contrast² /kən'trɑ:st/ vt gegenüberstellen (with dat) □ vi einen Kontrast bilden (with zu). ~ing *a* gegensätzlich; ⟨colour⟩ Kontrast-

contraven|e /kɒntrə'viːn/ *vt* verstoßen gegen. ~tion /-'venʃn/ *n* Verstoß *m* (of gegen)

contribut|e /kən'trɪbjuːt/ *vt/i* beitragen; beisteuern ⟨money⟩; ⟨donate⟩ spenden. ~ion /kɒntrɪ'bjuːʃn/ *n* Beitrag *m*; ⟨donation⟩ Spende *f*. ~or *n* Beitragende(r) *m/f*

contrite /kən'traɪt/ *a* reuig

contrivance /kən'traɪvəns/ *n* Vorrichtung *f*

contrive /kən'traɪv/ *vt* verfertigen; ~ to do sth es fertig bringen, etw zu tun

control /kən'trəʊl/ *n* Kontrolle *f*; ⟨mastery⟩ Beherrschung *f*; ⟨Techn⟩ Regler *m*; ~s *pl* (of car, plane) Steuerung *f*; get out of ~ außer Kontrolle geraten □ *vt* (pt/pp controlled) kontrollieren; ⟨restrain⟩ unter Kontrolle halten; ~ oneself sich beherrschen

controvers|ial /kɒntrə'vɜːʃl/ *a* umstritten. ~y /'kɒntrəvɜːsɪ/ *n* Kontroverse *f*

conundrum /kə'nʌndrəm/ *n* Rätsel *m*

conurbation /kɒnɜː'beɪʃn/ *n* Ballungsgebiet *nt*

convalesce /kɒnvə'les/ *vi* sich erholen. ~nce *n* Erholung *f*

convalescent /kɒnvə'lesnt/ *a* be ~ noch erholungsbedürftig sein. ~ home *n* Erholungsheim *nt*

convector /kən'vektə(r)/ *n* ~ [heater] Konvektor *m*

convene /kən'viːn/ *vt* einberufen □ *v* sich versammeln

convenience /kən'viːnɪəns/ *n* Bequemlichkeit *f*; [public] ~ öffentliche Toilette *f*; with all modern ~s mit allem Komfort

convenient /kən'viːnɪənt/ *a*, -ly *adv* günstig; be ~ for s.o. jdm gelegen sein *od* jdm passen; if it is ~ [for you] wenn es Ihnen passt

convent /'kɒnvənt/ *n* [Nonnen]kloster *nt*

convention /kən'venʃn/ *n* ⟨custom⟩ Brauch *m*, Sitte *f*; ⟨agreement⟩ Konvention *f*; ⟨assembly⟩ Tagung *f*. ~al *a*, -ly *adv* konventionell

converge /kən'vɜːdʒ/ *vi* zusammenlaufen

conversant /kən'vɜːsənt/ *a* ~ with vertraut mit

conversation /kɒnvə'seɪʃn/ *n* Gespräch *nt*; ⟨Sch⟩ Konversation *f*

converse¹ /kən'vɜːs/ *vi* sich unterhalten

converse² /'kɒnvɜːs/ *n* Gegenteil *nt*. ~ly *adv* umgekehrt

conversion /kən'vɜːʃn/ *n* Umbau *m*; ⟨Relig⟩ Bekehrung *f*; ⟨calculation⟩ Umrechnung *f*

convert¹ /'kɒnvɜːt/ *n* Bekehrte(r) *m/f*, Konvertit *m*

convert² /kən'vɜːt/ *vt* bekehren ⟨person⟩; ⟨change⟩ umwandeln (into in + *acc*); umbauen ⟨building⟩; ⟨calculate⟩ umrechnen; ⟨Techn⟩ umstellen. ~ible /-əbl/ *a* verwandelbar □ *n* ⟨Auto⟩ Kabriolett *nt*

convex /'kɒnveks/ *a* konvex

convey /kən'veɪ/ *vt* befördern; vermitteln ⟨idea, message⟩. ~ance *n* Beförderung *f*; ⟨vehicle⟩ Beförderungsmittel *nt*. ~or belt *n* Förderband *nt*

convict¹ /'kɒnvɪkt/ *n* Sträfling *m*

convict² /kən'vɪkt/ *vt* verurteilen (of wegen). ~ion /-ɪkʃn/ *n* Verurteilung *f*; ⟨belief⟩ Überzeugung *f*; previous ~ion Vorstrafe *f*

convinc|e /kən'vɪns/ *vt* überzeugen. ~ing *a*, -ly *adv* überzeugend

convivial /kən'vɪvɪəl/ *a* gesellig

convoluted /'kɒnvəluːtɪd/ *a* verschlungen; ⟨fig⟩ verwickelt

convoy /'kɒnvɔɪ/ *n* Konvoi *m*

convuls|e /kən'vʌls/ *vt* be ~edsich krümmen (with vor + *dat*). ~ion /-'ʌlʃn/ *n* Krampf *m*

coo /kuː/ *vi* gurren

cook /kʊk/ *n* Koch *m*/ Köchin *f* □ *vt/i* kochen; is it ~ed? ist es gar? ~ the books ⟨fam⟩ die Bilanz frisieren. ~book *n* ⟨Amer⟩ Kochbuch *nt*

cooker /'kʊkə(r)/ *n* [Koch]herd *m*; ⟨apple⟩ Kochapfel *m*. ~y *n* Kochen *nt*. ~y book *n* Kochbuch *nt*

cookie /'kʊkɪ/ *n* ⟨Amer⟩ Keks *m*

cool /kuːl/ *a* (-er, -est), -ly *adv* kühlen □ *n* Kühle *f* □ *vt* kühlen □ *vi* abkühlen. ~-box *n* Kühlbox *f*. ~ness *n* Kühle *f*

coop /kuːp/ *n* [Hühner]stall *m* □ *vt* ~ up einsperren

co-operat|e /kəʊ'ɒpəreɪt/ *vi* zusammenarbeiten. ~ion /-'reɪʃn/ *n* Kooperation *f*

co-operative /kəʊ'ɒpərətɪv/ *a* hilfsbereit □ *n* Genossenschaft *f*

co-opt /kəʊ'ɒpt/ *vt* hinzuwählen

co-ordinat|e /kəʊ'ɔːdɪneɪt/ *vt* koordinieren. ~ion /-'neɪʃn/ *n* Koordination *f*

cop /kɒp/ *n* ⟨fam⟩ Polizist *m*

cope /kəʊp/ *vi* ⟨fam⟩ zurechtkommen; ~ with fertig werden mit

copious /'kəʊpɪəs/ *a* reichlich

copper¹ /'kɒpə(r)/ *n* Kupfer *nt*; ~s *pl* Kleingeld *nt* □ *a* kupfern

copper² *n* ⟨fam⟩ Polizist *m*

copper 'beech *n* Blutbuche *f*

coppice /'kɒpɪs/ *n*, copse /kɒps/ *n* Gehölz *nt*

copulate /'kɒpjʊleɪt/ *vi* sich begatten

copy /'kɒpɪ/ *n* Kopie *f*; (*book*) Exemplar *nt* □ *vt* (*pt/pp* -ied) kopieren; (*imitate*) nachahmen; (*Sch*) abschreiben

copy: ~right *n* Copyright *nt*. ~-writer *n* Texter *m*

coral /'kɒrl/ *n* Koralle *f*

cord /kɔːd/ *n* Schnur *f*; (*fabric*) Cordsamt *m*; ~s *pl* Cordhose *f*

cordial /'kɔːdɪəl/ *a*, -ly *adv* herzlich □ *n* Fruchtsirup *m*

cordon /'kɔːdn/ *n* Kordon *m* □ *vt* ~ off absperren

corduroy /'kɔːdərɔɪ/ *n* Cordsamt *m*

core /kɔː(r)/ *n* Kern *m*; (*of apple, pear*) Kerngehäuse *nt*

cork /kɔːk/ *n* Kork *m*; (*for bottle*) Korken *m*. ~screw *n* Korkenzieher *m*

corn[1] /kɔːn/ *n* Korn *nt*; (*Amer: maize*) Mais *m*

corn[2] *n* (*Med*) Hühnerauge *nt*

cornea /'kɔːnɪə/ *n* Hornhaut *f*

corned beef /kɔːnd'biːf/ *n* Cornedbeef *nt*

corner /'kɔːnə(r)/ *n* Ecke *f*; (*bend*) Kurve *f*; (*football*) Eckball *m* □ *vt* (*fig*) in die Enge treiben; (*Comm*) monopolisieren (*market*). ~-stone *n* Eckstein *m*

cornet /'kɔːnɪt/ *n* (*Mus*) Kornett *nt*; (*for ice-cream*) [Eis]tüte *f*

corn: ~flour *n*, (*Amer*) ~starch *n* Stärkemehl *nt*

corny /'kɔːnɪ/ *a* (*fam*) abgedroschen

coronary /'kɒrənərɪ/ *a* & *n* ~ [thrombosis] Koronarthrombose *f*

coronation /kɒrə'neɪʃn/ *n* Krönung *f*

coroner /'kɒrənə(r)/ *n* Beamte(r) *m*, der verdächtige Todesfälle untersucht

coronet /'kɒrənet/ *n* Adelskrone *f*

corporal[1] /'kɔːpərəl/ *n* (*Mil*) Stabsunteroffizier *m*

corporal[2] *a* körperlich; ~ punishment körperliche Züchtigung *f*

corporate /'kɔːpərət/ *a* gemeinschaftlich

corporation /kɔːpə'reɪʃn/ *n* Körperschaft *f*; (*of town*) Stadtverwaltung *f*

corps /kɔː(r)/ *n* (*pl corps* /kɔːz/) Korps *nt*

corpse /kɔːps/ *n* Leiche *f*

corpulent /'kɔːpjʊlənt/ *a* korpulent

corpuscle /'kɔːpʌsl/ *n* Blutkörperchen *nt*

correct /kə'rekt/ *a*, -ly *adv* richtig; (*proper*) korrekt □ *vt* verbessern; (*Sch, Typ*) korrigieren. ~ion /-ekʃn/ *n* Verbesserung *f*; (*Typ*) Korrektur *f*

correlation /kɒrə'leɪʃn/ *n* Wechselbeziehung *f*

correspond /kɒrɪ'spɒnd/ *vi* entsprechen (to *dat*); (*two things:*) sich entsprechen;

(*write*) korrespondieren. ~ence *n* Briefwechsel *m*; (*Comm*) Korrespondenz *f*. ~ent *n* Korrespondent(in) *m(f)*. ~ing *a*, -ly *adv* entsprechend

corridor /'kɒrɪdɔː(r)/ *n* Gang *m*; (*Pol, Aviat*) Korridor *m*

corroborate /kə'rɒbəreɪt/ *vt* bestätigen

corro|de /kə'rəʊd/ *vt* zerfressen □ *vi* rosten. ~sion /-'rəʊʒn/ *n* Korrosion *f*

corrugated /'kɒrəgeɪtɪd/ *a* gewellt. ~ iron *n* Wellblech *nt*

corrupt /kə'rʌpt/ *a* korrupt □ *vt* korrumpieren; (*spoil*) verderben. ~ion /-ʌpʃn/ *n* Korruption *f*

corset /'kɔːsɪt/ *n* & -s *pl* Korsett *nt*

Corsica /'kɔːsɪkə/ *n* Korsika *f*

cortège /kɔː'teɪʒ/ *n* [funeral] ~ Leichenzug *m*

cosh /kɒʃ/ *n* Totschläger *m*

cosmetic /kɒz'metɪk/ *a* kosmetisch □ *n* ~s *pl* Kosmetika *pl*

cosmic /'kɒzmɪk/ *a* kosmisch

cosmonaut /'kɒzmənɔːt/ *n* Kosmonaut(in) *m(f)*

cosmopolitan /kɒzmə'pɒlɪtən/ *a* kosmopolitisch

cosmos /'kɒzmɒs/ *n* Kosmos *m*

cosset /'kɒsɪt/ *vt* verhätscheln

cost /kɒst/ *n* Kosten *pl*; ~s *pl* (*Jur*) Kosten; at all ~s um jeden Preis; I learnt to my ~ es ist mich teuer zu stehen gekommen □ *vt* (*pt/pp* cost) kosten; it ~ me £20 es hat mich £20 gekostet □ *vt* (*pt/pp* costed) ~ [out] die Kosten kalkulieren für

costly /'kɒstlɪ/ *a* (-ier, -iest) teuer

cost: ~ of ~ living *n* Lebenshaltungskosten *pl*. ~ price *n* Selbstkostenpreis *m*

costume /'kɒstjuːm/ *n* Kostüm *nt*; (*national*) Tracht *f*. ~ jewellery *n* Modeschmuck *m*

cosy /'kəʊzɪ/ *a* (-ier, -iest) gemütlich □ *n* (*tea-, egg-*) Wärmer *m*

cot /kɒt/ *n* Kinderbett *nt*; (*Amer: camp-bed*) Feldbett *nt*

cottage /'kɒtɪdʒ/ *n* Häuschen *nt*. ~ 'cheese *n* Hüttenkäse *m*

cotton /'kɒtn/ *n* Baumwolle *f*; (*thread*) Nähgarn *nt* □ *a* aus Baumwollen □ *vi* ~ on (*fam*) kapieren

cotton 'wool *n* Watte *f*

couch /kaʊtʃ/ *n* Liege *f*

couchette /kuː'ʃet/ *n* (*Rail*) Liegeplatz *m*

cough /kɒf/ *n* Husten *m* □ *vi* husten. ~ up *vt/i* husten; (*fam: pay*) blechen

'cough mixture *n* Hustensaft *m*

could /kʊd, unbetont kəd/ *see* can[1]

council /'kaʊnsl/ *n* Rat *m*; (*Admin*) Stadtverwaltung *f*; (*rural*) Gemeindeverwaltung *f*. ~ house *n* ≈ Sozialwohnung *f* councillor /'kaʊnsələ(r)/ n Stadtverordnete(r) m/f

'council tax n Gemeindesteuer f

counsel /'kaʊnsl/ n Rat m; (Jur) Anwalt m □ vt (pt/pp counselled) beraten. ~lor n Berater(in) m(f)

count¹ /kaʊnt/ n Graf m

count² n Zählung f; keep ~ zählen □ vt/i zählen. ~ on vt rechnen auf (+ acc)

countenance /'kaʊntənəns/ n Gesicht nt □ vt dulden

counter¹ /'kaʊntə(r)/ n (in shop) Ladentisch m; (in bank) Schalter m; (in café) Theke f; (Games) Spielmarke f

counter² adv ~ to gegen (+ acc) □ a Gegen- □ vt/i kontern

counter'act vt entgegenwirken (+ dat)

'counter-attack n Gegenangriff m

counter-'espionage n Spionageabwehr f

'counterfeit /-fɪt/ a gefälscht □ n Fälschung f □ vt fälschen

'counterfoil n Kontrollabschnitt m

'counterpart n Gegenstück nt

counter-pro'ductive a be ~ das Gegenteil bewirken

'countersign vt gegenzeichnen

countess /'kaʊntɪs/ n Gräfin f

countless /'kaʊntlɪs/ a unzählig

countrified /'kʌntrɪfaɪd/ a ländlich

country /'kʌntrɪ/ n Land nt; (native land) Heimat f; (countryside) Landschaft f; in the ~ auf dem Lande. ~man n [fellow] ~man Landsmann m. ~side n Landschaft f

county /'kaʊntɪ/ n Grafschaft f

coup /ku:/ n (Pol) Staatsstreich m

couple /'kʌpl/ n Paar nt; a ~ of (two) zwei □ vt verbinden; (Rail) koppeln

coupon /'ku:pɒn/ n Kupon m; (voucher) Gutschein m; (entry form) Schein m

courage /'kʌrɪdʒ/ n Mut m. ~ous /kə-'reɪdʒəs/ a, -ly adv mutig

courgettes /kʊə'ʒets/ npl Zucchini pl

courier /'kʊrɪə(r)/ n Bote m; (diplomatic) Kurier m; (for tourists) Reiseleiter(in) m(f)

course /kɔːs/ n (Naut, Sch) Kurs m; (Culin) Gang m; (for golf) Platz m; ~ of treatment (Med) Kur f; of ~ natürlich, selbstverständlich; in the ~ of im Lauf[e] (+ gen)

court /kɔːt/ n Hof m; (Sport) Platz m; (Jur) Gericht nt □ vt werben um; herausfordern (danger)

courteous /'kɜːtɪəs/ a, -ly adv höflich

courtesy /'kɜːtəsɪ/ n Höflichkeit f

court: ~ 'martial n (pl ~s martial) Militärgericht nt. ~ shoes npl Pumps pl. ~yard n Hof m

cousin /'kʌzn/ n Vetter m, Cousin m; (female) Kusine f

cove /kəʊv/ n kleine Bucht f

cover /'kʌvə(r)/ n Decke f, (cushion) Bezug m; (of umbrella) Hülle f; (of typewriter) Haube f; (of book; lid) Deckel m; (of magazine) Umschlag m; (protection) Deckung f, Schutz m; take ~ Deckung nehmen; under separate ~ mit getrennter Post □ vt bedecken; beziehen (cushion); decken (costs, needs); zurücklegen (distance); (Journ) berichten über (+ acc); (insure) versichern. ~ up vt zudecken; (fig) vertuschen

coverage /'kʌvərɪdʒ/ n (Journ) Berichterstattung f (of über + acc)

cover: ~ charge n Gedeck nt. ~ing n Decke f; (for floor) Belag m. ~-up n Vertuschung f

covet /'kʌvɪt/ vt begehren

cow /kaʊ/ n Kuh f

coward /'kaʊəd/ n Feigling m. ~ice /-ɪs/ n Feigheit f. ~ly a feige

'cowboy n Cowboy m; (fam) unsolider Handwerker m

cower /'kaʊə(r)/ vi sich [ängstlich] ducken

'cowshed n Kuhstall m

cox /kɒks/ n, coxswain /'kɒksn/ n Steuermann m

coy /kɔɪ/ a (-er, -est) gespielt schüchtern

crab /kræb/ n Krabbe f. ~-apple n Holzapfel m

crack /kræk/ n Riss m; (in china, glass) Sprung m; (noise) Knall m; (fam: joke) Witz m; (fam: attempt) Versuch m □ a (fam) erstklassig □ vt knacken (nut, code); einen Sprung machen in (+ acc) (china, glass); (fam) reißen (joke); (fam) lösen (problem) □ vi (china, glass:) springen; (whip:) knallen. ~ down vi (fam) durchgreifen

cracked /krækt/ a gesprungen; (rib) angebrochen; (fam: crazy) verrückt

cracker /'krækə(r)/ n (biscuit) Kräcker m; (firework) Knallkörper m; [Christmas] ~ Knallbonbon m. ~s a be ~s (fam) einen Knacks haben

crackle /'krækl/ vi knistern

cradle /'kreɪdl/ n Wiege f

craft¹ /krɑːft/ n inv (boat) [Wasser]fahrzeug nt

craft² n Handwerk nt; (technique) Fertigkeit f. ~sman n Handwerker m

crafty /'krɑːftɪ/ a (-ier, -iest) -ily adv gerissen

crag /kræg/ n Felszacken m. ~gy a felsig; (face) kantig

cram /kræm/ v (pt/pp crammed) □ vt hineinstopfen (into in + acc); vollstopfen (with mit) □ vi (for exams) pauken

cramp /kræmp/ n Krampf m. ~ed a eng

crampon /'kræmpən/ n Steigeisen nt

cranberry /'krænbəri/ n (Culin) Preiselbeere f

crane /krein/ n Kran m; (bird) Kranich m □ vt ~ one's neck den Hals recken

crank¹ /kræŋk/ n (fam) Exzentriker m

crank² n (Techn) Kurbel f. ~shaft n Kurbelwelle f

cranky /'kræŋki/ a exzentrisch; (Amer: irritable) reizbar

cranny /'kræni/ n Ritze f

crash /kræʃ/ n (noise) Krach m; (Auto) Zusammenstoß m; (Aviat) Absturz m □ vi krachen (into gegen); (cars:) zusammenstoßen; (plane:) abstürzen □ vt einen Unfall haben mit (car)

crash: ~ course n Schnellkurs m. ~-helmet n Sturzhelm m. ~-landing n Bruchlandung f

crate /kreit/ n Kiste f

crater /'kreitə(r)/ n Krater m

cravat /krə'væt/ n Halstuch nt

crav|e /kreiv/ vi ~e for sich sehnen nach. ~ing n Gelüst nt

crawl /krɔːl/ n (Swimming) Kraul nt; do the ~ kraulen; at a ~ im Kriechtempo □ vi kriechen; (baby:) krabbeln; ~ with wimmeln von. ~er lane n (Auto) Kriechspur f

crayon /'kreiən/ n Wachsstift m; (pencil) Buntstift m

craze /kreiz/ n Mode f

crazy /'kreizi/ a (-ier, -iest) verrückt; be ~ about verrückt sein nach

creak /kriːk/ n Knarren nt □ vi knarren

cream /kriːm/ n Sahne f; (Cosmetic, Med, Culin) Creme f □ a (colour) cremefarben □ vt (Culin) cremig rühren. ~ 'cheese n ≈ Quark m. ~y a sahnig; (smooth) cremig

crease /kriːs/ n Falte f; (unwanted) Knitterfalte f □ vt falten; (accidentally) zerknittern □ vi knittern. ~-resistant a knitterfrei

creat|e /kriː'eit/ vt schaffen. ~ion /-'eiʃn/ n Schöpfung f. ~ive /-tiv/ a schöpferisch. ~or n Schöpfer m

creature /'kriːtʃə(r)/ n Geschöpf nt

crèche /kreʃ/ n Kinderkrippe f

credentials /kri'denʃlz/ npl Beglaubigungsschreiben nt

credibility /kredə'biləti/ n Glaubwürdigkeit f

credible /'kredəbl/ a glaubwürdig

credit /'kredit/ n Kredit m; (honour) Ehre f □ vt glauben; ~ s.o. with sth (Comm)

jdm etw gutschreiben; (fig) jdm etw zuschreiben. ~able /-əbl/ a lobenswert

credit: ~ card n Kreditkarte f. ~or n Gläubiger m

creed /kriːd/ n Glaubensbekenntnis nt

creek /kriːk/ n enge Bucht f; (Amer: stream) Bach m

creep /kriːp/ vi (pt/pp crept) schleichen □ n (fam) fieser Kerl m; it gives me the ~s es ist mir unheimlich. ~er n Kletterpflanze f. ~y a gruselig

cremat|e /kri'meit/ vt einäschern. ~ion /-'eiʃn/ n Einäscherung f

crematorium /kremə'tɔːrɪəm/ n Krematorium nt

crêpe /kreip/ n Krepp m. ~ paper n Krepppapier nt

crept /krept/ see creep

crescent /'kresnt/ n Halbmond m

cress /kres/ n Kresse f

crest /krest/ n Kamm m; (coat of arms) Wappen nt

Crete /kriːt/ n Kreta nt

crevasse /kri'væs/ n [Gletscher]spalte f

crevice /'krevis/ n Spalte f

crew /kruː/ n Besatzung f; (gang) Bande f. ~ cut n Bürstenschnitt m

crib¹ /krib/ n Krippe f

crib² vt/i (pt/pp cribbed) (fam) abschreiben

crick /krik/ n ~ in the neck steifes Genick nt

cricket¹ /'krikit/ n (insect) Grille f

cricket² n Kricket nt. ~er n Kricketspieler m

crime /kraim/ n Verbrechen nt; (rate) Kriminalität f

criminal /'kriminl/ a kriminell, verbrecherisch; (law, court) Straf- □ n Verbrecher m

crimson /'krimzn/ a purpurrot

cringe /krindʒ/ vi sich [ängstlich] ducken

crinkle /'kriŋkl/ vt/i knittern

cripple /'kripl/ n Krüppel m □ vt zum Krüppel machen; (fig) lahm legen. ~d a verkrüppelt

crisis /'kraisis/ n (pl -ses /-siːz/) Krise f

crisp /krisp/ a (-er, -est) knusprig. ~bread n Knäckebrot nt. ~s npl Chips pl

criss-cross /'kris-/ a schräg gekreuzt

criterion /krai'tiəriən/ n (pl -ria /-riə/) Kriterium nt

critic /'kritik/ n Kritiker m. ~al a kritisch. ~ally adv kritisch; ~ally ill schwer krank

criticism /'kritisizm/ n Kritik f

criticize /'kritisaiz/ vt kritisieren

croak /krəʊk/ *vi* krächzen; ⟨*frog:*⟩ quaken

crochet /ˈkrəʊʃeɪ/ *n* Häkelarbeit *f* □ *vt/i* häkeln. ~-hook *n* Häkelnadel *f*

crock /krɒk/ *n* ⟨*fam:*⟩old ~ ⟨*person*⟩ Wrack *m*; ⟨*car*⟩ Klapperkiste *f*

crockery /ˈkrɒkərɪ/ *n* Geschirr *nt*

crocodile /ˈkrɒkədaɪl/ *n* Krokodil *nt*

crocus /ˈkrəʊkəs/ *n* (*pl* -es) Krokus *m*

crony /ˈkrəʊnɪ/ *n* Kumpel *m*

crook /krʊk/ *n* (*stick*) Stab *m*; ⟨*fam: criminal*⟩ Schwindler *m*, Gauner *m*

crooked /ˈkrʊkɪd/ *a* schief; ⟨*bent*⟩ krumm; ⟨*fam: dishonest*⟩ unehrlich

crop /krɒp/ *n* Feldfrucht *f*; ⟨*harvest*⟩ Ernte *f*; ⟨*of bird*⟩ Kropf *m* □ *v* (*pt/pp* cropped) □ *vt* stutzen □ *vi* ~ up ⟨*fam*⟩ zur Sprache kommen; (*occur*) dazwischenkommen

croquet /ˈkrəʊkeɪ/ *n* Krocket *nt*

croquette /krəʊˈket/ *n* Krokette *f*

cross /krɒs/ *a*, -ly *adv* (*annoyed*) böse (with auf + *acc*); talk at ~ purposes aneinander vorbeireden □ *n* Kreuz *nt*; ⟨*Bot, Zool*⟩ Kreuzung *f*; on the ~ schräg □ *vt* kreuzen ⟨*cheque, animals*⟩; überqueren ⟨*road*⟩; ~ oneself sich bekreuzigen; ~ one's arms die Arme verschränken; ~ one's legs die Beine übereinander schlagen; keep one's fingers ~ed for s.o. jdm die Daumen drücken; it ~ed my mind es fiel mir ein □ *vi* ⟨*go across*⟩ hinübergehen/-fahren; ⟨*lines:*⟩ sich kreuzen. ~ out *vt* durchstreichen

cross: ~bar *n* Querlatte *f*; ⟨*on bicycle*⟩ Stange *f*. ~-country *n* ⟨*Sport*⟩ Crosslauf *m*. ~-ex'amine *vt* ins Kreuzverhör nehmen. ~-exami'nation *n* Kreuzverhör *nt*. ~-'eyed *a* schielend; be ~-eyed schielen. ~fire *n* Kreuzfeuer *nt*. ~ing *n* Übergang *m*; ⟨*sea journey*⟩ Überfahrt *f*. ~'reference *n* Querverweis *m*. ~roads *n* ⟨*Straßen⟩*kreuzung *f*. ~'section *n* Querschnitt *m*. ~-stitch *n* Kreuzstich *m*. ~wise *adv* quer. ~word *n* ~word [puzzle] Kreuzworträtsel *nt*

crotchet /ˈkrɒtʃɪt/ *n* Viertelnote *f*

crotchety /ˈkrɒtʃɪtɪ/ *a* griesgrämig

crouch /kraʊtʃ/ *vi* kauern

crow /krəʊ/ *n* Krähe *f*; as the ~ flies Luftlinie □ *vi* krähen. ~bar *n* Brechstange *f*

crowd /kraʊd/ *n* [Menschen]menge *f* □ *vi* sich drängen. ~ed /ˈkraʊdɪd/ *a* [gedrängt] voll

crown /kraʊn/ *n* Krone *f* □ *vt* krönen; überkronen ⟨*tooth*⟩

crucial /ˈkruːʃl/ *a* höchst wichtig; ⟨*decisive*⟩ entscheidend (to für)

crucifix /ˈkruːsɪfɪks/ *n* Kruzifix *nt*

crucif|ixion /kruːsɪˈfɪkʃn/ *n* Kreuzigung *f*. ~y /ˈkruːsɪfaɪ/ *vt* (*pt/pp*-ied) kreuzigen

crude /kruːd/ *a* (-r, -st) ⟨*raw*⟩ roh

cruel /ˈkruːəl/ *a* (crueller, cruellest), -ly *adv* grausam (to gegen). ~ty *n* Grausamkeit *f*; ~ty to animals Tierquälerei *f*

cruis|e /kruːz/ *n* Kreuzfahrt *f* □ *vi* kreuzen; ⟨*car:*⟩ fahren. ~er *n* ⟨*Mil*⟩ Kreuzer *m*; (*motor boat*) Kajütboot *nt*. ~ing speed *n* Reisegeschwindigkeit *f*

crumb /krʌm/ *n* Krümel *m*

crumb|le /ˈkrʌmbl/ *vt/i* krümeln; ⟨*collapse*⟩ einstürzen. ~ly *a* krümelig

crumple /ˈkrʌmpl/ *vt* zerknittern □ *vi* knittern

crunch /krʌntʃ/ *n* ⟨*fam*⟩ when it comes to the ~ wenn es [wirklich] drauf ankommt □ *vt* mampfen □ *vi* knirschen

crusade /kruːˈseɪd/ *n* Kreuzzug *m*; ⟨*fig*⟩ Kampagne *f*. ~r *n* Kreuzfahrer *m*; ⟨*fig*⟩ Kämpfer *m*

crush /krʌʃ/ *n* ⟨*crowd*⟩ Gedränge *nt* □ *vt* zerquetschen; zerknittern ⟨*clothes*⟩; ⟨*fig: subdue*⟩ niederschlagen

crust /krʌst/ *n* Kruste *f*

crutch /krʌtʃ/ *n* Krücke *f*

crux /krʌks/ *n* ⟨*fig*⟩ springender Punkt *m*

cry /kraɪ/ *n* Ruf *m*; ⟨*shout*⟩ Schrei *m*; a far ~ from ⟨*fig*⟩ weit entfernt von □ *vi* (*pt/pp* cried) ⟨*weep*⟩ weinen; ⟨*baby:*⟩ schreien; (*call*) rufen

crypt /krɪpt/ *n* Krypta *f*. ~ic *a* rätselhaft

crystal /ˈkrɪstl/ *n* Kristall *m*; ⟨*glass*⟩ Kristall *nt*. ~lize *vi* [sich] kristallisieren

cub /kʌb/ *n* ⟨*Zool*⟩ Junge(s) *nt*; C~ ⟨Scout⟩ Wölfling *m*

Cuba /ˈkjuːbə/ *n* Kuba *nt*

cubby-hole /ˈkʌbɪ-/ *n* Fach *nt*

cub|e /kjuːb/ *n* Würfel *m*. ~ic *a* Kubik-

cubicle /ˈkjuːbɪkl/ *n* Kabine *f*

cuckoo /ˈkʊkuː/ *n* Kuckuck *m*. ~ clock *n* Kuckucksuhr *f*

cucumber /ˈkjuːkʌmbə(r)/ *n* Gurke *f*

cuddl|e /ˈkʌdl/ *vt* herzen □ *vi* ~e up to sich kuscheln an (+ *acc*). ~y *a* kuschelig. ~y 'toy *n* Plüschtier *nt*

cudgel /ˈkʌdʒl/ *n* Knüppel *m*

cue[1] /kjuː/ *n* Stichwort *nt*

cue[2] *n* (*Billiards*) Queue *nt*

cuff /kʌf/ *n* Manschette *f*; ⟨*Amer: turn-up*⟩ [Hosen]aufschlag *m*; ⟨*blow*⟩ Klaps *m*; off the ~ ⟨*fam*⟩ aus dem Stegreif □ *vt* einen Klaps geben (+ *dat*). ~-link *n* Manschettenknopf *m*

cul-de-sac /ˈkʌldəsæk/ *n* Sackgasse *f*

culinary /ˈkʌlɪnərɪ/ *a* kulinarisch

cull /kʌl/ vt pflücken ⟨flowers⟩; ⟨kill⟩ ausmerzen

culminat|e /'kʌlmɪneɪt/ vi gipfeln (in in + dat). ~ion /-'neɪʃn/ n Gipfelpunkt m

culottes /kju:'lɒts/ npl Hosenrock m

culprit /'kʌlprɪt/ n Täter m

cult /kʌlt/ n Kult m

cultivate /'kʌltɪveɪt/ vt anbauen ⟨crop⟩; bebauen ⟨land⟩

cultural /'kʌltʃərəl/ a kulturell

culture /'kʌltʃə(r)/ n Kultur f. ~d a kultiviert

cumbersome /'kʌmbəsəm/ a hinderlich; ⟨unwieldy⟩ unhandlich

cumulative /'kju:mjʊlətɪv/ a kumulativ

cunning /'kʌnɪŋ/ a listig □ n List f

cup /kʌp/ n Tasse f; ⟨prize⟩ Pokal m

cupboard /'kʌbəd/ n Schrank m

Cup 'Final n Pokalendspiel nt

Cupid /'kju:pɪd/ n Amor m

curable /'kjʊərəbl/ a heilbar

curate /'kjʊərət/ n Vikar m; ⟨Roman Catholic⟩ Kaplan m

curator /kjʊə'reɪtə(r)/ n Kustos m

curb /kɜ:b/ vt zügeln

curdle /'kɜ:dl/ vi gerinnen

cure /kjʊə(r)/ n ⟨Heil⟩mittel nt □ vt heilen; ⟨salt⟩ pökeln; ⟨smoke⟩ räuchern; gerben ⟨skin⟩

curfew /'kɜ:fju:/ n Ausgangssperre f

curio /'kjʊərɪəʊ/ n Kuriosität f

curiosity /kjʊərɪ'ɒsɪtɪ/ n Neugier f; ⟨object⟩ Kuriosität f

curious /'kjʊərɪəs/ a, -ly adv neugierig; ⟨strange⟩ merkwürdig, seltsam

curl /kɜ:l/ n Locke f □ vt locken □ vi sich locken. ~ up vi sich zusammenrollen

curler /'kɜ:lə(r)/ n Lockenwickler m

curly /'kɜ:lɪ/ a (-ier, -iest) lockig

currant /'kʌrənt/ n ⟨dried⟩ Korinthe f

currency /'kʌrənsɪ/ n Geläufigkeit f; ⟨money⟩ Währung f; foreign ~ Devisen pl

current /'kʌrənt/ a augenblicklich, gegenwärtig; ⟨in general use⟩ geläufig, gebräuchlich □ n Strömung f; ⟨Electr⟩ Strom m. ~ affairs or events npl Aktuelle(s) nt. ~ly adv zurzeit

curriculum /kə'rɪkjʊləm/ n Lehrplan m. ~ vitae /-'vi:taɪ/ n Lebenslauf m

curry /'kʌrɪ/ n Curry nt & m; ⟨meal⟩ Currygericht nt □ vt (pt/pp -ied) ~ favour sich einschmeicheln (with bei)

curse /kɜ:s/ n Fluch m □ vt verfluchen □ vi fluchen

cursory /'kɜ:sərɪ/ a flüchtig

curt /kɜ:t/ a, -ly adv barsch

curtail /kɜ:'teɪl/ vt abkürzen

curtain /'kɜ:tn/ n Vorhang m

curtsy /'kɜ:tsɪ/ n Knicks m □ vi (pt/pp -ied) knicksen

curve /kɜ:v/ n Kurve f □ vi einen Bogen machen; ~ to the right/left nach rechts/links biegen. ~d a gebogen

cushion /'kʊʃn/ n Kissen nt □ vt dämpfen; ⟨protect⟩ beschützen

cushy /'kʊʃɪ/ a (-ier, -iest) ⟨fam⟩ bequem

custard /'kʌstəd/ n Vanillesoße f

custodian /kʌ'stəʊdɪən/ n Hüter m

custody /'kʌstədɪ/ n Obhut f; ⟨of child⟩ Sorgerecht nt; ⟨imprisonment⟩ Haft f

custom /'kʌstəm/ n Brauch m; ⟨habit⟩ Gewohnheit f; ⟨Comm⟩ Kundschaft f. ~ary a üblich; ⟨habitual⟩ gewohnt. ~er n Kunde m/Kundin f

customs /'kʌstəmz/ npl Zoll m. ~ officer n Zollbeamte(r) m

cut /kʌt/ n Schnitt m; ⟨Med⟩ Schnittwunde f; ⟨reduction⟩ Kürzung f; ⟨in price⟩ Senkung f; ~ [of meat] [Fleisch]stück m □ vt/i (pt/pp cut, pres p cutting) schneiden; ⟨mow⟩ mähen; abheben ⟨cards⟩; ⟨reduce⟩ kürzen; senken ⟨price⟩; ~ one's finger sich in den Finger schneiden; ~ s.o.'s hair jdm die Haare schneiden; ~ short abkürzen. ~ back vt zurückschneiden; ⟨fig⟩ einschränken, kürzen. ~ down vt fällen; ⟨fig⟩ einschränken. ~ off vt abschneiden; ⟨disconnect⟩ abstellen; be ~ off ⟨Teleph⟩ unterbrochen werden. ~ out vt ausschneiden; ⟨delete⟩ streichen; be ~ out for ⟨fam⟩ geeignet sein zu. ~ up vt zerschneiden; ⟨slice⟩ aufschneiden

'cut-back n Kürzung f, Einschränkung f

cute /kju:t/ a (-r, -st) ⟨fam⟩ niedlich

cut 'glass n Kristall nt

cuticle /'kju:tɪkl/ n Nagelhaut f

cutlery /'kʌtlərɪ/ n Besteck nt

cutlet /'kʌtlɪt/ n Kotelett nt

'cut-price a verbilligt

cutting /'kʌtɪŋ/ a ⟨remark⟩ bissig □ n ⟨from newspaper⟩ Ausschnitt m; ⟨of plant⟩ Ableger m

CV abbr of curriculum vitae

cyclamen /'sɪkləmən/ n Alpenveilchen nt

cycl|e /'saɪkl/ n Zyklus m; ⟨bicycle⟩ [Fahr]rad nt □ vi mit dem Rad fahren. ~ing n Radfahren nt. ~ist n Radfahrer(in) m(f)

cyclone /'saɪkləʊn/ n Wirbelsturm m

cylind|er /'sɪlɪndə(r)/ n Zylinder m. ~rical /-'lɪndrɪkl/ a zylindrisch

cymbals /'sɪmblz/ npl ⟨Mus⟩ Becken nt

cynic /'sɪnɪk/ n Zyniker m. ~al a, -ly adv zynisch. ~ism /-sɪzm/ n Zynismus m cypress /'saɪprəs/ n Zypresse f

Cyprus /'saɪprəs/ n Zypern nt

cyst /sɪst/ n Zyste f. ~itis /-'taɪtɪs/ n Blasenentzündung f

Czech /tʃek/ a tschechisch □ n Tscheche m/ Tschechin f

Czechoslovak /tʃekə'sləʊvæk/ a tschechoslowakisch. ~ia /-'vækɪə/ n die Tschechoslowakei. ~ian /-'vækɪən/ a tschechoslowakisch

D

dab /dæb/ n Tupfer m; (of butter) Klecks m; a ~ of ein bisschen □ vt (pt/pp dabbed) abtupfen; betupfen (with mit)

dabble /'dæbl/ vi ~ in sth (fig) sich nebenbei mit etw befassen

dachshund /'dækshʊnd/ n Dackel m

dad[dy] /'dæd[ɪ]/ n (fam) Vati m

daddy-long-legs /'dædɪ/ n [Kohl]schnake f; (Amer: spider) Weberknecht m

daffodil /'dæfədɪl/ n Osterglocke f, gelbe Narzisse f

daft /dɑːft/ a (-er, -est) dumm

dagger /'dægə(r)/ n Dolch m; (Typ) Kreuz nt; be at ~s drawn (fam) auf Kriegsfuß stehen

dahlia /'deɪlɪə/ n Dahlie f

daily /'deɪlɪ/ a & adv täglich □ n (newspaper) Tageszeitung f; (fam: cleaner) Putzfrau f

dainty /'deɪntɪ/ a (-ier, -iest) zierlich

dairy /'deərɪ/ n Molkerei f; (shop) Milchgeschäft nt. ~ cow n Milchkuh f. ~ products pl Milchprodukte pl

dais /'deɪɪs/ n Podium nt

daisy /'deɪzɪ/ n Gänseblümchen nt

dale /deɪl/ n (liter) Tal nt

dally /'dælɪ/ vi (pt/pp -ied) trödeln

dam /dæm/ n [Stau]damm m □ vt (pt/pp dammed) eindämmen

damage /'dæmɪdʒ/ n Schaden m (to an + dat); ~es pl (Jur) Schadenersatz m □ vt beschädigen; (fig) beeinträchtigen. ~ing a schädlich

damask /'dæməsk/ n Damast m

dame /deɪm/ n (liter) Dame f; (Amer sl) Weib nt

damn /dæm/ a, int & adv (fam) verdammt □ n I don't care or give a ~ (fam) ich schere mich einen Dreck darum □ vt verdammen. ~ation /-'neɪʃn/ n Verdammnis f □ int (fam) verdammt!

damp /dæmp/ a (-er, -est) feucht □ n Feuchtigkeit f □ vt = dampen

damp|en vt anfeuchten; (fig) dämpfen. ~ness n Feuchtigkeit f

dance /dɑːns/ n Tanz m; (function) Tanzveranstaltung f □ vt/i tanzen. ~hall n Tanzlokal nt. ~ music n Tanzmusik f

dancer /'dɑːnsə(r)/ n Tänzer(in) m(f)

dandelion /'dændɪlaɪən/ n Löwenzahn m

dandruff /'dændrʌf/ n Schuppen pl

Dane /deɪn/ n Däne m/Dänin f; Great ~ [deutsche] Dogge f

danger /'deɪndʒə(r)/ n Gefahr f; in/out of ~ in/außer Gefahr. ~ous /-rəs/ a, -ly adv gefährlich. ~ously ill schwer erkrankt

dangle /'dæŋgl/ vi baumeln □ vt baumeln lassen

Danish /'deɪnɪʃ/ a dänisch. ~ 'pastry n Hefeteilchen nt, Plunderstück nt

dank /dæŋk/ a (-er, -est) nasskalt

Danube /'dænjuːb/ n Donau f

dare /deə(r)/ n Mutprobe f □ vt/i (challenge) herausfordern (to zu); ~ [to] do sth [es] wagen, etw zu tun; I ~ say! das mag wohl sein! ~devil n Draufgänger m

daring /'deərɪŋ/ a verwegen □ n Verwegenheit f

dark /dɑːk/ a (-er, -est) dunkel; ~ blue/ brown dunkelblau/-braun; ~ horse (fig) stilles Wasser nt; keep sth ~ (fig) etw geheim halten □ n Dunkelheit f; after ~ nach Einbruch der Dunkelheit; in the ~ im Dunkeln; keep in the ~ (fig) im Dunkeln lassen

dark|en /'dɑːkn/ vt verdunkeln □ vi dunkler werden. ~ness n Dunkelheit f

'dark-room n Dunkelkammer f

darling /'dɑːlɪŋ/ a allerliebst □ n Liebling m

darn /dɑːn/ vt stopfen. ~ing-needle n Stopfnadel f

dart /dɑːt/ n Pfeil m; (Sewing) Abnäher m; ~s sg (game) [Wurf]pfeil m □ vi flitzen

dash /dæʃ/ n (Typ) Gedankenstrich m; (in Morse) Strich m; a ~ of milk ein Schuss Milch; make a ~ losstürzen (for auf + acc) □ vi rennen □ vt schleudern. ~ off vi losstürzen □ vt (write quickly) hinwerfen

'dashboard n Armaturenbrett nt

dashing /'dæʃɪŋ/ a schneidig

data /'deɪtə/ npl & sg Daten pl. ~ processing n Datenverarbeitung f

date[1] /deɪt/ n (fruit) Dattel f

date² n Datum nt; (fam) Verabredung f; to ~ bis heute; out of ~ überholt; (expired) ungültig; be up to ~ auf dem Laufenden sein ▫ vt/i datieren; (Amer, fam: go out with) ausgehen mit; ~ back to zurückgehen auf (+ acc)

dated /'deɪtɪd/ a altmodisch

'date-line n Datumsgrenze f

dative /'deɪtɪv/ a & n (Gram) ~ [case] Dativ m

daub /dɔːb/ vt beschmieren (with with); schmieren (paint)

daughter /'dɔːtə(r)/ n Tochter f. ~-in-law n (pl ~s-in-law) Schwiegertochter f

daunt /dɔːnt/ vt entmutigen; nothing ~ed unverzagt. ~less a furchtlos

dawdle /'dɔːdl/ vi trödeln

dawn /dɔːn/ n Morgendämmerung f; at ~ bei Tagesanbruch ▫ vi anbrechen; it ~ed on me (fig) es ging mir auf

day /deɪ/ n Tag m; ~ by ~ Tag für Tag; ~ after ~ Tag um Tag; these ~s heutzutage; in those ~s zu der Zeit; it's had its ~ (fam) es hat ausgedient

day: ~break n at ~break bei Tagesanbruch m. ~dream n Tagtraum m ▫ vi [mit offenen Augen] träumen. ~light n Tageslicht nt. ~ re'turn n (ticket) Tagesrückfahrkarte f. ~time n in the ~time am Tage

daze /deɪz/ n in a ~ wie benommen. ~d a benommen

dazzle /'dæzl/ vt blenden

deacon /'diːkən/ n Diakon m

dead /ded/ a tot; (flower) verwelkt; (numb) taub; ~ body Leiche f; be ~ on time auf die Minute pünktlich kommen; ~ centre genau in der Mitte ▫ adv ~ tired todmüde; ~ slow sehr langsam; stop ~ stehen bleiben ▫ n the ~ pl die Toten; in the ~ of night mitten in der Nacht

deaden /'dedn/ vt dämpfen (sound); betäuben (pain)

dead: ~ 'end n Sackgasse f. ~ 'heat n totes Rennen nt. ~line n [letzter] Termin m. ~lock n reach ~lock (fig) sich festfahren

deadly /'dedlɪ/ a (-ier, -iest) tödlich; (fam: dreary) sterbenslangweilig; ~ sins pl Todsünden pl

deaf /def/ a (-er, -est) taub; ~ and dumb taubstumm. ~-aid n Hörgerät nt

deaf|en /'defn/ vt betäuben; (permanently) taub machen; ~ening a ohrenbetäubend. ~ness n Taubheit f

deal /diːl/ n (transaction) Geschäft nt; whose ~? (Cards) wer gibt? a good or great ~ eine Menge; get a raw ~ (fam) schlecht wegkommen ▫ v (pt/pp dealt

/delt/) ▫ vt (Cards) geben; ~ out austeilen; ~ s.o. a blow jdm einen Schlag versetzen ▫ vi ~ in handeln mit; ~ with zu tun haben mit; (handle) sich befassen mit; (cope with) fertig werden mit; (be about) handeln von; that's been dealt with das ist schon erledigt

deal|er /'diːlə(r)/ n Händler m; (Cards) Kartengeber m. ~ings npl have ~ings with zu tun haben mit

dean /diːn/ n Dekan m

dear /dɪə(r)/ a (-er, -est) lieb; (expensive) teuer; (in letter) liebe(r,s); (formal) sehr geehrte(r,s) ▫ n Liebe(r) m/f ▫ int oh ~! oje! ~ly adv (love) sehr; (pay) teuer

dearth /dɜːθ/ n Mangel m (of an + dat)

death /deθ/ n Tod m; three ~s drei Todesfälle. ~ certificate n Sterbeurkunde f. ~ duty n Erbschaftssteuer f

deathly a ~ silence Totenstille f ▫ adv ~ pale totenblass

death: ~ penalty n Todesstrafe f. ~'s head n Totenkopf m. ~-trap n Todesfalle f

debar /dɪ'bɑː(r)/ vt (pt/pp debarred) ausschließen

debase /dɪ'beɪs/ vt erniedrigen

debatable /dɪ'beɪtəbl/ a strittig

debate /dɪ'beɪt/ n Debatte f ▫ vt/i debattieren

debauchery /dɪ'bɔːtʃərɪ/ n Ausschweifung f

debility /dɪ'bɪlətɪ/ n Entkräftung f

debit /'debɪt/ n Schuldbetrag m; ~ [side] Soll nt ▫ vt (pt/pp debited) (Comm) belasten; abbuchen (sum)

debris /'debriː/ n Trümmer pl

debt /det/ n Schuld f; in ~ verschuldet. ~ or n Schuldner m

début /'deɪbuː/ n Debüt nt

decade /'dekeɪd/ n Jahrzehnt nt

decaden|ce /'dekədəns/ n Dekadenz f. ~t a dekadent

decaffeinated /dɪ'kæfɪneɪtɪd/ a koffeinfrei

decant /dɪ'kænt/ vt umfüllen. ~er n Karaffe f

decapitate /dɪ'kæpɪteɪt/ vt köpfen

decay /dɪ'keɪ/ n Verfall m; (rot) Verwesung f; (of tooth) Zahnfäule f ▫ vi verfallen; (rot) verwesen; (tooth:) schlecht werden

decease /dɪ'siːs/ n Ableben nt. ~d a verstorben ▫ n the ~d der/die Verstorbene

deceit /dɪ'siːt/ n Täuschung f. ~ful a, ~ly adv unaufrichtig

deceive /dɪ'siːv/ vt täuschen; (be unfaithful to) betrügen

December /dɪ'sembə(r)/ n Dezember m

decency /'di:sənsı/ n Anstand m

decent /'di:sənt/ a, -ly adv anständig

decentralize /di:'sentrəlaız/ vt dezentralisieren

decept|ion /dı'sepʃn/ n Täuschung f; (fraud) Betrug m. ~ive /-tıv/ a, -ly adv täuschend

decibel /'desıbel/ n Dezibel nt

decide /dı'saıd/ vt entscheiden □ vi sich entscheiden (on für)

decided /dı'saıdıd/ a, -ly adv entschieden

deciduous /dı'sıdjʊəs/ a ~ tree Laubbaum m

decimal /'desıml/ a Dezimal- □ n Dezimalzahl f. ~ 'point n Komma nt. ~ system n Dezimalsystem nt

decimate /'desımeıt/ vt dezimieren

decipher /dı'saıfə(r)/ vt entziffern

decision /dı'sıʒn/ n Entscheidung f; (firmness) Entschlossenheit f

decisive /dı'saısıv/ a ausschlaggebend; (firm) entschlossen

deck¹ /dek/ vt schmücken

deck² n (Naut) Deck nt; on ~ an Deck; top ~ (of bus) Oberdeck nt; ~ of cards (Amer) [Karten]spiel nt. ~chair n Liegestuhl m

declaration /deklə'reıʃn/ n Erklärung f

declare /dı'kleə(r)/ vt erklären; angeben (goods); anything to ~? etwas zu verzollen?

declension /dı'klenʃn/ n Deklination f

decline /dı'klaın/ n Rückgang m; (in health) Verfall m □ vt ablehnen; (Gram) deklinieren □ vi ablehnen; (fall) sinken; (decrease) nachlassen

decode /di:'kəʊd/ vt entschlüsseln

decompos|e /di:kəm'pəʊz/ vi sich zersetzen

décor /'deıkɔ:(r)/ n Ausstattung f

decorat|e /'dekəreıt/ vt (adorn) schmücken; verzieren (cake); (paint) streichen; (wallpaper) tapezieren; (award medal to) einen Orden verleihen (+ dat). ~ion /-'reıʃn/ n Verzierung f; (medal) Orden m; ~ions pl Schmuck m. ~ive /-rətıv/ a dekorativ. ~or n painter and ~or Maler und Tapezierer m

decorous /'dekərəs/ a, -ly adv schamhaft

decorum /dı'kɔ:rəm/ n Anstand m

decoy¹ /'di:kɔı/ n Lockvogel m

decoy² /dı'kɔı/ vt locken

decrease¹ /'di:kri:s/ n Verringerung f; (in number) Rückgang m; be on the ~ zurückgehen

decrease² /dı'kri:s/ vt verringern; herabsetzen (price) □ vi sich verringern; (price:) sinken

decree /dı'kri:/ n Erlass m □ vt (pt/pp decreed) verordnen

decrepit /dı'krepıt/ a altersschwach

dedicat|e /'dedıkeıt/ vt widmen; (Relig) weihen. ~ed a hingebungsvoll; (person) aufopfernd. ~ion /-'keıʃn/ n Hingabe f; (in book) Widmung f

deduce /dı'dju:s/ vt folgern (from aus)

deduct /dı'dʌkt/ vt abziehen

deduction /dı'dʌkʃn/ n Abzug m; (conclusion) Folgerung f

deed /di:d/ n Tat f; (Jur) Urkunde f

deem /di:m/ vt halten für

deep /di:p/ a (-er, -est), -ly adv tief; go off the ~ end (fam) auf die Palme gehen □ adv tief

deepen /'di:pn/ vt vertiefen □ vi tiefer werden; (fig) sich vertiefen

deep-'freeze n Gefriertruhe f; (upright) Gefrierschrank m

deer /dıə(r)/ n inv Hirsch m; (roe) Reh m

deface /dı'feıs/ vt beschädigen

defamat|ion /defə'meıʃn/ n Verleumdung f. ~ory /dı'fæmətərı/ a verleumderisch

default /dı'fɔ:lt/ n (Jur) Nichtzahlung f; (failure to appear) Nichterscheinen nt; win by ~ (Sport) kampflos gewinnen □ vi nicht zahlen; nicht erscheinen

defeat /dı'fi:t/ n Niederlage f; (defeating) Besiegung f; (rejection) Ablehnung f □ vt besiegen; ablehnen; (frustrate) vereiteln

defect¹ /dı'fekt/ vi (Pol) überlaufen

defect² /'di:fekt/ n Fehler m; (Techn) Defekt m. ~ive /dı'fektıv/ a fehlerhaft; (Techn) defekt

defence /dı'fens/ n Verteidigung f. ~less a wehrlos

defend /dı'fend/ vt verteidigen; (justify) rechtfertigen. ~ant n (Jur) Beklagte(r) m/f; (in criminal court) Angeklagte(r) m/f

defensive /dı'fensıv/ a defensiv □ n Defensive f

defer /dı'fɜ:(r)/ vt (pt/pp deferred) (postpone) aufschieben; ~ to s.o. sich jdm fügen

deferen|ce /'defərəns/ n Ehrerbietung f. ~tial /-'renʃl/ a, -ly adv ehrerbietig

defian|ce /dı'faıəns/ n Trotz m; in ~ce zum Trotz (+ dat). ~t a, -ly adv aufsässig

deficien|cy /dı'fıʃənsı/ n Mangel m. ~t a mangelhaft; he is ~t in ... ihm mangelt es an ... (dat)

deficit /'defısıt/ n Defizit nt

defile /dı'faıl/ vt (fig) schänden

define /dı'faın/ vt bestimmen, definieren (word)

definite /'defınıt/ a, -ly adv bestimmt; (certain) sicher

definition /defɪ'nɪʃn/ n Definition f; (Phot, TV) Schärfe f

definitive /dɪ'fɪnətɪv/ a endgültig; (authoritative) maßgeblich

deflat|e /dɪ'fleɪt/ vt die Luft auslassen aus. ~ion /-ɪʃn/ n (Comm) Deflation f

deflect /dɪ'flekt/ vt ablenken

deform|ed /dɪ'fɔːmd/ a missgebildet. ~ity n Missbildung f

defraud /dɪ'frɔːd/ vt betrügen (of um)

defray /dɪ'freɪ/ vt bestreiten

defrost /diː'frɒst/ vt entfrosten; abtauen (fridge); auftauen (food)

deft /deft/ a (-er, -est), -ly adv geschickt. ~ness n Geschicklichkeit f

defunct /dɪ'fʌŋkt/ a aufgelöst; (law) außer Kraft gesetzt

defuse /diː'fjuːz/ vt entschärfen

defy /dɪ'faɪ/ vt (pt/pp -ied) trotzen (+ dat); widerstehen (+ dat) (attempt)

degenerate[1] /dɪ'dʒenəreɪt/ vi degenerieren; ~ into (fig) ausarten in (+ acc)

degenerate[2] /dɪ'dʒenərət/ a degeneriert

degrading /dɪ'greɪdɪŋ/ a entwürdigend

degree /dɪ'griː/ n Grad m; (Univ) akademischer Grad m; 20 ~s 20 Grad

dehydrate /diː'haɪdreɪt/ vt Wasser entziehen (+ dat). ~d /-ɪd/ a ausgetrocknet

de-ice /diː'aɪs/ vt enteisen

deign /deɪn/ vi ~ to do sth sich herablassen, etw zu tun

deity /'diːɪtɪ/ n Gottheit f

dejected /dɪ'dʒektɪd/ a, -ly adv niedergeschlagen

delay /dɪ'leɪ/ n Verzögerung f; (of train, aircraft) Verspätung f; without ~ unverzüglich □ vt aufhalten; (postpone) aufschieben; be ~ed (person:) aufgehalten werden; (train, aircraft:) Verspätung haben □ vi zögern

delegate[1] /'delɪgət/ n Delegierte(r) m/f

delegat|e[2] /'delɪgeɪt/ vt delegieren. ~ion /-'geɪʃn/ n Delegation f

delet|e /dɪ'liːt/ vt streichen. ~ion /-iːʃn/ n Streichung f

deliberate[1] /dɪ'lɪbərət/ a, -ly adv absichtlich; (slow) bedächtig

deliberate[2] /dɪ'lɪbəreɪt/ vt/i überlegen. ~ion /-'reɪʃn/ n Überlegung f; with ~ion mit Bedacht

delicacy /'delɪkəsɪ/ n Feinheit f; Zartheit f; (food) Delikatesse f

delicate /'delɪkət/ a fein; (fabric, health) zart; (situation) heikel; (mechanism) empfindlich

delicatessen /delɪkə'tesn/ n Delikatessengeschäft nt

delicious /dɪ'lɪʃəs/ a köstlich

delight /dɪ'laɪt/ n Freude f □ vt entzücken □ vi ~ in sich erfreuen an (+ dat). ~ed a hocherfreut; be ~ed sich sehr freuen. ~ful a reizend

delinquen|cy /dɪ'lɪŋkwənsɪ/ n Kriminalität f. ~t a straffällig □ n Straffällige(r) m/f

deli|rious /dɪ'lɪrɪəs/ a be ~rious im Delirium sein. ~rium /-rɪəm/ n Delirium nt

deliver /dɪ'lɪvə(r)/ vt liefern; zustellen (post, newspaper); halten (speech); überbringen (message); versetzen (blow); (set free) befreien; ~ a baby ein Kind zur Welt bringen. ~ance n Erlösung f. ~y n Lieferung f; (of post) Zustellung f; (Med) Entbindung f; cash on ~y per Nachnahme

delta /'deltə/ n Delta nt

delude /dɪ'luːd/ vt täuschen; ~ oneself sich (dat) Illusionen machen

deluge /'deljuːdʒ/ n Flut f; (heavy rain) schwerer Guss m □ vt überschwemmen

delusion /dɪ'luːʒn/ n Täuschung f

de luxe /dɪ'lʌks/ a Luxus-

delve /delv/ vi hineingreifen (into in + acc); (fig) eingehen (into auf + acc)

demand /dɪ'mɑːnd/ n Forderung f; (Comm) Nachfrage f; in ~ gefragt; on ~ auf Verlangen □ vt verlangen, fordern (of/ from von). ~ing a anspruchsvoll

demarcation /diːmɑː'keɪʃn/ n Abgrenzung f

demean /dɪ'miːn/ vt ~ oneself sich erniedrigen

demeanour /dɪ'miːnə(r)/ n Verhalten nt

demented /dɪ'mentɪd/ a verrückt

demise /dɪ'maɪz/ n Tod m

demister /diː'mɪstə(r)/ n (Auto) Defroster m

demo /'deməʊ/ n (pl ~s) (fam) Demonstration f

demobilize /diː'məʊbɪlaɪz/ vt (Mil) entlassen

democracy /dɪ'mɒkrəsɪ/ n Demokratie f

democrat /'deməkræt/ n Demokrat m. ~ic /-'krætɪk/ a, -ally adv demokratisch

demo|lish /dɪ'mɒlɪʃ/ vt abbrechen; (destroy) zerstören. ~lition /demə'lɪʃn/ n Abbruch m

demon /'diːmən/ n Dämon m

demonstrat|e /'demənstreɪt/ vt beweisen; vorführen (appliance) □ vi (Pol) demonstrieren. ~ion /-'streɪʃn/ n Vorführung f; (Pol) Demonstration f

demonstrative /dɪ'mɒnstrətɪv/ a (Gram) demonstrativ; be ~ seine Gefühle zeigen

demonstrator /'demənstreɪtə(r)/ n Vorführer m; (Pol) Demonstrant m

demoralize /dɪˈmɒrəlaɪz/ vt demoralisieren

demote /dɪˈməʊt/ vt degradieren

demure /dɪˈmjʊə(r)/ a, -ly adv sittsam

den /den/ n Höhle f; (room) Bude f

denial /dɪˈnaɪəl/ n Leugnen nt; official ∼ Dementi nt

denigrate /ˈdenɪgreɪt/ vt herabsetzen

denim /ˈdenɪm/ n Jeansstoff m; ∼s pl Jeans pl

Denmark /ˈdenmɑːk/ n Dänemark nt

denomination /dɪnɒmɪˈneɪʃn/ n (Relig) Konfession f; (money) Nennwert m

denote /dɪˈnəʊt/ vt bezeichnen

denounce /dɪˈnaʊns/ vt denunzieren; (condemn) verurteilen

dens|e /dens/ a (-r, -st), -ly adv dicht; (fam: stupid) blöd[e]. ∼ity n Dichte f

dent /dent/ n Delle f, Beule f □ vt einbeulen; ∼ed /-ɪd/ verbeult

dental /ˈdentl/ a Zahn-; (treatment) zahnärztlich. ∼ floss /flɒs/ n Zahnseide f. ∼ surgeon n Zahnarzt m

dentist /ˈdentɪst/ n Zahnarzt m/-ärztin f. ∼ry n Zahnmedizin f

denture /ˈdentʃə(r)/ n Zahnprothese f; ∼s pl künstliches Gebiss nt

denude /dɪˈnjuːd/ vt entblößen

denunciation /dɪnʌnsɪˈeɪʃn/ n Denunziation f; (condemnation) Verurteilung f

deny /dɪˈnaɪ/ vt (pt/pp -ied) leugnen; (officially) dementieren; ∼ s.o. sth jdm etw verweigern

deodorant /diːˈəʊdərənt/ n Deodorant nt

depart /dɪˈpɑːt/ vi abfahren; (Aviat) abfliegen; (go away) weggehen/-fahren; (deviate) abweichen (from von)

department /dɪˈpɑːtmənt/ n Abteilung f; (Pol) Ministerium nt. ∼ store n Kaufhaus nt

departure /dɪˈpɑːtʃə(r)/ n Abfahrt f; (Aviat) Abflug m; (from rule) Abweichung f; new ∼ Neuerung f

depend /dɪˈpend/ vi abhängen (on von); (rely) sich verlassen (on auf + acc); it all ∼s das kommt darauf an. ∼able /-əbl/ a zuverlässig. ∼ant n Abhängige(r) m/f. ∼ence n Abhängigkeit f. ∼ent a abhängig (on von)

depict /dɪˈpɪkt/ vt darstellen

depilatory /dɪˈpɪlətərɪ/ n Enthaarungsmittel nt

deplete /dɪˈpliːt/ vt verringern

deplor|able /dɪˈplɔːrəbl/ a bedauerlich. ∼e vt bedauern

deploy /dɪˈplɔɪ/ vt (Mil) einsetzen □ vi sich aufstellen

depopulate /diːˈpɒpjʊleɪt/ vt entvölkern

deport /dɪˈpɔːt/ vt deportieren, ausweisen. ∼ation /diːpɔːˈteɪʃn/ n Ausweisung f

deportment /dɪˈpɔːtmənt/ n Haltung f

depose /dɪˈpəʊz/ vt absetzen

deposit /dɪˈpɒzɪt/ n Anzahlung f; (against damage) Kaution f; (on bottle) Pfand nt; (sediment) Bodensatz m; (Geol) Ablagerung f □ vt (pt/pp deposited) legen; (for safety) deponieren; (Geol) ablagern. ∼ account n Sparkonto nt

depot /ˈdepəʊ/ n Depot nt; (Amer: railway station) Bahnhof m

deprave /dɪˈpreɪv/ vt verderben. ∼d a verkommen. ∼ity /-ˈprævətɪ/ n Verderbtheit f

deprecate /ˈdeprəkeɪt/ vt missbilligen

depreciat|e /dɪˈpriːʃɪeɪt/ vi an Wert verlieren. ∼ion /-ˈeɪʃn/ n Wertminderung f; (Comm) Abschreibung f

depress /dɪˈpres/ vt deprimieren; (press down) herunterdrücken. ∼ed a deprimiert; ∼ed area Notstandsgebiet nt. ∼ing a deprimierend. ∼ion /-eʃn/ n Vertiefung f; (Med) Depression f; (Meteorol) Tief nt

deprivation /deprɪˈveɪʃn/ n Entbehrung f

deprive /dɪˈpraɪv/ vt entziehen; ∼ s.o. of sth jdm etw entziehen. ∼d a benachteiligt

depth /depθ/ n Tiefe f; in ∼ gründlich; in the ∼s of winter im tiefsten Winter

deputation /depjʊˈteɪʃn/ n Abordnung f

deputize /ˈdepjʊtaɪz/ vi ∼ for vertreten

deputy /ˈdepjʊtɪ/ n Stellvertreter m □ attrib stellvertretend

derail /dɪˈreɪl/ vt be ∼ed entgleisen. ∼ment n Entgleisung f

deranged /dɪˈreɪndʒd/ a geistesgestört

derelict /ˈderəlɪkt/ a verfallen; (abandoned) verlassen

deri|de /dɪˈraɪd/ vt verhöhnen. ∼sion /-ˈrɪʒn/ n Hohn m

derisive /dɪˈraɪsɪv/ a, -ly adv höhnisch

derisory /dɪˈraɪsərɪ/ a höhnisch; (offer) lächerlich

derivation /derɪˈveɪʃn/ n Ableitung f

derivative /dɪˈrɪvətɪv/ a abgeleitet □ n Ableitung f

derive /dɪˈraɪv/ vt/i (obtain) gewinnen (from aus); be ∼d from ⟨word:⟩ hergeleitet sein aus

dermatologist /dɜːməˈtɒlədʒɪst/ n Hautarzt m /-ärztin f

derogatory /dɪˈrɒgətrɪ/ a abfällig

derrick /ˈderɪk/ n Bohrturm m

derv /dɜːv/ n Diesel[kraftstoff] m

descend /dɪ'send/ vt/i hinunter-/herun-
tergehen; ⟨vehicle, lift:⟩ hinunter-/herun-
terfahren; be ~ed from abstammen von.
~ant n Nachkomme m

descent /dɪ'sent/ n Abstieg m; (lineage)
Abstammung f

describe /dɪ'skraɪb/ vt beschreiben

descrip|tion /dɪ'skrɪpʃn/ n Beschreibung
f; (sort) Art f. ~tive /-tɪv/ a beschreib-
end; (vivid) anschaulich

desecrat|e /'desɪkreɪt/ vt entweihen.
~ion /-'kreɪʃn/ n Entweihung f

desert¹ /'dezət/ n Wüste f ☐ a Wüsten-;
~ island verlassene Insel f

desert² /dɪ'zɜːt/ vt verlassen ☐ vt deser-
tieren. ~ed a verlassen. ~er n (Mil) De-
serteur m. ~ion /-ɜːʃn/ n Fahnenflucht f

deserts /dɪ'zɜːts/ npl get one's ~ seinen
verdienten Lohn bekommen

deserv|e /dɪ'zɜːv/ vt verdienen. ~edly
/-ɪdlɪ/ adv verdientermaßen. ~ing a ver-
dienstvoll; ~ing cause guter Zweck m

design /dɪ'zaɪn/ n Entwurf m; (pattern)
Muster m; (construction) Konstruktion f;
(aim) Absicht f ☐ vt entwerfen; (construct)
konstruieren; be ~ed for bestimmt sein
für

designat|e /'dezɪgneɪt/ vt bezeichnen; (ap-
point) ernennen. ~ion /-'neɪʃn/ n Be-
zeichnung f

designer /dɪ'zaɪnə(r)/ n Designer m;
(Techn) Konstrukteur m; (Theat) Bühnen-
bildner m

desirable /dɪ'zaɪrəbl/ a wünschenswert;
(sexually) begehrenswert

desire /dɪ'zaɪə(r)/ n Wunsch m; (longing)
Verlangen nt (for nach); (sexual) Begierde
f ☐ vt [sich (dat)] wünschen; (sexually) begehren

desk /desk/ n Schreibtisch m; (Sch) Pult
nt; (Comm) Kasse f; (in hotel) Rezeption f

desolat|e /'desələt/ a trostlos. ~ion
/-'leɪʃn/ n Trostlosigkeit f

despair /dɪ'speə(r)/ n Verzweiflung f; in
~ verzweifelt ☐ vi verzweifeln

desperat|e /'despərət/ a, -ly adv verzwei-
felt; (urgent) dringend; be ~e (criminal:)
zum Äußersten entschlossen sein; be ~e
for dringend brauchen. ~ion /-'reɪʃn/ n
Verzweiflung f; in ~ion aus Verzweiflung

despicable /dɪ'spɪkəbl/ a verachtenswert

despise /dɪ'spaɪz/ vt verachten

despite /dɪ'spaɪt/ prep trotz (+ gen)

despondent /dɪ'spɒndənt/ a niedergeschlagen

despot /'despɒt/ n Despot m

dessert /dɪ'zɜːt/ n Dessert nt, Nachtisch
m. ~ spoon n Dessertlöffel m

destination /destɪ'neɪʃn/ n [Reise]ziel nt;
(of goods) Bestimmungsort m

destine /'destɪn/ vt bestimmen

destiny /'destɪnɪ/ n Schicksal nt

destitute /'destɪtjuːt/ a völlig mittellos

destroy /dɪ'strɔɪ/ vt zerstören; (totally)
vernichten. ~er n (Naut) Zerstörer m

destruc|tion /dɪ'strʌkʃn/ n Zerstörung f;
Vernichtung f. ~tive /-tɪv/ a zerstöre-
risch; (fig) destruktiv

detach /dɪ'tætʃ/ vt abnehmen; (tear off)
abtrennen. ~able /-əbl/ a abnehmbar.
~ed a (fig) distanziert; ~ed house Ein-
zelhaus nt

detachment /dɪ'tætʃmənt/ n Distanz f;
(objectivity) Abstand m; (Mil) Sonderkommando nt

detail /'diːteɪl/ n Einzelheit f, Detail nt;
in ~ ausführlich ☐ vt einzeln aufführen;
(Mil) abkommandieren. ~ed a ausführlich

detain /dɪ'teɪn/ vt aufhalten; ⟨police:⟩ in
Haft behalten; (take into custody) in Haft
nehmen. ~ee /diːteɪ'niː/ n Häftling m

detect /dɪ'tekt/ vt entdecken; (perceive)
wahrnehmen. ~ion /-ekʃn/ n Entdeckung f

detective /dɪ'tektɪv/ n Detektiv m. ~
story n Detektivroman m

detector /dɪ'tektə(r)/ n Suchgerät nt; (for
metal) Metalldetektor m

detention /dɪ'tenʃn/ n Haft f; (Sch) Nachsitzen nt

deter /dɪ'tɜː(r)/ vt (pt/pp deterred)
abschrecken; (prevent) abhalten

detergent /dɪ'tɜːdʒənt/ n Waschmittel nt

deteriorat|e /dɪ'tɪərɪəreɪt/ vi sich versch-
lechtern. ~ion /-'reɪʃn/ n Ver-
schlechterung f

determination /dɪtɜːmɪ'neɪʃn/ n
Entschlossenheit f

determine /dɪ'tɜːmɪn/ vt bestimmen; ~
to (resolve) sich entschließen zu. ~d a
entschlossen

deterrent /dɪ'terənt/ n Abschreckungsmittel nt

detest /dɪ'test/ vt verabscheuen. ~able
/-əbl/ a abscheulich

detonat|e /'detəneɪt/ vt zünden ☐ vi ex-
plodieren. ~or n Zünder m

detour /'diːtʊə(r)/ n Umweg m, (for traffic)
Umleitung f

detract /dɪ'trækt/ vi ~ from beeinträchtigen

detriment /'detrɪmənt/ n to the ~ zum
Schaden (of gen). ~al /-'mentl/ a schädlich (to dat)

deuce /djuːs/ n (Tennis) Einstand m

devaluation /di:vælju'eɪʃn/ n Abwertung f

de'value vt abwerten ⟨currency⟩

devastat|e /'devəsteɪt/ vt verwüsten. ~ed /-ɪd/ a ⟨fam⟩ erschüttert. ~ing a verheerend. ~ion /-'steɪʃn/ n Verwüstung f

develop /dɪ'veləp/ vt entwickeln; bekommen ⟨illness⟩; erschließen ⟨area⟩ □ vi sich entwickeln (into zu). ~er n [property] ~er Bodenspekulant m

de'veloping country n Entwicklungsland nt

development /dɪ'veləpmənt/ n Entwicklung f

deviant /'di:vɪənt/ a abweichend

deviat|e /'di:vɪeɪt/ vi abweichen. ~ion /-'eɪʃn/ n Abweichung f

device /dɪ'vaɪs/ n Gerät nt; ⟨fig⟩ Mittel nt; leave s.o. to his own ~s jdn sich ⟨dat⟩ selbst überlassen

devil /'devl/ n Teufel m. ~ish a teuflisch

devious /'di:vɪəs/ a verschlagen; ~ route Umweg m

devise /dɪ'vaɪz/ vt sich ⟨dat⟩ ausdenken

devoid /dɪ'vɔɪd/ a ~ of ohne

devolution /di:və'lu:ʃn/ n Dezentralisierung f; ⟨of power⟩ Übertragung f

devot|e /dɪ'vəʊt/ vt widmen (to dat). ~ed a, -ly adv ergeben; ⟨care⟩ liebevoll; be ~ed to s.o. sehr an jdm hängen. ~ee /devə-'ti:/ n Anhänger(in) m(f)

devotion /dɪ'vəʊʃn/ n Hingabe f; ~s pl ⟨Relig⟩ Andacht f

devour /dɪ'vaʊə(r)/ vt verschlingen

devout /dɪ'vaʊt/ a fromm

dew /dju:/ n Tau m

dexterity /dek'sterətɪ/ n Geschicklichkeit f

diabet|es /daɪə'bi:ti:z/ n Zuckerkrankheit f. ~ic /-'betɪk/ a zuckerkrank □ n Zuckerkranke(r) m/f, Diabetiker(in) m(f)

diabolical /daɪə'bɒlɪkl/ a teuflisch

diagnose /daɪəg'nəʊz/ vt diagnostizieren

diagnosis /daɪəg'nəʊsɪs/ n (pl -oses /-si:z/) Diagnose f

diagonal /daɪ'ægənl/ a, -ly adv diagonal □ n Diagonale f

diagram /'daɪəgræm/ n Diagramm nt

dial /daɪəl/ n ⟨of clock⟩ Zifferblatt nt; ⟨Techn⟩ Skala f; ⟨Teleph⟩ Wählscheibe f □ vt/i ⟨pt/pp dialled⟩ ⟨Teleph⟩ wählen; ~ direct durchwählen

dialect /'daɪəlekt/ n Dialekt m

dialling: ~ code n Vorwahlnummer f. ~ tone n Amtszeichen nt

dialogue /'daɪəlɒg/ n Dialog m

'dial tone n ⟨Amer, Teleph⟩ Amtszeichen nt

diameter /daɪ'æmɪtə(r)/ n Durchmesser m

diametrically /daɪə'metrɪkəlɪ/ adv ~ opposed genau entgegengesetzt ⟨to dat⟩

diamond /'daɪəmənd/ n Diamant m; ⟨cut⟩ Brillant m; ⟨shape⟩ Raute f; ~s pl ⟨Cards⟩ Karo nt

diaper /'daɪəpə(r)/ n ⟨Amer⟩ Windel f

diaphragm /'daɪəfræm/ n ⟨Anat⟩ Zwerchfell nt; ⟨Phot⟩ Blende f

diarrhoea /daɪə'ri:ə/ n Durchfall m

diary /'daɪərɪ/ n Tagebuch nt; ⟨for appointments⟩ [Termin]kalender m

dice /daɪs/ n inv Würfel m □ vt ⟨Culin⟩ in Würfel schneiden

dicey /'daɪsɪ/ a ⟨fam⟩ riskant

dictat|e /dɪk'teɪt/ vt/i diktieren. ~ion /-'eɪʃn/ n Diktat nt

dictator /dɪk'teɪtə(r)/ n Diktator m. ~ial /-tə'tɔ:rɪəl/ a diktatorisch. ~ship n Diktatur f

diction /'dɪkʃn/ n Aussprache f

dictionary /'dɪkʃənrɪ/ n Wörterbuch nt

did /dɪd/ see do

didactic /dɪ'dæktɪk/ a didaktisch

diddle /'dɪdl/ vt ⟨fam⟩ übers Ohr hauen

didn't /'dɪdnt/ = did not

die¹ /daɪ/ n ⟨Techn⟩ Prägestempel m; ⟨metal mould⟩ Gussform f

die² vi ⟨pres p dying⟩ sterben ⟨of an + dat⟩; ⟨plant, animal:⟩ eingehen; ⟨flower:⟩ verwelken; be dying to do sth ⟨fam⟩ darauf brennen, etw zu tun; be dying for sth ⟨fam⟩ sich nach etw sehnen. ~ down vi nachlassen; ⟨fire:⟩ herunterbrennen. ~ out vi aussterben

diesel /'di:zl/ n Diesel m. ~ engine n Dieselmotor m

diet /'daɪət/ n Kost f; ⟨restricted⟩ Diät f; ⟨for slimming⟩ Schlankheitskur f; be on a ~ Diät leben; eine Schlankheitskur machen □ vi Diät leben; eine Schlankheitskur machen

dietician /daɪə'tɪʃn/ n Diätassistent(in) m(f)

differ /'dɪfə(r)/ vi sich unterscheiden; ⟨disagree⟩ verschiedener Meinung sein

differen|ce /'dɪfrəns/ n Unterschied m; ⟨disagreement⟩ Meinungsverschiedenheit f. ~t a andere(r,s); ⟨various⟩ verschiedene; be ~t anders sein (from als)

differential /dɪfə'renʃl/ a Differenzial- □ n Unterschied m; ⟨Techn⟩ Differenzial nt

differentiate /dɪfə'renʃɪeɪt/ vt/i unterscheiden ⟨between zwischen + dat⟩

differently /'dɪfrəntlɪ/ adv anders

difficult /'dɪfɪkəlt/ a schwierig, schwer. ~y n Schwierigkeit f

diffiden|ce /'dɪfɪdəns/ n Zaghaftigkeit f. ~t a zaghaft

diffuse¹ /dɪ'fjuːs/ a ausgebreitet; (wordy) langatmig

diffuse² /dɪ'fjuːz/ vt (Phys) streuen

dig /dɪg/ n (poke) Stoß m; (remark) spitze Bemerkung f; (Archaeol) Ausgrabung f; ~s pl (fam) möbliertes Zimmer nt □ vt/i (pt/pp dug, pres p digging) graben; umgraben ⟨garden⟩; ~ s.o. in the ribs jdm einen Rippenstoß geben. ~ out vt ausgraben. ~ up vt ausgraben; umgraben ⟨garden⟩; aufreißen ⟨street⟩

digest¹ /'daɪdʒest/ n Kurzfassung f

digest² /dɪ'dʒest/ vt verdauen. ~ible a verdaulich. ~ion /-estʃn/ n Verdauung f

digger /'dɪgə(r)/ n (Techn) Bagger m

digit /'dɪdʒɪt/ n Ziffer f; (finger) Finger m; (toe) Zehe f

digital /'dɪdʒɪtl/ a Digital-; ~ clock Digitaluhr f

dignified /'dɪgnɪfaɪd/ a würdevoll

dignitary /'dɪgnɪtərɪ/ n Würdenträger m

dignity /'dɪgnɪtɪ/ n Würde f

digress /daɪ'gres/ vi abschweifen. ~ion /-eʃn/ n Abschweifung f

dike /daɪk/ n Deich m; (ditch) Graben m

dilapidated /dɪ'læpɪdeɪtɪd/ a baufällig

dilate /daɪ'leɪt/ vt erweitern □ vi sich erweitern

dilatory /'dɪlətərɪ/ a langsam

dilemma /dɪ'lemə/ n Dilemma nt

dilettante /dɪlɪ'tæntɪ/ n Dilettant(in) m(f)

diligen|ce /'dɪlɪdʒəns/ n Fleiß m. ~t, -ly adv fleißig

dill /dɪl/ n Dill m

dilly-dally /'dɪlɪdælɪ/ vi (pt/pp -ied) (fam) trödeln

dilute /daɪ'luːt/ vt verdünnen

dim /dɪm/ a (dimmer, dimmest), -ly adv (weak) schwach; (dark) trüb[e]; (indistinct) undeutlich; (fam: stupid) dumm, (fam) doof □ v (pt/pp dimmed) □ vt dämpfen □ vi schwächer werden

dime /daɪm/ n (Amer) Zehncentstück nt

dimension /daɪ'menʃn/ n Dimension f; ~s pl Maße pl

diminish /dɪ'mɪnɪʃ/ vt verringern □ vi sich verringern

diminutive /dɪ'mɪnjʊtɪv/ a winzig □ n Verkleinerungsform f

dimple /'dɪmpl/ n Grübchen nt

din /dɪn/ n Krach m, Getöse nt

dine /daɪn/ vi speisen. ~r n Speisende(r) m/f; (Amer: restaurant) Esslokal nt

dinghy /'dɪŋgɪ/ n Dinghi f; (inflatable) Schlauchboot nt

dingy /'dɪndʒɪ/ a (-ier, -iest) trübe

dining /'daɪnɪŋ/: ~-car n Speisewagen m. ~-room n Esszimmer nt. ~-table n Esstisch m

dinner /'dɪnə(r)/ n Abendessen nt; (at midday) Mittagessen nt; (formal) Essen nt. ~-jacket n Smoking m

dinosaur /'daɪnəsɔː(r)/ n Dinosaurier m

dint /dɪnt/ n by ~ of durch (+ acc)

diocese /'daɪəsɪs/ n Diözese f

dip /dɪp/ n (in ground) Senke f; (Culin) Dip m; go for a ~ kurz schwimmen gehen □ v (pt/pp dipped) vt [ein]tauchen; ~ one's headlights (Auto) [die Scheinwerfer] abblenden □ vi sich senken

diphtheria /dɪf'θɪərɪə/ n Diphtherie f

diphthong /'dɪfθɒŋ/ n Diphthong m

diploma /dɪ'pləʊmə/ n Diplom nt

diplomacy /dɪ'pləʊməsɪ/ n Diplomatie f

diplomat /'dɪpləmæt/ n Diplomat m. ~ic /-'mætɪk/ a, -ally adv diplomatisch

'dip-stick n (Auto) Ölmessstab m

dire /'daɪə(r)/ a (-r, -st) bitter; (situation, consequences) furchtbar

direct /dɪ'rekt/ a & adv direkt □ vt (aim) richten (at auf / (fig) an + acc); (control) leiten; (order) anweisen; ~ s.o. (show the way) jdm den Weg zeigen; ~ a film/play bei einem Film/Theaterstück Regie führen. ~ 'current n Gleichstrom m

direction /dɪ'rekʃn/ n Richtung f; (control) Leitung f; (of play, film) Regie f; ~s pl Anweisungen pl; ~s for use Gebrauchsanweisung f

directly /dɪ'rektlɪ/ adv direkt; (at once) sofort □ conj (fam) sobald

director /dɪ'rektə(r)/ n (Comm) Direktor m; (of play, film) Regisseur m

directory /dɪ'rektərɪ/ n Verzeichnis nt; (Teleph) Telefonbuch nt

dirt /dɜːt/ n Schmutz m; (soil) Erde f; ~ cheap (fam) spottbillig

dirty /'dɜːtɪ/ a (-ier, -iest) schmutzig □ vt schmutzig machen

dis|a'bility /dɪs-/ n Behinderung f. ~abled /dɪs'eɪbld/ a [körper]behindert

disad'van|tage n Nachteil m; at a ~tage im Nachteil. ~taged a benachteiligt. ~tageous a nachteilig

disaf'fected a unzufrieden; (disloyal) illoyal

disa'gree vi nicht übereinstimmen (with mit); I ~ ich bin anderer Meinung; we ~ wir sind verschiedener Meinung; oysters ~ with me Austern bekommen mir nicht

disa'greeable a unangenehm

disa'greement n Meinungsverschiedenheit f

disap'pear vi verschwinden. ~ance n Verschwinden nt

disap'point vt enttäuschen. ~ment n Enttäuschung f

disap'proval n Missbilligung f

disap'prove vi dagegen sein; ~ of missbilligen

dis'arm vt entwaffnen □ vi (Mil) abrüsten. ~ment n Abrüstung f. ~ing a entwaffnend

disar'ray n Unordnung f

disast|er /dɪˈzɑːstə(r)/ n Katastrophe f; (accident) Unglück nt. ~rous /-rəs/ a katastrophal

dis'band vt auflösen □ vi sich auflösen

disbe'lief n Ungläubigkeit f; in ~ ungläubig

disc /dɪsk/ n Scheibe f; (record) [Schall]platte f; (CD) CD f

discard /dɪˈskɑːd/ vt ablegen; (throw away) wegwerfen

discern /dɪˈsɜːn/ vt wahrnehmen. ~ible a wahrnehmbar. ~ing a anspruchsvoll

'discharge¹ n Ausstoßen nt; (Naut, Electr) Entladung f; (dismissal) Entlassung f; (Jur) Freispruch m; (Med) Ausfluss m

dis'charge² vt ausstoßen; (Naut, Electr) entladen; (dismiss) entlassen; (Jur) freisprechen (accused); ~ a duty sich einer Pflicht entledigen

disciple /dɪˈsaɪpl/ n Jünger m; (fig) Schüler m

disciplinary /ˈdɪsɪplɪnərɪ/ a disziplinarisch

discipline /ˈdɪsɪplɪn/ n Disziplin f □ vt Disziplin beibringen (+ dat); (punish) bestrafen

'disc jockey n Diskjockey m

dis'claim vt abstreiten. ~er n Verzichterklärung f

dis'clos|e vt enthüllen. ~ure n Enthüllung f

disco /ˈdɪskəʊ/ n (fam) Disko f

dis'colour vt verfärben □ vi sich verfärben

dis'comfort n Beschwerden pl; (fig) Unbehagen nt

disconcert /dɪskənˈsɜːt/ vt aus der Fassung bringen

discon'nect vt trennen; (Electr) ausschalten; (cut supply) abstellen

disconsolate /dɪsˈkɒnsələt/ a untröstlich

discon'tent n Unzufriedenheit f. ~ed a unzufrieden

discon'tinue vt einstellen; (Comm) nicht mehr herstellen

'discord n Zwietracht f; (Mus & fig) Missklang m. ~ant /dɪsˈkɔːdənt/ a ~ant note Missklang m

discothèque /ˈdɪskətek/ n Diskothek f

'discount¹ n Rabatt m

dis'count² vt außer Acht lassen

dis'courage vt entmutigen; (dissuade) abraten (+ dat)

'discourse n Rede f

dis'courteous a, -ly adv unhöflich

discover /dɪˈskʌvə(r)/ vt entdecken. ~y n Entdeckung f

dis'credit n Misskredit m □ vt in Misskredit bringen

discreet /dɪˈskriːt/ a, -ly adv diskret

discrepancy /dɪˈskrepənsɪ/ n Diskrepanz f

discretion /dɪˈskreʃn/ n Diskretion f; (judgement) Ermessen nt

discriminat|e /dɪˈskrɪmɪneɪt/ vi unterscheiden (between zwischen + dat); ~e against diskriminieren. ~ing a anspruchsvoll. ~ion /-ˈneɪʃn/ n Diskriminierung f; (quality) Urteilskraft f

discus /ˈdɪskəs/ n Diskus m

discuss /dɪˈskʌs/ vt besprechen; (examine critically) diskutieren. ~ion /-ˈʌʃn/ n Besprechung f; Diskussion f

disdain /dɪsˈdeɪn/ n Verachtung f □ vt verachten. ~ful a verächtlich

disease /dɪˈziːz/ n Krankheit f. ~d a krank

disem'bark vi an Land gehen

disen'chant vt ernüchtern. ~ment n Ernüchterung f

disen'gage vt losmachen; ~ the clutch (Auto) auskuppeln

disen'tangle vt entwirren

dis'favour n Ungnade f; (disapproval) Missfallen nt

dis'figure vt entstellen

dis'gorge vt ausspeien

dis'grace n Schande f; in ~ in Ungnade □ vt Schande machen (+ dat). ~ful a schändlich

disgruntled /dɪsˈɡrʌntld/ a verstimmt

disguise /dɪsˈɡaɪz/ n Verkleidung f; in ~ verkleidet □ vt verkleiden; verstellen (voice); (conceal) verhehlen

disgust /dɪsˈɡʌst/ n Ekel m; in ~ empört □ vt anekeln; (appal) empören. ~ing a eklig; (appalling) abscheulich

dish /dɪʃ/ n Schüssel f; (shallow) Schale f; (small) Schälchen nt; (food) Gericht nt. ~ out austeilen. ~ up auftragen

'dishcloth n Spültuch nt

dis'hearten vt entmutigen. ~ing a entmutigend

dishevelled /dɪˈʃevld/ a zerzaust

dis'honest a, -ly adv unehrlich. ~y n Unehrlichkeit f

dis'honour *n* Schande *f* □ *vt* entehren; nicht honorieren (*cheque*). ~able *a*, -bly *adv* unehrenhaft

'dishwasher *n* Geschirrspülmaschine *f*

disil'lusion *vt* ernüchtern. ~ment *n* Ernüchterung *f*

disin'fect *vt* desinfizieren. ~ant *n* Desinfektionsmittel *nt*

disin'herit *vt* enterben

dis'integrate *vi* zerfallen

dis'interested *a* unvoreingenommen; (*uninterested*) uninteressiert

dis'jointed *a* unzusammenhängend

disk /dɪsk/ *n* = disc

dis'like *n* Abneigung *f* □ *vt* nicht mögen

dislocate /'dɪsləkeɪt/ *vt* ausrenken; ~ one's shoulder sich (*dat*) den Arm auskugeln

dis'lodge *vt* entfernen

dis'loyal *a*, -ly *adv* illoyal. ~ty *n* Illoyalität *f*

dismal /'dɪzməl/ *a* trüb[e]; (*person*) trübselig; (*fam: poor*) kläglich

dismantle /dɪs'mæntl/ *vt* auseinander nehmen; (*take down*) abbauen

dis'may *n* Bestürzung *f*. ~ed *a* bestürzt

dis'miss *vt* entlassen; (*reject*) zurückweisen. ~al *n* Entlassung *f*; Zurückweisung *f*

dis'mount *vi* absteigen

diso'bedien|ce *n* Ungehorsam *m*. ~t *a* ungehorsam

diso'bey *vt/i* nicht gehorchen (+ *dat*); nicht befolgen (*rule*)

dis'order *n* Unordnung *f*; (*Med*) Störung *f*. ~ly *a* unordentlich; ~ly conduct ungebührliches Benehmen *nt*

dis'organized *a* unorganisiert

dis'orientate *vt* verwirren; be ~d die Orientierung verloren haben

dis'own *vt* verleugnen

disparaging /dɪ'spærɪdʒɪŋ/ *a*, -ly *adv* abschätzig

disparity /dɪ'spærətɪ/ *n* Ungleichheit *f*

dispassionate /dɪs'pæʃənət/ *a*, -ly *adv* gelassen; (*impartial*) unparteiisch

dispatch /dɪ'spætʃ/ *n* (*Comm*) Versand *m*; (*Mil*) Nachricht *f*; (*report*) Bericht *m*; with ~ prompt □ *vt* [ab]senden; (*deal with*) erledigen; (*kill*) töten. ~-rider *n* Meldefahrer *m*

dispel /dɪ'spel/ *vt* (*pt/pp* dispelled) vertreiben

dispensable /dɪ'spensəbl/ *a* entbehrlich

dispensary /dɪ'spensərɪ/ *n* Apotheke *f*

dispense /dɪ'spens/ *vt* austeilen; ~ with verzichten auf (+ *acc*). ~r *n* Apotheker(in) *m(f)*; (*device*) Automat *m*

dispers|al /dɪ'spɜːsl/ *n* Zerstreuung *f*. ~e /dɪ'spɜːs/ *vt* zerstreuen □ *vi* sich zerstreuen

dispirited /dɪ'spɪrɪtɪd/ *a* entmutigt

dis'place *vt* verschieben; ~d person Vertriebene(r) *m/f*

display /dɪ'spleɪ/ *n* Ausstellung *f*; (*Comm*) Auslage *f*; (*performance*) Vorführung *f* □ *vt* zeigen; ausstellen (*goods*)

dis'please *vt* missfallen (+ *dat*)

dis'pleasure *n* Missfallen *nt*

disposable /dɪ'spəʊzəbl/ *a* Wegwerf-; (*income*) verfügbar

disposal /dɪ'spəʊzl/ *n* Beseitigung *f*; be at s.o.'s ~ jdm zur Verfügung stehen

dispose /dɪ'spəʊz/ *vi* ~ of beseitigen; (*deal with*) erledigen; be well ~d wohlgesinnt sein (to *dat*)

disposition /dɪspə'zɪʃn/ *n* Veranlagung *f*; (*nature*) Wesensart *f*

disproportionate /dɪsprə'pɔːʃənət/ *a*, -ly *adv* unverhältnismäßig

dis'prove *vt* widerlegen

dispute /dɪ'spjuːt/ *n* Disput *m*; (*quarrel*) Streit *m* □ *vt* bestreiten

disqualifi'cation *n* Disqualifikation *f*

dis'qualify *vt* disqualifizieren; ~ s.o. from driving jdm den Führerschein entziehen

disquieting /dɪs'kwaɪətɪŋ/ *a* beunruhigend

disre'gard *n* Nichtbeachtung *f* □ *vt* nicht beachten, ignorieren

disre'pair *n* fall into ~ verfallen

dis'reputable *a* verrufen

disre'pute *n* Verruf *m*

disre'spect *n* Respektlosigkeit *f*. ~ful *a*, -ly *adv* respektlos

disrupt /dɪs'rʌpt/ *vt* stören. ~ion /-'ʌpʃn/ *n* Störung *f*. ~ive /-ɪv/ *a* störend

dissatis'faction *n* Unzufriedenheit *f*

dis'satisfied *a* unzufrieden

dissect /dɪ'sekt/ *vt* zergliedern; (*Med*) sezieren. ~ion /-ekʃn/ *n* Zergliederung *f*; (*Med*) Sektion *f*

disseminat|e /dɪ'semɪneɪt/ *vt* verbreiten. ~ion /-'neɪʃn/ *n* Verbreitung *f*

dissent /dɪ'sent/ *n* Nichtübereinstimmung *f* □ *vi* nicht übereinstimmen

dissertation /dɪsə'teɪʃn/ *n* Dissertation *f*

dis'service *n* schlechter Dienst *m*

dissident /'dɪsɪdənt/ *n* Dissident *m*

dis'similar *a* unähnlich (to *dat*)

dissociate /dɪ'səʊʃɪeɪt/ *vt* trennen; ~ oneself sich distanzieren (from von)

dissolute /'dɪsəluːt/ *a* zügellos; (*life*) ausschweifend

dissolution /dɪsə'lu:ʃn/ n Auflösung f

dissolve /dɪ'zɒlv/ vt auflösen □ vi sich auflösen

dissuade /dɪ'sweɪd/ vt abbringen (from von)

distance /'dɪstəns/ n Entfernung f; long/short ~ lange/kurze Strecke f; in the/from a ~ in/aus der Ferne

distant /'dɪstənt/ a fern; (aloof) kühl; ⟨relative⟩ entfernt

dis'taste n Abneigung f. ~ful a unangenehm

distend /dɪ'stend/ vi sich [auf]blähen

distil /dɪ'stɪl/ vt (pt/pp distilled) brennen; (Chem) destillieren. ~lation /-'leɪʃn/ n Destillation f. ~lery /-ərɪ/ n Brennerei f

distinct /dɪ'stɪŋkt/ a deutlich; (different) verschieden. ~ion /-ɪŋkʃn/ n Unterschied m; (Sch) Auszeichnung f. ~ive /-tɪv/ a kennzeichnend; (unmistakable) unverwechselbar. ~ly adv deutlich

distinguish /dɪ'stɪŋgwɪʃ/ vt/i unterscheiden; (make out) erkennen; ~ oneself sich auszeichnen. ~ed a angesehen; (appearance) distinguiert

distort /dɪ'stɔ:t/ vt verzerren; (fig) verdrehen. ~ion /-ɔ:ʃn/ n Verzerrung f; (fig) Verdrehung f

distract /dɪ'strækt/ vt ablenken. ~ed /-ɪd/ a [völlig] aufgelöst. ~ion /-ækʃn/ n Ablenkung f; (despair) Verzweiflung f

distraught /dɪ'strɔ:t/ a [völlig] aufgelöst

distress /dɪ'stres/ n Kummer m; (pain) Schmerz m; (poverty, danger) Not f □ vt Kummer/Schmerz bereiten (+ dat); (sadden) bekümmern; (shock) erschüttern. ~ing a schmerzlich; (shocking) erschütternd. ~ signal n Notsignal nt

distribut|e /dɪ'strɪbju:t/ vt verteilen; (Comm) vertreiben. ~ion /-'bju:ʃn/ n Verteilung f; Vertrieb m. ~or n Verteiler m

district /'dɪstrɪkt/ n Gegend f; (Admin) Bezirk m. ~ nurse n Gemeindeschwester f

dis'trust n Misstrauen n □ vt misstrauen (+ dat). ~ful a misstrauisch

disturb /dɪ'stɜ:b/ vt stören; (perturb) beunruhigen; (touch) anrühren. ~ance n Unruhe f; (interruption) Störung f. ~ed a beunruhigt; [mentally] ~ed geistig gestört. ~ing a beunruhigend

dis'used a stillgelegt; (empty) leer

ditch /dɪtʃ/ n Graben m □ vt (fam: abandon) fallen lassen ⟨plan⟩; wegschmeißen ⟨thing⟩

dither /'dɪðə(r)/ vi zaudern

ditto /'dɪtəʊ/ n dito; (fam) ebenfalls

divan /dɪ'væn/ n Polsterbett nt

dive /daɪv/ n [Kopf]sprung m; (Aviat) Sturzflug m; (fam: place) Spelunke f □ vi einen Kopfsprung machen; (when in water) tauchen; (Aviat) einen Sturzflug machen; (fam: rush) stürzen

diver /'daɪvə(r)/ n Taucher m; (Sport) [Kunst]springer m

diver|ge /daɪ'vɜ:dʒ/ vi auseinander gehen. ~gent /-ənt/ a abweichend

diverse /daɪ'vɜ:s/ a verschieden

diversify /daɪ'vɜ:sɪfaɪ/ vt/i (pt/pp -ied) variieren; (Comm) diversifizieren

diversion /daɪ'vɜ:ʃn/ n Umleitung f; (distraction) Ablenkung f

diversity /daɪ'vɜ:sətɪ/ n Vielfalt f

divert /daɪ'vɜ:t/ vt umleiten; ablenken ⟨attention⟩; (entertain) unterhalten

divest /daɪ'vest/ vt sich entledigen (of + gen); (fig) entkleiden

divide /dɪ'vaɪd/ vt teilen; (separate) trennen; (Math) dividieren (by durch) □ vi sich teilen

dividend /'dɪvɪdend/ n Dividende f

divine /dɪ'vaɪn/ a göttlich

diving /'daɪvɪŋ/ n (Sport) Kunstspringen nt. ~-board n Sprungbrett nt. ~-suit n Taucheranzug m

divinity /dɪ'vɪnətɪ/ n Göttlichkeit f; (subject) Theologie f

divisible /dɪ'vɪzɪbl/ a teilbar (by durch)

division /dɪ'vɪʒn/ n Teilung f; (separation) Trennung f; (Math, Mil) Division f; (Parl) Hammelsprung m; (line) Trennlinie f; (group) Abteilung f

divorce /dɪ'vɔ:s/ n Scheidung f □ vt sich scheiden lassen von. □ a geschieden; get ~d sich scheiden lassen

divorcee /dɪvɔ:'si:/ n Geschiedene(r) m/f

divulge /daɪ'vʌldʒ/ vt preisgeben

DIY abbr of do-it-yourself

dizziness /'dɪzɪnɪs/ n Schwindel m

dizzy /'dɪzɪ/ a (-ier, -iest) schwindlig; I feel ~ mir ist schwindlig

do /du:/ n (pl dos or do's) (fam) Veranstaltung f □ v (3 sg pres tense does; pt did; pp done) □ vt/i tun, machen; (be suitable) passen; (be enough) reichen, genügen; (cook) kochen; (clean) putzen; (Sch: study) durchnehmen; (fam: cheat) beschwindeln (out of um); do without auskommen ohne; do away with abschaffen; be done (Culin) gar sein; well done gut gemacht! (Culin) gut durchgebraten; done in (fam) kaputt, fertig; done for (fam) verloren, erledigt; do the flowers die Blumen arrangieren; do the potatoes die Kartoffeln schälen; do the washing up abwaschen, spülen; do one's hair sich frisieren; do well/badly gut/schlecht abschneiden;

how is he doing? wie geht es ihm? this won't do das geht nicht; are you doing anything today? haben Sie heute etwas vor? I could do with a spanner ich könnte einen Schraubenschlüssel gebrauchen □ *v aux* do you speak German? sprechen Sie Deutsch? yes, I do ja; (*emphatic*) doch; no, I don't nein; I don't smoke ich rauche nicht; don't you/ doesn't he? nicht [wahr]? so do I ich auch; do come in kommen Sie doch herein; how do you do? guten Tag. do in *vt* (*fam*) um die Ecke bringen. do up *vt* (*fasten*) zumachen; (*renovate*) renovieren; (*wrap*) einpacken

docile /'dəʊsaɪl/ *a* fügsam

dock[1] /dɒk/ *n* (*Jur*) Anklagebank *f*

dock[2] *n* Dock *nt* □ *vi* anlegen, docken □ *vt* docken. ~er *n* Hafenarbeiter *m*. ~yard *n* Werft *f*

doctor /'dɒktə(r)/ *n* Arzt *m*/ Ärztin *f*; (*Univ*) Doktor *m* □ *vt* kastrieren; (*spay*) sterilisieren. ~ate /-ət/ *n* Doktorwürde *f*

doctrine /'dɒktrɪn/ *n* Lehre *f*, Doktrin *f*

document /'dɒkjʊmənt/ *n* Dokument *nt*. ~ary /-'mentərɪ/ *a* Dokumentar- □ *n* Dokumentarbericht *m*; (*film*) Dokumentarfilm *m*

doddery /'dɒdərɪ/ *a* (*fam*) tatterig

dodge /dɒdʒ/ *n* (*fam*) Trick *m*, Kniff *m* □ *vt/i* ausweichen (+ *dat*); ~ out of the way zur Seite springen

dodgems /'dɒdʒəmz/ *npl* Autoskooter *pl*

dodgy /'dɒdʒɪ/ *a* (-ier, -iest) (*fam*) (*awkward*) knifflig; (*dubious*) zweifelhaft

doe /dəʊ/ *n* Ricke *f*; (*rabbit*) [Kaninchen]weibchen *nt*

does /dʌz/ *see* do

doesn't /'dʌznt/ = does not

dog /dɒg/ *n* Hund *m* □ *vt* (*pt/pp* dogged) verfolgen

dog: ~-biscuit *n* Hundekuchen *m*. ~-collar *n* Hundehalsband *nt*; (*Relig, fam*) Kragen *m* eines Geistlichen. ~-eared *a* be ~-eared Eselsohren haben

dogged /'dɒgɪd/ *a*, -ly *adv* beharrlich

dogma /'dɒgmə/ *n* Dogma *nt*. ~tic /-'mætɪk/ *a* dogmatisch

'dogsbody *n* (*fam*) Mädchen *nt* für alles

doily /'dɔɪlɪ/ *n* Deckchen *nt*

do-it-yourself /duːɪtjə'self/ *n* Heimwerken *nt*. ~ shop *n* Heimwerkerladen *m*

doldrums /'dɒldrəmz/ *npl* be in the ~ niedergeschlagen sein; (*business:*) danlederliegen

dole /dəʊl/ *n* (*fam*) Stempelgeld *nt*; be on the ~ arbeitslos sein □ *vt* ~ out austeilen

doleful /'dəʊlfʊl/ *a*, -ly *adv* trauervoll

doll /dɒl/ *n* Puppe *f* □ *vt* (*fam*) ~ oneself up sich herausputzen

dollar /'dɒlə(r)/ *n* Dollar *m*

dollop /'dɒləp/ *n* (*fam*) Klecks *m*

dolphin /'dɒlfɪn/ *n* Delphin *m*

domain /də'meɪn/ *n* Gebiet *nt*

dome /dəʊm/ *n* Kuppel *f*

domestic /də'mestɪk/ *a* häuslich; (*Pol*) Innen-; (*Comm*) Binnen-. ~ animal *n* Haustier *nt*

domesticated /də'mestɪkeɪtɪd/ *a* häuslich; (*animal*) zahm

domestic: ~ flight *n* Inlandflug *m*. ~ 'servant *n* Hausangestellte(r) *m/f*

dominant /'dɒmɪnənt/ *a* vorherrschend

dominat|e /'dɒmɪneɪt/ *vt* beherrschen □ *vi* dominieren; ~e over beherrschen. ~ion /-'neɪʃn/ *n* Vorherrschaft *f*

domineer /dɒmɪ'nɪə(r)/ *vi* ~ over tyrannisieren. ~ing *a* herrschsüchtig

dominion /də'mɪnjən/ *n* Herrschaft *f*

domino /'dɒmɪnəʊ/ *n* (*pl* -es) Dominostein *m*; ~es *sg* (*game*) Domino *nt*

don[1] /dɒn/ *vt* (*pt/pp* donned) (*liter*) anziehen

don[2] *n* [Universitäts]dozent *m*

donat|e /dəʊ'neɪt/ *vt* spenden. ~ion /-eɪʃn/ *n* Spende *f*

done /dʌn/ *see* do

donkey /'dɒŋkɪ/ *n* Esel *m*; ~'s years (*fam*) eine Ewigkeit. ~-work *n* Routinearbeit *f*

donor /'dəʊnə(r)/ *n* Spender(in) *m(f)*

don't /dəʊnt/ = do not

doodle /'duːdl/ *vi* kritzeln

doom /duːm/ *n* Schicksal *nt*; (*ruin*) Verhängnis *nt* □ *vt* be ~ed to failure zum Scheitern verurteilt sein

door /dɔː(r)/ *n* Tür *f*; out of ~s im Freien

door: ~man *n* Portier *m*. ~mat *n* [Fuß]abtreter *m*. ~step *n* Türschwelle *f*; on the ~step vor der Tür. ~way *n* Türöffnung *f*

dope /dəʊp/ *n* (*fam*) Drogen *pl*; (*fam: information*) Informationen *pl*; (*fam: idiot*) Trottel *m* □ *vt* betäuben; (*Sport*) dopen

dopey /'dəʊpɪ/ *a* (*fam*) benommen; (*stupid*) blöd[e]

dormant /'dɔːmənt/ *a* ruhend

dormer /'dɔːmə(r)/ *n* ~ [window] Mansardenfenster *nt*

dormitory /'dɔːmɪtərɪ/ *n* Schlafsaal *m*

dormouse /'dɔː-/ *n* Haselmaus *f*

dosage /'dəʊsɪdʒ/ *n* Dosierung *f*

dose /dəʊs/ *n* Dosis *f*

doss /dɒs/ *vi* (*sl*) pennen. ~er *n* Penner *m*. ~-house *n* Penne *f*

dot /dɒt/ *n* Punkt *m*; on the ~ pünktlich

dote /dəʊt/ vi ~ on vernarrt sein in (+ acc)

dotted /'dɒtɪd/ a ~ line punktierte Linie f; be ~ with bestreut sein mit

dotty /'dɒtɪ/ a (-ier, -iest) (fam) verdreht

double /'dʌbl/ a & adv doppelt; ⟨bed, chin⟩ Doppel-; ⟨flower⟩ gefüllt □ n das Doppelte; ⟨person⟩ Doppelgänger m; ~s pl (Tennis) Doppel nt; at the ~ im Laufschritt □ vt verdoppeln; ⟨fold⟩ falten □ vi sich verdoppeln. ~ back vi zurückgehen. ~ up vi sich krümmen (with vor + dat)

double: ~'bass n Kontrabass m. ~ breasted a zweireihig. ~'cross vt ein Doppelspiel treiben mit. ~'decker n Doppeldecker m. ~ 'Dutch n (fam) Kauderwelsch nt. ~ 'glazing n Doppelverglasung f. ~ 'room n Doppelzimmer nt

doubly /'dʌblɪ/ adv doppelt

doubt /daʊt/ n Zweifel m □ vt bezweifeln. ~ful a, -ly adv zweifelhaft; ⟨disbelieving⟩ skeptisch. ~less adv zweifellos

dough /dəʊ/ n ⟨fester⟩ Teig m; (fam: money) Pinke f. ~nut n Berliner [Pfannkuchen] m, Krapfen m

douse /daʊs/ vt übergießen; ausgießen ⟨flames⟩

dove /dʌv/ n Taube f. ~tail n (Techn) Schwalbenschwanz m

dowdy /'daʊdɪ/ a (-ier, -iest) unschick

down¹ /daʊn/ n ⟨feathers⟩ Daunen pl

down² /daʊn/ adv unten; ⟨with movement⟩ nach unten; go ~ hinuntergehen; come ~ herunterkommen; ~ there da unten; £50 ~ £50 Anzahlung; ~! (to dog) Platz! ~ with ...! nieder mit ...! □ prep ~ the road/stairs die Straße/Treppe hinunter; ~ the river den Fluss abwärts; be ~ the pub (fam) in der Kneipe sein □ vt (fam) ⟨drink⟩ runterkippen; ~ tools die Arbeit niederlegen

down: ~and-'out n Penner m. ~cast a niedergeschlagen. ~fall n Sturz m; ⟨ruin⟩ Ruin m. ~'grade vt niedriger einstufen. ~'hearted a entmutigt. ~'hill adv bergab. ~ payment n Anzahlung f. ~pour n Platzregen m. ~right a & adv ausgesprochen. ~'stairs adv unten; ⟨go⟩ nach unten □ a /'--/ im Erdgeschoss. ~'stream adv stromabwärts. ~to-'earth a sachlich. ~town adv (Amer) im Stadtzentrum. ~trodden a unterdrückt. ~ward a nach unten; ⟨slope⟩ abfallend □ adv ~[s] abwärts, nach unten

downy /'daʊnɪ/ a (-ier, -iest) flaumig

dowry /'daʊrɪ/ n Mitgift f

doze /dəʊz/ n Nickerchen nt □ vi dösen. ~ off vi einnicken

dozen /'dʌzn/ n Dutzend nt

Dr abbr of doctor

draft¹ /drɑːft/ n Entwurf m; (Comm) Tratte f; (Amer Mil) Einberufung f □ vt entwerfen; (Amer Mil) einberufen

draft² n (Amer) = draught

drag /dræg/ n (fam) Klotz m am Bein; in ~ (fam) ⟨man⟩ als Frau gekleidet □ vt (pt/pp dragged) schleppen; absuchen ⟨river⟩. ~ on vi sich in die Länge ziehen

dragon /'drægən/ n Drache m. ~fly n Libelle f

'drag show n Transvestitenshow f

drain /dreɪn/ n Abfluss m; ⟨underground⟩ Kanal m; the ~s die Kanalisation □ vt entwässern ⟨land⟩; ablassen ⟨liquid⟩; das Wasser ablassen aus ⟨tank⟩; abgießen ⟨vegetables⟩; austrinken ⟨glass⟩ □ vi ~ [away] ablaufen; leave sth to ~ etw abtropfen lassen

drain|age /'dreɪnɪdʒ/ n Kanalisation f; (of land) Dränage f. ~ing board n Abtropfbrett nt. ~pipe n Abflussrohr nt

drake /dreɪk/ n Enterich m

drama /'drɑːmə/ n Drama nt; (quality) Dramatik f

dramatic /drə'mætɪk/ a, -ally adv dramatisch

dramat|ist /'dræmətɪst/ n Dramatiker m. ~ize vt für die Bühne bearbeiten; (fig) dramatisieren

drank /dræŋk/ see drink

drape /dreɪp/ n (Amer) Vorhang m □ vt drapieren

drastic /'dræstɪk/ a, -ally adv drastisch

draught /drɑːft/ n [Luft]zug m; ~s sg (game) Damespiel nt; there is a ~ es zieht

draught: ~ beer n Bier nt vom Fass. ~sman n technischer Zeichner m

draughty /'drɑːftɪ/ a zugig; it's ~ es zieht

draw /drɔː/ n Attraktion f; (Sport) Unentschieden nt; (in lottery) Ziehung f □ v (pt drew, pp drawn) □ vt ⟨attract⟩ anziehen; zeichnen ⟨picture⟩; abheben ⟨money⟩; holen ⟨water⟩; ~ the curtains die Vorhänge zuziehen; ⟨back⟩ aufziehen; ~ lots losen (for um) □ vi ⟨tea:⟩ ziehen; (Sport) unentschieden spielen. ~ back vt zurückziehen □ vi ⟨recoil⟩ zurückweichen. ~ in vt einziehen □ vi ⟨days:⟩ kürzer werden. ~ out vt herausziehen; abheben ⟨money⟩ □ vi ausfahren; ⟨days:⟩ länger werden. ~ up vt aufsetzen ⟨document⟩; heranrücken ⟨chair⟩; ~ oneself up sich aufrichten □ vi [an]halten

draw: ~back n Nachteil m. ~bridge n Zugbrücke f

drawer /drɔː(r)/ n Schublade f

drawing /'drɔːɪŋ/ n Zeichnung f

drawing: ∼board *n* Reißbrett *nt.* ∼-pin *n* Reißzwecke *f.* ∼-room *n* Wohnzimmer *nt*

drawl /drɔːl/ *n* schleppende Aussprache *f*

drawn /drɔːn/ *see* draw

dread /dred/ *n* Furcht *f* (of vor + *dat*) □ *vt* fürchten. ∼ful *a,* -fully *adv* fürchterlich

dream /driːm/ *n* Traum *m* □ *attrib* Traum- □ *vt/i* (*pt/pp* dreamt /dremt/ *or* dreamed) träumen (about/of von)

dreary /ˈdrɪərɪ/ *a* (-ier, -iest) trüb[e]; (*boring*) langweilig

dredge /dredʒ/ *vt/i* baggern. ∼r *n* [Nass]bagger *m*

dregs /dregz/ *npl* Bodensatz *m*

drench /drentʃ/ *vt* durchnässen

dress /dres/ *n* Kleid *nt*; (*clothing*) Kleidung *f* □ *vt* anziehen; (*decorate*) schmücken; (*Culin*) anmachen; (*Med*) verbinden; ∼ oneself, get ∼ed sich anziehen □ *vi* sich anziehen. ∼ up *vi* sich schön anziehen; (*in disguise*) sich verkleiden (as als)

dress: ∼ circle *n* (*Theat*) erster Rang *m.* ∼er *n* (*furniture*) Anrichte *f*; (*Amer: dressing-table*) Frisiertisch *m*

dressing *n* (*Culin*) Soße *f*; (*Med*) Verband *m*

dressing: ∼ down *n* (*fam*) Standpauke *f.* ∼-gown *n* Morgenmantel *m.* ∼-room *n* Ankleidezimmer *nt*; (*Theat*) [Künstler]- garderobe *f.* ∼-table *n* Frisiertisch *m*

dress: ∼maker *n* Schneiderin *f.* ∼mak- ing *n* Damenschneiderei *f.* ∼ rehearsal *n* Generalprobe *f*

dressy /ˈdresɪ/ *a* (-ier, -iest) schick

drew /druː/ *see* draw

dribble /ˈdrɪbl/ *vi* sabbern; (*Sport*) drib- beln

dried /draɪd/ *a* getrocknet; ∼ fruit Dörr- obst *nt*

drier /ˈdraɪə(r)/ *n* Trockner *m*

drift /drɪft/ *n* Abtrift *f*; (*of snow*) Schneewehe *f*; (*meaning*) Sinn *m* □ *vi* treiben; (*off course*) abtreiben; (*snow:*) We- hen bilden; (*fig/person:*) sich treiben las- sen; ∼ apart (*persons:*) sich auseinander leben. ∼wood *n* Treibholz *nt*

drill /drɪl/ *n* Bohrer *m*; (*Mil*) Drill *m* □ *vt/i* bohren (for nach); (*Mil*) drillen

drily /ˈdraɪlɪ/ *adv* trocken

drink /drɪŋk/ *n* Getränk *nt*; (*alcoholic*) Drink *m*; (*alcohol*) Alkohol *m*; have a ∼ etwas trinken □ *vt/i* (*pt* drank, *pp* drunk) trinken. ∼ up *vt/i* austrinken

drink|able /ˈdrɪŋkəbl/ *a* trinkbar. ∼er *n* Trinker *m*

'drinking-water *n* Trinkwasser *nt*

drip /drɪp/ *n* Tropfen *nt*; (*drop*) Tropfen *m*; (*Med*) Tropf *m*; (*fam: person*) Niete *f* □ *vi*

(*pt/pp* dripped) tropfen. ∼-'dry *a* bügel- frei. ∼ping *n* Schmalz *nt*

drive /draɪv/ *n* [Auto]fahrt *f*; (*entrance*) Einfahrt *f*; (*energy*) Elan *m*; (*Psych*) Trieb *m*; (*Pol*) Aktion *f*; (*Sport*) Treibschlag *m*; (*Techn*) Antrieb *m* □ *v* (*pt* drove, *pp* driven) □ *vt* treiben; fahren (*car*); (*Sport: hit*) schlagen; (*Techn*) antreiben; ∼ s.o. mad (*fam*) jdn verrückt machen; what are you driving at? (*fam*) worauf willst du hinaus? □ *vi* fahren. ∼ away *vt* ver- treiben □ *vi* abfahren. ∼ in *vt* hinein-/ hereinfahren. ∼ off *vt* vertreiben □ *vi* abfahren. ∼ on *vi* weiterfahren. ∼ up *vi* vorfahren

'drive-in *a* ∼ cinema Autokino *nt*

drivel /ˈdrɪvl/ *n* (*fam*) Quatsch *m*

driven /ˈdrɪvn/ *see* drive

driver /ˈdraɪvə(r)/ *n* Fahrer(in) *m(f)*; (*of train*) Lokführer *m*

driving /ˈdraɪvɪŋ/ *a* (*rain*) peitschend; (*force*) treibend

driving: ∼ lesson *n* Fahrstunde *f.* ∼ li- cence *n* Führerschein *m.* ∼ school *n* Fahrschule *f.* ∼ test Fahrprüfung *f*; take one's ∼ test den Führerschein machen

drizzle /ˈdrɪzl/ *n* Nieselregen *m* □ *vi* nie- seln

drone /drəʊn/ *n* Drohne *f*; (*sound*) Brum- men *nt*

droop /druːp/ *vi* herabhängen; (*flowers:*) die Köpfe hängen lassen

drop /drɒp/ *n* Tropfen *m*; (*fall*) Fall *m*; (*in price, temperature*) Rückgang *m* □ *v* (*pt/pp* dropped) □ *vt* fallen lassen; abwerfen (*bomb*); (*omit*) auslassen; (*give up*) auf- geben □ *vi* fallen; (*fall lower*) sinken; (*wind:*) nachlassen. ∼ in *vi* vorbeikom- men. ∼ off *vt* absetzen (*person*) □ *vi* abfallen; (*fall asleep*) einschlafen. ∼ out *vi* herausfallen; (*give up*) aufgeben

'drop-out *n* Aussteiger *m*

droppings /ˈdrɒpɪŋz/ *npl* Kot *m*

drought /draʊt/ *n* Dürre *f*

drove /drəʊv/ *see* drive

droves /drəʊvz/ *npl* in ∼ in Scharen

drown /draʊn/ *vi* ertrinken □ *vt* er- tränken; übertönen (*noise*); be ∼ed er- trinken

drowsy /ˈdraʊzɪ/ *a* schläfrig

drudgery /ˈdrʌdʒərɪ/ *n* Plackerei *f*

drug /drʌg/ *n* Droge *f* □ *vt* (*pt/pp* drugged) betäuben

drug: ∼ addict *n* Drogenabhängige(r) *m/f.* ∼gist *n* (*Amer*) Apotheker *m.* ∼store *n* (*Amer*) Drogerie *f*; (*dispensing*) Apotheke *f*

drum /drʌm/ *n* Trommel *f*; (*for oil*) Tonne *f* □ *v* (*pt/pp* drummed) □ *vi* trommeln

□ *vt* ~sth into s.o. (*fam*) jdm etw einbläuen. ~mer *n* Trommler *m*; (*in pop-
group*) Schlagzeuger *m*. ~stick *n* Trom-
melschlägel *m*; (*Culin*) Keule *f*

drunk /drʌŋk/ *see* drink □ *a* betrunken;
get ~ sich betrinken □ *n* Betrunkene(r)
m

drunk|ard /'drʌŋkəd/ *n* Trinker *m*. ~en
a betrunken; ~en driving Trunkenheit
f am Steuer

dry /draɪ/ *a* (drier, driest) trocken □ *vt/i*
trocknen; ~ one's eyes sich *dat* die
Tränen abwischen. ~ up *vi* austrocknen;
(*fig*) versiegen □ *vt* austrocknen; abtrocknen ⟨dishes⟩

dry: ~'clean *vt* chemisch reinigen. ~
'cleaner's *n* (*shop*) chemische Reinigung
f. ~ness *n* Trockenheit *f*

dual /'dju:əl/ *a* doppelt

dual: ~ 'carriageway *n* ≈ Schnellstraße
f. ~'purpose *a* zweifach verwendbar

dub /dʌb/ *vt* (*pt/pp* dubbed) synchronisieren ⟨film⟩; kopieren ⟨tape⟩; (*name*)
nennen

dubious /'dju:bɪəs/ *a* zweifelhaft; be ~
about Zweifel haben über (+ *acc*)

duchess /'dʌtʃɪs/ *n* Herzogin *f*

duck /dʌk/ *n* Ente *f* □ *vt* (*in water*) untertauchen; ~ one's head den Kopf ein-
ziehen □ *vi* sich ducken. ~ling *n* Entchen
nt; (*Culin*) Ente *f*

duct /dʌkt/ *n* Rohr *nt*; (*Anat*) Gang *m*

dud /dʌd/ *a* (*fam*) nutzlos; ⟨coin⟩ falsch;
⟨cheque⟩ ungedeckt; (*forged*) gefälscht □ *n*
(*fam*) ⟨banknote⟩ Blüte *f*; (*Mil*: *shell*)
Blindgänger *m*

due /dju:/ *a* angemessen; be ~ fällig sein;
⟨baby:⟩ erwartet werden; ⟨train:⟩ planmäßig ankommen; ~ to (*owing to*) wegen
(+ *gen*); be ~ to zurückzuführen sein auf
(+ *acc*); in ~ course im Laufe der Zeit;
⟨write:⟩ zu gegebener Zeit □ *adv* ~ west
genau westlich

duel /'dju:əl/ *n* Duell *nt*

dues /dju:z/ *npl* Gebühren *pl*

duet /dju:'et/ *n* Duo *nt*; (*vocal*) Duett *nt*

dug /dʌg/ *see* dig

duke /dju:k/ *n* Herzog *m*

dull /dʌl/ *a* (-er, -est) (*overcast, not bright*)
trüb[e]; (*not shiny*) matt; ⟨sound⟩ dumpf;
(*boring*) langweilig; (*stupid*) schwerfällig
□ *vt* betäuben; abstumpfen ⟨mind⟩

duly /'dju:lɪ/ *adv* ordnungsgemäß

dumb /dʌm/ *a* (-er, -est) stumm; (*fam:
stupid*) dumm. ~founded *a* sprachlos

dummy /'dʌmɪ/ *n* (*tailor's*) [Schneider]-
puppe *f*; (*for baby*) Schnuller *m*; (*Comm*)
Attrappe *f*

dump /dʌmp/ *n* Abfallhaufen *m*; (*for refuse*) Müllhalde *f*, Deponie *f*; (*fam: town*)
Kaff *nt*; be down in the ~s (*fam*) deprimiert sein □ *vt* abladen; (*fam: put down*)
hinwerfen (on auf + *acc*)

dumpling /'dʌmplɪŋ/ *n* Kloß *m*, Knödel
m

dunce /dʌns/ *n* Dummkopf *m*

dune /dju:n/ *n* Düne *f*

dung /dʌŋ/ *n* Mist *m*

dungarees /dʌŋgə'ri:z/ *npl* Latzhose *f*

dungeon /'dʌndʒən/ *n* Verlies *nt*

dunk /dʌŋk/ *vt* eintunken

duo /'dju:əʊ/ *n* Paar *nt*; (*Mus*) Duo *nt*

dupe /dju:p/ *n* Betrogene(r) *m/f* □ *vt* betrügen

duplicate[1] /'dju:plɪkət/ *a* Zweit- □ *n* Doppel *nt*; (*document*) Duplikat *nt*; in ~ in
doppelter Ausfertigung

duplicat|e[2] /'dju:plɪkeɪt/ *vt* kopieren;
(*do twice*) zweimal machen. ~or *n*
Vervielfältigungsapparat *m*

durable /'djʊərəbl/ *a* haltbar

duration /djʊə'reɪʃn/ *n* Dauer *f*

duress /djʊə'res/ *n* Zwang *m*

during /'djʊərɪŋ/ *prep* während (+ *gen*)

dusk /dʌsk/ *n* [Abend]dämmerung *f*

dust /dʌst/ *n* Staub *m* □ *vt* abstauben;
(*sprinkle*) bestäuben (with mit) □ *vi* Staub
wischen

dust: ~bin *n* Mülltonne *f*. ~cart *n*
Müllwagen *m*. ~er *n* Staubtuch *nt*. ~
jacket *n* Schutzumschlag *m*. ~man *n*
Müllmann *m*. ~pan *n* Kehrschaufel *f*

dusty /'dʌstɪ/ *a* (-ier, -iest) staubig

Dutch /dʌtʃ/ *a* holländisch; go ~ (*fam*)
getrennte Kasse machen □ *n* (*Lang*) Holländisch *nt*; the ~ *pl* die Holländer.
~man *n* Holländer *m*

dutiable /'dju:tɪəbl/ *a* zollpflichtig

dutiful /'dju:tɪfl/ *a*, -ly *adv* pflicht-
bewusst; (*obedient*) gehorsam

duty /'dju:tɪ/ *n* Pflicht *f*; (*task*) Aufgabe *f*;
(*tax*) Zoll *m*; be on ~ Dienst haben. ~
free *a* zollfrei

duvet /'du:veɪ/ *n* Steppdecke *f*

dwarf /dwɔ:f/ *n* (*pl* -s or dwarves) Zwerg
m

dwell /dwel/ *vi* (*pt/pp* dwelt) (*liter*)
wohnen. ~ on (*fig*) verweilen bei. ~ing
n Wohnung *f*

dwindle /'dwɪndl/ *vi* abnehmen, schwind-
en

dye /daɪ/ *n* Farbstoff *m* □ *vt* (*pres p* dyeing)
färben

dying /'daɪɪŋ/ *see* die[2]

dynamic /daɪ'næmɪk/ *a* dynamisch. ~s *n*
Dynamik *f*

dynamite /'daɪnəmaɪt/ n Dynamit nt
dynamo /'daɪnəməʊ/ n Dynamo m
dynasty /'dɪnəsti/ n Dynastie f
dysentery /'dɪsəntri/ n Ruhr f
dyslex|ia /dɪs'leksɪə/ n Legasthenie f. ~ic
a legasthenisch; be ~ic Legastheniker
sein

E

each /i:tʃ/ a & pron jede(r,s); (per) je; ~
other einander; £1 ~ £1 pro Person/ (for
thing) pro Stück
eager /'i:gə(r)/ a, -ly adv eifrig; be ~ to
do sth etw gerne machen wollen. ~ness
n Eifer m
eagle /'i:gl/ n Adler m
ear¹ /ɪə(r)/ n (of corn) Ähre f
ear² n Ohr nt. ~ache n Ohrenschmerzen
pl. ~drum n Trommelfell nt
earl /ɜ:l/ n Graf m
early /'ɜ:lɪ/ a & adv (-ier, -iest) früh; (reply) baldig; be ~ früh dran sein; ~ in the
morning früh am Morgen
'earmark vt ~ for bestimmen für
earn /ɜ:n/ vt verdienen
earnest /'ɜ:nɪst/ a, -ly adv ernsthaft □ n
in ~ im Ernst
earnings /'ɜ:nɪŋz/ npl Verdienst m
ear: ~phones npl Kopfhörer pl. ~ring n
Ohrring m; (clip-on) Ohrklips m. ~shot n
within/out of ~shot in/außer Hörweite
earth /ɜ:θ/ n Erde f; (of fox) Bau m; where/
what on ~? wo/was in aller Welt? □ vt
(Electr) erden
earthenware /'ɜ:θn-/ n Tonwaren pl
earthly /'ɜ:θlɪ/ a irdisch; be no ~ use
(fam) völlig nutzlos sein
'earthquake n Erdbeben nt
earthy /'ɜ:θɪ/ a erdig; (coarse) derb
earwig /'ɪəwɪg/ n Ohrwurm m
ease /i:z/ n Leichtigkeit f; at ~!(Mil) rührt
euch! be or feel ill at ~ ein ungutes Gefühl haben o mit erleichtern; lindern (pain)
□ vi (pain:) nachlassen; (situation:) sich
entspannen
easel /'i:zl/ n Staffelei f
easily /'i:zɪlɪ/ adv leicht, mit Leichtigkeit
east /i:st/ n Osten m; to the ~ of östlich
von □ a Ost-, ost- □ adv nach Osten
Easter /'i:stə(r)/ n Ostern nt □ attrib
Oster-. ~ egg n Osterei nt
east|erly /'i:stəlɪ/ a östlich. ~ern a
östlich. ~ward[s] /-wəd[z]/ adv nach Ost-
en

easy /'i:zɪ/ a (-ier, -iest) leicht; take it ~
(fam) sich schonen; take it ~! beruhige
dich! go ~ with (fam) sparsam umgehen
mit
easy: ~ chair n Sessel m. ~'going a gelassen; too ~going lässig
eat /i:t/ vt/i (pt ate, pp eaten) essen; (animal:) fressen. ~ up vt aufessen
eat|able /'i:təbl/ a genießbar. ~er n
(apple) Essapfel m
eau-de-Cologne /əʊdəkə'ləʊn/ n Köl-
nischwasser nt
eaves /i:vz/ npl Dachüberhang m. ~drop
vi (pt/pp dropped) [heimlich]
lauschen; ~drop on belauschen
ebb /eb/ n (tide) Ebbe f; at a low ~ (fig) auf
einem Tiefstand □ vi zurückgehen; (fig)
verebben
ebony /'ebənɪ/ n Ebenholz nt
ebullient /ɪ'bʌlɪənt/ a überschwänglich
EC abbr (European Community) EG f
eccentric /ɪk'sentrɪk/ a exzentrisch □ n
Exzentriker m
ecclesiastical /ɪkli:zɪ'æstɪkl/ a kirchlich
echo /'ekəʊ/ n (pl -es) Echo nt, Widerhall
m □ v (pt/pp echoed, pres p echoing) □ vt
zurückwerfen; (imitate) nachsagen □ vi
widerhallen (with von)
eclipse /ɪ'klɪps/ n (Astr) Finsternis f □ vt
(fig) in den Schatten stellen
ecolog|ical /i:kə'lɒdʒɪkl/ a ökologisch.
~y /i:'kɒlədʒɪ/ n Ökologie f
economic /i:kə'nɒmɪk/ a wirtschaftlich.
~al a sparsam. ~ally adv wirtschaftlich;
(thriftily) sparsam. ~s n Volkswirtschaft
f
economist /ɪ'kɒnəmɪst/ n Volkswirt m;
(Univ) Wirtschaftswissenschaftler m
economize /ɪ'kɒnəmaɪz/ vi sparen (on an
+ dat)
economy /ɪ'kɒnəmɪ/ n Wirtschaft f;
(thrift) Sparsamkeit f
ecstasy /'ekstəsɪ/ n Ekstase f
ecstatic /ɪk'stætɪk/ a, -ally adv ekstatisch
ecu /'eɪkju:/ n Ecu m
ecumenical /i:kju'menɪkl/ a ökumenisch
eczema /'eksɪmə/ n Ekzem nt
eddy /'edɪ/ n Wirbel m
edge /edʒ/ n Rand m; (of table, lawn) Kante
f; (of knife) Schneide f; on ~ (fam) nervös; have the ~ on (fam) etwas besser
sein als □ vt einfassen. ~ forward vi sich
nach vorn schieben
edging /'edʒɪŋ/ n Einfassung f
edgy /'edʒɪ/ a (fam) nervös
edible /'edɪbl/ a essbar
edict /'i:dɪkt/ n Erlass m
edifice /'edɪfɪs/ n [großes] Gebäude nt

edify /'edɪfaɪ/ vt (pt/pp -ied) erbauen. ∼ing a erbaulich

edit /'edɪt/ vt (pt/pp edited) redigieren; herausgeben ⟨anthology, dictionary⟩; schneiden ⟨film, tape⟩

edition /ɪ'dɪʃn/ n Ausgabe f; ⟨impression⟩ Auflage f

editor /'edɪtə(r)/ n Redakteur m; ⟨of anthology, dictionary⟩ Herausgeber m; ⟨of newspaper⟩ Chefredakteur m; ⟨of film⟩ Cutter(in) m(f)

editorial /edɪ'tɔ:rɪəl/ a redaktionell, Redaktions- □ n ⟨Journ⟩ Leitartikel m

educate /'edjʊkeɪt/ vt erziehen; be ∼d at X auf die X-Schule gehen. ∼d a gebildet

education /edjʊ'keɪʃn/ n Erziehung f; ⟨culture⟩ Bildung f. ∼al a pädagogisch; ⟨visit⟩ kulturell

eel /i:l/ n Aal m

eerie /'ɪərɪ/ a (-ier, -iest) unheimlich

effect /ɪ'fekt/ n Wirkung f, Effekt m; in ∼ in Wirklichkeit; take ∼ in Kraft treten □ vt bewirken

effective /ɪ'fektɪv/ a, -ly adv wirksam, effektiv; ⟨striking⟩ wirkungsvoll, effektvoll; ⟨actual⟩ tatsächlich. ∼ness n Wirksamkeit f

effeminate /ɪ'femɪnət/ a unmännlich

effervescent /efə'vesnt/ a sprudelnd

efficiency /ɪ'fɪʃənsɪ/ n Tüchtigkeit f; ⟨of machine, organization⟩ Leistungsfähigkeit f

efficient /ɪ'fɪʃənt/ a tüchtig; ⟨machine, organization⟩ leistungsfähig; ⟨method⟩ rationell. ∼ly adv gut; ⟨function⟩ rationell

effigy /'efɪdʒɪ/ n Bildnis nt

effort /'efət/ n Anstrengung f; make an ∼ sich ⟨dat⟩ Mühe geben. ∼less a, -ly adv mühelos

effrontery /ɪ'frʌntərɪ/ n Unverschämtheit f

effusive /ɪ'fju:sɪv/ a, -ly adv überschwänglich

e.g. abbr (exempli gratia) z.B.

egalitarian /ɪgælɪ'teərɪən/ a egalitär

egg[1] /eg/ vt ∼ on ⟨fam⟩ anstacheln

egg[2] n Ei nt. ∼cup n Eierbecher m. ∼shell n Eierschale f. ∼-timer n Eieruhr f

ego /'i:gəʊ/ n Ich nt. ∼centric /-'sentrɪk/ a egozentrisch. ∼ism n Egoismus m. ∼ist n Egoist m. ∼tism n Ichbezogenheit f. ∼tist n ichbezogener Mensch m

Egypt /'i:dʒɪpt/ n Ägypten nt. ∼ian /ɪ'dʒɪpʃn/ a ägyptisch □ n Ägypter(in) m(f)

eiderdown /'aɪdə-/ n ⟨quilt⟩ Daunendecke f

eigh|t /eɪt/ a acht □ n Acht f; ⟨boat⟩ Achter m. ∼'teen a achtzehn. ∼'teenth a achtzehnte(r,s)

eighth /eɪtθ/ a achte(r,s) □ n Achtel nt

eightieth /'eɪtɪɪθ/ a achtzigste(r,s)

eighty /'eɪtɪ/ a achtzig

either /'aɪðə(r)/ a & pron ∼ [of them] einer von [den] beiden; ⟨both⟩ beide; on ∼ side auf beiden Seiten □ adv I don't ∼ ich auch nicht □ conj ∼ ... or entweder ... oder

eject /ɪ'dʒekt/ vt hinauswerfen

eke /i:k/ vt ∼ out strecken; ⟨increase⟩ ergänzen; ∼ out a living sich kümmerlich durchschlagen

elaborate[1] /ɪ'læbərət/ a, -ly adv kunstvoll; ⟨fig⟩ kompliziert

elaborate[2] /ɪ'læbəreɪt/ vi ausführlicher sein; ∼ on näher ausführen

elapse /ɪ'læps/ vi vergehen

elastic /ɪ'læstɪk/ a elastisch □ n Gummiband nt. ∼ 'band n Gummiband nt

elasticity /ɪlæs'tɪsətɪ/ n Elastizität f

elated /ɪ'leɪtɪd/ a überglücklich

elbow /'elbəʊ/ n Ellbogen m

elder[1] /'eldə(r)/ n Holunder m

elder[2] a ältere(r,s) □ n the ∼er der/die Ältere. ∼erly a alt. ∼est a älteste(r,s) □ n the ∼est der/die Älteste

elect /ɪ'lekt/ a the president ∼ der designierte Präsident □ vt wählen; ∼ to do sth sich dafür entscheiden, etw zu tun. ∼ion /-ekʃn/ n Wahl f

elector /ɪ'lektə(r)/ n Wähler(in) m(f). ∼al a Wahl-; ∼al roll Wählerverzeichnis nt. ∼ate /-rət/ n Wählerschaft f

electric /ɪ'lektrɪk/ a, -ally adv elektrisch

electrical /ɪ'lektrɪkl/ a elektrisch; ∼ engineering Elektrotechnik f

electric: ∼ 'blanket n Heizdecke f. ∼ 'fire n elektrischer Heizofen m

electrician /ɪlek'trɪʃn/ n Elektriker m

electricity /ɪlek'trɪsətɪ/ n Elektrizität f; ⟨supply⟩ Strom m

electrify /ɪ'lektrɪfaɪ/ vt (pt/pp -ied) elektrifizieren. ∼ing a ⟨fig⟩ elektrisierend

electrocute /ɪ'lektrəkju:t/ vt durch einen elektrischen Schlag töten; ⟨execute⟩ auf dem elektrischen Stuhl hinrichten

electrode /ɪ'lektrəʊd/ n Elektrode f

electron /ɪ'lektrɒn/ n Elektron nt

electronic /ɪlek'trɒnɪk/ a elektronisch. ∼s n Elektronik f

elegance /'elɪgəns/ n Eleganz f

elegant /'elɪgənt/ a, -ly adv elegant

elegy /'elɪdʒɪ/ n Elegie f

element /'elɪmənt/ n Element nt. ~ary /-
'mentərɪ/ a elementar

elephant /'elɪfənt/ n Elefant m

elevat|e /'elɪveɪt/ vt heben; (fig) erheben.
~ion /-'veɪʃn/ n Erhebung f

elevator /'elɪveɪtə(r)/ n (Amer) Aufzug m,
Fahrstuhl m

eleven /ɪ'levn/ a elf □ n Elf f. ~th a elf-
te(r,s); at the ~th hour (fam) in letzter
Minute

elf /elf/ n (pl elves) Elfe f

elicit /ɪ'lɪsɪt/ vt herausbekommen

eligible /'elɪdʒəbl/ a berechtigt; ~ young
man gute Partie f

eliminate /ɪ'lɪmɪneɪt/ vt ausschalten;
(excrete) ausscheiden

élite /eɪ'li:t/ n Elite f

ellips|e /ɪ'lɪps/ n Ellipse f. ~tical a ellip-
tisch

elm /elm/ n Ulme f

elocution /elə'kju:ʃn/ n Sprecherziehung
f

elongate /'i:lɒŋgeɪt/ vt verlängern

elope /ɪ'ləʊp/ vi durchbrennen (fam)

eloquen|ce /'eləkwəns/ n Beredsamkeit f.
~t a, ~ly adv beredt

else /els/ adv sonst; who ~? wer sonst?
nothing ~ sonst nichts; or ~ oder;
(otherwise) sonst; someone/somewhere
~ jemand/irgendwo anders; anyone ~
jeder andere; (as question) sonst noch jemand? anything ~ alles andere; (as question) sonst noch etwas? ~where adv
woanders

elucidate /ɪ'lu:sɪdeɪt/ vt erläutern

elude /ɪ'lu:d/ vt entkommen (+ dat);
(avoid) ausweichen (+ dat)

elusive /ɪ'lu:sɪv/ a be ~ schwer zu fassen
sein

emaciated /ɪ'meɪsɪeɪtɪd/ a abgezehrt

emanate /'eməneɪt/ vi ausgehen (from
von)

emancipat|ed /ɪ'mænsɪpeɪtɪd/ a emanzi-
piert. ~ion /-'peɪʃn/ n Emanzipation f;
(of slaves) Freilassung f

embalm /ɪm'bɑ:m/ vt einbalsamieren

embankment /ɪm'bæŋkmənt/ n Böschung f; (of railway) Bahndamm m

embargo /em'bɑ:gəʊ/ n (pl -es) Embargo
nt

embark /ɪm'bɑ:k/ vi sich einschiffen; ~
on anfangen mit. ~ation /embɑ:'keɪʃn/ n
Einschiffung f

embarrass /ɪm'bærəs/ vt in Verlegenheit
bringen. ~ed a verlegen. ~ing a peinlich.
~ment n Verlegenheit f

embassy /'embəsɪ/ n Botschaft f

embedded /ɪm'bedɪd/ a be deeply ~ in
tief stecken in (+ dat)

embellish /ɪm'belɪʃ/ vt verzieren; (fig)
ausschmücken

embers /'embəz/ npl Glut f

embezzle /ɪm'bezl/ vt unterschlagen.
~ment n Unterschlagung f

embitter /ɪm'bɪtə(r)/ vt verbittern

emblem /'embləm/ n Emblem nt

embodiment /ɪm'bɒdɪmənt/ n Verkör-
perung f

embody /ɪm'bɒdɪ/ vt (pt/pp -ied) verkörpern; (include) enthalten

emboss /ɪm'bɒs/ vt prägen

embrace /ɪm'breɪs/ n Umarmung f □ vt
umarmen; (fig) umfassen □ vi sich umarmen

embroider /ɪm'brɔɪdə(r)/ vt besticken;
sticken (design); (fig) ausschmücken □ vi
sticken. ~y n Stickerei f

embroil /ɪm'brɔɪl/ vt become ~ed in sth
in etw (acc) verwickelt werden

embryo /'embrɪəʊ/ n Embryo m

emerald /'emərəld/ n Smaragd m

emer|ge /ɪ'mɜ:dʒ/ vi auftauchen (from
aus); (become known) sich herausstellen;
(come into being) entstehen. ~gence
/-əns/ n Auftauchen nt; Entstehung f

emergency /ɪ'mɜ:dʒənsɪ/ n Notfall m; in
an ~ im Notfall. ~ exit n Notausgang m

emery-paper /'emərɪ-/ n Schmirgelpa-
pier nt

emigrant /'emɪgrənt/ n Auswanderer m

emigrat|e /'emɪgreɪt/ vi auswandern.
~ion /-'greɪʃn/ n Auswanderung f

eminent /'emɪnənt/ a, -ly adv eminent

emission /ɪ'mɪʃn/ n Ausstrahlung f; (of
pollutant) Emission f

emit /ɪ'mɪt/ vt (pt/pp emitted) ausstrahlen
⟨light, heat⟩; ausstoßen ⟨smoke, fumes, cry⟩

emotion /ɪ'məʊʃn/ n Gefühl nt. ~al a
emotional; become ~al sich erregen

emotive /ɪ'məʊtɪv/ a emotional

empath|ize /'empəθaɪz/ vi ~ize with s.o.
sich in jdn einfühlen. ~y n Einfühlungs-
vermögen nt

emperor /'empərə(r)/ n Kaiser m

emphasis /'emfəsɪs/ n Betonung f

emphasize /'emfəsaɪz/ vt betonen

emphatic /ɪm'fætɪk/ a, -ally adv nachdrücklich

empire /'empaɪə(r)/ n Reich nt

empirical /em'pɪrɪkl/ a empirisch

employ /ɪm'plɔɪ/ vt beschäftigen; (appoint) einstellen; (fig) anwenden. ~ee
/emplɔɪ'i:/ n Beschäftigte(r) m/f; (in contrast to employer) Arbeitnehmer m. ~er
n Arbeitgeber m. ~ment n Beschäftigung

f; (work) Arbeit f. ~ment agency n Stellenvermittlung f

empower /ɪm'paʊə(r)/ vt ermächtigen

empress /'emprɪs/ n Kaiserin f

empties /'emptɪz/ npl leere Flaschen pl

emptiness /'emptɪnɪs/ n Leere f

empty /'emptɪ/ a leer □ vt leeren; ausleeren ⟨container⟩ □ vi sich leeren

emulate /'emjʊleɪt/ vt nacheifern (+ dat)

emulsion /ɪ'mʌlʃn/ n Emulsion f

enable /ɪ'neɪbl/ vt ~ s.o. to es jdm möglich machen, zu

enact /ɪ'nækt/ vt (Theat) aufführen

enamel /ɪ'næml/ n Email nt; (on teeth) Zahnschmelz m; (paint) Lack m □ vt (pt/pp enamelled) emaillieren

enamoured /ɪ'næməd/ a be ~ of sehr angetan sein von

enchant /ɪn'tʃɑːnt/ vt bezaubern. ~ing a bezaubernd. ~ment n Zauber m

encircle /ɪn'sɜːkl/ vt einkreisen

enclave /'enkleɪv/ n Enklave f

enclos|e /ɪn'kləʊz/ vt einschließen; (in letter) beilegen (with dat). ~ure /-ʒə(r)/ n (at zoo) Gehege nt; (in letter) Anlage f

encompass /ɪn'kʌmpəs/ vt umfassen

encore /'ɒŋkɔː(r)/ n Zugabe f □ int bravo!

encounter /ɪn'kaʊntə(r)/ n Begegnung f; (battle) Zusammenstoß m □ vt begegnen (+ dat); (fig) stoßen auf (+ acc)

encourag|e /ɪn'kʌrɪdʒ/ vt ermutigen; (promote) fördern. ~ement n Ermutigung f. ~ing a ermutigend

encroach /ɪn'krəʊtʃ/ vi ~ on eindringen in (+ acc) ⟨land⟩; beanspruchen ⟨time⟩

encumb|er /ɪn'kʌmbə(r)/ vt belasten (with mit). ~rance /-rəns/ n Belastung f

encyclopaed|ia /ɪnsaɪklə'piːdɪə/ n Enzyklopädie f, Lexikon nt. ~ic a enzyklopädisch

end /end/ n Ende nt; (purpose) Zweck m; in the ~ schließlich; at the ~ of May Ende Mai; for days on ~ tagelang; make ~s meet (fam) [gerade] auskommen; no ~ of (fam) unheimlich viel(e) □ vt beenden □ vi enden; ~ up in (fam: arrive at) landen in (+ dat)

endanger /ɪn'deɪndʒə(r)/ vt gefährden

endear|ing /ɪn'dɪərɪŋ/ a liebenswert. ~ment n term of ~ment Kosewort nt

endeavour /ɪn'devə(r)/ n Bemühung f □ vi sich bemühen (to zu)

ending /'endɪŋ/ n Schluss m, Ende nt; (Gram) Endung f

endive /'endaɪv/ n Endivie f

endless /'endlɪs/ a, -ly adv endlos

endorse /ɪn'dɔːs/ vt (Comm) indossieren; (confirm) bestätigen. ~ment n (Comm) Indossament nt; (fig) Bestätigung f; (on driving licence) Strafvermerk m

endow /ɪn'daʊ/ vt stiften; be ~ed with (fig) haben. ~ment n Stiftung f

endur|able /ɪn'djʊərəbl/ a erträglich. ~ance /-rəns/ n Durchhaltevermögen nt; beyond ~ance unerträglich

endur|e /ɪn'djʊə(r)/ vt ertragen □ vi [lange] bestehen. ~ing a dauernd

enemy /'enəmɪ/ n Feind m □ attrib feindlich

energetic /enə'dʒetɪk/ a tatkräftig; be ~ voller Energie sein

energy /'enədʒɪ/ n Energie f

enforce /ɪn'fɔːs/ vt durchsetzen. ~d a unfreiwillig

engage /ɪn'geɪdʒ/ vt einstellen ⟨staff⟩; (Theat) engagieren; (Auto) einlegen ⟨gear⟩ □ vi sich beteiligen (in an + dat); (Techn) ineinander greifen. ~d a besetzt; ⟨person⟩ beschäftigt; (to be married) verlobt; get ~d sich verloben (to mit). ~ment n Verlobung f; (appointment) Verabredung f; (Mil) Gefecht nt

engaging /ɪn'geɪdʒɪŋ/ a einnehmend

engender /ɪn'dʒendə(r)/ vt (fig) erzeugen

engine /'endʒɪn/ n Motor m; (Naut) Maschine f; (Rail) Lokomotive f; (of jetplane) Triebwerk nt. ~-driver n Lokomotivführer m

engineer /endʒɪ'nɪə(r)/ n Ingenieur m; (service, installation) Techniker m; (Naut) Maschinist m; (Amer) Lokomotivführer m □ vt (fig) organisieren. ~ing n [mechanical] ~ing Maschinenbau m

England /'ɪŋglənd/ n England nt

English /'ɪŋglɪʃ/ a englisch; the ~ Channel der Ärmelkanal □ n (Lang) Englisch nt; in ~ auf Englisch; into ~ ins Englische; the ~ pl die Engländer. ~man n Engländer m. ~woman n Engländerin f

engrav|e /ɪn'greɪv/ vt eingravieren. ~ing n Stich m

engross /ɪn'grəʊs/ vt be ~ed in vertieft sein in (+ acc)

engulf /ɪn'gʌlf/ vt verschlingen

enhance /ɪn'hɑːns/ vt verschönern; (fig) steigern

enigma /ɪ'nɪgmə/ n Rätsel nt. ~tic /-ɪg'mætɪk/ a rätselhaft

enjoy /ɪn'dʒɔɪ/ vt genießen; ~ oneself sich amüsieren; ~ cooking/painting gern kochen/malen; I ~ed it es hat mir gut gefallen; ⟨food:⟩ geschmeckt. ~able /-əbl/ a angenehm, nett. ~ment n Vergnügen nt

enlarge /ɪnˈlɑːdʒ/ *vt* vergrößern □ *vi* ~ upon sich näher auslassen über (+ *acc*). ~ment *n* Vergrößerung *f*

enlighten /ɪnˈlaɪtn/ *vt* aufklären. ~ment *n* Aufklärung *f*

enlist /ɪnˈlɪst/ *vt* (*Mil*) einziehen; ~ s.o.'s help jdn zur Hilfe heranziehen □ *vi* (*Mil*) sich melden

enliven /ɪnˈlaɪvn/ *vt* beleben

enmity /ˈenmətɪ/ *n* Feindschaft *f*

enormity /ɪˈnɔːmətɪ/ *n* Ungeheuerlichkeit *f*

enormous /ɪˈnɔːməs/ *a*, -ly *adv* riesig

enough /ɪˈnʌf/ *a*, *adv* & *n* genug; be ~ reichen; funnily ~ komischerweise; I've had ~! (*fam*) jetzt reicht's mir aber!

enquir|e /ɪnˈkwaɪə(r)/ *vi* sich erkundigen (about nach) □ *vt* sich erkundigen nach. ~y *n* Erkundigung *f*; (*investigation*) Untersuchung *f*

enrage /ɪnˈreɪdʒ/ *vt* wütend machen

enrich /ɪnˈrɪtʃ/ *vt* bereichern; (*improve*) anreichern

enrol /ɪnˈrəʊl/ *v* (*pt/pp* -rolled) □ *vt* einschreiben □ *vi* sich einschreiben. ~ment *n* Einschreibung *f*

ensemble /ɒnˈsɒmbl/ *n* (*clothing & Mus*) Ensemble *nt*

ensign /ˈensaɪn/ *n* Flagge *f*

enslave /ɪnˈsleɪv/ *vt* versklaven

ensue /ɪnˈsjuː/ *vi* folgen; (*result*) sich ergeben (from aus)

ensure /ɪnˈʃʊə(r)/ *vt* sicherstellen; ~ that dafür sorgen, dass

entail /ɪnˈteɪl/ *vt* erforderlich machen; what does it ~? was ist damit verbunden?

entangle /ɪnˈtæŋgl/ *vt* get ~d sich verfangen (in in + *dat*); (*fig*) sich verstricken (in in + *acc*)

enter /ˈentə(r)/ *vt* eintreten/⟨*vehicle:*⟩ einfahren in (+ *acc*), einreisen in (+ *acc*) ⟨*country*⟩; (*register*) eintragen; (*enter as competitor*) sich anmelden zu ⟨*competition*⟩ □ *vi* eintreten; ⟨*vehicle:*⟩ einfahren; (*Theat*) auftreten; (*register as competitor*) sich anmelden; (*take part*) sich beteiligen (in an + *dat*)

enterpris|e /ˈentəpraɪz/ *n* Unternehmen *nt*; (*quality*) Unternehmungsgeist *m*. ~ing *a* unternehmend

entertain /entəˈteɪn/ *vt* unterhalten; (*invite*) einladen; (*to meal*) bewirten ⟨*guest*⟩; (*fig*) in Erwägung ziehen □ *vi* unterhalten; (*have guests*) Gäste haben. ~er *n* Unterhalter *m*. ~ment *n* Unterhaltung *f*

enthral /ɪnˈθrɔːl/ *vt* (*pt/pp* enthralled) be ~led gefesselt sein (by von)

enthuse /ɪnˈθjuːz/ *vi* ~ over schwärmen von

enthusias|m /ɪnˈθjuːzɪæzm/ *n* Begeisterung *f*. ~t *n* Enthusiast *m*. ~tic /-ˈæstɪk/ *a*, -ally *adv* begeistert

entice /ɪnˈtaɪs/ *vt* locken. ~ment *n* Anreiz *m*

entire /ɪnˈtaɪə(r)/ *a* ganz. ~ly *adv* ganz, völlig. ~ty /-rətɪ/ *n* in its ~ty in seiner Gesamtheit

entitle /ɪnˈtaɪtl/ *vt* berechtigen; ~d . . . mit dem Titel . . .; be ~d to sth das Recht auf etw (*acc*) haben. ~ment *n* Berechtigung *f*; (*claim*) Anspruch *m* (to auf + *acc*)

entity /ˈentətɪ/ *n* Wesen *nt*

entomology /entəˈmɒlədʒɪ/ *n* Entomologie *f*

entourage /ˈɒntʊrɑːʒ/ *n* Gefolge *nt*

entrails /ˈentreɪlz/ *npl* Eingeweide *pl*

entrance¹ /ɪnˈtrɑːns/ *vt* bezaubern

entrance² /ˈentrəns/ *n* Eintritt *m*; (*Theat*) Auftritt *m*; (*way in*) Eingang *m*; (*for vehicle*) Einfahrt *f*. ~ examination *n* Aufnahmeprüfung *f*. ~ fee *n* Eintrittsgebühr *f*

entrant /ˈentrənt/ *n* Teilnehmer(in) *m(f)*

entreat /ɪnˈtriːt/ *vt* anflehen (for um)

entrench /ɪnˈtrentʃ/ *vt* be ~ed in verwurzelt sein in (+ *dat*)

entrust /ɪnˈtrʌst/ *vt* ~ s.o. with sth, ~ sth to s.o. jdm etw anvertrauen

entry /ˈentrɪ/ *n* Eintritt *m*; (*into country*) Einreise *f*; (*on list*) Eintrag *m*; no ~ Zutritt/ (*Auto*) Einfahrt verboten. ~-form *n* Anmeldeformular *nt*. ~ visa *n* Einreisevisum *nt*

enumerate /ɪˈnjuːməreɪt/ *vt* aufzählen

enunciate /ɪˈnʌnsɪeɪt/ *vt* [deutlich] aussprechen; (*state*) vorbringen

envelop /ɪnˈveləp/ *vt* (*pt/pp* enveloped) einhüllen

envelope /ˈenvələʊp/ *n* [Brief]umschlag *m*

enviable /ˈenvɪəbl/ *a* beneidenswert

envious /ˈenvɪəs/ *a*, -ly *adv* neidisch (of auf + *acc*)

environment /ɪnˈvaɪərənmənt/ *n* Umwelt *f*

environmental /ɪnvaɪərənˈmentl/ *a* Umwelt-. ~ist *n* Umweltschützer *m*. ~ly *adv* ~ly friendly umweltfreundlich

envisage /ɪnˈvɪzɪdʒ/ *vt* sich (*dat*) vorstellen

envoy /ˈenvɔɪ/ *n* Gesandte(r) *m*

envy /ˈenvɪ/ *n* Neid *m* □ *vt* (*pt/pp* -ied) ~ s.o. sth jdn um etw beneiden

enzyme /ˈenzaɪm/ *n* Enzym *nt*

epic /ˈepɪk/ *a* episch □ *n* Epos *nt*

epidemic /epɪˈdemɪk/ *n* Epidemie *f*

epilep|sy /ˈepɪlepsɪ/ n Epilepsie f. ~tic /-ˈleptɪk/ a epileptisch □ n Epileptiker(in) m(f)

epilogue /ˈepɪlɒg/ n Epilog m

episode /ˈepɪsəʊd/ n Episode f; (instalment) Folge f

epistle /ɪˈpɪsl/ n (liter) Brief m

epitaph /ˈepɪtɑːf/ n Epitaph nt

epithet /ˈepɪθet/ n Beiname m

epitom|e /ɪˈpɪtəmɪ/ n Inbegriff m. ~ize vt verkörpern

epoch /ˈiːpɒk/ n Epoche f. ~-making a epochemachend

equal /ˈiːkwl/ a gleich (to dat); be ~ to a task einer Aufgabe gewachsen sein □ n Gleichgestellte(r) m/f □ vt (pt/pp equalled) gleichen (+ dat); (fig) gleichkommen (+ dat). ~ity /ɪˈkwɒlətɪ/ n Gleichheit f

equalize /ˈiːkwəlaɪz/ vt/i ausgleichen. ~r n (Sport) Ausgleich[streffer] m

equally /ˈiːkwəlɪ/ adv gleich; (divide) gleichmäßig; (just as) genauso

equanimity /ekwəˈnɪmətɪ/ n Gleichmut m

equat|e /ɪˈkweɪt/ vt gleichsetzen (with mit). ~ion /-eɪʒn/ n (Math) Gleichung f

equator /ɪˈkweɪtə(r)/ n Äquator m. ~ial /ekwəˈtɔːrɪəl/ a Äquator-

equestrian /ɪˈkwestrɪən/ a Reit-

equilibrium /iːkwɪˈlɪbrɪəm/ n Gleichgewicht nt

equinox /ˈiːkwɪnɒks/ n Tagundnachtgleiche f

equip /ɪˈkwɪp/ vt (pt/pp equipped) ausrüsten; (furnish) ausstatten. ~ment n Ausrüstung f; Ausstattung f

equitable /ˈekwɪtəbl/ a gerecht

equity /ˈekwətɪ/ n Gerechtigkeit f

equivalent /ɪˈkwɪvələnt/ a gleichwertig; (corresponding) entsprechend □ n Äquivalent nt; (value) Gegenwert m; (counterpart) Gegenstück nt

equivocal /ɪˈkwɪvəkl/ a zweideutig

era /ˈɪərə/ n Ära f, Zeitalter nt

eradicate /ɪˈrædɪkeɪt/ vt ausrotten

erase /ɪˈreɪz/ vt ausradieren; (from tape) löschen; (fig) auslöschen. ~r n Radiergummi m

erect /ɪˈrekt/ a aufrecht □ vt errichten. ~ion /-ekʃn/ n Errichtung f; (building) Bau m; (Biol) Erektion f

ermine /ˈɜːmɪn/ n Hermelin m

ero|de /ɪˈrəʊd/ vt (water:) auswaschen; (acid:) angreifen. ~sion /-əʊʒn/ n Erosion f

erotic /ɪˈrɒtɪk/ a erotisch. ~ism /-tɪsɪzm/ n Erotik f

err /ɜː(r)/ vi sich irren; (sin) sündigen

errand /ˈerənd/ n Botengang m

erratic /ɪˈrætɪk/ a unregelmäßig; (person) unberechenbar

erroneous /ɪˈrəʊnɪəs/ a falsch; (belief, assumption) irrig. ~ly adv fälschlich; irrigerweise

error /ˈerə(r)/ n Irrtum m; (mistake) Fehler m; in ~ irrtümlicherweise

erudit|e /ˈeruːdaɪt/ a gelehrt. ~ion /-ˈdɪʃn/ n Gelehrsamkeit f

erupt /ɪˈrʌpt/ vi ausbrechen. ~ion /-ʌpʃn/ n Ausbruch m

escalat|e /ˈeskəleɪt/ vt/i eskalieren. ~ion /-ˈleɪʃn/ n Eskalation f. ~or n Rolltreppe f

escapade /ˈeskəpeɪd/ n Eskapade f

escape /ɪˈskeɪp/ n Flucht f; (from prison) Ausbruch m; have a narrow ~ gerade noch davonkommen □ vi flüchten; (prisoner:) ausbrechen; entkommen (from aus; from s.o. jdm); (gas:) entweichen □ vt ~ notice unbemerkt bleiben; the name ~s me der Name entfällt mir

escapism /ɪˈskeɪpɪzm/ n Flucht f vor der Wirklichkeit, Eskapismus m

escort¹ /ˈeskɔːt/ n (of person) Begleiter m; (Mil) Eskorte f; under ~ unter Bewachung

escort² /ɪˈskɔːt/ vt begleiten; (Mil) eskortieren

Eskimo /ˈeskɪməʊ/ n Eskimo m

esoteric /esəˈterɪk/ a esoterisch

especial /ɪˈspeʃl/ a besondere(r,s). ~ly adv besonders

espionage /ˈespɪənɑːʒ/ n Spionage f

essay /ˈeseɪ/ n Aufsatz m

essence /ˈesns/ n Wesen nt; (Chem, Culin) Essenz f; in ~ im Wesentlichen

essential /ɪˈsenʃl/ a wesentlich; (indispensable) unentbehrlich □ n the ~s das Wesentliche; (items) das Nötigste. ~ly adv im Wesentlichen

establish /ɪˈstæblɪʃ/ vt gründen; (form) bilden; (prove) beweisen. ~ment n (firm) Unternehmen nt

estate /ɪˈsteɪt/ n Gut nt; (possessions) Besitz m; (after death) Nachlass m; (housing) [Wohn]siedlung f. ~ agent n Immobilienmakler m. ~ car n Kombi[wagen] m

esteem /ɪˈstiːm/ n Achtung f □ vt hochschätzen

estimate¹ /ˈestɪmət/ n Schätzung f; (Comm) [Kosten]voranschlag m; at a rough ~ grob geschätzt

estimat|e² /ˈestɪmeɪt/ vt schätzen. ~ion /-ˈmeɪʃn/ n Einschätzung f; (esteem) Achtung f; in my ~ion meiner Meinung nach estuary /'estjʊərɪ/ n Mündung f

etc. /et'setərə/ abbr (et cetera) und so weiter, usw.

etching /'etʃɪŋ/ n Radierung f

eternal /ɪ'tɜ:nl/ a, -ly adv ewig

eternity /ɪ'tɜ:nətɪ/ n Ewigkeit f

ether /'i:θə(r)/ n Äther m

ethic /'eθɪk/ n Ethik f. ~al a ethisch; (morally correct) moralisch einwandfrei. ~s n Ethik f

Ethiopia /i:θɪ'əʊpɪə/ n Äthiopien nt

ethnic /'eθnɪk/ a ethnisch

etiquette /'etɪket/ n Etikette f

etymology /etɪ'mɒlədʒɪ/ n Etymologie f

eucalyptus /ju:kə'lɪptəs/ n Eukalyptus m

eulogy /'ju:lədʒɪ/ n Lobrede f

euphemis|m /'ju:fəmɪzm/ n Euphemismus m. ~tic /-'mɪstɪk/ a, -ally adv verhüllend

euphoria /ju:'fɔ:rɪə/ n Euphorie f

Euro /'jʊərəʊ/ n Euro m. ~cheque n Euroscheck m. ~passport n Europaß m

Europe /'jʊərəp/ n Europa m

European /jʊərə'pi:ən/ a europäisch; ~ Community Europäische Gemeinschaft f □ n Europäer(in) m(f)

evacuat|e /ɪ'vækjʊeɪt/ vt evakuieren; räumen (building, area). ~ion /-'eɪʃn/ n Evakuierung f; Räumung f

evade /ɪ'veɪd/ vt sich entziehen (+ dat); hinterziehen (taxes); ~ the issue ausweichen

evaluate /ɪ'væljʊeɪt/ vt einschätzen

evangel|ical /i:væn'dʒelɪkl/ a evangelisch. ~list /ɪ'vændʒəlɪst/ n Evangelist m

evaporat|e /ɪ'væpəreɪt/ vi verdunsten; ~ed milk Kondensmilch f, Dosenmilch f. ~ion /-'reɪʃn/ n Verdampfung f

evasion /ɪ'veɪʒn/ n Ausweichen nt; ~ of taxes Steuerhinterziehung f

evasive /ɪ'veɪsɪv/ a, -ly adv ausweichend; be ~ ausweichen

eve /i:v/ n (liter) Vorabend m

even /'i:vn/ a (level) eben; (same, equal) gleich; (regular) gleichmäßig; (number) gerade; get ~ with (fam) es jdm heimzahlen □ adv sogar, selbst; ~ so trotzdem; not ~ nicht einmal □ vt ~ up vt ausgleichen □ vi sich ausgleichen

evening /'i:vnɪŋ/ n Abend m; this ~ heute Abend; in the ~ abends, am Abend. ~ class n Abendkurs m

evenly /'i:vnlɪ/ adv gleichmäßig

event /ɪ'vent/ n Ereignis nt; (function) Veranstaltung f; (Sport) Wettbewerb m; in

the ~ of im Falle (+ gen); in the ~ wie es sich ergab. ~ful a ereignisreich

eventual /ɪ'ventjʊəl/ a his ~ success der Erfolg, der ihm schließlich zuteil wurde. ~ity /-'ælətɪ/ n Eventualität f, Fall m. ~ly adv schließlich

ever /'evə(r)/ adv je[mals]; not ~ nie; for ~ für immer; hardly ~ fast nie; ~ since seitdem; ~ so (fam) sehr, furchtbar (fam)

'evergreen n immergrüner Strauch m/ (tree) Baum m

ever'lasting a ewig

every /'evrɪ/ a jede(r,s); ~ one jede(r,s) Einzelne; ~ other day jeden zweiten Tag

every|body pron jede[rmann]; alle pl. ~day a alltäglich. ~ one pron jeder [-mann]; alle pl. ~thing pron alles. ~where adv überall

evict /ɪ'vɪkt/ vt [aus der Wohnung] hinausweisen. ~ion /-ɪkʃn/ n Ausweisung f

eviden|ce /'evɪdəns/ n Beweise pl; (Jur) Beweismaterial nt; (testimony) Aussage f; give ~ce aussagen. ~t a, -ly adv offensichtlich

evil /'i:vl/ a böse □ n Böse nt

evocative /ɪ'vɒkətɪv/ a be ~ of heraufbeschwören

evoke /ɪ'vəʊk/ vt heraufbeschwören

evolution /i:və'lu:ʃn/ n Evolution f

evolve /ɪ'vɒlv/ vt entwickeln □ vi sich entwickeln

ewe /ju:/ n [Mutter]schaf nt

exacerbate /ek'sæsəbeɪt/ vt verschlimmern; verschärfen (situation)

exact /ɪg'zækt/ a, -ly adv genau; not ~ly nicht gerade □ vt erzwingen. ~ing a anspruchsvoll. ~itude /-ɪtju:d/ n, ~ness f Genauigkeit f

exaggerat|e /ɪg'zædʒəreɪt/ vt/i übertreiben. ~ion /-'reɪʃn/ n Übertreibung f

exalt /ɪg'zɔ:lt/ vt erheben; (praise) preisen

exam /ɪg'zæm/ n (fam) Prüfung f

examination /ɪgzæmɪ'neɪʃn/ n Untersuchung f; (Sch) Prüfung f

examine /ɪg'zæmɪn/ vt untersuchen; (Sch) prüfen; (Jur) verhören. ~r n (Sch) Prüfer m

example /ɪg'zɑ:mpl/ n Beispiel nt (of für); for ~ zum Beispiel; make an ~ of ein Exempel statuieren an (+ dat)

exasperat|e /ɪg'zæspəreɪt/ vt zur Verzweiflung treiben. ~ion /-'reɪʃn/ n Verzweiflung f

excavat|e /'ekskəveɪt/ vt ausschachten; (Archaeol) ausgraben. ~ion /-'veɪʃn/ n Ausgrabung f

exceed /ɪk'si:d/ vt übersteigen. ~ingly adv äußerst

excel /ɪkˈsel/ v (pt/pp excelled) vi sich auszeichnen □ vt ~ oneself sich selbst übertreffen

excellen|ce /ˈeksələns/ n Vorzüglichkeit f. E ~cy n (title) Exzellenz f. ~t a, ~ly adv ausgezeichnet, vorzüglich

except /ɪkˈsept/ prep außer (+ dat); ~ for abgesehen von □ vt ausnehmen. ~ing prep außer (+ dat)

exception /ɪkˈsepʃn/ n Ausnahme f; take ~ to Anstoß nehmen an (+ dat). ~al a, ~ly adv außergewöhnlich

excerpt /ˈeksɜ:pt/ n Auszug m

excess /ɪkˈses/ n Übermaß n (of an + dat); (surplus) Überschuss m; ~es pl Exzesse pl; in ~ of über (+ dat)

excess 'fare /ekses-/ n Nachlösegebühr f

excessive /ɪkˈsesɪv/ a, ~ly adv übermäßig

exchange /ɪksˈtʃeɪndʒ/ n Austausch m; (Teleph) Fernsprechamt nt; (Comm) [Geld]wechsel m; [stock] ~ Börse f; in ~ dafür □ vt austauschen (for gegen); tauschen ⟨places, greetings, money⟩. ~ rate n Wechselkurs m

exchequer /ɪksˈtʃekə(r)/ n (Pol) Staatskasse f

excise¹ /ˈeksaɪz/ n ~ duty Verbrauchssteuer f

excise² /ekˈsaɪz/ vt herausschneiden

excitable /ɪkˈsaɪtəbl/ a [leicht] erregbar

excit|e /ɪkˈsaɪt/ vt aufregen; (cause) erregen. ~ed a, ~ly adv aufgeregt; get ~ed sich aufregen. ~ement n Aufregung f; Erregung f. ~ing a aufregend; ⟨story⟩ spannend

exclaim /ɪkˈskleɪm/ vt/i ausrufen

exclamation /ekskləˈmeɪʃn/ n Ausruf m. ~ mark n, (Amer) ~ point n Ausrufezeichen nt

exclu|de /ɪkˈsklu:d/ vt ausschließen. ~ding prep ausschließlich (+ gen). ~sion /-ʒn/ n Ausschluss m

exclusive /ɪkˈsklu:sɪv/ a, ~ly adv ausschließlich; (select) exklusiv; ~ of aus-schließlich (+ gen)

excommunicate /ekskəˈmju:nɪkeɪt/ vt exkommunizieren

excrement /ˈekskrɪmənt/ n Kot m

excrete /ɪkˈskri:t/ vt ausscheiden

excruciating /ɪkˈskru:ʃɪeɪtɪŋ/ a grässlich

excursion /ɪkˈskɜ:ʃn/ n Ausflug m

excusable /ɪkˈskju:zəbl/ a entschuldbar

excuse¹ /ɪkˈskju:s/ n Entschuldigung f; (pretext) Ausrede f

excuse² /ɪkˈskju:z/ vt entschuldigen; ~ from freistellen von; ~ me! Entschuldigung!

ex-di'rectory a be ~ nicht im Telefonbuch stehen

execute /ˈeksɪkju:t/ vt ausführen; (put to death) hinrichten

execution /eksɪˈkju:ʃn/ n (see execute) Ausführung f; Hinrichtung f. ~er n Scharfrichter m

executive /ɪgˈzekjʊtɪv/ a leitend □ n leitende(r) Angestellte(r) m/f; (Pol) Exekutive f

executor /ɪgˈzekjʊtə(r)/ n (Jur) Testamentsvollstrecker m

exemplary /ɪgˈzemplərɪ/ a beispielhaft; (as a warning) exemplarisch

exemplify /ɪgˈzemplɪfaɪ/ vt (pt/pp -ied) veranschaulichen

exempt /ɪgˈzempt/ a befreit □ vt befreien (from von). ~ion /-empʃn/ n Befreiung f

exercise /ˈeksəsaɪz/ n Übung f; physical ~ körperliche Bewegung f; take ~ sich bewegen □ vt (use) ausüben; bewegen ⟨horse⟩; spazieren führen ⟨dog⟩ □ vi sich bewegen. ~ book n [Schul]heft nt

exert /ɪgˈzɜ:t/ vt ausüben; ~ oneself sich anstrengen. ~ion /-ɜ:ʃn/ n Anstrengung f

exhale /eksˈheɪl/ vt/i ausatmen

exhaust /ɪgˈzɔ:st/ n (Auto) Auspuff m; (pipe) Auspuffrohr nt; (fumes) Abgase pl □ vt erschöpfen. ~ed a erschöpft. ~ing a anstrengend. ~ion /-ɔ:stʃn/ n Erschöpfung f. ~ive /-ɪv/ a (fig) erschöpfend

exhibit /ɪgˈzɪbɪt/ n Ausstellungsstück nt; (Jur) Beweisstück n □ vt ausstellen; (fig) zeigen

exhibition /eksɪˈbɪʃn/ n Ausstellung f; (Univ) Stipendium nt. ~ist n Exhibitionist(in) m(f)

exhibitor /ɪgˈzɪbɪtə(r)/ n Aussteller m

exhilarat|ed /ɪgˈzɪləreɪtɪd/ a beschwingt. ~ing a berauschend. ~ion /-ˈreɪʃn/ n Hochgefühl nt

exhort /ɪgˈzɔ:t/ vt ermahnen

exhume /ɪgˈzju:m/ vt exhumieren

exile /ˈeksaɪl/ n Exil nt; (person) im Exil Lebende(r) m/f □ vt ins Exil schicken

exist /ɪgˈzɪst/ vi bestehen, existieren. ~ence /-əns/ n Existenz f; be in ~ence existieren

exit /ˈeksɪt/ n Ausgang m; (Auto) Ausfahrt f; (Theat) Abgang m □ vi (Theat) abgehen. ~ visa n Ausreisevisum nt

exonerate /ɪgˈzɒnəreɪt/ vt entlasten

exorbitant /ɪgˈzɔ:bɪtənt/ a übermäßig hoch

exorcize /ˈeksɔ:saɪz/ vt austreiben

exotic /ɪgˈzɒtɪk/ a exotisch

expand /ɪkˈspænd/ vt ausdehnen; (explain better) weiter ausführen □ vi sich ausdehnen; (Comm) expandieren; ~ on (fig) weiter ausführen expans|e /ɪk'spæns/ n Weite f. ~ion /-ænʃn/ n Ausdehnung f; (Techn, Pol, Comm) Expansion f. ~ive /-ɪv/ a mitteilsam

expatriate /eks'pætrɪət/ n be an ~ im Ausland leben

expect /ɪk'spekt/ vt erwarten; (suppose) annehmen; I ~ so wahrscheinlich; we ~ to arrive on Monday wir rechnen damit, dass wir am Montag ankommen

expectan|cy /ɪk'spektənsɪ/ n Erwartung f. ~t a, -ly adv erwartungsvoll; ~t mother werdende Mutter f

expectation /ekspek'teɪʃn/ n Erwartung f; ~ of life Lebenserwartung f

expedient /ɪk'spi:dɪənt/ a zweckdienlich

expedite /'ekspɪdaɪt/ vt beschleunigen

expedition /ekspɪ'dɪʃn/ n Expedition f. ~ary /-ərɪ/ a (Mil) Expeditions-

expel /ɪk'spel/ vt (pt/pp expelled) ausweisen (from aus); (from school) von der Schule verweisen

expend /ɪk'spend/ vt aufwenden. ~able /-əbl/ a entbehrlich

expenditure /ɪk'spendɪtʃə(r)/ n Ausgaben pl

expense /ɪk'spens/ n Kosten pl; business ~s pl Spesen pl; at my ~ auf meine Kosten; at the ~ of (fig) auf Kosten (+ gen)

expensive /ɪk'spensɪv/ a, -ly adv teuer

experience /ɪk'spɪərɪəns/ n Erfahrung f; (event) Erlebnis nt □ vt erleben. ~d a erfahren

experiment /ɪk'sperɪmənt/ n Versuch m, Experiment nt □ /-ment/ vi experimentieren. ~al /-'mentl/ a experimentell

expert /'ekspɜ:t/ a, -ly adv fachmännisch □ n Fachmann m, Experte m

expertise /ekspɜ:'ti:z/ n Sachkenntnis f; (skill) Geschick nt

expire /ɪk'spaɪə(r)/ vi ablaufen

expiry /ɪk'spaɪərɪ/ n Ablauf m. ~ date n Verfallsdatum nt

explain /ɪk'spleɪn/ vt erklären

explana|tion /eksplə'neɪʃn/ n Erklärung f. ~tory /ɪk'splænətərɪ/ a erklärend

expletive /ɪk'spli:tɪv/ n Kraftausdruck m

explicit /ɪk'splɪsɪt/ a, -ly adv deutlich

explode /ɪk'spləʊd/ vi explodieren □ vt zur Explosion bringen

exploit¹ /'eksplɔɪt/ n [Helden]tat f

exploit² /ɪk'splɔɪt/ vt ausbeuten. ~ation /eksplɔɪ'teɪʃn/ n Ausbeutung f

explora|tion /eksplə'reɪʃn/ n Erforschung f. ~tory /ɪk'splɒrətərɪ/ a Probe-

explore /ɪk'splɔ:(r)/ vt erforschen. ~r n Forschungsreisende(r) m

explos|ion /ɪk'spləʊʒn/ n Explosion f. ~ive /-sɪv/ a explosiv □ n Sprengstoff m

exponent /ɪk'spəʊnənt/ n Vertreter m

export¹ /'ekspɔ:t/ n Export m, Ausfuhr f

export² /ɪk'spɔ:t/ vt exportieren, ausführen. ~er n Exporteur m

expos|e /ɪk'spəʊz/ vt freilegen; (to danger) aussetzen (to dat); (reveal) aufdecken; (Phot) belichten. ~ure /-ʒə(r)/ n Aussetzung f; (Med) Unterkühlung f; (Phot) Belichtung f; 24 ~ures 24 Aufnahmen

expound /ɪk'spaʊnd/ vt erläutern

express /ɪk'spres/ a ausdrücklich; (purpose) fest □ adv (send) per Eilpost □ n (train) Schnellzug m □ vt ausdrücken; ~ oneself sich ausdrücken. ~ion /-ʃn/ n Ausdruck m. ~ive /-ɪv/ a ausdrucksvoll. ~ly adv ausdrücklich

expulsion /ɪk'spʌlʃn/ n Ausweisung f; (Sch) Verweisung f von der Schule

expurgate /'ekspɜ:geɪt/ vt zensieren

exquisite /ek'skwɪzɪt/ a erlesen

ex-'serviceman n Veteran m

extempore /ɪk'stempərɪ/ adv (speak) aus dem Stegreif

extend /ɪk'stend/ vt verlängern; (stretch out) ausstrecken; (enlarge) vergrößern □ vi sich ausdehnen; (table:) sich ausziehen lassen

extension /ɪk'stenʃn/ n Verlängerung f; (to house) Anbau m; (Teleph) Nebenanschluss m; ~ 7 Apparat 7

extensive /ɪk'stensɪv/ a weit; (fig) umfassend. ~ly adv viel

extent /ɪk'stent/ n Ausdehnung f; (scope) Ausmaß nt, Umfang m; to a certain ~ in gewissem Maße

extenuating /ɪk'stenjʊeɪtɪŋ/ a mildernd

exterior /ɪk'stɪərɪə(r)/ a äußere(r,s) □ n the ~ das Äußere

exterminat|e /ɪk'stɜ:mɪneɪt/ vt ausrotten. ~ion /-'neɪʃn/ n Ausrottung f

external /ɪk'stɜ:nl/ a äußere(r,s); for ~ use only (Med) nur äußerlich. ~ly adv äußerlich

extinct /ɪk'stɪŋkt/ a ausgestorben; (volcano) erloschen. ~ion /-ɪŋkʃn/ n Aussterben nt

extinguish /ɪk'stɪŋgwɪʃ/ vt löschen. ~er n Feuerlöscher m

extol /ɪk'stəʊl/ vt (pt/pp extolled) preisen

extort /ɪk'stɔ:t/ vt erpressen. ~ion /-ɔ:ʃn/ n Erpressung f

extortionate /ɪk'stɔ:ʃənət/ a übermäßig hoch

extra /'ekstrə/ a zusätzlich □ adv extra; (especially) besonders; ~ strong extrastark □ n (Theat) Statist(in) m(f); ~s pl Nebenkosten pl; (Auto) Extras pl

extract¹ /'ekstrækt/ n Auszug m; (Culin) Extrakt m

extract² /ɪk'strækt/ vt herausziehen; ziehen ⟨tooth⟩; (fig) erzwingen. ~or [fan] n Entlüfter m

extradit|e /'ekstrədaɪt/ vt (Jur) ausliefern. ~ion /-'dɪʃn/ n (Jur) Auslieferung f.

extra'marital a außerehelich

extraordinary /ɪk'strɔːdɪnərɪ/ a, -ily adv außerordentlich; ⟨strange⟩ seltsam

extravagan|ce /ɪk'strævəgəns/ n Verschwendung f; an ~ce ein Luxus m. ~t a verschwenderisch; ⟨exaggerated⟩ extravagant

extrem|e /ɪk'striːm/ a äußerste(r,s); (fig) extrem □ n Extrem nt; in the ~e im höchsten Grade. ~ely adv äußerst. ~ist n Extremist m

extremit|y /ɪk'stremətɪ/ n ⟨distress⟩ Not f; the ~ies pl die Extremitäten pl

extricate /'ekstrɪkeɪt/ vt befreien

extrovert /'ekstrəvɜːt/ n extravertierter Mensch m

exuberant /ɪg'zjuːbərənt/ a überglücklich

exude /ɪg'zjuːd/ vt absondern; (fig) ausstrahlen

exult /ɪg'zʌlt/ vi frohlocken

eye /aɪ/ n Auge nt; ⟨of needle⟩ Öhr nt; ⟨for hook⟩ Öse f; keep an ~ on aufpassen auf (+ acc); see ~ to ~ einer Meinung sein □ vt (pt/pp eyed, pres p ey[e]ing) ansehen

eye: ~ball n Augapfel m. ~brow n Augenbraue f. ~lash n Wimper f. ~let /-lɪt/ n Öse f. ~lid n Augenlid nt. ~-shadow n Lidschatten m. ~sight n Sehkraft f. ~sore n (fam) Schandfleck m. ~tooth n Eckzahn m. ~witness n Augenzeuge m

F

fable /'feɪbl/ n Fabel f

fabric /'fæbrɪk/ n Stoff m; (fig) Gefüge nt

fabrication /fæbrɪ'keɪʃn/ n Erfindung f

fabulous /'fæbjʊləs/ a (fam) phantastisch

façade /fə'sɑːd/ n Fassade f

face /feɪs/ n Gesicht nt; ⟨grimace⟩ Grimasse f; ⟨surface⟩ Fläche f; ⟨of clock⟩ Zifferblatt nt; pull ~s Gesichter schneiden; in the ~ of angesichts (+ gen); on the ~ of it allem Anschein nach □ vt/i gegenüberstehen (+ dat); ~ north ⟨house:⟩ nach Norden liegen; ~ me! sieh mich an! ~ the fact that sich damit abfinden, dass; ~ up to s.o. jdm die Stirn bieten

face: ~flannel n Waschlappen m. ~less a anonym. ~-lift n Gesichtsstraffung f

facet /'fæsɪt/ n Facette f; (fig) Aspekt m

facetious /fə'siːʃəs/ a, -ly adv spöttisch

'face value n Nennwert m

facial /'feɪʃl/ a Gesichts-

facile /'fæsaɪl/ a oberflächlich

facilitate /fə'sɪlɪteɪt/ vt erleichtern

facilit|y /fə'sɪlətɪ/ n Leichtigkeit f; ⟨skill⟩ Gewandtheit f; ~ies pl Einrichtungen pl

facing /'feɪsɪŋ/ n Besatz m

facsimile /fæk'sɪməlɪ/ n Faksimile nt

fact /fækt/ n Tatsache f; in ~ tatsächlich; ⟨actually⟩ eigentlich

faction /'fækʃn/ n Gruppe f

factor /'fæktə(r)/ n Faktor m

factory /'fæktərɪ/ n Fabrik f

factual /'fæktʃʊəl/ a, -ly adv sachlich

faculty /'fækəltɪ/ n Fähigkeit f; (Univ) Fakultät f

fad /fæd/ n Fimmel m

fade /feɪd/ vi verblassen; ⟨material:⟩ verbleichen; ⟨sound:⟩ abklingen; ⟨flower:⟩ verwelken. ~ in/out vt (Radio, TV) ein-/ausblenden

fag /fæg/ n ⟨chore⟩ Plage f; ⟨fam: cigarette⟩ Zigarette f; ⟨Amer sl⟩ Homosexuelle(r) m

fagged /fægd/ a ~ out (fam) völlig erledigt

Fahrenheit /'færənhaɪt/ a Fahrenheit

fail /feɪl/ n without ~ unbedingt □ vi ⟨attempt:⟩ scheitern; ⟨grow weak⟩ nachlassen; ⟨break down⟩ versagen; (in exam) durchfallen; ~ to do sth etw nicht tun; he ~ed to break the record es gelang ihm nicht, den Rekord zu brechen □ vt nicht bestehen ⟨exam⟩; durchfallen lassen ⟨candidate⟩; ⟨disappoint⟩ enttäuschen; words ~ me ich weiß nicht, was ich sagen soll

failing /'feɪlɪŋ/ n Fehler m □ prep ~ that andernfalls

failure /'feɪljə(r)/ n Misserfolg m; ⟨breakdown⟩ Versagen nt; ⟨person⟩ Versager m

faint /feɪnt/ a (-er, -est), -ly adv schwach; I feel ~ mir ist schwach □ n Ohnmacht f □ vi ohnmächtig werden

faint: ~'hearted a zaghaft. ~ness n Schwäche f

fair¹ /feə(r)/ n Jahrmarkt m; (Comm) Messe f

fair² a (-er, -est) ⟨hair⟩ blond; ⟨skin⟩ hell; ⟨weather⟩ heiter; ⟨just⟩ gerecht, fair; ⟨quite good⟩ ziemlich gut; (Sch) genügend; a ~ amount ziemlich viel □ adv play ~ fair sein. ~ly adv gerecht; ⟨rather⟩ ziemlich. ~ness n Blondheit f; Helle f; Gerechtigkeit f; (Sport) Fairness f

fairy /ˈfeərɪ/ n Elfe f; good/wicked ~ gute/böse Fee f. ~ story, ~-tale n Märchen nt

faith /feɪθ/ n Glaube m; (trust) Vertrauen nt (in zu); in good ~ in gutem Glauben

faithful /ˈfeɪθfl/ a, -ly adv treu; (exact) genau; Yours ~ly Hochachtungsvoll. ~ness n Treue f; Genauigkeit f

'faith-healer n Gesundbeter(in) m(f)

fake /feɪk/ a falsch ● n Fälschung f; (person) Schwindler m ● vt fälschen; (pretend) vortäuschen

falcon /ˈfɔːlkən/ n Falke m

fall /fɔːl/ n Fall m; (heavy) Sturz m; (in prices) Fallen nt; (Amer: autumn) Herbst m; have a ~ fallen ● vi (pt fell, pp fallen) fallen; (heavily) stürzen; ⟨night:⟩ anbrechen; ~ in love sich verlieben; ~ back on zurückgreifen auf (+ acc); ~ for s.o. (fam) sich in jdn verlieben; ~ for sth (fam) auf etw (acc) hereinfallen. ~ about vi (with laughter) sich [vor Lachen] kringeln. ~ down vi umfallen; ⟨thing:⟩ herunterfallen; ⟨building:⟩ einstürzen. ~ in vi hineinfallen; (collapse) einfallen; (Mil) antreten; ~ in with sich anschließen (+ dat). ~ off vi herunterfallen; (diminish) abnehmen. ~ out vi herausfallen; ⟨hair:⟩ ausfallen; (quarrel) sich überwerfen. ~ over vi hinfallen. ~ through vi durchfallen; ⟨plan:⟩ ins Wasser fallen

fallacy /ˈfæləsɪ/ n Irrtum m

fallible /ˈfæləbl/ a fehlbar

'fall-out n [radioaktiver] Niederschlag m

fallow /ˈfæləʊ/ a lie ~ brachliegen

false /fɔːls/ a falsch; (artificial) künstlich; ~ start Fehlstart m. ~hood n Unwahrheit f. ~ly adv falsch. ~ness n Falschheit f

false 'teeth npl [künstliches] Gebiss nt

falsify /ˈfɔːlsɪfaɪ/ vt (pt/pp -ied) fälschen; (misrepresent) verfälschen

falter /ˈfɔːltə(r)/ vi zögern; (stumble) straucheln

fame /feɪm/ n Ruhm m. ~d a berühmt

familiar /fəˈmɪljə(r)/ a vertraut; (known) bekannt; too ~ familiär. ~ity /-lɪˈærətɪ/ n Vertrautheit f. ~ize vt vertraut machen (with mit)

family /ˈfæməlɪ/ n Familie f

family: ~ al'lowance n Kindergeld nt. ~ 'doctor n Hausarzt m. ~ 'life n Familienleben nt. ~ 'planning n Familienplanung f. ~ 'tree n Stammbaum m

famine /ˈfæmɪn/ n Hungersnot f

famished /ˈfæmɪʃt/ a sehr hungrig

famous /ˈfeɪməs/ a berühmt

fan¹ /fæn/ n Fächer m; (Techn) Ventilator m ● v (pt/pp fanned) ● vt fächeln; ~ oneself sich fächeln ● vi ~ out sich fächerförmig ausbreiten

fan² n (admirer) Fan m

fanatic /fəˈnætɪk/ n Fanatiker m. ~al a, -ly adv fanatisch. ~ism /-sɪzm/ n Fanatismus m

'fan belt n Keilriemen m

fanciful /ˈfænsɪfl/ a phantastisch; (imaginative) phantasiereich

fancy /ˈfænsɪ/ n Phantasie f; have a ~ to Lust haben, zu; I have taken a real ~ to him er hat es mir angetan ● a ausgefallen; ~ cakes and biscuits Feingebäck nt ● vt (believe) meinen; (imagine) sich (dat) einbilden; (fam: want) Lust haben auf (+ acc); ~ that! stell dir vor! (really) tatsächlich! ~ 'dress n Kostüm nt

fanfare /ˈfænfeə(r)/ n Fanfare f

fang /fæŋ/ n Fangzahn m; (of snake) Giftzahn m

fan: ~ heater n Heizlüfter m. ~light n Oberlicht nt

fantas|ize /ˈfæntəsaɪz/ vi phantasieren. ~tic /-ˈtæstɪk/ a phantastisch. ~y n Phantasie f; (Mus) Fantasie f

far /fɑː(r)/ adv weit; (much) viel; by ~ bei weitem; ~ away weit weg; as ~ as I know soviel ich weiß; as ~ as the church bis zur Kirche ● a at the ~ end am anderen Ende; the F~ East der Ferne Osten

farc|e /fɑːs/ n Farce f. ~ical a lächerlich

fare /feə(r)/ n Fahrpreis m; (money) Fahrgeld nt; (food) Kost f; air ~ Flugpreis m. ~-dodger /-dɒdʒə(r)/ n Schwarzfahrer m

farewell /feəˈwel/ int (liter) lebe wohl! ● n Lebewohl nt; ~ dinner Abschiedsessen nt

far-'fetched a weit hergeholt; be ~ an den Haaren herbeigezogen sein

farm /fɑːm/ n Bauernhof m ● vi Landwirtschaft betreiben ● vt bewirtschaften ⟨land⟩. ~er n Landwirt m

farm: ~house n Bauernhaus nt. ~ing n Landwirtschaft f. ~yard n Hof m

far: ~-'reaching a weit reichend. ~-'sighted a (fig) umsichtig; (Amer: longsighted) weitsichtig

fart /fɑːt/ n (vulg) Furz m ● vi (vulg) furzen

farther /ˈfɑːðə(r)/ adv weiter; ~ off weiter entfernt ● a at the ~ end am anderen Ende

fascinat|e /ˈfæsɪneɪt/ vt faszinieren. ~ing a faszinierend. ~ion /-ˈneɪʃn/ n Faszination f

fascis|m /ˈfæʃɪzm/ n Faschismus m. ~t n Faschist m ● a faschistisch

fashion /'fæʃn/ n Mode f; (manner) Art f
□ vt machen; (mould) formen. ~able
/-əbl/ a, -bly adv modisch; be ~able
Mode sein

fast¹ /fɑːst/ a & adv (-er, -est) schnell;
(firm) fest; (colour) waschecht; be ~
(clock:) vorgehen; be ~ asleep fest schlafen

fast² n Fasten nt □ vi fasten

'fastback n (Auto) Fließheck m

fasten /'fɑːsn/ vt zumachen; (fix) befestigen (to an + dat); ~ one's seatbelt sich
anschnallen. ~er n, ~ing n Verschluss
m

fastidious /fə'stɪdɪəs/ a wählerisch; (particular) penibel

fat /fæt/ a (fatter, fattest) dick; (meat) fett
□ n Fett nt

fatal /'feɪtl/ a tödlich; (error) verhängnis-
voll. ~ism /-təlɪzm/ n Fatalismus m. ~ist
/-təlɪst/ n Fatalist m. ~ity /fə'tælətɪ/ n
Todesopfer nt. ~ly /-təlɪ/ adv tödlich

fate /feɪt/ n Schicksal nt. ~ful a verhäng-
nisvoll

'fat-head n (fam) Dummkopf m

father /'fɑːðə(r)/ n Vater m; F~
Christmas der Weihnachtsmann □ vt
zeugen

father: ~hood n Vaterschaft f. ~-in-law
n (pl ~s-in-law) Schwiegervater m. ~ly
a väterlich

fathom /'fæðəm/ n (Naut) Faden m □ vt
verstehen; ~ out ergründen

fatigue /fə'tiːg/ n Ermüdung f □ vt ermüden

fatten /'fætn/ vt mästen (animal). ~ing a
cream is ~ing Sahne macht dick

fatty /'fætɪ/ a fett; (foods) fetthaltig

fatuous /'fætjʊəs/ a, -ly adv albern

faucet /'fɔːsɪt/ n (Amer) Wasserhahn m

fault /fɔːlt/ n Fehler m; (Techn) Defekt m;
(Geol) Verwerfung f; at ~ im Unrecht;
find ~ with etwas auszusetzen haben an
(+ dat); it's your ~ du bist schuld □ vt
etwas auszusetzen haben an (+ dat).
~less a, -ly adv fehlerfrei

faulty /'fɔːltɪ/ a fehlerhaft

fauna /'fɔːnə/ n Fauna f

favour /'feɪvə(r)/ n Gunst f; I am in ~ ich
bin dafür; do s.o. a ~ jdm einen Gefallen
tun □ vt begünstigen; (prefer) bevorzugen.
~able /-əbl/ a, -bly adv günstig; (reply)
positiv

favourit|e /'feɪvərɪt/ a Lieblings- □ n
Liebling m; (Sport) Favorit(in) m(f). ~ism
n Bevorzugung f

fawn¹ /fɔːn/ a rehbraun □ n Hirschkalb nt

fawn² vi sich einschmeicheln (on bei)

fax /fæks/ n Fax nt □ vt faxen (s.o. jdm). ~
machine n Faxgerät nt

fear /fɪə(r)/ n Furcht f, Angst f (of vor
+ dat); no ~! (fam) keine Angst! □ vt/i
fürchten

fear|ful /'fɪəfl/ a besorgt; (awful) furcht-
bar. ~less a, -ly adv furchtlos. ~some
/-səm/ a Furcht erregend

feas|ibility /fiːzə'bɪlətɪ/ n Durchführbar-
keit f. ~ible a durchführbar; (possible)
möglich

feast /fiːst/ n Festmahl nt; (Relig) Fest nt
□ vi ~ [on] schmausen

feat /fiːt/ n Leistung f

feather /'feðə(r)/ n Feder f

feature /'fiːtʃə(r)/ n Gesichtszug m;
(quality) Merkmal nt; (Journ) Feature nt
□ vt darstellen; (film:) in der Hauptrolle
zeigen. ~ film n Hauptfilm m

February /'februərɪ/ n Februar m

feckless /'feklɪs/ a verantwortungslos

fed /fed/ see feed □ a be ~ up (fam) die
Nase voll haben (with von)

federal /'fedərəl/ a Bundes-

federation /fedə'reɪʃn/ n Föderation f

fee /fiː/ n Gebühr f; (professional) Honorar
nt

feeble /'fiːbl/ a (-r, -st), -bly adv schwach

feed /fiːd/ n Futter nt; (for baby) Essen
nt □ v (pt/pp fed) □ vt füttern; (support)
ernähren; (into machine) eingeben;
speisen (computer) □ vi sich ernähren (on
von)

'feedback n Feedback nt

feel /fiːl/ v (pt/pp felt) □ vt fühlen; (experience) empfinden; (think) meinen □ vi sich
fühlen; ~ soft/hard sich weich/hart an-
fühlen; I ~ hot/ill mir ist heiß/schlecht;
I don't ~ like it ich habe keine Lust dazu.
~er n Fühler m. ~ing n Gefühl nt; no
hard ~ings nichts für ungut

feet /fiːt/ see foot

feign /feɪn/ vt vortäuschen

feint /feɪnt/ n Finte f

feline /'fiːlaɪn/ a Katzen-; (catlike) katzen-
artig

fell¹ /fel/ vt fällen

fell² see fall

fellow /'feləʊ/ n (of society) Mitglied nt;
(fam: man) Kerl m

fellow: ~-countryman n Landsmann m.
~ men pl Mitmenschen pl. ~ship n Kameradschaft f; (group) Gesellschaft f

felony /'felənɪ/ n Verbrechen nt

felt¹ /felt/ see feel

felt² n Filz m. ~[-tipped] 'pen n Filzstift
m

female /'fi:meɪl/ a weiblich □ nt Weibchen nt; (pej: woman) Weib nt

femin|ine /'femɪnɪn/ a weiblich □ n (Gram) Femininum nt. ~inity /-'nɪnətɪ/ n Weiblichkeit f. ~ist a feministisch □ n Feminist(in) m(f)

fenc|e /fens/ n Zaun m; (fam: person) Hehler m □ vi (Sport) fechten □ vt ~e in einzäunen. ~er n Fechter m. ~ing n Zaun m; (Sport) Fechten nt

fend /fend/ vi ~ for oneself sich allein durchschlagen. ~ off vt abwehren

fender /'fendə(r)/ n Kaminvorsetzer m; (Naut) Fender m; (Amer: wing) Kotflügel m

fennel /'fenl/ n Fenchel m

ferment¹ /'fɜ:ment/ n Erregung f

ferment² /fə'ment/ vi gären □ vt gären lassen. ~ation /fɜ:men'teɪʃn/ n Gärung f

fern /fɜ:n/ n Farn m

feroc|ious /fə'rəʊʃəs/ a wild. ~ity /-'rɒsətɪ/ n Wildheit f

ferret /'ferɪt/ n Frettchen nt

ferry /'ferɪ/ n Fähre f □ vt ~ [across] übersetzen

fertil|e /'fɜ:taɪl/ a fruchtbar. ~ity /fɜ:-'tɪlətɪ/ n Fruchtbarkeit f

fertilize /'fɜ:təlaɪz/ vt befruchten; düngen ⟨land⟩. ~r n Dünger m

fervent /'fɜ:vənt/ a leidenschaftlich

fervour /'fɜ:və(r)/ n Leidenschaft f

fester /'festə(r)/ vi eitern

festival /'festɪvl/ n Fest nt; (Mus, Theat) Festspiele pl

festiv|e /'festɪv/ a festlich; ~e season Festzeit. f. ~ities /fe'stɪvətɪz/ npl Feierlichkeiten pl

festoon /fe'stu:n/ vt behängen (with mit)

fetch /fetʃ/ vt holen; (collect) abholen; (be sold for) einbringen

fetching /'fetʃɪŋ/ a anziehend

fête /feɪt/ n Fest nt □ vt feiern

fetish /'fetɪʃ/ n Fetisch m

fetter /'fetə(r)/ vt fesseln

fettle /'fetl/ n in fine ~ in bester Form

feud /fju:d/ n Fehde f

feudal /'fju:dl/ a Feudal-

fever /'fi:və(r)/ n Fieber nt. ~ish a fiebrig; (fig) fieberhaft

few /fju:/ a (-er, -est) wenige; every ~ days alle paar Tage □ n a ~ ein paar; quite a ~ ziemlich viele

fiancé /fɪ'ɒnseɪ/ n Verlobte(r) m. fiancée n Verlobte f

fiasco /fɪ'æskəʊ/ n Fiasko nt

fib /fɪb/ n kleine Lüge; tell a ~ schwindeln

fibre /'faɪbə(r)/ n Faser f

fickle /'fɪkl/ a unbeständig

fiction /'fɪkʃn/ n Erfindung f; [works of] ~ Erzählungsliteratur f. ~al a erfunden

fictitious /fɪk'tɪʃəs/ a [frei] erfunden

fiddle /'fɪdl/ n (fam) Geige f; (cheating) Schwindel m □ vi herumspielen (with mit) □ vt (fam) frisieren ⟨accounts⟩; (arrange) arrangieren

fiddly /'fɪdlɪ/ a knifflig

fidelity /fɪ'delətɪ/ n Treue f

fidget /'fɪdʒɪt/ vi zappeln. ~y a zappelig

field /fi:ld/ n Feld nt; (meadow) Wiese f; (subject) Gebiet nt

field: ~ events npl Sprung- und Wurfdisziplinen pl. ~glasses npl Feldstecher m. F~ 'Marshal n Feldmarschall m. ~work n Feldforschung f

fiend /fi:nd/ n Teufel m. ~ish a teuflisch

fierce /fɪəs/ a (-r, -st), -ly adv wild; (fig) heftig. ~ness n Wildheit f; (fig) Heftigkeit f

fiery /'faɪərɪ/ a (-ier, -iest) feurig

fifteen /fɪf'ti:n/ a fünfzehn □ n Fünfzehn f. ~th a fünfzehnte(r,s)

fifth /fɪfθ/ a fünfte(r,s)

fiftieth /'fɪftɪɪθ/ a fünfzigste(r,s)

fifty /'fɪftɪ/ a fünfzig

fig /fɪg/ n Feige f

fight /faɪt/ n Kampf m; (brawl) Schlägerei f; (between children, dogs) Rauferei f □ v (pt/pp fought) □ vt kämpfen gegen; (fig) bekämpfen □ vi kämpfen; (brawl) sich schlagen; ⟨children, dogs:⟩ sich raufen. ~er n Kämpfer m; (Aviat) Jagdflugzeug nt. ~ing n Kampf m

figment /'fɪgmənt/ n ~ of the imagination Hirngespinst nt

figurative /'fɪgjərətɪv/ a, -ly adv bildlich, übertragen

figure /'fɪgə(r)/ n (digit) Ziffer f; (number) Zahl f; (sum) Summe f; (carving, sculpture, woman's) Figur f; (form) Gestalt f; (illustration) Abbildung f; ~ of speech Redefigur f; good at ~s gut im Rechnen □ vi (appear) erscheinen □ vt (Amer: think) glauben. ~ out vt ausrechnen

figure: ~head n Galionsfigur f; (fig) Repräsentationsfigur f. ~ skating n Eiskunstlauf m

filament /'fɪləmənt/ n Faden m; (Electr) Glühfaden m

filch /fɪltʃ/ vt (fam) klauen

file¹ /faɪl/ n Akte f; (for documents) [Akten]ordner m □ vt ablegen ⟨documents⟩; (Jur) einreichen

file² n (line) Reihe f; in single ~ im Gänsemarsch

file³ n (Techn) Feile f □ vt feilen

filigree /'fɪlɪgri:/ n Filigran nt

filings /'faɪlɪŋz/ npl Feilspäne pl

fill /fɪl/ n eat one's ~ sich satt essen □ vt füllen; plombieren ⟨tooth⟩ □ vi sich füllen. ~ in vt auffüllen; ausfüllen ⟨form⟩. ~ out vt ausfüllen ⟨form⟩. ~ up vi sich füllen □ vt vollfüllen; ⟨Auto⟩ volltanken; ausfüllen ⟨form⟩

fillet /ˈfɪlɪt/ n Filet nt □ vt ⟨pt/pp filleted⟩ entgräten

filling /ˈfɪlɪŋ/ n Füllung f; ⟨of tooth⟩ Plombe f. ~ station n Tankstelle f

filly /ˈfɪlɪ/ n junge Stute f

film /fɪlm/ n Film m; ⟨Culin⟩ [cling] ~ Klarsichtfolie f □ vt/i filmen; verfilmen ⟨book⟩. ~ star n Filmstar m

filter /ˈfɪltə(r)/ n Filter m □ vt filtern. ~ through vi durchsickern. ~ tip n Filter m; ⟨cigarette⟩ Filterzigarette f

filth /fɪlθ/ n Dreck m. ~y a (-ier, -iest) dreckig

fin /fɪn/ n Flosse f

final /ˈfaɪnl/ a letzte(r,s); ⟨conclusive⟩ endgültig. ~ result Endresultat nt □ n ⟨Sport⟩ Finale nt, Endspiel nt; ~s pl ⟨Univ⟩ Abschlussprüfung f

finale /fɪˈnɑːlɪ/ n Finale nt

final|ist /ˈfaɪnəlɪst/ n Finalist(in) m(f). ~ity /-ˈnælətɪ/ n Endgültigkeit f

final|ize /ˈfaɪnəlaɪz/ vt endgültig festlegen. ~ly adv schließlich

finance /faɪˈnæns/ n Finanz f □ vt finanzieren

financial /faɪˈnænʃl/ a, -ly adv finanziell

finch /fɪntʃ/ n Fink m

find /faɪnd/ n Fund m □ vt ⟨pt/pp found⟩ finden; ⟨establish⟩ feststellen; go and ~ holen; try to ~ suchen; ~ guilty ⟨Jur⟩ schuldig sprechen. ~ out vt herausfinden; ⟨learn⟩ erfahren □ vi ⟨enquire⟩ sich erkundigen

findings /ˈfaɪndɪŋz/ npl Ergebnisse pl

fine[1] /faɪn/ n Geldstrafe f □ vt zu einer Geldstrafe verurteilen

fine[2] a (-r, -st,) -ly adv fein; ⟨weather⟩ schön; he's ~ es geht ihm gut □ adv gut; cut it ~ ⟨fam⟩ sich ⟨dat⟩ wenig Zeit lassen. ~ arts npl schöne Künste pl

finery /ˈfaɪnərɪ/ n Putz m, Staat m

finesse /fɪˈnes/ n Gewandtheit f

finger /ˈfɪŋgə(r)/ n Finger m □ vt anfassen

finger: ~mark n Fingerabdruck m. ~nail n Fingernagel m. ~print n Fingerabdruck m. ~tip n Fingerspitze f; have sth at one's ~tips etw im kleinen Finger haben

finicky /ˈfɪnɪkɪ/ a knifflig; ⟨choosy⟩ wählerisch

finish /ˈfɪnɪʃ/ n Schluss m; ⟨Sport⟩ Finish nt; ⟨line⟩ Ziel nt; ⟨of product⟩ Ausführung f □ vt beenden; ⟨use up⟩ aufbrauchen; ~

one's drink austrinken; ~ reading zu Ende lesen □ vi fertig werden; ⟨performance:⟩ zu Ende sein; ⟨runner:⟩ durchs Ziel gehen

finite /ˈfaɪnaɪt/ a begrenzt

Finland /ˈfɪnlənd/ n Finnland nt

Finn /fɪn/ n Finne m/ Finnin f. ~ish a finnisch

fiord /fjɔːd/ n Fjord m

fir /fɜː(r)/ n Tanne f

fire /ˈfaɪə(r)/ n Feuer nt; ⟨forest, house⟩ Brand m; be on ~ brennen; catch ~ Feuer fangen; set ~ to anzünden; ⟨arsonist:⟩ in Brand stecken; under ~ unter Beschuss □ vt brennen ⟨pottery⟩; abfeuern ⟨shot⟩; schießen mit ⟨gun⟩; ⟨fam: dismiss⟩ feuern □ vi schießen (at auf + acc); ⟨engine:⟩ anspringen

fire: ~ alarm n Feueralarm m; ⟨apparatus⟩ Feuermelder m. ~arm n Schusswaffe f. ~ brigade n Feuerwehr f. ~-engine n Löschfahrzeug nt. ~-escape n Feuertreppe f. ~ extinguisher n Feuerlöscher m. ~man n Feuerwehrmann m. ~place n Kamin m. ~side n by or at the ~side am Kamin. ~ station n Feuerwache f. ~wood n Brennholz nt. ~work n Feuerwerkskörper m; ~works pl ⟨display⟩ Feuerwerk nt

'**firing squad** n Erschießungskommando nt

firm[1] /fɜːm/ n Firma f

firm[2] a (-er, -est), -ly adv fest; ⟨resolute⟩ entschlossen; ⟨strict⟩ streng

first /fɜːst/ a & n erste(r,s); at ~ zuerst; who's ~? wer ist der Erste? at ~ sight auf den ersten Blick; for the ~ time zum ersten Mal; from the ~ von Anfang an □ adv zuerst; ⟨firstly⟩ erstens

first: ~ 'aid n erste Hilfe. ~-'aid kit n Verbandkasten m. ~-class a erstklassig; ⟨Rail⟩ erster Klasse □. ~-class adv erster Klasse. ~ e'dition n Erstausgabe f. ~ 'floor n erster Stock; ⟨Amer: ground floor⟩ Erdgeschoss nt. ~ly adv erstens. ~ name n Vorname m. ~-rate a erstklassig

fish /fɪʃ/ n Fisch m □ vt/i fischen; ⟨with rod⟩ angeln. ~ out vt herausfischen

fish: ~bone n Gräte f. ~erman n Fischer m. ~-farm n Fischzucht f. ~ 'finger n Fischstäbchen n

fishing /ˈfɪʃɪŋ/ n Fischerei f. ~ boat n Fischerboot m. ~-rod n Angel[rute] f

fish: ~monger /-mʌŋgə(r)/ n Fischhändler m. ~slice n Fischheber m. ~y a ⟨fam: suspicious⟩ verdächtig

fission /ˈfɪʃn/ n ⟨Phys⟩ Spaltung f

fist /fɪst/ n Faust f

fit[1] /fɪt/ n ⟨attack⟩ Anfall m

fit² a (fitter, fittest) (suitable) geeignet; (healthy) gesund; (Sport) fit; ~ to eat essbar; keep ~ sich fit halten; see ~ es für angebracht halten (to zu)

fit³ n (of clothes) Sitz m; be a good ~ gut passen □ v (pt/pp fitted) □ vi (be the right size) passen □ vt anbringen (to an + dat); (install) einbauen; ⟨clothes:⟩ passen (+ dat); ~ with versehen mit. ~ in vi hineinpassen; ⟨person⟩ sich einfügen (with in + acc) □ vt (accommodate) unterbringen

fit|ful /'fɪtfl/ a, -ly adv ⟨sleep⟩ unruhig. ~ment n Einrichtungsgegenstand m; (attachment) Zusatzgerät nt. ~ness n Eignung f; (physical) Gesundheit f; (Sport) Fitness f. ~ted a eingebaut; ⟨garment⟩ tailliert

fitted: ~ 'carpet n Teppichboden m. ~ 'cupboard n Einbauschrank m. ~ 'kitchen n Einbauküche f. ~ 'sheet n Spannlaken nt

fitter /'fɪtə(r)/ n Monteur m

fitting /'fɪtɪŋ/ a passend □ n (of clothes) Anprobe f; (of shoes) Weite f; (Techn) Zubehörteil nt; ~s pl Zubehör nt. ~-room n Anprobekabine f

five /faɪv/ a fünf □ n Fünf f. ~r n Fünfpfundschein m

fix /fɪks/ n ⟨sl: drugs⟩ Fix m; be in a ~ ⟨fam⟩ in der Klemme sitzen □ vt befestigen (to an + dat); (arrange) festlegen; (repair) reparieren; (Phot) fixieren; ~ a meal ⟨Amer⟩ Essen machen

fixation /fɪk'seɪʃn/ n Fixierung f

fixed /fɪkst/ a fest

fixture /'fɪkstʃə(r)/ n (Sport) Veranstaltung f; ~s and fittings zu einer Wohnung gehörende Einrichtungen pl

fizz /fɪz/ vi sprudeln

fizzle /'fɪzl/ vi ~ out verpuffen

fizzy /'fɪzɪ/ a sprudelnd. ~ drink n Brause-[limonade] f

flabbergasted /'flæbəgɑːstɪd/ a be ~ platt sein ⟨fam⟩

flabby /'flæbɪ/ a schlaff

flag¹ /flæg/ n Fahne f; (Naut) Flagge f □ vt (pt/pp flagged) ~ down anhalten ⟨taxi⟩

flag² vi (pt/pp flagged) ermüden

flagon /'flægən/ n Krug m

'flag-pole n Fahnenstange f

flagrant /'fleɪgrənt/ a flagrant

flagstone n [Pflaster]platte f

flair /fleə(r)/ n Begabung f

flake /fleɪk/ n Flocke f □ vi ~ [off] abblättern

flaky /'fleɪkɪ/ a blättrig. ~ pastry n Blätterteig m

flamboyant /flæm'bɔɪənt/ a extravagant

flame /fleɪm/ n Flamme f

flammable /'flæməbl/ a feuergefährlich

flan /flæn/ n ⟨fruit⟩ ~ Obsttorte f

flank /flæŋk/ n Flanke f □ vt flankieren

flannel /'flænl/ n Flanell m; (for washing) Waschlappen m

flannelette /flænə'let/ n (Tex) Biber m

flap /flæp/ n Klappe f; in a ~ ⟨fam⟩ aufgeregt □ v (pt/pp flapped) vi flattern; ⟨fam⟩ sich aufregen □ vt ~ its wings mit den Flügeln schlagen

flare /fleə(r)/ n Leuchtsignal nt □ vi ~ up auflodern; ⟨fam: get angry⟩ aufbrausen. ~d a ⟨garment⟩ ausgestellt

flash /flæʃ/ n Blitz m; in a ~ ⟨fam⟩ im Nu □ vi blitzen; (repeatedly) blinken; ~ past vorbeirasen □ vt aufleuchten lassen; ~ one's headlights die Lichthupe betätigen

flash: ~back n Rückblende f. ~bulb n (Phot) Blitzbirne f. ~er n (Auto) Blinker m. ~light n (Phot) Blitzlicht nt; ⟨Amer: torch⟩ Taschenlampe f. ~y a auffällig

flask /flɑːsk/ n Flasche f; (Chem) Kolben m; ⟨vacuum ~⟩ Thermosflasche (P) f

flat /flæt/ a (flatter, flattest) flach; ⟨surface⟩ eben; ⟨refusal⟩ glatt; ⟨beer⟩ schal; ⟨battery⟩ verbraucht; (Auto) leer; ⟨tyre⟩ platt; (Mus) A ~ As nt; B ~ B nt □ n Wohnung f; (Mus) Erniedrigungszeichen nt; ⟨fam: puncture⟩ Reifenpanne f

flat: ~ 'feet npl Plattfüße pl. ~-fish n Plattfisch m. ~ly adv ⟨refuse⟩ glatt. ~ rate n Einheitspreis m

flatten /'flætn/ vt platt drücken

flatter /'flætə(r)/ vt schmeicheln (+ dat). ~y n Schmeichelei f

flat 'tyre n Reifenpanne f

flatulence /'flætjʊləns/ n Blähungen pl

flaunt /flɔːnt/ vt prunken mit

flautist /'flɔːtɪst/ n Flötist(in) m(f)

flavour /'fleɪvə(r)/ n Geschmack m □ vt abschmecken. ~ing n Aroma nt

flaw /flɔː/ n Fehler m. ~less a tadellos; ⟨complexion⟩ makellos

flax /flæks/ n Flachs m. ~en a flachsblond

flea /fliː/ n Floh m. ~ market n Flohmarkt m

fleck /flek/ n Tupfen m

fled /fled/ see flee

flee /fliː/ v (pt/pp fled) □ vi fliehen (from vor + dat) □ vt flüchten aus

fleec|e /fliːs/ n Vlies nt □ vt ⟨fam⟩ schröpfen. ~y a flauschig

fleet /fliːt/ n Flotte f; (of cars) Wagenpark m

fleeting /'fliːtɪŋ/ a flüchtig

Flemish /'flemɪʃ/ a flämisch

flesh /fleʃ/ n Fleisch nt; in the ~ ⟨fam⟩ in Person. ~y a fleischig flew /fluː/ *see* fly²

flex¹ /fleks/ *vt* anspannen ⟨muscle⟩

flex² *n* ⟨Electr⟩ Schnur *f*

flexib|ility /fleksə'bɪlətɪ/ *n* Biegsamkeit *f*; ⟨fig⟩ Flexibilität *f*. ~le *a* biegsam; ⟨fig⟩ flexibel

'flexitime /'fleksɪ-/ *n* Gleitzeit *f*

flick /flɪk/ *vt* schnippen. ~ through *vi* schnell durchblättern

flicker /'flɪkə(r)/ *vi* flackern

flier /'flaɪə(r)/ *n* = flyer

flight¹ /flaɪt/ *n* ⟨fleeing⟩ Flucht *f*; take ~ die Flucht ergreifen

flight² *n* ⟨flying⟩ Flug *m*; ~ of stairs Treppe *f*

flight: ~ path *n* Flugschneise *f*. ~ recorder *n* Flugschreiber *m*

flighty /'flaɪtɪ/ *a* (-ier, -iest) flatterhaft

flimsy /'flɪmzɪ/ *a* (-ier, -iest) dünn; ⟨excuse⟩ fadenscheinig

flinch /flɪntʃ/ *vi* zurückzucken

fling /flɪŋ/ *n* have a ~ ⟨fam⟩ sich austoben □ *vt* (pt/pp flung) schleudern

flint /flɪnt/ *n* Feuerstein *m*

flip /flɪp/ *vt/i* schnippen; ~ through durchblättern

flippant /'flɪpənt/ *a*, -ly *adv* leichtfertig

flipper /'flɪpə(r)/ *n* Flosse *f*

flirt /flɜːt/ *n* kokette Frau *f* □ *vi* flirten

flirtat|ion /flɜː'teɪʃn/ *n* Flirt *m*. ~ious /-ʃəs/ *a* kokett

flit /flɪt/ *vi* (pt/pp flitted) flattern

float /fləʊt/ *n* Schwimmer *m*; ⟨in procession⟩ Festwagen *m*; ⟨money⟩ Wechselgeld *nt* □ *vi* ⟨thing:⟩ schwimmen; ⟨person:⟩ sich treiben lassen; ⟨in air⟩ schweben; ⟨Comm⟩ floaten

flock /flɒk/ *n* Herde *f*; ⟨of birds⟩ Schwarm *m* □ *vi* strömen

flog /flɒg/ *vt* (pt/pp flogged) auspeitschen; ⟨fam: sell⟩ verkloppen

flood /flʌd/ *n* Überschwemmung *f*; ⟨fig⟩ Flut *f*; be in ~ ⟨river:⟩ Hochwasser führen □ *vt* überschwemmen □ *vi* ⟨river:⟩ über die Ufer treten

'floodlight *n* Flutlicht *nt* □ *vt* (pt/pp floodlit) anstrahlen

floor /flɔː(r)/ *n* Fußboden *m*; ⟨storey⟩ Stock *m* □ *vt* ⟨baffle⟩ verblüffen

floor: ~ board *n* Dielenbrett *nt*. ~cloth *n* Scheuertuch *nt*. ~polish *n* Bohnerwachs *nt*. ~ show *n* Kabarettvorstellung *f*

flop /flɒp/ *n* ⟨fam⟩ Reinfall *m*; ⟨Theat⟩ Durchfall *m* □ *vi* (pt/pp flopped) ⟨fam⟩ ⟨fail⟩ durchfallen; ~ down sich plumpsen lassen

floppy /'flɒpɪ/ *a* schlapp. ~ 'disc *n* Diskette *f*

flora /'flɔːrə/ *n* Flora *f*

floral /'flɔːrl/ *a* Blumen-

florid /'flɒrɪd/ *a* ⟨complexion⟩ gerötet; ⟨style⟩ blumig

florist /'flɒrɪst/ *n* Blumenhändler(in) *m(f)*

flounce /flaʊns/ *n* Volant *m* □ *vi* ~ out hinausstolzieren

flounder¹ /'flaʊndə(r)/ *vi* zappeln

flounder² *n* ⟨fish⟩ Flunder *f*

flour /'flaʊə(r)/ *n* Mehl *nt*

flourish /'flʌrɪʃ/ *n* große Geste *f*; ⟨scroll⟩ Schnörkel *m* □ *vi* gedeihen; ⟨fig⟩ blühen □ *vt* schwenken

floury /'flaʊərɪ/ *a* mehlig

flout /flaʊt/ *vt* missachten

flow /fləʊ/ *n* Fluss *m*; ⟨of traffic, blood⟩ Strom *m* □ *vi* fließen

flower /'flaʊə(r)/ *n* Blume *f* □ *vi* blühen

flower: ~-bed *n* Blumenbeet *nt*. ~ed *a* geblümt. ~pot *n* Blumentopf *m*. ~y *a* blumig

flown /fləʊn/ *see* fly²

flu /fluː/ *n* ⟨fam⟩ Grippe *f*

fluctuat|e /'flʌktjʊeɪt/ *vi* schwanken. ~ion /-'eɪʃn/ *n* Schwankung *f*

fluent /'fluːənt/ *a*, -ly *adv* fließend

fluff /flʌf/ *n* Fusseln *pl*; ⟨down⟩ Flaum *m*. ~y *a* (-ier, -iest) flauschig

fluid /'fluːɪd/ *a* flüssig; ⟨fig⟩ veränderlich □ *n* Flüssigkeit *f*

fluke /fluːk/ *n* [glücklicher] Zufall *m*

flung /flʌŋ/ *see* fling

flunk /flʌŋk/ *vt/i* ⟨Amer, fam⟩ durchfallen (in + dat)

fluorescent /flʊə'resnt/ *a* fluoreszierend; ~ lighting Neonbeleuchtung *f*

fluoride /'flʊəraɪd/ *n* Fluor *nt*

flurry /'flʌrɪ/ *n* ⟨snow⟩ Gestöber *nt*; ⟨fig⟩ Aufregung *f*

flush /flʌʃ/ *n* ⟨blush⟩ Erröten *nt* □ *vi* rot werden □ *vt* spülen □ *a* in einer Ebene (with mit); ⟨fam: affluent⟩ gut bei Kasse

flustered /'flʌstəd/ *a* nervös

flute /fluːt/ *n* Flöte *f*

flutter /'flʌtə(r)/ *n* Flattern *nt* □ *vi* flattern

flux /flʌks/ *n* in a state of ~ im Fluss

fly¹ /flaɪ/ *n* (pl flies) Fliege *f*

fly² *v* (pt flew, pp flown) □ *vi* fliegen; ⟨flag:⟩ wehen; ⟨rush⟩ sausen □ *vt* fliegen; führen ⟨flag⟩

fly³ *n* & flies *pl* ⟨on trousers⟩ Hosenschlitz *m*

flyer /'flaɪə(r)/ *n* Flieger(in) *m(f)*; ⟨Amer: leaflet⟩ Flugblatt *nt*

flying: ~ 'buttress *n* Strebebogen *m*. ~ 'saucer *n* fliegende Untertasse *f*. ~ 'visit *n* Stippvisite *f*

fly: ~leaf n Vorsatzblatt nt. ~over n
Überführung f

foal /fəʊl/ n Fohlen nt

foam /fəʊm/ n Schaum m; (synthetic)
Schaumstoff m □ vi schäumen. ~ 'rubber
n Schaumgummi m

fob /fɒb/ vt (pt/pp fobbed) ~ sth off etw
andrehen (on s.o. jdm); ~ s.o. off abspeisen (with mit)

focal /'fəʊkl/ n Brenn-

focus /'fəʊkəs/ n Brennpunkt m; in ~
scharf eingestellt □ v (pt/pp focused or
focussed) □ vt einstellen (on auf + acc);
(fig) konzentrieren (on auf + acc) □ vi
(fig) sich konzentrieren (on auf + acc)

fodder /'fɒdə(r)/ n Futter nt

foe /fəʊ/ n Feind m

foetus /'fiːtəs/ n (pl-tuses) Fötus m

fog /fɒg/ n Nebel m

foggy /'fɒgɪ/ a (foggier, foggiest) neblig

'fog-horn n Nebelhorn nt

fogy /'fəʊgɪ/ n old ~ alter Knacker m

foible /'fɔɪbl/ n Eigenart f

foil¹ /fɔɪl/ n Folie f; (Culin) Alufolie f

foil² vt (thwart) vereiteln

foil³ n (Fencing) Florett nt

foist /fɔɪst/ vt andrehen (on s.o. jdm)

fold¹ /fəʊld/ n (for sheep) Pferch m

fold² n Falte f; (in paper) Kniff m □ vt
falten; ~ one's arms die Arme verschränken □ vi sich falten lassen; (fail) eingehen. ~ up vt zusammenfalten;
zusammenklappen (chair) □ vi sich zu-
sammenfalten/-klappen lassen; (fam)
(business:) eingehen

fold|er /'fəʊldə(r)/ n Mappe f. ~ing a
Klapp-

foliage /'fəʊlɪɪdʒ/ n Blätter pl; (of tree)
Laub nt

folk /fəʊk/ npl Leute pl

folk: ~dance n Volkstanz m. ~lore n Folklore f. ~song n Volkslied nt

follow /'fɒləʊ/ vt/i folgen (+ dat); (pursue)
verfolgen; (in vehicle) nachfahren (+ dat);
~ suit (fig) dasselbe tun. ~ up vt nachgehen (+ dat)

follow|er /'fɒləʊə(r)/ n Anhänger(in)
m(f). ~ing a folgend □ n Folgende(s) nt;
(supporters) Anhängerschaft f □ prep im
Anschluss an (+ acc)

folly /'fɒlɪ/ n Torheit f

fond /fɒnd/ a (-er, -est), -ly adv liebevoll;
be ~ of gern haben; gern essen (food)

fondle /'fɒndl/ vt liebkosen

fondness /'fɒndnɪs/ n Liebe f (for zu)

font /fɒnt/ n Taufstein m

food /fuːd/ n Essen nt; (for animals) Futter
nt; (groceries) Lebensmittel pl

food: ~ mixer n Küchenmaschine f. ~
poisoning n Lebensmittelvergiftung f. ~
processor n Küchenmaschine f. ~ value
n Nährwert m

fool¹ /fuːl/ n (Culin) Fruchtcreme f

fool² n Narr m; you are a ~ du bist dumm;
make a ~ of oneself sich lächerlich
machen □ vt hereinlegen □ vi ~ around
herumalbern

'fool|hardy a tollkühn. ~ish a, -ly adv
dumm. ~ishness n Dummheit f. ~proof
a narrensicher

foot /fʊt/ n (pl feet) Fuß m; (measure) Fuß
m (30,48 cm); (of bed) Fußende nt; on ~ zu
Fuß; on one's feet auf den Beinen; put
one's ~ in it (fam) ins Fettnäpfchen treten

foot: ~-and-'mouth disease n Maul- und
Klauenseuche f. ~ball n Fußball m.
~baller n Fußballspieler m. ~ball pools
npl Fußballtoto nt. ~brake n Fußbremse
f. ~bridge n Fußgängerbrücke f. ~hills
npl Vorgebirge nt. ~hold n Halt m. ~ing
n Halt m; (fig) Basis f. ~lights npl Rampenlicht nt. ~man n Lakai m. ~note n
Fußnote f. ~path n Fußweg m. ~print n
Fußabdruck m. ~step n Schritt m; follow
in s.o.'s ~steps (fig) in jds Fußstapfen
treten. ~stool n Fußbank f. ~wear n
Schuhwerk nt

for /fə(r), betont fɔː(r)/ prep für (+ acc);
(send, long) nach; (ask, fight) um; what
~? wozu? ~ supper zum Abendessen; ~
nothing umsonst; ~ all that trotz allem;
~ this reason aus diesem Grund; ~ a
month einen Monat; I have lived here
~ ten years ich wohne seit zehn Jahren
hier □ conj denn

forage /'fɒrɪdʒ/ n Futter nt □ vi ~ for
suchen nach

forbade /fə'bæd/ see forbid

forbear|ance /fɔː'beərəns/ n Nachsicht
f. ~ing a nachsichtig

forbid /fə'bɪd/ vt (pt forbade, pp forbidden) verbieten (s.o. jdm). ~ding a bedrohlich; (stern) streng

force /fɔːs/ n Kraft f; (of blow) Wucht f;
(violence) Gewalt f; in ~ gültig; (in large
numbers) in großer Zahl; come into ~ in
Kraft treten; the ~s pl die Streitkräfte pl
□ vt zwingen; (break open) aufbrechen; ~
sth on s.o. jdm etw aufdrängen

forced /fɔːst/ a gezwungen; ~ landing
Notlandung f

force: ~'feed vt (pt/pp -fed) zwangser-
nähren. ~ful a, -ly adv energisch

forceps /'fɔːseps/ n inv Zange f

forcibl|e /'fɔːsəbl/ a gewaltsam. ~y adv mit Gewalt

ford /fɔːd/ n Furt f □ vt durchwaten; (in vehicle) durchfahren

fore /fɔː(r)/ a vordere(r,s) □ n to the ~ im Vordergrund

fore: ~arm n Unterarm m. ~boding /-'bəʊdɪŋ/ n Vorahnung f. ~cast n Voraussage f; (for weather) Vorhersage f □ vt (pt/pp ~cast) voraussagen, vorhersagen. ~court n Vorhof m. ~fathers npl Vorfahren pl. ~finger n Zeigefinger m. ~front n to be in the ~front führend sein. ~gone a be a ~gone conclusion von vornherein feststehen. ~ground n Vordergrund m. ~head /'fɔrɪd/ n Stirn f. ~hand n Vorhand f

foreign /'fɒrən/ a ausländisch; (country) fremd; he is ~ er ist Ausländer. ~ currency n Devisen pl. ~er n Ausländer(in) m(f). ~ language n Fremdsprache f

Foreign: ~ Office n ≈ Außenministerium nt. ~ 'Secretary n ≈ Außenminister m

fore: ~leg n Vorderbein nt. ~man n Vorarbeiter m. ~most a führend □ adv first and ~most zuallerest. ~name n Vorname m

forensic /fə'rensɪk/ a ~ medicine Gerichtsmedizin f

'forerunner n Vorläufer m

fore'see vt (pt -saw, pp -seen) voraussehen, vorhersehen. ~able /-'əbl/ a in the ~able future in absehbarer Zeit

'foresight n Weitblick m

forest /'fɒrɪst/ n Wald m. ~er n Förster m

fore'stall vt zuvorkommen (+ dat)

forestry /'fɒrɪstrɪ/ n Forstwirtschaft f

'foretaste n Vorgeschmack m

fore'tell vt (pt/pp -told) vorhersagen

forever /fə'revə(r)/ adv für immer

fore'warn vt vorher warnen

foreword /'fɔːwɜːd/ n Vorwort nt

forfeit /'fɔːfɪt/ n (in game) Pfand nt □ vt verwirken

forgave /fə'geɪv/ see forgive

forge¹ /fɔːdʒ/ vi ~ ahead (fig) Fortschritte machen

forge² n Schmiede f □ vt schmieden; (counterfeit) fälschen. ~r n Fälscher m. ~ry n Fälschung f

forget /fə'get/ vt/i (pt-got, pp-gotten) vergessen; verlernen (language, skill). ~ful a vergesslich. ~fulness n Vergesslichkeit f. ~-me-not n Vergissmeinnicht nt

forgive /fə'gɪv/ vt (pt -gave, pp -given) ~ s.o. for sth jdm etw vergeben od verzeihen. ~ness n Vergebung f, Verzeihung f

forgo /fɔː'gəʊ/ vt (pt -went, pp -gone) verzichten auf (+ acc)

forgot(ten) /fə'gɒt(n)/ see forget

fork /fɔːk/ n Gabel f; (in road) Gabelung f □ vi (road:) sich gabeln; ~ right rechts abzweigen. ~ out vt (fam) blechen

fork-lift 'truck n Gabelstapler m

forlorn /fə'lɔːn/ a verlassen; (hope) schwach

form /fɔːm/ n Form f; (document) Formular nt; (bench) Bank f; (Sch) Klasse f □ vt formen (into zu); (create) bilden □ vi sich bilden; (idea:) Gestalt annehmen

formal /'fɔːml/ a, -ly adv formell, förmlich. ~ity /-'mælətɪ/ n Förmlichkeit f; (requirement) Formalität f

format /'fɔːmæt/ n Format nt

formation /fɔː'meɪʃn/ n Formation f

formative /'fɔːmətɪv/ a ~ years Entwicklungsjahre pl

former /'fɔːmə(r)/ a ehemalig; the ~ der/die/das Erstere. ~ly adv früher

formidable /'fɔːmɪdəbl/ a gewaltig

formula /'fɔːmjʊlə/ n (pl -ae /-liː/ or -s) Formel f

formulate /'fɔːmjʊleɪt/ vt formulieren

forsake /fə'seɪk/ vt (pt -sook /-sʊk/, pp -saken) verlassen

fort /fɔːt/ n (Mil) Fort nt

forte /'fɔːteɪ/ n Stärke f

forth /fɔːθ/ adv back and ~ hin und her; and so ~ und so weiter

forth: ~coming a bevorstehend; (fam: communicative) mitteilsam. ~right a direkt. ~with adv umgehend

fortieth /'fɔːtɪɪθ/ a vierzigste(r,s)

fortification /fɔːtɪfɪ'keɪʃn/ n Befestigung f

fortify /'fɔːtɪfaɪ/ vt (pt/pp -ied) befestigen; (fig) stärken

fortitude /'fɔːtɪtjuːd/ n Standhaftigkeit f

fortnight /'fɔːt-/ n vierzehn Tage pl. ~ly a vierzehntäglich □ adv alle vierzehn Tage

fortress /'fɔːtrɪs/ n Festung f

fortuitous /fɔː'tjuːɪtəs/ a, -ly adv zufällig

fortunate /'fɔːtʃənət/ a glücklich; be ~ Glück haben. ~ly adv glücklicherweise

fortune /'fɔːtʃuːn/ n Glück nt; (money) Vermögen nt. ~-teller n Wahrsagerin f

forty /'fɔːtɪ/ a vierzig; have ~ winks (fam) ein Nickerchen machen □ n Vierzig f

forum /'fɔːrəm/ n Forum nt

forward /'fɔːwəd/ adv vorwärts; (to the front) nach vorn □ a Vorwärts-; (presumptuous) anmaßend □ n (Sport) Stürmer m □ vt nachsenden (letter). ~s adv vorwärts

fossil /'fosl/ n Fossil nt. ~ized a versteinert

foster /'fostə(r)/ vt fördern; in Pflege nehmen ⟨child⟩. ~-child n Pflegekind nt. ~-mother n Pflegemutter f

fought /fɔːt/ see fight

foul /faul/ a (-er, -est) widerlich; ⟨language⟩ unflätig; ~ play ⟨Jur⟩ Mord m □ n ⟨Sport⟩ Foul nt □ vt verschmutzen; ⟨obstruct⟩ blockieren; ⟨Sport⟩ foulen. ~-smelling a übel riechend

found[1] /faund/ see find

found[2] vt gründen

foundation /faun'deɪʃn/ n ⟨basis⟩ Grundlage f; ⟨charitable⟩ Stiftung f; ~s pl Fundament nt. ~-stone n Grundstein m

founder[1] /'faundə(r)/ n Gründer(in) m(f)

founder[2] vi ⟨ship:⟩ sinken; ⟨fig⟩ scheitern

foundry /'faundri/ n Gießerei f

fountain /'fauntɪn/ n Brunnen m. ~-pen n Füllfederhalter m

four /fɔː(r)/ a vier □ n Vier f

four: ~-'poster n Himmelbett nt. ~some /'fɔːsəm/ n in a ~some zu viert. ~-'teen a vierzehn □ n Vierzehn f. ~-'teenth a vierzehnte(r,s)

fourth /fɔːθ/ a vierte(r,s)

fowl /faul/ n Geflügel nt

fox /foks/ n Fuchs m □ vt ⟨puzzle⟩ verblüffen

foyer /'fɔɪeɪ/ n Foyer nt; ⟨in hotel⟩ Empfangshalle f

fraction /'frækʃn/ n Bruchteil m; ⟨Math⟩ Bruch m

fracture /'fræktʃə(r)/ n Bruch m □ vt/i brechen

fragile /'frædʒaɪl/ a zerbrechlich

fragment /'frægmənt/ n Bruchstück nt, Fragment nt. ~ary a bruchstückhaft

fragran|ce /'freɪgrəns/ n Duft m. ~t a duftend

frail /freɪl/ a (-er, -est) gebrechlich

frame /freɪm/ n Rahmen m; ⟨of spectacles⟩ Gestell nt; ⟨Anat⟩ Körperbau m; ~ of mind Gemütsverfassung f □ vt einrahmen; ⟨fig⟩ formulieren; ⟨sl⟩ ein Verbrechen anhängen (+ dat). ~-work n Gerüst nt; ⟨fig⟩ Gerippe nt

franc /fræŋk/ n ⟨French, Belgian⟩ Franc m; ⟨Swiss⟩ Franken m

France /frɑːns/ n Frankreich nt

franchise /'fræntʃaɪz/ n ⟨Pol⟩ Wahlrecht nt; ⟨Comm⟩ Franchise nt

frank[1] /fræŋk/ vt frankieren

frank[2] a, -ly adv offen

frankfurter /'fræŋkfɜːtə(r)/ n Frankfurter f

frantic /'fræntɪk/ a, -ally adv verzweifelt; be ~ außer sich ⟨dat⟩ sein (with vor)

fraternal /frə'tɜːnl/ a brüderlich

fraud /frɔːd/ n Betrug m; ⟨person⟩ Betrüger(in) m(f). ~ulent /-jʊlənt/ a betrügerisch

fraught /frɔːt/ a ~ with danger gefahrvoll

fray[1] /freɪ/ n Kampf m

fray[2] vi ausfransen

freak /friːk/ n Missbildung f; ⟨person⟩ Missgeburt f; ⟨phenomenon⟩ Ausnahmeerscheinung f □ a anormal. ~ish a anormal

freckle /'frekl/ n Sommersprosse f. ~d a sommersprossig

free /friː/ a (freer, freest) frei; ⟨ticket, copy, time⟩ Frei-; ⟨lavish⟩ freigebig; ~ [of charge] kostenlos; set ~ freilassen; ⟨rescue⟩ befreien; you are ~ to ... es steht Ihnen frei, zu ... □ vt ⟨pt/pp freed⟩ freilassen; ⟨rescue⟩ befreien; ⟨disentangle⟩ freibekommen

free: ~dom n Freiheit f. ~hand adv aus freier Hand. ~hold n [freier] Grundbesitz m. ~ 'kick n Freistoß m. ~lance a & adv freiberuflich. ~ly adv frei; ⟨voluntarily⟩ freiwillig; ⟨generously⟩ großzügig. F~mason n Freimaurer m. F~masonry n Freimaurerei f. ~-range a ~-range eggs Landeier pl. ~ 'sample n Gratisprobe f. ~style n Freistil m. ~way n ⟨Amer⟩ Autobahn f. ~-'wheel vi im Freilauf fahren

freez|e /friːz/ vt ⟨pt froze, pp frozen⟩ einfrieren; stoppen ⟨wages⟩ □ vi gefrieren; it's ~ing es friert

freez|er /'friːzə(r)/ n Gefriertruhe f; ⟨upright⟩ Gefrierschrank m. ~ing a eiskalt □ n below ~ing unter Null

freight /freɪt/ n Fracht f. ~er n Frachter m. ~ train n ⟨Amer⟩ Güterzug m

French /frentʃ/ a französisch □ n ⟨Lang⟩ Französisch nt; the ~ pl die Franzosen

French: ~ 'beans npl grüne Bohnen pl. ~ 'bread n Stangenbrot m. ~ 'fries npl Pommes frites pl. ~man n Franzose m. ~ 'window n Terrassentür f. ~woman n Französin f

frenzied /'frenzɪd/ a rasend

frenzy /'frenzi/ n Raserei f

frequency /'friːkwənsi/ n Häufigkeit f; ⟨Phys⟩ Frequenz f

frequent[1] /'friːkwənt/ a, -ly adv häufig

frequent[2] /frɪ'kwent/ vt regelmäßig besuchen

fresco /'freskəʊ/ n Fresko nt

fresh /freʃ/ a (-er, -est), -ly adv frisch; ⟨new⟩ neu; ⟨Amer: cheeky⟩ frech

freshen /'freʃn/ vi ⟨wind:⟩ auffrischen. ~ up vt auffrischen □ vi sich frisch machen

freshness /'freʃnɪs/ n Frische f

'freshwater a Süßwasser-

fret /fret/ vi ⟨pt/pp fretted⟩ sich grämen. ~ful a weinerlich

'fretsaw n Laubsäge f

friar /'fraɪə(r)/ n Mönch m

friction /'frɪkʃn/ n Reibung f; ⟨fig⟩ Reibereien pl

Friday /'fraɪdeɪ/ n Freitag m

fridge /frɪdʒ/ n Kühlschrank m

fried /fraɪd/ see fry² □ a gebraten; ~ egg Spiegelei nt

friend /frend/ n Freund(in) m(f). ~liness n Freundlichkeit f. ~ly a (-ier, -iest) freundlich; ~ly with befreundet mit. ~ship n Freundschaft f

frieze /fri:z/ n Fries m

fright /fraɪt/ n Schreck m

frighten /'fraɪtn/ vt Angst machen (+ dat); ⟨startle⟩ erschrecken; be ~ed Angst haben (of vor + dat). ~ing a Angst erregend

frightful /'fraɪtfl/ a, -ly adv schrecklich

frigid /'frɪdʒɪd/ a frostig; ⟨Psych⟩ frigide. ~ity /-'dʒɪdətɪ/ n Frostigkeit f; Frigidität f

frill /frɪl/ n Rüsche f; ⟨paper⟩ Manschette f. ~y a rüschenbesetzt

fringe /frɪndʒ/ n Fransen pl; ⟨of hair⟩ Pony m; ⟨fig: edge⟩ Rand m. ~ benefits npl zusätzliche Leistungen pl

frisk /frɪsk/ vi herumspringen □ vt ⟨search⟩ durchsuchen, ⟨fam⟩ filzen

frisky /'frɪskɪ/ a (-ier, -iest) lebhaft

fritter /'frɪtə(r)/ vt ~ [away] verplempern ⟨fam⟩

frivol|ity /frɪ'vɒlətɪ/ n Frivolität f. ~ous /'frɪvələs/ a, -ly adv frivol, leichtfertig

frizzy /'frɪzɪ/ a kraus

fro /frəʊ/ adv to and ~ hin und her

frock /frɒk/ n Kleid nt

frog /frɒg/ n Frosch m. ~man n Froschmann m. ~-spawn n Froschlaich m

frolic /'frɒlɪk/ vi ⟨pt/pp frolicked⟩ herumtollen

from /frɒm/ prep von (+ dat); ⟨out of⟩ aus (+ dat); ⟨according to⟩ nach (+ dat); ~ Monday ab Montag; ~ that day seit dem Tag

front /frʌnt/ n Vorderseite f; ⟨fig⟩ Fassade f; ⟨of garment⟩ Vorderteil nt; ⟨sea-⟩ Strandpromenade f; ⟨Mil, Pol, Meteorol⟩ Front f; in ~ of vor; in or at the ~ vorne; to the

~ nach vorne □ a vordere(r,s); ⟨page, row⟩ erste(r,s); ⟨tooth, wheel⟩ Vorder-

frontal /'frʌntl/ a Frontal-

front: ~ 'door n Haustür f. ~ 'garden n Vorgarten m

frontier /'frʌntɪə(r)/ n Grenze f

front-wheel 'drive n Vorderradantrieb m

frost /frɒst/ n Frost m; ⟨hoar-⟩ Raureif m; ten degrees of ~ zehn Grad Kälte. ~bite n Erfrierung f. ~bitten a erfroren

frost|ed /'frɒstɪd/ a ~ed glass Mattglas nt. ~ing n ⟨Amer Culin⟩ Zuckerguss m. ~y a, -ily adv frostig

froth /frɒθ/ n Schaum m □ vi schäumen. ~y a schaumig

frown /fraʊn/ n Stirnrunzeln nt □ vi die Stirn runzeln; ~ on missbilligen

froze /frəʊz/ see freeze

frozen /'frəʊzn/ see freeze □ a gefroren; ⟨Culin⟩ tiefgekühlt; I'm ~ ⟨fam⟩ mir ist eiskalt. ~ food n Tiefkühlkost f

frugal /'fru:gl/ a, -ly adv sparsam; ⟨meal⟩ frugal

fruit /fru:t/ n Frucht f; ⟨collectively⟩ Obst nt. ~ cake n englischer [Tee]kuchen m

fruit|erer /'fru:tərə(r)/ n Obsthändler m. ~ful a fruchtbar

fruition /fru:'ɪʃn/ n come to ~ sich verwirklichen

fruit: ~ juice n Obstsaft m. ~less a, -ly adv fruchtlos. ~ machine n Spielautomat m. ~ 'salad n Obstsalat m

fruity /'fru:tɪ/ a fruchtig

frumpy /'frʌmpɪ/ a unmodisch

frustrat|e /frʌ'streɪt/ vt vereiteln; ⟨psych⟩ frustrieren. ~ing a frustrierend. ~ion /-eɪʃn/ n Frustration f

fry¹ /fraɪ/ n inv small ~ ⟨fig⟩ kleine Fische pl

fry² vt/i ⟨pt/pp fried⟩ [in der Pfanne] braten. ~ing-pan n Bratpfanne f

fuck /fʌk/ vt/i ⟨vulg⟩ ficken. ~ing a ⟨vulg⟩ Scheiß-

fuddy-duddy /'fʌdɪdʌdɪ/ n ⟨fam⟩ verknöcherter Kerl m

fudge /fʌdʒ/ n weiche Karamellen pl

fuel /'fju:əl/ n Brennstoff m; ⟨for car⟩ Kraftstoff m; ⟨for aircraft⟩ Treibstoff m

fugitive /'fju:dʒətɪv/ n Flüchtling m

fugue /fju:g/ n ⟨Mus⟩ Fuge f

fulfil /fʊl'fɪl/ vt ⟨pt/pp -filled⟩ erfüllen. ~ment n Erfüllung f

full /fʊl/ a & adv (-er, -est) voll; ⟨detailed⟩ ausführlich; ⟨skirt⟩ weit; ~ of voll von (+ dat), voller (+ gen); at ~ speed in voller Fahrt □ n in ~ vollständig full: ~ 'moon n Vollmond m. ~-scale a (model) in Originalgröße; (rescue, alert) groß angelegt. ~ 'stop n Punkt m. ~-time a ganztägig □ adv ganztags

fully /'fʊlɪ/ adv völlig; (in detail) ausführlich

fulsome /'fʊlsəm/ a übertrieben

fumble /'fʌmbl/ vi herumfummeln (with an + dat)

fume /fjuːm/ vi vor Wut schäumen

fumes /fjuːmz/ npl Dämpfe pl; (from car) Abgase pl

fumigate /'fjuːmɪgeɪt/ vt ausräuchern

fun /fʌn/ n Spaß m; for ~ aus od zum Spaß; make ~ of sich lustig machen über (+ acc); have ~! viel Spaß!

function /'fʌŋkʃn/ n Funktion f; (event) Veranstaltung f □ vi funktionieren; (serve) dienen (as als). ~al a zweckmäßig

fund /fʌnd/ n Fonds m; (fig) Vorrat m; ~s pl Geldmittel pl □ vt finanzieren

fundamental /fʌndə'mentl/ a grundlegend; (essential) wesentlich

funeral /'fjuːnərl/ n Beerdigung f; (cremation) Feuerbestattung f

funeral: ~ directors pl, (Amer) ~ home n Bestattungsinstitut nt. ~ march n Trauermarsch m. ~ parlour n (Amer) Bestattungsinstitut nt. ~ service n Trauergottesdienst m

'funfair n Jahrmarkt m, Kirmes f

fungus /'fʌŋgəs/ n (pl -gi /-gaɪ/) Pilz m

funicular /fjuː'nɪkjʊlə(r)/ n Seilbahn f

funnel /'fʌnl/ n Trichter m; (on ship, train) Schornstein m

funnily /'fʌnɪlɪ/ adv komisch; ~ enough komischerweise

funny /'fʌnɪ/ a (-ier, -iest) komisch. ~-bone n (fam) Musikantenknochen m

fur /fɜː(r)/ n Fell nt; (for clothing) Pelz m; (in kettle) Kesselstein m. ~ 'coat n Pelzmantel m

furious /'fjʊərɪəs/ a, -ly adv wütend (with auf + acc)

furnace /'fɜːnɪs/ n (Techn) Ofen m

furnish /'fɜːnɪʃ/ vt einrichten; (supply) liefern. ~ed a ~ed room möbliertes Zimmer m. ~ings npl Einrichtungsgegenstände pl

furniture /'fɜːnɪtʃə(r)/ n Möbel pl

furred /fɜːd/ a (tongue) belegt

furrow /'fʌrəʊ/ n Furche f

furry /'fɜːrɪ/ a (animal) Pelz-; (toy) Plüsch-

further /'fɜːðə(r)/ a weitere(r,s); at the ~ end am anderen Ende; until ~ notice bis auf weiteres □ adv weiter; ~ off weiter entfernt □ vt fördern

further: ~ edu'cation n Weiterbildung f. ~'more adv überdies

furthest /'fɜːðɪst/ a am weitesten entfernt □ adv am weitesten

furtive /'fɜːtɪv/ a, -ly adv verstohlen

fury /'fjʊərɪ/ n Wut f

fuse¹ /fjuːz/ n (of bomb) Zünder m; (cord) Zündschnur f

fuse² n (Electr) Sicherung f □ vt/i verschmelzen; the lights have ~d die Sicherung [für das Licht] ist durchgebrannt. ~-box n Sicherungskasten m

fuselage /'fjuːzəlɑːʒ/ n (Aviat) Rumpf m

fusion /'fjuːʒn/ n Verschmelzung f, Fusion f

fuss /fʌs/ n Getue nt; make a ~ of verwöhnen; (caress) liebkosen □ vi Umstände machen

fussy /'fʌsɪ/ a (-ier, -iest) wählerisch; (particular) penibel

fusty /'fʌstɪ/ a moderig

futile /'fjuːtaɪl/ a zwecklos. ~ity /-'tɪlətɪ/ n Zwecklosigkeit f

future /'fjuːtʃə(r)/ a zukünftig □ n Zukunft f; (Gram) [erstes] Futur nt; ~ perfect zweites Futur nt; in ~ in Zukunft

futuristic /fjuːtʃə'rɪstɪk/ a futuristisch

fuzz /fʌz/ n the ~ (sl) die Bullen pl

fuzzy /'fʌzɪ/ a (-ier, -iest) (hair) kraus; (blurred) verschwommen

G

gab /gæb/ n (fam) have the gift of the ~ gut reden können

gabble /'gæbl/ vi schnell reden

gable /'geɪbl/ n Giebel m

gad /gæd/ vi (pt/pp gadded) ~ about dauernd ausgehen

gadget /'gædʒɪt/ n [kleines] Gerät nt

Gaelic /'geɪlɪk/ n Gälisch nt

gaffe /gæf/ n Fauxpas m

gag /gæg/ n Knebel m; (joke) Witz m; (Theat) Gag m □ vt (pt/pp gagged) knebeln

gaiety /'geɪətɪ/ n Fröhlichkeit f

gaily /'geɪlɪ/ adv fröhlich

gain /geɪn/ n Gewinn m; (increase) Zunahme f □ vt gewinnen; (obtain) erlangen; ~ weight zunehmen □ vi (clock:) vorgehen. ~ful a ~ful employment Erwerbstätigkeit f

gait /geɪt/ n Gang m

gala /'gɑːlə/ n Fest nt; swimming ~ Schwimmfest nt □ attrib Gala-

galaxy /'gæləksɪ/ n Galaxie f; the G~ die Milchstraße

gale /geɪl/ n Sturm m

gall /gɔːl/ n Galle f; (impudence) Frechheit f

gallant /'gælənt/ a, -ly adv tapfer; (chivalrous) galant. ~ry n Tapferkeit f

'gall-bladder n Gallenblase f

gallery /'gælərɪ/ n Galerie f

galley /'gælɪ/ n (ship's kitchen) Kombüse f; ~ [proof] [Druck]fahne f

gallivant /'gælɪvænt/ vi (fam) ausgehen

gallon /'gælən/ n Gallone f (= 4,5 l; Amer = 3,785 l)

gallop /'gæləp/ n Galopp m □ vi galoppieren

gallows /'gæləʊz/ n Galgen m

'gallstone n Gallenstein m

galore /gə'lɔː(r)/ adv in Hülle und Fülle

galvanize /'gælvənaɪz/ vt galvanisieren

gambit /'gæmbɪt/ n Eröffnungsmanöver nt

gamble /'gæmbl/ n (risk) Risiko nt □ vi [um Geld] spielen; ~ on (rely) sich verlassen auf (+ acc). ~r n Spieler(in) m(f)

game /geɪm/ n Spiel nt; (animals, birds) Wild nt; ~s (Sch) Sport m □ a (brave) tapfer; (willing) bereit (for zu). ~keeper n Wildhüter m

gammon /'gæmən/ n [geräucherter] Schinken m

gamut /'gæmət/ n Skala f

gander /'gændə(r)/ n Gänserich m

gang /gæŋ/ n Bande f; (of workmen) Kolonne f □ vi ~ up sich zusammenrotten (on gegen)

gangling /'gæŋglɪŋ/ a schlaksig

gangrene /'gæŋgriːn/ n Wundbrand m

gangster /'gæŋstə(r)/ n Gangster m

gangway /'gæŋweɪ/ n Gang m; (Naut, Aviat) Gangway f

gaol /dʒeɪl/ n Gefängnis nt □ vt ins Gefängnis sperren. ~er n Gefängniswärter m

gap /gæp/ n Lücke f; (interval) Pause f; (difference) Unterschied m

gape /geɪp/ vi gaffen; ~e at anstarren. ~ing a klaffend

garage /'gærɑːʒ/ n Garage f; (for repairs) Werkstatt f; (for petrol) Tankstelle f

garb /gɑːb/ n Kleidung f

garbage /'gɑːbɪdʒ/ n Müll m. ~ can n (Amer) Mülleimer m

garbled /'gɑːbld/ a verworren

garden /'gɑːdn/ n Garten m; [public] ~s pl [öffentliche] Anlagen pl □ vi im Garten arbeiten. ~er n Gärtner(in) m(f). ~ing n Gartenarbeit f

gargle /'gɑːgl/ n (liquid) Gurgelwasser nt □ vi gurgeln

gargoyle /'gɑːgɔɪl/ n Wasserspeier m

garish /'geərɪʃ/ a grell

garland /'gɑːlənd/ n Girlande f

garlic /'gɑːlɪk/ n Knoblauch m

garment /'gɑːmənt/ n Kleidungsstück nt

garnet /'gɑːnɪt/ n Granat m

garnish /'gɑːnɪʃ/ n Garnierung f □ vt garnieren

garret /'gærɪt/ n Dachstube f

garrison /'gærɪsn/ n Garnison f

garrulous /'gærʊləs/ a geschwätzig

garter /'gɑːtə(r)/ n Strumpfband nt; (Amer: suspender) Strumpfhalter m

gas /gæs/ n Gas nt; (Amer fam: petrol) Benzin nt □ v (pt/pp gassed) □ vt vergasen □ vi (fam) schwatzen. ~ cooker n Gasherd m. ~ 'fire n Gasofen m

gash /gæʃ/ n Schnitt m; (wound) klaffende Wunde f □ vt ~ one's arm sich (dat) den Arm aufschlitzen

gasket /'gæskɪt/ n (Techn) Dichtung f

gas: ~ mask n Gasmaske f. ~-meter n Gaszähler m

gasoline /'gæsəliːn/ n (Amer) Benzin nt

gasp /gɑːsp/ vi keuchen; (in surprise) hörbar die Luft einziehen

'gas station n (Amer) Tankstelle f

gastric /'gæstrɪk/ a Magen-. ~ 'flu n Darmgrippe f. ~ 'ulcer n Magengeschwür nt

gastronomy /gæ'strɒnəmɪ/ n Gastronomie f

gate /geɪt/ n Tor nt; (to field) Gatter nt; (barrier) Schranke f; (at airport) Flugsteig m

gâteau /'gætəʊ/ n Torte f

gate: ~crasher n ungeladener Gast m. ~way n Tor nt

gather /'gæðə(r)/ vt sammeln; (pick) pflücken; (conclude) folgern (from aus); (Sewing) kräuseln; ~ speed schneller werden □ vi sich versammeln; ⟨storm:⟩ sich zusammenziehen. ~ing n family ~ing Familientreffen nt

gaudy /'gɔːdɪ/ a (-ier, -iest) knallig

gauge /geɪdʒ/ n Stärke f; (Rail) Spurweite f; (device) Messinstrument nt □ vt messen; (estimate) schätzen

gaunt /gɔːnt/ a hager

gauntlet /'gɔːntlɪt/ n run the ~ Spießruten laufen

gauze /gɔːz/ n Gaze f

gave /geɪv/ *see* give

gawky /'gɔːkɪ/ *a* (-ier, -iest) schlaksig

gawp /gɔːp/ *vi* (*fam*) glotzen; ∼ at anglotzen

gay /geɪ/ *a* (-er, -est) fröhlich; (*fam*) homosexuell, (*fam*) schwul

gaze /geɪz/ *n* [langer] Blick *m* □ *vi* sehen; ∼ at ansehen

gazelle /gə'zel/ *n* Gazelle *f*

GB *abbr of* Great Britain

gear /gɪə(r)/ *n* Ausrüstung *f*; (*Techn*) Getriebe *nt*; (*Auto*) Gang *m*; in ∼ mit eingelegtem Gang; change ∼ schalten □ *vt* anpassen (to *dat*)

gear: ∼box *n* (*Auto*) Getriebe *nt*. ∼lever *n*, (*Amer*) ∼shift *n* Schalthebel *m*

geese /giːs/ *see* goose

geezer /'giːzə(r)/ *n* (*sl*) Typ *m*

gel /dʒel/ *n* Gel *nt*

gelatine /'dʒelətɪn/ *n* Gelatine *f*

gelignite /'dʒelɪgnaɪt/ *n* Gelatinedynamit *nt*

gem /dʒem/ *n* Juwel *nt*

Gemini /'dʒemɪnaɪ/ *n* (*Astr*) Zwillinge *pl*

gender /'dʒendə(r)/ *n* (*Gram*) Geschlecht *nt*

gene /dʒiːn/ *n* Gen *nt*

genealogy /dʒiːnɪ'ælədʒɪ/ *n* Genealogie *f*

general /'dʒenrəl/ *a* allgemein □ *n* General *m*; in ∼ im Allgemeinen. ∼ e'lection *n* allgemeine Wahlen *pl*

generaliz|ation /dʒenrəlaɪ'zeɪʃn/ *n* Verallgemeinerung *f*. ∼e /'dʒenrəlaɪz/ *vi* verallgemeinern

generally /'dʒenrəlɪ/ *adv* im Allgemeinen

general prac'titioner *n* praktischer Arzt *m*

generate /'dʒenəreɪt/ *vt* erzeugen

generation /dʒenə'reɪʃn/ *n* Generation *f*

generator /'dʒenəreɪtə(r)/ *n* Generator *m*

generic /dʒɪ'nerɪk/ *a* ∼ term Oberbegriff *m*

generosity /dʒenə'rɒsɪtɪ/ *n* Großzügigkeit *f*

generous /'dʒenərəs/ *a*, -ly *adv* großzügig

genetic /dʒɪ'netɪk/ *a* genetisch. ∼ engineering *n* Gentechnologie *f*. ∼s *n* Genetik *f*

Geneva /dʒɪ'niːvə/ *n* Genf *nt*

genial /'dʒiːnɪəl/ *a*, -ly *adv* freundlich

genitals /'dʒenɪtlz/ *pl* [äußere] Geschlechtsteile *pl*

genitive /'dʒenɪtɪv/ *a & n* ∼ [case] Genitiv *m*

genius /'dʒiːnɪəs/ *n* (*pl* -uses) Genie *nt*; (*quality*) Genialität *f*

genocide /'dʒenəsaɪd/ *n* Völkermord *m*

genre /'ʒãrə/ *n* Gattung *f*, Genre *nt*

gent /dʒent/ *n* (*fam*) Herr *m*; the ∼s *sg* die Herrentoilette *f*

genteel /dʒen'tiːl/ *a* vornehm

gentle /'dʒentl/ *a* (-r, -st) sanft

gentleman /'dʒentlmən/ *n* Herr *m*; (*well-mannered*) Gentleman *m*

gent|leness /'dʒentlnɪs/ *n* Sanftheit *f*. ∼ly *adv* sanft

genuine /'dʒenjʊɪn/ *a* echt; (*sincere*) aufrichtig. ∼ly *adv* (*honestly*) ehrlich

genus /'dʒiːnəs/ *n* (*Biol*) Gattung *f*

geograph|ical /dʒɪə'græfɪkl/ *a*, -ly *adv* geographisch. ∼y /dʒɪ'ɒgrəfɪ/ *n* Geographie *f*, Erdkunde *f*

geological /dʒɪə'lɒdʒɪkl/ *a*, -ly *adv* geologisch

geolog|ist /dʒɪ'ɒlədʒɪst/ *n* Geologe *m* /-gin *f*. ∼y *n* Geologie *f*

geometr|ic(al) /dʒɪə'metrɪk(l)/ *a* geometrisch. ∼y /dʒɪ'ɒmətrɪ/ *n* Geometrie *f*

geranium /dʒə'reɪnɪəm/ *n* Geranie *f*

geriatric /dʒerɪ'ætrɪk/ *a* geriatrisch □ *n* geriatrischer Patient *m*. ∼s *n* Geriatrie *f*

germ /dʒɜːm/ *n* Keim *m*; ∼s *pl* (*fam*) Bazillen *pl*

German /'dʒɜːmən/ *a* deutsch □ *n* (*person*) Deutsche(r) *m*/*f*; (*Lang*) Deutsch *nt*; in ∼ auf Deutsch; into ∼ ins Deutsche

Germanic /dʒə'mænɪk/ *a* germanisch

German: ∼ 'measles *n* Röteln *pl*. ∼ 'shepherd [dog] *n* [deutscher] Schäferhund *m*

Germany /'dʒɜːmənɪ/ *n* Deutschland *nt*

germinate /'dʒɜːmɪneɪt/ *vi* keimen

gesticulate /dʒe'stɪkjʊleɪt/ *vi* gestikulieren

gesture /'dʒestʃə(r)/ *n* Geste *f*

get /get/ *v* (*pt*/*pp* got, *pp Amer also* gotten, *pres p* getting) □ *vt* bekommen, (*fam*) kriegen; (*procure*) besorgen; (*buy*) kaufen; (*fetch*) holen; (*take*) bringen; (*on telephone*) erreichen; (*fam: understand*) kapieren; machen ⟨*meal*⟩; ∼ s.o. to do sth jdn dazu bringen, etw zu tun □ *vi* (*become*) werden; ∼ to kommen zu/nach ⟨*town*⟩; (*reach*) erreichen; ∼ dressed sich anziehen; ∼ married heiraten. ∼ at *vt* herankommen an (+ *acc*); what are you ∼ting at? worauf willst du hinaus? ∼ away *vi* (*leave*) weggehen; (*escape*) entkommen. ∼ back *vi* zurückkommen □ *vt* (*recover*) zurückbekommen; one's own back sich revanchieren. ∼ by *vi* vorbeikommen; (*manage*) sein Auskommen haben. ∼ down *vi* heruntersteigen; ∼ down to sich [heran]machen an (+ *acc*) □ *vt* (*depress*) deprimieren. ∼ in *vi* einsteigen □ *vt* (*fetch*) hereinholen. ∼ off *vi* (*dismount*) absteigen; (*from bus*) aussteigen; (*leave*) wegkommen, (*Jur*) freigesprochen werden □ *vt* (*remove*) abbekommen. ~ on *vi* (*mount*) aufsteigen; (*to bus*) einsteigen; (*be on good terms*) gut auskommen (with mit); (*make progress*) Fortschritte machen; how are you ~ting on? wie geht's? ~ out *vi* herauskommen; (*of car*) aussteigen; ~ out of (*avoid doing*) sich drücken um □ *vt* herausholen; herauskommen (*cork, stain*). ~ over *vi* hinübersteigen □ *vt* (*fig*) hinwegkommen über (+ *acc*). ~ round *vi* herumkommen; I never ~ round to it ich komme nie dazu □ *vt* herumkriegen; (*avoid*) umgehen. ~ through *vi* durchkommen. ~ up *vi* aufstehen

get: ~away *n* Flucht *f*. ~-up *n* Aufmachung *f*

geyser /'giːzə(r)/ *n* Durchlauferhitzer *m*; (*Geol*) Geysir *m*

ghastly /'gɑːstlɪ/ *a* (-ier, -iest) grässlich; (*pale*) blass

gherkin /'gɜːkɪn/ *n* Essiggurke *f*

ghetto /'getəʊ/ *n* Getto *nt*

ghost /gəʊst/ *n* Geist *m*, Gespenst *nt*. ~ly *a* geisterhaft

ghoulish /'guːlɪʃ/ *a* makaber

giant /'dʒaɪənt/ *n* Riese *m* □ *a* riesig

gibberish /'dʒɪbərɪʃ/ *n* Kauderwelsch *nt*

gibe /dʒaɪb/ *n* spöttische Bemerkung *f* □ *vi* spotten (at über + *acc*)

giblets /'dʒɪblɪts/ *npl* Geflügelklein *nt*

giddiness /'gɪdɪnɪs/ *n* Schwindel *m*

giddy /'gɪdɪ/ *a* (-ier, -iest) schwindlig; I feel ~ mir ist schwindlig

gift /gɪft/ *n* Geschenk *nt*; (*to charity*) Gabe *f*; (*talent*) Begabung *f*. ~ed /-ɪd/ *a* begabt. ~-wrap *vt* als Geschenk einpacken

gig /gɪg/ *n* (*fam, Mus*) Gig *m*

gigantic /dʒaɪˈgæntɪk/ *a* riesig, riesengroß

giggle /'gɪgl/ *n* Kichern *nt* □ *vi* kichern

gild /gɪld/ *vt* vergolden

gills /gɪlz/ *npl* Kiemen *pl*

gilt /gɪlt/ *a* vergoldet □ *n* Vergoldung *f*. ~-edged *a* (*Comm*) mündelsicher

gimmick /'gɪmɪk/ *n* Trick *m*

gin /dʒɪn/ *n* Gin *m*

ginger /'dʒɪndʒə(r)/ *a* rotblond; (*cat*) rot □ *n* Ingwer *m*. ~bread *n* Pfefferkuchen *m*

gingerly /'dʒɪndʒəlɪ/ *adv* vorsichtig

gipsy /'dʒɪpsɪ/ *n* = gypsy

giraffe /dʒɪˈrɑːf/ *n* Giraffe *f*

girder /'gɜːdə(r)/ *n* (*Techn*) Träger *m*

girdle /'gɜːdl/ *n* Bindegürtel *m*; (*corset*) Hüfthalter *m*

girl /gɜːl/ *n* Mädchen *nt*; (*young woman*) junge Frau *f*. ~friend *n* Freundin *f*. ~ish *a*, -ly *adv* mädchenhaft

giro /'dʒaɪərəʊ/ *n* Giro *nt*; (*cheque*) Postscheck *m*

girth /gɜːθ/ *n* Umfang *m*; (*for horse*) Bauchgurt *m*

gist /dʒɪst/ *n* the ~ das Wesentliche

give /gɪv/ *n* Elastizität *f* □ *v* (*pt* gave, *pp* given) □ *vt* geben; (*as present*) schenken (to *dat*); (*donate*) spenden; (*lecture*) halten; (*one's name*) angeben □ *vi* geben; (*yield*) nachgeben. ~ away *vt* verschenken; (*betray*) verraten; (*distribute*) verteilen; ~ away the bride ≈ Brautführer sein. ~ back *vt* zurückgeben. ~ in *vt* einreichen □ *vi* (*yield*) nachgeben. ~ off *vt* abgeben. ~ up *vt/i* aufgeben; ~ oneself up *vt* sich stellen. ~ way *vi* nachgeben; (*Auto*) die Vorfahrt beachten

given /'gɪvn/ *see* give □ *a* ~ name Vorname *m*

glacier /'glæsɪə(r)/ *n* Gletscher *m*

glad /glæd/ *a* froh (of über + *acc*). ~den /'glædn/ *vt* erfreuen

glade /gleɪd/ *n* Lichtung *f*

gladly /'glædlɪ/ *adv* gern[e]

glamorous /'glæmərəs/ *a* glanzvoll; (*film star*) glamourös

glamour /'glæmə(r)/ *n* [betörender] Glanz *m*

glance /glɑːns/ *n* [flüchtiger] Blick *m* □ *vi* ~ at einen Blick werfen auf (+ *acc*). ~ up *vi* aufblicken

gland /glænd/ *n* Drüse *f*

glandular /'glændjʊlə(r)/ *a* Drüsen-

glare /gleə(r)/ *n* grelles Licht *nt*; (*look*) ärgerlicher Blick *m* □ *vi* ~ at böse ansehen

glaring /'gleərɪŋ/ *a* grell; (*mistake*) krass

glass /glɑːs/ *n* Glas *nt*; (*mirror*) Spiegel *m*; ~es *pl* (*spectacles*) Brille *f*. ~y *a* glasig

glaze /gleɪz/ *n* Glasur *f* □ *vt* verglasen; (*Culin, Pottery*) glasieren

glazier /'gleɪzɪə(r)/ *n* Glaser *m*

gleam /gliːm/ *n* Schein *m* □ *vi* glänzen

glean /gliːn/ *vi* Ähren lesen □ *vt* (*learn*) erfahren

glee /gliː/ *n* Frohlocken *nt*. ~ful *a*, -ly *adv* frohlockend

glen /glen/ *n* [enges] Tal *nt*

glib /glɪb/ *a*, -ly *adv* (*pej*) gewandt

glid|e /glaɪd/ *vi* gleiten; (*through the air*) schweben. ~er *n* Segelflugzeug *nt*. ~ing *n* Segelfliegen *nt*

glimmer /'glɪmə(r)/ *n* Glimmen *nt* □ *vi* glimmen

glimpse /glɪmps/ *n* catch a ~ of flüchtig sehen □ *vt* flüchtig sehen

glint /glɪnt/ n Blitzen nt ◻ vi blitzen

glisten /'glɪsn/ vi glitzern

glitter /'glɪtə(r)/ vi glitzern

gloat /gləʊt/ vi schadenfroh sein; ~ over sich weiden an (+ dat)

global /'gləʊbl/ a, -ly adv global

globe /gləʊb/ n Kugel f; (map) Globus m

gloom /gluːm/ n Düsterkeit f; (fig) Pessimismus m

gloomy /'gluːmɪ/ a (-ier, -iest), -ily adv düster; (fig) perssimistisch

glorif|y /'glɔːrɪfaɪ/ vt (pt/pp -ied) verherrlichen; a ~ied waitress eine bessere Kellnerin f

glorious /'glɔːrɪəs/ a herrlich; ⟨deed, hero⟩ glorreich

glory /'glɔːrɪ/ n Ruhm m; (splendour) Pracht f ◻ vi ~ in genießen

gloss /glɒs/ n Glanz m ◻ a Glanz- ◻ vi ~ over beschönigen

glossary /'glɒsərɪ/ n Glossar nt

glossy /'glɒsɪ/ a (-ier, -iest) glänzend

glove /glʌv/ n Handschuh m. ~ compartment n (Auto) Handschuhfach nt

glow /gləʊ/ n Glut f; (of candle) Schein m ◻ vi glühen; ⟨candle:⟩ scheinen. ~ing a glühend; ⟨account⟩ begeistert

'glow-worm n Glühwürmchen nt

glucose /'gluːkəʊs/ n Traubenzucker m, Glukose f

glue /gluː/ n Klebstoff m ◻ vt (pres p gluing) kleben (to an + acc)

glum /glʌm/ a (glummer, glummest), -ly adv niedergeschlagen

glut /glʌt/ n Überfluss m (of an + dat); ~ of fruit Obstschwemme f

glutton /'glʌtən/ n Vielfraß m. ~ous /-əs/ a gefräßig. ~y n Gefräßigkeit f

gnarled /nɑːld/ a knorrig; ⟨hands⟩ knotig

gnash /næʃ/ vt ~ one's teeth mit den Zähnen knirschen

gnat /næt/ n Mücke f

gnaw /nɔː/ vt/i nagen (at an + dat)

gnome /nəʊm/ n Gnom m

go /gəʊ/ n (pl goes) Energie f; (attempt) Versuch m; on the go auf Trab; at one go auf einmal; it's your go du bist dran; make a go of it Erfolg haben ◻ vi (pt went, pp gone) gehen; (in vehicle) fahren; (leave) weggehen; (on journey) abfahren; ⟨time:⟩ vergehen; (vanish) verschwinden; (fail) versagen; (become) werden; (belong) kommen; go swimming/shopping schwimmen/einkaufen gehen; where are you going? wo gehst du hin? it's all gone es ist nichts mehr übrig; I am not going to ich werde es nicht tun; 'to go' (Amer) 'zum Mitnehmen'. go away vi weggehen/ -fahren. go back vi zurückgehen/-fahren.

go by vi vorbeigehen/-fahren; ⟨time:⟩ vergehen. go down vi hinuntergehen/ -fahren; ⟨sun, ship:⟩ untergehen; ⟨prices:⟩ fallen; ⟨temperature, swelling:⟩ zurückgehen. go for vt holen; ⟨fam: attack⟩ losgehen auf (+ acc). go in vi hineingehen/ -fahren; go in for teilnehmen an (+ dat) ⟨competition⟩; (take up) sich verlegen auf (+ acc). go off vi weggehen/-fahren; ⟨alarm:⟩ klingeln; ⟨gun, bomb:⟩ losgehen; (go bad) schlecht werden; go off well gut verlaufen. go on vi weitergehen/-fahren; (continue) weitermachen; (talking) fortfahren; (happen) vorgehen; go on at (fam) herumnörgeln an (+ dat). go out vi ausgehen; (leave) hinausgehen/-fahren. go over vi hinübergehen/-fahren ◻ vt (check) durchgehen. go round vi herumgehen/-fahren; (visit) vorbeigehen; (turn) sich drehen; (be enough) reichen. go through vi durchgehen/-fahren ◻ vt (suffer) durchmachen; (check) durchgehen. go under vi untergehen; (fail) scheitern. go up vi hinaufgehen/-fahren; ⟨lift:⟩ hochfahren; ⟨prices:⟩ steigen. go without vt verzichten auf (+ acc) ◻ vi darauf verzichten

goad /gəʊd/ vt anstacheln (into zu); (taunt) reizen

'go-ahead a fortschrittlich; (enterprising) unternehmend ◻ n (fig) grünes Licht nt

goal /gəʊl/ n Ziel nt; (sport) Tor nt. ~keeper n Torwart m. ~-post n Torpfosten m

goat /gəʊt/ n Ziege f

gobble /'gɒbl/ vt hinunterschlingen

'go-between n Vermittler(in) m(f)

goblet /'gɒblɪt/ n Pokal m; (glass) Kelchglas nt

goblin /'gɒblɪn/ n Kobold m

God, god /gɒd/ n Gott m

god: ~child n Patenkind nt. ~daughter n Patentochter f. ~dess n Göttin f. ~father n Pate m. G~-forsaken a gottverlassen. ~mother n Patin f. ~parents npl Paten pl. ~send n Segen m. ~son n Patensohn m

goggle /'gɒgl/ vi (fam) ~ at anglotzen. ~s npl Schutzbrille f

going /'gəʊɪŋ/ a ⟨price, rate⟩ gängig; ⟨concern⟩ gut gehend ◻ n it is hard ~ es ist schwierig; while the ~ is good solange es noch geht. ~s-'on npl [seltsame] Vorgänge pl

gold /gəʊld/ n Gold nt ◻ a golden

golden /'gəʊldn/ a golden. ~ 'handshake n hohe Abfindungssumme f. ~ 'wedding n goldene Hochzeit f

gold: ~fish n inv Goldfisch m. ~-mine n Goldgrube f. ~-plated a vergoldet. ~smith n Goldschmied m golf /gɒlf/ n Golf nt

golf: ~club n Golfklub m; (implement) Golfschläger m. ~course n Golfplatz m. ~er m Golfspieler(in) m(f)

gondo|la /'gɒndələ/ n Gondel f. ~lier /-'lɪə(r)/ n Gondoliere m

gone /gɒn/ see go

gong /gɒŋ/ n Gong m

good /gʊd/ a (better, best) gut; (well-behaved) brav, artig; ~ at gut in (+ dat); a ~ deal ziemlich viel; as ~ as so gut wie; (almost) fast; ~ morning/evening guten Morgen/Abend; ~ afternoon guten Tag; ~ night gute Nacht □ n the ~ das Gute; for ~ für immer; do ~ Gutes tun; do s.o. ~ jdm gut tun; it's no ~ es ist nutzlos; (hopeless) da ist nichts zu machen; be up to no ~ nichts Gutes im Schilde führen

goodbye /gʊd'baɪ/ int auf Wiedersehen; (Teleph, Radio) auf Wiederhören

good: ~-for-nothing a nichtsnutzig □ n Taugenichts m. G~ 'Friday n Karfreitag m. ~-'looking a gut aussehend. ~-'natured a gutmütig

goodness /'gʊdnɪs/ n Güte f; my ~! du meine Güte! thank ~! Gott sei Dank!

goods /gʊdz/ npl Waren pl. ~ train n Güterzug m

good'will n Wohlwollen nt; (Comm) Goodwill m

goody /'gʊdɪ/ n (fam) Gute(r) m/f. ~-goody n Musterkind n

gooey /'guːɪ/ a (fam) klebrig

goof /guːf/ vi (fam) einen Schnitzer machen

goose /guːs/ n (pl geese) Gans f

gooseberry /'gʊzbərɪ/ n Stachelbeere f

goose /guːs/: ~-flesh n, ~-pimples npl Gänsehaut f

gore¹ /gɔː(r)/ n Blut nt

gore² vt mit den Hörnern aufspießen

gorge /gɔːdʒ/ n (Geog) Schlucht f □ vt ~ oneself sich vollessen

gorgeous /'gɔːdʒəs/ a prachtvoll; (fam) herrlich

gorilla /gə'rɪlə/ n Gorilla m

gormless /'gɔːmlɪs/ a (fam) doof

gorse /gɔːs/ n inv Stechginster m

gory /'gɔːrɪ/ a (-ier, -iest) blutig; (story) blutrünstig

gosh /gɒʃ/ int (fam) Mensch!

go-'slow n Bummelstreik m

gospel /'gɒspl/ n Evangelium nt

gossip /'gɒsɪp/ n Klatsch m; (person) Klatschbase f □ vi klatschen. ~y a geschwätzig

got /gɒt/ see get; have ~ haben; have ~ to müssen; have ~ to do sth etw tun müssen

Gothic /'gɒθɪk/ a gotisch

gotten /'gɒtn/ see get

gouge /gaʊdʒ/ vt ~ out aushöhlen

goulash /'guːlæʃ/ n Gulasch nt

gourmet /'ɡʊəmeɪ/ n Feinschmecker m

gout /gaʊt/ n Gicht f

govern /'gʌvn/ vt/i regieren; (determine) bestimmen. ~ess n Gouvernante f

government /'gʌvnmənt/ n Regierung f. ~al /-'mentl/ a Regierungs-

governor /'gʌvnə(r)/ n Gouverneur m; (on board) Vorstandsmitglied nt; (of prison) Direktor m; (fam: boss) Chef m

gown /gaʊn/ n [elegantes] Kleid nt; (Univ, Jur) Talar m

GP abbr of general practitioner

grab /græb/ vt (pt/pp grabbed) ergreifen; ~ [hold of] packen

grace /greɪs/ n Anmut f; (before meal) Tischgebet nt; (Relig) Gnade f; with good ~ mit Anstand; say ~ [vor dem Essen] beten; three days' ~ drei Tage Frist. ~ful a, -ly adv anmutig

gracious /'greɪʃəs/ a gnädig; (elegant) vornehm

grade /greɪd/ n Stufe f; (Comm) Güteklasse f; (Sch) Note f; (Amer, Sch: class) Klasse f; (Amer) = gradient □ vt einstufen; (Comm) sortieren. ~ crossing n (Amer) Bahnübergang m

gradient /'greɪdɪənt/ n Steigung f; (downward) Gefälle nt

gradual /'grædjʊəl/ a, -ly adv allmählich

graduate¹ /'grædjʊət/ n Akademiker(in) m(f)

graduate² /'grædjʊeɪt/ vi (Univ) sein Examen machen. ~d a abgestuft; (container) mit Maßeinteilung

graffiti /grə'fiːtɪ/ npl Graffiti pl

graft /grɑːft/ n (Bot) Pfropfreis nt; (Med) Transplantat nt; (fam: hard work) Plackerei f □ vt (Bot) aufpfropfen; (Med) übertragen

grain /greɪn/ n (sand, salt, rice) Korn n; (cereals) Getreide nt; (in wood) Maserung f; against the ~ (fig) gegen den Strich

gram /græm/ n Gramm nt

grammar /'græmə(r)/ n Grammatik f. ~ school n ≈ Gymnasium nt

grammatical /grə'mætɪkl/ a, -ly adv grammatisch

granary /'grænərɪ/ n Getreidespeicher m

grand /grænd/ a (-er, -est) großartig

grandad /'grændæd/ n (fam) Opa m

'grandchild n Enkelkind nt

'granddaughter n Enkelin f

grandeur /'grændʒə(r)/ n Pracht f

'**grandfather** n Großvater m. ~ **clock** n Standuhr f

grandiose /'grændɪəʊs/ a grandios

grand: ~**mother** n Großmutter f. ~**parents** npl Großeltern pl. ~**pi'ano** n Flügel m. ~**son** n Enkel m. ~**stand** n Tribüne f

granite /'grænɪt/ n Granit m

granny /'grænɪ/ n (fam) Oma f

grant /grɑːnt/ n Subvention f; (Univ) Studienbeihilfe f □ vt gewähren; (admit) zugeben; **take sth for** ~**ed** etw als selbstverständlich hinnehmen

granular /'grænjʊlə(r)/ a körnig

granulated /'grænjʊleɪtɪd/ a ~ **sugar** Kristallzucker m

granule /'grænjuːl/ n Körnchen nt

grape /greɪp/ n [Wein]traube f; **bunch of** ~**s** [ganze] Weintraube f

grapefruit /'greɪp-/ n invar Grapefruit f, Pampelmuse f

graph /grɑːf/ n Kurvendiagramm nt

graphic /'græfɪk/ a, -**ally** adv grafisch; (vivid) anschaulich. ~**s** n (design) grafische Gestaltung f

'**graph paper** n Millimeterpapier nt

grapple /'græpl/ vi ringen

grasp /grɑːsp/ n Griff m □ vt ergreifen; (understand) begreifen. ~**ing** a habgierig

grass /grɑːs/ n Gras nt; (lawn) Rasen m; **at the** ~ **roots** an der Basis. ~**hopper** n Heuschrecke f. ~**land** n Weideland nt

grassy /'grɑːsɪ/ a grasig

grate[1] /greɪt/ n Feuerrost m; (hearth) Kamin m

grate[2] vt (Culin) reiben; ~ **one's teeth** mit den Zähnen knirschen

grateful /'greɪtfl/ a, -**ly** adv dankbar (to dat)

grater /'greɪtə(r)/ n (Culin) Reibe f

gratify /'grætɪfaɪ/ vt (pt/pp -ied) befriedigen. ~**ing** a erfreulich

grating /'greɪtɪŋ/ n Gitter nt

gratis /'grɑːtɪs/ adv gratis

gratitude /'grætɪtjuːd/ n Dankbarkeit f

gratuitous /grə'tjuːɪtəs/ a (uncalled for) überflüssig

gratuity /grə'tjuːɪt/ n (tip) Trinkgeld nt

grave[1] /greɪv/ a (-r, -st), -**ly** adv ernst; ~**ly ill** schwer krank

grave[2] n Grab nt. ~**digger** n Totengräber m

gravel /'grævl/ n Kies m

grave: ~**stone** n Grabstein m. ~**yard** n Friedhof m

gravitate /'grævɪteɪt/ vi gravitieren

gravity /'grævətɪ/ n Ernst m; (force) Schwerkraft f

gravy /'greɪvɪ/ n [Braten]soße f

gray /greɪ/ a (Amer) = **grey**

graze[1] /greɪz/ vi ⟨animal:⟩ weiden

graze[2] n Schürfwunde f □ vt ⟨car⟩ streifen; ⟨knee⟩ aufschürfen

grease /griːs/ n Fett nt; (lubricant) Schmierfett nt □ vt einfetten; (lubricate) schmieren. ~**proof** '**paper** n Pergamentpapier nt

greasy /'griːsɪ/ a (-ier, -iest) fettig

great /greɪt/ a (-er, -est) groß; (fam: marvellous) großartig

great: ~**'aunt** n Großtante f. G~ '**Britain** n Großbritannien nt. ~**'grandchildren** npl Urenkel pl. ~**'grandfather** n Urgroßvater m. ~**'grandmother** n Urgroßmutter f

great|**ly** /'greɪtlɪ/ adv sehr. ~**ness** n Größe f

great-'uncle n Großonkel m

Greece /griːs/ n Griechenland nt

greed /griːd/ n [Hab]gier f

greedy /'griːdɪ/ a (-ier, -iest), -**ily** adv gierig; **don't be** ~ sei nicht so unbescheiden

Greek /griːk/ a griechisch □ n Grieche m/Griechin f; (Lang) Griechisch nt

green /griːn/ a (-er, -est) grün; (fig) unerfahren □ n Grün nt; (grass) Wiese f; ~**s** pl Kohl m; **the G**~**s** pl (Pol) die Grünen pl

greenery /'griːnərɪ/ n Grün nt

'**greenfly** n Blattlaus f

greengage /'griːngeɪdʒ/ n Reneklode f

green: ~**grocer** n Obst- und Gemüsehändler m. ~**house** n Gewächshaus nt. ~**house effect** n Treibhauseffekt m

Greenland /'griːnlənd/ n Grönland nt

greet /griːt/ vt grüßen; (welcome) begrüßen. ~**ing** n Gruß m; (welcome) Begrüßung f. ~**ings card** n Glückwunschkarte f

gregarious /grɪ'geərɪəs/ a gesellig

grenade /grɪ'neɪd/ n Granate f

grew /gruː/ see **grow**

grey /greɪ/ a (-er, -est) grau □ n Grau nt □ vi grau werden. ~**hound** n Windhund m

grid /grɪd/ n Gitter nt; (on map) Gitternetz nt; (Electr) Überlandleitungsnetz nt

grief /griːf/ n Trauer f; **come to** ~ scheitern

grievance /'griːvəns/ n Beschwerde f

grieve /griːv/ vt betrüben □ vi trauern (for um)

grievous /'griːvəs/ a, -**ly** adv schwer

grill /grɪl/ n Gitter nt; (Culin) Grill m; **mixed** ~ Gemischtes nt vom Grill □ vt/i grillen; (interrogate) [streng] verhören

grille /grɪl/ n Gitter nt

grim /grɪm/ a (grimmer, grimmest), **-ly** adv ernst; ⟨determination⟩ verbissen

grimace /grɪ'meɪs/ n Grimasse f ◻ vi Grimassen schneiden

grime /graɪm/ n Schmutz m

grimy /'graɪmɪ/ a (-ier, -iest) schmutzig

grin /grɪn/ n Grinsen nt ◻ vi (pt/pp grinned) grinsen

grind /graɪnd/ n (fam: hard work) Plackerei f ◻ vt (pt/pp ground) mahlen; ⟨smooth, sharpen⟩ schleifen; ⟨Amer: mince⟩ durchdrehen; ~ one's teeth mit den Zähnen knirschen

grip /grɪp/ n Griff m; ⟨bag⟩ Reisetasche f ◻ vt (pt/pp gripped) ergreifen; ⟨hold⟩ festhalten; fesseln ⟨interest⟩

gripe /graɪp/ vi (sl: grumble) meckern

gripping /'grɪpɪŋ/ a fesselnd

grisly /'grɪzlɪ/ a (-ier, -iest) grausig

gristle /'grɪsl/ n Knorpel m

grit /grɪt/ n (grober) Sand m; (for roads) Streugut nt; (courage) Mut m ◻ vt (pt/pp gritted) streuen ⟨road⟩; ~ one's teeth die Zähne zusammenbeißen

grizzle /'grɪzl/ vi quengeln

groan /grəʊn/ n Stöhnen nt ◻ vi stöhnen

grocer /'grəʊsə(r)/ n Lebensmittelhändler m; ~'s [shop] Lebensmittelgeschäft nt. ~ies npl Lebensmittel pl

groggy /'grɒgɪ/ a schwach; (unsteady) wackelig [auf den Beinen]

groin /grɔɪn/ n (Anat) Leiste f

groom /gru:m/ n Bräutigam m; (for horse) Pferdepfleger(in) m(f) ◻ vt striegeln ⟨horse⟩

groove /gru:v/ n Rille f

grope /grəʊp/ vi tasten (for nach)

gross /grəʊs/ a (-er, -est) fett; (coarse) derb; (glaring) grob; (Comm) brutto; ⟨salary, weight⟩ Brutto- ◻ n inv Gros nt. ~ly adv (very) sehr

grotesque /grəʊ'tesk/ a, **-ly** adv grotesk

grotto /'grɒtəʊ/ n (pl -es) Grotte f

grotty /'grɒtɪ/ a (fam) mies

ground[1] /graʊnd/ see grind

ground[2] n Boden m; (terrain) Gelände nt; (reason) Grund m; (Amer, Electr) Erde f; ~s pl (park) Anlagen pl; (of coffee) Satz m ◻ vi ⟨ship:⟩ auflaufen ◻ vt aus dem Verkehr ziehen ⟨aircraft⟩; (Amer, Electr) erden

ground: ~ floor n Erdgeschoss nt. ~ing n Grundlage f. ~less a grundlos. ~'meat n (Amer) Hackfleisch nt. ~sheet n Bodenplane f. ~work n Vorarbeiten pl

group /gru:p/ n Gruppe f ◻ vt gruppieren ◻ vi sich gruppieren

grouse[1] /graʊs/ n inv schottisches Moorschneehuhn nt

grouse[2] vi (fam) meckern

grovel /'grɒvl/ vi (pt/pp grovelled) kriechen. ~ling a kriecherisch

grow /grəʊ/ v (pt grew, pp grown) ◻ vi wachsen; (become) werden; (increase) zunehmen ◻ vt anbauen; ~ one's hair sich (dat) die Haare wachsen lassen. ~ up vi aufwachsen; ⟨town:⟩ entstehen

growl /graʊl/ n Knurren nt ◻ vi knurren

grown /grəʊn/ see grow. ~-up a erwachsen ◻ n Erwachsene(r) m/f

growth /grəʊθ/ n Wachstum nt; (increase) Zunahme f; (Med) Gewächs nt

grub /grʌb/ n (larva) Made f; (fam: food) Essen nt

grubby /'grʌbɪ/ a (-ier, -iest) schmuddelig

grudg|e /grʌdʒ/ n Groll m; bear s.o. a ~e einen Groll gegen jdn hegen ◻ vt ~e s.o. sth jdm etw missgönnen. ~ing a, **-ly** adv widerwillig

gruelling /'gru:əlɪŋ/ a strapaziös

gruesome /'gru:səm/ a grausig

gruff /grʌf/ a, **-ly** adv barsch

grumble /'grʌmbl/ vi schimpfen (at mit)

grumpy /'grʌmpɪ/ a (-ier, -iest) griesgrämig

grunt /grʌnt/ n Grunzen nt ◻ vi grunzen

guarant|ee /gærən'ti:/ n Garantie f; (document) Garantieschein m ◻ vt garantieren; garantieren für ⟨quality, success⟩; be ~eed ⟨product:⟩ Garantie haben. ~or n Bürge m

guard /gɑ:d/ n Wache f; (security) Wächter m; (on train) ≈ Zugführer m; (Techn) Schutz m; be on ~ Wache stehen; on one's ~ auf der Hut ◻ vt bewachen; (protect) schützen ◻ vi ~ against sich hüten vor (+ dat). ~-dog n Wachhund m

guarded /'gɑ:dɪd/ a vorsichtig

guardian /'gɑ:dɪən/ n Vormund m

guerrilla /gə'rɪlə/ n Guerillakämpfer m. ~ warfare n Partisanenkrieg m

guess /ges/ n Vermutung f ◻ vt erraten ◻ vi raten; (Amer: believe) glauben. ~work n Vermutung f

guest /gest/ n Gast m. ~-house n Pension f

guffaw /gʌ'fɔ:/ n derbes Lachen nt ◻ vi derb lachen

guidance /'gaɪdəns/ n Führung f, Leitung f; (advice) Beratung f

guide /gaɪd/ n Führer(in) m(f); (book) Führer m; [Girl] G~ Pfadfinderin f ◻ vt führen, leiten. ~book n Führer m

guided /'gaɪdɪd/ a ~ missile Fernlenkgeschoss nt; ~ tour Führung f

guide: ~-dog n Blindenhund m. ~lines npl Richtlinien pl

guild /gɪld/ n Gilde f, Zunft f

guile /gaɪl/ n Arglist f

guillotine /'gɪlətiːn/ n Guillotine f; (for paper) Papierschneidemaschine f

guilt /gɪlt/ n Schuld f. ~ily adv schuldbewusst

guilty /'gɪlti/ a (-ier, -iest) a schuldig (of gen); (look) schuldbewusst; (conscience) schlecht

guinea-pig /'gɪnɪ-/ n Meerschweinchen nt; (person) Versuchskaninchen nt

guise /gaɪz/ n in the ~ of in Gestalt (+ gen)

guitar /gɪ'tɑː(r)/ n Gitarre f. ~ist n Gitarrist(in) m(f)

gulf /gʌlf/ n (Geog) Golf m; (fig) Kluft f

gull /gʌl/ n Möwe f

gullet /'gʌlɪt/ n Speiseröhre f; (throat) Kehle f

gullible /'gʌlɪbl/ a leichtgläubig

gully /'gʌlɪ/ n Schlucht f; (drain) Rinne f

gulp /gʌlp/ n Schluck m □ vi schlucken □ vt ~ down hinunterschlucken

gum[1] /gʌm/ n & -s pl (Anat) Zahnfleisch nt

gum[2] n Gummi[harz] nt; (glue) Klebstoff m; (chewing-gum) Kaugummi m □ vt (pt/pp gummed) kleben (to an + acc). ~boot n Gummistiefel m

gummed /gʌmd/ see gum[2] □ a (label) gummiert

gumption /'gʌmpʃn/ n (fam) Grips m

gun /gʌn/ n Schusswaffe f; (pistol) Pistole f; (rifle) Gewehr nt; (cannon) Geschütz nt □ vt (pt/pp gunned) ~ down niederschießen

gun: ~fire n Geschützfeuer nt. ~man bewaffneter Bandit m

gunner /'gʌnə(r)/ n Artillerist m

gun: ~powder n Schießpulver nt. ~shot n Schuss m

gurgle /'gɜːgl/ vi gluckern; (of baby) glucksen

gush /gʌʃ/ vi strömen; (enthuse) schwärmen (over von). ~ out n herausströmen

gusset /'gʌsɪt/ n Zwickel m

gust /gʌst/ n (of wind) Windstoß m; (Naut) Bö f

gusto /'gʌstəʊ/ n with ~ mit Schwung

gusty /'gʌstɪ/ a böig

gut /gʌt/ n Darm m; ~s pl Eingeweide pl; (fam: courage) Schneid m □ vt (pt/pp gutted) (Culin) ausnehmen; ~ted by fire ausgebrannt

gutter /'gʌtə(r)/ n Rinnstein m; (fig) Gosse f; (on roof) Dachrinne f

guttural /'gʌtərl/ a guttural

guy /gaɪ/ n (fam) Kerl m

guzzle /'gʌzl/ vt/i schlingen; (drink) schlürfen

gym /dʒɪm/ n (fam) Turnhalle f; (gymnastics) Turnen nt

gymnasium /dʒɪm'neɪzɪəm/ n Turnhalle f

gymnast /'dʒɪmnæst/ n Turner(in) m(f). ~ics /-'næstɪks/ n Turnen nt

gym: ~ shoes pl Turnschuhe pl. ~-slip n (Sch) Trägerkleid nt

gynaecolog|ist /gaɪnɪ'kɒlədʒɪst/ n Frauenarzt m /-ärztin f. ~y n Gynäkologie f

gypsy /'dʒɪpsɪ/ n Zigeuner(in) m(f)

gyrate /dʒaɪə'reɪt/ vi sich drehen

H

haberdashery /'hæbədæʃərɪ/ n Kurzwaren pl; (Amer) Herrenmoden pl

habit /'hæbɪt/ n Gewohnheit f; (Relig: costume) Ordenstracht f; be in the ~ die Angewohnheit haben (of zu)

habitable /'hæbɪtəbl/ a bewohnbar

habitat /'hæbɪtæt/ n Habitat nt

habitation /hæbɪ'teɪʃn/ n unfit for human ~ für Wohnzwecke ungeeignet

habitual /hə'bɪtjʊəl/ a gewohnt; (inveterate) gewohnheitsmäßig. ~ly adv gewohnheitsmäßig; (constantly) ständig

hack[1] /hæk/ n (writer) Schreiberling m; (hired horse) Mietpferd m

hack[2] vt hacken; ~ to pieces zerhacken

hackneyed /'hæknɪd/ a abgedroschen

'hacksaw n Metallsäge f

had /hæd/ see have

haddock /'hædək/ n inv Schellfisch m

haemorrhage /'hemərɪdʒ/ n Blutung f

haemorrhoids /'hemərɔɪdz/ npl Hämorrhoiden pl

hag /hæg/ n old ~ alte Hexe f

haggard /'hægəd/ a abgehärmt

haggle /'hægl/ vi feilschen (over um)

hail[1] /heɪl/ vt begrüßen; herbeirufen (taxi) □ vi ~ from kommen aus

hail[2] n Hagel m □ vi hageln. ~stone n Hagelkorn nt

hair /heə(r)/ n Haar nt; wash one's ~ sich (dat) die Haare waschen

hair: ~brush n Haarbürste f. ~cut n Haarschnitt m; have a ~cut sich (dat) die Haare schneiden lassen. ~-do n (fam) Frisur f. ~dresser n Friseur m /Friseuse f. ~drier n Haartrockner m; (hand-held)

Föhn m. ~-grip n [Haar]klemme f. ~pin n Haarnadel f. ~pin 'bend n Haarnadelkurve f. ~-raising a haarsträubend. ~-style n Frisur f

hairy /'heərɪ/ a (-ier, -iest) behaart; (excessively) haarig; (fam: frightening) brenzlig

hake /heɪk/ n inv Seehecht m

hale /heɪl/ a ~ and hearty gesund und munter

half /hɑ:f/ n (pl halves) Hälfte f; cut in ~ halbieren; one and a ~ eineinhalb, anderthalb; a ~ a dozen ein halbes Dutzend; ~ an hour eine halbe Stunde □ a & adv halb; ~ past two halb drei; [at] ~ price zum halben Preis

half: ~-board n Halbpension f. ~-caste n Mischling m. ~-hearted a lustlos. ~-'hourly a & adv halbstündlich. ~-'mast n at ~-mast auf halbmast. ~-measure n Halbheit f. ~-'term n schulfreie Tage nach dem halben Trimester. ~-'timbered a Fachwerk-. ~-time n (Sport) Halbzeit f. ~-'way a the ~-way mark/stage die Hälfte □ adv auf halbem Weg; get ~-way den halben Weg zurücklegen; (fig) bis zur Hälfte kommen. ~-wit n Idiot m

halibut /'hælɪbət/ n inv Heilbutt m

hall /hɔ:l/ n Halle f; (room) Saal m; (Sch) Aula f; (entrance) Flur m; (mansion) Gutshaus nt; ~ of residence (Univ) Studentenheim nt

'hallmark n [Feingehalts]stempel m; (fig) Kennzeichen nt (of für) □ vt stempeln

hallo /hə'ləʊ/ int [guten] Tag! (fam) hallo!

Hallowe'en /hæləʊ'i:n/ n der Tag vor Allerheiligen

hallucination /həlu:sɪ'neɪʃn/ n Halluzination f

halo /'heɪləʊ/ n (pl -es) Heiligenschein m; (Astr) Hof m

halt /hɔ:lt/ n Halt m; come to a ~ stehen bleiben; (traffic:) zum Stillstand kommen □ vi Halt machen; ~! halt! ~ing a, adv -ly zögernd

halve /hɑ:v/ vt halbieren; (reduce) um die Hälfte reduzieren

ham /hæm/ n Schinken m

hamburger /'hæmbɜ:gə(r)/ n Hamburger m

hamlet /'hæmlɪt/ n Weiler m

hammer /'hæmə(r)/ n Hammer m □ vt/i hämmern (at an + acc)

hammock /'hæmək/ n Hängematte f

hamper[1] /'hæmpə(r)/ n Picknickkorb m; [gift] ~ Geschenkkorb m

hamper[2] vt behindern

hamster /'hæmstə(r)/ n Hamster m

hand /hænd/ n Hand f; (of clock) Zeiger m; (writing) Handschrift f; (worker) Arbeiter(in) m(f); (Cards) Blatt nt; all ~s (Naut) alle Mann; at ~ in der Nähe; on the one/other ~ einer-/andererseits; out of ~ außer Kontrolle; (summarily) kurzerhand; in ~ unter Kontrolle; (available) verfügbar; give s.o. a ~ jdm behilflich sein □ vt reichen (to dat). ~ in vt abgeben. ~ out vt austeilen. ~ over vt überreichen

hand: ~bag n Handtasche f. ~book n Handbuch nt. ~brake n Handbremse f. ~cuffs npl Handschellen pl. ~ful n Handvoll f; be [quite] a ~ful (fam) nicht leicht zu haben sein

handicap /'hændɪkæp/ n Behinderung f; (Sport & fig) Handikap nt. ~ped a mentally/physically ~ped geistig/körperlich behindert

handi|craft /'hændɪkrɑ:ft/ n Basteln nt; (Sch) Werken nt. ~work n Werk nt

handkerchief /'hæŋkətʃɪf/ n (pl ~s & -chieves) Taschentuch nt

handle /'hændl/ n Griff m; (of door) Klinke f; (of cup) Henkel m; (of broom) Stiel m; fly off the ~ (fam) aus der Haut fahren □ vt handhaben; (treat) umgehen mit; (touch) anfassen. ~bars npl Lenkstange f

hand: ~luggage n Handgepäck nt. ~made a handgemacht. ~out n Prospekt m; (money) Unterstützung f. ~rail n Handlauf m. ~shake n Händedruck m

handsome /'hænsəm/ a gut aussehend; (generous) großzügig; (large) beträchtlich

hand: ~stand n Handstand m. ~writing n Handschrift f. ~'written a handgeschrieben

handy /'hændɪ/ a (-ier, -iest) handlich; (person) geschickt; have/keep ~ griffbereit haben/halten. ~man n [home] ~man Heimwerker m

hang /hæŋ/ vt/i (pt/pp hung) hängen; ~ wallpaper tapezieren □ vt (pt/pp hanged) hängen (criminal). ~ oneself sich erhängen □ n get the ~ of it (fam) den Dreh herauskriegen. ~ about vi sich herumdrücken. ~ on vi sich festhalten (to an + dat); (fam: wait) warten. ~ out vi heraushängen; (fam: live) wohnen □ vt draußen aufhängen (washing). ~ up vt/i aufhängen

hangar /'hæŋə(r)/ n Flugzeughalle f

hanger /'hæŋə(r)/ n [Kleider]bügel m

hang: ~-glider n Drachenflieger m. ~-gliding n Drachenfliegen nt. ~man n Henker m. ~over n (fam) Kater m (fam). ~-up n (fam) Komplex m

hanker /'hæŋkə(r)/ vi ~ after sth sich (dat) etw wünschen

hanky /'hæŋkı/ n (fam) Taschentuch nt

hanky-panky /'hæŋkı'pæŋkı/ n (fam) Mauscheleien pl

haphazard /hæp'hæzəd/ a, -ly adv planlos

happen /'hæpn/ vi geschehen, passieren; as it ~s zufälligerweise; I ~ed to be there ich war zufällig da; what has ~ed to him? was ist mit ihm los? (become of) was ist aus ihm geworden? ~ing n Ereignis nt

happi|ly /'hæpılı/ adv glücklich; (fortunately) glücklicherweise. ~ness n Glück nt

happy /'hæpı/ a (-ier, -iest) glücklich. ~go-'lucky a sorglos

harass /'hærəs/ vt schikanieren. ~ed a abgehetzt. ~ment n Schikane f; (sexual) Belästigung f

harbour /'hɑ:bə(r)/ n Hafen m □ vt Unterschlupf gewähren (+ dat); hegen ⟨grudge⟩

hard /hɑ:d/ a (-er, -est) hart; (difficult) schwer; ~ of hearing schwerhörig □ adv hart; ⟨work⟩ schwer; ⟨pull⟩ kräftig; ⟨rain, snow⟩ stark; think ~! denk mal nach! be ~ up (fam) knapp bei Kasse sein; be ~ done by (fam) ungerecht behandelt werden

hard: ~back n gebundene Ausgabe f. ~board n Hartfaserplatte f. ~-boiled a hart gekocht

harden /'hɑ:dn/ vi hart werden

hard-'hearted a hartherzig

hard|ly /'hɑ:dlı/ adv kaum; ~ly ever kaum [jemals]. ~ness n Härte f. ~ship n Not f

hard: ~ 'shoulder n (Auto) Randstreifen m. ~ware n Haushaltswaren pl; (Computing) Hardware f. ~'wearing a strapazierfähig. ~'working a fleißig

hardy /'hɑ:dı/ a (-ier, -iest) abgehärtet; ⟨plant⟩ winterhart

hare /heə(r)/ n Hase m. ~ 'lip n Hasenscharte f

hark /hɑ:k/ vi ~! hört! ~ back vi ~ back to (fig) zurückkommen auf (+ acc)

harm /hɑ:m/ n Schaden m; out of ~'s way in Sicherheit; it won't do any ~ es kann nichts schaden □ vt ~ s.o. jdm etwas antun. ~ful a schädlich. ~less a harmlos

harmonica /hɑ:'mɒnıkə/ n Mundharmonika f

harmonious /hɑ:'məʊnıəs/ a, -ly adv harmonisch

harmon|ize /'hɑ:mənaız/ vi (fig) harmonieren. ~y n Harmonie f

harness /'hɑ:nıs/ n Geschirr nt; (of parachute) Gurtwerk nt □ vt anschirren ⟨horse⟩; (use) nutzbar machen

harp /hɑ:p/ n Harfe f □ vi ~ on [about] (fam) herumreiten auf (+ dat). ~ist n Harfenist(in) m(f)

harpoon /hɑ:'pu:n/ n Harpune f

harpsichord /'hɑ:psıkɔ:d/ n Cembalo nt

harrow /'hærəʊ/ n Egge f. ~ing a grauenhaft

harsh /hɑ:ʃ/ a (-er, -est), -ly adv hart; ⟨voice⟩ rau; ⟨light⟩ grell. ~ness n Härte f; Rauheit f

harvest /'hɑ:vıst/ n Ernte f □ vt ernten

has /hæz/ see have

hash /hæʃ/ n (Culin) Haschee nt; make a ~ of (fam) verpfuschen

hashish /'hæʃıʃ/ n Haschisch nt

hassle /'hæsl/ n (fam) Ärger m □ vt schikanieren

hassock /'hæsək/ n Kniekissen nt

haste /heɪst/ n Eile f; make ~ sich beeilen

hasten /'heɪsn/ vi sich beeilen (to zu); (go quickly) eilen □ vt beschleunigen

hasty /'heɪstı/ a (-ier, -iest), -ily adv hastig; ⟨decision⟩ voreilig

hat /hæt/ n Hut m; (knitted) Mütze f

hatch¹ /hætʃ/ n (for food) Durchreiche f; (Naut) Luke f

hatch² vi ~ [out] ausschlüpfen □ vt ausbrüten

'hatchback n (Auto) Modell nt mit Hecktür

hatchet /'hætʃıt/ n Beil nt

hate /heɪt/ n Hass m □ vt hassen. ~ful a abscheulich

hatred /'heɪtrıd/ n Hass m

haughty /'hɔ:tı/ a (-ier, -iest), -ily adv hochmütig

haul /hɔ:l/ n (fish) Fang m; (loot) Beute f □ vt/i ziehen (on an + dat). ~age /-ıdʒ/ n Transport m. ~ier /-ıə(r)/ n Spediteur m

haunt /hɔ:nt/ n Lieblingsaufenthalt m □ vt umgehen in (+ dat); this house is ~ed in diesem Haus spukt es

have /hæv/ vt (3 sg pres tense has; pt/pp had) haben; bekommen ⟨baby⟩; holen ⟨doctor⟩; ~ a meal/drink etwas essen/trinken; ~ lunch zu Mittag essen; ~ a walk spazieren gehen; ~ a dream träumen; ~ a rest sich ausruhen; ~ a swim schwimmen; ~ sth done etw machen lassen; ~ sth made sich ⟨dat⟩ etw machen lassen; ~ to do sth etw tun müssen; ~ it out with jdn zur Rede stellen; so I ~! tatsächlich! he has [got] two houses er hat zwei Häuser; you have got the money, haven't you? du hast das Geld, nicht [wahr]? □ v aux haben; (with verbs of motion & some others) sein; I ~ seen him ich habe ihn gesehen; he has never been there er ist nie da gewesen. ~ on vt (be wearing) anhaben; (dupe) anführen

haven /'heɪvn/ n (fig) Zuflucht f

haversack /'hævə-/ n Rucksack m

havoc /'hævək/ n Verwüstung f; play ~ with (fig) völlig durcheinander bringen

haw /hɔ:/ see hum

hawk¹ /hɔ:k/ n Falke m

hawk² vt hausieren mit. ~er n Hausierer m

hawthorn /'hɔ:-/ n Hagedorn m

hay /heɪ/ n Heu nt. ~ fever n Heuschnupfen m. ~stack n Heuschober m

haywire a (fam) go ~ verrückt spielen; (plans:) über den Haufen geworfen werden

hazard /'hæzəd/ n Gefahr f; (risk) Risiko nt □ vt riskieren. ~ous a gefährlich; (risky) riskant. ~ [warning] lights npl (Auto) Warnblinkanlage f

haze /heɪz/ n Dunst m

hazel /'heɪzl/ n Haselbusch m. ~nut n Haselnuss f

hazy /'heɪzɪ/ a (-ier, -iest) dunstig; (fig) unklar

he /hi:/ pron er

head /hed/ n Kopf m; (chief) Oberhaupt nt; (of firm) Chef(in) m(f); (of school) Schulleiter(in) m(f); (on beer) Schaumkrone f; (of bed) Kopfende nt; 20 ~ of cattle 20 Stück Vieh; ~ first kopfüber □ vt anführen; (Sport) köpfen (ball) □ vi ~ for zusteuern auf (+ acc). ~ache n Kopfschmerzen pl. ~-dress n Kopfschmuck m

head|er /'hedə(r)/ n Kopfball m; (dive) Kopfsprung m. ~ing n Überschrift f

head: ~lamp n (Auto) Scheinwerfer m. ~land n Landspitze f. ~light n (Auto) Scheinwerfer m. ~line n Schlagzeile f. ~long adv kopfüber. ~master n Schulleiter m. ~mistress n Schulleiterin f. ~on a & adv frontal. ~phones npl Kopfhörer m. ~quarters npl Hauptquartier nt; (Pol) Zentrale f. ~rest n Kopfstütze f. ~room n lichte Höhe f. ~scarf n Kopftuch nt. ~strong a eigenwillig. ~waiter n Oberkellner m. ~way n make ~way Fortschritte machen. ~wind n Gegenwind m. ~word n Stichwort nt

heady /'hedɪ/ a berauschend

heal /hi:l/ vt/i heilen

health /helθ/ n Gesundheit f

health: ~ farm n Schönheitsfarm f. ~ foods npl Reformkost f. ~ food shop n Reformhaus nt. ~ insurance n Krankenversicherung f

healthy /'helθɪ/ a (-ier, -iest) -ily adv gesund

heap /hi:p/ n Haufen m; ~s (fam) jede Menge □ vt ~ [up] häufen; ~ed teaspoon gehäufter Teelöffel

hear /hɪə(r)/ vt/i (pt/pp heard) hören; ~, ~! hört, hört! he would not ~ of it er ließ es nicht zu

hearing /'hɪərɪŋ/ n Gehör nt; (Jur) Verhandlung f. ~-aid n Hörgerät nt

hearsay /'hɪəseɪ/ n from ~ vom Hörensagen

hearse /hɜ:s/ n Leichenwagen m

heart /hɑ:t/ n Herz nt; (courage) Mut m; ~s pl (Cards) Herz nt; by ~ auswendig

heart: ~ache n Kummer m. ~ attack n Herzanfall m. ~beat n Herzschlag m. ~break n Leid nt. ~breaking a herzzerreißend. ~broken a untröstlich. ~burn n Sodbrennen nt. ~en vt ermutigen. ~felt a herzlich[st]

hearth /hɑ:θ/ n Herd m; (fireplace) Kamin m. ~rug n Kaminvorleger m

heart|ily /'hɑ:tɪlɪ/ adv herzlich; (eat) viel. ~less a, -ly adv herzlos. ~y a herzlich; (meal) groß; (person) burschikos

heat /hi:t/ n Hitze f; (Sport) Vorlauf m □ vt heiß machen; heizen (room). ~ed a geheizt; (swimming pool) beheizt; (discussion) hitzig. ~er n Heizgerät nt; (Auto) Heizanlage f

heath /hi:θ/ n Heide f

heathen /'hi:ðn/ a heidnisch □ n Heide m/Heidin f

heather /'heðə(r)/ n Heidekraut nt

heating /'hi:tɪŋ/ n Heizung f

heat: ~stroke n Hitzschlag m. ~wave n Hitzewelle f

heave /hi:v/ vt/i ziehen; (lift) heben; (fam: throw) schmeißen; ~ a sigh einen Seufzer ausstoßen

heaven /'hevn/ n Himmel m. ~ly a himmlisch

heavy /'hevɪ/ a (-ier, -iest), -ily adv schwer; (traffic, rain) stark; (sleep) tief. ~weight n Schwergewicht nt

Hebrew /'hi:bru:/ a hebräisch

heckle /'hekl/ vt [durch Zwischenrufe] unterbrechen. ~r n Zwischenrufer m

hectic /'hektɪk/ a hektisch

hedge /hedʒ/ n Hecke f □ vi (fig) ausweichen. ~hog n Igel m

heed /hi:d/ n pay ~ to Beachtung schenken (+ dat) □ vt beachten. ~less a ungeachtet (of gen)

heel¹ /hi:l/ n Ferse f; (of shoe) Absatz m; down at ~ heruntergekommen; take to one's ~s (fam) Fersengeld geben

heel² vi ~ over (Naut) sich auf die Seite legen

hefty /'heftɪ/ a (-ier, -iest) kräftig; (heavy) schwer

heifer /'hefə(r)/ n Färse f

height /haɪt/ n Höhe f; (of person) Größe f. ~en vt (fig) steigern

heir /eə(r)/ n Erbe m. ~ess n Erbin f. ~loom n Erbstück nt

held /held/ see hold²

helicopter /'helɪkɒptə(r)/ n Hubschrauber m

hell /hel/ n Hölle f; go to ~! (sl) geh zum Teufel! □ int verdammt!

hello /hə'ləʊ/ int [guten] Tag! (fam) hallo!

helm /helm/ n [Steuer]ruder nt; at the ~ (fig) am Ruder

helmet /'helmɪt/ n Helm m

help /help/ n Hilfe f; (employees) Hilfskräfte pl; that's no ~ das nützt nichts □ vt/i helfen (s.o. jdm); ~ oneself to sth sich (dat) etw nehmen; ~ yourself (at table) greif zu; I could not ~ laughing ich musste lachen; it cannot be ~ed es lässt sich nicht ändern; I can't ~ it ich kann nichts dafür

help|er /'helpə(r)/ n Helfer(in) m(f). ~ful a, -ly adv hilfsbereit; (advice) nützlich. ~ing n Portion f. ~less a, -ly adv hilflos

helter-skelter /heltə'skeltə(r)/ adv holterdiepolter □ n Rutschbahn f

hem /hem/ n Saum m □ vt (pt/pp hemmed) säumen; ~ in umzingeln

hemisphere /'hemɪ-/ n Hemisphäre f

'hem-line n Rocklänge f

hemp /hemp/ n Hanf m

hen /hen/ n Henne f; (any female bird) Weibchen nt

hence /hens/ adv daher; five years ~ in fünf Jahren. ~'forth adv von nun an

henchman /'hentʃmən/ n (pej) Gefolgsmann m

'henpecked a ~ husband Pantoffelheld m

her /hɜː(r)/ a ihr □ pron (acc) sie; (dat) ihr; I know ~ ich kenne sie; give ~ the money gib ihr das Geld

herald /'herəld/ vt verkünden. ~ry n Wappenkunde f

herb /hɜːb/ n Kraut nt

herbaceous /hɜː'beɪʃəs/ a krautartig; ~ border Staudenrabatte f

herd /hɜːd/ n Herde f □ vt (tend) hüten; (drive) treiben. ~ together vi sich zusammendrängen □ vt zusammentreiben

here /hɪə(r)/ adv hier; (to this place) hierher; in ~ hier drinnen; come/bring ~ herkommen/herbringen. ~'after adv im Folgenden. ~'by adv hiermit

heredit|ary /hə'redɪtərɪ/ a erblich. ~y n Vererbung f

here|sy /'herəsɪ/ n Ketzerei f. ~tic n Ketzer(in) m(f)

here'with adv (Comm) beiliegend

heritage /'herɪtɪdʒ/ n Erbe nt

hermetic /hɜː'metɪk/ a, -ally adv hermetisch

hermit /'hɜːmɪt/ n Einsiedler m

hernia /'hɜːnɪə/ n Bruch m, Hernie f

hero /'hɪərəʊ/ n (pl -es) Held m

heroic /hɪ'rəʊɪk/ a, -ally adv heldenhaft

heroin /'herəʊɪn/ n Heroin nt

hero|ine /'herəʊɪn/ n Heldin f. ~ism n Heldentum nt

heron /'herən/ n Reiher m

herring /'herɪŋ/ n Hering m; red ~ (fam) falsche Spur f. ~bone n (pattern) Fischgrätenmuster nt

hers /hɜːz/ poss pron ihre(r), ihrs; a friend of ~ ein Freund von ihr; that is ~ das gehört ihr

her'self pron selbst; (refl) sich; by ~ allein

hesitant /'hezɪtənt/ a, -ly adv zögernd

hesitat|e /'hezɪteɪt/ vi zögern. ~ion /-'teɪʃn/ n Zögern nt; without ~ion ohne zu zögern

het /het/ a ~ up (fam) aufgeregt

hetero'sexual /hetərəʊ-/ a heterosexuell

hew /hjuː/ vt (pt hewed, pp hewed or hewn) hauen

hexagonal /hek'sægənl/ a sechseckig

heyday /'heɪ-/ n Glanzzeit f

hi /haɪ/ int he! (hallo!) Tag!

hiatus /haɪ'eɪtəs/ n (pl -tuses) Lücke f

hibernat|e /'haɪbəneɪt/ vi Winterschlaf halten. ~ion /-'neɪʃn/ n Winterschlaf m

hiccup /'hɪkʌp/ n Hick m; (fam: hitch) Panne f; have the ~s den Schluckauf haben □ vi hick machen

hid /hɪd/, **hidden** see hide²

hide¹ /haɪd/ n (Comm) Haut f; (leather) Leder nt

hide² v (pt hid, pp hidden) □ vt verstecken; (keep secret) verheimlichen □ vi sich verstecken. ~-and-seek n play ~-and-seek Versteck spielen

hideous /'hɪdɪəs/ a, -ly adv hässlich; (horrible) grässlich

'hide-out n Versteck nt

hiding¹ /'haɪdɪŋ/ n (fam) give s.o. a ~ jdn verdreschen

hiding² n go into ~ untertauchen

hierarchy /'haɪərɑːkɪ/ n Hierarchie f

hieroglyphics /haɪərə'glɪfɪks/ npl Hieroglyphen pl

higgledy-piggledy /hɪgldɪ'pɪgldɪ/ adv kunterbunt durcheinander

high /haɪ/ a (-er, -est) hoch; attrib hohe(r,s); (meat) angegangen; (wind) stark;

(on *drugs*) high; it's ~ time es ist höchste Zeit □ *adv* hoch; ~ and low überall □ *n* Hoch *nt*; (*temperature*) Höchsttemperatur *f*

high: ~brow *a* intellektuell. ~ **chair** *n* Kinderhochstuhl *m*. ~'handed *a* selbstherrlich. ~'heeled *a* hochhackig. ~ **jump** *n* Hochsprung *m*

'**highlight** *n* (*fig*) Höhepunkt *m*; ~s *pl* (*in hair*) helle Strähnen *pl* □ *vt* (*emphasize*) hervorheben

highly /'haɪlɪ/ *adv* hoch; speak ~ of loben; think ~ of sehr schätzen. ~'strung *a* nervös

Highness /'haɪnɪs/ *n* Hoheit *f*

high: ~rise *a* ~rise flats *pl* Wohnturm *m*. ~ season *n* Hochsaison *f*. ~ street *n* Hauptstraße *f*. ~ tide *n* Hochwasser *nt*. ~way *n* public ~way öffentliche Straße

hijack /'haɪdʒæk/ *vt* entführen. ~er *n* Entführer *m*

hike /haɪk/ *n* Wanderung *f* □ *vi* wandern. ~r *n* Wanderer *m*

hilarious /hɪ'leərɪəs/ *a* sehr komisch

hill /hɪl/ *n* Berg *m*; (*mound*) Hügel *m*; (*slope*) Hang *m*

hill: ~billy *n* (*Amer*) Hinterwäldler *m*. ~side *n* Hang *m*. ~y *a* hügelig

hilt /hɪlt/ *n* Griff *m*; to the ~ (*fam*) voll und ganz

him /hɪm/ *pron* (*acc*) ihn; (*dat*) ihm; I know ~ ich kenne ihn; give ~ the money gib ihm das Geld. ~'self *pron* selbst; (*refl*) sich; by ~self allein

hind /haɪnd/ *a* Hinter-

hind|er /'hɪndə(r)/ *vt* hindern. ~rance /-rəns/ *n* Hindernis *nt*

hindsight /'haɪnd-/ *n* with ~ rückblickend

Hindu /'hɪndu:/ *n* Hindu *m* □ *a* Hindu-. ~ism *n* Hinduismus *m*

hinge /hɪndʒ/ *n* Scharnier *nt*; (*on door*) Angel *f* □ *vi* ~ on (*fig*) ankommen auf (+ *acc*)

hint /hɪnt/ *n* Wink *m*, Andeutung *f*; (*advice*) Hinweis *m*; (*trace*) Spur *f* □ *vi* ~ at anspielen auf (+ *acc*)

hip /hɪp/ *n* Hüfte *f*

hippie /'hɪpɪ/ *n* Hippie *m*

hip 'pocket *n* Gesäßtasche *f*

hippopotamus /hɪpə'pɒtəməs/ *n* (*pl* -muses *or* -mi /-maɪ/) Nilpferd *nt*

hire /'haɪə(r)/ *vt* mieten (*car*); leihen (*suit*); einstellen (*person*); ~ [out] vermieten; verleihen □ *n* Mieten *nt*; Leihen *nt*. ~car *n* Leihwagen *m*

his /hɪz/ *a* sein □ *poss pron* seiner; seins; a friend of ~ ein Freund von ihm; that is ~ das gehört ihm

hiss /hɪs/ *n* Zischen *nt* □ *vt*/*i* zischen

historian /hɪ'stɔ:rɪən/ *n* Historiker(in) *m(f)*

historic /hɪ'stɒrɪk/ *a* historisch. ~al, -ly *adv* geschichtlich, historisch

history /'hɪstərɪ/ *n* Geschichte *f*

hit /hɪt/ *n* (*blow*) Schlag *m*; (*fam: success*) Erfolg *m*; direct ~ Volltreffer *m* □ *vt*/*i* (*pt*/*pp* hit, *pres p* hitting) schlagen; (*knock against, collide with, affect*) treffen; ~ the target das Ziel treffen; ~ on (*fig*) kommen auf (+ *acc*); ~ it off gut auskommen (with mit); ~ one's head on sth sich (*dat*) den Kopf an etw (*dat*) stoßen

hitch /hɪtʃ/ *n* Problem *nt*; technical ~ Panne *f* □ *vt* festmachen (to + *dat*); ~ up hochziehen; ~ a lift per Anhalter fahren, (*fam*) trampen. ~hike *vi* per Anhalter fahren, (*fam*) trampen. ~hiker *n* Anhalter(in) *m(f)*

hither /'hɪðə(r)/ *adv* hierher; ~ and thither hin und her. ~'to *adv* bisher

hive /haɪv/ *n* Bienenstock *m*. ~ off *vt* (*Comm*) abspalten

hoard /hɔ:d/ *n* Hort *m* □ *vt* horten, hamstern

hoarding /'hɔ:dɪŋ/ *n* Bauzaun *m*; (*with advertisements*) Reklamewand *f*

hoar-frost /'hɔ:-/ *n* Raureif *m*

hoarse /hɔ:s/ *a* (-r, -st), -ly *adv* heiser. ~ness *n* Heiserkeit *f*

hoax /həʊks/ *n* übler Scherz *m*; (*false alarm*) blinder Alarm *m*

hob /hɒb/ *n* Kochmulde *f*

hobble /'hɒbl/ *vi* humpeln

hobby /'hɒbɪ/ *n* Hobby *nt*. ~-horse *n* (*fig*) Lieblingsthema *nt*

hobnailed /'hɒb-/ *a* ~ boots *pl* genagelte Schuhe *pl*

hock /hɒk/ *n* [weißer] Rheinwein *m*

hockey /'hɒkɪ/ *n* Hockey *nt*

hoe /həʊ/ *n* Hacke *f* □ *vt* (*pres p* hoeing) hacken

hog /hɒg/ *n* [Mast]schwein *nt* □ *vt* (*pt*/*pp* hogged) (*fam*) mit Beschlag belegen

hoist /hɔɪst/ *n* Lastenaufzug *m* □ *vt* hochziehen; hissen (*flag*)

hold[1] /həʊld/ *n* (*Naut*) Laderaum *m*

hold[2] *n* Halt *m*; (*Sport*) Griff *m*; (*fig: influence*) Einfluss *m*; get ~ of fassen; (*fam: contact*) erreichen □ *v* (*pt*/*pp* held) □ *vt* halten; (*container:*) fassen; (*believe*) meinen; (*possess*) haben; anhalten (*breath*); ~ one's tongue den Mund halten □ *vi* (*rope:*) halten; (*weather:*) sich halten; not ~ with (*fam*) nicht einverstanden sein mit. ~ back *vt* zurückhalten □ *vi* zögern. ~ on *vi* (*wait*) warten; (*on telephone*) am Apparat bleiben; ~ on to (*keep*) behalten; (*cling to*) sich festhalten an (+ *dat*). ~ out *vt* hinhalten □ *vi* (*resist*) aushalten. ~ up *vt* hochhalten; (*delay*) aufhalten; (*rob*) überfallen

'**hold|all** *n* Reisetasche *f*. ~er *n* Inhaber(in) *m(f)*; (*container*) Halter *m*. ~-up *n* Verzögerung *f*; (*attack*) Überfall *m*

hole /həʊl/ *n* Loch *nt*

holiday /'hɒlədeɪ/ *n* Urlaub *m*; (*Sch*) Ferien *pl*; (*public*) Feiertag *m*; (*day off*) freier Tag *m*; go on ~ in Urlaub fahren. ~maker *n* Urlauber(in) *m(f)*

holiness /'həʊlɪnɪs/ *n* Heiligkeit *f*

Holland /'hɒlənd/ *n* Holland *nt*

hollow /'hɒləʊ/ *a* hohl; (*promise*) leer □ *n* Vertiefung *f*; (*in ground*) Mulde *f*. ~ out *vt* aushöhlen

holly /'hɒlɪ/ *n* Stechpalme *f*

'**hollyhock** *n* Stockrose *f*

hologram /'hɒləgræm/ *n* Hologramm *nt*

holster /'həʊlstə(r)/ *n* Pistolentasche *f*

holy /'həʊlɪ/ *a* (-ier, -est) heilig. H~ Ghost *or* Spirit *n* Heiliger Geist *m*. ~ water *n* Weihwasser *nt*. H~ Week *n* Karwoche *f*

homage /'hɒmɪdʒ/ *n* Huldigung *f*; pay ~ to huldigen (+ *dat*)

home /həʊm/ *n* Zuhause *nt*; (*house*) Haus *nt*; (*institution*) Heim *nt*; (*native land*) Heimat *f* □ *adv* at ~ zu Hause; come/go ~ nach Hause kommen/gehen

home: ~ ad'dress *n* Heimatanschrift *f*. ~ com'puter *n* Heimcomputer *m*. ~ game *n* Heimspiel *nt*. ~ help *n* Haushaltshilfe *f*. ~land *n* Heimatland *nt*. ~less *a* obdachlos

homely /'həʊmlɪ/ *a* (-ier, -iest) *a* gemütlich; (*Amer: ugly*) unscheinbar

home: ~'made *a* selbst gemacht. H~ Office *n* Innenministerium *nt*. H~ 'Secretary Innenminister *m*. ~sick *a* be ~ sick Heimweh haben (for nach). ~ sickness *n* Heimweh *nt*. ~ 'town *n* Heimatstadt *f*. ~work *n* (*Sch*) Hausaufgaben *pl*

homicide /'hɒmɪsaɪd/ *n* Totschlag *m*; (*murder*) Mord *m*

homoeopath|ic /həʊmɪə'pæθɪk/ *a* homöopathisch. ~y /-'ɒpəθɪ/ *n* Homöopathie *f*

homogeneous /hɒmə'dʒiːnɪəs/ *a* homogen

homo'sexual *a* homosexuell □ *n* Homosexuelle(r) *m/f*

honest /'ɒnɪst/ *a*, -ly *adv* ehrlich. ~y *n* Ehrlichkeit *f*

honey /'hʌnɪ/ *n* Honig *m*; (*fam: darling*) Schatz *m*

honey: ~comb *n* Honigwabe *f*. ~moon *n* Flitterwochen *pl*; (*journey*) Hochzeitsreise *f*. ~suckle *n* Geißblatt *nt*

honk /hɒŋk/ *vi* hupen

honorary /'ɒnərərɪ/ *a* ehrenamtlich; (*member, doctorate*) Ehren-

honour /'ɒnə(r)/ *n* Ehre *f* □ *vt* ehren; honorieren (*cheque*). ~able /-əbl/ *a*, -bly *adv* ehrenhaft

hood /hʊd/ *n* Kapuze *f*; (*of pram*) [Klapp]verdeck *nt*; (*over cooker*) Abzugshaube *f*; (*Amer, Auto*) Kühlerhaube *f*

hoodlum /'huːdləm/ *n* Rowdy *m*

'**hoodwink** /'hʊd-/ *vt* (*fam*) reinlegen

hoof /huːf/ *n* (*pl* ~s *or* hooves) Huf *m*

hook /hʊk/ *n* Haken *m*; by ~ or by crook mit allen Mitteln □ *vt* festhaken (to an + *acc*)

hook|ed /hʊkt/ *a* ~ed nose Hakennase *f*; ~ed on (*fam*) abhängig von; (*keen on*) besessen von. ~er *n* (*Amer, sl*) Nutte *f*

hookey /'hʊkɪ/ *n* play ~ (*Amer, fam*) schwänzen

hooligan /'huːlɪgən/ *n* Rowdy *m*. ~ism *n* Rowdytum *nt*

hoop /huːp/ *n* Reifen *m*

hooray /hʊ'reɪ/ *int* & *n* = hurrah

hoot /huːt/ *n* Ruf *m*; ~s of laughter schallendes Gelächter *nt* □ *vi* (*owl:*) rufen; (*car:*) hupen; (*jeer*) johlen. ~er *n* (*of factory*) Sirene *f*; (*Auto*) Hupe *f*

hoover /'huːvə(r)/ *n* H~ (P) Staubsauger *m* □ *vt/i* [staub]saugen

hop[1] /hɒp/ *n*, & ~s *pl* Hopfen *m*

hop[2] /hɒp/ *n* Hüpfer *m*; catch s.o. on the ~ (*fam*) jdm ungelegen kommen □ *vi* (*pt/pp* hopped) hüpfen; ~ it! (*fam*) hau ab! ~ in *vi* (*fam*) einsteigen. ~ out *vi* (*fam*) aussteigen

hope /həʊp/ *n* Hoffnung *f*; (*prospect*) Aussicht *f* (of auf + *acc*) □ *vt/i* hoffen (for auf + *acc*); I ~ so hoffentlich

hope|ful /'həʊpfl/ *a* hoffnungsvoll; be ~ful that hoffen, dass. ~fully *adv* hoffnungsvoll; (*it is hoped*) hoffentlich. ~less *a*, -ly *adv* hoffnungslos; (*useless*) nutzlos; (*incompetent*) untauglich

horde /hɔːd/ *n* Horde *f*

horizon /hə'raɪzn/ *n* Horizont *m*; on the ~ am Horizont

horizontal /hɒrɪ'zɒntl/ *a*, -ly *adv* horizontal. ~ 'bar *n* Reck *nt*

horn /hɔːn/ *n* Horn *nt*; (*Auto*) Hupe *f*

hornet /'hɔːnɪt/ *n* Hornisse *f*

horny /'hɔːnɪ/ *a* schwielig

horoscope /'hɒrəskəʊp/ *n* Horoskop *nt*

horrible /'hɒrɪbl/ *a*, -bly *adv* schrecklich

horrid /'hɒrɪd/ *a* grässlich

horrific /hə'rɪfɪk/ *a* entsetzlich

horrify /'hɒrɪfaɪ/ *vt* (*pt/pp* -ied) entsetzen

horror /'hɒrə(r)/ n Entsetzen nt. ~ film n Horrorfilm m

hors-d'œuvre /ɔː'dɜːvr/ n Vorspeise f

horse /hɔːs/ n Pferd nt

horse: ~back n on ~back zu Pferde. ~-'chestnut n [Ross]kastanie f. ~man n Reiter m. ~play n Toben nt. ~power n Pferdestärke f. ~-racing n Pferderennen nt. ~radish n Meerrettich m. ~shoe n Hufeisen nt

horti'cultural /hɔːtɪ-/ a Garten-

'horticulture n Gartenbau m

hose /həʊz/ n (pipe) Schlauch m □ vt ~ down abspritzen

hosiery /'həʊʒərɪ/ n Strumpfwaren pl

hospice /'hɒspɪs/ n Heim nt; (for the terminally ill) Sterbeklinik f

hospitable /hɒ'spɪtəbl/ a, -bly adv gastfreundlich

hospital /'hɒspɪtl/ n Krankenhaus nt

hospitality /hɒspɪ'tælətɪ/ n Gastfreundschaft f

host¹ /həʊst/ n a ~ of eine Menge von

host² n Gastgeber m

host³ n (Relig) Hostie f

hostage /'hɒstɪdʒ/ n Geisel f

hostel /'hɒstl/ n [Wohn]heim nt

hostess /'həʊstɪs/ n Gastgeberin f

hostile /'hɒstaɪl/ a feindlich; (unfriendly) feindselig

hostilit|y /hɒ'stɪlətɪ/ n Feindschaft f; ~ies pl Feindseligkeiten pl

hot /hɒt/ a (hotter, hottest) heiß; (meal) warm; (spicy) scharf; I am or feel ~ mir ist heiß

'hotbed n (fig) Brutstätte f

hotchpotch /'hɒtʃpɒtʃ/ n Mischmasch m

hotel /həʊ'tel/ n Hotel nt. ~ier /-ɪə(r)/ n Hotelier m

hot: ~head n Hitzkopf m. ~-'headed a hitzköpfig. ~house n Treibhaus nt. ~ly adv (fig) heiß, heftig. ~plate n Tellerwärmer m; (of cooker) Kochplatte f. ~ tap n Warmwasserhahn m. ~-tempered a jähzornig. ~-'water bottle n Wärmflasche f

hound /haʊnd/ n Jagdhund m □ vt (fig) verfolgen

hour /'aʊə(r)/ n Stunde f. ~ly a & adv stündlich; ~ly pay or rate Stundenlohn m

house¹ /haʊs/ n Haus nt; at my ~ bei mir

house² /haʊz/ vt unterbringen

house /haʊs/: ~boat n Hausboot nt. ~breaking n Einbruch m. ~hold n Haushalt m. ~holder n Hausinhaber(in) m(f). ~keeper n Haushälterin f. ~keeping n Hauswirtschaft f; (money) Haushaltsgeld

nt. ~plant n Zimmerpflanze f. ~trained a stubenrein. ~warming n have a ~warming party Einstand feiern. ~wife n Hausfrau f. ~work n Hausarbeit f

housing /'haʊzɪŋ/ n Wohnungen pl; (Techn) Gehäuse nt. ~estate n Wohnsiedlung f

hovel /'hɒvl/ n elende Hütte f

hover /'hɒvə(r)/ vi schweben; (be undecided) schwanken; (linger) herumstehen. ~craft n Luftkissenfahrzeug nt

how /haʊ/ adv wie; ~ do you do? guten Tag! ~ many wie viele; ~ much wie viel; and ~! und ob!

how'ever adv (in question) wie; (nevertheless) jedoch, aber; ~ small wie klein es auch sein mag

howl /haʊl/ n Heulen nt □ vi heulen; (baby:) brüllen. ~er n (fam) Schnitzer m

hub /hʌb/ n Nabe f; (fig) Mittelpunkt m

hubbub /'hʌbʌb/ n Stimmengewirr nt

'hub-cap n Radkappe f

huddle /'hʌdl/ vi ~ together sich zusammendrängen

hue¹ /hjuː/ n Farbe f

hue² n ~ and cry Aufruhr m

huff /hʌf/ n in a ~ beleidigt

hug /hʌg/ n Umarmung f □ vt (pt/pp hugged) umarmen

huge /hjuːdʒ/ a, -ly adv riesig

hulking /'hʌlkɪŋ/ a (fam) ungeschlacht

hull /hʌl/ n (Naut) Rumpf m

hullo /hə'ləʊ/ int = hallo

hum /hʌm/ n Summen nt; Brummen nt □ vt/i (pt/pp hummed) summen; (motor:) brummen; ~ and haw nicht mit der Sprache herauswollen

human /'hjuːmən/ a menschlich □ n Mensch m. ~ 'being n Mensch m

humane /hjuː'meɪn/ a, -ly adv human

humanitarian /hjuːmænɪ'teərɪən/ a humanitär

humanit|y /hjuː'mænətɪ/ n Menschheit f; ~ies pl (Univ) Geisteswissenschaften pl

humble /'hʌmbl/ a (-r, -st), -bly adv demütig □ vt demütigen

'humdrum a eintönig

humid /'hjuːmɪd/ a feucht. ~ity /-'mɪdətɪ/ n Feuchtigkeit f

humiliat|e /hjuː'mɪlɪeɪt/ vt demütigen. ~ion /-'eɪʃn/ n Demütigung f

humility /hjuː'mɪlətɪ/ n Demut f

'humming-bird n Kolibri m

humorous /'hjuːmərəs/ a, -ly adv humorvoll; (story) humoristisch humour /'hju:mə(r)/ n Humor m; (mood) Laune f; have a sense of ~ Humor haben □ vt ~ s.o jdm seinen Willen lassen

hump /hʌmp/ n Buckel m; (of camel) Höcker m □ vt schleppen

hunch /hʌntʃ/ n (idea) Ahnung f

'hunch|back n Bucklige(r) m/f. ~ed a ~ed up gebeugt

hundred /'hʌndrəd/ a one/a ~ [ein]hundert □ n Hundert nt; (written figure) Hundert f. ~th a hundertste(r,s) □ n Hunderstel nt. ~weight n ≈ Zentner m

hung /hʌŋ/ see hang

Hungarian /hʌŋ'geəriən/ a ungarisch □ n Ungar(in) m(f)

Hungary /'hʌŋgəri/ n Ungar nt

hunger /'hʌŋgə(r)/ n Hunger m. ~-strike n Hungerstreik m

hungry /'hʌŋgri/ a (-ier, -iest), -ily adv hungrig; be ~ Hunger haben

hunk /hʌŋk/ n [großes] Stück nt

hunt /hʌnt/ n Jagd f; (for criminal) Fahndung f □ vt/i jagen; fahnden nach (criminal); ~ for suchen. ~er n Jäger m; (horse) Jagdpferd nt. ~ing n Jagd f

hurdle /'hɜ:dl/ n (Sport & fig) Hürde f. ~r n Hürdenläufer(in) m(f)

hurl /hɜ:l/ vt schleudern

hurrah /hʊ'rɑ:/, hurray /hʊ'reɪ/ int hurra! □ n Hurra nt

hurricane /'hʌrɪkən/ n Orkan m

hurried /'hʌrɪd/ a, -ly adv eilig; (superficial) flüchtig

hurry /'hʌrɪ/ n Eile f; be in a ~ es eilig haben □ vi (pt/pp -ied) sich beeilen; (go quickly) eilen. ~ up vi sich beeilen □ vt antreiben

hurt /hɜ:t/ n Schmerz m □ vt/i (pt/pp hurt) weh tun (+ dat); (injure) verletzen; (offend) kränken. ~ful a verletzend

hurtle /'hɜ:tl/ vi ~ along rasen

husband /'hʌzbənd/ n [Ehe]mann m

hush /hʌʃ/ n Stille f □ vt ~ up vertuschen. ~ed a gedämpft. ~-'hush a (fam) streng geheim

husk /hʌsk/ n Spelze f

husky /'hʌskɪ/ a (-ier, -iest) heiser; (burly) stämmig

hustle /'hʌsl/ vt drängen □ n Gedränge nt; ~ and bustle geschäftiges Treiben nt

hut /hʌt/ n Hütte f

hutch /hʌtʃ/ n [Kaninchen]stall m

hybrid /'haɪbrɪd/ a hybrid □ n Hybride f

hydrangea /haɪ'dreɪndʒə/ n Hortensie f

hydrant /'haɪdrənt/ n [fire] ~ Hydrant m

hydraulic /haɪ'drɔ:lɪk/ a, -ally adv hydraulisch

hydrochloric /haɪdrə'klɔ:rɪk/ a ~ acid Salzsäure f

hydroe'lectric /haɪdrəʊ-/ a hydroelektrisch. ~ power station n Wasserkraftwerk nt

hydrofoil /'haɪdrə-/ n Tragflügelboot nt

hydrogen /'haɪdrədʒən/ n Wasserstoff m

hyena /haɪ'i:nə/ n Hyäne f

hygien|e /'haɪdʒi:n/ n Hygiene f. ~ic /haɪ'dʒi:nɪk/ a, -ally adv hygienisch

hymn /hɪm/ n Kirchenlied nt. ~-book n Gesangbuch nt

hyphen /'haɪfn/ n Bindestrich m. ~ate vt mit Bindestrich schreiben

hypno|sis /hɪp'nəʊsɪs/ n Hypnose f. ~tic /-'nɒtɪk/ a hypnotisch

hypno|tism /'hɪpnətɪzm/ n Hypnotik f. ~tist /-tɪst/ n Hypnotiseur m. ~tize vt hypnotisieren

hypochondriac /haɪpə'kɒndrɪæk/ a hypochondrisch □ n Hypochonder m

hypocrisy /hɪ'pɒkrəsɪ/ n Heuchelei f

hypocrit|e /'hɪpəkrɪt/ n Heuchler(in) m(f). ~ical /-'krɪtɪkl/ a, -ly adv heuchlerisch

hypodermic /haɪpə'dɜ:mɪk/ a & n ~ [syringe] Injektionsspritze f

hypothe|sis /haɪ'pɒθəsɪs/ n Hypothese f. ~tical /-ə'θetɪkl/ a, -ly adv hypothetisch

hyster|ia /hɪ'stɪərɪə/ n Hysterie f. ~ical /-'sterɪkl/ a, -ly adv hysterisch. ~ics /hɪ-'sterɪks/ npl hysterischer Anfall m

I

I /aɪ/ pron ich

ice /aɪs/ n Eis nt □ vt mit Zuckerguss überziehen (cake)

ice: ~ age n Eiszeit f. ~-axe n Eispickel m. ~berg /-bɜ:g/ n Eisberg m. ~-box n (Amer) Kühlschrank m. ~-'cream n [Speise]eis nt. ~-'cream parlour n Eisdiele f. ~-cube n Eiswürfel m

Iceland /'aɪslənd/ n Island nt

ice: ~-'lolly n Eis nt am Stiel. ~ rink n Eisbahn f

icicle /'aɪsɪkl/ n Eiszapfen m

icing /'aɪsɪŋ/ n Zuckerguss m. ~ sugar n Puderzucker m

icon /'aɪkɒn/ n Ikone f

icy /'aɪsɪ/ a (-ier, -iest), -ily adv eisig; (road) vereist

idea /aɪ'dɪə/ n Idee f; (conception) Vorstellung f; I have no ~! ich habe keine Ahnung!

ideal /aɪˈdɪəl/ a ideal ▫ n Ideal nt. ∼ism n Idealismus m. ∼ist n Idealist(in) m(f). ∼istic /-ˈlɪstɪk/ a idealistisch. ∼ize vt idealisieren. ∼ly adv ideal; (in ideal circumstances) idealerweise

identical /aɪˈdentɪkl/ a identisch; ⟨twins⟩ eineiig

identi|fication /aɪdentɪfɪˈkeɪʃn/ n Identifizierung f; (proof of identity) Ausweispapiere pl. ∼fy /aɪˈdentɪfaɪ/ vt (pt/pp -ied) identifizieren

identity /aɪˈdentətɪ/ n Identität f. ∼ card n [Personal]ausweis m

ideological /aɪdɪəˈlɒdʒɪkl/ a ideologisch. ∼y /aɪdɪˈɒlədʒɪ/ n Ideologie f

idiom /ˈɪdɪəm/ n [feste] Redewendung f. ∼atic /-ˈmætɪk/ a, -ally adv idiomatisch

idiosyncrasy /ɪdɪəˈsɪŋkrəsɪ/ n Eigenart f

idiot /ˈɪdɪət/ n Idiot m. ∼ic /-ˈɒtɪk/ a idiotisch

idle /ˈaɪdl/ a (-r, -st), -ly adv untätig; (lazy) faul; (empty) leer; ⟨machine⟩ nicht in Betrieb ▫ vi faulenzen; ⟨engine:⟩ leer laufen. ∼ness n Untätigkeit f; Faulheit f

idol /ˈaɪdl/ n Idol nt. ∼ize /ˈaɪdəlaɪz/ vt vergöttern

idyllic /ɪˈdɪlɪk/ a idyllisch

i.e. abbr (id est) d.h.

if /ɪf/ conj wenn; (whether) ob; as if als ob

ignite /ɪgˈnaɪt/ vt entzünden ▫ vi sich entzünden

ignition /ɪgˈnɪʃn/ n (Auto) Zündung f. ∼ key n Zündschlüssel m

ignoramus /ɪgnəˈreɪməs/ n Ignorant m

ignoran|ce /ˈɪgnərəns/ n Unwissenheit f. ∼t a unwissend; (rude) ungehobelt

ignore /ɪgˈnɔː(r)/ vt ignorieren

ilk /ɪlk/ n (fam) of that ∼ von der Sorte

ill /ɪl/ a krank; (bad) schlecht; feel ∼ at ease sich unbehaglich fühlen ▫ adv schlecht ▫ n Schlechte[s] nt; (evil) Übel nt. ∼-advised a unklug. ∼-bred a schlecht erzogen

illegal /ɪˈliːgl/ a, -ly adv illegal

illegible /ɪˈledʒəbl/ a, -bly adv unleserlich

illegitima|cy /ɪlɪˈdʒɪtɪməsɪ/ n Unehelichkeit f. ∼te /-mət/ a unehelich; ⟨claim⟩ unberechtigt

illicit /ɪˈlɪsɪt/ a, -ly adv illegal

illitera|cy /ɪˈlɪtərəsɪ/ n Analphabetentum nt. ∼te /-rət/ a be ∼te nicht lesen und schreiben können ▫ n Analphabet(in) m(f)

illness /ˈɪlnɪs/ n Krankheit f

illogical /ɪˈlɒdʒɪkl/ a, -ly adv unlogisch

ill-treat /ɪlˈtriːt/ vt misshandeln. ∼ment n Misshandlung f

illuminat|e /ɪˈluːmɪneɪt/ vt beleuchten. ∼ing a aufschlussreich. ∼ion /-ˈneɪʃn/ n Beleuchtung f

illusion /ɪˈluːʒn/ n Illusion f; be under the ∼ that sich (dat) einbilden, dass

illusory /ɪˈluːsərɪ/ a illusorisch

illustrat|e /ˈɪləstreɪt/ vt illustrieren. ∼ion /-ˈstreɪʃn/ n Illustration f

illustrious /ɪˈlʌstrɪəs/ a berühmt

image /ˈɪmɪdʒ/ n Bild nt; (statue) Standbild nt; (figure) Figur f; (exact likeness) Ebenbild nt; [public] ∼ Image nt

imagin|able /ɪˈmædʒɪnəbl/ a vorstellbar. ∼ary /-ərɪ/ a eingebildet

imaginat|ion /ɪmædʒɪˈneɪʃn/ n Phantasie f; (fancy) Einbildung f. ∼ive /ɪˈmædʒɪnətɪv/ a, -ly adv phantasievoll; (full of ideas) einfallsreich

imagine /ɪˈmædʒɪn/ vt sich (dat) vorstellen; (wrongly) sich (dat) einbilden

im'balance n Unausgeglichenheit f

imbecile /ˈɪmbəsiːl/ n Schwachsinnige(r) m/f; (pej) Idiot m

imbibe /ɪmˈbaɪb/ vt trinken; (fig) aufnehmen

imbue /ɪmˈbjuː/ vt be ∼d with erfüllt sein von

imitat|e /ˈɪmɪteɪt/ vt nachahmen, imitieren. ∼ion /-ˈteɪʃn/ n Nachahmung f, Imitation f

immaculate /ɪˈmækjʊlət/ a, -ly adv tadellos; (Relig) unbefleckt

imma'terial a (unimportant) unwichtig, unwesentlich

imma'ture a unreif

immediate /ɪˈmiːdɪət/ a sofortig; (nearest) nächste(r,s). ∼ly adv sofort; ∼ly next to unmittelbar neben ▫ conj sobald

immemorial /ɪməˈmɔːrɪəl/ a from time ∼ seit Urzeiten

immense /ɪˈmens/ a, -ly adv riesig; (fam) enorm; (extreme) äußerst

immers|e /ɪˈmɜːs/ vt untertauchen; be ∼ed in (fig) vertieft sein in (+ acc). ∼ion /-ʒn/ n Untertauchen nt. ∼ion heater n Heißwasserbereiter m

immigrant /ˈɪmɪgrənt/ n Einwanderer m

immigrat|e /ˈɪmɪgreɪt/ vi einwandern. ∼ion /-ˈgreɪʃn/ n Einwanderung f

imminent /ˈɪmɪnənt/ a be ∼ unmittelbar bevorstehen

immobil|e /ɪˈməʊbaɪl/ a unbeweglich. ∼ize /-bəlaɪz/ vt (fig) lähmen; (Med) ruhig stellen

immoderate /ɪˈmɒdərət/ a übermäßig

immodest /ɪˈmɒdɪst/ a unbescheiden

immoral /ɪˈmɒrəl/ a, -ly adv unmoralisch. ∼ity /ɪməˈrælətɪ/ n Unmoral f

immortal /ɪˈmɔːtl/ a unsterblich. ∼ity /-ˈtælətɪ/ n Unsterblichkeit f. ∼ize vt verewigen

immovable /ɪˈmuːvəbl/ a unbeweglich; (fig) fest

immune /ɪˈmjuːn/ a immun (to/from gegen). ∼ system n Abwehrsystem nt

immunity /ɪˈmjuːnətɪ/ n Immunität f

immunize /ˈɪmjʊnaɪz/ vt immunisieren

imp /ɪmp/ n Kobold m

impact /ˈɪmpækt/ n Aufprall m; (collision) Zusammenprall m; (of bomb) Einschlag m; (fig) Auswirkung f

impair /ɪmˈpeə(r)/ vt beeinträchtigen

impale /ɪmˈpeɪl/ vt aufspießen

impart /ɪmˈpɑːt/ vt übermitteln (to dat); vermitteln (knowledge)

im'parti|al a unparteiisch. ∼'ality n Unparteilichkeit f

im'passable a unpassierbar

impasse /æmˈpɑːs/ n (fig) Sackgasse f

impassioned /ɪmˈpæʃnd/ a leidenschaftlich

im'passive a, -ly adv unbeweglich

im'patien|ce n Ungeduld f. ∼t a, -ly adv ungeduldig

impeach /ɪmˈpiːtʃ/ vt anklagen

impeccable /ɪmˈpekəbl/ a, -bly adv tadellos

impede /ɪmˈpiːd/ vt behindern

impediment /ɪmˈpedɪmənt/ n Hindernis nt; (in speech) Sprachfehler m

impel /ɪmˈpel/ vt (pt/pp impelled) treiben; feel ∼led sich genötigt fühlen (to zu)

impending /ɪmˈpendɪŋ/ a bevorstehend

im'penetrable /ɪmˈpenɪtrəbl/ a undurchdringlich

imperative /ɪmˈperətɪv/ a be ∼ dringend notwendig sein □ n (Gram) Imperativ m, Befehlsform f

imper'ceptible a nicht wahrnehmbar

im'perfect a unvollkommen; (faulty) fehlerhaft □ n (Gram) Imperfekt nt. ∼ion /-ˈfekʃn/ n Unvollkommenheit f; (fault) Fehler m

imperial /ɪmˈpɪərɪəl/ a kaiserlich. ∼ism n Imperialismus m

imperil /ɪmˈperəl/ vt (pt/pp imperilled) gefährden

imperious /ɪmˈpɪərɪəs/ a, -ly adv herrisch

im'personal a unpersönlich

impersonat|e /ɪmˈpɜːsəneɪt/ vt sich ausgeben als; (Theat) nachmachen, imitieren. ∼or n Imitator m

impertinen|ce /ɪmˈpɜːtɪnəns/ n Frechheit f. ∼t a frech

imperturbable /ɪmpəˈtɜːbəbl/ a unerschütterlich

impervious /ɪmˈpɜːvɪəs/ a ∼ to (fig) unempfänglich für

impetuous /ɪmˈpetjʊəs/ a, -ly adv ungestüm

impetus /ˈɪmpɪtəs/ n Schwung m

impish /ˈɪmpɪʃ/ a schelmisch

implacable /ɪmˈplækəbl/ a unerbittlich

im'plant[1] /ɪmˈplɑːnt/ vt einpflanzen

'implant[2] n Implantat nt

implement[1] /ˈɪmplɪmənt/ n Gerät nt

implement[2] /ˈɪmplɪment/ vt ausführen

implicat|e /ˈɪmplɪkeɪt/ vt verwickeln. ∼ion /-ˈkeɪʃn/ n Verwicklung f; ∼ions pl Auswirkungen pl; by ∼ion implizit

implicit /ɪmˈplɪsɪt/ a, -ly adv unausgesprochen; (absolute) unbedingt

implore /ɪmˈplɔː(r)/ vt anflehen

imply /ɪmˈplaɪ/ vt (pt/pp -ied) andeuten; what are you ∼ing? was wollen Sie damit sagen?

impo'lite a, -ly adv unhöflich

import[1] /ˈɪmpɔːt/ n Import m, Einfuhr f; (importance) Wichtigkeit f; (meaning) Bedeutung f

import[2] /ɪmˈpɔːt/ vt importieren, einführen

importan|ce /ɪmˈpɔːtns/ n Wichtigkeit f. ∼t a wichtig

importer /ɪmˈpɔːtə(r)/ n Importeur m

impos|e /ɪmˈpəʊz/ vt auferlegen (on dat) □ vi sich aufdrängen (on dat). ∼ing a eindrucksvoll. ∼ition /ɪmpəˈzɪʃn/ n be an ∼ition eine Zumutung sein

impossi'bility n Unmöglichkeit f

im'possible a, -bly adv unmöglich

impostor /ɪmˈpɒstə(r)/ n Betrüger(in) m(f)

impoten|ce /ˈɪmpətəns/ n Machtlosigkeit f; (Med) Impotenz f. ∼t a machtlos; (Med) impotent

impound /ɪmˈpaʊnd/ vt beschlagnahmen

impoverished /ɪmˈpɒvərɪʃt/ a verarmt

im'practicable a undurchführbar

im'practical a unpraktisch

impre'cise a ungenau

impregnable /ɪmˈpregnəbl/ a uneinnehmbar

impregnate /ˈɪmpregneɪt/ vt tränken; (Biol) befruchten

im'press vt beeindrucken; ∼ sth [up]on s.o. jdm etw einprägen

impression /ɪmˈpreʃn/ n Eindruck m; (imitation) Nachahmung f; (imprint) Abdruck m; (edition) Auflage f. ∼ism n Impressionismus m

impressive /ɪmˈpresɪv/ a eindrucksvoll

'imprint¹ n Abdruck m

im'print² vt prägen; (fig) einprägen (on dat)

im'prison vt gefangen halten; (put in prison) ins Gefängnis sperren

im'probable a unwahrscheinlich

impromptu /ɪm'prɒmptju:/ a improvisiert □ adv aus dem Stegreif

im'proper a, -ly adv inkorrekt; (indecent) unanständig

impro'priety n Unkorrektheit f

improve /ɪm'pru:v/ vt verbessern; verschönern ⟨appearance⟩ □ vi sich bessern; ~ [up]on übertreffen. ~ment /-mənt/ n Verbesserung f; (in health) Besserung f

improvise /'ɪmprəvaɪz/ vt/i improvisieren

im'prudent a unklug

impuden|ce /'ɪmpjʊdəns/ n Frechheit f. ~t a, -ly adv frech

impuls|e /'ɪmpʌls/ n Impuls m; on [an] ~e impulsiv. ~ive /-'pʌlsɪv/ a, -ly adv impulsiv

impunity /ɪm'pju:nəti/ n with ~ ungestraft

im'pur|e a unrein. ~ity n Unreinheit f; ~ities pl Verunreinigungen pl

impute /ɪm'pju:t/ vt zuschreiben (to dat)

in /ɪn/ prep in (+ dat/(into) + acc); sit in the garden im Garten sitzen; go in the garden in den Garten gehen; in May im Mai; in the summer/winter im Sommer/Winter; in 1992 [im Jahre] 1992; in this heat bei dieser Hitze; in the rain/sun im Regen/in der Sonne; in the evening am Abend; in the sky am Himmel; in the world auf der Welt; in the street auf der Straße; deaf in one ear auf einem Ohr taub; in the army beim Militär; in English/German auf Englisch/Deutsch; in ink/pencil mit Tinte/Bleistift; in a soft/loud voice mit leiser/lauter Stimme; in doing this, he ... indem er das tut/tat, ... er □ adv (at home) zu Hause; (indoors) drinnen; he's not in yet er ist noch nicht da; all in alles inbegriffen; (fam: exhausted) kaputt; day in, day out tagaus, tagein; keep in with s.o. sich mit jdm gut stellen; have it in for s.o. (fam) es auf jdn abgesehen haben; let oneself in for sth sich auf etw (acc) einlassen; send/go in hineinschicken/-gehen; come/bring in hereinkommen/-bringen □ a (fam: in fashion) in □ n the ins and outs alle Einzelheiten pl

ina'bility n Unfähigkeit f

inac'cessible a unzugänglich

in'accura|cy n Ungenauigkeit f. ~te a, -ly adv ungenau

in'ac|tive a untätig. ~'tivity n Untätigkeit f

in'adequate a, -ly adv unzulänglich; feel ~ sich der Situation nicht gewachsen fühlen

inad'missable a unzulässig

inad'vertently /ɪnəd'vɜ:təntlɪ/ adv versehentlich

inad'visable a nicht ratsam

inane /ɪ'neɪn/ a, -ly adv albern

in'animate a unbelebt

in'applicable a nicht zutreffend

inap'propriate a unangebracht

inar'ticulate a undeutlich; be ~ sich nicht gut ausdrücken können

inat'tentive a unaufmerksam

in'audible a, -bly adv unhörbar

inaugural /ɪ'nɔ:gjʊrl/ a Antritts-

inaugurat|e /ɪ'nɔ:gjʊreɪt/ vt [feierlich] in sein Amt einführen. ~ion /-'reɪʃn/ n Amtseinführung f

inau'spicious a ungünstig

inborn /'ɪnbɔ:n/ a angeboren

inbred /ɪn'bred/ a angeboren

incalculable /ɪn'kælkjʊləbl/ a nicht berechenbar; (fig) unabsehbar

in'capable a unfähig; be ~ of doing sth nicht fähig sein, etw zu tun

incapacitate /ɪnkə'pæsɪteɪt/ vt unfähig machen

incarcerate /ɪn'kɑ:səreɪt/ vt einkerkern

incarnat|e /ɪn'kɑ:nət/ a the devil ~e der leibhaftige Satan. ~ion /-'neɪʃn/ n Inkarnation f

incendiary /ɪn'sendɪəri/ a & n ~ [bomb] Brandbombe f

incense¹ /'ɪnsens/ n Weihrauch m

incense² /ɪn'sens/ vt wütend machen

incentive /ɪn'sentɪv/ n Anreiz m

inception /ɪn'sepʃn/ n Beginn m

incessant /ɪn'sesnt/ a, -ly adv unaufhörlich

incest /'ɪnsest/ n Inzest m, Blutschande f

inch /ɪntʃ/ n Zoll m □ vi ~ forward sich ganz langsam vorwärts schieben

inciden|ce /'ɪnsɪdəns/ n Vorkommen nt. ~t n Zwischenfall m

incidental /ɪnsɪ'dentl/ a nebensächlich; ⟨remark⟩ beiläufig; ⟨expenses⟩ Neben-. ~ly adv übrigens

incinerat|e /ɪn'sɪnəreɪt/ vt verbrennen. ~or n Verbrennungsofen m

incipient /ɪn'sɪpɪənt/ a angehend

incision /ɪn'sɪʒn/ n Einschnitt m

incisive /ɪn'saɪsɪv/ a scharfsinnig

incisor /ɪn'saɪzə(r)/ n Schneidezahn m

incite /ɪn'saɪt/ vt aufhetzen. ~ment n Aufhetzung f

inci'vility n Unhöflichkeit f

in'clement a rau

inclination /ɪnklɪ'neɪʃn/ n Neigung f

incline¹ /ɪn'klaɪn/ vt neigen; be ~d to do sth dazu neigen, etw zu tun □ vi sich neigen

incline² /'ɪnklaɪn/ n Neigung f

inclu|de /ɪn'kluːd/ vt einschließen; (contain) enthalten; (incorporate) aufnehmen (in in + acc). ~ding prep einschließlich (+ gen). ~sion /-'ʒn/ n Aufnahme f

inclusive /ɪn'kluːsɪv/ a Inklusiv-; ~ of einschließlich (+ gen) □ adv inklusive

incognito /ɪnkɒg'niːtəʊ/ adv inkognito

inco'herent a, -ly adv zusammenhanglos; (incomprehensible) unverständlich

income /'ɪnkʌm/ n Einkommen nt. ~ tax n Einkommensteuer f

'incoming a ankommend; (mail, call) eingehend. ~ tide n steigende Flut f

in'comparable a unvergleichlich

incom'patible a unvereinbar; be ~ ⟨people:⟩ nicht zueinander passen

in'competen|ce n Unfähigkeit f. ~t a unfähig

incom'plete a unvollständig

incompre'hensible a unverständlich

incon'ceivable a undenkbar

incon'clusive a nicht schlüssig

incongruous /ɪn'kɒŋgrʊəs/ a unpassend

inconsequential /ɪnkɒnsɪ'kwenʃl/ a unbedeutend

incon'siderate a rücksichtslos

incon'sisten|t a, -ly adv widersprüchlich; (illogical) inkonsequent; be ~ nicht übereinstimmen

inconsolable /ɪnkən'səʊləbl/ a untröstlich

incon'spicuous a unauffällig

inconti'nen|ce /ɪn'kɒntɪnəns/ n Inkontinenz f. ~t a inkontinent

incon'venien|ce n Unannehmlichkeit f; (drawback) Nachteil m; put s.o. to ~ce jdm Umstände machen. ~t a, -ly adv ungünstig; be ~t for s.o. jdm nicht passen

incorporate /ɪn'kɔːpəreɪt/ vt aufnehmen; (contain) enthalten

incor'rect a, -ly adv inkorrekt

incorrigible /ɪn'kɒrɪdʒəbl/ a unverbesserlich

incorruptible /ɪnkə'rʌptəbl/ a unbestechlich

increase¹ /'ɪnkriːs/ n Zunahme f; (rise) Erhöhung f; be on the ~ zunehmen

increas|e² /ɪn'kriːs/ vt vergrößern; (raise) erhöhen □ vi zunehmen; (rise) sich erhöhen. ~ing a, -ly adv zunehmend

in'credible a, -bly adv unglaublich

incredulous /ɪn'kredjʊləs/ a ungläubig

increment /'ɪnkrɪmənt/ n Gehaltszulage f

incriminate /ɪn'krɪmɪneɪt/ vt (Jur) belasten

incubat|e /'ɪŋkjʊbeɪt/ vt ausbrüten. ~ion /-'beɪʃn/ n Ausbrüten nt. ~ion period n (Med) Inkubationszeit f. ~or n (for baby) Brutkasten m

inculcate /'ɪnkʌlkeɪt/ vt einprägen (in dat)

incumbent /ɪn'kʌmbənt/ a be ~ on s.o. jds Pflicht sein

incur /ɪn'kɜː(r)/ vt (pt/pp incurred) sich (dat) zuziehen; machen ⟨debts⟩

in'curable a, -bly adv unheilbar

incursion /ɪn'kɜːʃn/ n Einfall m

indebted /ɪn'detɪd/ a verpflichtet (to dat)

in'decent a, -ly adv unanständig

inde'cision n Unentschlossenheit f

inde'cisive a ergebnislos; ⟨person⟩ unentschlossen

indeed /ɪn'diːd/ adv in der Tat, tatsächlich; yes ~! allerdings! ~ I am/do oh doch! very much ~ sehr; thank you very much ~ vielen herzlichen Dank

indefatigable /ɪndɪ'fætɪgəbl/ a unermüdlich

in'definite a unbestimmt. ~ly adv unbegrenzt; ⟨postpone⟩ auf unbestimmte Zeit

indelible /ɪn'delɪbl/ a, -bly adv nicht zu entfernen; (fig) unauslöschlich

indemni|fy /ɪn'demnɪfaɪ/ vt (pt/pp -ied) versichern; (compensate) entschädigen. ~ty n Versicherung f; Entschädigung f

indent /ɪn'dent/ vt (Typ) einrücken. ~ation /-'teɪʃn/ n Einrückung f; (notch) Kerbe f

inde'penden|ce n Unabhängigkeit f; (self-reliance) Selbstständigkeit f. ~t a, -ly adv unabhängig; selbstständig

indescribable /ɪndɪ'skraɪbəbl/ a, -bly adv unbeschreiblich

indestructible /ɪndɪ'strʌktəbl/ a unzerstörbar

indeterminate /ɪndɪ'tɜːmɪnət/ a unbestimmt

index /'ɪndeks/ n Register nt

index: ~ card n Karteikarte f. ~ finger n Zeigefinger m. ~-linked a ⟨pension⟩ dynamisch

India /'ɪndɪə/ n Indien nt. ~n a indisch; (American) indianisch □ n Inder(in) m(f); (American) Indianer(in) m(f)

Indian: ~ 'ink n Tusche f. ~ 'summer n Nachsommer m

indicat|e /'ɪndɪkeɪt/ vt zeigen; (point at) zeigen auf (+ acc); (hint) andeuten; (register) anzeigen ▫ vi (Auto) blinken. ~ion /-'keɪʃn/ n Anzeichen nt

indicative /ɪn'dɪkətɪv/ a be ~ of schließen lassen auf (+ acc) ▫ n (Gram) Indikativ m

indicator /'ɪndɪkeɪtə(r)/ n (Auto) Blinker m

indict /ɪn'daɪt/ vt anklagen. ~ment n Anklage f

in'differen|ce n Gleichgültigkeit f. ~t a, -ly adv gleichgültig; (not good) mittelmäßig

indigenous /ɪn'dɪdʒɪnəs/ a einheimisch

indi'gest|ible a unverdaulich; (difficult to digest) schwer verdaulich. ~ion n Magenverstimmung f

indigna|nt /ɪn'dɪgnənt/ a, -ly adv entrüstet, empört. ~tion /-'neɪʃn/ n Entrüstung f, Empörung f

in'dignity n Demütigung f

indi'rect a, -ly adv indirekt

indi'screet a indiskret

indis'cretion n Indiskretion f

indiscriminate /ɪndɪ'skrɪmɪnət/ a, -ly adv wahllos

indi'spensable a unentbehrlich

indisposed /ɪndɪ'spəʊzd/ a indisponiert

indisputable /ɪndɪ'spjuːtəbl/ a, -bly adv unbestreitbar

indi'stinct a, -ly adv undeutlich

indistinguishable /ɪndɪ'stɪŋgwɪʃəbl/ a be ~ nicht zu unterscheiden sein; (not visible) nicht erkennbar sein

individual /ɪndɪ'vɪdjʊəl/ a, -ly adv individuell; (single) einzeln ▫ n Individuum nt. ~ity /-'ælətɪ/ n Individualität f

indi'visible a unteilbar

indoctrinate /ɪn'dɒktrɪneɪt/ vt indoktrinieren

indolen|ce /'ɪndələns/ n Faulheit f. ~t a faul

indomitable /ɪn'dɒmɪtəbl/ a unbeugsam

indoor /'ɪndɔː(r)/ a Innen-; (clothes) Haus-; (plant) Zimmer-; (Sport) Hallen-. ~s /-'dɔːz/ adv im Haus, drinnen; go ~s ins Haus gehen

induce /ɪn'djuːs/ vt dazu bewegen (to zu); (produce) herbeiführen. ~ment n (incentive) Anreiz m

indulge /ɪn'dʌldʒ/ vt frönen (+ dat); verwöhnen (child) ▫ vi ~ in frönen (+ dat). ~nce /-əns/ n Nachgiebigkeit f; (leniency) Nachsicht f. ~nt a [zu] nachgiebig; nachsichtig

industrial /ɪn'dʌstrɪəl/ a Industrie-; take ~ action streiken. ~ist n Industrielle(r) m. ~ized a industrialisiert

industr|ious /ɪn'dʌstrɪəs/ a, -ly adv fleißig. ~y /'ɪndəstrɪ/ n Industrie f; (zeal) Fleiß m

inebriated /ɪ'niːbrɪeɪtɪd/ a betrunken

in'edible a nicht essbar

inef'fective a, -ly adv unwirksam; (person) untauglich

ineffectual /ɪnɪ'fektjʊəl/ a unwirksam; (person) untauglich

inef'ficient a unfähig; (organization) nicht leistungsfähig; (method) nicht rationell

in'eligible a nicht berechtigt

inept /ɪ'nept/ a ungeschickt

ine'quality n Ungleichheit f

inert /ɪ'nɜːt/ a unbeweglich; (Phys) träge. ~ia /ɪ'nɜːʃə/ n Trägheit f

inescapable /ɪnɪ'skeɪpəbl/ a unvermeidlich

inestimable /ɪn'estɪməbl/ a unschätzbar

inevitab|le /ɪn'evɪtəbl/ a unvermeidlich. ~ly adv zwangsläufig

ine'xact a ungenau

inex'cusable a unverzeihlich

inexhaustible /ɪnɪg'zɔːstəbl/ a unerschöpflich

inexorable /ɪn'eksərəbl/ a unerbittlich

inex'pensive a, -ly adv preiswert

inex'perience n Unerfahrenheit f. ~d a unerfahren

inexplicable /ɪnɪk'splɪkəbl/ a unerklärlich

in'fallible a unfehlbar

infam|ous /'ɪnfəməs/ a niederträchtig; (notorious) berüchtigt. ~y n Niederträchtigkeit f

infan|cy /'ɪnfənsɪ/ n frühe Kindheit f; (fig) Anfangsstadium nt. ~t n Kleinkind nt. ~tile a kindisch

infantry /'ɪnfəntrɪ/ n Infanterie f

infatuated /ɪn'fætjʊeɪtɪd/ a vernarrt (with in + acc)

infect /ɪn'fekt/ vt anstecken, infizieren; become ~ed (wound:) sich infizieren. ~ion /-'fekʃn/ n Infektion f. ~ious /-'fekʃəs/ a ansteckend

infer /ɪn'fɜː(r)/ vt (pt/pp inferred) folgern (from aus); (imply) andeuten. ~ence /'ɪnfərəns/ n Folgerung f

inferior /ɪn'fɪərɪə(r)/ a minderwertig; (in rank) untergeordnet ▫ n Untergebene(r) m|f

inferiority /ɪnfɪərɪ'ɒrɪtɪ/ n Minderwertigkeit f. ~ complex n Minderwertigkeitskomplex m

infern|al /ɪnˈfɜ:nl/ a höllisch. ∼o n flammendes Inferno nt

in'fer|tile a unfruchtbar. ∼'tility n Unfruchtbarkeit f

infest /ɪnˈfest/ vt be ∼ed with befallen sein von; ⟨place⟩ verseucht sein mit

infi'delity n Untreue f

infighting /ˈɪnfaɪtɪŋ/ n (fig) interne Machtkämpfe pl

infiltrate /ˈɪnfɪltreɪt/ vt infiltrieren; (Pol) unterwandern

infinite /ˈɪnfɪnət/ a, -ly adv unendlich

infinitesimal /ɪnfɪnɪˈtesɪml/ a unendlich klein

infinitive /ɪnˈfɪnətɪv/ n (Gram) Infinitiv m

infinity /ɪnˈfɪnəti/ n Unendlichkeit f

infirm /ɪnˈfɜ:m/ a gebrechlich. ∼ary n Krankenhaus nt. ∼ity n Gebrechlichkeit f

inflame /ɪnˈfleɪm/ vt entzünden; become ∼d sich entzünden. ∼d a entzündet

in'flammable a feuergefährlich

inflammation /ɪnfləˈmeɪʃn/ n Entzündung f

inflammatory /ɪnˈflæmətrɪ/ a aufrührerisch

inflatable /ɪnˈfleɪtəbl/ a aufblasbar

inflat|e /ɪnˈfleɪt/ vt aufblasen; ⟨with pump⟩ aufpumpen. ∼ion /-eɪʃn/ n Inflation f. ∼ionary /-eɪʃənərɪ/ a inflationär

in'flexible a starr; ⟨person⟩ unbeugsam

inflexion /ɪnˈflekʃn/ n Tonfall m; (Gram) Flexion f

inflict /ɪnˈflɪkt/ vt zufügen (on dat); versetzen ⟨blow⟩ (on dat)

influen|ce /ˈɪnflʊəns/ n Einfluss m □ vt beeinflussen. ∼tial /-ˈenʃl/ a einflussreich

influenza /ɪnflʊˈenzə/ n Grippe f

influx /ˈɪnflʌks/ n Zustrom m

inform /ɪnˈfɔ:m/ vt benachrichtigen; ⟨officially⟩ informieren; ∼ s.o. of sth jdm etw mitteilen; keep s.o. ∼ed jdn auf dem Laufenden halten □ vi ∼ against denunzieren

in'for|mal a, -ly adv zwanglos; ⟨unofficial⟩ inoffiziell. ∼'mality n Zwanglosigkeit f

informant /ɪnˈfɔ:mənt/ n Gewährsmann m

informat|ion /ɪnfəˈmeɪʃn/ n Auskunft f; a piece of ∼ion eine Auskunft. ∼ive /ɪnˈfɔ:mətɪv/ a aufschlussreich; ⟨instructive⟩ lehrreich

informer /ɪnˈfɔ:mə(r)/ n Spitzel m; (Pol) Denunziant m

infra-'red /ɪnfrə-/ a infrarot

in'frequent a, -ly adv selten

infringe /ɪnˈfrɪndʒ/ vt/i ∼ [on] verstoßen gegen. ∼ment n Verstoß m

infuriat|e /ɪnˈfjʊərɪeɪt/ vt wütend machen. ∼ing a ärgerlich; he is ∼ing er kann einen zur Raserei bringen

infusion /ɪnˈfju:ʒn/ n Aufguss m

ingenious /ɪnˈdʒi:nɪəs/ a erfinderisch; ⟨thing⟩ raffiniert

ingenuity /ɪndʒɪˈnju:ətɪ/ n Geschicklichkeit f

ingenuous /ɪnˈdʒenjʊəs/ a unschuldig

ingot /ˈɪŋgət/ n Barren m

ingrained /ɪnˈgreɪnd/ a eingefleischt; be ∼ ⟨dirt⟩ tief sitzen

ingratiate /ɪnˈgreɪʃɪeɪt/ vt ∼ oneself sich einschmeicheln (with bei)

in'gratitude n Undankbarkeit f

ingredient /ɪnˈgri:dɪənt/ n (Culin) Zutat f

ingrowing /ˈɪngrəʊɪŋ/ a ⟨nail⟩ eingewachsen

inhabit /ɪnˈhæbɪt/ vt bewohnen. ∼ant n Einwohner(in) m(f)

inhale /ɪnˈheɪl/ vt/i einatmen; (Med & when smoking) inhalieren

inherent /ɪnˈhɪərənt/ a natürlich

inherit /ɪnˈherɪt/ vt erben. ∼ance /-əns/ n Erbschaft f, Erbe nt

inhibit /ɪnˈhɪbɪt/ vt hemmen. ∼ed a gehemmt. ∼ion /-ˈbɪʃn/ n Hemmung f

inho'spitable a ungastlich

in'human a unmenschlich

inimitable /ɪˈnɪmɪtəbl/ a unnachahmlich

iniquitous /ɪˈnɪkwɪtəs/ a schändlich; (unjust) ungerecht

initial /ɪˈnɪʃl/ a anfänglich, Anfangs- □ n Anfangsbuchstabe m; my ∼s meine Initialen □ vt (pt/pp initialled) abzeichnen; (Pol) paraphieren. ∼ly adv anfangs, am Anfang

initiat|e /ɪˈnɪʃɪeɪt/ vt einführen. ∼ion /-ˈeɪʃn/ n Einführung f

initiative /ɪˈnɪʃətɪv/ n Initiative f

inject /ɪnˈdʒekt/ vt einspritzen, injizieren. ∼ion /-ekʃn/ n Spritze f, Injektion f

injunction /ɪnˈdʒʌŋkʃn/ n gerichtliche Verfügung f

injur|e /ˈɪndʒə(r)/ vt verletzen. ∼y n Verletzung f

in'justice n Ungerechtigkeit f; do s.o. an ∼ jdm unrecht tun

ink /ɪŋk/ n Tinte f

inkling /ˈɪŋklɪŋ/ n Ahnung f

inlaid /ɪnˈleɪd/ a eingelegt

inland /ˈɪnlənd/ a Binnen- □ adv landeinwärts. I ∼ Revenue n ≈ Finanzamt nt

in-laws /ˈɪnlɔ:z/ npl (fam) Schwiegereltern pl

inlay /'ınleı/ n Einlegearbeit f

inlet /'ınlet/ n schmale Bucht f; (Techn) Zuleitung f

inmate /'ınmeıt/ n Insasse m

inn /ın/ n Gasthaus nt

innards /'ınədz/ npl (fam) Eingeweide pl

innate /ı'neıt/ a angeboren

inner /'ınə(r)/ a innere(r,s). ~most a in-nerste(r,s)

'innkeeper n Gastwirt m

innocen|ce /'ınəsəns/ n Unschuld f. ~t a unschuldig. ~tly adv in aller Unschuld

innocuous /ı'nɒkjuəs/ a harmlos

innovat|e /'ınəveıt/ vi neu einführen. ~ion /-'veıʃn/ n Neuerung f. ~or n Neu-erer m

innuendo /ınju:'endəʊ/ n (pl -es) [verste-ckte] Anspielung f

innumerable /ı'nju:mərəbl/ a unzählig

inoculat|e /ı'nɒkjuleıt/ vt impfen. ~ion /-'leıʃn/ n Impfung f

inof'fensive a harmlos

in'operable a nicht operierbar

in'opportune a unpassend

inordinate /ı'nɔ:dınət/ a, -ly adv über-mäßig

inor'ganic a anorganisch

'in-patient n [stationär behandelter] Krankenhauspatient m

input /'ınpʊt/ n Input m & nt

inquest /'ınkwest/ n gerichtliche Untersu-chung f

inquir|e /ın'kwaıə(r)/ vi sich erkundigen (about nach); ~e into untersuchen □ vt sich erkundigen nach. ~y n Erkundigung f; (investigation) Untersuchung f

inquisitive /ın'kwızətıv/ a, -ly adv neu-gierig

inroad /'ınrəʊd/ n Einfall m; make ~s into sth etw angreifen

in'sane a geisteskrank; (fig) wahnsinnig

in'sanitary a unhygienisch

in'sanity n Geisteskrankheit f

insatiable /ın'seıʃəbl/ a unersättlich

inscri|be /ın'skraıb/ vt eingravieren. ~ption /-'skrıpʃn/ n Inschrift f

inscrutable /ın'skru:təbl/ a unergründ-lich; (expression) undurchdringlich

insect /'ınsekt/ n Insekt nt. ~icide /-'sektı-saıd/ n Insektenvertilgungsmittel nt

inse'cur|e a nicht sicher; (fig) unsicher. ~ity n Unsicherheit f

insemination /ınsemı'neıʃn/ n Besa-mung f; (Med) Befruchtung f

in'sensible a (unconscious) bewusstlos

in'sensitive a gefühllos; ~ to un-empfindlich gegen

in'separable a untrennbar; (people) un-zertrennlich

insert[1] /'ınsɜ:t/ n Einsatz m

insert[2] /ın'sɜ:t/ vt einfügen, einsetzen; einstecken (key); einwerfen (coin). ~ion /-ɜ:ʃn/ n (insert) Einsatz m; (in text) Einfü-gung f

inside /ın'saıd/ n Innenseite f; (of house) Innere(s) nt □ attrib Innen- □ adv innen; (indoors) drinnen; go ~ hineingehen; come ~ hereinkommen; ~ out links [herum]; know sth ~ out etw in- und auswendig kennen □ prep ~ [of] in (+ dat) (into) + acc)

insidious /ın'sıdıəs/ a, -ly adv heimtü-ckisch

insight /'ınsaıt/ n Einblick m (into in + acc); (understanding) Einsicht f

insignia /ın'sıgnıə/ npl Insignien pl

insig'nificant a unbedeutend

insin'cere a unaufrichtig

insinuat|e /ın'sınjueıt/ vt andeuten. ~ion /-'eıʃn/ n Andeutung f

insipid /ın'sıpıd/ a fade

insist /ın'sıst/ vi darauf bestehen; ~ on bestehen auf (+ dat) □ vt ~ that darauf bestehen, dass. ~ence n Bestehen nt. ~ent a, -ly adv beharrlich; be ~ent da-rauf bestehen

'insole n Einlegesohle f

insolen|ce /'ınsələns/ n Unverschämtheit f. ~t a, -ly adv unverschämt

in'soluble a unlöslich; (fig) unlösbar

in'solvent a zahlungsunfähig

insomnia /ın'sɒmnıə/ n Schlaflosigkeit f

inspect /ın'spekt/ vt inspizieren; (test) prüfen; kontrollieren (ticket). ~ion /-ekʃn/ n Inspektion f. ~or n Inspektor m; (of tickets) Kontrolleur m

inspiration /ınspə'reıʃn/ n Inspiration f

inspire /ın'spaıə(r)/ vt inspirieren; ~ sth in s.o. jdm etw einflößen

insta'bility n Unbeständigkeit f; (of per-son) Labilität f

install /ın'stɔ:l/ vt installieren; [in ein Amt] einführen (person). ~ation /-stə-'leıʃn/ n Installation f; Amtseinführung f

instalment /ın'stɔ:lmənt/ n (Comm) Rate f; (of serial) Fortsetzung f; (Radio, TV) Folge f

instance /'ınstəns/ n Fall m; (example) Bei-spiel nt; in the first ~ zunächst; for ~ zum Beispiel

instant /'ınstənt/ a sofortig; (Culin) Inst-ant- □ n Augenblick m, Moment m. ~aneous /-'teınıəs/ a unverzüglich, un-mittelbar; death was ~aneous der Tod trat sofort ein

instant 'coffee n Pulverkaffee m

instantly /'ɪnstəntlɪ/ adv sofort

instead /ɪn'sted/ adv statt dessen; ~ of statt (+ gen), anstelle von; ~ of me an meiner Stelle; ~ of going anstatt zu gehen

'instep n Spann m, Rist m

instigat|e /'ɪnstɪgeɪt/ vt anstiften; einleiten ⟨proceedings⟩. ~ion /-'geɪʃn/ n Anstiftung f; at his ~ion auf seine Veranlassung. ~or n Anstifter(in) m(f)

instil /ɪn'stɪl/ vt (pt/pp instilled) einprägen (into s.o. jdm)

instinct /'ɪnstɪŋkt/ n Instinkt m. ~ive /ɪn'stɪŋktɪv/ a, -ly adv instinktiv

institut|e /'ɪnstɪtjuːt/ n Institut nt ◻ vt einführen; einleiten ⟨search⟩. ~ion /-'tjuːʃn/ n Institution f; (home) Anstalt f

instruct /ɪn'strʌkt/ vt unterrichten; ⟨order⟩ anweisen. ~ion /-ʌkʃn/ n Unterricht m; Anweisung f; ~ions pl for use Gebrauchsanweisung f. ~ive /-ɪv/ a lehrreich. ~or n Lehrer(in) m(f); (Mil) Ausbilder m

instrument /'ɪnstrʊmənt/ n Instrument nt. ~al /-'mentl/ a Instrumental-; be ~al in eine entscheidende Rolle spielen bei

insu'bordi|nate a ungehorsam. ~nation /-'neɪʃn/ n Ungehorsam m; (Mil) Insubordination f

in'sufferable a unerträglich

insuf'ficient a, -ly adv nicht genügend

insular /'ɪnsjʊlə(r)/ a (fig) engstirnig

insulat|e /'ɪnsjʊleɪt/ vt isolieren. ~ing tape n Isolierband nt. ~ion /-'leɪʃn/ n Isolierung f

insulin /'ɪnsjʊlɪn/ n Insulin nt

insult¹ /'ɪnsʌlt/ n Beleidigung f

insult² /ɪn'sʌlt/ vt beleidigen

insuperable /ɪn'suːpərəbl/ a unüberwindlich

insur|ance /ɪn'ʃʊərəns/ n Versicherung f. ~e vt versichern

insurrection /ɪnsə'rekʃn/ n Aufstand m

intact /ɪn'tækt/ a unbeschädigt; (complete) vollständig

'intake n Aufnahme f

in'tangible a nicht greifbar

integral /'ɪntɪgrl/ a wesentlich

integrat|e /'ɪntɪgreɪt/ vt integrieren ◻ vi sich integrieren. ~ion /-'greɪʃn/ n Integration f

integrity /ɪn'tegrətɪ/ n Integrität f

intellect /'ɪntəlekt/ n Intellekt m. ~ual /-'lektjʊəl/ a intellektuell

intelligen|ce /ɪn'telɪdʒəns/ n Intelligenz f; (Mil) Nachrichtendienst m; (information) Meldungen pl. ~t a, -ly adv intelligent

intelligentsia /ɪntelɪ'dʒentsɪə/ n Intelligenz f

intelligible /ɪn'telɪdʒəbl/ a verständlich

intend /ɪn'tend/ vt beabsichtigen; be ~ed for bestimmt sein für

intense /ɪn'tens/ a intensiv; ⟨pain⟩ stark. ~ly adv äußerst; ⟨study⟩ intensiv

intensi|fication /ɪntensɪfɪ'keɪʃn/ n Intensivierung f. ~fy /-'tensɪfaɪ/ v (pt/pp -ied) ◻ vt intensivieren ◻ vi zunehmen

intensity /ɪn'tensətɪ/ n Intensität f

intensive /ɪn'tensɪv/ a, -ly adv intensiv; be in ~ care auf der Intensivstation sein

intent /ɪn'tent/ a, -ly adv aufmerksam; ~ on (absorbed in) vertieft in (+ acc); be ~ on doing sth fest entschlossen sein, etw zu tun ◻ n Absicht f; to all ~s and purposes im Grunde

intention /ɪn'tenʃn/ n Absicht f. ~al a, -ly adv absichtlich

inter /ɪn't3ː(r)/ vt (pt/pp interred) bestatten

inter'action n Wechselwirkung f

intercede /ɪntə'siːd/ vi Fürsprache einlegen (on behalf of für)

intercept /ɪntə'sept/ vt abfangen

'interchange¹ n Austausch m; (Auto) Autobahnkreuz nt

inter'change² vt austauschen. ~able a austauschbar

intercom /'ɪntəkɒm/ n [Gegen]sprechanlage f

'intercourse n Verkehr m; (sexual) Geschlechtsverkehr m

interest /'ɪntrəst/ n Interesse nt; (Comm) Zinsen pl; have an ~ (Comm) beteiligt sein (in an + dat) ◻ vt interessieren; be ~ed sich interessieren (in für). ~ing a interessant. ~ rate n Zinssatz m

interfere /ɪntə'fɪə(r)/ vi sich einmischen. ~nce /-əns/ n Einmischung f; (Radio, TV) Störung f

interim /'ɪntərɪm/ a Zwischen-; (temporary) vorläufig ◻ n in the ~ in der Zwischenzeit

interior /ɪn'tɪərɪə(r)/ a innere(r,s), Innen- ◻ n Innere(s) nt

interject /ɪntə'dʒekt/ vt einwerfen. ~ion /-ekʃn/ n Interjektion f; (remark) Einwurf m

inter'lock vi ineinander greifen

interloper /'ɪntələʊpə(r)/ n Eindringling m

interlude /'ɪntəluːd/ n Pause f; (performance) Zwischenspiel nt

inter'marry vi untereinander heiraten; ⟨different groups:⟩ Mischehen schließen

intermediary /ɪntə'miːdɪərɪ/ n Vermittler(in) m(f)

intermediate /ɪntəˈmiːdɪət/ a Zwischen-

interminable /ɪnˈtɜːmɪnəbl/ a endlos [lang]

intermission /ɪntəˈmɪʃn/ n Pause f

intermittent /ɪntəˈmɪtənt/ a in Abständen auftretend

intern /ɪnˈtɜːn/ vt internieren

internal /ɪnˈtɜːnl/ a innere(r,s); ⟨matter, dispute⟩ intern. ~ly adv innerlich; ⟨deal with⟩ intern

inter'national a, -ly adv international □ n Länderspiel nt; ⟨player⟩ Nationalspieler(in) m(f)

internist /ɪnˈtɜːnɪst/ n (Amer) Internist m

internment /ɪnˈtɜːnmənt/ n Internierung f

'interplay n Wechselspiel nt

interpolate /ɪnˈtɜːpəleɪt/ vt einwerfen

interpret /ɪnˈtɜːprɪt/ vt interpretieren; auslegen ⟨text⟩; deuten ⟨dream⟩; ⟨translate⟩ dolmetschen □ vi dolmetschen. ~ation /-ˈteɪʃn/ n Interpretation f. ~er n Dolmetscher(in) m(f)

interre'lated a verwandt; ⟨facts⟩ zusammenhängend

interrogat|e /ɪnˈterəgeɪt/ vt verhören. ~ion /-ˈgeɪʃn/ n Verhör n

interrogative /ɪntəˈrɒgətɪv/ a & n ~ [pronoun] Interrogativpronomen nt

interrupt /ɪntəˈrʌpt/ vt/i unterbrechen; don't ~! nicht dazwischen! ~ion /-ˈʌpʃn/ n Unterbrechung f

intersect /ɪntəˈsekt/ vi sich kreuzen; (Geom) sich schneiden. ~ion /-ˈekʃn/ n Kreuzung f

interspersed /ɪntəˈspɜːst/ a ~ with durchsetzt mit

inter'twine vi sich ineinander schlingen

interval /ˈɪntəvl/ n Abstand m; (Theat) Pause f; (Mus) Intervall nt; at hourly ~s alle Stunde; bright ~s pl Aufheiterungen pl

interven|e /ɪntəˈviːn/ vi eingreifen; ⟨occur⟩ dazwischenkommen. ~tion /-ˈvenʃn/ n Eingreifen nt; (Mil, Pol) Intervention f

interview /ˈɪntəvjuː/ n (Journ) Interview nt; (for job) Vorstellungsgespräch nt; go for an ~ sich vorstellen □ vt interviewen; ein Vorstellungsgespräch führen mit. ~er n Interviewer(in) m(f)

intestine /ɪnˈtestɪn/ n Darm m

intimacy /ˈɪntɪməsɪ/ n Vertrautheit f; (sexual) Intimität f

intimate¹ /ˈɪntɪmət/ a, -ly adv vertraut; ⟨friend⟩ eng; (sexually) intim

intimate² /ˈɪntɪmeɪt/ vt zu verstehen geben; (imply) andeuten

intimidat|e /ɪnˈtɪmɪdeɪt/ vt einschüchtern. ~ion /-ˈdeɪʃn/ n Einschüchterung f

into /ˈɪntə, vor einem Vokal ˈɪntʊ/ prep in (+ acc); go ~ the house ins Haus [hinein]gehen; be ~ (fam) sich auskennen mit; 7 ~ 21 21 [geteilt] durch 7

in'tolerable a unerträglich

in'toleran|ce n Intoleranz f. ~t a intolerant

intonation /ɪntəˈneɪʃn/ n Tonfall m

intoxicat|ed /ɪnˈtɒksɪkeɪtɪd/ a betrunken; (fig) berauscht. ~ion /-ˈkeɪʃn/ n Rausch m

intractable /ɪnˈtræktəbl/ a widerspenstig; ⟨problem⟩ hartnäckig

intransigent /ɪnˈtrænsɪdʒənt/ a unnachgiebig

in'transitive a, -ly adv intransitiv

intravenous /ɪntrəˈviːnəs/ a, -ly adv intravenös

intrepid /ɪnˈtrepɪd/ a kühn, unerschrocken

intricate /ˈɪntrɪkət/ a kompliziert

intrigu|e /ɪnˈtriːg/ n Intrige f □ vi faszinieren □ vi intrigieren. ~ing a faszinierend

intrinsic /ɪnˈtrɪnsɪk/ a ~ value Eigenwert m

introduce /ɪntrəˈdjuːs/ vt vorstellen; ⟨bring in, insert⟩ einführen

introduct|ion /ɪntrəˈdʌkʃn/ n Einführung f; (to person) Vorstellung f; (to book) Einleitung f. ~ory /-tərɪ/ a einleitend

introspective /ɪntrəˈspektɪv/ a in sich (acc) gerichtet

introvert /ˈɪntrəvɜːt/ n introvertierter Mensch m

intru|de /ɪnˈtruːd/ vi stören. ~der n Eindringling m. ~sion /-ˈuːʒn/ n Störung f

intuit|ion /ɪntjuːˈɪʃn/ n Intuition f. ~ive /-ˈtjuːɪtɪv/ a, -ly adv intuitiv

inundate /ˈɪnəndeɪt/ vt überschwemmen

invade /ɪnˈveɪd/ vt einfallen in (+ acc). ~r n Angreifer m

invalid¹ /ˈɪnvəlɪd/ n Kranke(r) m/f

invalid² /ɪnˈvælɪd/ a ungültig. ~ate vt ungültig machen

in'valuable a unschätzbar; ⟨person⟩ unersetzlich

in'variab|le a unveränderlich. ~ly adv immer

invasion /ɪnˈveɪʒn/ n Invasion f

invective /ɪnˈvektɪv/ n Beschimpfungen pl

invent /ɪnˈvent/ vt erfinden. ~ion /-enʃn/ n Erfindung f. ~ive /-tɪv/ a erfinderisch. ~or n Erfinder m

inventory /'ɪnvəntrɪ/ n Bestandsliste f; make an ∼ ein Inventar aufstellen

inverse /ɪn'vɜːs/ a, -ly adv umgekehrt □ n Gegenteil nt

invert /ɪn'vɜːt/ vt umkehren. ∼ed commas npl Anführungszeichen pl

invest /ɪn'vest/ vt investieren, anlegen; ∼ in (fam: buy) sich (dat) zulegen

investigat|e /ɪn'vestɪgeɪt/ vt untersuchen. ∼ion /-'geɪʃn/ n Untersuchung f

invest|ment /ɪn'vestmənt/ n Anlage f; be a good ∼ment (fig) sich bezahlt machen. ∼or n Kapitalanleger m

inveterate /ɪn'vetərət/ a Gewohnheits-; ⟨liar⟩ unverbesserlich

invidious /ɪn'vɪdɪəs/ a unerfreulich; (unfair) ungerecht

invigilate /ɪn'vɪdʒɪleɪt/ vi (Sch) Aufsicht führen

invigorate /ɪn'vɪgəreɪt/ vt beleben

invincible /ɪn'vɪnsəbl/ a unbesiegbar

inviolable /ɪn'vaɪələbl/ a unantastbar

in'visible a unsichtbar. ∼ mending n Kunststopfen nt

invitation /ɪnvɪ'teɪʃn/ n Einladung f

invit|e /ɪn'vaɪt/ vt einladen. ∼ing a einladend

invoice /'ɪnvɔɪs/ n Rechnung f □ vt ∼ s.o. jdm eine Rechnung schicken

invoke /ɪn'vəʊk/ vt anrufen

in'voluntary a, -ily adv unwillkürlich

involve /ɪn'vɒlv/ vt beteiligen; (affect) betreffen; (implicate) verwickeln; (entail) mit sich bringen; (mean) bedeuten; be ∼d in beteiligt sein an (+ dat); (implicated) verwickelt sein in (+ acc); get ∼d with s.o. sich mit jdm einlassen. ∼d a kompliziert

in'vulnerable a unverwundbar; ⟨position⟩ unangreifbar

inward /'ɪnwəd/ a innere(r,s). ∼ly adv innerlich. ∼s adv nach innen

iodine /'aɪədiːn/ n Jod nt

iota /aɪ'əʊtə/ n Jota nt, (fam) Funke m

IOU abbr (I owe you) Schuldschein m

Iran /ɪ'rɑːn/ n der Iran

Iraq /ɪ'rɑːk/ n der Irak

irascible /ɪ'ræsəbl/ a aufbrausend

irate /aɪ'reɪt/ a wütend

Ireland /'aɪələnd/ n Irland nt

iris /'aɪərɪs/ n (Anat) Regenbogenhaut f, Iris f; (Bot) Schwertlilie f

Irish /'aɪərɪʃ/ a irisch □ n the ∼ pl die Iren. ∼man n Ire m. ∼woman n Irin f

irk /ɜːk/ vt ärgern. ∼some /-səm/ a lästig

iron /'aɪən/ a Eisen-; (fig) eisern □ n Eisen nt; (appliance) Bügeleisen nt □ vt/i bügeln. ∼ out vt ausbügeln

ironic[al] /aɪ'rɒnɪk[l]/ a ironisch

ironing /'aɪənɪŋ/ n Bügeln nt; (articles) Bügelwäsche f; do the ∼ bügeln. ∼board n Bügelbrett nt

ironmonger /'-mʌŋgə(r)/ n ∼'s [shop] Haushaltswarengeschäft nt

irony /'aɪərənɪ/ n Ironie f

irradiate /ɪ'reɪdɪeɪt/ vt bestrahlen

irrational /ɪ'ræʃənl/ a irrational

irreconcilable /ɪ'rekənsaɪləbl/ a unversöhnlich

irrefutable /ɪrɪ'fjuːtəbl/ a unwiderlegbar

irregular /ɪ'regjʊlə(r)/ a, -ly adv unregelmäßig; (against rules) regelwidrig. ∼ity /-'lærətɪ/ n Unregelmäßigkeit f; Regelwidrigkeit f

irrelevant /ɪ'reləvənt/ a irrelevant

irreparable /ɪ'repərəbl/ a unersetzlich; be ∼ nicht wieder gutzumachen sein

irreplaceable /ɪrɪ'pleɪsəbl/ a unersetzlich

irrepressible /ɪrɪ'presəbl/ a unverwüstlich; be ∼ ⟨person⟩ nicht unterzukriegen sein

irresistible /ɪrɪ'zɪstəbl/ a unwiderstehlich

irresolute /ɪ'rezəluːt/ a unentschlossen

irrespective /ɪrɪ'spektɪv/ a ∼ of ungeachtet (+ gen)

irresponsible /ɪrɪ'spɒnsəbl/ a, -bly adv unverantwortlich; ⟨person⟩ verantwortungslos

irreverent /ɪ'revərənt/ a, -ly adv respektlos

irreversible /ɪrɪ'vɜːsəbl/ a unwiderruflich; (Med) irreversibel

irrevocable /ɪ'revəkəbl/ a, -bly adv unwiderruflich

irrigat|e /'ɪrɪgeɪt/ vt bewässern. ∼ion /-'geɪʃn/ n Bewässerung f

irritability /ɪrɪtə'bɪlətɪ/ n Gereiztheit f

irritable /'ɪrɪtəbl/ a reizbar

irritant /'ɪrɪtənt/ n Reizstoff m

irritat|e /'ɪrɪteɪt/ vt irritieren; (Med) reizen. ∼ion /-'teɪʃn/ n Ärger m; (Med) Reizung f

is /ɪz/ see be

Islam /'ɪzlɑːm/ n der Islam. ∼ic /-'læmɪk/ a islamisch

island /'aɪlənd/ n Insel f. ∼er n Inselbewohner(in) m(f)

isle /aɪl/ n Insel f

isolat|e /'aɪsəleɪt/ vt isolieren. ∼ed a (remote) abgelegen; (single) einzeln. ∼ion /-'leɪʃn/ n Isoliertheit f; (Med) Isolierung f

Israel /'ɪzreɪl/ n Israel nt. ∼i /ɪz'reɪlɪ/ a israelisch □ n Israeli m/f

issue /'ɪʃuː/ n Frage f; (outcome) Ergebnis nt; (of magazine, stamps) Ausgabe f; (offspring) Nachkommen pl; what is at ~? worum geht es? take ~ with s.o. jdm widersprechen □ vt ausgeben; ausstellen (passport); erteilen (order); herausgeben (book); be ~d with sth etw erhalten □ vi ~ from herausströmen aus

isthmus /'ɪsməs/ n (pl -muses) Landenge f

it /ɪt/ pron es; (m)er; (f) sie; (as direct object) es; (m) ihn; (f) sie; (as indirect object) ihm; (f) ihr; it is raining es regnet; it's me ich bin's; who is it? wer ist da? of/from it davon; with it damit; out of it daraus

Italian /ɪ'tæljən/ a italienisch □ n Italiener(in) m(f); (Lang) Italienisch nt

italic /ɪ'tælɪk/ a kursiv. ~s npl Kursivschrift f; in ~s kursiv

Italy /'ɪtəlɪ/ n Italien nt

itch /ɪtʃ/ n Juckreiz m; I have an ~ es juckt mich □ vi jucken; I'm ~ing (fam) es juckt mich (to zu). ~y a juckend

item /'aɪtəm/ n Gegenstand m; (Comm) Artikel m; (on agenda) Punkt m; (on invoice) Posten m; (act) Nummer f; ~ [of news] Nachricht f. ~ize vt einzeln aufführen; spezifizieren (bill)

itinerant /aɪ'tɪnərənt/ a Wander-

itinerary /aɪ'tɪnərərɪ/ n [Reise]route f

its /ɪts/ poss pron sein; (f) ihr

it's = it is, it has

itself /ɪt'self/ pron selbst; (refl) sich; by ~ von selbst; (alone) allein

ivory /'aɪvərɪ/ n Elfenbein nt □ attrib Elfenbein-

ivy /'aɪvɪ/ n Efeu m

J

jab /dʒæb/ n Stoß m; (fam: injection) Spritze f □ vt (pt/pp jabbed) stoßen

jabber /'dʒæbə(r)/ vi plappern

jack /dʒæk/ n (Auto) Wagenheber m; (Cards) Bube m □ vt ~ up (Auto) aufbocken

jackdaw /'dʒækdɔː/ n Dohle f

jacket /'dʒækɪt/ n Jacke f; (of book) Schutzumschlag m. ~ po'tato n in der Schale gebackene Kartoffel f

'jackpot n hit the ~ das große Los ziehen

jade /dʒeɪd/ n Jade m

jaded /'dʒeɪdɪd/ a abgespannt

jagged /'dʒægɪd/ a zackig

jail /dʒeɪl/ = gaol

jalopy /dʒə'lɒpɪ/ n (fam) Klapperkiste f

jam¹ /dʒæm/ n Marmelade f

jam² n Gedränge nt; (Auto) Stau m; (fam: difficulty) Klemme f □ v (pt/pp jammed) □ vt klemmen (in in + acc); stören (broadcast) □ vi klemmen

Jamaica /dʒə'meɪkə/ n Jamaika nt

jangle /'dʒæŋgl/ vi klimpern □ vt klimpern mit

janitor /'dʒænɪtə(r)/ n Hausmeister m

January /'dʒænjʊərɪ/ n Januar m

Japan /dʒə'pæn/ n Japan nt. ~ese /dʒæpə'niːz/ a japanisch □ n Japaner(in) m(f); (Lang) Japanisch nt

jar¹ /dʒɑː(r)/ n Glas nt; (earthenware) Topf m

jar² v (pt/pp jarred) vi stören □ vt erschüttern

jargon /'dʒɑːgən/ n Jargon m

jaundice /'dʒɔːndɪs/ n Gelbsucht f. ~d a (fig) zynisch

jaunt /dʒɔːnt/ n Ausflug m

jaunty /'dʒɔːntɪ/ a (-ier, -iest) -ily adv keck

javelin /'dʒævlɪn/ n Speer m

jaw /dʒɔː/ n Kiefer m; ~s pl Rachen m □ vi (fam) quatschen

jay /dʒeɪ/ n Eichelhäher m. ~-walker n achtloser Fußgänger m

jazz /dʒæz/ n Jazz m. ~y a knallig

jealous /'dʒeləs/ a, -ly adv eifersüchtig (of auf + acc). ~y n Eifersucht f

jeans /dʒiːnz/ npl Jeans pl

jeer /dʒɪə(r)/ n Johlen nt □ vi johlen; ~ at verhöhnen

jell /dʒel/ vi gelieren

jelly /'dʒelɪ/ n Gelee nt; (dessert) Götterspeise f. ~fish n Qualle f

jemmy /'dʒemɪ/ n Brecheisen nt

jeopar|dize /'dʒepədaɪz/ vt gefährden. ~dy /-dɪ/ n in ~dy gefährdet

jerk /dʒɜːk/ n Ruck m □ vt stoßen; (pull) reißen □ vi rucken; (limb, muscle:) zucken. ~ily adv ruckweise. ~y a ruckartig

jersey /'dʒɜːzɪ/ n Pullover m; (Sport) Trikot nt; (fabric) Jersey m

jest /dʒest/ n Scherz m; in ~ im Spaß □ vi scherzen

jet¹ /dʒet/ n (Miner) Jett m

jet² n (of water) [Wasser]strahl m; (nozzle) Düse f; (plane) Düsenflugzeug nt

jet: ~-'black a pechschwarz. ~lag n Jetlag nt. ~-pro'pelled a mit Düsenantrieb

jettison /'dʒetɪsn/ vt über Bord werfen

jetty /'dʒetɪ/ n Landesteg m; (breakwater) Buhne f

Jew /dʒuː/ n Jude m /Jüdin f

jewel /'dʒuːəl/ n Edelstein m; (fig) Juwel nt. ∼ler n Juwelier m; ∼ler's [shop] Juweliergeschäft nt. ∼lery n Schmuck m

Jew|ess /'dʒuːɪs/ n Jüdin f. ∼ish a jüdisch

jib /dʒɪb/ vi (pt/pp jibbed) (fig) sich sträuben (at gegen)

jiffy /'dʒɪfɪ/ n (fam) in a ∼ in einem Augenblick

jigsaw /'dʒɪgsɔː/ n ∼ [puzzle] Puzzlespiel nt

jilt /dʒɪlt/ vt sitzen lassen

jingle /'dʒɪŋgl/ n (rhyme) Versehen nt □ vi klimpern □ vt klimpern mit

jinx /dʒɪŋks/ n (fam) it's got a ∼ on it es ist verhext

jitter|s /'dʒɪtəz/ npl (fam) have the ∼s nervös sein. ∼y a (fam) nervös

job /dʒɒb/ n Aufgabe f; (post) Stelle f, (fam) Job m; be a ∼ (fam) nicht leicht sein; it's a good ∼ that es ist [nur] gut, dass. ∼ centre n Arbeitsvermittlungsstelle f. ∼less a arbeitslos

jockey /'dʒɒkɪ/ n Jockei m

jocular /'dʒɒkjʊlə(r)/ a, -ly adv spaßhaft

jog /dʒɒg/ n Stoß m; at a ∼ im Dauerlauf □ vi (pt/pp jogged) □ vt anstoßen; ∼ s.o.'s memory jds Gedächtnis nachhelfen □ vi (Sport) joggen. ∼ging n Jogging nt

john /dʒɒn/ n (Amer, fam) Klo nt

join /dʒɔɪn/ n Nahtstelle f □ vt verbinden (to mit); sich anschließen (+ dat) (person); (become member of) beitreten (+ dat); eintreten (+ acc) (firm); sich (dat) treffen. ∼ in vi mitmachen. ∼ up vi (Mil) Soldat werden □ vt zusammenfügen

joiner /'dʒɔɪnə(r)/ n Tischler m

joint /dʒɔɪnt/ a, -ly adv gemeinsam □ n Gelenk nt; (in wood, brickwork) Fuge f; (Culin) Braten m; (fam: bar) Lokal nt

joist /dʒɔɪst/ n Dielenbalken m

jok|e /dʒəʊk/ n Scherz m; (funny story) Witz m; (trick) Streich m □ vi scherzen. ∼er n Witzbold m; (Cards) Joker m. ∼ing n ∼ing apart Spaß beiseite. ∼ingly adv im Spaß

jollity /'dʒɒlətɪ/ n Lustigkeit f

jolly /'dʒɒlɪ/ a (-ier, -iest) lustig □ adv (fam) sehr

jolt /dʒəʊlt/ n Ruck m □ vt einen Ruck versetzen (+ dat) □ vi holpern

Jordan /'dʒɔːdn/ n Jordanien nt

jostle /'dʒɒsl/ vt anrempeln □ vi drängeln

jot /dʒɒt/ n Jota nt □ vt (pt/pp jotted) ∼ [down] sich (dat) notieren. ∼ter n Notizblock m

journal /'dʒɜːnl/ n Zeitschrift f; (diary) Tagebuch nt. ∼ese /-ə'liːz/ n Zeitungsjargon m. ∼ism n Journalismus m. ∼ist n Journalist(in) m(f)

journey /'dʒɜːnɪ/ n Reise f

jovial /'dʒəʊvɪəl/ a lustig

joy /dʒɔɪ/ n Freude f. ∼ful a, -ly adv freudig, froh. ∼ride n (fam) Spritztour f [im gestohlenen Auto]

jubil|ant /'dʒuːbɪlənt/ a überglücklich. ∼ation /-'leɪʃn/ n Jubel m

jubilee /'dʒuːbɪliː/ n Jubiläum nt

Judaism /'dʒuːdeɪɪzm/ n Judentum nt

judder /'dʒʌdə(r)/ vi rucken

judge /dʒʌdʒ/ n Richter m; (of competition) Preisrichter m □ vt beurteilen; (estimate) [ein]schätzen □ vi urteilen (by nach). ∼ment n Beurteilung f; (Jur) Urteil nt; (fig) Urteilsvermögen nt

judic|ial /dʒuː'dɪʃl/ a gerichtlich. ∼iary /-ʃərɪ/ n Richterstand m. ∼ious /-ʃəs/ a klug

judo /'dʒuːdəʊ/ n Judo nt

jug /dʒʌg/ n Kanne f; (small) Kännchen nt; (for water, wine) Krug m

juggernaut /'dʒʌgənɔːt/ n (fam) Riesenlaster m

juggle /'dʒʌgl/ vi jonglieren. ∼r n Jongleur m

juice /dʒuːs/ n Saft m. ∼ extractor n Entsafter m

juicy /'dʒuːsɪ/ a (-ier, -iest) saftig; (fam) (story) pikant

juke-box /'dʒuːk-/ n Musikbox f

July /dʒʊ'laɪ/ n Juli m

jumble /'dʒʌmbl/ n Durcheinander nt □ vt ∼ [up] durcheinander bringen. ∼ sale n [Wohltätigkeits]basar m

jumbo /'dʒʌmbəʊ/ n ∼ [jet] Jumbo[jet] m

jump /dʒʌmp/ n Sprung m; (in prices) Anstieg m; (in horse racing) Hindernis nt □ vi springen; (start) zusammenzucken; make s.o. ∼ jdn erschrecken; ∼ at (fig) sofort zugreifen bei (offer); ∼ to conclusions voreilige Schlüsse ziehen □ vt überspringen; ∼ the gun (fig) vorschnell handeln. ∼ up vi aufspringen

jumper /'dʒʌmpə(r)/ n Pullover m, Pulli m

jumpy /'dʒʌmpɪ/ a nervös

junction /'dʒʌŋkʃn/ n Kreuzung f; (Rail) Knotenpunkt m

juncture /'dʒʌŋktʃə(r)/ n at this ∼ zu diesem Zeitpunkt

June /dʒuːn/ n Juni m

jungle /'dʒʌŋgl/ n Dschungel m

junior /'dʒuːnɪə(r)/ a jünger; (in rank) untergeordnet; (Sport) Junioren- □ n Junior m. ∼ school n Grundschule f

juniper /'dʒuːnɪpə(r)/ n Wacholder m

junk /dʒʌŋk/ n Gerümpel nt, Trödel m

junkie /'dʒʌŋkɪ/ n (sl) Fixer m

'junk-shop n Trödelladen m

juris|diction /dʒʊərɪs'dɪkʃn/ n Gerichtsbarkeit f. ∼'prudence n Rechtswissenschaft f

juror /'dʒʊərə/ n Geschworene(r) m/f

jury /'dʒʊərɪ/ n the ∼ die Geschworenen pl; (for competition) die Jury

just /dʒʌst/ a gerecht □ adv gerade; (only) nur; (simply) einfach; (exactly) genau; ∼ as tall ebenso groß; ∼ listen! hör doch mal! I'm ∼ going ich gehe schon; ∼ put it down stell es nur hin

justice /'dʒʌstɪs/ n Gerechtigkeit f; do ∼ to gerecht werden (+ dat); J∼ of the Peace ≈ Friedensrichter m

justifiab|le /'dʒʌstɪfaɪəbl/ a berechtigt. ∼ly adv berechtigterweise

justi|fication /dʒʌstɪfɪ'keɪʃn/ n Rechtfertigung f. ∼fy /'dʒʌstɪfaɪ/ vt (pt/pp -ied) rechtfertigen

justly /'dʒʌstlɪ/ adv zu Recht

jut /dʒʌt/ vi (pt/pp jutted) ∼ out vorstehen

juvenile /'dʒu:vənaɪl/ a jugendlich; (childish) kindisch □ n Jugendliche(r) m/f. ∼ delinquency n Jugendkriminalität f

juxtapose /dʒʌkstə'pəʊz/ vt nebeneinander stellen

K

kangaroo /kæŋgə'ru:/ n Känguru nt

karate /kə'rɑ:tɪ/ n Karate nt

kebab /kɪ'bæb/ n (Culin) Spießchen nt

keel /ki:l/ n Kiel m □ vi ∼ over umkippen; (Naut) kentern

keen /ki:n/ a (-er, -est) (sharp) scharf; (intense) groß; (eager) eifrig, begeistert; ∼ on (fam) erpicht auf (+ acc); ∼ on s.o. von jdm sehr angetan; be ∼ to do sth etw gerne machen wollen. ∼ly adv tief. ∼ness n Eifer m, Begeisterung f

keep /ki:p/ n (maintenance) Unterhalt m; (of castle) Bergfried m; for ∼s für immer □ v (pt/pp kept) □ vt behalten; (store) aufbewahren; (not throw away) aufheben; (support) unterhalten; (detain) aufhalten; freihalten (seat); halten (promise, animals); führen, haben (shop); einhalten (law, rules); ∼ sth hot etw warm halten; ∼ s.o. from doing sth jdn davon abhalten, etw zu tun; ∼ s.o. waiting jdn warten lassen; ∼ sth to oneself etw nicht weitersagen; where do you ∼ the sugar? wo hast du den Zucker? □ vi (remain) bleiben; (food:) sich halten; ∼ left/right

sich links/rechts halten; ∼ doing sth etw dauernd machen; ∼ on doing sth etw weitermachen; ∼ in with sich gut stellen mit. ∼ up vi Schritt halten □ vt (continue) weitermachen

keep|er /'ki:pə(r)/ n Wärter(in) m(f). ∼ing n Obhut f; be in ∼ing with passen zu. ∼sake n Andenken f

keg /keg/ n kleines Fass nt

kennel /'kenl/ n Hundehütte f; ∼s pl (boarding) Hundepension f; (for breeding) Zwinger m

Kenya /'kenjə/ n Kenia nt

kept /kept/ see keep

kerb /kɜ:b/ n Bordstein m

kernel /'kɜ:nl/ n Kern m

kerosene /'kerəsi:n/ n (Amer) Petroleum nt

ketchup /'ketʃʌp/ n Ketchup m

kettle /'ketl/ n [Wasser]kessel m; put the ∼ on Wasser aufsetzen; a pretty ∼ of fish (fam) eine schöne Bescherung f

key /ki:/ n Schlüssel m; (Mus) Tonart f; (of piano, typewriter) Taste f □ vt ∼ in eintasten

key: ∼board n Tastatur f; (Mus) Klaviatur f. ∼boarder n Taster(in) m(f). ∼hole n Schlüsselloch nt. ∼ring n Schlüsselring m

khaki /'kɑ:kɪ/ a khakifarben □ n Khaki nt

kick /kɪk/ n [Fuß]tritt m; for ∼s (fam) zum Spaß □ vt treten; ∼ the bucket (fam) abkratzen □ vi (animal:) ausschlagen. ∼off n (Sport) Anstoß m

kid /kɪd/ n Kitz nt; (fam: child) Kind nt □ vt (pt/pp kidded) (fam) ∼ s.o. jdm etwas vormachen. ∼ gloves npl Glacéhandschuhe pl

kidnap /'kɪdnæp/ vt (pt/pp -napped) entführen. ∼per n Entführer m. ∼ping n Entführung f

kidney /'kɪdnɪ/ n Niere f. ∼ machine n künstliche Niere f

kill /kɪl/ vt töten; (fam) totschlagen (time); ∼ two birds with one stone zwei Fliegen mit einer Klappe schlagen. ∼er n Mörder(in) m(f). ∼ing n Tötung f; (murder) Mord m

'killjoy n Spielverderber m

kiln /kɪln/ n Brennofen m

kilo /'ki:ləʊ/ n Kilo nt

kilo /'kɪlə/: ∼gram n Kilogramm nt. ∼hertz /-h3:ts/ n Kilohertz nt. ∼metre /-mi:tə/ n Kilometer m. ∼watt n Kilowatt nt

kilt /kɪlt/ n Schottenrock m

kin /kɪn/ n Verwandtschaft f; next of ∼ nächster Verwandter m/nächste Verwandte f

kind¹ /kaɪnd/ n Art f; (*brand, type*) Sorte f; what ~ of car? was für ein Auto? ~ of (*fam*) irgendwie

kind² a (-er, -est) nett; ~ to animals gut zu Tieren; ~ regards herzliche Grüße

kindergarten /'kɪndəgɑːtn/ n Vorschule f

kindle /'kɪndl/ vt anzünden

kind|ly /'kaɪndlɪ/ a (-ier, -iest) nett □ adv netterweise; (*if you please*) gefälligst. ~ness n Güte f; (*favour*) Gefallen m

kindred /'kɪndrɪd/ a ~ spirit Gleichgesinnte(r) m/f

kinetic /kɪ'netɪk/ a kinetisch

king /kɪŋ/ n König m; (*Draughts*) Dame f. ~dom n Königreich nt; (*fig & Relig*) Reich nt

king: ~fisher n Eisvogel m. ~sized a extragroß

kink /kɪŋk/ n Knick m. ~y a (*fam*) pervers

kiosk /'kiːɒsk/ n Kiosk m

kip /kɪp/ n have a ~ (*fam*) pennen □ vi (*pt/pp* kipped) (*fam*) pennen

kipper /'kɪpə(r)/ n Räucherhering m

kiss /kɪs/ n Kuss m □ vt/i küssen

kit /kɪt/ n Ausrüstung f; (*tools*) Werkzeug nt; (*construction* ~) Bausatz m □ vt (*pt/pp* kitted) ~ out ausrüsten. ~bag n See sack m

kitchen /'kɪtʃɪn/ n Küche f □ attrib Küchen-. ~ette /kɪtʃɪ'net/ n Kochnische f

kitchen: ~ 'garden n Gemüsegarten m. ~ 'sink n Spülbecken nt

kite /kaɪt/ n Drachen m

kith /kɪθ/ n with ~ and kin mit der ganzen Verwandtschaft

kitten /'kɪtn/ n Kätzchen nt

kitty /'kɪtɪ/ n (*money*) [gemeinsame] Kasse f

kleptomaniac /klɛptə'meɪnɪæk/ n Kleptomane m/ -manin f

knack /næk/ n Trick m, Dreh m

knapsack /'næp-/ n Tornister m

knead /niːd/ vt kneten

knee /niː/ n Knie nt. ~cap n Kniescheibe f

kneel /niːl/ vi (*pt/pp* knelt) knien; ~ [down] sich [nieder]knien

knelt /nelt/ see kneel

knew /njuː/ see know

knickers /'nɪkəz/ npl Schlüpfer m

knick-knacks /'nɪknæks/ npl Nippsachen pl

knife /naɪf/ n (*pl* knives) Messer nt □ vt einen Messerstich versetzen (+ *dat*); (*to death*) erstechen

knight /naɪt/ n Ritter m; (*Chess*) Springer m □ vt adeln

knit /nɪt/ vt/i (*pt/pp* knitted) stricken; ~ one, purl one eine rechts eine links; ~ one's brow die Stirn runzeln. ~ting n Stricken nt; (*work*) Strickzeug nt. ~ting-needle n Stricknadel f. ~wear n Strickwaren pl

knives /naɪvz/ npl see knife

knob /nɒb/ n Knopf m; (*on door*) Knauf m; (*small lump*) Beule f; (*small piece*) Stückchen nt. ~bly a knorrig; (*bony*) knochig

knock /nɒk/ n Klopfen nt; (*blow*) Schlag m; there was a ~ at the door es klopfte □ vt anstoßen; (*at door*) klopfen an (+ *acc*); (*fam:criticize*) heruntermachen; ~ a hole in sth ein Loch in etw (*acc*) schlagen; ~ one's head sich (*dat*) den Kopf stoßen (on an + *dat*) □ vi klopfen. ~ about vt schlagen □ vi (*fam*) herumkommen. ~ down vt herunterwerfen; (*with fist*) niederschlagen; (*in car*) anfahren; (*demolish*) abreißen; (*fam: reduce*) herabsetzen. ~ off vt herunterwerfen; (*fam: steal*) klauen; (*fam: complete quickly*) hinhauen □ vi (*fam: cease work*) Feierabend machen. ~ out vt ausschlagen; (*make unconscious*) bewusstlos schlagen; (*Boxing*) k.o. schlagen. ~ over vt umwerfen; (*in car*) anfahren

knock: ~down a ~-down prices Schleuderpreise pl. ~er n Türklopfer m. ~-kneed /-'niːd/ a X-beinig. ~-out n (*Boxing*) K.o. m

knot /nɒt/ n Knoten m □ vt (*pt/pp* knotted) knoten

knotty /'nɒtɪ/ a (-ier, -iest) verwickelt

know /nəʊ/ vt/i (*pt* knew, *pp* known) wissen; kennen (*person*); können (*language*); get to ~ kennen lernen □ n in the ~ (*fam*) im Bild

know: ~-all n (*fam*) Alleswisser m. ~how n (*fam*) [Sach]kenntnis f. ~ing a wissend. ~ingly adv wissend; (*intentionally*) wissentlich

knowledge /'nɒlɪdʒ/ n Kenntnis f (of von/gen); (*general*) Wissen nt; (*specialized*) Kenntnisse pl. ~able /-əbl/ a be ~able viel wissen

known /nəʊn/ see know □ a bekannt

knuckle /'nʌkl/ n [Finger]knöchel m; (*Culin*) Hachse f □ vi ~ under sich fügen; ~ down sich dahinter klemmen

kosher /'kəʊʃə(r)/ a koscher

kowtow /kaʊ'taʊ/ vi Kotau machen (to vor + *dat*)

kudos /'kjuːdɒs/ n (*fam*) Prestige nt

L

lab /læb/ n (fam) Labor nt

label /'leɪbl/ n Etikett nt □ vt (pt/pp labelled) etikettieren

laboratory /lə'bɒrətrɪ/ n Labor nt

laborious /lə'bɔːrɪəs/ a, -ly adv mühsam

labour /'leɪbə(r)/ n Arbeit f; (workers) Arbeitskräfte pl; (Med) Wehen pl; L~ (Pol) die Labourpartei □ attrib Labour- □ vi arbeiten □ vt (fig) sich lange auslassen über (+ acc). ~er n Arbeiter m

'labour-saving a arbeitssparend

laburnum /lə'bɜːnəm/ n Goldregen m

labyrinth /'læbərɪnθ/ n Labyrinth nt

lace /leɪs/ n Spitze f; (of shoe) Schnürsenkel m □ vt schnüren; ~d with rum mit einem Schuss Rum

lacerate /'læsəreɪt/ vt zerreißen

lack /læk/ n Mangel m (of an + dat) □ vt I ~ the time mir fehlt die Zeit □ vi be ~ing fehlen

lackadaisical /lækə'deɪzɪkl/ a lustlos

laconic /lə'kɒnɪk/ a, -ally adv lakonisch

lacquer /'lækə(r)/ n Lack m; (for hair) [Haar]spray m

lad /læd/ n Junge m

ladder /'lædə(r)/ n Leiter f; (in fabric) Laufmasche f

laden /'leɪdn/ a beladen

ladle /'leɪdl/ n [Schöpf]kelle f □ vt schöpfen

lady /'leɪdɪ/ n Dame f; (title) Lady f

lady: ~bird n, (Amer) ~bug n Marienkäfer m. ~like a damenhaft

lag¹ /læg/ vi (pt/pp lagged) ~ behind zurückbleiben; (fig) nachhinken

lag² vt (pt/pp lagged) umwickeln (pipes)

lager /'lɑːgə(r)/ n Lagerbier nt

lagoon /lə'guːn/ n Lagune f

laid /leɪd/ see lay³

lain /leɪn/ see lie²

lair /leə(r)/ n Lager nt

laity /'leɪətɪ/ n Laienstand m

lake /leɪk/ n See m

lamb /læm/ n Lamm nt

lame /leɪm/ a (-r, -st) lahm

lament /lə'ment/ n Klage f; (song) Klagelied nt □ vt beklagen □ vi klagen. ~able /'læməntəbl/ a beklagenswert

laminated /'læmɪneɪtɪd/ a laminiert

lamp /læmp/ n Lampe f; (in street) Laterne f. ~post n Laternenpfahl m. ~shade n Lampenschirm m

lance /lɑːns/ n Lanze f □ vt (Med) aufschneiden. ~'corporal n Gefreite(r) m

land /lænd/ n Land nt; plot of ~ Grundstück nt □ vt/i landen; ~ s.o. with sth (fam) jdm etw aufhalsen

landing /'lændɪŋ/ n Landung f; (top of stairs) Treppenflur m. ~-stage n Landesteg m

land: ~lady n Wirtin f. ~locked a ~locked country Binnenstaat m. ~lord n Wirt m; (of land) Grundbesitzer m; (of building) Hausbesitzer m. ~mark n Erkennungszeichen nt; (fig) Meilenstein m. ~owner n Grundbesitzer m. ~scape /-skeɪp/ n Landschaft f. ~slide n Erdrutsch m

lane /leɪn/ n kleine Landstraße f; (Auto) Spur f; (Sport) Bahn f; 'get in ~' (Auto) 'bitte einordnen'

language /'læŋgwɪdʒ/ n Sprache f; (speech, style) Ausdrucksweise f. ~ laboratory n Sprachlabor nt

languid /'læŋgwɪd/ a, -ly adv träge

languish /'læŋgwɪʃ/ vi schmachten

lank /læŋk/ a (hair) strähnig

lanky /'læŋkɪ/ a (-ier, -iest) schlaksig

lantern /'læntən/ n Laterne f

lap¹ /læp/ n Schoß m

lap² n (Sport) Runde f; (of journey) Etappe f □ vi (pt/pp lapped) plätschern (against gegen)

lap³ vt (pt/pp lapped) ~ up aufschlecken

lapel /lə'pel/ n Revers nt

lapse /læps/ n Fehler m; (moral) Fehltritt m; (of time) Zeitspanne f □ vi (expire) erlöschen; ~ into verfallen in (+ acc)

larceny /'lɑːsənɪ/ n Diebstahl m

lard /lɑːd/ n [Schweine]schmalz nt

larder /'lɑːdə(r)/ n Speisekammer f

large /lɑːdʒ/ a (-r, -st) & adv groß; by and ~ im Großen und Ganzen; at ~ auf freiem Fuß; (in general) im Allgemeinen. ~ly adv großenteils

lark¹ /lɑːk/ n (bird) Lerche f

lark² n (joke) Jux m □ vi ~ about herumalbern

larva /'lɑːvə/ n (pl -vae /-viː/) Larve f

laryngitis /lærɪn'dʒaɪtɪs/ n Kehlkopfentzündung f

larynx /'lærɪŋks/ n Kehlkopf m

lascivious /lə'sɪvɪəs/ a lüstern

laser /'leɪzə(r)/ n Laser m

lash /læʃ/ n Peitschenhieb m; (eyelash) Wimper f □ vt peitschen; (tie) festbinden (to an + acc). ~ out vi um sich schlagen; (spend) viel Geld ausgeben (on für)

lashings /'læʃɪŋz/ npl ~ of (fam) eine Riesenmenge von

lass /læs/ n Mädchen nt

lasso /lə'su:/ n Lasso nt

last[1] /lɑːst/ n (for shoe) Leisten m

last[2] a & n letzte(r,s); ~ night heute od gestern Nacht; (evening) gestern Abend; at ~ endlich; the ~ time das letzte Mal; for the ~ time zum letzten Mal; the ~ but one der/die/das vorletzte; that's the ~ straw (fam) das schlägt dem Fass den Boden aus □ adv zuletzt; (last time) das letzte Mal; do sth ~ etw zuletzt od als Letztes machen; he/she went ~ er/sie ging als Letzter/Letzte □ vi dauern; (weather:) sich halten; (relationship:) halten. ~ing a dauerhaft. ~ly adv schließlich, zum Schluss

latch /lætʃ/ n [einfache] Klinke f; on the ~ nicht verschlossen

late /leɪt/ a & adv (-r, -st) spät; (delayed) verspätet; (deceased) verstorben; the ~st news die neuesten Nachrichten; stay up ~ bis spät aufbleiben; of ~ in letzter Zeit; arrive ~ zu spät ankommen; I am ~ ich komme zu spät od habe mich verspätet; the train is ~ der Zug hat Verspätung. ~comer n Zuspätkommende(r) m/f. ~ly adv in letzter Zeit. ~ness n Zuspätkommen nt; (delay) Verspätung f

latent /'leɪtnt/ a latent

later /'leɪtə(r)/ a & adv später; ~ on nachher

lateral /'lætərəl/ a seitlich

lathe /leɪð/ n Drehbank f

lather /'lɑːðə(r)/ n [Seifen]schaum m □ vt einseifen □ vi schäumen

Latin /'lætɪn/ a lateinisch □ n Latein nt. ~ A'merica n Lateinamerika nt

latitude /'lætɪtjuːd/ n (Geog) Breite f; (fig) Freiheit f

latter /'lætə(r)/ a & n the ~ der/die/das Letztere. ~ly adv in letzter Zeit

lattice /'lætɪs/ n Gitter nt

Latvia /'lætvɪə/ n Lettland nt

laudable /'lɔːdəbl/ a lobenswert

laugh /lɑːf/ n Lachen nt; with a ~ lachend □ vi lachen (at/about über + acc); ~ at s.o. (mock) jdn auslachen. ~able /-əbl/ a lachhaft, lächerlich. ~ing-stock n Gegenstand m des Spottes

laughter /'lɑːftə(r)/ n Gelächter nt

launch[1] /lɔːntʃ/ n (boat) Barkasse f

launch[2] n Stapellauf m; (of rocket) Abschuss m; (of product) Lancierung f □ vt vom Stapel lassen (ship); zu Wasser lassen (lifeboat); abschießen (rocket); starten (attack); (Comm) lancieren (product)

launder /'lɔːndə(r)/ vt waschen. ~ette /-'dret/ n Münzwäscherei f

laundry /'lɔːndrɪ/ n Wäscherei f; (clothes) Wäsche f

laurel /'lɒrl/ n Lorbeer m

lava /'lɑːvə/ n Lava f

lavatory /'lævətrɪ/ n Toilette f

lavender /'lævəndə(r)/ n Lavendel m

lavish /'lævɪʃ/ a, -ly adv großzügig; (wasteful) verschwenderisch; on a ~ scale mit viel Aufwand □ vt ~ sth on s.o. jdn mit etw überschütten

law /lɔː/ n Gesetz nt; (system) Recht nt; study ~ Jura studieren; ~ and order Recht und Ordnung

law: ~-abiding a gesetzestreu. ~court n Gerichtshof m. ~ful a rechtmäßig. ~less a gesetzlos

lawn /lɔːn/ n Rasen m. ~-mower n Rasenmäher m

law suit n Prozess m

lawyer /'lɔːjə(r)/ n Rechtsanwalt m /-anwältin f

lax /læks/ a lax, locker

laxative /'læksətɪv/ n Abführmittel nt

laxity /'læksətɪ/ n Laxheit f

lay[1] /leɪ/ a Laien-

lay[2] see **lie**[2]

lay[3] vt (pt/pp laid) legen; decken (table); ~ a trap eine Falle stellen. ~ down vt hinlegen; festlegen (rules, conditions). ~ off vt entlassen (workers) □ vi (fam: stop) aufhören. ~ out vt hinlegen; aufbahren (corpse); anlegen (garden); (Typ) gestalten

lay: ~about n Faulenzer m. ~-by n Parkbucht f; (on motorway) Rastplatz m

layer /'leɪə(r)/ n Schicht f

layette /leɪ'et/ n Babyausstattung f

lay: ~man n Laie m. ~out n Anordnung f; (design) Gestaltung f; (Typ) Layout nt. ~'preacher n Laienprediger m

laze /leɪz/ vi ~ [about] faulenzen

laziness /'leɪzɪnɪs/ n Faulheit f

lazy /'leɪzɪ/ a (-ier, -iest) faul. ~-bones n Faulenzer m

lb /paʊnd/ abbr (pound) Pfd.

lead[1] /led/ n Blei nt; (of pencil) [Blei-stift]mine f

lead[2] /liːd/ n Führung f; (leash) Leine f; (flex) Schnur f; (clue) Hinweis m, Spur f; (Theat) Hauptrolle f; (distance ahead) Vorsprung m; be in the ~ in Führung liegen □ vt/i (pt/pp led) führen; leiten (team); (induce) bringen; (at cards) ausspielen; ~ the way vorangehen; ~ up to sth (fig) etw (dat) vorangehen. ~ away vt wegführen

leaded /'ledɪd/ a verbleit

leader /'liːdə(r)/ n Führer m; (of expedition, group) Leiter(in) m(f); (of orchestra) Konzertmeister m; (in newspaper) Leitartikel m. ∼ship n Führung f; Leitung f

leading /'liːdɪŋ/ a führend; ∼ lady Hauptdarstellerin f; ∼ question Suggestivfrage f

leaf /liːf/ n (pl leaves) Blatt nt; (of table) Ausziehplatte f □ vi ∼ through sth etw durchblättern. ∼ let n Merkblatt nt; (advertising) Reklameblatt nt; (political) Flugblatt nt

league /liːg/ n Liga f; be in ∼ with unter einer Decke stecken mit

leak /liːk/ n (hole) undichte Stelle f; (Naut) Leck nt; (of gas) Gasausfluss m □ vi undicht sein; ⟨ship.⟩ leck sein, lecken; ⟨liquid:⟩ auslaufen; ⟨gas:⟩ ausströmen □ vt auslaufen lassen; ∼ sth to s.o. (fig) jdm etw zuspielen. ∼y a undicht; (Naut) leck

lean[1] /liːn/ a (-er, -est) mager

lean[2] v (pt/pp leaned or leant /lent/) □ vt lehnen (against/on an + acc) □ vi ⟨person⟩ sich lehnen (against/on an + acc); (not be straight) sich neigen; be ∼ing against lehnen an (+ dat); ∼ on s.o. (depend) bei jdm festen Halt finden. ∼ back vi sich zurücklehnen. ∼ forward vi sich vorbeugen. ∼ out vi sich hinauslehnen. ∼ over vi sich vorbeugen

leaning /'liːnɪŋ/ a schief □ n Neigung f

leap /liːp/ n Sprung m □ vi (pt/pp leapt /lept/ or leaped) springen; he leapt at it (fam) er griff sofort zu. ∼-frog n Bockspringen nt. ∼ year n Schaltjahr nt

learn /lɜːn/ vt/i (pt/pp learnt or learned) lernen; (hear) erfahren; ∼ to swim schwimmen lernen

learn|ed /'lɜːnɪd/ a gelehrt. ∼er n Anfänger m; ∼er [driver] Fahrschüler(in) m(f). ∼ing n Gelehrsamkeit f

lease /liːs/ n Pacht f; (contract) Mietvertrag m; (Comm) Pachtvertrag m □ vt pachten; ∼ [out] verpachten

leash /liːʃ/ n Leine f

least /liːst/ a geringste(r,s); have ∼ time am wenigsten Zeit haben □ n the ∼ das wenigste; at ∼ wenigstens, mindestens; not in the ∼ nicht im Geringsten □ adv am wenigsten

leather /'leðə(r)/ n Leder nt. ∼y a ledrig; (tough) zäh

leave /liːv/ n Erlaubnis f; (holiday) Urlaub m; on ∼ auf Urlaub; take one's ∼ sich verabschieden □ v (pt/pp left) □ vt lassen; (go out of, abandon) verlassen; (forget) liegen lassen; (bequeath) vermachen (to dat); ∼ it to me! überlassen Sie es mir! there is nothing left es ist nichts mehr übrig □ vi [weg]gehen/-fahren; ⟨train, bus:⟩ abfahren. ∼ behind vt zurücklassen; (forget) liegen lassen. ∼ out vt liegen lassen; (leave outside) draußen lassen; (omit) auslassen

leaves /liːvz/ see leaf

Lebanon /'lebənən/ n Libanon m

lecherous /'letʃərəs/ a lüstern

lectern /'lektən/ n [Lese]pult nt

lecture /'lektʃə(r)/ n Vortrag m; (Univ) Vorlesung f; (reproof) Strafpredigt f □ vi einen Vortrag/eine Vorlesung halten (on über + acc) □ vt ∼ s.o. jdm eine Strafpredigt halten. ∼r n Vortragende(r) m/f; (Univ) Dozent(in) m(f)

led /led/ see lead[2]

ledge /ledʒ/ n Leiste f; (shelf, of window) Sims m; (in rock) Vorsprung m

ledger /'ledʒə(r)/ n Hauptbuch nt

lee /liː/ n (Naut) Lee f

leech /liːtʃ/ n Blutegel m

leek /liːk/ n Stange f Porree; ∼s pl Porree m

leer /lɪə(r)/ n anzügliches Grinsen nt □ vi anzüglich grinsen

lee|ward /'liːwəd/ adv nach Lee. ∼way n (fig) Spielraum m

left[1] /left/ see leave

left[2] a linke(r,s) □ adv links; (go) nach links □ n linke Seite f; on the ∼ links; from/to the ∼ von/nach links; the ∼ (Pol) die Linke

left: ∼-'handed a linkshändig. ∼-'luggage [office] n Gepäckaufbewahrung f. ∼overs npl Reste pl. ∼-'wing a (Pol) linke(r,s)

leg /leg/ n Bein nt; (Culin) Keule f; (of journey) Etappe f

legacy /'legəsɪ/ n Vermächtnis nt, Erbschaft f

legal /'liːgl/ a, -ly adv gesetzlich; ⟨matters⟩ rechtlich; ⟨department, position⟩ Rechts-; be ∼ [gesetzlich] erlaubt sein; take ∼ action gerichtlich vorgehen

legality /lɪ'gælɪtɪ/ n Legalität f

legalize /'liːgəlaɪz/ vt legalisieren

legend /'ledʒənd/ n Legende f. ∼ary a legendär

legible /'ledʒəbl/ a, -bly adv leserlich

legion /'liːdʒn/ n Legion f

legislat|e /'ledʒɪsleɪt/ vi Gesetze erlassen. ∼ion /-'leɪʃn/ n Gesetzgebung f; (laws) Gesetze pl

legislat|ive /'ledʒɪslətɪv/ a gesetzgebend. ∼ure /-leɪtʃə(r)/ n Legislative f

legitimate /lɪ'dʒɪtɪmət/ a rechtmäßig; (justifiable) berechtigt; ⟨child⟩ ehelich

leisure /'leʒə(r)/ n Freizeit f; at your ∼ wenn Sie Zeit haben. ∼ly a gemächlich

lemon /'lemən/ n Zitrone f. ~ade /-'neɪd/ n Zitronenlimonade f

lend /lend/ vt (pt/pp lent) leihen; ~ s.o. sth jdm etw leihen; ~ a hand (fam) helfen. ~ing library n Leihbücherei f

length /leŋθ/ n Länge f; (piece) Stück nt; (of wallpaper) Bahn f; (of time) Dauer f; at ~ ausführlich; (at last) endlich

length|en /'leŋθən/ vt länger machen □ vi länger werden. ~ways adv der Länge nach, längs

lengthy /'leŋθɪ/ a (-ier, -iest) langwierig

lenien|ce /'li:nɪəns/ n Nachsicht f. ~t a, -ly adv nachsichtig

lens /lenz/ n Linse f; (Phot) Objektiv nt; (of spectacles) Glas nt

lent /lent/ see lend

Lent n Fastenzeit f

lentil /'lentl/ n (Bot) Linse f

Leo /'li:əʊ/ n (Astr) Löwe m

leopard /'lepəd/ n Leopard m

leotard /'li:əta:d/ n Trikot nt

leper /'lepə(r)/ n Leprakranke(r) m/f; (Bible & fig) Aussätzige(r) m/f

leprosy /'leprəsɪ/ n Lepra f

lesbian /'lezbɪən/ a lesbisch □ n Lesbierin f

lesion /'li:ʒn/ n Verletzung f

less /les/ a, adv, n & prep weniger; ~ and ~ immer weniger; not any the ~ um nichts weniger

lessen /'lesn/ vt verringern □ vi nachlassen; (value:) abnehmen

lesser /'lesə(r)/ a geringere(r,s)

lesson /'lesn/ n Stunde f; (in text-book) Lektion f; (Relig) Lesung f; teach s.o. a ~ (fig) jdm eine Lehre erteilen

lest /lest/ conj (liter) damit ... nicht

let /let/ vt (pt/pp let, pres p letting) lassen; (rent) vermieten; ~ alone (not to mention) geschweige denn; 'to ~' 'zu vermieten'; ~ us go gehen wir; ~ me know sagen Sie mir Bescheid; ~ him do it lass ihn das machen; just ~ him! soll er doch! ~ s.o. sleep/win jdn schlafen/gewinnen lassen; ~ oneself in for sth (fam) sich (dat) etw einbrocken. ~ down vt hinunter-/herunterlassen; (lengthen) länger machen; ~ s.o. down (fam) jdn im Stich lassen; (disappoint) jdn enttäuschen. ~ in vt hereinlassen. ~ off vt abfeuern (gun); hochgehen lassen (firework, bomb); (emit) ausstoßen; (excuse from) befreien von; (not punish) frei ausgehen lassen. ~ out vt hinaus-/herauslassen; (make larger) auslassen. ~ through vt durchlassen. ~ up vi (fam) nachlassen

'let-down n Enttäuschung f, (fam) Reinfall m

lethal /'li:θl/ a tödlich

letharg|ic /lɪ'θɑ:dʒɪk/ a lethargisch. ~y /'leθədʒɪ/ n Lethargie f

letter /'letə(r)/ n Brief m; (of alphabet) Buchstabe m; by ~ brieflich. ~-box n Briefkasten m. ~-head n Briefkopf m. ~ing n Beschriftung f

lettuce /'letɪs/ n [Kopf]salat m

'let-up n (fam) Nachlassen nt

leukaemia /lu:'ki:mɪə/ n Leukämie f

level /'levl/ a eben; (horizontal) waagerecht; (in height) auf gleicher Höhe; (spoonful) gestrichen; draw ~ with gleichziehen mit; one's ~ best sein Möglichstes □ n Höhe f; (fig) Ebene f, Niveau nt; (stage) Stufe f; on the ~ (fam) ehrlich □ vt (pt/pp levelled) einebnen; (aim) richten (at auf + acc)

level: ~ 'crossing n Bahnübergang m. ~-'headed a vernünftig

lever /'li:və(r)/ n Hebel m □ vt ~ up mit einem Hebel anheben. ~age /-rɪdʒ/ n Hebelkraft f

levity /'levɪtɪ/ n Heiterkeit f; (frivolity) Leichtfertigkeit f

levy /'levɪ/ vt (pt/pp levied) erheben (tax)

lewd /lju:d/ a (-er, -est) anstößig

liabilit|y /laɪə'bɪlətɪ/ n Haftung f; ~ies pl Verbindlichkeiten pl

liable /'laɪəbl/ a haftbar; be ~ to do sth leicht etw tun können

liaise /lɪ'eɪz/ vi (fam) Verbindungsperson sein

liaison /lɪ'eɪzɒn/ n Verbindung f; (affair) Verhältnis nt

liar /'laɪə(r)/ n Lügner(in) m(f)

libel /'laɪbl/ n Verleumdung f □ vt (pt/pp libelled) verleumden. ~lous a verleumderisch

liberal /'lɪbərl/ a, -ly adv tolerant; (generous) großzügig. L~ a (Pol) liberal □ n Liberale(r) m/f

liberat|e /'lɪbəreɪt/ vt befreien. ~ed a (woman) emanzipiert. ~ion /-'reɪʃn/ n Befreiung f. ~or n Befreier m

liberty /'lɪbətɪ/ n Freiheit f; take the ~ of doing sth sich (dat) erlauben, etw zu tun; take liberties sich (dat) Freiheiten erlauben

Libra /'li:brə/ n (Astr) Waage f

librarian /laɪ'breərɪən/ n Bibliothekar(in) m(f)

library /'laɪbrərɪ/ n Bibliothek f

Libya /'lɪbɪə/ n Libyen nt

lice /laɪs/ see louse

licence /'laɪsns/ n Genehmigung f; (Comm) Lizenz f; (for TV) ≈ Fernsehgebühr f; (for driving) Führerschein m; (for

alcohol) Schankkonzession *f;* *(freedom)*
Freiheit *f*

license /'laɪsns/ *vt* eine Genehmigung/*(Comm)* Lizenz erteilen (+ *dat*); be ~d *(car.:)* zugelassen sein; *(restaurant:)* Schankkonzession haben. ~-plate *n* Nummernschild *nt*

licentious /laɪˈsenʃəs/ *a* lasterhaft

lichen /'laɪkən/ *n (Bot)* Flechte *f*

lick /lɪk/ *n* Lecken *nt;* a ~ of paint ein bisschen Farbe ◻ *vt* lecken; *(fam: defeat)* schlagen

lid /lɪd/ *n* Deckel *m; (of eye)* Lid *nt*

lie[1] /laɪ/ *n* Lüge *f;* tell a ~ lügen ◻ *vi* (pt/pp lied, pres p lying) lügen; ~ to belügen

lie[2] *vi* (pt lay, pp lain, pres p lying) liegen; here ~s ... hier ruht ... ~ down *vi* sich hinlegen

Liège /lɪˈeɪʒ/ *n* Lüttich *nt*

'**lie-in** *n* have a ~ [sich] ausschlafen

lieu /ljuː/ *n* in ~ of statt (+ *gen*)

lieutenant /lefˈtenənt/ *n* Oberleutnant *m*

life /laɪf/ *n* (pl lives) Leben *nt; (biography)* Biographie *f;* lose one's ~ ums Leben kommen

life: ~belt *n* Rettungsring *m.* ~-boat *n* Rettungsboot *nt.* ~-buoy *n* Rettungsring *m.* ~-guard *n* Lebensretter *m.* ~-jacket *n* Schwimmweste *f.* ~less *a* leblos. ~-like *a* naturgetreu. ~-line *n* Rettungsleine *f.* ~-long *a* lebenslang. ~-preserver *n (Amer)* Rettungsring *m.* ~-size(d) *a* ... in Lebensgröße. ~-time *n* Leben *nt;* in s.o.'s ~-time zu jds Lebzeiten; the chance of a ~-time eine einmalige Gelegenheit

lift /lɪft/ *n* Aufzug *m,* Lift *m;* give s.o. a ~ jdn mitnehmen; get a ~ mitgenommen werden ◻ *vt* heben; aufheben *(restrictions)* ◻ *vi (fog:)* sich lichten. ~ up *vt* hochheben

'**lift-off** *n* Abheben *nt*

ligament /'lɪɡəmənt/ *n (Anat)* Band *nt*

light[1] /laɪt/ *a* (-er, -est) *(not dark)* hell; ~ blue hellblau □ *n* Licht *nt; (lamp)* Lampe *f;* in the ~ of *(fig)* angesichts (+ *gen*); have you [got] a ~? haben Sie Feuer? ◻ *vt* (pt/pp lit or lighted) anzünden *(fire, cigarette);* anmachen *(lamp); (illuminate)* beleuchten. ~ up *vi (face:)* sich erhellen

light[2] *a* (-er, -est) *(not heavy)* leicht; ~ sentence milde Strafe □ *adv* travel ~ mit wenig Gepäck reisen

'**light-bulb** *n* Glühbirne *f*

lighten[1] /'laɪtn/ *vt* heller machen □ *vi* heller werden

lighten[2] *vt* leichter machen *(load)*

lighter /'laɪtə(r)/ *n* Feuerzeug *nt*

light: ~-headed *a* benommen. ~-hearted *a* unbekümmert. ~house *n* Leuchtturm *m.* ~ing *n* Beleuchtung *f.*

~ly *adv* leicht; *(casually)* leichthin; get off ~ly glimpflich davonkommen

lightning /'laɪtnɪŋ/ *n* Blitz *m.* ~-conductor *n* Blitzableiter *m*

'**lightweight** *a* leicht □ *n (Boxing)* Leichtgewicht *nt*

like[1] /laɪk/ *a* ähnlich; *(same)* gleich □ *prep* wie; *(similar to)* ähnlich (+ *dat*); ~ this so; a man ~ that so ein Mann; what's he ~? wie ist er denn? □ *conj (fam: as)* wie; *(Amer: as if)* als ob

like[2] *vt* mögen; I should/would ~ ich möchte; I ~ the car das Auto gefällt mir; I ~ chocolate ich esse gern Schokolade; ~ dancing/singing tanzen/singen; I ~ that! *(fam)* das ist doch die Höhe! □ *n* ~s and dislikes *pl* Vorlieben und Abneigungen *pl*

like|able /'laɪkəbl/ *a* sympathisch. ~-lihood /-lihʊd/ *n* Wahrscheinlichkeit *f.* ~ly *a* (-ier, -iest) & *adv* wahrscheinlich; not ~ly! *(fam)* auf gar keinen Fall!

'**like-minded** *a* gleich gesinnt

liken /'laɪkən/ *vt* vergleichen (to mit)

like|ness /'laɪknɪs/ *n* Ähnlichkeit *f.* ~wise *adv* ebenso

liking /'laɪkɪŋ/ *n* Vorliebe *f;* is it to your ~? gefällt es Ihnen?

lilac /'laɪlək/ *n* Flieder *m* □ *a* fliederfarben

lily /'lɪlɪ/ *n.* Lilie *f.* ~ of the valley *n* Maiglöckchen *nt*

limb /lɪm/ *n* Glied *nt*

limber /'lɪmbə(r)/ *vi* ~ up Lockerungsübungen machen

lime[1] /laɪm/ *n (fruit)* Limone *f; (tree)* Linde *f*

lime[2] *n* Kalk *m.* ~light *n* be in the ~light im Rampenlicht stehen. ~stone *n* Kalkstein *m*

limit /'lɪmɪt/ *n* Grenze *f; (limitation)* Beschränkung *f;* that's the ~! *(fam)* das ist doch die Höhe! □ *vt* beschränken (to auf + *acc*). ~ation /-ɪˈteɪʃn/ *n* Beschränkung *f;* ~ed *a* beschränkt; ~ed company Gesellschaft *f* mit beschränkter Haftung

limousine /'lɪməziːn/ *n* Limousine *f*

limp[1] /lɪmp/ *n* Hinken *nt;* have a ~ hinken □ *vi* hinken

limp[2] *a* (-er -est), -ly *adv* schlaff

limpet /'lɪmpɪt/ *n* like a ~ *(fig)* wie eine Klette

limpid /'lɪmpɪd/ *a* klar

linctus /'lɪŋktəs/ *n* [cough] ~ Hustensirup *m*

line[1] /laɪn/ *n* Linie *f; (length of rope, cord)* Leine *f; (Teleph)* Leitung *f; (of writing)* Zeile *f; (row)* Reihe *f; (wrinkle)* Falte *f; (of business)* Branche *f; (Amer: queue)* Schlange *f;* in ~ with gemäß (+ *dat*) □ *vt* säumen ⟨street⟩. ~ up *vi* sich aufstellen □ *vt* aufstellen

line² *vt* füttern ⟨garment⟩; (Techn) auskleiden

lineage /'lɪnɪdʒ/ *n* Herkunft *f*

linear /'lɪnɪə(r)/ *a* linear

lined¹ /laɪnd/ *a* ⟨paper⟩ liniert; ⟨wrinkled⟩ faltig

lined² *a* ⟨garment⟩ gefüttert

linen /'lɪnɪn/ *n* Leinen *nt*; (articles) Wäsche *f*

liner /'laɪnə(r)/ *n* Passagierschiff *nt*

'linesman *n* (Sport) Linienrichter *m*

linger /'lɪŋɡə(r)/ *vi* [zurück]bleiben

lingerie /'læʒərɪ/ *n* Damenunterwäsche *f*

linguist /'lɪŋɡwɪst/ *n* Sprachkundige(r) *m/f*

linguistic /lɪŋ'ɡwɪstɪk/ *a*, **-ally** *adv* sprachlich. ~s *n* Linguistik *f*

lining /'laɪnɪŋ/ *n* ⟨of garment⟩ Futter *nt*; (Techn) Auskleidung *f*

link /lɪŋk/ *n* ⟨of chain⟩ Glied *nt* ⟨fig⟩ Verbindung *f* □ *vt* verbinden; ~ arms sich unterhaken

links /lɪŋks/ *n or npl* Golfplatz *m*

lino /'laɪnəʊ/ *n*, linoleum /lɪ'nəʊlɪəm/ *n* Linoleum *nt*

lint /lɪnt/ *n* Verbandstoff *m*

lion /'laɪən/ *n* Löwe *m*; ~'s share ⟨fig⟩ Löwenanteil *m*. ~ess *n* Löwin *f*

lip /lɪp/ *n* Lippe *f*; ⟨edge⟩ Rand *m*; ⟨of jug⟩ Schnabel *m*

lip: ~-reading *n* Lippenlesen *nt*. ~-service *n* pay ~-service ein Lippenbekenntnis ablegen (to zu). ~stick *n* Lippenstift *m*

liquefy /'lɪkwɪfaɪ/ *vt* ⟨pt/pp -ied⟩ verflüssigen □ *vi* sich verflüssigen

liqueur /lɪ'kjʊə(r)/ *n* Likör *m*

liquid /'lɪkwɪd/ *n* Flüssigkeit *f* □ *a* flüssig

liquidat|e /'lɪkwɪdeɪt/ *vt* liquidieren. ~ion /-'deɪʃn/ *n* Liquidation *f*

liquidize /'lɪkwɪdaɪz/ *vt* [im Mixer] pürieren. ~r *n* (Culin) Mixer *m*

liquor /'lɪkə(r)/ *n* Alkohol *m*; ⟨juice⟩ Flüssigkeit *f*

liquorice /'lɪkərɪs/ *n* Lakritze *f*

'liquor store *n* (Amer) Spirituosengeschäft *nt*

lisp /lɪsp/ *n* Lispeln *nt* □ *vt/i* lispeln

list¹ /lɪst/ *n* Liste *f* □ *vt* aufführen

list² *vi* ⟨ship:⟩ Schlagseite haben

listen /'lɪsn/ *vi* zuhören (to *dat*); ~ to the radio Radio hören. ~er *n* Zuhörer(in) *m(f)*; (Radio) Hörer(in) *m(f)*

listless /'lɪstlɪs/ *a*, **-ly** *adv* lustlos

lit /lɪt/ *see* light¹

litany /'lɪtənɪ/ *n* Litanei *f*

literacy /'lɪtərəsɪ/ *n* Lese- und Schreibfertigkeit *f*

literal /'lɪtərl/ *a* wörtlich. ~ly *adv* buchstäblich

literary /'lɪtərərɪ/ *a* literarisch

literate /'lɪtərət/ *a* be ~ lesen und schreiben können

literature /'lɪtrətʃə(r)/ *n* Literatur *f*; ⟨fam⟩ Informationsmaterial *nt*

lithe /laɪð/ *a* geschmeidig

Lithuania /lɪθjʊ'eɪnɪə/ *n* Litauen *nt*

litigation /lɪtɪ'ɡeɪʃn/ *n* Rechtsstreit *m*

litre /'liːtə(r)/ *n* Liter *m* & *nt*

litter /'lɪtə(r)/ *n* Abfall *m*; ⟨Zool⟩ Wurf *m* □ *vt* be ~ed with übersät sein mit. ~-bin *n* Abfalleimer *m*

little /'lɪtl/ *a* klein; (not much) wenig □ *adv* & *n* wenig; a ~ ein bisschen/wenig; ~ by ~ nach und nach

liturgy /'lɪtədʒɪ/ *n* Liturgie *f*

live¹ /laɪv/ *a* lebendig; ⟨ammunition⟩ scharf; ~ broadcast Live-Sendung *f*; be ~ ⟨Electr⟩ unter Strom stehen □ *adv* ⟨Radio, TV⟩ live

live² /lɪv/ *vi* leben; ⟨reside⟩ wohnen; ~ up to gerecht werden (+ *dat*). ~ on *vt* leben von; ⟨eat⟩ sich ernähren von □ *vi* weiterleben

liveli|hood /'laɪvlɪhʊd/ *n* Lebensunterhalt *m*. ~ness *n* Lebendigkeit *f*

lively /'laɪvlɪ/ *a* (-ier, -iest) lebhaft, lebendig

liven /'laɪvn/ *v* ~ up *vt* beleben □ *vi* lebhaft werden

liver /'lɪvə(r)/ *n* Leber *f*

lives /laɪvz/ *see* life

livestock /'laɪv-/ *n* Vieh *nt*

livid /'lɪvɪd/ *a* ⟨fam⟩ wütend

living /'lɪvɪŋ/ *a* lebend *n* earn one's ~ seinen Lebensunterhalt verdienen; the ~ *pl* die Lebenden. ~-room *n* Wohnzimmer *nt*

lizard /'lɪzəd/ *n* Eidechse *f*

load /ləʊd/ *n* Last *f*; ⟨quantity⟩ Ladung *f*; ⟨Electr⟩ Belastung *f*; ~s of ⟨fam⟩ jede Menge □ *vt* laden ⟨goods, gun⟩; beladen ⟨vehicle⟩; ~ a camera einen Film in eine Kamera einlegen. ~ed *a* beladen; ⟨fam: rich⟩ steinreich; ~ed question Fangfrage *f*

loaf¹ /ləʊf/ *n* ⟨pl loaves⟩ Brot *nt*

loaf² *vi* faulenzen

loan /ləʊn/ *n* Leihgabe *f*; ⟨money⟩ Darlehen *nt*; on ~ geliehen □ *vt* leihen (to *dat*)

loath /ləʊθ/ *a* be ~ to do sth etw ungern tun

loath|e /ləʊð/ vt verabscheuen. ~**ing** n Abscheu m. ~**some** a abscheulich

loaves /ləʊvz/ see loaf[1]

lobby /'lɒbɪ/ n Foyer nt; (ante-room) Vorraum m; (Pol) Lobby f

lobe /ləʊb/ n (of ear) Ohrläppchen nt

lobster /'lɒbstə(r)/ n Hummer m

local /'ləʊkl/ a hiesig; (time, traffic) Orts-; under ~ anaesthetic unter örtlicher Betäubung; I'm not ~ ich bin nicht von hier □ n Hiesige(r) m/f; (fam: public house) Stammkneipe f. ~ au'thority n Kommunalbehörde f. ~ call n (Teleph) Ortsgespräch nt

locality /ləʊ'kælətɪ/ n Gegend f

localized /'ləʊkəlaɪzd/ a lokalisiert

locally /'ləʊkəlɪ/ adv am Ort

locat|e /ləʊ'keɪt/ vt ausfindig machen; be ~ed sich befinden. ~**ion** /-'keɪʃn/ n Lage f; filmed on ~**ion** als Außenaufnahme gedreht

lock[1] /lɒk/ n (hair) Strähne f

lock[2] n (on door) Schloss nt; (on canal) Schleuse f □ vt abschließen □ vi sich abschließen lassen. ~ **in** vt einschließen. ~ **out** vt ausschließen. ~ **up** vt abschließen; einsperren (person) □ vi zuschließen

locker /'lɒkə(r)/ n Schließfach nt; (Mil) Spind m; (in hospital) kleiner Schrank m

locket /'lɒkɪt/ n Medaillon nt

lock: ~**out** n Aussperrung f. ~**smith** n Schlosser m

locomotion /ləʊkə'məʊʃn/ n Fortbewegung f

locomotive /ləʊkə'məʊtɪv/ n Lokomotive f

locum /'ləʊkəm/ n Vertreter(in) m(f)

locust /'ləʊkəst/ n Heuschrecke f

lodge /lɒdʒ/ n (porter's) Pförtnerhaus nt; (masonic) Loge f □ vt (submit) einreichen; (deposit) deponieren □ vi zur Untermiete wohnen (with bei); (become fixed) stecken bleiben. ~r n Untermieter(in) m(f)

lodging /'lɒdʒɪŋ/ n Unterkunft f; ~s npl möbliertes Zimmer nt

loft /lɒft/ n Dachboden m

lofty /'lɒftɪ/ a (-ier, -iest) hoch; (haughty) hochmütig

log /lɒg/ n Baumstamm m; (for fire) [Holz]scheit nt; sleep like a ~ (fam) wie ein Murmeltier schlafen

logarithm /'lɒgərɪðm/ n Logarithmus m

'log-book n (Naut) Logbuch nt

loggerheads /'lɒgə-/ npl be at ~ (fam) sich in den Haaren liegen

logic /'lɒdʒɪk/ n Logik f. ~**al** a, -ly adv logisch

logistics /lə'dʒɪstɪks/ npl Logistik f

logo /'ləʊgəʊ/ n Symbol nt, Logo nt

loin /lɔɪn/ n (Culin) Lende f

loiter /'lɔɪtə(r)/ vi herumlungern

loll /lɒl/ vi sich lümmeln

loll|ipop /'lɒlɪpɒp/ n Lutscher m. ~**y** n Lutscher m; (fam: money) Moneten pl

London /'lʌndən/ n London nt □ attrib Londoner. ~**er** n Londoner(in) m(f)

lone /ləʊn/ a einzeln. ~**liness** n Einsamkeit f

lonely /'ləʊnlɪ/ a (-ier, -iest) einsam

lone|r /'ləʊnə(r)/ n Einzelgänger m. ~**some** a einsam

long[1] /lɒŋ/ a (-er /'lɒŋgə(r)/, -est /'lɒŋgɪst/) lang; (journey) weit; a ~ time lange; a ~ way weit; in the ~ run auf lange Sicht; (in the end) letzten Endes □ adv lange; all day ~ den ganzen Tag; not ~ ago vor kurzem; before ~ bald; no ~ er nicht mehr; as or so ~ as solange; so ~! (fam) tschüs! will you be ~? dauert es noch lange [bei dir]? it won't take ~ es dauert nicht lange

long[2] vi ~ for sich sehnen nach

long-'distance a Fern-; (Sport) Langstrecken-

longevity /lɒn'dʒevətɪ/ n Langlebigkeit f

'longhand n Langschrift f

longing /'lɒŋɪŋ/ a, -ly adv sehnsüchtig □ n Sehnsucht f

longitude /'lɒŋgɪtjuːd/ n (Geog) Länge f

long: ~ **jump** n Weitsprung m. ~**-life 'milk** n H-Milch f. ~**-lived** /-lɪvd/ a langlebig. ~**-range** a (Mil, Aviat) Langstrecken-; (forecast) langfristig. ~**-sighted** a weitsichtig. ~**-sleeved** a langärmelig. ~**-suffering** a langmütig. ~**-term** a langfristig. ~ **wave** n Langwelle f. ~**-winded** /-'wɪndɪd/ a langatmig

loo /luː/ n (fam) Klo nt

look /lʊk/ n Blick m; (appearance) Aussehen nt; [good] ~s pl Aussehen nt; have a ~ at sich (dat) ansehen; go and have a ~ sieh mal nach □ vi sehen; (search) nachsehen; (seem) aussehen; don't ~ sieh nicht hin; ~ here! hören Sie mal! ~ **at** ansehen; ~ **for** suchen; ~ **forward to** sich freuen auf (+ acc); ~ **in** on vorbeischauen bei; ~ **into** (examine) nachgehen (+ dat); ~ **like** aussehen wie; ~ **on to** (room:) gehen auf (+ acc). ~ **after** vt betreuen. ~ **down** vi hinuntersehen; ~ **down on s.o.** (fig) auf jdn herabsehen. ~ **out** vi hinaus-/heraussehen; (take care) aufpassen; ~ **out for** Ausschau halten nach; ~ **out!** Vorsicht! ~ **round** vi sich umsehen. ~ **up** vi aufblicken; ~ **up to s.o.** (fig) zu jdm aufsehen □ vt nachschlagen (word) 'look-out n Wache f; (prospect) Aussicht f; be on the ~ for Ausschau halten nach

loom¹ /luːm/ n Webstuhl m

loom² vi auftauchen; (fig) sich abzeichnen

loony /'luːnɪ/ a (fam) verrückt

loop /luːp/ n Schlinge f; (in road) Schleife f; (on garment) Aufhänger m □ vt schlingen. ~hole n Hintertürchen nt; (in the law) Lücke f

loose /luːs/ a (-r, -st), -ly adv lose; (not tight enough) locker; (inexact) frei; be at a ~ end nichts zu tun haben; set ~ freilassen; run ~ frei herumlaufen. ~ 'change n Kleingeld nt. ~ 'chippings npl Rollsplit m

loosen /'luːsn/ vt lockern □ vi sich lockern

loot /luːt/ n Beute f □ vt/i plündern. ~er n Plünderer m

lop /lɒp/ vt (pt/pp lopped) stutzen. ~ off vt abhacken

lop'sided a schief

loquacious /lə'kweɪʃəs/ a redselig

lord /lɔːd/ n Herr m; (title) Lord m; House of L~s = Oberhaus nt; the L~'s Prayer das Vaterunser; good L~! du liebe Zeit!

lore /lɔː(r)/ n Überlieferung f

lorry /'lɒrɪ/ n Last[kraft]wagen m

lose /luːz/ v (pt/pp lost) □ vt verlieren; (miss) verpassen □ vi verlieren; (clock:) nachgehen; get lost verloren gehen; (person:) sich verlaufen. ~r n Verlierer m

loss /lɒs/ n Verlust m; be at a ~ nicht mehr weiter wissen; be at a ~ for words nicht wissen, was man sagen soll

lost /lɒst/ see lose. ~ 'property office n Fundbüro nt

lot¹ /lɒt/ n Los nt; (at auction) Posten m; draw ~s losen (for um)

lot² n the ~ alle; (everything) alles; a ~ [of] viel; (many) viele; ~s of (fam) eine Menge; it has changed a ~ es hat sich sehr verändert

lotion /'ləʊʃn/ n Lotion f

lottery /'lɒtərɪ/ n Lotterie f. ~ ticket n Los nt

loud /laʊd/ a (-er, -est), -ly adv laut; (colours) grell □ adv [out] ~ laut. ~ 'hailer n Megaphon nt. ~'speaker n Lautsprecher m

lounge /laʊndʒ/ n Wohnzimmer nt; (in hotel) Aufenthaltsraum m. □ vi sich lümmeln. ~ suit n Straßenanzug m

louse /laʊs/ n (pl lice) Laus f

lousy /'laʊzɪ/ a (-ier, -iest) (fam) lausig

lout /laʊt/ n Flegel m, Lümmel m. ~ish a flegelhaft

lovable /'lʌvəbl/ a liebenswert

love /lʌv/ n Liebe f; (Tennis) null; in ~ verliebt □ vt lieben; ~ doing sth etw sehr gerne machen; I ~ chocolate ich esse sehr gerne Schokolade. ~affair n Liebesverhältnis nt. ~ letter n Liebesbrief m

lovely /'lʌvlɪ/ a (-ier, -iest) schön; we had a ~ time es war sehr schön

lover /'lʌvə(r)/ n Liebhaber m

love: ~ song n Liebeslied nt. ~ story n Liebesgeschichte f

loving /'lʌvɪŋ/ a, -ly adv liebevoll

low /ləʊ/ a (-er, -est) niedrig; (cloud, note) tief; (voice) leise; (depressed) niedergeschlagen □ adv niedrig; (fly, sing) tief; (speak) leise; feel ~ deprimiert sein □ n (Meteorol) Tief nt; (fig) Tiefstand m

low: ~brow a geistig anspruchslos. ~-cut a (dress) tief ausgeschnitten

lower /'ləʊə(r)/ a & adv see low □ vt niedriger machen; (let down) herunterlassen; (reduce) senken; ~ oneself sich herabwürdigen

low: ~-fat a fettarm. ~-'grade a minderwertig. ~lands /-ləndz/ npl Tiefland nt. ~ 'tide n Ebbe f

loyal /'lɔɪəl/ a, -ly adv treu. ~ty n Treue f

lozenge /'lɒzɪndʒ/ n Pastille f

Ltd abbr (Limited) GmbH

lubricant /'luːbrɪkənt/ n Schmiermittel nt

lubricat|e /'luːbrɪkeɪt/ vt schmieren. ~ion /-'keɪʃn/ n Schmierung f

lucid /'luːsɪd/ a klar. ~ity /-'sɪdətɪ/ n Klarheit f

luck /lʌk/ n Glück nt; bad ~ Pech nt; good ~! viel Glück! ~ily adv glücklicherweise, zum Glück

lucky /'lʌkɪ/ a (-ier, -iest) glücklich; (day, number) Glücks-; be ~ Glück haben; (thing:) Glück bringen. ~ 'charm n Amulett nt

lucrative /'luːkrətɪv/ a einträglich

ludicrous /'luːdɪkrəs/ a lächerlich

lug /lʌg/ vt (pt/pp lugged) (fam) schleppen

luggage /'lʌgɪdʒ/ n Gepäck nt

luggage: ~-rack in Gepäckablage f. ~ trolley n Kofferkuli m. ~-van n Gepäckwagen m

lugubrious /luː'guːbrɪəs/ a traurig

lukewarm /'luːk-/ a lauwarm

lull /lʌl/ n Pause f □ vt ~ to sleep einschläfern

lullaby /'lʌləbaɪ/ n Wiegenlied nt

lumbago /lʌm'beɪgəʊ/ n Hexenschuss m

lumber /'lʌmbə(r)/ n Gerümpel nt; (Amer: timber) Bauholz nt □ vt ~ s.o. with sth jdm etw aufhalsen. ~jack n (Amer) Holzfäller m

luminous /'luːmɪnəs/ a leuchtend; be ~ leuchten

M

lump¹ /lʌmp/ n Klumpen m; (of sugar) Stück nt; (swelling) Beule f; (in breast) Knoten m; (tumour) Geschwulst f; a ~ in one's throat (fam) ein Kloß im Hals □ vt ~ together zusammentun

lump² vt ~ it (fam) sich damit abfinden

lump: ~ sugar n Würfelzucker m. ~ 'sum n Pauschalsumme f

lumpy /'lʌmpɪ/ a (-ier, -iest) klumpig

lunacy /'lu:nəsɪ/ n Wahnsinn m

lunar /'lu:nə(r)/ a Mond-

lunatic /'lu:nətɪk/ n Wahnsinnige(r) m/f

lunch /lʌntʃ/ n Mittagessen nt □ vi zu Mittag essen

luncheon /'lʌntʃən/ n Mittagessen nt. ~ meat n Frühstücksfleisch nt. ~ voucher n Essensbon m

lunch: ~-hour n Mittagspause f. ~-time n Mittagszeit f

lung /lʌŋ/ n Lungenflügel m; ~s pl Lunge f. ~ cancer n Lungenkrebs m

lunge /lʌndʒ/ vi sich stürzen (at auf + acc)

lurch¹ /lɜ:tʃ/ n leave in the ~ (fam) im Stich lassen

lurch² vi schleudern; ⟨person:⟩ torkeln

lure /ljʊə(r)/ n Lockung f; (bait) Köder m □ vt locken

lurid /'lʊərɪd/ a grell; (sensational) reißerisch

lurk /lɜ:k/ vi lauern

luscious /'lʌʃəs/ a lecker, köstlich

lush /lʌʃ/ a üppig

lust /lʌst/ n Begierde f □ vi ~ after gieren nach. ~ful a lüstern

lustre /'lʌstə(r)/ n Glanz m

lusty /'lʌstɪ/ a (-ier, -iest) kräftig

lute /lu:t/ n Laute f

luxuriant /lʌg'ʒʊərɪənt/ a üppig

luxurious /lʌg'ʒʊərɪəs/ a, -ly adv luxuriös

luxury /'lʌkʃərɪ/ n Luxus m □ attrib Luxus-

lying /'laɪɪŋ/ see lie¹, lie²

lymph gland /'lɪmf-/ n Lymphdrüse f

lynch /lɪntʃ/ vt lynchen

lynx /lɪŋks/ n Luchs m

lyric /'lɪrɪk/ a lyrisch. ~al a lyrisch; (fam: enthusiastic) schwärmerisch. ~ poetry n Lyrik f. ~s npl [Lied]text m

mac /mæk/ n (fam) Regenmantel m

macabre /mə'ka:br/ a makaber

macaroni /mækə'rəʊnɪ/ n Makkaroni pl

macaroon /mækə'ru:n/ n Makrone f

mace¹ /meɪs/ n Amtsstab m

mace² n (spice) Muskatblüte f

machinations /mækɪ'neɪʃnz/ pl Machenschaften pl

machine /mə'ʃi:n/ n Maschine f □ vt (sew) mit der Maschine nähen; (Techn) maschinell bearbeiten. ~gun n Maschinengewehr nt

machinery /mə'ʃi:nərɪ/ n Maschinerie f

machine tool n Werkzeugmaschine f

machinist /mə'ʃi:nɪst/ n Maschinist m; (on sewing machine) Maschinennäherin f

mackerel /'mækrl/ n inv Makrele f

mackintosh /'mækɪntɒʃ/ n Regenmantel m

mad /mæd/ a (madder, maddest) verrückt; (dog) tollwütig; (fam: angry) böse (at auf + acc)

madam /'mædəm/ n gnädige Frau f

madden /'mædn/ vt (make angry) wütend machen

made /meɪd/ see make; ~ to measure maßgeschneidert

Madeira cake /mə'dɪərə-/ n Sandkuchen m

mad|ly /'mædlɪ/ adv (fam) wahnsinnig. ~man n Irre(r) m. ~ness n Wahnsinn m

madonna /mə'dɒnə/ n Madonna f

magazine /mægə'zi:n/ n Zeitschrift f; (Mil, Phot) Magazin nt

maggot /'mægət/ n Made f. ~y a madig

Magi /'meɪdʒaɪ/ npl the ~ die Heiligen Drei Könige

magic /'mædʒɪk/ n Zauber m; (tricks) Zauberkunst f □ a magisch; ⟨word, wand, flute⟩ Zauber-. ~al a zauberhaft

magician /mə'dʒɪʃn/ n Zauberer m; (entertainer) Zauberkünstler m

magistrate /'mædʒɪstreɪt/ n ≈ Friedensrichter m

magnanim|ity /mægnə'nɪmətɪ/ n Großmut f. ~ous /-'nænɪməs/ a großmütig

magnesia /mæg'ni:ʃə/ n Magnesia f

magnet /'mægnɪt/ n Magnet m. ~ic /-'netɪk/ a magnetisch. ~ism n Magnetismus m. ~ize vt magnetisieren

magnification /mægnɪfɪ'keɪʃn/ n Vergrößerung f

magnifice|nce /mæg'nɪfɪsəns/ n Großartigkeit f. ~t a, -ly adv großartig

magnify /'mægnɪfaɪ/ vt (pt/pp -ied) vergrößern; (exaggerate) übertreiben. ~ing glass n Vergrößerungsglas nt

magnitude /'mægnɪtjuːd/ n Größe f; (importance) Bedeutung f

magpie /'mægpaɪ/ n Elster f

mahogany /mə'hogənɪ/ n Mahagoni nt

maid /meɪd/ n Dienstmädchen nt; (liter: girl) Maid f; old ~ (pej) alte Jungfer f

maiden /'meɪdn/ n (liter) Maid f □ a ⟨speech, voyage⟩ Jungfern-. ~ 'aunt n unverheiratete Tante f. ~ name n Mädchenname m

mail¹ /meɪl/ n Kettenpanzer m

mail² n Post f □ vt mit der Post schicken; (send off) abschicken

mail: ~bag n Postsack m. ~box n (Amer) Briefkasten m. ~ing list n Postversandliste f. ~man n (Amer) Briefträger m. ~order firm n Versandhaus nt

maim /meɪm/ vt verstümmeln

main¹ /meɪn/ n (water, gas, electricity) Hauptleitung f

main² a Haupt-. □ n in the ~ im Großen und Ganzen

main: ~land /-lənd/ n Festland nt. ~ly adv hauptsächlich. ~stay n (fig) Stütze f. ~ street n Hauptstraße f

maintain /meɪn'teɪn/ vt aufrechterhalten; (keep in repair) instand halten; (support) unterhalten; (claim) behaupten

maintenance /'meɪntənəns/ n Aufrechterhaltung f; (care) Instandhaltung f; (allowance) Unterhalt m

maisonette /meɪzə'net/ n Wohnung f [auf zwei Etagen]

maize /meɪz/ n Mais m

majestic /mə'dʒestɪk/ a, -ally adv majestätisch

majesty /'mædʒəstɪ/ n Majestät f

major /'meɪdʒə(r)/ a größer □ n (Mil) Major m; (Mus) Dur nt □ vi (Amer) ~ in als Hauptfach studieren

Majorca /mə'jɔːkə/ n Mallorca nt

majority /mə'dʒɒrətɪ/ n Mehrheit f; in the ~ in der Mehrzahl

major road n Hauptverkehrsstraße f

make /meɪk/ n (brand) Marke f □ v (pt/pp made) □ vt machen; (force) zwingen; (earn) verdienen; halten ⟨speech⟩; treffen ⟨decision⟩; erreichen ⟨destination⟩ □ vi ~ as if to Miene machen zu. ~ do vi zurechtkommen (with mit). ~ for vi zusteuern auf (+ acc). ~ off vi sich davonmachen (with mit). ~ out vt (distinguish) ausmachen; (write out) ausstellen; (assert) behaupten. ~ over vt überschreiben (to auf

+ acc). ~ up vt (constitute) bilden; (invent) erfinden; (apply cosmetics to) schminken; ~ up one's mind sich entschließen □ vi sich versöhnen; ~ up for sth etw wieder gutmachen; ~ up for lost time verlorene Zeit aufholen

'make-believe n Phantasie f

maker /'meɪkə(r)/ n Hersteller m

make: ~shift a behelfsmäßig □ n Notbehelf m. ~-up n Make-up nt

making /'meɪkɪŋ/ n have the ~s of das Zeug haben zu

maladjusted /mælə'dʒʌstɪd/ a verhaltensgestört

malaise /mə'leɪz/ n (fig) Unbehagen nt

male /meɪl/ a männlich □ n Mann m; (animal) Männchen nt. ~ nurse n Krankenpfleger m. ~ voice 'choir n Männerchor m

malevolen|ce /mə'levələns/ n Bosheit f. ~t a boshaft

malfunction /mæl'fʌŋkʃn/ n technische Störung f, (Med) Funktionsstörung f □ vi nicht richtig funktionieren

malice /'mælɪs/ n Bosheit f; bear s.o. ~ einen Groll gegen jdn hegen

malicious /mə'lɪʃəs/ a, -ly adv böswillig

malign /mə'laɪn/ vt verleumden

malignan|cy /mə'lɪgnənsɪ/ n Bösartigkeit f. ~t a bösartig

malinger /mə'lɪŋgə(r)/ vi simulieren, sich krank stellen. ~er n Simulant m

malleable /'mælɪəbl/ a formbar

mallet /'mælɪt/ n Holzhammer m

malnu'trition /mæl-/ n Unterernährung f

mal'practice n Berufsvergehen n

malt /mɔːlt/ n Malz nt

mal'treat /mæl-/ vt misshandeln. ~ment n Misshandlung f

mammal /'mæml/ n Säugetier nt

mammoth /'mæməθ/ a riesig □ n Mammut nt

man /mæn/ n (pl men) Mann m; (mankind) der Mensch; (chess) Figur f; (draughts) Stein m □ vt (pt/pp manned) bemannen ⟨ship⟩; bedienen ⟨pump⟩; besetzen ⟨counter⟩

manacle /'mænəkl/ vt fesseln (to an + acc); ~d in Handschellen

manage /'mænɪdʒ/ vt leiten; verwalten ⟨estate⟩; (cope with) fertig werden mit; ~ to do sth es schaffen, etw zu tun □ vi zurechtkommen; ~ on auskommen mit. ~able /-əbl/ a ⟨tool⟩ handlich; ⟨person⟩ fügsam. ~ment /-mənt/ n the ~ment die Geschäftsleitung f

manager /'mænɪdʒə(r)/ n Geschäftsführer m; (of bank) Direktor m; (of estate)

Verwalter m; (Sport) [Chef]trainer m. ~ess n Geschäftsführerin f. ~ial /-'dʒɪərɪəl/ a ~ial staff Führungskräfte pl

managing /'mænɪdʒɪŋ/ a ~ director Generaldirektor m

mandarin /'mændərɪn/ n ~ [orange] Mandarine f

mandat|e /'mændeɪt/ n Mandat nt. ~ory /-dətrɪ/ a obligatorisch

mane /meɪn/ n Mähne f

manful /'mænfl/ a, -ly adv mannhaft

manger /'meɪndʒə(r)/ n Krippe f

mangle¹ /'mæŋgl/ n Wringmaschine f; (for smoothing) Mangel f

mangle² vt (damage) verstümmeln

mango /'mæŋgəʊ/ n (pl -es) Mango f

mangy /'meɪndʒɪ/ a (dog) räudig

man: ~handle vt grob behandeln (person). ~hole n Kanalschacht m. ~hole cover n Kanaldeckel m. ~hood n Mannesalter nt; (quality) Männlichkeit f. ~hour n Arbeitsstunde f. ~hunt n Fahndung f

man|ia /'meɪnɪə/ n Manie f. ~iac /-ɪæk/ n Wahnsinnige(r) m/f

manicur|e /'mænɪkjʊə(r)/ n Maniküre f □ vt maniküren. ~ist n Maniküre f

manifest /'mænɪfest/ a, -ly adv offensichtlich □ vt itself sich manifestieren

manifesto /mænɪ'festəʊ/ n Manifest nt

manifold /'mænɪfəʊld/ a mannigfaltig

manipulat|e /mə'nɪpjʊleɪt/ vt handhaben; (pej) manipulieren. ~ion /-'leɪʃn/ n Manipulation f

mankind n die Menschheit

manly /'mænlɪ/ a männlich

man-made a künstlich. ~ fibre n Kunstfaser f

manner /'mænə(r)/ n Weise f; (kind, behaviour) Art f; in this ~ auf diese Weise; [good/bad] ~s [gute/schlechte] Manieren pl. ~ism n Angewohnheit f

mannish /'mænɪʃ/ a männlich

manœuvrable /mə'nu:vrəbl/ a manövrierfähig

manœuvre /mə'nu:və(r)/ n Manöver nt □ vt/i manövrieren

manor /'mænə(r)/ n Gutshof m; (house) Gutshaus nt

man: ~power n Arbeitskräfte pl. ~servant n (pl menservants) Diener m

mansion /'mænʃn/ n Villa f

manslaughter n Totschlag m

mantelpiece /'mæntl-/ n Kaminsims m & nt

manual /'mænjʊəl/ a Hand- □ n Handbuch nt

manufacture /mænjʊ'fæktʃə(r)/ vt herstellen □ n Herstellung f. ~r n Hersteller m

manure /mə'njʊə(r)/ n Mist m

manuscript /'mænjʊskrɪpt/ n Manuskript nt

many /'menɪ/ a viele; ~ a time oft □ n a good/great ~ sehr viele

map /mæp/ n Landkarte f; (of town) Stadtplan m □ vt (pt/pp mapped) ~ out (fig) ausarbeiten

maple /'meɪpl/ n Ahorn m

mar /mɑ:(r)/ vt (pt/pp marred) verderben

marathon /'mærəθən/ n Marathon m

marauding /mə'rɔ:dɪŋ/ a plündernd

marble /'mɑ:bl/ n Marmor m; (for game) Murmel f

March /mɑ:tʃ/ n März m

march n Marsch m □ vi marschieren □ vt marschieren lassen; ~ s.o. off jdn abführen

mare /meə(r)/ n Stute f

margarine /mɑ:dʒə'ri:n/ n Margarine f

margin /'mɑ:dʒɪn/ n Rand m; (leeway) Spielraum m; (Comm) Spanne f. ~al a, -ly adv geringfügig

marigold /'mærɪgəʊld/ n Ringelblume f

marijuana /mærɪ'hwɑ:nə/ n Marihuana nt

marina /mə'ri:nə/ n Jachthafen m

marinade /mærɪ'neɪd/ n Marinade f □ vt marinieren

marine /mə'ri:n/ a Meeres- □ n Marine f; (sailor) Marineinfanterist m

marionette /mærɪə'net/ n Marionette f

marital /'mærɪtl/ a ehelich. ~ status n Familienstand m

maritime /'mærɪtaɪm/ a See-

marjoram /'mɑ:dʒərəm/ n Majoran m

mark¹ /mɑ:k/ n (currency) Mark f

mark² n Fleck m; (sign) Zeichen nt; (trace) Spur f; (target) Ziel nt; (Sch) Note f □ vt markieren; (spoil) beschädigen; (characterize) kennzeichnen; (Sch) korrigieren; (Sport) decken; ~ time (Mil) auf der Stelle treten; (fig) abwarten; ~ my words das [eine] will ich dir sagen. ~ out vt markieren

marked /mɑ:kt/ a, -ly /-kɪdlɪ/ adv deutlich; (pronounced) ausgeprägt

marker /'mɑ:kə(r)/ n Marke f; (of exam) Korrektor(in) m(f)

market /'mɑ:kɪt/ n Markt m □ vt vertreiben; (launch) auf den Markt bringen. ~ing n Marketing nt. ~ re'search n Marktforschung f

marking /'mɑ:kɪŋ/ n Markierung f; (on animal) Zeichnung f

marksman /'mɑːksmən/ n Scharfschütze m

marmalade /'mɑːməleɪd/ n Orangenmarmelade f

marmot /'mɑːmət/ n Murmeltier nt

maroon /mə'ruːn/ a dunkelrot

marooned /mə'ruːnd/ a (fig) von der Außenwelt abgeschnitten

marquee /mɑː'kiː/ n Festzelt nt; (Amer: awning) Markise f

marquetry /'mɑːkɪtrɪ/ n Einlegearbeit f

marquis /'mɑːkwɪs/ n Marquis m

marriage /'mærɪdʒ/ n Ehe f; (wedding) Hochzeit f. ~able f. -əbl/ a heiratsfähig

married /'mærɪd/ see marry □ a verheiratet. ~ life n Eheleben nt

marrow /'mærəʊ/ n (Anat) Mark nt; (vegetable) Kürbis m

marr|y /'mærɪ/ vt/i (pt/pp married) heiraten; (unite) trauen; get ~ied heiraten

marsh /mɑːʃ/ n Sumpf m

marshal /'mɑːʃl/ n Marschall m; (steward) Ordner m □ vt (pt/pp marshalled) (Mil) formieren; (fig) ordnen

marshy /'mɑːʃɪ/ a sumpfig

marsupial /mɑː'suːpɪəl/ n Beuteltier nt

martial /'mɑːʃl/ a kriegerisch. ~ 'law n Kriegsrecht nt

martyr /'mɑːtə(r)/ n Märtyrer(in) m(f) □ vt zum Märtyrer machen. ~dom /-dəm/ n Martyrium nt

marvel /'mɑːvl/ n Wunder nt □ vi (pt/pp marvelled) staunen (at über + acc). ~lous /-vələs/ a, -ly adv wunderbar

Marxis|m /'mɑːksɪzm/ n Marxismus m. ~t a marxistisch □ n Marxist(in) m(f)

marzipan /'mɑːzɪpæn/ n Marzipan nt

mascara /mæ'skɑːrə/ n Wimperntusche f

mascot /'mæskɒt/ n Maskottchen nt

masculin|e /'mæskjʊlɪn/ a männlich □ n (Gram) Maskulinum nt. ~ity /-'lɪnətɪ/ n Männlichkeit f

mash /mæʃ/ n (fam, Culin) Kartoffelpüree nt □ vt stampfen. ~ed potatoes npl Kartoffelpüree nt

mask /mɑːsk/ n Maske f □ vt maskieren

masochis|m /'mæsəkɪzm/ n Masochismus m. ~t /-ɪst/ n Masochist m

mason /'meɪsn/ n Steinmetz m

Mason n Freimaurer m. ~ic /mə'sɒnɪk/ a freimaurerisch

masonry /'meɪsnrɪ/ n Mauerwerk nt

masquerade /mæskə'reɪd/ n (fig) Maskerade f □ vi ~ as (pose) sich ausgeben als

mass¹ /mæs/ n (Relig) Messe f

mass² n Masse f □ vi sich sammeln; (Mil) sich massieren

massacre /'mæsəkə(r)/ n Massaker nt □ vt niedermetzeln

massage /'mæsɑːʒ/ n Massage f □ vt massieren

masseu|r /mæ'sɜː(r)/ n Masseur m. ~se /-'sɜːz/ n Masseuse f

massive /'mæsɪv/ a massiv; (huge) riesig

mass: ~ 'media npl Massenmedien pl. ~ pro'duce vt in Massenproduktion herstellen. ~pro'duction n Massenproduktion f

mast /mɑːst/ n Mast m

master /'mɑːstə(r)/ n Herr m; (teacher) Lehrer m; (craftsman, artist) Meister m; (of ship) Kapitän m □ vt meistern; beherrschen (language)

master: ~key n Hauptschlüssel m. ~ly a meisterhaft. ~mind n führender Kopf m □ vt der führende Kopf sein von. ~piece n Meisterwerk nt. ~y n (of subject) Beherrschung f

masturbat|e /'mæstəbeɪt/ vi masturbieren. ~ion /-'beɪʃn/ n Masturbation f

mat /mæt/ n Matte f; (on table) Untersatz m

match¹ /mætʃ/ n Wettkampf m; (in ball games) Spiel nt; (Tennis) Match nt; (marriage) Heirat f; be a good ~ ⟨colours:⟩ gut zusammenpassen; be no ~ for s.o. jdm nicht gewachsen sein □ vt (equal) gleichkommen (+ dat); (be like) passen zu; (find sth similar) etwas Passendes finden zu □ vi zusammenpassen

match² n Streichholz nt. ~box n Streichholzschachtel f

matching /'mætʃɪŋ/ a [zusammen]passend

mate¹ /meɪt/ n Kumpel m; (assistant) Gehilfe m; (Naut) Maat m; (Zool) Männchen nt; (female) Weibchen nt □ vi sich paaren □ vt paaren

mate² n (Chess) Matt nt

material /mə'tɪərɪəl/ n Material nt; (fabric) Stoff m; raw ~s Rohstoffe pl □ a materiell

material|ism /mə'tɪərɪəlɪzm/ n Materialismus m. ~istic /-'lɪstɪk/ a materialistisch. ~ize /-laɪz/ vi sich verwirklichen

maternal /mə'tɜːnl/ a mütterlich

maternity /mə'tɜːnɪtɪ/ n Mutterschaft f. ~ clothes npl Umstandskleidung f. ~ward n Entbindungsstation f

matey /'meɪtɪ/ a (fam) freundlich

mathematic|al /mæθə'mætɪkl/ a, -ly adv mathematisch. ~ian /-mə'tɪʃn/ n Mathematiker(in) m(f)

mathematics /mæθə'mætɪks/ n Mathematik f

maths /mæθs/ n (fam) Mathe f

matinée /'mætɪneɪ/ n (Theat) Nachmittagsvorstellung f

matriculat|e /mə'trɪkjuleɪt/ vi sich immatrikulieren. ∼ion /-'leɪʃn/ n Immatrikulation f

matrimon|ial /mætrɪ'məʊnɪəl/ a Ehe-. ∼y /'mætrɪmənɪ/ n Ehe f

matrix /'meɪtrɪks/ n (pl matrices /-siːz/) n (Techn: mould) Matrize f

matron /'meɪtrən/ n (of hospital) Oberin f; (of school) Hausmutter f. ∼ly a matronenhaft

matt /mæt/ a matt

matted /'mætɪd/ a verfilzt

matter /'mætə(r)/ n (affair) Sache f; (pus) Eiter m; (Phys: substance) Materie f; money ∼s Geldangelegenheiten pl; as a ∼ of fact eigentlich; what is the ∼? was ist los? ∼ vi wichtig sein; ∼ to s.o. jdm etwas ausmachen; it doesn't ∼ es macht nichts. ∼-of-fact a sachlich

matting /'mætɪŋ/ n Matten pl

mattress /'mætrɪs/ n Matratze f

matur|e /mə'tjʊə(r)/ a reif; (Comm) fällig □ vi reifen; (person:) reifer werden; (Comm) fällig werden □ vt reifen lassen. ∼ity n Reife f; (Comm) Fälligkeit f

maul /mɔːl/ vt übel zurichten

Maundy /'mɔːndɪ/ n ∼ Thursday Gründonnerstag m

mauve /məʊv/ a lila

mawkish /'mɔːkɪʃ/ a rührselig

maxim /'mæksɪm/ n Maxime f

maximum /'mæksɪməm/ a maximal □ n (pl -ima) Maximum nt. ∼ speed n Höchstgeschwindigkeit f

may /meɪ/ v aux (nur Präsens) (be allowed to) dürfen; (be possible) können; may I come in? darf ich reinkommen? may he succeed möge es ihm gelingen; I may as well stay am besten bleibe ich hier; it may be true es könnte wahr sein

May /meɪ/ n Mai m

maybe /'meɪbi:/ adv vielleicht

'May Day n der Erste Mai

mayonnaise /meɪə'neɪz/ n Mayonnaise f

mayor /'meə(r)/ n Bürgermeister m. ∼ess n Bürgermeisterin f; (wife of mayor) Frau Bürgermeister f

maze /meɪz/ n Irrgarten m; (fig) Labyrinth nt

me /mi:/ pron (acc) mich; (dat) mir; he knows ∼ er kennt mich; give ∼ the money gib mir das Geld; it's ∼ (fam) ich bin es

meadow /'medəʊ/ n Wiese f

meagre /'mi:gə(r)/ a dürftig

meal¹ /mi:l/ n Mahlzeit f; (food) Essen nt

meal² n (grain) Schrot m

mealy-mouthed /mi:lɪ'maʊðd/ a heuchlerisch

mean¹ /mi:n/ a (-er, -est) geizig; (unkind) gemein; (poor) schäbig

mean² a mittlere(r,s) □ n (average) Durchschnitt m; the golden ∼ die goldene Mitte

mean³ vt (pt/pp meant) heißen; (signify) bedeuten; (intend) beabsichtigen; I ∼ it das ist mein Ernst; ∼ well es gut meinen; be meant for (present:) bestimmt sein für; (remark:) gerichtet sein an (+ acc)

meander /mɪ'ændə(r)/ vi sich schlängeln; (person:) schlendern

meaning /'mi:nɪŋ/ n Bedeutung f. ∼ful a bedeutungsvoll. ∼less a bedeutungslos

means /mi:nz/ n Möglichkeit f, Mittel nt; ∼ of transport Verkehrsmittel nt; by ∼ of durch; by all ∼! aber natürlich! by no ∼ keineswegs □ npl (resources) [Geld]mittel pl. ∼ test n Bedürftigkeitsnachweis m

meant /ment/ see mean³

'meantime n in the ∼ in der Zwischenzeit □ adv inzwischen

'meanwhile adv inzwischen

measles /'mi:zlz/ n Masern pl

measly /'mi:zlɪ/ a (fam) mickerig

measurable /'meʒərəbl/ a messbar

measure /'meʒə(r)/ n Maß nt; (action) Maßnahme f □ vt/i messen; ∼ up to (fig) herankommen an (+ acc). ∼d a gemessen. ∼ment /-mənt/ n Maß nt

meat /mi:t/ n Fleisch nt. ∼ ball n (Culin) Klops m. ∼ loaf n falscher Hase m

mechan|ic /mɪ'kænɪk/ n Mechaniker m. ∼ical a, -ly adv mechanisch. ∼ical engineering Maschinenbau m. ∼ics n Mechanik f □ n pl Mechanismus m

mechan|ism /'mekənɪzm/ n Mechanismus m. ∼ize vt mechanisieren

medal /'medl/ n Orden m; (Sport) Medaille f

medallion /mɪ'dælɪən/ n Medaillon nt

medallist /'medəlɪst/ n Medaillengewinner(in) m(f)

meddle /'medl/ vi sich einmischen (in in + acc); (tinker) herumhantieren (with an + acc)

media /'mi:dɪə/ see medium □ n pl the ∼ die Medien pl

median /'mi:dɪən/ a ∼ strip (Amer) Mittelstreifen m

mediat|e /'mi:dɪeɪt/ vi vermitteln. ∼or n Vermittler(in) m(f)

medical /'medɪkl/ a medizinisch; (treatment) ärztlich □ n ärztliche Untersuchung f. ∼ insurance n Krankenversicherung f. ∼ student n Medizinstudent m medicat|ed /'medɪkeɪtɪd/ a medizinisch. ∼ion /-'keɪʃn/ n ⟨drugs⟩ Medikamente pl

medicinal /mɪ'dɪsɪnl/ a medizinisch; ⟨plant⟩ heilkräftig

medicine /'medsən/ n Medizin f; ⟨preparation⟩ Medikament nt

medieval /medi'i:vl/ a mittelalterlich

mediocr|e /mi:dɪ'əʊkə(r)/ a mittelmäßig. ∼ity /-'bkrɒtɪ/ n Mittelmäßigkeit f

meditat|e /'medɪteɪt/ vi nachdenken (on über + acc); ⟨Relig⟩ meditieren. ∼ion /-'teɪʃn/ n Meditation f

Mediterranean /medɪtə'reɪnɪən/ n Mittelmeer nt ▫ a Mittelmeer-

medium /'mi:dɪəm/ a mittlere(r,s); ⟨steak⟩ medium; of ∼ size von mittlerer Größe ▫ n ⟨pl media⟩ Medium nt; ⟨means⟩ Mittel nt ▫ ⟨pl -s⟩ ⟨person⟩ Medium nt

medium: ∼-sized a mittelgroß. ∼ wave n Mittelwelle f

medley /'medlɪ/ n Gemisch nt; ⟨Mus⟩ Potpourri nt

meek /mi:k/ a (-er, -est), -ly adv sanftmütig; ⟨unprotesting⟩ widerspruchslos

meet /mi:t/ v ⟨pt/pp met⟩ ▫ vt treffen; ⟨by chance⟩ begegnen (+ dat); ⟨at station⟩ abholen; ⟨make the acquaintance of⟩ kennen lernen; stoßen auf (+ acc) ⟨problem⟩; bezahlen ⟨bill⟩; erfüllen ⟨requirements⟩ ▫ vi sich treffen; ⟨for the first time⟩ sich kennen lernen; ∼ with stoßen auf (+ acc) ⟨problem⟩; sich treffen mit ⟨person⟩ ▫ n Jagdtreffen nt

meeting /'mi:tɪŋ/ n Treffen nt; ⟨by chance⟩ Begegnung f; ⟨discussion⟩ Besprechung f; ⟨of committee⟩ Sitzung f; ⟨large⟩ Versammlung f

megalomania /megələ'meɪnɪə/ n Größenwahnsinn m

megaphone /'megəfəʊn/ n Megaphon nt

melancholy /'melənkəlɪ/ a melancholisch ▫ n Melancholie f

mellow /'meləʊ/ a(-er, -est) ⟨fruit⟩ ausgereift; ⟨sound, person⟩ sanft ▫ vi reifer werden

melodic /mɪ'lɒdɪk/ a melodisch

melodious /mɪ'ləʊdɪəs/ a melodiös

melodrama /'melə-/ n Melodrama nt. ∼tic /-drə'mætɪk/ a, -ally adv melodramatisch

melody /'melədɪ/ n Melodie f

melon /'melən/ n Melone f

melt /melt/ vt/i schmelzen. ∼ down vt einschmelzen. ∼ing-pot n ⟨fig⟩ Schmelztiegel m

member /'membə(r)/ n Mitglied nt; ⟨of family⟩ Angehörige(r) m/f; M∼ of Parliament Abgeordnete(r) m/f. ∼ship n Mitgliedschaft f; ⟨members⟩ Mitgliederzahl f

membrane /'membreɪn/ n Membran f

memento /mɪ'mentəʊ/ n Andenken nt

memo /'meməʊ/ n Mitteilung f

memoirs /'memwɑ:z/ n pl Memoiren pl

memorable /'memərəbl/ a denkwürdig

memorandum /memə'rændəm/ n Mitteilung f

memorial /mɪ'mɔ:rɪəl/ n Denkmal nt. ∼ service n Gedenkfeier f

memorize /'memərɑɪz/ vt sich ⟨dat⟩ einprägen

memory /'memərɪ/ n Gedächtnis nt; ⟨thing remembered⟩ Erinnerung f; ⟨of computer⟩ Speicher m; from ∼ auswendig; in ∼ of zur Erinnerung an (+ acc)

men /men/ see man

menac|e /'menɪs/ n Drohung f; ⟨nuisance⟩ Plage f ▫ vt bedrohen. ∼ing a, ∼ly adv drohend

mend /mend/ vt reparieren; ⟨patch⟩ flicken; ausbessern ⟨clothes⟩ ▫ n on the ∼ auf dem Weg der Besserung

'menfolk n pl Männer pl

menial /'mi:nɪəl/ a niedrig

meningitis /menɪn'dʒaɪtɪs/ n Hirnhautentzündung f, Meningitis f

menopause /'menə-/ n Wechseljahre pl

menstruat|e /'menstrʊeɪt/ vi menstruieren. ∼ion /-'eɪʃn/ n Menstruation f

mental /'mentl/ a, -ly adv geistig; ⟨fam: mad⟩ verrückt. ∼ a'rithmetic n Kopfrechnen nt. ∼ 'illness n Geisteskrankheit f

mentality /men'tælətɪ/ n Mentalität f

mention /'menʃn/ n Erwähnung f ▫ vt erwähnen; don't ∼ it keine Ursache; bitte

menu /'menju:/ n Speisekarte f

mercantile /'mɜ:kəntaɪl/ a Handels-

mercenary /'mɜ:sɪnərɪ/ a geldgierig ▫ n Söldner m

merchandise /'mɜ:tʃəndaɪz/ n Ware f

merchant /'mɜ:tʃənt/ n Kaufmann m; ⟨dealer⟩ Händler m. ∼ 'navy n Handelsmarine f

merci|ful /'mɜ:sɪfl/ a barmherzig. ∼fully adv ⟨fam⟩ glücklicherweise. ∼less a, -ly adv erbarmungslos

mercury /'mɜ:kjʊrɪ/ n Quecksilber nt

mercy /'mɜ:sɪ/ n Barmherzigkeit f, Gnade f; be at s.o.'s ∼ jdm ausgeliefert sein

mere /mɪə(r)/ a, -ly adv bloß

merest /'mɪərɪst/ a kleinste(r,s)

merge /mɜ:dʒ/ vi zusammenlaufen; ⟨Comm⟩ fusionieren ▫ vt ⟨Comm⟩ zusammenschließen

merger /'mɜ:dʒə(r)/ n Fusion f

meridian /mə'rɪdɪən/ n Meridian m

meringue /mə'ræŋ/ n Baiser nt

merit /'merɪt/ n Verdienst nt; (advantage) Vorzug m; (worth) Wert m □ vt verdienen

mermaid /'mɜːmeɪd/ n Meerjungfrau f

merri|ly /'merɪlɪ/ adv fröhlich. ~ment /-mənt/ n Fröhlichkeit f; (laughter) Gelächter nt

merry /'merɪ/ a (-ier, -iest) fröhlich; ~ Christmas! fröhliche Weihnachten!

merry: ~-go-round n Karussell nt. ~making n Feiern nt

mesh /meʃ/ n Masche f; (size) Maschenweite f; (fig: network) Netz nt

mesmerize /'mezməraɪz/ vt hypnotisieren. ~d a (fig) [wie] gebannt

mess /mes/ n Durcheinander nt; (trouble) Schwierigkeiten pl; (something spilt) Bescherung f (dirt); (Mil) Messe f; make a ~ of (botch) verpfuschen □ vt ~ up in Unordnung bringen; (botch) verpfuschen □ vi ~ about herumalbern; (tinker) herumspielen (with mit)

message /'mesɪdʒ/ n Nachricht f; give s.o. a ~ jdm etwas ausrichten

messenger /'mesɪndʒə(r)/ n Bote m

Messiah /mɪ'saɪə/ n Messias m

Messrs /'mesəz/ n pl see Mr; (on letter) ~ Smith Firma Smith

messy /'mesɪ/ a (-ier, -iest) schmutzig; (untidy) unordentlich

met /met/ see meet

metabolism /mɪ'tæbəlɪzm/ n Stoffwechsel m

metal /'metl/ n Metall nt □ a Metall-. ~lic /mɪ'tælɪk/ a metallisch. ~lurgy /mɪ'tælədʒɪ/ n Metallurgie f

metamorphosis /metə'mɔːfəsɪs/ n (pl -phoses /-siːz/) Metamorphose f

metaphor /'metəfə(r)/ n Metapher f. ~ical /-'forɪkl/ a, -ly adv metaphorisch

meteor /'miːtɪə(r)/ n Meteor m. ~ic /-'ɒrɪk/ a kometenhaft

meteorological /miːtɪərə'lɒdʒɪkl/ a Wetter-

meteorolog|ist /miːtɪə'rɒlədʒɪst/ n Meteorologe m/ -gin f. ~y n Meteorologie f

meter¹ /'miːtə(r)/ n Zähler m

meter² n (Amer) = metre

method /'meθəd/ n Methode f; (Culin) Zubereitung f

methodical /mɪ'θɒdɪkl/ a, -ly adv systematisch, methodisch

Methodist /'meθədɪst/ n Methodist(in) m(f)

meths /meθs/ n (fam) Brennspiritus m

methylated /'meθɪleɪtɪd/ a ~ spirit[s] Brennspiritus m

meticulous /mɪ'tɪkjʊləs/ a, -ly adv sehr genau

metre /'miːtə(r)/ n Meter m & n; (rhythm) Versmaß nt

metric /'metrɪk/ a metrisch

metropolis /mɪ'trɒpəlɪs/ n Metropole f

metropolitan /metrə'pɒlɪtən/ a hauptstädtisch; (international) weltstädtisch

mettle /'metl/ n Mut m

mew /mjuː/ n Miau nt □ vi miauen

Mexican /'meksɪkən/ a mexikanisch □ n Mexikaner(in) m(f). 'Mexico n Mexiko nt

miaow /mɪ'aʊ/ n Miau nt □ vi miauen

mice /maɪs/ see mouse

microbe /'maɪkrəʊb/ n Mikrobe f

micro /'maɪkrəʊ/: ~chip n Mikrochip nt. ~computer n Mikrocomputer m. ~film n Mikrofilm m. ~phone n Mikrofon m. ~processor n Mikroprozessor m. ~scope /-skəʊp/ n Mikroskop nt. ~scopic /-'skɒpɪk/ a mikroskopisch. ~wave n Mikrowelle f. ~wave [oven] n Mikrowellenherd m

mid /mɪd/ a ~ May Mitte Mai; in ~ air in der Luft

midday /mɪd'deɪ/ n Mittag m

middle /'mɪdl/ a mittlere(r,s); the M~ Ages das Mittelalter; the ~ class[es] der Mittelstand; the M~ East der Nahe Osten □ n Mitte f; in the ~ of the night mitten in der Nacht

middle: ~-aged a mittleren Alters. ~class a bürgerlich. ~man n (Comm) Zwischenhändler m

middling /'mɪdlɪŋ/ a mittelmäßig

midge /mɪdʒ/ n [kleine] Mücke f

midget /'mɪdʒɪt/ n Liliputaner(in) m(f)

Midlands /'mɪdləndz/ npl the ~ Mittelengland n

midnight n Mitternacht f

midriff /'mɪdrɪf/ n (fam) Taille f

midst /mɪdst/ n in the ~ of mitten in (+ dat); in our ~ unter uns

mid: ~summer n Hochsommer m; (solstice) Sommersonnenwende f. ~way adv auf halbem Wege. ~wife n Hebamme f. ~wifery /-wɪfrɪ/ n Geburtshilfe f. ~'winter n Mitte f des Winters

might¹ /maɪt/ v aux I ~ vielleicht; it ~ be true es könnte wahr sein; I ~ as well stay am besten bleibe ich hier; he asked if he ~ go er fragte, ob er gehen dürfte; you ~ have drowned du hättest ertrinken können

might² n Macht f

mighty /'maɪtɪ/ a (-ier, -iest) mächtig

migraine /'miːgreɪn/ n Migräne f

migrant /'maɪgrənt/ a Wander- □ n (bird) Zugvogel m

migrat|e /maɪ'greɪt/ vi abwandern; ⟨birds:⟩ ziehen. ∼ion /-'greɪʃn/ n Wanderung f; (of birds) Zug m

mike /maɪk/ n (fam) Mikrofon nt

mild /maɪld/ a (-er, -est) mild

mildew /'mɪldju:/ n Schimmel m; (Bot) Mehltau m

mild|ly /'maɪldlɪ/ adv leicht; to put it ∼ly gelinde gesagt. ∼ness n Milde f

mile /maɪl/ n Meile f (= 1,6 km); ∼s too big (fam) viel zu groß

mile|age /-ɪdʒ/ n Meilenzahl f; (of car) Meilenstand m. ∼stone n Meilenstein m

militant /'mɪlɪtənt/ a militant

military /'mɪlɪtrɪ/ a militärisch. ∼ service n Wehrdienst m

militate /'mɪlɪteɪt/ vi ∼ against sprechen gegen

militia /mɪ'lɪʃə/ n Miliz f

milk /mɪlk/ n Milch f ▢ vt melken

milk: ∼man n Milchmann m. ∼ shake n Milchmixgetränk nt. ∼ tooth n Milchzahn m

milky /'mɪlkɪ/ a (-ier, -iest) milchig. M∼ Way n (Astr) Milchstraße f

mill /mɪl/ n Mühle f; (factory) Fabrik f ▢ vt/i mahlen; (Techn) fräsen. ∼ about, ∼ around vi umherlaufen

millenium /mɪ'lenɪəm/ n Jahrtausend nt

miller /'mɪlə(r)/ n Müller m

millet /'mɪlɪt/ n Hirse f

milli|gram /'mɪlɪ-/ n Milligramm nt. ∼metre n Millimeter m & nt

milliner /'mɪlɪnə(r)/ n Modistin f; (man) Hutmacher m. ∼y n Damenhüte pl

million /'mɪljən/ n Million f; a ∼ pounds eine Million Pfund. ∼aire /-'neə(r)/ n Millionär(in) m(f)

'**millstone** n Mühlstein m

mime /maɪm/ n Pantomime f ▢ vt pantomimisch darstellen

mimic /'mɪmɪk/ n Imitator m ▢ vt (pt/pp mimicked) nachahmen. ∼ry n Nachahmung f

mimosa /mɪ'məʊzə/ n Mimose f

mince /mɪns/ n Hackfleisch nt ▢ vt (Culin) durchdrehen; not ∼ one's words kein Blatt vor den Mund nehmen

mince: ∼meat n Masse f aus Korinthen, Zitronat usw; make ∼ meat of (fig) vernichtend schlagen. ∼'pie n mit 'mincemeat' gefülltes Pastetchen nt

mincer /'mɪnsə(r)/ n Fleischwolf m

mind /maɪnd/ n Geist m; (sanity) Verstand m; to my ∼ meiner Meinung nach; give s.o. a piece of one's ∼ jdm gehörig die Meinung sagen; make up one's ∼ sich entschließen; be out of one's ∼ nicht bei Verstand sein; have sth in ∼ etw im Sinn haben; bear sth in ∼ an etw (acc) denken; have a good ∼ to große Lust haben, zu; I have changed my ∼ ich habe es mir anders überlegt ▢ vt aufpassen auf (+ acc); I don't ∼ the noise der Lärm stört mich nicht; ∼ the step! Achtung Stufe! ▢ vi (care) sich kümmern (about um); I don't ∼ mir macht es nichts aus; never ∼! macht nichts! do you ∼ if? haben Sie etwas dagegen, wenn? ∼ out vi aufpassen

mind|ful a ∼ful of eingedenk (+ gen). ∼less a geistlos

mine¹ /maɪn/ poss pron meine(r), meins; a friend of ∼ ein Freund von mir; that is ∼ das gehört mir

mine² n Bergwerk nt; (explosive) Mine f ▢ vt abbauen; (Mil) verminen. ∼ detector n Minensuchgerät nt. ∼field n Minenfeld nt

miner /'maɪnə(r)/ n Bergarbeiter m

mineral /'mɪnərl/ n Mineral nt. ∼ogy /-'rælədʒɪ/ n Mineralogie f. ∼ water n Mineralwasser nt

minesweeper /'maɪn-/ n Minenräumboot nt

mingle /'mɪŋgl/ vi ∼ with sich mischen unter (+ acc)

miniature /'mɪnɪtʃə(r)/ a Klein- ▢ n Miniatur f

mini|bus /'mɪnɪ-/ n Kleinbus m. ∼cab n Taxi nt

minim /'mɪnɪm/ n (Mus) halbe Note f

minim|al /'mɪnɪməl/ a minimal. ∼ize vt auf ein Minimum reduzieren. ∼um n (pl -ima) Minimum nt ▢ a Mindest-

mining /'maɪnɪŋ/ n Bergbau m

miniskirt /'mɪnɪ-/ n Minirock m

minist|er /'mɪnɪstə(r)/ n Minister m; (Relig) Pastor m. ∼erial /-'stɪərɪəl/ a ministeriell

ministry /'mɪnɪstrɪ/ n (Pol) Ministerium nt; the ∼ (Relig) das geistliche Amt

mink /mɪŋk/ n Nerz m

minor /'maɪnə(r)/ a kleiner; (less important) unbedeutend ▢ n Minderjährige(r) m/f; (Mus) Moll nt

minority /maɪ'nɒrɪtɪ/ n Minderheit f; (age) Minderjährigkeit f

minor road n Nebenstraße f

mint¹ /mɪnt/ n Münzstätte f ▢ a ⟨stamp⟩ postfrisch; in ∼ condition wie neu ▢ vt prägen

mint² n (herb) Minze f; (sweet) Pfefferminzbonbon m & nt

minuet /mɪnjʊ'et/ n Menuett nt

minus /'maɪnəs/ prep minus, weniger; (fam: without) ohne ▢ n [sign] Minuszeichen nt minute¹ /'mɪnɪt/ n Minute f; in a ~ (*shortly*) gleich; ~s pl (*of meeting*) Protokoll nt

minute² /maɪ'njuːt/ a winzig; (*precise*) genau

mirac|le /'mɪrəkl/ n Wunder nt. ~ulous /-'rækjʊləs/ a wunderbar

mirage /'mɪrɑːʒ/ n Fata Morgana f

mire /'maɪə(r)/ n Morast m

mirror /'mɪrə(r)/ n Spiegel m ▫ vt widerspiegeln

mirth /mɜːθ/ n Heiterkeit f

misad'venture /mɪs-/ n Missgeschick nt

misanthropist /mɪ'zænθrəpɪst/ n Menschenfeind m

misappre'hension n Missverständnis nt; be under a ~ sich irren

misbe'hav|e vi sich schlecht benehmen. ~iour n schlechtes Benehmen nt

mis'calcu|late vt falsch berechnen ▫ vi sich verrechnen. ~'lation n Fehlkalkulation f

'miscarriage n Fehlgeburt f; ~ of justice Justizirrtum m. mis'carry vi eine Fehlgeburt haben

miscellaneous /mɪsə'leɪnɪəs/ a vermischt

mischief /'mɪstʃɪf/ n Unfug m; (*harm*) Schaden m

mischievous /'mɪstʃɪvəs/ a, -ly adv schelmisch; (*malicious*) boshaft

miscon'ception n falsche Vorstellung f

mis'conduct n unkorrektes Verhalten nt; (*adultery*) Ehebruch m

miscon'strue vt missdeuten

mis'deed n Missetat f

misde'meanour n Missetat f; (*teacher*)

miser /'maɪzə(r)/ n Geizhals m

miserable /'mɪzrəbl/ a, -bly adv unglücklich; (*wretched*) elend

miserly /'maɪzəlɪ/ adv geizig

misery /'mɪzərɪ/ n Elend nt; (*fam: person*) Miesepeter m

mis'fire vi fehlzünden; (*go wrong*) fehlschlagen

'misfit n Außenseiter(in) m(f)

mis'fortune n Unglück nt

mis'givings npl Bedenken pl

mis'guided a töricht

mishap /'mɪshæp/ n Missgeschick nt

misin'form vt falsch unterrichten

misin'terpret vt missdeuten

mis'judge vt falsch beurteilen; (*estimate wrongly*) falsch einschätzen

mis'lay vt (pt/pp -laid) verlegen

mis'lead vt (pt/pp -led) irreführen. ~ing a irreführend

mis'manage vt schlecht verwalten. ~ment n Misswirtschaft f

misnomer /mɪs'nəʊmə(r)/ n Fehlbezeichnung f

'misprint n Druckfehler m

mis'quote vt falsch zitieren

misrepre'sent vt falsch darstellen

miss /mɪs/ n Fehltreffer m ▫ vt verpassen; (*fail to hit or find*) verfehlen; (*fail to attend*) versäumen; (*fail to notice*) übersehen; (*feel the loss of*) vermissen ▫ vi (*fail to hit*) nicht treffen. ~ out vt auslassen

Miss n (pl -es) Fräulein nt

misshapen /mɪs'ʃeɪpən/ a missgestaltet

missile /'mɪsaɪl/ n [Wurf]geschoss nt; (*Mil*) Rakete f

missing /'mɪsɪŋ/ a fehlend (*lost*) verschwunden; (*Mil*) vermisst; be ~ fehlen

mission /'mɪʃn/ n Auftrag m; (*Mil*) Einsatz m; (*Relig*) Mission f

missionary /'mɪʃənrɪ/ n Missionar(in) m(f)

mis'spell vt (pt/pp -spelt or -spelled) falsch schreiben

mist /mɪst/ n Dunst m; (*fog*) Nebel m; (*on window*) Beschlag m ▫ vi ~ up beschlagen

mistake /mɪ'steɪk/ n Fehler m; by ~ aus Versehen ▫ vt (pt mistook, pp mistaken) missverstehen; ~ for verwechseln mit

mistaken /mɪ'steɪkən/ a falsch; be ~ sich irren; ~ identity Verwechslung f. ~ly adv irrtümlicherweise

mistletoe /'mɪsltəʊ/ n Mistel f

mistress /'mɪstrɪs/ n Herrin f; (*teacher*) Lehrerin f; (*lover*) Geliebte f

mis'trust n Misstrauen nt ▫ vt misstrauen (+ dat)

misty /'mɪstɪ/ a (-ier, -iest) dunstig; (*foggy*) neblig; (*fig*) unklar

misunder'stand vt (pt/pp -stood) missverstehen. ~ing n Missverständnis nt

misuse¹ /mɪs'juːz/ vt missbrauchen

misuse² /mɪs'juːs/ n Missbrauch m

mite /maɪt/ n (*Zool*) Milbe f; little ~ (*child*) kleines Ding nt

mitigat|e /'mɪtɪgeɪt/ vt mildern. ~ing a mildernd

mitten /'mɪtn/ n Fausthandschuh m

mix /mɪks/ n Mischung f ▫ vt mischen ▫ vi sich mischen; ~ with (*associate with*) verkehren mit. ~ up vt mischen; (*muddle*) durcheinander bringen; (*mistake for*) verwechseln (with mit)

mixed /mɪkst/ a gemischt; be ~ up durcheinander sein

mixer /'mɪksə(r)/ n Mischmaschine f; (*Culin*) Küchenmaschine f mixture /ˈmɪkstʃə(r)/ n Mischung f; (medicine) Mixtur f; (Culin) Teig m

'mix-up n Durcheinander nt; (confusion) Verwirrung f; (mistake) Verwechslung f

moan /məʊn/ n Stöhnen nt □ vi stöhnen; (complain) jammern

moat /məʊt/ n Burggraben m

mob /mɒb/ n Horde f; (rabble) Pöbel m; (fam: gang) Bande f □ vt (pt/pp mobbed) herfallen über (+ acc); belagern (celebrity)

mobile /ˈməʊbaɪl/ a beweglich □ n Mobile nt; (telephone) Handy nt. ~ 'home n Wohnwagen m. ~ 'phone n Mobiltelefon nt, Handy nt

mobility /məˈbɪlətɪ/ n Beweglichkeit f

mobilization /məʊbɪlaɪˈzeɪʃn/ n Mobilisierung f. ~lize /ˈməʊbɪlaɪz/ vt mobilisieren

mocha /ˈmɒkə/ n Mokka m

mock /mɒk/ a Schein- □ vt verspotten. ~ery n Spott m

'mock-up n Modell nt

modal /ˈməʊdl/ a ~ auxiliary Modalverb nt

mode /məʊd/ n [Art und] Weise f; (fashion) Mode f

model /ˈmɒdl/ n Modell nt; (example) Vorbild nt; [fashion] ~ Mannequin nt □ a Modell-; (exemplary) Muster- □ v (pt/pp modelled) □ vt formen, modellieren; vorführen (clothes) □ vi Mannequin sein; (for artist) Modell stehen

moderate¹ /ˈmɒdəreɪt/ vt mäßigen □ vi sich mäßigen

moderate² /ˈmɒdərət/ a mäßig; (opinion) gemäßigt □ n (Pol) Gemäßigte(r) m/f. ~ly adv mäßig; (fairly) einigermaßen

moderation /mɒdəˈreɪʃn/ n Mäßigung f; in ~ mit Maß[en]

modern /ˈmɒdn/ a modern. ~ize vt modernisieren. ~ 'languages npl neuere Sprachen pl

modest /ˈmɒdɪst/ a bescheiden; (decorous) schamhaft. ~y n Bescheidenheit f

modicum /ˈmɒdɪkəm/ n a ~ of ein bisschen

modification /mɒdɪfɪˈkeɪʃn/ n Abänderung f. ~y /ˈmɒdɪfaɪ/ vt (pt/pp -fied) abändern

modulate /ˈmɒdjʊleɪt/ vt/i modulieren

moist /mɔɪst/ a (-er, -est) feucht

moisten /ˈmɔɪsn/ vt befeuchten

moisture /ˈmɔɪstʃə(r)/ n Feuchtigkeit f. ~izer n Feuchtigkeitscreme f

molar /ˈməʊlə(r)/ n Backenzahn m

molasses /məˈlæsɪz/ n (Amer) Sirup m

mole¹ /məʊl/ n Leberfleck m

mole² n (Zool) Maulwurf m

mole³ n (breakwater) Mole f

molecule /ˈmɒlɪkjuːl/ n Molekül nt

'molehill n Maulwurfshaufen m

molest /məˈlest/ vt belästigen

mollify /ˈmɒlɪfaɪ/ vt (pt/pp -ied) besänftigen

mollusc /ˈmɒləsk/ n Weichtier nt

mollycoddle /ˈmɒlɪkɒdl/ vt verzärteln

molten /ˈməʊltən/ a geschmolzen

mom /mɒm/ n (Amer fam) Mutti f

moment /ˈməʊmənt/ n Moment m, Augenblick m; at the ~ im Augenblick, augenblicklich. ~ary a vorübergehend

momentous /məˈmentəs/ a bedeutsam

momentum /məˈmentəm/ n Schwung m

monarch /ˈmɒnək/ n Monarch(in) m(f). ~y n Monarchie f

monastery /ˈmɒnəstrɪ/ n Kloster nt. ~ic /məˈnæstɪk/ a Kloster-

Monday /ˈmʌndeɪ/ n Montag m

money /ˈmʌnɪ/ n Geld nt

money: ~-box n Sparbüchse f. ~-lender n Geldverleiher m. ~ order n Zahlungsanweisung f

mongrel /ˈmʌŋgrəl/ n Promenadenmischung f

monitor /ˈmɒnɪtə(r)/ n (Techn) Monitor m □ vt überwachen (progress); abhören (broadcast)

monk /mʌŋk/ n Mönch m

monkey /ˈmʌŋkɪ/ n Affe m. ~-nut n Erdnuss f. ~-wrench n (Techn) Engländer m

mono /ˈmɒnəʊ/ n Mono nt

monocle /ˈmɒnəkl/ n Monokel nt

monogram /ˈmɒnəgræm/ n Monogramm nt

monologue /ˈmɒnəlɒg/ n Monolog m

monopolize /məˈnɒpəlaɪz/ vt monopolisieren. ~y n Monopol nt

monosyllabic /mɒnəsɪˈlæbɪk/ a einsilbig. ~able /ˈmɒnəsɪləbl/ n einsilbiges Wort nt

monotone /ˈmɒnətəʊn/ n in a ~ mit monotoner Stimme

monotonous /məˈnɒtənəs/ a, -ly adv eintönig, monoton; (tedious) langweilig. ~y n Eintönigkeit f, Monotonie f

monsoon /mɒnˈsuːn/ n Monsun m

monster /ˈmɒnstə(r)/ n Ungeheuer nt; (cruel person) Unmensch m

monstrosity /mɒnˈstrɒsətɪ/ n Monstrosität f

monstrous /ˈmɒnstrəs/ a ungeheuer; (outrageous) ungeheuerlich

montage /mɒnˈtɑːʒ/ n Montage f

month /mʌnθ/ n Monat m. ~ly a & adv monatlich □ n (periodical) Monatszeitschrift f

monument /'mɒnjʊmənt/ n Denkmal nt.
~al /-'mentl/ a (fig) monumental

moo /muː/ n Muh nt □ vi (pt/pp mooed)
muhen

mooch /muːtʃ/ vi ~ about (fam)
herumschleichen

mood /muːd/ n Laune f; be in a good/bad
~ gute/schlechte Laune haben

moody /'muːdɪ/ a (-ier, -iest) launisch

moon /muːn/ n Mond m; over the ~ (fam)
überglücklich

moon: ~light n Mondschein m. ~light-
ing n (fam) ≈ Schwarzarbeit f. ~lit a
mondhell

moor¹ /mʊə(r)/ n Moor nt

moor² vt (Naut) festmachen □ vi anlegen.
~ings npl (chains) Verankerung f; (place)
Anlegestelle f

moose /muːs/ n Elch m

moot /muːt/ a it's a ~ point darüber lässt
sich streiten □ vt aufwerfen (question)

mop /mɒp/ n Mopp m; ~ of hair Wuschelk-
opf m □ vt (pt/pp mopped) wischen. ~ up
vt aufwischen

mope /məʊp/ vi Trübsal blasen

moped /'məʊped/ n Moped nt

moral /'mɒrl/ a, -ly adv moralisch,
sittlich; (virtuous) tugendhaft □ n Moral
f; ~s pl Moral f

morale /mə'rɑːl/ n Moral f

morality /mə'rælətɪ/ n Sittlichkeit f

moralize /'mɒrəlaɪz/ vi moralisieren

morbid /'mɔːbɪd/ a krankhaft; (gloomy)
trübe

more /mɔː(r)/ a, adv & n mehr; (in addition) noch; a few ~ noch ein paar; any ~
noch etwas; once ~ noch einmal; ~ or
less mehr oder weniger; some ~ tea?
noch etwas Tee? ~ interesting inter-
essanter; ~ [and ~] quickly [immer]
schneller; no ~, thank you, nichts mehr,
danke; no ~ bread kein Brot mehr; no ~
apples keine Äpfel mehr

moreover /mɔː'rəʊvə(r)/ adv außerdem

morgue /mɔːg/ n Leichenschauhaus nt

moribund /'mɒrɪbʌnd/ a sterbend

morning /'mɔːnɪŋ/ n Morgen m; in the ~
morgens, am Morgen; (tomorrow) morgen
früh

Morocco /mə'rɒkəʊ/ n Marokko nt

moron /'mɔːrɒn/ n (fam) Idiot m

morose /mə'rəʊs/ a, -ly adv mürrisch

morphine /'mɔːfiːn/ n Morphium nt

Morse /mɔːs/ n ~ [code] Morsealphabet
nt

morsel /'mɔːsl/ n (food) Happen m

mortal /'mɔːtl/ a sterblich; (fatal) tödlich
□ n Sterbliche(r) m/f. ~ity /mɔː'tælətɪ/ n
Sterblichkeit f. ~ly adv tödlich

mortar /'mɔːtə(r)/ n Mörtel m

mortgage /'mɔːgɪdʒ/ n Hypothek f □ vt
hypothekarisch belasten

mortify /'mɔːtɪfaɪ/ vt (pt/pp -ied) demütigen

mortuary /'mɔːtjʊərɪ/ n Leichenhalle f;
(public) Leichenschauhaus nt; (Amer: undertaker's) Bestattungsinstitut nt

mosaic /məʊ'zeɪɪk/ n Mosaik nt

Moscow /'mɒskəʊ/ n Moskau nt

Moselle /məʊ'zel/ n Mosel f; (wine) Mo-
selwein m

mosque /mɒsk/ n Moschee f

mosquito /mɒs'kiːtəʊ/ n (pl -es)
[Stech]mücke f, Schnake f; (tropical)
Moskito m

moss /mɒs/ n Moos nt. ~y a moosig

most /məʊst/ a der/die/das meiste;
(majority) die meisten; for the ~ part
zum größten Teil □ adv am meisten; (very)
höchst; the ~ interesting day der inte-
ressanteste Tag; ~ unlikely höchst unwahrscheinlich □ n das meiste; ~ of them
die meisten [von ihnen]; at [the] ~ höchstens; ~ of the time die meiste Zeit. ~ly
adv meist

MOT n ≈ TÜV m

motel /məʊ'tel/ n Motel nt

moth /mɒθ/ n Nachtfalter m; [clothes-]~
Motte f

moth: ~ball n Mottenkugel f. ~-eaten a
mottenzerfressen

mother /'mʌðə(r)/ n Mutter f; M~'s Day
Muttertag m □ vt bemuttern

mother: ~hood n Mutterschaft f. ~-in-
law n (pl ~s-in-law) Schwiegermutter f.
~land n Mutterland nt. ~ly a mütterlich.
~-of-pearl n Perlmutter f. ~-to-be n werdende Mutter f. ~ tongue n Muttersprache f

mothproof /'mɒθ-/ a mottenfest

motif /məʊ'tiːf/ n Motiv nt

motion /'məʊʃn/ n Bewegung f; (proposal) Antrag m □ vt/i ~ [to] s.o. jdm ein
Zeichen geben (to zu). ~less a, -ly adv
bewegungslos

motivate /'məʊtɪveɪt/ vt motivieren.
~ion /-'veɪʃn/ n Motivation f

motive /'məʊtɪv/ n Motiv nt

motley /'mɒtlɪ/ a bunt

motor /'məʊtə(r)/ n Motor m; (car) Auto
nt □ a Motor-; (Anat) motorisch □ vi [mit
dem Auto] fahren

Motorail /'məʊtəreɪl/ n Autozug m

motor: ~ bike n (fam) Motorrad nt. ~
boat n Motorboot nt. ~cade /-keɪd/ n
(Amer) Autokolonne f. ~ car n Auto nt,

Wagen m. ∼ cycle n Motorrad nt. ∼cyc-
list n Motorradfahrer m. ∼ing n Auto-
fahren nt. ∼ist n Autofahrer(in) m(f).
∼ize vt motorisieren. ∼ vehicle n
Kraftfahrzeug nt. ∼way n Autobahn f

mottled /'mɒtld/ a gesprenkelt

motto /'mɒtəʊ/ n (pl -es) Motto nt

mould[1] /məʊld/ n (fungus) Schimmel m

mould[2] n Form f □ vt formen (into zu).
∼ing n (Archit) Fries m

mouldy /'məʊldɪ/ a schimmelig; (fam:
worthless) schäbig

moult /məʊlt/ vi (bird:) sich mausern; (animal:) sich haaren

mound /maʊnd/ n Hügel m; (of stones)
Haufen m

mount[1] /maʊnt/ n Berg m

mount[2] n (animal) Reittier nt; (of jewel)
Fassung f; (of photo, picture) Passepartout
nt □ vt (get on) steigen auf (+ acc); (on
pedestal) montieren auf (+ acc); besteigen
(horse); fassen (jewel); aufziehen (photo,
picture) □ vi aufsteigen; (increase) steigen.
∼ up vi sich häufen; (add up) sich anhäufen; (increase) steigen

mountain /'maʊntɪn/ n Berg m

mountaineer /maʊntɪ'nɪə(r)/ n Bergstei-
ger(in) m(f). ∼ing n Bergsteigen nt

mountainous /'maʊntɪnəs/ a bergig, ge-
birgig

mourn /mɔːn/ vt betrauern □ vi trauern
(for um). ∼er n Trauernde(r) m/f. ∼ful
a, -ly adv trauervoll. ∼ing n Trauer f

mouse /maʊs/ n (pl mice) Maus f. ∼trap
n Mausefalle f

mousse /muːs/ n Schaum m; (Culin)
Mousse f

moustache /mə'stɑːʃ/ n Schnurrbart m

mousy /'maʊsɪ/ a graubraun; (person)
farblos

mouth[1] /maʊð/ vt ∼ sth etw lautlos mit
den Lippen sagen

mouth[2] /maʊθ/ n Mund m; (of animal)
Maul nt; (of river) Mündung f

mouth: ∼ful n Mundvoll m; (bite) Bissen
m. ∼organ n Mundharmonika f. ∼piece
n Mundstück nt; (fig: person) Sprachrohr
nt. ∼wash n Mundwasser nt

movable /'muːvəbl/ a beweglich

move /muːv/ n Bewegung f; (fig) Schritt
m; (moving house) Umzug m; (in board-
game) Zug m; on the ∼ unterwegs; get a
∼ on (fam) sich beeilen □ vt bewegen;
(emotionally) rühren; (move along) rücken; (in board-game) ziehen; (take away)
wegnehmen; wegfahren (car); (rearrange)
umstellen; (transfer) versetzen (office);
verlegen (office) □ vi sich bewegen; (move

house) umziehen; don't ∼! stillhalten!
(stop) stillstehen! ∼ along vt/i weiterrü-
cken. ∼ away vt/i wegrücken; (move
house) wegziehen. ∼ forward vt/i vorrücken; (vehicle) vorwärts fahren. ∼ in vi
einziehen. ∼ off vi (vehicle:) losfahren. ∼
out vi ausziehen. ∼ over vt/i [zur Seite]
rücken. ∼ up vi aufrücken

movement /'muːvmənt/ n Bewegung f;
(Mus) Satz m; (of clock) Uhrwerk nt

movie /'muːvɪ/ n (Amer) Film m; go to the
∼s ins Kino gehen

moving /'muːvɪŋ/ a beweglich; (touching)
rührend

mow /məʊ/ vt (pt mowed, pp mown or
mowed) mähen. ∼ down vt (destroy) nie-
dermähen

mower /'məʊə(r)/ n Rasenmäher m

MP abbr see Member of Parliament

Mr /'mɪstə(r)/ n (pl Messrs) Herr m

Mrs /'mɪsɪz/ n Frau f

Ms /mɪz/ n Frau f

much /mʌtʃ/ a, adv & n viel; as ∼ as so
viel wie; very ∼ loved/interested sehr
geliebt/interessiert

muck /mʌk/ n Mist m; (fam: filth) Dreck
m. ∼ about vi herumalbern; (tinker)
herumspielen (with mit). ∼ in vt (fam)
mitmachen. ∼ out vt ausmisten. ∼ up vt
(fam) vermasseln; (make dirty) schmutzig
machen

mucky /'mʌkɪ/ a (-ier, -iest) dreckig

mucus /'mjuːkəs/ n Schleim m

mud /mʌd/ n Schlamm m

muddle /'mʌdl/ n Durcheinander nt; (confusion) Verwirrung f □ vt ∼ [up] durcheinander bringen

muddy /'mʌdɪ/ a (-ier, -iest) schlammig;
(shoes) schmutzig

mudguard /'mʌdgɑːd/ n Kotflügel m; (on bicycle)
Schutzblech nt

muesli /'mjuːzlɪ/ n Müsli nt

muff /mʌf/ n Muff m

muffle /'mʌfl/ vt dämpfen (sound); ∼ [up]
(for warmth) einhüllen (in in + acc)

muffler /'mʌflə(r)/ n Schal m; (Amer,
Auto) Auspufftopf m

mufti /'mʌftɪ/ n in ∼ in Zivil

mug[1] /mʌg/ n Becher m; (for beer) Bier-
krug m; (fam: face) Visage f; (fam:
simpleton) Trottel m

mug[2] vt (pt/pp mugged) überfallen. ∼ger
n Straßenräuber m. ∼ging n Straßenraub
m

muggy /'mʌgɪ/ a (-ier, -iest) schwül

mule[1] /mjuːl/ n Maultier nt

mule[2] n (slipper) Pantoffel m

mull /mʌl/ vt ∼ over nachdenken über (+
acc)

mulled /mʌld/ a ∼ wine Glühwein m

multi /'mʌltɪ/: ~coloured a vielfarbig, bunt. ~lingual /-'lɪŋgwəl/ a mehrsprachig. ~national a multinational

multiple /'mʌltɪpl/ a vielfach; (with pl) mehrere □ n Vielfache(s) nt

multiplication /mʌltɪplɪ'keɪʃn/ n Multiplikation f

multiply /'mʌltɪplaɪ/ v (pt/pp -ied) □ vt multiplizieren (by mit) □ vi sich vermehren

multi-storey a ~ car park Parkhaus nt

mum¹ /mʌm/ a keep ~ (fam) den Mund halten

mum² n (fam) Mutti f

mumble /'mʌmbl/ vt/i murmeln

mummy¹ /'mʌmɪ/ n (fam) Mutti f

mummy² n (Archaeol) Mumie f

mumps /mʌmps/ n Mumps m

munch /mʌntʃ/ vt/i mampfen

mundane /mʌn'deɪn/ a banal; (worldly) weltlich

municipal /mju:'nɪsɪpl/ a städtisch

munitions /mju:'nɪʃnz/ npl Kriegsmaterial nt

mural /'mjʊərəl/ n Wandgemälde nt

murder /'mɜ:də(r)/ n Mord m □ vt ermorden; (fam: ruin) verhunzen. ~er n Mörder m. ~ess n Mörderin f. ~ous /-rəs/ a mörderisch

murky /'mɜ:kɪ/ a (-ier, -iest) düster

murmur /'mɜ:mə(r)/ n Murmeln nt □ vt/i murmeln

muscle /'mʌsl/ n Muskel m

muscular /'mʌskjʊlə(r)/ a Muskel-; (strong) muskulös

muse /mju:z/ vi nachsinnen (on über + acc)

museum /mju:'zɪəm/ n Museum nt

mush /mʌʃ/ n Brei m

mushroom /'mʌʃrʊm/ n (essbarer) Pilz m, esp Champignon m □ vi (fig) wie Pilze aus dem Boden schießen

mushy /'mʌʃɪ/ a breiig

music /'mju:zɪk/ n Musik f; (written) Noten pl; set to ~ vertonen

musical /'mju:zɪkl/ a musikalisch □ n Musical nt. ~ box n Spieldose f. ~ instrument n Musikinstrument nt

'music-hall n Varieté nt

musician /mju:'zɪʃn/ n Musiker(in) m(f)

'music-stand n Notenständer m

Muslim /'mʊzlɪm/ a mohammedanisch □ n Mohammedaner(in) m(f)

muslin /'mʌzlɪn/ n Musselin m

mussel /'mʌsl/ n [Mies]muschel f

must /mʌst/ v aux (nur Präsens) müssen; (with negative) dürfen □ n a ~ (fam) ein Muss nt

mustard /'mʌstəd/ n Senf m

muster /'mʌstə(r)/ vt versammeln; aufbringen (strength) □ vi sich versammeln

musty /'mʌstɪ/ a (-ier, -iest) muffig

mutation /mju:'teɪʃn/ n Veränderung f; (Biol) Mutation f

mute /mju:t/ a stumm

muted /'mju:tɪd/ a gedämpft

mutilat|e /'mju:tɪleɪt/ vt verstümmeln. ~ion /-'leɪʃn/ n Verstümmelung f

mutin|ous /'mju:tɪnəs/ a meuterisch. ~y n Meuterei f □ vi (pt/pp -ied) meutern

mutter /'mʌtə(r)/ n Murmeln nt □ vt/i murmeln

mutton /'mʌtn/ n Hammelfleisch nt

mutual /'mju:tjʊəl/ a gegenseitig; (fam: common) gemeinsam. ~ly adv gegenseitig

muzzle /'mʌzl/ n (of animal) Schnauze f; (of firearm) Mündung f; (for dog) Maulkorb m □ vt einen Maulkorb anlegen (+ dat)

my /maɪ/ a mein

myopic /maɪ'ɒpɪk/ a kurzsichtig

myself /maɪ'self/ pron selbst; (refl) mich; by ~ allein; I thought to ~ ich habe mir gedacht

mysterious /mɪ'stɪərɪəs/ a, -ly adv geheimnisvoll; (puzzling) mysteriös, rätselhaft

mystery /'mɪstərɪ/ n Geheimnis nt; (puzzle) Rätsel nt; ~ [story] Krimi m

mysti|c[al] /'mɪstɪk[l]/ a mystisch. ~cism /-sɪzm/ n Mystik f

mystification /mɪstɪfɪ'keɪʃn/ n Verwunderung f

mystified /'mɪstɪfaɪd/ a be ~ vor einem Rätsel stehen

mystique /mɪ'sti:k/ n geheimnisvoller Zauber m

myth /mɪθ/ n Mythos m; (fam: untruth) Märchen nt. ~ical a mythisch; (fig) erfunden

mythology /mɪ'θɒlədʒɪ/ n Mythologie f

N

nab /næb/ vt (pt/pp nabbed) (fam) erwischen

nag¹ /næg/ n (horse) Gaul m

nag² vt/i (pp/pp nagged) herumnörgeln (s.o. an jdm). ~ging a (pain) nagend □ n Nörgelei f

nail /neɪl/ n (Anat, Techn) Nagel m; on the ~ (fam) sofort ▫ vt nageln (to an + acc). ~ down vt festnageln; (close) zunageln

nail: ~brush n Nagelbürste f. ~file n Nagelfeile f. ~ polish n Nagellack m. ~ scissors npl Nagelschere f. ~ varnish n Nagellack m

naïve /naɪˈiːv/ a, -ly adv naiv. ~ty /-ətɪ/ n Naivität f

naked /ˈneɪkɪd/ a nackt; (flame) offen; with the ~ eye mit bloßem Auge. ~ness n Nacktheit f

name /neɪm/ n Name m; (reputation) Ruf m; by ~ dem Namen nach; by the ~ of namens; call s.o. ~s (fam) jdn beschimpfen ▫ vt nennen; (give a name to) einen Namen geben (+ dat); (announce publicly) den Namen bekannt geben von. ~less a namenlos. ~ly adv nämlich

name: ~plate n Namensschild nt. ~sake n Namensvetter m/Namensschwester f

nanny /ˈnænɪ/ n Kindermädchen nt. ~ goat n Ziege f

nap /næp/ n Nickerchen nt; have a ~ ein Nickerchen machen ▫ vi catch s.o. ~ping jdn überrumpeln

nape /neɪp/ n ~ [of the neck] Nacken m

napkin /ˈnæpkɪn/ n Serviette f; (for baby) Windel f

nappy /ˈnæpɪ/ n Windel f

narcotic /nɑːˈkɒtɪk/ a betäubend ▫ n Narkotikum nt; (drug) Rauschgift nt

narrat|e /nəˈreɪt/ vt erzählen. ~ion /-eɪʃn/ n Erzählung f

narrative /ˈnærətɪv/ a erzählend ▫ n Erzählung f

narrator /nəˈreɪtə(r)/ n Erzähler(in) m(f)

narrow /ˈnærəʊ/ a (-er, -est) schmal; (restricted) eng; (margin, majority) knapp; (fig) beschränkt; have a ~ escape, ~ly escape mit knapper Not davonkommen ▫ vi sich verengen. ~'minded a engstirnig

nasal /ˈneɪzl/ a nasal; (Med & Anat) Nasen-

nastily /ˈnɑːstɪlɪ/ adv boshaft

nasturtium /nəˈstɜːʃəm/ n Kapuzinerkresse f

nasty /ˈnɑːstɪ/ a (-ier, -iest) übel; (unpleasant) unangenehm; (unkind) boshaft; (serious) schlimm; turn ~ gemein werden

nation /ˈneɪʃn/ n Nation f; (people) Volk nt

national /ˈnæʃənl/ a national; (newspaper) überregional; (campaign) landesweit ▫ n Staatsbürger(in) m(f)

national: ~ 'anthem n Nationalhymne f. N~ 'Health Service n staatlicher Gesundheitsdienst m. N~ In'surance n Sozialversicherung f

nationalism /ˈnæʃənəlɪzm/ n Nationalismus m

nationality /næʃəˈnælətɪ/ n Staatsangehörigkeit f

national|ization /næʃənəlaɪˈzeɪʃn/ n Verstaatlichung f. ~ize /ˈnæʃənəlaɪz/ vt verstaatlichen. ~ly /ˈnæʃənəlɪ/ adv landesweit

'nation-wide a landesweit

native /ˈneɪtɪv/ a einheimisch; (innate) angeboren ▫ n Eingeborene(r) m(f); (local inhabitant) Einheimische(r) m(f); a ~ of Vienna ein gebürtiger Wiener

native: ~ 'land n Heimatland nt. ~ 'language n Muttersprache f

Nativity /nəˈtɪvətɪ/ n the ~ Christi Geburt f. ~ play n Krippenspiel nt

natter /ˈnætə(r)/ n have a ~ (fam) einen Schwatz halten ▫ vi (fam) schwatzen

natural /ˈnætʃrəl/ a, -ly adv natürlich; ~[-coloured] naturfarben

natural: ~ 'gas n Erdgas nt. ~ 'history n Naturkunde f

naturalist /ˈnætʃrəlɪst/ n Naturforscher m

natural|ization /nætʃrəlaɪˈzeɪʃn/ n Einbürgerung f. ~ize /ˈnætʃrəlaɪz/ vt einbürgern

nature /ˈneɪtʃə(r)/ n Natur f; (kind) Art f; by ~ von Natur aus. ~ reserve n Naturschutzgebiet nt

naturism /ˈneɪtʃərɪzm/ n Freikörperkultur f

naught /nɔːt/ n = nought

naughty /ˈnɔːtɪ/ a (-ier, -iest), -ily adv unartig; (slightly indecent) gewagt

nausea /ˈnɔːzɪə/ n Übelkeit f

nause|ate /ˈnɔːzɪeɪt/ vt anekeln. ~ating a ekelhaft. ~ous /-ɪəs/ a I feel ~ous mir ist übel

nautical /ˈnɔːtɪkl/ a nautisch. ~ mile n Seemeile f

naval /ˈneɪvl/ a Marine-

nave /neɪv/ n Kirchenschiff nt

navel /ˈneɪvl/ n Nabel m

navigable /ˈnævɪgəbl/ a schiffbar

navigat|e /ˈnævɪgeɪt/ vi navigieren ▫ vt befahren (river). ~ion /-ˈgeɪʃn/ n Navigation f. ~or n Navigator m

navvy /ˈnævɪ/ n Straßenarbeiter m

navy /ˈneɪvɪ/ n [Kriegs]marine f ▫ a ~ [blue] marineblau

near /nɪə(r)/ a (-er, -est) nah[e]; the ~est bank die nächste Bank ▫ adv nahe; ~ by nicht weit weg; ~ at hand in der Nähe; draw ~ sich nähern ▫ prep nahe an (+ dat/acc); in der Nähe von; ~ to tears den Tränen nahe; go ~ [to] sth nahe an etw (acc) herangehen ▫ vt sich nähern (+ dat)

near: ∼**by** *a* nahe gelegen, nahe liegend □ *adv* /-'-/ nicht weit weg. ∼**ly** *adv* fast, beinahe; **not** ∼**ly** bei weitem nicht. ∼**ness** *n* Nähe *f*. ∼**side** *n* Beifahrerseite *f*. ∼**sighted** *a* (*Amer*) kurzsichtig

neat /niːt/ *a* (-er, -est), -**ly** *adv* adrett; (*tidy*) ordentlich; (*clever*) geschickt; (*undiluted*) pur. ∼**ness** *n* Ordentlichkeit *f*

necessarily /'nesəsərəlɪ/ *adv* notwendigerweise; **not** ∼ nicht unbedingt

necessary /'nesəsərɪ/ *a* nötig, notwendig

necessit|ate /nɪ'sesɪteɪt/ *vt* notwendig machen. ∼**y** *n* Notwendigkeit *f*; **she works from** ∼**y** sie arbeitet, weil sie es nötig hat

neck /nek/ *n* Hals *m*; ∼ **and** ∼ Kopf an Kopf

necklace /'neklɪs/ *n* Halskette *f*

neck: ∼**line** *n* Halsausschnitt *m*. ∼**tie** *n* Schlips *m*

nectar /'nektə(r)/ *n* Nektar *m*

née /neɪ/ *a* ∼ **Brett** geborene Brett

need /niːd/ *n* Bedürfnis *nt*; (*misfortune*) Not *f*; **be in** ∼ Not leiden; **be in** ∼ **of** brauchen; **in case of** ∼ notfalls; **if** ∼ **be** wenn nötig; **there is a** ∼ **for** es besteht ein Bedarf an (+ *dat*); **there is no** ∼ **for that** das ist nicht nötig; **there is no** ∼ **for you to go** du brauchst nicht zu gehen □ *vt* brauchen; **you** ∼ **not go** du brauchst nicht zu gehen; ∼ **I come?** muss ich kommen? **I** ∼ **to know** ich muss es wissen; **it** ∼**s to be done** es muss gemacht werden

needle /'niːdl/ *n* Nadel *f* □ *vt* (*annoy*) ärgern

needless /'niːdlɪs/ *a*, -**ly** *adv* unnötig; ∼ **to say** selbstverständlich, natürlich

'**needlework** *n* Nadelarbeit *f*

needy /'niːdɪ/ *a* (-ier, -iest) bedürftig

negation /nɪ'ɡeɪʃn/ *n* Verneinung *f*

negative /'neɡətɪv/ *a* negativ □ *n* Verneinung *f*; (*photo*) Negativ *nt*

neglect /nɪ'ɡlekt/ *n* Vernachlässigung *f*; **state of** ∼ verwahrloster Zustand *m* □ *vt* vernachlässigen; (*omit*) versäumen (**to** zu). ∼**ed** *a* verwahrlost. ∼**ful** *a* nachlässig; **be** ∼**ful of** vernachlässigen

negligen|ce /'neɡlɪdʒəns/ *n* Nachlässigkeit *f*; (*Jur*) Fahrlässigkeit *f*. ∼**t** *a*, -**ly** *adv* nachlässig; (*Jur*) fahrlässig

negligible /'neɡlɪdʒəbl/ *a* unbedeutend

negotiable /nɪ'ɡəʊʃəbl/ *a* (*road*) befahrbar; (*Comm*) unverbindlich; **not** ∼ nicht übertragbar

negotiat|e /nɪ'ɡəʊʃɪeɪt/ *vt* aushandeln; (*Auto*) nehmen (*bend*) □ *vi* verhandeln. ∼**ion** /-'eɪʃn/ *n* Verhandlung *f*. ∼**or** *n* Unterhändler(in) *m(f)*

Negro /'niːɡrəʊ/ *a* Neger- □ *n* (*pl* -**es**) Neger *m*

neigh /neɪ/ *vi* wiehern

neighbour /'neɪbə(r)/ *n* Nachbar(in) *m(f)*. ∼**hood** *n* Nachbarschaft *f*; **in the** ∼**hood of** in der Nähe von; (*fig*) um ... herum. ∼**ing** *a* Nachbar-. ∼**ly** *a* [gut]nachbarlich

neither /'naɪðə(r)/ *a* & *pron* keine(r, s) [von beiden] □ *adv* ∼... **nor** weder ... **noch** □ *conj* auch nicht

neon /'niːɒn/ *n* Neon *nt*. ∼ **light** *n* Neonlicht *nt*

nephew /'nevjuː/ *n* Neffe *m*

nepotism /'nepətɪzm/ *n* Vetternwirtschaft *f*

nerve /nɜːv/ *n* Nerv *m*; (*fam: courage*) Mut *m*; (*fam: impudence*) Frechheit *f*; **lose one's** ∼ den Mut verlieren. ∼**racking** *a* nervenaufreibend

nervous /'nɜːvəs/ *a*, -**ly** *adv* (*afraid*) ängstlich; (*highly strung*) nervös; (*Anat, Med*) Nerven-; **be** ∼ Angst haben. ∼ '**breakdown** *n* Nervenzusammenbruch *m*. ∼**ness** *n* Ängstlichkeit *f*; (*Med*) Nervosität *f*

nervy /'nɜːvɪ/ *a* (-ier, -iest) nervös; (*Amer: impudent*) frech

nest /nest/ *n* Nest *nt* □ *vi* nisten. ∼-**egg** *n* Notgroschen *m*

nestle /'nesl/ *vi* sich schmiegen (**against** an + *acc*)

net¹ /net/ *n* Netz *nt*; (*curtain*) Store *m* □ *vt* (*pt/pp* netted) (*catch*) [mit dem Netz] fangen

net² *a* netto; (*salary, weight*) Netto- □ *vt* (*pt/pp* netted) netto einnehmen; (*yield*) einbringen

'**netball** *n* ≈ Korbball *m*

Netherlands /'neðələndz/ *npl* **the** ∼ die Niederlande *pl*

netting /'netɪŋ/ *n* [wire] ∼ Maschendraht *m*

nettle /'netl/ *n* Nessel *f*

'**network** *n* Netz *nt*

neuralgia /njʊə'rældʒə/ *n* Neuralgie *f*

neurolog|ist /njʊə'rɒlədʒɪst/ *n* Neurologe *m*/ -gin *f*. ∼**y** *n* Neurologie *f*

neur|osis /njʊə'rəʊsɪs/ *n* (*pl* -**oses** /-siːz/) Neurose *f*. ∼**otic** /-'rɒtɪk/ *a* neurotisch

neuter /'njuːtə(r)/ *a* (*Gram*) sächlich □ *n* (*Gram*) Neutrum *nt* □ *vt* kastrieren; (*spay*) sterilisieren

neutral /'njuːtrl/ *a* neutral □ *n* **in** ∼ (*Auto*) im Leerlauf. ∼**ity** /-'trælətɪ/ *n* Neutralität *f*. ∼**ize** *vt* neutralisieren

never /'nevə(r)/ *adv* nie, niemals; (*fam: not*) nicht; ∼ **mind** macht nichts; **well I** ∼! ja so was! ∼-**ending** *a* endlos

nevertheless /nevəðə'les/ *adv* dennoch, trotzdem

new /nju:/ *a* (-er, -est) neu

new: ~born *n* neugeboren. ~comer *n* Neuankömmling *m*. ~fangled /-'fæŋgld/ *a* (pej) neumodisch. ~-laid *a* frisch gelegt

'**newly** *adv* frisch. ~-weds *npl* Jungverheiratete *pl*

new: ~'moon *n* Neumond *m*. ~ness *n* Neuheit *f*

news /nju:z/ *n* Nachricht *f*; (Radio, TV) Nachrichten *pl*; piece of ~ Neuigkeit *f*

news: ~agent *n* Zeitungshändler *m*. ~bulletin *n* Nachrichtensendung *f*. ~caster *n* Nachrichtensprecher(in) *m(f)*. ~flash *n* Kurzmeldung *f*. ~letter *n* Mitteilungsblatt *nt*. ~paper *n* Zeitung *f*; (material) Zeitungspapier *nt*. ~reader *n* Nachrichtensprecher(in) *m(f)*

newt /nju:t/ *n* Molch *m*

New: ~ Year's Day *n* Neujahr *nt*. ~ Year's Eve *n* Silvester *m*. ~ Zealand /'zi:lənd/ *n* Neuseeland *nt*

next /nekst/ *a* *adv* nächste(r, s); who's ~? wer kommt als Nächster dran? the ~ best das nächstbeste; ~ door nebenan; my ~ of kin mein nächster Verwandter; ~ to nothing fast gar nichts; the week after ~ übernächste Woche □ *adv* als Nächstes; ~ to neben

NHS *abbr* see National Health Service

nib /nɪb/ *n* Feder *f*

nibble /'nɪbl/ *vt/i* knabbern (at an + dat)

nice /naɪs/ *a* (-r, -st) nett; ⟨day, weather⟩ schön; ⟨food⟩ gut; ⟨distinction⟩ fein. ~ly *adv* nett; ⟨well⟩ gut. ~ties /'naɪsətɪz/ *npl* Feinheiten *pl*

niche /ni:ʃ/ *n* Nische *f*; (fig) Platz *m*

nick /nɪk/ *n* Kerbe *f*; (fam: prison) Knast *m*; (fam: police station) Revier *nt*; in the ~ of time (fam) gerade noch rechtzeitig; in good ~ (fam) in gutem Zustand □ *vt* einkerben; (steal) klauen; (fam: arrest) schnappen

nickel /'nɪkl/ *n* Nickel *nt*; (Amer) Fünfcentstück *nt*

'**nickname** *n* Spitzname *m*

nicotine /'nɪkəti:n/ *n* Nikotin *nt*

niece /ni:s/ *n* Nichte *f*

Nigeria /naɪ'dʒɪərɪə/ *n* Nigeria *nt*. ~n *a* nigerianisch □ *n* Nigerianer(in) *m(f)*

niggardly /'nɪgədlɪ/ *a* knauserig

niggling /'nɪglɪŋ/ *a* gering; (petty) kleinlich; ⟨pain⟩ quälend

night /naɪt/ *n* Nacht *f*; (evening) Abend *m*; at ~ nachts; Monday ~ Montag Nacht/Abend

night: ~cap *n* Schlafmütze *f*; (drink) Schlaftrunk *m*. ~club *n* Nachtklub *m*. ~dress *n* Nachthemd *nt*. ~fall *n* at ~fall bei Einbruch der Dunkelheit. ~gown *n*, (fam) ~ie /'naɪtɪ/ *n* Nachthemd *nt*

nightingale /'naɪtɪŋgeɪl/ *n* Nachtigall *f*

night: ~-life *n* Nachtleben *nt*. ~ly *a* nächtlich □ *adv* jede Nacht. ~mare *n* Alptraum *m*. ~shade *n* (Bot) deadly ~shade Tollkirsche *f*. ~time *n* at ~time bei Nacht. ~'watchman *n* Nachtwächter *m*

nil /nɪl/ *n* null

nimble /'nɪmbl/ *a* (-r, -st), -bly *adv* flink

nine /naɪn/ *a* neun □ *n* Neun *f*. ~teen *a* neunzehn. ~teenth *a* neunzehnte(r, s)

ninetieth /'naɪntɪɪθ/ *a* neunzigste(r, s)

ninety /'naɪntɪ/ *a* neunzig

ninth /naɪnθ/ *a* neunte(r, s)

nip /nɪp/ *n* Kniff *m*; (bite) Biss *m* □ *vt* kneifen; (bite) beißen; ~ in the bud (fig) im Keim ersticken □ *vi* (fam: run) laufen

nipple /'nɪpl/ *n* Brustwarze *f*; (Amer: on bottle) Sauger *m*

nippy /'nɪpɪ/ *a* (-ier, -iest) (fam) (cold) frisch; (quick) flink

nitrate /'naɪtreɪt/ *n* Nitrat *nt*

nitrogen /'naɪtrədʒən/ *n* Stickstoff *m*

nitwit /'nɪtwɪt/ *n* (fam) Dummkopf *m*

no /nəʊ/ *adv* nein □ *n* (pl noes) Nein *nt* □ *a* kein(e); (pl) keine; in no time [sehr] schnell; no parking/smoking Parken/Rauchen verboten; no one = nobody

nobility /nəʊ'bɪlətɪ/ *n* Adel *m*

noble /'nəʊbl/ *a* (-r, -st) edel; (aristocratic) adlig. ~man *n* Adlige(r) *m*

nobody /'nəʊbədɪ/ *pron* niemand, keiner; he knows ~ er kennt niemanden *od* keinen □ *n* a ~ ein Niemand *m*

nocturnal /nɒk'tɜ:nl/ *a* nächtlich; ⟨animal, bird⟩ Nacht-

nod /nɒd/ *n* Nicken *nt* □ *v* (pt/pp nodded) □ *vi* nicken □ *vt* ~ one's head mit dem Kopf nicken. ~ off *vi* einnicken

nodule /'nɒdju:l/ *n* Knötchen *nt*

noise /nɔɪz/ *n* Geräusch *nt*; (loud) Lärm *m*. ~less *a*, -ly *adv* geräuschlos

noisy /'nɔɪzɪ/ *a* (-ier, -iest), -ily *adv* laut; ⟨eater⟩ geräuschvoll

nomad /'nəʊmæd/ *n* Nomade *m*. ~ic /-'mædɪk/ *a* nomadisch; ⟨life, tribe⟩ Nomaden-

nominal /'nɒmɪnl/ *a*, -ly *adv* nominell

nominat|e /'nɒmɪneɪt/ *vt* nominieren, aufstellen; (appoint) ernennen. ~ion /-'neɪʃn/ *n* Nominierung *f*; Ernennung *f*

nominative /'nɒmɪnətɪv/ *a* & *n* (Gram) ~ [case] Nominativ *m*

nonchalant /'nɒnʃələnt/ *a*, -ly *adv* nonchalant; ⟨gesture⟩ lässig non-com'missioned /nɒn-/ a ~ officer Unteroffizier m

non-com'mittal a unverbindlich; be ~ sich nicht festlegen

nondescript /'nɒndɪskrɪpt/ a unbestimmbar; (person) unscheinbar`

none /nʌn/ pron keine(r)/keins; ~ of us keiner von uns; ~ of it/this nichts davon □ adv ~ too nicht gerade; ~ too soon [um] keine Minute zu früh; ~ the wiser um nichts klüger; ~ the less dennoch

nonentity /nɒ'nentəti/ n Null f

non-ex'istent a nicht vorhanden; be ~ nicht vorhanden sein

non-'fiction n Sachliteratur f

non-'iron a bügelfrei

nonplussed /nɒn'plʌst/ a verblüfft

nonsens|e /'nɒnsəns/ n Unsinn m. ~ical /'-sensɪkl/ a unsinnig

non-'smoker n Nichtraucher m; (compartment) Nichtraucherabteil nt

non-'stop adv ununterbrochen; (fly) nonstop; ~ 'flight Nonstopflug m

non-'swimmer n Nichtschwimmer m

non-'violent a gewaltlos

noodles /'nu:dlz/ npl Bandnudeln pl

nook /nʊk/ n Eckchen nt, Winkel m

noon /nu:n/ n Mittag m; at ~ um 12 Uhr mittags

noose /nu:s/ n Schlinge f

nor /nɔ:(r)/ adv noch □ conj auch nicht

Nordic /'nɔ:dɪk/ a nordisch

norm /nɔ:m/ n Norm f

normal /'nɔ:ml/ a normal. ~ity /-'mæləti/ n Normalität f. ~ly adv normal; (usually) normalerweise

north /nɔ:θ/ n Norden m; to the ~ of nördlich von □ a Nord-, nord- □ adv nach Norden

north: N~ America n Nordamerika nt. ~-east a Nordost- □ n Nordosten m

norther|ly /'nɔ:ðəlɪ/ a nördlich. ~n a nördlich. N~n Ireland n Nordirland nt

north: N~ 'Pole n Nordpol m. N~ 'Sea n Nordsee f. ~ward[s] /-wəd[z]/ adv nach Norden. ~-west a Nordwest- □ n Nordwesten m

Nor|way /'nɔ:weɪ/ n Norwegen nt. ~wegian /-'wi:dʒn/ a norwegisch □ n Norweger(in) m(f)

nose /nəʊz/ n Nase f □ vi ~ about herumschnüffeln

nose: ~bleed n Nasenbluten nt. ~dive n (Aviat) Sturzflug m

nostalg|ia /nɒ'stældʒɪə/ n Nostalgie f. ~ic a nostalgisch

nostril /'nɒstrəl/ n Nasenloch nt; (of horse) Nüster f

nosy /'nəʊzɪ/ a (-ier, -iest) (fam) neugierig

not /nɒt/ adv nicht; ~ a kein(e); if ~ wenn nicht; ~ at all gar nicht; ~ a bit kein bisschen; ~ even nicht mal; ~ yet noch nicht; he is ~ a German er ist kein Deutscher

notab|le /'nəʊtəbl/ a bedeutend; (remarkable) bemerkenswert. ~ly adv insbesondere

notary /'nəʊtərɪ/ n ~ 'public ≈ Notar m

notation /nəʊ'teɪʃn/ n Notation f; (Mus) Notenschrift f

notch /nɒtʃ/ n Kerbe f. ~ up vt (score) erzielen

note /nəʊt/ n (written comment) Notiz f, Anmerkung f; (short letter) Briefchen nt, Zettel m; (bank ~) Banknote f, Schein m; (Mus) Note f; (sound) Ton m; (on piano) Taste f; eighth/quarter ~ (Amer) Achtel-/Viertelnote f; half/whole ~ (Amer) halbe/ganze Note f; of ~ von Bedeutung; make a ~ of notieren □ vt beachten; (notice) bemerken (that dass). ~ down vt notieren

'notebook n Notizbuch nt

noted /'nəʊtɪd/ a bekannt (for für)

note: ~paper n Briefpapier nt. ~worthy a beachtenswert

nothing /'nʌθɪŋ/ n, pron & adv nichts; for ~ umsonst; ~ but nichts als; ~ much nicht viel; ~ interesting nichts Interessantes; it's ~ to do with you das geht dich nichts an

notice /'nəʊtɪs/ n (on board) Anschlag m, Bekanntmachung f; (announcement) Anzeige f; (review) Kritik f; (termination of lease, employment) Kündigung f; [advance] ~ Bescheid m; give [in one's] ~ kündigen; give s.o. ~ jdm kündigen; take no ~ of keine Notiz nehmen von; take no ~! ignoriere es! □ vt bemerken. ~able /-əbl/ a, -bly adv merklich. ~board n Anschlagbrett nt

noti|fication /nəʊtɪfɪ'keɪʃn/ n Benachrichtigung f. ~fy /'nəʊtɪfaɪ/ vt (pt/pp -ied) benachrichtigen

notion /'nəʊʃn/ n Idee f; ~s pl (Amer: haberdashery) Kurzwaren pl

notorious /nəʊ'tɔ:rɪəs/ a berüchtigt

notwith'standing prep trotz (+ gen) □ adv trotzdem, dennoch

nought /nɔ:t/ n Null f

noun /naʊn/ n Substantiv nt

nourish /'nʌrɪʃ/ vt nähren. ~ing a nahrhaft. ~ment n Nahrung f

novel /'nɒvl/ a neu[artig] □ n Roman m. ~ist n Romanschriftsteller(in) m(f). ~ty n Neuheit f; ~ties pl kleine Geschenkartikel pl

November /nəʊ'vembə(r)/ n November m

novice /'nɒvɪs/ n Neuling m; (Relig) Novize m/Novizin f

now /naʊ/ adv & conj jetzt; ~ [that] jetzt; wo; just ~ gerade, eben; right ~ sofort; ~ and again hin und wieder; now, now! na, na!

nowadays adv heutzutage

nowhere /'nəʊ-/ adv nirgendwo, nirgends

noxious /'nɒkʃəs/ a schädlich

nozzle /'nɒzl/ n Düse f

nuance /'nju:ãs/ n Nuance f

nuclear /'nju:klɪə(r)/ a Kern-. ~ de'terrent n nukleares Abschreckungsmittel nt

nucleus /'nju:klɪəs/ n (pl -lei /-lɪaɪ/) Kern m

nude /nju:d/ a nackt □ n (Art) Akt m; in the ~ nackt

nudge /nʌdʒ/ n Stups m □ vt stupsen

nudist /'nju:dɪst/ n Nudist m. ~ity n Nacktheit f

nugget /'nʌgɪt/ n [Gold]klumpen m

nuisance /'nju:sns/ n Ärgernis nt; (pest) Plage f; be a ~ ärgerlich sein; (person:) lästig sein; what a ~! wie ärgerlich!

null /nʌl/ a ~ and void null und nichtig. ~ify /'nʌlɪfaɪ/ vt (pt/pp -ied) für nichtig erklären

numb /nʌm/ a gefühllos, taub; ~ with cold taub vor Kälte □ vt betäuben

number /'nʌmbə(r)/ n Nummer f; (amount) Anzahl f; (Math) Zahl f □ vt nummerieren; (include) zählen (among zu). ~-plate n Nummernschild nt

numeral /'nju:mərl/ n Ziffer f

numerate /'nju:mərət/ a be ~ rechnen können

numerical /nju:'merɪkl/ a, -ly adv numerisch; in ~ order zahlenmäßig geordnet

numerous /'nju:mərəs/ a zahlreich

nun /nʌn/ n Nonne f

nuptial /'nʌpʃl/ a Hochzeits-. ~s npl (Amer) Hochzeit f

nurse /nɜ:s/ n [Kranken]schwester f; (male) Krankenpfleger m; children's ~ Kindermädchen nt □ vt pflegen. ~maid n Kindermädchen nt

nursery /'nɜ:səri/ n Kinderzimmer nt; (Hort) Gärtnerei f; [day] ~ Kindertagesstätte f. ~ rhyme n Kinderreim m. ~ school n Kindergarten m

nursing /'nɜ:sɪŋ/ n Krankenpflege f. ~ home n Pflegeheim nt

nurture /'nɜ:tʃə/ vt nähren; (fig) hegen

nut /nʌt/ n Nuss f; (Techn) [Schrauben]-mutter f; (fam: head) Birne f (fam); be ~s (fam) spinnen (fam). ~crackers npl Nussknacker m. ~meg n Muskat m

nutrient /'nju:trɪənt/ n Nährstoff m

nutrit|ion /nju:'trɪʃn/ n Ernährung f. ~ious /-ʃəs/ a nahrhaft

nutshell n Nussschale f; in a ~ (fig) kurz gesagt

nuzzle /'nʌzl/ vt beschnüffeln

nylon /'naɪlɒn/ n Nylon nt; ~s pl Nylonstrümpfe pl

nymph /nɪmf/ n Nymphe f

O

O /əʊ/ n (Teleph) null

oaf /əʊf/ n (pl oafs) Trottel m

oak /əʊk/ n Eiche f □ attrib Eichen-

OAP abbr (old-age pensioner) Rentner(in) m(f)

oar /ɔ:(r)/ n Ruder nt. ~sman n Ruderer m

oasis /əʊ'eɪsɪs/ n (pl oases /-si:z/) Oase f

oath /əʊθ/ n Eid m; (swear-word) Fluch m

oatmeal /'əʊt-/ n Hafermehl nt

oats /əʊts/ npl Hafer m; (Culin) [rolled] ~ Haferflocken pl

obedien|ce /ə'bi:dɪəns/ n Gehorsam m. ~t a, -ly adv gehorsam

obese /əʊ'bi:s/ a fettleibig. ~ity n Fettleibigkeit f

obey /ə'beɪ/ vt/i gehorchen (+ dat); befolgen (instructions, rules)

obituary /ə'bɪtjʊərɪ/ n Nachruf m; (notice) Todesanzeige f

object[1] /'ɒbdʒɪkt/ n Gegenstand m; (aim) Zweck m; (intention) Absicht f; (Gram) Objekt nt; money is no ~ Geld spielt keine Rolle

object[2] /əb'dʒekt/ vi Einspruch erheben (to gegen); (be against) etwas dagegen haben

objection /əb'dʒekʃn/ n Einwand m; have no ~s nichts dagegen haben. ~able /-əbl/ a anstößig; (person) unangenehm

objectiv|e /əb'dʒektɪv/ a, -ly adv objektiv □ n Ziel nt. ~ity /-'tɪvətɪ/ n Objektivität f

objector /əb'dʒektə(r)/ n Gegner m

obligation /ɒblɪ'geɪʃn/ n Pflicht f; be under an ~ verpflichtet sein; without ~ unverbindlich

obligatory /ə'blɪgətrɪ/ a obligatorisch; be ~ Vorschrift sein

oblig|e /ə'blaɪdʒ/ vt verpflichten; (compel) zwingen; (do a small service) einen Gefallen tun (+ dat); much ~ed! vielen Dank! ~ing a entgegenkommend

oblique /ə'bli:k/ a schräg; ⟨angle⟩ schief; ⟨fig⟩ indirekt. ~ **stroke** n Schrägstrich m

obliterate /ə'blɪtəreɪt/ vt auslöschen

oblivion /ə'blɪvɪən/ n Vergessenheit f

oblivious /ə'blɪvɪəs/ a be ~ sich ⟨dat⟩ nicht bewusst sein (of or to gen)

oblong /'ɒblɒŋ/ a rechteckig ◻ n Rechteck nt

obnoxious /əb'nɒkʃəs/ a widerlich

oboe /'əʊbəʊ/ n Oboe f

obscen|e /əb'si:n/ a obszön; ⟨atrocious⟩ abscheulich. ~ity /-'senɪtɪ/ n Obszönität f; Abscheulichkeit f

obscur|e /əb'skjʊə(r)/ a dunkel; ⟨unknown⟩ unbekannt ◻ vt verdecken; ⟨confuse⟩ verwischen. ~ity n Dunkelheit f; Unbekanntheit f

obsequious /əb'si:kwɪəs/ a unterwürfig

observa|nce /əb'zɜ:vns/ n ⟨of custom⟩ Einhaltung f. ~nt a aufmerksam. ~tion /ɒbzə'veɪʃn/ n Beobachtung f; ⟨remark⟩ Bemerkung f

observatory /əb'zɜ:vətrɪ/ n Sternwarte f; ⟨weather⟩ Wetterwarte f

observe /əb'zɜ:v/ vt beobachten; ⟨say, notice⟩ bemerken; ⟨keep, celebrate⟩ feiern; ⟨obey⟩ einhalten. ~r n Beobachter m

obsess /əb'ses/ vt be ~ed by besessen sein von. ~ion /-eʃn/ n Besessenheit f; ⟨persistent idea⟩ fixe Idee f. ~ive /-ɪv/ a, ~ly adv zwanghaft

obsolete /'ɒbsəli:t/ a veraltet

obstacle /'ɒbstəkl/ n Hindernis nt

obstetrician /ɒbstə'trɪʃn/ n Geburtshelfer m. **obstetrics** /-'stetrɪks/ n Geburtshilfe f

obstina|cy /'ɒbstɪnəsɪ/ n Starrsinn m. ~te /-nət/ a, ~ly adv starrsinnig; ⟨refusal⟩ hartnäckig

obstreperous /əb'strepərəs/ a widerspenstig

obstruct /əb'strʌkt/ vt blockieren; ⟨hinder⟩ behindern. ~ion /-ʌkʃn/ n Blockierung f; Behinderung f; ⟨obstacle⟩ Hindernis nt. ~ive /-ɪv/ a be ~ive Schwierigkeiten bereiten

obtain /əb'teɪn/ vt erhalten, bekommen ◻ vi gelten. ~able /-əbl/ a erhältlich

obtrusive /əb'tru:sɪv/ a aufdringlich; ⟨thing⟩ auffällig

obtuse /əb'tju:s/ a ⟨Geom⟩ stumpf; ⟨stupid⟩ begriffsstutzig

obviate /'ɒbvɪeɪt/ vt beseitigen

obvious /'ɒbvɪəs/ a, ~ly adv offensichtlich, offenbar

occasion /ə'keɪʒn/ n Gelegenheit f; ⟨time⟩ Mal nt; ⟨event⟩ Ereignis nt; ⟨cause⟩ Anlass m, Grund m; on ~ gelegentlich, hin und wieder; on the ~ of anlässlich (+ gen) ◻ vt veranlassen

occasional /ə'keɪʒənl/ a gelegentlich; he has the ~ glass of wine or trinkt gelegentlich ein Glas Wein. ~ly adv gelegentlich, hin und wieder

occult /ɒ'kʌlt/ a okkult

occupant /'ɒkjʊpənt/ n Bewohner(in) m(f); ⟨of vehicle⟩ Insasse m

occupation /ɒkjʊ'peɪʃn/ n Beschäftigung f; ⟨job⟩ Beruf m; ⟨Mil⟩ Besetzung f; ⟨period⟩ Besatzung f. ~al a Berufs-. ~al therapy n Beschäftigungstherapie f

occupier /'ɒkjʊpaɪə(r)/ n Bewohner(in) m(f)

occupy /'ɒkjʊpaɪ/ vt (pt/pp occupied) besetzen ⟨seat, (Mil) country⟩; einnehmen ⟨space⟩; in Anspruch nehmen ⟨time⟩; ⟨live in⟩ bewohnen; ⟨fig⟩ bekleiden ⟨office⟩; ⟨keep busy⟩ beschäftigen; ~ oneself sich beschäftigen

occur /ə'kɜ:(r)/ vi (pt/pp occurred) geschehen; ⟨exist⟩ vorkommen, auftreten; it ~red to me that es fiel mir ein, dass. ~rence /ə'kʌrəns/ n Auftreten nt; ⟨event⟩ Ereignis nt

ocean /'əʊʃn/ n Ozean m

o'clock /ə'klɒk/ adv [at] 7 ~ [um] 7 Uhr

octagonal /ɒk'tægənl/ a achteckig

octave /'ɒktɪv/ n ⟨Mus⟩ Oktave f

October /ɒk'təʊbə(r)/ n Oktober m

octopus /'ɒktəpəs/ n (pl -puses) Tintenfisch m

odd /ɒd/ a (-ier, -est) seltsam, merkwürdig; ⟨number⟩ ungerade; ⟨not of set⟩ einzeln; forty ~ über vierzig; ~ jobs Gelegenheitsarbeiten pl; the ~ one out die Ausnahme; at ~ moments zwischendurch; have the ~ glass of wine gelegentlich ein Glas Wein trinken

odd|ity /'ɒdɪtɪ/ n Kuriosität f. ~ly adv merkwürdig; ~ly enough merkwürdigerweise. ~ment n ⟨of fabric⟩ Rest m

odds /ɒdz/ npl ⟨chances⟩ Chancen pl; at ~ uneinig; ~ and ends Kleinkram m; it makes no ~ es spielt keine Rolle

ode /əʊd/ n Ode f

odious /'əʊdɪəs/ a widerlich, abscheulich

odour /'əʊdə(r)/ n Geruch m. ~less a geruchlos

oesophagus /i:'sɒfəgəs/ n Speiseröhre f

of /ɒv, unbetont əv/ prep von (+ dat); ⟨made of⟩ aus (+ dat); the two of us wir zwei; a child of three ein dreijähriges Kind; the fourth of January der vierte Januar; a pound of butter ein Pfund Butter; a cup of tea/coffee eine Tasse Tee/Kaffee; a bottle of wine eine Flasche Wein; half of it die Hälfte davon; the whole of the room das ganze Zimmer

off /ɒf/ *prep* von (+ *dat*); £10 ~ the price £10 Nachlass; ~ the coast vor der Küste; get ~ the ladder/bus von der Leiter/aus dem Bus steigen; take/leave the lid ~ the saucepan den Topf abdecken/nicht zudecken ◻ *adv* weg; ⟨*button, lid, handle*⟩ ab; ⟨*light*⟩ aus; ⟨*brake*⟩ los; ⟨*machine*⟩ abgeschaltet; ⟨*tap*⟩ zu; ⟨*on appliance*⟩ 'off' 'aus'; 2 kilometres ~ 2 Kilometer entfernt; a long way ~ weit weg; ⟨*time*⟩ noch lange hin; ~ and on hin und wieder; with his hat/coat ~ ohne Hut/Mantel; with the light/lid ~ ohne Licht/Deckel; 20% ~ 20% Nachlass; be ~ ⟨*leave*⟩ [weg]gehen; ⟨*Sport*⟩ starten; ⟨*food:*⟩ schlecht/⟨*all gone*⟩ alle sein; be better/worse ~ besser/schlechter dran sein; be well ~ gut dran sein; ⟨*financially*⟩ wohlhabend sein; have a day ~ einen freien Tag haben; go/drive ~ weggehen/-fahren; turn/take sth ~ etw abdrehen/-nehmen

offal /ˈɒfl/ *n* ⟨*Culin*⟩ Innereien *pl*

offence /əˈfens/ *n* ⟨*illegal act*⟩ Vergehen *nt*; give/take ~ Anstoß erregen/nehmen (at an + *dat*)

offend /əˈfend/ *vt* beleidigen. ~er *n* ⟨*Jur*⟩ Straftäter *m*

offensive /əˈfensɪv/ *a* anstößig; ⟨*Mil, Sport*⟩ offensiv ◻ *n* Offensive *f*

offer /ˈɒfə(r)/ *n* Angebot *nt*; on special ~ im Sonderangebot ◻ *vt* anbieten (to *dat*); leisten ⟨*resistance*⟩. ~ s.o. sth jdm etw anbieten; ~ to do sth sich anbieten, etw zu tun. ~ing *n* Gabe *f*

off·hand *a* brüsk; ⟨*casual*⟩ lässig ◻ *adv* so ohne weiteres

office /ˈɒfɪs/ *n* Büro *nt*; ⟨*post*⟩ Amt *nt*; in ~ im Amt; ~ hours *pl* Dienststunden *pl*

officer /ˈɒfɪsə(r)/ *n* Offizier *m*; ⟨*official*⟩ Beamte(r) *m*/ Beamtin *f*; ⟨*police*⟩ Polizeibeamte(r) *m*/-beamtin *f*

official /əˈfɪʃl/ *a* offiziell, amtlich ◻ *n* Beamte(r) *m*/ Beamtin *f*; ⟨*Sport*⟩ Funktionär *m*. ~ly *adv* offiziell

officiate /əˈfɪʃɪeɪt/ *vi* amtieren

officious /əˈfɪʃəs/ *a*, -ly *adv* übereifrig

offing *n* in the ~ in Aussicht

off·licence *n* Wein- und Spirituosenhandlung *f*

off·load *vt* ausladen

off·putting *a* ⟨*fam*⟩ abstoßend

off·set *vt* (*pt/pp* -set, *pres p* -setting) ausgleichen

offshoot *n* Schössling *m*; ⟨*fig*⟩ Zweig *m*

offshore *a* offshore-. ~ rig *n* Bohrinsel *f*

off·side *a* ⟨*Sport*⟩ abseits

offspring *n* Nachwuchs *m*

off·stage *adv* hinter den Kulissen

off·white *a* fast weiß

often /ˈɒfn/ *adv* oft; every so ~ von Zeit zu Zeit

ogle /ˈəʊgl/ *vt* beäugeln

ogre /ˈəʊgə(r)/ *n* Menschenfresser *m*

oh /əʊ/ *int* oh! ach! oh dear! o weh!

oil /ɔɪl/ *n* Öl *nt*; ⟨*petroleum*⟩ Erdöl *nt* ◻ *vt* ölen

oil: ~cloth *n* Wachstuch *nt*. ~field *n* Ölfeld *nt*. ~painting *n* Ölgemälde *nt*. ~refinery *n* [Erdöl]raffinerie *f*. ~skins *npl* Ölzeug *nt*. ~slick *n* Ölteppich *m*. ~tanker *n* Öltanker *m*. ~ well *n* Ölquelle *f*

oily /ˈɔɪlɪ/ *a* (-ier, -iest) ölig

ointment /ˈɔɪntmənt/ *n* Salbe *f*

OK /əʊˈkeɪ/ *a & int* ⟨*fam*⟩ in Ordnung; okay ◻ *adv* ⟨*well*⟩ gut ◻ *vt* ⟨*auch* okay⟩ ⟨*pt/pp* okayed⟩ genehmigen

old /əʊld/ *a* (-er, -est) alt; ⟨*former*⟩ ehemalig

old: ~ 'age *n* Alter *nt*. ~-age 'pensioner *n* Rentner(in) *m(f)*. ~ boy *n* ehemaliger Schüler. ~-fashioned *a* altmodisch. ~ girl *n* ehemalige Schülerin *f*. ~ 'maid *n* alte Jungfer *f*

olive /ˈɒlɪv/ *n* Olive *f*; ⟨*colour*⟩ Oliv *nt* ◻ *a* olivgrün. ~ branch *n* Ölzweig *m*; ⟨*fig*⟩ Friedensangebot *nt*. ~ 'oil *n* Olivenöl *nt*

Olympic /əˈlɪmpɪk/ *a* olympisch ◻ *n* the ~s die Olympischen Spiele *pl*

omelette /ˈɒmlɪt/ *n* Omelett *nt*

omen /ˈəʊmən/ *n* Omen *nt*

ominous /ˈɒmɪnəs/ *a* bedrohlich

omission /əˈmɪʃn/ *n* Auslassung *f*; ⟨*failure to do*⟩ Unterlassung *f*

omit /əˈmɪt/ *vt* ⟨*pt/pp* omitted⟩ auslassen; ~ to do sth es unterlassen, etw zu tun

omnipotent /ɒmˈnɪpətənt/ *a* allmächtig

on /ɒn/ *prep* auf (+ *dat*/⟨*on to*⟩ + *acc*); ⟨*on vertical surface*⟩ an (+ *dat*/⟨*on to*⟩ + *acc*); ⟨*about*⟩ über (+ *acc*); on Monday ⟨am⟩ Montag; on Mondays montags; on the first of May am ersten Mai; on arriving als ich ankam; on one's finger am Finger; on the right/left rechts/links; on the Rhine/Thames am Rhein/an der Themse; on the radio/television im Radio/Fernsehen; on the bus/train im Bus/Zug; go on the bus/train mit dem Bus/Zug fahren; get on the bus/train in den Bus/Zug einsteigen; on me ⟨*with me*⟩ bei mir; it's on me ⟨*fam*⟩ das spendiere ich ◻ *adv* ⟨*further on*⟩ weiter; ⟨*switched on*⟩ an; ⟨*brake*⟩ angezogen; ⟨*machine*⟩ angeschaltet; ⟨*on appliance*⟩ 'on' 'ein'; with/without his hat/coat on mit/ohne Hut/Mantel; with/without the lid on mit/ohne Deckel; be on ⟨*film:*⟩ laufen; ⟨*event:*⟩ stattfinden; be at ⟨*fam*⟩ bedrängen (zu to); it's not on ⟨*fam*⟩ das geht nicht; on and on immer weiter; on and off hin und wieder; **and so on** und so weiter; **later on** später; **drive on** weiterfahren; **stick/sew on** ankleben/-nähen; **from then on** von da an

once /wʌns/ *adv* einmal; *(formerly)* früher; **at ~** sofort; *(at the same time)* gleichzeitig; **~ and for all** ein für alle Mal □ *conj* wenn; *(with past tense)* als. **~over** *n* *(fam)* give s.o./sth the **~-over** sich *(dat)* jdn/etw kurz ansehen

'**oncoming** *a* ~ traffic Gegenverkehr *m*

one /wʌn/ *a* ein(e); *(only)* einzig; **not ~** kein(e); **~ day/evening** eines Tages/Abends □ *n* Eins *f* □ *pron* eine(r)/eins; *(impersonal)* man; **which ~** welche(r,s); **~ another** einander; **~ by ~** einzeln; **~ never knows** man kann nie wissen

one: ~-**eyed** *a* einäugig. ~-**parent** 'family *n* Einelternfamilie *f*. ~'**self** *pron* selbst; *(refl)* sich; **by ~self** allein. ~-**sided** *a* einseitig. ~-**way** *(street)* Einbahn-; *(ticket)* einfach

onion /'ʌnjən/ *n* Zwiebel *f*

'**onlooker** *n* Zuschauer(in) *m(f)*

only /'əʊnlɪ/ *a* einzige(r,s); an **~ child** ein Einzelkind *nt* □ *adv* & *conj* nur; **~ just** gerade erst; *(barely)* gerade noch

'**onset** *n* Beginn *m*; *(of winter)* Einsetzen *nt*

'**onslaught** /'ɒnslɔːt/ *n* heftiger Angriff *m*

onus /'əʊnəs/ *n* the ~ is on me es liegt an mir (to zu)

onward[s] /'ɒnwəd[z]/ *adv* vorwärts; **from then ~** von der Zeit an

ooze /uːz/ *vi* sickern

opal /'əʊpl/ *n* Opal *m*

opaque /əʊ'peɪk/ *a* undurchsichtig

open /'əʊpən/ *a*, -**ly** *adv* offen; **be ~** *(shop:)* geöffnet sein; **in the ~ air** im Freien □ *n* **in the ~** im Freien □ *vt* öffnen, aufmachen; *(start, set up)* eröffnen □ *vi* sich öffnen; *(flower:)* aufgehen; *(shop:)* öffnen, aufmachen; *(be started)* eröffnet werden. **~ up** *vt* öffnen, aufmachen; *(fig)* eröffnen □ *vi* sich öffnen; *(fig)* sich eröffnen

open: ~-'**air** 'swimming pool *n* Freibad *nt*. ~ **day** *n* Tag *m* der offenen Tür

opener /'əʊpənə(r)/ *n* Öffner *m*

opening /'əʊpənɪŋ/ *n* Öffnung *f*; *(beginning)* Eröffnung *f*; *(job)* Einstiegsmöglichkeit *f*. ~ **hours** *npl* Öffnungszeiten *pl*

open: ~-'**minded** *a* aufgeschlossen. ~-**plan** *a* **~-plan office** Großraumbüro *nt*. ~ '**sandwich** *n* belegtes Brot *nt*

opera /'ɒprə/ *n* Oper *f*

operable /'ɒpərəbl/ *a* operierbar

opera: ~-**glasses** *npl* Opernglas *nt*. ~-**house** *n* Opernhaus *nt*. ~-**singer** *n* Opernsänger(in) *m(f)*

operate /'ɒpəreɪt/ *vt* bedienen *(machine, lift)*; betätigen *(lever, brake)*; *(fig: run)* betreiben □ *vi* *(Techn)* funktionieren; *(be in action)* in Betrieb sein; *(Mil & fig)* operieren; **~ [on]** *(Med)* operieren

operatic /ɒpə'rætɪk/ *a* Opern-

operation /ɒpə'reɪʃn/ *n* *(see operate)* Bedienung *f*; Betätigung *f*; Operation *f*; **in ~** *(Techn)* in Betrieb; **come into ~** *(fig)* in Kraft treten; **have an ~** *(Med)* operiert werden. **~al** *a* **be ~al** in Betrieb sein; *(law:)* in Kraft sein

operative /'ɒpərətɪv/ *a* wirksam

operator /'ɒpəreɪtə(r)/ *n* *(user)* Bedienungsperson *f*; *(Teleph)* Vermittlung *f*

operetta /ɒpə'retə/ *n* Operette *f*

opinion /ə'pɪnjən/ *n* Meinung *f*; **in my ~** meiner Meinung nach. **~ated** *a* rechthaberisch

opium /'əʊpɪəm/ *n* Opium *nt*

opponent /ə'pəʊnənt/ *n* Gegner(in) *m(f)*

opportun|e /'ɒpətjuːn/ *a* günstig. **~ist** /-'tjuːnɪst/ *a* opportunistisch □ *n* Opportunist *m*

opportunity /ɒpə'tjuːnətɪ/ *n* Gelegenheit *f*

oppos|e /ə'pəʊz/ *vt* Widerstand leisten (+ *dat)*; *(argue against)* sprechen gegen; **be ~ed to sth** gegen etw sein; **as ~ed to** im Gegensatz zu. **~ing** *a* gegnerisch; *(opposite)* entgegengesetzt

opposite /'ɒpəzɪt/ *a* entgegengesetzt; *(house, side)* gegenüberliegend; **~ number** *(fig)* Gegenstück *nt*; **the ~ sex** das andere Geschlecht □ *n* Gegenteil *nt* □ *adv* gegenüber □ *prep* gegenüber (+ *dat)*

opposition /ɒpə'zɪʃn/ *n* Widerstand *m*; *(Pol)* Opposition *f*

oppress /ə'pres/ *vt* unterdrücken. **~ion** /-eʃn/ *n* Unterdrückung *f*. **~ive** /-ɪv/ *a* tyrannisch; *(heat)* drückend. **~or** *n* Unterdrücker *m*

opt /ɒpt/ *vi* **~ for** sich entscheiden für; **~ out** ausscheiden (of aus)

optical /'ɒptɪkl/ *a* optisch; **~ illusion** optische Täuschung *f*

optician /ɒp'tɪʃn/ *n* Optiker *m*

optics /'ɒptɪks/ *n* Optik *f*

optimis|m /'ɒptɪmɪzm/ *n* Optimismus *m*. **~t** /-mɪst/ *n* Optimist *m*. **~tic** /-'mɪstɪk/ *a*, -**ally** *adv* optimistisch

optimum /'ɒptɪməm/ *a* optimal □ *n* *(pl* -ima) Optimum *nt*

option /'ɒpʃn/ *n* Wahl *f*; *(Comm)* Option *f*. **~al** *a* auf Wunsch erhältlich; *(subject)* wahlfrei; **~al extras** *pl* Extras *pl*

opulen|ce /'ɒpjʊləns/ *n* Prunk *m*; *(wealth)* Reichtum *m*. **~t** *a* prunkvoll; *(wealthy)* sehr reich

or /ɔː(r)/ *conj* oder; *(after negative)* noch; or [else] sonst; in a year or two in ein bis zwei Jahren

oracle /ˈɒrəkl/ *n* Orakel *nt*

oral /ˈɔːrl/ *a*, **-ly** *adv* mündlich; *(Med)* oral □ *n (fam)* Mündliche(s) *nt*

orange /ˈɒrɪndʒ/ *n* Apfelsine *f*, Orange *f*; *(colour)* Orange *nt* □ *a* orangefarben. **~ade** /-ˈdʒeɪd/ *n* Orangeade *f*

oration /əˈreɪʃn/ *n* Rede *f*

orator /ˈɒrətə(r)/ *n* Redner *m*

oratorio /ɒrəˈtɔːrɪəʊ/ *n* Oratorium *nt*

oratory /ˈɒrətərɪ/ *n* Redekunst *f*

orbit /ˈɔːbɪt/ *n* Umlaufbahn *f* □ *vt* umkreisen. **~al** *a* **~al road** Ringstraße *f*

orchard /ˈɔːtʃəd/ *n* Obstgarten *m*

orches|tra /ˈɔːkɪstrə/ *n* Orchester *nt*. **~tral** /ˈkestrəl/ *a* Orchester-. **~trate** *vt* orchestrieren

orchid /ˈɔːkɪd/ *n* Orchidee *f*

ordain /ɔːˈdeɪn/ *vt* bestimmen; *(Relig)* ordinieren

ordeal /ɔːˈdiːl/ *n (fig)* Qual *f*

order /ˈɔːdə(r)/ *n* Ordnung *f*; *(sequence)* Reihenfolge *f*; *(condition)* Zustand *m*; *(command)* Befehl *m*; *(in restaurant)* Bestellung *f*; *(Comm)* Auftrag *m*; *(Relig, medal)* Orden *m*; out of **~** *(machine)* außer Betrieb; in **~** that damit; in **~** to help um zu helfen; take holy **~s** Geistlicher werden □ *vt (put in* **~***)* ordnen; *(command)* befehlen (+ *dat*); *(Comm, in restaurant)* bestellen; *(prescribe)* verordnen

orderly /ˈɔːdəlɪ/ *a* ordentlich; *(not unruly)* friedlich □ *n (Mil, Med)* Sanitäter *m*

ordinary /ˈɔːdɪnərɪ/ *a* gewöhnlich, normal; *(meeting)* ordentlich

ordination /ɔːdɪˈneɪʃn/ *n (Relig)* Ordination *f*

ore /ɔː(r)/ *n* Erz *nt*

organ /ˈɔːgən/ *n (Biol & fig)* Organ *nt*; *(Mus)* Orgel *f*

organic /ɔːˈgænɪk/ *a*, **-ally** *adv* organisch; *(without chemicals)* biodynamisch; *(crop)* biologisch angebaut; *(food)* Bio-; **~ally** grown biologisch angebaut. **~** farm *n* Biohof *m*. **~** farming *n* biologischer Anbau *m*

organism /ˈɔːgənɪzm/ *n* Organismus *m*

organist /ˈɔːgənɪst/ *n* Organist *m*

organization /ɔːgənaɪˈzeɪʃn/ *n* Organisation *f*

organize /ˈɔːgənaɪz/ *vt* organisieren; veranstalten *(event)*. **~r** *n* Organisator *m*; Veranstalter *m*

orgasm /ˈɔːgæzm/ *n* Orgasmus *m*

orgy /ˈɔːdʒɪ/ *n* Orgie *f*

Orient /ˈɔːrɪənt/ *n* Orient *m*. **o~al** /-ˈentl/ *a* orientalisch; **~al carpet** Orientteppich *m* □ *n* Orientale *m*, Orientalin *f*

orient|ate /ˈɔːrɪənteɪt/ *vt* **~ate oneself** sich orientieren. **~ation** /-ˈteɪʃn/ *n* Orientierung *f*

orifice /ˈɒrɪfɪs/ *n* Öffnung *f*

origin /ˈɒrɪdʒɪn/ *n* Ursprung *m*; *(of person, goods)* Herkunft *f*

original /əˈrɪdʒənl/ *a* ursprünglich; *(not copied)* original; *(new)* original □ *n* Original *nt*. **~ity** /-ˈnælətɪ/ *n* Originalität *f*. **~ly** *adv* ursprünglich

originat|e /əˈrɪdʒɪneɪt/ *vi* entstehen □ *vt* hervorbringen. **~or** *n* Urheber *m*

ornament /ˈɔːnəmənt/ *n* Ziergegenstand *m*; *(decoration)* Verzierung *f*. **~al** /-ˈmentl/ *a* dekorativ. **~ation** /-ˈteɪʃn/ *n* Verzierung *f*

ornate /ɔːˈneɪt/ *a* reich verziert

ornithology /ɔːnɪˈθɒlədʒɪ/ *n* Vogelkunde *f*

orphan /ˈɔːfn/ *n* Waisenkind *nt*, Waise *f* □ *vt* zur Waise machen; **~ed** verwaist. **~age** /-ɪdʒ/ *n* Waisenhaus *nt*

orthodox /ˈɔːθədɒks/ *a* orthodox

orthography /ɔːˈθɒgrəfɪ/ *n* Rechtschreibung *f*

orthopaedic /ɔːθəˈpiːdɪk/ *a* orthopädisch

oscillate /ˈɒsɪleɪt/ *vi* schwingen

ostensible /ɒˈstensəbl/ *a*, **-bly** *adv* angeblich

ostentat|ion /ɒsten'teɪʃn/ *n* Protzerei *f (fam)*. **~ious** /-ʃəs/ *a* protzig *(fam)*

osteopath /ˈɒstɪəpæθ/ *n* Osteopath *m*

ostracize /ˈɒstrəsaɪz/ *vt* ächten

ostrich /ˈɒstrɪtʃ/ *n* Strauß *m*

other /ˈʌðə(r)/ *a, pron & n* andere(r,s); the **~** [one] der/die/das andere; the **~** two die zwei anderen; two **~s** zwei andere; *(more)* noch zwei; no **~s** sonst keine; any **~** questions? sonst noch Fragen? every **~** day jeden zweiten Tag; the **~** day neulich; the **~** evening neulich abends; someone/something or **~** irgendjemand/-etwas □ *adv* anders; **~** than him außer ihm; somehow/somewhere or **~** irgendwie/irgendwo

'otherwise *adv* sonst; *(differently)* anders

otter /ˈɒtə(r)/ *n* Otter *m*

ouch /aʊtʃ/ *int* autsch

ought /ɔːt/ *v aux* I/we **~** to stay ich sollte/wir sollten eigentlich bleiben; he **~** not to have done it er hätte es nicht machen sollen; that **~** to be enough das sollte eigentlich genügen

ounce /aʊns/ *n* Unze *f (28, 35 g)*

our /ˈaʊə(r)/ *a* unser

ours /ˈaʊəz/ *poss pron* unsere(r,s); a friend of ~ ein Freund von uns; that is ~ das gehört uns

ourselves /aʊəˈselvz/ *pron* selbst; (*refl*) uns; by ~ allein

oust /aʊst/ *vt* entfernen

out /aʊt/ *adv* (*not at home*) weg; (*outside*) draußen; (*not alight*) aus; (*unconscious*) bewusstlos; be ~ (*sun:*) scheinen; (*flower*) blühen; (*workers*) streiken; (*calculation:*) nicht stimmen; (*Sport*) aus sein; (*fig: not feasible*) nicht infrage kommen; ~ and about unterwegs; have it ~ with s.o. (*fam*) jdn zur Rede stellen; get ~! (*fam*) raus! ~ with it! (*fam*) heraus damit! □/ send ~ hinausgehen/-schicken; come/ bring ~ herauskommen/-bringen □ *prep* ~ of aus (+ *dat*); go ~ of the door zur Tür hinausgehen; be ~ of bed/ the room nicht im Bett/im Zimmer sein; ~ of breath/danger außer Atem/Gefahr; ~ of work arbeitslos; nine ~ of ten neun von zehn; be ~ of sugar/bread keinen Zucker/kein Brot mehr haben □ *prep* aus (+ *dat*); go ~ the door zur Tür hinausgehen

out'bid *vt* (*pt/pp* -bid, *pres p* -bidding) überbieten

'outboard *a* ~ motor Außenbordmotor *m*

'outbreak *n* Ausbruch *m*

'outbuilding *n* Nebengebäude *nt*

'outburst *n* Ausbruch *m*

'outcast *n* Ausgestoßene(r) *m/f*

'outcome *n* Ergebnis *nt*

'outcry *n* Aufschrei *m* [der Entrüstung]

out'dated *a* überholt

out'do *vt* (*pt* -did, *pp* -done) übertreffen, übertrumpfen

'outdoor *a* (*life, sports*) im Freien; ~ shoes *pl* Straßenschuhe *pl*; ~ swimming pool Freibad *nt*

out'doors *adv* draußen; go ~ nach draußen gehen

'outer *a* äußere(r,s)

'outfit *n* Ausstattung *f*; (*clothes*) Ensemble *nt*; (*fam: organization*) Betrieb *m*; (*fam*) Laden *m*. ~ter *n* men's ~ter's Herrenbekleidungsgeschäft *nt*

'outgoing *a* ausscheidend; (*mail*) ausgehend; (*sociable*) kontaktfreudig. ~s *npl* Ausgaben *pl*

out'grow *vi* (*pt* -grew, *pp* -grown) herauswachsen aus

'outhouse *n* Nebengebäude *nt*

outing /ˈaʊtɪŋ/ *n* Ausflug *m*

outlandish /aʊtˈlændɪʃ/ *a* ungewöhnlich

'outlaw *n* Geächtete(r) *m/f* □ *vt* ächten

'outlay *n* Auslagen *pl*

'outlet *n* Abzug *m*; (*for water*) Abfluss *m*; (*fig*) Ventil *nt*; (*Comm*) Absatzmöglichkeit *f*

'outline *n* Umriss *m*; (*summary*) kurze Darstellung *f* □ *vt* umreißen

out'live *vt* überleben

'outlook *n* Aussicht *f*; (*future prospect*) Aussichten *pl*; (*attitude*) Einstellung *f*

'outlying *a* entlegen; ~ areas *pl* Außengebiete *pl*

out'moded *a* überholt

out'number *vt* zahlenmäßig überlegen sein (+ *dat*)

'out-patient *n* ambulanter Patient *m*; ~s' department Ambulanz *f*

'outpost *n* Vorposten *m*

'output *n* Leistung *f*; Produktion *f*

'outrage *n* Gräueltat *f*; (*fig*) Skandal *m*; (*indignation*) Empörung *f* □ *vt* empören. ~ous /-ˈreɪdʒəs/ *a* empörend

'outright[1] *a* völlig, total; (*refusal*) glatt

out'right[2] *adv* ganz; (*at once*) sofort; (*frankly*) offen

'outset *n* Anfang *m*; from the ~ von Anfang an

'outside[1] *a* äußere(r,s); ~ wall Außenwand *f* □ *n* Außenseite *f*; from the ~ von außen; at the ~ höchstens

out'side[2] *adv* außen; (*out of doors*) draußen; go ~ nach draußen gehen □ *prep* außerhalb (+ *gen*); (*in front of*) vor (+ *dat/acc*)

out'sider *n* Außenseiter *m*

'outsize *a* übergroß

'outskirts *npl* Rand *m*

out'spoken *a* offen; be ~ kein Blatt vor den Mund nehmen

out'standing *a* hervorragend; (*conspicuous*) bemerkenswert; (*not settled*) unerledigt; (*Comm*) ausstehend

'outstretched *a* ausgestreckt

out'strip *vt* (*pt/pp* -stripped) davonlaufen (+ *dat*); (*fig*) übertreffen

out'vote *vt* überstimmen

'outward /-wəd/ *a* äußerlich; ~ journey Hinreise *f* □ *adv* nach außen; be ~ bound (*ship:*) auslaufen. ~ly *adv* nach außen hin, äußerlich. ~s *adv* nach außen

out'weigh *vt* überwiegen

out'wit *vt* (*pt/pp* -witted) überlisten

oval /ˈəʊvl/ *a* oval □ *n* Oval *nt*

ovary /ˈəʊvəri/ *n* (*Anat*) Eierstock *m*

ovation /əʊˈveɪʃn/ *n* Ovation *f*

oven /ˈʌvn/ *n* Backofen *m*. ~-ready *a* bratfertig

over /ˈəʊvə(r)/ *prep* über (+ *acc/dat*); ~ dinner beim Essen; ~ the weekend übers Wochenende; ~ the phone am Telefon; ~ the page auf der nächsten Seite; all ~ Germany in ganz Deutschland; ⟨travel⟩ durch ganz Deutschland; all ~ the place ⟨fam⟩ überall ▫ adv ⟨remaining⟩ übrig; ⟨ended⟩ zu Ende; ~ again noch einmal; ~ and ~ immer wieder; ~ here/there hier/da drüben; all ~ ⟨everywhere⟩ überall; it's all ~ es ist vorbei; I ache all ~ mir tut alles weh; go/drive ~ hinübergehen/-fahren; come/bring ~ herüberkommen/-bringen; turn ~ herumdrehen

overall[1] /'əʊvərɔːl/ n Kittel m; ~s pl Overall m

overall[2] /əʊvər'ɔːl/ a gesamt; ⟨general⟩ allgemein ▫ adv insgesamt

over'awe vt ⟨fig⟩ überwältigen

over'balance vi das Gleichgewicht verlieren

over'bearing a herrisch

'overboard adv ⟨Naut⟩ über Bord

'overcast a bedeckt

over'charge vt ~ s.o. jdm zu viel berechnen ▫ vi zu viel verlangen

'overcoat n Mantel m

over'come vt ⟨pt -came, pp -come⟩ überwinden; be ~ by überwältigt werden von

over'crowded a überfüllt

over'do vt ⟨pt -did, pp -done⟩ übertreiben; ⟨cook too long⟩ zu lange kochen; ~ it ⟨fam: do too much⟩ sich übernehmen

'overdose n Überdosis f

'overdraft n [Konto]überziehung f; have an ~ sein Konto überzogen haben

over'draw vt ⟨pt -drew, pp -drawn⟩ ⟨Comm⟩ überziehen

over'due a überfällig

over'estimate vt überschätzen

'overflow[1] n Überschuss m; ⟨outlet⟩ Überlauf m

over'flow[2] vi überlaufen

over'grown a ⟨garden⟩ überwachsen

'overhang[1] n Überhang m

over'hang[2] vt/i ⟨pt/pp -hung⟩ überhängen (über + acc)

'overhaul[1] n Überholung f

over'haul[2] vt ⟨Techn⟩ überholen

'overhead[1] adv oben

'overhead[2] a Ober-; ⟨ceiling⟩ Decken-. ~s npl allgemeine Unkosten pl

over'hear vt ⟨pt/pp -heard⟩ mit anhören ⟨conversation⟩; I overheard him saying it ich hörte zufällig, wie er das sagte

over'heat vi zu heiß werden ▫ vt zu stark erhitzen

over'joyed a überglücklich

'overland a & adv /--'-/ auf dem Landweg; ~ route Landroute f

over'lap v ⟨pt/pp -lapped⟩ ▫ vi sich überschneiden ▫ vt überlappen

over'leaf adv umseitig

over'load vt überladen; ⟨Electr⟩ überlasten

'overlook[1] n ⟨Amer⟩ Aussichtspunkt m

over'look[2] vt überblicken; ⟨fail to see, ignore⟩ übersehen

overly /'əʊvlɪ/ adv übermäßig

over'night[1] adv über Nacht; stay ~ übernachten

'overnight[2] a Nacht-; ~ stay Übernachtung f

'overpass n Überführung f

over'pay vt ⟨pt/pp -paid⟩ überbezahlen

over'populated a übervölkert

over'power vt überwältigen. ~ing a überwältigend

over'priced a zu teuer

overpro'duce vt überproduzieren

over'rate vt überschätzen. ~d a überbewertet

over'reach vt ~ oneself sich übernehmen

overre'act vi überreagieren. ~ion n Überreaktion f

over'rid|e vt ⟨pt -rode, pp -ridden⟩ sich hinwegsetzen über (+ acc). ~ing a Haupt-

over'rule vt ablehnen; we were ~d wir wurden überstimmt

over'run vt ⟨pt -ran, pp -run, pres p -running⟩ überrennen; überschreiten ⟨time⟩; be ~ with überlaufen sein von

over'seas[1] adv in Übersee; go ~ nach Übersee gehen

'overseas[2] a Übersee-

over'see vt ⟨pt -saw, pp -seen⟩ beaufsichtigen

'overseer /-sɪə(r)/ n Aufseher m

over'shadow vt überschatten

over'shoot vt ⟨pt/pp -shot⟩ hinausschießen über (+ acc)

'oversight n Versehen nt

over'sleep vi ⟨pt/pp -slept⟩ [sich] verschlafen

over'step vt ⟨pt/pp -stepped⟩ überschreiten

over'strain vt überanstrengen

overt /əʊ'vɜːt/ a offen

over'tak|e vt/i ⟨pt -took, pp -taken⟩ überholen. ~ing n Überholen nt; no ~ing Überholverbot nt

over'tax vt zu hoch besteuern; ⟨fig⟩ überfordern

'overthrow[1] n ⟨Pol⟩ Sturz m

over'throw[2] vt ⟨pt -threw, pp -thrown⟩ ⟨Pol⟩ stürzen

'**overtime** n Überstunden pl □ adv work ~ Überstunden machen

over'**tired** a übermüdet

over'**tone** n (fig) Unterton m

overture /'ɔʊvətjʊə(r)/ n (Mus) Ouvertüre f; ~s pl (fig) Annäherungsversuche pl

over'**turn** vt umstoßen □ vi umkippen

over'**weight** a übergewichtig; be ~ Übergewicht haben

over**whelm** /-'welm/ vt überwältigen. ~ing a überwältigend

over'**work** n Überarbeitung f □ vt überfordern □ vi sich überarbeiten

over'**wrought** a überreizt

ovulation /ɒvjʊ'leɪʃn/ n Eisprung m

ow|e /əʊ/ vt schulden/ (fig) verdanken ([to] s.o. jdm); ~e s.o. sth jdm etw schuldig sein; be ~ing (money:) ausstehen. '~ing to prep wegen (+ gen)

owl /aʊl/ n Eule f

own¹ /əʊn/ a & pron eigen; it's my ~ es gehört mir; a car of my ~ mein eigenes Auto; on one's ~ allein; hold one's ~ sich behaupten; get one's ~ back (fam) sich revanchieren

own² vt besitzen; (confess) zugeben; I don't ~ it es gehört mir nicht. ~ up vi es zugeben

owner /'əʊnə(r)/ n Eigentümer(in) m(f), Besitzer(in) m(f); (of shop) Inhaber(in) m(f). ~ship n Besitz m

ox /ɒks/ n (pl oxen) Ochse m

oxide /'ɒksaɪd/ n Oxid nt

oxygen /'ɒksɪdʒən/ n Sauerstoff m

oyster /'ɔɪstə(r)/ n Auster f

ozone /'əʊzəʊn/ n Ozon nt. ~-'friendly a ≈ ohne FCKW. ~ layer n Ozonschicht f

P

pace /peɪs/ n Schritt m; (speed) Tempo nt; keep ~ with Schritt halten mit □ vi ~ up and down auf und ab gehen. ~-maker n (Sport & Med) Schrittmacher m

Pacific /pə'sɪfɪk/ a & n the ~ [Ocean] der Pazifik

pacifier /'pæsɪfaɪə(r)/ n (Amer) Schnuller m

pacifist /'pæsɪfɪst/ n Pazifist m

pacify /'pæsɪfaɪ/ vt (pt/pp -ied) beruhigen

pack /pæk/ n Packung f; (Mil) Tornister m; (of cards) [Karten]spiel nt; (gang) Bande f; (of hounds) Meute f; (of wolves) Rudel nt; a ~ of lies ein Haufen Lügen □ vt/i packen;

einpacken (article); be ~ed (crowded) [gedrängt] voll sein; send s.o. ~ing (fam) jdn wegschicken. ~ up vt einpacken □ vi (fam) (machine:) kaputtgehen; (person:) einpacken (fam)

package /'pækɪdʒ/ n Paket nt □ vt verpacken. ~ holiday n Pauschalreise f

packed 'lunch n Lunchpaket nt

packet /'pækɪt/ n Päckchen nt; cost a ~ (fam) einen Haufen Geld kosten

packing /'pækɪŋ/ n Verpackung f

pact /pækt/ n Pakt m

pad¹ /pæd/ n Polster nt; (for writing) [Schreib]block m; (fam: home) Wohnung f □ vt (pt/pp padded) polstern

pad² vi (pt/pp padded) tappen

padding /'pædɪŋ/ n Polsterung f; (in written work) Füllwerk nt

paddle¹ /'pædl/ n Paddel nt □ vt (row) paddeln

paddle² vi waten

paddock /'pædək/ n Koppel f

padlock /'pædlɒk/ n Vorhängeschloss nt □ vt mit einem Vorhängeschloss verschließen

paediatrician /piːdɪə'trɪʃn/ n Kinderarzt m /-ärztin f

pagan /'peɪgən/ a heidnisch □ n Heide m/Heidin f

page¹ /peɪdʒ/ n Seite f

page² n (boy) Page m □ vt ausrufen (person)

pageant /'pædʒənt/ n Festzug m. ~ry n Prunk m

paid /peɪd/ see pay □ a bezahlt; put ~ to (fam) zunichte machen

pail /peɪl/ n Eimer m

pain /peɪn/ n Schmerz m; be in ~ Schmerzen haben; take ~s sich (dat) Mühe geben; ~ in the neck (fam) Nervensäge f □ vt (fig) schmerzen

pain: ~ful a schmerzhaft; (fig) schmerzlich. ~-killer n schmerzstillendes Mittel nt. ~less a, -ly adv schmerzlos

painstaking /'peɪnzteɪkɪŋ/ a sorgfältig

paint /peɪnt/ n Farbe f □ vt/i streichen; (artist:) malen. ~brush n Pinsel m. ~er n Maler m; (decorator) Anstreicher m. ~ing n Malerei f; (picture) Gemälde nt

pair /peə(r)/ n Paar nt; ~ of trousers Hose f; ~ of scissors Schere f □ vt paaren □ vi ~ off Paare bilden

pajamas /pə'dʒɑːməz/ n pl (Amer) Schlafanzug m

Pakistan /pɑːkɪ'stɑːn/ n Pakistan nt. ~i a pakistanisch □ n Pakistaner(in) m(f)

pal /pæl/ n Freund(in) m(f)

palace /'pælɪs/ n Palast m

palatable /'pælətəbl/ a schmackhaft

palate /'pælət/ n Gaumen m

palatial /pə'leɪʃl/ a palastartig

palaver /pə'lɑːvə(r)/ n (fam: fuss) Theater nt (fam)

pale¹ /peɪl/ n (stake) Pfahl m; beyond the ~ (fam) unmöglich

pale² a (-r, -st) blass ◻ vi blass werden. ~ness n Blässe f

Palestin|e /'pælɪstaɪn/ n Palästina nt. ~ian /pælə'stɪnɪən/ a palästinensisch ◻ n Palästinenser(in) m(f)

palette /'pælɪt/ n Palette f

pall /pɔːl/ n Sargtuch nt; (fig) Decke f ◻ vi an Reiz verlieren

pall|id /'pælɪd/ a bleich. ~or n Blässe f

palm /pɑːm/ n Handfläche f; (tree, symbol) Palme f ◻ vt ~ sth off on s.o. jdm etw andrehen. P~ 'Sunday n Palmsonntag m

palpable /'pælpəbl/ a tastbar; (perceptible) spürbar

palpitat|e /'pælpɪteɪt/ vi klopfen. ~ions /-'teɪʃnz/ npl Herzklopfen nt

paltry /'pɔːltrɪ/ a (-ier, -iest) armselig

pamper /'pæmpə(r)/ vt verwöhnen

pamphlet /'pæmflɪt/ n Broschüre f

pan /pæn/ n Pfanne f; (saucepan) Topf m; (of scales) Schale f ◻ vt (pt/pp panned) (fam) verreißen

panacea /pænə'siːə/ n Allheilmittel nt

panache /pə'næʃ/ n Schwung m

'pancake n Pfannkuchen m

pancreas /'pæŋkrɪəs/ n Bauchspeicheldrüse f

panda /'pændə/ n Panda m. ~ car n Streifenwagen m

pandemonium /pændɪ'məʊnɪəm/ n Höllenlärm m

pander /'pændə(r)/ vi ~ to s.o. jdm zu sehr nachgeben

pane /peɪn/ n [Glas]scheibe f

panel /'pænl/ n Tafel f, Platte f; ~ of experts Expertenrunde f; ~ of judges Jury f. ~ling n Täfelung f

pang /pæŋ/ n ~s of hunger Hungergefühl nt; ~s of conscience Gewissensbisse pl

panic /'pænɪk/ n Panik f ◻ vi (pt/pp panicked) in Panik geraten. ~-stricken a von Panik ergriffen

panorama /pænə'rɑːmə/ n Panorama nt. ~ic /-'ræmɪk/ a Panorama-

pansy /'pænzɪ/ n Stiefmütterchen nt

pant /pænt/ vi keuchen; ⟨dog:⟩ hecheln

pantechnicon /pæn'teknɪkən/ n Möbelwagen m

panther /'pænθə(r)/ n Panther m

panties /'pæntɪz/ npl [Damen]slip m

pantomime /'pæntəmaɪm/ n [zu Weihnachten aufgeführte] Märchenvorstellung f

pantry /'pæntrɪ/ n Speisekammer f

pants /pænts/ npl Unterhose f; (woman's) Schlüpfer m; (trousers) Hose f

'pantyhose n (Amer) Strumpfhose f

papal /'peɪpl/ a päpstlich

paper /'peɪpə(r)/ n Papier nt; (wall~) Tapete f; (newspaper) Zeitung f; (exam ~) Testbogen m; (exam) Klausur f; (treatise) Referat nt; ~s pl (documents) Unterlagen pl; (for identification) [Ausweis]papiere pl; on ~ schriftlich ◻ vt tapezieren

paper: ~back n Taschenbuch nt. ~-clip n Büroklammer f. ~-knife n Brieföffner m. ~weight n Briefbeschwerer m. ~work n Schreibarbeit f

par /pɑː(r)/ n (Golf) Par nt; on a ~ gleichwertig (with dat); feel below ~ sich nicht ganz auf der Höhe fühlen

parable /'pærəbl/ n Gleichnis nt

parachut|e /'pærəʃuːt/ n Fallschirm m ◻ vi [mit dem Fallschirm] abspringen. ~ist n Fallschirmspringer m

parade /pə'reɪd/ n Parade f; (procession) Festzug m ◻ vi marschieren ◻ vt (show off) zur Schau stellen

paradise /'pærədaɪs/ n Paradies nt

paradox /'pærədɒks/ n Paradox nt. ~ical a /-'dɒksɪkl/ paradox

paraffin /'pærəfɪn/ n Paraffin nt

paragon /'pærəgən/ n ~ of virtue Ausbund m der Tugend

paragraph /'pærəgrɑːf/ n Absatz m

parallel /'pærəlel/ a & adv parallel ◻ n (Geog) Breitenkreis m; (fig) Parallele f

paralyse /'pærəlaɪz/ vt lähmen; (fig) lahm legen

paralysis /pə'ræləsɪs/ n (pl -ses /-siːz/) Lähmung f

paramount /'pærəmaʊnt/ a überragend; be ~ vorgehen

paranoid /'pærənɔɪd/ a [krankhaft] misstrauisch

parapet /'pærəpɪt/ n Brüstung f

paraphernalia /pærəfə'neɪlɪə/ n Kram m

paraphrase /'pærəfreɪz/ n Umschreibung f ◻ vt umschreiben

paraplegic /pærə'pliːdʒɪk/ a querschnittsgelähmt ◻ n Querschnittsgelähmte(r) m/f

parasite /'pærəsaɪt/ n Parasit m, Schmarotzer m

parasol /'pærəsɒl/ n Sonnenschirm m

paratrooper /'pærətruːpə(r)/ n Fallschirmjäger m

parcel /'pɑːsl/ n Paket nt

parch /pɑːtʃ/ vt austrocknen; be ~ed 〈person:〉 furchtbaren Durst haben

parchment /'pɑːtʃmənt/ n Pergament nt

pardon /'pɑːdn/ n Verzeihung f; (Jur) Begnadigung f; ~? 〈fam〉 bitte? I beg your ~ wie bitte? 〈sorry〉 Verzeihung! □ vt verzeihen; (Jur) begnadigen

pare /peə(r)/ vt 〈peel〉 schälen

parent /'peərənt/ n Elternteil m; ~s pl Eltern pl. ~al /pə'rentl/ a elterlich

parenthesis /pə'renθəsɪs/ n (pl -ses /-siːz/) Klammer f

parish /'pærɪʃ/ n Gemeinde f. ~ioner /pə'rɪʃənə(r)/ n Gemeindemitglied nt

parity /'pærətɪ/ n Gleichheit f

park /pɑːk/ n Park m □ vt/i parken

parking /'pɑːkɪŋ/ n Parken nt; 'no ~' 'Parken verboten'. ~-lot n (Amer) Parkplatz m. ~-meter n Parkuhr f. ~ space n Parkplatz m

parliament /'pɑːləmənt/ n Parlament nt. ~ary /-'mentərɪ/ a parlamentarisch

parlour /'pɑːlə(r)/ n Wohnzimmer nt

parochial /pə'rəʊkɪəl/ a Gemeinde-; (fig) beschränkt

parody /'pærədɪ/ n Parodie f □ vt (pt/pp -ied) parodieren

parole /pə'rəʊl/ n on ~ auf Bewährung

paroxysm /'pærəksɪzm/ n Anfall m

parquet /'pɑːkeɪ/ n ~ floor Parkett nt

parrot /'pærət/ n Papagei m

parry /'pærɪ/ vt (pt/pp -ied) abwehren 〈blow〉; (Fencing) parieren

parsimonious /pɑːsɪ'məʊnɪəs/ a geizig

parsley /'pɑːslɪ/ n Petersilie f

parsnip /'pɑːsnɪp/ n Pastinake f

parson /'pɑːsn/ n Pfarrer m

part /pɑːt/ n Teil m; (Techn) Teil nt; (area) Gegend f; (Theat) Rolle f; (Mus) Part m; spare ~ Ersatzteil nt; for my ~ meinerseits; on the ~ of vonseiten (+ gen); take s.o.'s ~ für jdn Partei ergreifen; take ~ in teilnehmen an (+ dat) □ adv teils □ vt trennen; scheiteln 〈hair〉 □ vi 〈people:〉 sich trennen; ~ with sich trennen von

partake /pɑː'teɪk/ vi (pt -took, pp -taken) teilnehmen; ~ of 〈eat〉 zu sich nehmen

part-ex'change n take in ~ in Zahlung nehmen

partial /'pɑːʃl/ a Teil-; be ~ to mögen. ~ity /-ʃɪ'ælətɪ/ n Voreingenommenheit f; 〈liking〉 Vorliebe f. ~ly adv teilweise

particip|ant /pɑː'tɪsɪpənt/ n Teilnehmer(in) m(f). ~ate /-peɪt/ vi teilnehmen (in an + dat). ~ation /-'peɪʃn/ n Teilnahme f

participle /'pɑːtɪsɪpl/ n Partizip nt; present/past ~ erstes/zweites Partizip

particle /'pɑːtɪkl/ n Körnchen nt; (Phys) Partikel nt; (Gram) Partikel f

particular /pə'tɪkjʊlə(r)/ a besondere(r,s); (precise) genau; (fastidious) penibel; in ~ besonders. ~ly adv besonders. ~s npl nähere Angaben pl

parting /'pɑːtɪŋ/ n Abschied m; (in hair) Scheitel m □ attrib Abschieds-

partition /pɑː'tɪʃn/ n Trennwand f; (Pol) Teilung f □ vt teilen. ~ off vt abtrennen

partly /'pɑːtlɪ/ adv teilweise

partner /'pɑːtnə(r)/ n Partner(in) m(f); (Comm) Teilhaber m. ~ship n Partnerschaft f; (Comm) Teilhaberschaft f

partridge /'pɑːtrɪdʒ/ n Rebhuhn nt

part-time a & adv Teilzeit-; be or work ~ Teilzeitarbeit machen

party /'pɑːtɪ/ n Party f, Fest nt; (group) Gruppe f; (Pol, Jur) Partei f; be ~ to sich beteiligen an (+ dat)

'party line¹ n (Teleph) Gemeinschaftsanschluss m

party 'line² n (Pol) Parteilinie f

pass /pɑːs/ n Ausweis m; (Geog, Sport) Pass m; (Sch) ≈ ausreichend; get a ~ bestehen □ vt vorbeigehen/-fahren an (+ dat); (overtake) überholen; 〈hand〉 reichen; (Sport) abgeben, abspielen; (approve) annehmen; (exceed) übersteigen; bestehen 〈exam〉; machen 〈remark〉; fällen 〈judgement〉; (Jur) verhängen 〈sentence〉; ~ water Wasser lassen; ~ the time sich 〈dat〉 die Zeit vertreiben; ~ sth off as etw als etw ausgeben; ~ one's hand over sth mit der Hand über etw 〈acc〉 fahren □ vi vorbeigehen/-fahren; 〈get by〉 vorbeikommen; (overtake) überholen; 〈time:〉 vergehen; (in exam) bestehen; let sth ~ 〈fig〉 etw übergehen; [I] ~! [ich] passe! ~ away vi sterben. ~ down vt herunterreichen; 〈fig〉 weitergeben. ~ out vi ohnmächtig werden. ~ round vt herumreichen. ~ up vt heraufreichen; 〈fam: miss〉 vorübergehen lassen

passable /'pɑːsəbl/ a 〈road〉 befahrbar; (satisfactory) passabel

passage /'pæsɪdʒ/ n Durchgang m; (corridor) Gang m; (voyage) Überfahrt f; (in book) Passage f

passenger /'pæsɪndʒə(r)/ n Fahrgast m; (Naut, Aviat) Passagier m; (in car) Mitfahrer m. ~ seat n Beifahrersitz m

passer-by /pɑːsə'baɪ/ n (pl -s-by) Passant(in) m(f)

'passing place n Ausweichstelle f

passion /'pæʃn/ n Leidenschaft f. ~ate /-ət/ a, ~ly adv leidenschaftlich

passive /'pæsɪv/ a passiv □ n Passiv nt

Passover /'pɑːsəʊvə(r)/ n Passah nt

pass: ~port n [Reise]pass m. ~word n Kennwort nt; (Mil) Losung f

past /pɑːst/ a vergangene(r,s); (former) ehemalig; in the ~ few days in den letzten paar Tagen; that's all ~ das ist jetzt vorbei □ n Vergangenheit f □ prep an (+ dat) . . . vorbei; (after) nach; at ten ~ two um zehn nach zwei □ adv vorbei; go/come ~ vorbeigehen/-kommen

pasta /'pæstə/ n Nudeln pl

paste /peɪst/ n Brei m; (dough) Teig m; (fish-, meat-) Paste f; (adhesive) Kleister m; (jewellery) Strass m □ vt kleistern

pastel /'pæstl/ n Pastellfarbe f; (crayon) Pastellstift m; (drawing) Pastell nt □ attrib Pastell-

pasteurize /'pɑːstʃəraɪz/ vt pasteurisieren

pastille /'pæstɪl/ n Pastille f

pastime /'pɑːstaɪm/ n Zeitvertreib m

pastoral /'pɑːstərl/ a ländlich; (care) seelsorgerisch

pastr|y /'peɪstrɪ/ n Teig m; cakes and ~ies Kuchen und Gebäck

pasture /'pɑːstʃə(r)/ n Weide f

pasty¹ /'pæstɪ/ n Pastete f

pasty² /'peɪstɪ/ a blass, (fam) käsig

pat /pæt/ n Klaps m; (of butter) Stückchen nt □ adv have sth off ~ etw aus dem Effeff können □ vt (pp patted) tätscheln; ~ s.o. on the back jdm auf die Schulter klopfen

patch /pætʃ/ n Flicken m; (spot) Fleck m; not a ~ on (fam) gar nicht zu vergleichen mit ~ vt flicken. ~ up vt [zusammen]flicken; beilegen (quarrel)

patchy /'pætʃɪ/ a ungleichmäßig

pâté /'pæteɪ/ n Pastete f

patent /'peɪtnt/ a, -ly adv offensichtlich □ n Patent nt □ vt patentieren. ~ leather n Lackleder nt

patern|al /pə'tɜːnl/ a väterlich. ~ity n Vaterschaft f

path /pɑːθ/ n (pl ~s /pɑːðz/) [Fuß]weg m, Pfad m; (orbit, track) Bahn f; (fig) Weg m

pathetic /pə'θetɪk/ a mitleiderregend; (attempt) erbärmlich

patholog|ical /pæθə'lɒdʒɪkl/ a pathologisch. ~ist /pə'θɒlədʒɪst/ n Pathologe m

pathos /'peɪθɒs/ n Rührseligkeit f

patience /'peɪʃns/ n Geduld f; (game) Patience f

patient /'peɪʃnt/ a, -ly adv geduldig □ n Patient|in m(f)

patio /'pætɪəʊ/ n Terrasse f

patriot /'pætrɪət/ n Patriot(in) m(f). ~ic /-'ɒtɪk/ a patriotisch. ~ism n Patriotismus m

Patrol /pə'trəʊl/ n Patrouille f □ vt/i patrouillieren [in (+ dat)]; (police:) auf Streife gehen/fahren [in (+ dat)]. ~ car n Streifenwagen m

patron /'peɪtrən/ n Gönner m; (of charity) Schirmherr m; (of the arts) Mäzen m; (customer) Kunde m/Kundin f; (Theat) Besucher m. ~age /'pætrənɪdʒ/ n Schirmherrschaft f

patroniz|e /'pætrənaɪz/ vt (fig) herablassend behandeln. ~ing a, -ly adv gönnerhaft

patter¹ /'pætə(r)/ n Getrippel nt; (of rain) Plätschern nt □ vi trippeln; plätschern

patter² n (speech) Gerede nt

pattern /'pætn/ n Muster nt

paunch /pɔːntʃ/ n [Schmer]bauch m

pauper /'pɔːpə(r)/ n Arme(r) m/f

pause /pɔːz/ n Pause f □ vi innehalten

pave /peɪv/ vt pflastern; ~ the way den Weg bereiten (for dat). ~ment n Bürgersteig m

pavilion /pə'vɪljən/ n Pavillon m; (Sport) Klubhaus nt

paw /pɔː/ n Pfote f; (of large animal) Pranke f, Tatze f

pawn¹ /pɔːn/ n (Chess) Bauer m; (fig) Schachfigur f

pawn² vt verpfänden □ n in ~ verpfändet. ~broker n Pfandleiher m. ~shop n Pfandhaus nt

pay /peɪ/ n Lohn m; (salary) Gehalt nt; be in the ~ of bezahlt werden von □ v (pt/pp paid) □ vt bezahlen; zahlen (money); ~ s.o. a visit jdm einen Besuch abstatten; ~ s.o. a compliment jdm ein Kompliment machen □ vi zahlen; (be profitable) sich bezahlt machen; (fig) sich lohnen; ~ for sth etw bezahlen. ~ back vt zurückzahlen. ~ in vt einzahlen. ~ off vt abzahlen (debt) □ vi (fig) sich auszahlen. ~ up vi zahlen

payable /'peɪəbl/ a zahlbar; make ~ to ausstellen auf (+ acc)

payee /peɪ'iː/ n [Zahlungs]empfänger m

payment /'peɪmənt/ n Bezahlung f; (amount) Zahlung f

pay: ~ packet n Lohntüte f. ~phone n Münzfernsprecher m

pea /piː/ n Erbse f

peace /piːs/ n Frieden m; for my ~ of mind zu meiner eigenen Beruhigung

peace|able /'piːsəbl/ a friedlich. ~ful a, -ly adv friedlich. ~maker n Friedensstifter m

peach /piːtʃ/ n Pfirsich m

peacock /'piːkɒk/ n Pfau m

peak /piːk/ n Gipfel m; (fig) Höhepunkt m. ~ed 'cap n Schirmmütze f. ~ hours npl

Hauptbelastungszeit *f*; (*for traffic*) Hauptverkehrszeit *f*

peaky /'pi:kı/ *a* kränklich

peal /pi:l/ *n* (*of bells*) Glockengeläut *nt*; ~s of laughter schallendes Gelächter *n*

'**peanut** *n* Erdnuss *f*; for ~s (*fam*) für einen Apfel und ein Ei

pear /peə(r)/ *n* Birne *f*

pearl /pɜ:l/ *n* Perle *f*

peasant /'peznt/ *n* Bauer *m*

peat /pi:t/ *n* Torf *m*

pebble /'pebl/ *n* Kieselstein *m*

peck /pek/ *n* Schnabelhieb *m*; (*kiss*) flüchtiger Kuss *m* □ *vt/i* picken/(*nip*) hacken (at nach). ~ing order *n* Hackordnung *f*

peckish /'pekıʃ/ *a* be ~ (*fam*) Hunger haben

peculiar /pı'kju:lıə(r)/ *a* eigenartig, seltsam; ~ to eigentümlich (+ *dat*). ~ity /-'ærətı/ *n* Eigenart *f*

pedal /'pedl/ *n* Pedal *nt* □ *vt* fahren ⟨bicycle⟩ □ *vi* treten. ~ bin *n* Treteimer *m*

pedantic /pı'dæntık/ *a*, **-ally** *adv* pedantisch

peddle /'pedl/ *vt* handeln mit

pedestal /'pedıstl/ *n* Sockel *m*

pedestrian /pı'destrıən/ *n* Fußgänger(in) *m(f)* □ *a* (*fig*) prosaisch. ~ 'crossing *n* Fußgängerüberweg *m*. ~ 'precinct *n* Fußgängerzone *f*

pedicure /'pedıkjʊə(r)/ *n* Pediküre *f*

pedigree /'pedıgri:/ *n* Stammbaum *m* □ *attrib* ⟨animal⟩ Rasse-

pedlar /'pedlə(r)/ *n* Hausierer *m*

pee /pi:/ *vi* (*pt/pp* peed) (*fam*) pinkeln

peek /pi:k/ *vi* (*fam*) gucken

peel /pi:l/ *n* Schale *f* □ *vt* schälen; □ *vi* ⟨skin:⟩ sich schälen; ⟨paint:⟩ abblättern. ~ings *npl* Schalen *pl*

peep /pi:p/ *n* kurzer Blick *m* □ *vi* gucken. ~-hole *n* Guckloch *nt*. P~ing 'Tom *n* (*fam*) Spanner *m*

peer[1] /pıə(r)/ *vi* ~ at forschend ansehen

peer[2] *n* Peer *m*; his ~s *pl* seinesgleichen

peev|ed /pi:vd/ *a* (*fam*) ärgerlich. ~ish *a* reizbar

peg /peg/ *n* (*hook*) Haken *m*; (*for tent*) Pflock *m*, Hering *m*; (*for clothes*) [Wäsche]klammer *f*; off the ~ (*fam*) von der Stange □ *vt* (*pt/pp* pegged) anpflocken; anklammern ⟨washing⟩

pejorative /pı'dʒɒrətıv/ *a*, **-ly** *adv* abwertend

pelican /'pelıkən/ *n* Pelikan *m*

pellet /'pelıt/ *n* Kügelchen *nt*

pelt[1] /pelt/ *n* ⟨skin⟩ Pelz *m*, Fell *nt*

pelt[2] *vt* bewerfen □ *vi* (*fam: run fast*) rasen; ~ [down] ⟨rain:⟩ [hernieder]prasseln

pelvis /'pelvıs/ *n* (*Anat*) Becken *nt*

pen[1] /pen/ *n* (*for animals*) Hürde *f*

pen[2] *n* Federhalter *m*; (*ball-point*) Kugelschreiber *m*

penal /'pi:nl/ *a* Straf-. ~ize *vt* bestrafen; (*fig*) benachteiligen

penalty /'penltı/ *n* Strafe *f*; (*fine*) Geldstrafe *f*; (*Sport*) Strafstoß *m*; (*Football*) Elfmeter *m*

penance /'penəns/ *n* Buße *f*

pence /pens/ *see* penny

pencil /'pensıl/ *n* Bleistift *m* □ *vt* (*pt/pp* pencilled) mit Bleistift schreiben. ~-sharpener *n* Bleistiftspitzer *m*

pendant /'pendənt/ *n* Anhänger *m*

pending /'pendıŋ/ *a* unerledigt □ *prep* bis zu

pendulum /'pendjʊləm/ *n* Pendel *nt*

penetrat|e /'penıtreıt/ *vt* durchdringen; ~e [into] eindringen in (+ *acc*). ~ing *a* durchdringend. ~ion /-'treıʃn/ *n* Durchdringen *nt*

'**penfriend** *n* Brieffreund(in) *m(f)*

penguin /'pengwın/ *n* Pinguin *m*

penicillin /penı'sılın/ *n* Penizillin *nt*

peninsula /pə'nınsʊlə/ *n* Halbinsel *f*

penis /'pi:nıs/ *n* Penis *m*

peniten|ce /'penıtəns/ *n* Reue *f*. ~t *a* reuig □ *n* Büßer *m*

penitentiary /penı'tenʃərı/ *n* (*Amer*) Gefängnis *nt*

pen: ~knife *n* Taschenmesser *nt*. ~-name *n* Pseudonym *nt*

pennant /'penənt/ *n* Wimpel *m*

penniless /'penılıs/ *a* mittellos

penny /'penı/ *n* (*pl* pence; *single coins* pennies) Penny *m*; (*Amer*) Centstück *nt*; spend a ~ (*fam*) mal verschwinden; the ~'s dropped (*fam*) der Groschen ist gefallen

pension /'penʃn/ *n* Rente *f*; (*of civil servant*) Pension *f*. ~er *n* Rentner(in) *m(f)*; Pensionär(in) *m(f)*

pensive /'pensıv/ *a* nachdenklich

Pentecost /'pentıkɒst/ *n* Pfingsten *nt*

pent-up /'pentʌp/ *a* angestaut

penultimate /pe'nʌltımət/ *a* vorletzte(r,s)

penury /'penjʊrı/ *n* Armut *f*

peony /'pıənı/ *n* Pfingstrose *f*

people /'pi:pl/ *npl* Leute *pl*, Menschen *pl*; (*citizens*) Bevölkerung *f*; the ~ das Volk; English ~ die Engländer; ~ say man sagt; for four ~ für vier Personen □ *vt* bevölkern

pep /pep/ *n* (*fam*) Schwung *m*

pepper /'pepə(r)/ n Pfeffer m; (vegetable) Paprika m; a ~ (fruit) eine Paprika[schote] □ vt (Culin) pfeffern

pepper: ~corn n Pfefferkorn nt. ~mint n Pfefferminz nt; (Bot) Pfefferminze f. ~pot n Pfefferstreuer m

per /pɜ:(r)/ prep pro; ~ cent Prozent nt

perceive /pə'si:v/ vt wahrnehmen

percentage /pə'sentɪdʒ/ n Prozentsatz m; (part) Teil m

perceptible /pə'septəbl/ a wahrnehmbar

percept|ion /pə'sepʃn/ n Wahrnehmung f. ~ive /-tɪv/ a feinsinnig

perch¹ /pɜ:tʃ/ n Stange f □ vi (bird:) sich niederlassen

perch² n inv (fish) Barsch m

percolat|e /'pɜ:kəleɪt/ vi durchsickern. ~or n Kaffeemaschine f

percussion /pə'kʌʃn/ n Schlagzeug nt. ~ instrument n Schlaginstrument nt

peremptory /pə'remptərɪ/ a herrisch

perennial /pə'renɪəl/ a (problem) immer wiederkehrend □ n (Bot) mehrjährige Pflanze f

perfect¹ /'pɜ:fɪkt/ a perfekt, vollkommen; (fam: utter) völlig □ n (Gram) Perfekt nt

perfect² /pə'fekt/ vt vervollkommnen. ~ion /-ekʃn/ n Vollkommenheit f; to ~ion perfekt

perfectly /'pɜ:fɪktlɪ/ adv perfekt; (completely) vollkommen, völlig

perforate /'pɜ:fəreɪt/ vt perforieren; (make a hole in) durchlöchern. ~d a perforiert

perform /pə'fɔ:m/ vt ausführen; erfüllen (duty); (Theat) aufführen (play); spielen (role) □ vi (Theat) auftreten; (Techn) laufen. ~ance n Aufführung f; (at theatre, cinema) Vorstellung f; (Techn) Leistung f. ~er n Künstler(in) m(f)

perfume /'pɜ:fju:m/ n Parfüm nt; (smell) Duft m

perfunctory /pə'fʌŋktərɪ/ a flüchtig

perhaps /pə'hæps/ adv vielleicht

peril /'perəl/ n Gefahr f. ~ous /-əs/ a gefährlich

perimeter /pə'rɪmɪtə(r)/ n [äußere] Grenze f; (Geom) Umfang m

period /'pɪərɪəd/ n Periode f; (Sch) Stunde f; (full stop) Punkt m □ attrib (costume) zeitgenössisch; (furniture) antik. ~ic /-'ɒdɪk/ a, ~ally adv periodisch. ~ical /-'ɒdɪkl/ n Zeitschrift f

peripher|al /pə'rɪfərl/ a nebensächlich. ~y n Peripherie f

periscope /'perɪskəʊp/ n Periskop nt

perish /'perɪʃ/ vi (rubber:) verrotten; (food:) verderben; (die) ums Leben kommen. ~able /-əbl/ a leicht verderblich. ~ing a (fam: cold) eiskalt

perjur|e /'pɜ:dʒə(r)/ vt ~e oneself einen Meineid leisten. ~y n Meineid m

perk¹ /pɜ:k/ n (fam) [Sonder]vergünstigung f

perk² vi ~ up munter werden

perky /'pɜ:kɪ/ a munter

perm /pɜ:m/ n Dauerwelle f □ vt ~ s.o.'s hair jdm eine Dauerwelle machen

permanent /'pɜ:mənənt/ a ständig; (job, address) fest. ~ly adv ständig; (work, live) dauernd, permanent; (employed) fest

permeable /'pɜ:mɪəbl/ a durchlässig

permeate /'pɜ:mɪeɪt/ vt durchdringen

permissible /pə'mɪsəbl/ a erlaubt

permission /pə'mɪʃn/ n Erlaubnis f

permissive /pə'mɪsɪv/ a (society) permissiv

permit¹ /pə'mɪt/ vt (pt/pp -mitted) erlauben (s.o. jdm); ~ me! gestatten Sie!

permit² /'pɜ:mɪt/ n Genehmigung f

pernicious /pə'nɪʃəs/ a schädlich; (Med) perniziös

perpendicular /pɜ:pən'dɪkjʊlə(r)/ a senkrecht □ n Senkrechte f

perpetrat|e /'pɜ:pɪtreɪt/ vt begehen. ~or n Täter m

perpetual /pə'petjʊəl/ a, ~ly adv ständig, dauernd

perpetuate /pə'petjʊeɪt/ vt bewahren; verewigen (error)

perplex /pə'pleks/ vt verblüffen. ~ed a verblüfft. ~ity n Verblüffung f

persecut|e /'pɜ:sɪkju:t/ vt verfolgen. ~ion /-'kju:ʃn/ n Verfolgung f

perseverance /pɜ:sɪ'vɪərəns/ n Ausdauer f

persever|e /pɜ:sɪ'vɪə(r)/ vi beharrlich weitermachen. ~ing a ausdauernd

Persia /'pɜ:ʃə/ n Persien nt

Persian /'pɜ:ʃn/ a persisch; (cat, carpet) Perser-

persist /pə'sɪst/ vi beharrlich weitermachen; (continue) anhalten; (view:) weiter bestehen; ~ in doing sth dabei bleiben, etw zu tun. ~ence n Beharrlichkeit f. ~ent a, ~ly adv beharrlich; (continuous) anhaltend

person /'pɜ:sn/ n Person f; in ~ persönlich

personal /'pɜ:sənl/ a, ~ly adv persönlich. ~ 'hygiene n Körperpflege f

personality /pɜ:sə'nælətɪ/ n Persönlichkeit f

personify /pəˈsɒnɪfaɪ/ vt (pt/pp -ied) personifizieren, verkörpern

personnel /pɜːsəˈnel/ n Personal nt

perspective /pəˈspektɪv/ n Perspektive f

perspicacious /pɜːspɪˈkeɪʃəs/ a scharfsichtig

persp|iration /pɜːspɪˈreɪʃn/ n Schweiß m. ~ire /-ˈspaɪə(r)/ vi schwitzen

persua|de /pəˈsweɪd/ vt überreden; (convince) überzeugen. ~sion /-eɪʒn/ n Überredung f; (powers of ~sion) Überredungskunst f; (belief) Glaubensrichtung f

persuasive /pəˈsweɪsɪv/ a, -ly adv beredsam; (convincing) überzeugend

pert /pɜːt/ a, -ly adv kess

pertain /pəˈteɪn/ vi ~ to betreffen; (belong) gehören zu

pertinent /ˈpɜːtɪnənt/ a relevant (to für)

perturb /pəˈtɜːb/ vt beunruhigen

peruse /pəˈruːz/ vt lesen

perva|de /pəˈveɪd/ vt durchdringen. ~sive /-sɪv/ a durchdringend

pervers|e /pəˈvɜːs/ a eigensinnig. ~ion /-ʒn/ n Perversion f

pervert¹ /pəˈvɜːt/ vt verdrehen; verführen (person)

pervert² /ˈpɜːvɜːt/ n Perverse(r) m

perverted /pəˈvɜːtɪd/ a abartig

pessimis|m /ˈpesɪmɪzm/ n Pessimismus m. ~t /-mɪst/ n Pessimist m. ~tic /-ˈmɪstɪk/ a, -ally adv pessimistisch

pest /pest/ n Schädling m; (fam: person) Nervensäge f

pester /ˈpestə(r)/ vt belästigen; ~ s.o. for sth jdm wegen etw in den Ohren liegen

pesticide /ˈpestɪsaɪd/ n Schädlingsbekämpfungsmittel nt

pet /pet/ n Haustier nt; (favourite) Liebling m □ vt (pt/pp petted) liebkosen

petal /ˈpetl/ n Blütenblatt nt

peter /ˈpiːtə(r)/ vi ~ out allmählich aufhören; (stream:) versickern

petite /pəˈtiːt/ a klein und zierlich

petition /pəˈtɪʃn/ n Bittschrift f □ vt eine Bittschrift richten an (+ acc)

pet ˈname n Kosename m

petrify /ˈpetrɪfaɪ/ vt/i (pt/pp -ied) versteinern; ~ied (frightened) vor Angst wie versteinert

petrol /ˈpetrl/ n Benzin nt

petroleum /pɪˈtrəʊlɪəm/ n Petroleum nt

petrol: ~-pump n Zapfsäule f. ~ station n Tankstelle f. ~ tank n Benzintank m

ˈpet shop n Tierhandlung f

petticoat /ˈpetɪkəʊt/ n Unterrock m

petty /ˈpetɪ/ a (-ier, -iest) kleinlich. ~ ˈcash n Portokasse f

petulant /ˈpetjʊlənt/ a gekränkt

pew /pjuː/ n [Kirchen]bank f

pewter /ˈpjuːtə(r)/ n Zinn nt

phantom /ˈfæntəm/ n Gespenst nt

pharmaceutical /fɑːməˈsjuːtɪkl/ a pharmazeutisch

pharmac|ist /ˈfɑːməsɪst/ n Apotheker(in) m(f). ~y n Pharmazie f; (shop) Apotheke f

phase /feɪz/ n Phase f □ vt ~ in/out allmählich einführen/abbauen

Ph.D. (abbr of Doctor of Philosophy) Dr. phil.

pheasant /ˈfeznt/ n Fasan m

phenomen|al /fɪˈnɒmɪnl/ a phänomenal. ~on n (pl -na) Phänomen nt

phial /ˈfaɪəl/ n Fläschchen nt

philanderer /fɪˈlændərə(r)/ n Verführer m

philanthrop|ic /fɪlənˈθrɒpɪk/ a menschenfreundlich. ~ist /fɪˈlænθrəpɪst/ n Philanthrop m

philately /fɪˈlætəlɪ/ n Philatelie f, Briefmarkenkunde f

philharmonic /fɪləˈmɒnɪk/ n (orchestra) Philharmoniker pl

Philippines /ˈfɪlɪpiːnz/ npl Philippinen pl

philistine /ˈfɪlɪstaɪn/ n Banause m

philosoph|er /fɪˈlɒsəfə(r)/ n Philosoph m. ~ical /fɪləˈsɒfɪkl/ a, -ly adv philosophisch. ~y n Philosophie f

phlegm /flem/ n (Med) Schleim m

phlegmatic /fleɡˈmætɪk/ a phlegmatisch

phobia /ˈfəʊbɪə/ n Phobie f

phone /fəʊn/ n Telefon nt; be on the ~ Telefon haben; (be phoning) telefonieren □ vt anrufen □ vi telefonieren. ~ back vt/i zurückrufen. ~ book n Telefonbuch nt. ~ box n Telefonzelle f. ~ card n Telefonkarte f. ~-in n (Radio) Hörersendung f. ~ number n Telefonnummer f

phonetic /fəˈnetɪk/ a phonetisch. ~s n Phonetik f

phoney /ˈfəʊnɪ/ a (-ier, -iest) falsch; (forged) gefälscht

phosphorus /ˈfɒsfərəs/ n Phosphor m

photo /ˈfəʊtəʊ/ n Foto nt, Aufnahme f. ~copier n Fotokopiergerät nt. ~copy n Fotokopie f □ vt fotokopieren

photogenic /fəʊtəʊˈdʒenɪk/ a fotogen

photograph /ˈfəʊtəɡrɑːf/ n Fotografie f, Aufnahme f □ vt fotografieren

photograph|er /fəˈtɒɡrəfə(r)/ n Fotograf(in) m(f). ~ic /fəʊtəˈɡræfɪk/ a, -ally adv fotografisch. ~y n Fotografie f

phrase /freɪz/ n Redensart f □ vt formulieren. ~-book n Sprachführer m

physical /'fızıkl/ *a*, -ly *adv* körperlich; (*geography, law*) physikalisch. ~ edu'ca-tion *n* Turnen *nt*

physician /fı'zıʃn/ *n* Arzt *m*/ Ärztin *f*

physic|ist /'fızısıst/ *n* Physiker(in) *m(f)*. ~s *n* Physik *f*

physiology /fızı'ɒlədʒı/ *n* Physiologie *f*

physio'therap|ist /fızıəʊ-/ *n* Physio-therapeut(in) *m(f)*. ~y *n* Physiotherapie *f*

physique /fı'ziːk/ *n* Körperbau *m*

pianist /'pıənıst/ *n* Klavierspieler(in) *m(f)*; (*professional*) Pianist(in) *m(f)*

piano /pı'ænəʊ/ *n* Klavier *nt*

pick¹ /pık/ *n* Spitzhacke *f*

pick² *n* Auslese *f*; take one's ~ sich (*dat*) aussuchen □ *vt/i* (*pluck*) pflücken; (*select*) wählen, sich (*dat*) aussuchen; ~ and choose wählerisch sein; ~ one's nose in der Nase bohren; ~ a quarrel einen Streit anfangen; ~ a hole in etw ein Loch in etw (*acc*) machen; ~ holes in (*fam*) kriti-sieren; ~ at one's food im Essen herum-stochern. ~ on *vt* wählen; (*fam: find fault with*) herumhacken auf (+ *dat*). ~ up *vt* in die Hand nehmen; (*off the ground*) aufheben; hochnehmen (*baby*); (*learn*) lernen; (*acquire*) erwerben; (*buy*) kaufen; (*Teleph*) abnehmen (*receiver*); auffangen (*signal*); (*collect*) abholen; aufgreifen (*criminal*); sich holen (*illness*); (*fam*) aufgabeln (*girl*); ~ oneself up aufstehen □ *vi* (*improve*) sich bessern

'pickaxe *n* Spitzhacke *f*

picket /'pıkıt/ *n* Streikposten *m* □ *vt* Streikposten aufstellen vor (+ *dat*). ~ line *n* Streikpostenkette *f*

pickle /'pıkl/ *n* (*Amer: gherkin*) Essig-gurke *f*; ~s *pl* [Mixed] Pickles *pl* □ *vt* ein-legen

pick: ~pocket *n* Taschendieb *m*. ~up *n* (*truck*) Lieferwagen *m*; (*on record-player*) Tonabnehmer *m*

picnic /'pıknık/ *n* Picknick *nt* □ *vi* (*pt/pp* -nicked*) picknicken

pictorial /pık'tɔːrıəl/ *a* bildlich

picture /'pıktʃə(r)/ *n* Bild *nt*; (*film*) Film *m*; as pretty as a ~ bildhübsch; put s.o. in the ~ (*fig*) jdn ins Bild setzen □ *vt* (*imagine*) sich (*dat*) vorstellen

picturesque /pıktʃə'resk/ *a* malerisch

pie /paı/ *n* Pastete *f*; (*fruit* ~) Kuchen *m*

piece /piːs/ *n* Stück *nt*; (*of set*) Teil *nt*; (*in game*) Stein *m*; (*Journ*) Artikel *m*; a ~ of bread/paper ein Stück Brot/Papier; a ~ of news/advice eine Nachricht/ein Rat; take to ~s auseinander nehmen □ *vt* ~ together zusammensetzen; (*fig*)

zusammenstückeln. ~meal *adv* stück-weise. ~work *n* Akkordarbeit *f*

pier /pıə(r)/ *n* Pier *m*; (*pillar*) Pfeiler *m*

pierc|e /pıəs/ *vt* durchstechen; ~e a hole in sth ein Loch in etw (*acc*) stechen. ~ing *a* durchdringend

piety /'paıətı/ *n* Frömmigkeit *f*

piffle /'pıfl/ *n* (*fam*) Quatsch *m*

pig /pıg/ *n* Schwein *nt*

pigeon /'pıdʒın/ *n* Taube *f*. ~hole *n* Fach *nt*

piggy /'pıgı/ *n* (*fam*) Schweinchen *nt*. ~back *n* give s.o. a ~back jdn hucke-pack tragen. ~ bank *n* Sparschwein *nt*

pig'headed *a* (*fam*) starrköpfig

pigment /'pıgmənt/ *n* Pigment *nt*. ~ation /-men'teıʃn/ *n* Pigmentierung *f*

pig: ~skin *n* Schweinsleder *nt*. ~sty *n* Schweinestall *m*. ~tail *n* (*fam*) Zopf *m*

pike /paık/ *n inv* (*fish*) Hecht *m*

pilchard /'pıltʃəd/ *n* Sardine *f*

pile¹ /paıl/ *n* (*of fabric*) Flor *m*

pile² *n* Haufen *m* □ *vt* ~ sth on to sth etw auf etw (*acc*) häufen. ~ up *vt* aufhäufen □ *vi* sich häufen

piles /paılz/ *npl* Hämorrhoiden *pl*

'pile-up *n* Massenkarambolage *f*

pilfer /'pılfə(r)/ *vt/i* stehlen

pilgrim /'pılgrım/ *n* Pilger(in) *m(f)*. ~age /-ıdʒ/ *n* Pilgerfahrt *f*, Wallfahrt *f*

pill /pıl/ *n* Pille *f*

pillage /'pılıdʒ/ *vt* plündern

pillar /'pılə(r)/ *n* Säule *f*. ~-box *n* Briefkasten *m*

pillion /'pılıən/ *n* Sozius[sitz] *m*

pillory /'pılərı/ *n* Pranger *m* □ *vt* (*pt/pp* -ied*) anprangern

pillow /'pıləʊ/ *n* Kopfkissen *nt*. ~case *n* Kopfkissenbezug *m*

pilot /'paılət/ *n* Pilot *m*; (*Naut*) Lotse *m* □ *vt* fliegen (*plane*); lotsen (*ship*). ~-light *n* Zündflamme *f*

pimp /pımp/ *n* Zuhälter *m*

pimple /'pımpl/ *n* Pickel *m*

pin /pın/ *n* Stecknadel *f*; (*Techn*) Bolzen *m*, Stift *m*; (*Med*) Nagel *m*; I have ~s and needles in my leg (*fam*) mein Bein ist eingeschlafen □ *vt* (*pt/pp* pinned*) anste-cken (to/on an + *acc*); (*sewing*) stecken; (*hold down*) festhalten; ~ sth on s.o. (*fam*) jdm etw anhängen. ~ up *vt* hochste-cken; (*on wall*) anheften, anschlagen

pinafore /'pınəfɔː(r)/ *n* Schürze *f*. ~ dress *n* Kleiderrock *m*

pincers /'pınsəz/ *npl* Kneifzange *f*; (*Zool*) Scheren *pl*

pinch /pıntʃ/ *n* Kniff *m*; (*of salt*) Prise *f*; at a ~ (*fam*) zur Not □ *vt* kneifen, zwicken;

(*fam: steal*) klauen; ~ one's finger sich (*dat*) den Finger klemmen ▯ *vi* ⟨*shoe:*⟩ drücken

'**pincushion** *n* Nadelkissen *nt*

pine[1] /paɪn/ *n* ⟨*tree*⟩ Kiefer *f*

pine[2] *vi* ~ for sich sehnen nach; ~ away sich verzehren

pineapple /'paɪn-/ *n* Ananas *f*

ping /pɪŋ/ *n* Klingeln *nt*

'**ping-pong** *n* Tischtennis *nt*

pink /pɪŋk/ *a* rosa

pinnacle /'pɪnəkl/ *n* Gipfel *m*; ⟨*on roof*⟩ Turmspitze *f*

pin: ~**point** *vt* genau festlegen. ~**stripe** *n* Nadelstreifen *m*

pint /paɪnt/ *n* Pint *nt* (*0,571, Amer: 0,47 l*)

'**pin-up** *n* Pin-up-Girl *nt*

pioneer /paɪə'nɪə(r)/ *n* Pionier *m* ▯ *vt* bahnbrechende Arbeit leisten für

pious /'paɪəs/ *a*, **-ly** *adv* fromm

pip[1] /pɪp/ *n* ⟨*seed*⟩ Kern *m*

pip[2] *n* ⟨*sound*⟩ Tonsignal *nt*

pipe /paɪp/ *n* Pfeife *f*; ⟨*for water, gas*⟩ Rohr *nt* ▯ *vt* in Rohren leiten; ⟨*Culin*⟩ spritzen. ~ **down** *vi* (*fam*) den Mund halten

pipe: ~**dream** *n* Luftschloss *nt*. ~**line** *n* Pipeline *f*; in the ~**line** (*fam*) in Vorbereitung

piper /'paɪpə(r)/ *n* Pfeifer *m*

piping /'paɪpɪŋ/ *a* ~ hot kochend heiß

piquant /'piːkənt/ *a* pikant

pique /piːk/ *n* in a fit of ~ beleidigt

pirate /'paɪərət/ *n* Pirat *m*

Pisces /'paɪsiːz/ *n* ⟨*Astr*⟩ Fische *pl*

piss /pɪs/ *vi* (*sl*) pissen

pistol /'pɪstl/ *n* Pistole *f*

piston /'pɪstən/ *n* ⟨*Techn*⟩ Kolben *m*

pit /pɪt/ *n* Grube *f*; ⟨*for orchestra*⟩ Orchestergraben *m* ▯ *vt* (*pt/pp* **pitted**) (*fig*) messen (**against** mit)

pitch[1] /pɪtʃ/ *n* ⟨*steepness*⟩ Schräge *f*; ⟨*of voice*⟩ Stimmlage *f*; ⟨*of sound*⟩ [Ton]höhe *f*; ⟨*Sport*⟩ Feld *nt*; ⟨*of street-trader*⟩ Standplatz *m*; ⟨*fig: degree*⟩ Grad *m* ▯ *vt* werfen; aufschlagen ⟨*tent*⟩ ▯ *vi* fallen

pitch[2] *n* ⟨*tar*⟩ Pech *nt*. ~'**black** *a* pechschwarz. ~'**dark** *a* stockdunkel

pitcher /'pɪtʃə(r)/ *n* Krug *m*

'**pitchfork** *n* Heugabel *f*

piteous /'pɪtɪəs/ *a* erbärmlich

'**pitfall** *n* (*fig*) Falle *f*

pith /pɪθ/ *n* ⟨*Bot*⟩ Mark *nt*; ⟨*of orange*⟩ weiße Haut *f*; (*fig*) Wesentliche(s) *nt*

pithy /'pɪθɪ/ *a* (**-ier, -iest**) (*fig*) prägnant

piti|ful /'pɪtɪfl/ *a* bedauernswert. ~**less** *a* mitleidslos

pittance /'pɪtns/ *n* Hungerlohn *m*

pity /'pɪtɪ/ *n* Mitleid *nt*, Erbarmen *nt*; [what a] ~! [wie] schade! take ~ on sich erbarmen über (+ *acc*) ▯ *vt* bemitleiden

pivot /'pɪvət/ *n* Drehzapfen *m*; (*fig*) Angelpunkt *m* ▯ *vi* sich drehen (**on** um)

pixie /'pɪksɪ/ *n* Kobold *m*

pizza /'piːtsə/ *n* Pizza *f*

placard /'plækɑːd/ *n* Plakat *nt*

placate /plə'keɪt/ *vt* beschwichtigen

place /pleɪs/ *n* Platz *m*; ⟨*spot*⟩ Stelle *f*; ⟨*town, village*⟩ Ort *m*; (*fam: house*) Haus *nt*; out of ~ fehl am Platze; take ~ stattfinden; all over the ~ überall ▯ *vt* setzen; ⟨*upright*⟩ stellen; ⟨*flat*⟩ legen; (*remember*) unterbringen (*fam*); ~ an order eine Bestellung aufgeben; be ~**d** (*in race*) sich platzieren. ~**mat** *n* Set *nt*

placid /'plæsɪd/ *a* gelassen

plagiar|ism /'pleɪdʒərɪzm/ *n* Plagiat *nt*. ~**ize** *vt* plagiieren

plague /pleɪg/ *n* Pest *f* ▯ *vt* plagen

plaice /pleɪs/ *n inv* Scholle *f*

plain /pleɪn/ *a* (**-er, -est**) klar; ⟨*simple*⟩ einfach; (*not pretty*) nicht hübsch; (*not patterned*) einfarbig; ⟨*chocolate*⟩ zartbitter; in ~ clothes in Zivil ▯ *adv* ⟨*simply*⟩ einfach ▯ *n* Ebene *f*; ⟨*Knitting*⟩ rechte Masche *f*. ~**ly** *adv* klar, deutlich; ⟨*simply*⟩ einfach; (*obviously*) offensichtlich

plaintiff /'pleɪntɪf/ *n* ⟨*Jur*⟩ Kläger(in) *m(f)*

plaintive /'pleɪntɪv/ *a*, **-ly** *adv* klagend

plait /plæt/ *n* Zopf *m* ▯ *vt* flechten

plan /plæn/ *n* Plan *m* ▯ *vt* (*pt/pp* **planned**) planen; (*intend*) vorhaben

plane[1] /pleɪn/ *n* ⟨*tree*⟩ Platane *f*

plane[2] *n* Flugzeug *nt*; ⟨*Geom & fig*⟩ Ebene *f*

plane[3] *n* ⟨*Techn*⟩ Hobel *m* ▯ *vt* hobeln

planet /'plænɪt/ *n* Planet *m*

plank /plæŋk/ *n* Brett *nt*; ⟨*thick*⟩ Planke *f*

planning /'plænɪŋ/ *n* Planung *f*. ~ permission *n* Baugenehmigung *f*

plant /plɑːnt/ *n* Pflanze *f*; ⟨*Techn*⟩ Anlage *f*; ⟨*factory*⟩ Werk *nt* ▯ *vt* pflanzen; ⟨*place in position*⟩ setzen; ~ oneself in front of s.o. sich vor jdn hinstellen. ~**ation** /plæn'teɪʃn/ *n* Plantage *f*

plaque /plɑːk/ *n* [Gedenk]tafel *f*; ⟨*on teeth*⟩ Zahnbelag *m*

plasma /'plæzmə/ *n* Plasma *nt*

plaster /'plɑːstə(r)/ *n* Verputz *m*; ⟨*sticking* ~⟩ Pflaster *nt*; ~ [of Paris] Gips *m* ▯ *vt* verputzen ⟨*wall*⟩; (*cover*) bedecken mit. ~**ed** *a* (*sl*) besoffen. ~**er** *n* Gipser *m*

plastic /'plæstɪk/ *n* Kunststoff *m*, Plastik *nt* ▯ *a* Kunststoff-, Plastik-; ⟨*malleable*⟩ formbar, plastisch

Plasticine (P) /'plæstɪsiːn/ *n* Knetmasse *f*

plastic 'surgery n plastische Chirurgie f

plate /pleɪt/ n Teller m; (flat sheet) Platte f; (with name, number) Schild nt; (gold and silverware) vergoldete/versilberte Ware f; (in book) Tafel f □ vt (with gold) vergolden; (with silver) versilbern

plateau /'plætəʊ/ n (pl ~x /-əʊz/) Hochebene f

platform /'plætfɔ:m/ n Plattform f; (stage) Podium nt; (Rail) Bahnsteig m; ~ 5 Gleis 5

platinum /'plætɪnəm/ n Platin nt

platitude /'plætɪtju:d/ n Plattitüde f

platonic /plə'tɒnɪk/ a platonisch

platoon /plə'tu:n/ n (Mil) Zug m

platter /'plætə(r)/ n Platte f

plausible /'plɔ:zəbl/ a plausibel

play /pleɪ/ n Spiel nt; [Theater]stück nt; (Radio) Hörspiel nt; (TV) Fernsehspiel nt; ~ on words Wortspiel nt □ vt/i spielen; ausspielen (card); ~ safe sichergehen. ~ down vt herunterspielen. ~ up vi (fam) Mätzchen machen

play: ~boy n Playboy m. ~er n Spieler(in) m(f). ~ful a, -ly adv verspielt. ~ground n Spielplatz m; (Sch) Schulhof m. ~group n Kindergarten m

playing: ~card n Spielkarte f. ~field n Sportplatz m

play: ~mate n Spielkamerad m. ~pen n Laufstall m, Laufgitter nt. ~thing n Spielzeug nt. ~wright /-raɪt/ n Dramatiker m

plc abbr (public limited company) ≈ GmbH

plea /pli:/ n Bitte f; make a ~ for bitten um

plead /pli:d/ vt vorschützen; (Jur) vertreten (case) □ vi flehen (for um); ~ guilty sich schuldig bekennen; ~ with s.o. jdn anflehen

pleasant /'plezənt/ a angenehm; (person) nett. ~ly adv angenehm; (say, smile) freundlich

please /pli:z/ adv bitte □ vt gefallen (+ dat); ~ e s.o. jdm eine Freude machen; ~ oneself tun, was man will. ~ed a erfreut; be ~ed with/about sth sich über etw (acc) freuen. ~ing a erfreulich

pleasurable /'pleʒərəbl/ a angenehm

pleasure /'pleʒə(r)/ n Vergnügen nt; (joy) Freude f; with ~ gern[e]

pleat /pli:t/ n Falte f □ vt fälteln. ~ed 'skirt n Faltenrock m

plebiscite /'plebɪsɪt/ n Volksabstimmung f

pledge /pledʒ/ n Pfand nt; (promise) Versprechen nt □ vt verpfänden; versprechen

plentiful /'plentɪfl/ a reichlich; be ~ reichlich vorhanden sein

plenty /'plentɪ/ n eine Menge; (enough) reichlich; ~ of money/people viel Geld/viele Leute

pleurisy /'plʊərəsɪ/ n Rippenfellentzündung f

pliable /'plaɪəbl/ a biegsam

pliers /'plaɪəz/ npl [Flach]zange f

plight /plaɪt/ n [Not]lage f

plimsolls /'plɪmsəlz/ npl Turnschuhe pl

plinth /plɪnθ/ n Sockel m

plod /plɒd/ vi (pt/pp plodded) trotten; (work hard) sich abmühen

plonk /plɒŋk/ n (fam) billiger Wein m

plot /plɒt/ n Komplott nt; (of novel) Handlung f; ~ of land Stück nt Land □ vt einzeichnen □ vi ein Komplott schmieden

plough /plaʊ/ n Pflug m □ vt/i pflügen. ~ back vt (Comm) wieder investieren

ploy /plɔɪ/ n (fam) Trick m

pluck /plʌk/ n Mut m □ vt zupfen; rupfen (bird); pflücken (flower); ~ up courage Mut fassen

plucky /'plʌkɪ/ a (-ier, -iest) tapfer, mutig

plug /plʌg/ n Stöpsel m; (wood) Zapfen m; (cotton wool) Bausch m; (Electr) Stecker m; (Auto) Zündkerze f; (fam: advertisement) Schleichwerbung f □ vt zustopfen; (fam: advertise) Schleichwerbung machen für. ~ in vt (Electr) einstecken

plum /plʌm/ n Pflaume f

plumage /'plu:mɪdʒ/ n Gefieder nt

plumb /plʌm/ a Lot nt □ adv lotrecht □ vt loten. ~ in vt installieren

plumb|er /'plʌmə(r)/ n Klempner m. ~ing n Wasserleitungen pl

'plumb-line n [Blei]lot nt

plume /plu:m/ n Feder f

plummet /'plʌmɪt/ vi herunterstürzen

plump /plʌmp/ a (-er, -est) mollig, rundlich □ vt ~ for wählen

plunder /'plʌndə(r)/ n Beute f □ vt plündern

plunge /plʌndʒ/ n Sprung m; take the ~ (fam) den Schritt wagen □ vt/i tauchen

plu'perfect /plu:-/ n Plusquamperfekt nt

plural /'plʊərəl/ a pluralisch □ n Mehrzahl f, Plural m

plus /plʌs/ prep plus (+ dat) □ a Plus- □ n Pluszeichen nt; (advantage) Plus nt

plush[y] /'plʌʃ[ɪ]/ a luxuriös

ply /plaɪ/ vt (pt/pp plied) ausüben (trade); ~ s.o. with drink jdm an den anderen eingießen. ~wood n Sperrholz nt

p.m. adv (abbr of post meridiem) nachmittags

pneumatic /nju:'mætɪk/ a pneumatisch. ~ 'drill n Presslufthammer m

pneumonia /nju:'məʊnɪə/ n Lungenentzündung f

poach /pəʊtʃ/ vt (Culin) pochieren; (steal) wildern. ~er n Wilddieb m

pocket /'pɒkɪt/ n Tasche f; ~ of resistance Widerstandsnest nt; be out of ~ [an einem Geschäft] verlieren □ vt einstecken. ~book n Notizbuch nt; (wallet) Brieftasche f. ~-money n Taschengeld nt

pock-marked /'pɒk-/ a pockennarbig

pod /pɒd/ n Hülse f

podgy /'pɒdʒɪ/ a (-ier, -iest) dick

poem /'pəʊɪm/ n Gedicht nt

poet /'pəʊɪt/ n Dichter(in) m(f). ~ic /-'etɪk/ a dichterisch

poetry /'pəʊɪtrɪ/ n Dichtung f

poignant /'pɔɪnjənt/ a ergreifend

point /pɔɪnt/ n Punkt m; (sharp end) Spitze f; (meaning) Sinn m; (purpose) Zweck m; (Electr) Steckdose f; ~s pl (Rail) Weiche f; ~ of view Standpunkt m; good/ bad ~s gute/schlechte Seiten; what is the ~? wozu? the ~ is es geht darum; I don't see the ~ das sehe ich nicht ein; up to a ~ bis zu einem gewissen Grade; be on the ~ of doing sth im Begriff sein, etw zu tun □ vt richten (at auf + acc); ausfugen (brickwork) □ vi deuten (at/to auf + acc); (with finger) mit dem Finger zeigen. ~ out vt zeigen auf (+ acc); ~ sth out to s.o. jdn auf etw (acc) hinweisen

point-'blank a aus nächster Entfernung; (fig) rundweg

point|ed /'pɔɪntɪd/ a spitz; (question) gezielt. ~er n (hint) Hinweis m. ~less a zwecklos, sinnlos

poise /pɔɪz/ n Haltung f. ~d a (confident) selbstsicher; ~d to bereit zu

poison /'pɔɪzn/ n Gift nt □ vt vergiften. ~ous a giftig

poke /pəʊk/ n Stoß m □ vt stoßen; schüren (fire); (put) stecken; ~ fun at sich lustig machen über (+ acc)

poker[1] /'pəʊkə(r)/ n Schüreisen nt

poker[2] n (Cards) Poker nt

poky /'pəʊkɪ/ a (-ier, -iest) eng

Poland /'pəʊlənd/ n Polen nt

polar /'pəʊlə(r)/ a Polar-. ~ 'bear n Eisbär m. ~ize vt polarisieren

Pole /pəʊl/ n Pole m/Polin f

pole[1] n Stange f

pole[2] n (Geog, Electr) Pol m

'polecat n Iltis m

'pole-star n Polarstern m

'pole-vault n Stabhochsprung m

police /pə'li:s/ npl Polizei f □ vt polizeilich kontrollieren

police: ~man n Polizist m. ~ state n Polizeistaat m. ~ station n Polizeiwache f. ~woman n Polizistin f

policy[1] /'pɒlɪsɪ/ n Politik f

policy[2] n (insurance) Police f

polio /'pəʊlɪəʊ/ n Kinderlähmung f

Polish /'pəʊlɪʃ/ a polnisch

polish /'pɒlɪʃ/ n (shine) Glanz m; (for shoes) [Schuh]creme f; (for floor) Bohnerwachs m; (for furniture) Politur f; (for silver) Putzmittel nt; (for nails) Lack m; (fig) Schliff m □ vt polieren; bohnern (floor). ~ off vt (fam) verputzen (food); erledigen (task)

polisher /'pɒlɪʃə(r)/ n (machine) Poliermaschine f; (for floor) Bohnermaschine f

polite /pə'laɪt/ a, -ly adv höflich. ~ness n Höflichkeit f

politic /'pɒlɪtɪk/ a ratsam

politic|al /pə'lɪtɪkl/ a, -ly adv politisch. ~ian /pɒlɪ'tɪʃn/ n Politiker(in) m(f)

politics /'pɒlɪtɪks/ n Politik f

polka /'pɒlkə/ n Polka f

poll /pəʊl/ n Abstimmung f; (election) Wahl f; [opinion] ~ [Meinungs]umfrage f; go to the ~s wählen □ vt erhalten (votes)

pollen /'pɒlən/ n Blütenstaub m, Pollen m

polling /'pəʊlɪŋ/: ~-booth n Wahlkabine f. ~-station n Wahllokal nt

'poll tax n Kopfsteuer f

pollutant /pə'lu:tənt/ n Schadstoff m

pollut|e /pə'lu:t/ vt verschmutzen. ~ion /-u:ʃn/ n Verschmutzung f

polo /'pəʊləʊ/ n Polo nt. ~-neck n Rollkragen m. ~ shirt n Polohemd nt

polyester /pɒlɪ'estə(r)/ n Polyester m

polystyrene /pɒlɪ'staɪri:n/ n Polystyrol nt; (for packing) Styropor (P) nt

polytechnic /pɒlɪ'teknɪk/ n ≈ technische Hochschule f

polythene /'pɒlɪθi:n/ n Polyäthylen nt. ~ bag n Plastiktüte f

polyun'saturated a mehrfach ungesättigt

pomegranate /'pɒmɪɡrænɪt/ n Granatapfel m

pomp /pɒmp/ n Pomp m

pompon /'pɒmpɒn/ n Pompon m

pompous /'pɒmpəs/ a, -ly adv großspurig

pond /pɒnd/ n Teich m

ponder /'pɒndə(r)/ vi nachdenken

ponderous /'pɒndərəs/ a schwerfällig

pong /pɒŋ/ n (fam) Mief m

pony /'pəʊnɪ/ n Pony nt. ~tail n Pferdeschwanz m. ~-trekking n Ponyreiten nt

poodle /'pu:dl/ n Pudel m

pool¹ /puːl/ n [Schwimm]becken nt; (pond) Teich m; (of blood) Lache f

pool² n (common fund) [gemeinsame] Kasse f; ~s pl [Fußball]toto nt □ vt zusammenlegen

poor /pʊə(r)/ a (-er, -est) arm; (not good) schlecht; in ~ health nicht gesund □ npl the ~ die Armen. ~ly a be ~ly krank sein □ adv ärmlich; (badly) schlecht

pop¹ /pɒp/ n Knall m; (drink) Brause f □ v (pt/pp popped) □ vt (fam: put) stecken (in in + acc) □ vi knallen; (burst) platzen. ~ in vi (fam) reinschauen. ~ out vi (fam) kurz rausgehen

pop² n (fam) Popmusik f, Pop m □ attrib Pop-

'popcorn n Puffmais m

pope /pəʊp/ n Papst m

poplar /'pɒplə(r)/ n Pappel f

poppy /'pɒpɪ/ n Mohn m

popular /'pɒpjʊlə(r)/ a beliebt, populär; (belief) volkstümlich. ~ity /-'lærətɪ/ n Beliebtheit f, Popularität f

populat|e /'pɒpjʊleɪt/ vt bevölkern. ~ion /-'leɪʃn/ n Bevölkerung f

porcelain /'pɔːsəlɪn/ n Porzellan nt

porch /pɔːtʃ/ n Vorbau m; (Amer) Veranda f

porcupine /'pɔːkjʊpaɪn/ n Stachelschwein nt

pore¹ /pɔː(r)/ n Pore f

pore² vi ~ over studieren

pork /pɔːk/ n Schweinefleisch nt

porn /pɔːn/ n (fam) Porno m

pornograph|ic /pɔːnə'græfɪk/ a pornographisch. ~y /-'nɒgrəfɪ/ n Pornographie f

porous /'pɔːrəs/ a porös

porpoise /'pɔːpəs/ n Tümmler m

porridge /'pɒrɪdʒ/ n Haferbrei m

port¹ /pɔːt/ n Hafen m; (town) Hafenstadt f

port² n (Naut) Backbord nt

port³ n (wine) Portwein m

portable /'pɔːtəbl/ a tragbar

porter /'pɔːtə(r)/ n Pförtner m; (for luggage) Gepäckträger m

portfolio /pɔːt'fəʊlɪəʊ/ n Mappe f; (Comm) Portefeuille nt

'porthole n Bullauge nt

portion /'pɔːʃn/ n Portion f; (part, share) Teil m

portly /'pɔːtlɪ/ a (-ier, -iest) beleibt

portrait /'pɔːtrɪt/ n Porträt nt

portray /pɔː'treɪ/ vt darstellen. ~al n Darstellung f

Portug|al /'pɔːtjʊgl/ n Portugal nt. ~uese /-'giːz/ a portugiesisch □ n Portugiese m /-giesin f

pose /pəʊz/ n Pose f □ vt aufwerfen (problem); stellen (question) □ vi posieren; (for painter) Modell stehen; ~ as sich ausgeben als

posh /pɒʃ/ a (fam) feudal

position /pə'zɪʃn/ n Platz m; (posture) Haltung f; (job) Stelle f; (situation) Lage f, Situation f; (status) Stellung f □ vt platzieren; ~ oneself sich stellen

positive /'pɒzətɪv/ a, -ly adv positiv; (definite) eindeutig; (real) ausgesprochen □ n Positiv nt

possess /pə'zes/ vt besitzen. ~ion /pə'zeʃn/ n Besitz m; ~ions pl Sachen pl

possess|ive /pə'zesɪv/ a Possessiv-; be ~ive zu sehr an jdm hängen. ~or n Besitzer m

possibility /pɒsə'bɪlətɪ/ n Möglichkeit f

possib|le /'pɒsəbl/ a möglich. ~ly adv möglicherweise; not ~ly unmöglich

post¹ /pəʊst/ n (pole) Pfosten m □ vt anschlagen (notice)

post² n (place of duty) Posten m; (job) Stelle f □ vt postieren; (transfer) versetzen

post³ n (mail) Post f; by ~ mit der Post □ vt aufgeben (letter); (send by ~) mit der Post schicken; keep s.o. ~ed jdn auf dem Laufenden halten

postage /'pəʊstɪdʒ/ n Porto nt. ~ stamp n Briefmarke f

postal /'pəʊstl/ a Post-. ~ order n ≈ Geldanweisung f

post: ~box n Briefkasten m. ~card n Postkarte f; (picture) Ansichtskarte f. ~code n Postleitzahl f. ~'date vt vordatieren

poster /'pəʊstə(r)/ n Plakat nt

posterior /pɒ'stɪərɪə(r)/ a hintere(r,s) □ n (fam) Hintern m

posterity /pɒ'sterətɪ/ n Nachwelt f

posthumous /'pɒstjʊməs/ a, -ly adv postum

post: ~man n Briefträger m. ~mark n Poststempel m

post-mortem /-'mɔːtəm/ n Obduktion f

'post office n Post f

postpone /pəʊst'pəʊn/ vt aufschieben; ~ until verschieben auf (+ acc). ~ment n Verschiebung f

postscript /'pəʊstskrɪpt/ n Nachschrift f

posture /'pɒstʃə(r)/ n Haltung f

post-'war a Nachkriegs-

posy /'pəʊzɪ/ n Sträußchen nt

pot /pɒt/ n Topf m; (for tea, coffee) Kanne f; ~s of money (fam) eine Menge Geld; go to ~ (fam) herunterkommen potassium /pə'tæsɪəm/ n Kalium nt

potato /pə'teɪtəʊ/ n (pl -es) Kartoffel f

poten|cy /'pəʊtənsɪ/ n Stärke f. ~t a stark

potential /pə'tenʃl/ a, -ly adv potenziell □ n Potenzial nt

pot: ~hole n Höhle f; (in road) Schlagloch nt. ~holer n Höhlenforscher m. ~shot n take a ~shot at schießen auf (+ acc)

potted /'pɒtɪd/ a eingemacht; (shortened) gekürzt. ~ 'plant n Topfpflanze f

potter¹ /'pɒtə(r)/ vi ~ [about] herumwerkeln

potter² n Töpfer(in) m(f). ~y n Töpferei f; (articles) Töpferwaren pl

potty /'pɒtɪ/ a (-ier, -iest) (fam) verrückt □ n Töpfchen nt

pouch /paʊtʃ/ n Beutel m

pouffe /puːf/ n Sitzkissen nt

poultry /'pəʊltrɪ/ n Geflügel nt

pounce /paʊns/ vi zuschlagen; ~ on sich stürzen auf (+ acc)

pound¹ /paʊnd/ n (money & 0,454 kg) Pfund nt

pound² vt hämmern □ vi (heart:) hämmern; (run heavily) stampfen

pour /pɔː(r)/ vt gießen; einschenken (drink) □ vi strömen; (with rain) gießen. ~ out vi ausströmen □ vt ausschütten; einschenken (drink)

pout /paʊt/ vi einen Schmollmund machen

poverty /'pɒvətɪ/ n Armut f

powder /'paʊdə(r)/ n Pulver nt; (cosmetic) Puder m □ vt pudern. ~y a pulverig

power /'paʊə(r)/ n Macht f; (strength) Kraft f; (Electr) Strom m; (nuclear) Energie f; (Math) Potenz f. ~ cut n Stromsperre f. ~ed a betrieben (by mit); ~ed by electricity mit Elektroantrieb. ~ful a mächtig; (strong) stark. ~less a machtlos. ~-station n Kraftwerk nt

practicable /'præktɪkəbl/ a durchführbar, praktikabel

practical /'præktɪkl/ a, -ly adv praktisch. ~ 'joke n Streich m

practice /'præktɪs/ n Praxis f; (custom) Brauch m; (habit) Gewohnheit f; (exercise) Übung f; (Sport) Training nt; in ~ (in reality) in der Praxis; out of ~ außer Übung; put into ~ ausführen

practise /'præktɪs/ vt üben; (carry out) praktizieren; ausüben (profession) □ vi üben; (doctor:) praktizieren. ~d a geübt

pragmatic /præg'mætɪk/ a, ~ally adv pragmatisch

praise /preɪz/ n Lob nt □ vt loben. ~worthy a lobenswert

pram /præm/ n Kinderwagen m

prance /prɑːns/ vi herumhüpfen; (horse:) tänzeln

prank /præŋk/ n Streich m

prattle /'prætl/ vi plappern

prawn /prɔːn/ n Garnele f, Krabbe f. ~ 'cocktail n Krabbencocktail m

pray /preɪ/ vi beten. ~er /preə(r)/ n Gebet nt; ~ers pl (service) Andacht f

preach /priːtʃ/ vt/i predigen. ~er n Prediger m

preamble /priː'æmbl/ n Einleitung f

pre-ar'range /priː-/ vt im Voraus arrangieren

precarious /prɪ'keərɪəs/ a, -ly adv unsicher

precaution /prɪ'kɔːʃn/ n Vorsichtsmaßnahme f; as a ~ zur Vorsicht. ~ary a Vorsichts-

precede /prɪ'siːd/ vt vorangehen (+ dat)

preceden|ce /'presɪdəns/ n Vorrang m. ~t n Präzedenzfall m

preceding /prɪ'siːdɪŋ/ a vorhergehend

precinct /'priːsɪŋkt/ n Bereich m; (traffic-free) Fußgängerzone f; (Amer: district) Bezirk m

precious /'preʃəs/ a kostbar; (style) preziös □ adv (fam) ~ little recht wenig

precipice /'presɪpɪs/ n Steilabfall m

precipitate¹ /prɪ'sɪpɪtət/ a voreilig

precipitat|e² /prɪ'sɪpɪteɪt/ vt schleudern; (fig: accelerate) beschleunigen. ~ion /-'teɪʃn/ n (Meteorol) Niederschlag m

précis /'preɪsiː/ n (pl précis /-siːz/) Zusammenfassung f

precis|e /prɪ'saɪs/ a, -ly adv genau. ~ion /-'sɪʒn/ n Genauigkeit f

preclude /prɪ'kluːd/ vt ausschließen

precocious /prɪ'kəʊʃəs/ a frühreif

pre|con'ceived /priː-/ a vorgefasst. ~con'ception n vorgefasste Meinung f

precursor /priː'kɜːsə(r)/ n Vorläufer m

predator /'predətə(r)/ n Raubtier m

predecessor /'priːdɪsesə(r)/ n Vorgänger(in) m(f)

predicament /prɪ'dɪkəmənt/ n Zwangslage f

predicat|e /'predɪkət/ n (Gram) Prädikat nt. ~ive /prɪ'dɪkətɪv/ a, -ly adv prädikativ

predict /prɪ'dɪkt/ vt voraussagen. ~able /-əbl/ a voraussehbar; (person) berechenbar. ~ion /-'dɪkʃn/ n Voraussage f

pre'dominant /prɪ-/ a vorherrschend. ~antly adv hauptsächlich, überwiegend. ~ate vi vorherrschen

pre-'eminent /priː-/ a hervorragend

pre-empt /priː'empt/ vt zuvorkommen (+ dat)

preen /priːn/ vt putzen; ~ oneself (fig) selbstgefällig tun

pre|fab /'pri:fæb/ n (fam) [einfaches] Fertighaus nt. ~'fabricated a vorgefertigt

preface /'prefis/ n Vorwort nt

prefect /'pri:fekt/ n Präfekt m

prefer /prɪ'fɜ:(r)/ vt (pt/pp preferred) vorziehen; I ~ to walk ich gehe lieber zu Fuß; I ~ wine ich trinke lieber Wein

prefera|ble /'prefərəbl/ a be ~ble vorzuziehen sein (to dat). ~bly adv vorzugsweise

preferen|ce /'prefərəns/ n Vorzug m. ~tial /-'renʃl/ a bevorzugt

prefix /'pri:fɪks/ n Vorsilbe f

pregnan|cy /'pregnənsɪ/ n Schwangerschaft f. ~t a schwanger; (animal) trächtig

prehi'storic /pri:-/ a prähistorisch

prejudice /'predʒʊdɪs/ n Vorurteil nt; (bias) Voreingenommenheit f □ vt einnehmen (against gegen). ~d a voreingenommen

preliminary /prɪ'lɪmɪnərɪ/ a Vor-

prelude /'prelju:d/ n Vorspiel nt

pre-'marital a vorehelich

premature /'premətjʊə(r)/ a vorzeitig; ⟨birth⟩ Früh-. ~ly adv zu früh

pre'meditated /pri:-/ a vorsätzlich

premier /'premɪə(r)/ a führend □ n (Pol) Premier[minister] m

première /'premɪeə(r)/ n Premiere f

premises /'premɪsɪz/ npl Räumlichkeiten pl; on the ~ im Haus

premiss /'premɪs/ n Prämisse f

premium /'pri:mɪəm/ n Prämie f; be at a ~ hoch im Kurs stehen

premonition /premə'nɪʃn/ n Vorahnung f

preoccupied /prɪ'ɒkjʊpaɪd/ a [in Gedanken] beschäftigt

prep /prep/ n (Sch) Hausaufgaben pl

pre-'packed /pri:-/ a abgepackt

preparation /prepə'reɪʃn/ n Vorbereitung f; (substance) Präparat nt

preparatory /prɪ'pærətrɪ/ a Vor- □ adv ~ to vor (+ dat)

prepare /prɪ'peə(r)/ vt vorbereiten; anrichten ⟨meal⟩ □ vi sich vorbereiten (for auf + acc); ~d to bereit zu

pre'pay /pri:-/ vt (pt/pp -paid) im Voraus bezahlen

preposition /prepə'zɪʃn/ n Präposition f

prepossessing /pri:pə'zesɪŋ/ a ansprechend

preposterous /prɪ'pɒstərəs/ a absurd

prerequisite /pri:'rekwɪzɪt/ n Voraussetzung f

prerogative /prɪ'rɒgətɪv/ n Vorrecht nt

Presbyterian /prezbɪ'tɪərɪən/ a presbyterianisch □ n Presbyterian(in) m(f)

prescribe /prɪ'skraɪb/ vt vorschreiben; (Med) verschreiben

prescription /prɪ'skrɪpʃn/ n (Med) Rezept nt

presence /'prezns/ n Anwesenheit f, Gegenwart f; ~ of mind Geistesgegenwart f

present[1] /'preznt/ a gegenwärtig; be ~ anwesend sein; (occur) vorkommen □ n Gegenwart f; (Gram) Präsens nt; at ~ zurzeit; for the ~ vorläufig

present[2] n (gift) Geschenk nt

present[3] /prɪ'zent/ vt überreichen; (show) zeigen; vorlegen ⟨cheque⟩; (introduce) vorstellen; ~ s.o. with sth jdm etw überreichen. ~able /-əbl/ a be ~able sich zeigen lassen können

presentation /prezn'teɪʃn/ n Überreichung f. ~ ceremony n Verleihungszeremonie f

presently /'prezntlɪ/ adv nachher; (Amer: now) zurzeit

preservation /prezə'veɪʃn/ n Erhaltung f

preservative /prɪ'zɜ:vətɪv/ n Konservierungsmittel nt

preserve /prɪ'zɜ:v/ vt erhalten; (Culin) konservieren; (bottle) einmachen □ n (Hunting & fig) Revier nt; (jam) Konfitüre f

preside /prɪ'zaɪd/ vi den Vorsitz haben (over bei)

presidency /'prezɪdənsɪ/ n Präsidentschaft f

president /'prezɪdənt/ n Präsident m; (Amer: chairman) Vorsitzende(r) m/f. ~ial /-'denʃl/ a Präsidenten-; (election) Präsidentschafts-

press /pres/ n Presse f □ vt/i drücken; drücken auf (+ acc) ⟨button⟩; pressen ⟨flower⟩; (iron) bügeln; (urge) bedrängen; ~ for drängen auf (+ acc); be ~ed for time in Zeitdruck sein. ~ on vi weitergehen; -fahren] weitermachen

press: ~ cutting n Zeitungsausschnitt m. ~ing a dringend. ~-stud n Druckknopf m. ~-up n Liegestütz m

pressure /'preʃə(r)/ n Druck m □ vt = pressurize. ~-cooker n Schnellkochtopf m. ~ group n Interessengruppe f

pressurize /'preʃəraɪz/ vt Druck ausüben auf (+ acc). ~d a Druck-

prestig|e /pre'sti:ʒ/ n Prestige nt. ~ious /-'stɪdʒəs/ a Prestige-

presumably /prɪ'zju:məblɪ/ adv vermutlich

presume /prɪ'zjuːm/ vt vermuten; ~ to do sth sich (dat) anmaßen, etw zu tun □ vi ~ on ausnutzen

presumpt|ion /prɪ'zʌmpʃn/ n Vermutung f; (boldness) Anmaßung f. ~uous /-'zʌmptjʊəs/ a, -ly adv anmaßend

presup'pose /priː-/ vt voraussetzen

pretence /prɪ'tens/ n Verstellung f; (pretext) Vorwand m; it's all ~ das ist alles gespielt

pretend /prɪ'tend/ vt (claim) vorgeben; ~ that so tun, als ob; ~ to be sich ausgeben als

pretentious /prɪ'tenʃəs/ a protzig

pretext /'priːtekst/ n Vorwand m

pretty /'prɪtɪ/ a (-ier, -iest), ~ily adv hübsch □ adv (fam: fairly) ziemlich

pretzel /'pretsl/ n Brezel f

prevail /prɪ'veɪl/ vi siegen; (custom:) vorherrschen; ~ on s.o. to do sth jdn dazu bringen, etw zu tun

prevalen|ce /'prevələns/ n Häufigkeit f. ~t a vorherrschend

prevent /prɪ'vent/ vt verhindern, verhüten; ~ s.o. [from] doing sth jdn daran hindern, etw zu tun. ~able /-əbl/ a vermeidbar. ~ion /-enʃn/ n Verhinderung f, Verhütung f. ~ive /-ɪv/ a vorbeugend

preview /'priːvjuː/ n Voraufführung f

previous /'priːvɪəs/ a vorhergehend; ~ to vor (+ dat). ~ly adv vorher, früher

pre-'war /priː-/ a Vorkriegs-

prey /preɪ/ n Beute f; bird of ~ Raubvogel m □ vi ~ on Jagd machen auf (+ acc); ~ on s.o.'s mind jdm schwer auf der Seele liegen

price /praɪs/ n Preis m □ vt (Comm) auszeichnen. ~less a unschätzbar; (fig) unbezahlbar

prick /prɪk/ n Stich m □ vt/i stechen; ~ up one's ears die Ohren spitzen

prickl|e /'prɪkl/ n Stachel m; (thorn) Dorn m. ~y a stachelig; (sensation) stechend

pride /praɪd/ n Stolz m; (arrogance) Hochmut m; (of lions) Rudel nt □ vt ~ oneself on stolz sein auf (+ acc)

priest /priːst/ n Priester m

prig /prɪg/ n Tugendbold m

prim /prɪm/ a (primmer, primmest) prüde

primarily /'praɪmərɪlɪ/ adv hauptsächlich, in erster Linie

primary /'praɪmərɪ/ a Haupt-. ~ school n Grundschule f

prime¹ /praɪm/ a Haupt-; (first-rate) erstklassig □ n be in one's ~ in den besten Jahren sein

prime² vt scharf machen (bomb); grundieren (surface); (fig) instruieren

Prime Minister /praɪ'mɪnɪstə(r)/ n Premierminister(in) m(f)

primeval /praɪ'miːvl/ a Ur-

primitive /'prɪmɪtɪv/ a primitiv

primrose /'prɪmrəʊz/ n gelbe Schlüsselblume f

prince /prɪns/ n Prinz m

princess /prɪn'ses/ n Prinzessin f

principal /'prɪnsəpl/ a Haupt- □ n (Sch) Rektor(in) m(f)

principality /prɪnsɪ'pælətɪ/ n Fürstentum nt

principally /'prɪnsəplɪ/ adv hauptsächlich

principle /'prɪnsəpl/ n Prinzip nt, Grundsatz m; in/on ~ im/aus Prinzip

print /prɪnt/ n Druck m; (Phot) Abzug m; in ~ gedruckt; (available) erhältlich; out of ~ vergriffen □ vt drucken; (write in capitals) in Druckschrift schreiben; (Computing) ausdrucken; (Phot) abziehen. ~ed matter n Drucksache f

print|er /'prɪntə(r)/ n Drucker m. ~ing n Druck m

'printout n (Computing) Ausdruck m

prior /'praɪə(r)/ a frühere(r,s); ~ to vor (+ dat)

priority /praɪ'ɒrətɪ/ n Priorität f, Vorrang m; (matter) vordringliche Sache f

prise /praɪz/ vt ~ open/up aufstemmen/ hochstemmen

prism /'prɪzm/ n Prisma nt

prison /'prɪzn/ n Gefängnis nt. ~er n Gefangene(r) m(f)

pristine /'prɪstiːn/ a tadellos

privacy /'prɪvəsɪ/ n Privatsphäre f; have no ~ nie für sich sein

private /'praɪvət/ a, -ly adv privat; (confidential) vertraulich; (car, secretary, school) Privat- □ n (Mil) [einfacher] Soldat m; in ~ privat; (confidentially) vertraulich

privation /praɪ'veɪʃn/ n Entbehrung f

privatize /'praɪvətaɪz/ vt privatisieren

privilege /'prɪvɪlɪdʒ/ n Privileg nt. ~d a privilegiert

privy /'prɪvɪ/ a be ~ to wissen

prize /praɪz/ n Preis m □ vt schätzen. ~giving n Preisverleihung f. ~-winner n Preisgewinner(in) m(f)

pro /prəʊ/ n (fam) Profi m; the ~s and cons das Für und Wider

probability /prɒbə'bɪlətɪ/ n Wahrscheinlichkeit f

probable /'prɒbəbl/ a, -bly adv wahrscheinlich

probation /prə'beɪʃn/ n (Jur) Bewährung f. ~ary a Probe-; ~ary period Probezeit f

probe /prəʊb/ n Sonde f; (fig: investigation) Untersuchung f □ vt/i ∼ [into] untersuchen

problem /'prɒbləm/ n Problem nt; (Math) Textaufgabe f. ∼atic /-'mætɪk/ a problematisch

procedure /prə'si:dʒə(r)/ n Verfahren nt

proceed /prə'si:d/ vi gehen; (in vehicle) fahren; (continue) weitergehen/-fahren; (speaking) fortfahren; (act) verfahren □ vt ∼ to do sth anfangen, etw zu tun

proceedings /prə'si:dɪŋz/ npl Verfahren nt; (Jur) Prozess m

proceeds /'prəʊsi:dz/ npl Erlös m

process /'prəʊses/ n Prozess m; (procedure) Verfahren nt; in the ∼ dabei □ vt verarbeiten; (Admin) bearbeiten; (Phot) entwickeln

procession /prə'seʃn/ n Umzug m, Prozession f

proclaim /prə'kleɪm/ vt ausrufen

proclamation /prɒklə'meɪʃn/ n Proklamation f

procure /prə'kjʊə(r)/ vt beschaffen

prod /prɒd/ n Stoß m □ vt stoßen; (fig) einen Stoß geben (+ dat)

prodigal /'prɒdɪgl/ a verschwenderisch

prodigious /prə'dɪdʒəs/ a gewaltig

prodigy /'prɒdɪdʒɪ/ n [infant] ∼ Wunderkind nt

produce[1] /'prɒdju:s/ n landwirtschaftliche Erzeugnisse pl

produce[2] /prə'dju:s/ vt erzeugen, produzieren; (manufacture) herstellen; (bring out) hervorholen; (cause) hervorrufen; inszenieren; (play), (Radio, TV) redigieren. ∼r n Erzeuger m, Produzent m; Hersteller m; (Theat) Regisseur m; (Radio, TV) Redakteur(in) m(f)

product /'prɒdʌkt/ n Erzeugnis nt, Produkt nt. ∼ion /prə'dʌkʃn/ n Produktion f; (Theat) Inszenierung f

productiv|e /prə'dʌktɪv/ a produktiv; ⟨land, talks⟩ fruchtbar. ∼ity /-'tɪvətɪ/ n Produktivität f

profan|e /prə'feɪn/ a weltlich; (blasphemous) [gottes]lästerlich. ∼ity /-'fænətɪ/ n (oath) Fluch m

profess /prə'fes/ vt behaupten; bekennen ⟨faith⟩

profession /prə'feʃn/ n Beruf m. ∼al a, -ly adv beruflich; (not amateur) Berufs-; (expert) fachmännisch; (Sport) professionell □ n Fachmann m; (Sport) Profi m

professor /prə'fesə(r)/ n Professor m

proficien|cy /prə'fɪʃnsɪ/ n Können nt. ∼t a be ∼t in beherrschen

profile /'prəʊfaɪl/ n Profil nt; (character study) Porträt nt

profit /'prɒfɪt/ n Gewinn m, Profit m □ vi ∼ from profitieren von. ∼able /-əbl/ a, -bly adv gewinnbringend; (fig) nutzbringend

profound /prə'faʊnd/ a, -ly adv tief

profus|e /prə'fju:s/ a, -ly adv üppig; (fig) überschwenglich. ∼ion /-ju:ʒn/ n in ∼ion in großer Fülle

progeny /'prɒdʒənɪ/ n Nachkommenschaft f

program /'prəʊgræm/ n Programm nt; □ vt (pt/pp programmed) programmieren

programme /'prəʊgræm/ n Programm nt; (Radio, TV) Sendung f. ∼r n (Computing) Programmierer(in) m(f)

progress[1] /'prəʊgres/ n Vorankommen nt; (fig) Fortschritt m; in ∼ im Gange; make ∼ (fig) Fortschritte machen

progress[2] /prə'gres/ vi vorankommen; (fig) fortschreiten. ∼ion /-eʃn/ n Folge f; (development) Entwicklung f

progressive /prə'gresɪv/ a fortschrittlich; ⟨disease⟩ fortschreitend. ∼ly adv zunehmend

prohibit /prə'hɪbɪt/ vt verbieten (s.o. jdm). ∼ive /-ɪv/ a unerschwinglich

project[1] /'prɒdʒekt/ n Projekt nt; (Sch) Arbeit f

project[2] /prə'dʒekt/ vt projizieren ⟨film⟩; (plan) planen □ vi (jut out) vorstehen

projectile /prə'dʒektaɪl/ n Geschoss nt

projector /prə'dʒektə(r)/ n Projektor m

proletariat /prəʊlɪ'teərɪət/ n Proletariat nt

prolific /prə'lɪfɪk/ a fruchtbar; (fig) produktiv

prologue /'prəʊlɒg/ n Prolog m

prolong /prə'lɒŋ/ vt verlängern

promenade /prɒmə'nɑ:d/ n Promenade f □ vi spazieren gehen

prominent /'prɒmɪnənt/ a vorstehend; (important) prominent; (conspicuous) auffällig; (place) gut sichtbar

promiscu|ity /prɒmɪ'skju:ətɪ/ n Promiskuität f. ∼ous /prə'mɪskjʊəs/ a be ∼ous häufig den Partner wechseln

promis|e /'prɒmɪs/ n Versprechen nt □ vt/i versprechen (s.o. jdm); the P∼ed Land das Gelobte Land. ∼ing a viel versprechend

promot|e /prə'məʊt/ vt befördern; (advance) fördern; (publicize) Reklame machen für; be ∼ed (Sport) aufsteigen. ∼ion /-əʊʃn/ n Beförderung f; (Sport) Aufstieg m; (Comm) Reklame f

prompt /prɒmpt/ a prompt, unverzüglich; (punctual) pünktlich □ adv pünktlich

□ *vt/i* veranlassen (to zu); (*Theat*) soufflieren (+ *dat*). ∼er *n* Souffleur *m*/Souffleuse *f*. ∼ly *adv* prompt

prone /prəʊn/ *a* be or lie ∼ auf dem Bauch liegen; be ∼ to neigen zu; be ∼ to do sth dazu neigen, etw zu tun

prong /prɒŋ/ *n* Zinke *f*

pronoun /'prəʊnaʊn/ *n* Fürwort *nt*, Pronomen *nt*

pronounce /prə'naʊns/ *vt* aussprechen; (*declare*) erklären. ∼d *a* ausgeprägt; (*noticeable*) deutlich. ∼ment *n* Erklärung *f*

pronunciation /prənʌnsɪ'eɪʃn/ *n* Aussprache *f*

proof /pruːf/ *n* Beweis *m*; (*Typ*) Korrekturbogen *m* □ *a* ∼ against water/theft wasserfest/diebessicher. ∼-reader *n* Korrektor *m*

prop[1] /prɒp/ *n* Stütze *f* □ *vt* (*pt/pp* propped) ∼ open offen halten; ∼ against (*lean*) lehnen an (+ *acc*). ∼ up *vt* stützen

prop[2] *n* (*Theat, fam*) Requisit *nt*

propaganda /prɒpə'gændə/ *n* Propaganda *f*

propagate /'prɒpəgeɪt/ *vt* vermehren; (*fig*) verbreiten, propagieren

propel /prə'pel/ *vt* (*pt/pp* propelled) [an]treiben. ∼ler *n* Propeller *m*. ∼ling 'pencil *n* Drehbleistift *m*

propensity /prə'pensətɪ/ *n* Neigung *f* (for zu)

proper /'prɒpə(r)/ *a*, -ly *adv* richtig; (*decent*) anständig. ∼ 'name, ∼ 'noun *n* Eigenname *m*

property /'prɒpətɪ/ *n* Eigentum *nt*; (*quality*) Eigenschaft *f*; (*Theat*) Requisit *nt*; (*land*) [Grund]besitz *m*; (*house*) Haus *nt*. ∼ market *n* Immobilienmarkt *m*

prophecy /'prɒfəsɪ/ *n* Prophezeiung *f*

prophesy /'prɒfɪsaɪ/ *vt* (*pt/pp* -ied) prophezeien

prophet /'prɒfɪt/ *n* Prophet *m*. ∼ic /prə'fetɪk/ *a* prophetisch

proportion /prə'pɔːʃn/ *n* Verhältnis *nt*; (*share*) Teil *m*; ∼s *pl* Proportionen; (*dimensions*) Maße. ∼al *a*, -ly *adv* proportional

proposal /prə'pəʊzl/ *n* Vorschlag *m*; (*of marriage*) [Heirats]antrag *m*

propose /prə'pəʊz/ *vt* vorschlagen; (*intend*) vorhaben; einbringen (*motion*); ausbringen (*toast*) □ *vi* einen Heiratsantrag machen

proposition /prɒpə'zɪʃn/ *n* Vorschlag *m*

propound /prə'paʊnd/ *vt* darlegen

proprietor /prə'praɪətə(r)/ *n* Inhaber(in) *m(f)*

propriety /prə'praɪətɪ/ *n* Korrektheit *f*; (*decorum*) Anstand *m*

propulsion /prə'pʌlʃn/ *n* Antrieb *m*

prosaic /prə'zeɪk/ *a* prosaisch

prose /prəʊz/ *n* Prosa *f*

prosecut|e /'prɒsɪkjuːt/ *vt* strafrechtlich verfolgen. ∼ion /-'kjuːʃn/ *n* strafrechtliche Verfolgung *f*; the ∼ion die Anklage. ∼or *n* [Public] P∼or Staatsanwalt *m*

prospect[1] /'prɒspekt/ *n* Aussicht *f*

prospect[2] /prə'spekt/ *vi* suchen (for nach)

prospect|ive /prə'spektɪv/ *a* (*future*) zukünftig. ∼or *n* Prospektor *m*

prospectus /prə'spektəs/ *n* Prospekt *m*

prosper /'prɒspə(r)/ *vi* gedeihen, florieren; (*person*) Erfolg haben. ∼ity /-'sperətɪ/ *n* Wohlstand *m*

prosperous /'prɒspərəs/ *a* wohlhabend

prostitut|e /'prɒstɪtjuːt/ *n* Prostituierte *f*. ∼ion /-'tjuːʃn/ *n* Prostitution *f*

prostrate /'prɒstreɪt/ *a* ausgestreckt; ∼ with grief (*fig*) vor Kummer gebrochen

protagonist /prəʊ'tægənɪst/ *n* Kämpfer *m*; (*fig*) Protagonist *m*

protect /prə'tekt/ *vt* schützen (from vor + *dat*); beschützen (*person*). ∼ion /-ʃn/ *n* Schutz *m*. ∼ive /-ɪv/ *a* Schutz-; (*fig*) beschützend. ∼or *n* Beschützer *m*

protégé /'prɒtɪʒeɪ/ *n* Schützling *m*, Protegé *m*

protein /'prəʊtiːn/ *n* Eiweiß *nt*

protest[1] /'prəʊtest/ *n* Protest *m*

protest[2] /prə'test/ *vi* protestieren

Protestant /'prɒtɪstənt/ *a* protestantisch, evangelisch □ *n* Protestant(in) *m(f)*, Evangelische(r) *m/f*

protester /prə'testə(r)/ *n* Protestierende(r) *m/f*

protocol /'prəʊtəkɒl/ *n* Protokoll *m*

prototype /'prəʊtə-/ *n* Prototyp *m*

protract /prə'trækt/ *vt* verlängern. ∼or *n* Winkelmesser *m*

protrude /prə'truːd/ *vi* [her]vorstehen

proud /praʊd/ *a*, -ly *adv* stolz (of auf + *acc*)

prove /pruːv/ *vt* beweisen □ *vi* ∼ to be sich erweisen als

proverb /'prɒvɜːb/ *n* Sprichwort *nt*. ∼ial /prə'vɜːbɪəl/ *a* sprichwörtlich

provide /prə'vaɪd/ *vt* zur Verfügung stellen; spenden (*shade*); ∼ s.o. with sth jdn mit etw versorgen *od* versehen □ *vi* ∼ for sorgen für

provided /prə'vaɪdɪd/ *conj* ∼ [that] vorausgesetzt [dass]

providing /prə'vaɪdɪŋ/ *conj* = provided

provid|ence /'prɒvɪdəns/ *n* Vorsehung *f*. ∼tial /-'denʃl/ *a* be ∼tial ein Glück sein

provinc|e /'prɒvɪns/ *n* Provinz *f*; (*fig*) Bereich *m*. ∼ial /prə'vɪnʃl/ *a* provinziell

provision /prə'vɪʒn/ n Versorgung f (of mit); ~s pl Lebensmittel pl. ~al a, -ly adv vorläufig

proviso /prə'vaɪzəʊ/ n Vorbehalt m

provocat|ion /prɒvə'keɪʃn/ n Provokation f. ~ive /prə'vɒkətɪv/ a, -ly adv provozierend; (sexually) aufreizend

provoke /prə'vəʊk/ vt provozieren; (cause) hervorrufen

prow /praʊ/ n Bug m

prowess /'praʊɪs/ n Kraft f

prowl /praʊl/ vi herumschleichen □ n be on the ~ herumschleichen

proximity /prɒk'sɪmətɪ/ n Nähe f

proxy /'prɒksɪ/ n Stellvertreter(in) m(f); (power) Vollmacht f

prude /pruːd/ n be a ~ prüde sein

pruden|ce /'pruːdns/ n Umsicht f. ~t a, -ly adv umsichtig; (wise) klug

prudish /'pruːdɪʃ/ a prüde

prune[1] /pruːn/ n Backpflaume f

prune[2] vt beschneiden

pry /praɪ/ vi (pt/pp pried) neugierig sein

psalm /sɑːm/ n Psalm m

pseudonym /'sjuːdənɪm/ n Pseudonym nt

psychiatric /saɪkɪ'ætrɪk/ a psychiatrisch

psychiatr|ist /saɪ'kaɪətrɪst/ n Psychiater(in) m(f). ~y n Psychiatrie f

psychic /'saɪkɪk/ a übersinnlich; I'm not ~ ich kann nicht hellsehen

psycho|'analyse /saɪkəʊ-/ vt psychoanalysieren. ~'nalysis n Psychoanalyse f. ~'analyst Psychoanalytiker(in) m(f)

psychological /saɪkə'lɒdʒɪkl/ a, -ly adv psychologisch; (illness) psychisch

psycholog|ist /saɪ'kɒlədʒɪst/ n Psychologe m/ -login f. ~y n Psychologie f

psychopath /'saɪkəpæθ/ n Psychopath(in) m(f)

P.T.O. abbr (please turn over) b.w.

pub /pʌb/ n (fam) Kneipe f

puberty /'pjuːbətɪ/ n Pubertät f

public /'pʌblɪk/ a, -ly adv öffentlich; make ~ publik machen □ n the ~ die Öffentlichkeit; in ~ in aller Öffentlichkeit

publican /'pʌblɪkən/ n [Gast]wirt m

publication /pʌblɪ'keɪʃn/ n Veröffentlichung f

public: ~ con'venience n öffentliche Toilette f. ~ 'holiday n gesetzlicher Feiertag m. ~ 'house n [Gast]wirtschaft f

publicity /pʌb'lɪsətɪ/ n Publicity f; (advertising) Reklame f

publicize /'pʌblɪsaɪz/ vt Reklame machen für

public: ~ 'library n öffentliche Bücherei f. ~ 'school n Privatschule f; (Amer)

staatliche Schule f. ~-'spirited a be ~-spirited Gemeinsinn haben. ~ 'transport n öffentliche Verkehrsmittel pl

publish /'pʌblɪʃ/ vt veröffentlichen. ~er n Verleger(in) m(f); (firm) Verlag m. ~ing n Verlagswesen nt

pucker /'pʌkə(r)/ vt kräuseln

pudding /'pʊdɪŋ/ n Pudding m; (course) Nachtisch m

puddle /'pʌdl/ n Pfütze f

puerile /'pjʊəraɪl/ a kindisch

puff /pʌf/ n (of wind) Hauch m; (of smoke) Wölkchen nt; (for powder) Quaste f □ vt blasen, pusten; ~ out ausstoßen □ vi keuchen; ~ at paffen an (+ dat) (pipe). ~ed a (out of breath) aus der Puste. ~ pastry n Blätterteig m

puffy /'pʌfɪ/ a geschwollen

pugnacious /pʌg'neɪʃəs/ a, -ly adv aggressiv

pull /pʊl/ n Zug m; (jerk) Ruck m; (fam: influence) Einfluss m □ vt ziehen; ziehen an (+ dat) (rope); ~ a muscle sich (dat) einen Muskel zerren; ~ oneself together sich zusammennehmen; ~ one's weight tüchtig mitarbeiten; ~ s.o.'s leg (fam) jdn auf den Arm nehmen. ~ down vt herunterziehen; (demolish) abreißen. ~ in vt hereinziehen □ vi (Auto) einscheren. ~ off vt abziehen; (fam) schaffen. ~ out vt herausziehen □ vi (Auto) ausscheren. ~ through vt durchziehen □ vi (recover) durchkommen. ~ up vt heraufziehen; ausziehen (plant); (reprimand) zurechtweisen □ vi (Auto) anhalten

pulley /'pʊlɪ/ n (Techn) Rolle f

pullover /'pʊləʊvə(r)/ n Pullover m

pulp /pʌlp/ n Brei m; (of fruit) [Frucht]fleisch nt

pulpit /'pʊlpɪt/ n Kanzel f

pulsate /pʌl'seɪt/ vi pulsieren

pulse /pʌls/ n Puls m

pulses /'pʌlsɪz/ npl Hülsenfrüchte pl

pulverize /'pʌlvəraɪz/ vt pulverisieren

pumice /'pʌmɪs/ n Bimsstein m

pummel /'pʌml/ vt (pt/pp pummelled) mit den Fäusten bearbeiten

pump /pʌmp/ n Pumpe f □ vt pumpen; (fam) aushorchen. ~ up vt hochpumpen; (inflate) aufpumpen

pumpkin /'pʌmpkɪn/ n Kürbis m

pun /pʌn/ n Wortspiel nt

punch[1] /pʌntʃ/ n Faustschlag m; (device) Locher m □ vt boxen; lochen (ticket); stanzen (hole)

punch[2] n (drink) Bowle f

punch: ~ line n Pointe f. ~-up n Schlägerei f

punctual /'pʌŋktjuəl/ a, -ly adv pünktlich. ~ity /-'ælətɪ/ n Pünktlichkeit f

punctuat|e /'pʌŋktjueɪt/ vt mit Satzzeichen versehen. ~ion /-'eɪʃn/ n Interpunktion f. ~ion mark n Satzzeichen nt

puncture /'pʌŋktʃə(r)/ n Loch nt; (tyre) Reifenpanne f □ vt durchstechen

pundit /'pʌndɪt/ n Experte m

pungent /'pʌndʒənt/ a scharf

punish /'pʌnɪʃ/ vt bestrafen. ~able /-əbl/ a strafbar. ~ment n Strafe f

punitive /'pju:nɪtɪv/ a Straf-

punnet /'pʌnɪt/ n Körbchen nt

punt /pʌnt/ n (boat) Stechkahn m

punter /'pʌntə(r)/ n (gambler) Wetter m; (client) Kunde m

puny /'pju:nɪ/ a (-ier, -iest) mickerig

pup /pʌp/ n = puppy

pupil /'pju:pl/ n Schüler(in) m(f); (of eye) Pupille f

puppet /'pʌpɪt/ n Puppe f; (fig) Marionette f

puppy /'pʌpɪ/ n junger Hund m

purchase /'pɜ:tʃəs/ n Kauf m; (leverage) Hebelkraft f □ vt kaufen. ~r n Käufer m

pure /pjʊə(r)/ a (-r, -st,) -ly adv rein

purée /'pjʊəreɪ/ n Püree nt, Brei m

purgatory /'pɜ:gətrɪ/ n (Relig) Fegefeuer nt; (fig) Hölle f

purge /pɜ:dʒ/ n (Pol) Säuberungsaktion f □ vt reinigen; (Pol) säubern

puri|fication /pjʊərɪfɪ'keɪʃn/ n Reinigung f. ~fy /'pjʊərɪfaɪ/ vt (pt/pp -ied) reinigen

puritanical /pjʊərɪ'tænɪkl/ a puritanisch

purity /'pjʊərɪtɪ/ n Reinheit f

purl /pɜ:l/ n (Knitting) linke Masche f □ vt/i links stricken

purple /'pɜ:pl/ a (dunkel)lila

purport /pə'pɔ:t/ vt vorgeben

purpose /'pɜ:pəs/ n Zweck m; (intention) Absicht f; (determination) Entschlossenheit f; on ~ absichtlich; to no ~ unnützerweise. ~ful a, -ly adv entschlossen. ~ly adv absichtlich

purr /pɜ:(r)/ vi schnurren

purse /pɜ:s/ n Portemonnaie nt; (Amer: handbag) Handtasche f □ vt schürzen ⟨lips⟩

pursue /pə'sju:/ vt verfolgen; (fig) nachgehen (+ dat). ~r /-ə(r)/ n Verfolger m

pursuit /pə'sju:t/ n Verfolgung f; Jagd f; (pastime) Beschäftigung f; in ~ hinterher

pus /pʌs/ n Eiter m

push /pʊʃ/ n Stoß m, (fam) Schubs m; get the ~ (fam) hinausfliegen □ vt/i schieben; (press) drücken; (roughly) stoßen; be

~ed for time (fam) unter Zeitdruck stehen. ~ off vt hinunterstoßen □ vi (fam: leave) abhauen. ~ on vi (continue) weitergehen/-fahren; (with activity) weitermachen. ~ up vt hochschieben; hochtreiben ⟨price⟩

push: ~-button n Druckknopf m. ~-chair n [Kinder]sportwagen m. ~-over n (fam) Kinderspiel nt. ~-up n (Amer) Liegestütz m

pushy /'pʊʃɪ/ a (fam) aufdringlich

puss /pʊs/ n, **pussy** /'pʊsɪ/ n Mieze f

put /pʊt/ vt (pt/pp put, pres p putting) tun; (place) setzen; (upright) stellen; (flat) legen; (express) ausdrücken; (say) sagen; (estimate) schätzen (at auf + acc); ~ aside or by beiseite legen; ~ one's foot down (fam) energisch werden; (Auto) Gas geben □ vi ~ to sea auslaufen □ a stay = bleiben. ~ away vt wegräumen. ~ back vt wieder hinsetzen/-stellen; zurückstellen ⟨clock⟩. ~ down vt hinsetzen/ -stellen/-legen; (suppress) niederschlagen; (kill) töten; (write) niederschreiben; (attribute) zuschreiben (to dat). ~ forward vt vorbringen; vorstellen ⟨clock⟩. ~ in vt hineinsetzen/-stellen/-legen; (insert) einstecken; (submit) einreichen □ vi ~ in for beantragen. ~ off vt ausmachen ⟨light⟩; (postpone) verschieben; ~ s.o. off (disconcert) jdn abbestellen; (disconcert) jdn aus der Fassung bringen; ~ s.o. off sth jdm etw verleiden. ~ on vt anziehen ⟨clothes, brake⟩; sich (dat) aufsetzen ⟨hat⟩; (Culin) aufsetzen; anmachen ⟨light⟩; aufführen ⟨play⟩; annehmen ⟨accent⟩; ~ on weight zunehmen. ~ out vt hinaussetzen/ -stellen/-legen; ausmachen ⟨fire, light⟩; ausstrecken ⟨hand⟩; (disconcert) aus der Fassung bringen; ~ s.o./oneself out jdm/sich Umstände machen. ~ through vt durchstecken; (Teleph) verbinden (to mit). ~ up vt errichten ⟨building⟩; aufschlagen ⟨tent⟩; aufspannen ⟨umbrella⟩; anschlagen ⟨notice⟩; erhöhen ⟨price⟩; unterbringen ⟨guest⟩; ~ s.o. up to sth jdn zu etw anstiften □ vi (at hotel) absteigen in (+ dat); ~ up with sth sich (dat) etw bieten lassen

putrefy /'pju:trɪfaɪ/ vi (pt/pp -ied) verwesen

putrid /'pju:trɪd/ a faulig

putty /'pʌtɪ/ n Kitt m

put-up /'pʊtʌp/ a a ~ job ein abgekartetes Spiel nt

puzzl|e /'pʌzl/ n Rätsel nt; (jigsaw) Puzzlespiel nt □ vt it ~es me es ist mir rätselhaft □ vi ~e over sich (dat) den Kopf zerbrechen über (+ acc). ~ing a rätselhaft

pyjamas /pə'dʒɑ:məz/ npl Schlafanzug m

pylon /'paɪlən/ n Mast m

pyramid /'pɪrəmɪd/ n Pyramide f

python /'paɪθn/ n Pythonschlange f

Q

quack[1] /kwæk/ n Quaken nt □ vi quaken

quack[2] n (doctor) Quacksalber m

quad /kwɒd/ n (fam: court) Hof m; ~s pl = quadruplets

quadrangle /'kwɒdræŋgl/ n Viereck nt; (court) Hof m

quadruped /'kwɒdrʊped/ n Vierfüßer m

quadruple /'kwɒdrʊpl/ a vierfach □ vt vervierfachen □ vi sich vervierfachen. ~ts /-plɪts/ npl Vierlinge pl

quagmire /'kwɒgmaɪə(r)/ n Sumpf m

quaint /kweɪnt/ a (-er, -est) malerisch; (odd) putzig

quake /kweɪk/ n (fam) Erdbeben nt □ vi beben; (with fear) zittern

Quaker /'kweɪkə(r)/ n Quäker(in) m(f)

qualif|ication /kwɒlɪfɪ'keɪʃn/ n Qualifikation f; (reservation) Einschränkung f. ~ied /-faɪd/ a qualifiziert; (trained) ausgebildet; (limited) bedingt

qualify /'kwɒlɪfaɪ/ v (pt/pp -ied) □ vt qualifizieren; (entitle) berechtigen; (limit) einschränken □ vi sich qualifizieren

quality /'kwɒlɪtɪ/ n Qualität f; (characteristic) Eigenschaft f

qualm /kwɑ:m/ n Bedenken pl

quandary /'kwɒndərɪ/ n Dilemma nt

quantity /'kwɒntətɪ/ n Quantität f, Menge f; in ~ in großen Mengen

quarantine /'kwɒrənti:n/ n Quarantäne f

quarrel /'kwɒrl/ n Streit m □ vi (pt/pp quarrelled) sich streiten. ~some a streitsüchtig

quarry[1] /'kwɒrɪ/ n (prey) Beute f

quarry[2] n Steinbruch m

quart /kwɔ:t/ n Quart nt

quarter /'kwɔ:tə(r)/ n Viertel nt; (of year) Vierteljahr nt; (Amer) 25-Cent-Stück nt; ~s pl Quartier nt; at [a] ~ to six um Viertel vor sechs; from all ~s aus allen Richtungen □ vt vierteln; (Mil) einquartieren (on bei). ~-'final n Viertelfinale nt

quarterly /'kwɔ:təlɪ/ a & adv vierteljährlich

quartet /kwɔ:'tet/ n Quartett nt

quartz /kwɔ:ts/ n Quarz m. ~ watch n Quarzuhr f

quash /kwɒʃ/ vt aufheben; niederschlagen ⟨rebellion⟩

quaver /'kweɪvə(r)/ n (Mus) Achtelnote f □ vi zittern

quay /ki:/ n Kai m

queasy /'kwi:zɪ/ a I feel ~ mir ist übel

queen /kwi:n/ n Königin f; (Cards, Chess) Dame f

queer /kwɪə(r)/ a (-er, -est) eigenartig; (dubious) zweifelhaft; (ill) unwohl; (fam: homosexual) schwul □ n (fam) Schwule(r) m

quell /kwel/ vt unterdrücken

quench /kwentʃ/ vt löschen

query /'kwɪərɪ/ n Frage f; (question mark) Fragezeichen nt □ vt (pt/pp -ied) infrage stellen; reklamieren ⟨bill⟩

quest /kwest/ n Suche f (for nach)

question /'kwestʃn/ n Frage f; (for discussion) Thema nt; out of the ~ ausgeschlossen; without ~ ohne Frage; the person in ~ die fragliche Person □ vt infrage stellen; ~ s.o. jdn ausfragen; (police:) jdn verhören. ~able a zweifelhaft. ~ mark n Fragezeichen nt

questionnaire /kwestʃə'neə(r)/ n Fragebogen m

queue /kju:/ n Schlange f □ vi ~ [up] Schlange stehen, sich anstellen (for nach)

quibble /'kwɪbl/ vi Haarspalterei treiben

quick /kwɪk/ a (-er, -est), -ly adv schnell; be ~! mach schnell! have a ~ meal schnell etwas essen □ adv schnell □ n cut to the ~ (fig) bis ins Mark getroffen. ~en vt beschleunigen □ vi sich beschleunigen

quick: ~sand n Treibsand m. ~-tempered a aufbrausend

quid /kwɪd/ n inv (fam) Pfund nt

quiet /'kwaɪət/ a (-er, -est), -ly adv still; (calm) ruhig; (soft) leise; keep ~ about ⟨fam⟩ nichts sagen von □ n Stille f, Ruhe f; on the ~ heimlich

quiet|en /'kwaɪətn/ vt beruhigen □ vi ~en down ruhig werden. ~ness n (see quiet) Stille f; Ruhe f

quill /kwɪl/ n Feder f; (spine) Stachel m

quilt /kwɪlt/ n Steppdecke f. ~ed a Steppquince /kwɪns/ n Quitte f

quins /kwɪnz/ npl (fam) = quintuplets

quintet /kwɪn'tet/ n Quintett nt

quintuplets /'kwɪntjʊplɪts/ npl Fünflinge pl

quip /kwɪp/ n Scherz m □ vi (pt/pp quipped) scherzen

quirk /kwɜ:k/ n Eigenart f

quit /kwɪt/ v (pt/pp quitted or quit) □ vt verlassen; (give up) aufgeben; ~ doing sth aufhören, etw zu tun □ vi gehen; give s.o. notice to ~ jdm die Wohnung kündigen

quite /kwaɪt/ adv ganz; (really) wirklich; ~ [so]! genau! ~ a few ziemlich viele

quits /kwɪts/ a quitt

quiver /'kwɪvə(r)/ vi zittern

quiz /kwɪz/ n Quiz nt □ vt (pt/pp quizzed) ausfragen. ~zical a, -ly adv fragend

quorum /'kwɔːrəm/ n have a ~ beschlussfähig sein

quota /'kwəʊtə/ n Anteil m; (Comm) Kontingent nt

quotation /kwəʊ'teɪʃn/ n Zitat nt; (price) Kostenvoranschlag m; (of shares) Notierung f. ~ marks npl Anführungszeichen pl

quote /kwəʊt/ n (fam) = quotation; in ~s in Anführungszeichen □ vt/i zitieren

R

rabbi /'ræbaɪ/ n Rabbiner m; (title) Rabbi m

rabbit /'ræbɪt/ n Kaninchen nt

rabble /'ræbl/ n the ~ der Pöbel

rabid /'ræbɪd/ a fanatisch; (animal) tollwütig

rabies /'reɪbiːz/ n Tollwut f

race¹ /reɪs/ n Rasse f

race² n Rennen nt; (fig) Wettlauf m □ vi [am Rennen] teilnehmen; (athlete, horse:) laufen; (fam: rush) rasen □ vt um die Wette laufen mit; an einem Rennen teilnehmen lassen (horse)

race: ~course n Rennbahn f. ~horse n Rennpferd nt. ~track n Rennbahn f

racial /'reɪʃl/ a, -ly adv rassisch; (discrimination, minority) Rassen-

racing /'reɪsɪŋ/ n Rennsport m; (horse-) Pferderennen nt. ~ car n Rennwagen m. ~ driver n Rennfahrer m

racis|m /'reɪsɪzm/ n Rassismus m. ~t /-ɪst/ a rassistisch □ n Rassist m

rack¹ /ræk/ n Ständer m; (for plates) Gestell nt □ vt ~ one's brains sich (dat) den Kopf zerbrechen

rack² n go to ~ and ruin verfallen; (fig) herunterkommen

racket¹ /'rækɪt/ n (Sport) Schläger m

racket² n (din) Krach m; (swindle) Schwindelgeschäft nt

racy /'reɪsɪ/ a (-ier, -iest) schwungvoll; (risqué) gewagt

radar /'reɪdɑː(r)/ n Radar m

radian|ce /'reɪdɪəns/ n Strahlen nt. ~ly adv strahlend

radiat|e /'reɪdɪeɪt/ vt ausstrahlen □ vi (heat:) ausgestrahlt werden; (roads:) strahlenförmig ausgehen. ~ion /-'eɪʃn/ n Strahlung f

radiator /'reɪdɪeɪtə(r)/ n Heizkörper m; (Auto) Kühler m

radical /'rædɪkl/ a, -ly adv radikal □ n Radikale(r) m/f

radio /'reɪdɪəʊ/ n Radio nt; by ~ über Funk □ vt funken (message)

radio|'active a radioaktiv. ~ac'tivity n Radioaktivität f

radiography /reɪdɪ'ɒɡrəfɪ/ n Röntgenographie f

'radio ham n Hobbyfunker m

radio'therapy n Strahlenbehandlung f

radish /'rædɪʃ/ n Radieschen nt

radius /'reɪdɪəs/ n (pl -dii /-dɪaɪ/) Radius m, Halbmesser m

raffle /'ræfl/ n Tombola f □ vt verlosen

raft /rɑːft/ n Floß nt

rafter /'rɑːftə(r)/ n Dachsparren m

rag¹ /ræɡ/ n Lumpen m; (pej: newspaper) Käseblatt nt; in ~s in Lumpen

rag² vt (pt/pp ragged) (fam) aufziehen

rage /reɪdʒ/ n Wut f; all the ~ (fam) der letzte Schrei □ vi rasen; (storm:) toben

ragged /'ræɡɪd/ a zerlumpt; (edge) ausgefranst

raid /reɪd/ n Überfall m; (Mil) Angriff m; (police) Razzia f □ vt überfallen; (Mil) angreifen; (police) eine Razzia durchführen in (+ dat); (break in) eindringen in (+ acc). ~er n Eindringling m; (of bank) Bankräuber m

rail /reɪl/ n Schiene f; (pole) Stange f; (hand~) Handlauf m; (Naut) Reling f; by ~ mit der Bahn

railings /'reɪlɪŋz/ npl Geländer nt

'railroad n (Amer) = railway

'railway n [Eisen]bahn f. ~man n Eisenbahner m. ~ station n Bahnhof m

rain /reɪn/ n Regen m □ vi regnen

rain: ~bow n Regenbogen m. ~check n (Amer) take a ~check on aufschieben. ~coat n Regenmantel m. ~fall n Niederschlag m

rainy /'reɪnɪ/ a (-ier, -iest) regnerisch

raise /reɪz/ n (Amer) Lohnerhöhung f □ vt erheben; (upright) aufrichten; (make higher) erhöhen; (lift) [hoch]heben; lüften (hat); aufziehen (children, animals); aufwerfen (question); aufbringen (money)

raisin /'reɪzn/ n Rosine f

rake /reɪk/ n Harke f, Rechen m □ vt harken, rechen. ~ up vt zusammenharken; (fam) wieder aufführen 'rake-off *n (fam)* Prozente *pl*

rally /'rælɪ/ *n* Versammlung *f*; *(Auto)* Rallye *f*; *(Tennis)* Ballwechsel *m* □ *vt* sammeln; □ *vi* sich sammeln; *(recover strength)* sich erholen

ram /ræm/ *n* Schafbock *m*; *(Astr)* Widder *m* □ *vt (pt/pp* rammed) rammen

rambl|e /'ræmbl/ *n* Wanderung *f* □ *vi* wandern; *(in speech)* irrereden. ~er *n* Wanderer *m*; *(rose)* Kletterrose *f*. ~ing *a* weitschweifig; *(club)* Wander-

ramp /ræmp/ *n* Rampe *f*; *(Aviat)* Gangway *f*

rampage¹ /'ræmpeɪdʒ/ *n* be/go on the ~ randalieren

rampage² /ræm'peɪdʒ/ *vi* randalieren

rampant /'ræmpənt/ *a* weit verbreitet; *(in heraldry)* aufgerichtet

rampart /'ræmpɑ:t/ *n* Wall *m*

ramshackle /'ræmʃækl/ *a* baufällig

ran /ræn/ *see* run

ranch /rɑ:ntʃ/ *n* Ranch *f*

rancid /'rænsɪd/ *a* ranzig

rancour /'ræŋkə(r)/ *n* Groll *m*

random /'rændəm/ *a* willkürlich; a ~ sample eine Stichprobe □ *n* at ~ aufs Geratewohl; *(choose)* willkürlich

randy /'rændɪ/ *a (-ier, -iest) (fam)* geil

rang /ræŋ/ *see* ring²

range /reɪndʒ/ *n* Serie *f*, Reihe *f*; *(Comm)* Auswahl *f*, Angebot *nt* (of an + *dat*); *(of mountains)* Kette *f*; *(Mus)* Umfang *m*; *(distance)* Reichweite *f*; *(for shooting)* Schießplatz *m*; *(stove)* Kohlenherd *m*; at a ~ of auf eine Entfernung von; ~ from ... to gehen von ... bis. ~r *n* Aufseher *m*

rank¹ /ræŋk/ *n (row)* Reihe *f*; *(Mil)* Rang *m*; *(social position)* Stand *m*; the ~ and file die breite Masse; the ~s *pl* die gemeinen Soldaten □ *vt/i* einstufen; ~ among zählen zu

rank² *a (bad)* übel; *(plants)* üppig; *(fig)* krass

ransack /'rænsæk/ *vt* durchwühlen; *(pillage)* plündern

ransom /'rænsəm/ *n* Lösegeld *nt*; hold s.o. to ~ Lösegeld für jdn fordern

rant /rænt/ *vi* rasen

rap /ræp/ *n* Klopfen *nt*; *(blow)* Schlag *m* □ *v (pt/pp* rapped) □ *vt* klopfen auf (+ *acc*) □ *vi* ~ at/on klopfen an/auf (+ *acc*)

rape¹ /reɪp/ *n (Bot)* Raps *m*

rape² *n* Vergewaltigung *f* □ *vt* vergewaltigen

rapid /'ræpɪd/ *a, -ly adv* schnell. ~ity /rə'pɪdətɪ/ *n* Schnelligkeit *f*

rapids /'ræpɪdz/ *npl* Stromschnellen *pl*

rapist /'reɪpɪst/ *n* Vergewaltiger *m*

rapport /ræ'pɔ:(r)/ *n* [innerer] Kontakt *m*

rapt /ræpt/ *a, -ly adv* gespannt; *(look)* andächtig; ~ in versunken in (+ *acc*)

raptur|e /'ræptʃə(r)/ *n* Entzücken *nt*. ~ous /-rəs/ *a, -ly adv* begeistert

rare¹ /reə(r)/ *a (-r, -st), -ly adv* selten

rare² *a (Culin)* englisch gebraten

rarefied /'reərɪfaɪd/ *a* dünn

rarity /'reərətɪ/ *n* Seltenheit *f*

rascal /'rɑ:skl/ *n* Schlingel *m*

rash¹ /ræʃ/ *n (Med)* Ausschlag *m*

rash² *a (-er, -est), -ly adv* voreilig

rasher /'ræʃə(r)/ *n* Speckscheibe *f*

rasp /rɑ:sp/ *n* Raspel *f*

raspberry /'rɑ:zbərɪ/ *n* Himbeere *f*

rat /ræt/ *n* Ratte *f*; *(person)* Schuft *m*; smell a ~ *(fam)* Lunte riechen

rate /reɪt/ *n* Rate *f*; *(speed)* Tempo *nt*; *(of payment)* Satz *m*; *(of exchange)* Kurs *m*; ~s *pl (taxes)* ≈ Grundsteuer *f*; at any ~ auf jeden Fall; at this ~ auf diese Weise □ *vt* einschätzen; ~ among zählen zu □ *vi* ~ as gelten als

rather /'rɑ:ðə(r)/ *adv* lieber; *(fairly)* ziemlich; ~! und ob!

rati|fication /rætɪfɪ'keɪʃn/ *n* Ratifizierung *f*. ~fy /'rætɪfaɪ/ *vt (pt/pp* -ied) ratifizieren

rating /'reɪtɪŋ/ *n* Einschätzung *f*; *(class)* Klasse *f*; *(sailor)* [einfacher] Matrose *m*; ~s *pl (Radio, TV)* ≈ Einschaltquote *f*

ratio /'reɪʃɪəʊ/ *n* Verhältnis *nt*

ration /'ræʃn/ *n* Ration *f* □ *vt* rationieren

rational /'ræʃənl/ *a, -ly adv* rational. ~ize *vt/i* rationalisieren

'rat race *n (fam)* Konkurrenzkampf *m*

rattle /'rætl/ *n* Rasseln *nt*; *(of china, glass)* Klirren *nt*; *(of windows)* Klappern *nt*; *(toy)* Klapper *f* □ *vi* rasseln; klirren; klappern □ *vt* rasseln mit; *(shake)* schütteln. ~ off *vt* herunterrasseln

'rattlesnake *n* Klapperschlange *f*

raucous /'rɔ:kəs/ *a* rau

ravage /'rævɪdʒ/ *vt* verwüsten, verheeren

rave /reɪv/ *vi* toben; ~ about schwärmen von

raven /'reɪvn/ *n* Rabe *m*

ravenous /'rævənəs/ *a* heißhungrig

ravine /rə'vi:n/ *n* Schlucht *f*

raving /'reɪvɪŋ/ *a* ~ mad *(fam)* total verrückt

ravishing /'rævɪʃɪŋ/ *a* hinreißend

raw /rɔ:/ *a (-er, -est)* roh; *(not processed)* Roh-; *(skin)* wund; *(weather)* nasskalt; *(inexperienced)* unerfahren; get a ~ deal *(fam)* schlecht wegkommen. ~ ma'terials *npl* Rohstoffe *pl* ray /reɪ/ n Strahl m; ~ of hope Hoffnungs-schimmer m

raze /reɪz/ vt ~ to the ground dem Erd-boden gleichmachen

razor /'reɪzə(r)/ n Rasierapparat m. ~blade n Rasierklinge f

re /riː/ prep betreffs (+ gen)

reach /riːtʃ/ n Reichweite f; (of river) Stre-cke f; within/out of ~ within/außer Reichweite; within easy ~ leicht erreich-bar □ vt erreichen; (arrive at) ankommen in (+ dat); (~ as far as) reichen bis zu; kommen zu ⟨decision, conclusion⟩; (pass) reichen □ vi reichen (to bis zu); ~ for greifen nach; I can't ~ ich komme nicht daran

re'act /rɪ-/ vi reagieren (to auf + acc)

re'action /rɪ-/ n Reaktion f. ~ary a reak-tionär

reactor /rɪ'æktə(r)/ n Reaktor m

read /riːd/ vt/i (pt/pp read /red/) lesen; (aloud) vorlesen (to dat); (Univ) studieren; ablesen ⟨meter⟩. ~ out vt vorlesen

readable /'riːdəbl/ a lesbar

reader /'riːdə(r)/ n Leser(in) m(f); (book) Lesebuch nt

readi|ly /'redɪlɪ/ adv bereitwillig; (easily) leicht. ~ness n Bereitschaft f; in ~ness bereit

reading /'riːdɪŋ/ n Lesen nt; (Pol, Relig) Lesung f

rea'djust /riː-/ vt neu einstellen □ vi sich umstellen (to auf + acc)

ready /'redɪ/ a (-ier, -iest) fertig; (willing) bereit; (quick) schnell; get ~ sich fertig machen; (prepare to) sich bereitmachen

ready: ~-'made a fertig. ~ 'money n Bar-geld nt. ~-to-'wear a Konfektions-

real /rɪəl/ a wirklich; (genuine) echt; (ac-tual) eigentlich □ adv ⟨Amer, fam⟩ echt. ~ estate n Immobilien pl

realis|m /'rɪəlɪzm/ n Realismus m. ~t /-lɪst/ n Realist m. ~tic /-'lɪstɪk/ a, -ally adv realistisch

reality /rɪ'ælətɪ/ n Wirklichkeit f, Realität f

realization /rɪəlaɪ'zeɪʃn/ n Erkenntnis f

realize /'rɪəlaɪz/ vt einsehen; (become aware) gewahr werden; verwirklichen ⟨hopes, plans⟩; (Comm) realisieren; ein-bringen ⟨price⟩; I didn't ~ das wusste ich nicht

really /'rɪəlɪ/ adv wirklich; (actually) ei-gentlich

realm /relm/ n Reich nt

realtor /'riːəltə(r)/ n (Amer) Immobilien-makler m

reap /riːp/ vt ernten

reap'pear /riː-/ vi wiederkommen

rear[1] /rɪə(r)/ a Hinter-; (Auto) Heck- □ n the ~ der hintere Teil; from the ~ von hinten

rear[2] vt aufziehen □ vi ~ [up] ⟨horse:⟩ sich aufbäumen

'rear-light n Rücklicht nt

re'arm /riː-/ vi wieder aufrüsten

rear'range /riː-/ vt umstellen

rear-view 'mirror n (Auto) Rückspiegel m

reason /'riːzn/ n Grund m; (good sense) Vernunft f; (ability to think) Verstand m; within ~ in vernünftigen Grenzen □ vi argumentieren; ~ with s.o. jdm gut zu-reden. ~able /-əbl/ a vernünftig; (not expen-sive) preiswert. ~ably /-əblɪ/ adv (fairly) ziemlich

reas'sur|ance /riː-/ n Beruhigung f; Ver-sicherung f. ~e vt beruhigen; ~e s.o. of sth jdm etw ⟨gen⟩ versichern

rebate /'riːbeɪt/ n Rückzahlung f; (dis-count) Nachlass m

rebel[1] /'rebl/ n Rebell m

rebel[2] /rɪ'bel/ vi (pt/pp rebelled) re-bellieren. ~lion /-lɪən/ n Rebellion f. ~li-ous /-lɪəs/ a rebellisch

re'bound[1] /rɪ-/ vi abprallen

'rebound[2] /riː-/ n Rückprall m

rebuff /rɪ'bʌf/ n Abweisung f □ vt abweisen; eine Abfuhr erteilen (s.o. jdm)

re'build /riː-/ vt (pt/pp -built) wieder auf-bauen

rebuke /rɪ'bjuːk/ n Tadel m □ vt tadeln

rebuttal /rɪ'bʌtl/ n Widerlegung f

re'call /rɪ-/ n Erinnerung f; beyond ~ unwiderruflich □ vt zurückrufen; ab-berufen ⟨diplomat⟩; vorzeitig einberufen ⟨parliament⟩; (remember) sich erinnern an (+ acc)

recant /rɪ'kænt/ vi widerrufen

recap /'riːkæp/ vt/i (fam) = recapitulate

recapitulate /riːkə'pɪtjʊleɪt/ vt/i zusam-menfassen; rekapitulieren

re'capture /riː-/ vt wieder gefangen neh-men ⟨person⟩; wieder einfangen ⟨animal⟩

recede /rɪ'siːd/ vi zurückgehen. ~ing a ⟨forehead, chin⟩ fliehend; ~ing hair lichter werdendes Haar Stirnglatze f

receipt /rɪ'siːt/ n Quittung f; (receiving) Empfang m; ~s pl (Comm) Einnahmen pl

receive /rɪ'siːv/ vt erhalten, bekommen; empfangen ⟨guests⟩. ~r n (Teleph) Hörer m; (Radio, TV) Empfänger m; (of stolen goods) Hehler m

recent /'riːsnt/ a kürzlich erfolgte(r,s). ~ly adv in letzter Zeit; (the other day) kürzlich, vor kurzem

receptacle /rɪ'septəkl/ n Behälter m

reception /rɪ'sepʃn/ n Empfang m; ~
[desk] (in hotel) Rezeption f. ~ist n
Empfangsdame f

receptive /rɪ'septɪv/ a aufnahmefähig; ~
to empfänglich für

recess /rɪ'ses/ n Nische f; (holiday) Ferien
pl; (Amer, Sch) Pause f

recession /rɪ'seʃn/ n Rezession f

re'charge /rɪ-/ vt [wieder] aufladen

recipe /'resɪpɪ/ n Rezept nt

recipient /rɪ'sɪpɪənt/ n Empfänger m

recipro|cal /rɪ'sɪprəkl/ a gegenseitig.
~cate /-keɪt/ vt erwidern

recital /rɪ'saɪtl/ n (of poetry, songs) Vortrag
m; (on piano) Konzert nt

recite /rɪ'saɪt/ vt aufsagen; (before audience) vortragen; (list) aufzählen

reckless /'reklɪs/ a, -ly adv leichtsinnig;
(careless) rücksichtslos. ~ness n Leichtsinn m; Rücksichtslosigkeit f

reckon /'rekn/ vt zählen; (consider)
glauben □ vi ~ on/with rechnen mit

re'claim /rɪ-/ vt zurückfordern; zurück-
gewinnen (land)

reclin|e /rɪ'klaɪn/ vi liegen. ~ing seat n
Liegesitz m

recluse /rɪ'klu:s/ n Einsiedler(in) m(f)

recognition /rekəg'nɪʃn/ n Erkennen nt;
(acknowledgement) Anerkennung f; in ~
als Anerkennung (of gen); be beyond ~
nicht wieder zu erkennen sein

recognize /'rekəgnaɪz/ vt erkennen;
(know again) wieder erkennen; (acknowledge) anerkennen

re'coil /rɪ-/ vi zurückschnellen; (in fear)
zurückschrecken

recollect /rekə'lekt/ vt sich erinnern an
(+ acc). ~ion /-ekʃn/ n Erinnerung f

recommend /rekə'mend/ vt empfehlen.
~ation /-'deɪʃn/ n Empfehlung f

recompense /'rekəmpens/ n Entschädigung f □ vt entschädigen

recon|cile /'rekənsaɪl/ vt versöhnen;
~cile oneself to sich abfinden mit. ~
ciliation /-sɪlɪ'eɪʃn/ n Versöhnung f

recon'dition /ri:-/ vt generalüberholen.
~ed engine n Austauschmotor m

reconnaissance /rɪ'kɒnɪsns/ n (Mil) Aufklärung f

reconnoitre /rekə'nɔɪtə(r)/ vi (pres p
-tring) auf Erkundung ausgehen

recon'sider /ri:-/ vt sich (dat) noch einmal überlegen

recon'struct /ri:-/ vt wieder aufbauen;
rekonstruieren (crime). ~ion n Wiederaufbau m; Rekonstruktion f

record¹ /rɪ'kɔ:d/ vt aufzeichnen; (register)
registrieren; (on tape) aufnehmen

record² /'rekɔ:d/ n Aufzeichnung f; (Jur)
Protokoll nt; (Mus) [Schall]platte f;
(Sport) Rekord m; ~s pl Unterlagen pl;
keep a ~ of sich (dat) notieren; off the
~ inoffiziell; have a [criminal] ~ vorbestraft sein

recorder /rɪ'kɔ:də(r)/ n (Mus) Blockflöte
f

recording /rɪ'kɔ:dɪŋ/ n Aufzeichnung f,
Aufnahme f

'record-player n Plattenspieler m

recount /rɪ'kaunt/ vt erzählen

re-'count¹ /ri:-/ vt nachzählen

're-count² /ri:-/ n (Pol) Nachzählung f

recoup /rɪ'ku:p/ vt wieder einbringen;
ausgleichen (losses)

recourse /rɪ'kɔ:s/ n have ~ to Zuflucht
nehmen zu

re-'cover /ri:-/ vt neu beziehen

recover /rɪ'kʌvə(r)/ vt zurückbekommen;
bergen (wreck) □ vi sich erholen. ~y n
Wiedererlangung f; Bergung f; (of health)
Erholung f

recreation /rekrɪ'eɪʃn/ n Erholung f;
(hobby) Hobby nt. ~al a Freizeit-; be ~al
erholsam sein

recrimination /rɪkrɪmɪ'neɪʃn/ n Gegen-
beschuldigung f

recruit /rɪ'kru:t/ n (Mil) Rekrut m; new
~ (member) neues Mitglied nt; (worker)
neuer Mitarbeiter m □ vt anwerben;
anwerben (staff). ~ment n Rekrutierung
f; Anwerbung f

rectang|le /'rektæŋgl/ n Rechteck nt. ~u-
lar /-'tæŋgjʊlə(r)/ a rechteckig

rectify /'rektɪfaɪ/ vt (pt/pp -ied) berichtigen

rector /'rektə(r)/ n Pfarrer m; (Univ)
Rektor m. ~y n Pfarrhaus nt

recuperat|e /rɪ'kju:pəreɪt/ vi sich er-
holen. ~ion /-'reɪʃn/ n Erholung f

recur /rɪ'kɜ:(r)/ vi (pt/pp recurred) sich
wiederholen; (illness:) wiederkehren

recurren|ce /rɪ'kʌrəns/ n Wiederkehr f.
~t a wiederkehrend

recycle /ri:'saɪkl/ vt wieder verwerten. ~d
paper n Umweltschutzpapier nt

red /red/ a (redder, reddest) rot □ n Rot
nt. ~currant n rote Johannisbeere f

redd|en /'redn/ vt röten □ vi rot werden.
~ish a rötlich

re'decorate /ri:-/ vt renovieren; (paint)
neu streichen; (wallpaper) neu tapezieren

redeem /rɪ'di:m/ vt einlösen; (Relig) erlö-
sen

redemption /rɪ'dempʃn/ n Erlösung f

rede'ploy /ri:-/ vt an anderer Stelle einsetzen

red: ~-haired *a* rothaarig. ~-'handed *a* catch s.o. ~-handed jdn auf frischer Tat ertappen. ~ 'herring *n* falsche Spur *f*. ~-hot *a* glühend heiß. R~ 'Indian *n* Indianer(in) *m(f)*

redi'rect /ri-/ *vt* nachsenden ⟨*letter*⟩; umleiten ⟨*traffic*⟩

red: ~ 'light *n* (*Auto*) rote Ampel *f*. ~ness *n* Röte *f*

re'do /ri:-/ *vt* (*pt* -did, *pp* -done) noch einmal machen

re'double /ri:-/ *vt* verdoppeln

redress /rɪ'dres/ *n* Entschädigung *f* □ *vt* wieder gutmachen; wiederherstellen ⟨*balance*⟩

red 'tape *n* (*fam*) Bürokratie *f*

reduc|e /rɪ'dju:s/ *vt* verringern, vermindern; (*in size*) verkleinern; ermäßigen ⟨*costs*⟩; herabsetzen ⟨*price, goods*⟩; (*Culin*) einkochen lassen. ~tion /-'dʌkʃn/ *n* Verringerung *f*; (*in price*) Ermäßigung *f*; (*in size*) Verkleinerung *f*

redundan|cy /rɪ'dʌndənsɪ/ *n* Beschäftigungslosigkeit *f*; ⟨*payment*⟩ Abfindung *f*. ~t *a* überflüssig; make ~t entlassen; be made ~t beschäftigungslos werden

reed /ri:d/ *n* [Schilf]rohr *nt*; ~s *pl* Schilf *nt*

reef /ri:f/ *n* Riff *nt*

reek /ri:k/ *vi* riechen (of nach)

reel /ri:l/ *n* Rolle *f*, Spule *f* □ *vi* (*stagger*) taumeln □ *vt* ~ off ⟨*fig*⟩ herunterrasseln

refectory /rɪ'fektərɪ/ *n* Refektorium *nt*; (*Univ*) Mensa *f*

refer /rɪ'fɜ:/ *v* (*pt/pp* referred) □ *vt* verweisen (to an + *acc*); übergeben, weiterleiten ⟨*matter*⟩ (to an + *acc*) □ *vi* ~ to sich beziehen auf (+ *acc*); (*mention*) erwähnen; (*concern*) betreffen; (*consult*) sich wenden an (+ *acc*); nachschlagen in (+ *dat*) ⟨*book*⟩; are you ~ring to me? meinen Sie mich?

referee /refə'ri:/ *n* Schiedsrichter *m*; (*Boxing*) Ringrichter *m*; (*for job*) Referenz *f* □ *vt/i* (*pt/pp* refereed) Schiedsrichter/ Ringrichter sein (bei)

reference /'refərəns/ *n* Erwähnung *f*; (*in book*) Verweis *m*; (*for job*) Referenz *f*; (*Comm*) 'your ~' Ihr Zeichen'; with ~ to in Bezug auf (+ *acc*) □ *vt* ansehen, betrachten (as als); as ~ in Bezug auf (+ *acc*). ~ book *n* Nachschlagewerk *nt*. ~ number *n* Aktenzeichen *nt*

referendum /refə'rendəm/ *n* Volksabstimmung *f*

re'fill¹ /ri:-/ *vt* nachfüllen

'refill² /ri:-/ *vt* (*for pen*) Ersatzmine *f*

refine /rɪ'faɪn/ *vt* raffinieren. ~d *a* fein, vornehm. ~ment *n* Vornehmheit *f*;

(*Techn*) Verfeinerung *f*. ~ry /-ərɪ/ *n* Raffinerie *f*

reflect /rɪ'flekt/ *vt* reflektieren; ⟨*mirror:*⟩ [wider]spiegeln; be ~ed in sich spiegeln in (+ *dat*) □ *vi* nachdenken (on über + *acc*); ~ badly upon s.o. ⟨*fig*⟩ jdn in ein schlechtes Licht stellen. ~ion /-ekʃn/ *n* Reflexion *f*; (*image*) Spiegelbild *nt*; on ~ion nach nochmaliger Überlegung. ~ive /-ɪv/ *a*, -ly *adv* nachdenklich. ~or *n* Rückstrahler *m*

reflex /'ri:fleks/ *n* Reflex *m* □ *attrib* Reflex-

reflexive /rɪ'fleksɪv/ *a* reflexiv

reform /rɪ'fɔ:m/ *n* Reform *f* □ *vt* reformieren □ *vi* sich bessern. R~ation /refə'meɪʃn/ *n* (*Relig*) Reformation *f*. ~er *n* Reformer *m*; (*Relig*) Reformator *m*

refract /rɪ'frækt/ *vt* (*Phys*) brechen

refrain¹ /rɪ'freɪn/ *n* Refrain *m*

refrain² *vi* ~ from doing sth etw nicht tun

refresh /rɪ'freʃ/ *vt* erfrischen. ~ing *a* erfrischend. ~ments *npl* Erfrischungen *f*

refrigerat|e /rɪ'frɪdʒəreɪt/ *vt* kühlen. ~or *n* Kühlschrank *m*

re'fuel /ri:-/ *vt/i* (*pt/pp* -fuelled) auftanken

refuge /'refju:dʒ/ *n* Zuflucht *f*; take ~ in Zuflucht nehmen in (+ *dat*)

refugee /refjʊ'dʒi:/ *n* Flüchtling *m*

re'fund¹ /ri:-/ get a ~ sein Geld zurückbekommen

re'fund² /rɪ-/ *vt* zurückerstatten

refurbish /ri:'fɜ:bɪʃ/ *vt* renovieren

refusal /rɪ'fju:zl/ *n* (*see* refuse¹) Ablehnung *f*, Weigerung *f*

refuse¹ /rɪ'fju:z/ *vt* ablehnen; (*not grant*) verweigern; ~ to do sth sich weigern, etw zu tun □ *vi* ablehnen; sich weigern

refuse² /'refju:s/ *n* Müll *m*, Abfall *m*. ~ collection *n* Müllabfuhr *f*

refute /rɪ'fju:t/ *vt* widerlegen

re'gain /rɪ-/ *vt* wiedergewinnen

regal /'ri:gl/ *a*, -ly *adv* königlich

regalia /rɪ'geɪlɪə/ *npl* Insignien *pl*

regard /rɪ'gɑ:d/ *n* (*heed*) Rücksicht *f*; (*respect*) Achtung *f*; ~s *pl* Grüße *pl*; with ~ to in Bezug auf (+ *acc*) □ *vt* ansehen, betrachten (as als); as ~ in Bezug auf (+ *acc*). ~ing *prep* bezüglich (+ *gen*). ~less *adv* ohne Rücksicht (of auf + *acc*)

regatta /rɪ'gætə/ *n* Regatta *f*

regenerate /rɪ'dʒenəreɪt/ *vt* regenerieren □ *vi* sich regenerieren

regime /reɪ'ʒi:m/ *n* Regime *nt*

regiment /'redʒɪmənt/ *n* Regiment *nt*. ~al /-'mentl/ *a* Regiments-. ~ation /-'teɪʃn/ *n* Reglementierung *f* region /ˈriːdʒən/ n Region f; in the ~ of (fig) ungefähr. ~al a, -ly adv regional

register /ˈredʒɪstə(r)/ n Register nt; (Sch) Anwesenheitsliste f □ vt registrieren; (report) anmelden; einschreiben ⟨letter⟩; aufgeben ⟨luggage⟩ □ vi (report) sich anmelden; it didn't ~ (fig) ich habe es nicht registriert

registrar /redʒɪˈstrɑː(r)/ n Standesbeamte(r) m

registration /redʒɪˈstreɪʃn/ n Registrierung f; Anmeldung f. ~ number n Autonummer f

registry office /ˈredʒɪstrɪ-/ n Standesamt nt

regret /rɪˈgret/ n Bedauern nt □ vt (pt/pp regretted) bedauern. ~fully adv mit Bedauern

regrettab|le /rɪˈgretəbl/ a bedauerlich. ~ly adv bedauerlicherweise

regular /ˈregjʊlə(r)/ a, -ly adv regelmäßig; (usual) üblich; (Mil) Berufs- □ n Berufssoldat m; (in pub) Stammgast m; (in shop) Stammkunde m. ~ity /-ˈlærətɪ/ n Regelmäßigkeit f

regulat|e /ˈregjʊleɪt/ vt regulieren. ~ion /-ˈleɪʃn/ n (rule) Vorschrift f

rehabilitat|e /riːhəˈbɪlɪteɪt/ vt rehabilitieren. ~ion /-ˈteɪʃn/ n Rehabilitation f

rehears|al /rɪˈhɜːsl/ n (Theat) Probe f. ~e vt/i proben

reign /reɪn/ n Herrschaft f □ vi herrschen, regieren

reimburse /riːɪmˈbɜːs/ vt ~ s.o. for sth jdm etw zurückerstatten

rein /reɪn/ n Zügel m

reincarnation /riːɪnkɑːˈneɪʃn/ f Reinkarnation f, Wiedergeburt f

reindeer /ˈreɪndɪə(r)/ n inv Rentier nt

reinforce /riːɪnˈfɔːs/ vt verstärken. ~d 'concrete n Stahlbeton m. ~ment n Verstärkung f; send ~ments Verstärkung schicken

reinstate /riːɪnˈsteɪt/ vt wieder einstellen; (to office) wieder einsetzen

reiterate /riːˈɪtəreɪt/ vt wiederholen

reject /rɪˈdʒekt/ vt ablehnen. ~ion /-ekʃn/ n Ablehnung f

rejects /ˈriːdʒekts/ npl (Comm) Ausschussware f

rejoic|e /rɪˈdʒɔɪs/ vi (liter) sich freuen. ~ing n Freude f

re'join /rɪ-/ vt sich wieder anschließen (+ dat); wieder beitreten (+ dat) ⟨club, party⟩; (answer) erwidern

rejuvenate /rɪˈdʒuːvəneɪt/ vt verjüngen

relapse /rɪˈlæps/ n Rückfall m □ vi einen Rückfall erleiden

relate /rɪˈleɪt/ vt (tell) erzählen; (connect) verbinden □ vi zusammenhängen (to mit). ~d a verwandt (to mit)

relation /rɪˈleɪʃn/ n Beziehung f; (person) Verwandte(r) m/f. ~ship n Beziehung f; (link) Verbindung f; (blood tie) Verwandtschaft f; (affair) Verhältnis nt

relative /ˈrelətɪv/ n Verwandte(r) m/f □ a relativ; (Gram) Relativ-. ~ly adv relativ, verhältnismäßig

relax /rɪˈlæks/ vt lockern, entspannen □ vi sich lockern, sich entspannen. ~ation /-ˈseɪʃn/ n Entspannung f. ~ing a entspannend

relay[1] /ˈriːˈleɪ/ vt (pt/pp -layed) weitergeben; (Radio, TV) übertragen

relay[2] /ˈriːleɪ/ n (Electr) Relais nt; work in ~s sich die Arbeit abteilen. ~ [race] n Staffel f

release /rɪˈliːs/ n Freilassung f, Entlassung f; (Techn) Auslöser m □ vt freilassen; (let go of) loslassen; (Techn) auslösen; veröffentlichen ⟨information⟩

relegate /ˈrelɪgeɪt/ vt verbannen; be ~d (Sport) absteigen

relent /rɪˈlent/ vi nachgeben. ~less a, -ly adv erbarmungslos; (unceasing) unaufhörlich

relevan|ce /ˈreləvəns/ n Relevanz f. ~t a relevant (to für)

reliab|ility /rɪlaɪəˈbɪlətɪ/ n Zuverlässigkeit f. ~le /-ˈlaɪəbl/ a, -ly adv zuverlässig

relian|ce /rɪˈlaɪəns/ n Abhängigkeit f (on von). ~t a angewiesen (on auf + acc)

relic /ˈrelɪk/ n Überbleibsel nt; (Relig) Reliquie f

relief /rɪˈliːf/ n Erleichterung f; (assistance) Hilfe f; (distraction) Abwechslung f; (replacement) Ablösung f; (Art) Relief nt; in ~ im Relief. ~ map n Reliefkarte f. ~ train n Entlastungszug m

relieve /rɪˈliːv/ vt erleichtern; (take over from) ablösen; ~ of entlasten von

religion /rɪˈlɪdʒən/ n Religion f

religious /rɪˈlɪdʒəs/ a religiös. ~ly adv (conscientiously) gewissenhaft

relinquish /rɪˈlɪŋkwɪʃ/ vt loslassen; (give up) aufgeben

relish /ˈrelɪʃ/ n Genuss m; (Culin) Würze f □ vt genießen

relo'cate /riː-/ vt verlegen

reluctan|ce /rɪˈlʌktəns/ n Widerstreben nt. ~t a widerstrebend; be ~t zögern (to zu). ~tly adv ungern, widerstrebend

rely /rɪˈlaɪ/ vi (pt/pp -ied) ~ on sich verlassen auf (+ acc); (be dependent on) angewiesen sein auf (+ acc)

remain /rɪˈmeɪn/ vi bleiben; (be left) übrig bleiben. ~der n Rest m. ~ing a restlich.

~s *npl* Reste *pl*; [mortal] ~s [sterbliche] Überreste *pl*

remand /rɪˈmɑːnd/ *n* on ~ in Untersuchungshaft ◻ *vt* ~ in custody in Untersuchungshaft schicken

remark /rɪˈmɑːk/ *n* Bemerkung *f* ◻ *vt* bemerken. ~**able** /-əbl/ *a*, -**bly** *adv* bemerkenswert

re'**marry** /riː-/ *vi* wieder heiraten

remedial /rɪˈmiːdɪəl/ *a* Hilfs-; (*Med*) Heil-

remedy /ˈremədɪ/ *n* [Heil]mittel *nt* (for gegen); (*fig*) Abhilfe *f* ◻ *vt* (*pt/pp* -ied) abhelfen (+ *dat*); beheben ⟨*fault*⟩

remember /rɪˈmembə(r)/ *vt* sich erinnern an (+ *acc*); ~ to do sth daran denken, etw zu tun; ~er me to him grüßen Sie ihn von mir ◻ *vi* sich erinnern. ~**rance** *n* Erinnerung *f*

remind /rɪˈmaɪnd/ *vt* erinnern (of an + *acc*). ~**er** *n* Andenken *nt*; (*letter, warning*) Mahnung *f*

reminisce /remɪˈnɪs/ *vi* sich seinen Erinnerungen hingeben. ~**nces** /-sɪz/ *npl* Erinnerungen *pl*. ~**nt** *a* be ~**nt** of erinnern an (+ *acc*)

remiss /rɪˈmɪs/ *a* nachlässig

remission /rɪˈmɪʃn/ *n* Nachlass *m*; (*of sentence*) [Straf]erlass *m*; (*Med*) Remission *f*

remit /rɪˈmɪt/ *vt* (*pt/pp* remitted) überweisen ⟨*money*⟩. ~**tance** *n* Überweisung *f*

remnant /ˈremnənt/ *n* Rest *m*

remonstrate /ˈremənstreɪt/ *vi* protestieren; ~ with s.o. jdm Vorhaltungen machen

remorse /rɪˈmɔːs/ *n* Reue *f*. ~**ful** *a*, -**ly** *adv* reumütig. ~**less** *a*, -**ly** *adv* unerbittlich

remote /rɪˈməʊt/ *a* fern; (*isolated*) abgelegen; (*slight*) gering. ~ con'**trol** *n* Fernsteuerung *f*; (*for TV*) Fernbedienung *f*. ~con'**trolled** *a* ferngesteuert; fernbedient

remotely /rɪˈməʊtlɪ/ *adv* entfernt; not ~ nicht im Entferntesten

re'**movable** /rɪ-/ *a* abnehmbar

removal /rɪˈmuːvl/ *n* Entfernung *f*; (*from house*) Umzug *m*. ~ van *n* Möbelwagen *m*

remove /rɪˈmuːv/ *vt* entfernen; (*take off*) abnehmen; (*take out*) herausnehmen

remunerate /rɪˈmjuːnəreɪt/ *vt* bezahlen. ~**ion** /-ˈreɪʃn/ *n* Bezahlung *f*. ~**ive** /-ətɪv/ *a* einträglich

render /ˈrendə(r)/ *vt* machen; erweisen ⟨*service*⟩; (*translate*) wiedergeben; (*Mus*) vortragen

renegade /ˈrenɪgeɪd/ *n* Abtrünnige(r) *m/f*

renew /rɪˈnjuː/ *vt* erneuern; verlängern ⟨*contract*⟩. ~**al** *n* Erneuerung *f*; Verlängerung *f*

renounce /rɪˈnaʊns/ *vt* verzichten auf (+ *acc*); (*Relig*) abschwören (+ *dat*)

renovate /ˈrenəveɪt/ *vt* renovieren. ~**ion** /-ˈveɪʃn/ *n* Renovierung *f*

renown /rɪˈnaʊn/ *n* Ruf *m*. ~**ed** *a* berühmt

rent /rent/ *n* Miete *f* ◻ *vt* mieten; (*hire*) leihen; ~ [out] vermieten; verleihen. ~**al** *n* Mietgebühr *f*; Leihgebühr *f*

renunciation /rɪnʌnsɪˈeɪʃn/ *n* Verzicht *m*

re'**open** /riː-/ *vt/i* wieder aufmachen

re'**organize** /riː-/ *vt* reorganisieren

rep /rep/ *n* (*fam*) Vertreter *m*

repair /rɪˈpeə(r)/ *n* Reparatur *f*; in good/ bad ~ in gutem/schlechtem Zustand ◻ *vt* reparieren

repartee /repɑːˈtiː/ *n* piece of ~ schlagfertige Antwort *f*

repatriate /riːˈpætrɪeɪt/ *vt* repatriieren. ~**ion** /-ˈeɪʃn/ *n* Repatriierung *f*

re'**pay** /riː-/ *vt* (*pt/pp* -paid) zurückzahlen; ~ s.o. for sth jdm etw zurückzahlen. ~**ment** *n* Rückzahlung *f*

repeal /rɪˈpiːl/ *n* Aufhebung *f* ◻ *vt* aufheben

repeat /rɪˈpiːt/ *n* Wiederholung *f* ◻ *vt/i* wiederholen; ~ after me sprechen Sie mir nach. ~**ed** *a*, -**ly** *adv* wiederholt

repel /rɪˈpel/ *vt* (*pt/pp* repelled) abwehren; (*fig*) abstoßen. ~**lent** *a* abstoßend

repent /rɪˈpent/ *vi* Reue zeigen. ~**ance** *n* Reue *f*. ~**ant** *a* reuig

repercussions /riːpəˈkʌʃnz/ *npl* Auswirkungen *pl*

repertoire /ˈrepətwɑː(r)/ *n* Repertoire *nt*

repertory /ˈrepətrɪ/ *n* Repertoire *nt*

repetition /repɪˈtɪʃn/ *n* Wiederholung *f*. ~**ive** /rɪˈpetɪtɪv/ *a* eintönig

re'**place** /rɪ-/ *vt* zurücktun; (*take the place of*) ersetzen; (*exchange*) austauschen, auswechseln. ~**ment** *n* Ersatz *m*. ~**ment part** *n* Ersatzteil *nt*

re'**play** /riː-/ *n* (*Sport*) Wiederholungsspiel *nt*; [action] ~ Wiederholung *f*

replenish /rɪˈplenɪʃ/ *vt* auffüllen ⟨*stocks*⟩; (*refill*) nachfüllen

replete /rɪˈpliːt/ *a* gesättigt

replica /ˈreplɪkə/ *n* Nachbildung *f*

reply /rɪˈplaɪ/ *n* Antwort *f* (to auf + *acc*) ◻ *vt/i* (*pt/pp* replied) antworten

report /rɪˈpɔːt/ *n* Bericht *m*; (*Sch*) Zeugnis *nt*; (*rumour*) Gerücht *nt*; (*of gun*) Knall *m* ◻ *vt* berichten; (*notify*) melden; ~ s.o. to the police jdn anzeigen ◻ *vi* berichten (on über + *acc*); (*present oneself*) sich melden (to bei). ~**er** *n* Reporter(in) *m(f)*

repose /rɪˈpəʊz/ *n* Ruhe *f*

repos'sess /riː-/ *vt* wieder in Besitz nehmen

reprehensible /reprɪ'hensəbl/ a tadelnswert

represent /reprɪ'zent/ vt darstellen; (act for) vertreten, repräsentieren. ~ation /-'teɪʃn/ n Darstellung f; make ~ations to vorstellig werden bei

representative /reprɪ'zentətɪv/ a repräsentativ (of für) □ n Bevollmächtigte(r) m/(f); (Comm) Vertreter(in) m/(f); (Amer, Pol) Abgeordnete(r) m/f

repress /rɪ'pres/ vt unterdrücken. ~ion /-eʃn/ n Unterdrückung f. ~ive /-ɪv/ a repressiv

reprieve /rɪ'priːv/ n Begnadigung f; (postponement) Strafaufschub m; (fig) Gnadenfrist f □ vt begnadigen

reprimand /'reprɪmɑːnd/ n Tadel m □ vt tadeln

'reprint¹ /riː-/ n Nachdruck m

re'print² /riː-/ vt neu auflegen

reprisal /rɪ'praɪzl/ n Vergeltungsmaßnahme f

reproach /rɪ'prəʊtʃ/ n Vorwurf m □ vt Vorwürfe pl machen (+ dat). ~ful a, -ly adv vorwurfsvoll

repro'duc|e /riː-/ vt wiedergeben, reproduzieren □ vi sich fortpflanzen. ~tion /-'dʌkʃn/ n Reproduktion f; (Biol) Fortpflanzung f. ~tion furniture n Stilmöbel pl. ~tive /-'dʌktɪv/ a Fortpflanzungs-

reprove /rɪ'pruːv/ vt tadeln

reptile /'reptaɪl/ n Reptil nt

republic /rɪ'pʌblɪk/ n Republik f. ~an a republikanisch □ n Republikaner(in) m(f)

repudiate /rɪ'pjuːdɪeɪt/ vt zurückweisen

repugnan|ce /rɪ'pʌgnəns/ n Widerwille m. ~t a widerlich

repuls|e /rɪ'pʌls/ vt abwehren; (fig) abweisen. ~ion /-'ʌlʃn/ n Widerwille m. ~ive /-ɪv/ a abstoßend, widerlich

reputable /'repjʊtəbl/ a (firm) von gutem Ruf; (respectable) anständig

reputation /repjʊ'teɪʃn/ n Ruf m

repute /rɪ'pjuːt/ n Ruf m. ~d /-ɪd/ a, -ly adv angeblich

request /rɪ'kwest/ n Bitte f □ vt bitten. ~ stop n Bedarfshaltestelle f

require /rɪ'kwaɪə(r)/ vt (need) brauchen; (demand) erfordern; be ~d to do sth etw tun müssen. ~ment n Bedürfnis nt; (condition) Erfordernis nt

requisite /'rekwɪzɪt/ a erforderlich □ n toilet/travel ~s pl Toiletten-/Reiseartikel pl

requisition /rekwɪ'zɪʃn/ n ~ [order] Anforderung f □ vt anfordern

re'sale /riː-/ n Weiterverkauf m

rescind /rɪ'sɪnd/ vt aufheben

rescue /'reskjuː/ n Rettung f □ vt retten. ~r n Retter m

research /rɪ'sɜːtʃ/ n Forschung f □ vt erforschen; (Journ) recherchieren □ vi ~ into erforschen. ~er n Forscher m; (Journ) Rechercheur m

resem|blance /rɪ'zembləns/ n Ähnlichkeit f. ~ble /-bl/ vt ähneln (+ dat)

resent /rɪ'zent/ vt übel nehmen; einen Groll hegen gegen (person). ~ful a, -ly adv verbittert. ~ment n Groll m

reservation /rezə'veɪʃn/ n Reservierung f; (doubt) Vorbehalt m; (enclosure) Reservat nt

reserve /rɪ'zɜːv/ n Reserve f; (for animals) Reservat nt; (Sport) Reservespieler(in) m(f) □ vt reservieren; (client:) reservieren lassen; (keep) aufheben; sich (dat) vorbehalten (right). ~d a reserviert

reservoir /'rezəvwɑː(r)/ n Reservoir nt

re'shape /riː-/ vt umformen

re'shuffle /riː-/ n (Pol) Umbildung f □ vt (Pol) umbilden

reside /rɪ'zaɪd/ vi wohnen

residence /'rezɪdəns/ n Wohnsitz m; (official) Residenz f; (stay) Aufenthalt m. ~ permit n Aufenthaltsgenehmigung f

resident /'rezɪdənt/ a ansässig (in in + dat); (housekeeper, nurse) im Haus wohnend □ n Bewohner(in) m(f); (of street) Anwohner m. ~ial /-'denʃl/ a Wohn-

residue /'rezɪdjuː/ n Rest m; (Chem) Rückstand m

resign /rɪ'zaɪn/ vt ~ oneself to sich abfinden mit □ vi kündigen; (from public office) zurücktreten. ~ation /rezɪg'neɪʃn/ n Resignation f; (from job) Kündigung f; Rücktritt m. ~ed a, -ly adv resigniert

resilient /rɪ'zɪlɪənt/ a federnd; (fig) widerstandsfähig

resin /'rezɪn/ n Harz nt

resist /rɪ'zɪst/ vt/i sich widersetzen (+ dat); (fig) widerstehen (+ dat). ~ance n Widerstand m. ~ant a widerstandsfähig

resolut|e /'rezəluːt/ a, -ly adv entschlossen. ~ion /-'luːʃn/ n Entschlossenheit f; (intention) Vorsatz m; (Pol) Resolution f

resolve /rɪ'zɒlv/ n Entschlossenheit f; (decision) Beschluss m □ vt beschließen; (solve) lösen. ~d a entschlossen (to zu)

resonan|ce /'rezənəns/ n Resonanz f. ~t a klangvoll

resort /rɪ'zɔːt/ n (place) Urlaubsort m; as a last ~ wenn alles andere fehlschlägt □ vi ~ to (fig) greifen zu

resound /rɪ'zaʊnd/ vi widerhallen. ~ing a widerhallend; (loud) laut; (notable) groß resource /rɪˈsɔːs/ n ~s pl Ressourcen pl. ~ful a findig. ~fulness n Findigkeit f

respect /rɪˈspekt/ n Respekt m, Achtung f (for vor + dat); (aspect) Hinsicht f; with ~ to in Bezug auf (+ acc) □ vt respektieren, achten

respectability /rɪspektəˈbɪlətɪ/ n (see respectable) Ehrbarkeit f; Anständigkeit f

respect|able /rɪˈspektəbl/ a, -bly adv ehrbar; (decent) anständig; (considerable) ansehnlich. ~ful a, -ly adv respektvoll

respective /rɪˈspektɪv/ a jeweilig. ~ly adv beziehungsweise

respiration /respəˈreɪʃn/ n Atmung f

respite /ˈrespaɪt/ n [Ruhe]pause f; (delay) Aufschub m

resplendent /rɪˈsplendənt/ a glänzend

respond /rɪˈspɒnd/ vi antworten; (react) reagieren (to auf + acc); (patient:) ansprechen (to auf + acc)

response /rɪˈspɒns/ n Antwort f; Reaktion f

responsibility /rɪspɒnsɪˈbɪlətɪ/ n Verantwortung f; (duty) Verpflichtung f

responsib|le /rɪˈspɒnsəbl/ a verantwortlich; (trustworthy) verantwortungsvoll. ~ly adv verantwortungsbewusst

responsive /rɪˈspɒnsɪv/ a be ~ reagieren

rest¹ /rest/ n Ruhe f; (holiday) Erholung f; (interval & Mus) Pause f; have a ~ eine Pause machen; (rest) sich ausruhen □ vt ausruhen; (lean) lehnen (on an/auf + acc) □ vi ruhen; (have a rest) sich ausruhen

rest² n the ~ der Rest; (people) die Übrigen pl □ vi it ~s with you es ist an Ihnen (to zu)

restaurant /ˈrestərɒnt/ n Restaurant nt, Gaststätte f. ~ car n Speisewagen m

restful /ˈrestfl/ a erholsam

restitution /restɪˈtjuːʃn/ n Entschädigung f; (return) Rückgabe f

restive /ˈrestɪv/ a unruhig

restless /ˈrestlɪs/ a, -ly adv unruhig

restoration /restəˈreɪʃn/ n (of building) Restaurierung f

restore /rɪˈstɔː(r)/ vt wiederherstellen; restaurieren (building); (give back) zurückgeben

restrain /rɪˈstreɪn/ vt zurückhalten; ~ oneself sich beherrschen. ~ed a zurückhaltend. ~t n Zurückhaltung f

restrict /rɪˈstrɪkt/ vt einschränken; ~ to beschränken auf (+ acc). ~ion /-ɪkʃn/ n Einschränkung f; Beschränkung f. ~ive /-ɪv/ a einschränkend

ˈrest room n (Amer) Toilette f

result /rɪˈzʌlt/ n Ergebnis nt, Resultat nt; (consequence) Folge f; as a ~ als Folge (of gen) □ vi sich ergeben (from aus); ~ in enden in (+ dat); (lead to) führen zu

resume /rɪˈzjuːm/ vt wieder aufnehmen; wieder einnehmen (seat) □ vi wieder beginnen

résumé /ˈrezʊmeɪ/ n Zusammenfassung f

resumption /rɪˈzʌmpʃn/ n Wiederaufnahme f

resurgence /rɪˈsɜːdʒəns/ n Wiederaufleben nt

resurrect /rezəˈrekt/ vt (fig) wieder beleben. ~ion /-ekʃn/ n the R~ion (Relig) die Auferstehung

resuscitat|e /rɪˈsʌsɪteɪt/ vt wieder beleben. ~ion /-ˈteɪʃn/ n Wiederbelebung f

retail /ˈriːteɪl/ n Einzelhandel m □ a Einzelhandels. □ adv im Einzelhandel □ vt im Einzelhandel verkaufen □ vi ~ at im Einzelhandel kosten. ~er n Einzelhändler m. ~ price n Ladenpreis m

retain /rɪˈteɪn/ vt behalten

retaliat|e /rɪˈtælɪeɪt/ vi zurückschlagen. ~ion /-ˈeɪʃn/ n Vergeltung f; in ~ion als Vergeltung

retarded /rɪˈtɑːdɪd/ a zurückgeblieben

retentive /rɪˈtentɪv/ a (memory) gut

reticen|ce /ˈretɪsns/ n Zurückhaltung f. ~t a zurückhaltend

retina /ˈretɪnə/ n Netzhaut f

retinue /ˈretɪnjuː/ n Gefolge nt

retire /rɪˈtaɪə(r)/ vi in den Ruhestand treten; (withdraw) sich zurückziehen. ~d a im Ruhestand. ~ment n Ruhestand m; since my ~ment seit ich nicht mehr arbeite

retiring /rɪˈtaɪərɪŋ/ a zurückhaltend

retort /rɪˈtɔːt/ n scharfe Erwiderung f; (Chem) Retorte f □ vt scharf erwidern

re'touch /riː-/ vt (Phot) retuschieren

re'trace /rɪ-/ vt zurückverfolgen; ~ one's steps denselben Weg zurückgehen

retract /rɪˈtrækt/ vt einziehen; zurücknehmen (remark) □ vt widerrufen

re'train /riː-/ vt umschulen □ vi umgeschult werden

retreat /rɪˈtriːt/ n Rückzug m; (place) Zufluchtsort m □ vi sich zurückziehen

re'trial /riː-/ n Wiederaufnahmeverfahren nt

retribution /retrɪˈbjuːʃn/ n Vergeltung f

retrieve /rɪˈtriːv/ vt zurückholen; (from wreckage) bergen; (Computing) wieder auffinden; (dog:) apportieren

retrograde /ˈretrəgreɪd/ a rückschrittlich

retrospect /ˈretrəspekt/ n in ~ rückblickend. ~ive /-ɪv/ a, -ly adv rückwirkend; (looking back) rückblickend return /rɪ'tɜ:n/ n Rückkehr f; (giving back) Rückgabe f; (Comm) Ertrag m; (ticket) Rückfahrkarte f; (Aviat) Rückflugschein m; by ~ [of post] postwendend; in ~ dafür; in ~ for für; many happy ~s! herzlichen Glückwunsch zum Geburtstag! □ vt zurückgehen/-fahren; (come back) zurückkommen □ vt zurückgeben; (put back) zurückstellen/-legen; (send back) zurückschicken; (elect) wählen

return- ~ flight n Rückflug m. ~ match n Rückspiel m. ~ ticket n Rückfahrkarte f; (Aviat) Rückflugschein m

reunion /ri:'ju:nɪən/ n Wiedervereinigung f; (social gathering) Treffen nt

reunite /ri:ju:'naɪt/ vt wieder vereinigen □ vi sich wieder vereinigen

re'us|able /ri:-/ a wieder verwendbar. ~e vt wieder verwenden

rev /rev/ n (Auto, fam) Umdrehung f □ vt/i ~ [up] den Motor auf Touren bringen

reveal /rɪ'vi:l/ vt zum Vorschein bringen; (fig) enthüllen. ~ing a (fig) aufschlussreich

revel /'revl/ vi (pt/pp revelled) ~ in sth etw genießen

revelation /revə'leɪʃn/ n Offenbarung f, Enthüllung f

revelry /'revlrɪ/ n Lustbarkeit f

revenge /rɪ'vendʒ/ n Rache f; (fig & Sport) Revanche f □ vt rächen

revenue /'revənju:/ n [Staats]einnahmen pl

reverberate /rɪ'vɜ:bəreɪt/ vi nachhallen

revere /rɪ'vɪə(r)/ vt verehren. ~nce /'revərəns/ n Ehrfurcht f

Reverend /'revərənd/ a the ~ X Pfarrer X; (Catholic) Hochwürden X

reverent /'revərənt/ a, -ly adv ehrfürchtig

reverie /'revərɪ/ n Träumerei f

revers /rɪ'vɪə/ n (pl revers /-z/) Revers nt

reversal /rɪ'vɜ:sl/ n Umkehrung f

reverse /rɪ'vɜ:s/ a umgekehrt □ n Gegenteil nt; (back) Rückseite f; (Auto) Rückwärtsgang m □ vt umkehren; (Auto) zurücksetzen; ~ the charges (Teleph) ein R-Gespräch führen □ vi zurücksetzen

revert /rɪ'vɜ:t/ vi ~ to zurückfallen an (+ acc); zurückkommen auf (+ acc) (topic)

review /rɪ'vju:/ n Rückblick m (of auf + acc); (re-examination) Überprüfung f; (Mil) Truppenschau f; (of book, play) Kritik f, Rezension f □ vt zurückblicken auf (+ acc); überprüfen (situation); (Mil) besichtigen; kritisieren, rezensieren (book, play). ~er n Kritiker m, Rezensent m

revile /rɪ'vaɪl/ vt verunglimpfen

revis|e /rɪ'vaɪz/ vt revidieren; (for exam) wiederholen. ~ion /-'vɪʒn/ n Revision f; Wiederholung f

revival /rɪ'vaɪvl/ n Wiederbelebung f

revive /rɪ'vaɪv/ vt wieder beleben; (fig) wieder aufleben lassen □ vi wieder aufleben

revoke /rɪ'vəʊk/ vt aufheben; widerrufen (command, decision)

revolt /rɪ'vəʊlt/ n Aufstand m □ vi rebellieren □ vt anwidern. ~ing a widerlich, eklig

revolution /revə'lu:ʃn/ n Revolution f; (Auto) Umdrehung f. ~ary /-ərɪ/ a revolutionär. ~ize vt revolutionieren

revolve /rɪ'vɒlv/ vi sich drehen; ~ around kreisen um

revolv|er /rɪ'vɒlvə(r)/ n Revolver m. ~ing a Dreh-

revue /rɪ'vju:/ n Revue f; (satirical) Kabarett nt

revulsion /rɪ'vʌlʃn/ n Abscheu m

reward /rɪ'wɔ:d/ n Belohnung f □ vt belohnen. ~ing a lohnend

re'write /ri:-/ vt (pt rewrote, pp rewritten) noch einmal [neu] schreiben; (alter) umschreiben

rhapsody /'ræpsədɪ/ n Rhapsodie f

rhetoric /'retərɪk/ n Rhetorik f. ~al /rɪ'tɒrɪkl/ a rhetorisch

rheuma|tic /ru:'mætɪk/ a rheumatisch. ~tism /'ru:mətɪzm/ n Rheumatismus m, Rheuma nt

Rhine /raɪn/ n Rhein m

rhinoceros /raɪ'nɒsərəs/ n Nashorn nt, Rhinozeros nt

rhubarb /'ru:bɑ:b/ n Rhabarber m

rhyme /raɪm/ n Reim m □ vt reimen □ vi sich reimen

rhythm /'rɪðm/ n Rhythmus m. ~ic[al] a, -ally adv rhythmisch

rib /rɪb/ n Rippe f □ vt (pt/pp ribbed) (fam) aufziehen (fam)

ribald /'rɪbld/ a derb

ribbon /'rɪbən/ n Band nt; (for typewriter) Farbband nt; in ~s in Fetzen

rice /raɪs/ n Reis m

rich /rɪtʃ/ a (-er, -est), -ly adv reich; (food) gehaltvoll; (heavy) schwer □ n the ~ pl die Reichen; ~es pl Reichtum m

rickets /'rɪkɪts/ n Rachitis f

rickety /'rɪkɪtɪ/ a wackelig

ricochet /'rɪkəʃeɪ/ vi abprallen

rid /rɪd/ vt (pt/pp rid, pres p ridding) befreien (of von); get ~ of loswerden

riddance /'rɪdns/ n good ~! auf Nimmerwiedersehen!

ridden /'rɪdn/ see ride

riddle /'rɪdl/ n Rätsel nt

riddled /'rɪdld/ a ~ with durchlöchert mit

ride /raɪd/ n Ritt m; (in vehicle) Fahrt f; take s.o. for a ~ (fam) jdn reinlegen □ v (pt rode, pp ridden) □ vt reiten ⟨horse⟩; fahren mit ⟨bicycle⟩ □ vi reiten; (in vehicle) fahren. ~r n Reiter(in) m(f); (on bicycle) Fahrer(in) m(f); (in document) Zusatzklausel f

ridge /rɪdʒ/ n Erhebung f; (on roof) First m; (of mountain) Grat m, Kamm m; (of high pressure) Hochdruckkeil m

ridicule /'rɪdɪkjuːl/ n Spott m □ vt verspotten, spotten über (+ acc)

ridiculous /rɪ'dɪkjʊləs/ a, -ly adv lächerlich

riding /'raɪdɪŋ/ n Reiten nt □ attrib Reit-

rife /raɪf/ a be ~ weit verbreitet sein

riff-raff /'rɪfræf/ n Gesindel nt

rifle /'raɪfl/ n Gewehr nt □ vt plündern; ~ through durchwühlen

rift /rɪft/ n Spalt m; (fig) Riss m

rig¹ /rɪg/ n Ölbohrturm m; (at sea) Bohrinsel f □ vt (pt/pp rigged) ~ out ausrüsten; ~ up aufbauen

rig² vt (pt/pp rigged) manipulieren

right /raɪt/ a richtig; (not left) rechte(r,s); be ~ ⟨person:⟩ Recht haben; ⟨clock:⟩ richtig gehen; put ~ wieder in Ordnung bringen; (fig) richtig stellen; that's ~! das stimmt! □ adv richtig; (directly) direkt; (completely) ganz; (not left) rechts; ⟨go⟩ nach rechts; ~ away sofort □ n Recht nt; (not left) rechte Seite f; on the ~ rechts; from/to the ~ von/nach rechts; be in the ~ Recht haben; by ~s eigentlich; the R~ (Pol) die Rechte. ~ angle n rechter Winkel m

righteous /'raɪtʃəs/ a rechtschaffen

rightful /'raɪtfl/ a, -ly adv rechtmäßig

right: ~-handed a rechtshändig. ~-hand 'man n (fig) rechte Hand f

rightly /'raɪtlɪ/ adv mit Recht

right: ~ of way n Durchgangsrecht nt; (path) öffentlicher Fuß weg m; (Auto) Vorfahrt f. ~-wing a (Pol) rechte(r,s)

rigid /'rɪdʒɪd/ a starr; (strict) streng. ~ity /-'dʒɪdətɪ/ n Starrheit f; Strenge f

rigmarole /'rɪgmərəʊl/ n Geschwätz nt; (procedure) Prozedur f

rigorous /'rɪgərəs/ a, -ly adv streng

rigour /'rɪgə(r)/ n Strenge f

rile /raɪl/ vt (fam) ärgern

rim /rɪm/ n Rand m; (of wheel) Felge f

rind /raɪnd/ n (on fruit) Schale f; (on cheese) Rinde f; (on bacon) Schwarte f

ring¹ /rɪŋ/ n Ring m; (for circus) Manege f; stand in a ~ im Kreis stehen □ vt umringen; ~ in red rot einkreisen

ring² n Klingeln nt; give s.o. a ~ (Teleph) jdn anrufen □ v (pt rang, pp rung) □ vt läuten; ~ [up] (Teleph) anrufen □ vi läuten, klingeln. ~ back vt/i (Teleph) zurückrufen. ~ off vi (Teleph) auflegen

ring: ~leader n Rädelsführer m. ~ road n Umgehungsstraße f

rink /rɪŋk/ n Eisbahn f

rinse /rɪns/ n Spülung f; (hair colour) Tönung f □ vt spülen; tönen ⟨hair⟩. ~ off vt abspülen

riot /'raɪət/ n Aufruhr m; ~s pl Unruhen pl; ~ of colours bunte Farbenpracht f; run ~ randalieren □ vi randalieren. ~er n Randalierer m. ~ous /-əs/ a aufrührerisch; (boisterous) wild

rip /rɪp/ n Riss m □ v/i (pt/pp ripped) zerreißen; ~ open aufreißen. ~ off vt (fam) neppen

ripe /raɪp/ a (-r, -st) reif

ripen /'raɪpn/ vi reifen □ vt reifen lassen

ripeness /'raɪpnɪs/ n Reife f

'rip-off n (fam) Nepp m

ripple /'rɪpl/ n kleine Welle f □ vt kräuseln □ vi sich kräuseln

rise /raɪz/ n Anstieg m; (fig) Aufstieg m; (increase) Zunahme f; (in wages) Lohnerhöhung f; (in salary) Gehaltserhöhung f; give ~ to Anlass geben zu □ vi (pt rose, pp risen) steigen; ⟨ground:⟩ ansteigen; ⟨sun, dough:⟩ aufgehen; ⟨river:⟩ entspringen; (get up) aufstehen; (fig) aufsteigen (to zu); (rebel) sich erheben; ⟨court:⟩ sich vertagen. ~r n early ~r Frühaufsteher m

rising /'raɪzɪŋ/ a steigend; ⟨sun⟩ aufgehend; the ~ generation die heranwachsende Generation □ n (revolt) Aufstand m

risk /rɪsk/ n Risiko nt; at one's own ~ auf eigene Gefahr □ vt riskieren

risky /'rɪskɪ/ a (-ier, -iest) riskant

risqué /'rɪskeɪ/ a gewagt

rissole /'rɪsəʊl/ n Frikadelle f

rite /raɪt/ n Ritus m; last ~s Letzte Ölung f

ritual /'rɪtjʊəl/ a rituell □ n Ritual nt

rival /'raɪvl/ a rivalisierend □ n Rivale m/Rivalin f; ~s pl (Comm) Konkurrenten pl □ vt (pt/pp rivalled) gleichkommen (+ dat); (compete with) rivalisieren mit. ~ry n Rivalität f; (Comm) Konkurrenzkampf m

river /'rɪvə(r)/ n Fluss m. ~-bed n Flussbett nt

rivet /'rɪvɪt/ n Niete f □ vt [ver]nieten; ~ed by (fig) gefesselt von

road /rəʊd/ n Straße f; (fig) Weg m

road: ~-block n Straßensperre f. ~-hog n (fam) Straßenschreck m. ~-map n Straßenkarte f. ~ safety n Verkehrssicherheit f. ~ sense n Verkehrssinn m. ~side n Straßenrand m. ~way n Fahrbahn f. ~works npl Straßenarbeiten pl. ~worthy a verkehrssicher

roam /rəʊm/ vi wandern

roar /rɔː(r)/ n Gebrüll nt; ~s of laughter schallendes Gelächter ▫ vi brüllen; (with laughter) schallend lachen. ~ing a (fire) prasselnd; do a ~ing trade (fam) ein Bombengeschäft machen

roast /rəʊst/ a gebraten, Brat-; ~ beef/pork Rinder-/Schweinebraten m ▫ n Braten m ▫ vt/i braten; rösten (coffee, chestnuts)

rob /rɒb/ vt (pt/pp robbed) berauben (of gen); ausrauben (bank). ~ber n Räuber m. ~bery n Raub m

robe /rəʊb/ n Robe f; (Amer: bathrobe) Bademantel m

robin /ˈrɒbɪn/ n Rotkehlchen nt

robot /ˈrəʊbɒt/ n Roboter m

robust /rəʊˈbʌst/ a robust

rock[1] /rɒk/ n Fels m; stick of ~ Zuckerstange f; on the ~s (ship) aufgelaufen; (marriage) kaputt; (drink) mit Eis

rock[2] vt/i schaukeln

rock[3] n (Mus) Rock m

rock-ˈbottom n Tiefpunkt m

rockery /ˈrɒkərɪ/ n Steingarten m

rocket /ˈrɒkɪt/ n Rakete f ▫ vi in die Höhe schießen

rocking: ~-chair n Schaukelstuhl m. ~-horse n Schaukelpferd nt

rocky /ˈrɒkɪ/ a (-ier, -iest) felsig; (unsteady) wackelig

rod /rɒd/ n Stab m; (stick) Rute f; (for fishing) Angel[rute] f

rode /rəʊd/ see ride

rodent /ˈrəʊdnt/ n Nagetier nt

roe[1] /rəʊ/ n Rogen m; (soft) Milch f

roe[2] n (pl roe or roes) ~[-deer] Reh nt

rogue /rəʊg/ n Gauner m

role /rəʊl/ n Rolle f

roll /rəʊl/ n Rolle f; (bread) Brötchen nt; (list) Liste f; (of drum) Wirbel m ▫ vi rollen; be ~ing in money (fam) Geld wie Heu haben ▫ vt rollen; walzen (lawn); ausrollen (pastry). ~ over vi sich auf die andere Seite rollen. ~ up vt aufrollen; hochkrempeln (sleeves) ▫ vi (fam) auftauchen

ˈroll-call n Namensaufruf m; (Mil) Appell m

roller /ˈrəʊlə(r)/ n Rolle f; (lawn, road) Walze f; (hair) Lockenwickler m. ~ blind n Rollo nt. ~-coaster n Berg-und-Tal-Bahn f. ~-skate n Rollschuh m

ˈrolling-pin n Teigrolle f

Roman /ˈrəʊmən/ a römisch ▫ n Römer(in) m(f)

romance /rəˈmæns/ n Romantik f; (love-affair) Romanze f; (book) Liebesgeschichte f

Romania /rəʊˈmeɪnɪə/ n Rumänien nt. ~n a rumänisch ▫ n Rumäne m/-nin f

romantic /rəʊˈmæntɪk/ a, -ally adv romantisch. ~ism /-tɪsɪzm/ n Romantik f

Rome /rəʊm/ n Rom nt

romp /rɒmp/ n Tollen nt ▫ vi (herum)tollen. ~ers npl Strampelhöschen nt

roof /ruːf/ n Dach nt; (of mouth) Gaumen m ▫ vt ~ over überdachen. ~-rack n Dachgepäckträger m. ~-top n Dach nt

rook /rʊk/ n Saatkrähe f; (Chess) Turm m ▫ vt (fam: swindle) schröpfen

room /ruːm/ n Zimmer nt; (for functions) Saal m; (space) Platz m. ~y a geräumig

roost /ruːst/ n Hühnerstange f ▫ vi schlafen

root[1] /ruːt/ n Wurzel f; take ~ anwachsen ▫ vi Wurzeln schlagen. ~ out vt (fig) ausrotten

root[2] vi ~ about wühlen; ~ for s.o. (Amer, fam) für jdn sein

rope /rəʊp/ n Seil nt; know the ~s (fam) sich auskennen. ~ in vt (fam) einspannen

rope-ˈladder n Strickleiter f

rosary /ˈrəʊzərɪ/ n Rosenkranz m

rose[1] /rəʊz/ n Rose f; (of watering-can) Brause f

rose[2] see rise

rosemary /ˈrəʊzmərɪ/ n Rosmarin m

rosette /rəʊˈzet/ n Rosette f

roster /ˈrɒstə(r)/ n Dienstplan m

rostrum /ˈrɒstrəm/ n Podest nt, Podium nt

rosy /ˈrəʊzɪ/ a (-ier, -iest) rosig

rot /rɒt/ n Fäulnis f; (fam: nonsense) Quatsch m ▫ vi (pt/pp rotted) [ver]faulen

rota /ˈrəʊtə/ n Dienstplan m

rotary /ˈrəʊtərɪ/ a Dreh-; (Techn) Rotations-

rotat|e /rəʊˈteɪt/ vt drehen; im Wechsel anbauen (crops) ▫ vi sich drehen; (Techn) rotieren. ~ion /-eɪʃn/ n Drehung f; (of crops) Fruchtfolge f; in ~ion im Wechsel

rote /rəʊt/ n by ~ auswendig

rotten /ˈrɒtn/ a faul; (fam) mies; (person) fies

rotund /rəʊˈtʌnd/ a rundlich

rough /rʌf/ a (-er, -est) rau; (uneven) uneben; (coarse, not gentle) grob; (brutal) roh; (turbulent) stürmisch; (approximate) ungefähr □ *adv* sleep ~ im Freien übernachten; play ~ holzen □ do sth in ~ etw ins Unreine schreiben □ *vt* ~ it primitiv leben. ~ out *vt* im Groben entwerfen

roughage /'rʌfidʒ/ *n* Ballaststoffe *pl*

rough 'draft *n* grober Entwurf *m*

rough|ly /'rʌflɪ/ *adv* (*see* rough) rau; grob; roh; ungefähr. ~ness *n* Rauheit *f*

'rough paper *n* Konzeptpapier *nt*

round /raʊnd/ *a* (-er, -est) rund □ *n* Runde *f*; (*slice*) Scheibe *f*; do one's ~s seine Runde machen □ *prep* um (+ *acc*); ~ the clock rund um die Uhr □ *adv* all ~ ringsherum; ~ and ~ im Kreis; ask s.o. ~ jdn einladen; turn/look ~ sich umdrehen/ umsehen □ *vt* biegen um (*corner*) □ *vi* ~ on s.o. jdn anfahren. ~ off *vt* abrunden. ~ up *vt* aufrunden; zusammentreiben (*animals*); festnehmen (*criminals*)

roundabout /'raʊndəbaʊt/ *a* umständlich □ *n* Umweg *m* □ *n* Karussell *nt*; (*for traffic*) Kreisverkehr *m*

round: ~'shouldered *a* mit einem runden Rücken. ~ 'trip *n* Rundreise *f*

rous|e /raʊz/ *vt* wecken; (*fig*) erregen. ~ing *a* mitreißend

route /ruːt/ *n* Route *f*; (*of bus*) Linie *f*

routine /ruː'tiːn/ *a*, -ly *adv* routinemäßig □ *n* Routine *f*; (*Theat*) Nummer *f*

roux /ruː/ *n* Mehlschwitze *f*

rove /rəʊv/ *vi* wandern

row[1] /rəʊ/ *n* (*line*) Reihe *f*; in a ~ (*one after the other*) nacheinander

row[2] *vt*/*i* rudern

row[3] /raʊ/ *n* (*fam*) Krach *m* □ *vi* (*fam*) sich streiten

rowan /'rəʊən/ *n* Eberesche *f*

rowdy /'raʊdɪ/ *a* (-ier, -iest) laut

rowing boat /'rəʊɪŋ-/ *n* Ruderboot *nt*

royal /'rɔɪəl/ *a*, -ly *adv* königlich

royal|ty /'rɔɪəltɪ/ *n* Königtum *nt*; (*persons*) Mitglieder *pl* der königlichen Familie; -ies *pl* (*payments*) Tantiemen *pl*

rub /rʌb/ *n* give sth a ~ etw reiben; (*polish*) polieren □ *vt* (*pt*/*pp* rubbed) reiben; (*polish*) polieren; don't ~ it in (*fam*) reib es mir nicht unter die Nase. ~ off *vt* abreiben □ *vi* abgehen; ~ off on abfärben auf (+ *acc*). ~ out *vt* ausradieren

rubber /'rʌbə(r)/ *n* Gummi *m*; (*eraser*) Radiergummi *m*. ~ band *n* Gummiband *nt*. ~y *a* gummiartig

rubbish /'rʌbɪʃ/ *n* Abfall *m*, Müll *m*; (*fam: nonsense*) Quatsch *m*; (*fam: junk*) Plunder *m*, Kram *m* □ *vt* (*fam*) schlecht machen. ~ bin *n* Mülleimer *m*, Abfalleimer *m*. ~

dump *n* Abfallhaufen *m*; (*official*) Müllhalde *f*

rubble /'rʌbl/ *n* Trümmer *pl*, Schutt *m*

ruby /'ruːbɪ/ *n* Rubin *m*

rucksack /'rʌksæk/ *n* Rucksack *m*

rudder /'rʌdə(r)/ *n* [Steuer]ruder *nt*

ruddy /'rʌdɪ/ *a* (-ier, -iest) rötlich; (*sl*) verdammt

rude /ruːd/ *a* (-r, -st), -ly *adv* unhöflich; (*improper*) unanständig. ~ness *n* Unhöflichkeit *f*

rudiment /'ruːdɪmənt/ *n* ~s *pl* Anfangsgründe *pl*. ~ary /-'mentərɪ/ *a* elementar; (*Biol*) rudimentär

rueful /'ruːfl/ *a*, -ly *adv* reumütig

ruffian /'rʌfɪən/ *n* Rüpel *m*

ruffle /'rʌfl/ *n* Rüsche *f* □ *vt* zerzausen

rug /rʌg/ *n* Vorleger *m*, (kleiner) Teppich *m*; (*blanket*) Decke *f*

rugged /'rʌgɪd/ *a* (*coastline*) zerklüftet

ruin /'ruːɪn/ *n* Ruine *f*; (*fig*) Ruin *m* □ *vt* ruinieren. ~ous /-əs/ *a* ruinös

rule /ruːl/ *n* Regel *f*; (*control*) Herrschaft *f*; (*government*) Regierung *f*; (*for measuring*) Lineal *nt*; as a ~ in der Regel □ *vt* regieren, herrschen über (+ *acc*); (*fig*) beherrschen; (*decide*) entscheiden; (*line*) □ *vi* regieren, herrschen. ~ out *vt* ausschließen

ruled /ruːld/ *a* (*paper*) liniert

ruler /'ruːlə(r)/ *n* Herrscher(in) *m*(*f*); (*measure*) Lineal *nt*

ruling /'ruːlɪŋ/ *a* herrschend; (*factor*) entscheidend; (*Pol*) regierend □ *n* Entscheidung *f*

rum /rʌm/ *n* Rum *m*

rumble /'rʌmbl/ *n* Grollen *nt* □ *vi* grollen; (*stomach:*) knurren

ruminant /'ruːmɪnənt/ *n* Wiederkäuer *m*

rummage /'rʌmɪdʒ/ *vi* wühlen; ~ through durchwühlen

rummy /'rʌmɪ/ *n* Rommé *nt*

rumour /'ruːmə(r)/ *n* Gerücht *nt* □ *vt* it is ~ed that es geht das Gerücht, dass

rump /rʌmp/ *n* Hinterteil *nt*. ~ steak *n* Rumpsteak *nt*

rumpus /'rʌmpəs/ *n* (*fam*) Spektakel *m*

run /rʌn/ *n* Lauf *m*; (*journey*) Fahrt *f*; (*series*) Serie *f*, Reihe *f*; (*Theat*) Laufzeit *f*; (*Skiing*) Abfahrt *f*; (*enclosure*) Auslauf *m*; (*Amer: ladder*) Laufmasche *f*; at a ~ im Laufschritt; ~ of bad luck Pechsträhne *f*; be on the ~ flüchtig sein; have the ~ of sth etw zu seiner freien Verfügung haben; in the long ~ auf lange Sicht □ *vi* (*pt* ran, *pp* run, *pres p* running) □ *vi* laufen; (*flow*) fließen; (*eyes:*) tränen; (*bus:*) verkehren, fahren; (*butter, ink:*) zerfließen; (*colours:*) [ab]färben; (*in election*)

kandidieren; ~ across s.o./sth auf jdn/
etw stoßen □ *vt* laufen lassen; einlaufen
lassen 〈*bath*〉; 〈*manage*〉 führen, leiten;
〈*drive*〉 fahren; eingehen 〈*risk*〉; 〈*Journ*〉
bringen 〈*article*〉; ~ one's hand over sth
mit der Hand über etw 〈*acc*〉 fahren. ~
away *vi* weglaufen. ~ down *vi* hinunter-/
herunterlaufen; 〈*clockwork*:〉 ablaufen;
〈*stocks*:〉 sich verringern □ *vt* 〈*run over*〉
überfahren; 〈*reduce*〉 verringern; 〈*fam*:
criticize〉 heruntermachen. ~ in *vi* hinein-/
hereinlaufen. ~ off *vi* weglaufen □ *vt* abziehen 〈*copies*〉. ~ out *vi* hinaus-/heraus-
laufen; 〈*supplies, money*:〉 ausgehen; I've
~ out of sugar Ich habe keinen Zucker
mehr. ~ over *vi* hinüber-/herüberlaufen;
〈*overflow*〉 überlaufen □ *vt* überfahren. ~
through *vi* durchlaufen. ~ up *vi* hinauf-/
herauflaufen; 〈*towards*〉 hinlaufen □ *vt*
machen 〈*debts*〉 auflaufen lassen 〈*bill*〉;
〈*sew*〉 schnell nähen

'runaway *n* Ausreißer *m*
run-'down *a* 〈*area*〉 verkommen
rung¹ /rʌŋ/ *n* 〈*of ladder*〉 Sprosse *f*
rung² *see* ring²
runner /'rʌnə(r)/ *n* Läufer *m*; 〈*Bot*〉 Ausläufer *m*; 〈*on sledge*〉 Kufe *f*. ~ bean *n*
Stangenbohne *f*. ~'up *n* Zweite(r) *m/f*
running /'rʌnɪŋ/ *a* laufend; 〈*water*〉
fließend; four times ~ viermal nacheinander □ *n* Laufen *nt*; 〈*management*〉
Führung *f*, Leitung *f*; be/not be in the
~ eine/keine Chance haben. ~ 'commentary *n* fortlaufender Kommentar *m*
runny /'rʌnɪ/ *a* flüssig
run-:-of-the-'mill *a* gewöhnlich. ~-up *n*
〈*Sport*〉 Anlauf *m*; 〈*to election*〉 Zeit *f* vor
der Wahl. ~way *n* Start- und Landebahn
f, Piste *f*
rupture /'rʌptʃə(r)/ *n* Bruch *m* □ *vt*/*i*
brechen; ~ oneself sich 〈*dat*〉 einen
Bruch heben
rural /'rʊərəl/ *a* ländlich
ruse /ruːz/ *n* List *f*
rush¹ /rʌʃ/ *n* 〈*Bot*〉 Binse *f*
rush² *n* Hetze *f*; in a ~ in Eile □ *vi* sich
hetzen; 〈*run*〉 rasen; 〈*water*:〉 rauschen □ *vt*
hetzen, drängen; ~ s.o. to hospital jdn
schnellstens ins Krankenhaus bringen.
~-hour *n* Hauptverkehrszeit *f*, Stoßzeit
f
rusk /rʌsk/ *n* Zwieback *m*
Russia /'rʌʃə/ *n* Russland *nt*. ~n *a* rus-
sisch □ *n* Russe *m*/Russin *f*; 〈*Lang*〉 Rus-
sisch *nt*
rust /rʌst/ *n* Rost *m* □ *vi* rosten
rustic /'rʌstɪk/ *a* bäuerlich; 〈*furniture*〉
rustikal

rustle /'rʌsl/ *vi* rascheln □ *vt* rascheln mit;
〈*Amer*〉 stehlen 〈*cattle*〉. ~ up *vt* 〈*fam*〉 improvisieren
'rustproof *a* rostfrei
rusty /'rʌstɪ/ *a* 〈-ier, -iest〉 rostig
rut /rʌt/ *n* Furche *f*; be in a ~ 〈*fam*〉 aus
dem alten Trott nicht herauskommen
ruthless /'ruːθlɪs/ *a*, -ly *adv* rücksichtslos.
~ness *n* Rücksichtslosigkeit *f*
rye /raɪ/ *n* Roggen *m*

S

sabbath /'sæbəθ/ *n* Sabbat *m*
sabbatical /sə'bætɪkl/ *n* 〈*Univ*〉 For-
schungsurlaub *m*
sabot|age /'sæbətɑːʒ/ *n* Sabotage *f* □ *vt*
sabotieren. ~eur /-'tɜː(r)/ *n* Saboteur *m*
sachet /'sæfeɪ/ *n* Beutel *m*; 〈*scented*〉
Kissen *nt*
sack¹ /sæk/ *vt* 〈*plunder*〉 plündern
sack² *n* Sack *m*; get the ~ 〈*fam*〉 rausge-
schmissen werden □ *vt* 〈*fam*〉 rausschmeißen. ~ing *n* Sackleinen *nt*; 〈*fam*:
dismissal〉 Rausschmiss *m*
sacrament /'sækrəmənt/ *n* Sakrament *nt*
sacred /'seɪkrɪd/ *a* heilig
sacrifice /'sækrɪfaɪs/ *n* Opfer *nt* □ *vt* op-
fern
sacrilege /'sækrɪlɪdʒ/ *n* Sakrileg *nt*
sad /sæd/ *a* 〈sadder, saddest〉 traurig;
〈*loss, death*〉 schmerzlich. ~den *vt* traurig
machen
saddle /'sædl/ *n* Sattel *m* □ *vt* satteln; ~
s.o. with sth 〈*fam*〉 jdm etw aufhalsen
sadis|m /'seɪdɪzm/ *n* Sadismus *m*. ~t
/-dɪst/ *n* Sadist *m*. ~tic /sə'dɪstɪk/ *a*,
-ally *adv* sadistisch
sad|ly /'sædlɪ/ *adv* traurig; 〈*unfortunately*〉
leider. ~ness *n* Traurigkeit *f*
safe /seɪf/ *a* 〈-r, -st〉 sicher; 〈*journey*〉 gut;
〈*not dangerous*〉 ungefährlich; ~ and
sound gesund und wohlbehalten □ *n* Safe
m. ~guard *n* Schutz *m* □ *vt* schützen. ~ly
adv sicher; 〈*arrive*〉 gut
safety /'seɪftɪ/ *n* Sicherheit *f*. ~-belt *n*
Sicherheitsgurt *m*. ~-pin *n* Sicherheits-
nadel *f*. ~-valve *n* [Sicherheits]ventil *nt*
sag /sæg/ *vi* 〈*pt/pp* sagged〉 durchhängen
saga /'sɑːgə/ *n* Saga *f*; 〈*fig*〉 Geschichte *f*
sage¹ /seɪdʒ/ *n* 〈*herb*〉 Salbei *m*
sage² *a* weise □ *n* Weise(r) *m*
Sagittarius /sædʒɪ'teərɪəs/ *n* 〈*Astr*〉
Schütze *m*

said /sed/ *see* say

sail /seɪl/ *n* Segel *nt*; (*trip*) Segelfahrt *f* ◻ *vi* segeln; (*on liner*) fahren; (*leave*) abfahren (for nach) ◻ *vt* segeln mit

'sailboard *n* Surfbrett *nt*. ∼ing *n* Windsurfen *nt*

sailing /'seɪlɪŋ/ *n* Segelsport *m*. ∼-boat *n* Segelboot *nt*. ∼-ship *n* Segelschiff *nt*

sailor /'seɪlə(r)/ *n* Seemann *m*; (*in navy*) Matrose *m*

saint /seɪnt/ *n* Heilige(r) *m/f*. ∼ly *a* heilig

sake /seɪk/ *n* for the ∼ of ... um ... (*gen*) willen; for my/your ∼ um meinet-/deinetwillen

salad /'sæləd/ *n* Salat *m*. ∼ cream *n* ≈ Mayonnaise *f*. ∼-dressing *n* Salatsoße *f*

salary /'sæləri/ *n* Gehalt *nt*

sale /seɪl/ *n* Verkauf *m*; (*event*) Basar *m*; (*at reduced prices*) Schlussverkauf *m*; for ∼ zu verkaufen

sales|man *n* Verkäufer *m*. ∼woman *n* Verkäuferin *f*

salient /'seɪlɪənt/ *a* wichtigste(r,s)

saliva /sə'laɪvə/ *n* Speichel *m*

sallow /'sæləʊ/ *a* (-er, -est) bleich

salmon /'sæmən/ *n* Lachs *m*. ∼-pink *a* lachsrosa

saloon /sə'luːn/ *n* Salon *m*; (*Auto*) Limousine *f*; (*Amer: bar*) Wirtschaft *f*

salt /sɔːlt/ *n* Salz *nt* ◻ *a* salzig; (*water, meat*) Salz- ◻ *vt* salzen; (*cure*) pökeln; streuen (*road*). ∼-cellar *n* Salzfass *nt*. ∼'water *n* Salzwasser *nt*. ∼y *a* salzig

salutary /'sæljʊtəri/ *a* heilsam

salute /sə'luːt/ *n* (*Mil*) Gruß *m* ◻ *vt/i* (*Mil*) grüßen

salvage /'sælvɪdʒ/ *n* (*Naut*) Bergung *f* ◻ *vt* bergen

salvation /sæl'veɪʃn/ *n* Rettung *f*; (*Relig*) Heil *nt*. S∼ 'Army *n* Heilsarmee *f*

salvo /'sælvəʊ/ *n* Salve *f*

same /seɪm/ *a & pron* the ∼ der/die/das gleiche; (*pl*) die gleichen; (*identical*) der-/die-/dasselbe; (*pl*) dieselben ◻ *adv* the ∼ gleich; all the ∼ trotzdem; the ∼ to you gleichfalls

sample /'sɑːmpl/ *n* Probe *f*; (*Comm*) Muster *nt* ◻ *vt* probieren, kosten

sanatorium /sænə'tɔːrɪəm/ *n* Sanatorium *nt*

sanctify /'sæŋktɪfaɪ/ *vt* (*pt/pp* -fied) heiligen

sanctimonious /sæŋktɪ'məʊnɪəs/ *a*, -ly *adv* frömmlerisch

sanction /'sæŋkʃn/ *n* Sanktion *f* ◻ *vt* sanktionieren

sanctity /'sæŋktəti/ *n* Heiligkeit *f*

sanctuary /'sæŋktjʊərɪ/ *n* (*Relig*) Heiligtum *nt*; (*refuge*) Zuflucht *f*; (*for wildlife*) Tierschutzgebiet *nt*

sand /sænd/ *n* Sand *m* ◻ *vt* ∼ [down] [ab]schmirgeln

sandal /'sændl/ *n* Sandale *f*

sand: ∼bank *n* Sandbank *f*. ∼paper *n* Sandpapier *nt* ◻ *vt* [ab]schmirgeln. ∼-pit *n* Sandkasten *m*

sandwich /'sænwɪdʒ/ *n* ≈ belegtes Brot *nt*; Sandwich *m* ◻ *vt* ∼ed between eingeklemmt zwischen

sandy /'sændɪ/ *a* (-ier, -iest) sandig; (*beach, soil*) Sand-; (*hair*) rotblond

sane /seɪn/ *a* (-r, -st) geistig normal; (*sensible*) vernünftig

sang /sæŋ/ *see* sing

sanitary /'sænɪtərɪ/ *a* hygienisch; (*system*) sanitär. ∼ napkin *n* (*Amer*), ∼ towel *n* [Damen]binde *f*

sanitation /sænɪ'teɪʃn/ *n* Kanalisation und Abfallbeseitigung *pl*

sanity /'sænɪtɪ/ *n* [gesunder] Verstand *m*

sank /sæŋk/ *see* sink

sap /sæp/ *n* (*Bot*) Saft *m* ◻ *vt* (*pt/pp* sapped) schwächen

sapphire /'sæfaɪə(r)/ *n* Saphir *m*

sarcas|m /'sɑːkæzm/ *n* Sarkasmus *m*. ∼tic /-'kæstɪk/ *a*, -ally *adv* sarkastisch

sardine /sɑː'diːn/ *n* Sardine *f*

Sardinia /sɑː'dɪnɪə/ *n* Sardinien *nt*

sardonic /sɑː'dɒnɪk/ *a*, -ally *adv* höhnisch; (*smile*) sardonisch

sash /sæʃ/ *n* Schärpe *f*

sat /sæt/ *see* sit

satanic /sə'tænɪk/ *a* satanisch

satchel /'sætʃl/ *n* Ranzen *m*

satellite /'sætəlaɪt/ *n* Satellit *m*. ∼ dish *n* Satellitenschüssel *f*. ∼ television *n* Satellitenfernsehen *nt*

satin /'sætɪn/ *n* Satin *m*

satire /'sætaɪə(r)/ *n* Satire *f*

satirical /sə'tɪrɪkl/ *a*, -ly *adv* satirisch

satir|ist /'sætərɪst/ *n* Satiriker(in) *m(f)*. ∼ize *vt* satirisch darstellen; (*book:*) eine Satire sein auf (+ *acc*)

satisfaction /sætɪs'fækʃn/ *n* Befriedigung *f*; to my ∼ zu meiner Zufriedenheit

satisfactory /sætɪs'fæktərɪ/ *a*, -ily *adv* zufrieden stellend

satisf|y /'sætɪsfaɪ/ *vt* (*pp/pp* -fied) befriedigen; zufrieden stellen (*customer*); (*convince*) überzeugen; be ∼ied zufrieden sein. ∼ying *a* befriedigend; (*meal*) sättigend

saturat|e /'sætʃəreɪt/ *vt* durchtränken; (*Chem & fig*) sättigen. ∼ed *a* durchnässt; (*fat*) gesättigt

Saturday /'sætədeɪ/ n Samstag m, Sonnabend m

sauce /sɔːs/ n Soße f; (cheek) Frechheit f. ~pan n Kochtopf m

saucer /'sɔːsə(r)/ n Untertasse f

saucy /'sɔːʃɪ/ a (-ier, -iest) frech

Saudi Arabia /saʊdɪə'reɪbɪə/ n Saudi-Arabien f

sauna /'sɔːnə/ n Sauna f

saunter /'sɔːntə(r)/ vi schlendern

sausage /'sɒsɪdʒ/ n Wurst f

savage /'sævɪdʒ/ a wild; (fierce) scharf; (brutal) brutal □ n Wilde(r) m/f □ vt anfallen. ~ry n Brutalität f

save /seɪv/ n (Sport) Abwehr f □ vt retten (from vor + dat); (keep) aufheben; (not waste) sparen; (collect) sammeln; (avoid) ersparen; (Sport) abwehren (shot); verhindern (goal) □ vi ~ [up] sparen □ prep außer (+ dat), mit Ausnahme (+ gen)

saver /'seɪvə(r)/ n Sparer m

saving /'seɪvɪŋ/ n (see save) Rettung f; Sparen nt; Ersparnis f; ~s pl (money) Ersparnisse pl. ~s account n Sparkonto nt. ~s bank n Sparkasse f

saviour /'seɪvjə(r)/ n Retter m

savour /'seɪvə(r)/ n Geschmack m □ vt auskosten. ~y a herzhaft, würzig; (fig) angenehm

saw¹ /sɔː/ see see¹

saw² n Säge f □ vt/i (pt sawed, pp sawn or sawed) sägen. ~dust n Sägemehl nt

saxophone /'sæksəfəʊn/ n Saxophon nt

say /seɪ/ n Mitspracherecht nt; have one's ~ seine Meinung sagen □ vt/i (pt/pp said) sagen; sprechen (prayer); that is to ~ das heißt; that goes without ~ing das versteht sich von selbst; when all is said and done letzten Endes; I ~! (attracting attention) hallo! ~ing n Redensart f

scab /skæb/ n Schorf m; (pej) Streikbrecher m

scaffold /'skæfəld/ n Schafott nt. ~ing n Gerüst nt

scald /skɔːld/ vt verbrühen

scale¹ /skeɪl/ n (of fish) Schuppe f

scale² n Skala f; (Mus) Tonleiter f; (ratio) Maßstab m; on a grand ~ in großem Stil □ vt (climb) erklettern. ~ down vt verkleinern

scales /skeɪlz/ npl (for weighing) Waage f

scalp /skælp/ n Kopfhaut f □ vt skalpieren

scalpel /'skælpl/ n Skalpell nt

scam /skæm/ n (fam) Schwindel m

scamper /'skæmpə(r)/ vi huschen

scan /skæn/ n (Med) Szintigramm nt □ v (pt/pp scanned) □ vt absuchen; (quickly) flüchtig ansehen; (Med) szintigraphisch

untersuchen □ vi (poetry:) das richtige Versmaß haben

scandal /'skændl/ n Skandal m; (gossip) Skandalgeschichten pl. ~ize /-dəlaɪz/ vt schockieren. ~ous /-əs/ a skandalös

Scandinavia /skændɪ'neɪvɪə/ n Skandinavien nt. ~n a skandinavisch □ n Skandinavier(in) m/f

scant /skænt/ a wenig

scanty /'skæntɪ/ a (-ier, -iest), -ily adv spärlich; (clothing) knapp

scapegoat /'skeɪp-/ n Sündenbock m

scar /skɑː(r)/ n Narbe f □ vt (pt/pp scarred) eine Narbe hinterlassen auf (+ dat)

scarc|e /skeəs/ a (-r, -st) knapp; make oneself ~e (fam) sich aus dem Staub machen. ~ely adv kaum. ~ity n Knappheit f

scare /skeə(r)/ n Schreck m; (panic) [allgemeine] Panik f; (bomb ~) Bombendrohung f □ vt Angst machen (+ dat); be ~d Angst haben (of vor + dat)

'scarecrow n Vogelscheuche f

scarf /skɑːf/ n (pl scarves) Schal m; (square) Tuch nt

scarlet /'skɑːlət/ a scharlachrot. ~ 'fever n Scharlach m

scary /'skeərɪ/ a unheimlich

scathing /'skeɪðɪŋ/ a bissig

scatter /'skætə(r)/ vt verstreuen; (disperse) zerstreuen □ vi sich zerstreuen. ~brained a (fam) schusselig. ~ed a verstreut; (showers) vereinzelt

scatty /'skætɪ/ a (-ier, -iest) (fam) verrückt

scavenge /'skævɪndʒ/ vi [im Abfall] Nahrung suchen; (animal:) Aas fressen. ~r n Aasfresser m

scenario /sɪ'nɑːrɪəʊ/ n Szenario nt

scene /siːn/ n (sight) Anblick m; (place of event) Schauplatz m; behind the ~s hinter den Kulissen; ~ of the crime Tatort m

scenery /'siːnərɪ/ n Landschaft f; (Theat) Szenerie f

scenic /'siːnɪk/ a landschaftlich schön; (Theat) Bühnen-

scent /sent/ n Duft m; (trail) Fährte f; (perfume) Parfüm nt. ~ed a parfümiert

sceptic|al /'skeptɪkl/ a, -ly adv skeptisch. ~ism /-tɪsɪzm/ n Skepsis f

schedule /'ʃedjuːl/ n Programm nt; (of work) Zeitplan m; (timetable) Fahrplan m; behind ~ im Rückstand; according to ~ planmäßig □ vt planen. ~d flight n Linienflug m

scheme /skiːm/ n Programm nt; (plan) Plan m; (plot) Komplott nt □ vi Ränke schmieden

schizophren|ia /ˌskɪtsə'fri:nɪə/ n Schizophrenie f. ~ic /-'frenɪk/ a schizophren

scholar /'skɒlə(r)/ n Gelehrte(r) m/f. ~ly a gelehrt. ~ship n Gelehrtheit f; (grant) Stipendium nt

school /sku:l/ n Schule f; (Univ) Fakultät f □ vt schulen; dressieren (animal)

school: ~boy n Schüler m. ~girl n Schülerin f. ~ing n Schulbildung f. ~master n Lehrer m. ~mistress n Lehrerin f. ~teacher n Lehrer(in) m(f)

sciatica /saɪ'ætɪkə/ n Ischias m

scien|ce /'saɪəns/ n Wissenschaft f. ~tific /-'tɪfɪk/ a wissenschaftlich. ~tist n Wissenschaftler m

scintillating /'sɪntɪleɪtɪŋ/ a sprühend

scissors /'sɪzəz/ npl Schere f; a pair of ~ eine Schere

scoff[1] /skɒf/ vi ~ at spotten über (+ acc)

scoff[2] vt (fam) verschlingen

scold /skəʊld/ vt ausschimpfen

scoop /sku:p/ n Schaufel f; (Culin) Portionierer m; (Journ) Exklusivmeldung f □ vt ~ out aushöhlen; (remove) auslöffeln; ~ up schaufeln; schöpfen (liquid)

scoot /sku:t/ vi (fam) rasen. ~er n Roller m

scope /skəʊp/ n Bereich m; (opportunity) Möglichkeiten pl

scorch /skɔ:tʃ/ vt versengen. ~ing a glühend heiß

score /skɔ:(r)/ n [Spiel]stand m; (individual) Punktzahl f; (Mus) Partitur f; (Cinema) Filmmusik f; a ~ [of] (twenty) zwanzig; keep [the] ~ zählen; (written) aufschreiben; on that ~ was das betrifft □ vt erzielen; schießen (goal); (cut) einritzen □ vi Punkte erzielen; (Sport) ein Tor schießen; (keep score) Punkte zählen. ~r n Punktezähler m; (of goals) Torschütze m

scorn /skɔ:n/ n Verachtung f □ vt verachten. ~ful a, -ly adv verächtlich

Scorpio /'skɔ:pɪəʊ/ n (Astr) Skorpion m

Scorpion /'skɔ:pɪən/ n Skorpion m

Scot /skɒt/ n Schotte m/Schottin f

Scotch /skɒtʃ/ a schottisch □ n (whisky) Scotch m

scotch vt unterbinden

scot-'free a get off ~ straffrei ausgehen

Scot|land /'skɒtlənd/ n Schottland nt. ~s, ~tish a schottisch

scoundrel /'skaʊndrl/ n Schurke m

scour[1] /'skaʊə(r)/ vt (search) absuchen

scour[2] vt (clean) scheuern

scourge /skɜ:dʒ/ n Geißel f

scout /skaʊt/ n (Mil) Kundschafter m □ vi ~ for Ausschau halten nach

Scout n [Boy] ~ Pfadfinder m

scowl /skaʊl/ n böser Gesichtsausdruck m □ vi ein böses Gesicht machen

scraggy /'skrægɪ/ a (-ier, -iest) (pej) dürr, hager

scram /skræm/ vi (fam) abhauen

scramble /'skræmbl/ n Gerangel nt □ vi klettern; ~ for sich drängen nach □ vt (Teleph) verschlüsseln. ~d 'egg[s] n[pl] Rührei nt

scrap[1] /skræp/ n (fam: flight) Rauferei f □ vi sich raufen

scrap[2] n Stückchen nt; (metal) Schrott m; ~s pl Reste; not a ~ kein bisschen □ vt (pt/pp scrapped) aufgeben

'**scrap-book** n Sammelalbum nt

scrape /skreɪp/ vt schaben; (clean) abkratzen; (damage) [ver]schrammen. ~ through vi gerade noch durchkommen. ~ together vt zusammenkriegen

scraper /'skreɪpə(r)/ n Kratzer m

'**scrap iron** n Alteisen nt

'**scrappy** /'skræpɪ/ a lückenhaft

'**scrap-yard** n Schrottplatz m

scratch /skrætʃ/ n Kratzer m; start from ~ von vorne anfangen; not be up to ~ zu wünschen übrig lassen □ vt/i kratzen; (damage) zerkratzen

scrawl /skrɔ:l/ n Gekrakel nt □ vt/i krakeln

scrawny /'skrɔ:nɪ/ a (-ier, -iest) (pej) dürr, hager

scream /skri:m/ n Schrei m □ vt/i schreien

screech /skri:tʃ/ n Kreischen nt □ vt/i kreischen

screen /skri:n/ n Schirm m; (Cinema) Leinwand f; (TV) Bildschirm m □ vt schützen; (conceal) verdecken; vorführen (film); (examine) überprüfen (Med) untersuchen. ~ing n (Med) Reihenuntersuchung f. ~play n Drehbuch nt

screw /skru:/ n Schraube f □ vt schrauben; ~ up vt festschrauben; (crumple) zusammenknüllen; zusammenkneifen (eyes); (sl: bungle) vermasseln; ~ up one's courage seinen Mut zusammennehmen

'**screwdriver** n Schraubenzieher m

screwy /'skru:ɪ/ a (-ier, -iest) (fam) verrückt

scribble /'skrɪbl/ n Gekritzel nt □ vt/i kritzeln

script /skrɪpt/ n Schrift f; (of speech, play) Text m; (Radio, TV) Skript nt; (of film) Drehbuch nt

Scripture /'skrɪptʃə(r)/ n (Sch) Religion f; the ~s pl die Heilige Schrift f

scroll /skrəʊl/ n Schriftrolle f; (decoration) Volute f

scrounge /skraʊndʒ/ vt/i schnorren. ~r n Schnorrer m

scrub¹ /skrʌb/ n (land) Buschland nt, Gestrüpp nt

scrub² vt/i (pt/pp scrubbed) schrubben; (fam: cancel) absagen; fallen lassen (plan)

scruff /skrʌf/ n by the ~ of the neck beim Genick

scruffy /ˈskrʌfɪ/ a (-ier, -iest) vergammelt

scrum /skrʌm/ n Gedränge nt

scruple /ˈskruːpl/ n Skrupel m

scrupulous /ˈskruːpjʊləs/ a, -ly adv gewissenhaft

scrutinize /ˈskruːtɪnaɪz/ vt (genau) ansehen. ~y n (look) prüfender Blick m

scuff /skʌf/ vt abstoßen

scuffle /ˈskʌfl/ n Handgemenge nt

scullery /ˈskʌlərɪ/ n Spülküche f

sculptor /ˈskʌlptə(r)/ n Bildhauer(in) m(f). ~ure /-tʃə(r)/ n Bildhauerei f; (piece of work) Skulptur f, Plastik f

scum /skʌm/ n Schmutzschicht f; (people) Abschaum m

scurrilous /ˈskʌrɪləs/ a niederträchtig

scurry /ˈskʌrɪ/ vi (pt/pp -ied) huschen

scuttle¹ /ˈskʌtl/ n Kohleneimer m

scuttle² vt versenken ⟨ship⟩

scuttle³ vi schnell krabbeln

scythe /saɪð/ n Sense f

sea /siː/ n Meer nt, See f; at ~ auf See; by ~ mit dem Schiff. ~board n Küste f. ~food n Meeresfrüchte pl. ~gull n Möwe f

seal¹ /siːl/ n (Zool) Seehund m

seal² n Siegel nt; (Techn) Dichtung f ⟹ vt versiegeln; (Techn) abdichten; (fig) besiegeln. ~ off vt abriegeln

'sea-level n Meeresspiegel m

seam /siːm/ n Naht f; (of coal) Flöz nt

'seaman n Seemann m; (sailor) Matrose m

seamless /ˈsiːmlɪs/ a nahtlos

seance /ˈseɪɑːns/ n spiritistische Sitzung f

sea: ~plane n Wasserflugzeug nt. ~port n Seehafen m

search /sɜːtʃ/ n Suche f; (official) Durchsuchung f ⟹ vt durchsuchen; absuchen ⟨area⟩ ⟹ vi suchen (for nach). ~ing a prüfend, forschend

search: ~light n [Such]scheinwerfer m. ~party n Suchmannschaft f

sea: ~sick a seekrank. ~side n at/to the ~side am/ans Meer

season /ˈsiːzn/ n Jahreszeit f; (social, tourist, sporting) Saison f ⟹ vt (flavour) würzen. ~able /-əbl/ a der Jahreszeit

gemäß. ~al a Saison-. ~ing n Gewürze pl

'season ticket n Dauerkarte f

seat /siːt/ n Sitz m; (place) Sitzplatz m; (bottom) Hintern m; take a ~ Platz nehmen ⟹ vt setzen; (have seats for) Sitzplätze bieten (+ dat); remain ~ed sitzen bleiben. ~belt n Sicherheitsgurt m; fasten one's ~belt sich anschnallen

sea: ~weed n [See]tang m. ~worthy a seetüchtig

secateurs /sekəˈtɜːz/ npl Gartenschere f

seclude /sɪˈkluːd/ vt absondern. ~ded a abgelegen. ~sion /-ʒn/ n Zurückgezogenheit f

second¹ /sɪˈkɒnd/ vt (transfer) [vorübergehend] versetzen

second² /ˈsekənd/ a zweite(r,s); on ~ thoughts nach weiterer Überlegung ⟹ n Sekunde f; (Sport) Sekundant m; ~s pl (goods) Waren zweiter Wahl; the ~ der/die/das Zweite ⟹ adv (in race) an zweiter Stelle ⟹ vt unterstützen (proposal)

secondary /ˈsekəndrɪ/ a zweitrangig; (Phys) Sekundär-. ~ school n höhere Schule f

second: ~-best a zweitbeste(r,s). ~ 'class adv (travel, send) zweiter Klasse. ~-class a zweitklassig

'second hand n (on clock) Sekundenzeiger m

second-'hand a gebraucht ⟹ adv aus zweiter Hand

secondly /ˈsekəndlɪ/ adv zweitens

second-'rate a zweitklassig

secrecy /ˈsiːkrəsɪ/ n Heimlichkeit f

secret /ˈsiːkrɪt/ a geheim; (agent, police) Geheim-; (drinker, lover) heimlich ⟹ n Geheimnis nt; in ~ heimlich

secretarial /sekrəˈteərɪəl/ a Sekretärinnen-; (work, staff) Sekretariats-

secretary /ˈsekrətərɪ/ n Sekretär(in) m(f)

secrete /sɪˈkriːt/ vt absondern. ~ion /-iːʃn/ n Absonderung f

secretive /ˈsiːkrətɪv/ a geheimtuerisch. ~ness n Heimlichtuerei f

secretly /ˈsiːkrɪtlɪ/ adv heimlich

sect /sekt/ n Sekte f

section /ˈsekʃn/ n Teil m; (of text) Abschnitt m; (of firm) Abteilung f; (of organization) Sektion f

sector /ˈsektə(r)/ n Sektor m

secular /ˈsekjʊlə(r)/ a weltlich

secure /sɪˈkjʊə(r)/ a, -ly adv sicher; (firm) fest; (emotionally) geborgen ⟹ vt sichern; (fasten) festmachen; (obtain) sich (dat) sichern

security /sɪˈkjʊərətɪ/ n Sicherheit f; (emotional) Geborgenheit f; ~ies pl Wertpapiere pl; (Fin) Effekten pl

sedan /sɪˈdæn/ n (Amer) Limousine f

sedate[1] /sɪˈdeɪt/ a, -ly adv gesetzt

sedate[2] vt sedieren

sedation /sɪˈdeɪʃn/ n Sedierung f; be under ~ sediert sein

sedative /ˈsedətɪv/ a beruhigend □ n Beruhigungsmittel nt

sedentary /ˈsedəntərɪ/ a sitzend

sediment /ˈsedɪmənt/ n [Boden]satz m

seduce /sɪˈdjuːs/ vt verführen

seduct|ion /sɪˈdʌkʃn/ n Verführung f. ~ive /-tɪv/ a, -ly adv verführerisch

see[1] /siː/ v (pt saw, pp seen) □ vt sehen; (understand) einsehen; (imagine) sich (dat) vorstellen; (escort) begleiten; go and ~ nachsehen; (visit) besuchen; ~ you later! bis nachher! ~ing that da □ vi sehen; (check) nachsehen; ~ about sich kümmern um. ~ off vt verabschieden; (chase away) vertreiben. ~ through vi durchsehen □ vt (fig) ~ through s.o. jdn durchschauen

see[2] n (Relig) Bistum nt

seed /siːd/ n Samen m; (of grape) Kern m; (fig) Saat f; (Tennis) gesetzter Spieler m; go to ~ Samen bilden; (fig) herunterkommen. ~ed a (Tennis) gesetzt. ~ling n Sämling m

seedy /ˈsiːdɪ/ a (-ier, -iest) schäbig; (area) heruntergekommen

seek /siːk/ vt (pt/pp sought) suchen

seem /siːm/ vi scheinen. ~ingly adv scheinbar

seemly /ˈsiːmlɪ/ a schicklich

seen /siːn/ see see[1]

seep /siːp/ vi sickern

see-saw /ˈsiːsɔː/ n Wippe f

seethe /siːð/ vi ~ with anger vor Wut schäumen

'see-through a durchsichtig

segment /ˈsegmənt/ n Teil m; (of worm) Segment nt; (of orange) Spalte f

segregat|e /ˈsegrɪgeɪt/ vt trennen. ~ion /-ˈgeɪʃn/ n Trennung f

seize /siːz/ vt ergreifen; (Jur) beschlagnahmen; ~ s.o. by the arm jdn am Arm packen. ~ up vi (Techn) sich festfressen

seizure /ˈsiːʒə(r)/ n (Jur) Beschlagnahme f; (Med) Anfall m

seldom /ˈseldəm/ adv selten

select /sɪˈlekt/ a ausgewählt; (exclusive) exklusiv □ vt auswählen; aufstellen (team). ~ion /-ekʃn/ n Auswahl f. ~ive /-ɪv/ a, -ly adv selektiv; (choosy) wählerisch

self /self/ n (pl selves) Ich nt

self: ~-ad'dressed a adressiert. ~-ad'hesive a selbstklebend. ~-as'surance n Selbstsicherheit f. ~-as'sured a selbstsicher. ~-'catering n Selbstversorgung f. ~-'centred a egozentrisch. ~-'confidence n Selbstbewusstsein nt, Selbstvertrauen nt. ~-'confident a selbstbewusst. ~-'conscious a befangen. ~-con'tained a (flat) abgeschlossen. ~-con'trol n Selbstbeherrschung f. ~-de'fence n Selbstverteidigung f; (Jur) Notwehr f. ~-de'nial n Selbstverleugnung f. ~-determi'nation n Selbstbestimmung f. ~-em'ployed selbstständig. ~-e'steem n Selbstachtung f. ~-'evident a offensichtlich. ~-'governing a selbst verwaltet. ~-'help n Selbsthilfe f. ~-in'dulgent a maßlos. ~-'interest n Eigennutz m

self|ish /ˈselfɪʃ/ a, -ly adv egoistisch, selbstsüchtig. ~less a, -ly adv selbstlos

self: ~-'pity n Selbstmitleid nt. ~-'portrait n Selbstporträt nt. ~-pos'sessed a selbstbeherrscht. ~-preser'vation n Selbsterhaltung f. ~-re'spect n Selbstachtung f. ~-'righteous a selbstgerecht. ~-'sacrifice n Selbstaufopferung f. ~-'satisfied a selbstgefällig. ~-'service n Selbstbedienung f □ attrib Selbstbedienungs-. ~-suf'ficient a selbstständig. ~-'willed a eigenwillig

sell /sel/ v (pt/pp sold) □ vt verkaufen; be sold out ausverkauft sein □ vi sich verkaufen. ~ off vt verkaufen

seller /ˈselə(r)/ n Verkäufer m

Sellotape (P) /ˈseləʊ-/ n ≈ Tesafilm (P) m

'sell-out n be a ~ ausverkauft sein; (fam: betrayal) Verrat sein

selves /selvz/ see self

semblance /ˈsembləns/ n Anschein m

semen /ˈsiːmən/ n (Anat) Samen m

semester /sɪˈmestə(r)/ n (Amer) Semester nt

semi|breve /ˈsemɪbriːv/ n (Mus) ganze Note f. ~circle n Halbkreis m. ~circular a halbkreisförmig. ~colon n Semikolon nt. ~-de'tached a & n ~-detached [house] Doppelhaushälfte f. ~-'final n Halbfinale nt

seminar /ˈseminɑː(r)/ n Seminar nt. -y /-nərɪ/ n Priesterseminar nt

'semitone n (Mus) Halbton m

semolina /seməˈliːnə/ n Grieß m

senat|e /ˈsenət/ n Senat m. ~or n Senator m

send /send/ vt/i (pt/pp sent) schicken; ~ one's regards grüßen lassen; ~ for kommen lassen (person); sich (dat) schicken lassen (thing). ~er n Absender m. ~off n Verabschiedung f

senil|e /'si:naɪl/ a senil. ~ity /sɪ'nɪlətɪ/ n Senilität f

senior /'si:nɪə(r)/ a älter; (in rank) höher □ n Ältere(r) m/f; (in rank) Vorgesetzte(r) m/f. ~ 'citizen n Senior(in) m(f)

seniority /si:nɪ'ɒrətɪ/ n höheres Alter nt; (in rank) höherer Rang m

sensation /sen'seɪʃn/ n Sensation f; (feeling) Gefühl nt. ~al a, -ly adv sensationell

sense /sens/ n Sinn m; (feeling) Gefühl nt; (common ~) Verstand m; in a ~ in gewisser Hinsicht; make ~ Sinn ergeben □ vt spüren. ~less a, -ly adv sinnlos; (unconscious) bewusstlos

sensible /'sensəbl/ a, -bly adv vernünftig; (suitable) zweckmäßig

sensitiv|e /'sensətɪv/ a, -ly adv empfindlich; (understanding) einfühlsam. ~ity /-'tɪvətɪ/ n Empfindlichkeit f

sensory /'sensərɪ/ a Sinnes-

sensual /'sensjʊəl/ a sinnlich. ·ity /-'ælətɪ/ n Sinnlichkeit f

sensuous /'sensjʊəs/ a sinnlich

sent /sent/ see send

sentence /'sentəns/ n Satz m; (Jur) Urteil nt; (punishment) Strafe f □ vt verurteilen

sentiment /'sentɪmənt/ n Gefühl nt; (opinion) Meinung f; (sentimentality) Sentimentalität f. ~al /-'mentl/ a sentimental. ~ality /-'tælɪtɪ/ n Sentimentalität f

sentry /'sentrɪ/ n Wache f

separable /'sepərəbl/ a trennbar

separate[1] /'sepərət/ a, -ly adv getrennt, separat

separat|e[2] /'sepəreɪt/ vt trennen □ vi sich trennen. ~ion /-'reɪʃn/ n Trennung f

September /sep'tembə(r)/ n September m

septic /'septɪk/ a vereitert; go ~ vereitern

sequel /'si:kwl/ n Folge f; (fig) Nachspiel nt

sequence /'si:kwəns/ n Reihenfolge f

sequin /'si:kwɪn/ n Paillette f

serenade /serə'neɪd/ n Ständchen nt □ vt ~ s.o. jdm ein Ständchen bringen

seren|e /sɪ'ri:n/ a, -ly adv gelassen. ~ity /-'renətɪ/ n Gelassenheit f

sergeant /'sɑ:dʒənt/ n (Mil) Feldwebel m; (in police) Polizeimeister m

serial /'sɪərɪəl/ n Fortsetzungsgeschichte f; (Radio, TV) Serie f. ~ize vt in Fortsetzungen veröffentlichen/(Radio, TV) senden

series /'sɪərɪz/ n inv Serie f

serious /'sɪərɪəs/ a, -ly adv ernst; (illness, error) schwer. ~ness n Ernst m

sermon /'sɜ:mən/ n Predigt f

serpent /'sɜ:pənt/ n Schlange f

serrated /se'reɪtɪd/ a gezackt

serum /'sɪərəm/ n Serum nt

servant /'sɜ:vənt/ n Diener(in) m(f)

serve /sɜ:v/ n (Tennis) Aufschlag m □ vt dienen (+ dat); bedienen (customer, guest); servieren (food); (Jur) zustellen (on s.o. jdm); verbüßen (sentence); ~ its purpose seinen Zweck erfüllen; it ~s you right! das geschieht dir recht! ~s two für zwei Personen □ vi dienen; (Tennis) aufschlagen

service /'sɜ:vɪs/ n Dienst m; (Relig) Gottesdienst m; (in shop, restaurant) Bedienung f; (transport) Verbindung f; (maintenance) Wartung f; (set of crockery) Service nt; (Tennis) Aufschlag m; ~s pl Dienstleistungen pl; (on motorway) Tankstelle und Raststätte f; in the ~s beim Militär; be of ~ nützlich sein; out of/in ~ (machine·) außer/in Betrieb □ vt (Techn) warten. ~able /-əbl/ a nützlich; (durable) haltbar

service: ~ area n Tankstelle und Raststätte f. ~ charge n Bedienungszuschlag m. ~man n Soldat m. ~ station n Tankstelle f

serviette /sɜ:vɪ'et/ n Serviette f

servile /'sɜ:vaɪl/ a unterwürfig

session /'seʃn/ n Sitzung f; (Univ) Studienjahr nt

set /set/ n Satz m; (of crockery) Service nt; (of cutlery) Garnitur f; (TV, Radio) Apparat m; (Math) Menge f; (Theat) Bühnenbild nt; (Cinema) Szenenaufbau m; (of people) Kreis m; shampoo and ~ Waschen und Legen □ a (ready) fertig, bereit; (rigid) fest; (book) vorgeschrieben; be ~ on doing sth entschlossen sein, etw zu tun; be ~ in one's ways in seinen Gewohnheiten festgefahren sein □ v (pt/pp set, pres p setting) □ vt setzen; (adjust) einstellen; stellen (task, alarm clock); festsetzen, festlegen (date, limit); aufgeben (homework); zusammenstellen (questions); [ein]fassen (gem); einrichten (bone); legen (hair); decken (table) □ vi (sun·) untergehen; (become hard) fest werden; ~ about sth sich an etw (acc) machen; ~ about doing sth sich daranmachen, etw zu tun. ~ back vt zurücksetzen; (hold up) aufhalten; (fam: cost) kosten. ~ off vi losgehen (in vehicle) losfahren □ vt auslösen (alarm); explodieren lassen (bomb). ~ out vi losgehen (in vehicle) losfahren; ~ out to do sth sich vornehmen, etw zu tun □ vt auslegen (state) darlegen. ~ up vt aufbauen; (fig) gründen

set 'meal n Menü nt

settee /se'ti:/ n Sofa nt, Couch f

setting /'setɪŋ/ n Rahmen m; ⟨surroundings⟩ Umgebung f; ⟨of sun⟩ Untergang m; ⟨of jewel⟩ Fassung f

settle /'setl/ vt ⟨decide⟩ entscheiden; ⟨agree⟩ regeln; ⟨fix⟩ festsetzen; ⟨calm⟩ beruhigen; ⟨pay⟩ bezahlen □ vi sich niederlassen; ⟨snow, dust:⟩ liegen bleiben; ⟨subside⟩ sich senken; ⟨sediment:⟩ sich absetzen. ~ down vi sich beruhigen; ⟨permanently⟩ sesshaft werden. ~ up vi abrechnen

settlement /'setlmənt/ n ⟨see settle⟩ Entscheidung f; Regelung f; Bezahlung f; ⟨Jur⟩ Vergleich m; ⟨colony⟩ Siedlung f

settler /'setlə(r)/ n Siedler m

'set-to n ⟨fam⟩ Streit m

'set-up n System nt

seven /'sevn/ a sieben. ~teen a siebzehn. ~'teenth a siebzehnte(r,s)

seventh /'sevnθ/ a siebte(r,s)

seventieth /'sevntɪɪθ/ a siebzigste(r,s)

seventy /'sevntɪ/ a siebzig

sever /'sevə(r)/ vt durchtrennen; abbrechen ⟨relations⟩

several /'sevrl/ a & pron mehrere, einige

sever|e /sɪ'vɪə(r)/ a (-r, -st,) -ly adv streng; ⟨pain⟩ stark; ⟨illness⟩ schwer. ~ity /-'verətɪ/ n Strenge f; Schwere f

sew /səʊ/ vt/i ⟨pt sewed, pp sewn or sewed⟩ nähen. ~ up vt zunähen

sewage /'su:ɪdʒ/ n Abwasser nt

sewer /'su:ə(r)/ n Abwasserkanal m

sewing /'səʊɪŋ/ n Nähen nt; ⟨work⟩ Näharbeit f. ~ machine n Nähmaschine f

sewn /səʊn/ see sew

sex /seks/ n Geschlecht nt; ⟨sexuality, intercourse⟩ Sex m. ~ist a sexistisch. ~ offender n Triebverbrecher m

sexual /'seksjʊəl/ a, -ly adv sexuell. ~ 'intercourse n Geschlechtsverkehr m

sexuality /seksjʊ'ælətɪ/ n Sexualität f

sexy /'seksɪ/ a (-ier, -iest) sexy

shabby /'ʃæbɪ/ a (-ier, -iest), -ily adv schäbig

shack /ʃæk/ n Hütte f

shackles /'ʃæklz/ npl Fesseln pl

shade /ʃeɪd/ n Schatten m; ⟨of colour⟩ [Farb]ton m; ⟨for lamp⟩ [Lampen]schirm m; ⟨Amer: window-blind⟩ Jalousie f □ vt beschatten; ⟨draw lines on⟩ schattieren

shadow /'ʃædəʊ/ n Schatten m □ vt ⟨follow⟩ beschatten. ~y a schattenhaft

shady /'ʃeɪdɪ/ a (-ier, -iest) schattig; ⟨fam: disreputable⟩ zwielichtig

shaft /ʃɑ:ft/ n Schaft m; ⟨Techn⟩ Welle f; ⟨of light⟩ Strahl m; ⟨of lift⟩ Schacht m; ~s pl ⟨of cart⟩ Gabeldeichsel f

shaggy /'ʃægɪ/ a (-ier, -iest) zottig

shake /ʃeɪk/ n Schütteln nt □ v ⟨pt shook, pp shaken⟩ □ vt schütteln; ⟨cause to tremble, shock⟩ erschüttern; ~ hands with s.o. jdm die Hand geben □ vi wackeln; ⟨tremble⟩ zittern. ~ off vt abschütteln

shaky /'ʃeɪkɪ/ a (-ier, -iest) wackelig; ⟨hand, voice⟩ zittrig

shall /ʃæl/ v aux I ~ go ich werde gehen; we ~ see wir werden sehen; what ~ I do? was soll ich machen? I'll come too, ~ I? ich komme mit, ja? thou shalt not kill ⟨liter⟩ du sollst nicht töten

shallow /'ʃæləʊ/ a (-er, -est) seicht; ⟨dish⟩ flach; ⟨fig⟩ oberflächlich

sham /ʃæm/ a unecht □ n Heuchelei f; ⟨person⟩ Heuchler(in) m(f) □ vt ⟨pt/pp shammed⟩ vortäuschen

shambles /'ʃæmblz/ n Durcheinander nt

shame /ʃeɪm/ n Scham f; ⟨disgrace⟩ Schande f; be a ~ schade sein; what a ~! wie schade! ~-faced a betreten

shame|ful /'ʃeɪmfl/ a, -ly adv schändlich. ~less a, -ly adv schamlos

shampoo /ʃæm'pu:/ n Shampoo nt □ vt schamponieren

shandy /'ʃændɪ/ n Radler m

shan't /ʃɑ:nt/ = shall not

shape /ʃeɪp/ n Form f; ⟨figure⟩ Gestalt f; take ~ Gestalt annehmen □ vt formen ⟨into zu⟩ □ vi ~ up sich entwickeln. ~less a formlos; ⟨clothing⟩ unförmig

shapely /'ʃeɪplɪ/ a (-ier, -iest) wohlgeformt

share /ʃeə(r)/ n [An]teil m; ⟨Comm⟩ Aktie f □ vt/i teilen. ~holder n Aktionär(in) m(f)

shark /ʃɑ:k/ n Hai[fisch] m

sharp /ʃɑ:p/ a (-er, -est), -ly adv scharf; ⟨pointed⟩ spitz; ⟨severe⟩ heftig; ⟨sudden⟩ steil; ⟨alert⟩ clever; ⟨unscrupulous⟩ gerissen □ adv scharf; ⟨Mus⟩ zu hoch; at six o'clock ~ Punkt sechs Uhr; look ~! beeil dich! □ n ⟨Mus⟩ Kreuz nt. ~en vt schärfen; [an]spitzen ⟨pencil⟩

shatter /'ʃætə(r)/ vt zertrümmern; ⟨fig⟩ zerstören; be ~ed ⟨person:⟩ erschüttert sein; ⟨fam: exhausted⟩ kaputt sein □ vi zersplittern

shave /ʃeɪv/ n Rasur f; have a ~ sich rasieren □ vt rasieren □ vi sich rasieren. ~r n Rasierapparat m

shaving /'ʃeɪvɪŋ/ n Rasieren nt. ~-brush n Rasierpinsel m

shawl /ʃɔ:l/ n Schultertuch nt

she /ʃi:/ pron sie

sheaf /ʃi:f/ n (pl sheaves) Garbe f; ⟨of papers⟩ Bündel nt

shear /ʃɪə(r)/ vt (pt sheared, pp shorn or sheared) scheren

shears /ʃɪəz/ npl [große] Schere f

sheath /ʃiːθ/ n (pl ~s /ʃiːðz/) Scheide f

sheaves /ʃiːvz/ see sheaf

shed¹ /ʃed/ n Schuppen m; (for cattle) Stall m

shed² vt (pt/pp shed, pres p shedding) verlieren; vergießen ⟨blood, tears⟩; ~ light on Licht bringen in (+ acc)

sheen /ʃiːn/ n Glanz m

sheep /ʃiːp/ n inv Schaf nt. ~-dog n Hütehund m

sheepish /ʃiːpɪʃ/ a, -ly adv verlegen

'sheepskin n Schaffell nt

sheer /ʃɪə(r)/ a rein; (steep) steil; (transparent) hauchdünn ⬜ adv steil

sheet /ʃiːt/ n Laken nt, Betttuch nt; (of paper) Blatt nt; (of glass, metal) Platte f

sheikh /ʃeɪk/ n Scheich m

shelf /ʃelf/ n (pl shelves) Brett nt, Bord nt; (set of shelves) Regal nt

shell /ʃel/ n Schale f; (of snail) Haus nt; (of tortoise) Panzer m; (on beach) Muschel f; (of unfinished building) Rohbau m; (Mil) Granate f ⬜ vt pellen; enthülsen ⟨peas⟩; (Mil) [mit Granaten] beschießen. ~ out vi (fam) blechen

'shellfish n inv Schalentiere pl; (Culin) Meeresfrüchte pl

shelter /ʃeltə(r)/ n Schutz m; (air-raid~) Luftschutzraum m ⬜ vt schützen (from vor + dat) ⬜ vi sich unterstellen. ~ed a geschützt; ⟨life⟩ behütet

shelve /ʃelv/ vt auf Eis legen; (abandon) aufgeben ⬜ vi ⟨slope:⟩ abfallen

shelves /ʃelvz/ see shelf

shelving /ʃelvɪŋ/ n (shelves) Regale pl

shepherd /ʃepəd/ n Schäfer m; (Relig) Hirte m ⬜ vt führen. ~ess n Schäferin f. ~'s pie n Auflauf m aus mit Kartoffelbrei bedecktem Hackfleisch

sherry /ʃerɪ/ n Sherry m

shield /ʃiːld/ n Schild m; (for eyes) Schirm m; (Techn & fig) Schutz m ⬜ vt schützen (from vor + dat)

shift /ʃɪft/ n Verschiebung f; (at work) Schicht f; make ~ sich (dat) behelfen (with mit) ⬜ vt rücken; (take away) wegnehmen; (rearrange) umstellen, schieben ⟨blame⟩ (on to auf + acc) ⬜ vi sich verschieben; (fam: move quickly) rasen

'shift work n Schichtarbeit f

shifty /ʃɪftɪ/ a (-ier, -iest) (pej) verschlagen

shilly-shally /ʃɪlɪʃælɪ/ vi fackeln (fam)

shimmer /ʃɪmə(r)/ n Schimmer m ⬜ vi schimmern

shin /ʃɪn/ n Schienbein nt

shine /ʃaɪn/ n Glanz m ⬜ v (pt/pp shone) ⬜ vi leuchten; (reflect light) glänzen; ⟨sun:⟩ scheinen ⬜ vt ~ a light on beleuchten

shingle /ʃɪŋgl/ n (pebbles) Kiesel pl

shingles /ʃɪŋglz/ n (Med) Gürtelrose f

shiny /ʃaɪnɪ/ a (-ier, -iest) glänzend

ship /ʃɪp/ n Schiff nt ⬜ vt (pt/pp shipped) verschiffen

ship: ~building n Schiffbau m. ~ment n Sendung f. ~per n Spediteur m. ~ping n Versand m; (traffic) Schifffahrt f. ~shape a & adv in Ordnung. ~wreck n Schiffbruch m. ~wrecked a schiffbrüchig. ~yard n Werft f

shirk /ʃɜːk/ vt sich drücken vor (+ dat). ~er n Drückeberger m

shirt /ʃɜːt/ n [Ober]hemd nt; (for woman) Hemdbluse f

shit /ʃɪt/ n (vulg) Scheiße f ⬜ vi (pt/pp shit) (vulg) scheißen

shiver /ʃɪvə(r)/ n Schauder m ⬜ vi zittern

shoal /ʃəʊl/ n (of fish) Schwarm m

shock /ʃɒk/ n Schock m; (Electr) Schlag m; (impact) Erschütterung f ⬜ vt einen Schock versetzen (+ dat); (scandalize) schockieren. ~ing a schockierend; (fam: dreadful) fürchterlich

shod /ʃɒd/ see shoe

shoddy /ʃɒdɪ/ a (-ier, -iest) minderwertig

shoe /ʃuː/ n Schuh m; (of horse) Hufeisen nt ⬜ vt (pt/pp shod, pres p shoeing) beschlagen ⟨horse⟩

shoe: ~horn n Schuhanzieher m. ~lace n Schnürsenkel m. ~maker n Schuhmacher m. ~-string n on a ~-string (fam) mit ganz wenig Geld

shone /ʃɒn/ see shine

shoo /ʃuː/ vt scheuchen ⬜ int sch!

shook /ʃʊk/ see shake

shoot /ʃuːt/ n (Bot) Trieb m; (hunt) Jagd f ⬜ v (pt/pp shot) ⬜ vt schießen; (kill) erschießen; drehen ⟨film⟩ ⬜ vi schießen. ~ down vt abschießen. ~ out vi (rush) herausschießen. ~ up vi (grow) in die Höhe schießen/⟨prices:⟩ schnellen

'shooting-range n Schießstand m

shop /ʃɒp/ n Laden m, Geschäft nt; (workshop) Werkstatt f; talk ~ (fam) fachsimpeln ⬜ vi (pt/pp shopped, pres p shopping) einkaufen; go ~ping einkaufen gehen

shop: ~ assistant n Verkäufer(in) m(f). ~keeper n Ladenbesitzer(in) m(f). ~lifter n Ladendieb m. ~lifting n Ladendiebstahl m

shopping /ʃɒpɪŋ/ n Einkaufen nt; (articles) Einkäufe pl; do the ~ einkaufen. ~ bag n Einkaufstasche f ~ centre n

Einkaufszentrum nt. ~ trolley n Einkaufswagen m

shop: ~ 'steward n [gewerkschaftlicher] Vertrauensmann m. ~-'window n Schaufenster nt

shore /ʃɔː(r)/ n Strand m; (of lake) Ufer nt

shorn /ʃɔːn/ see shear

short /ʃɔːt/ (er, -est) kurz; (person) klein; (curt) schroff; a ~ time ago vor kurzem; be ~ of ... zu wenig ... haben; be in ~ supply knapp sein □ adv kurz; (abruptly) plötzlich; (curtly) kurz angebunden; in ~ kurzum; ~ of (except) außer; go ~ Mangel leiden; stop ~ of doing sth davor zurückschrecken, etw zu tun

shortage /ʃɔːtɪdʒ/ n Mangel m (of an + dat); (scarcity) Knappheit f

short: ~bread n ≈ Mürbekekse pl. ~-'circuit n Kurzschluss m. ~coming n Fehler m. ~ 'cut n Abkürzung f

shorten /ʃɔːtn/ vt [ab]kürzen; kürzer machen (garment)

short: ~hand n Kurzschrift f, Stenographie f. ~-'handed a be ~handed zu wenig Personal haben. ~hand 'typist n Stenotypistin f. ~ list n engere Auswahl f. ~-lived /-lɪvd/ a kurzlebig

short|ly /ʃɔːtlɪ/ adv in Kürze; ~ly before/after kurz vorher/danach. ~ness n Kürze f; (of person) Kleinheit f

shorts /ʃɔːts/ npl kurze Hose f, Shorts pl

short: ~-'sighted a kurzsichtig. ~-sleeved a kurzärmelig. ~-'staffed a be ~-staffed zu wenig Personal haben. ~ 'story n Kurzgeschichte f. ~-'tempered a aufbrausend. ~-term a kurzfristig. ~ wave n Kurzwelle f

shot /ʃɒt/ see shoot □ n Schuss m; (pellets) Schrot m; (person) Schütze m; (Phot) Aufnahme f; (injection) Spritze f; (fam: attempt) Versuch m; like a ~ (fam) sofort. ~gun n Schrotflinte f. ~-putting n (Sport) Kugelstoßen nt

should /ʃʊd/ v aux you ~ go du solltest gehen; I ~ have seen him ich hätte ihn sehen sollen; I ~ like it ich möchte; this ~ be enough das müsste eigentlich reichen; if he ~ be there falls er da sein sollte

shoulder /ʃəʊldə(r)/ n Schulter f □ vt schultern; (fig) auf sich (acc) nehmen. ~-blade n Schulterblatt nt. ~-strap n Tragriemen m; (on garment) Träger m

shout /ʃaʊt/ n Schrei m □ vt/i schreien. ~down vt niederschreien

shouting /ʃaʊtɪŋ/ n Geschrei nt

shove /ʃʌv/ n Stoß m; (fam) Schubs m □ vt stoßen; (fam) schubsen; (fam: put) tun □ vi drängeln. ~ off vi (fam) abhauen

shovel /ʃʌvl/ n Schaufel f □ vt (pt/pp shovelled) schaufeln

show /ʃəʊ/ n (display) Pracht f; (exhibition) Ausstellung f, Schau f; (performance) Vorstellung f; (Theat, TV) Show f; on ~ ausgestellt □ v (pt showed, pp shown) □ vt zeigen; (put on display) ausstellen; vorführen (film) □ vi sichtbar sein; (film:) gezeigt werden. ~ in vt hereinführen. ~ off vi (fam) angeben □ vt vorführen; (flaunt) angeben mit. ~ up vi [deutlich] zu sehen sein; (fam: arrive) auftauchen □ vt deutlich zeigen; (fam:embarrass) blamieren

'show-down n Entscheidungskampf m

shower /ʃaʊə(r)/ n Dusche f; (of rain) Schauer m; have a ~ duschen □ vt ~ with überschütten mit □ vi duschen. ~proof a regendicht. ~y a regnerisch

'show-jumping n Springreiten nt

shown /ʃəʊn/ see show

show: ~-off n Angeber(in) m(f). ~-piece n Paradestück nt. ~room n Ausstellungsraum m

showy /ʃəʊɪ/ a protzig

shrank /ʃræŋk/ see shrink

shred /ʃred/ n Fetzen m; (fig) Spur f □ vt (pt/pp shredded) zerkleinern; (Culin) schnitzeln. ~der n Reißwolf m; (Culin) Schnitzelwerk nt

shrewd /ʃruːd/ a (-er, -est), -ly adv klug. ~ness n Klugheit f

shriek /ʃriːk/ n Schrei m □ vt/i schreien

shrift /ʃrɪft/ n give s.o. short ~ jdn kurz abfertigen

shrill /ʃrɪl/ a, -y adv schrill

shrimp /ʃrɪmp/ n Garnele f, Krabbe f

shrine /ʃraɪn/ n Heiligtum nt

shrink /ʃrɪŋk/ vi (pt shrank, pp shrunk) schrumpfen; (garment:) einlaufen; (draw back) zurückschrecken (from vor + dat)

shrivel /ʃrɪvl/ vi (pt/pp shrivelled) verschrumpeln

shroud /ʃraʊd/ n Leichentuch nt; (fig) Schleier m

Shrove /ʃrəʊv/ n ~ 'Tuesday Fastnachtsdienstag m

shrub /ʃrʌb/ n Strauch m

shrug /ʃrʌg/ n Achselzucken nt □ vt/i (pt/pp shrugged) ~ [one's shoulders] die Achseln zucken

shrunk /ʃrʌŋk/ see shrink. ~en a geschrumpft

shudder /ʃʌdə(r)/ n Schauder m □ vi schaudern; (tremble) zittern

shuffle /ʃʌfl/ vi schlurfen □ vt mischen (cards)

shun /ʃʌn/ vt (pt/pp shunned) meiden

shunt /ʃʌnt/ vt rangieren

shush /ʃʊʃ/ int sch!

shut /ʃʌt/ v (pt/pp shut, pres p shutting) □ vt zumachen, schließen; ~ one's finger in the door sich (dat) den Finger in der Tür einklemmen □ vi sich schließen; ⟨shop:⟩ schließen, zumachen. ~ down vt schließen; stillegen ⟨factory⟩ □ vi schließen; ⟨factory:⟩ stillgelegt werden. ~ up vt abschließen; ⟨lock in⟩ einsperren □ vi ⟨fam⟩ den Mund halten

'shut-down n Stillegung f

shutter /'ʃʌtə(r)/ n [Fenster]laden m; ⟨Phot⟩ Verschluss m

shuttle /'ʃʌtl/ n ⟨Tex⟩ Schiffchen nt □ vi pendeln

shuttle: ~cock n Federball m. ~ service n Pendelverkehr m

shy /ʃaɪ/ a (-er, -est), -ly adv schüchtern; ⟨timid⟩ scheu □ vi ⟨pt/pp shied⟩ ⟨horse:⟩ scheuen. ~ness n Schüchternheit f

Siamese /saɪə'miːz/ a siamesisch

siblings /'sɪblɪŋz/ npl Geschwister pl

Sicily /'sɪsɪlɪ/ n Sizilien nt

sick /sɪk/ a krank; ⟨humour⟩ makaber; be ~ ⟨vomit⟩ sich übergeben; be ~ of sth ⟨fam⟩ etw satt haben; I feel ~ mir ist schlecht

sicken /'sɪkn/ vt anwidern □ vi be ~ing for something krank werden

sickle /'sɪkl/ n Sichel f

sick|ly /'sɪklɪ/ a (-ier, -iest) kränklich. ~ness n Krankheit f; ⟨vomiting⟩ Erbrechen nt

'sick-room n Krankenzimmer nt

side /saɪd/ n Seite f; on the ~ ⟨as sideline⟩ nebenbei; ~ by ~ nebeneinander; ⟨fig⟩ Seite an Seite; take ~s Partei ergreifen ⟨with für⟩; to be on the safe ~ vorsichtshalber □ attrib Seiten- □ vi ~ with Partei ergreifen für

side: ~board n Anrichte f. ~burns npl Koteletten pl. ~-effect n Nebenwirkung f. ~lights npl Standlicht nt. ~line n Nebenbeschäftigung f. ~-show n Nebenattraktion f. ~step vt ausweichen (+ dat). ~-track vt ablenken. ~walk n ⟨Amer⟩ Bürgersteig m. ~ways adv seitwärts

siding /'saɪdɪŋ/ n Abstellgleis nt

sidle /'saɪdl/ vi sich heranschleichen (up to an + acc)

siege /siːdʒ/ n Belagerung f; ⟨by police⟩ Umstellung f

sieve /sɪv/ n Sieb nt □ vt sieben

sift /sɪft/ vt sieben; ⟨fig⟩ durchsehen

sigh /saɪ/ n Seufzer m □ vi seufzen

sight /saɪt/ n Sicht f; ⟨faculty⟩ Sehvermögen nt; ⟨spectacle⟩ Anblick m; ⟨on gun⟩ Visier nt; ~s pl Sehenswürdigkeiten pl; at first ~ auf den ersten Blick; within/out of ~ in/außer Sicht; lose ~ of aus

dem Auge verlieren; know by ~ vom Sehen kennen; have bad ~ schlechte Augen haben □ vt sichten

'sightseeing n go ~ die Sehenswürdigkeiten besichtigen

sign /saɪn/ n Zeichen nt; ⟨notice⟩ Schild nt □ vt/i unterschreiben; ⟨author, artist:⟩ signieren. ~ on vi ⟨as unemployed⟩ sich arbeitslos melden; ⟨Mil⟩ sich verpflichten

signal /'sɪgnl/ n Signal nt □ vt/i ⟨pt/pp signalled⟩ signalisieren; ~ to s.o. jdm ein Signal geben ⟨to zu⟩. ~-box n Stellwerk nt

signature /'sɪgnətʃə(r)/ n Unterschrift f; ⟨of artist⟩ Signatur f. ~ tune n Kennmelodie f

signet-ring /'sɪgnɪt-/ n Siegelring m

significan|ce /sɪg'nɪfɪkəns/ n Bedeutung f. ~t a, -ly adv bedeutungsvoll; ⟨important⟩ bedeutend

signify /'sɪgnɪfaɪ/ vt ⟨pt/pp -ied⟩ bedeuten

signpost /'saɪn-/ n Wegweiser m

silence /'saɪləns/ n Stille f; ⟨of person⟩ Schweigen nt □ vt zum Schweigen bringen. ~r n ⟨on gun⟩ Schalldämpfer m; ⟨Auto⟩ Auspufftopf m

silent /'saɪlənt/ a, -ly adv still; ⟨without speaking⟩ schweigend; remain ~ schweigen. ~ film n Stummfilm m

silhouette /sɪlu'et/ n Silhouette f; ⟨picture⟩ Schattenriss m □ vt be ~d sich als Silhouette abheben

silicon /'sɪlɪkən/ n Silizium nt

silk /sɪlk/ n Seide f □ attrib Seiden-. ~worm n Seidenraupe f

silky /'sɪlkɪ/ a (-ier, -iest) seidig

sill /sɪl/ n Sims m & nt

silly /'sɪlɪ/ a (-ier, -iest) dumm, albern

silo /'saɪləʊ/ n Silo m

silt /sɪlt/ n Schlick m

silver /'sɪlvə(r)/ a silbern; ⟨coin, paper⟩ Silber- □ n Silber nt

silver: ~-plated a versilbert. ~ware n Silber nt. ~ 'wedding n Silberhochzeit f

similar /'sɪmɪlə(r)/ a, -ly adv ähnlich. ~ity /-'lærətɪ/ n Ähnlichkeit f

simile /'sɪmɪlɪ/ n Vergleich m

simmer /'sɪmə(r)/ vi leise kochen, ziehen □ vt ziehen lassen

simple /'sɪmpl/ a (-r, -st) einfach; ⟨person⟩ einfältig. ~-'minded a einfältig. ~ton /'sɪmpltən/ n Einfaltspinsel m

simplicity /sɪm'plɪsətɪ/ n Einfachheit f

simpli|fication /sɪmplɪfɪ'keɪʃn/ n Vereinfachung f. ~fy /'sɪmplɪfaɪ/ vt ⟨pt/pp -ied⟩ vereinfachen

simply /'sɪmplɪ/ adv einfach

simulat|e /'sɪmjʊleɪt/ vt vortäuschen; (Techn) simulieren. ~ion /-'leɪʃn/ n Vortäuschung f; Simulation f

simultaneous /sɪml'teɪnɪəs/ a, -ly adv gleichzeitig; (interpreting) Simultan-

sin /sɪn/ n Sünde f □ vi (pt sinned) sündigen

since /sɪns/ prep seit (+ dat) □ adv seitdem □ conj seit; (because) da

sincere /sɪn'sɪə(r)/ a aufrichtig; (heartfelt) herzlich. ~ly adv aufrichtig; Yours ~ly Mit freundlichen Grüßen

sincerity /sɪn'serətɪ/ n Aufrichtigkeit f

sinew /'sɪnju:/ n Sehne f

sinful /'sɪnfl/ a sündhaft

sing /sɪŋ/ vt/i (pt sang, pp sung) singen

singe /sɪndʒ/ vt (pres p singeing) versengen

singer /'sɪŋə(r)/ n Sänger(in) m(f)

single /'sɪŋgl/ a einzeln; (one only) einzig; (unmarried) ledig; (ticket) einfach; (room, bed) Einzel- □ n (ticket) einfache Fahrkarte f; (record) Single f; ~s pl (Tennis) Einzel nt □ vt ~ out auswählen

single: ~-breasted a einreihig. ~handed a & adv allein. ~-minded a zielstrebig. ~ parent n Alleinerziehende(r) m/f

singlet /'sɪŋglɪt/ n Unterhemd nt

singly /'sɪŋglɪ/ adv einzeln

singular /'sɪŋgjʊlə(r)/ a eigenartig; (Gram) im Singular □ n Singular m. ~ly adv außerordentlich

sinister /'sɪnɪstə(r)/ a finster

sink /sɪŋk/ n Spülbecken nt □ v (pt sank, pp sunk) vi sinken □ vt versenken ⟨ship⟩; senken ⟨shaft⟩. ~ in vi einsinken; (fam: be understood) kapiert werden

'sink unit n Spüle f

sinner /'sɪnə(r)/ n Sünder(in) m(f)

sinus /'saɪnəs/ n Nebenhöhle f

sip /sɪp/ n Schlückchen n □ vt (pt/pp sipped) in kleinen Schlucken trinken

siphon /'saɪfn/ n (bottle) Siphon m. ~ off vt mit einem Saugheber ablassen

sir /sɜː(r)/ n mein Herr; S~ (title) Sir; Dear S~s Sehr geehrte Herren

siren /'saɪrən/ n Sirene f

sissy /'sɪsɪ/ n Waschlappen m

sister /'sɪstə(r)/ n Schwester f; (nurse) Oberschwester f. ~-in-law (pl ~s-in-law) Schwägerin f. ~ly a schwesterlich

sit /sɪt/ v (pt/pp sat, pres p sitting) vi sitzen; (sit down) sich setzen; ⟨committee:⟩ tagen □ vt setzen; machen ⟨exam⟩. ~ back vi sich zurücklehnen. ~ down vi sich setzen. ~ up vi [aufrecht] sitzen; (rise) sich aufsetzen; (not slouch) gerade sitzen; (stay up) aufbleiben

site /saɪt/ n Gelände nt; (for camping) Platz m; (Archaeol) Stätte f □ vt legen

sitting /'sɪtɪŋ/ n Sitzung f; (for meals) Schub m

situat|e /'sɪtjʊeɪt/ vt legen; be ~ed liegen. ~ion /-'eɪʃn/ n Lage f; (circumstances) Situation f; (job) Stelle f

six /sɪks/ a sechs. ~teen a sechzehn. ~teenth a sechzehnte(r,s)

sixth /sɪksθ/ a sechste(r,s)

sixtieth /'sɪkstɪɪθ/ a sechzigste(r,s)

sixty /'sɪkstɪ/ a sechzig

size /saɪz/ n Größe f □ vt ~ up (fam) taxieren

sizeable /'saɪzəbl/ a ziemlich groß

sizzle /'sɪzl/ vi brutzeln

skate¹ /skeɪt/ n inv (fish) Rochen m

skate² n Schlittschuh m; (roller-) Rollschuh m □ vi Schlittschuh/Rollschuh laufen. ~r n Eisläufer(in) m(f); Rollschuhläufer(in) m(f)

skating /'skeɪtɪŋ/ n Eislaufen nt. ~-rink n Eisbahn f

skeleton /'skelɪtn/ n Skelett nt. ~ 'key n Dietrich m. ~ 'staff n Minimalbesetzung f

sketch /sketʃ/ n Skizze f; (Theat) Sketch m □ vt skizzieren

sketchy /'sketʃɪ/ a (-ier, -iest), -ily adv skizzenhaft

skew /skju:/ n on the ~ schräg

skewer /'skjʊə(r)/ n [Brat]spieß m

ski /ski:/ n Ski m □ vi (pt/pp skied, pres p skiing) Ski fahren or laufen

skid /skɪd/ n Schleudern nt □ vi (pt/pp skidded) schleudern

skier /'ski:ə(r)/ n Skiläufer(in) m(f)

skiing /'ski:ɪŋ/ n Skilaufen nt

skilful /'skɪlfl/ a, -ly adv geschickt

skill /skɪl/ n Geschick nt. ~ed a geschickt; (trained) ausgebildet

skim /skɪm/ vt (pt/pp skimmed) entrahmen ⟨milk⟩. ~ off vt abschöpfen. ~ through vt überfliegen

skimp /skɪmp/ vt sparen an (+ dat)

skimpy /'skɪmpɪ/ a (-ier, -iest) knapp

skin /skɪn/ n Haut f; (on fruit) Schale f □ vt (pt/pp skinned) häuten; schälen ⟨fruit⟩

skin: ~-deep a oberflächlich. ~-diving n Sporttauchen nt

skinflint /'skɪnflɪnt/ n Geizhals m

skinny /'skɪnɪ/ a (-ier, -iest) dünn

skip¹ /skɪp/ n Container m

skip² n Hüpfer m □ v (pt/pp skipped) vi hüpfen; (with rope) seilspringen □ vt überspringen

skipper /'skɪpə(r)/ n Kapitän m

'skipping-rope n Sprungseil nt

skirmish /'skɜːmɪʃ/ n Gefecht nt

skirt /skɜːt/ n Rock m □ vt herumgehen um

skit /skɪt/ n parodistischer Sketch m

skittle /'skɪtl/ n Kegel m

skive /skaɪv/ vi (fam) blaumachen

skulk /skʌlk/ vi lauern

skull /skʌl/ n Schädel m

skunk /skʌŋk/ n Stinktier nt

sky /skaɪ/ n Himmel m. ~light n Dachluke f. ~scraper n Wolkenkratzer m

slab /slæb/ n Platte f; (slice) Scheibe f; (of chocolate) Tafel f

slack /slæk/ a (-er, -est) schlaff, locker; ⟨person⟩ nachlässig; (Comm) flau □ vi bummeln

slacken /'slækn/ vi sich lockern; (diminish) nachlassen; (speed:) sich verringern □ vt lockern; (diminish) verringern

slacks /slæks/ npl Hose f

slag /slæg/ n Schlacke f

slain /sleɪn/ see slay

slake /sleɪk/ vt löschen

slam /slæm/ v (pt/pp slammed) □ vt zuschlagen; (put) knallen (fam); (fam: criticize) verreißen □ vi zuschlagen

slander /'slɑːndə(r)/ n Verleumdung f □ vt verleumden. ~ous /-rəs/ a verleumderisch

slang /slæŋ/ n Slang m. ~y a salopp

slant /slɑːnt/ n Schräge f; on the ~ schräg □ vt abschrägen; (fig) färben ⟨report⟩ □ vi sich neigen

slap /slæp/ n Schlag m □ vt (pt/pp slapped) schlagen; (put) knallen (fam) □ adv direkt

slap: ~dash a (fam) schludrig; ~-up a (fam) toll

slash /slæʃ/ n Schlitz m □ vt aufschlitzen; [drastisch] reduzieren ⟨prices⟩

slat /slæt/ n Latte f

slate /sleɪt/ n Schiefer m □ vt (fam) heruntermachen; verreißen ⟨performance⟩

slaughter /'slɔːtə(r)/ n Schlachten nt; (massacre) Gemetzel nt □ vt schlachten; abschlachten. ~house n Schlachthaus nt

Slav /slɑːv/ a slawisch □ n Slawe m/ Slawin f

slave /sleɪv/ n Sklave m/ Sklavin f □ vi ~ [away] schuften. ~-driver n Leuteschinder m

slavery /'sleɪvərɪ/ n Sklaverei f. ~ish a, -ly adv sklavisch

Slavonic /slə'vɒnɪk/ a slawisch

slay /sleɪ/ vt (pt slew, pp slain) ermorden

sleazy /'sliːzɪ/ a (-ier, -iest) schäbig

sledge /sledʒ/ n Schlitten m. ~-hammer n Vorschlaghammer m

sleek /sliːk/ a (-er, -est) seidig; (well-fed) wohlgenährt

sleep /sliːp/ n Schlaf m; go to ~ einschlafen; put to ~ einschläfern □ v (pt/pp slept) □ vi schlafen □ vt (accommodate) Unterkunft bieten für. ~er n Schläfer(in) m(f); (Rail) Schlafwagen m; (on track) Schwelle f

sleeping: ~-bag n Schlafsack m. ~-car n Schlafwagen m. ~-pill n Schlaftablette f

sleep: ~less a schlaflos. ~-walking n Schlafwandeln nt

sleepy /'sliːpɪ/ a (-ier, -iest), -ily adv schläfrig

sleet /sliːt/ n Schneeregen m □ vi it is ~ing es gibt Schneeregen

sleeve /sliːv/ n Ärmel m; (for record) Hülle f. ~less a ärmellos

sleigh /sleɪ/ n [Pferde]schlitten m

sleight /slaɪt/ n ~ of hand Taschenspielerei f

slender /'slendə(r)/ a schlank; (fig) gering

slept /slept/ see sleep

sleuth /sluːθ/ n Detektiv m

slew[1] /sluː/ vi schwenken

slew[2] see slay

slice /slaɪs/ n Scheibe f □ vt in Scheiben schneiden; ~d bread Schnittbrot nt

slick /slɪk/ a clever □ n (of oil) Ölteppich m

slid|e /slaɪd/ n Rutschbahn f; (for hair) Spange f; (Phot) Dia nt □ v (pt/pp slid) □ vi rutschen □ vt schieben. ~ing a gleitend; ⟨door, seat⟩ Schiebe-

slight /slaɪt/ a (-er, -est), -ly adv leicht; ⟨importance⟩ gering; ⟨acquaintance⟩ flüchtig; (slender) schlank; not in the ~est nicht im Geringsten; ~ly better ein bisschen besser □ vt kränken, beleidigen □ n Beleidigung f

slim /slɪm/ a (slimmer, slimmest) schlank; ⟨volume⟩ schmal; (fig) gering □ vi eine Schlankheitskur machen

slim|e /slaɪm/ n Schleim m. ~y a schleimig

sling /slɪŋ/ n (Med) Schlinge f □ vt (pt/pp slung) (fam) schmeißen

slip /slɪp/ n (mistake) Fehler m, (fam) Patzer m; (petticoat) Unterrock m; (for pillow) Bezug m; (paper) Zettel m; give s.o. the ~ (fam) jdm entwischen; ~ of the tongue Versprecher m □ v (pt/pp slipped) □ vi rutschen; (fall) ausrutschen; (go quickly) schlüpfen; (decline) nachlassen □ vt schieben; ~ s.o.'s mind jdm entfallen. ~ away vi sich fortschleichen; ⟨time:⟩ verfliegen. ~ up vi (fam) einen Schnitzer machen

slipped 'disc n (Med) Bandscheibenvorfall m

slipper /'slɪpə(r)/ n Hausschuh m

slippery /'slɪpərɪ/ a glitschig; ⟨surface⟩ glatt

slipshod /'slɪpʃɒd/ a schludrig

'slip-up n (fam) Schnitzer m

slit /slɪt/ n Schlitz m □ vt (pt/pp slit) aufschlitzen

slither /'slɪðə(r)/ vi rutschen

sliver /'slɪvə(r)/ n Splitter m

slobber /'slɒbə(r)/ vi sabbern

slog /slɒg/ n [hard] ~ Schinderei f □ vi (pt/pp slogged) □ vi schuften □ vt schlagen

slogan /'sləʊgən/ n Schlagwort nt; ⟨advertising⟩ Werbespruch m

slop /slɒp/ v (pt/pp slopped) □ vt verschütten □ vi ~ over überschwappen. ~s npl Schmutzwasser nt

slop|e /sləʊp/ n Hang m; ⟨inclination⟩ Neigung f □ vi sich neigen. ~ing a schräg

sloppy /'slɒpɪ/ a (-ier, -iest) schludrig; ⟨sentimental⟩ sentimental

slosh /slɒʃ/ vi (fam) platschen; ⟨water:⟩ schwappen □ vt (fam: hit) schlagen

slot /slɒt/ n Schlitz m; (TV) Sendezeit f □ v (pt/pp slotted) □ vt einfügen □ vi sich einfügen (in in + acc)

sloth /sləʊθ/ n Trägheit f

'slot-machine n Münzautomat m; (for gambling) Spielautomat m

slouch /slaʊtʃ/ vi sich schlecht halten

slovenly /'slʌvnlɪ/ a schlampig

slow /sləʊ/ a (-er, -est), -ly adv langsam; be ~ ⟨clock:⟩ nachgehen; in ~ motion in Zeitlupe □ adv langsam □ vt verlangsamen □ vi ~ down, ~ up langsamer werden

slow: ~coach n (fam) Trödler m. ~ness n Langsamkeit f

sludge /slʌdʒ/ n Schlamm m

slug /slʌg/ n Nacktschnecke f

sluggish /'slʌgɪʃ/ a, -ly adv träge

sluice /sluːs/ n Schleuse f

slum /slʌm/ n ⟨house⟩ Elendsquartier nt; ~s pl Elendsviertel nt

slumber /'slʌmbə(r)/ n Schlummer m □ vi schlummern

slump /slʌmp/ n Sturz m □ vi fallen; ⟨crumple⟩ zusammensacken; ⟨prices:⟩ stürzen; ⟨sales:⟩ zurückgehen

slung /slʌŋ/ see sling

slur /slɜː(r)/ n ⟨discredit⟩ Schande f □ vt (pt/pp slurred) undeutlich sprechen

slurp /slɜːp/ vt/i schlürfen

slush /slʌʃ/ n [Schnee]matsch m; ⟨fig⟩ Kitsch m. ~ fund n Fonds m für Bestechungsgelder

slushy /'slʌʃɪ/ a matschig; ⟨sentimental⟩ kitschig

slut /slʌt/ n Schlampe f (fam)

sly /slaɪ/ a (-er, -est), -ly adv verschlagen □ n on the ~ heimlich

smack[1] /smæk/ n Schlag m, Klaps m □ vt schlagen; ~ one's lips mit den Lippen schmatzen □ adv (fam) direkt

smack[2] vi ~ of ⟨fig⟩ riechen nach

small /smɔːl/ a (-er, -est) klein; in the ~ hours in den frühen Morgenstunden □ adv chop up ~ klein hacken □ n ~ of the back Kreuz nt

small: ~ ads npl Kleinanzeigen pl. ~ 'change n Kleingeld nt. ~-holding n landwirtschaftlicher Kleinbetrieb m. ~pox n Pocken pl. ~ talk n leichte Konversation f

smarmy /'smɑːmɪ/ a (-ier, -iest) (fam) ölig

smart /smɑːt/ a (-er, -est), -ly adv schick; ⟨clever⟩ schlau, clever; ⟨brisk⟩ flott; ⟨Amer fam: cheeky⟩ frech □ vi brennen

smarten /'smɑːtn/ vt ~ oneself up mehr auf sein Äußeres achten

smash /smæʃ/ n Krach m; ⟨collision⟩ Zusammenstoß m; (Tennis) Schmetterball m □ vt zerschlagen; ⟨strike⟩ schlagen; (Tennis) schmettern □ vi zerschmettern; ⟨crash⟩ krachen (into gegen). ~ing a (fam) toll

smattering /'smætərɪŋ/ n a ~ of German ein paar Brocken Deutsch

smear /smɪə(r)/ n verschmierter Fleck m; (Med) Abstrich m; ⟨fig⟩ Verleumdung f □ vt schmieren; ⟨coat⟩ beschmieren (with mit); ⟨fig⟩ verleumden □ vi schmieren

smell /smel/ n Geruch m; ⟨sense⟩ Geruchssinn m □ v (pt/pp smelt or smelled) □ vt riechen; ⟨sniff⟩ riechen an (+ dat) □ vi riechen (of nach)

smelly /'smelɪ/ a (-ier, -iest) übel riechend

smelt[1] /smelt/ see smell

smelt[2] vt schmelzen

smile /smaɪl/ n Lächeln nt □ vi lächeln; ~ at anlächeln

smirk /smɜːk/ vi feixen

smith /smɪθ/ n Schmied m

smithereens /smɪðə'riːnz/ npl smash to ~ in tausend Stücke schlagen

smitten /'smɪtn/ a ~ with sehr angetan von

smock /smɒk/ n Kittel m

smog /smɒg/ n Smog m

smoke /sməʊk/ n Rauch m □ vt/i rauchen; (Culin) räuchern. ~less a rauchfrei; ⟨fuel⟩ rauchlos

smoker /'sməʊkə(r)/ n Raucher m; (Rail) Raucherabteil nt

'smoke-screen n [künstliche] Nebelwand f

smoking /'sməʊkɪŋ/ n Rauchen nt; 'no ~' 'Rauchen verboten'

smoky /'sməʊkɪ/ a (-ier, -iest) verraucht; (taste) rauchig

smooth /smuːð/ a (-er, -est), -ly adv glatt □ vt glätten. ~ out vt glatt streichen

smother /'smʌðə(r)/ vt ersticken; (cover) bedecken; (suppress) unterdrücken

smoulder /'sməʊldə(r)/ vi schwelen

smudge /smʌdʒ/ n Fleck m □ vt verwischen □ vi schmieren

smug /smʌg/ a (smugger, smuggest), -ly adv selbstgefällig

smuggl|e /'smʌgl/ vt schmuggeln. ~er n Schmuggler m. ~ing n Schmuggel m

smut /smʌt/ n Rußflocke f; (mark) Rußfleck m; (fig) Schmutz m

smutty /'smʌtɪ/ a (-ier, -iest) schmutzig

snack /snæk/ n Imbiss m. ~-bar n Imbissstube f

snag /snæg/ n Schwierigkeit f, (fam) Haken m

snail /sneɪl/ n Schnecke f; at a ~'s pace im Schneckentempo

snake /sneɪk/ n Schlange f

snap /snæp/ n Knacken nt; (photo) Schnappschuss m □ attrib (decision) plötzlich □ v (pt/pp snapped) □ vi [entzwei]brechen; ~ at (bite) schnappen nach; (speak sharply) [scharf] anfahren □ vt zerbrechen; (say) fauchen; (Phot) knipsen. ~ up vt wegschnappen

snappy /'snæpɪ/ a (-ier, -iest) bissig; (smart) flott; make it ~! ein bisschen schnell!

'snapshot n Schnappschuss m

snare /sneə(r)/ n Schlinge f

snarl /snɑːl/ vi [mit gefletschten Zähnen] knurren

snatch /snætʃ/ n (fragment) Fetzen pl; (theft) Raub m; make a ~ at greifen nach □ vt schnappen; (steal) klauen; entführen (child); ~ sth from s.o. jdm etw entreißen

sneak /sniːk/ n (fam) Petze f □ vi schleichen; (fam: tell tales) petzen □ vt (take) mitgehen lassen □ vi ~ in/out sich hinein-/hinausschleichen

sneakers /'sniːkəz/ npl (Amer) Turnschuhe pl

sneaking /'sniːkɪŋ/ a heimlich; (suspicion) leise

sneaky /'sniːkɪ/ a hinterhältig

sneer /snɪə(r)/ vi höhnisch lächeln; (mock) spotten

sneeze /sniːz/ n Niesen nt □ vi niesen

snide /snaɪd/ a (fam) abfällig

sniff /snɪf/ vi schnüffeln □ vt schnüffeln an (+ dat); schnüffeln (glue)

snigger /'snɪgə(r)/ vi [boshaft] kichern

snip /snɪp/ n Schnitt m; (fam: bargain) günstiger Kauf m □ vt/i ~ [at] schnippeln an (+ dat)

snipe /snaɪp/ vi ~ at aus dem Hinterhalt schießen auf (+ acc); (fig) anschießen. ~r n Heckenschütze m

snippet /'snɪpɪt/ n Schnipsel m; (of information) Bruchstück nt

snivel /'snɪvl/ vi (pt/pp snivelled) flennen

snob /snɒb/ n Snob m. ~bery n Snobismus m. ~bish a snobistisch

snoop /snuːp/ vi (fam) schnüffeln

snooty /'snuːtɪ/ a (fam) hochnäsig

snooze /snuːz/ n Nickerchen nt □ vi dösen

snore /snɔː(r)/ vi schnarchen

snorkel /'snɔːkl/ n Schnorchel m

snort /snɔːt/ vi schnauben

snout /snaʊt/ n Schnauze f

snow /snəʊ/ n Schnee m □ vi schneien; ~ed under with (fig) überhäuft mit

snow: ~ball n Schneeball m □ vi lawinenartig anwachsen. ~drift n Schneewehe f. ~drop n Schneeglöckchen nt. ~fall n Schneefall m. ~flake n Schneeflocke f. ~ flurry n Schneegestöber nt. ~man n Schneemann m. ~plough n Schneepflug m. ~storm n Schneesturm m

snub /snʌb/ n Abfuhr f □ vt (pt/pp snubbed) brüskieren

'snub-nosed a stupsnasig

snuff¹ /snʌf/ n Schnupftabak m

snuff² vt ~ [out] löschen

snuffle /'snʌfl/ vi schnüffeln

snug /snʌg/ a (snugger, snuggest) behaglich, gemütlich

snuggle /'snʌgl/ vi sich kuscheln (up to an + acc)

so /səʊ/ adv so; not so fast nicht so schnell; so am I ich auch; so does he er auch; so I see das sehe ich; that is so das stimmt; so much the better umso besser; so it is tatsächlich; if so wenn ja; so as to um zu; so long! (fam) tschüs! □ pron I hope so hoffentlich; I think so ich glaube schon; I told you so ich hab's dir gleich gesagt; because I say so weil ich es sage; I'm afraid so leider ja; so saying/doing, he/she … indem er/sie das sagte/tat, …; an hour or so eine Stunde oder so; very much so durchaus □ conj (therefore) also; so that damit; so there! fertig! so what! na und! so you see wie du siehst; so where have you been? wo warst du denn?

soak /səʊk/ vt nass machen; (steep) einweichen; (fam: fleece) schröpfen □ vi weichen; (liquid:) sickern. ~ up vt aufsaugen

soaking /ˈsəʊkɪŋ/ a & adv ~ [wet] patschnass (fam)

soap /səʊp/ n Seife f. ~ opera n Seifenoper f. ~ powder n Seifenpulver nt

soapy /ˈsəʊpɪ/ a (-ier, -iest) seifig

soar /sɔː(r)/ vi aufsteigen; (prices:) in die Höhe schnellen

sob /sɒb/ n Schluchzer m □ vi (pt/pp sobbed) schluchzen

sober /ˈsəʊbə(r)/ a, -ly adv nüchtern; (serious) ernst; (colour:) gedeckt. ~ up vi nüchtern werden

'so-called a sogenannt

soccer /ˈsɒkə(r)/ n (fam) Fußball m

sociable /ˈsəʊʃəbl/ a gesellig

social /ˈsəʊʃl/ a gesellschaftlich; (Admin, Pol, Zool) sozial

socialis|m /ˈsəʊʃəlɪzm/ n Sozialismus m. ~t /-ɪst/ a sozialistisch □ n Sozialist m

socialize /ˈsəʊʃəlaɪz/ vi [gesellschaftlich] verkehren

socially /ˈsəʊʃəlɪ/ adv gesellschaftlich; know ~ privat kennen

social: ~ se'curity n Sozialhilfe f. ~ work n Sozialarbeit f. ~ worker n Sozialarbeiter(in) m(f)

society /səˈsaɪətɪ/ n Gesellschaft f; (club) Verein m

sociolog|ist /səʊsɪˈɒlədʒɪst/ n Soziologe m. ~y n Soziologie f

sock[1] /sɒk/ n Socke f; (knee-length) Kniestrumpf m

sock[2] n (fam) Schlag m □ vt (fam) hauen

socket /ˈsɒkɪt/ n (of eye) Augenhöhle f; (of joint) Gelenkpfanne f; (wall plug) Steckdose f; (for bulb) Fassung f

soda /ˈsəʊdə/ n Soda nt; (Amer) Limonade f. ~ water n Sodawasser nt

sodden /ˈsɒdn/ a durchnässt

sodium /ˈsəʊdɪəm/ n Natrium nt

sofa /ˈsəʊfə/ n Sofa nt. ~ bed n Schlafcouch f

soft /sɒft/ a (-er, -est), -ly adv weich; (quiet) leise; (gentle) sanft; (fam: silly) dumm; have a ~ spot for s.o. jdn mögen. ~ drink n alkoholfreies Getränk nt

soften /ˈsɒfn/ vt weich machen; (fig) mildern □ vi weich werden

soft: ~ toy n Stofftier nt. ~ware n Software f

soggy /ˈsɒgɪ/ a (-ier, -iest) aufgeweicht

soil[1] /sɔɪl/ n Erde f, Boden m

soil[2] vt verschmutzen

solace /ˈsɒləs/ n Trost m

solar /ˈsəʊlə(r)/ a Sonnen-

sold /səʊld/ see sell

solder /ˈsəʊldə(r)/ n Lötmetall nt □ vt löten

soldier /ˈsəʊldʒə(r)/ n Soldat m □ vi ~ on [unbeirrt] weitermachen

sole[1] /səʊl/ n Sohle f

sole[2] n (fish) Seezunge f

sole[3] a einzig. ~ly adv einzig und allein

solemn /ˈsɒləm/ a, -ly adv feierlich; (serious) ernst. ~ity /səˈlemnətɪ/ n Feierlichkeit f; Ernst m

solicit /səˈlɪsɪt/ vt bitten um □ vi (prostitute:) sich an Männer heranmachen

solicitor /səˈlɪsɪtə(r)/ n Rechtsanwalt m /-anwältin f

solicitous /səˈlɪsɪtəs/ a besorgt

solid /ˈsɒlɪd/ a fest; (sturdy) stabil; (not hollow, of same substance) massiv; (unanimous) einstimmig; (complete) ganz □ n (Geom) Körper m; ~s pl (food) feste Nahrung f

solidarity /sɒlɪˈdærətɪ/ n Solidarität f

solidify /səˈlɪdɪfaɪ/ vi (pt/pp -ied) fest werden

soliloquy /səˈlɪləkwɪ/ n Selbstgespräch nt

solitary /ˈsɒlɪtərɪ/ a einsam; (sole) einzig. ~ con'finement n Einzelhaft f

solitude /ˈsɒlɪtjuːd/ n Einsamkeit f

solo /ˈsəʊləʊ/ n Solo nt □ a Solo-; (flight) Allein- □ adv solo. ~ist n Solist(in) m(f)

solstice /ˈsɒlstɪs/ n Sonnenwende f

soluble /ˈsɒljʊbl/ a löslich; (solvable) lösbar

solution /səˈluːʃn/ n Lösung f

solvable /ˈsɒlvəbl/ a lösbar

solve /sɒlv/ vt lösen

solvent /ˈsɒlvənt/ a zahlungsfähig; (Chem) lösend □ n Lösungsmittel nt

sombre /ˈsɒmbə(r)/ a dunkel; (mood) düster

some /sʌm/ a & pron etwas; (a little) ein bisschen; (with pl noun) einige; (a few) ein paar; (certain) manche(r,s); (one or the other) [irgend]ein; ~ day eines Tages; I want ~ ich möchte etwas/(pl) welche; will you have ~ wine? möchten Sie Wein? I need ~ money/books ich brauche Geld/Bücher; do ~ shopping einkaufen

some: ~body /-bədɪ/ pron & n jemand; (emphatic) irgendjemand. ~how adv irgendwie. ~one pron & n = somebody

somersault /ˈsʌməsɔːlt/ n Purzelbaum m (fam); (Sport) Salto m; turn a ~ einen Purzelbaum schlagen/einen Salto springen

'something pron & adv etwas; (emphatic) irgendetwas; ~ different etwas anderes;

~ like so etwas wie; see ~ of s.o. jdn mal sehen

some: ~time adv irgendwann □ a ehemalig. ~times adv manchmal. ~what adv ziemlich. ~where adv irgendwo; ⟨go⟩ irgendwohin

son /sʌn/ n Sohn m

sonata /sə'nɑːtə/ n Sonate f

song /sɒŋ/ n Lied nt. ~bird n Singvogel m

sonic /'sɒnɪk/ a Schall-. ~ 'boom n Überschallknall m

'son-in-law n (pl ~s-in-law) Schwiegersohn m

soon /suːn/ adv (-er, -est) bald; ⟨quickly⟩ schnell; too ~ zu früh; as ~ as sobald; as ~ as possible so bald wie möglich; ~er or later früher oder später; no ~er had I arrived than ... kaum war ich angekommen, da ...; I would ~er stay in würde lieber bleiben

soot /sʊt/ n Ruß m

sooth|e /suːð/ vt beruhigen; lindern ⟨pain⟩. ~ing a, -ly adv beruhigend; lindernd

sooty /'sʊtɪ/ a rußig

sop /sɒp/ n Beschwichtigungsmittel nt

sophisticated /sə'fɪstɪkeɪtɪd/ a weltgewandt; ⟨complex⟩ hoch entwickelt

soporific /sɒpə'rɪfɪk/ a einschläfernd

sopping /'sɒpɪŋ/ a & adv ~ [wet] durchnässt

soppy /'sɒpɪ/ a (-ier, -iest) ⟨fam⟩ rührselig

soprano /sə'prɑːnəʊ/ n Sopran m; ⟨woman⟩ Sopranistin f

sordid /'sɔːdɪd/ a schmutzig

sore /sɔː(r)/ a (-r, -st) wund; ⟨painful⟩ schmerzhaft; have a ~ throat Halsschmerzen haben □ n wunde Stelle f. ~ly adv sehr

sorrow /'sɒrəʊ/ n Kummer m, Leid nt. ~ful a traurig

sorry /'sɒrɪ/ a (-ier, -iest) ⟨sad⟩ traurig; ⟨wretched⟩ erbärmlich; I am ~ es tut mir Leid; she is or feels ~ for him er tut ihr Leid; I am ~ to say leider; ~! Entschuldigung!

sort /sɔːt/ n Art f; ⟨brand⟩ Sorte f; he's a good ~ ⟨fam⟩ er ist in Ordnung; be out of ~s ⟨fam⟩ nicht auf der Höhe sein □ vt sortieren.~ out vt sortieren; ⟨fig⟩ klären

sought /sɔːt/ see seek

soul /səʊl/ n Seele f. ~ful a gefühlvoll

sound¹ /saʊnd/ a (-er, -est) gesund; ⟨sensible⟩ vernünftig; ⟨secure⟩ solide; ⟨thorough⟩ gehörig □ adv be ~ asleep fest schlafen

sound² vt ⟨Naut⟩ loten. ~ out vt ⟨fig⟩ aushorchen

sound³ n ⟨strait⟩ Meerenge f

sound⁴ n Laut m; ⟨noise⟩ Geräusch nt; ⟨Phys⟩ Schall m; ⟨Radio, TV⟩ Ton m; ⟨of bells, music⟩ Klang m; I don't like the ~ of it ⟨fam⟩ das hört sich nicht gut an □ vi [er]tönen; ⟨seem⟩ sich anhören □ vt ⟨pronounce⟩ aussprechen; schlagen ⟨alarm⟩; ⟨Med⟩ abhorchen ⟨chest⟩. ~ barrier n Schallmauer f. ~less a, -ly adv lautlos

soundly /'saʊndlɪ/ adv solide; ⟨sleep⟩ fest; ⟨defeat⟩ vernichtend

'soundproof a schalldicht

soup /suːp/ n Suppe f. ~ed-up a ⟨fam⟩ ⟨engine⟩ frisiert

soup: ~plate n Suppenteller m. ~spoon n Suppenlöffel m

sour /saʊə(r)/ a (-er, -est) sauer; ⟨bad-tempered⟩ griesgrämig, verdrießlich

source /sɔːs/ n Quelle f

south /saʊθ/ n Süden m; to the ~ of südlich von □ a Süd-, süd- □ adv nach Süden

south: S~ 'Africa n Südafrika nt. S~ A'merica n Südamerika nt. ~-'east n Südosten m

southerly /'sʌðəlɪ/ a südlich

southern /'sʌðən/ a südlich

South 'Pole n Südpol m

'southward[s] /-wəd[z]/ adv nach Süden

souvenir /suːvə'nɪə(r)/ n Andenken nt, Souvenir nt

sovereign /'sɒvrɪn/ a souverän □ n Souverän m. ~ty n Souveränität f

Soviet /'səʊvɪət/ a sowjetisch; ~ Union Sowjetunion f

sow¹ /saʊ/ n Sau f

sow² /səʊ/ vt (pt sowed, pp sown or sowed) säen

soya /'sɔɪə/ n ~ bean Sojabohne f

spa /spɑː/ n Heilbad nt

space /speɪs/ n Raum m; ⟨gap⟩ Platz m; ⟨Astr⟩ Weltraum m; leave/clear a ~ Platz lassen/schaffen □ vt ~ [out] [in Abständen] verteilen

space: ~craft n Raumfahrzeug nt. ~ship n Raumschiff nt

spacious /'speɪʃəs/ a geräumig

spade /speɪd/ n Spaten m; ⟨for child⟩ Schaufel f; ~s pl ⟨Cards⟩ Pik nt; call a ~ a ~ das Kind beim rechten Namen nennen. ~work n Vorarbeit f

Spain /speɪn/ n Spanien nt

span¹ /spæn/ n Spanne f; ⟨of arch⟩ Spannweite f □ vt (pp spanned) überspannen; umspannen ⟨time⟩

span² see spick

Span|iard /'spænjəd/ n Spanier(in) m(f). ~ish a spanisch □ n ⟨Lang⟩ Spanisch nt; the ~ish pl die Spanier

spank /spæŋk/ vt verhauen

spanner /'spænə(r)/ n Schraubenschlüssel m

spar /spɑ:(r)/ vi (pt/pp sparred) (Sport) sparren; (argue) sich zanken

spare /speə(r)/ a (surplus) übrig; (additional) zusätzlich; (seat, time) frei; (room) Gäste-; (bed, cup) Ersatz- □ n (part) Ersatzteil nt □ vt ersparen; (not hurt) verschonen; (do without) entbehren; (afford to give) erübrigen; to ~ (surplus) übrig. ~ 'wheel n Reserverad nt

sparing /'speərɪŋ/ a, -ly adv sparsam

spark /spɑ:k/ n Funke nt □ vt ~ off zünden; (fig) auslösen. ~ing-plug n (Auto) Zündkerze f

sparkl|e /'spɑ:kl/ n Funkeln nt □ vi funkeln. ~ing a funkelnd; (wine) Schaum-

sparrow /'spærəʊ/ n Spatz m

sparse /spɑ:s/ a spärlich. ~ly adv spärlich; (populated) dünn

Spartan /'spɑ:tn/ a spartanisch

spasm /'spæzm/ n Anfall m; (cramp) Krampf m. ~odic /-'mɒdɪk/ a, -ally adv sporadisch; (Med) krampfartig

spastic /'spæstɪk/ a spastisch [gelähmt] □ n Spastiker(in) m(f)

spat /spæt/ see spit²

spate /speɪt/ n Flut f; (series) Serie f; be in full ~ Hochwasser führen

spatial /'speɪʃl/ a räumlich

spatter /'spætə(r)/ vt spritzen; ~ with bespritzen mit

spatula /'spætjʊlə/ n Spachtel m; (Med) Spatel m

spawn /spɔ:n/ n Laich m □ vi laichen □ vt (fig) hervorbringen

spay /speɪ/ vt sterilisieren

speak /spi:k/ v (pt spoke, pp spoken) □ vi sprechen (to mit) □ ~ing! (Teleph) am Apparat! □ vt sprechen; sagen (truth). ~ up vi lauter sprechen; ~ up for oneself seine Meinung äußern

speaker /'spi:kə(r)/ n Sprecher(in) m(f); (in public) Redner(in) m(f); (loudspeaker) Lautsprecher m

spear /spɪə(r)/ n Speer m □ vt aufspießen. ~head vt (fig) anführen

spec /spek/ n on ~ (fam) auf gut Glück

special /'speʃl/ a besondere(r,s), speziell. ~ist n Spezialist m; (Med) Facharzt m /-ärztin f. ~ity /-ʃi'ælətɪ/ n Spezialität f

special|ize /'speʃəlaɪz/ vi sich spezialisieren (in auf + acc). ~ly adv speziell; (particularly) besonders

species /'spi:ʃi:z/ n Art f

specific /spə'sɪfɪk/ a bestimmt; (precise) genau; (Phys) spezifisch. ~ally adv ausdrücklich

specification /spesɪfɪ'keɪʃn/ n & ~s pl genaue Angaben pl

specify /'spesɪfaɪ/ vt (pt/pp -ied) [genau] angeben

specimen /'spesɪmən/ n Exemplar nt; (sample) Probe f; (of urine) Urinprobe f

speck /spek/ n Fleck m; (particle) Teilchen nt

speckled /'spekld/ a gesprenkelt

specs /speks/ npl (fam) Brille f

spectacle /'spektəkl/ n (show) Schauspiel nt; (sight) Anblick m. ~s npl Brille f

spectacular /spek'tækjʊlə(r)/ a spektakulär

spectator /spek'teɪtə(r)/ n Zuschauer(in) m(f)

spectre /'spektə(r)/ n Gespenst nt; (fig) Schreckgespenst nt

spectrum /'spektrəm/ n (pl -tra) Spektrum nt

speculat|e /'spekjʊleɪt/ vi spekulieren. ~ion /-'leɪʃn/ n Spekulation f. ~or n Spekulant m

sped /sped/ see speed

speech /spi:tʃ/ n Sprache f; (address) Rede f. ~less a sprachlos

speed /spi:d/ n Geschwindigkeit f; (rapidity) Schnelligkeit f; (gear) Gang m; at ~ mit hoher Geschwindigkeit □ vi (pt/pp sped) schnell fahren □ (pt/pp speeded) (go too fast) zu schnell fahren. ~ up (pt/pp speeded up) □ vt beschleunigen □ vi schneller werden; (vehicle:) schneller fahren

speed: ~boat n Rennboot nt. ~ing n Geschwindigkeitsüberschreitung f. ~ limit n Geschwindigkeitsbeschränkung f

speedometer /spi:'dɒmɪtə(r)/ n Tachometer m

speedy /'spi:dɪ/ a (-ier, -iest), -ily adv schnell

spell¹ /spel/ n Weile f; (of weather) Periode f

spell² v (pt/pp spelled or spelt) □ vt schreiben; (aloud) buchstabieren; (fig: mean) bedeuten □ vi richtig schreiben; (aloud) buchstabieren. ~ out vt buchstabieren; (fig) genau erklären

spell³ n Zauber m; (words) Zauberspruch m. ~bound a wie verzaubert

spelling /'spelɪŋ/ n Schreibweise f; (orthography) Rechtschreibung f

spelt /spelt/ see spell²

spend /spend/ vt/i (pt/pp spent) ausgeben; verbringen (time)

spent /spent/ see spend

sperm /spɜ:m/ n Samen m

spew /spju:/ vt speien

spher|e /sfɪə(r)/ n Kugel f; (fig) Sphäre f. ~ical /'sferɪkl/ a kugelförmig

spice /spaɪs/ n Gewürz nt; (fig) Würze f

spick /spɪk/ a ~ and span blitzsauber

spicy /'spaɪsɪ/ a würzig, pikant

spider /'spaɪdə(r)/ n Spinne f

spik|e /spaɪk/ n Spitze f; (Bot, Zool) Stachel m; (on shoe) Spike m. ~y a stachelig

spill /spɪl/ v (pt/pp spilt or spilled) □ vt verschütten; vergießen ⟨blood⟩ □ vi überlaufen

spin /spɪn/ v (pt/pp spun, pres p spinning) □ vt drehen; spinnen ⟨wool⟩; schleudern ⟨washing⟩ □ vi sich drehen. ~ out vt in die Länge ziehen

spinach /'spɪnɪdʒ/ n Spinat m

spinal /'spaɪnl/ a Rückgrat-. ~ 'cord n Rückenmark nt

spindl|e /'spɪndl/ n Spindel f. ~y a spindeldürr

spin-'drier n Wäscheschleuder f

spine /spaɪn/ n Rückgrat nt; (of book) [Buch]rücken m; (Bot, Zool) Stachel m. ~less a (fig) rückgratlos

spinning /'spɪnɪŋ/ n Spinnen nt. ~-wheel n Spinnrad nt

'spin-off n Nebenprodukt nt

spinster /'spɪnstə(r)/ n ledige Frau f

spiral /'spaɪrl/ a spiralig □ n Spirale f □ vi (pt/pp spiralled) sich hochwinden; ⟨smoke:⟩ in einer Spirale aufsteigen. ~ 'staircase n Wendeltreppe f

spire /spaɪə(r)/ n Turmspitze f

spirit /'spɪrɪt/ n Geist m; (courage) Mut m; ~s pl (alcohol) Spirituosen pl; in high ~s in gehobener Stimmung; in low ~s niedergedrückt. ~ away vt verschwinden lassen

spirited /'spɪrɪtɪd/ a lebhaft; (courageous) beherzt

spirit: ~-level n Wasserwaage f. ~ stove n Spirituskocher m

spiritual /'spɪrɪtjʊəl/ a geistig; (Relig) geistlich. ~ism /-ɪzm/ n Spiritismus m. ~ist /-ɪst/ a spiritistisch □ n Spiritist m

spit¹ /spɪt/ n (for roasting) [Brat]spieß m

spit² n Spucke f □ vt/i (pt/pp spat, pres p spitting) spucken; ⟨cat:⟩ fauchen; ⟨fat:⟩ spritzen; it's ~ting with rain es tröpfelt; be the ~ting image of s.o. jdm wie aus dem Gesicht geschnitten sein

spite /spaɪt/ n Boshaftigkeit f; in ~ of trotz (+ gen) □ vt ärgern. ~ful a, -ly adv gehässig

spittle /'spɪtl/ n Spucke f

splash /splæʃ/ n Platschen nt; (fam: drop) Schuss m; ~ of colour Farbfleck m □ vt spritzen; ~ s.o. with sth jdn mit etw bespritzen □ vi spritzen. ~ about vi planschen

spleen /spliːn/ n Milz f

splendid /'splendɪd/ a herrlich, großartig

splendour /'splendə(r)/ n Pracht f

splint /splɪnt/ n (Med) Schiene f

splinter /'splɪntə(r)/ n Splitter m □ vi zersplittern

split /splɪt/ n Spaltung f; (Pol) Bruch m; (tear) Riss m □ v (pt/pp split, pres p splitting) □ vt spalten; (share) teilen; (tear) zerreißen; ~ one's sides sich kaputtlachen □ vi sich spalten; (tear) zerreißen; ~ on s.o. (fam) jdn verpfeifen. ~ up vt aufteilen □ vi ⟨couple:⟩ sich trennen

splutter /'splʌtə(r)/ vi prusten

spoil /spɔɪl/ n ~s pl Beute f □ v (pt/pp spoilt or spoiled) □ vt verderben; verwöhnen ⟨person⟩ □ vi verderben. ~sport n Spielverderber m

spoke¹ /spəʊk/ n Speiche f

spoke², **spoken** /'spəʊkn/ see speak

'spokesman n Sprecher m

sponge /spʌndʒ/ n Schwamm m □ vt abwaschen □ vi ~ on schmarotzen bei. ~-bag n Waschbeutel m. ~-cake n Biskuitkuchen m

spong|er /'spʌndʒə(r)/ n Schmarotzer m. ~y a schwammig

sponsor /'spɒnsə(r)/ n Sponsor m; (godparent) Pate m/Patin f; (for membership) Bürge m □ vt sponsern; bürgen für

spontaneous /spɒn'teɪnɪəs/ a, -ly adv spontan

spoof /spuːf/ n (fam) Parodie f

spooky /'spuːkɪ/ a (-ier, -iest) (fam) gespenstisch

spool /spuːl/ n Spule f

spoon /spuːn/ n Löffel m □ vt löffeln. ~feed vt (pt/pp -fed) (fig) alles vorkauen (+ dat). ~ful n Löffel m

sporadic /spə'rædɪk/ a, -ally adv sporadisch

sport /spɔːt/ n Sport m; (amusement) Spaß m □ vt (stolz) tragen. ~ing a sportlich; a ~ing chance eine faire Chance

sports: ~car n Sportwagen m. ~ coat n, ~ jacket n Sakko m. ~man n Sportler m. ~woman n Sportlerin f

sporty /'spɔːtɪ/ a (-ier, -iest) sportlich

spot /spɒt/ n Fleck m; (place) Stelle f; (dot) Punkt m; (drop) Tropfen m; (pimple) Pickel m; ~s pl (rash) Ausschlag m; a ~ of (fam) ein bisschen; on the ~ auf der Stelle; be in a tight ~ (fam) in der Klemme sitzen □ vt (pt/pp spotted) entdecken

spot: ~'check *n* Stichprobe *f*. ~less *a* makellos; (*fam: very clean*) blitzsauber. ~light *n* Scheinwerfer *m*; (*fig*) Rampenlicht *nt*

spotted /'spɒtɪd/ *a* gepunktet

spotty /'spɒtɪ/ *a* (-ier, -iest) fleckig; (*pimply*) pickelig

spouse /spauz/ *n* Gatte *m*/Gattin *f*

spout /spaut/ *n* Schnabel *m*, Tülle *f* □ *vi* schießen (from aus)

sprain /spreɪn/ *n* Verstauchung *f* □ *vt* verstauchen

sprang /spræŋ/ *see* spring²

sprat /spræt/ *n* Sprotte *f*

sprawl /sprɔ:l/ *vi* sich ausstrecken; (*fall*) der Länge nach hinfallen

spray¹ /spreɪ/ *n* (*of flowers*) Strauß *m*

spray² *n* Sprühnebel *m*; (*from sea*) Gischt *m*; (*device*) Spritze *f*; (*container*) Sprühdose *f*; (*preparation*) Spray *nt* □ *vt* spritzen; (*with aerosol*) sprühen

spread /spred/ *n* Verbreitung *f*; (*paste*) Aufstrich *m*; (*fam: feast*) Festessen *nt* □ *v* (*pt/pp* spread) □ *vt* ausbreiten; streichen ⟨*butter, jam*⟩; bestreichen ⟨*bread, surface*⟩; streuen ⟨*sand, manure*⟩; verbreiten ⟨*news, disease*⟩; verteilen ⟨*payments*⟩ □ *vi* sich ausbreiten. ~ **out** *vt* ausbreiten; (*space out*) verteilen □ *vi* sich verteilen

spree /spri:/ *n* (*fam*) go on a shopping ~ groß einkaufen gehen

sprig /sprɪg/ *n* Zweig *m*

sprightly /'spraɪtlɪ/ *a* (-ier, -iest) rüstig

spring¹ /sprɪŋ/ *n* Frühling *m* □ *attrib* Frühlings-

spring² *n* (*jump*) Sprung *m*; (*water*) Quelle *f*; (*device*) Feder *f*; (*elasticity*) Elastizität *f* □ *v* (*pt* sprang, *pp* sprung) □ *vi* springen; (*arise*) entspringen (from *dat*) □ *vt* ~ sth on s.o. jdn mit etw überfallen

spring: ~**board** *n* Sprungbrett *nt*. ~'cleaning *n* Frühjahrsputz *m*. ~**time** *n* Frühling *m*

sprinkl|e /'sprɪŋkl/ *vt* sprengen; (*scatter*) streuen; bestreuen ⟨*surface*⟩. ~**er** *n* Sprinkler *m*; (*Hort*) Sprenger *m*. ~**ing** *n* dünne Schicht *f*

sprint /sprɪnt/ *n* Sprint *m* □ *vi* rennen; (*Sport*) sprinten. ~**er** *n* Kurzstreckenläufer(in) *m(f)*

sprout /spraut/ *n* Trieb *m*; [Brussels] ~s *pl* Rosenkohl *m* □ *vi* sprießen

spruce /spru:s/ *a* gepflegt □ *n* Fichte *f*

sprung /sprʌŋ/ *see* spring² □ *a* gefedert

spry /spraɪ/ *a* (-ier, -iest) rüstig

spud /spʌd/ *n* (*fam*) Kartoffel *f*

spun /spʌn/ *see* spin

spur /spɜ:(r)/ *n* Sporn *m*; (*stimulus*) Ansporn *m*; (*road*) Nebenstraße *f*; on the ~

of the moment ganz spontan □ *vt* (*pt/pp* spurred) ~ [on] (*fig*) anspornen

spurious /'spjʊərɪəs/ *a*, -ly *adv* falsch

spurn /spɜ:n/ *vt* verschmähen

spurt /spɜ:t/ *n* Strahl *m*; (*Sport*) Spurt *m*; put on a ~ spurten □ *vi* spritzen

spy /spaɪ/ *n* Spion(in) *m(f)* □ *vi* spionieren; ~ on s.o. jdm nachspionieren □ *vt* (*fam: see*) sehen. ~ **out** *vt* auskundschaften

spying /'spaɪɪŋ/ *n* Spionage *f*

squabble /'skwɒbl/ *n* Zank *m* □ *vi* sich zanken

squad /skwɒd/ *n* Gruppe *f*; (*Sport*) Mannschaft *f*

squadron /'skwɒdrən/ *n* (*Mil*) Geschwader *nt*

squalid /'skwɒlɪd/ *a*, -ly *adv* schmutzig

squall /skwɔ:l/ *n* Bö *f* □ *vi* brüllen

squalor /'skwɒlə(r)/ *n* Schmutz *m*

squander /'skwɒndə(r)/ *vt* vergeuden

square /skweə(r)/ *a* quadratisch; ⟨*metre, mile*⟩ Quadrat-; ⟨*meal*⟩ anständig; all ~ (*fam*) quitt □ *n* Quadrat *nt*; (*area*) Platz *m*; (*on chessboard*) Feld *nt* □ *vt* (*settle*) klären; (*Math*) quadrieren □ *vi* (*agree*) übereinstimmen

squash /skwɒʃ/ *n* Gedränge *nt*; (*drink*) Fruchtsaftgetränk *nt*; (*Sport*) Squash *nt* □ *vt* zerquetschen; (*suppress*) niederschlagen. ~**y** *a* weich

squat /skwɒt/ *a* gedrungen □ *n* (*fam*) besetztes Haus *nt* □ *vi* (*pt/pp* squatted) hocken; ~ in a house ein Haus besetzen. ~**ter** *n* Hausbesetzer *m*

squawk /skwɔ:k/ *vi* krächzen

squeak /skwi:k/ *n* Quieken *nt*; (*of hinge, brakes*) Quietschen *nt* □ *vi* quieken; quietschen

squeal /skwi:l/ *n* Schrei *m*; (*screech*) Kreischen *nt* □ *vi* schreien; kreischen

squeamish /'skwi:mɪʃ/ *a* empfindlich

squeeze /skwi:z/ *n* Druck *m*; (*crush*) Gedränge *nt* □ *vt* drücken; (*to get juice*) ausdrücken; (*force*) zwängen; (*fam: extort*) herauspressen (from aus) □ *vi* ~ in/out sich hinein-/hinauszwängen

squelch /skweltʃ/ *vi* quatschen

squid /skwɪd/ *n* Tintenfisch *m*

squiggle /'skwɪgl/ *n* Schnörkel *m*

squint /skwɪnt/ *n* Schielen *nt* □ *vi* schielen

squire /'skwaɪə(r)/ *n* Gutsherr *m*

squirm /skwɜ:m/ *vi* sich winden

squirrel /'skwɪrl/ *n* Eichhörnchen *nt*

squirt /skwɜ:t/ *n* Spritzer *m* □ *vt/i* spritzen

St *abbr* (Saint) St.; (Street) Str.

stab /stæb/ *n* Stich *m*; (*fam: attempt*) Versuch *m* □ *vt* (*pt/pp* stabbed) stechen; (*to death*) erstechen

stability /stə'bɪlətɪ/ n Stabilität f

stabilize /'steɪbɪlaɪz/ vt stabilisieren □ vi sich stabilisieren

stable[1] /'steɪbl/ a (-r, -st) stabil

stable[2] n Stall m; (establishment) Reitstall m

stack /stæk/ n Stapel m; (of chimney) Schornstein m; (fam: large quantity) Haufen m □ vt stapeln

stadium /'steɪdɪəm/ n Stadion nt

staff /stɑːf/ n (stick & Mil) Stab m □ (& pl) (employees) Personal nt; (Sch) Lehrkräfte pl □ vt mit Personal besetzen. ~-room n (Sch) Lehrerzimmer nt

stag /stæg/ n Hirsch m

stage /steɪdʒ/ n Bühne f; (in journey) Etappe f; (in process) Stadium nt; by or in ~s in Etappen □ vt aufführen; (arrange) veranstalten

stage: ~ door n Bühneneingang m. ~ fright n Lampenfieber nt

stagger /'stægə(r)/ vi taumeln □ vt staffeln (holidays); versetzt anordnen (seats); I was ~ed es hat mir die Sprache verschlagen. ~ing a unglaublich

stagnant /'stægnənt/ a stehend; (fig) stagnierend

stagnate /stæg'neɪt/ vi (fig) stagnieren. ~ion /-'neɪʃn/ n Stagnation f

staid /steɪd/ a gesetzt

stain /steɪn/ n Fleck m; (for wood) Beize f □ vt färben; beizen (wood); (fig) beflecken; ~ed glass farbiges Glas nt. ~less a fleckenlos; (steel) rostfrei. ~ remover n Fleckentferner m

stair /steə(r)/ n Stufe f; ~s pl Treppe f. ~case n Treppe f

stake /steɪk/ n Pfahl m; (wager) Einsatz m; (Comm) Anteil m; be at ~ auf dem Spiel stehen □ vt [an einem Pfahl] anbinden; (wager) setzen; ~ a claim to sth Anspruch auf etw (acc) erheben

stale /steɪl/ a (-r, -st) alt; (air) verbraucht. ~mate n Patt nt

stalk[1] /stɔːk/ n Stiel m, Stängel m

stalk[2] vt pirschen auf (+ acc) □ vi stolzieren

stall /stɔːl/ n Stand m; ~s pl (Theat) Parkett nt □ vi (engine:) stehen bleiben; (fig) ausweichen □ vt abwürgen (engine)

stallion /'stæljən/ n Hengst m

stalwart /'stɔːlwət/ a treu □ n treuer Anhänger m

stamina /'stæmɪnə/ n Ausdauer f

stammer /'stæmə(r)/ n Stottern nt □ vt/i stottern

stamp /stæmp/ n Stempel m; (postage ~) [Brief]marke f □ vt stempeln; (impress) prägen; (put postage on) frankieren; ~

one's feet mit den Füßen stampfen □ vi stampfen. ~ out vt [aus]stanzen; (fig) ausmerzen

stampede /stæm'piːd/ n wilde Flucht f; (fam) Ansturm m □ vi in Panik fliehen

stance /stɑːns/ n Haltung f

stand /stænd/ n Stand m; (rack) Ständer m; (pedestal) Sockel m; (Sport) Tribüne f; (fig) Einstellung f □ v (pt/pp stood) □ vi stehen; (rise) aufstehen; (be candidate) kandidieren; (stay valid) gültig bleiben; ~ still stillstehen; ~ firm (fig) festbleiben; ~ together zusammenhalten; ~ to lose/ gain gewinnen/verlieren können; ~ to reason logisch sein; ~ in for vertreten; ~ for (mean) bedeuten; I won't ~ for that das lasse ich mir nicht bieten □ vt stellen; (withstand) standhalten (+ dat); (endure) ertragen; vertragen (climate); (put up with) aushalten; haben (chance); ~ one's ground nicht nachgeben; ~ the test of time sich bewähren; ~ s.o. a beer jdm ein Bier spendieren; I can't ~ her (fam) ich kann sie nicht ausstehen. ~ by vi daneben stehen; (be ready) sich bereithalten □ vt by s.o. (fig) zu jdm stehen. ~ down vi (retire) zurücktreten. ~ out vi hervorstehen; (fig) herausragen. ~ up vi aufstehen; ~ up for eintreten für; ~ up to sich wehren gegen

standard /'stændəd/ a Normal-; be ~ practice allgemein üblich sein □ n Maßstab m; (Techn) Norm f; (level) Niveau nt; (flag) Standarte f; ~s pl (morals) Prinzipien pl; ~ of living Lebensstandard m. ~ize vt standardisieren; (Techn) normen

'**standard lamp** n Stehlampe f

'**standard-in** n Ersatz m

standing /'stændɪŋ/ a (erect) stehend; (permanent) ständig □ n Rang m; (duration) Dauer f. ~ 'order n Dauerauftrag m. ~-room n Stehplätze pl

stand: ~-offish /stænd'ɒfɪʃ/ a distanziert. ~point n Standpunkt m. ~still n Stillstand m; come to a ~still zum Stillstand kommen

stank /stæŋk/ see stink

staple[1] /'steɪpl/ a Grund- □ n (product) Haupterzeugnis nt

staple[2] n Heftklammer f □ vt heften. ~r n Heftmaschine f

star /stɑː(r)/ n Stern m; (asterisk) Sternchen nt; (Theat, Sport) Star m □ vi (pt/pp starred) die Hauptrolle spielen

starboard /'stɑːbəd/ n Steuerbord nt

starch /stɑːtʃ/ n Stärke f □ vt stärken. ~y a stärkehaltig; (fig) steif

stare /steə(r)/ n Starren nt □ vt starren; ~ at anstarren

'**starfish** n Seestern m

stark /stɑːk/ a (-er, -est) scharf; ⟨contrast⟩ krass □ adv ~ naked splitternackt

starling /'stɑːlɪŋ/ n Star m

'starlit a sternhell

starry /'stɑːrɪ/ a sternklar

start /stɑːt/ n Anfang m, Beginn m; ⟨departure⟩ Aufbruch m; ⟨Sport⟩ Start m; from the ~ von Anfang an; for a ~ erstens □ vi anfangen, beginnen; ⟨set out⟩ aufbrechen; ⟨engine:⟩ anspringen; ⟨Auto, Sport⟩ starten; ⟨jump⟩ aufschrecken; to ~ with zuerst □ vt anfangen, beginnen; ⟨cause⟩ verursachen; ⟨found⟩ gründen; starten ⟨car, race⟩; in Umlauf setzen ⟨rumour⟩. ~er n ⟨Culin⟩ Vorspeise f; ⟨Auto, Sport⟩ Starter m. ~ing-point n Ausgangspunkt m

startle /'stɑːtl/ vt erschrecken

starvation /stɑː'veɪʃn/ n Verhungern nt

starve /stɑːv/ vi hungern; ⟨to death⟩ verhungern □ vt verhungern lassen

stash /stæʃ/ vt ⟨fam⟩ ~ [away] beiseite schaffen

state /steɪt/ n Zustand m; ⟨grand style⟩ Prunk m; ⟨Pol⟩ Staat m; ~ of play Spielstand m; be in a ~ ⟨person:⟩ aufgeregt sein; lie in ~ feierlich aufgebahrt sein □ attrib Staats-, staatlich □ vt erklären; ⟨specify⟩ angeben. ~-aided a staatlich gefördert. ~less a staatenlos

stately /'steɪtlɪ/ a (-ier, -iest) stattlich. ~ 'home n Schloss nt

statement /'steɪtmənt/ n Erklärung f; ⟨Jur⟩ Aussage f; ⟨Banking⟩ Auszug m

'statesman n Staatsmann m

static /'stætɪk/ a statisch; remain ~ unverändert bleiben

station /'steɪʃn/ n Bahnhof m; ⟨police⟩ Wache f; ⟨radio⟩ Sender m; ⟨space, weather⟩ Station f; ⟨Mil⟩ Posten m; ⟨status⟩ Rang m □ vt stationieren; ⟨post⟩ postieren. ~ary /-ərɪ/ a stehend; be ~ary stehen

stationer /'steɪʃənə(r)/ n ~'s [shop] Schreibwarengeschäft nt. ~y n Briefpapier nt; ⟨writing-materials⟩ Schreibwaren pl

'station-wagon n ⟨Amer⟩ Kombi[wagen] n

statistic /stə'tɪstɪk/ n statistische Tatsache f. ~al a, -ly adv statistisch. ~s n & pl Statistik f

statue /'stætjuː/ n Statue f

stature /'stætʃə(r)/ n Statur f; ⟨fig⟩ Format nt

status /'steɪtəs/ n Status m, Rang m. ~ symbol n Statussymbol nt

statut|e /'stætjuːt/ n Statut nt. ~ory a gesetzlich

staunch /stɔːntʃ/ a (-er, -est), -ly adv treu

stave /steɪv/ vt ~ off abwenden

stay /steɪ/ n Aufenthalt m □ vi bleiben; ⟨reside⟩ wohnen; ~ the night übernachten; ~ put dableiben □ vt ~ the course durchhalten. ~ away vi wegbleiben. ~ behind vi zurückbleiben. ~ in vi zu Hause bleiben; ⟨Sch⟩ nachsitzen. ~ up vi oben bleiben; ⟨upright⟩ stehen bleiben; ⟨on wall⟩ hängen bleiben; ⟨person:⟩ aufbleiben

stead /sted/ n in his ~ an seiner Stelle; stand s.o. in good ~ jdm zustatten kommen. ~fast a, -ly adv standhaft

steadily /'stedɪlɪ/ adv fest; ⟨continually⟩ stetig

steady /'stedɪ/ a (-ier, -iest) fest; ⟨not wobbly⟩ stabil; ⟨hand⟩ ruhig; ⟨regular⟩ regelmäßig; ⟨dependable⟩ zuverlässig

steak /steɪk/ n Steak nt

steal /stiːl/ vt/i (pt stole, pp stolen) stehlen (from dat). ~ in/out vi sich hinein-/hinausstehlen

stealth /stelθ/ n Heimlichkeit f; by ~ heimlich. ~y a heimlich

steam /stiːm/ n Dampf m; under one's own ~ ⟨fam⟩ aus eigener Kraft □ vt ⟨Culin⟩ dämpfen, dünsten □ vi dampfen. ~ up vi beschlagen

'steam-engine n Dampfmaschine f; ⟨Rail⟩ Dampflokomotive f

steamer /'stiːmə(r)/ n Dampfer m

'steamroller n Dampfwalze f

steamy /'stiːmɪ/ a dampfig

steel /stiːl/ n Stahl m □ vt ~ oneself allen Mut zusammennehmen

steep¹ /stiːp/ vt ⟨soak⟩ einweichen

steep² a, -ly adv steil; ⟨fam: exorbitant⟩ gesalzen

steeple /'stiːpl/ n Kirchturm m. ~chase n Hindernisrennen nt

steer /stɪə(r)/ vt/i steuern; ~ clear of s.o./sth jdm/ etw aus dem Weg gehen. ~ing n ⟨Auto⟩ Steuerung f. ~ing-wheel n Lenkrad nt

stem¹ /stem/ n Stiel m; ⟨of word⟩ Stamm m □ vi (pt/pp stemmed) ~ from zurückzuführen sein auf (+ acc)

stem² vt (pt/pp stemmed) eindämmen; stillen ⟨bleeding⟩

stench /stentʃ/ n Gestank m

stencil /'stensl/ n Schablone f; ⟨for typing⟩ Matrize f

step /step/ n Schritt m; ⟨stair⟩ Stufe f; ~s pl ⟨ladder⟩ Trittleiter f; in ~ im Schritt; ~ by ~ Schritt für Schritt; take ~s ⟨fig⟩ Schritte unternehmen □ vi (pt/pp stepped) treten; ~ in ⟨fig⟩ eingreifen; ~ into s.o.'s shoes in jds Stelle treten; ~ out of line aus der Reihe tanzen. ~ up *vi* hinaufsteigen □ *vt* (*increase*) erhöhen, steigern; verstärken (*efforts*)

step: ~**brother** *n* Stiefbruder *m*. ~**child** *n* Stiefkind *nt*. ~**daughter** *n* Stieftochter *f*. ~**father** *n* Stiefvater *m*. ~**ladder** *n* Trittleiter *f*. ~**mother** *n* Stiefmutter *f*

'**stepping-stone** *n* Trittstein *m*; (*fig*) Sprungbrett *nt*

step: ~**sister** *n* Stiefschwester *f*. ~**son** *n* Stiefsohn *m*

stereo /'steriəʊ/ *n* Stereo *nt*; (*equipment*) Stereoanlage *f*; in ~ stereo. ~**phonic** /-'fɒnɪk/ *a* stereophon

stereotype /'steriətaɪp/ *n* stereotype Figur *f*. ~**d** *a* stereotyp

steril|e /'steraɪl/ *a* steril. ~**ity** /stə'rɪlətɪ/ *n* Sterilität *f*

steriliz|ation /sterəlaɪ'zeɪʃn/ *n* Sterilisation *f*. ~**e** *vt* sterilisieren

sterling /'stɜːlɪŋ/ *a* Sterling-; (*fig*) gediegen □ *n* Sterling *m*

stern¹ /stɜːn/ *a* (-er, -est), -**ly** *adv* streng

stern² *n* (*of boat*) Heck *nt*

stew /stjuː/ *n* Eintopf *m*; in a ~ (*fam*) aufgeregt □ *vt/i* schmoren; ~**ed fruit** Kompott *nt*

steward /'stjuːəd/ *n* Ordner *m*; (*on ship, aicraft*) Steward *m*. ~**ess** *n* Stewardess *f*

stick¹ /stɪk/ *n* Stock *m*; (*of chalk*) Stück *nt*; (*of rhubarb*) Stange *f*; (*Sport*) Schläger *m*

stick² *v* (*pt/pp* **stuck**) □ *vt* stecken; (*stab*) stechen; (*glue*) kleben; (*fam: put*) tun; (*fam: endure*) aushalten □ *vi* stecken; (*adhere*) kleben, haften (**to** an + *dat*); (*jam*) klemmen; ~ **to sth** (*fig*) bei etw bleiben; ~ **at it** (*fam*) dranbleiben; ~ **at nothing** (*fam*) vor nichts zurückschrecken; ~ **up for** (*fam*) eintreten für; **be stuck** nicht weiterkönnen; (*vehicle:*) festsitzen, festgefahren sein; (*drawer:*) klemmen; **be stuck with** sth (*fam*) etw am Hals haben. ~ **out** *vi* abstehen; (*project*) vorstehen □ *vt* (*fam*) hinausstrecken; herausstrecken (*tongue*)

sticker /'stɪkə(r)/ *n* Aufkleber *m*

'**sticking plaster** *n* Heftpflaster *nt*

stickler /'stɪklə(r)/ *n* **be a** ~ **for** es sehr genau nehmen mit

sticky /'stɪkɪ/ *a* (-ier, -iest) klebrig; (*adhesive*) Klebe-

stiff /stɪf/ *a* (-er, -est), -**ly** *adv* steif; (*brush*) hart; (*dough*) fest; (*difficult*) schwierig; (*penalty*) schwer; **be bored** ~ (*fam*) sich zu Tode langweilen. ~**en** *vt* steif machen □ *vi* steif werden. ~**ness** *n* Steifheit *f*

stifl|e /'staɪfl/ *vt* ersticken; (*fig*) unterdrücken. ~**ing** *a* **be** ~**ing** zum Ersticken sein

stigma /'stɪgmə/ *n* Stigma *nt*

stile /staɪl/ *n* Zauntritt *m*

stiletto /stɪ'letəʊ/ *n* Stilett *nt*; (*heel*) Bleistiftabsatz *m*

still¹ /stɪl/ *n* Destillierapparat *m*

still² *a* still; (*drink*) ohne Kohlensäure; **keep** ~ stillhalten; **stand** ~ stillstehen □ *n* Stille *f* □ *adv* noch; (*emphatic*) immer noch; (*nevertheless*) trotzdem; ~ **not** immer noch nicht

'**stillborn** *a* tot geboren

still 'life *n* Stilleben *nt*

stilted /'stɪltɪd/ *a* gestelzt, geschraubt

stilts /stɪlts/ *npl* Stelzen *pl*

stimulant /'stɪmjʊlənt/ *n* Anregungsmittel *nt*

stimulat|e /'stɪmjʊleɪt/ *vt* anregen. ~**ion** /-'leɪʃn/ *n* Anregung *f*

stimulus /'stɪmjʊləs/ *n* (*pl* -**li** /-laɪ/) Reiz *m*

sting /stɪŋ/ *n* Stich *m*; (*from nettle, jellyfish*) Brennen *nt*; (*organ*) Stachel *m* □ *v* (*pt/pp* **stung**) □ *vt* stechen □ *vi* brennen; (*insect:*) stechen. ~**ing nettle** *n* Brennnessel *f*

stingy /'stɪndʒɪ/ *a* (-ier, -iest) geizig, (*fam*) knauserig

stink /stɪŋk/ *n* Gestank *m* □ *vi* (*pt* **stank**, *pp* **stunk**) stinken (**of** nach)

stint /stɪnt/ *n* Pensum *nt* □ *vi* ~ **on** sparen an (+ *dat*)

stipulat|e /'stɪpjʊleɪt/ *vt* vorschreiben. ~**ion** /-'leɪʃn/ *n* Bedingung *f*

stir /stɜː(r)/ *n* (*commotion*) Aufregung *f* □ *v* (*pt/pp* **stirred**) *vt* rühren □ *vi* sich rühren

stirrup /'stɪrəp/ *n* Steigbügel *m*

stitch /stɪtʃ/ *n* Stich *m*; (*Knitting*) Masche *f*; (*pain*) Seitenstechen *nt*; **be in** ~**es** (*fam*) sich kaputtlachen □ *vt* nähen

stoat /stəʊt/ *n* Hermelin *nt*

stock /stɒk/ *n* Vorrat *m* (**of** an + *dat*); (*in shop*) [Waren]bestand *m*; (*livestock*) Vieh *nt*; (*lineage*) Abstammung *f*; (*Finance*) Wertpapiere *pl*; (*Culin*) Brühe *f*; (*plant*) Levkoje *f*; **in/out of** ~ vorrätig/nicht vorrätig; **take** ~ (*fig*) Bilanz ziehen □ *a* Standard- □ *vt* (*shop:*) führen; auffüllen (*shelves*). ~ **up** *vi* sich eindecken (**with** mit)

stock: ~**broker** *n* Börsenmakler *m*. ~**cube** *n* Brühwürfel *m*. **S**~ **Exchange** *n* Börse *f*

stocking /'stɒkɪŋ/ *n* Strumpf *m*

stockist /'stɒkɪst/ *n* Händler *m*

stock: ~**market** *n* Börse *f*. ~**pile** *vt* horten; anhäufen (*weapons*). ~'**still** *a* bewegungslos. ~**taking** *n* (*Comm*) Inventur *f*

stocky /'stɒkɪ/ *a* (-ier, -iest) untersetzt

stodgy /'stɒdʒɪ/ *a* pappig [und schwer verdaulich]

stoical /'stəʊɪkl/ a, -ly adv stoisch

stoke /stəʊk/ vt heizen

stole¹ /stəʊl/ n Stola f

stole², stolen /'stəʊlən/ see steal

stolid /'stɒlɪd/ a, -ly adv stur

stomach /'stʌmək/ n Magen m □ vt vertragen. ~ache n Magenschmerzen pl

stone /stəʊn/ n Stein m; (weight) 6,35kg □ a steinern; (wall, Age) Stein- □ vt mit Steinen bewerfen; entsteinen (fruit). ~-cold a eiskalt. ~-'deaf n (fam) stocktaub

stony /'stəʊnɪ/ a steinig

stood /stʊd/ see stand

stool /stuːl/ n Hocker m

stoop /stuːp/ n walk with a ~ gebeugt gehen □ vi sich bücken; (fig) sich erniedrigen

stop /stɒp/ n Halt m; (break) Pause f; (for bus) Haltestelle f; (for train) Station f; (Gram) Punkt m; (on organ) Register nt; come to a ~ stehen bleiben; put a ~ to sth etw unterbinden □ v (pt/pp stopped) □ vt anhalten, stoppen; (switch off) abstellen; (plug, block) zustopfen; (prevent) verhindern; ~ s.o. doing sth jdn daran hindern, etw zu tun; ~ doing sth aufhören, etw zu tun; ~ that! hör auf damit! lass das sein! □ vi anhalten; (cease) aufhören; (clock:) stehen bleiben; (fam: stay) bleiben (with bei) □ int halt! stopp!

stop: ~gap n Notlösung f. ~over n Zwischenaufenthalt m; (Aviat) Zwischenlandung f

stoppage /'stɒpɪdʒ/ n Unterbrechung f; (strike) Streik m; (deduction) Abzug m

stopper /'stɒpə(r)/ n Stöpsel m

stop: ~-press n letzte Meldungen pl. ~-watch n Stoppuhr f

storage /'stɔːrɪdʒ/ n Aufbewahrung f; (in warehouse) Lagerung f; (Computing) Speicherung f

store /stɔː(r)/ n (stock) Vorrat m; (shop) Laden m; (department ~) Kaufhaus nt; (depot) Lager nt; in ~ auf Lager; put in ~ lagern; set great ~ by großen Wert legen auf (+ acc); be in ~ for s.o. (fig) jdm bevorstehen □ vt aufbewahren; (in warehouse) lagern; (Computing) speichern. ~room n Lagerraum m

storey /'stɔːrɪ/ n Stockwerk nt

stork /stɔːk/ n Storch m

storm /stɔːm/ n Sturm m; (with thunder) Gewitter nt □ vt/i stürmen. ~y a stürmisch

story /'stɔːrɪ/ n Geschichte f; (in newspaper) Artikel m; (fam: lie) Märchen nt

stout /staʊt/ a (-er, -est) beleibt; (strong) fest

stove /stəʊv/ n Ofen m; (for cooking) Herd m

stow /stəʊ/ vt verstauen. ~away n blinder Passagier m

straddle /'strædl/ vt rittlings sitzen auf (+ dat); (standing) mit gespreizten Beinen stehen über (dat)

straggl|e /'strægl/ vi hinterherhinken. ~er n Nachzügler m. ~y a strähnig

straight /streɪt/ a (-er, -est) gerade; (direct) direkt; (clear) klar; (hair) glatt; (drink) pur; be ~ (tidy) in Ordnung sein □ adv gerade; (directly) direkt, geradewegs; (clearly) klar; ~ away sofort; ~ on or ahead geradeaus; ~ out (fig) geradeheraus; go ~ (fam) ein ehrliches Leben führen; put sth ~ etw in Ordnung bringen; sit/stand up ~ gerade sitzen/stehen

straighten /'streɪtn/ vt gerade machen; (put straight) gerade richten □ vi gerade werden; ~ [up] (person:) sich aufrichten. ~ out vt gerade biegen

straight'forward a offen; (simple) einfach

strain¹ /streɪn/ n Rasse f; (Bot) Sorte f; (of virus) Art f

strain² n Belastung f; ~s pl (of music) Klänge pl □ vt belasten; (overexert) überanstrengen; (injure) zerren (muscle); (Culin) durchseihen; abgießen (vegetables) □ vi sich anstrengen. ~ed a (relations) gespannt. ~er n Sieb nt

strait /streɪt/ n Meerenge f; in dire ~s in großen Nöten. ~-jacket n Zwangsjacke f. ~-'laced a puritanisch

strand¹ /strænd/ n (of thread) Faden m; (of beads) Kette f; (of hair) Strähne f

strand² vt be ~ed festsitzen

strange /streɪndʒ/ a (-r, -st) fremd; (odd) seltsam, merkwürdig. ~r n Fremde(r) m|f

strangely /'streɪndʒlɪ/ adv seltsam, merkwürdig; ~ enough seltsamerweise

strangle /'strængl/ vt erwürgen; (fig) unterdrücken

strangulation /ˌstrængjʊ'leɪʃn/ n Erwürgen nt

strap /stræp/ n Riemen m; (for safety) Gurt m; (to grasp in vehicle) Halteriemen m; (of watch) Armband nt; (shoulder-) Träger m □ vt (pt/pp strapped) schnallen; ~ in or down festschnallen

strapping /'stræpɪŋ/ a stramm

strata /'strɑːtə/ npl see stratum

stratagem /'strætədʒəm/ n Kriegslist f

strategic /strə'tiːdʒɪk/ a, -ally adv strategisch

strategy /'strætədʒɪ/ n Strategie f

stratum /'strɑːtəm/ n (pl strata) Schicht f

straw /strɔː/ n Stroh nt; (single piece, drinking) Strohhalm m; that's the last ~ jetzt reicht's aber

strawberry /'strɔːbəri/ n Erdbeere f

stray /streɪ/ a streunend □ n streunendes Tier nt □ vi sich verirren; (deviate) abweichen

streak /striːk/ n Streifen m; (in hair) Strähne f; (fig: trait) Zug m □ vi flitzen. ~y a streifig; (bacon) durchwachsen

stream /striːm/ n Bach m; (flow) Strom m; (current) Strömung f; (Sch) Parallelzug m □ vi strömen; ~ in/out hinaus-/herausströmen

streamer /'striːmə(r)/ n Luftschlange f; (flag) Wimpel m

'**streamline** vt (fig) rationalisieren. ~d a stromlinienförmig

street /striːt/ n Straße f. ~car n (Amer) Straßenbahn f. ~lamp n Straßenlaterne f

strength /streŋθ/ n Stärke f; (power) Kraft f; on the ~ of auf Grund (+ gen). ~en vt stärken; (reinforce) verstärken

strenuous /'strenjʊəs/ a anstrengend

stress /stres/ n (emphasis) Betonung f; (strain) Belastung f; (mental) Stress m □ vt betonen; (put a strain on) belasten. ~ful a stressig (fam)

stretch /stretʃ/ n (of road) Strecke f; (elasticity) Elastizität f; at a ~ ohne Unterbrechung; a long ~ eine lange Zeit; have a ~ sich strecken □ vt strecken; (widen) dehnen; (spread) ausbreiten; fordern (person); ~ one's legs sich (dat) die Beine vertreten □ vt sich erstrecken; (become wider) sich dehnen; (person:) sich strecken. ~er n Tragbahre f

strew /struː/ vt (pp strewn or strewed) streuen

stricken /'strɪkn/ a betroffen; ~ with heimgesucht von

strict /strɪkt/ a (-er, -est), -ly adv streng; ~ly speaking streng genommen

stride /straɪd/ n [großer] Schritt m; make great ~s (fig) große Fortschritte machen; take sth in one's ~ mit etw gut fertig werden □ vi (pt strode, pp stridden) [mit großen Schritten] gehen

strident /'straɪdnt/ a, -ly adv schrill; (colour) grell

strife /straɪf/ n Streit m

strike /straɪk/ n Streik m; (Mil) Angriff m; be on ~ streiken □ v (pt/pp struck) vt schlagen; (knock against, collide with) treffen; prägen (coin); anzünden (match); stoßen auf (+ acc) (oil, gold); abbrechen (camp); (delete) streichen; (impress)

beeindrucken; (occur to) einfallen (+ dat); (Mil) angreifen; ~ s.o. a blow jdm einen Schlag versetzen □ vi treffen; (lightning:) einschlagen; (clock:) schlagen; (attack) zuschlagen; (workers:) streiken; ~ lucky Glück haben. ~breaker n Streikbrecher m

striker /'straɪkə(r)/ n Streikende(r) m/f

striking /'straɪkɪŋ/ a auffallend

string /strɪŋ/ n Schnur f; (thin) Bindfaden m; (of musical instrument, racket) Saite f; (of bow) Sehne f; (of pearls) Kette f; the ~s (Mus) die Streicher pl; pull ~s (fam) seine Beziehungen spielen lassen; ~ed Fäden ziehen □ vt (pt/pp strung) (thread) aufziehen (beads). ~ed a (Mus) Saiten-; (played with bow) Streich-

stringent /'strɪndʒnt/ a streng

strip /strɪp/ n Streifen m □ v (pt/pp stripped) □ vt ablösen; ausziehen (clothes); abziehen (bed); abbeizen (wood, furniture); auseinander nehmen (machine); (deprive) berauben (of gen); ~ sth off sth etw von etw entfernen □ vi (undress) sich ausziehen. ~ club n Stripteaselokal nt

stripe /straɪp/ n Streifen m. ~d a gestreift

'**striplight** n Neonröhre f

stripper /'strɪpə(r)/ n Stripperin f; (male) Stripper m

strip-'tease n Striptease m

strive /straɪv/ vi (pt strove, pp striven) sich bemühen (to zu); ~ for streben nach

strode /strəʊd/ see **stride**

stroke[1] /strəʊk/ n Schlag m; (of pen) Strich m; (Swimming) Zug m; (style) Stil m; (Med) Schlaganfall m; ~ of luck Glücksfall m; put s.o. off his ~ jdn aus dem Konzept bringen

stroke[2] □ vt streicheln

stroll /strəʊl/ n Spaziergang m, (fam) Bummel m □ vi spazieren, (fam) bummeln. ~er n (Amer: push-chair) [Kinder]sportwagen m

strong /strɒŋ/ a (-er, -ger(r), -est -gist/), -ly adv stark; (powerful, healthy) kräftig; (severe) streng; (sturdy) stabil; (convincing) gut

strong: ~box n Geldkassette f. ~hold n Festung f; (fig) Hochburg f. ~-minded a willensstark. ~room n Tresorraum m

stroppy /'strɒpi/ a widerspenstig

strove /strəʊv/ see **strive**

struck /strʌk/ see **strike**

structural /'strʌktʃərl/ a, -ly adv baulich

structure /'strʌktʃə(r)/ n Struktur f; (building) Bau m

struggle /'strʌgl/ n Kampf m; with a ~ mit Mühe □ vt kämpfen; ~ for breath nach Atem ringen; ~ to do sth sich abmühen, etw zu tun; ~ to one's feet mühsam aufstehen

strum /strʌm/ v (pt/pp strummed) ◻ vt klimpern auf (+ dat) ◻ vi klimpern

strung /strʌŋ/ see string

strut[1] /strʌt/ n Strebe f

strut[2] vi (pt/pp strutted) stolzieren

stub /stʌb/ n Stummel m; (counterfoil) Abschnitt m ◻ vt (pt/pp stubbed) ~ one's toe sich (dat) den Zeh stoßen (on an + dat). ~ out vt ausdrücken (cigarette)

stubb|le /stʌbl/ n Stoppeln pl. ~ly a stoppelig

stubborn /stʌbən/ a, -ly adv starrsinnig; (refusal) hartnäckig

stubby /stʌbɪ/ a (-ier, -iest) kurz und dick

stucco /stʌkəʊ/ n Stuck m

stuck /stʌk/ see stick[2]. ~-up a (fam) hochnäsig

stud[1] /stʌd/ n Nagel m; (on clothes) Niete f; (for collar) Kragenknopf m; (for ear) Ohrstecker m

stud[2] n (of horses) Gestüt nt

student /stju:dnt/ n Student(in) m(f); (Sch) Schüler(in) m(f). ~ nurse n Lernschwester f

studied /stʌdɪd/ a gewollt

studio /stju:dɪəʊ/ n Studio nt; (for artist) Atelier nt

studious /stju:dɪəs/ a lerneifrig; (earnest) ernsthaft

stud|y /stʌdɪ/ n Studie f; (room) Studierzimmer nt; (investigation) Untersuchung f; ~ies pl Studium nt ◻ v (pt/pp studied) ◻ vt studieren; (examine) studieren ◻ vi lernen; (at university) studieren

stuff /stʌf/ n Stoff m; (fam: things) Zeug nt ◻ vt vollstopfen; (with padding, Culin) füllen; ausstopfen (animal); ~ sth into sth etw in etw (acc) [hinein]stopfen. ~ing n Füllung f

stuffy /stʌfɪ/ a (-ier, -iest) stickig; (old-fashioned) spießig

stumb|le /stʌmbl/ vi stolpern; ~e across zufällig stoßen auf (+ acc). ~ing-block n Hindernis nt

stump /stʌmp/ n Stumpf m ◻ ~ up vt/i (fam) blechen. ~ed a (fam) überfragt

stun /stʌn/ vt (pt/pp stunned) betäuben; ~ned by (fig) wie betäubt von

stung /stʌŋ/ see sting

stunk /stʌŋk/ see stink

stunning /stʌnɪŋ/ a (fam) toll

stunt[1] /stʌnt/ n (fam) Kunststück nt

stunt[2] vt hemmen. ~ed a verkümmert

stupendous /stju:pendəs/ a, -ly adv enorm

stupid /stju:pɪd/ a dumm. ~ity /-pɪdətɪ/ n Dummheit f. ~ly adv dumm; ~ly [enough] dummerweise

stupour /stju:pə(r)/ n Benommenheit f

sturdy /stɜ:dɪ/ a (-ier, -iest) stämmig; (furniture) stabil; (shoes) fest

stutter /stʌtə(r)/ n Stottern nt ◻ vt/i stottern

sty[1] /staɪ/ n (pl sties) Schweinestall m

sty[2], **stye** n (pl styes) (Med) Gerstenkorn nt

style /staɪl/ n Stil m; (fashion) Mode f; (sort) Art f; (hair~) Frisur f; in ~ in großem Stil

stylish /staɪlɪʃ/ a, -ly adv stilvoll

stylist /staɪlɪst/ n Friseur m/ Friseuse f. ~ic /-lɪstɪk/ a, -ally adv stilistisch

stylized /staɪlaɪzd/ a stilisiert

stylus /staɪləs/ n (on record-player) Nadel f

suave /swɑ:v/ a (pej) gewandt

sub·conscious /sʌb-/ a, -ly adv unterbewusst ◻ n Unterbewusstsein nt

sub·con·tract vt [vertraglich] weitervergeben (to an + acc)

'subdivi|de vt unterteilen. ~sion n Unterteilung f

subdue /səbdju:/ vt unterwerfen; (make quieter) beruhigen. ~d a gedämpft; (person) still

subject[1] /sʌbdʒɪkt/ a be ~ to sth etw (dat) unterworfen sein ◻ n Staatsbürger(in) m(f); (of ruler) Untertan m; (theme) Thema nt; (of investigation) Gegenstand m; (Sch) Fach nt; (Gram) Subjekt nt

subject[2] /səbdʒekt/ vt unterwerfen (to dat); (expose) aussetzen (to dat)

subjective /səbdʒektɪv/ a, -ly adv subjektiv

subjugate /sʌbdʒʊgeɪt/ vt unterjochen

subjunctive /səbdʒʌŋktɪv/ n Konjunktiv m

sub·let vt (pt/pp -let) untervermieten

sublime /səblaɪm/ a, -ly adv erhaben

subliminal /sʌblɪmɪnl/ a unterschwellig

sub-ma·chine-gun n Maschinenpistole f

subma·rine n Unterseeboot nt

submerge /səbmɜ:dʒ/ vt untertauchen; be ~d unter Wasser stehen ◻ vi tauchen

submiss|ion /səbmɪʃn/ n Unterwerfung f. ~ive /-sɪv/ a gehorsam; (pej) unterwürfig

submit /səbmɪt/ v (pt/pp -mitted, pres p -mitting) ◻ vt vorlegen (to dat); (hand in) einreichen ◻ vi sich unterwerfen (to dat)

subordinate[1] /səbɔ:dɪnət/ a untergeordnet ◻ n Untergebene(r) m/f

subordinate² /sə'bɔːdɪneɪt/ vt unterordnen (to dat)

subscribe /səb'skraɪb/ vi spenden; ∼ to abonnieren ⟨newspaper⟩; (fig) sich anschließen (+ dat). ∼r n Spender m; Abonnent m

subscription /səb'skrɪpʃn/ n (to club) [Mitglieds]beitrag m; (to newspaper) Abonnement nt; by ∼ mit Spenden; ⟨buy⟩ im Abonnement

subsequent /'sʌbsɪkwənt/ a, -ly adv folgend; ⟨later⟩ später

subservient /səb'sɜːvɪənt/ a, -ly adv untergeordnet; ⟨servile⟩ unterwürfig

subside /səb'saɪd/ vi sinken; ⟨ground:⟩ sich senken; ⟨storm:⟩ nachlassen

subsidiary /səb'sɪdɪərɪ/ a untergeordnet ▫ n Tochtergesellschaft f

subsid|ize /'sʌbsɪdaɪz/ vt subventionieren. ∼y n Subvention f

subsist /səb'sɪst/ vi leben (on von). ∼ence n Existenz f

substance /'sʌbstəns/ n Substanz f

sub'standard a unzulänglich; ⟨goods⟩ minderwertig

substantial /səb'stænʃl/ a solide; ⟨meal⟩ reichhaltig; ⟨considerable⟩ beträchtlich. ∼ly adv solide; ⟨essentially⟩ im Wesentlichen

substantiate /səb'stænʃɪeɪt/ vt erhärten

substitut|e /'sʌbstɪtjuːt/ n Ersatz m; ⟨Sport⟩ Ersatzspieler(in) m(f) ▫ vt ∼e A for B B durch A ersetzen ▫ vi ∼e for s.o. jdn vertreten. ∼ion /-'tjuːʃn/ n Ersetzung f

subterfuge /'sʌbtəfjuːdʒ/ n List f

subterranean /sʌbtə'reɪnɪən/ a unterirdisch

'subtitle n Untertitel m

subtle /'sʌtl/ a (-r, -st), -tly adv fein; (fig) subtil

subtract /səb'trækt/ vt abziehen, subtrahieren. ∼ion /-ækʃn/ n Subtraktion f

suburb /'sʌbɜːb/ n Vorort m; in the ∼s am Stadtrand. ∼an /sə'bɜːbən/ a Vorort-; (pej) spießig. ∼ia /sə'bɜːbɪə/ n die Vororte pl

subversive /səb'vɜːsɪv/ a subversiv

subway /'sʌbweɪ/ n Unterführung f; (Amer: railway) U-Bahn f

succeed /sək'siːd/ vi Erfolg haben; ⟨plan:⟩ gelingen; ⟨follow⟩ nachfolgen (+ dat); I ∼ed es ist mir gelungen; he ∼ed in escaping es gelang ihm zu entkommen ▫ vt folgen (+ dat). ∼ing a folgend

success /sək'ses/ n Erfolg m. ∼ful a, -ly adv erfolgreich

succession /sək'seʃn/ n Folge f; ⟨series⟩ Serie f; ⟨to title, office⟩ Nachfolge f; ⟨to

throne⟩ Thronfolge f; in ∼ hintereinander

successive /sək'sesɪv/ a aufeinander folgend. ∼ly adv hintereinander

successor /sək'sesə(r)/ n Nachfolger(in) m(f)

succinct /sək'sɪŋkt/ a, -ly adv prägnant

succulent /'sʌkjʊlənt/ a saftig

succumb /sə'kʌm/ vi erliegen (to dat)

such /sʌtʃ/ a solche(r,s); ∼ a book ein solches od solch ein Buch; ∼ a thing so etwas; ∼ a long time so lange; there is no ∼ thing das gibt es gar nicht; there is no ∼ person eine solche Person gibt es nicht ▫ pron as ∼ als solche(r,s); ⟨strictly speaking⟩ an sich; ∼ as wie [zum Beispiel]; and ∼ und dergleichen. ∼like pron (fam) dergleichen

suck /sʌk/ vt/i saugen; lutschen ⟨sweet⟩. ∼ up vt aufsaugen ▫ vi ∼ up to s.o. (fam) sich bei jdm einschmeicheln

sucker /'sʌkə(r)/ n ⟨Bot⟩ Ausläufer m; (fam: person) Dumme(r) m/f

suckle /'sʌkl/ vt säugen

suction /'sʌkʃn/ n Saugwirkung f

sudden /'sʌdn/ a, -ly adv plötzlich; ⟨abrupt⟩ jäh ▫ n all of a ∼ auf einmal

sue /suː/ vt (pres p suing) verklagen (for auf + acc) ▫ vi klagen

suede /sweɪd/ n Wildleder nt

suet /'suːɪt/ n [Nieren]talg m

suffer /'sʌfə(r)/ vi leiden (from an + dat) ▫ vt erleiden; ⟨tolerate⟩ dulden. ∼ance /-əns/ n on ∼ance bloß geduldet. ∼ing n Leiden nt

suffice /sə'faɪs/ vi genügen

sufficient /sə'fɪʃnt/ a, -ly adv genug, genügend; be ∼ genügen

suffix /'sʌfɪks/ n Nachsilbe f

suffocat|e /'sʌfəkeɪt/ vt/i ersticken. ∼ion /-'keɪʃn/ n Ersticken nt

sugar /'ʃʊgə(r)/ n Zucker m ▫ vt zuckern; (fig) versüßen. ∼ basin, ∼-bowl n Zuckerschale f. ∼y a süß; (fig) süßlich

suggest /sə'dʒest/ vt vorschlagen; ⟨indicate, insinuate⟩ andeuten. ∼ion /-estʃn/ n Vorschlag m; Andeutung f; ⟨trace⟩ Spur f. ∼ive a, -ly adv anzüglich; be ∼ive of schließen lassen auf (+ acc)

suicidal /suːɪ'saɪdl/ a selbstmörderisch

suicide /'suːɪsaɪd/ n Selbstmord m

suit /suːt/ n Anzug m; ⟨woman's⟩ Kostüm nt; ⟨Cards⟩ Farbe f; ⟨Jur⟩ Prozess m; follow ∼ (fig) das Gleiche tun ▫ vt ⟨adapt⟩ anpassen (to dat); ⟨be convenient for⟩ passen (+ dat); ⟨go with⟩ passen zu; ⟨clothing:⟩ stehen (s.o. jdm); be ∼ed for geeignet sein für; ∼ yourself! wie du willst!

suit|able /'suːtəbl/ a geeignet; ⟨convenient⟩ passend; ⟨appropriate⟩ angemessen;

(*for weather, activity*) zweckmäßig. ~**ably** *adv* angemessen; zweckmäßig

'suitcase *n* Koffer *m*

suite /swiːt/ *n* Suite *f*; (*of furniture*) Garnitur *f*

sulk /sʌlk/ *vi* schmollen. ~**y** *a* schmollend

sullen /'sʌlən/ *a*, **-ly** *adv* mürrisch

sulphur /'sʌlfə(r)/ *n* Schwefel *f*. ~**ic** /-'fjʊərɪk/ *a* ~ic acid Schwefelsäure *f*

sultana /sʌl'tɑːnə/ *n* Sultanine *f*

sultry /'sʌltrɪ/ *a* (-ier, -iest) ⟨*weather*⟩ schwül

sum /sʌm/ *n* Summe *f*; (*Sch*) Rechenaufgabe *f* □ *vt/i* (*pt/pp* summed) ~ **up** zusammenfassen; (*assess*) einschätzen

summar|ize /'sʌməraɪz/ *vt* zusammenfassen. ~**y** *n* Zusammenfassung *f* □ *a*, **-ily** *adv* summarisch; ⟨*dismissal*⟩ fristlos

summer /'sʌmə(r)/ *n* Sommer *m*. ~**house** *n* [Garten]laube *f*. ~**time** *n* Sommer *m*

summery /'sʌmərɪ/ *a* sommerlich

summit /'sʌmɪt/ *n* Gipfel *m*. ~ **conference** *n* Gipfelkonferenz *f*

summon /'sʌmən/ *vt* rufen; holen ⟨*help*⟩; (*Jur*) vorladen. ~ **up** *vt* aufbringen

summons /'sʌmənz/ *n* (*Jur*) Vorladung *f* □ *vt* vorladen

sump /sʌmp/ *n* (*Auto*) Ölwanne *f*

sumptuous /'sʌmptjʊəs/ *a*, **-ly** *adv* prunkvoll; ⟨*meal*⟩ üppig

sun /sʌn/ *n* Sonne *f* □ *vt* (*pt/pp* sunned) ~ oneself sich sonnen

sun: ~**bathe** *vi* sich sonnen. ~**bed** *n* Sonnenbank *f*. ~**burn** *n* Sonnenbrand *m*

sundae /'sʌndeɪ/ *n* Eisbecher *m*

Sunday /'sʌndeɪ/ *n* Sonntag *m*

'sundial *n* Sonnenuhr *f*

sundry /'sʌndrɪ/ *a* verschiedene *pl*; all and ~ alle *pl*

'sunflower *n* Sonnenblume *f*

sung /sʌŋ/ *see* sing

'sun-glasses *npl* Sonnenbrille *f*

sunk /sʌŋk/ *see* sink

sunken /'sʌŋkn/ *a* gesunken; ⟨*eyes*⟩ eingefallen

sunny /'sʌnɪ/ *a* (-ier, -iest) sonnig

sun: ~**rise** *n* Sonnenaufgang *m*. ~**roof** *n* (*Auto*) Schiebedach *nt*. ~**set** *n* Sonnenuntergang *m*. ~**shade** *n* Sonnenschirm *m*. ~**shine** *n* Sonnenschein *m*. ~**stroke** *n* Sonnenstich *m*. ~**tan** *n* [Sonnen]bräune *f*. ~**tanned** *a* braun [gebrannt]. ~**tan oil** *n* Sonnenöl *nt*

super /'suːpə(r)/ *a* (*fam*) prima, toll

superb /su'pɜːb/ *a* erstklassig

supercilious /suːpə'sɪlɪəs/ *a* überlegen

superficial /suːpə'fɪʃl/ *a*, **-ly** *adv* oberflächlich

superfluous /su'pɜːflʊəs/ *a* überflüssig

super'human *a* übermenschlich

superintendent /suːpərɪn'tendənt/ *n* (*of police*) Kommissar *m*

superior /suː'pɪərɪə(r)/ *a* überlegen; (*in rank*) höher □ *n* Vorgesetzte(r) *m/f*. ~**ity** /-'ɒrətɪ/ *n* Überlegenheit *f*

superlative /suː'pɜːlətɪv/ *a* unübertrefflich □ *n* Superlativ *m*

'superman *n* Übermensch *m*

'supermarket *n* Supermarkt *m*

super'natural *a* übernatürlich

'superpower *n* Supermacht *f*

supersede /suːpə'siːd/ *vt* ersetzen

super'sonic *a* Überschall-

superstiti|on /suːpə'stɪʃn/ *n* Aberglaube *m*. ~**ous** /-'stɪʃəs/ *a*, **-ly** *adv* abergläubisch

supervis|e /'suːpəvaɪz/ *vt* beaufsichtigen; überwachen ⟨*work*⟩. ~**ion** /-'vɪʒn/ *n* Aufsicht *f*; Überwachung *f*. ~**or** *n* Aufseher(in) *m(f)*

supper /'sʌpə(r)/ *n* Abendessen *nt*

supple /'sʌpl/ *a* geschmeidig

supplement /'sʌplɪmənt/ *n* Ergänzung *f*; (*addition*) Zusatz *m*; (*to fare*) Zuschlag *m*; (*book*) Ergänzungsband *m*; (*to newspaper*) Beilage *f* □ *vt* ergänzen. ~**ary** /-'mentərɪ/ *a* zusätzlich

supplier /sə'plaɪə(r)/ *n* Lieferant *m*

supply /sə'plaɪ/ *n* Vorrat *m*; supplies *pl* (*Mil*) Nachschub *m* □ *vt* (*pt/pp* -ied) liefern; ~ s.o. with sth jdn mit etw versorgen

support /sə'pɔːt/ *n* Stütze *f*; (*fig*) Unterstützung *f* □ *vt* stützen; (*bear weight of*) tragen; (*keep*) ernähren; (*give money to*) unterstützen; (*speak in favour of*) befürworten; (*Sport*) Fan sein von. ~**er** *n* Anhänger(in) *m(f)*; (*Sport*) Fan *m*. ~**ive** /-ɪv/ *a* be ~ive [to s.o.] [jdm] eine große Stütze sein

suppose /sə'pəʊz/ *vt* annehmen; (*presume*) vermuten; (*imagine*) sich vorstellen; be ~d to do sth etw tun sollen; not be ~d to (*fam*) nicht dürfen; I ~ so vermutlich. ~**dly** /-ɪdlɪ/ *adv* angeblich

supposition /sʌpə'zɪʃn/ *n* Vermutung *f*

suppository /sʌ'pɒzɪtrɪ/ *n* Zäpfchen *nt*

suppress /sə'pres/ *vt* unterdrücken. ~**ion** /-eʃn/ *n* Unterdrückung *f*

supremacy /suː'preməsɪ/ *n* Vorherrschaft *f*

supreme /suːˈpriːm/ a höchste(r,s); ⟨court⟩ oberste(r,s)

surcharge /ˈsɜːtʃɑːdʒ/ n Zuschlag m

sure /ʃʊə(r)/ a (-r, -st) sicher; make ~ sich vergewissern (of gen); (check) nachprüfen; be ~ to do it sieh zu, dass du es tust □ adv (Amer, fam) klar; ~ enough tatsächlich. ~ly adv sicher; (for emphasis) doch; (Amer: gladly) gern

surety /ˈʃʊərətɪ/ n Bürgschaft f; stand ~ for bürgen für

surf /sɜːf/ n Brandung f

surface /ˈsɜːfɪs/ n Oberfläche f □ vi (emerge) auftauchen. ~ mail n by ~ mail auf dem Land-/Seeweg

'surfboard n Surfbrett nt

surfeit /ˈsɜːfɪt/ n Übermaß nt;

surfing /ˈsɜːfɪŋ/ n Surfen nt

surge /sɜːdʒ/ n (of sea) Branden nt; (fig) Welle f □ vi branden; ~ forward nach vorn drängen

surgeon /ˈsɜːdʒən/ n Chirurg(in) m(f)

surgery /ˈsɜːdʒərɪ/ n Chirurgie f; (place) Praxis f; (room) Sprechzimmer nt; (hours) Sprechstunde f; have ~ operiert werden

surgical /ˈsɜːdʒɪkl/ a, -ly adv chirurgisch

surly /ˈsɜːlɪ/ a (-ier, -iest) mürrisch

surmise /səˈmaɪz/ vt mutmaßen

surmount /səˈmaʊnt/ vt überwinden

surname /ˈsɜːneɪm/ n Nachname m

surpass /səˈpɑːs/ vt übertreffen

surplus /ˈsɜːpləs/ a überschüssig; be ~ to requirements nicht benötigt werden □ n Überschuss m (of an + dat)

surpris|e /səˈpraɪz/ n Überraschung f □ vt überraschen; be ~ed sich wundern (at über + acc). ~ing a, -ly adv überraschend

surrender /səˈrendə(r)/ n Kapitulation f □ vi sich ergeben; (Mil) kapitulieren □ vt aufgeben

surreptitious /sʌrəpˈtɪʃəs/ a, -ly adv heimlich, verstohlen

surrogate /ˈsʌrəgət/ n Ersatz m. ~ 'mother n Leihmutter f

surround /səˈraʊnd/ vt umgeben; (encircle) umzingeln; ~ed by umgeben von. ~ing a umliegend. ~ings npl Umgebung f

surveillance /səˈveɪləns/ n Überwachung f; be under ~ überwacht werden

survey¹ /ˈsɜːveɪ/ n Überblick m; (poll) Umfrage f; (investigation) Untersuchung f; (of land) Vermessung f; (of house) Gutachten nt

survey² /səˈveɪ/ vt betrachten; vermessen ⟨land⟩; begutachten ⟨building⟩. ~or n Landvermesser m; Gutachter m

survival /səˈvaɪvl/ n Überleben nt; (of tradition) Fortbestand m

surviv|e /səˈvaɪv/ vt überleben □ vi überleben; ⟨tradition:⟩ erhalten bleiben. ~or n Überlebende(r) m/f; be a ~or (fam) nicht unterzukriegen sein

susceptible /səˈseptəbl/ a empfänglich/ (Med) anfällig (to für)

suspect¹ /səˈspekt/ vt verdächtigen; (assume) vermuten; he ~s nothing er ahnt nichts

suspect² /ˈsʌspekt/ a verdächtig □ n Verdächtige(r) m/f

suspend /səˈspend/ vt aufhängen; (stop) [vorläufig] einstellen; (from duty) vorläufig beurlauben. ~er belt n Strumpfbandgürtel m. ~ers npl Strumpfbänder pl; (Amer: braces) Hosenträger pl

suspense /səˈspens/ n Spannung f

suspension /səˈspenʃn/ n (Auto) Federung f. ~ bridge n Hängebrücke f

suspici|on /səˈspɪʃn/ n Verdacht m; (mistrust) Misstrauen nt; (trace) Spur f. ~ous /-ɪʃəs/ a, -ly adv misstrauisch; (arousing suspicion) verdächtig

sustain /səˈsteɪn/ vt tragen; (fig) aufrechterhalten; erhalten ⟨life⟩; erleiden ⟨injury⟩

sustenance /ˈsʌstɪnəns/ n Nahrung f

swab /swɒb/ n (Med) Tupfer m; (specimen) Abstrich m

swagger /ˈswægə(r)/ vi stolzieren

swallow¹ /ˈswɒləʊ/ vt/i schlucken. ~ up vt verschlucken; verschlingen ⟨resources⟩

swallow² n (bird) Schwalbe f

swam /swæm/ see swim

swamp /swɒmp/ n Sumpf m □ vt überschwemmen. ~y a sumpfig

swan /swɒn/ n Schwan m

swank /swæŋk/ vi (fam) angeben

swap /swɒp/ n (fam) Tausch m □ vt/i (pt/pp swapped) (fam) tauschen (for gegen)

swarm /swɔːm/ n Schwarm m □ vi schwärmen; be ~ing with wimmeln von

swarthy /ˈswɔːðɪ/ a (-ier, -iest) dunkel

swastika /ˈswɒstɪkə/ n Hakenkreuz nt

swat /swɒt/ vt (pt/pp swatted) totschlagen

sway /sweɪ/ n (fig) Herrschaft f □ vi schwanken; (gently) sich wiegen □ vt wiegen; (influence) beeinflussen

swear /sweə(r)/ v (pt swore, pp sworn) □ vt schwören □ vi schwören (by auf + acc); (curse) fluchen. ~-word n Kraftausdruck m

sweat /swet/ n Schweiß m □ vi schwitzen

sweater /ˈswetə(r)/ n Pullover m

sweaty /ˈswetɪ/ a verschwitzt

swede /swiːd/ n Kohlrübe f

Swed|e n Schwede m /-din f. ~en n Schweden nt. ~ish a schwedisch sweep /swiːp/ n Schornsteinfeger m; (curve) Bogen m; (movement) ausholende Bewegung f; make a clean ~ (fig) gründlich aufräumen □ v (pt/pp swept) □ vt fegen, kehren □ vi (go swiftly) rauschen; (wind:) fegen. ~ up vt zusammenfegen/-kehren

sweeping /'swiːpɪŋ/ a ausholend; (statement) pauschal; (changes) weit reichend

sweet /swiːt/ a (-er, -est) süß; have a ~ tooth gern Süßes mögen □ n Bonbon m & nt; (dessert) Nachtisch m. ~ corn n [Zucker]mais m

sweeten /'swiːtn/ vt süßen. ~er n Süßstoff m; (fam: bribe) Schmiergeld nt

sweet: ~heart n Schatz m. ~shop n Süßwarenladen m. ~ness n Süße f; (fig) Liebreiz m. ~ 'pea n Wicke f

swell /swel/ n Dünung f □ v (pt swelled, pp swollen or swelled) □ vi [an]schwellen; (sails:) sich blähen; (wood:) aufquellen □ vt anschwellen lassen; (increase) vergrößern. ~ing n Schwellung f

swelter /'sweltə(r)/ vi schwitzen

swept /swept/ see sweep

swerve /swɜːv/ vi einen Bogen machen

swift /swɪft/ a (-er, -est), -ly adv schnell

swig /swɪg/ n (fam) Schluck m, Zug m □ vt (pt/pp swigged) (fam) [herunter]kippen

swill /swɪl/ n (for pigs) Schweinefutter nt □ vt ~ [out] [aus]spülen

swim /swɪm/ n have a ~ schwimmen □ vi (pt swam, pp swum) schwimmen; my head is ~ming mir dreht sich der Kopf. ~mer n Schwimmer(in) m(f)

swimming /'swɪmɪŋ/ n Schwimmen nt. ~-baths npl Schwimmbad nt. ~-pool n Schwimmbecken nt; (private) Swimming-pool m

'swim-suit n Badeanzug m

swindle /'swɪndl/ n Schwindel m, Betrug m □ vt betrügen. ~r n Schwindler m

swine /swaɪn/ n Schwein nt

swing /swɪŋ/ n Schwung m; (shift) Schwenk m; (seat) Schaukel f; in full ~ in vollem Gange □ v (pt/pp swung) □ vi schwingen; (on swing) schaukeln; (sway) schwanken; (dangle) baumeln; (turn) schwenken □ vt schwingen; (influence) beeinflussen. ~-'door n Schwingtür f

swingeing /'swɪndʒɪŋ/ a hart; (fig) drastisch

swipe /swaɪp/ n (fam) Schlag m □ vt (fam) knallen; (steal) klauen

swirl /swɜːl/ n Wirbel m □ vt/i wirbeln

swish /swɪʃ/ a (fam) schick □ vi zischen

Swiss /swɪs/ a Schweizer, schweizerisch □ n Schweizer(in) m(f); the ~ pl die Schweizer. ~ 'roll n Biskuitrolle f

switch /swɪtʃ/ n Schalter m; (change) Wechsel m; (Amer, Rail) Weiche f □ vt wechseln; (exchange) tauschen □ vi wechseln; ~ to umstellen auf (+ acc). ~ off vt ausschalten; abschalten (engine). ~ on vt einschalten, anschalten

switch: ~back n Achterbahn f. ~board n [Telefon]zentrale f

Switzerland /'swɪtsələnd/ n die Schweiz

swivel /'swɪvl/ v (pt/pp swivelled) □ vt drehen □ vi sich drehen

swollen /'swəʊlən/ see swell □ a geschwollen. ~-'headed a eingebildet

swoop /swuːp/ n Sturzflug m; (by police) Razzia f □ vi ~ down herabstoßen

sword /sɔːd/ n Schwert nt

swore /swɔː(r)/ see swear

sworn /swɔːn/ see swear

swot /swɒt/ n (fam) Streber m □ vt (pt/pp swotted) (fam) büffeln

swum /swʌm/ see swim

swung /swʌŋ/ see swing

syllable /'sɪləbl/ n Silbe f

syllabus /'sɪləbəs/ n Lehrplan m; (for exam) Studienplan m

symbol /'sɪmbl/ n Symbol nt (of für). ~ic /-'bɒlɪk/ a, -ally adv symbolisch ~ism /-ɪzm/ n Symbolik f. ~ize vt symbolisieren

symmetr|ical /sɪ'metrɪkl/ a, -ly adv symmetrisch. ~y /'sɪmɪtrɪ/ n Symmetrie f

sympathetic /sɪmpə'θetɪk/ a, -ally adv mitfühlend; (likeable) sympathisch

sympathize /'sɪmpəθaɪz/ vi mitfühlen. ~r n (Pol) Sympathisant m

sympathy /'sɪmpəθɪ/ n Mitgefühl nt; (condolences) Beileid nt

symphony /'sɪmfənɪ/ n Sinfonie f

symptom /'sɪmptəm/ n Symptom nt. ~atic /-'mætɪk/ a symptomatisch (of für)

synagogue /'sɪnəgɒg/ n Synagoge f

synchronize /'sɪŋkrənaɪz/ vt synchronisieren

syndicate /'sɪndɪkət/ n Syndikat nt

syndrome /'sɪndrəʊm/ n Syndrom nt

synonym /'sɪnənɪm/ n Synonym nt. ~ous /-'nɒnɪməs/ a, -ly adv synonym

synopsis /sɪ'nɒpsɪs/ n (pl -opses /-siːz/) Zusammenfassung f; (of opera, ballet) Inhaltsangabe f

syntax /'sɪntæks/ n Syntax f

synthesis /'sɪnθəsɪs/ n (pl -ses /-siːz/) Synthese f

synthetic /sɪn'θetɪk/ a synthetisch □ n Kunststoff m

Syria /'sɪrɪə/ n Syrien nt

syringe /sɪ'rɪndʒ/ n Spritze f □ vt spritzen; ausspritzen (ears) syrup /'sɪrəp/ n Sirup m

system /'sɪstəm/ n System nt. ~atic /ɪ-'mætɪk/ a, -ally adv systematisch

T

tab /tæb/ n (projecting) Zunge f; (with name) Namensschild nt; (loop) Aufhänger m; keep ~s on (fam) [genau] beobachten; pick up the ~ (fam) bezahlen

tabby /'tæbɪ/ n getigerte Katze f

table /'teɪbl/ n Tisch m; (list) Tabelle f; at [the] ~ bei Tisch □ vt einbringen. ~cloth n Tischdecke f, Tischtuch nt. ~spoon n Servierlöffel m

tablet /'tæblɪt/ n Tablette f; (of soap) Stück nt; (slab) Tafel f

'table tennis n Tischtennis nt

tabloid /'tæblɔɪd/ n kleinformatige Zeitung f; (pej) Boulevardzeitung f

taboo /tə'buː/ a tabu □ n Tabu nt

tacit /'tæsɪt/ a, -ly adv stillschweigend

taciturn /'tæsɪtɜːn/ a wortkarg

tack /tæk/ n (nail) Stift m; (stitch) Heftstich m; (Naut & fig) Kurs m □ vt festnageln; (sew) heften □ vi (Naut) kreuzen

tackle /'tækl/ n Ausrüstung f □ vt angehen

tacky /'tækɪ/ a klebrig

tact /tækt/ n Takt m, Taktgefühl nt. ~ful a, -ly adv taktvoll

tactic|al /'tæktɪkl/ a, -ly adv taktisch. ~s npl Taktik f

tactless /'tæktlɪs/ a, -ly adv taktlos. ~ness n Taktlosigkeit f

tadpole /'tædpəʊl/ n Kaulquappe f

tag¹ /tæg/ n (label) Schild nt □ vi (pt/pp tagged) ~ along mitkommen

tag² n (game) Fangen nt

tail /teɪl/ n Schwanz m; ~s pl (tailcoat) Frack m; heads or ~s? Kopf oder Zahl? □ vt (fam: follow) beschatten □ vi ~ off zurückgehen

tail: ~back n Rückstau m. ~coat n Frack m. ~end n Ende nt. ~ light n Rücklicht nt

tailor /'teɪlə(r)/ n Schneider m. ~-made a maßgeschneidert

'tail wind n Rückenwind m

taint /teɪnt/ vt verderben

take /teɪk/ v (pt took, pp taken) □ vt nehmen; (with one) mitnehmen; (take to a place) bringen; (steal) stehlen; (win) gewinnen; (capture) einnehmen; (require) brauchen; (last) dauern; (teach) geben; machen ⟨exam, subject holiday, photograph⟩; messen ⟨pulse, temperature⟩; ~ s.o. home jdn nach Hause bringen; ~ sth to the cleaner's etw in die Reinigung bringen; ~ s.o. prisoner jdn gefangen nehmen; be ~n ill krank werden; ~ sth calmly etw gelassen aufnehmen □ vi ⟨plant:⟩ angehen; ~ after s.o. jdm nachschlagen; (in looks) jdm ähnlich sehen; ~ to (like) mögen; (as a habit) sich ⟨dat⟩ angewöhnen. ~ away vt wegbringen; (remove) wegnehmen; (subtract) abziehen; 'to ~ away' 'zum Mitnehmen'. ~ back vt zurücknehmen; (return) zurückbringen. ~ down vt herunternehmen; (remove) abnehmen; (write down) aufschreiben. ~ in vt hineinbringen; (bring indoors) hereinholen; (to one's home) aufnehmen; (understand) begreifen; (deceive) hereinlegen; (make smaller) enger machen. ~ off vt abnehmen; ablegen ⟨coat⟩; sich ⟨dat⟩ ausziehen ⟨clothes⟩; (deduct) abziehen; (mimic) nachmachen; ~ time off sich ⟨dat⟩ freinehmen; ~ oneself off [fort]gehen □ vi (Aviat) starten. ~ on vt annehmen; (undertake) übernehmen; (engage) einstellen; (as opponent) antreten gegen. ~ out vt hinausbringen; (for pleasure) ausgehen mit; ausführen ⟨dog⟩; (remove) herausnehmen; (withdraw) abheben ⟨money⟩; (from library) ausleihen; ~ out a subscription to sth etw abonnieren; ~ it out on s.o. (fam) seinen Ärger an jdm auslassen. ~ over vt hinüberbringen; übernehmen ⟨firm, control⟩ □ vi ~ over from s.o. jdn ablösen. ~ up vt hinaufbringen; annehmen ⟨offer⟩; ergreifen ⟨profession⟩; sich ⟨dat⟩ zulegen ⟨hobby⟩; in Anspruch nehmen ⟨time⟩; einnehmen ⟨space⟩; aufreißen ⟨floorboards⟩; ~ sth up with s.o. mit jdm über etw (acc) sprechen □ vi ~ up with s.o. sich mit jdm einlassen

take: ~-away n Essen nt zum Mitnehmen; (restaurant) Restaurant nt mit Straßenverkauf. ~-off n (Aviat) Start m, Abflug m. ~-over n Übernahme f

takings /'teɪkɪŋz/ npl Einnahmen pl

talcum /'tælkəm/ n ~ [powder] Körperpuder m

tale /teɪl/ n Geschichte f

talent /'tælənt/ n Talent nt. ~ed a talentiert

talk /tɔːk/ n Gespräch nt; (lecture) Vortrag m; make small ~ Konversation machen □ vi reden, sprechen (to/with mit) □ vt reden; ~ s.o. into sth jdn zu etw überreden. ~ over vt besprechen

talkative /'tɔːkətɪv/ a gesprächig

'talking-to n Standpauke f

tall /tɔːl/ a (-er, -est) groß; ⟨building, tree⟩ hoch; that's a ~ order das ist ziemlich viel verlangt. ~boy n hohe Kommode f. ~ 'story n übertriebene Geschichte f

tally /'tælɪ/ n keep a ~ of Buch führen über (+ acc) □ vi übereinstimmen

talon /'tælən/ n Klaue f

tambourine /tæmbə'riːn/ n Tamburin nt

tame /teɪm/ a (-r, -st), -ly adv zahm; ⟨dull⟩ lahm (fam) □ vt zähmen. ~r n Dompteur m

tamper /'tæmpə(r)/ vi ~ with sich (dat) zu schaffen machen an (+ dat)

tampon /'tæmpɒn/ n Tampon m

tan /tæn/ a gelbbraun □ n Gelbbraun nt; (from sun) Bräune f □ vt gerben ⟨hide⟩ □ vi braun werden

tang /tæŋ/ n herber Geschmack m; (smell) herber Geruch m

tangent /'tændʒənt/ n Tangente f; go off at a ~ (fam) vom Thema abschweifen

tangible /'tændʒɪbl/ a greifbar

tangle /'tæŋgl/ n Gewirr nt; (in hair) Verfilzung f □ vt ~ [up] verheddern □ vi sich verheddern

tango /'tæŋgəʊ/ n Tango m

tank /tæŋk/ n Tank m; (Mil) Panzer m

tankard /'tæŋkəd/ n Krug m

tanker /'tæŋkə(r)/ n Tanker m; (lorry) Tank[last]wagen m

tantaliz|e /'tæntəlaɪz/ vt quälen. ~ing a verlockend

tantamount /'tæntəmaʊnt/ a be ~ to gleichbedeutend sein mit

tantrum /'tæntrəm/ n Wutanfall m

tap /tæp/ n Hahn m; (knock) Klopfen nt; on ~ zur Verfügung □ v (pt/pp tapped) □ vt klopfen an (+ acc); anzapfen ⟨barrel, tree⟩; erschließen ⟨resources⟩; abhören ⟨telephone⟩ □ vi klopfen. ~dance n Stepptanz m □ vi Stepp tanzen, steppen

tape /teɪp/ n Band nt; (adhesive) Klebstreifen m; (for recording) Tonband nt □ vt mit Klebstreifen zukleben; (record) auf Band aufnehmen

'tape-measure n Bandmaß nt

taper /'teɪpə(r)/ n dünne Wachskerze f □ vi sich verjüngen

'tape recorder n Tonbandgerät nt

tapestry /'tæpɪstrɪ/ n Gobelinstickerei f

tapeworm n Bandwurm m

'tap water n Leitungswasser nt

tar /tɑː(r)/ n Teer m □ vt (pt/pp tarred) teeren

tardy /'tɑːdɪ/ a (-ier, -iest) langsam; (late) spät

target /'tɑːgɪt/ n Ziel nt; (board) [Ziel]-scheibe f

tariff /'tærɪf/ n Tarif m; (duty) Zoll m

tarnish /'tɑːnɪʃ/ vi anlaufen

tarpaulin /tɑː'pɔːlɪn/ n Plane f

tarragon /'tærəgən/ n Estragon m

tart¹ /tɑːt/ a (-er, -est) sauer; (fig) scharf

tart² n ≈ Obstkuchen m; (individual) Törtchen nt; (sl: prostitute) Nutte f □ vt ~ oneself up (fam) sich auftakeln

tartan /'tɑːtn/ n Schottenmuster nt; (cloth) Schottenstoff m □ attrib schottisch kariert

tartar /'tɑːtə(r)/ n (on teeth) Zahnstein m

tartar 'sauce /tɑːtə-/ n ≈ Remouladensoße f

task /tɑːsk/ n Aufgabe f; take s.o. to ~ jdm Vorhaltungen machen. ~ force n Sonderkommando nt

tassel /'tæsl/ n Quaste f

taste /teɪst/ n Geschmack m; (sample) Kostprobe f □ vt kosten, probieren; schmecken ⟨flavour⟩ □ vi schmecken (of nach). ~ful a, -ly adv (fig) geschmackvoll. ~less a, -ly adv geschmacklos

tasty /'teɪstɪ/ a (-ier, -iest) lecker, schmackhaft

tat /tæt/ see tit²

tatter|ed /'tætəd/ a zerlumpt; ⟨pages⟩ zerfleddert. ~s npl in ~s in Fetzen

tattoo¹ /tə'tuː/ n Tätowierung f □ vt tätowieren

tattoo² n (Mil) Zapfenstreich m

tatty /'tætɪ/ a (-ier, -iest) schäbig; ⟨book⟩ zerfleddert

taught /tɔːt/ see teach

taunt /tɔːnt/ n höhnische Bemerkung f □ vt verhöhnen

Taurus /'tɔːrəs/ n (Astr) Stier m

taut /tɔːt/ a straff

tavern /'tævən/ n (liter) Schenke f

tawdry /'tɔːdrɪ/ a (-ier, -iest) billig und geschmacklos

tawny /'tɔːnɪ/ a gelbbraun

tax /tæks/ n Steuer f □ vt besteuern; (fig) strapazieren; ~ with beschuldigen (+ gen). ~able /-əbl/ a steuerpflichtig. ~ation /-'seɪʃn/ n Besteuerung f. ~free a steuerfrei

taxi /'tæksɪ/ n Taxi nt □ vi (pt/pp taxied, pres p taxiing) ⟨aircraft⟩ rollen. ~driver n Taxifahrer m. ~ rank n Taxistand m

taxpayer n Steuerzahler m

tea /tiː/ n Tee m. ~bag n Teebeutel m. ~break n Teepause f

teach /tiːtʃ/ vt/i (pt/pp taught) unterrichten; ~ s.o. sth jdm etw beibringen. ~er n Lehrer(in) m(f)

tea: ~cloth n (for drying) Geschirrtuch nt. ~cup n Teetasse f teak /tiːk/ n Teakholz nt

team /tiːm/ n Mannschaft f; ⟨fig⟩ Team nt; ⟨of animals⟩ Gespann nt □ vi ~ up sich zusammentun

'team-work n Teamarbeit f

'teapot n Teekanne f

tear¹ /teə(r)/ n Riss m □ v ⟨pt tore, pp torn⟩ □ vt reißen; ⟨damage⟩ zerreißen; ~ open aufreißen; ~ oneself away sich losreißen □ vi [zer]reißen; ⟨run⟩ rasen. ~ up vt zerreißen

tear² /tɪə(r)/ n Träne f. ~ful a weinend. ~fully adv unter Tränen. ~gas n Tränengas nt

tease /tiːz/ vt necken

tea: ~-set n Teeservice nt. ~shop n Café nt. ~spoon n Teelöffel m. ~-strainer n Teesieb nt

teat /tiːt/ n Zitze f; ⟨on bottle⟩ Sauger m

'tea-towel n Geschirrtuch nt

technical /'teknɪkl/ a technisch; ⟨specialized⟩ fachlich. ~ity /-'kælətɪ/ n technisches Detail nt; ⟨Jur⟩ Formfehler m. ~ly adv technisch; ⟨strictly⟩ streng genommen. ~ term n Fachausdruck m

technician /tek'nɪʃn/ n Techniker m

technique /tek'niːk/ n Technik f

technological /teknə'lɒdʒɪkl/ a, -ly adv technologisch

technology /tek'nɒlədʒɪ/ n Technologie f

teddy /'tedɪ/ n ~ [bear] Teddybär m

tedious /'tiːdɪəs/ a langweilig

tedium /'tiːdɪəm/ n Langeweile f

teem /tiːm/ vi ⟨rain⟩ in Strömen gießen; be ~ing with ⟨full of⟩ wimmeln von

teenage /'tiːneɪdʒ/ a Teenager-; ~ boy/girl Junge m/Mädchen nt im Teenageralter. ~r n Teenager m

teens /tiːnz/ npl the ~ die Teenagerjahre pl

teeny /'tiːnɪ/ a (-ier, -iest) winzig

teeter /'tiːtə(r)/ vi schwanken

teeth /tiːθ/ see tooth

teeth|e /tiːð/ vi zahnen. ~ing troubles npl ⟨fig⟩ Anfangsschwierigkeiten pl

teetotal /tiː'təʊtl/ a abstinent. ~ler n Abstinenzler m

telecommunications /telɪkəmjuːnɪ-'keɪʃnz/ npl Fernmeldewesen nt

telegram /'telɪgræm/ n Telegramm nt

telegraph /'telɪgrɑːf/ n Telegraf m. ~ic /-'græfɪk/ a telegrafisch. ~ pole n Telegrafenmast m

telepathy /tɪ'lepəθɪ/ n Telepathie f; by ~ telepathisch

telephone /'telɪfəʊn/ n Telefon nt; be on the ~ Telefon haben; ⟨be telephoning⟩ telefonieren □ vt anrufen □ vi telefonieren

telephone: ~ book n Telefonbuch nt. ~ booth n, ~ box n Telefonzelle f. ~ directory n Telefonbuch nt. ~ number n Telefonnummer f

telephonist /tɪ'lefənɪst/ n Telefonist(in) m(f)

tele'photo /telɪ-/ a ~ lens Teleobjektiv nt

teleprinter /'telɪ-/ n Fernschreiber m

telescop|e /'telɪskəʊp/ n Teleskop nt, Fernrohr nt. ~ic /-'skɒpɪk/ a teleskopisch; ⟨collapsible⟩ ausziehbar

televise /'telɪvaɪz/ vt im Fernsehen übertragen

television /'telɪvɪʒn/ n Fernsehen nt; watch ~ fernsehen. ~ set n Fernsehapparat m, Fernseher m

telex /'teleks/ n Telex nt □ vt telexen

tell /tel/ vt/i ⟨pt/pp told⟩ sagen ⟨s.o. jdm⟩; ⟨relate⟩ erzählen; ⟨know⟩ wissen; ⟨distinguish⟩ erkennen; ~ the time die Uhr lesen; time will ~ das wird man erst sehen; his age is beginning to ~ sein Alter macht sich bemerkbar; don't ~ me sag es mir nicht; you mustn't ~ du darfst nichts sagen. ~ off vt ausschimpfen

teller /'telə(r)/ n ⟨cashier⟩ Kassierer(in) m(f)

telly /'telɪ/ n ⟨fam⟩ = television

temerity /tɪ'merətɪ/ n Kühnheit f

temp /temp/ n ⟨fam⟩ Aushilfssekretärin f

temper /'tempə(r)/ n ⟨disposition⟩ Naturell nt; ⟨mood⟩ Laune f; ⟨anger⟩ Wut f; lose one's ~ wütend werden □ vt ⟨fig⟩ mäßigen

temperament /'temprəmənt/ n Temperament nt. ~al /-'mentl/ a temperamentvoll; ⟨moody⟩ launisch

temperance /'tempərəns/ n Mäßigung f; ⟨abstinence⟩ Abstinenz f

temperate /'tempərət/ a gemäßigt

temperature /'temprətʃə(r)/ n Temperatur f; have or run a ~ Fieber haben

tempest /'tempɪst/ n Sturm m. ~uous /-'pestjʊəs/ a stürmisch

template /'templɪt/ n Schablone f

temple¹ /'templ/ n Tempel m

temple² n ⟨Anat⟩ Schläfe f

tempo /'tempəʊ/ n Tempo nt

temporary /'tempərərɪ/ a, -ly adv vorübergehend; ⟨measure, building⟩ provisorisch

tempt /tempt/ vt verleiten; ⟨Relig⟩ versuchen; herausfordern ⟨fate⟩; ⟨entice⟩ [ver]locken; be ~ed versucht sein ⟨to zu⟩; I am ~ed by it es lockt mich. ~ation /-'teɪʃn/ n Versuchung f. ~ing a verlockend

ten /ten/ a zehn

tenable /'tenəbl/ a (fig) haltbar

tenacious /tɪ'neɪʃəs/ a, **-ly** adv hartnäckig. **~ty** /-'næsətɪ/ n Hartnäckigkeit f

tenant /'tenənt/ n Mieter(in) m(f); (Comm) Pächter(in) m(f)

tend¹ /tend/ vt (look after) sich kümmern um

tend² vi ~ to do sth dazu neigen, etw zu tun

tendency /'tendənsɪ/ n Tendenz f; (inclination) Neigung f

tender¹ /'tendə(r)/ n □(Comm) Angebot nt; legal ~ gesetzliches Zahlungsmittel nt □ vt anbieten; einreichen (resignation)

tender² a zart; (loving) zärtlich; (painful) empfindlich. **~ly** adv zärtlich. **~ness** n Zartheit f; Zärtlichkeit f

tendon /'tendən/ n Sehne f

tenement /'tenəmənt/ n Mietshaus nt

tenet /'tenɪt/ n Grundsatz m

tenner /'tenə(r)/ n (fam) Zehnpfundschein m

tennis /'tenɪs/ n Tennis nt. **~-court** n Tennisplatz m

tenor /'tenə(r)/ n Tenor m

tense¹ /tens/ n (Gram) Zeit f

tense² a (-r, -st) gespannt □ vt anspannen (muscle)

tension /'tenʃn/ n Spannung f

tent /tent/ n Zelt nt

tentacle /'tentəkl/ n Fangarm m

tentative /'tentətɪv/ a, **-ly** adv vorläufig; (hesitant) zaghaft

tenterhooks /'tentəhʊks/ npl be on ~ wie auf glühenden Kohlen sitzen

tenth /tenθ/ a zehnte(r,s) □ n Zehntel nt

tenuous /'tenjʊəs/ a (fig) schwach

tepid /'tepɪd/ a lauwarm

term /tɜːm/ n Zeitraum m; (Sch) Halbjahr nt; (Univ) ≈ Semester nt; (expression) Ausdruck m; ~s pl (conditions) Bedingungen pl; ~ of office Amtszeit f; in the short/long ~ kurz-/langfristig; be on good/bad ~s gut/nicht gut miteinander auskommen; come to ~s with sich abfinden mit

terminal /'tɜːmɪnl/ a End-; (Med) unheilbar □ n (Aviat) Terminal m; (of bus) Endstation f; (on battery) Pol m; (Computing) Terminal nt

terminat|e /'tɜːmɪneɪt/ vt beenden; lösen (contract); unterbrechen (pregnancy) □ vi enden. **~ion** /-'neɪʃn/ n Beendigung f; (Med) Schwangerschaftsabbruch m

terminology /tɜːmɪ'nɒlədʒɪ/ n Terminologie f

terminus /'tɜːmɪnəs/ n (pl -ni /-naɪ/) Endstation f

terrace /'terəs/ n Terrasse f; (houses) serreihe f; the ~s (Sport) die [Steh]ränge pl. **~d house** n Reihenhaus nt

terrain /te'reɪn/ n Gelände nt

terrible /'terəbl/ a, **-bly** adv schrecklich

terrier /'terɪə(r)/ n Terrier m

terrific /tə'rɪfɪk/ a (fam) (excellent) sagenhaft; (huge) riesig

terri|fy /'terɪfaɪ/ vt (pt/pp -ied) Angst machen (+ dat); be **~fied** Angst haben. **~fying** a Furcht erregend

territorial /terɪ'tɔːrɪəl/ a Territorial-

territory /'terɪtərɪ/ n Gebiet nt

terror /'terə(r)/ n [panische] Angst f; (Pol) Terror m. **~ism** /-ɪzm/ n Terrorismus m. **~ist** /-ɪst/ n Terrorist m. **~ize** vt terrorisieren

terse /tɜːs/ a, **-ly** adv kurz, knapp

test /test/ n Test m; (Sch) Klassenarbeit f; put to the ~ auf die Probe stellen □ vt prüfen; (examine) untersuchen (for auf + acc)

testament /'testəmənt/ n Testament nt; Old/New T~ Altes/Neues Testament nt

testicle /'testɪkl/ n Hoden m

testi|fy /'testɪfaɪ/ v (pt/pp -ied) □ vt beweisen; ~ that bezeugen, dass □ vi aussagen; ~ to bezeugen

testimonial /testɪ'məʊnɪəl/ n Zeugnis nt

testimony /'testɪmənɪ/ n Aussage f

'test-tube n Reagenzglas nt. ~ 'baby n (fam) Retortenbaby nt

testy /'testɪ/ a gereizt

tetanus /'tetənəs/ n Tetanus m

tetchy /'tetʃɪ/ a gereizt

tether /'teðə(r)/ n be at the end of one's ~ am Ende seiner Kraft sein □ vt anbinden

text /tekst/ n Text m. **~book** n Lehrbuch nt

textile /'tekstaɪl/ a Textil- □ n ~s pl Textilien pl

texture /'tekstʃə(r)/ n Beschaffenheit f; (Tex) Struktur f

Thai /taɪ/ a thailändisch. **~land** n Thailand nt

Thames /temz/ n Themse f

than /ðən, betont ðæn/ conj als; older ~ me älter als ich

thank /θæŋk/ vt danken (+ dat); ~ you [very much] danke [schön]. **~ful** a, **-ly** adv dankbar. **~less** a undankbar

thanks /θæŋks/ npl Dank m; ~! (fam) danke! ~ to dank (+ dat or gen)

that /ðæt/ a & pron (pl those) der/die/das; (pl) die; ~ one der/die/das da; I'll take ~ ich nehme den/die/das; I don't like those die mag ich nicht; ~ is das heißt; is ~ you? bist du es? who is ~? wer ist da? with/after ∼ damit/danach; like ∼ so; a man like ∼ so ein Mann; ∼ is why deshalb; ∼'s it! genau! all ∼ I know alles was ich weiß; the day ∼ I saw him an dem Tag, als ich ihn sah □ *adv* so; ∼ good/ hot so gut/heiß □ *conj* dass

thatch /θætʃ/ *n* Strohdach *nt*. ∼ed *a* strohgedeckt

thaw /θɔ:/ *n* Tauwetter *nt* □ *vt/i* auftauen; it's ∼ing es taut

the /ðə, *vor einem Vokal* ði:/ *def art* der/ die/das; (*pl*) die; play ∼ piano/violin Klavier/Geige spielen □ *adv* ∼ more ∼ better je mehr, desto besser; all ∼ better umso besser

theatre /'θɪətə(r)/ *n* Theater *nt*; (*Med*) Operationssaal *m*

theatrical /θɪ'ætrɪkl/ *a* Theater-; (*showy*) theatralisch

theft /θeft/ *n* Diebstahl *m*

their /ðeə(r)/ *a* ihr

theirs /ðeəz/ *poss pron* ihre(r), ihrs; a friend of ∼ ein Freund von ihnen; those are ∼ die gehören ihnen

them /ðem/ *pron* (*acc*) sie; (*dat*) ihnen; I know ∼ ich kenne sie; give ∼ the money gib ihnen das Geld

theme /θi:m/ *n* Thema *nt*

them'selves *pron* selbst; (*refl*) sich; by ∼ allein

then /ðen/ *adv* dann; (*at that time in past*) damals; by ∼ bis dahin; since ∼ seitdem; before ∼ vorher; from ∼ on von da an; now and ∼ dann und wann; there and ∼ auf der Stelle □ *a* damalig

theolog|ian /θɪə'ləʊdʒɪən/ *n* Theologe *m*. ∼y /-'ɒlədʒɪ/ *n* Theologie *f*

theorem /'θɪərəm/ *n* Lehrsatz *m*

theoretical /θɪə'retɪkl/ *a*, -ly *adv* theoretisch

theory /'θɪərɪ/ *n* Theorie *f*; in ∼ theoretisch

therapeutic /θerə'pju:tɪk/ *a* therapeutisch

therap|ist /'θerəpɪst/ *n* Therapeut(in) *m(f)*. ∼y *n* Therapie *f*

there /ðeə(r)/ *adv* da; (*with movement*) dahin, dorthin; down/up ∼ da unten/oben; ∼ is/are da ist/sind; (*in existence*) es gibt; ∼ he/she is da ist er/sie; send/take ∼ hinschicken/-bringen □ *int* there, there! nun, nun!

there: ∼abouts *adv* da [in der Nähe]; or ∼abouts (*roughly*) ungefähr. ∼'after *adv* danach. ∼by *adv* dadurch. ∼fore /-fɔ:(r)/ *adv* deshalb, also

thermal /'θɜ:ml/ *a* Thermal-; ∼ 'underwear *n* Thermowäsche *f*

thermometer /θə'mɒmɪtə(r)/ *n* Thermometer *nt*

Thermos (P) /'θɜ:məs/ *n* ∼ [flask] Thermosflasche (P) *f*

thermostat /'θɜ:məstæt/ *n* Thermostat *m*

these /ði:z/ *see* this

thesis /'θi:sɪs/ *n* (*pl* -ses /-si:z/) Dissertation *f*; (*proposition*) These *f*

they /ðeɪ/ *pron* sie; ∼ say (*generalizing*) man sagt

thick /θɪk/ *a* (-er, -est), -ly *adv* dick; (*dense*) dicht; (*liquid*) dickflüssig; (*fam: stupid*) dumm □ dick *a n* in the ∼ of mitten in (+ *dat*). ∼en *vt* dicker machen; eindicken (*sauce*) □ *vi* dicker werden; (*fog:*) dichter werden; (*plot:*) kompliziert werden. ∼ness *n* Dicke *f*; Dichte *f*; Dickflüssigkeit *f*

thick: ∼set *a* untersetzt. ∼-'skinned *a* (*fam*) dickfellig

thief /θi:f/ *n* (*pl* thieves) Dieb(in) *m(f)*

thieving /'θi:vɪŋ/ *a* diebisch □ *n* Stehlen *nt*

thigh /θaɪ/ *n* Oberschenkel *m*

thimble /'θɪmbl/ *n* Fingerhut *m*

thin /θɪn/ *a* (thinner, thinnest), -ly *adv* dünn □ *adv* dünn □ *v* (*pt/pp* thinned) □ *vt* verdünnen (*liquid*) □ *vi* sich lichten. ∼ out *vt* ausdünnen

thing /θɪŋ/ *n* Ding *nt*; (*subject, affair*) Sache *f*; ∼s *pl* (*belongings*) Sachen *pl*; for one ∼ erstens; the right ∼ das Richtige; just the ∼! genau das Richtige! how are ∼s? wie geht's? the latest ∼ (*fam*) der letzte Schrei; the best ∼ would be am besten wäre es

think /θɪŋk/ *vt/i* (*pt/pp* thought) denken (about/of an + *acc*); (*believe*) meinen; (*consider*) nachdenken; (*regard as*) halten für; I ∼ so ich glaube schon; what do you ∼? was meinen Sie? what do you ∼ of it? was halten Sie davon? ∼ better of it es sich (*dat*) anders überlegen. ∼ over *vt* sich (*dat*) überlegen. ∼ up *vt* sich (*dat*) ausdenken

third /θɜ:d/ *a* dritte(r,s) □ *n* Drittel *nt*. ∼ly *adv* drittens. ∼-rate *a* drittrangig

thirst /θɜ:st/ *n* Durst *m*. ∼y *a*, -ily *adv* durstig; be ∼y Durst haben

thirteen /θɜ:'ti:n/ *a* dreizehn. ∼th *a* dreizehnte(r,s)

thirtieth /'θɜ:tɪɪθ/ *a* dreißigste(r,s)

thirty /'θɜ:tɪ/ *a* dreißig

this /ðɪs/ *a* (*pl* these) diese(r,s); (*pl*) diese; ∼ one diese(r,s) da; I'll take ∼ ich nehme diesen/diese/ dieses; ∼ evening/morning heute Abend/Morgen; these days heutzutage □ *pron* (*pl* these) das, dies[es]; (*pl*) die, diese; ∼ and that dies und das; ∼ or that dieses oder das da; like ∼ so;

~ is Peter das ist Peter; (*Teleph*) hier [spricht] Peter; who is ~? wer ist das? (*Amer, Teleph*) wer ist am Apparat?

thistle /'θɪsl/ *n* Distel *f*

thorn /θɔːn/ *n* Dorn *m*. ~**y** *a* dornig

thorough /'θʌrə/ *a* gründlich

thorough: ~**bred** *n* reinrassiges Tier *nt*; (*horse*) Rassepferd *nt*. ~**fare** *n* Durchfahrtsstraße *f*; 'no ~**fare**' 'keine Durchfahrt'

thorough|**ly** /'θʌrəlɪ/ *adv* gründlich; (*completely*) völlig; (*extremely*) äußerst. ~**ness** *n* Gründlichkeit *f*

those /ðəʊz/ *see* **that**

though /ðəʊ/ *conj* obgleich, obwohl; as ~ als ob □ *adv* (*fam*) doch

thought /θɔːt/ *see* **think** □ *n* Gedanke *m*; (*thinking*) Denken *nt*. ~**ful** *a*, -**ly** *adv* nachdenklich; (*considerate*) rücksichtsvoll. ~**less** *a*, -**ly** *adv* gedankenlos

thousand /'θaʊznd/ *a* one/a ~ [ein]tausend □ *n* Tausend *nt*; ~**s** of Tausende von. ~**th** *a* tausendste(r,s) □ *n* Tausendstel *nt*

thrash /θræʃ/ *vt* verprügeln; (*defeat*) [vernichtend] schlagen. ~ **about** *vi* sich herumwerfen; (*fish:*) zappeln. ~ **out** *vt* ausdiskutieren

thread /θred/ *n* Faden *m*; (*of screw*) Gewinde *nt* □ *vt* einfädeln; auffädeln (*beads*); ~ one's way through sich schlängeln durch. ~**bare** *a* fadenscheinig

threat /θret/ *n* Drohung *f*; (*danger*) Bedrohung *f*

threaten /'θretn/ *vt* drohen (+ *dat*); (*with weapon*) bedrohen; ~ to do sth drohen, etw zu tun; ~ s.o. with sth jdm etw androhen □ *vi* drohen. ~**ing** *a*, -**ly** *adv* drohend; (*ominous*) bedrohlich

three /θriː/ *a* drei. ~**fold** *a* & *adv* dreifach. ~**some** /-səm/ *n* Trio *nt*

thresh /θreʃ/ *vt* dreschen

threshold /'θreʃəʊld/ *n* Schwelle *f*

threw /θruː/ *see* **throw**

thrift /θrɪft/ *n* Sparsamkeit *f*. ~**y** *a* sparsam

thrill /θrɪl/ *n* Erregung *f*; (*fam*) Nervenkitzel *m* □ *vt* (*excite*) erregen; be ~ed with sich sehr freuen über (+ *acc*). ~**er** *n* Thriller *m*. ~**ing** *a* aufregend

thrive /θraɪv/ *vi* (*pt* thrived *or* throve, *pp* thrived *or* thriven /'θrɪvn/) gedeihen (on bei); (*business:*) florieren

throat /θrəʊt/ *n* Hals *m*; sore ~ Halsschmerzen *pl*; cut s.o.'s ~ jdm die Kehle durchschneiden

throb /θrɒb/ *n* Pochen *nt* □ *vi* (*pt/pp* throbbed) pochen; (*vibrate*) vibrieren

throes /θrəʊz/ *npl* in the ~ of (*fig*) mitten in (+ *dat*)

thrombosis /θrɒm'bəʊsɪs/ *n* Thrombose *f*

throne /θrəʊn/ *n* Thron *m*

throng /θrɒŋ/ *n* Menge *f*

throttle /'θrɒtl/ *vt* erdrosseln

through /θruː/ *prep* durch (+ *acc*); (*during*) während (+ *gen*); (*Amer: up to & including*) bis einschließlich □ *adv* durch; all ~ die ganze Zeit; ~ and ~ durch und durch; wet ~ durch und durch nass; read sth ~ etw durchlesen; let/walk ~ durchlassen/-gehen □ *a* (*train*) durchgehend; be ~ (*finished*) fertig sein; (*Teleph*) durch sein

throughout /θruː'aʊt/ *prep* ~ the country im ganzen Land; ~ the night die Nacht durch □ *adv* ganz; (*time*) die ganze Zeit

throve /θrəʊv/ *see* **thrive**

throw /θrəʊ/ *n* Wurf *m* □ *vt* (*pt* threw, *pp* thrown) werfen; schütten (*liquid*); betätigen (*switch*); abwerfen (*rider*); (*fam: disconcert*) aus der Fassung bringen; (*party*) geben (*party*); ~ sth to s.o. jdm etw zuwerfen; ~ sth at s.o. etw nach jdm werfen; (*pelt with*) jdn mit etw bewerfen. ~ **away** *vt* wegwerfen. ~ **out** *vt* hinauswerfen; (~ *away*) wegwerfen; verwerfen (*plan*). ~ **up** *vt* hochwerfen □ *vi* (*fam*) sich übergeben

'**throw-away** *a* Wegwerf-

thrush /θrʌʃ/ *n* Drossel *f*

thrust /θrʌst/ *n* Stoß *m*; (*Phys*) Schub *m* □ *vt* (*pt/pp* thrust) stoßen; (*insert*) stecken; ~ [up]on aufbürden (s.o. jdm)

thud /θʌd/ *n* dumpfer Schlag *m*

thug /θʌg/ *n* Schläger *m*

thumb /θʌm/ *n* Daumen *m*; rule of ~ Faustregel *f*; under s.o.'s ~ unter jds Fuchtel □ *vt* ~ a lift (*fam*) per Anhalter fahren. ~**index** *n* Daumenregister *nt*. ~**tack** *n* (*Amer*) Reißzwecke *f*

thump /θʌmp/ *n* Schlag *m*; (*noise*) dumpfer Schlag *m* □ *vt* schlagen □ *vi* hämmern (on an/auf + *acc*); (*heart:*) pochen

thunder /'θʌndə(r)/ *n* Donner *m* □ *vi* donnern. ~**clap** *n* Donnerschlag *m*. ~**storm** *n* Gewitter *nt*. ~**y** *a* gewittrig

Thursday /'θɜːzdeɪ/ *n* Donnerstag *m*

thus /ðʌs/ *adv* so

thwart /θwɔːt/ *vt* vereiteln; ~ s.o. jdm einen Strich durch die Rechnung machen

thyme /taɪm/ *n* Thymian *m*

thyroid /'θaɪrɔɪd/ *n* Schilddrüse *f*

tiara /tɪ'ɑːrə/ *n* Diadem *nt*

tick¹ /tɪk/ *n* on ~ (*fam*) auf Pump

tick² (*sound*) Ticken *nt*; (*mark*) Häkchen *nt*; (*fam: instant*) Sekunde *f* □ *vi* ticken

□ *vt* abhaken. ~ off *vt* abhaken; (*fam*) rüffeln. ~ over *vi* ⟨*engine:*⟩ im Leerlauf laufen

ticket /'tɪkɪt/ *n* Karte *f*; (*for bus, train*) Fahrschein *m*; (*Aviat*) Flugschein *m*; (*for lottery*) Los *nt*; (*for article deposited*) Schein *m*; (*label*) Schild *nt*; (*for library*) Lesekarte *f*; (*fine*) Strafzettel *m*. ~-collector *n* Fahrkartenkontrolleur *m*. ~-office *n* Fahrkartenschalter *m*; (*for entry*) Kasse *f*

tick|le /'tɪkl/ *n* Kitzeln *nt* □ *vt/i* kitzeln. ~lish /'tɪklɪʃ/ *a* kitzlig

tidal /'taɪdl/ *a* ⟨*river, harbour*⟩ Tide-. ~ wave *n* Flutwelle *f*

tiddly-winks /'tɪdlɪwɪŋks/ *n* Flohspiel *nt*

tide /taɪd/ *n* Gezeiten *pl*; (*of events*) Strom *m*; the ~ is in/out es ist Flut/Ebbe □ *vt* ~ s.o. over jdm über die Runden helfen

tidiness /'taɪdɪnɪs/ *n* Ordentlichkeit *f*

tidy /'taɪdɪ/ *a* (-ier, -iest) -ily *adv* ordentlich □ *vt* ~ [up] aufräumen; ~ oneself up sich zurechtmachen

tie /taɪ/ *n* Krawatte *f*; Schlips *m*; (*cord*) Schnur *f*; (*fig: bond*) Band *nt*; (*restriction*) Bindung *f*; (*Sport*) Unentschieden *nt*; (*in competition*) Punktgleichheit *f* □ *v* (*pres p* tying) □ *vt* binden; machen ⟨*knot*⟩ □ *vi* (*Sport*) unentschieden spielen; (*have equal scores, votes*) punktgleich sein; ~ in with passen zu. ~ up *vt* festbinden; verschnüren ⟨*parcel*⟩; fesseln ⟨*person*⟩; be ~d up (*busy*) beschäftigt sein

tier /tɪə(r)/ *n* Stufe *f*; (*of cake*) Etage *f*; (*in stadium*) Rang *m*

tiff /tɪf/ *n* Streit *m*, (*fam*) Krach *m*

tiger /'taɪgə(r)/ *n* Tiger *m*

tight /taɪt/ *a* (-er, -est), -ly *adv* fest; (*taut*) straff; ⟨*clothes*⟩ eng; ⟨*control*⟩ streng; (*fam: drunk*) blau; in a ~ corner (*fam*) in der Klemme □ *adv* fest

tighten /'taɪtn/ *vt* fester ziehen; straffen ⟨*rope*⟩; anziehen ⟨*screw*⟩; verschärfen ⟨*control*⟩ □ *vi* sich spannen

tight: ~-fisted *a* knauserig. ~rope *n* Hochseil *nt*

tights /taɪts/ *npl* Strumpfhose *f*

tile /taɪl/ *n* Fliese *f*; (*on wall*) Kachel *f*; (*on roof*) [Dach]ziegel *m* □ *vt* mit Fliesen auslegen; kacheln ⟨*wall*⟩; decken ⟨*roof*⟩

till[1] /tɪl/ *prep & conj* = until

till[2] *n* Kasse *f*

tiller /'tɪlə(r)/ *n* Ruderpinne *f*

tilt /tɪlt/ *n* Neigung *f*; at full ~ mit voller Wucht □ *vt* kippen; [zur Seite] neigen ⟨*head*⟩ □ *vi* sich neigen

timber /'tɪmbə(r)/ *n* [Nutz]holz *nt*

time /taɪm/ *n* Zeit *f*; (*occasion*) Mal *nt*; (*rhythm*) Takt *m*; ~s (*Math*) mal; at any ~ jederzeit; this ~ dieses Mal, diesmal; at ~s manchmal; ~ and again immer wieder; two at a ~ zwei auf einmal; on ~ pünktlich; in ~ rechtzeitig; (*eventually*) mit der Zeit; in no ~ im Handumdrehen; in a year's ~ in einem Jahr; behind ~ verspätet; behind the ~s rückständig; for the ~ being vorläufig; what is the ~? wie spät ist es? wie viel Uhr ist es? by the ~ we arrive bis wir ankommen; did you have a nice ~? hat es dir gut gefallen? have a good ~! viel Vergnügen! □ *vt* stoppen ⟨*race*⟩; be well ~d gut abgepaßt sein

time: ~ bomb *n* Zeitbombe *f*. ~-lag *n* Zeitdifferenz *f*. ~-less *a* zeitlos. ~ly *a* rechtzeitig. ~-switch *n* Zeitschalter *m*. ~-table *n* Fahrplan *m*; (*Sch*) Stundenplan *m*

timid /'tɪmɪd/ *a*, -ly *adv* scheu; (*hesitant*) zaghaft

timing /'taɪmɪŋ/ *n* Wahl *f* des richtigen Zeitpunkts; (*Sport, Techn*) Timing *nt*

tin /tɪn/ *n* Zinn *nt*; (*container*) Dose *f* □ *vt* (*pt/pp* tinned) in Dosen *od* Büchsen konservieren. ~ foil *n* Stanniol *nt*; (*Culin*) Alufolie *f*

tinge /tɪndʒ/ *n* Hauch *m* □ *vt* ~d with mit einer Spur von

tingle /'tɪŋgl/ *vi* kribbeln

tinker /'tɪŋkə(r)/ *vi* herumbasteln (with an + *dat*)

tinkle /'tɪŋkl/ *n* Klingeln *nt* □ *vi* klingeln

tinned /tɪnd/ *a* Dosen-, Büchsen-

'tin opener *n* Dosen-/Büchsenöffner *m*

'tinpot *a* (*pej*) ⟨*firm*⟩ schäbig

tinsel /'tɪnsl/ *n* Lametta *nt*

tint /tɪnt/ *n* Farbton *m* □ *vt* tönen

tiny /'taɪnɪ/ *a* (-ier, -iest) winzig

tip[1] /tɪp/ *n* Spitze *f*

tip[2] *n* (*money*) Trinkgeld *nt*; (*advice*) Rat *m*, (*fam*) Tipp *m*; (*for rubbish*) Müllhalde *f* □ *v* (*pt/pp* tipped) □ *vt* (*tilt*) kippen; (*reward*) Trinkgeld geben (s.o. jdm) □ *vi* kippen. ~ off *vt* ~ s.o. off jdm einen Hinweis geben. ~ out *vt* auskippen. ~ over *vt/i* umkippen

'tip-off *n* Hinweis *m*

tipped /tɪpt/ *a* Filter-

tipsy /'tɪpsɪ/ *a* (*fam*) beschwipst

tiptoe /'tɪptəʊ/ *n* on ~ auf Zehenspitzen

tiptop /tɪp'tɒp/ *a* (*fam*) erstklassig

tire /'taɪə(r)/ *vt/i* ermüden. ~ *a* müde; be ~d of sth etw satt haben; ~d out [völlig] erschöpft. ~less *a*, -ly *adv* unermüdlich. ~some /-səm/ *a* lästig

tiring /'taɪrɪŋ/ *a* ermüdend

tissue /'tɪʃu:/ n Gewebe nt; (handkerchief) Papiertaschentuch nt. ~-paper n Seidenpapier nt

tit¹ /tɪt/ n (bird) Meise f

tit² /tɪt/ n ~ for tat wie du mir, so ich dir

'titbit n Leckerbissen m

titilate /'tɪtɪleɪt/ vt erregen

title /'taɪtl/ n Titel m. ~-role n Titelrolle f

tittle-tattle /'tɪtltætl/ n Klatsch m

titular /'tɪtjʊlə(r)/ a nominell

to /tu:, unbetont tə/ prep zu (+ dat); (with place, direction) nach; (to cinema, theatre) in (+ acc); (to wedding, party) auf (+ acc); ⟨address, send, fasten⟩ an (+ acc); (per) pro; (up to, until) bis; to the station zum Bahnhof; to Germany/Switzerland nach Deutschland/ in die Schweiz; to the toilet/one's room auf die Toilette/sein Zimmer; to the office/an exhibition ins Büro/ in eine Ausstellung; to university auf die Universität; twenty/quarter to eight zwanzig/Viertel vor acht; 5 to 6 pounds 5 bis 6 Pfund; to the end bis zum Schluss; to this day bis heute; to the best of my knowledge nach meinem besten Wissen; give/say sth to s.o. jdm etw geben/sagen; go/come to s.o. zu jdm gehen/kommen; I've never been to Berlin ich war noch nie in Berlin; there's nothing to it es ist nichts dabei □ verbal construction to go gehen; to stay bleiben; learn to swim schwimmen lernen; want to/have to go gehen wollen/müssen; be easy/difficult to forget leicht/schwer zu vergessen sein; too ill/tired to go zu krank/müde, um zu gehen; he did it to annoy me er tat es, um mich zu ärgern; you have to du musst; I don't want to ich will nicht; I'd love to gern; I forgot to ich habe es vergessen; he wants to be a teacher er will Lehrer werden; live to be 90 90 werden; he was the last to arrive er kam als Letzter; to be honest ehrlich gesagt □ adv pull to anlehnen; to and fro hin und her

toad /təʊd/ n Kröte f. ~stool n Giftpilz m

toast /təʊst/ n Toast m □ vt toasten ⟨bread⟩; ⟨drink a ~ to⟩ trinken auf (+ acc). ~er n Toaster m

tobacco /tə'bækəʊ/ n Tabak m. ~nist's [shop] n Tabakladen m

toboggan /tə'bɒgən/ n Schlitten m □ vi Schlitten fahren

today /tə'deɪ/ n & adv heute; ~ week heute in einer Woche; ~'s paper die heutige Zeitung

toddler /'tɒdlə(r)/ n Kleinkind nt

to-do /tə'du:/ n (fam) Getue nt, Theater nt

toe /təʊ/ n Zeh m; (of footwear) Spitze f □ vt ~ the line spuren. ~nail n Zehennagel m

toffee /'tɒfɪ/ n Karamellbonbon m & nt

together /tə'geðə(r)/ adv zusammen; (at the same time) gleichzeitig

toil /tɔɪl/ n [harte] Arbeit f □ vi schwer arbeiten

toilet /'tɔɪlɪt/ n Toilette f. ~ bag n Kulturbeutel m. ~ paper n Toilettenpapier nt

toiletries /'tɔɪlɪtrɪz/ npl Toilettenartikel pl

toilet: ~ roll n Rolle f Toilettenpapier. ~-water n Toilettenwasser nt

token /'təʊkən/ n Zeichen nt; (counter) Marke f; (voucher) Gutschein m □ attrib symbolisch

told /təʊld/ see tell □ all ~ insgesamt

tolerable /'tɒlərəbl/ a, -bly adv erträglich; (not bad) leidlich

toleran|ce /'tɒlərəns/ n Toleranz f. ~t a, -ly adv tolerant

tolerate /'tɒləreɪt/ vt dulden, tolerieren; (bear) ertragen

toll¹ /təʊl/ n Gebühr f; (for road) Maut f (Aust); death ~ Zahl f der Todesopfer; take a heavy ~ einen hohen Tribut fordern

toll² vi läuten

tom /tɒm/ n (cat) Kater m

tomato /tə'mɑ:təʊ/ n (pl -es) Tomate f. ~ purée n Tomatenmark nt

tomb /tu:m/ n Grabmal nt

tomboy /'tɒm-/ n Wildfang m

'tombstone n Grabstein m

'tom-cat n Kater m

tome /təʊm/ n dicker Band m

tomfoolery /tɒm'fu:lərɪ/ n Blödsinn m

tomorrow /tə'mɒrəʊ/ n & adv morgen; ~ morning morgen früh; the day after ~ übermorgen; see you ~! bis morgen!

ton /tʌn/ n Tonne f. ~s of (fam) jede Menge

tone /təʊn/ n Ton m; (colour) Farbton m □ vt ~ down dämpfen; (fig) mäßigen. ~ up vt kräftigen; straffen ⟨muscles⟩

tongs /tɒŋz/ npl Zange f

tongue /tʌŋ/ n Zunge f; ~ in cheek (fam) nicht ernst. ~-twister n Zungenbrecher m

tonic /'tɒnɪk/ n Tonikum nt; (for hair) Haarwasser nt; (fig) Wohltat f; ~ [water] n Tonic nt

tonight /tə'naɪt/ n & adv heute Nacht; (evening) heute Abend

tonne /tʌn/ n Tonne f

tonsil /'tɒnsl/ n (Anat) Mandel f. ~litis /-sə'laɪtɪs/ n Mandelentzündung f too /tu:/ adv zu; (also) auch; ∼ much/little zu viel/zu wenig

took /tʊk/ see take

tool /tu:l/ n Werkzeug nt; (for gardening) Gerät nt

toot /tu:t/ n Hupsignal nt □ vi tuten; (Auto) hupen

tooth /tu:θ/ n (pl teeth) Zahn m

tooth: ∼ache n Zahnschmerzen pl. ∼brush n Zahnbürste f. ∼less a zahnlos. ∼paste n Zahnpasta f. ∼pick n Zahnstocher m

top¹ /tɒp/ n (toy) Kreisel m

top² n oberer Teil m; (apex) Spitze f; (summit) Gipfel m; (Sch) Erste(r) m/f; (top part or half) Oberteil nt; (head) Kopfende nt; (of road) oberes Ende nt; (upper surface) Oberfläche f; (lid) Deckel m; (of bottle) Verschluss m; (garment) Top nt; at the/on ∼ oben; on ∼ of oben auf (+ dat/acc); on ∼ of that (besides) obendrein; from ∼ to bottom von oben bis unten □ a oberste(r,s); (highest) höchste(r,s); (best) beste(r,s) □ vt (pp topped) an erster Stelle stehen auf (+ dat) (list); (exceed) übersteigen; (remove the ∼ of) die Spitze abschneiden von. ∼ up vt nachfüllen, auffüllen

top: ∼ hat n Zylinder[hut] m. ∼-heavy a kopflastig

topic /'tɒpɪk/ n Thema nt. ∼al a aktuell

top: ∼less a & adv oben ohne. ∼most a oberste(r,s)

topple /'tɒpl/ vt/i umstürzen. ∼ off vi stürzen

top-'secret a streng geheim

topsy-turvy /tɒpsɪ'tɜ:vɪ/ adv völlig durcheinander

torch /tɔ:tʃ/ n Taschenlampe f; (flaming) Fackel f

tore /tɔ:(r)/ see tear¹

torment¹ /'tɔ:ment/ n Qual f

torment² /tɔ:'ment/ vt quälen

torn /tɔ:n/ see tear¹ □ a zerrissen

tornado /tɔ:'neɪdəʊ/ n (pl -es) Wirbelsturm m

torpedo /tɔ:'pi:dəʊ/ n (pl -es) Torpedo m □ vt torpedieren

torrent /'tɒrənt/ n reißender Strom m. ∼ial /-'renʃl/ a (rain) wolkenbruchartig

torso /'tɔ:səʊ/ n Rumpf m; (Art) Torso m

tortoise /'tɔ:təs/ n Schildkröte f. ∼shell n Schildpatt nt

tortuous /'tɔ:tjʊəs/ a verschlungen; (fig) umständlich

torture /'tɔ:tʃə(r)/ n Folter f; (fig) Qual f □ vt foltern; (fig) quälen

toss /tɒs/ vt werfen; (into the air) hochwerfen; (shake) schütteln; (unseat)

abwerfen; mischen (salad); wenden (pancake); ∼ a coin mit einer Münze losen □ vi ∼ and turn (in bed) sich [schlaflos] im Bett wälzen. ∼ up vi [mit einer Münze] losen

tot¹ /tɒt/ n kleines Kind nt; (fam: of liquor) Gläschen nt

tot² vt (pt/pp totted) ∼ up (fam) zusammenzählen

total /'təʊtl/ a gesamt; (complete) völlig, total □ n Gesamtzahl f; (sum) Gesamtsumme f □ vt (pt/pp totalled) zusammenzählen; (amount to) sich belaufen auf (+ acc)

totalitarian /təʊtælɪ'teərɪən/ a totalitär

totally /'təʊtəlɪ/ adv völlig, total

totter /'tɒtə(r)/ vi taumeln; (rock) schwanken. ∼y a wackelig

touch /tʌtʃ/ n Berührung f; (sense) Tastsinn m; (Mus) Anschlag m; (contact) Kontakt m; (trace) Spur f; (fig) Anflug m; get/be in ∼ sich in Verbindung setzen/in Verbindung stehen (with mit) □ vt berühren; (get hold of) anfassen; (lightly) tippen auf/an (+ acc); (brush against) streifen [gegen]; (reach) erreichen; (equal) herankommen an (+ acc); (fig: move) rühren; anrühren (food, subject); don't ∼ that! fass das nicht an! □ vi sich berühren; ∼ on (fig) berühren. ∼ down vi (Aviat) landen. ∼ up vt ausbessern

touch|ing /'tʌtʃɪŋ/ a rührend. ∼y a empfindlich; (subject) heikel

tough /tʌf/ a (-er, -est) zäh; (severe, harsh) hart; (difficult) schwierig; (durable) strapazierfähig

toughen /'tʌfn/ vt härten; ∼ up abhärten

tour /tʊə(r)/ n Reise f, Tour f; (of building, town) Besichtigung f; (Theat, Sport) Tournee f; (of duty) Dienstzeit f □ vt fahren durch; besichtigen (building) □ vi herumreisen

touris|m /'tʊərɪzm/ n Tourismus m, Fremdenverkehr m. ∼t /-rɪst/ n Tourist(in) m(f) □ attrib Touristen-. ∼t office n Fremdenverkehrsbüro nt

tournament /'tʊənəmənt/ n Turnier nt

'tour operator n Reiseveranstalter m

tousle /'taʊzl/ vt zerzausen

tout /taʊt/ n Anreißer m; (ticket ∼) Kartenschwarzhändler m □ vi ∼ for customers Kunden werben

tow /təʊ/ n give s.o./a car a ∼ jdn/ein Auto abschleppen; 'on ∼' 'wird geschleppt'; in ∼ (fam) im Schlepptau □ vt schleppen; ziehen (trailer). ∼ away vt abschleppen

toward[s] /tə'wɔ:d(z)/ prep zu (+ dat); (with direction) nach; (with time) gegen (+ acc); (with respect to) gegenüber (+ dat)

towel /ˈtauəl/ n Handtuch nt. ~ling n (Tex) Frottee nt

tower /ˈtauə(r)/ n Turm m ◻ vi ~ above überragen. ~ block n Hochhaus nt. ~ing a hoch aufragend

town /taun/ n Stadt f. ~ 'hall n Rathaus nt

tow: ~-path n Treidelpfad m. ~-rope n Abschleppseil nt

toxic /ˈtɒksɪk/ a giftig. ~ 'waste n Giftmüll m

toxin /ˈtɒksɪn/ n Gift nt

toy /tɔɪ/ n Spielzeug nt ◻ vi ~ with spielen mit; stochern in (+ dat) ⟨food⟩. ~shop n Spielwarengeschäft nt

trac|e /treɪs/ n Spur f ◻ vt folgen (+ dat); ⟨find⟩ finden; ⟨draw⟩ zeichnen; ⟨with tracing-paper⟩ durchpausen. ~ing-paper n Pauspapier nt

track /træk/ n Spur f; ⟨path⟩ [unbefestigter] Weg m; ⟨Sport⟩ Bahn f; ⟨Rail⟩ Gleis nt; keep ~ of im Auge behalten ◻ vt verfolgen. ~ down vt aufspüren; ⟨find⟩ finden

'tracksuit n Trainingsanzug m

tract¹ /trækt/ n ⟨land⟩ Gebiet nt

tract² n ⟨pamphlet⟩ [Flug]schrift f

tractor /ˈtræktə(r)/ n Traktor m

trade /treɪd/ n Handel m; ⟨line of business⟩ Gewerbe nt; ⟨business⟩ Geschäft nt; ⟨craft⟩ Handwerk nt; by ~ von Beruf ◻ vt tauschen; ~ in ⟨give in part exchange⟩ in Zahlung geben ◻ vi handeln (in mit)

'trade mark n Warenzeichen nt

trader /ˈtreɪdə(r)/ n Händler m

trade: ~ 'union n Gewerkschaft f. ~ 'unionist n Gewerkschaftler(in) m(f)

trading /ˈtreɪdɪŋ/ n Handel m. ~ estate n Gewerbegebiet nt. ~ stamp n Rabattmarke f

tradition /trəˈdɪʃn/ n Tradition f. ~al a, -ly adv traditionell

traffic /ˈtræfɪk/ n Verkehr m; ⟨trading⟩ Handel m ◻ vi handeln (in mit)

traffic: ~ circle n ⟨Amer⟩ Kreisverkehr m. ~ jam n [Verkehrs]stau m. ~ lights npl [Verkehrs]ampel f. ~ warden n ≈ Hilfspolizist m; ⟨woman⟩ Politesse f

tragedy /ˈtrædʒədɪ/ n Tragödie f

tragic /ˈtrædʒɪk/ a, -ally adv tragisch

trail /treɪl/ n Spur f; ⟨path⟩ Weg m, Pfad m ◻ vi schleifen; ⟨plant:⟩ sich ranken; ~ [behind] zurückbleiben; ⟨Sport⟩ zurückliegen ◻ vt verfolgen, folgen (+ dat); ⟨drag⟩ schleifen

trailer /ˈtreɪlə(r)/ n ⟨Auto⟩ Anhänger m; ⟨Amer: caravan⟩ Wohnwagen m; ⟨film⟩ Vorschau f

train /treɪn/ n Zug m; ⟨of dress⟩ Schleppe f; ~ of thought Gedankengang m ◻ vt ausbilden; ⟨Sport⟩ trainieren; ⟨aim⟩ richten auf (+ acc); erziehen ⟨child⟩; abrichten/⟨to do tricks⟩ dressieren ⟨animal⟩; ziehen ⟨plant⟩ ◻ vi eine Ausbildung machen; ⟨Sport⟩ trainieren. ~ed a ausgebildet

trainee /treɪˈniː/ n Auszubildende(r) m/f; ⟨Techn⟩ Praktikant(in) m(f)

train|er /ˈtreɪnə(r)/ n ⟨Sport⟩ Trainer m; ⟨in circus⟩ Dompteur m. ~ers pl Trainingsschuhe pl. ~ing n Ausbildung f; ⟨Sport⟩ Training nt; ⟨of animals⟩ Dressur f

traipse /treɪps/ vi ⟨fam⟩ latschen

trait /treɪt/ n Eigenschaft f

traitor /ˈtreɪtə(r)/ n Verräter m

tram /træm/ n Straßenbahn f. ~-lines npl Straßenbahnschienen pl

tramp /træmp/ n Landstreicher m; ⟨hike⟩ Wanderung f ◻ vi stapfen; ⟨walk⟩ marschieren

trample /ˈtræmpl/ vt/i trampeln (on auf + acc)

trampoline /ˈtræmpəliːn/ n Trampolin nt

trance /trɑːns/ n Trance f

tranquil /ˈtræŋkwɪl/ a ruhig. ~lity /-ˈkwɪlətɪ/ n Ruhe f

tranquillizer /ˈtræŋkwɪlaɪzə(r)/ n Beruhigungsmittel nt

transact /trænˈzækt/ vt abschließen. ~ion /-ækʃn/ n Transaktion f

transcend /trænˈsend/ vt übersteigen

transcript /ˈtrænskrɪpt/ n Abschrift f; ⟨of official proceedings⟩ Protokoll nt. ~ion /-ˈskrɪpʃn/ n Abschrift f

transept /ˈtrænsept/ n Querschiff nt

transfer¹ /ˈtrænsfɜː(r)/ n ⟨see transfer²⟩ Übertragung f; Verlegung f; Versetzung f; Überweisung f; ⟨Sport⟩ Transfer m; ⟨design⟩ Abziehbild nt

transfer² /trænsˈfɜː(r)/ v ⟨pt/pp transferred⟩ ◻ vt übertragen; verlegen ⟨firm, prisoners⟩; versetzen ⟨employee⟩; überweisen ⟨money⟩; ⟨Sport⟩ transferieren ◻ vi [über]wechseln; ⟨when travelling⟩ umsteigen. ~able /-əbl/ a übertragbar

transform /trænsˈfɔːm/ vt verwandeln. ~ation /-fəˈmeɪʃn/ n Verwandlung f. ~er n Transformator m

transfusion /trænsˈfjuːʒn/ n Transfusion f

transient /ˈtrænzɪənt/ a kurzlebig; ⟨life⟩ kurz

transistor /trænˈzɪstə(r)/ n Transistor m

transit /ˈtrænsɪt/ n Transit m; ⟨of goods⟩ Transport m; in ~ ⟨goods⟩ auf dem Transport

transition /træn'sɪʒn/ n Übergang m. ~al a Übergangs-

transitive /'trænsɪtɪv/ a, -ly adv transitiv

transitory /'trænsɪtərɪ/ a vergänglich; ⟨life⟩ kurz

translat|e /træns'leɪt/ vt übersetzen. ~ion /-'leɪʃn/ n Übersetzung f. ~or n Übersetzer(in) m(f)

translucent /trænz'luːsnt/ a durchscheinend

transmission /trænz'mɪʃn/ n Übertragung f

transmit /trænz'mɪt/ vt (pt/pp transmitted) übertragen. ~ter n Sender m

transparen|cy /træns'pærənsɪ/ n (Phot) Dia nt. ~t a durchsichtig

transpire /træn'spaɪə(r)/ vi sich herausstellen; (fam: happen) passieren

transplant¹ /'trænsplɑːnt/ n Verpflanzung f, Transplantation f

transplant² /træns'plɑːnt/ vt umpflanzen; (Med) verpflanzen

transport¹ /'trænspɔːt/ n Transport m

transport² /træn'spɔːt/ vt transportieren. ~ation /-'teɪʃn/ n Transport m

transpose /træns'pəʊz/ vt umstellen

transvestite /trænz'vestaɪt/ n Transvestit m

trap /træp/ n Falle f; (fam: mouth) Klappe f; pony and ~ Einspänner m □ vt (pt/pp trapped) [mit einer Falle] fangen; (jam) einklemmen; be ~ped festsitzen; (shut in) eingeschlossen sein; (cut off) abgeschnitten sein. ~door n Falltür f

trapeze /trə'piːz/ n Trapez nt

trash /træʃ/ n Schund m; (rubbish) Abfall m; (nonsense) Quatsch m. ~can n (Amer) Mülleimer m. ~y a Schund-

trauma /'trɔːmə/ n Trauma nt. ~tic /-'mætɪk/ a traumatisch

travel /'trævl/ n Reisen nt □ v (pt/pp travelled) □ vi reisen; (go in vehicle) fahren; (light, sound:) sich fortpflanzen; (Techn) sich bewegen □ vt bereisen; fahren (distance). ~ agency n Reisebüro nt. ~ agent n Reisebürokaufmann m

traveller /'trævələ(r)/ n Reisende(r) m/f; (Comm) Vertreter m; ~s pl (gypsies) fahrendes Volk. ~'s cheque n Reisescheck m

trawler /'trɔːlə(r)/ n Fischdampfer m

tray /treɪ/ n Tablett nt; (for oven) [Back]-blech nt; (for documents) Ablagekorb m

treacher|ous /'tretʃərəs/ a treulos; (dangerous) tückisch. ~y n Verrat m

treacle /'triːkl/ n Sirup m

tread /tred/ n Schritt m; (step) Stufe f; (of tyre) Profil nt □ v (pt trod, pp trodden)

□ vi (walk) gehen; ~ on/in treten auf/ in (+ acc) □ vt treten

treason /'triːzn/ n Verrat m

treasure /'treʒə(r)/ n Schatz m □ vt in Ehren halten. ~r n Kassenwart m

treasury /'treʒərɪ/ n Schatzkammer f; the T~ das Finanzministerium

treat /triːt/ n [besonderes] Vergnügen nt; give s.o. a ~ jdm etwas Besonderes bieten □ vt behandeln; ~ s.o. to sth jdm etw spendieren

treatise /'triːtɪz/ n Abhandlung f

treatment /'triːtmənt/ n Behandlung f

treaty /'triːtɪ/ n Vertrag m

treble /'trebl/ a dreifach; ~ the amount dreimal so viel □ n (Mus) Diskant m; (voice) Sopran m □ vt verdreifachen □ vi sich verdreifachen. ~ clef n Violinschlüssel m

tree /triː/ n Baum m

trek /trek/ n Marsch m □ vi (pt/pp trekked) latschen

trellis /'trelɪs/ n Gitter nt

tremble /'trembl/ vi zittern

tremendous /trɪ'mendəs/ a, -ly adv gewaltig; (fam: excellent) großartig

tremor /'tremə(r)/ n Zittern nt; [earth] ~ Beben nt

trench /trentʃ/ n Graben m; (Mil) Schützengraben m

trend /trend/ n Tendenz f; (fashion) Trend m. ~y a (-ier, -iest) (fam) modisch

trepidation /trepɪ'deɪʃn/ n Beklommenheit f

trespass /'trespəs/ vi ~ on unerlaubt betreten. ~er n Unbefugte(r) m/f

trial /'traɪəl/ n (Jur) [Gerichts]verfahren nt, Prozess m; (test) Probe f; (ordeal) Prüfung f; be on ~ auf Probe sein, (Jur) angeklagt sein (for wegen); by ~ and error durch Probieren

triang|le /'traɪæŋgl/ n Dreieck nt; (Mus) Triangel m. ~ular /-'æŋgjʊlə(r)/ a dreieckig

tribe /traɪb/ n Stamm m

tribulation /trɪbjʊ'leɪʃn/ n Kummer m

tribunal /traɪ'bjuːnl/ n Schiedsgericht nt

tributary /'trɪbjʊtərɪ/ n Nebenfluss m

tribute /'trɪbjuːt/ n Tribut m; pay ~ Tribut zollen (to dat)

trice /traɪs/ n in a ~ im Nu

trick /trɪk/ n Trick m; (joke) Streich m; (Cards) Stich m; (feat of skill) Kunststück nt; that should do the ~ (fam) damit dürfte es klappen □ vt täuschen, (fam) hereinlegen

trickle /'trɪkl/ vi rinnen

trick|ster /'trɪkstə(r)/ n Schwindler m.
~y a (-ier, -iest) a schwierig

tricycle /'traɪsɪkl/ n Dreirad nt

tried /traɪd/ see try

trifl|e /'traɪfl/ n Kleinigkeit f; (Culin) Trifle nt. ~ing a unbedeutend

trigger /'trɪgə(r)/ n Abzug m; (fig)
Auslöser m □ vt ~ [off] auslösen

trigonometry /trɪgə'nɒmɪtrɪ/ n Trigonometrie f

trim /trɪm/ a (trimmer, trimmest) gepflegt □ n (cut) Nachschneiden nt; (decoration) Verzierung f; (condition) Zustand m
□ vt schneiden; (decorate) besetzen; (Naut)
trimmen. ~ming n Besatz m; ~mings
pl (accessories) Zubehör m; ~mings
pl (decorations) Verzierungen pl; with all the ~mings
mit allem Drum und Dran

Trinity /'trɪnətɪ/ n the [Holy] ~ die [Heilige] Dreieinigkeit f

trinket /'trɪŋkɪt/ n Schmuckgegenstand m

trio /'tri:əʊ/ n Trio nt

trip /trɪp/ n Reise f; (excursion) Ausflug m
□ v (pt/pp tripped) □ vt ~ s.o. up jdm ein
Bein stellen □ vi stolpern (on/over über + acc)

tripe /traɪp/ n Kaldaunen pl; (nonsense)
Quatsch m

triple /'trɪpl/ a dreifach □ vt verdreifachen
□ vi sich verdreifachen

triplets /'trɪplɪts/ npl Drillinge pl

triplicate /'trɪplɪkət/ n in ~ in dreifacher
Ausfertigung

tripod /'traɪpɒd/ n Stativ nt

tripper /'trɪpə(r)/ n Ausflügler m

trite /traɪt/ a banal

triumph /'traɪʌmf/ n Triumph m □ vi triumphieren (over über + acc). ~ant
/-'ʌmfnt/ a, -ly adv triumphierend

trivial /'trɪvɪəl/ a belanglos. ~ity
/-'ælɪtɪ/ n Belanglosigkeit f

trod, trodden /trɒd, 'trɒdn/ see tread

trolley /'trɒlɪ/ n (for serving food) Servierwagen m; (for shopping) Einkaufswagen
m; (for luggage) Kofferkuli m; (Amer:
tram) Straßenbahn f. ~ bus n O-Bus m

trombone /trɒm'bəʊn/ n Posaune f

troop /tru:p/ n Schar f; ~s pl Truppen pl
□ vi ~ in/out hinein-/hinausströmen

trophy /'trəʊfɪ/ n Trophäe f; (in competition) ≈ Pokal m

tropic /'trɒpɪk/ n Wendekreis m; ~s pl
Tropen pl. ~al a tropisch; (fruit) Südfrucht

trot /trɒt/ n Trab m □ vi (pt/pp trotted)
traben

trouble /'trʌbl/ n Ärger m; (difficulties)
Schwierigkeiten pl; (inconvenience) Mühe
f; (conflict) Unruhe f; (Med) Beschwerden
pl; (Techn) Probleme pl; get into ~ Ärger

bekommen; take ~ sich (dat) Mühe geben
□ vt (disturb) stören; (worry) beunruhigen
□ vi sich bemühen. ~-maker n Unruhestifter m. ~some /-səm/ a schwierig;
(flies, cough) lästig

trough /trɒf/ n Trog m

trounce /traʊns/ vt vernichtend schlagen;
(thrash) verprügeln

troupe /tru:p/ n Truppe f

trousers /'traʊzəz/ npl Hose f

trousseau /'tru:səʊ/ n Aussteuer f

trout /traʊt/ n inv Forelle f

trowel /'traʊəl/ n Kelle f; (for gardening)
Pflanzkelle f

truant /'tru:ənt/ n play ~ die Schule
schwänzen

truce /tru:s/ n Waffenstillstand m

truck /trʌk/ n Last[kraft]wagen m; (Rail)
Güterwagen m

truculent /'trʌkjʊlənt/ a aufsässig

trudge /trʌdʒ/ n [mühseliger] Marsch m
□ vi latschen

true /tru:/ a (-r, -st) wahr; (loyal) treu; (genuine) echt; come ~ in Erfüllung gehen; is
that ~? stimmt das?

truism /'tru:ɪzm/ n Binsenwahrheit f

truly /'tru:lɪ/ adv wirklich; (faithfully)
treu; Yours ~ Hochachtungsvoll

trump /trʌmp/ n (Cards) Trumpf m □ vt
übertrumpfen. ~ up vt (fam) erfinden

trumpet /'trʌmpɪt/ n Trompete f. ~er n
Trompeter m

truncheon /'trʌntʃn/ n Schlagstock m

trundle /'trʌndl/ vt/i rollen

trunk /trʌŋk/ n [Baum]stamm m; (body)
Rumpf m; (of elephant) Rüssel m; (for
travelling) [Übersee]koffer m; (for storage) Truhe f; (Amer: of car) Kofferraum
m; ~s pl Badehose f

truss /trʌs/ n (Med) Bruchband nt

trust /trʌst/ n Vertrauen nt; (group of companies) Trust m; (organization)
Treuhandgesellschaft f; (charitable) Stiftung f □ vt trauen (+ dat), vertrauen (+
dat); (hope) hoffen □ vi vertrauen (in/to
auf + acc)

trustee /trʌs'ti:/ n Treuhänder m

trust|ful /'trʌstfl/ a, -ly adv vertrauensvoll. ~ing a vertrauensvoll.
~worthy a vertrauenswürdig

truth /tru:θ/ n (pl -s /tru:ðz/) Wahrheit f.
~ful a, -ly adv ehrlich

try /traɪ/ n Versuch m □ v (pt/pp tried) □ vt
versuchen; (sample, taste) probieren; (be
a strain on) anstrengen; (Jur) vor Gericht
stellen; verhandeln (case) □ vi versuchen;
(make an effort) sich bemühen. ~ on vt
anprobieren; aufprobieren (hat). ~ out vt
ausprobieren

trying /'traɪɪŋ/ a schwierig

T-shirt /'tiː-/ n T-Shirt nt

tub /tʌb/ n Kübel m; (carton) Becher m; (bath) Wanne f

tuba /'tjuːbə/ n (Mus) Tuba f

tubby /'tʌbɪ/ a (-ier, -iest) rundlich

tube /tjuːb/ n Röhre f; (pipe) Rohr nt; (flexible) Schlauch m; (of toothpaste) Tube f; (Rail, fam) U-Bahn f

tuber /'tjuːbə(r)/ n Knolle f

tuberculosis /tjuːbɜːkjʊ'ləʊsɪs/ n Tuberkulose f

tubing /'tjuːbɪŋ/ n Schlauch m

tubular /'tjuːbjʊlə(r)/ a röhrenförmig

tuck /tʌk/ n Saum m; (decorative) Biese f □ vt (put) stecken. ~ in vt hineinstecken; ~ s.o. in jdn zudecken □ vi (fam: eat) zulangen. ~ up vt hochkrempeln (sleeves); (in bed) zudecken

Tuesday /'tjuːzdeɪ/ n Dienstag m

tuft /tʌft/ n Büschel nt

tug /tʌg/ n Ruck m; (Naut) Schleppdampfer m □ v (pt/pp tugged) □ vt ziehen □ vi zerren (at an + dat). ~ of war n Tauziehen nt

tuition /tjuː'ɪʃn/ n Unterricht m

tulip /'tjuːlɪp/ n Tulpe f

tumble /'tʌmbl/ n Sturz m □ vi fallen; ~ to sth (fam) etw kapieren. ~down a verfallen. ~drier n Wäschetrockner m

tumbler /'tʌmblə(r)/ n Glas nt

tummy /'tʌmɪ/ n (fam) Magen m; (abdomen) Bauch m

tumour /'tjuːmə(r)/ n Geschwulst f, Tumor m

tumult /'tjuːmʌlt/ n Tumult m. ~uous /-'mʌltjʊəs/ a stürmisch

tuna /'tjuːnə/ n Thunfisch m

tune /tjuːn/ n Melodie f; out of ~ (instrument) verstimmt; to the ~ of (fam) in Höhe von □ vt stimmen; (Techn) einstellen. ~ in vt einstellen □ vi ~ in to a station einen Sender einstellen. ~ up vi (Mus) stimmen

tuneful /'tjuːnfl/ a melodisch

tunic /'tjuːnɪk/ n (Mil) Uniformjacke f; (Sch) Trägerkleid nt

Tunisia /tjuː'nɪzɪə/ n Tunesien nt

tunnel /'tʌnl/ n Tunnel m □ vi (pt/pp tunnelled) einen Tunnel graben

turban /'tɜːbən/ n Turban m

turbine /'tɜːbaɪn/ n Turbine f

turbot /'tɜːbət/ n Steinbutt m

turbulen|ce /'tɜːbjʊləns/ n Turbulenz f. ~t a stürmisch

tureen /tjʊə'riːn/ n Terrine f

turf /tɜːf/ n Rasen m; (segment) Rasenstück nt. ~ out vt (fam) rausschmeißen

'turf accountant n Buchmacher m

Turk /tɜːk/ n Türke m/Türkin f

turkey /'tɜːkɪ/ n Pute f, Truthahn m

Turk|ey n die Türkei. ~ish a türkisch

turmoil /'tɜːmɔɪl/ n Aufruhr m; (confusion) Durcheinander n

turn /tɜːn/ n (rotation) Drehung f; (in road) Kurve f; (change of direction) Wende f; (short walk) Runde f; (Theat) Nummer f; (fam: attack) Anfall m; do s.o. a good ~ jdm einen guten Dienst erweisen; take ~s sich abwechseln; in ~ der Reihe nach; out of ~ außer der Reihe; it's your ~ du bist an der Reihe □ vt drehen; (~ over) wenden; (reverse) umdrehen; (Techn) drechseln (wood); ~ the page umblättern; ~ the corner um die Ecke biegen □ vi sich drehen; (~ round) sich umdrehen; (car) wenden; (leaves) sich färben; (weather) umschlagen; (become) werden; ~ right/left nach rechts/links abbiegen; ~ to s.o. sich an jdn wenden; have ~ed against s.o. gegen jdn sein. ~ away vt abweisen □ vi sich abwenden. ~ down vt herunterschlagen (collar); herunterdrehen (heat, gas); leiser stellen (sound); (reject) ablehnen; abweisen (person). ~ in vt einschlagen (edges) □ vi (car:) einbiegen; (fam: go to bed) ins Bett gehen. ~ off vt zudrehen (tap); ausschalten (light, radio); abstellen (water, gas, engine, machine) □ vi abbiegen. ~ on vt aufdrehen (tap); einschalten (light, radio); anstellen (water, gas, engine, machine). ~ out vt (expel) vertreiben, (fam) hinauswerfen; ausschalten (light); abdrehen (gas); (produce) produzieren; (empty) ausleeren; [gründlich] aufräumen (room, cupboard) □ vi (go out) hinausgehen; (transpire) sich herausstellen; ~ out well/badly gut/schlecht gehen. ~ over vt umdrehen □ vi sich umdrehen. ~ up vt hochschlagen (collar); aufdrehen (heat, gas); lauter stellen (sound, radio) □ vi auftauchen

turning /'tɜːnɪŋ/ n Abzweigung f. ~point n Wendepunkt m

turnip /'tɜːnɪp/ n weiße Rübe f

turn: ~out n (of people) Teilnahme f, Beteiligung f; (of goods) Produktion f. ~over n (Comm) Umsatz m; (of staff) Personalwechsel m. ~pike n (Amer) gebührenpflichtige Autobahn f. ~stile n Drehkreuz nt. ~table n Drehscheibe f; (on record-player) Plattenteller m. ~up n [Hosen]aufschlag m

turpentine /'tɜːpəntaɪn/ n Terpentin nt

turquoise /'tɜːkwɔɪz/ a türkis[farben] □ n (gem) Türkis m

turret /'tʌrɪt/ n Türmchen nt

turtle /'tɜːtl/ n Seeschildkröte f

tusk /tʌsk/ n Stoßzahn m

tussle /'tʌsl/ n Balgerei f; (fig) Streit m ▢ vi sich balgen

tutor /'tju:tə(r)/ n [Privat]lehrer m

tuxedo /tʌk'si:dəʊ/ n (Amer) Smoking m

TV /ti:'vi:/ abbr of television

twaddle /'twɒdl/ n Geschwätz nt

twang /twæŋ/ n (in voice) Näseln nt ▢ vt zupfen

tweed /twi:d/ n Tweed m

tweezers /'twi:zəz/ npl Pinzette f

twelfth /twelfθ/ a zwölfter(r,s)

twelve /twelv/ a zwölf

twentieth /'twentɪɪθ/ a zwanzigste(r,s)

twenty /'twentɪ/ a zwanzig

twerp /twɜ:p/ n (fam) Trottel m

twice /twaɪs/ adv zweimal

twiddle /'twɪdl/ vt drehen an (+ dat)

twig¹ /twɪg/ n Zweig m

twig² vt/i (pt/pp twigged) (fam) kapieren

twilight /'twaɪ-/ n Dämmerlicht nt

twin /twɪn/ n Zwilling m ▢ attrib Zwillings-. ~ beds npl zwei Einzelbetten pl

twine /twaɪn/ n Bindfaden m ▢ vi sich winden; (plant:) sich ranken

twinge /twɪndʒ/ n Stechen nt; ~ of conscience Gewissensbisse pl

twinkle /'twɪŋkl/ n Funkeln nt ▢ vi funkeln

twin 'town n Partnerstadt f

twirl /twɜ:l/ vt/i herumwirbeln

twist /twɪst/ n Drehung f; (curve) Kurve f; (unexpected occurrence) überraschende Wendung f ▢ vt drehen; (distort) verdrehen; (fam: swindle) beschummeln; ~ one's ankle sich (dat) den Knöchel verrenken ▢ vi sich drehen; (road:) sich winden. ~er n (fam) Schwindler m

twit /twɪt/ n (fam) Trottel m

twitch /twɪtʃ/ n Zucken nt ▢ vi zucken

twitter /'twɪtə(r)/ n Zwitschern nt ▢ vi zwitschern

two /tu:/ a zwei

two: ~-faced a falsch. ~-piece a zweiteilig. ~some /-səm/ n Paar nt. ~-way a ~-way traffic Gegenverkehr m

tycoon /taɪ'ku:n/ n Magnat m

tying /'taɪŋ/ see tie

type /taɪp/ n Art f, Sorte f; (person) Typ m; (printing) Type f ▢ vt mit der Maschine schreiben, (fam) tippen; ~d letter maschinegeschriebener Brief ▢ vi Maschine schreiben, (fam) tippen. ~writer n Schreibmaschine f. ~written a maschinegeschrieben

typhoid /'taɪfɔɪd/ n Typhus m

typical /'tɪpɪkl/ a, -ly adv typisch (of für)

typify /'tɪpɪfaɪ/ vt (pt/pp -ied) typisch sein für

typing /'taɪpɪŋ/ n Maschineschreiben nt. ~ paper n Schreibmaschinenpapier nt

typist /'taɪpɪst/ n Schreibkraft f

typography /taɪ'pɒgrəfɪ/ n Typographie f

tyrannical /tɪ'rænɪkl/ a tyrannisch

tyranny /'tɪrənɪ/ n Tyrannei f

tyrant /'taɪrənt/ n Tyrann m

tyre /'taɪə(r)/ n Reifen m

U

ubiquitous /ju:'bɪkwɪtəs/ a allgegenwärtig; be ~ überall zu finden sein

udder /'ʌdə(r)/ n Euter nt

ugl|iness /'ʌglɪnɪs/ n Hässlichkeit f. ~y a (-ier, -iest) hässlich; (nasty) übel

UK abbr see United Kingdom

ulcer /'ʌlsə(r)/ n Geschwür nt

ulterior /ʌl'tɪərɪə(r)/ a ~ motive Hintergedanke m

ultimate /'ʌltɪmət/ a letzte(r,s); (final) endgültig; (fundamental) grundlegend, eigentlich. ~ly adv schließlich

ultimatum /ʌltɪ'meɪtəm/ n Ultimatum nt

ultrasound /'ʌltrə-/ n (Med) Ultraschall m

ultra'violet a ultraviolett

umbilical /ʌm'bɪlɪkl/ a ~ cord Nabelschnur f

umbrella /ʌm'brelə/ n [Regen]schirm m

umpire /'ʌmpaɪə(r)/ n Schiedsrichter m ▢ vt/i Schiedsrichter sein (bei)

umpteen /ʌmp'ti:n/ a (fam) zig. ~th a (fam) zigste(r,s); for the ~th time zum zigsten Mal

un'able /ʌn-/ a be ~ to do sth etw nicht tun können

una'bridged a ungekürzt

unac'companied a ohne Begleitung; (luggage) unbegleitet

unac'countab|le a unerklärlich. ~y adv unerklärlicherweise

unac'customed a ungewohnt; be ~ to sth etw nicht gewohnt sein

una'dulterated a unverfälscht, rein; (utter) völlig

un'aided a ohne fremde Hilfe

unalloyed /ʌnə'lɔɪd/ a (fig) ungetrübt

unanimity /ju:nə'nɪmətɪ/ n Einstimmigkeit f

unanimous /ju:'nænɪməs/ a, -ly adv einmütig; (vote, decision) einstimmig un'armed a unbewaffnet; ~ combat Kampf m ohne Waffen

unas'suming a bescheiden

unat'tached a nicht befestigt; ⟨person⟩ ungebunden

unat'tended a unbeaufsichtigt

un'authorized a unbefugt

una'voidable a unvermeidlich

una'ware a be ~ of sth sich (dat) etw (gen) nicht bewusst sein. ~s /-ɛəz/ adv catch s.o. ~s jdn überraschen

un'balanced a unausgewogen; (mentally) unausgeglichen

un'bearable a, -bly adv unerträglich

unbeat|able /ʌn'biːtəbl/ a unschlagbar. ~en a ungeschlagen; ⟨record⟩ ungebrochen

unbeknown /ʌnbɪ'nəʊn/ a (fam) ~ to me ohne mein Wissen

unbe'lievable a unglaublich

un'bend vi (pt/pp -bent) (relax) aus sich herausgehen

un'biased a unvoreingenommen

un'block vt frei machen

un'bolt vt aufriegeln

un'breakable a unzerbrechlich

unbridled /ʌn'braɪdld/ a ungezügelt

un'burden vt ~ oneself (fig) sich aussprechen

un'button vt aufknöpfen

uncalled-for /ʌn'kɔːldfɔː(r)/ a unangebracht

un'canny a unheimlich

un'ceasing a unaufhörlich

uncere'monious a, -ly adv formlos; (abrupt) brüsk

un'certain a (doubtful) ungewiss; ⟨origins⟩ unbestimmt; be ~ nicht sicher sein; in no ~ terms ganz eindeutig. ~ty n Ungewissheit f

un'changed a unverändert

un'charitable a lieblos

uncle /'ʌŋkl/ n Onkel m

un'comfortable a, -bly adv unbequem; feel ~ (fig) sich nicht wohl fühlen

un'common a ungewöhnlich

un'compromising a kompromisslos

uncon'ditional a, ~ly adv bedingungslos

un'conscious a bewusstlos; (unintended) unbewusst; be ~ of sth sich (dat) etw (gen) nicht bewusst sein. ~ly adv unbewusst

uncon'ventional a unkonventionell

unco'operative a nicht hilfsbereit

un'cork vt entkorken

uncouth /ʌn'kuːθ/ a ungehobelt

un'cover vt aufdecken

unctuous /'ʌŋktjʊəs/ a, -ly adv salbungsvoll

unde'cided a unentschlossen; (not settled) nicht entschieden

undeniable /ʌndɪ'naɪəbl/ a, -bly adv unbestreitbar

under /'ʌndə(r)/ prep unter (+ dat/acc); ~ it darunter; ~ there da drunter; ~ repair in Reparatur; ~ construction im Bau; ~ age minderjährig; ~ way unterwegs; (fig) im Gange □ adv darunter

'undercarriage n (Aviat) Fahrwerk nt, Fahrgestell nt

'underclothes npl Unterwäsche f

under'cover a geheim

'undercurrent n Unterströmung f; (fig) Unterton m

under'cut vt (pt/pp -cut) (Comm) unterbieten

'underdog n Unterlegene(r) m

under'done a nicht gar; (rare) nicht durchgebraten

under'estimate vt unterschätzen

under'fed a unterernährt

under'foot adv am Boden; trample ~ zertrampeln

under'go vt (pt -went, pp -gone) durchmachen; sich unterziehen (+ dat) ⟨operation, treatment⟩; ~ repairs repariert werden

under'graduate n Student(in) m(f)

under'ground¹ adv unter der Erde; ⟨mining⟩ unter Tage

'underground² a unterirdisch; (secret) Untergrund- □ n (railway) U-Bahn f. ~ car park n Tiefgarage f

'undergrowth n Unterholz nt

'underhand a hinterhältig

'underlay n Unterlage f

under'lie vt (pt -lay, pp -lain, pres p -lying) (fig) zugrunde liegen (+ dat)

under'line vt unterstreichen

underling /'ʌndəlɪŋ/ n (pej) Untergebene(r) m/f

under'lying a (fig) eigentlich

under'mine vt (fig) unterminieren, untergraben

underneath /ʌndə'niːθ/ prep unter (+ dat/acc); ~ it darunter □ adv darunter

'underpants npl Unterhose f

'underpass n Unterführung f

under'privileged a unterprivilegiert

under'rate vt unterschätzen

'underseal n (Auto) Unterbodenschutz m

'undershirt n (Amer) Unterhemd nt

understaffed /-'stɑːft/ a unterbesetzt

under'stand vt/i (pt/pp -stood) verstehen; I ~ that . . . (have heard) ich habe gehört, dass . . . ~able /-əbl/ a verständlich. ~ably /-əblɪ/ adv verständlicherweise

under'standing a verständnisvoll □ n Verständnis nt; (agreement) Vereinbarung f; reach an ~ sich verständigen; on the ~ that unter der Voraussetzung, dass

'understatement n Untertreibung f

'understudy n (Theat) Ersatzspieler(in) m(f)

under'take vt (pt-took, pp-taken) unternehmen; ~ to do sth sich verpflichten, etw zu tun

'undertaker n Leichenbestatter m; [firm of] ~s Bestattungsinstitut n

under'taking n Unternehmen nt; (promise) Versprechen nt

'undertone n (fig) Unterton m; in an ~ mit gedämpfter Stimme

under'value vt unterbewerten

'underwater¹ a Unterwasser-

under'water² adv unter Wasser

'underwear n Unterwäsche f

'underweight a untergewichtig; be ~ Untergewicht haben

'underworld n Unterwelt f

'underwriter n Versicherer m

unde'sirable a unerwünscht

undies /'ʌndɪz/ npl (fam) [Damen]unterwäsche f

un'dignified a würdelos

un'do vt (pt -did, pp -done) aufmachen; (fig) ungeschehen machen; (ruin) zunichte machen

un'done a offen; (not accomplished) unerledigt

un'doubted a unzweifelhaft. ~ly adv zweifellos

un'dress vt ausziehen; get ~ed sich ausziehen □ vi sich ausziehen

un'due a übermäßig

undulating /'ʌndjʊleɪtɪŋ/ a Wellen-; (country) wellig

un'duly adv übermäßig

un'dying a ewig

un'earth vt ausgraben; (fig) zutage bringen. ~ly a unheimlich; at an ~ly hour (fam) in aller Herrgottsfrühe

un'eas|e n Unbehagen nt. ~y a unbehaglich; I feel ~y mir ist unbehaglich zumute

un'eatable a ungenießbar

uneco'nomic a, -ally adv unwirtschaftlich

uneco'nomical a verschwenderisch

unem'ployed a arbeitslos □ npl the ~ die Arbeitslosen

unem'ployment n Arbeitslosigkeit f. ~ benefit n Arbeitslosenunterstützung f

un'ending a endlos

un'equal a unterschiedlich; (struggle) ungleich; be ~ to a task einer Aufgabe nicht gewachsen sein. ~ly adv ungleichmäßig

unequivocal /ʌnɪ'kwɪvəkl/ a, -ly adv eindeutig

unerring /ʌn'ɜːrɪŋ/ a unfehlbar

un'ethical a unmoralisch; be ~ gegen das Berufsethos verstoßen

un'even a uneben; (unequal) ungleich; (not regular) ungleichmäßig; (number) ungerade. ~ly adv ungleichmäßig

unex'pected a, -ly adv unerwartet

un'failing a nie versagend

un'fair a, -ly adv ungerecht, unfair. ~ness n Ungerechtigkeit f

un'faithful a untreu

unfa'miliar a ungewohnt; (unknown) unbekannt

un'fasten vt aufmachen; (detach) losmachen

un'favourable a ungünstig

un'feeling a gefühllos

un'finished a unvollendet; (business) unerledigt

un'fit a ungeeignet; (incompetent) unfähig; (Sport) nicht fit; ~ for work arbeitsunfähig

unflinching /ʌn'flɪntʃɪŋ/ a unerschrocken

un'fold vt auseinander falten, entfalten; (spread out) ausbreiten □ vi sich entfalten

unfore'seen a unvorhergesehen

unforgettable /ʌnfə'getəbl/ a unvergesslich

unforgivable /ʌnfə'gɪvəbl/ a unverzeihlich

un'fortunate a unglücklich; (unfavourable) ungünstig; (regrettable) bedauerlich; be ~ (person.) Pech haben. ~ly adv leider

un'founded a unbegründet

unfurl /ʌn'fɜːl/ vt entrollen □ vi sich entrollen

un'furnished a unmöbliert

ungainly /ʌn'geɪnlɪ/ a unbeholfen

ungodly /ʌn'gɒdlɪ/ a gottlos; at an ~ hour (fam) in aller Herrgottsfrühe

un'grateful a, -ly adv undankbar

un'happi|ly adv unglücklich; (unfortunately) leider. ~ness n Kummer m

un'happy a unglücklich; (not content) unzufrieden

un'harmed a unverletzt

un'healthy a ungesund

un'hook *vt* vom Haken nehmen; aufhaken 〈*dress*〉

un'hurt *a* unverletzt

unhy'gienic *a* unhygienisch

unicorn /'juːnɪkɔːn/ *n* Einhorn *nt*

unification /juːnɪfɪ'keɪʃn/ *n* Einigung *f*

uniform /'juːnɪfɔːm/ *a, -ly adv* einheitlich □ *n* Uniform *f*

unify /'juːnɪfaɪ/ *vt (pt/pp* -ied) einigen

uni'lateral /juːnɪ-/ *a, -ly adv* einseitig

unim'aginable *a* unvorstellbar

unim'portant *a* unwichtig

unin'habited *a* unbewohnt

unin'tentional *a, -ly adv* unabsichtlich

union /'juːnɪən/ *n* Vereinigung *f*; (*Pol*) Union *f*; (*trade* ~) Gewerkschaft *f*. ~ist *n (Pol)* Unionist *m*

unique /juː'niːk/ *a* einzigartig. ~ly *adv* einmalig

unison /'juːnɪsn/ *n* in ~ einstimmig

unit /'juːnɪt/ *n* Einheit *f*; (*Math*) Einer *m*; (*of furniture*) Teil *m*, Element *nt*

unite /juː'naɪt/ *vt* vereinigen □ *vi* sich vereinigen

united /juː'naɪtɪd/ *a* einig. U~ 'Kingdom *n* Vereinigtes Königreich *nt*. U~ 'Nations *n* Vereinte Nationen *pl*. U~ States [of America] *n* Vereinigte Staaten *pl* [von Amerika]

unity /'juːnəti/ *n* Einheit *f*; (*harmony*) Einigkeit *f*

universal /juːnɪ'vɜːsl/ *a, -ly adv* allgemein

universe /'juːnɪvɜːs/ *n* [Welt]all *nt*, Universum *nt*

university /juːnɪ'vɜːsəti/ *n* Universität *f* □ *attrib* Universitäts-

un'just *a, -ly adv* ungerecht

unkempt /ʌn'kempt/ *a* ungepflegt

un'kind *a, -ly adv* unfreundlich; (*harsh*) hässlich. ~ness *n* Unfreundlichkeit *f*; Hässlichkeit *f*

un'known *a* unbekannt

un'lawful *a, -ly adv* gesetzwidrig

unleaded /ʌn'ledɪd/ *a* bleifrei

un'leash *vt (fig)* entfesseln

unless /ən'les/ *conj* wenn ... nicht; ~ I am mistaken wenn ich mich nicht irre

un'like *a* nicht ähnlich, unähnlich; (*not the same*) ungleich □ *prep* im Gegensatz zu (+ *dat*)

un'likely *a* unwahrscheinlich

un'limited *a* unbegrenzt

un'load *vt* entladen; ausladen 〈*luggage*〉

un'lock *vt* aufschließen

un'lucky *a* unglücklich; 〈*day, number*〉 Unglücks-; be ~ Pech haben; 〈*thing:*〉 Unglück bringen

un'manned *a* unbemannt

un'married *a* unverheiratet. ~ 'mother *n* ledige Mutter *f*

un'mask *vt (fig)* entlarven

unmistakable /ʌnmɪ'steɪkəbl/ *a*, -bly *adv* unverkennbar

un'mitigated *a* vollkommen

un'natural *a, -ly adv* unnatürlich; (*not normal*) nicht normal

un'necessary *a, -ily adv* unnötig

un'noticed *a* unbemerkt

unob'tainable *a* nicht erhältlich

unob'trusive *a, -ly adv* unaufdringlich; 〈*thing*〉 unauffällig

unof'ficial *a, -ly adv* inoffiziell

un'pack *vt/i* auspacken

un'paid *a* unbezahlt

un'palatable *a* ungenießbar

un'paralleled *a* beispiellos

un'pick *vt* auftrennen

un'pleasant *a*, -ly *adv* unangenehm. ~ness *n (bad feeling)* Ärger *m*

un'plug *vt (pt/pp* -plugged) den Stecker herausziehen von

un'popular *a* unbeliebt

un'precedented *a* beispiellos

unpre'dictable *a* unberechenbar

unpre'meditated *a* nicht vorsätzlich

unpre'pared *a* nicht vorbereitet

unprepos'sessing *a* wenig attraktiv

unpre'tentious *a* bescheiden

un'principled *a* skrupellos

unpro'fessional *a* be ~ gegen das Berufsethos verstoßen; (*Sport*) unsportlich sein

un'profitable *a* unrentabel

un'qualified *a* unqualifiziert; (*fig: absolute*) uneingeschränkt

un'questionable *a* unbezweifelbar; 〈*right*〉 unbestreitbar

unravel /ʌn'rævl/ *vt (pt/pp* -ravelled) entwirren; (*Knitting*) aufziehen

un'real *a* unwirklich

un'reasonable *a* unvernünftig; be ~ zu viel verlangen

unre'lated *a* unzusammenhängend; be ~ nicht verwandt sein; 〈*events:*〉 nicht miteinander zusammenhängen

unre'liable *a* unzuverlässig

unrequited /ʌnrɪ'kwaɪtɪd/ *a* unerwidert

unre'servedly /ʌnrɪ'zɜːvɪdlɪ/ *adv* uneingeschränkt; (*frankly*) offen

un'rest *n* Unruhen *pl*

un'rivalled *a* unübertroffen

un'roll *vt* aufrollen □ *vi* sich aufrollen

unruly /ʌn'ruːlɪ/ *a* ungebärdig

un'safe *a* nicht sicher

un'said *vt* ungesagt

un'salted *a* ungesalzen

unsatis'factory *a* unbefriedigend

un'savoury *a* unangenehm; ⟨*fig*⟩ unerfreulich

unscathed /ʌnˈskeɪðd/ *a* unversehrt

un'screw *vt* abschrauben

un'scrupulous *a* skrupellos

un'seemly *a* unschicklich

un'selfish *a* selbstlos

un'settled *a* ungeklärt; nicht gesund; ⟨*weather*⟩ unbeständig; ⟨*bill*⟩ unbezahlt

unshakeable /ʌnˈʃeɪkəbl/ *a* unerschütterlich

unshaven /ʌnˈʃeɪvn/ *a* unrasiert

un'sightly /ʌnˈsaɪtlɪ/ *a* unansehnlich

un'skilled *a* ungelernt; ⟨*work*⟩ unqualifiziert

un'sociable *a* ungesellig

unso'phisticated *a* einfach

un'sound *a* krank, nicht gesund; ⟨*building*⟩ nicht sicher; ⟨*advice*⟩ unzuverlässig; ⟨*reasoning*⟩ nicht stichhaltig; of ∼ mind unzurechnungsfähig

unspeakable /ʌnˈspiːkəbl/ *a* unbeschreiblich

un'stable *a* nicht stabil; ⟨*mentally*⟩ labil

un'steady *a*, -ily *adv* unsicher; ⟨*wobbly*⟩ wackelig

un'stuck *a* come ∼ sich lösen; ⟨*fam: fail*⟩ scheitern

unsuc'cessful *a*, -ly *adv* erfolglos; be ∼ keinen Erfolg haben

un'suitable *a* ungeeignet; ⟨*inappropriate*⟩ unpassend; ⟨*for weather, activity*⟩ unzweckmäßig

unsu'specting *a* ahnungslos

un'sweetened *a* ungesüßt

unthinkable /ʌnˈθɪŋkəbl/ *a* unvorstellbar

un'tidiness *n* Unordentlichkeit *f*

un'tidy *a*, -ily *adv* unordentlich

un'tie *vt* aufbinden; losbinden ⟨*person, boat, horse*⟩

until /ənˈtɪl/ *prep* bis (+ *acc*); not ∼ erst; ∼ the evening bis zum Abend; ∼ his arrival bis zu seiner Ankunft □ *conj* bis; not ∼ erst wenn; ⟨*in past*⟩ erst als

untimely /ʌnˈtaɪmlɪ/ *a* ungelegen; ⟨*premature*⟩ vorzeitig

un'tiring *a* unermüdlich

un'told *a* unermesslich

unto'ward *a* ungünstig; ⟨*unseemly*⟩ ungehörig; if nothing ∼ happens wenn nichts dazwischenkommt

un'true *a* unwahr; that's ∼ das ist nicht wahr

unused[1] /ʌnˈjuːzd/ *a* unbenutzt; ⟨*not utilized*⟩ ungenutzt

unused[2] /ʌnˈjuːst/ *a* be ∼ to sth etw nicht gewohnt sein

un'usual *a*, -ly *adv* ungewöhnlich

un'veil *vt* enthüllen

un'versed *a* nicht bewandert (in in + *dat*)

un'wanted *a* unerwünscht

un'warranted *a* ungerechtfertigt

un'welcome *a* unwillkommen

un'well *a* be *or* feel ∼ sich nicht wohl fühlen

unwieldy /ʌnˈwiːldɪ/ *a* sperrig

un'willing *a*, -ly *adv* widerwillig; be ∼ to do sth etw nicht tun wollen

un'wind *v* ⟨*pt/pp* unwound⟩ □ *vt* abwickeln □ *vi* sich abwickeln; ⟨*fam: relax*⟩ sich entspannen

un'wise *a*, -ly *adv* unklug

unwitting /ʌnˈwɪtɪŋ/ *a*, -ly *adv* unwissentlich

un'worthy *a* unwürdig

un'wrap *vt* ⟨*pt/pp* -wrapped⟩ auswickeln; auspacken ⟨*present*⟩

un'written *a* ungeschrieben

up /ʌp/ *adv* oben; ⟨*with movement*⟩ nach oben; ⟨*not in bed*⟩ auf; ⟨*collar*⟩ hochgeklappt; ⟨*road*⟩ aufgerissen; ⟨*price*⟩ gestiegen; ⟨*curtains*⟩ aufgehängt; ⟨*shelves*⟩ angebracht; ⟨*notice*⟩ angeschlagen; ⟨*tent*⟩ aufgebaut; ⟨*building*⟩ gebaut; be up for sale zu verkaufen sein; up there da oben; up to ⟨*as far as*⟩ bis; time's up die Zeit ist um; what's up? ⟨*fam*⟩ was ist los? what's he up to? ⟨*fam*⟩ was hat er vor? I don't feel up to it ich fühle mich dem nicht gewachsen; be one up on s.o. ⟨*fam*⟩ jdm etwas voraushaben; go up hinaufgehen; come up heraufkommen □ *prep* be up on sth [oben] auf etw ⟨*dat*⟩ sein; up the mountain oben am Berg; ⟨*movement*⟩ den Berg hinauf; be up the tree oben im Baum sein; up the road die Straße entlang; up the river stromaufwärts; go up the stairs die Treppe hinaufgehen; be up the pub ⟨*fam*⟩ in der Kneipe sein

'upbringing *n* Erziehung *f*

up'date *vt* auf den neuesten Stand bringen

up'grade *vt* aufstufen

upheaval /ʌpˈhiːvl/ *n* Unruhe *f*; ⟨*Pol*⟩ Umbruch *m*

up'hill *a* ⟨*fig*⟩ mühsam □ *adv* bergauf

up'hold *vt* ⟨*pt/pp* upheld⟩ unterstützen; bestätigen ⟨*verdict*⟩

upholster /ʌpˈhəʊlstə(r)/ *vt* polstern. ∼er *n* Polsterer *m*. ∼y *n* Polsterung *f*

'upkeep *n* Unterhalt *m*

up-'market *a* anspruchsvoll

upon /əˈpɒn/ *prep* auf (+ *dat/acc*)

upper /'ʌpə(r)/ a obere(r,s); ⟨deck, jaw, lip⟩ Ober-; have the ~ hand die Oberhand haben ▢ n (of shoe) Obermaterial nt

upper-: ~ circle n zweiter Rang m. ~ class n Oberschicht f. ~most a oberste(r,s)

'**upright** a aufrecht ▢ n Pfosten m

'**uprising** n Aufstand m

'**uproar** n Aufruhr m

up'**root** vt entwurzeln

up'**set²** vt (pt/pp upset, pres p upsetting) umstoßen; ⟨spill⟩ verschütten; durcheinander bringen ⟨plan⟩; ⟨distress⟩ erschüttern; ⟨food:⟩ nicht bekommen (+ dat); get ~ about sth sich über etw (acc) ~ aufregen; be very ~ sehr bestürzt sein

'**upset²** n Aufregung f; have a stomach ~ einen verdorbenen Magen haben

'**upshot** n Ergebnis nt

upside 'down adv verkehrt herum; turn ~ umdrehen

up'**stairs¹** adv oben; ⟨go⟩ nach oben

'**upstairs²** a im Obergeschoss

'**upstart** n Emporkömmling m

up'**stream** adv stromaufwärts

'**upsurge** n Zunahme f

'**uptake** n slow on the ~ schwer von Begriff; be quick on the ~ schnell begreifen

up'**tight** a nervös

'**upturn** n Aufschwung m

upward /'ʌpwəd/ a nach oben; ⟨movement⟩ Aufwärts-; ~ slope Steigung f ▢ adv ~[s] aufwärts, nach oben

uranium /jʊ'reɪnɪəm/ n Uran nt

urban /'ɜːbən/ a städtisch

urbane /ɜː'beɪn/ a weltmännisch

urge /ɜːdʒ/ n Trieb m, Drang m ▢ vt drängen; ~ on antreiben

urgen|cy /'ɜːdʒənsɪ/ n Dringlichkeit f. ~t a, -ly adv dringend

urinate /'jʊərɪneɪt/ vi urinieren

urine /'jʊərɪn/ n Urin m, Harn m

urn /ɜːn/ n Urne f; (for tea) Teemaschine f

us /ʌs/ pron uns; it's us wir sind es

US[A] abbr USA pl

usable /'juːzəbl/ a brauchbar

usage /'juːzɪdʒ/ n Brauch m; (of word) [Sprach]gebrauch m

use¹ /juːs/ n (see use²) Benutzung f; Verwendung f; Gebrauch m; be of ~ nützlich sein; be of no ~ nichts nützen; make ~ of Gebrauch machen von; (exploit) ausnutzen; it is no ~ es hat keinen Zweck; what's the ~? wozu?

use² /juːz/ vt benutzen ⟨implement, room, lift⟩; verwenden ⟨ingredient, method, book, money⟩; gebrauchen ⟨words, force, brains⟩; ~ [up] aufbrauchen

used¹ /juːzd/ a benutzt; ⟨car⟩ Gebraucht-

used² /juːst/ pt be ~ to sth an etw (acc) gewöhnt sein; get ~ to sich gewöhnen an (+ acc); he ~ to say er hat immer gesagt; he ~ to live here er hat früher hier gewohnt

useful /'juːsfl/ a nützlich. ~ness n Nützlichkeit f

useless /'juːslɪs/ a nutzlos; (not usable) unbrauchbar; (pointless) zwecklos

user /'juːzə(r)/ n Benutzer(in) m(f). ~-'friendly a benutzerfreundlich

usher /'ʌʃə(r)/ n Platzanweiser m; (in court) Gerichtsdiener m ▢ vt ~ in hineinführen

usherette /ʌʃə'ret/ n Platzanweiserin f

USSR abbr UdSSR f

usual /'juːʒʊəl/ a üblich. ~ly adv gewöhnlich

usurp /juː'zɜːp/ vt sich (dat) widerrechtlich aneignen

utensil /juː'tensl/ n Gerät nt

uterus /'juːtərəs/ n Gebärmutter f

utilitarian /juːtɪlɪ'teərɪən/ a zweckmäßig

utility /juː'tɪlətɪ/ a Gebrauchs- ▢ n Nutzen m. ~ room n ≈ Waschküche f

utiliz|ation /juːtɪlaɪ'zeɪʃn/ n Nutzung f. ~e /'juːtɪlaɪz/ vt nutzen

utmost /'ʌtməʊst/ a äußerste(r,s), größte(r,s) ▢ n do one's ~ sein Möglichstes tun

utter¹ /'ʌtə(r)/ a, -ly adv völlig

utter² vt von sich geben ⟨sigh, sound⟩; sagen ⟨word⟩. ~ance /-əns/ n Äußerung f

U-turn /'juː-/ n (fig) Kehrtwendung f; 'no ~s' (Auto) 'Wenden verboten'

V

vacan|cy /'veɪkənsɪ/ n (job) freie Stelle f; (room) freies Zimmer nt; 'no ~cies' 'belegt'. ~t a frei; ⟨look⟩ [gedanken]leer

vacate /və'keɪt/ vt räumen

vacation /və'keɪʃn/ n (Univ & Amer) Ferien pl

vaccinat|e /'væksɪneɪt/ vt impfen. ~ion /-'neɪʃn/ n Impfung f

vaccine /'væksiːn/ n Impfstoff m

vacuum /'vækjʊəm/ n Vakuum nt, luftleerer Raum m ▢ vt saugen. ~ cleaner n Staubsauger m. ~ flask n Thermosflasche (P) f. ~-packed a vakuumverpackt

vagaries /'veɪgərɪz/ npl Launen pl

vagina /vəˈdʒaɪnə/ n (Anat) Scheide f

vagrant /ˈveɪgrənt/ n Landstreicher m

vague /veɪg/ a (-r,-st), -ly adv vage; ⟨outline⟩ verschwommen

vain /veɪn/ a (-er,-est) eitel; ⟨hope, attempt⟩ vergeblich; in ~ vergeblich. ~ly adv vergeblich

vale /veɪl/ n (liter) Tal nt

valet /ˈvæleɪ/ n Kammerdiener m

valiant /ˈvæliənt/ a, -ly adv tapfer

valid /ˈvælɪd/ a gültig; ⟨claim⟩ berechtigt; ⟨argument⟩ stichhaltig; ⟨reason⟩ triftig. ~ate vt ⟨confirm⟩ bestätigen. ~ity /vəˈlɪdəti/ n Gültigkeit f

valley /ˈvæli/ n Tal nt

valour /ˈvælə(r)/ n Tapferkeit f

valuable /ˈvæljʊəbl/ a wertvoll. ~s npl Wertsachen pl

valuation /væljʊˈeɪʃn/ n Schätzung f

value /ˈvælju:/ n Wert m; ⟨usefulness⟩ Nutzen m □ vt schätzen. ~ 'added tax n Mehrwertsteuer f

valve /vælv/ n Ventil nt; (Anat) Klappe f; (Electr) Röhre f

vampire /ˈvæmpaɪə(r)/ n Vampir m

van /væn/ n Lieferwagen m

vandal /ˈvændl/ n Rowdy n. ~ism /-ɪzm/ n mutwillige Zerstörung f. ~ize vt demolieren

vanilla /vəˈnɪlə/ n Vanille f

vanish /ˈvænɪʃ/ vi verschwinden

vanity /ˈvænəti/ n Eitelkeit f. ~ bag n Kosmetiktäschchen nt

vantage-point /ˈvɑ:ntɪdʒ-/ n Aussichtspunkt m

vapour /ˈveɪpə(r)/ n Dampf m

variable /ˈveəriəbl/ a unbeständig; (Math) variabel; ⟨adjustable⟩ regulierbar

variance /ˈveəriəns/ n be at ~ nicht übereinstimmen

variant /ˈveəriənt/ n Variante f

variation /veəriˈeɪʃn/ n Variation f; ⟨difference⟩ Unterschied m

varicose /ˈværɪkəʊs/ a ~ veins Krampfadern pl

varied /ˈveərɪd/ a vielseitig; ⟨diet:⟩ abwechslungsreich

variety /vəˈraɪəti/ n Abwechslung f; ⟨quantity⟩ Vielfalt f; (Comm) Auswahl f; ⟨type⟩ Art f; (Bot) Abart f; (Theat) Varieté nt

various /ˈveəriəs/ a verschieden. ~ly adv unterschiedlich

varnish /ˈvɑ:nɪʃ/ n Lack m □ vt lackieren

vary /ˈveəri/ v (pt/pp -ied) □ vi sich ändern; ⟨be different⟩ verschieden sein □ vt ⟨ver⟩ändern; ⟨add variety to⟩

abwechslungsreicher gestalten. ~ing a wechselnd; ⟨different⟩ unterschiedlich

vase /vɑ:z/ n Vase f

vast /vɑ:st/ a riesig; ⟨expanse⟩ weit. ~ly adv gewaltig

vat /væt/ n Bottich m

VAT /vi:eɪˈti:, væt/ abbr (value added tax) Mehrwertsteuer f, MwSt.

vault[1] /vɔ:lt/ n ⟨roof⟩ Gewölbe nt; (in bank) Tresor m; ⟨tomb⟩ Gruft f

vault[2] n Sprung m □ vt/i ~ [over] springen über (+ acc)

VDU abbr (visual display unit) Bildschirmgerät nt

veal /vi:l/ n Kalbfleisch nt □ attrib Kalbs-

veer /vɪə(r)/ vi sich drehen; (Naut) abdrehen; (Auto) ausscheren

vegetable /ˈvedʒtəbl/ n Gemüse nt; ~s pl Gemüse n □ attrib Gemüse-; ⟨oil, fat⟩ Pflanzen-

vegetarian /vedʒɪˈteəriən/ a vegetarisch □ n Vegetarier(in) m(f)

vegetat|e /ˈvedʒɪteɪt/ vi dahinvegetieren. ~ion /-ˈteɪʃn/ n Vegetation f

vehemen|ce /ˈvi:əməns/ n Heftigkeit f. ~t a, -ly adv heftig

vehicle /ˈvi:ɪkl/ n Fahrzeug nt; ⟨fig: medium⟩ Mittel nt

veil /veɪl/ n Schleier m □ vt verschleiern

vein /veɪn/ n Ader f; ⟨mood⟩ Stimmung f; ⟨manner⟩ Art f; ~s and arteries Venen und Arterien. ~ed a geädert

Velcro (P) /ˈvelkrəʊ/ n ~ fastening Klettverschluss m

velocity /vɪˈlɒsəti/ n Geschwindigkeit f

velvet /ˈvelvɪt/ n Samt m. ~y a samtig

vending-machine /ˈvendɪŋ-/ n [Verkaufs]automat m

vendor /ˈvendə(r)/ n Verkäufer(in) m(f)

veneer /vəˈnɪə(r)/ n Furnier nt; ⟨fig⟩ Tünche f. ~ed a furniert

venerable /ˈvenərəbl/ a ehrwürdig

venereal /vɪˈnɪəriəl/ a ~ disease Geschlechtskrankheit f

Venetian /vəˈni:ʃn/ a venezianisch. v~ blind n Jalousie f

vengeance /ˈvendʒəns/ n Rache f; with a ~ ⟨fam⟩ gewaltig

Venice /ˈvenɪs/ n Venedig nt

venison /ˈvenɪsn/ n (Culin) Wild nt

venom /ˈvenəm/ n Gift nt; ⟨fig⟩ Hass m. ~ous /-əs/ a giftig

vent[1] /vent/ n Öffnung f; ⟨fig⟩ Ventil nt; give ~ to Luft machen (+ dat) □ vt Luft machen (+ dat)

vent[2] n (in jacket) Schlitz m

ventilat|e /'ventɪleɪt/ vt belüften. ∼ion /-'leɪʃn/ n Belüftung f; (installation) Lüftung f. ∼or n Lüftungsvorrichtung f; (Med) Beatmungsgerät nt

ventriloquist /ven'trɪləkwɪst/ n Bauchredner m

venture /'ventʃə(r)/ n Unternehmung f □ vt wagen □ vi sich wagen

venue /'venju:/ n Treffpunkt m; (for event) Veranstaltungsort m

veranda /və'rændə/ n Veranda f

verb /vɜ:b/ n Verb nt. ∼al a, -ly adv mündlich; (Gram) verbal

verbatim /vɜ:'beɪtɪm/ a & adv [wort]wörtlich

verbose /vɜ:'bəʊs/ a weitschweifig

verdict /'vɜ:dɪkt/ n Urteil nt

verge /vɜ:dʒ/ n Rand m; be on the ∼ of doing sth im Begriff sein, etw zu tun □ vi ∼ on (fig) grenzen an (+ acc)

verger /'vɜ:dʒə(r)/ n Küster m

verify /'verɪfaɪ/ vt (pt/pp -ied) überprüfen; (confirm) bestätigen

vermin /'vɜ:mɪn/ n Ungeziefer nt

vermouth /'vɜ:məθ/ n Wermut m

vernacular /və'nækjʊlə(r)/ n Landessprache f

versatil|e /'vɜ:sətaɪl/ a vielseitig. ∼ity /-'tɪlətɪ/ n Vielseitigkeit f

verse /vɜ:s/ n Strophe f; (of Bible) Vers m; (poetry) Lyrik f

version /'vɜ:ʃn/ n Version f; (translation) Übersetzung f; (model) Modell nt

versus /'vɜ:səs/ prep gegen (+ acc)

vertebra /'vɜ:tɪbrə/ n (pl -brae /-bri:/) (Anat) Wirbel m

vertical /'vɜ:tɪkl/ a, -ly adv senkrecht □ n Senkrechte f

vertigo /'vɜ:tɪgəʊ/ n (Med) Schwindel m

verve /vɜ:v/ n Schwung m

very /'verɪ/ adv sehr; ∼ much sehr; (quantity) sehr viel; ∼ little sehr wenig; ∼ probably höchstwahrscheinlich; at the ∼ most allerhöchstens □ a (mere) bloß; the ∼ first der/die/das allererste; the ∼ thing genau das Richtige; at the ∼ end/beginning ganz am Ende/Anfang; only a ∼ little nur ein ganz kleines bisschen

vessel /'vesl/ n Schiff nt; (receptacle & Anat) Gefäß nt

vest /vest/ n [Unter]hemd nt; (Amer: waistcoat) Weste f □ vt ∼ sth in s.o. jdm etw verleihen; have a ∼ed interest in sth ein persönliches Interesse an etw (dat) haben

vestige /'vestɪdʒ/ n Spur f

vestment /'vestmənt/ n (Relig) Gewand nt

vestry /'vestrɪ/ n Sakristei f

vet /vet/ n Tierarzt m /-ärztin f □ vt (pt/pp vetted) überprüfen

veteran /'vetərən/ n Veteran m. ∼ car n Oldtimer m

veterinary /'vetərɪnərɪ/ a tierärztlich. ∼ surgeon n Tierarzt m /-ärztin f

veto /'vi:təʊ/ n (pl -es) Veto nt □ vt sein Veto einlegen gegen

vex /veks/ vt ärgern. ∼ation /-'seɪʃn/ n Ärger m. ∼ed a verärgert; ∼ed question viel diskutierte Frage f

VHF abbr (very high frequency) UKW

via /'vaɪə/ prep über (+ acc)

viable /'vaɪəbl/ a lebensfähig; (fig) realisierbar; (firm) rentabel

viaduct /'vaɪədʌkt/ n Viadukt m

vibrant /'vaɪbrənt/ a (fig) lebhaft

vibrat|e /vaɪ'breɪt/ vi vibrieren. ∼ion /-'breɪʃn/ n Vibrieren nt

vicar /'vɪkə(r)/ n Pfarrer m. ∼age /-rɪdʒ/ n Pfarrhaus nt

vicarious /vɪ'keərɪəs/ a nachempfunden

vice¹ /vaɪs/ n Laster nt

vice² /vaɪs/ n (Techn) Schraubstock m

vice 'chairman n stellvertretender Vorsitzender m

vice 'president n Vizepräsident m

vice versa /vaɪs'vɜ:sə/ adv umgekehrt

vicinity /vɪ'sɪnətɪ/ n Umgebung f; in the ∼ of in der Nähe von

vicious /'vɪʃəs/ a, -ly adv boshaft; (animal) bösartig. ∼ 'circle n Teufelskreis m

victim /'vɪktɪm/ n Opfer nt. ∼ize vt schikanieren

victor /'vɪktə(r)/ n Sieger m

victor|ious /vɪk'tɔ:rɪəs/ a siegreich. ∼y /'vɪktərɪ/ n Sieg m

video /'vɪdɪəʊ/ n Video nt; (recorder) Videorecorder m □ attrib Video- □ vt [auf Videoband] aufnehmen

video: ∼ cas'sette n Videokassette f. ∼ game n Videospiel nt. ∼ 'nasty n Horrorvideo nt. ∼ recorder n Videorecorder m

vie /vaɪ/ vi (pres p vying) wetteifern

Vienn|a /vɪ'enə/ n Wien nt. ∼ese /vɪə-'ni:z/ a Wiener

view /vju:/ n Sicht f; (scene) Aussicht f, Blick m; (picture, opinion) Ansicht f; in my ∼ meiner Ansicht nach; in ∼ of angesichts (+ gen); keep/have sth in ∼ etw im Auge behalten/haben; be on ∼ besichtigt werden können □ vt sich (dat) ansehen; besichtigen (house); (consider) betrachten □ vi (TV) fernsehen. ∼er n (TV) Zuschauer(in) m(f); (Phot) Diabetrachter m

view: ∼finder n (Phot) Sucher m. ∼point n Standpunkt m

vigil /'vɪdʒɪl/ n Wache f

vigilan|ce /'vɪdʒɪləns/ n Wachsamkeit f. ~t a, -ly adv wachsam

vigorous /'vɪgərəs/ a, -ly adv kräftig; (fig) heftig

vigour /'vɪgə(r)/ n Kraft f; (fig) Heftigkeit f

vile /vaɪl/ a abscheulich

villa /'vɪlə/ n (for holidays) Ferienhaus nt

village /'vɪlɪdʒ/ n Dorf nt. ~r n Dorfbewohner(in) m(f)

villain /'vɪlən/ n Schurke m; (in story) Bösewicht m

vim /vɪm/ n (fam) Schwung m

vindicat|e /'vɪndɪkeɪt/ vt rechtfertigen. ~ion /-'keɪʃn/ n Rechtfertigung f

vindictive /vɪn'dɪktɪv/ a nachtragend

vine /vaɪn/ n Weinrebe f

vinegar /'vɪnɪgə(r)/ n Essig m

vineyard /'vɪnjɑːd/ n Weinberg m

vintage /'vɪntɪdʒ/ a erlesen □ n (year) Jahrgang m. ~ 'car n Oldtimer m

viola /vɪ'əʊlə/ n (Mus) Bratsche f

violat|e /'vaɪəleɪt/ vt verletzen; (break) brechen; (disturb) stören; (defile) schänden. ~ion /-'leɪʃn/ n Verletzung f; Schändung f

violen|ce /'vaɪələns/ n Gewalt f; (fig) Heftigkeit f. ~t a gewalttätig; (fig) heftig. ~tly adv brutal; (fig) heftig

violet /'vaɪələt/ a violett □ n (flower) Veilchen nt

violin /vaɪə'lɪn/ n Geige f, Violine f. ~ist n Geiger(in) m(f)

VIP abbr (very important person) Prominente(r) m/f

viper /'vaɪpə(r)/ n Kreuzotter f; (fig) Schlange f

virgin /'vɜːdʒɪn/ a unberührt □ n Jungfrau f. ~ity /-'dʒɪnəti/ n Unschuld f

Virgo /'vɜːgəʊ/ n (Astr) Jungfrau f

viril|e /'vɪraɪl/ a männlich. ~ity /-'rɪləti/ n Männlichkeit f

virtual /'vɜːtjʊəl/ a a ... praktisch ein ... ~ly adv praktisch

virtue /'vɜːtjuː/ n Tugend f; (advantage) Vorteil m; by or in ~e of auf Grund (+ gen)

virtuoso /vɜːtjʊ'əʊzəʊ/ n (pl -si /-ziː/) Virtuose m

virtuous /'vɜːtjʊəs/ a tugendhaft

virulent /'vɪrʊlənt/ a bösartig; (poison) stark; (fig) scharf

virus /'vaɪərəs/ n Virus nt

visa /'viːzə/ n Visum nt

vis-à-vis /viːzɑː'viː/ adv & prep gegenüber (+ dat)

viscous /'vɪskəs/ a dickflüssig

visibility /vɪzə'bɪlətɪ/ n Sichtbarkeit f; (Meteorol) Sichtweite f

visible /'vɪzəbl/ a, -bly adv sichtbar

vision /'vɪʒn/ n Vision f; (sight) Sehkraft f; (foresight) Weitblick m

visit /'vɪzɪt/ n Besuch m □ vt besuchen; besichtigen (town, building). ~ing hours npl Besuchszeiten pl. ~or n Besucher(in) m(f); (in hotel) Gast m; have ~ors Besuch haben

visor /'vaɪzə(r)/ n Schirm m; (on helmet) Visier nt; (Auto) [Sonnen]blende f

vista /'vɪstə/ n Aussicht f

visual /'vɪzjʊəl/ a, -ly adv visuell; ~ly handicapped sehbehindert. ~ aids npl Anschauungsmaterial nt. ~ dis'play unit n Bildschirmgerät nt

visualize /'vɪzjʊəlaɪz/ vt sich (dat) vorstellen

vital /'vaɪtl/ a unbedingt notwendig; (essential to life) lebenswichtig. ~ity /vaɪ'tælətɪ/ n Vitalität f. ~ly /'vaɪtəlɪ/ adv äußerst

vitamin /'vɪtəmɪn/ n Vitamin nt

vitreous /'vɪtrɪəs/ a glasartig; (enamel) Glas-

vivaci|ous /vɪ'veɪʃəs/ a, -ly adv lebhaft. ~ty /-'væsətɪ/ n Lebhaftigkeit f

vivid /'vɪvɪd/ a, -ly adv lebhaft; (description) lebendig

vixen /'vɪksn/ n Füchsin f

vocabulary /və'kæbjʊlərɪ/ n Wortschatz m; (list) Vokabelverzeichnis nt; learn ~ Vokabeln lernen

vocal /'vəʊkl/ a, -ly adv stimmlich; (vociferous) lautstark. ~ cords npl Stimmbänder pl

vocalist /'vəʊkəlɪst/ n Sänger(in) m(f)

vocation /və'keɪʃn/ n Berufung f. ~al a Berufs-

vociferous /və'sɪfərəs/ a lautstark

vodka /'vɒdkə/ n Wodka m

vogue /vəʊg/ n Mode f; in ~ in Mode

voice /vɔɪs/ n Stimme f □ vt zum Ausdruck bringen

void /vɔɪd/ a leer; (not valid) ungültig; ~ of ohne □ n Leere f

volatile /'vɒlətaɪl/ a flüchtig; (person) sprunghaft

volcanic /vɒl'kænɪk/ a vulkanisch

volcano /vɒl'keɪnəʊ/ n Vulkan m

volition /və'lɪʃn/ n of one's own ~ aus eigenem Willen

volley /'vɒlɪ/ n (of gunfire) Salve f; (Tennis) Volley m

volt /vəʊlt/ n Volt nt. ~age /-ɪdʒ/ n (Electr) Spannung f

voluble /'vɒljʊbl/ a, -bly adv redselig; ⟨protest⟩ wortreich

volume /'vɒljuːm/ n ⟨book⟩ Band m; (Geom) Rauminhalt m; ⟨amount⟩ Ausmaß nt; (Radio, TV) Lautstärke f. ∼ control n Lautstärkeregler m

voluntary /'vɒləntərɪ/ a, -ily adv freiwillig

volunteer /vɒlən'tɪə(r)/ n Freiwillige(r) m/f □ vt anbieten; geben ⟨information⟩ □ vi sich freiwillig melden

voluptuous /və'lʌptjʊəs/ a sinnlich

vomit /'vɒmɪt/ n Erbrochene(s) nt □ vt erbrechen □ vi sich übergeben

voracious /və'reɪʃəs/ a gefräßig; ⟨appetite⟩ unbändig

vot|e /vəʊt/ n Stimme f; ⟨ballot⟩ Abstimmung f; ⟨right⟩ Wahlrecht nt; take a ∼e on abstimmen über (+ acc) □ vi abstimmen; (in election) wählen □ vt s.o. ∼e s.o. president jdn zum Präsidenten wählen. ∼er n Wähler(in) m(f)

vouch /vaʊtʃ/ vi ∼ for sich verbürgen für. ∼er n Gutschein m

vow /vaʊ/ n Gelöbnis nt; (Relig) Gelübde nt □ vt geloben

vowel /'vaʊəl/ n Vokal m

voyage /'vɔɪɪdʒ/ n Seereise f; (in space) Reise f, Flug m

vulgar /'vʌlgə(r)/ a vulgär, ordinär. ∼ity /-'gærətɪ/ n Vulgarität f

vulnerable /'vʌlnərəbl/ a verwundbar

vulture /'vʌltʃə(r)/ n Geier m

vying /'vaɪɪŋ/ see vie

W

wad /wɒd/ n Bausch m; ⟨bundle⟩ Bündel nt. ∼ding n Wattierung f

waddle /'wɒdl/ vi watscheln

wade /weɪd/ vi waten; ∼ through ⟨fam⟩ sich durchackern durch ⟨book⟩

wafer /'weɪfə(r)/ n Waffel f; (Relig) Hostie f

waffle[1] /'wɒfl/ vi ⟨fam⟩ schwafeln

waffle[2] n (Culin) Waffel f

waft /wɒft/ vt/i wehen

wag /wæg/ v (pt/pp wagged) □ vt wedeln mit; ∼ one's finger at s.o. jdm mit dem Finger drohen □ vi wedeln

wage[1] /weɪdʒ/ vt führen

wage[2] n, & ∼s pl Lohn m. ∼ packet n Lohntüte f

wager /'weɪdʒə(r)/ n Wette f

waggle /'wægl/ vt wackeln mit □ vi wackeln

wagon /'wægən/ n Wagen m; (Rail) Waggon m

wail /weɪl/ n ⟨klagender⟩ Schrei m □ vi heulen; ⟨lament⟩ klagen

waist /weɪst/ n Taille f. ∼coat /'weɪskəʊt/ n Weste f. ∼line n Taille f

wait /weɪt/ n Wartezeit f; lie in ∼ for auflauern (+ dat) □ vi warten (for auf + acc); (at table) servieren; ∼ on bedienen □ vt ∼ one's turn warten, bis man an der Reihe ist

waiter /'weɪtə(r)/ n Kellner m; ∼! Herr Ober!

waiting: ∼-list n Warteliste f. ∼-room n Warteraum m; (doctor's) Wartezimmer nt

waitress /'weɪtrɪs/ n Kellnerin f

waive /weɪv/ vt verzichten auf (+ acc)

wake[1] /weɪk/ n Totenwache f □ v (pt woke, pp woken) ∼ [up] □ vt [auf]wecken □ vi aufwachen

wake[2] n (Naut) Kielwasser nt; in the ∼ of im Gefolge (+ gen)

waken /'weɪkn/ vt [auf]wecken □ vi aufwachen

Wales /weɪlz/ n Wales nt

walk /wɔːk/ n Spaziergang m; ⟨gait⟩ Gang m; ⟨path⟩ Weg m; go for a ∼ spazieren gehen □ vi gehen; (not ride) laufen, zu Fuß gehen; ⟨ramble⟩ wandern; learn to ∼ laufen lernen □ vt ausführen ⟨dog⟩. ∼ out vi hinausgehen; ⟨workers:⟩ in den Streik treten; ∼ out on s.o. jdn verlassen

walker /'wɔːkə(r)/ n Spaziergänger(in) m(f); ⟨rambler⟩ Wanderer m/Wanderin f

walking /'wɔːkɪŋ/ n Gehen nt; ⟨rambling⟩ Wandern nt. ∼-stick n Spazierstock m

walk: ∼-out n Streik m. ∼-over n (fig) leichter Sieg m

wall /wɔːl/ n Wand f; (external) Mauer f; go to the ∼ (fam) eingehen; drive s.o. up the ∼ (fam) jdn auf die Palme bringen □ vt ∼ up zumauern

wallet /'wɒlɪt/ n Brieftasche f

wallflower n Goldlack m

wallop /'wɒləp/ n (fam) Schlag m □ vt (pt/pp walloped) ⟨fam⟩ schlagen

wallow /'wɒləʊ/ vi sich wälzen; ⟨fig⟩ schwelgen

wallpaper n Tapete f □ vt tapezieren

walnut /'wɔːlnʌt/ n Walnuss f

waltz /wɔːlts/ n Walzer m □ vi Walzer tanzen; come ∼ing up (fam) angetanzt kommen

wan /wɒn/ a bleich

wand /wɒnd/ n Zauberstab m

wander /'wɒndə(r)/ vi umherwandern, ⟨fam⟩ bummeln; ⟨fig: digress⟩ abschweifen. ∼ about vi umherwandern. ∼lust n Fernweh nt

wane /weɪn/ n be on the ∼ schwinden; ⟨moon:⟩ abnehmen □ vi schwinden; abnehmen

wangle /'wæŋgl/ vt ⟨fam⟩ organisieren

want /wɒnt/ n Mangel m (of an + dat); ⟨hardship⟩ Not f; ⟨desire⟩ Bedürfnis nt □ vt wollen; ⟨need⟩ brauchen; ∼ [to have] sth etw haben wollen; ∼ to do sth etw tun wollen; we ∼ to stay wir wollen bleiben; I ∼ you to go ich will, dass du gehst; it ∼s painting es müsste gestrichen werden; you ∼ to learn to swim du solltest schwimmen lernen □ vi he doesn't ∼ for anything ihm fehlt es an nichts. ∼ed a gesucht. ∼ing a be ∼ing fehlen; he is ∼ing in him fehlt es an (+ dat)

wanton /'wɒntən/ a, -ly adv mutwillig

war /wɔ:(r)/ n Krieg m; be at ∼ sich im Krieg befinden

ward /wɔ:d/ n [Kranken]saal m; ⟨unit⟩ Station f; ⟨of town⟩ Wahlbezirk m; ⟨child⟩ Mündel nt □ vt ∼ off abwehren

warden /'wɔ:dn/ n Heimleiter(in) m(f); ⟨of youth hostel⟩ Herbergsvater m; ⟨supervisor⟩ Aufseher(in) m(f)

warder /'wɔ:də(r)/ n Wärter(in) m(f)

wardrobe /'wɔ:drəʊb/ n Kleiderschrank m; ⟨clothes⟩ Garderobe f

warehouse /'weəhaʊs/ n Lager nt; ⟨building⟩ Lagerhaus n

wares /weəz/ npl Waren pl

war: ∼fare n Krieg m. ∼head n Sprengkopf m. ∼like a kriegerisch

warm /wɔ:m/ a (-er, -est), -ly adv warm; ⟨welcome⟩ herzlich; I am ∼ mir ist warm □ vt wärmen. ∼ up vt aufwärmen □ vi warm werden; ⟨Sport⟩ sich aufwärmen. ∼-hearted a warmherzig

warmth /wɔ:mθ/ n Wärme f

warn /wɔ:n/ vt warnen (of vor + dat). ∼ing n Warnung f; ⟨advance notice⟩ Vorwarnung f; ⟨caution⟩ Verwarnung f

warp /wɔ:p/ vt verbiegen □ vi sich verziehen

'war-path n on the ∼ auf dem Kriegspfad

warrant /'wɒrənt/ n ⟨for arrest⟩ Haftbefehl m; ⟨for search⟩ Durchsuchungsbefehl m □ vt ⟨justify⟩ rechtfertigen; ⟨guarantee⟩ garantieren

warranty /'wɒrəntɪ/ n Garantie f

warrior /'wɒrɪə(r)/ n Krieger m

'warship n Kriegsschiff n

wart /wɔ:t/ n Warze f

'wartime n Kriegszeit f

wary /'weərɪ/ a (-ier, -iest), -ily adv vorsichtig; ⟨suspicious⟩ misstrauisch

was /wɒz/ see be

wash /wɒʃ/ n Wäsche f; ⟨Naut⟩ Wellen pl; have a ∼ sich waschen □ vt waschen; spülen ⟨dishes⟩; aufwischen ⟨floor⟩; ⟨flow over⟩ bespülen; ∼ one's hands sich ⟨dat⟩ die Hände waschen □ vi sich waschen; ⟨fabric:⟩ sich waschen lassen. ∼ out vt auswaschen; ausspülen ⟨mouth⟩. ∼ up vt abwaschen, spülen □ vi abwaschen; ⟨Amer⟩ sich waschen

washable /'wɒʃəbl/ a waschbar

wash: ∼basin n Waschbecken nt. ∼cloth n ⟨Amer⟩ Waschlappen m

washed 'out a ⟨faded⟩ verwaschen; ⟨tired⟩ abgespannt

washer /'wɒʃə(r)/ n ⟨Techn⟩ Dichtungsring m; ⟨machine⟩ Waschmaschine f

washing /'wɒʃɪŋ/ n Wäsche f. ∼-machine n Waschmaschine f. ∼-powder n Waschpulver nt. ∼-'up n Abwasch m; do the ∼-up abwaschen, spülen. ∼-'up liquid n Spülmittel nt

wash: ∼-out n Pleite f; ⟨person⟩ Niete f. ∼-room n Waschraum m

wasp /wɒsp/ n Wespe f

wastage /'weɪstɪdʒ/ n Schwund m

waste /weɪst/ n Verschwendung f; ⟨rubbish⟩ Abfall m; ∼s pl Öde f; ∼ of time Zeitverschwendung f □ a ⟨product⟩ Abfall-; lay ∼ verwüsten □ vt verschwenden □ vi ∼ away immer mehr abmagern

waste: ∼-di'sposal unit n Müllzerkleinerer m. ∼ful a verschwenderisch. ∼land n Ödland nt. ∼'paper n Altpapier nt. ∼'paper basket n Papierkorb m

watch /wɒtʃ/ n Wache f; ⟨timepiece⟩ ⟨Armband⟩uhr f; be on the ∼ aufpassen □ vt beobachten; sich ⟨dat⟩ ansehen ⟨film, match⟩; ⟨be careful of, look after⟩ achten auf (+ acc); ∼ television fernsehen □ vi zusehen. ∼ out vi Ausschau halten ⟨for nach⟩; ⟨be careful⟩ aufpassen

watch: ∼dog n Wachhund m. ∼ful a, -ly adv wachsam. ∼maker n Uhrmacher m. ∼man n Wachmann m. ∼strap n Uhrarmband nt. ∼tower n Wachtturm m. ∼word n Parole f

water /'wɔ:tə(r)/ n Wasser nt; ∼s pl Gewässer pl □ vt gießen ⟨garden, plant⟩; ⟨dilute⟩ verdünnen; ⟨give drink to⟩ tränken □ vi ⟨eyes:⟩ tränen; my mouth was ∼ing mir lief das Wasser im Munde zusammen. ∼ down vt verwässern

water: ∼colour n Wasserfarbe f; ⟨painting⟩ Aquarell nt. ∼cress n Brunnenkresse f. ∼fall n Wasserfall m 'watering-can n Gießkanne f

water: ~-lily n Seerose f. ~logged a be ~logged ⟨ground:⟩ unter Wasser stehen. ~main n Hauptwasserleitung f. ~mark n Wasserzeichen nt. ~ polo n Wasserball m. ~power n Wasserkraft f. ~proof a wasserdicht. ~shed n Wasserscheide f; ⟨fig⟩ Wendepunkt m. ~skiing n Wasserskilaufen nt. ~tight a wasserdicht. ~way n Wasserstraße f

watery /'wɔːtəri/ a wässrig

watt /wɒt/ n Watt nt

wave /weiv/ n Welle f; ⟨gesture⟩ Handbewegung f; ⟨as greeting⟩ Winken nt □ vt winken mit; ⟨brandish⟩ schwingen; ⟨threateningly⟩ drohen mit; ⟨hair⟩; ~ one's hand winken □ vi winken (to dat); ⟨flag:⟩ wehen. ~length n Wellenlänge f

waver /'weivə(r)/ vi schwanken

wavy /'weivi/ a wellig

wax[1] /wæks/ vi ⟨moon:⟩ zunehmen; ⟨fig: become⟩ werden

wax[2] n Wachs nt; ⟨in ear⟩ Schmalz nt □ vt wachsen. ~works n Wachsfigurenkabinett nt

way /wei/ n Weg m; ⟨direction⟩ Richtung f; ⟨respect⟩ Hinsicht f; ⟨manner⟩ Art f; ⟨method⟩ Art und Weise f; ~s pl Gewohnheiten pl; in the ~ im Weg; on the ~ auf dem Weg (to nach/zu); ⟨under way⟩ unterwegs; a little/long ~ ein kleines/ganzes Stück; a long ~ off weit weg; this ~ hierher; ⟨like this⟩ so; which ~ in welche Richtung; ⟨how⟩ wie; by the ~ übrigens; in some ~s in gewisser Hinsicht; either ~ so oder so; in this ~ auf diese Weise; in a ~ in gewisser Weise; in a bad ~ ⟨person⟩ in schlechter Verfassung; lead the ~ vorausgehen; make ~ Platz machen (for dat); 'give ~' ⟨Auto⟩ 'Vorfahrt beachten'; go out of one's ~ ⟨fig⟩ sich ⟨dat⟩ besondere Mühe geben (to zu); get one's [own] ~ seinen Willen durchsetzen □ adv weit; ~ behind weit zurück. ~ in n Eingang m

way'lay vt ⟨pt/pp -laid⟩ überfallen; ⟨fam: intercept⟩ abfangen

way 'out n Ausgang m; ⟨fig⟩ Ausweg m

way-'out a ⟨fam⟩ verrückt

wayward /'weiwəd/ a eigenwillig

WC $abbr$ WC nt

we /wiː/ $pron$ wir

weak /wiːk/ a (-er, -est), -ly adv schwach; ⟨liquid⟩ dünn. ~en vt schwächen □ vi schwächer werden. ~ling n Schwächling m. ~ness n Schwäche f

wealth /welθ/ n Reichtum m; ⟨fig⟩ Fülle f (of an + dat). ~y a (-ier, -iest) reich

wean /wiːn/ vt entwöhnen

weapon /'wepən/ n Waffe f

wear /weə(r)/ n ⟨clothing⟩ Kleidung f; ~ and tear Abnutzung f, Verschleiß m □ v ⟨pt wore, pp worn⟩ □ vt tragen; ⟨damage⟩ abnutzen; ~ a hole in sth etw durchwetzen; what shall I ~? was soll ich anziehen? □ vi sich abnutzen; ⟨last⟩ halten. ~ off vi abgehen; ⟨effect:⟩ nachlassen. ~ out vt abnutzen; ⟨exhaust⟩ erschöpfen □ vi sich abnutzen

wearable /'weərəbl/ a tragbar

weary /'wiəri/ a (-ier, -iest), -ily adv müde □ v ⟨pt/pp wearied⟩ □ vt ermüden □ vi ~ of sth etw ⟨gen⟩ überdrüssig werden

weasel /'wiːzl/ n Wiesel nt

weather /'weðə(r)/ n Wetter nt; in this ~ bei diesem Wetter; under the ~ ⟨fam⟩ nicht ganz auf dem Posten □ vt abwettern ⟨storm⟩; ⟨fig⟩ überstehen

weather: ~-beaten a verwittert; wettergegerbt ⟨face⟩. ~cock n Wetterhahn m. ~forecast n Wettervorhersage f. ~-vane n Wetterfahne f

weave[1] /wiːv/ vi ⟨pt/pp weaved⟩ sich schlängeln (through durch)

weave[2] n ⟨Tex⟩ Bindung f □ vt ⟨pt wove, pp woven⟩ weben; ⟨plait⟩ flechten; ⟨fig⟩ einflechten (in in + acc). ~r n Weber m

web /web/ n Netz nt. ~bed feet npl Schwimmfüße pl

wed /wed/ vt/i ⟨pt/pp wedded⟩ heiraten. ~ding n Hochzeit f; ⟨ceremony⟩ Trauung f

wedding: ~ day n Hochzeitstag m. ~ dress n Hochzeitskleid nt. ~-ring n Ehering m, Trauring m

wedge /wedʒ/ n Keil m; ⟨of cheese⟩ [keilförmiges] Stück nt □ vt festklemmen

wedlock /'wedlɒk/ n ⟨liter⟩ Ehe f; in/out of ~ ehelich/unehelich

Wednesday /'wenzdei/ n Mittwoch m

wee /wiː/ a ⟨fam⟩ klein □ vi Pipi machen

weed /wiːd/ n & ~s pl Unkraut nt □ vt/i jäten. ~ out vt ⟨fig⟩ aussieben

'weed-killer n Unkrautvertilgungsmittel nt

weedy /'wiːdi/ a ⟨fam⟩ spillerig

week /wiːk/ n Woche f. ~day n Wochentag m. ~end n Wochenende nt

weekly /'wiːkli/ a & adv wöchentlich □ n Wochenzeitschrift f

weep /wiːp/ vi ⟨pt/pp wept⟩ weinen. ~ing 'willow n Trauerweide f

weigh /wei/ vt/i wiegen; ~ anchor den Anker lichten. ~ down vt ⟨fig⟩ niederdrücken. ~ up vt ⟨fig⟩ abwägen

weight /weit/ n Gewicht nt; put on/lose ~ zunehmen/abnehmen. ~ing n ⟨allowance⟩ Zulage f

weight /∼lessness n Schwerelosigkeit f. ∼-lifting n Gewichtheben nt

weighty /'weɪtɪ/ a (-ier, -iest) schwer; (important) gewichtig

weir /wɪə(r)/ n Wehr nt

weird /wɪəd/ a (-er, -est) unheimlich; (bizarre) bizarr

welcome /'welkəm/ a willkommen; you're ∼! nichts zu danken! you're ∼ to have it das können Sie gerne haben □ n Willkommen nt □ vt begrüßen

weld /weld/ vt schweißen. ∼er n Schweißer m

welfare /'welfeə(r)/ n Wohl nt; (Admin) Fürsorge f. W∼ State n Wohlfahrtsstaat m

well[1] /wel/ n Brunnen m; (oil ∼) Quelle f; (of staircase) Treppenhaus nt

well[2] adv (better, best) gut; as ∼ auch; as ∼ as (in addition) sowohl ... als auch; ∼ done! gut gemacht! □ a gesund; he is not ∼ es geht ihm nicht gut; get ∼ soon! gute Besserung! □ int nun, na

well: ∼-behaved a artig. ∼-being n Wohl nt. ∼-bred a wohlerzogen. ∼-heeled a (fam) gut betucht

wellingtons /'welɪŋtənz/ npl Gummistiefel pl

well: ∼-known a bekannt. ∼-meaning a wohlmeinend. ∼-meant a gut gemeint. ∼-off a wohlhabend; be ∼-off gut dran sein. ∼-read a belesen. ∼-to-do a wohlhabend

Welsh /welʃ/ a walisisch □ n (Lang) Walisisch nt; the ∼ pl die Waliser. ∼ man n Waliser m. ∼ rabbit n überbackenes Käsebrot nt

went /went/ see go

wept /wept/ see weep

were /wɜ:(r)/ see be

west /west/ n Westen m; to the ∼ of westlich von □ a West-, west- □ adv nach Westen; go ∼ (fam) flöten gehen. ∼erly a westlich. ∼ern a westlich □ n Western m

West: ∼ 'Germany n Westdeutschland nt. ∼ 'Indian a westindisch □ n Westindier(in) m(f). ∼ 'Indies /-'ɪndɪz/ npl Westindische Inseln pl

'westward[s] /-wəd[z]/ adv nach Westen

wet /wet/ a (wetter, wettest) nass; (fam: person) weichlich, lasch; '∼ paint' 'frisch gestrichen' □ vt (pt/pp wet or wetted) nass machen. ∼ 'blanket n Spaßverderber m

whack /wæk/ n (fam) Schlag m □ vt (fam) schlagen. ∼ed a (fam) kaputt

whale /weɪl/ n Wal m; have a ∼ of a time (fam) sich toll amüsieren

wharf /wɔ:f/ n Kai m

what /wɒt/ pron & int was; ∼ for? wozu? ∼ is it like? wie ist es? ∼ is your name? wie ist Ihr Name? ∼ is the weather like? wie ist das Wetter? ∼'s he talking about? wovon redet er? □ a welche(r,s); ∼ kind of a was für ein(e); at ∼ time? um wie viel Uhr?

what'ever a (egal) welche(r,s) □ pron was ... auch; ∼ is it? was ist das bloß? ∼ he does was er auch tut; ∼ happens was auch geschieht; nothing ∼ überhaupt nichts

whatso'ever pron & a ≈ whatever

wheat /wi:t/ n Weizen m

wheedle /'wi:dl/ vt gut zureden (+ dat); ∼ sth out of s.o. jdm etw ablocken

wheel /wi:l/ n Rad nt; (pottery) Töpferscheibe f; (steering ∼) Lenkrad nt; at the ∼ am Steuer □ vt (push) schieben □ vi kehrtmachen; (circle) kreisen

wheel: ∼barrow n Schubkarre f. ∼chair n Rollstuhl m. ∼clamp n Parkkralle f

wheeze /wi:z/ vi keuchen

when /wen/ adv wann; the day ∼ der Tag, an dem □ conj wenn; (in the past) als; (although) wo ... doch; ∼ swimming/reading beim Schwimmen/Lesen

whence /wens/ adv (liter) woher

when'ever conj & adv [immer] wenn; (at whatever time) wann immer; ∼ did it happen? wann ist das bloß passiert?

where /weə(r)/ adv & conj wo; ∼ [to] wohin; ∼ [from] woher

whereabouts[1] /weərə'baʊts/ adv wo

'whereabouts[2] n Verbleib m; (of person) Aufenthaltsort m

where'as conj während; (in contrast) wohingegen

where'by adv wodurch

whereu'pon adv worauf[hin]

wher'ever conj & adv wo immer; (to whatever place) wohin immer; (from whatever place) woher immer; (everywhere) überall wo; ∼ is he? wo ist er bloß? ∼ possible wenn irgend möglich

whet /wet/ vt (pt/pp whetted) wetzen; anregen (appetite)

whether /'weðə(r)/ conj ob

which /wɪtʃ/ a & pron welche(r,s); ∼ one welche(r,s) □ rel pron der/die/das, (pl) die; (after clause) was; after ∼ wonach; on ∼ worauf

which'ever a & pron [egal] welche(r,s); ∼ it is was es auch ist

whiff /wɪf/ n Hauch m

while /waɪl/ n Weile f; a long ∼ lange; be worth ∼ sich lohnen; its worth my ∼ es lohnt sich für mich □ conj während; (as

long as) solange; (*although*) obgleich ▢ *vt*
~ away sich (*dat*) vertreiben

whilst /waɪlst/ *conj* während

whim /wɪm/ *n* Laune *f*

whimper /ˈwɪmpə(r)/ *vi* wimmern; ⟨*dog:*⟩
winseln

whimsical /ˈwɪmzɪkl/ *a* skurril

whine /waɪn/ *n* Winseln *nt* ▢ *vi* winseln

whip /wɪp/ *n* Peitsche *f*; (*Pol*) Einpeitscher
m ▢ *vt* (*pt/pp* whipped) peitschen; (*Culin*)
schlagen; (*snatch*) reißen; (*fam: steal*)
klauen. ~ up *vt* (*incite*) anheizen; (*fam*)
schnell hinzaubern ⟨*meal*⟩. ~ped 'cream
n Schlagsahne *f*

whirl /wɜːl/ *n* Wirbel *m*; I am in a ~ mir
schwirrt der Kopf ▢ *vt/i* wirbeln. ~pool
n Strudel *m*. ~wind *n* Wirbelwind *m*

whirr /wɜː(r)/ *vi* surren

whisk /wɪsk/ *n* (*Culin*) Schneebesen *m* ▢ *vt*
(*Culin*) schlagen. ~ away *vt* wegreißen

whisker /ˈwɪskə(r)/ *n* Schnurrhaar *nt*; ~s
pl (*on man's cheek*) Backenbart *m*

whisky /ˈwɪskɪ/ *n* Whisky *m*

whisper /ˈwɪspə(r)/ *n* Flüstern *nt*;
(*rumour*) Gerücht *nt*; in a ~ im Flüsterton
▢ *vt/i* flüstern

whistle /ˈwɪsl/ *n* Pfiff *m*; (*instrument*)
Pfeife *f* ▢ *vt/i* pfeifen

white /waɪt/ *a* (*-r, -st*) weiß ▢ *n* Weiß *nt*;
(*of egg*) Eiweiß *nt*; (*person*) Weiße(r) *m/f*

white: ~'coffee *n* Kaffee *m* mit Milch. ~'
'collar worker *n* Angestellte(r) *m*. ~ 'lie
n Notlüge *f*

whiten /ˈwaɪtn/ *vt* weiß machen ▢ *vi* weiß
werden

whiteness /ˈwaɪtnɪs/ *n* Weiß *nt*

'whitewash *n* Tünche *f*; (*fig*) Schönfärberei *f* ▢ *vt* tünchen

Whitsun /ˈwɪtsn/ *n* Pfingsten *nt*

whittle /ˈwɪtl/ *vt* ~ down reduzieren;
kürzen ⟨*list*⟩

whiz[z] /wɪz/ *vi* (*pt/pp* whizzed) zischen.
~-kid *n* (*fam*) Senkrechtstarter *m*

who /huː/ *pron* wer; (*acc*) wen; (*dat*) wem
▢ *rel pron* der/die/das, (*pl*) die

who'ever *pron* wer [immer]; ~ he is wer
er auch ist; ~ is it? wer ist das bloß?

whole /həʊl/ *a* ganz; (*truth*) voll ▢ *n*
Ganze(s) *nt*; as a ~ als Ganzes; on the ~
im Großen und Ganzen; the ~ lot alle;
(*everything*) alles; the ~ of Germany
ganz Deutschland; the ~ time die ganze
Zeit

whole: ~food *n* Vollwertkost *f*. ~'
'hearted *a* rückhaltlos. ~meal *a*
Vollkorn-

'wholesale *a* Großhandels- ▢ *adv* en gros;
(*fig*) in Bausch und Bogen. ~r *n* Groß-
händler *m*

wholesome /ˈhəʊlsəm/ *a* gesund

wholly /ˈhəʊlɪ/ *adv* völlig

whom /huːm/ *pron* wen; to ~ wem ▢ *rel
pron* den/die/das, (*pl*) die; (*dat*) dem/der/
dem, (*pl*) denen

whooping cough /ˈhuːpɪŋ-/ *n*
Keuchhusten *m*

whopping /ˈwɒpɪŋ/ *a* (*fam*) Riesen-

whore /hɔː(r)/ *n* Hure *f*

whose /huːz/ *pron* wessen; ~ is that? wem
gehört das? ▢ *rel pron* dessen/
deren/dessen, (*pl*) deren

why /waɪ/ *adv* warum; (*for what purpose*)
wozu; that's ~ darum ▢ *int* na

wick /wɪk/ *n* Docht *m*

wicked /ˈwɪkɪd/ *a* böse; (*mischievous*)
frech, boshaft

wicker /ˈwɪkə(r)/ *n* Korbgeflecht *nt*
▢ *attrib* Korb-

wide /waɪd/ *a* (*-r, -st*) weit; (*broad*) breit;
(*fig*) groß; be ~ (*far from target*) daneben-
gehen ▢ *adv* weit; (*off target*) daneben; ~
awake hellwach; far and ~ weit und
breit. ~ly *adv* weit; (*known, accepted*)
weithin; (*differ*) stark

widen /ˈwaɪdn/ *vt* verbreitern; (*fig*) erweitern ▢ *vi* sich verbreitern

'widespread *a* weit verbreitet

widow /ˈwɪdəʊ/ *n* Witwe *f*. ~ed *a* verwitwet. ~er *n* Witwer *m*

width /wɪdθ/ *n* Weite *f*; (*breadth*) Breite *f*

wield /wiːld/ *vt* schwingen; ausüben
⟨*power*⟩

wife /waɪf/ *n* (*pl* wives) [Ehe]frau *f*

wig /wɪg/ *n* Perücke *f*

wiggle /ˈwɪgl/ *vi* wackeln ▢ *vt* wackeln mit

wild /waɪld/ *a* (*-er, -est*), *-ly adv* wild; (*animal*) wild lebend; (*flower*) wild wachsend;
(*furious*) wütend; be ~ about (*keen on*)
wild sein auf (+ *acc*) ▢ *adv* wild; run ~
frei herumlaufen ▢ *n* in the ~ wild; the
~s *pl* die Wildnis *f*

'wildcat strike *n* wilder Streik *m*

wilderness /ˈwɪldənɪs/ *n* Wildnis *f*; (*desert*) Wüste *f*

wild: ~-'goose chase *n* aussichtslose Suche *f*. ~life *n* Tierwelt *f*

wilful /ˈwɪlfl/ *a*, *-ly adv* mutwillig; (*self-
willed*) eigenwillig

will[1] /wɪl/ *v aux* wollen; (*forming future
tense*) werden; he ~ arrive tomorrow er
wird morgen kommen; ~ you go? gehst
du? you ~ be back soon, won't you? du
kommst doch bald wieder, nicht? he ~ be
there, won't he? er wird doch da sein?
she ~ be there by now sie wird jetzt
schon da sein; ~ you be quiet! willst du
wohl ruhig sein! ~ you have some wine?

möchten Sie Wein? the engine won't start der Motor will nicht anspringen

will² *n* Wille *m*; (*document*) Testament *nt*

willing /'wɪlɪŋ/ *a* willig; (*eager*) bereitwillig; be ~ bereit sein. ~ly *adv* bereitwillig; (*gladly*) gern. ~ness *n* Bereitwilligkeit *f*

willow /'wɪloʊ/ *n* Weide *f*

'will-power *n* Willenskraft *f*

willy-'nilly *adv* wohl oder übel

wilt /wɪlt/ *vi* welk werden, welken

wily /'waɪlɪ/ *a* (-ier, -iest) listig

wimp /wɪmp/ *n* Schwächling *m*

win /wɪn/ *n* Sieg *m*; have a ~ gewinnen □ *v* (*pt/pp* won; *pres p* winning) □ *vi* gewinnen; bekommen (*scholarship*) □ *vi* gewinnen; (*in battle*) siegen. ~ over *vt* auf seine Seite bringen

wince /wɪns/ *vi* zusammenzucken

winch /wɪntʃ/ *n* Winde *f* □ *vt* ~ up hochwinden

wind¹ /wɪnd/ *n* Wind *m*; (*breath*) Atem *m*; (*fam: flatulence*) Blähungen *pl*; have the ~ up (*fam*) Angst haben □ *vt* ~ s.o. jdm den Atem nehmen

wind² /waɪnd/ *v* (*pt/pp* wound) □ *vt* (*wrap*) wickeln; (*move by turning*) kurbeln; aufziehen (*clock*) □ *vi* (*road:*) sich winden. ~ up *vt* aufziehen (*clock*); schließen (*proceedings*)

wind /wɪnd/: ~fall *n* unerwarteter Glücksfall *m*; ~falls *pl* (*fruit*) Fallobst *pl*. ~ instrument *n* Blasinstrument *nt*. ~mill *n* Windmühle *f*

window /'wɪndoʊ/ *n* Fenster *nt*; (*of shop*) Schaufenster *nt*

window: ~box *n* Blumenkasten *m*. ~cleaner *n* Fensterputzer *m*. ~dresser *n* Schaufensterdekorateur(in) *m(f)*. ~dressing *n* Schaufensterdekoration *f*; (*fig*) Schönfärberei *f*. ~pane *n* Fensterscheibe *f*. ~shopping *n* Schaufensterbummel *m*. ~sill *n* Fensterbrett *nt*

'windpipe *n* Luftröhre *f*

'windscreen *n*, (*Amer*) **'windshield** *n* Windschutzscheibe *f*. ~ washer *n* Scheibenwaschanlage *f*. ~wiper *n* Scheibenwischer *m*

wind: ~ surfing *n* Windsurfen *nt*. ~swept *a* windgepeitscht; (*person*) zersaust

windy /'wɪndɪ/ *a* (-ier, -iest) windig; be ~ (*fam*) Angst haben

wine /waɪn/ *n* Wein *m*

wine: ~bar *n* Weinstube *f*. ~glass *n* Weinglas *nt*. ~list *n* Weinkarte *f*

winery /'waɪnərɪ/ *n* (*Amer*) Weingut *n*

'wine-tasting *n* Weinprobe *f*

wing /wɪŋ/ *n* Flügel *m*; (*Auto*) Kotflügel *m*; ~s *pl* (*Theat*) Kulissen *pl*

wink /wɪŋk/ *n* Zwinkern *nt*; not sleep a ~ kein Auge zutun □ *vi* zwinkern; (*light:*) blinken

winner /'wɪnə(r)/ *n* Gewinner(in) *m(f)*; (*Sport*) Sieger(in) *m(f)*

winning /'wɪnɪŋ/ *a* siegreich; (*smile*) gewinnend. ~-post *n* Zielpfosten *m*. ~s *npl* Gewinn *m*

winter /'wɪntə(r)/ *n* Winter *m*. ~ry *a* winterlich

wipe /waɪp/ *n* give sth a ~ etw abwischen □ *vt* abwischen; (*floor:*) (*dry*) abtrocknen. ~ off *vt* abwischen; (*erase*) auslöschen. ~ out *vt* (*cancel*) löschen; (*destroy*) ausrotten. ~ up *vt* aufwischen; abtrocknen (*dishes*)

wire /'waɪə(r)/ *n* Draht *m*. ~-haired *a* rauhaarig

wireless /'waɪəlɪs/ *n* Radio *nt*

wire 'netting *n* Maschendraht *m*

wiring /'waɪərɪŋ/ *n* [elektrische] Leitungen *pl*

wiry /'waɪərɪ/ *a* (-ier, -iest) drahtig

wisdom /'wɪzdəm/ *n* Weisheit *f*; (*prudence*) Klugheit *f*. ~ tooth *n* Weisheitszahn *m*

wise /waɪz/ *a* (-r, -st), -ly *adv* weise; (*prudent*) klug

wish /wɪʃ/ *n* Wunsch *m* □ *vt* wünschen; ~ s.o. well jdm alles Gute wünschen; I ~ you could stay ich wünschte, du könntest hier bleiben □ *vi* sich (*dat*) etwas wünschen. ~ful *a* ~ful thinking Wunschdenken *nt*

wishy-washy /'wɪʃɪwɒʃɪ/ *a* labberig; (*colour*) verwaschen; (*person*) lasch

wisp /wɪsp/ *n* Büschel *nt*; (*of hair*) Strähne *f*; (*of smoke*) Fahne *f*

wisteria /wɪs'tɪərɪə/ *n* Glyzinie *f*

wistful /'wɪstfl/ *a*, -ly *adv* wehmütig

wit /wɪt/ *n* Geist *m*, Witz *m*; (*intelligence*) Verstand *m*; (*person*) geistreicher Mensch *m*; be at one's ~s' end sich (*dat*) keinen Rat mehr wissen; scared out of one's ~s zu Tode erschrocken

witch /wɪtʃ/ *n* Hexe *f*. ~craft *n* Hexerei *f*. ~hunt *n* Hexenjagd *f*

with /wɪð/ *prep* mit (+ *dat*); ~ fear/cold vor Angst/Kälte; ~ it damit; I'm going ~ you ich gehe mit; take it ~ you nimm es mit; I haven't got it ~ me ich habe es nicht bei mir; I'm not ~ you (*fam*) ich komme nicht mit

with'draw *v* (*pt* -drew, *pp* -drawn) □ *vt* zurückziehen; abheben (*money*) □ *vi* sich zurückziehen. ~al *n* Zurückziehen *n*; (*of money*) Abhebung *f*; (*from drugs*) Entzug *m*. ~al symptoms *npl* Entzugserscheinungen *pl* with'drawn *see* withdraw □ *a* ⟨*person*⟩ verschlossen

wither /'wɪðə(r)/ *vi* [ver]welken

with'hold *vt* (*pt/pp* -held) vorenthalten (from s.o. jdm)

with'in *prep* innerhalb (+ *gen*); ~ the law im Rahmen des Gesetzes □ *adv* innen

with'out *prep* ohne (+ *acc*); ~ my noticing it ohne dass ich es merkte

with'stand *vt* (*pt/pp* -stood) standhalten (+ *dat*)

witness /'wɪtnɪs/ *n* Zeuge *m*/ Zeugin *f*; ⟨*evidence*⟩ Zeugnis *nt* □ *vt* Zeuge/Zeugin sein (+ *gen*); bestätigen ⟨*signature*⟩. ~box *n*, (*Amer*) ~stand *n* Zeugenstand *m*

witticism /'wɪtɪsɪzm/ *n* geistreicher Ausspruch *m*

wittingly /'wɪtɪŋlɪ/ *adv* wissentlich

witty /'wɪtɪ/ *a* (-ier, -iest) witzig, geistreich

wives /waɪvz/ *see* wife

wizard /'wɪzəd/ *n* Zauberer *m*. ~ry *n* Zauberei *f*

wizened /'wɪznd/ *a* verhutzelt

wobb|le /'wɒbl/ *vi* wackeln. ~ly *a* wackelig

woe /wəʊ/ *n* ⟨*liter*⟩ Jammer *m*; ~ is me! wehe mir!

woke, woken /wəʊk, 'wəʊkn/ *see* wake[1]

wolf /wʊlf/ *n* (*pl* wolves /wʊlvz/) Wolf *m* □ *vt* ~ [down] hinunterschlingen

woman /'wʊmən/ *n* (*pl* women) Frau *f*. ~izer *n* Schürzenjäger *m*. ~ly *a* fraulich

womb /wuːm/ *n* Gebärmutter *f*

women /'wɪmɪn/ *npl see* woman; W~'s Libber /'lɪbə(r)/ *n* Frauenrechtlerin *f*. W~'s Liberation *n* Frauenbewegung *f*

won /wʌn/ *see* win

wonder /'wʌndə(r)/ *n* Wunder *nt*; ⟨*surprise*⟩ Staunen *nt* □ *vt/i* sich fragen; ⟨*be surprised*⟩ sich wundern; I ~ da frage ich mich; I ~ whether she is ill ob sie wohl krank ist? ~ful *a*, -ly *adv* wunderbar

won't /wəʊnt/ = will not

woo /wuː/ *vt* ⟨*liter*⟩ werben um; ⟨*fig*⟩ umwerben

wood /wʊd/ *n* Holz *nt*; ⟨*forest*⟩ Wald *m*; touch ~! unberufen!

wood: ~cut *n* Holzschnitt *m*. ~ed /-ɪd/ *a* bewaldet. ~en *a* Holz-; ⟨*fig*⟩ hölzern. ~pecker *n* Specht *m*. ~wind *n* Holzbläser *pl*. ~work *n* ⟨*wooden parts*⟩ Holzteile *pl*; ⟨*craft*⟩ Tischlerei *f*. ~worm *n* Holzwurm *m*. ~y *a* holzig

wool /wʊl/ *n* Wolle *f* □ *attrib* Woll-. ~len *a* wollen. ~lens *npl* Wollsachen *pl*

woolly /'wʊlɪ/ *a* (-ier, -iest) wollig; ⟨*fig*⟩ unklar

word /wɜːd/ *n* Wort *nt*; ⟨*news*⟩ Nachricht *f*; by ~ of mouth mündlich; have a ~ with s.o. mit jdm sprechen; have ~s einen Wortwechsel haben. ~ing *n* Wortlaut *m*. ~ processor *n* Textverarbeitungssystem *nt*

wore /wɔː(r)/ *see* wear

work /wɜːk/ *n* Arbeit *f*; ⟨*Art, Literature*⟩ Werk *nt*; ~s *pl* ⟨*factory, mechanism*⟩ Werk *nt*; at ~ bei der Arbeit; out of ~ arbeitslos □ *vi* arbeiten; ⟨*machine, system:*⟩ funktionieren; ⟨*have effect*⟩ wirken; ⟨*study*⟩ lernen; it won't ~ ⟨*fig*⟩ es klappt nicht □ *vt* arbeiten lassen; bedienen ⟨*machine*⟩; betätigen ⟨*lever*⟩; ~ one's way through sth sich durch etw hindurcharbeiten. ~ off *vt* abarbeiten. ~ out *vt* ausrechnen; ⟨*solve*⟩ lösen □ *vi* gut gehen, ⟨*fam*⟩ klappen. ~ up *vt* aufbauen; sich ⟨*dat*⟩ holen ⟨*appetite*⟩; get ~ed up sich aufregen

workable /'wɜːkəbl/ *a* ⟨*feasible*⟩ durchführbar

workaholic /wɜːkə'hɒlɪk/ *n* arbeitswütiger Mensch *m*

worker /'wɜːkə(r)/ *n* Arbeiter(in) *m(f)*

working /'wɜːkɪŋ/ *a* berufstätig; ⟨*day, clothes*⟩ Arbeits-; be in ~ order funktionieren. ~ class *n* Arbeiterklasse *f*. ~-class *a* Arbeiter-; be ~-class zur Arbeiterklasse gehören

work: ~man *n* Arbeiter *m*; ⟨*craftsman*⟩ Handwerker *m*. ~manship *n* Arbeit *f*. ~out *n* [Fitness]training *nt*. ~shop *n* Werkstatt *f*

world /wɜːld/ *n* Welt *f*; in the ~ auf der Welt; a ~ of difference ein himmelweiter Unterschied; think the ~ of s.o. große Stücke auf jdn halten. ~ly *a* weltlich; ⟨*person*⟩ weltlich gesinnt. ~-wide *a & adv* /-'-/ weltweit

worm /wɜːm/ *n* Wurm *m* □ *vi* ~ one's way into s.o.'s confidence sich in jds Vertrauen einschleichen. ~-eaten *a* wurmstichig

worn /wɔːn/ *see* wear □ *a* abgetragen. ~out *a* abgetragen; ⟨*carpet*⟩ abgenutzt; ⟨*person*⟩ erschöpft

worried /'wʌrɪd/ *a* besorgt

worry /'wʌrɪ/ *n* Sorge *f* □ *v* (*pt/pp* worried) □ *vt* beunruhigen, Sorgen machen (+ *dat*); ⟨*bother*⟩ stören □ *vi* sich beunruhigen, sich ⟨*dat*⟩ Sorgen machen. ~ing *a* beunruhigend

worse /wɜːs/ *a & adv* schlechter; ⟨*more serious*⟩ schlimmer □ *n* Schlechtere(s) *nt*; Schlimmere(s) *nt*

worsen /'wɜːsn/ *vt* verschlechtern □ *vi* sich verschlechtern

worship /'wɜːʃɪp/ *n* Anbetung *f*; ⟨*service*⟩ Gottesdienst *m*; Your/His W~ ~ Euer/

Seine Ehren □ *v* (*pt/pp* -shipped) □ *vt* anbeten □ *vi* am Gottesdienst teilnehmen

worst /wɜ:st/ *a* schlechteste(r,s); (*most serious*) schlimmste(r,s) □ *adv* am schlechtesten; am schlimmsten □ *n* the ~ das Schlimmste; get the ~ of it den Kürzeren ziehen

worsted /ˈwʊstɪd/ *n* Kammgarn *m*

worth /wɜ:θ/ *n* Wert *m*; £10's ~ of petrol Benzin für £10 □ *a* be ~ £5 £5 wert sein; be ~ it (*fig*) sich lohnen. ~less *a* wertlos. ~while *a* lohnend

worthy /ˈwɜ:ðɪ/ *a* würdig

would /wʊd/ *v aux* I ~ do it ich würde es tun, ich täte es; ~ you go? würdest du gehen? he said he ~n't er sagte, er würde es nicht tun; what ~ you like? was möchten Sie?

wound[1] /wu:nd/ *n* Wunde *f* □ *vt* verwunden

wound[2] /waʊnd/ *see* wind[2]

wove, woven /wəʊv, ˈwəʊvn/ *see* weave[2]

wrangle /ˈræŋgl/ *n* Streit *m* □ *vi* sich streiten

wrap /ræp/ *n* Umhang *m* □ *vt* (*pt/pp* wrapped) ~ [up] wickeln; einpacken (*present*) □ *vi* ~ up warmly sich warm einpacken; be ~ped up in (*fig*) aufgehen in (+ *dat*). ~per *n* Hülle *f*. ~ping *n* Verpackung *f*. ~ping paper *n* Einwickelpapier *nt*

wrath /rɒθ/ *n* Zorn *m*

wreak /ri:k/ *vt* ~ havoc Verwüstungen anrichten

wreath /ri:θ/ *n* (*pl* ~s /-ðz/) Kranz *m*

wreck /rek/ *n* Wrack *nt* □ *vt* zerstören; zunichte machen (*plans*); zerrütten (*marriage*). ~age /-ɪdʒ/ *n* Wrackteile *pl*; (*fig*) Trümmer *pl*

wren /ren/ *n* Zaunkönig *m*

wrench /rentʃ/ *n* Ruck *m*; (*tool*) Schraubenschlüssel *m*; be a ~ (*fig*) weh tun □ *vt* reißen; ~sth from s.o. jdm etw entreißen

wrest /rest/ *vt* entwinden from s.o. jdm)

wrestl|e /ˈresl/ *vi* ringen. ~er *n* Ringer *m*. ~ing *n* Ringen *nt*

wretch /retʃ/ *n* Kreatur *f*. ~ed /-ɪd/ *a* elend; (*very bad*) erbärmlich

wriggle /ˈrɪgl/ *n* □ *vi* zappeln; (*move forward*) sich schlängeln; ~ out of sth (*fam*) sich vor etw (*dat*) drücken

wring /rɪŋ/ *vt* (*pt/pp* wrung) wringen; (~ *out*) auswringen; umdrehen (*neck*); ringen (*hands*); be ~ing wet tropfnass sein

wrinkle /ˈrɪŋkl/ *n* Falte *f*; (*on skin*) Runzel *f* □ *vt* kräuseln □ *vi* sich kräuseln, sich falten. ~d *a* runzlig

wrist /rɪst/ *n* Handgelenk *nt*. ~watch *n* Armbanduhr *f*

writ /rɪt/ *n* (*Jur*) Verfügung *f*

write /raɪt/ *vt/i* (*pt* wrote, *pp* written, *pres p* writing) schreiben. ~ down *vt* aufschreiben. ~ off *vt* abschreiben; zu Schrott fahren (*car*)

'write-off *n* ≈ Totalschaden *m*

writer /ˈraɪtə(r)/ *n* Schreiber(in) *m(f)*; (*author*) Schriftsteller(in) *m(f)*

'write-up *n* Bericht *m*; (*review*) Kritik *f*

writhe /raɪð/ *vi* sich winden

writing /ˈraɪtɪŋ/ *n* Schreiben *nt*; (*handwriting*) Schrift *f*; in ~ schriftlich. ~-paper *n* Schreibpapier *nt*

written /ˈrɪtn/ *see* write

wrong /rɒŋ/ *a*, -ly *adv* falsch; (*morally*) unrecht; (*not just*) ungerecht; be ~ nicht stimmen; (*person:*) Unrecht haben; what's ~? was ist los? □ *adv* falsch; go ~ (*person:*) etwas falsch machen; (*machine:*) kaputtgehen; (*plan:*) schief gehen □ *n* Unrecht *nt* □ *vt* Unrecht tun (+ *dat*). ~ful *a* ungerechtfertigt. ~fully *adv* (*accuse*) zu Unrecht

wrote /rəʊt/ *see* write

wrought 'iron /rɔ:t-/ *n* Schmiedeeisen *nt* □ *attrib* schmiedeeisern

wrung /rʌŋ/ *see* wring

wry /raɪ/ *a* (-er, -est) ironisch; (*humour*) trocken

X

xerox (P) /ˈzɪərɒks/ *vt* fotokopieren

Xmas /ˈkrɪsməs, ˈeksməs/ *n* (*fam*) Weihnachten *nt*

X-ray /ˈeks-/ *n* (*picture*) Röntgenaufnahme *f*; ~s *pl* Röntgenstrahlen *pl*; have an ~ geröntgt werden □ *vt* röntgen; durchleuchten (*luggage*)

Y

yacht /jɒt/ *n* Jacht *f*; (*for racing*) Segelboot *nt*. ~ing *n* Segeln *nt*

yank /jæŋk/ *vt* (*fam*) reißen

Yank *n* (*fam*) Amerikaner(in) *m(f)*, (*fam*) Ami *m*

yap /jæp/ *vi* (*pt/pp* yapped) (*dog:*) kläffen

yard[1] /jɑ:d/ *n* Hof *m*; (*for storage*) Lager *nt*

yard² n Yard nt (= 0,91 m). ~stick n (fig) Maßstab m

yarn /jɑːn/ n Garn m; (fam: tale) Geschichte f

yawn /jɔːn/ n Gähnen nt □ vi gähnen. ~ing a gähnend

year /jɪə(r)/ n Jahr nt; (of wine) Jahrgang m; for ~s jahrelang. ~book n Jahrbuch nt. ~ly a & adv jährlich

yearn /jɜːn/ vi sich sehnen (for nach). ~ing n Sehnsucht f

yeast /jiːst/ n Hefe f

yell /jel/ n Schrei m □ vi schreien

yellow /ˈjeləʊ/ a gelb □ n Gelb nt. ~ish a gelblich

yelp /jelp/ vi jaulen

yen /jen/ n Wunsch m (for nach)

yes /jes/ adv ja; (contradicting) doch □ n Ja nt

yesterday /ˈjestədeɪ/ n & adv gestern; ~'s paper die gestrige Zeitung; the day before ~ vorgestern

yet /jet/ adv noch; (in question) schon; (nevertheless) doch; as ~ bisher; not ~ noch nicht; the best ~ das bisher beste □ conj doch

yew /juː/ n Eibe f

Yiddish /ˈjɪdɪʃ/ n Jiddisch nt

yield /jiːld/ n Ertrag m □ vt bringen; abwerfen (profit) □ vi nachgeben; (Amer, Auto) die Vorfahrt beachten

yodel /ˈjəʊdl/ vi (pt/pp yodelled) jodeln

yoga /ˈjəʊgə/ n Yoga m

yoghurt /ˈjɒgət/ n Joghurt m

yoke /jəʊk/ n Joch nt; (of garment) Passe f

yokel /ˈjəʊkl/ n Bauerntölpel m

yolk /jəʊk/ n Dotter m, Eigelb nt

yonder /ˈjɒndə(r)/ adv (liter) dort drüben

you /juː/ pron du; (acc) dich; (dat) dir; (pl) ihr; (acc, dat) euch; (formal) (nom & acc, sg & pl) Sie; (dat, sg & pl) Ihnen; (one) man; (acc) einen; (dat) einem; all of ~ ihr/Sie alle; I know ~ ich kenne dich/euch/Sie; I'll give ~ the money ich gebe dir/euch/Ihnen das Geld; it does ~ good es tut einem gut; it's bad for ~ es ist ungesund

young /jʌŋ/ a (-er /-gə(r)/, -est /-gɪst/) jung □ npl (animals) Junge pl; the ~ die

Jugend f. ~ster n Jugendliche(r) m/f; (child) Kleine(r) m/f

your /jɔː(r)/ a dein; (pl) euer; (formal) Ihr

yours /jɔːz/ poss pron deine(r), deins; (pl) eure(r), euers; (formal, sg & pl) Ihre(r), Ihr[e]s; a friend of ~ ein Freund von dir/Ihnen/euch; that is ~ das gehört dir/Ihnen/euch

your'self pron (pl -selves) selbst; (refl) dich; (dat) dir; (pl) euch; (formal) sich; by ~ allein

youth /juːθ/ n (pl youths /-ðːz/) Jugend f; (boy) Jugendliche(r) m. ~ful a jugendlich. ~ hostel n Jugendherberge f

Yugoslav /ˈjuːgəslɑːv/ a jugoslawisch. ~ia /-ˈslɑːvɪə/ n Jugoslawien nt

Z

zany /ˈzeɪnɪ/ a (-ier, -iest) närrisch, verrückt

zeal /ziːl/ n Eifer m

zealous /ˈzeləs/ a, -ly adv eifrig

zebra /ˈzebrə/ n Zebra nt. ~ 'crossing n Zebrastreifen m

zenith /ˈzenɪθ/ n Zenit m; (fig) Gipfel m

zero /ˈzɪərəʊ/ n Null f

zest /zest/ n Begeisterung f

zigzag /ˈzɪgzæg/ n Zickzack m □ vi (pt/pp -zagged) im Zickzack laufen/ (in vehicle) fahren

zinc /zɪŋk/ n Zink nt

zip /zɪp/ n ~ [fastener] Reißverschluss m □ vt ~ [up] den Reißverschluss zuziehen an (+ dat)

'Zip code n (Amer) Postleitzahl f

zipper /ˈzɪpə(r)/ n Reißverschluss m

zither /ˈzɪðə(r)/ n Zither f

zodiac /ˈzəʊdɪæk/ n Tierkreis m

zombie /ˈzɒmbɪ/ n (fam) like a ~ ganz benommen

zone /zəʊn/ n Zone f

zoo /zuː/ n Zoo m

zoological /zəʊəˈlɒdʒɪkl/ a zoologisch

zoolog|ist /zəʊˈɒlədʒɪst/ n Zoologe m /-gin f. ~y Zoologie f

zoom /zuːm/ vi sausen. ~ lens n Zoomobjektiv nt

Phonetic symbols used for German words

a	Hand	hant	ŋ	lang	laŋ	
a:	Bahn	ba:n	o	Moral	mo'ra:l	
ɐ	Ober	'o:bɐ	o:	Boot	bo:t	
ɐ̯	Uhr	u:ɐ̯	ǫ	Foyer	fo̯a'je:	
ã	Conférencier	kõferã'sie̯	õ	Konkurs	kõ'kʊrs	
ã:	Abonnement	abɔnə'mã:	õ:	Ballon	ba'lõ:	
ai̯	weit	vai̯t	ɔ	Post	pɔst	
au̯	Haut	hau̯t	ø	Ökonom	øko'no:m	
b	Ball	bal	ø:	Öl	ø:l	
ç	ich	ɪç	œ	göttlich	'gœtlɪç	
d	dann	dan	ɔy	heute	'hɔy̯tə	
dʒ	Gin	dʒɪn	p	Pakt	pakt	
e	Metall	me'tal	r	Rast	rast	
e:	Beet	be:t	s	Hast	hast	
ɛ	mästen	'mɛstən	ʃ	Schal	ʃa:l	
ɛ:	wählen	'vɛ:lən	t	Tal	ta:l	
ɛ̃	Cousin	ku'zɛ̃:	ts	Zahl	tsa:l	
ə	Nase	'na:zə	tʃ	Couch	kau̯tʃ	
f	Faß	fas	u	kulant	ku'lant	
g	Gast	gast	u:	Hut	hu:t	
h	haben	'ha:bən	u̯	aktuell	ak'tu̯ɛl	
i	Rivale	ri'va:lə	ʊ	Pult	pʊlt	
i:	viel	fi:l	v	was	vas	
i̯	Aktion	ak'tsio̯:n	x	Bach	bax	
ɪ	Birke	'bɪrkə	y	Physik	fy'zi:k	
j	ja	ja:	y:	Rübe	'ry:bə	
k	kalt	kalt	ỹ	Nuance	'nỹã:sə	
l	Last	last	ʏ	Fülle	'fʏlə	
m	Mast	mast	z	Nase	'na:zə	
n	Naht	na:t	ʒ	Regime	re'ʒi:m	

ʔ	Glottal stop, e.g. Koordination /koʔɔrdina'tsio̯:n/.
:	Length sign after a vowel, e.g. Chrom /kro:m/.
'	Stress mark before stressed syllable, e.g. Balkon /bal'kõ:/.

Die für das Englische verwendeten Zeichen der Lautschrift

ɑː	barn	bɑːn		l	lot	lɒt
ã	nuance	'njuːãs		m	mat	mæt
æ	fat	fæt		n	not	nɒt
æ̃	lingerie	'læ̃ʒərɪ		ŋ	sing	sɪŋ
aɪ	fine	faɪn		ɒ	got	gɒt
aʊ	now	naʊ		ɔː	paw	pɔː
b	bat	bæt		ɔɪ	boil	bɔɪl
d	dog	dɒg		p	pet	pet
dʒ	jam	dʒæm		r	rat	ræt
e	met	met		s	sip	sɪp
eɪ	fate	feɪt		ʃ	ship	ʃɪp
eə	fairy	'feərɪ		t	tip	tɪp
əʊ	goat	gəʊt		tʃ	chin	tʃɪn
ə	ago	ə'gəʊ		θ	thin	θɪn
ɜː	fur	fɜː(r)		ð	the	ðə
f	fat	fæt		uː	boot	buːt
g	good	gʊd		ʊ	book	bʊk
h	hat	hæt		ʊə	tourism	'tʊərɪzm
ɪ	bit, happy	bɪt, 'hæpɪ		ʌ	dug	dʌg
ɪə	near	nɪə(r)		v	van	væn
iː	meet	miːt		w	win	wɪn
j	yet	jet		z	zip	zɪp
k	kit	kɪt		ʒ	vision	'vɪʒn

:   bezeichnet Länge des vorhergehenden Vokals, z. B. boot [buːt].

ˈ   Betonung, steht unmittelbar vor einer betonten Silbe, z. B. ago [ə'gəʊ].

(r)   Ein „r" in runden Klammern wird nur gesprochen, wenn im Textzusammenhang ein Vokal unmittelbar folgt, z. B. fire /'faɪə(r); fire at /'faɪər æt/.

Guide to German pronunciation

Consonants are pronounced as in English with the following exceptions:

b	as	p	*at the end of a word or syllable*
d	as	t	
g	as	k	

ch	as in Scottish lo<u>ch</u> *after a, o, u, au*	
	like an exaggerated h as in <u>h</u>uge	
		after i, e, ä, ö, ü, eu, ei

-chs	as	x	(as in bo<u>x</u>)
-ig	as	-ich /ɪç/	*when a suffix*
j	as	y	(as in <u>y</u>es)

ps		the p is pronounced
pn		

qu	as	k+v	
s	as	z	(as in <u>z</u>ero) *at the beginning of a word*
	as	s	(as in bu<u>s</u>) *at the end of a word or syllable, before a consonant, or when doubled*
sch	as	sh	
sp	as	shp	*at the beginning of a word*
st	as	sht	
v	as	f	(as in <u>f</u>or)
	as	v	(as in <u>v</u>ery) *within a word*
w	as	v	(as in <u>v</u>ery)
z	as	ts	

Vowels are approximately as follows:

a	short	as	u	(as in but)
	long	as	a	(as in car)
e	short	as	e	(as in pen)
	long	as	a	(as in paper)
i	short	as	i	(as in bit)
	long	as	ee	(as in queen)
o	short	as	o	(as in hot)
	long	as	o	(as in pope)
u	short	as	oo	(as in foot)
	long	as	oo	(as in boot)

Vowels are always short before a double consonant, and long when followed by an h or when double

ie	is pronounced ee	(as in keep)

Diphthongs

au	as	ow	(as in how)
ei ai	as	y	(as in my)
eu äu	as	oy	(as in boy)

German irregular verbs

1st, 2nd and 3rd person present are given after the infinitive, and past subjunctive after the past indicative, where there is a change of vowel or any other irregularity.

Compound verbs are only given if they do not take the same forms as the corresponding simple verb, e.g. *befehlen*, or if there is no corresponding simple verb, e.g. *bewegen*.

An asterisk (*) indicates a verb which is also conjugated regularly.

Infinitive	Past Tense	Past Participle
Infinitiv	Präteritum	2. Partizip
abwägen	wog (wöge) ab	abgewogen
ausbedingen	bedang (bedänge) aus	ausbedungen
*backen (du bäckst, er bäckt)	buk (büke)	gebacken
befehlen (du befiehlst, er befiehlt)	befahl (beföhle, befähle)	befohlen
beginnen	begann (begänne)	begonnen
beißen (du/er beißt)	biss (bisse)	gebissen
bergen (du birgst, er birgt)	barg (bärge)	geborgen
bersten (du/er birst)	barst (bärste)	geborsten
bewegen[2]	bewog (bewöge)	bewogen
biegen	bog (böge)	gebogen
bieten	bot (böte)	geboten
binden	band (bände)	gebunden
bitten	bat (bäte)	gebeten
blasen (du/er bläst)	blies	geblasen
bleiben	blieb	geblieben
*bleichen	blich	geblichen
braten (du brätst, er brät)	briet	gebraten
brechen (du brichst, er bricht)	brach (bräche)	gebrochen
brennen	brannte (brennte)	gebrannt
bringen	brachte (brächte)	gebracht
denken	dachte (dächte)	gedacht
dreschen (du drischst, er drischt)	drosch (drösche)	gedroschen

Infinitive Infinitiv	Past Tense Präteritum	Past Participle 2. Partizip
dringen	drang (dränge)	gedrungen
dürfen (ich/er darf, du darfst)	durfte (dürfte)	gedurft
empfehlen (du empfiehlst, er empfiehlt)	empfahl (empföhle)	empfohlen
erlöschen (du erlischst, er erlischt)	erlosch (erlösche)	erloschen
*erschallen	erscholl (erschölle)	erschollen
*erschrecken (du erschrickst, er erschrickt)	erschrak (erschräke)	erschrocken
erwägen	erwog (erwöge)	erwogen
essen (du/er isst)	aß (äße)	gegessen
fahren (du fährst, er fährt)	fuhr (führe)	gefahren
fallen (du fällst, er fällt)	fiel	gefallen
fangen (du fängst, er fängt)	fing	gefangen
fechten (du fichtst, er ficht)	focht (föchte)	gefochten
finden	fand (fände)	gefunden
flechten (du flichtst, er flicht)	flocht (flöchte)	geflochten
fliegen	flog (flöge)	geflogen
fliehen	floh (flöhe)	geflohen
fließen (du/er fließt)	floss (flösse)	geflossen
fressen (du/er frisst)	fraß (fräße)	gefressen
frieren	fror (fröre)	gefroren
*gären	gor (göre)	gegoren
gebären (du gebierst, sie gebiert)	gebar (gebäre)	geboren
geben (du gibst, er gibt)	gab (gäbe)	gegeben
gedeihen	gedieh	gediehen
gehen	ging	gegangen
gelingen	gelang (gelänge)	gelungen
gelten (du giltst, er gilt)	galt (gölte, gälte)	gegolten
genesen (du/er genest)	genas (genäse)	genesen
genießen (du/er genießt)	genoss (genösse)	genossen
geschehen (es geschieht)	geschah (geschähe)	geschehen
gewinnen	gewann (gewönne, gewänne)	gewonnen
gießen (du/er gießt)	goss (gösse)	gegossen
gleichen	glich	geglichen

Infinitive Infinitiv	Past Tense Präteritum	Past Participle 2. Partizip
gleiten	glitt	geglitten
glimmen	glomm (glömme)	geglommen
graben (du gräbst, er gräbt)	grub (grübe)	gegraben
greifen	griff	gegriffen
haben (du hast, er hat)	hatte (hätte)	gehabt
halten (du hältst, er hält)	hielt	gehalten
hängen[2]	hing	gehangen
hauen	haute	gehauen
heben	hob (höbe)	gehoben
heißen (du/er heißt)	hieß	geheißen
helfen (du hilfst, er hilft)	half (hülfe)	geholfen
kennen	kannte (kennte)	gekannt
klingen	klang (klänge)	geklungen
kneifen	kniff	gekniffen
kommen	kam (käme)	gekommen
können (ich/er kann, du kannst)	konnte (könnte)	gekonnt
kriechen	kroch (kröche)	gekrochen
laden (du lädst, er lädt)	lud (lüde)	geladen
lassen (du/er lässt)	ließ	gelassen
laufen (du läufst, er läuft)	lief	gelaufen
leiden	litt	gelitten
leihen	lieh	geliehen
lesen (du/er liest)	las (läse)	gelesen
liegen	lag (läge)	gelegen
lügen	log (löge)	gelogen
mahlen	mahlte	gemahlen
meiden	mied	gemieden
melken	molk (mölke)	gemolken
messen (du/er misst)	maß (mäße)	gemessen
misslingen	misslang (misslänge)	misslungen
mögen (ich/er mag, du magst)	mochte (möchte)	gemocht
müssen (ich/er muss, du musst)	musste (müsste)	gemusst
nehmen (du nimmst, er nimmt)	nahm (nähme)	genommen
nennen	nannte (nennte)	genannt
pfeifen	pfiff	gepfiffen
preisen (du/er preist)	pries	gepriesen
quellen (du quillst, er quillt)	quoll (quölle)	gequollen

Infinitive Infinitiv	Past Tense Präteritum	Past Participle 2. Partizip
raten (du rätst, er rät)	riet	geraten
reiben	rieb	gerieben
reißen (du/er reißt)	riss	gerissen
reiten	ritt	geritten
rennen	rannte (rennte)	gerannt
riechen	roch (röche)	gerochen
ringen	rang (ränge)	gerungen
rinnen	rann (ränne)	geronnen
rufen	rief	gerufen
*salzen (du/er salzt)	salzte	gesalzen
saufen (du säufst, er säuft)	soff (söffe)	gesoffen
*saugen	sog (söge)	gesogen
schaffen[1]	schuf (schüfe)	geschaffen
scheiden	schied	geschieden
scheinen	schien	geschienen
scheißen (du/er scheißt)	schiss	geschissen
schelten (du schiltst, er schilt)	schalt (schölte)	gescholten
scheren[1]	schor (schöre)	geschoren
schieben	schob (schöbe)	geschoben
schießen (du/er schießt)	schoss (schösse)	geschossen
schinden	schindete	geschunden
schlafen (du schläfst, er schläft)	schlief	geschlafen
schlagen (du schlägst, er schlägt)	schlug (schlüge)	geschlagen
schleichen	schlich	geschlichen
schleifen[2]	schliff	geschliffen
schließen (du/er schließt)	schloss (schlösse)	geschlossen
schlingen	schlang (schlänge)	geschlungen
schmeißen (du/er schmeißt)	schmiss (schmisse)	geschmissen
schmelzen (du/er schmilzt)	schmolz (schmölze)	geschmolzen
schneiden	schnitt	geschnitten
*schrecken (du schrickst, er schrickt)	schrak (schräke)	geschreckt
schreiben	schrieb	geschrieben
schreien	schrie	geschrie[e]n
schreiten	schritt	geschritten
schweigen	schwieg	geschwiegen
schwellen (du schwillst, er schwillt)	schwoll (schwölle)	geschwollen

Infinitive Infinitiv	Past Tense Präteritum	Past Participle 2. Partizip
schwimmen	schwamm (schwömme)	geschwommen
schwinden	schwand (schwände)	geschwunden
schwingen	schwang (schwänge)	geschwungen
schwören	schwor (schwüre)	geschworen
sehen (du siehst, er sieht)	sah (sähe)	gesehen
sein (ich bin, du bist, er ist, wir sind, ihr seid, sie sind)	war (wäre)	gewesen
senden[1]	sandte (sendete)	gesandt
sieden	sott (sötte)	gesotten
singen	sang (sänge)	gesungen
sinken	sank (sänke)	gesunken
sinnen	sann (sänne)	gesonnen
sitzen (du/er sitzt)	saß (säße)	gesessen
sollen (ich/er soll, du sollst)	sollte	gesollt
*spalten	spaltete	gespalten
speien	spie	gespie[e]n
spinnen	spann (spönne, spänne)	gesponnen
sprechen (du sprichst, er spricht)	sprach (spräche)	gesprochen
sprießen (du/er sprießt)	spross (sprösse)	gesprossen
springen	sprang (spränge)	gesprungen
stechen (du stichst, er sticht)	stach (stäche)	gestochen
stehen	stand (stünde, stände)	gestanden
stehlen (du stiehlst, er stiehlt)	stahl (stähle)	gestohlen
steigen	stieg	gestiegen
sterben (du stirbst, er stirbt)	starb (stürbe)	gestorben
stinken	stank (stänke)	gestunken
stoßen (du/er stößt)	stieß	gestoßen
streichen	strich	gestrichen
streiten	stritt	gestritten
tragen (du trägst, er trägt)	trug (trüge)	getragen
treffen (du triffst, er trifft)	traf (träfe)	getroffen
treiben	trieb	getrieben
treten (du trittst, er tritt)	trat (träte)	getreten
*triefen	troff (tröffe)	getroffen

Infinitive	Past Tense	Past Participle
Infinitiv	Präteritum	2. Partizip
trinken	trank (tränke)	getrunken
trügen	trog (tröge)	getrogen
tun (du tust, er tut)	tat (täte)	getan
verderben (du verdirbst, er verdirbt)	verdarb (verdürbe)	verdorben
vergessen (du/er vergisst)	vergaß (vergäße)	vergessen
verlieren	verlor (verlöre)	verloren
verschleißen (du/er verschleißt)	verschliss	verschlissen
verzeihen	verzieh	verziehen
wachsen¹ (du/er wächst)	wuchs (wüchse)	gewachsen
waschen (du wäschst, er wäscht)	wusch (wüsche)	gewaschen
weichen²	wich	gewichen
weisen (du/er weist)	wies	gewiesen
*wenden²	wandte (wendete)	gewandt
werben (du wirbst, er wirbt)	warb (würbe)	geworben
werden (du wirst, er wird)	wurde (würde)	geworden
werfen (du wirfst, er wirft)	warf (würfe)	geworfen
wiegen¹	wog (wöge)	gewogen
winden	wand (wände)	gewunden
wissen (ich/er weiß, du weißt)	wusste (wüsste)	gewusst
wollen (ich/er will, du willst)	wollte	gewollt
wringen	wrang (wränge)	gewrungen
ziehen	zog (zöge)	gezogen
zwingen	zwang (zwänge)	gezwungen